Why Maps?

HISTORICAL EVENTS DO NOT JUST "HAPPEN"

— they happen in a specific place. Since events are often dictated by a location's specifics it is important to learn all you can about that place, and a good map can help you do this. Your textbook may include different types of maps:

Demographic or Population Maps show which groups inhabited which regions and how that distribution changed over time.

Geographic-Political Maps show territories occupied by particular nations and empires and the borders between them.

Topographic Maps show natural physical features such as oceans, rivers, elevations, forests, and deserts and manmade features such as dams and canals.

Expedition Maps show the routes followed by explorers, migrants, invaders, and military forces.

Battle Maps show the encounters and maneuvers of contending armies and navies.

Here are some basic tips to help you to get the most out of a map:

- Always look at the scale, which allows you to determine the distance in miles or kilometers between locations on the map.

- Examine the legend carefully. It explains the colors and/or symbols used on the map.

- Note the locations of mountains, rivers, oceans, and other geographic features, and consider how these would affect such human activities as agriculture, commerce, travel, and warfare.

- Read the map caption thoroughly. It provides important information sometimes not covered in the text itself. The caption may also inform you of additional resources, such as interactive maps, which may be available online.

Discover EVEN MORE ABOUT THE PAST ONLINE!

FOR STUDENTS:

The Wadsworth World History Resource Center

Your comprehensive resource for media assets to accompany any World History course!

Explore by Topic, Type of Asset, or Time Period. This rich resource can help you better understand the cultures, conditions, and concepts you will encounter in your study of World History. Assets include Timelines, Images, Primary Sources, Simulations, Web Links, and more!

Timelines

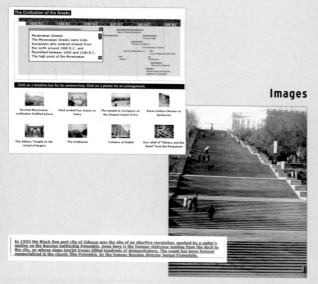

Images

In 1905 the Black Sea port city of Odessa was the site of an abortive revolution, marked by a sailor's mutiny on the Russian battleship Potemkin. Seen here is the famous staircase leading from the dock to the city, on whose steps tsarist troops killed hundreds of demonstrators. The event has been forever memorialized in the classic film Potemkin, by the famous Russian director Sergei Eisenstein.

FOR INSTRUCTORS:

Wadsworth HistoryFinder for World History

Create rich and exciting PowerPoint presentations for your World History course!

With **Wadsworth HistoryFinder for World History** you can quickly and easily download thousands of assets, including: Photographs, Maps, Art, Primary Sources, and Audio/Video Multimedia Clips.

Art

Akbar with Representatives of Various Religions at His Court
For years, the Mughal Emperor Akbar hosted weekly conversations among scholars and priests of numerous religions, including the Jesuits seen here on the left. Akbar sponsored the translation of varied religious texts, including the Christian Bible, into Persian, even though he himself was illiterate. When criticized by some Muslim scholars for his patronage of Hindu arts and his openness to other religious traditions, Akbar is said to have replied, "God loves beauty."

Maps

Major Sub-Saharan African Kingdoms and States, 1200–1600 C.E.
Many large kingdoms and states emerged in Intermediate Africa. Large empires dominated the Sudan in West Africa. Prosperous trading cities sharing a Swahili culture dotted the East Coast.

VOLUME II: SINCE 1500

SIXTH EDITION

THE ESSENTIAL WORLD HISTORY

WILLIAM J. DUIKER
The Pennsylvania State University

JACKSON J. SPIELVOGEL
The Pennsylvania State University

WADSWORTH
CENGAGE Learning™

Australia • Brazil • Japan • Korea • Mexico • Singapore • Spain • United Kingdom • United States

WADSWORTH
CENGAGE Learning

**The Essential World History,
Volume II: Since 1500: Sixth Edition**
William J. Duiker, Jackson J. Spielvogel

Senior Publisher: Suzanne Jeans

Senior Sponsoring Editor, History: Nancy Blaine

Senior Development Editor:
    Margaret McAndrew Beasley

Assistant Editor: Lauren Floyd

Editorial Assistant: Emma Goehring

Senior Media Editor: Lisa Ciccolo

Marketing Manager: Katherine Bates

Marketing Coordinator: Lorreen Pelletier

Marketing Communications Manager:
    Christine Dobberpuhl

Content Project Manager: Tiffany Kayes

Senior Art Director: Cate Rickard Barr

Production Technology Analyst: Lori Johnson

Print Buyer: Karen Hunt

Senior Rights Specialist, Text: Katie Huha

Production Service: John Orr Book Services

Text Designer: Shawn Girsberger

Photo Manager: Jennifer Meyer Dare

Cover Designer: Shawn Girsberger

Cover Image: Bibliotheque des Arts Decoratifs,
    Paris/Archives Charmet/The Bridgeman Art
    Library

Compositor: Glyph International

Library of Congress Control Number: 2010921089

ISBN-13: 978-0-495-90292-8
ISBN-10: 0-495-90292-6

Wadsworth
20 Channel Center Street
Boston, MA 02210
USA

Cengage Learning is a leading provider of customized learning solutions with office locations around the globe, including Singapore, the United Kingdom, Australia, Mexico, Brazil and Japan. Locate your local office at **international.cengage.com/region**.

Cengage Learning products are represented in Canada by Nelson Education, Ltd.

For your course and learning solutions, visit **www.cengage.com**.

Purchase any of our products at your local college store or at our preferred online store **www.CengageBrain.com**.

Printed in the United States of America
1 2 3 4 5 6 7 14 13 12 11 10

ABOUT THE AUTHORS

WILLIAM J. DUIKER is liberal arts professor emeritus of East Asian studies at The Pennsylvania State University. A former U.S. diplomat with service in Taiwan, South Vietnam, and Washington, D.C., he received his doctorate in Far Eastern history from Georgetown University in 1968, where his dissertation dealt with the Chinese educator and reformer Cai Yuanpei. At Penn State, he has written widely on the history of Vietnam and modern China, including the widely acclaimed *The Communist Road to Power in Vietnam* (revised edition, Westview Press, 1996), which was selected for a Choice Outstanding Academic Book Award in 1982–1983 and 1996–1997. Other recent books are *China and Vietnam: The Roots of Conflict* (Berkeley, 1987); *Sacred War: Nationalism and Revolution in a Divided Vietnam* (McGraw-Hill, 1995); and *Ho Chi Minh: A Life* (Hyperion, 2000), which was nominated for a Pulitzer Prize in 2001. While his research specialization is in the field of nationalism and Asian revolutions, his intellectual interests are considerably more diverse. He has traveled widely and has taught courses on the History of Communism and non-Western civilizations at Penn State, where he was awarded a Faculty Scholar Medal for Outstanding Achievement in the spring of 1996.

TO YVONNE,

FOR ADDING SPARKLE TO THIS BOOK, AND TO MY LIFE

W.J.D.

JACKSON J. SPIELVOGEL is associate professor emeritus of history at The Pennsylvania State University. He received his Ph.D. from The Ohio State University, where he specialized in Reformation history under Harold J. Grimm. His articles and reviews have appeared in such journals as *Moreana, Journal of General Education, Catholic Historical Review, Archiv für Reformationsgeschichte,* and *American Historical Review.* He has also contributed chapters or articles to *The Social History of the Reformation, The Holy Roman Empire: A Dictionary Handbook, Simon Wiesenthal Center Annual of Holocaust Studies,* and *Utopian Studies.* His work has been supported by fellowships from the Fulbright Foundation and the Foundation for Reformation Research. At Penn State, he helped inaugurate the Western civilization courses as well as a popular course on Nazi Germany. His book *Hitler and Nazi Germany* was published in 1987 (sixth edition, 2010). He is the author of *Western Civilization* published in 1991 (seventh edition, 2009). Professor Spielvogel has won five major university-wide teaching awards. During the year 1988–1989, he held the Penn State Teaching Fellowship, the university's most prestigious teaching award. In 1996, he won the Dean Arthur Ray Warnock Award for Outstanding Faculty Member and in 2000 received the Schreyer Honors College Excellence in Teaching Award.

TO DIANE,

WHOSE LOVE AND SUPPORT MADE IT ALL POSSIBLE

J.J.S.

BRIEF CONTENTS

DETAILED CONTENTS

DOCUMENTS

(continued on page 811)

MAPS

FEATURES

OPPOSING VIEWPOINTS

COMPARATIVE ESSAY

FILM & HISTORY

PREFACE

FOR SEVERAL MILLION YEARS after primates first appeared on the surface of the earth, human beings lived in small communities, seeking to survive by hunting, fishing, and foraging in a frequently hostile environment. Then suddenly, in the space of a few thousand years, there was an abrupt change of direction as human beings in a few widely scattered areas of the globe began to master the art of cultivating food crops. As food production increased, the population in those areas rose correspondingly, and people began to congregate in larger communities. Governments were formed to provide protection and other needed services to the local population. Cities appeared and became the focal point of cultural and religious development. Historians refer to this process as the beginnings of civilization.

For generations, historians in Europe and the United States pointed to the rise of such civilizations as marking the origins of the modern world. Courses on Western civilization conventionally began with a chapter or two on the emergence of advanced societies in Egypt and Mesopotamia and then proceeded to ancient Greece and the Roman Empire. From Greece and Rome, the road led directly to the rise of modern civilization in the West.

There is nothing inherently wrong with this approach. Important aspects of our world today can indeed be traced back to these early civilizations, and all human beings the world over owe a considerable debt to their achievements. But all too often this interpretation has been used to imply that the course of civilization has been linear in nature, leading directly from the emergence of agricultural societies in ancient Mesopotamia to the rise of advanced industrial societies in Europe and North America. Until recently, most courses on world history taught in the United States routinely focused almost exclusively on the rise of the West, with only a passing glance at other parts of the world, such as Africa, India, and East Asia. The contributions made by those societies to the culture and technology of our own time were often passed over in silence.

Two major reasons have been advanced to justify this approach. Some have argued that it is more important that young minds understand the roots of their own heritage than that of peoples elsewhere in the world. In many cases, however, the motivation for this Eurocentric approach has been the belief that since the time of Socrates and Aristotle Western civilization has been the sole driving force in the evolution of human society.

Such an interpretation, however, represents a serious distortion of the process. During most of the course of human history, the most advanced civilizations have been not in the West, but in East Asia or the Middle East. A relatively brief period of European dominance culminated with the era of imperialism in the late nineteenth century, when the political, military, and economic power of the advanced nations of the West spanned the globe. During recent generations, however, that dominance has gradually eroded, partly as a result of changes taking place within Western societies and partly because new centers of development are emerging elsewhere on the globe—notably in Asia, with the growing economic strength of China and India and many of their neighbors.

World history, then, has been a complex process in which many branches of the human community have taken an active part, and the dominance of any one area of the world has been a temporary rather than a permanent phenomenon. It will be our purpose in this book to present a balanced picture of this story, with all respect for the richness and diversity of the tapestry of the human experience. Due attention must be paid to the rise of the West, of course, since that has been the most dominant aspect of world history in recent centuries. But the contributions made by other peoples must be given adequate consideration as well, not only in the period prior to 1500 when the major centers of civilization were located in Asia, but also in our own day, when a multipolar picture of development is clearly beginning to emerge.

Anyone who wishes to teach or write about world history must decide whether to present the topic as an integrated whole or as a collection of different cultures. The world that we live in today, of course, is in many respects an interdependent one in terms of economics as well as culture and communications, a reality that is often expressed by the phrase "global village." The convergence of peoples across the surface of the earth into an integrated world system began in early times and intensified after the rise of capitalism in the early modern era. In growing recognition of this trend, historians trained in global history, as well as instructors in the growing number of world history courses, have now begun to speak and write of a "global approach" that turns attention away from the study of individual civilizations and focuses instead on the "big picture" or, as the world historian Fernand Braudel termed it, interpreting world history as a river with no banks.

On the whole, this development is to be welcomed as a means of bringing the common elements of the evolution of human society to our attention. But a problem is involved in this approach. For the vast majority of their time on earth, human beings have lived in partial or virtually total isolation from each other. Differences in climate, location, and geographic features have created human societies very different from each other in culture and historical experience. Only in relatively recent times—the commonly accepted date has long been the beginning of the age of European exploration at the end of the fifteenth century, but some would now push it back to the era of the Mongol Empire or even further—have cultural interchanges begun to create a common "world system," in which events taking place in one part of the world are rapidly transmitted throughout the globe, often with momentous consequences. In recent generations, of course, the process of global interdependence has been proceeding even more rapidly. Nevertheless, even now the process is by no means complete, as ethnic and regional differences continue to exist and to shape the course of world history. The tenacity of these differences and sensitivities is reflected not only in the rise of internecine conflicts in such divergent areas as Africa, India, and Eastern Europe, but also in the emergence in recent years of such regional organizations as the African Union, the Association for the Southeast Asian Nations, and the European Union.

The second problem is a practical one. College students today are all too often not well informed about the distinctive character of civilizations such as China and India and, without sufficient exposure to the historical evolution of such societies, will assume all too readily that the peoples in these countries have had historical experiences similar to ours and will respond to various stimuli in a similar fashion to those living in Western Europe or the United States. If it is a mistake to ignore those forces that link us together, it is equally a mistake to underestimate those factors that continue to divide us and to differentiate us into a world of diverse peoples.

Our response to this challenge has been to adopt a global approach to world history while at the same time attempting to do justice to the distinctive character and development of individual civilizations and regions of the world. The presentation of individual cultures is especially important in Parts I and II, which cover a time when it is generally agreed that the process of global integration was not yet far advanced. Later chapters begin to adopt a more comparative and thematic approach, in deference to the greater number of connections that have been established among the world's peoples since the fifteenth and sixteenth centuries. Part V consists of a series of chapters that center on individual regions of the world while at the same time focusing on common problems related to the Cold War and the rise of global problems such as overproduction and environmental pollution.

We have sought balance in another way as well. Many textbooks tend to simplify the content of history courses by emphasizing an intellectual or political perspective or, most recently, a social perspective, often at the expense of sufficient details in a chronological framework. This approach is confusing to students whose high school social studies programs have often neglected a systematic study of world history. We have attempted to write a well-balanced work in which political, economic, social, religious, intellectual, cultural, and military history have been integrated into a chronologically ordered synthesis.

Features of the Text

To enliven the past and let readers see for themselves the materials that historians use to create their pictures of the past, we have included **primary sources** (boxed documents) in each chapter that are keyed to the discussion in the text. The documents include examples of the religious, artistic, intellectual, social, economic, and political aspects of life in different societies and reveal in a vivid fashion what civilization meant to the individual men and women who shaped it by their actions. Questions at the end of each source aid students in analyzing the documents.

Each chapter has a **lengthy introduction and conclusion** to help maintain the continuity of the narrative and to provide a synthesis of important themes. Anecdotes in the chapter introductions more dramatically convey the major theme or themes of each chapter. **Timelines,** with thumbnail images illustrating major events and figures, at the end of each chapter enable students to see the major developments of an era at a glance and within cross-cultural categories, while the more **detailed chronologies** reinforce the events discussed in the text. An **annotated bibliography** at the end of each chapter reviews the most recent literature on each period and also gives references to some of the older, "classic" works in each field.

Updated maps and extensive illustrations serve to deepen the reader's understanding of the text. **Map captions** are designed to enrich students' awareness of the importance of geography to history, and numerous **spot maps** enable students to see at a glance the region or subject being discussed in the text. Map captions also include a question to guide students' reading of the map, as well as references to online interactive versions of the maps. To facilitate understanding of cultural movements, illustrations of artistic works discussed in the text are placed near the discussions. **Chapter outlines and focus questions, including critical thinking questions,** at the beginning of each chapter give students a useful overview and guide them to the main subjects of each chapter. The focus questions are then repeated at the beginning of each major section in the chapter. A **glossary of important terms** (boldfaced in the text when they are introduced and defined) and a **pronunciation guide** are provided at the back of the book to maximize reader comprehension.

Comparative essays, keyed to the seven major themes of world history (see p. 787), enable us to more concretely draw comparisons and contrasts across geographic, cultural, and chronological lines. Some new essays as well as illustrations for every essay have been added to the sixth edition. **Comparative illustrations,** also keyed to the seven major themes of world history, continue to be a feature in each chapter. We have also added focus questions to both the comparative essays and the comparative illustrations to help students develop their analytical skills. We hope that both the comparative essays and the comparative illustrations will assist instructors who wish to encourage their students to adopt a comparative approach to their understanding of the human experience.

New to This Edition

After reexamining the entire book and analyzing the comments and reviews of many colleagues who have found the book to be a useful instrument for introducing their students to world history, we have also made a number of other changes for the sixth edition. In the first place, we have reorganized some of the material. Chapter 7 now is devoted exclusively to the rise of Islam. Chapter 12, "The Making of Europe," now focuses entirely on medieval Europe to 1400. A new Chapter 13, "The Byzantine Empire and Crisis and Recovery in the West," covers the Byzantine Empire with new material as well as the crises in the fourteenth century and the Renaissance in Europe. Chapter 19 was reorganized and now deals with "The Beginnings of Modernization: Industrialization and Nationalism in the Nineteenth Century." Chapter 20 now covers "The Americas and Society and Culture in the West" in the nineteenth century. Also new to the sixth edition is an Epilogue, "Toward a Global Civilization," which focuses on the global economy, global culture, globalization and the environmental crisis, the social challenges of globalization, and new global movements.

We have also continued to strengthen the global framework of the book, but not at the expense of reducing the attention assigned to individual regions of the world. New material, including new comparative sections, has been added to most chapters to help students be aware of similar developments globally.

The enthusiastic response to the primary sources (boxed documents) led us to evaluate the content of each document carefully and add new documents throughout the text, including a new feature called **Opposing Viewpoints,** which presents a comparison of two or three primary sources in order to facilitate student analysis of historical documents. This feature appears in twenty-one chapters and includes such topics as "Roman Authorities and a Christian on Christianity;" "The Siege of Jerusalem: Christian and Muslim Perspectives;" "Advice to Women: Two Views;" "Action or Inaction: An Ideological Dispute in Medieval China;" "White Man's Burden, Black Man's Sorrow;" and "Who Started the Cold War? American and Soviet Perspectives." Focus questions are included to help students evaluate the documents.

An additional new feature is **Film & History,** which presents a brief analysis of the plot as well as the historical significance, value, and accuracy of fourteen films, including such movies as *Alexander, Marco Polo, The Mission, Khartoum, The Last Emperor, Gandhi,* and *Europa, Europa.*

Discovery sections at the end of every chapter provide assignable questions relating to primary source materials in the text. These sections engage students in "reading" and analyzing specific evidence—images, documents, maps, and timelines—to help them practice the skills of historical analysis and to connect the various threads of world history. A new section entitled "Studying from Primary Source Materials" appears in the front of the book to introduce students to the language and tools of analyzing historical evidence—documents, photos, artwork, and maps.

A number of new illustrations and maps have been added, and the bibliographies have been reorganized by topic and revised to take account of newly published material. The chronologies and maps have been fine-tuned as well to help the reader locate in time and space the multitude of individuals and place names that appear in the book. To keep up with the ever-growing body of historical scholarship, new or revised material has been added throughout the book on many topics.

Chapter-Specific Content Revisions

Chapter 1 New material on the Neolithic Age, early civilizations around the world, and Sumerian social classes; a new Opposing Viewpoints feature on Akhenaten's *Hymn to Aten* and Psalm 104 of the Hebrew Bible.

Chapter 2 Added material on the arrival of Indo-European peoples; a new document on the role of women in ancient India.

Chapter 3 New material on the arrival of *Homo sapiens* in East Asia, the "mother culture" hypothesis, and the origins of the Zhou dynasty; new information on jade, tea culture, bronze work, and the role of women in ancient

China; a revised chapter conclusion; a revised comparative illustration on the afterlife; a new Opposing Viewpoints feature on good and evil.

Chapter 4 New material on the Greek *polis;* a new Film & History feature, *Alexander;* a new comparative essay, "The Axial Age."

Chapter 5 A revised chapter conclusion; a new Opposing Viewpoints feature on Roman authorities and Christianity.

Chapter 6 A new introduction and new materials on the arrival of *Homo sapiens* in the Americas; additional material on Zapotec culture, the Olmecs, the "mother culture" hypothesis, and the Maya, including the writing system, city-state rivalries, and the causes of collapse; expanded coverage of Caral and early cultures in South America; the material on the arrival of the Spanish has been relocated to Chapter 14; two new maps—Map 6.1, Early Mesoamerica, and Map 6.2, The Maya Heartland—have been added, and other maps have been revised.

Chapter 7 A major expansion of the material on Islamic culture, with the relocation of Byzantine material to the new Chapter 13; new information on military tactics, the political and economic institutions of the Arab Empire, and the role of the environment; a major expansion of the material on Andalusian culture; new material on science and technology in the Islamic world; a new Film & History feature, *The Message,* on the life of Muhammad; a new Opposing Viewpoints feature on Christian and Muslim views of the Crusades; a new map—Map 7.1, The Middle East in the Time of Muhammad.

Chapter 8 Additional material on the role of trade in ancient Africa; new boxes on the gold trade and nomadic culture.

Chapter 9 An expanded section on science and technology; a new section on the spread of Polynesian culture in the Pacific.

Chapter 10 A major new section on the Mongol Empire, with a document and an illustration of Genghis Khan; a new Opposing Viewpoints feature on Taoist and Confucian attitudes; a new Film & History feature, *Marco Polo.*

Chapter 11 A new chapter introduction; new materials on the origins of Korean and Vietnamese civilizations and the universalist nature of Chinese civilization; a new Film & History feature, *Rashomon.*

Chapter 12 (Major Reorganization) Complete reorganization of the chapter so that it focuses entirely on medieval Europe to 1400, with the sections on "The Crises of the Late Middle Ages" and "Recovery: The Renaissance" moved to the new Chapter 13; a new section, "The Significance of Charlemagne;" a new section, "Effects of the Crusades;" new material on Viking expansion; two new document boxes, "Achievements of Charlemagne" and "University Students and Violence at Oxford;" a new Opposing Viewpoints

feature, "Two Views of Trade and Merchants;" a new Film & History feature, *The Lion in Winter;* a new comparative essay, "Cities in the Medieval World."

Chapter 13 (New) This is a new chapter with the following major sections: "From Eastern Roman to Byzantine Empire;" "The Zenith of Byzantine Civilization (750–1025);" "Decline and Fall of the Byzantine Empire (1025–1453);" "The Crises of the Fourteenth Century;" and "Recovery: The Renaissance." New material on the Byzantine Empire and educated women in the Renaissance; a new section, "The Black Death: From Asia to Europe," with a subsection on "The Role of the Mongols;" new document boxes, "The Achievements of Basil II" and "The Fall of Constantinople;" a new comparative essay, "The Role of Disease in History."

Chapter 14 A new Film & History feature, *Mutiny on the Bounty;* a new comparative illustration, "Spanish Conquest of the New World;" a new Opposing Viewpoints feaature, "The March of Civilization."

Chapter 15 New material on Zwingli and the Zwinglian Reformation; a new Opposing Viewpoints feature, "A Reformation Debate: Conflict at Marburg."

Chapter 16 A new Opposing Viewpoints feature, The Capture of Port Hoogly."

Chapter 17 Expanded material on Vietnam and additional information on technological developments in China.

Chapter 18 New material on Napoleon; a new Film & History feature, *The Mission.*

Chapter 19 (Major Reorganization) Reorganization of the chapter to focus on "The Beginnings of Modernization: Industrialization and Nationalism in the Nineteenth Century," with the following major sections: "The Industrial Revolution and Its Impact;" "The Growth of Industrial Prosperity;" "Reaction and Revolution: The Growth of Nationalism;" "National Unification and the National State, 1848–1871;" and "The European State, 1871–1914." New material on the principle of legitimacy; a new Opposing Viewpoints feature, "Response to Revolution: Two Perspectives."

Chapter 20 (Major Reorganization) Reorganized to focus on "The Americas and Society and Culture in the West," with the following major sections: "Latin America in the Nineteenth and Early Twentieth Centuries;" "The North American Neighbors: The United States and Canada;" "The Emergence of Mass Society in the West;" "Cultural Life: Romanticism and Realism in the Western World;" and "Toward the Modern Consciousness: Intellectual and Cultural Developments." New material on Latin America, including new sections, "The Wars for Independence" and "The Difficulties of Nation Building;" new material on the United States, especially a new section, "Slavery and the Coming of War," and new material on the Civil War and Reconstruction; new material on Canada and realism in South America; a new Opposing Viewpoints feature, "Advice to Women: Two Views;" a new document box, "Simón Bolívar on Government in Latin America."

Chapter 21 New material on direct rule in Africa; a new Film & History feature, *Khartoum*.

Chapter 22 A new Film & History feature, *The Last Emperor;* a new Opposing Viewpoints feature, "Two Views of the World."

Chapter 23 Clarified points on the Russian Revolution; a new document box, "Women in the Factories."

Chapter 24 Revised section on Palestine after World War I; expanded coverage of Japanese literature, Mexican politics, and Latin American culture; a new Film & History feature, *Gandhi;* a new Opposing Viewpoints feature, "Islam in the Modern World;" a new document box, "The Arranged Marriage."

Chapter 25 A revised section on "Aftermath of the War;" a new Opposing Viewpoints feature, "The Munich Conference;" a new Film & History feature, *Europa, Europa.*

Chapter 26 New material on the Vietnam War and Cold War rivalry in the Third World; two new Opposing Viewpoints features on the Cold War; a new Film & History feature, *The Missiles of October;* a new comparative illustration, "War in the Rice Paddies."

Chapter 27 Expanded and updated material on China; a new comparative illustration on sideline industries; a new document box on the Cultural Revolution in China.

Chapter 28 New material on France, Germany, and Great Britain since 1995; eastern Europe after communism; immigrants to Europe; and Canada, the United States, and Latin America since 1995; new material on art in the Age of Commerce.

Chapter 29 Expanded and updated material on Africa, including the Cold War and the role of international organizations; updated and expanded section on the Palestine issue; updated coverage on Africa and the Middle East; two new Opposing Viewpoints features, "An African Lament" and "Africa: Dark Continent or Radiant Land?;" a new Film & History feature, *Persepolis.*

Chapter 30 Expanded section on Pakistan; updated all sections; a new Film & History feature, *The Year of Living Dangerously.*

Epilogue: A Global Civilization (New) New to this edition; contains a new document box, "A Warning to Humanity."

Because courses in world history at American and Canadian colleges and universities follow different chronological divisions, a one-volume comprehensive edition, a two-volume edition of this text, and a volume covering events to 1500 are being made available to fit the needs of instructors. Teaching and learning ancillaries include:

Instructor Resources

PowerLecture CD-ROM with ExamView® This dual platform, all-in-one multimedia resource includes the Instructor's Resource Manual; Test Bank (includes key term identification, multiple-choice, essay, and true/false questions); and Microsoft® PowerPoint® slides of both lecture outlines and images and maps from the text that can be used as offered, or customized by importing personal lecture slides or other material. Also included is ExamView, an easy-to-use assessment and tutorial system that allows instructors to create, deliver, and customize tests in minutes. Instructors can build tests with as many as 250 questions using up to 12 question types, and using ExamView's complete word-processing capabilities, they can enter an unlimited number of new questions or edit existing ones.

HistoryFinder This searchable online database allows instructors to quickly and easily download thousands of assets, including art, photographs, maps, primary sources, and audio/video clips. Each asset downloads directly into a Microsoft® PowerPoint® slide, allowing instructors to easily create exciting PowerPoint presentations for their classrooms.

eInstructor's Resource Manual This manual has many features, including chapter outlines and summaries, lecture suggestions, discussion questions for primary sources, suggested debate and research topics, and suggested web links and video collections. Available on the instructor's companion website.

Student Resources

Book Companion Site A website for students that features a wide assortment of resources to help students master the subject matter. The website includes learning objectives, a glossary, flashcards, crossword puzzles, tutorial quizzes, critical thinking exercises, and web links.

CL eBook This interactive multimedia ebook links out to rich media assets such as web field trips. Through this ebook, students can also access self-test quizzes, chapter outlines, focus questions, critical thinking questions (for which the answers can be emailed to their instructors), primary source documents with critical thinking questions, and interactive (zoomable) maps. Available on iChapters.

iChapters Save your students time and money. Tell them about www.iChapters.com for choice in formats and savings and a better chance to succeed in your class. iChapters.com, Cengage Learning's online store, is a single destination for more than 10,000 new textbooks, eTextbooks, eChapters, study tools, and audio supplements. Students have the freedom to purchase a-la-carte exactly what they need when they need it. Students can save 50 percent on the electronic textbook, and can pay as little as $1.99 for an individual eChapter.

Wadsworth World History Resource Center   Wadsworth's World History Resource Center gives your students access to a "virtual reader" with hundreds of primary sources including speeches, letters, legal documents and transcripts, poems, maps, simulations, timelines, and additional images that bring history to life, along with interactive assignable exercises. A map feature including Google Earth™ coordinates and exercises will aid in student comprehension of geography and use of maps. Students can compare the traditional textbook map with an aerial view of the location today. It's an ideal resource for study, review, and research. In addition to this map feature, the resource center also provides blank maps for student review and testing.

Writing for College History, 1e   Prepared by Robert M. Frakes, Clarion University. This brief handbook for survey courses in American history, Western Civilization/European history, and world civilization guides students through the various types of writing assignments they encounter in a history class. Providing examples of student writing and candid assessments of student work, this text focuses on the rules and conventions of writing for the college history course.

The History Handbook, 1e   Prepared by Carol Berkin of Baruch College, City University of New York and Betty Anderson of Boston University. This book teaches students both basic and history-specific study skills such as how to read primary sources, research historical topics, and correctly cite sources. Substantially less expensive than comparable skill-building texts, *The History Handbook* also offers tips for Internet research and evaluating online sources.

Doing History: Research and Writing in the Digital Age, 1e Prepared by Michael J. Galgano, J. Chris Arndt, and Raymond M. Hyser of James Madison University. Whether you're starting down the path as a history major, or simply looking for a straightforward and systematic guide to writing a successful paper, you'll find this text to be an indispensable handbook to historical research. This text's "soup to nuts" approach to researching and writing about history addresses every step of the process, from locating your sources and gathering information, to writing clearly and making proper use of various citation styles to avoid plagiarism. You'll also learn how to make the most of every

tool available to you—especially the technology that helps you conduct the process efficiently and effectively.

The Modern Researcher, 6e   Prepared by Jacques Barzun and Henry F. Graff of Columbia University. This classic introduction to the techniques of research and the art of expression is used widely in history courses, but is also appropriate for writing and research methods courses in other departments. Barzun and Graff thoroughly cover every aspect of research, from the selection of a topic through the gathering, analysis, writing, revision, and publication of findings, presenting the process not as a set of rules but through actual cases that put the subtleties of research in a useful context. Part One covers the principles and methods of research; Part Two covers writing, speaking, and getting one's work published.

Reader Program   Cengage Learning publishes a number of readers, some containing exclusively primary sources, others a combination of primary and secondary sources, and some designed to guide students through the process of historical inquiry. Visit Cengage.com/history for a complete list of readers.

Rand McNally Historical Atlas of the World, 2e   This valuable resource features over 70 maps that portray the rich panoply of the world's history from preliterate times to the present. They show how cultures and civilizations were linked and how they interacted. The maps make it clear that history is not static. Rather, it is about change and movement across time. The maps show change by presenting the dynamics of expansion, cooperation, and conflict. This atlas includes maps that display the world from the beginning of civilization; the political development of all major areas of the world; expanded coverage of Africa, Latin America, and the Middle East; the current Islamic world; and the world population change from 1900 and 2000.

Custom Options

Nobody knows your students like you, so why not give them a text that is tailored to their needs. Cengage Learning offers custom solutions for your course—whether it is making a small modification to *The Essential World History* to match your syllabus or combining multiple sources to create something truly unique. You can pick and choose chapters, include your own material, and add additional map exercises along with the Rand McNally Atlas to create a text that fits the way you teach. Ensure that your students get the most out of their textbook dollar by giving them exactly what they need. Contact your Cengage Learning representative to explore custom solutions for your course.

ACKNOWLEDGMENTS

BOTH AUTHORS GRATEFULLY acknowledge that without the generosity of many others, this project could not have been completed.

William Duiker would like to thank Kumkum Chatterjee and On-cho Ng for their helpful comments about issues related to the history of India and premodern China. His longtime colleague Cyril Griffith, now deceased, was a cherished friend and a constant source of information about modern Africa. Art Goldschmidt has been of invaluable assistance in reading several chapters of the manuscript, as well as in unraveling many of the mysteries of Middle Eastern civilization. Finally, he remains profoundly grateful to his wife, Yvonne V. Duiker, Ph.D. She has not only given her usual measure of love and support when this appeared to be an insuperable task, but she has also contributed her own time and expertise to enrich the sections on art and literature, thereby adding life and sparkle to this, as well as the earlier editions of the book. To her, and to his daughters Laura and Claire, he will be forever thankful for bringing joy to his life.

Jackson Spielvogel would like to thank Art Goldschmidt, David Redles, and Christine Colin for their time and ideas. Daniel Haxall of Kutztown University and Kathryn Spielvogel of SUNY–Buffalo provided valuable assistance with materials on postwar art, popular culture, and Postmodern art and thought. Above all, he thanks his family for their support. The gifts of love, laughter, and patience from his daughters, Jennifer and Kathryn, his sons, Eric and Christian, and his daughters-in-law, Liz and Laurie, and his sons-in-law, Daniel and Eddie, were invaluable. He also wishes to acknowledge his grandchildren, Devyn, Bryn, Drew, Elena, Sean, and Emma, who bring great joy to his life. Diane, his wife and best friend, provided him with editorial assistance, wise counsel, and the loving support that made a project of this magnitude possible.

Thanks to Wadsworth's comprehensive review process, many historians were asked to evaluate our manuscript. We are grateful to the following for the innumerable suggestions that have greatly improved our work.

Henry Abramson
Florida Atlantic University

Eric H. Ash
Wayne State University

William Bakken
Rochester Community College

Suzanne Balch-Lindsay
Eastern New Mexico University

Michael E. Birdwell
Tennessee Technological University

Connie Brand
Meridien Community College

Eileen Brown
Norwalk Community College

Thomas Cardoza
University of California, San Diego

Alistair Chapman
Westmont College

Nupur Chaudhuri
Texas Southern University

Richard Crane
Greensboro College

Wade Dudley
East Carolina University

E. J. Fabyan
Vincennes University

Kenneth Faunce
Washington State University

Jamie Garcia
Hawaii Pacific University

Steven Gosch
University of Wisconsin—Eau Claire

Donald Harreld
Brigham Young University

Janine C. Hartman
University of Connecticut

Greg Havrilcsak
University of Michigan—Flint

Thomas Hegerty
University of Tampa

Sanders Huguenin
University of Science and Arts of Oklahoma

Ahmed Ibrahim
Southwest Missouri State University

C. Barden Keeler
Gulf Coast High School

Marilynn Fox Kokoszka
Orchard Ridge Campus, Oakland Community College

James Krippner-Martinez
Haverford College

Oscar Lansen
University of North Carolina—Charlotte

David Leinweber
Oxford College, Emory University

Susie Ling
Pasadena City College

Moira Maguire
University of Arkansas at Little Rock

Andrew McGreevy
Ohio University

Daniel Miller
Calvin College

Michael Murdock
Brigham Young University

Elsa A. Nystrom
Kennesaw State University

S. Mike Pavelec
Hawaii Pacific University

Randall L. Pouwels
University of Central Arkansas

Margaret Power
Illinois Institute of Technology

Pamela Sayre
Henry Ford Community College

Philip Curtis Skaggs
Grand Valley State University

Laura Smoller
University of Arkansas at Little Rock

Beatrice Spade
University of Southern Colorado

Jeremy Stahl
Middle Tennessee State University

Kate Transchel
California State University, Chico

Justin Vance
Hawaii Pacific University

Lorna VanMeter
Ball State University

Michelle White
University of Tennessee at Chattanooga

Edna Yahil
Washington State University—Swiss Center

The authors are truly grateful to the people who have helped us to produce this book. We especially want to thank Clark Baxter, whose faith in our ability to do this project was inspiring. Margaret McAndrew Beasley thoughtfully, wisely, efficiently, and pleasantly guided the overall development of this edition. We also thank Nancy Blaine for her valuable editorial insights. We want to express our gratitude to John Orr, whose good humor, well-advised suggestions, and generous verbal support made the production process easier. Pat Lewis was, as usual, a truly outstanding copyeditor. Abigail Baxter provided valuable assistance in obtaining illustrations and permissions for the illustrations.

THE PEOPLES OF MESOPOTAMIA AND EGYPT, like the peoples of India and China, built the first civilizations. Blessed with an abundant environment in their fertile river valleys, beginning around 3000 B.C.E. they built technologically advanced societies, developed cities, and struggled with the problems of organized states.

They developed writing to keep records and created literature. They constructed monumental architecture to please their gods, symbolize their power, and preserve their culture for all time. They developed new political, military, social, and religious structures to deal with the basic problems of human existence and organization. These first literate civilizations left detailed records that allow us to view how they grappled with three of the fundamental problems that humans have pondered: the nature of human relationships, the nature of the universe, and the role of divine forces in that cosmos. Although other peoples would provide different answers from those of the Mesopotamians and Egyptians, they posed the questions, gave answers, and wrote them down. Human memory begins with the creation of civilizations.

By the middle of the second millennium B.C.E., much of the creative impulse of the Mesopotamian and Egyptian civilizations was beginning to wane. Around 1200 B.C.E., the decline of the Hittites and Egyptians had created a power vacuum that allowed a number of small states to emerge and flourish temporarily. All of them were eventually overshadowed by the rise of the great empires of the Assyrians and Persians. The Assyrian Empire had been the first to unite almost all of the ancient Middle East. Even larger, however, was the empire of the Great Kings of Persia. The many years of peace that the Persian Empire brought to the Middle East facilitated trade and the general well-being of its peoples. It is no wonder that many peoples expressed their gratitude for being subjects of the Great Kings of Persia. Among these peoples were the Israelites, who created no empire but nevertheless left an important spiritual legacy. The evolution of monotheism created in Judaism one of the world's greatest religions; Judaism in turn influenced the development of both Christianity and Islam.

While the peoples of North Africa and the Middle East were actively building the first civilizations, a similar process was getting under way in India. The first civilization in India arose in the Indus River valley during the fourth millennium B.C.E. This Harappan civilization made significant political and social achievements for some two thousand years until the coming of the Aryans finally brought its end around 1500 B.C.E. The Aryans established political control throughout all of India and created a new Indian civilization. Two of the world's great religions, Hinduism and Buddhism, began in India. With its belief in reincarnation, Hinduism provided justification for the rigid class system of India. Buddhism was the product of one man, Siddhartha Gautama, whose simple message in the sixth century B.C.E. of achieving wisdom created a new spiritual philosophy that came to rival Hinduism.

With the rise of the Mauryan dynasty in the fourth century B.C.E., the distinctive features of a great civilization began to be clearly visible. It was extensive in its scope, embracing the entire Indian subcontinent and eventually, in the form of Buddhism and Hinduism, spreading to China and  Southeast Asia. But the underlying ethnic, linguistic, and cultural diversity of the Indian people posed a constant challenge to the unity of the state. After the collapse of the Mauryas, the subcontinent would not come under a single authority again for several hundred years.

In the meantime, another great experiment was taking place far to the northeast, across the Himalaya Mountains. Like many other civilizations of antiquity, the first Chinese state was concentrated on a major river system. Beginning around 1600 B.C.E., the Shang dynasty created the first flourishing Chinese civilization. Under the Shang, China developed organized government, a system of writing, and advanced skills in the making of bronze vessels. During the Zhou dynasty, China began to adopt many of the features that characterized Chinese civilization for centuries. Especially important politically was the "mandate from Heaven," which, it was believed, gave kings a divine right to rule. The family, with its ideal of filial piety, also emerged as a powerful economic and social unit.

Once embarked on its own path toward the creation of a complex society, China achieved results that were in all respects the equal of its counterparts elsewhere. A new dynasty—the Han—then established a vast empire that

lasted over four hundred years. During the glory years of the Han dynasty (202 B.C.E.–221 C.E.), China extended the boundaries of its empire far into the sands of central Asia and southward along the coast of the South China Sea into what is modern-day Vietnam. Chinese culture appeared to be unrivaled, and its scientific and technological achievements were unsurpassed.

Unlike the great centralized empires of the Persians and the Chinese, ancient Greece consisted of a larger number of small, independent city-states, most of which had populations of only a few thousand. Despite the small size of their city-states, these ancient Greeks created a civilization that was the fountainhead of Western culture. In Classical Greece (c. 500–338 B.C.E.), Socrates, Plato, and Aristotle established the foundations of Western philosophy. Western literary forms are largely derived from Greek poetry and drama. Greek notions of harmony, proportion, and beauty have remained the touchstones for all subsequent Western art. A rational method of inquiry, so important to modern science, was conceived in ancient

Greece. Many political terms are Greek in origin, and so too are concepts of the rights and duties of citizenship, especially as they were conceived in Athens, the first great democracy. The Greeks raised and debated the fundamental questions about the purpose of human existence, the structure of human society, and the nature of the universe that have concerned thinkers ever since.

For all of their brilliant accomplishments, however, the Greeks were unable to rise above the divisions and rivalries that caused them to fight each other and undermine their own civilization. Of course, their cultural contributions have outlived their political struggles. And the Hellenistic era, which emerged after the Greek city-states had lost their independence in 338 B.C.E. and Alexander the Great had defeated the Persian Empire and carved out a new kingdom in the Middle East, made possible the spread of Greek ideas to larger areas. New philosophical concepts captured the minds of many. Significant achievements were made in art, literature, and science. Greek culture spread throughout the Middle East and made an impact wherever it was carried. Although the Hellenistic world achieved a degree of political stability, by the late third century B.C.E. signs of decline were beginning to multiply, and the growing power of Rome would eventually endanger the Hellenistic world.

In the eighth and seventh centuries B.C.E., the Latin-speaking community of Rome emerged as an actual city. Between 509 and 264 B.C.E., the expansion of this city

brought about the union of almost all of Italy under Rome's control. Even more dramatically, between 264 and 133 B.C.E., Rome expanded to the west and east and became master of the Mediterranean Sea and its surrounding territories, creating one of the largest empires in antiquity. Rome's republican institutions proved inadequate for the task of ruling an empire, however, and after a series of bloody civil wars, Octavian created a new order that would rule the empire in an orderly fashion. His successors established a Roman imperial state.

The Roman Empire experienced a lengthy period of peace and prosperity between 14 and 180 C.E. During this era, trade flourished and the provinces were governed efficiently. In the course of the third century, however, the Roman Empire came near to collapse due to invasions, civil wars, and economic decline. Although the emperors Diocletian and Constantine brought new life to the so-called Late Empire, their efforts shored up the empire only temporarily. In its last two hundred years, as Christianity, with its new ideals of spiritual equality and respect for human life, grew, a slow transformation of the Roman world took place. The Germanic invasions greatly accelerated this process. Beginning in 395, the empire divided into western and eastern parts, and in 476, the Roman Empire in the west came to an end.

Although the western Roman Empire lived on only as an idea, Roman achievements were bequeathed to the future. The Romance languages of today (French, Italian, Spanish, Portuguese, and Romanian) are based on Latin. Western practices of impartial justice and trial by jury owe much to Roman law. As great builders, the Romans left monuments to their skills throughout Europe, some of which, such as aqueducts and roads, are still in use today.

The fall of ancient empires did not mark the end of civilization. After 500 C.E., new societies eventually rose on the ashes of the ancient empires, while new civilizations were on the verge of creation across the oceans in the continents of North and South America. The Maya and Aztecs were especially successful in developing advanced and prosperous civilizations in Central America. Both cultures built elaborate cities with pyramids, temples, and palaces. Both were polytheistic and practiced human sacrifice as a major part of their religions. Mayan civilization collapsed in the ninth century, whereas the Aztecs fell to Spanish invaders in the sixteenth century. In the fifteenth century, another remarkable civilization—that of

the Inka—flourished in South America. The Inkan Empire was carefully planned and regulated, which is especially evident in the extensive network of roads that connected all parts of the empire. However, the Inka, possessing none of the new weapons of the Spaniards, eventually fell to the foreign conquerors.

All of these societies in the Americas developed in apparently total isolation from their counterparts elsewhere in the world. This lack of contact with other human beings deprived them of access to developments taking place in Africa, Asia, and Europe. They did not know of the wheel, for example, and their written languages were not as sophisticated as those in other parts of the world. In other respects, however, their cultural achievements were the equal of those realized elsewhere. One development that the peoples of the Americas lacked was the knowledge of firearms. In a few short years, tiny bands of Spanish explorers were able to conquer the magnificent civilizations of the Americas and turn them into ruins.

After the collapse of Roman power in the west, the eastern Roman Empire, centered in Constantinople, continued in the eastern Mediterranean and eventually emerged as the unique Christian civilization known as the Byzantine Empire, which flourished for hundreds of years. One of the greatest challenges to the Byzantine Empire, however, came from a new force—Islam, a new religion that arose in the Arabian peninsula at the beginning of the seventh century C.E. and spread rapidly throughout the Middle East. It was the work of a man named Muhammad. After Muhammad's death, his successors organized the Arabs and set in motion a great expansion. Arab armies moved westward across North Africa and into Spain, as well as eastward into the Persian Empire, conquering Syria and Mesopotamia. Internal struggles, however, soon weakened the empire, although the Abbasid dynasty established an Arab empire in 750 that flourished for almost five hundred years.

Like other empires in the region, however, the Arab Empire did not last. Nevertheless, Islam brought a code of law and a written language to societies that had previously not had them. By creating a flourishing trade network stretching from West Africa to East Asia, Islam also brought untold wealth to thousands and a better life to millions. By the end of the thirteenth century, the Arab Empire was no more than a memory. But it left a powerful legacy in Islam, which remains one of the great religions of the world. In succeeding centuries, Islam began to penetrate into Africa and across the Indian Ocean into the islands of Southeast Asia.

The mastery of agriculture gave rise to three early civilizations in northern Africa: Egypt, Kush, and Axum. Later, new states emerged in different parts of Africa, some of them strongly influenced by the spread of Islam. Ghana, Mali, and Songhai were three prosperous trading states that flourished in West Africa between the twelfth and fifteenth centuries. Zimbabwe, which emerged around 1300, played an important role in the southern half of Africa. Africa was also an active participant in emerging regional and global trade with the Mediterranean world and across the Indian Ocean. Although the state-building process in sub-Saharan Africa was still in its early stages compared with the ancient civilizations of India, China, and Mesopotamia, in many respects the new African states were as impressive and sophisticated as their counterparts elsewhere in the world.

In the fifteenth century, a new factor came to affect Africa. Fleets from Portugal began to probe southward along the coast of West Africa. At first, their sponsors were in search of gold and slaves, but when Portuguese ships rounded the southern coast of Africa by 1500, they began to seek to dominate the trade of the Indian Ocean as well. The new situation posed a challenge to the peoples of Africa, whose states would be severely tested by the demands of the Europeans.

The peoples of Africa were not the only ones to confront a new threat from Europe at the beginning of the sixteenth century. When the Portuguese sailed across the Indian Ocean, they sought to reach India, where a new empire capable of rivaling the great kingdom of the Mauryas was in the throes of creation. Between 500 and 1500, Indian civilization had faced a number of severe challenges. One was an ongoing threat from beyond the mountains in the northwest. This challenge, which began in the eleventh century, led to the takeover of all of northern India in the eleventh century by Turkish warriors, who were Muslims. A second challenge came from the tradition of internal rivalry that had marked Indian civilization for hundreds of years and that continued almost without interruption down to the sixteenth century. The third challenge was the religious divisions between Hindus and Buddhists, and later between Hindus and Muslims, that existed throughout much of this period.

During the same period that Indian civilization faced these challenges at home, it was having a profound impact on the emerging states of Southeast Asia. Situated at the crossroads between two oceans and two great civilizations, Southeast Asia has long served as a bridge linking peoples and cultures. When complex societies began to appear in the region, they were strongly influenced by the older civilizations of neighboring China and India. All the young states throughout the region—Vietnam, Angkor, Thailand, the Burmese kingdom of Pagan, and several states on the Malayan peninsula and Indonesian archipelago—were affected by foreign ideas and adopted them as a part of their own cultures. At the same time, the Southeast Asian peoples, like the Japanese, put their own unique stamp

on the ideas that they adopted. The result was a region marked by cultural richness and diversity yet rooted in the local culture.

One of the civilizations that spread its shadow over the emerging societies of Southeast Asia was China. Between the sixth and fifteenth centuries, China was ruled by a series of strong dynasties and had advanced in many ways. The industrial and commercial sectors had grown considerably in size, complexity, and technological capacity. In the countryside, a flourishing agriculture bolstered China's economic prosperity. The civil service provided for a stable government bureaucracy and an avenue of upward mobility that was virtually unknown elsewhere in the world. China's achievements were unsurpassed throughout the world and made it a civilization that was the envy of its neighbors.

And yet some things had not changed. By 1500, China was still a predominantly agricultural society, with wealth based primarily on the ownership of land. Commercial activities flourished but remained under a high level of government regulation. China also remained a relatively centralized empire based on an official ideology that stressed the virtue of hard work, social conformity, and hierarchy. In foreign affairs, the long frontier struggle with the nomadic peoples along the northern and western frontiers continued unabated.

Along the fringes of Chinese civilization were a number of other agricultural societies that were beginning to follow a pattern of development similar to that of China, although somewhat later in time. All of these early agricultural societies were eventually influenced to some degree by their great neighbor. Vietnam remained under Chinese rule for a thousand years. Korea retained its separate existence but was long a tributary state of China and in many ways followed China's cultural example. Cut off from the mainland by 120 miles of ocean, the Japanese had little contact with the outside world during most

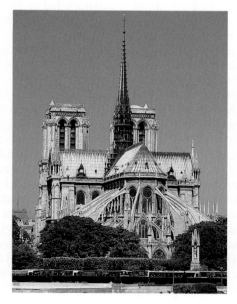

of their early development. However, once the Japanese became acquainted with Chinese culture, they were quick to take advantage of the opportunity. In the space of a few decades, the young state adopted many features of Chinese society and culture and thereby introduced major changes into the Japanese way of life. Nevertheless, Japan was a society that was able to make use of ideas imported from beyond its borders without endangering its customs, beliefs, and institutions. Japan retained both its political independence and its cultural uniqueness.

After the collapse of the Roman Empire in the fifth century, a new European civilization slowly began to emerge in western Europe. The coronation of Charlemagne, the descendant of a Germanic tribe converted to Christianity, as Roman emperor in 800 symbolized the fusion of the three chief components of the new European civilization: the German tribes, the Roman legacy, and the Christian church. Charlemagne's Carolingian Empire fostered the idea of a distinct European identity. With the disintegration of that empire, power fell into the hands of many different lords, who came to constitute a powerful group of nobles that dominated the political, economic, and social life of Europe. But quietly and surely, within this world of castles and private power, kings gradually began to extend their public power and laid the foundations for the European kingdoms that in one form or another have dominated European politics ever since.

European civilization began to flourish in the High Middle Ages (1000–1300). The revival of trade, the expansion of towns and cities, and the development of a money economy did not mean the end of a predominantly rural European society, but they did offer new opportunities for people to expand and enrich their lives. At the same time, the High Middle Ages also gave birth to an intellectual and spiritual revival that transformed European society. However, fourteenth-century Europe was challenged by an overwhelming number of disintegrative forces but proved remarkably resilient. Elements of recovery in the age of the Renaissance made the fifteenth century a period of significant artistic, intellectual, and political change in Europe. By the second half of the fifteenth century, the growth of strong, centralized monarchical states made possible the dramatic expansion of Europe into other parts of the world.

ASTRONOMERS INVESTIGATE THE universe through telescopes. Biologists study the natural world by collecting plants and animals in the field and then examining them with microscopes. Sociologists and psychologists study human behavior through observation and controlled laboratory experiments.

Historians study the past by examining historical "evidence" or "source" materials—church or town records, letters, treaties, advertisements, paintings, menus, literature, buildings, clothing—anything and everything written or created by our ancestors that give clues about their lives and the times in which they lived.

Historians refer to written materials as "documents." This textbook contains excerpts from more than one hundred documents—some in shaded boxes and others in the text narrative itself. Every chapter includes not only several selections from documents but also a number of photographs of buildings, paintings, and other kinds of historical evidence.

As you read each chapter, the more you examine all this "evidence," the better you will understand the main ideas of the course. This introduction to studying historical evidence and the Discovery features at the end of each chapter will help you learn how to look at evidence the way your instructor does. The better you become at reading and analyzing evidence, the better the grade you will earn in your course.

Source Material Comes in Two Main Types: Primary and Secondary

"Primary" evidence is material that comes to us exactly as it left the pen of the person who wrote or created it. Letters between King Louis XIV of France and the king of Tonkin (now Vietnam) are primary evidence (p. 354). So is the court transcript of a witchcraft trial in France (p. 372), a poem by Shakespeare, or a diagram of the solar system drawn by Copernicus (p. 437).

"Secondary" evidence is an account by someone about the life or activity of someone else. A story about Abraham Lincoln written by his secretary of war would give us primary source information about Lincoln by someone who knew him. Reflections about Lincoln's presidency written by a historian might give us insights into how, for example, Lincoln governed during wartime. But because the historian did not know Lincoln firsthand, we would consider this information a secondary source of information about Lincoln. Secondary sources such as historical essays (and textbooks!) can therefore be very helpful in understanding the past. But it is important to remember that a secondary source can reveal as much about its author as it does about its subject.

Reading Documents

We will turn to a specific document in a moment and analyze it in some detail. For now, however, the following are a few basic questions to consider—and to ask yourself—as you read any written document:

1. Who wrote it? The authors of this textbook answer this question for you at the beginning of each document in the book. But your instructors may give you other documents to read, and the authorship of each document is the first question you need to answer.
2. What do we know about the author of the document? The more you know about the author, the better and more reliable the information you can extract from the document.
3. Is it a primary or a secondary document?
4. When was the document written?
5. What is the purpose of the document? Closely tied to the question of document type is the document's purpose. A work of fiction might have been written to entertain, whereas an official document was written to convey a particular law or decree to subjects, citizens, or believers.
6. Who was the intended audience? A play was meant to be performed, whereas Martin Luther's Ninety-five Theses were posted publicly.
7. Can you detect a bias in the document? As the two documents on the siege of Jerusalem (p. 168) suggest, firsthand accounts of the Crusades written by Christians and Muslims tend to differ. Each may be "accurate" as far as the writer is concerned, but your job as a historian is to decide whether this written evidence gives a reliable account of what happened. You cannot always believe everything you read, but the more you read, the more you can decide what is, in fact, accurate.

"Reading" and Studying Photographs and Artwork

This book pays close attention to primary source and written documents, but contemporary illustrations can also be analyzed to provide understanding of a historical period.

A historian might study a painting like the one of a medieval town (p. 297) to learn more about life in a medieval town. The more you learn about medieval social history, the more information this painting will reveal. To help you look at and interpret art like a historian, ask yourself the following questions:

1. By looking closely at just the buildings, what do you learn about the nature of medieval town dwellings and the allotment of space within the town? Why were medieval towns arranged in this fashion? How does this differ from modern urban planning?
2. By examining the various activities shown, what do you learn about the kinds of groups that might be found in a medieval town? What do you learn about medieval methods of production? How do they differ from modern methods of production? What difference would this make in the nature of community organization and life?
3. Based on what the people in the street are wearing, what do you judge to be their economic status? Are they typical of people in a medieval town? Why or why not?
4. What do you think the artist who created this picture was trying to communicate about life in a medieval town? Based on your knowledge of medieval towns, would you agree with the artist's assessment? Why or why not?
5. What do you think was the social class of the artist? Why?

Reading and Studying Maps

Historical events do not just "happen." They happen in a specific place. It is important to learn all you can about that place, and a good map can help you do this.

Your textbook includes several kinds of maps. The pullout map of the world bound into the inside front cover of the textbook is a good place to start. Map basics include taking care to read and understand every label on each map you encounter. The textbook's pullout map has labels for the following kinds of information, each of which is important:

1. Names of countries
2. Names of major cities
3. Names of oceans and other large bodies of water
4. Names of rivers
5. Longitude and latitude. Lines of longitude extend from the North Pole to the South Pole; one such line intersects Iceland in the top left (or northwest) corner of the map. Lines of latitude circle the globe east to west and intersect lines of longitude. These imaginary lines place countries and oceans in their approximate setting on the face of the earth. Not every map includes latitude and longitude.
6. Mileage scale. A mileage scale shows how far, in miles and kilometers, each location is from other locations.

Most Maps Include Three Basic Types of Information

1. The boundaries of countries, cities, empires, and other kinds of "political" information. A good map shows each political division in a different color to make them all easy to find. The color of each region or country is the decision of the mapmaker (also known as a cartographer).
2. Mountains, oceans, rivers, and other "physical" or "topographic" information. The mountains on this map appear as wavy lines: Ethiopia and the western United States are mountainous; Sudan and Kazakhstan are flat.
3. Latitude, longitude, a mileage scale, and other information. These elements help the reader place the information in some kind of context. Some maps include an N with an arrow that points north. Most maps show northern areas (Alaska, Norway, etc.) at the top, but a map that does not do so is not wrong. But if an N arrow appears on the map, be sure you know where north is.

"Political" information tends to change a great deal over time. For example, after a major war, the boundaries of countries may change if the winners expand their territory. "Physical" information changes slowly. Latitude, north, distances, and the like do not change.

In addition, maps may include many other types of information such as the way a disease spread, the location of cathedrals and universities, or trade routes. There is hardly any limit to the kinds of information a map can show, and the more information a map can display clearly, the more useful it is. A good map will include a boxed "legend" stating the information that makes the map useful. The more detailed the map, the more information the mapmaker should provide in the legend.

Again, note that only the "physical" features shown on a map, such as the oceans, lakes, rivers, and

Ancient Italy

proximity of two or more ideas. Map 14.2 (p. 340) shows the routes of several voyages of the sixteenth and seventeenth centuries. Note that the boxed legend associates the color of a route (shown as a line) with its nation of origin. This map makes it possible to see a number of useful things at a glance that would otherwise take several maps to depict, including:

1. Where each voyage began. Note the places that launched the most voyages and those that launched none.
2. How long each voyage was. Note the mileage scale.
3. Which route each explorer took. Note the letters labeling each line.
4. The trading cities that were established. Which nation established the most?
5. The location of the trade winds. What effect would they have had on voyages, such as Vasco da Gama's?

Another kind of movement appears in Map 9.3 (p. 213). This map shows the spread of religions in southern and eastern Asia between 600 and 1900 C.E. Using the legend, trace the movement of each major religion.

Putting It Together: Reading and Studying Documents, Supported by Maps and Images

Learning to read a document is no different from learning to read a restaurant menu. The more you practice, the quicker your eyes will find the lobster and pastries.

Let's Explore a Pair of Primary Sources

As the introduction to the reading on the next page makes clear, King Louis XIV of France is writing to the king of

mountains, really exist in nature. As mentioned earlier, they are relatively changeless. All other features shown on maps are created by human beings and change fairly often. The maps you see here and on the next page all show the same familiar "boot," which we call Italy. But over the centuries all or part of this landmass has also been called Latium, Campania, the duchy of Benevento, the kingdom of Lothair, the Papal States, the kingdom of Sicily, Tuscany, Lombardy, Piedmont, Savoy, and finally, in 1870, Italy. People and places change; mountains and oceans do not, at least not very much or very quickly. Whenever you have trouble finding a region or a place on a map, look for a permanent feature to help you get your bearings.

In addition to kingdoms, cities, and mountains, maps can show movements, developments, or the physical

Europe in the High Middle Ages

Europe in 1763

Tonkin to ask permission to send Christian missionaries to Southeast Asia. But this exchange of letters tells a great deal more than that.

Before you read this document, take a careful look at the portrait of Louis XIV (p. 376). As this image makes clear, Louis lived during an age of flourishes and excess. Among many other questions, including some that appear later, you may ask yourself how Louis's manner of writing reflects the public presentation you see in his portrait.

Your textbook does not show a corresponding portrait of the king of Tonkin, but you might try to create a picture of him in your mind as you read his response to

The Unification of Italy

Map legend:
- Kingdom of Piedmont, before 1859
- To Kingdom of Piedmont, 1859
- To Kingdom of Piedmont, 1860
- To Kingdom of Italy, 1866, 1870

the letter he receives from his fellow king.

The following questions are the kinds of questions your instructor would ask about the document.

1. Why does Louis refer to the king of Tonkin, whom he had never met, as his "very dear and good friend" (line 2)? Do you think that this French king would have begun a conversation with, say, a French shopkeeper in quite the same way? If not, why does he identify more with a fellow king than with a fellow Frenchman?
2. How often do you think the king of France had to persuade

A Letter to the King of Tonkin from Louis XIV

1 Most high, most excellent, most mighty, and most magnanimous
2 Prince, our very dear and good friend, may it please God to increase
3 your greatness with a happy end!
4   We hear from our subjects who were in your Realm what pro-
5 tection you accorded them. We appreciate this all the more since
6 we have for you all the esteem that one can have for a prince as il-
7 lustrious through his military valor as he is commendable for the
8 justice which he exercises in his Realm. We have even been in-
9 formed that you have not been satisfied to extend this general
10 protection to our subjects but, in particular, that you gave effec-
11 tive proofs of it to Messrs. Deydier and de Bourges. We would
12 have wished that they might have been able to recognize all the
13 favors they received from you by having presents worthy of you
14 offered you; but since the war which we have had for several
15 years, in which all of Europe had banded together against us, pre-
16 vented our vessels from going to the Indies, at the present time,
17 when we are at peace after having gained many victories and ex-
18 panded our Realm through the conquest of several important
19 places, we have immediately given orders to the Royal Company
20 to establish itself in your kingdom as soon as possible, and have
21 commanded Messrs. Deydier and de Bourges to remain with you
22 in order to maintain a good relationship between our subjects and
23 yours, also to warn us on occasions that might present themselves
24 when we might be able to give you proofs of our esteem and of
25 our wish to concur with your satisfaction as well as with your best
26 interests.
27   By way of initial proof, we have given orders to have brought
28 to you some presents which we believe might be agreeable to you.
29 But the one thing in the world which we desire most, both for you
30 and for your Realm, would be to obtain for your subjects who have
31 already embraced the law of the only true God of heaven and earth,
32 the freedom to profess it, since this law is the highest, the noblest,
33 the most sacred, and especially the most suitable to have kings reign
34 absolutely over the people.
35   We are even quite convinced that, if you knew the truths and
36 the maxims which it teaches, you would give first of all to your sub-
37 jects the glorious example of embracing it. We wish you this

38 incomparable blessing together with a long and happy reign, and we
39 pray God that it may please Him to augment your greatness with
40 the happiest of endings.
41   Written at Saint-Germain-en-Laye, the 10th day of
42 January, 1681,
43
44   Your very dear and good friend,
                                                Louis

Answer from the King of Tonkin to Louis XIV

45 The King of Tonkin sends to the King of France a letter to express
46 to him his best sentiments, saying that he was happy to learn that
47 fidelity is a durable good of man and that justice is the most im-
48 portant of things. Consequently practicing of fidelity and justice
49 cannot but yield good results. Indeed, though France and our
50 Kingdom differ as to mountains, rivers, and boundaries, if fidelity
51 and justice reign among our villages, our conduct will express all
52 of our good feelings and contain precious gifts. Your communica-
53 tion, which comes from a country which is a thousand leagues
54 away, and which proceeds from the heart as a testimony of your
55 sincerity, merits repeated consideration and infinite praise. Polite-
56 ness toward strangers is nothing unusual in our country. There is
57 not a stranger who is not well received by us. How then could we
58 refuse a man from France, which is the most celebrated among
59 the kingdoms of the world and which for love of us wishes to fre-
60 quent us and bring us merchandise? These feelings of fidelity and
61 justice are truly worthy to be applauded. As regards your wish
62 that we should cooperate in propagating your religion, we do not
63 dare to permit it, for there is an ancient custom, introduced by
64 edicts, which formally forbids it. Now, edicts are promulgated
65 only to be carried out faithfully; without fidelity nothing is stable.
66 How could we disdain a well-established custom to satisfy a pri-
67 vate friendship? . . .
68   We beg you to understand well that this is our communication
69 concerning our mutual acquaintance. This then is my letter. We
70 send you herewith a modest gift, which we offer you with a glad
71 heart.
72   This letter was written at the beginning of winter and on a
73 beautiful day.

people to do what he wanted rather than order them to do so? Who might the people that he had to persuade have been?

3. Note that Louis uses what is known as the "royal 'we'" and refers to himself in the third person singular. When does the king of Tonkin refer to himself in the first person ("I"), and when does he refer to himself in the third person ("we")?

4. Why does Louis say that he is writing at this time, rather than earlier (lines 13–18)?

5. Why does Louis say that Christian missionaries will be good for Tonkin and its people (lines 28–33)? What reason in Louis's own letter makes you wonder if converting the people of Tonkin to Christianity is "the one thing in the world which we desire most"?

6. Does the king of Tonkin seem pleased to hear from Louis and by his request (lines 45–55)? How does he refer to the gift Louis offers him?

7. Louis mentions his gratitude for the good treatment of some French subjects when they were "in your realm." What do you think the French were actually doing in Tonkin? Do you think they were invited, or did they arrive on their own? How does the king of Tonkin respond to Louis's expression of appreciation for the "protection" the French were accorded (lines 55–60)? And protection from what?

8. What reason does the king of Tonkin give for refusing Louis's offer of Christian missionaries (lines 61–67)? He takes care to explain to Louis that "edicts are promulgated . . . nothing is stable." What does this suggest about the king of Tonkin's attitude toward Louis and the "incomparable blessing" of faith in the Christian God? How many French people (or Europeans, for that matter) is the king of Tonkin likely to have met? What French person or persons might have already given the king ideas about Louis and his offer?

9. Compare the final lines of the two letters. What significance do you draw from the fact that Louis names the day, month, and year, and the location in which he writes? Apart from later historians, who in particular is most likely to have been interested in having this information? What is the significance of the king of Tonkin's closing lines?

If you can propose thoughtful answers to these questions, you will have understood the material very well and will be ready for whatever examinations and papers await you in your course.

HISTORIANS OFTEN REFER to the period from the sixteenth through eighteenth centuries as the early modern era. During these years, several factors were at work that created the conditions of our own time.

From a global perspective, perhaps the most noteworthy event of the period was the extension of the maritime trade network throughout the entire populated world. The Chinese had inaugurated the process with their groundbreaking voyages to East Africa in the early fifteenth century. Muslim traders had contributed their part by extending their mercantile network as far as China and the Spice Islands in Southeast Asia. The final instrument of that expansion was a resurgent Europe, which exploded onto the world scene with the initial explorations of the Portuguese and the Spanish at the end of the fifteenth century and then gradually came to dominate shipping on international trade routes during the next three centuries.

Some contemporary historians argue that it was this sudden burst of energy from Europe that created the first truly global economic network. According to Immanuel Wallerstein, one of the leading proponents of this theory, the Age of Exploration led to the creation of a new "world system" characterized by the emergence of global trade networks dominated by the rising force of European capitalism, which now began to scour the periphery of the system for access to markets and cheap raw materials.

Other historians, however, qualify Wallerstein's view and point to the Mongol expansion beginning in the thirteenth century or even to the rise of the Arab Empire in the Middle East a few centuries earlier as signs of the creation of a global communications network enabling goods and ideas to travel from one end of the Eurasian supercontinent to the other.

Whatever the truth of this debate, there are still many reasons for considering the end of the fifteenth century as a crucial date in world history. In the most basic sense, it marked the end of the long isolation of the Western Hemisphere from the rest of the inhabited world. In so doing, it led to the creation of the first truly global network of ideas and commodities, which would introduce plants, ideas, and (unfortunately) many new diseases to all humanity (see the comparative essay in Chapter 14). Second, the period gave birth to a stunning increase in trade and manufacturing that stimulated major economic changes not only in Europe but in other parts of the world as well.

The period from 1500 to 1800, then, was an incubation period for the modern world and the launching pad for an era of European domination that would reach fruition in the nineteenth century. To understand why the West emerged as the leading force in the world at that time, it is necessary to grasp what factors were at work in Europe and why they were absent in other major civilizations around the globe.

Historians have identified improvements in navigation, shipbuilding, and weaponry that took place in Europe in the early modern era as essential elements in the Age of Exploration. As we have seen, many of these technological advances were based on earlier discoveries that had taken place elsewhere—in China, India, and the Middle East—and had

© The Art Archive

then been brought to Europe on Muslim ships or along the trade routes through Central Asia. But it was the capacity and the desire of the Europeans to enhance their wealth and power by making practical use of the discoveries of others that was the significant factor in the equation and enabled them to dominate international sea-lanes and create vast colonial empires in the Western Hemisphere.

European expansion was not fueled solely by economic considerations, however. As had been the case with the rise of Islam, religion played a major role in motivating the European Age of Exploration in the early modern era. Although Christianity was by no means a new religion in the sixteenth century (as Islam had been at the moment of Arab expansion), the world of Christendom was in the midst of a major period of conflict with the forces of Islam, a rivalry that had been exacerbated by the conquest of the Byzantine Empire by the Ottoman Turks in 1453.

Although the claims of Portuguese and Spanish adventurers that their activities were motivated primarily by a desire to bring the word of God to non-Christian peoples undoubtedly included a considerable measure of hypocrisy, there is no doubt that religious motives played a major part in the European Age of Exploration. Religious motives were less evident in the activities of the non-Catholic powers that entered the competition in the seventeenth century. English and Dutch merchants and officials were more inclined to be motivated purely by the pursuit of economic profit.

Conditions in many areas of Asia were less conducive to these economic and political developments. In China, a centralized monarchy continued to rely on a prosperous agricultural sector as the economic foundation of the empire. In Japan, power was centralized under the powerful Tokugawa shogunate, and the era of peace and stability that ensued saw an increase in manufacturing and commercial activity. But Japanese elites, after initially expressing interest in the outside world, abruptly shut the door on European trade and ideas in an effort to protect the "land of the gods" from external contamination.

In India and the Middle East, commerce and manufacturing had played a vital role in the life of societies since the emergence of the Indian Ocean trade network in the first centuries C.E. But beginning in the eleventh century, the area had suffered through an extended period of political instability, marked by invasions by nomadic peoples from Central Asia. The violence of the period and the local rulers' lack of experience in promoting maritime commerce had a severe depressing effect on urban manufacturing and commerce.

In the early modern era, then, Europe was best placed to take advantage of the technological innovations that had become increasingly available. It possessed the political stability, the capital, and the "modernizing elite" that spurred efforts to wrest the greatest benefit from the new conditions. Whereas other regions were beset by internal obstacles or had deliberately turned inward to seek their destiny, Europe now turned outward to seek a new and dominant position in the world. Nevertheless, significant changes were taking place in other parts of the world as well, and many of these changes had relatively little to do with the situation in the West. As we shall see, the impact of European expansion on the rest of the world was still limited at the end of the eighteenth century. While European political authority was firmly established in a few key areas, such as the Spice Islands and Latin America, traditional societies remained relatively intact in most regions of Africa and Asia. And processes at work in these societies were often operating independently of events in Europe and would later give birth to forces that acted to restrict or shape the Western impact. One of these forces was the progressive emergence of centralized states, some of them built on the concept of ethnic unity. ✿

CHAPTER 14

NEW ENCOUNTERS: THE CREATION OF A WORLD MARKET

The port of Calicut in the mid-1500s

WHEN, IN THE SPRING OF 1498, the Portuguese fleet arrived at the town of Calicut (now known as Kozhikode), on the western coast of India, fleet commander Vasco da Gama ordered a landing party to go ashore to contact the local authorities. The first to greet them, a Muslim merchant from Tunisia, said, "May the Devil take thee! What brought thee hither?" "Christians and spices," replied the visitors. "A lucky venture, a lucky venture," replied the Muslim. "Plenty of rubies, plenty of emeralds! You owe great thanks to God, for having brought you to a country holding such riches!"[1]

Such words undoubtedly delighted the Portuguese, who sent a landing party ashore and concluded that the local population appeared to be Christians. Although it later turned out that they were mistaken—the local faith was a form of Hinduism—their spirits were probably not seriously dampened, for God was undoubtedly of less immediate importance than gold and glory to sailors who had gone through considerable hardship to become the first Europeans since the ancient Greeks to sail across the Indian Ocean. They left two months later with a cargo of spices and the determination to return soon with a second and larger fleet.

Vasco da Gama's maiden voyage to India inaugurated an extended period of European expansion into Asia, led by merchant adventurers and missionaries, that lasted several hundred years and had effects that are still felt today. Eventually, it resulted in a Western takeover of existing trade routes in the Indian Ocean and the establishment of colonies throughout Asia, Africa, and Latin America. In later years, Western historians would react to these events by describing the era as an "Age of Discovery" that significantly broadened the maritime trade network and set the stage for the emergence of the modern world.

In fact, however, the voyages of Vasco da Gama and his European successors were only the latest stage in a process that had begun generations earlier, at a time when European explorations were still restricted to the stormy waters of the North Atlantic Ocean. As we have seen in Chapter 10, Chinese fleets had roamed the Indian Ocean for several years during the early fifteenth century, linking the Middle Kingdom with societies as distant as the Middle East and the coast of East Africa. Although the voyages of Zhenghe were short in duration and had few lasting effects, the world of Islam was also on the march, as Muslim traders blazed new trails into Southeast Asia and across the Sahara to the civilizations that flourished along the banks of the Niger River. It was, after all, a Muslim from North Africa who had greeted the Portuguese when they first appeared off the coast of India. In this chapter, we turn our attention to the stunning expansion in the scope and volume of commercial and cultural contacts that took place in the generations preceding and following da Gama's historic voyage to India, as well as to the factors that brought about this expansion. ✿

An Age of Exploration and Expansion

Q Focus Question: How did Muslim merchants expand the world trade network at the end of the fifteenth century?

The voyage of Vasco da Gama has customarily been seen as a crucial step in the opening of trade routes to the East. In the sense that the voyage was a harbinger of future European participation in the spice trade, this view undoubtedly has merit. In fact, however, as has been pointed out in earlier chapters, the Indian Ocean had been a busy thoroughfare for centuries. The spice trade had been carried on by sea in the region since the days of the legendary Queen of Sheba, and Chinese junks had sailed to the area in search of cloves and nutmeg since the Tang dynasty (see Chapter 10).

Islam and the Spice Trade

By the fourteenth century, a growing percentage of the spice trade was being transported in Muslim ships sailing from ports in India or the Middle East. Muslims, either Arabs or Indian converts, had taken part in the Indian Ocean trade for centuries, and by the thirteenth century, Islam had established a presence in seaports on the islands of Sumatra and Java and was gradually moving inland. In 1292, the Venetian traveler Marco Polo observed that Muslims were engaging in missionary activity in northern Sumatra: "This kingdom is so much frequented by the Saracen merchants that they have converted the natives to the Law of Mahomet—I mean the townspeople only, for the hill people live for all the world like beasts, and eat human flesh, as well as other kinds of flesh, clean or unclean."[2]

But the major impetus for the spread of Islam in Southeast Asia came in the early fifteenth century, with the foundation of a new sultanate at Malacca, on the strait that today bears the same name. The founder was Paramesvara, a vassal of the Hindu state of Majapahit on Java, whose original base of operations had been at Palembang, on the island of Sumatra. In 1390, he had moved his base to Tumasik (modern Singapore), at the tip of the Malay peninsula, hoping to enhance his ability to play a role in the commerce passing through the region. Under pressure from the expanding power of the Thai state of Ayuthaya (see "Southeast Asia in the Era of the Spice Trade" later in this chapter), in the early fifteenth century Paramesvara moved once again to Malacca. The latter's potential strategic importance was confirmed in the sixteenth century by a visitor from Portugal, who noted that Malacca "is a city that was made for commerce; . . . the trade and commerce between the different nations for a thousand leagues on every hand must come to Malacca."[3]

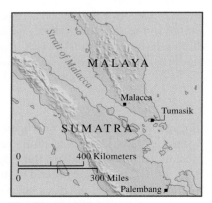

The Strait of Malacca

Shortly after its founding, Malacca was visited by a Chinese fleet under the command of Admiral Zhenghe (see Chapter 10). In order to protect his patrimony from local rivals, Paramesvara accepted Chinese vassalage and cemented the new relationship by making an official visit to the Ming emperor in Beijing (see the box on p. 336). More importantly, perhaps, he also converted to Islam. The move was undoubtedly undertaken with a view to enhancing Malacca's ability to participate in the trade that passed through the strait, much of which was dominated by Muslim merchants. Within a few years, Malacca had become the leading economic power in the region and helped to promote the spread of Islam to trading ports

A CHINESE DESCRIPTION OF MALACCA

 Malacca, located on the west coast of the Malay peninsula, first emerged as a major trading port in the early fifteenth century, when its sultan, Paramesvara, avoided Thai rule with the aid of the emperor of China. This description of the area was written by a naval officer who served in one of the famous Chinese fleets that visited the city in the early fifteenth century.

Ma Huan, *Description of a Starry Raft*

This place did not formerly rank as a kingdom. It can be reached from Palembang on the monsoon in eight days. The coast is rocky and desolate, the population sparse. The country (used to) pay an annual tax of 40 taels of gold to Siam. The soil is infertile and yields low. In the interior there is a mountain from (the slopes of) which a river takes its rise. The (local) folk pan the sands (of this river) to obtain tin, which they melt into ingots called *tou*. These weigh 1 kati 4 taels standard weight. (The inhabitants) also weave banana fiber into mats. Apart from tin, no other product enters into (foreign) trade. The climate is hot during the day but cool at night. (Both) sexes coil their hair into a knot. Their skin resembles black lacquer, but there are (some) white-complexioned folk among them

who are of Chinese descent. The people esteem sincerity and honesty. They make a living by panning tin and catching fish. Their houses are raised above the ground. (When constructing them) they refrain from joining planks and restrict the building to the length of a (single) piece of timber. When they wish to retire, they spread their bedding side by side. They squat on their haunches when taking their meals. The kitchen and all its appurtenances is (also) raised (on the stilts). The goods (used in trading at Malacca) are blue and white porcelain, colored beads, colored taffetas, gold and silver. In the seventh year of Yung-lo (1409), the imperial envoy, the eunuch Cheng-Ho, and his lieutenants conferred (on the ruler), by Imperial command, a pair of silver seals, and a headdress, girdle and robe. They also set up a tablet (stating that) Malacca had been raised to the rank of a kingdom, but at first Siam refused to recognize it. In the thirteenth year (of Yung-lo) (1415), the ruler (of Malacca, desirous of) showing his gratitude for the Imperial bounty, crossed the ocean and, accompanied by his consort and son, came to court with tribute. The Emperor rewarded him (appropriately), whereupon (the ruler of Malacca) returned to his (own) country.

Q *Why was Malacca such an important center of world trade?*

---

throughout the islands of Southeast Asia, including Java, Borneo, Sulawesi, and the Philippines. Adoption of the Muslim faith was eased by the popularity of Sufism, a form of Islam that expressed a marked tolerance for mysticism and local religious beliefs.

The Spread of Islam in West Africa

In the meantime, Muslim trade and religious influence continued to expand south of the Sahara into the Niger River valley in West Africa. The area had been penetrated by traders from across the Sahara since ancient times, and contacts undoubtedly increased after the establishment of Muslim control over the Mediterranean coastal regions. Muslim traders crossed the desert carrying Islamic values, political culture, and legal traditions along with their goods. The early stage of state formation had culminated with the kingdom of Mali, symbolized by the renowned Mansa Musa, whose pilgrimage to Mecca in the fourteenth century had left an indelible impression on observers (see Chapter 8).

The Kingdom of Songhai   With the decline of Mali in the late fifteenth century, a new power eventually appeared with the creation of the kingdom of Songhai. The founder of Songhai was Sonni Ali, a local chieftain who

seized Timbuktu from its Berber overlords in 1468 and then sought to restore the formidable empire of his predecessors. Rumored to possess magical powers, Sonni Ali was criticized by Muslim scholars for supporting traditional religious practices, but under his rule, Songhai emerged as a major trading state in the region (see Map 14.1). When he died in 1492, his son ascended to the throne, but was deposed shortly thereafter by one of his military commanders, who seized power as king under the name Askia Mohammed (r. 1493–1528).

Under the new ruler, a fervent Muslim, Songhai increasingly relied on Islamic institutions and ideology to strengthen national unity and centralize authority. Askia Mohammed himself embarked on a pilgrimage to Mecca and was recognized by the caliph of Cairo as the Muslim ruler of the Niger River valley. On his return from Mecca, he tried to revive Timbuktu as a major center of Islamic learning, but had less success in converting his subjects, many of whom—especially in rural regions—continued to resist conversion to Islam. He did preside over a significant increase in trans-Saharan trade (notably in salt and gold), which provided a steady source of income to Songhai and other kingdoms in the region. Despite the efforts of Askia Mohammed and his successors, however, centrifugal forces within Songhai eventually led to its breakup after his death.

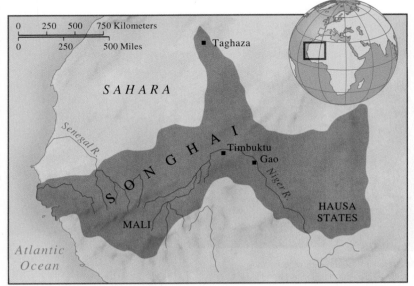

MAP 14.1 **The Songhai Empire.** Songhai was the last of the great states to dominate the region of the Niger River valley prior to the European takeover in the nineteenth century.

Q What were the predecessors of the Songhai Empire in the region? What explains the importance of the area in African history?

A New Player: Europe

For almost a millennium, Catholic Europe had been confined to one area. Its one major attempt to expand beyond those frontiers, the Crusades, had largely failed. Of course, Europe had never completely lost contact with the outside world: the goods of Asia and Africa made their way into medieval castles, the works of Muslim philosophers were read in medieval universities, and the Vikings in the ninth and tenth centuries had even explored the eastern fringes of North America. Nevertheless, Europe's contacts with non-European civilizations remained limited until the fifteenth century, when Europeans began to embark on a remarkable series of overseas journeys. What caused European seafarers to undertake such dangerous voyages to the ends of the earth?

Europeans had long been attracted to the East. In the Middle Ages, myths and legends of an exotic land of great riches and magic were widespread. The most famous medieval travelers to the East were the Polos of Venice. In 1271, Nicolò and Maffeo, merchants from Venice, accompanied by Nicolò's son Marco, undertook the lengthy journey to the court of the great Mongol ruler Khubilai Khan (see Chapter 10). As one of the Great Khan's ambassadors, Marco traveled to Japan as well and did not return to Italy until 1295. An account of his experiences, the *Travels,* proved to be the most informative of all the descriptions of Asia by medieval European travelers. Others, like the Franciscan friar John Plano Carpini, had

preceded the Polos, but in the fourteenth century, the conquests of the Ottoman Turks and then the breakup of the Mongol Empire reduced Western traffic to the East. With the closing of the overland routes, a number of people in Europe became interested in the possibility of reaching Asia by sea.

The Motives An economic motive thus looms large in Renaissance European expansion (see Chapter 13). The rise of capitalism in Europe was undoubtedly a powerful spur to the process. Merchants, adventurers, and government officials had high hopes of finding precious metals and expanding the areas of trade, especially for the spices of the East. Spices continued to be transported to Europe via Arab intermediaries but were outrageously expensive. Adventurous Europeans did not hesitate to express their desire to share in the wealth. As one Spanish conquistador explained, he and his kind went to the Americas to "serve God and His Majesty, to give light to those who were in darkness, and to grow rich, as all men desire to do."[4]

This statement expresses another major reason for the overseas voyages—religious zeal. A crusading mentality was particularly strong in Portugal and Spain, where the Muslims had largely been driven out in the Middle Ages. Contemporaries of Prince Henry the Navigator of Portugal, an outspoken advocate of European expansion, said that he was motivated by "his great desire to make increase in the faith of our Lord Jesus Christ and to bring him all the souls that should be saved." Although most scholars believe that the religious motive was secondary to economic considerations, it would be foolish to overlook the genuine desire on the part of both explorers and conquistadors, let alone missionaries, to convert the heathen to Christianity. Hernán Cortés, the conqueror of Mexico, asked his Spanish rulers if it was not their duty to ensure that the native Mexicans were "introduced into and instructed in the holy Catholic faith."[5]

The Means If "God, glory, and gold" were the primary motives, what made the voyages possible? First of all, the expansion of Europe was a state enterprise, tied to the growth of centralized monarchies during the Renaissance. By the second half of the fifteenth century, European monarchies had increased both their authority and their resources and were in a position to turn their energies beyond their borders. That meant the invasion of Italy for France, but for Portugal, a state not strong enough to

European Warships During the Age of Exploration. Prior to the fifteenth century, most European ships were either small craft with triangular, lateen sails used in the Mediterranean or slow, unwieldy square-rigged vessels operating in the North Atlantic. By the sixteenth century, European naval architects began to build caravels (left), ships that combined the maneuverability and speed offered by lateen sails (widely used by sailors in the Indian Ocean—see the inset) with the carrying capacity and seaworthiness of the square-riggers. For a century, caravels were the feared "raiders of the oceans." Eventually, as naval technology progressed, European warships developed in size and firepower, as the illustration of Portuguese carracks on the right shows.

pursue power in Europe, it meant going abroad. The Spanish scene was more complex, since the Spanish monarchy was strong enough by the sixteenth century to pursue power both on the Continent and beyond.

At the same time, by the end of the fifteenth century, European states had a level of knowledge and technology that enabled them to achieve a regular series of voyages beyond Europe. Although the highly schematic and symbolic medieval maps were of little help to sailors, the *portolani,* or detailed charts made by medieval navigators and mathematicians in the thirteenth and fourteenth centuries, were more useful. With details on coastal contours, distances between ports, and compass readings, they proved of great value for voyages in European waters. But because the *portolani* were drawn on a flat surface and took no account of the curvature of the earth, they were of little use for longer overseas voyages. Only when seafarers began to venture beyond the coasts of Europe did they begin to accumulate information about the actual shape of the earth. By the end of the fifteenth century, cartography had developed to the point that Europeans possessed fairly accurate maps of the known world.

In addition, Europeans had developed remarkably seaworthy ships as well as new navigational techniques. European shipbuilders had mastered the use of the sternpost rudder (an import from China) and had learned how to combine the use of lateen sails with a square rig. With these innovations, they could construct ships mobile enough to sail against the wind and engage in naval warfare and also large enough to mount heavy cannons and carry a substantial amount of goods over long distances. Previously, sailors had used a quadrant and their knowledge of the position of the polestar to ascertain their latitude. Below the equator, however, this technique was useless. Only with the assistance of new navigational aids such as the compass (a Chinese invention) and the astrolabe (an astronomical instrument, reportedly devised by Arab sailors, that was used to measure the altitude of the sun and the stars above the horizon) were they able to explore the high seas with confidence.

The Portuguese Maritime Empire

Q Focus Question: Why where the Portuguese so successful in taking over the spice trade?

Portugal took the lead in exploration when it began exploring the coast of Africa under the sponsorship of Prince Henry the Navigator (1394–1460). Prince Henry's motives were a blend of seeking a Christian kingdom as an ally against the Muslims and acquiring new trade opportunities for Portugal. In 1419, he founded a school

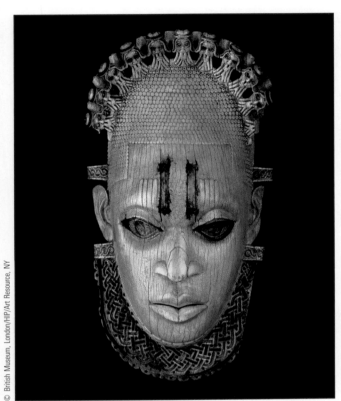

An Ivory Mask from Benin. By the end of the fifteenth century, the West African state of Benin had developed into an extensive and powerful empire enjoying trade with many of its neighbors, as well as with the state of Portugal. With the latter it traded ivory, forest products, and slaves in exchange for textiles and other European manufactured goods. This life-size ivory mask was probably intended to be worn by the king of Benin as a belt ornament in a gesture of gratitude to his mother, who had allegedly used her magical powers to help defeat his enemies. On the crest of the crown are carvings of Portuguese figures, providing one of the first examples in African art of the new trade relationship between that continent and Europe.

for navigators on the southwestern coast of Portugal. Shortly thereafter, Portuguese fleets began probing southward along the western coast of Africa in search of gold. In 1441, Portuguese ships reached the Senegal River, just north of Cape Verde, and brought home a cargo of black Africans, most of whom were sold as slaves to wealthy buyers elsewhere in Europe. Within a few years, an estimated thousand slaves were shipped annually from the area back to Lisbon.

Continuing southward, in 1471 the Portuguese discovered a new source of gold along the southern coast of the hump of West Africa (an area that would henceforth be known to Europeans as the Gold Coast). To facilitate trade in gold, ivory, and slaves (some slaves were brought back to Lisbon and others were bartered to local merchants for gold), the Portuguese leased land from local rulers and built stone forts along the coast.

The Portuguese in India

Hearing reports of a route to India around the southern tip of Africa, Portuguese sea captains continued their probing (see Map 14.2). In 1487, Bartolomeu Dias took advantage of westerly winds in the South Atlantic to round the Cape of Good Hope, but he feared a mutiny from his crew and returned home without continuing onward. Ten years later, a fleet under the command of Vasco da Gama rounded the cape and stopped at several ports controlled by Muslim merchants along the coast of East Africa, including Sofala, Kilwa, and Mombasa. Then da Gama's fleet crossed the Arabian Sea and arrived off the port of Calicut on the southwestern coast of India, on May 18, 1498. The Portuguese crown had sponsored da Gama's voyage with the clear objective of destroying the Muslim monopoly over the spice trade, a monopoly that had been intensified by the Ottoman conquest of Constantinople in 1453 (see Chapter 13). Calicut was a major entrepôt on the long route from the Spice Islands to the Mediterranean Sea, but the ill-informed Europeans believed it was the source of the spices themselves. Although he lost two ships en route, da Gama's remaining vessels returned to Europe with their holds filled with ginger and cinnamon, a cargo that earned the investors a profit of several thousand percent.

The Search for Spices

During the next years, the Portuguese set out to gain control of the spice trade. In 1510, Admiral Afonso de Albuquerque established his headquarters at Goa, on the western coast of India south of present-day Mumbai. From there, the Portuguese raided Arab shippers, provoking the following comment from an Arab source: "[The Portuguese] took about seven vessels, killing those on board and making some prisoner. This was their first action, may God curse them."[6] In 1511, Albuquerque attacked Malacca itself.

For Albuquerque, control of Malacca would serve two purposes. It could help to destroy the Arab spice trade network by blocking passage through the Strait of Malacca, and it could also provide the Portuguese with a way station en route to the Spice Islands and other points east. After a short but bloody battle, the Portuguese seized the city

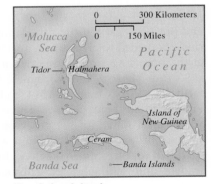

The Spice Islands

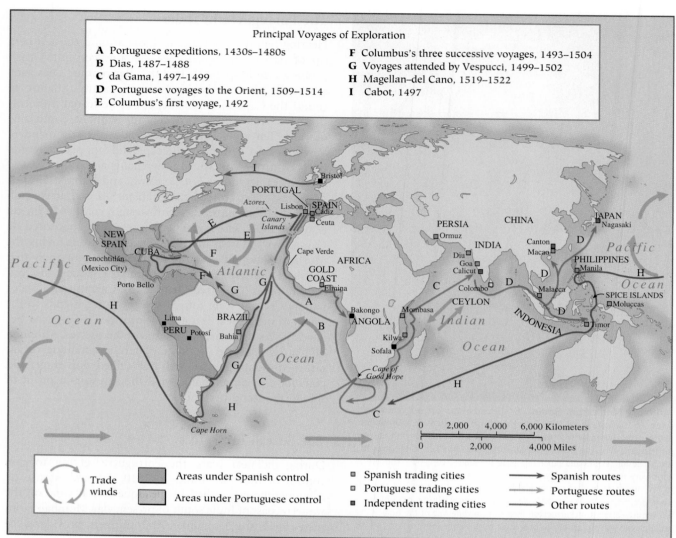

Principal Voyages of Exploration

A Portuguese expeditions, 1430s–1480s
B Dias, 1487–1488
C da Gama, 1497–1499
D Portuguese voyages to the Orient, 1509–1514
E Columbus's first voyage, 1492

F Columbus's three successive voyages, 1493–1504
G Voyages attended by Vespucci, 1499–1502
H Magellan–del Cano, 1519–1522
I Cabot, 1497

Trade winds	Areas under Spanish control	Spanish trading cities	Spanish routes
	Areas under Portuguese control	Portuguese trading cities	Portuguese routes
		Independent trading cities	Other routes

MAP 14.2 European Voyages and Possessions in the Sixteenth and Seventeenth Centuries. This map indicates the most important voyages launched by Europeans during their momentous Age of Exploration in the sixteenth and seventeenth centuries.
Q Why did Vasco da Gama sail so far into the South Atlantic on his voyage to Asia?
View an animated version of this map or related maps at www.cengage.com/history/duikspiel/essentialworld6e

and put the local Muslim population to the sword. They then proceeded to erect a fort, a factory (a common term at the time for a warehouse), and a church.

From Malacca, the Portuguese launched expeditions farther east, to China in 1514 and the Moluccas, then known as the Spice Islands. There they signed a treaty with a local sultan for the purchase and export of cloves to the European market. Within a few years, they had managed to seize control of the spice trade from Muslim traders and had garnered substantial profits for the Portuguese monarchy.

Why were the Portuguese so successful? Basically, their success was a matter of guns and seamanship. The first Portuguese fleet to arrive in Indian waters was relatively modest in size. It consisted of three ships and twenty guns, a force sufficient for self-defense and intimidation but not for serious military operations. Sixteenth-century Portuguese fleets were more heavily armed and were capable of inflicting severe defeats if necessary on local naval and land forces. The Portuguese by no means possessed a monopoly on the use of firearms and explosives, but they used the maneuverability of their light ships to maintain their distance while bombarding the enemy with their powerful cannons. Such tactics gave them a military superiority over lightly armed rivals that they were able to exploit until the arrival of other European forces several decades later.

Spanish Conquests in the "New World"

Q Focus Question: How did Portugal and Spain acquire their overseas empires, and how did their methods differ?

While the Portuguese were seeking access to the spice trade of the Indies by sailing eastward through the Indian Ocean, the Spanish attempted to reach the same destination by sailing westward across the Atlantic. Although the Spanish came to overseas discovery and exploration later than the Portuguese, their greater resources enabled them to establish a far grander overseas empire.

The Voyages

An important figure in the history of Spanish exploration was an Italian from Genoa, Christopher Columbus (1451–1506). Knowledgeable Europeans were aware that the world was round but had little understanding of its size or the extent of the continent of Asia. Convinced that the circumference of the earth was smaller than contemporaries believed and that Asia was larger, Columbus felt that Asia could be reached by sailing due west instead of eastward around Africa. After being rejected by the Portuguese, he persuaded Queen Isabella of Spain to finance his exploratory expedition, which reached the Americas in October 1492 and explored the coastline of Cuba and the northern shores of the neighboring island of Hispaniola. Columbus believed that he had reached Asia and in three subsequent voyages (1493, 1498, and 1502) sought in vain to find a route through the outer islands to the Asian mainland. In his four voyages, Columbus reached all the major islands of the Caribbean, which he called the Indies, as well as Honduras in Central America.

Although Columbus clung to his belief until his death, other navigators soon realized that he had discovered a new frontier altogether. State-sponsored explorers joined the race to what Europeans began to call the "New World." A Venetian seafarer, John Cabot, explored the New England coastline of the Americas under a license from King Henry VII of England. The continent of South America was discovered accidentally by the Portuguese sea captain Pedro Cabral in 1500. Amerigo Vespucci, a Florentine, accompanied several voyages and wrote a series of letters describing the geography of the New World. The publication of these letters led to the use of the name "America" (after Amerigo) for the new lands.

The Conquests

The newly discovered territories were referred to as the New World, even though they possessed flourishing civilizations populated by millions of people when the Europeans arrived. But the Americas were new to the Europeans, who quickly saw opportunities for conquest and exploitation. The Spanish, in particular, were interested because in 1494 the Treaty of Tordesillas had divided the newly discovered world into separate Portuguese and Spanish spheres of influence. Thereafter the route east around the Cape of Good Hope was to be reserved for the Portuguese, while the route across the Atlantic (except for the eastern hump of South America) was assigned to Spain. The Spanish conquistadors, as they were called, were a hardy lot of mostly upper-class individuals motivated by a typical sixteenth-century blend of glory, greed, and religious crusading zeal. Although sanctioned by the Castilian crown, these groups were financed and outfitted privately, not by the government.

Their superior weapons, organizational skills, and determination brought the conquistadors incredible success. Beginning in 1519 with a small band of men, Hernán Cortés took three years to overthrow the mighty Aztec Empire in central Mexico, led by the chieftain Moctezuma (see Chapter 6). By 1550, the Spanish had gained control of northern Mexico. Between 1531 and 1536, another expedition led by a hardened and somewhat corrupt soldier, Francisco Pizarro (1470–1541), destroyed the Inka Empire high in the Peruvian Andes. The Spanish conquests were undoubtedly facilitated by the previous arrival of European diseases, which had decimated the local population. Although it took another three decades before the western part of Latin America was brought under Spanish control (the Portuguese took over Brazil), already by 1535, the Spanish had created a system of colonial

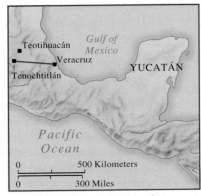

The Arrival of Hernán Cortés in Mexico

© North Wind Picture Archives

© Bildarchiv Preussischer Kulturbesitz/Art Resource, NY

COMPARATIVE ILLUSTRATION

The Spaniards Conquer a New World. The perspective that the Spanish brought to their first arrival in the Americas was quite different from that of the indigenous peoples. In the European painting shown on the left, the encounter was a peaceful one, and the upturned eyes of Columbus and his fellow voyagers imply that their motives were spiritual rather than material. The image below, drawn by an Aztec artist, expresses a dramatically different point of view, as the Spanish invaders, assisted by their Indian allies, use superior weapons against the bows and arrows of their adversaries to bring about the conquest of Mexico.

Q What does the Aztec painting show the viewer about the nature of the conflict between the two contending armies?

administration that made the New World an extension of the old—at least in European eyes.

Governing the Empire

Spanish policy toward the inhabitants of the Americas, whom the Europeans called Indians, was a combination of confusion, misguided paternalism, and cruel exploitation (see the comparative illustration above). Confusion arose over the nature of the Indians. Queen Isabella declared the Indians to be subjects of Castile and instituted the *encomienda* **system,** which permitted the conquering Spaniards to collect tribute from the natives and use them as laborers. In return, the holders of an *encomienda* were

supposed to protect the Indians and supervise their spiritual and material needs. In practice, this meant that the settlers were free to implement the system as they pleased. Three thousand miles from Spain, Spanish settlers largely ignored their government and brutally used the Indians to pursue their own economic interests. Indians were put to work on sugar plantations and in the lucrative gold and silver mines. Forced labor, starvation, and especially disease took a fearful toll on Indian lives. With little or no natural resistance to European diseases, the Indians of America were ravaged by smallpox, measles, and typhus brought by the explorers and the conquistadors. Although scholarly estimates of native populations vary drastically, a reasonable guess is that at least half of the natives died of European diseases. On Hispaniola alone, out of an initial population of 100,000 natives when Columbus arrived in 1493, only 300 Indians survived by 1570. In 1542, largely in response to the publications of Bartolomé de Las Casas, a Dominican monk who championed the Indians, the government abolished the *encomienda* system and provided more protection for the natives.

The chief organ of colonial administration was the Council of the Indies. The council nominated colonial viceroys, oversaw their activities, and kept an eye on ecclesiastical affairs in the colonies. Spanish possessions in the Americas were initially divided between New Spain (Mexico, Central America, and the Caribbean islands), with its center in Mexico City, and Peru (western South America), with its capital at Lima. Each area was governed

Christopher Columbus's first voyage to the Americas	1492
Last voyages of Columbus	1502–1504
Spanish conquest of Mexico	1519–1522
Francisco Pizarro's conquest of the Inkas	1531–1536

by a viceroy who served as the king's chief civil and military officer.

By papal agreement, the Catholic monarchs of Spain were given extensive rights over ecclesiastical affairs in the Americas. They could nominate church officials, build churches, collect fees, and supervise the various religious orders that conducted missionary activities. Catholic monks had remarkable success converting and baptizing hundreds of thousands of Indians in the early years of the conquest. Soon after the missionaries came the establishment of dioceses, parishes, schools, and hospitals—all the trappings of a European society.

The Impact of European Expansion

Q **Focus Question:** What were some of the consequences of the arrival of the European traders and missionaries for the peoples of Asia and the Americas?

The arrival of the Europeans had an enormous impact on both the conquerors and the conquered. The native American civilizations, which (as we discussed in Chapter 6) had their own unique qualities and a degree of sophistication rarely appreciated by the conquerors, were virtually destroyed, while the native populations were ravaged by diseases introduced by the Europeans. Ancient social and political structures were ripped up and replaced by European institutions, religion, language, and culture.

How does one evaluate the psychological impact of colonization on the colonizers? The relatively easy European success in dominating native peoples undoubtedly reinforced the Europeans' belief in the inherent superiority of their civilization. The Scientific Revolution of the seventeenth century, to be followed by the era of imperialism a century later, then served to strengthen the Eurocentric perspective that has long pervaded Western civilization in its relationship with the rest of the world.

European expansion also affected the conquerors in the economic arena. Wherever they went in the Americas, Europeans sought gold and silver. One Aztec observer commented that the Spanish conquerors "longed and lusted for gold. Their bodies swelled with greed, and their hunger was ravenous; they hungered like pigs for that gold."[7] Rich silver deposits were found and exploited in Mexico and southern Peru (modern Bolivia). When the mines at Potosí in Peru were opened in 1545, the value of precious metals imported into Europe quadrupled. It has been estimated that between 1503 and 1650, some 16 million kilograms of silver and 185,000 kilograms of gold entered the port of Seville, fueling a price revolution that affected the Spanish economy.

But gold and silver were only two of the products sent to Europe from the Western Hemisphere. Into Seville flowed sugar, dyes, cotton, vanilla, and hides from livestock raised on the South American pampas. New agricultural products native to the Americas, such as potatoes, cacao, corn, manioc, and tobacco, were also imported (see the comparative essay "The Columbian Exchange" on p. 344). Because of its trading posts in Asia, Portugal soon challenged the Italian states as the chief entry point of the eastern trade in spices, jewels, silk, carpets, ivory, leather, and perfumes. Economic historians believe that the increase in the volume and area of European trade and the rise in fluid capital due to this expansion were crucial factors in producing a new era of commercial capitalism that represented the first step toward the world economy that has characterized the modern era.

New Rivals

Portugal's efforts to dominate the trade of the Indian Ocean were never totally successful. The Portuguese lacked both the numbers and the wealth to overcome local resistance and colonize the Asian regions. Moreover, their massive investments in ships and laborers for their empire (hundreds of ships and hundreds of thousands of workers in shipyards and overseas bases) proved very costly. Disease, shipwreck, and battles took a heavy toll of life. The empire was simply too large and Portugal too small to maintain it, and by the end of the sixteenth century, the Portuguese were being severely challenged by rivals.

Europeans in Asia The Spanish had established themselves in Asia in the early 1520s, when Ferdinand Magellan, seeking a western route to the Spice Islands across the Pacific Ocean, had sailed around the

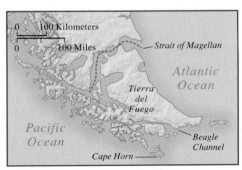
Cape Horn and the Strait of Magellan

COMPARATIVE ESSAY
THE COLUMBIAN EXCHANGE

In the Western world, the discovery of the Americas has traditionally been viewed essentially in a positive sense, as the first step in a process that expanded the global trade network and eventually led to economic well-being and the spread of civilization throughout the world. In recent years, however, that view has come under sharp attack from some observers, who claim that for the peoples of the Americas, the primary legacy of the European conquest was not improved living standards but harsh colonial exploitation and the spread of pestilential diseases that decimated the local population. The brunt of such criticism has been directed at Christopher Columbus, one of the chief initiators of the discovery and conquest of the Americas. Taking issue with the prevailing image of Columbus as a heroic figure in world history, critics view him as a symbol of Spanish colonial repression and a prime mover in the virtual extinction of the peoples and cultures of the Americas.

There is no doubt that the record of the European conquistadors in the Western Hemisphere leaves much to be desired, and certainly the voyages of Columbus were not of universal benefit to his contemporaries or to the generations later to come. They not only resulted in the destruction of vibrant civilizations that were evolving in the Americas but also led ultimately to the enslavement of millions of Africans, who were separated from their families and shipped to a new world in conditions of inhuman bestiality.

But to focus solely on the evils that were committed in the name of civilization misses a larger point and distorts the historical realities of the era.

The age of European expansion that began with Prince Henry the Navigator and Christopher Columbus was only the latest in a series of population movements that included the spread of nomadic peoples across Central Asia and the expansion of Islam from the Middle East after the death of the prophet Muhammad. In fact, the migration of peoples in search of survival and a better livelihood has been a central theme in the evolution of the human race since the dawn of prehistory. Virtually all of these migrations involved acts of unimaginable cruelty and the forcible displacement of peoples and societies.

Even more important, it seems clear that the consequences of such population movements are too complex to be summed up in moral or ideological simplifications. The European expansion into the Americas, for example, not only brought the destruction of cultures and the introduction of dangerous new diseases but also initiated exchanges of plant and animal species that have ultimately been of widespread benefit to peoples throughout the globe. The introduction of the horse, cow, and various grain crops vastly increased food productivity in the Western Hemisphere. The cultivation of corn, manioc, and the potato, all of them products of the Americas, have had the same effect in Asia, Africa, and Europe.

Christopher Columbus was a man of his time, with many of the character traits and prejudices common to his era. Whether he was hero or a villain is a matter of debate. That he and his contemporaries played a key role in the emergence of the modern world is a matter of which there can be no doubt.

Q *Why did the expansion of the global trade network into the Western Hemisphere have a greater impact than had previously occurred elsewhere in the world?*

Collections of the Library of Congress, USA

Massacre of the Indians. This sixteenth-century engraving is an imaginative treatment of what was probably an all-too-common occurrence as the Spanish attempted to enslave the American peoples and convert them to Christianity.

southern tip of South America, crossed the Pacific, and landed on the island of Cebu in the Philippine Islands. Although Magellan and some forty of his crew were killed in a skirmish with the local population, one of the two remaining ships sailed on to Tidor, in the Moluccas, and thence around the world via the Cape of Good Hope. In the words of a contemporary historian, they arrived in Cádiz "with precious cargo and fifteen men surviving out of a fleet of five sail."[8]

As it turned out, the Spanish could not follow up on Magellan's accomplishment, and in 1529, they sold their rights in Tidor to the Portuguese. But Magellan's voyage was not a total loss. In the absence of concerted resistance from the local population, the Spanish managed to consolidate their control over the Philippines, which eventually became a major Spanish base in the carrying trade across the Pacific.

The primary threat to the Portuguese toehold in Southeast Asia, however, came from the English and the Dutch. In 1591, the first English expedition to the Indies through the Indian Ocean arrived in London with a cargo of pepper. Nine years later, a private joint-stock company, the East India Company, was founded to provide a stable source of capital for future voyages. In 1608, an English fleet landed at Surat, on the northwestern coast of India. Trade with Southeast Asia soon followed.

The Dutch were quick to follow suit, and the first Dutch fleet arrived in India in 1595. In 1602, the Dutch East India Company was established under government sponsorship and was soon actively competing with the English and the Portuguese in the region.

Europeans in the Americas The Dutch, the French, and the English also began to make inroads on Spanish and Portuguese possessions in the Americas. War and steady pressure from their Dutch and English rivals eroded Portuguese trade in both the West and the East, although Portugal continued to profit from its large colonial empire in Brazil. A formal administration system had been instituted in Brazil in 1549, and Portuguese migrants had established massive plantations there to produce sugar for export to the Old World. The Spanish also maintained an enormous South American empire, but Spain's importance as a commercial power declined rapidly in the seventeenth century because of a drop in the output of the silver mines and the poverty of the Spanish monarchy.

The Dutch formed their own Dutch West India Company in 1621 to compete with Spanish and Portuguese interests in the Americas. But although it made some inroads in Portuguese Brazil and the Caribbean (see Map 14.3), the company's profits were never large enough to compensate for the expenditures. Dutch settlements were also established on the North American continent. The mainland colony of New Netherland stretched from the mouth of the Hudson River as far north as present-day Albany, New York. In the meantime, French colonies appeared in the Lesser Antilles and in Louisiana, at the mouth of the Mississippi River.

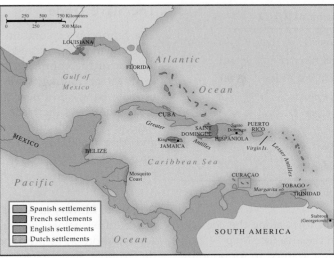

MAP 14.3 European Possessions in the West Indies. After the first voyage of Christopher Columbus, other European adventurers followed on his trail, seeking their share of the alleged riches of the Americas.
Q Where else did the French, Dutch, and English settle that proved more profitable for them?

In the second half of the seventeenth century, however, rivalry and years of warfare with the English and the French (who had also become active in North America) brought the decline of the Dutch commercial empire in the Americas. In 1664, the English seized the colony of New Netherland and renamed it New York, and the Dutch West India Company soon went bankrupt. In 1663, Canada became the property of the French crown and was administered like a French province. But the French failed to provide adequate men or money, allowing their continental wars to take precedence over the conquest of the North American continent. By the early eighteenth century, the French began to cede some of their American possessions to their English rival.

The English, meanwhile, had proceeded to create a colonial empire along the Atlantic seaboard of North America. The desire to escape from religious oppression combined with economic interests made successful colonization possible, as the Massachusetts Bay Company demonstrated. The Massachusetts colony had only 4,000 settlers in its early years, but by 1660, their number had swelled to 40,000.

Africa in Transition

Q **Focus Question:** What were the main features of the African slave trade, and what effects did European participation have on traditional African practices?

Although the primary objective of the Portuguese in rounding the Cape of Good Hope was to find a sea route to the Spice Islands, they soon discovered that profits were to be made en route, along the eastern coast of Africa.

Europeans in Africa

In the early sixteenth century, a Portuguese fleet seized a number of East African port cities, including Kilwa,

Life of Prince Henry the Navigator	1394–1460
Portuguese ships reach the Senegal River	1441
Bartolomeu Dias sails around the tip of Africa	1487
First boatload of slaves to the Americas	1518
Dutch way station established at Cape of Good Hope	1652
Ashanti kingdom established in West Africa	1680
Portuguese expelled from Mombasa	1728

Sofala, and Mombasa, and built forts along the coast in an effort to control the trade in the area (see Map 14.2 on p. 340). Above all, the Portuguese wanted to monopolize the trade in gold, which was mined by Bantu workers in the hills along the upper Zambezi River and then shipped to Sofala on the coast (see Chapter 8). For centuries, the gold trade had been monopolized by local Bantu-speaking Shona peoples at Zimbabwe. In the fifteenth century, it had come under the control of a Shona dynasty known as the Mwene Metapa. The Portuguese opened treaty relations with the Mwene Metapa, and Jesuit priests were eventually posted to the court in 1561. At first, the Mwene Metapa found the Europeans useful as an ally against local rivals, but by the end of the sixteenth century, the Portuguese had established a protectorate and forced the local ruler to grant title to large tracts of land to European officials and private individuals living in the area. The Portuguese lacked the personnel, the capital, and the expertise to dominate local trade, however, and in the late seventeenth century, a vassal of the Mwene Metapa succeeded in driving them from the plateau; his descendants maintained control of the area for the next two hundred years.

The first Europeans to settle in southern Africa were the Dutch. After an unsuccessful attempt to seize the Portuguese settlement on the island of Mozambique off the East African coast, in 1652 the Dutch set up a way station at the Cape of Good Hope to serve as a base for their fleets en route to the East Indies. At first, the new settlement was intended simply to provide food and other supplies to Dutch ships, but eventually it developed into a permanent colony. Dutch farmers, known as Boers and speaking a Dutch dialect that evolved into Afrikaans, began to settle in the sparsely occupied areas outside the city of Cape Town. The temperate climate and the absence of tropical diseases made the territory near the cape practically the only land south of the Sahara that the Europeans had found suitable for habitation.

The Slave Trade

The European exploration of the African coastline had little apparent significance for most peoples living in the interior of the continent, except for a few who engaged in direct or indirect trade with the foreigners. But for peoples living on or near the coast, the impact was often great indeed. As the trade in slaves increased during the sixteenth through the eighteenth centuries, thousands, and then millions, were removed from their homes and forcibly exported to plantations in the Western Hemisphere.

Origins of Slavery in Africa   Traffic in slaves had existed for centuries before the arrival of Portuguese fleets along African shores. The primary market for African slaves was the Middle East, where most were used as domestic servants. Slavery also existed in many European countries, where a few slaves from Africa or war captives from the regions north of the Black Sea were used for domestic purposes or as agricultural workers in the lands adjacent to the Mediterranean.

At first, the Portuguese simply replaced European slaves with African ones. During the second half of the fifteenth century, about a thousand slaves were taken to Portugal each year; the vast majority were apparently destined to serve as domestic servants for affluent families throughout Europe. But the discovery of the Americas in the 1490s and the subsequent planting of sugarcane in South America and the islands of the Caribbean changed the situation. Cane sugar was native to Indonesia and had first been introduced to Europeans from the Middle East during the Crusades. By the fifteenth century, it was grown (often by slaves from Africa or the region of the Black Sea) in modest amounts on Cyprus, Sicily, and southern regions of the Iberian peninsula. But when the Ottoman Empire seized much of the eastern Mediterranean (see Chapter 16), the Europeans needed to seek out new areas suitable for cultivation. Demand increased as sugar gradually replaced honey as a sweetener, especially in northern Europe.

The primary impetus to the sugar industry came from the colonization of the Americas. During the sixteenth century, plantations were established along the eastern coast of Brazil and on several islands in the Caribbean. Because the cultivation of cane sugar is an arduous process demanding both skill and large quantities of labor, the new plantations required more workers than could be provided by the Indian population in the Americas, many of whom had died of diseases imported from Europe and Africa. Since the climate and soil of much of West Africa were not especially conducive to the cultivation of sugar, African slaves began to be shipped to

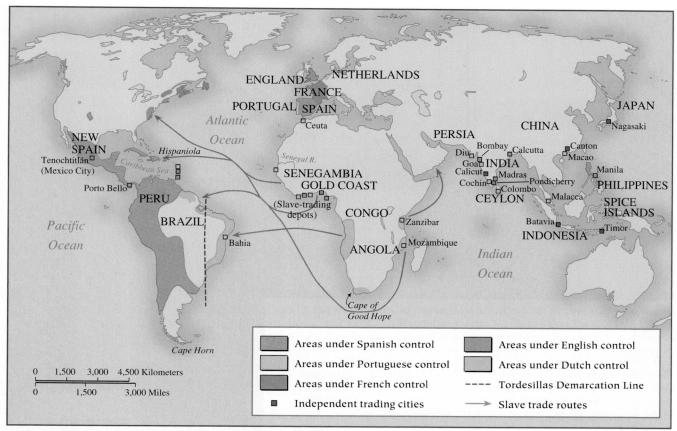

MAP 14.4 The Slave Trade. Beginning in the sixteenth century, the trade in African slaves to the Americas became a major source of profit to European merchants. This map traces the routes taken by slave-trading ships, as well as the territories and ports of call of European powers in the seventeenth century.

Q What were the major destinations for the slave trade?

View an animated version of this map or related maps at www.cengage.com/history/
duikspiel/essentialworld6e

Brazil and the Caribbean to work on the plantations. The first were sent from Portugal, but in 1518, a Spanish ship carried the first boatload of African slaves directly from Africa to the Americas.

Growth of the Slave Trade During the next two centuries, the trade in slaves increased by massive proportions (see Map 14.4). An estimated 275,000 enslaved Africans were exported to other countries during the sixteenth century, with 2,000 going annually to the Americas alone. The total climbed to over a million during the next century and jumped to six million in the eighteenth century, when the trade spread from West and Central Africa to East Africa. It has been estimated that altogether as many as ten million African slaves were transported to the Americas between the early sixteenth and the late nineteenth centuries. As many as

two million were exported to other areas during the same period.

The Middle Passage One reason for these astonishing numbers, of course, was the tragically high death rate. In what is often called the **Middle Passage,** the arduous voyage from Africa to the Americas, losses were frequently appalling. Although figures on the number of slaves who died on the journey are almost entirely speculative, during the first shipments, up to one-third of the human cargo may have died of disease or malnourishment. Even among crew members, mortality rates were sometimes as high as one in four. Later merchants became more efficient and reduced losses to about 10 percent. Still, the future slaves were treated in an inhumane manner, chained together in the holds of ships reeking with the stench of human waste and diseases carried by vermin.

Gateway to Slavery. Of the 12 million slaves shipped from Africa to other parts of the world, a good number passed through this doorway (right) on Gorée (top), a small island in a bay just off the coast of Senegal, near Cape Verde. Beginning in the sixteenth century, European traders began to ship Africans from this region to the Americas to be used as slave labor on sugar plantations. Some victims were kept in a prison on the island, which was occupied first by the Portuguese and later by the Dutch, the British, and the French. Gorée also served as an entrepôt and a source of supplies for ships passing along the western coast of Africa. The sign by the doorway reads, "From this door, they would embark on a voyage with no return, eyes fixed on an infinity of suffering."

Ironically, African slaves who survived the brutal voyage fared somewhat better than whites after their arrival. Mortality rates for Europeans in the West Indies, in fact, were ten to twenty times higher than in Europe, and death rates for those newly arrived in the islands averaged more than 125 per 1,000 annually. But the figure for Africans, many of whom had developed at least a partial immunity to yellow fever, was only about 30 per 1,000.

The reason for these staggering death rates was clearly more than maltreatment, although that was certainly a factor. As we have seen, the transmission of diseases from one continent to another brought high death rates among those lacking immunity. African slaves were somewhat less susceptible to European diseases than the American Indian populations. Indeed, they seem to have possessed a degree of immunity, perhaps because their ancestors had developed antibodies to "white people's diseases" owing to the trans-Saharan trade. The Africans would not have had immunity to native American diseases, however.

Sources of Slaves Slaves were obtained by traditional means. Before the coming of the Europeans in the fifteenth century, most slaves in Africa were prisoners or war captives or had inherited their status. Many served as domestic servants or as wageless workers for the local ruler. When Europeans first began to take part in the slave trade, they would normally purchase slaves from local African merchants at the infamous slave markets in exchange for gold, guns, or other European manufactured goods such as textiles or copper or iron utensils (see the box on p. 349). At first, local slave traders obtained their supply from immediately surrounding regions, but as demand increased, they had to move farther inland to locate their victims. In a few cases, local rulers became concerned about the impact of the slave trade on the political and social well-being of their societies. In a letter to the king of Portugal in 1526, King Affonso of Congo (Bakongo) complained that "so great, Sire, is the corruption and licentiousness that our country is being completely depopulated."[9] As a general rule, however, local monarchs viewed the slave trade as a source of income, and many launched forays against defenseless villages in search of unsuspecting victims.

A SLAVE MARKET IN AFRICA

FAMILY & SOCIETY

Traffic in slaves had been carried on in Africa since the kingdom of the pharaohs in ancient Egypt. But the slave trade increased dramatically after the arrival of European ships off the coast of West Africa. The following passage by a Dutch observer describes a slave market in Africa and the conditions on the ships that carried the slaves to the Americas. Note the difference in tone between this account and the far more critical views expressed in Chapter 21.

Slavery in Africa: A Firsthand Report

Not a few in our country fondly imagine that parents here sell their children, men their wives, and one brother the other. But those who think so deceive themselves, for this never happens on any other account but that of necessity, or some great crime; most of the slaves that are offered to us are prisoners of war, who are sold by the victors as their booty.

When these slaves come to Fida, they are put in prison all together; and when we treat concerning buying them, they are brought out into a large plain. There, by our surgeons, whose province it is, they are thoroughly examined, even to the smallest member, and that naked too, both men and women, without the least distinction or modesty. Those that are approved as good are set on one side; and the lame or faulty are set by as invalids. . . .

The invalids and the maimed being thrown out, . . . the remainder are numbered, and it is entered who delivered them. In the meanwhile, a burning iron, with the arms or name of the companies, lies in the fire, with which ours are marked on the breast. This is done that we may distinguish them from the slaves of the English, French, or others (which are also marked with their mark), and to prevent the Negroes exchanging them for worse, at which they have a good hand.

I doubt not but this trade seems very barbarous to you, but since it is followed by mere necessity, it must go on; but we take all possible care that they are not burned too hard, especially the women, who are more tender than the men.

When we have agreed with the owners of the slaves, they are returned to their prison. There from that time forward they are kept at our charge, costing us two pence a day a slave; which serves to subsist them, like our criminals, on bread and water. To save charges, we send them on board our ships at the very first opportunity, before which their masters strip them of all they have on their backs so that they come aboard stark naked, women as well as men. In this condition they are obliged to continue, if the master of the ship is not so charitable (which he commonly is) as to bestow something on them to cover their nakedness.

You would really wonder to see how these slaves live on board, for though their number sometimes amounts to six or seven hundred, yet by the careful management of our masters of ships, they are so regulated that it seems incredible. And in this particular our nation exceeds all other Europeans, for the French, Portuguese and English slave ships are always foul and stinking; on the contrary, ours are for the most part clean and neat.

The slaves are fed three times a day with indifferent good victuals, and much better than they eat in their own country. Their lodging place is divided into two parts, one of which is appointed for the men, the other for the women, each sex being kept apart. Here they lie as close together as it is possible for them to be crowded.

We are sometimes sufficiently plagued with a parcel of slaves which come from a far inland country who very innocently persuade one another that we buy them only to fatten and afterward eat them as a delicacy. When we are so unhappy as to be pestered with many of this sort, they resolve and agree together (and bring over the rest to their party) to run away from the ship, kill the Europeans, and set the vessel ashore, by which means they design to free themselves from being our food.

I have twice met with this misfortune; and the first time proved very unlucky to me, I not in the least suspecting it, but the uproar was quashed by the master of the ship and myself by causing the abettor to be shot through the head, after which all was quiet.

Q *What is the author's overall point of view with respect to the institution of slavery? Does he justify the practice? How does he think Dutch behavior compares with that of other European countries?*

The Effects of the Slave Trade The effects of the slave trade varied from area to area. It might be assumed that apart from the tragic effects on the lives of individual victims and their families, the practice would have led to the depopulation of vast areas of the continent. This did occur in some areas, notably in modern Angola, south of the Congo River basin, and in thinly populated areas in East Africa, but it was less true in West Africa. There high birthrates were often able to counterbalance the loss of able-bodied adults, and the introduction of new crops from the Western Hemisphere, such as maize, peanuts, and manioc, led to an increase in food production that made it possible to support a larger population. One of the many cruel ironies of history is that while the institution of slavery was a tragedy for many, it benefited others.

Still, there is no denying the reality that from a moral point of view, the slave trade represented a tragic loss for millions of Africans, not only for the individual

Manioc, Food for the Millions. One of the plants native to the Americas that European adventurers would take back to the Old World was manioc (also known as cassava or yuca). A tuber like the potato, manioc is a prolific crop that grows well in poor, dry soils, but it lacks the high nutrient value of grain crops such as wheat and rice and for that reason never became popular in Europe (except as a source of tapioca). It was introduced to Africa in the seventeenth century and eventually became a staple food for up to one-third of the population of that continent. Shown on the left is a manioc plant in East Africa. On the right, a Brazilian farmer on the Amazon River sifts peeled lengths of manioc into fine grains that will be dried into flour.

victims, but also for their families. One of the more poignant aspects of the trade is that as many as 20 percent of those sold to European slavers were children, a statistic that may be partly explained by the fact that many European countries had enacted regulations that permitted more children than adults to be transported aboard the ships.

How did Europeans justify cruelty of such epidemic proportions? Some rationalized that slave traders were only carrying on a tradition that had existed for centuries throughout the Mediterranean and African world. In fact, African intermediaries were active in the process and were often able to dictate the price, volume, and availability of slaves to European purchasers. Other Europeans eased their consciences by noting that slaves brought from Africa would now be exposed to the Christian faith and would be able to replace American Indian workers, many of whom were considered too physically fragile for the heavy human labor involved in cutting sugarcane.

Political and Social Structures in a Changing Continent

Of course, the Western economic penetration of Africa had other dislocating effects. As in other parts of the non-Western world, the importation of manufactured goods from Europe undermined the foundations of local cottage industry and impoverished countless families. The demand for slaves and the introduction of firearms intensified political instability and civil strife. At the same time, the impact of the Europeans should not be exaggerated. Only in a few isolated areas, such as South Africa and Mozambique, were permanent European settlements established. Elsewhere, at the insistence of African rulers and merchants, European influence generally did not penetrate beyond the coastal regions.

Nevertheless, inland areas were often affected by events taking place elsewhere. In the western Sahara, for example, the diversion of trade routes toward the coast led to the weakening of the old Songhai trading empire and its eventual conquest by a vigorous new Moroccan dynasty in the late sixteenth century. In 1590, Moroccan forces defeated Songhai's army at Gao, on the Niger River, and then occupied the great caravan center of Timbuktu.

European influence had a more direct impact along the coast of West Africa, especially in the vicinity of European forts such as Dakar and Sierra Leone, but no European colonies were established there before 1800. Most of the numerous African states in the area from Cape Verde to the delta of the Niger River were sufficiently strong to resist Western encroachments, and they often allied with each other to force European purchasers to respect their monopoly over trading operations. Some, like the powerful Ashanti kingdom, established in 1680 on the Gold Coast, profited substantially from the rise in seaborne commerce. Some states, particularly along the so-called Slave Coast, in what is now Benin and Togo, or in the densely populated Niger River delta, took an active part in the slave trade. The demands of slavery and the temptations of economic profit, however, also contributed to the increase in conflict among the states in the area.

This was especially true in the region of the Congo River, where Portuguese activities eventually led to the splintering of the Congo Empire and two centuries of rivalry and internal strife among the successor states in the area. A similar pattern developed in East Africa, where Portuguese activities led to the decline and eventual collapse of the Mwene Metapa. Northward along the coast, in present-day Kenya and Tanzania, African rulers, assisted by Arab forces from Oman and Muscat in the Arabian peninsula, expelled the Portuguese from Mombasa in 1728. Swahili culture now regained some of the dynamism it had possessed before the arrival of Vasco da Gama and his successors. But with much shipping now diverted southward to the route around the Cape of Good Hope, the commerce of the area never completely recovered and was increasingly dependent on the export of slaves and ivory obtained through contacts with African states in the interior.

Southeast Asia in the Era of the Spice Trade

> Q **Focus Question:** What were the main characteristics of Southeast Asian societies, and how were they affected by the coming of Islam and the Europeans?

In Southeast Asia, the encounter with the West that began with the arrival of Portuguese fleets in the Indian Ocean at the end of the fifteenth century eventually resulted in the breakdown of traditional societies and the advent of colonial rule. The process was a gradual one, however.

The Arrival of the West

As we have seen, the Spanish soon followed the Portuguese into Southeast Asia. By the seventeenth century, the Dutch, English, and French had begun to join the scramble for rights to the lucrative spice trade.

Within a short time, the Dutch, through the aggressive and well-financed Dutch East India Company (Vereenigde Oost-Indische Compagnie, or VOC), had not only succeeded in elbowing their rivals out of the spice trade but had also begun to consolidate their political and military control over the area. On the island of Java,

where they established a fort at Batavia (today's Jakarta) in 1619 (see the illustration on p. 333), the Dutch found that it was necessary to bring the inland regions under their control to protect their position. Rather than establishing a formal colony, however, they tried to rule as much as possible through the local landed aristocracy. On Java and the neighboring island of Sumatra, the VOC established pepper plantations, which soon became the source of massive profits for Dutch merchants in Amsterdam. Elsewhere they attempted to monopolize the clove trade by limiting cultivation of the crop to one island. By the end of the eighteenth century, the Dutch had succeeded in bringing almost the entire Indonesian archipelago under their control.

Competition among the European naval powers for territory and influence, however, continued to intensify throughout the region. In the countless island groups scattered throughout the Pacific Ocean, native rulers found it difficult to resist the growing European presence. The results were sometimes tragic, as indigenous cultures were quickly overwhelmed under the impact of Western material civilization, often leaving a sense of rootlessness and psychic stress in their wake (see the Film & History feature on p. 352).

The arrival of the Europeans had somewhat less impact in the Indian subcontinent and in mainland Southeast Asia, where cohesive monarchies in Burma, Thailand, and Vietnam resisted foreign encroachment. In addition, the coveted spices did not thrive on the mainland, so the Europeans' efforts there were far less determined than in the islands. The Portuguese did establish limited trade relations with several mainland states, including the Thai kingdom at Ayuthaya, Burma, Vietnam, and the remnants of the old Angkor kingdom in Cambodia. By the early seventeenth century, other nations had followed and had begun to compete actively for trade and missionary privileges. As was the case elsewhere, the Europeans soon became involved in local factional disputes as a means of obtaining political and economic advantages.

In Vietnam, the arrival of Western merchants and missionaries coincided with a period of internal conflict among ruling groups in the country. After their arrival in the mid-seventeenth century, the European powers characteristically began to intervene in local politics, with the Portuguese and the Dutch supporting rival factions. By the end of the century, when it became clear that economic opportunities were limited, most European states abandoned their factories (trading stations) in the area. French missionaries attempted to remain, but their efforts were hampered by the local authorities, who viewed the Catholic insistence that converts give their primary loyalty to the pope as a threat to the legal status

The film *Mutiny on the Bounty* is a dramatic re-creation of the most famous mutiny in British naval history. Based on the historical novel by Charles Nordhoff and James Norman Hall, the film portrays events that took place during an abortive British naval mission to the South Pacific in the late eighteenth century. The objective of the mission was to ship seedlings of the breadfruit tree, an edible tropical plant, to the island of Jamaica in the Caribbean, where it was hoped they could be used to feed African slaves working on the sugar plantations there.

On one level, the film is the account of a titanic conflict over authority between Captain William Bligh—played by veteran British actor Trevor Howard—and his first mate, Fletcher Christian, portrayed by the enigmatic American actor Marlon Brando. When Bligh's cruel treatment of his men leads to unrest, Christian takes command of the ship, forcing Bligh and his supporters into a small sloop, where they are left to fend for themselves in the vast Pacific Ocean.

Behind the tension between two strong personalities lies a broader tale of cultural collision between two worlds. Landing on the South Seas island of Tahiti in 1789, the men of the *Bounty* discover a society with a set of customs and beliefs vastly different from their own. The clash of cultures that ensues, leading inexorably to the gradual erosion and eventual destruction of Polynesian civilization, is an unspoken subtext of the film. When the mutineers leave Tahiti to find a new home on the isolated rock known today as Pitcairn Island, they take several Polynesian men and women with them to serve their needs, thus perpetuating the conflict in a new location.

Although the film does not dwell on this aspect of the story, the end is tragic, as several of the Polynesian islanders—angered at their treatment at the hands of the mutineers—turn on the latter and massacre them, almost to the last man. When a European

Captain Bligh (center, Trevor Howard) blocks Fletcher Christian (Marlon Brando, left) from giving a seaman a drink of water. In the background, Seaman John Mills (Richard Harris), who will start the mutiny, looks on.

MGM/The Kobal Collection

sailing ship accidentally discovers the island many years later, only one of the mutineers, along with a new generation of mixed-blood islanders, remains alive.

The 1962 film version of the book (a previous black-and-white version had been produced in 1935) has a number of historical weaknesses. Recent research suggests that Captain Bligh's treatment of his men was not exceptional in the context of the time and that Christian's role in provoking the mutiny has been underestimated. More important for our purposes here, the incipient culture clash between the European sailors and their Tahitian hosts is only hinted at in the film. Still, *Mutiny on the Bounty* retains its appeal as a swashbuckling sea story with dramatic characters set against the backdrop of a stunning tropical island in the vast emptiness of the Pacific Ocean.

and prestige of the Vietnamese emperor (see the box on p. 354).

State and Society in Precolonial Southeast Asia

Between 1400 and 1800, Southeast Asia experienced the last flowering of traditional culture before the advent of European rule in the nineteenth century. Although the coming of the Europeans had an immediate and direct impact in some areas, notably the Philippines and parts of

the Malay world, in most areas Western influence was still relatively limited.

Nevertheless, Southeast Asian societies were changing in several subtle ways—in their trade patterns, their means of livelihood, and their religious beliefs. In some ways, these changes accentuated the differences between individual states in the region. Yet beneath these differences was an underlying commonality of life for most people. Despite the diversity of cultures and religious beliefs in the area, Southeast Asians were in most respects closer to

A Pepper Plantation. During the Age of Exploration, pepper was one of the spices most desired by European adventurers. Unlike cloves and nutmeg, pepper could be grown in parts of mainland Asia as well as in the Indonesian archipelago. Shown here is a French pepper plantation in southern India. Eventually, the French were driven out of the Indian subcontinent by the British and retained only a few tiny enclaves along the coast.

each other than they were to peoples outside the region. For the most part, the states and peoples of Southeast Asia were still in control of their own destiny.

Religion and Kingship   During the early modern era, both Buddhism and Islam became well established in Southeast Asia, and Christianity began to attract some converts, especially in the Philippines. Buddhism was dominant in lowland areas on the mainland, from Burma to Vietnam. At first, Muslim influence was felt mainly on the Malay peninsula and along the northern coast of Java and Sumatra, where local merchants encountered their Muslim counterparts from foreign lands on a regular basis.

Buddhism and Islam also helped shape Southeast Asian political institutions. As the political systems began to mature, they evolved into four main types: Buddhist kings, Javanese kings, Islamic sultans, and Vietnamese emperors (for Vietnam, which was strongly influenced by China, see Chapter 11). In each case, institutions and concepts imported from abroad were adapted to local circumstances.

The Buddhist style of kingship took shape between the eleventh and the fifteenth centuries. It became the predominant political system in the Buddhist states of mainland Southeast Asia—Burma, Ayuthaya, Laos, and Cambodia. Perhaps the dominant feature of the Buddhist model was the godlike character of the monarch, who was considered by virtue of his *karma* to be innately superior to other human beings and served as a link between human society and the cosmos.

The Javanese model was a blend of Buddhist and Islamic political traditions. Like their Buddhist counterparts, Javanese monarchs possessed a sacred quality and maintained the balance between the sacred and the material world.

The Islamic model was found mainly on the Malay peninsula and along the coast of the Indonesian archipelago. In this pattern, the head of state was a sultan, who was viewed as a mortal, although he still possessed some magical qualities.

The Economy   During the early period of European penetration, the economy of most Southeast Asian societies was based on agriculture, as it had been for thousands of years. Still, by the sixteenth century, commerce was beginning to affect daily life, especially in the cities that were beginning to proliferate along the coasts or on

An Exchange of Royal Correspondence

 INTERACTION & EXCHANGE In 1681, King Louis XIV of France wrote a letter to the "king of Tonkin" (the Trinh family head, then acting as viceroy to the Vietnamese ruler) requesting permission for Christian missionaries to proselytize in Vietnam. The latter politely declined the request on the grounds that such activity was prohibited by ancient custom. In fact, Christian missionaries had been active in Vietnam for years, and their intervention in local politics had aroused the anger of the court in Hanoi.

A Letter to the King of Tonkin from Louis XIV

Most high, most excellent, most mighty, and most magnanimous Prince, our very dear and good friend, may it please God to increase your greatness with a happy end!

We hear from our subjects who were in your Realm what protection you accorded them. We appreciate this all the more since we have for you all the esteem that one can have for a prince as illustrious through his military valor as he is commendable for the justice which he exercises in his Realm. We have even been informed that you have not been satisfied to extend this general protection to our subjects but, in particular, that you gave effective proofs of it to Messrs. Deydier and de Bourges. We would have wished that they might have been able to recognize all the favors they received from you by having presents worthy of you offered you; but since the war which we have had for several years, in which all of Europe had banded together against us, prevented our vessels from going to the Indies, at the present time, when we are at peace after having gained many victories and expanded our Realm through the conquest of several important places, we have immediately given orders to the Royal Company to establish itself in your kingdom as soon as possible, and have commanded Messrs. Deydier and de Bourges to remain with you in order to maintain a good relationship between our subjects and yours, also to warn us on occasions that might present themselves when we might be able to give you proofs of our esteem and of our wish to concur with your satisfaction as well as with your best interests.

By way of initial proof, we have given orders to have brought to you some presents which we believe might be agreeable to you. But the one thing in the world which we desire most, both for you and for your Realm, would be to obtain for your subjects who have already embraced the law of the only true God of heaven and earth, the freedom to profess it, since this law is the highest, the noblest, the most sacred, and especially the most suitable to have kings reign absolutely over the people.

We are even quite convinced that, if you knew the truths and the maxims which it teaches, you would give first of all to your subjects the glorious example of embracing it. We wish you this incomparable blessing together with a long and happy reign, and we pray God that it may please Him to augment your greatness with the happiest of endings.

Written at Saint-Germain-en-Laye, the 10th day of January, 1681,

Your very dear and good friend,
Louis

Answer from the King of Tonkin to Louis XIV

The King of Tonkin sends to the King of France a letter to express to him his best sentiments, saying that he was happy to learn that fidelity is a durable good of man and that justice is the most important of things. Consequently practicing of fidelity and justice cannot but yield good results. Indeed, though France and our Kingdom differ as to mountains, rivers, and boundaries, if fidelity and justice reign among our villages, our conduct will express all of our good feelings and contain precious gifts. Your communication, which comes from a country which is a thousand leagues away, and which proceeds from the heart as a testimony of your sincerity, merits repeated consideration and infinite praise. Politeness toward strangers is nothing unusual in our country. There is not a stranger who is not well received by us. How then could we refuse a man from France, which is the most celebrated among the kingdoms of the world and which for love of us wishes to frequent us and bring us merchandise? These feelings of fidelity and justice are truly worthy to be applauded. As regards your wish that we should cooperate in propagating your religion, we do not dare to permit it, for there is an ancient custom, introduced by edicts, which formally forbids it. Now, edicts are promulgated only to be carried out faithfully; without fidelity nothing is stable. How could we disdain a well-established custom to satisfy a private friendship? . . .

We beg you to understand well that this is our communication concerning our mutual acquaintance. This then is my letter. We send you herewith a modest gift, which we offer you with a glad heart.

This letter was written at the beginning of winter and on a beautiful day.

Q *Compare the king of Tonkin's response to Louis XIV with the answer that the Mongol emperor Kuyuk Khan gave to the pope in 1244 (see p. 249). Which do you think was more conciliatory?*

CHRONOLOGY   The Spice Trade

Vasco da Gama lands at Calicut in southwestern India	1498
Albuquerque establishes base at Goa	1510
Portuguese seize Malacca	1511
Portuguese ships land in southern China	1514
Magellan's voyage around the world	1519–1522
English East India Company established	1600
Dutch East India Company established	1602
English arrive at Surat in northwestern India	1608
Dutch fort established at Batavia	1619

exchange for manufactured goods, ceramics, and high-quality textiles such as silk from China.

Society

In general, Southeast Asians probably enjoyed a somewhat higher living standard than most of their contemporaries elsewhere in Asia. Although most of the population was poor by modern Western standards, hunger was not a widespread problem. Several factors help explain this relative prosperity. In the first place, most of Southeast Asia has been blessed by a salubrious climate. The uniformly high temperatures and the abundant rainfall enable as many as two or even three crops to be grown each year. Second, although the soil in some areas is poor, the alluvial deltas on the mainland are fertile, and the volcanoes of Indonesia periodically spew forth rich volcanic ash that renews the mineral resources of the soil of Sumatra and Java. Finally, with some exceptions, most of Southeast Asia was relatively thinly populated.

Social institutions tended to be fairly homogeneous throughout Southeast Asia. Compared with China and India, there was little social stratification, and the nuclear family predominated. In general, women fared better in the region than anywhere else in Asia. Daughters often had the same inheritance rights as sons, and family property was held jointly between husband and wife. Wives were often permitted to divorce their husbands,

navigable rivers. In part, this was because agriculture itself was becoming more commercialized as cash crops like sugar and spices replaced subsistence farming in rice or other cereals in some areas.

Regional and interregional trade were already expanding before the coming of the Europeans. The central geographic location of Southeast Asia enabled it to become a focal point in a widespread trading network. Spices, of course, were the mainstay of the interregional trade, but Southeast Asia exchanged other products as well. The region exported tin (mined in Malaya since the tenth century), copper, gold, tropical fruits and other agricultural products, cloth, gems, and luxury goods in

© William J. Duiker

In a Buddhist Wonderland. The Shwedagon Pagoda is the most sacred site in Myanmar (Burma). Located on a hill in today's capital of Yangon (formerly Rangoon), the pagoda was originally erected on the site of an earlier Buddhist structure sometime in the late first millennium C.E. Its centerpiece is a magnificent stupa covered in gold leaf that stands more than 320 feet high. The platform at the base of the stupa contains a multitude of smaller shrines and stupas covered with marble carvings and fragments of cut glass. It is no surprise that for centuries, the Buddhist faithful have visited the site, and the funds they have donated have made the Shwedagon stupa one of the wonders of the world.

OPPOSING VIEWPOINTS
THE MARCH OF CIVILIZATION

As Europeans began to explore new parts of the world beginning in the fifteenth century, they were convinced that it was their duty to introduce civilized ways to the heathen peoples of Asia, Africa, and the Americas. Such was the message of Spanish captain Vasco Núñez one September morning in 1513, when from a hill on the Isthmus of Panama he first laid eyes on the Pacific Ocean. Two centuries later, however, the intrepid British explorer James Cook, during his last visit to the island of Tahiti in 1777, expressed in his private journal his growing doubts that Europeans had brought lasting benefits to the Polynesian islanders. Such disagreements over the alleged benefits of Western civilization to non-Western peoples would continue to spark debate during the centuries that followed and remain with us today (see the comparative essay "Imperialism: The Balance Sheet" in Chapter 21).

Gonzalo Fernández de Ovieda, *Historia General y Natural de las Indias*

On Tuesday, the twenty-fifth of September of the year 1513, at ten o'clock in the morning, Captain Vasco Núñez, having gone ahead of his company, climbed a hill with a bare summit, and from the top of this hill saw the South Sea. Of all the Christians in his company, he was the first to see it. He turned back toward his people, full of joy, lifting his hands and his eyes to Heaven, praising Jesus Christ and his glorious Mother the Virgin, Our Lady. Then he fell upon his knees on the ground and gave great thanks to God for the mercy He had shown him, in allowing him to discover that sea, and thereby to render so great a service to God and to the most serene Catholic Kings of Castile, our sovereigns. . . .

And he told all the people with him to kneel also, to give the same thanks to God, and to beg Him fervently to allow them to see and discover the secrets and great riches of that sea and coast, for the greater glory and increase of the Christian faith, for the conversion of the Indians, natives of those southern regions, and for the fame and prosperity of the royal throne of Castile and of its sovereigns present and to come. All the people cheerfully and willingly did as they were bidden; and the Captain made them fell a big tree and make from it a tall cross, which they erected in that same place, at the top of the hill from which the South Sea had first been seen. And they all sang together the hymn of the glorious holy fathers of the Church, Ambrose and Augustine, led by a devout priest Andrés de Vera, who was with them, saying with tears of joyful devotion *Te Deum laudamus, Te Dominum confitemur.*

Maori Tiki god, South Pacific

© William J. Duiker

Journal of Captain James Cook

I cannot avoid expressing it as my real opinion that it would have been far better for these poor people never to have known our superiority in the accommodations and arts that make life comfortable, than after once knowing it, to be again left and abandoned in their original incapacity of improvement. Indeed they cannot be restored to that happy mediocrity in which they lived before we discovered them, if the intercourse between us should be discontinued. It seems to me that it has become, in a manner, incumbent on the Europeans to visit them once in three or four years, in order to supply them with those conveniences which we have introduced among them, and have given them a predilection for. The want of such occasional supplies will, probably, be felt very heavily by them, when it may be too late to go back to their old, less perfect, contrivances, which they now despise, and have discontinued since the introduction of ours. For, by the time that the iron tools, of which they are now possessed, are worn out, they will have almost lost the knowledge of their own. A stone hatchet is, at present, as rare a thing amongst them, as an iron one was eight years ago, and a chisel of bone or stone is not to be seen.

Q *Why does James Cook express regret that the peoples of Tahiti had been exposed to European influence? How might Captain Núñez have responded to Cook?*

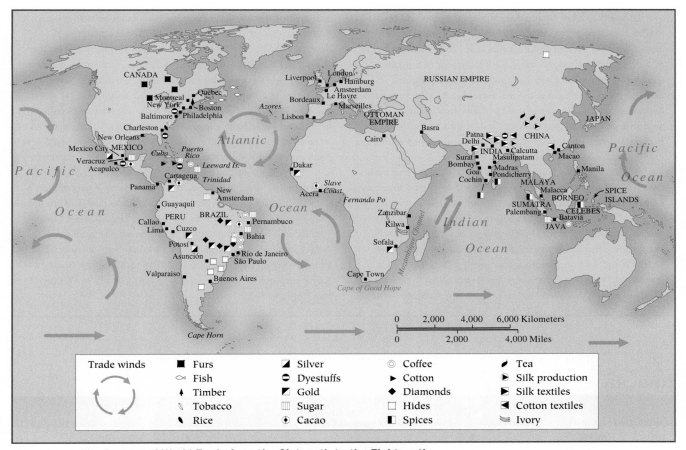

MAP 14.5 **The Pattern of World Trade from the Sixteenth to the Eighteenth Centuries.** This map shows the major products that were traded by European merchants throughout the world during the era of European exploration. Prevailing wind patterns in the oceans are also shown on the map.

Q What were the primary sources of gold and silver, so sought after by Columbus and his successors?

🐚 **View an animated version of this map or related maps at** www.cengage.com/history/ duikspiel/essentialworld6e

and monogamy was the rule rather than the exception. Although women were usually restricted to specialized work, such as making ceramics, weaving, or transplanting the rice seedlings into the main paddy fields, and rarely possessed legal rights equal to those of men, they enjoyed a comparatively high degree of freedom and status in most societies in the region and were sometimes involved in commerce.

CONCLUSION

DURING THE FIFTEENTH CENTURY, the pace of international commerce increased dramatically. Chinese fleets visited the Indian Ocean while Muslim traders extended their activities into the Spice Islands and sub-Saharan West Africa. Then the Europeans burst onto the world scene. Beginning with the seemingly modest ventures of the Portuguese ships that sailed southward along the West African coast, the process accelerated with the epoch-making voyages of Christopher Columbus to the Americas and Vasco da Gama to the Indian Ocean in the 1490s. Soon a number of other European states had entered the scene, and by the end of the eighteenth century, they had created a global trade network dominated by Western ships and Western power that distributed foodstuffs, textile goods, spices, and precious minerals from one end of the globe to the other (see Map 14.5).

In less than three hundred years, the European Age of Exploration changed the face of the world. In some areas, such as the Americas and the Spice Islands, it led to the destruction of indigenous civilizations and the establishment of European colonies. In others, as in Africa, South Asia, and mainland Southeast Asia, it left native regimes intact but had a strong impact on local societies and regional trade patterns. In some areas, it led to an irreversible decline in traditional institutions and values, setting in motion a corrosive process that has not been reversed to this day (see the box on p. 356).

At the time, many European observers viewed the process in a favorable light. Not only did it expand world trade and foster the exchange of new crops and discoveries between the Americas and the rest of the world, but it also introduced Christianity to "heathen peoples" around the globe. Many modern historians have been much more critical, concluding that European activities during the sixteenth and seventeenth centuries created a "tributary mode of production" based on European profits from unequal terms of trade that foreshadowed the exploitative relationship characteristic of the later colonial period. Other scholars have questioned that contention, however, and argue that although Western commercial operations had a significant impact on global trade patterns, they did not—at least not before the eighteenth century—freeze out non-European participants. Muslim merchants, for example, were long able to evade European efforts to eliminate them from the spice trade, and the trans-Saharan caravan trade was relatively unaffected by European merchant shipping along the West African coast. In some cases, the European presence may even have encouraged new economic activity, as in the Indian subcontinent (see Chapter 16).

By the same token, the Age of Exploration did not, as some have claimed, usher in an era of Western dominance over the rest of the world. In the Middle East, powerful empires continued to hold sway over the lands washed by the Muslim faith. Beyond the Himalayas, Chinese emperors in their new northern capital of Beijing retained proud dominion over all the vast territory of continental East Asia. We shall deal with these regions, and how they confronted the challenges of a changing world, in Chapters 16 and 17.

TIMELINE

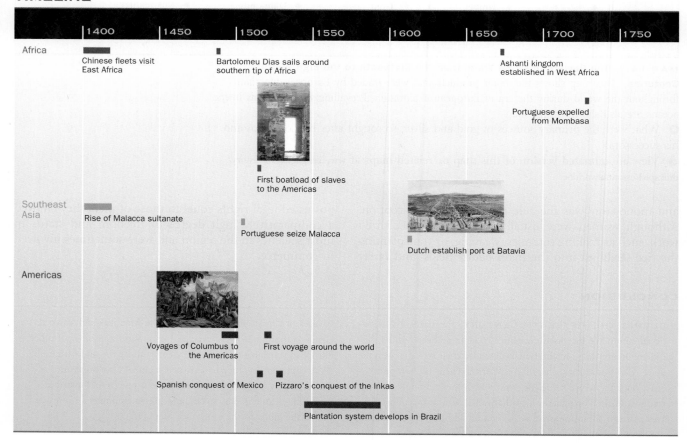

| | 1400 | 1450 | 1500 | 1550 | 1600 | 1650 | 1700 | 1750 |

Africa
Chinese fleets visit East Africa
Bartolomeu Dias sails around southern tip of Africa
Ashanti kingdom established in West Africa
Portuguese expelled from Mombasa
First boatload of slaves to the Americas

Southeast Asia
Rise of Malacca sultanate
Portuguese seize Malacca
Dutch establish port at Batavia

Americas
Voyages of Columbus to the Americas
First voyage around the world
Spanish conquest of Mexico
Pizzaro's conquest of the Inkas
Plantation system develops in Brazil

SUGGESTED READING

European Expansion On the technological aspects of European expansion, see **C. M. Cipolla, *Guns, Sails, and Empires: Technological Innovation and the Early Phases of European Expansion, 1400–1700*** (New York, 1965); **F. Fernandez-Armesto, ed., *The Times Atlas of World Exploration*** (New York, 1991); and **R. C. Smith, *Vanguard of Empire: Ships of Exploration in the Age of Columbus*** (Oxford, 1993); also see **A. Pagden, *Lords of All the World: Ideologies of Empire in Spain, Britain, and France, c. 1500–c. 1800*** (New Haven, Conn., 1995). For an overview of the impact of European expansion in the Indian Ocean, see **K. N. Chaudhuri, *Trade and Civilization in the Indian Ocean: An Economic History from the Rise of Islam to 1750*** (Cambridge, 1985). For a series of stimulating essays reflecting modern scholarship, see **J. D. Tracy, *The Rise of Merchant Empires: Long-Distance Trade in the Early Modern World, 1350–1750*** (Cambridge, 1990).

Spanish Activities in the Americas A gripping work on the conquistadors is **H. Thomas, *Conquest: Montezuma, Cortés, and the Fall of Old Mexico*** (New York, 1993). The human effects of the interaction of New and Old World cultures are examined thoughtfully in **A. W. Crosby, *The Columbian Exchange: Biological and Cultural Consequences of 1492*** (Westport, Conn., 1972).

Spain's Rivals On Portuguese expansion, the fundamental work is **C. R. Boxer, *The Portuguese Seaborne Empire, 1415–1825*** (New York, 1969). On the Dutch, see **J. I. Israel, *Dutch Primacy in World Trade, 1585–1740*** (Oxford, 1989). British activities are chronicled in **S. Sen, *Empire of Free Trade: The East India Company and the Making of the Colonial Marketplace*** (Philadelphia, 1998), and **Anthony Wild's** elegant work ***The East India Company: Trade and Conquest from 1600*** (New York, 2000).

The Spice Trade The effects of European trade in Southeast Asia are discussed in **A. Reid, *Southeast Asia in the Age of Commerce, 1450–1680*** (New Haven, Conn., 1989). On the spice trade, see **A. Dalby, *Dangerous Tastes: The Story of Spices*** (Berkeley, Calif., 2000), and **J. Turner, *Spice: The History of a Temptation*** (New York, 2004).

The Slave Trade On the African slave trade, the standard work is **P. Curtin, *The African Slave Trade: A Census*** (Madison, Wis., 1969). For more recent treatments, see **P. E. Lovejoy, *Transformations in Slavery: A History of Slavery in Africa*** (Cambridge, 1983), and **P. Manning, *Slavery and African Life*** (Cambridge, 1990); **H. Thomas, *The Slave Trade*** (New York, 1997), provides a useful overview. Also see **C. Palmer, *Human Cargoes: The British Slave Trade to Spanish America, 1700–1739*** (Urbana, Ill., 1981), and **K. F. Kiple, *The Caribbean Slave: A Biological History*** (Cambridge, 1984).

Women For a brief introduction to women's experiences during the Age of Exploration and global trade, see **S. Hughes** and **B. Hughes, *Women in World History,*** vol. 2 (Armonk, N.Y., 1997). For a more theoretical discussion of violence and gender in the early modern period, consult **R. Trexler, *Sex and Conquest: Gendered Violence, Political Order, and the European Conquest of the Americas*** (Ithaca, N.Y., 1995). The native American female experience with the European encounter is presented in **R. Gutierrez, *When Jesus Came the Corn Mothers Went Away: Marriage, Sexuality, and Power in New Mexico, 1500–1846*** (Stanford, Calif., 1991), and **K. Anderson, *Chain Her by One Foot: The Subjugation of Women in Seventeenth-Century New France*** (London, 1991).

WORLD HISTORY RESOURCES

Visit the website for *The Essential World History* **to access study aids such as Flashcards, Critical Thinking Exercises, and Chapter Quizzes:**
www.cengage.com/history/duikspiel/essentialworld6e

DISCOVERY

How was European expansion into the rest of the world both a positive and a negative experience for Europeans and non-Europeans?

In thinking about this question, begin by breaking it down into the components shown below. A discussion of each component should appear in your answer.

POLITICS AND GOVERNMENT   Look back at the exchange of correspondence between King Louis XIV and the king of Tonkin (document, p. 354). What social and cultural effects of French overseas expansion can you find in these letters? Why did Louis XIV want to send missionaries, and why did the king of Tonkin oppose Louis's request? In what ways did Louis see his culture as superior to the king of Tonkin's? Compare the closing sentences of the letters. How do they differ? What do these differences tell you about European and East Asian culture in the 1600s?

INTERACTION AND EXCHANGE   Based on the fanciful image of Columbus's landing (p. 342) and the comparative essay (p. 344), including its illustration, what do you think was the European attitude toward native peoples? Columbus has recently become a controversial figure in world history. Why do you think this is so, and how would you evaluate his contribution to the modern world?

Look at the maps below showing European voyages in the Age of Exploration and patterns of world trade. Compare the key areas of European exploration with what became key centers of trade. What were the major products valued by the Europeans? Note the areas of the world trade map that do not show any trade products. What does this indicate about the flow of products in the world trade of the sixteenth to eighteenth centuries? Who controlled this trade, and who benefited? Compare the patterns shown here with the development of major economies and centers of economic power in the modern world.

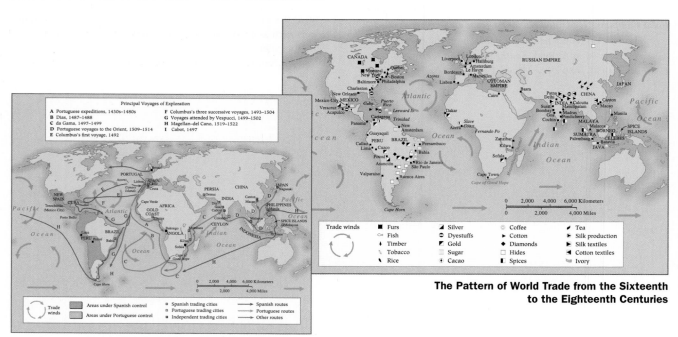

The Pattern of World Trade from the Sixteenth to the Eighteenth Centuries

European Voyages and Possessions in the Sixteenth and Seventeenth Centuries

CHAPTER 15

EUROPE TRANSFORMED: REFORM AND STATE BUILDING

A sixteenth-century engraving of Martin Luther in front of Charles V at the Diet of Worms

© The Bridgeman Art Library

ON APRIL 18, 1521, A LOWLY MONK stood before the emperor and princes of Germany in the city of Worms. He had been called before this august gathering to answer charges of heresy, charges that could threaten his very life. The monk was confronted with a pile of his books and asked if he wished to defend them all or reject a part. Courageously, Martin Luther defended them all and asked to be shown where any part was in error on the basis of "Scripture and plain reason." The emperor was outraged by Luther's response and made his own position clear the next day: "Not only I, but you of this noble German nation, would be forever disgraced if by our negligence not only heresy but the very suspicion of heresy were to survive. After having heard yesterday the obstinate defense of Luther, I regret that I have so long delayed in proceeding against him and his false teaching. I will have no more to do with him." Luther's appearance at Worms set the stage for a serious challenge to the authority of the Catholic church. This was by no means the first crisis in the church's fifteen-hundred-year history, but its consequences were more far-reaching than anyone at Worms in 1521 could have imagined.

After the disintegrative patterns of the fourteenth century, Europe began a remarkable recovery that encompassed a revival of arts and letters in the fifteenth century, known as the Renaissance, and a religious renaissance in the sixteenth century, known as the Reformation. The religious division of Europe (Catholics versus Protestants) that was a result of the Reformation was instrumental in beginning a series of wars that dominated much of European history from 1560 to 1650 and exacerbated the economic and social crises that were besetting the region.

One of the responses to the crises of the seventeenth century was a search for order. The most general trend was an extension of monarchical power as a stablizing force. This development, which historians have called absolutism or absolute monarchy, was most evident in France during the flamboyant reign of Louis XIV, regarded by some as the perfect embodiment of an absolute monarch.

But absolutism was not the only response to the search for order in the seventeenth century. Other states, such as England, reacted very differently to domestic crisis, and another very different system emerged where monarchs were limited by the power of their representative assemblies. Absolute and limited monarchy were the two poles of seventeenth-century state building. ❀

The Reformation of the Sixteenth Century

Q **Focus Question:** What were the main tenets of Lutheranism and Calvinism, and how did they differ from each other and from Catholicism?

The **Protestant Reformation** is the name given to the religious reform movement that divided the western Christian church into Catholic and Protestant groups. Although Martin Luther began the Reformation in the early sixteenth century, several earlier developments had set the stage for religious change.

Background to the Reformation

Changes in the fifteenth century—the age of the Renaissance—helped prepare the way for the dramatic upheavals in sixteenth-century Europe.

The Growth of State Power In the first half of the fifteenth century, European states had continued the disintegrative patterns of the previous century. In the second half of the fifteenth century, however, recovery had set in, and attempts had been made to reestablish the centralized power of monarchical governments. To characterize the results, some historians have used the label "Renaissance states"; others have spoken of the "**new monarchies,**" especially those of France, England, and Spain at the end of the fifteenth century (see Chapter 13).

Although appropriate, the term *new monarch* can also be misleading. What was new about these Renaissance monarchs was their concentration of royal authority, their attempts to suppress the nobility, their efforts to control the church in their lands, and their desire to obtain new sources of revenue in order to increase royal power and enhance the military forces at their disposal. Like the rulers of fifteenth-century Italian states, the Renaissance monarchs were often crafty men obsessed with the acquisition and expansion of political power. Of course, none of these characteristics was entirely new; a number of medieval monarchs, especially in the thirteenth century, had also exhibited them. Nevertheless, the Renaissance period does mark the further extension of centralized royal authority.

No one gave better expression to the Renaissance preoccupation with political power than Niccolò Machiavelli (1469–1527), an Italian who wrote *The Prince* (1513), one of the most influential works on political power in the Western world. Machiavelli's major concerns in *The Prince* were the acquisition, maintenance, and expansion of political power as the means to restore and maintain order in his time. In the Middle Ages, many political theorists stressed the ethical side of a prince's activity—how a ruler ought to behave based on Christian moral principles. Machiavelli bluntly contradicted this approach: "For the gap between how people actually behave and how they ought to behave is so great that anyone who ignores everyday reality in order to live up to an ideal will soon discover he had been taught how to destroy himself, not how to preserve himself."[1] Machiavelli was among the first Western thinkers to abandon morality as the basis for the analysis of political activity. The same emphasis on the ends justifying the means, or on achieving results regardless of the methods employed, had in fact been expressed a thousand years earlier by a court official in India named Kautilya in his treatise on politics, the *Arthasastra* (see Chapter 2).

Social Changes in the Renaissance Social changes in the fifteenth century also had an impact on the Reformation of the sixteenth century. After the severe economic reversals and social upheavals of the fourteenth century, the European economy gradually recovered as manufacturing and trade increased in volume.

As noted in Chapter 12, society in the Middle Ages was divided into three estates: the clergy, or first estate, whose preeminence was grounded in the belief that people should be guided to spiritual ends; the nobility, or second estate, whose privileges rested on the principle that nobles provided security and justice for society; and the peasants and inhabitants of the towns and cities, the third estate. Although this social order continued into the Renaissance, some changes also became evident.

Throughout much of Europe, the landholding nobles faced declining real incomes during most of the fourteenth and fifteenth centuries. Many members of the old nobility survived, however, and new blood also infused their ranks. By 1500, the nobles, old and new, who constituted between 2 and 3 percent of the population in most countries, managed to dominate society, as they had done in the Middle Ages, holding important political posts and serving as advisers to the king.

Except in the heavily urban areas of northern Italy and Flanders, peasants made up the overwhelming mass of the third estate—they constituted 85 to 90 percent of the total European population. Serfdom decreased as the manorial system continued its decline. Increasingly, the labor dues owed by peasants to their lord were converted into rents paid in money. By 1500, especially in western Europe, more and more peasants were becoming legally free. At the same time, peasants in many areas resented their social superiors and sought a greater share of the benefits coming from their labor. In the sixteenth century, the grievances of peasants, especially in Germany, led many of them to support religious reform movements.

The remainder of the third estate consisted of the inhabitants of towns and cities, originally merchants and artisans. But by the fifteenth century, the Renaissance town or city had become more complex. At the top of urban society were the patricians, whose wealth from capitalistic enterprises in trade, industry, and banking enabled them to dominate their urban communities economically, socially, and politically. Below them were the petty burghers—the shopkeepers, artisans, guildmasters, and guildsmen—who were largely concerned with providing goods and services for local consumption. Below these two groups were the propertyless workers earning pitiful wages and the unemployed, living squalid and miserable lives. These poor city-dwellers constituted 30 to 40 percent of the urban population. The pitiful conditions of the lower groups in urban society often led them to support calls for radical religious reform in the sixteenth century.

The Impact of Printing   The Renaissance witnessed the development of printing, which made an immediate impact on European intellectual life and thought. Printing from hand-carved wooden blocks had been done in the West since the twelfth century and in China even before that. What was new in the fifteenth century in Europe was multiple printing with movable metal type. The development of printing from movable type was a gradual process that culminated sometime between 1445 and 1450; Johannes Gutenberg of Mainz played an

important role in bringing the process to completion. Gutenberg's Bible, completed in 1455 or 1456, was the first true book produced from movable type.

By 1500, there were more than a thousand printers in Europe, who collectively had published almost 40,000 titles (between eight and ten million copies). Probably half of these books were religious—Bibles and biblical commentaries, books of devotion, and sermons.

The printing of books encouraged scholarly research and the desire to attain knowledge. Printing also stimulated the growth of an ever-expanding lay reading public, a development that had an enormous impact on European society. Indeed, without the printing press, the new religious ideas of the Reformation would never have spread as rapidly as they did in the sixteenth century. Moreover, printing allowed European civilization to compete for the first time with the civilization of China.

Prelude to Reformation   During the second half of the fifteenth century, the new Classical learning of the Italian Renaissance spread to the European countries north of the Alps and spawned a movement called **Christian humanism** or **northern Renaissance humanism,** whose major goal was the reform of Christendom. The Christian humanists believed in the ability of human beings to reason and improve themselves and thought that through education in the sources of Classical, and especially Christian, antiquity, they could instill an inner piety or an inward religious feeling that would bring about a reform of the church and society. To change society, they must first change the human beings who compose it.

The most influential of all the Christian humanists was Desiderius Erasmus (1466–1536), who formulated and popularized the reform program of Christian humanism. He called his conception of religion "the philosophy of Christ," by which he meant that Christianity should be a guiding philosophy for the direction of daily life rather than the system of dogmatic beliefs and practices that the medieval church seemed to stress. No doubt his work helped prepare the way for the Reformation; as contemporaries proclaimed, "Erasmus laid the egg that Luther hatched."

Church and Religion on the Eve of the Reformation   Corruption in the Catholic church was another factor that encouraged people to want reform. Between 1450 and 1520, a series of popes—called the Renaissance popes—failed to meet the church's spiritual needs. The popes were supposed to be the spiritual leaders of the Catholic church, but as rulers of the Papal States, they were all too often involved in worldly interests. Julius II (1503–1513), the fiery "warrior-pope," personally led armies against his enemies, much to the disgust of pious

Christians, who viewed the pope as a spiritual leader. As one intellectual wrote, "How, O bishop standing in the room of the Apostles, dare you teach the people the things that pertain to war?" Many high church officials regarded their church offices mainly as opportunities to advance their careers and their wealth, and many ordinary parish priests seemed ignorant of their spiritual duties.

While the leaders of the church were failing to meet their responsibilities, ordinary people were clamoring for meaningful religious expression and certainty of salvation. As a result, for some the process of salvation became almost mechanical. Collections of **relics** grew as more and more people sought certainty of salvation through the veneration of objects associated with the saints and martyrs or with Jesus himself. Frederick the Wise, elector of Saxony and Martin Luther's prince, had amassed more than five thousand relics to which were attached **indulgences** that could reduce one's time in purgatory by 1,443 years. (An indulgence is a remission, after death, of all or part of the punishment due to sin.)

Martin Luther and the Reformation in Germany

Martin Luther (1483–1546) was a monk and a professor at the University of Wittenberg, where he lectured on the Bible. Probably sometime between 1513 and 1516, through his study of the Bible, he arrived at an answer to a problem—the assurance of salvation—that had disturbed him since his entry into the monastery.

Catholic doctrine had emphasized that both faith and good works were required for a Christian to achieve personal salvation. In Luther's eyes, human beings, weak and powerless in the sight of an almighty God, could never do enough good works to merit salvation. Through his study of the Bible, Luther came to believe that humans are saved not through their good works but through faith in the promises of God, made possible by the sacrifice of Jesus on the cross. This doctrine of salvation, or justification by grace through faith alone, became the primary doctrine of the Protestant Reformation (**justification by faith** is the act by which a person is made deserving of salvation). Because Luther had arrived at this doctrine from his study of the Bible, the Bible became for Luther as for all other Protestants the chief guide to religious truth.

Luther did not see himself as a rebel, but he was greatly upset by the widespread selling of indulgences. Especially offensive in his eyes was the monk Johann Tetzel, who hawked indulgences with the slogan: "As soon as the coin in the coffer [money box] rings, the soul from purgatory springs." Greatly angered, in 1517 Luther issued a stunning indictment of the abuses in the sale of indulgences, known as the Ninety-five Theses. Thousands of copies were printed and quickly spread to all parts of Germany.

Unable to accept Luther's ideas, the church excommunicated him in January 1521. He had also been summoned to appear before the imperial diet or Reichstag of the Holy Roman Empire, convened by the newly elected Emperor Charles V (1519–1556). Ordered to recant the heresies he had espoused, Luther refused and made the famous reply that became the battle cry of the Reformation:

> Unless I am convicted by Scripture and plain reason—I do not accept the authority of popes and councils, for they have contradicted each other—my conscience is captive to the Word of God. I cannot and I will not recant anything, for to go against conscience is neither right nor safe. Here I stand, I cannot do otherwise. God help me. Amen.[2]

Members of the Reichstag were outraged and demanded that Luther be captured and delivered to the emperor. But Luther's ruler, Elector Frederick of Saxony, stepped in and protected him.

During the next few years, Luther's religious movement became a revolution. Luther was able to gain the support of many of the German rulers among the three hundred or so states that made up the Holy Roman Empire. These rulers quickly took control of the churches in their territories. The Lutheran churches in Germany (and later in Scandinavia) quickly became territorial or state churches in which the state supervised the affairs of the church. As part of the development of these state-dominated churches, Luther also instituted new religious services to replace the Catholic Mass. These focused on Bible reading, preaching the word of God, and song.

Politics and Religion in the German Reformation From its very beginning, the fate of Luther's movement was closely tied to political affairs. In 1519, Charles I, king of Spain and the grandson of Emperor Maximilian, was elected Holy Roman Emperor as Charles V. Charles V ruled over an immense empire, consisting of Spain and its overseas possessions, the traditional Austrian Habsburg lands, Bohemia, Hungary, the Low Countries, and the kingdom of Naples in southern Italy. Politically, Charles wanted to maintain his enormous empire; religiously, he hoped to preserve the unity of his empire in the Catholic faith.

The internal political situation in the Holy Roman Empire was not in Charles's favor, however. Although all the German states owed loyalty to the emperor, in the Middle Ages these states had become quite independent of imperial authority. By the time Charles V was able to bring military forces to Germany in 1546, Lutheranism

Luther versus the Pope. In the 1520s, after Luther's return to Wittenberg, his teachings began to spread rapidly, ending ultimately in a reform movement supported by state authorities. Pamphlets containing picturesque woodcuts were important in the spread of Luther's ideas. In the woodcut shown here, the crucified Jesus attends Luther's service on the left, while on the right the pope is at a table selling indulgences.

had become well established, and the Lutheran princes were well organized. Unable to defeat them, Charles was forced to negotiate a truce. Religious warfare in Germany came to an end in 1555 with the Peace of Augsburg. The division of Christianity was formally acknowledged; Lutheran states were to have the same legal rights as Catholic states. Although the German states were now free to choose between Catholicism and Lutheranism, the peace settlement did not recognize the principle of religious toleration for individuals. The right of each German ruler to determine the religion of his subjects was accepted, but not the right of the subjects to choose their own religion. With the Peace of Augsburg, what had at first been merely feared was now certain: the ideal of Christian unity was forever lost. The rapid spread of new Protestant groups made this a certainty.

The Spread of the Protestant Reformation

Switzerland was home to two major Reformation movements: Zwinglianism and Calvinism. Ulrich Zwingli (1484–1531) was ordained a priest in 1506 and accepted an appointment as a cathedral priest in the Great Minster of Zürich in 1518. Zwingli's preaching aroused such discontent with the existing practices that in 1523 the city council decided to institute evangelical reforms. Relics and images were abolished; all paintings and decorations were removed from the churches and replaced by whitewashed

walls. The Mass was replaced by a new liturgy consisting of Scripture reading, prayer, and sermons. Monasticism, pilgrimages, the veneration of saints, clerical celibacy, and the pope's authority were all abolished as remnants of papal Christianity.

As his movement began to spread to other cities in Switzerland, Zwingli sought an alliance with Martin Luther and the German reformers. Although both the German and the Swiss reformers realized the need for unity to defend against the opposition of the Catholic authorities, they were unable to agree on the interpretation of the Lord's Supper, the sacrament of Communion (see the box on p. 366). Zwingli believed that the scriptural words "This is my body, this is my blood" should be taken figuratively, not literally, and refused to accept Luther's insistence on the real presence of the body and blood of Christ "in, with, and under the bread and wine." In October 1531, war erupted between the Swiss Protestant and Catholic states. Zürich's army was routed, and Zwingli was found wounded on the battlefield. His enemies killed him, cut up his body, burned the pieces, and scattered the ashes. The leadership of Swiss Protestantism now passed to John Calvin, the systematic theologian and organizer of the Protestant movement.

Calvin and Calvinism John Calvin (1509–1564) was educated in his native France but after his conversion to Protestantism was forced to flee to the safety of Switzerland. In 1536, he published the first edition of the *Institutes of the Christian Religion,* a masterful synthesis of Protestant thought that immediately secured Calvin's reputation as one of the new leaders of Protestantism.

On most important doctrines, Calvin stood very close to Luther. He adhered to the doctrine of justification by faith alone to explain how humans achieved salvation. But Calvin also placed much emphasis on the absolute sovereignty of God or the all-powerful nature of God—what Calvin called the "power, grace, and glory of God." One of the ideas derived from his emphasis on the absolute sovereignty of God—**predestination**—gave a unique cast to Calvin's teachings. This "eternal decree,"

OPPOSING VIEWPOINTS
A REFORMATION DEBATE: CONFLICT AT MARBURG

RELIGION & PHILOSOPHY

Debates played a crucial role in the Reformation period. They were a primary instrument for introducing the Reformation in innumerable cities as well as a means of resolving differences among like-minded Protestant groups. This selection contains an excerpt from the vivacious and often brutal debate between Luther and Zwingli over the sacrament of the Lord's Supper at Marburg in 1529. The two protagonists failed to reach agreement.

The Marburg Colloquy, 1529

THE HESSIAN CHANCELLOR FEIGE: My gracious prince and lord [Landgrave Philip of Hesse] has summoned you for the express and urgent purpose of settling the dispute over the sacrament of the Lord's Supper.... Let everyone on both sides present his arguments in a spirit of moderation, as becomes such matters.... Now then, Doctor Luther, you may proceed.

LUTHER: Noble prince, gracious lord! Undoubtedly the colloquy is well intentioned.... Although I have no intention of changing my mind, which is firmly made up, I will nevertheless present the grounds of my belief and show where the others are in error.... Your basic contentions are these: In the last analysis you wish to prove that a body cannot be in two places at once, and you produce arguments about the unlimited body which are based on natural reason. I do not question how Christ can be God and man and how the two natures can be joined. For God is more powerful than all our ideas, and we must submit to his word.

Prove that Christ's body is not there where the Scripture says, "This is my body!" Rational proofs I will not listen to.... God is beyond all mathematics and the words of God are to be revered and carried out in awe. It is God who commands, "Take, eat, this is my body." I request, therefore, valid scriptural proof to the contrary.

Luther writes on the table in chalk, "This is my body," and covers the words with a velvet cloth.

OECOLAMPADIUS [leader of the reform movement in Basel and a Zwinglian partisan]: The sixth chapter of John clarifies the other scriptural passages. Christ is not speaking there about a local presence. "The flesh is of no avail," he says. It is not my intention to employ rational, or geometrical, arguments—neither am I denying the power of God—but as long as I have the complete faith I will speak from that. For Christ is risen; he sits at the right hand of God; and so he cannot be present in the bread. Our view is neither new nor sacrilegious, but is based on faith and Scripture....

ZWINGLI: I insist that the words of the Lord's Supper must be figurative. This is ever apparent, and even required by the article of faith: "taken up into heaven, seated at the right hand of the Father." Otherwise, it would be absurd to look for him in the Lord's Supper at the same time that Christ is telling us that he is in heaven. One and the same body cannot possibly be in different places....

LUTHER: I call upon you as before: your basic contentions are shaky. Give way, and give glory to God!

ZWINGLI: And we call upon you to give glory to God and to quit begging the question! The issue at stake is this: Where is the proof of your position? I am willing to consider your words carefully—no harm meant! You're trying to outwit me. I stand by this passage in the sixth chapter of John, verse 63, and shall not be shaken from it. You'll have to sing another tune.

LUTHER: You're being obnoxious.

ZWINGLI: (*excitedly*) Don't you believe that Christ was attempting in John 6 to help those who did not understand?

LUTHER: You're trying to dominate things! You insist on passing judgment! Leave that to someone else!... It is your point that must be proved, not mine. But let us stop this sort of thing. It serves no purpose.

ZWINGLI: It certainly does! It is for you to prove that the passage in John 6 speaks of a physical repast.

LUTHER: You express yourself poorly and make about as much progress as a cane standing in a corner. You're going nowhere.

ZWINGLI: No, no, no! This is the passage that will break your neck!

LUTHER: Don't be so sure of yourself. Necks don't break this way. You're in Hesse, not Switzerland.

Q *What were the differences in the positions of Zwingli and Luther on the sacrament of the Lord's Supper? What was the purpose of this debate? Based on this example, why do you think Reformation debates led to further hostility rather than compromise and unity between religious and sectarian opponents? What implication did this have for the future of the Protestant Reformation?*

as Calvin called it, meant that God had predestined some people to be saved (the elect) and others to be damned (the reprobate). According to Calvin, "He has once for all determined, both whom He would admit to salvation, and whom He would condemn to destruction."[3] Although Calvin stressed that there could be no absolute certainty of salvation, his followers did not always make this distinction. The practical psychological effect of predestination was to give later Calvinists an unshakable conviction that they were doing God's work on earth, making Calvinism a dynamic and activist faith.

In 1536, Calvin began working to reform the city of Geneva. He was able to fashion a tightly organized church order that employed both clergy and laymen in the service of the church. The Consistory, a special body for enforcing moral discipline, functioned as a court to oversee the moral life, daily behavior, and doctrinal orthodoxy of Genevans and to admonish and correct deviants. Citizens of Geneva were punished for such varied "crimes" as dancing, singing obscene songs, drunkenness, swearing, and playing cards.

Calvin's success in Geneva enabled the city to become a vibrant center of Protestantism. Following Calvin's lead, missionaries trained in Geneva were sent to all parts of Europe. Calvinism became established in France, the Netherlands, Scotland, and central and eastern Europe, and by the mid-sixteenth century, Calvin's Geneva stood as the fortress of the Reformation.

The English Reformation The English Reformation was rooted in politics, not religion. King Henry VIII (1509–1547) had a strong desire to divorce his first wife, Catherine of Aragon, with whom he had a daughter, Mary, but no male heir. He wanted to marry Anne Boleyn, with whom he had fallen in love. Impatient with the pope's unwillingness to grant him an annulment of his marriage, Henry turned to England's own church courts. As archbishop of Canterbury and head of the highest church court in England, Thomas Cranmer ruled in May 1533 that the king's marriage to Catherine was "absolutely void." At the beginning of June, Anne was crowned queen, and three months later a child was born, a girl (the future queen Elizabeth I), much to the king's disappointment.

In 1534, at Henry's request, Parliament moved to finalize the break of the Church of England with Rome. The Act of Supremacy of 1534 declared that the king was "the only supreme head on earth of the Church of England," a position that gave him control of doctrine, clerical appointments, and discipline. Although Henry VIII had broken with the papacy, little change occurred in matters of doctrine, theology, and ceremony. Some of his supporters, including Archbishop Cranmer, sought a religious reformation as well as an administrative one, but Henry was unyielding. But he died in 1547 and was succeeded by his son, the underage and sickly Edward VI (1547–1553), and during Edward's reign, Cranmer and others inclined toward Protestant doctrines were able to move the Church of England (or Anglican Church) in a more Protestant direction. New acts of Parliament gave the clergy the right to marry and created a new Protestant church service.

Edward VI was succeeded by Mary (1553–1558), a Catholic who attempted to return England to Catholicism. Her actions aroused much anger, however, especially when "bloody Mary" burned more than three hundred Protestant heretics. By the end of Mary's reign, England was more Protestant than it had been at the beginning.

The Social Impact of the Protestant Reformation

The Protestants were especially important in developing a new view of the family (see the comparative essay "Marriage in the Early Modern World" on p. 368). Because Protestantism had eliminated any idea of special holiness for celibacy and had abolished both monasticism and a celibate clergy, the family could be placed at the center of human life, and a new stress on "mutual love between man and wife" could be extolled.

But were doctrine and reality the same? Most often, reality reflected the traditional roles of husband as the ruler and wife as the obedient servant whose chief duty was to please her husband. Luther stated it clearly:

> The rule remains with the husband, and the wife is compelled to obey him by God's command. He rules the home and the state, wages war, defends his possessions, tills the soil, builds, plants, etc. The woman on the other hand is like a nail driven into the wall ... so the wife should stay at home and look after the affairs of the household, as one who has been deprived of the ability of administering those affairs that are outside and that concern the state. She does not go beyond her most personal duties.[4]

Obedience to her husband was not a wife's only role; her other important duty was to bear children. To Calvin and Luther, this function of women was part of the divine plan, and for most Protestant women, family life was their only destiny. Overall, the Protestant Reformation did not noticeably alter women's subordinate place in society.

The Catholic Reformation

By the mid-sixteenth century, Lutheranism had become established in Germany and Scandinavia and Calvinism in Scotland, Switzerland, France, the Netherlands, and eastern Europe. In England, the split from Rome had resulted in the creation of a national church. The situation in Europe did not look particularly favorable for the Roman Catholic Church. Nevertheless, the Catholic church also underwent a revitalization in the sixteenth century, giving it new strength. There were three chief

COMPARATIVE ESSAY
MARRIAGE IN THE EARLY MODERN WORLD

Marriage is an ancient institution. In China, mythical stories about the beginnings of Chinese civilization maintain that the rites of marriage began with the primordial couple Fuxi and Nugun and that these rites actually preceded such discoveries as fire, farming, and medicine. In the early modern world, family and marriage were inseparable and at the center of all civilizations.

In the early modern period, the family was still at the heart of Europe's social organization. For the most part, people thought of the family in traditional terms, as a patriarchal institution with the husband dominating his wife and children. The upper classes in particular regarded the family as a "house," an association whose collective interests were more important than those of its individual members. Parents (especially fathers) generally selected marriage partners for their children, based on the interests of the family. When one French nobleman's son asked about his upcoming marriage, the father responded, "Mind your own business." Details were worked out well in advance, sometimes when children were only two or three years old, and reinforced by a legally binding contract. The most important aspect of the contract was the size of the dowry, money presented by the wife's family to the husband upon marriage. The dowry could involve large sums and was expected of all families.

Arranged marriages were not unique to Europe but were common throughout the world. In China, marriages were normally arranged for the benefit of the family, often by a go-between, and the groom and bride were usually not consulted. Frequently, they did not meet until the marriage ceremony. Love was obviously not a reason for marriage and in fact was often viewed as a detriment because it might distract the married couple from their responsibilities to the larger family unit. In Japan too, marriages were arranged, often by the heads of dominant families in rural areas, and the new wife moved in with the family of her husband. In India, not only were marriages arranged, but it was not uncommon for women to be married before the age of ten. In colonial Latin America, parents also selected the spouse and often chose a dwelling for the couple as well. The process of selection was frequently complicated by the need for the lower classes to present gifts to powerful landlords who dominated their regions in order to gain their permission to marry. These nobles often stopped unmarried women from marrying in order to keep them as servants.

Arranged marriages were the logical result of a social system in which men dominated and women's primary role was to bear

Marriage Ceremony. This eighteenth-century painting shows the wedding of the Spanish nobleman Martin de Loyola to the Inka princess Nusta Beatriz.

children, manage the household, and work in the fields. Not until the nineteenth century did a feminist movement emerge in Europe to improve the rights of women. By the beginning of the twentieth century, that movement had spread to other parts of the world. The New Culture Movement in China, for example, advocated the free choice of spouses. Despite the progress that has been made throughout the world in allowing people to choose their spouses, in some places, especially in rural areas, families still play an active role in the selection of marriage partners.

Q *In what ways was the practice of marriage similar in the West and East during the early modern period? Were there any significant differences?*

Ignatius of Loyola. The Jesuits became the most important new religious order of the Catholic Reformation. Shown here in a sixteenth-century painting by an unknown artist is Ignatius of Loyola, founder of the Society of Jesus. Loyola is seen kneeling before Pope Paul III, who officially recognized the Jesuits in 1540.

pillars of the **Catholic Reformation:** the Jesuits, a reformed papacy, and the Council of Trent.

The Society of Jesus   The Society of Jesus, known as the Jesuits, was founded by a Spanish nobleman, Ignatius of Loyola (1491–1556). Loyola gathered together a small group of individuals who were recognized as a religious order by the pope in 1540. The new order was grounded on the principles of absolute obedience to the papacy, a strict hierarchical order for the society, the use of education to achieve its goals, and a dedication to engage in "conflict for God." A special vow of absolute obedience to the pope made the Jesuits an important instrument for papal policy. Jesuit missionaries proved singularly successful in restoring Catholicism to parts of Germany and eastern Europe.

Another prominent Jesuit activity was the propagation of the Catholic faith among non-Christians. Francis Xavier (1506–1552), one of the original members of the Society of Jesus, carried the message of Catholic Christianity to the East. After converting tens of thousands in India, he traveled to Malacca and the Moluccas before finally reaching Japan in 1549. He spoke highly of the Japanese: "They are a people of excellent morals—good in general and not malicious."[5] Thousands of Japanese, especially in the southernmost islands, became Christians. In 1552, Xavier set out for China but died of fever before he reached the mainland.

Although conversion efforts in Japan proved short-lived, Jesuit activity in China, especially that of the Italian Matteo Ricci, was more long-lasting. Recognizing the

Chinese pride in their own culture, the Jesuits attempted to draw parallels between Christian and Confucian concepts and to show the similarities between Christian morality and Confucian ethics. For their part, the missionaries were much impressed with many aspects of Chinese civilization, and reports of their experiences heightened European curiosity about this great society on the other side of the world.

A Reformed Papacy   A reformed papacy was another important factor in the development of the Catholic Reformation. The involvement of Renaissance popes in dubious finances and Italian political and military affairs had created numerous sources of corruption. It took the jolt of the Protestant Reformation to bring about serious reform. Pope Paul III (1534–1549) perceived the need for change and took the audacious step of appointing a reform commission to ascertain the church's ills. The commission's report in 1537 blamed the church's problems on the corrupt policies of popes and cardinals. Paul III also formally recognized the Jesuits and summoned the Council of Trent.

The Council of Trent   In March 1545, a group of high church officials met in the city of Trent on the border between Germany and Italy and initiated the Council of Trent, which met intermittently from 1545 to 1563 in three major sessions. The final decrees of the Council of Trent reaffirmed traditional Catholic teachings in opposition to Protestant beliefs. Scripture and tradition were affirmed as equal authorities in religious matters; only the church could interpret Scripture. Both faith and good works were declared necessary for salvation. Belief in purgatory and in the use of indulgences was strengthened, although the selling of indulgences was prohibited.

By the mid-sixteenth century, the Roman Catholic Church had become one Christian denomination among many. Nevertheless, after the Council of Trent, the Catholic church possessed a clear body of doctrine and a unified church under the acknowledged supremacy of the popes. With a new spirit of confidence, the Catholic church entered a new phase of its history.

Europe in Crisis, 1560–1650

Q Focus Question: Why is the period between 1560 and 1650 in Europe called an age of crisis?

Between 1560 and 1650, Europe experienced religious wars, revolutions and constitutional crises, economic and social disintegration, and a witchcraft craze. It was truly an age of crisis.

Politics and the Wars of Religion in the Sixteenth Century

By 1560, Calvinism and Catholicism had become activist religions dedicated to spreading the word of God as they interpreted it. Although their struggle for the minds and hearts of Europeans was at the center of the religious wars of the sixteenth century, economic, social, and political forces also played an important role in these conflicts.

The French Wars of Religion (1562–1598)

Religion was central to the French civil wars of the sixteenth century. The growth of Calvinism had led to persecution by the French kings, but the latter did little to stop the spread of Calvinism. Huguenots (as the French Calvinists were called) constituted only about 7 percent of the population, but 40 to 50 percent of the French nobility became Huguenots, including the house of Bourbon, which stood next to the Valois in the royal line of succession. The conversion of so many nobles made the Huguenots a potentially dangerous political threat to monarchical power. Still, the Calvinist minority was greatly outnumbered by the Catholic majority, and the Valois monarchy was staunchly Catholic.

For thirty years, battles raged in France between Catholic and Calvinist parties. Finally, in 1589, Henry of Navarre, the political leader of the Huguenots and a member of the Bourbon dynasty, succeeded to the throne as Henry IV (1589–1610). Realizing, however, that he would never be accepted by Catholic France, Henry converted to Catholicism. With his coronation in 1594, the Wars of Religion had finally come to an end. The Edict of Nantes in 1598 solved the religious problem by acknowledging Catholicism as the official religion of France while guaranteeing the Huguenots the right to worship and to enjoy all political privileges, including the holding of public offices.

Philip II and Militant Catholicism

The greatest advocate of militant Catholicism in the second half of the sixteenth century was King Philip II of Spain (1556–1598), the son and heir of Charles V. Philip's reign ushered in an age of Spanish greatness, both politically and culturally. Philip II had inherited from his father Spain, the Netherlands, and possessions in Italy and the Americas. To strengthen his control, Philip insisted on strict conformity to Catholicism and strong monarchical authority. Achieving the latter was not an easy task, because each of the lands of his empire had its own structure of government.

Philip's attempt to strengthen his control over the Spanish Netherlands, which consisted of seventeen provinces (the modern Netherlands and Belgium), soon led to a revolt. The nobles, who stood to lose the most politically, strongly opposed Philip's efforts. Religion also became a major catalyst for rebellion when Philip attempted to crush Calvinism. Violence erupted in 1566, and the revolt became organized, especially in the northern provinces, where the Dutch, under the leadership of William of Nassau, the prince of Orange, offered growing resistance. The struggle dragged on for decades until 1609, when the war ended with a twelve-year truce that virtually recognized the independence of the northern provinces. These seven northern provinces, which called themselves the United Provinces of the Netherlands, became the core of the modern Dutch state.

At the beginning of the seventeenth century, most Europeans still regarded Spain as the greatest power of the age, but the reality was quite different. The Spanish treasury was empty, the armed forces were obsolescent, and the government was inefficient. Spain continued to play the role of a great power, but real power had shifted to England.

The England of Elizabeth

When Elizabeth Tudor, the daughter of Henry VIII and Anne Boleyn, ascended the throne in 1558, England was home to fewer than four million people. Yet during her reign, the small island kingdom became the leader of the Protestant nations of Europe and laid the foundations for a world empire.

Intelligent, cautious, and self-confident, Elizabeth moved quickly to solve the difficult religious problem she inherited from her half-sister, Queen Mary. Elizabeth's religious policy was based on moderation and compromise. She repealed the Catholic laws of Mary's reign, and a new Act of Supremacy designated Elizabeth as "the only supreme governor" of both church and state. The Church of England under Elizabeth was basically Protestant, but it was of a moderate bent that kept most people satisfied.

Caution and moderation also dictated Elizabeth's foreign policy. Gradually, however, Elizabeth was drawn into conflict with Spain. Having resisted for years the idea of invading England as too impractical, Philip II of Spain was finally persuaded to do so by advisers who assured him that the people of England would rise against their queen when the Spaniards arrived. A successful invasion of England would mean the overthrow of heresy and the return of England to Catholicism. Philip ordered preparations for a fleet of warships, the Armada, to spearhead the invasion of England.

The Armada was a disaster. The Spanish fleet that finally set sail had neither the ships nor the manpower that Philip had planned to send. Battered by a number of encounters with the English, the Spanish fleet sailed back to Spain by a northward route around Scotland and Ireland, where it was further pounded by storms.

Procession of Queen Elizabeth I. Intelligent and learned, Elizabeth Tudor was familiar with Latin and Greek and spoke several European languages. Served by able administrators, Elizabeth ruled for nearly forty-five years and generally avoided open military action against any major power. This picture, painted near the end of her reign, shows the queen in a ceremonial procession.

Economic and Social Crises

The period of European history from 1560 to 1650 witnessed severe economic and social crises as well as political upheaval. Economic contraction began to be evident in some parts of Europe by the 1620s. In the 1630s and 1640s, as imports of silver from the Americas declined, economic recession intensified, especially in the Mediterranean area.

Population Decline   Population trends of the sixteenth and seventeenth centuries also reveal Europe's worsening conditions. The population of Europe increased from 60 million in 1500 to 85 million by 1600, the first major recovery of the European population since the devastation of the Black Death in the mid-fourteenth century. By 1650, however, records also indicate a decline in the population, especially in central and southern Europe. Europe's longtime adversaries—war, famine, and plague—continued to affect population levels. Europe's problems created social tensions, some of which were manifested in an obsession with witches.

Witchcraft Mania   Hysteria over witchcraft affected the lives of many Europeans in the sixteenth and seventeenth centuries. Perhaps more than 100,000 people were prosecuted throughout Europe on charges of witchcraft. As more and more people were brought to trial, the fear of witches, as well as the fear of being accused of witchcraft, escalated to frightening levels (see the box on p. 372).

Common people—usually those who were poor and without property—were more likely to be accused of witchcraft. Indeed, where lists are given, those mentioned most often are milkmaids, peasant women, and servant girls. In the witchcraft trials of the sixteenth and seventeenth centuries, more than 75 percent of the accused were women, most of them single or widowed and many over fifty years old.

That women should be the chief victims of witchcraft trials was hardly accidental. Nicholas Rémy, a witchcraft judge in France in the 1590s, found it "not unreasonable that this scum of humanity, i.e., witches, should be drawn chiefly from the feminine sex." To another judge, it came as no surprise that witches would confess to sexual experiences with Satan: "The Devil uses them so, because he knows that women love carnal pleasures, and he means to bind them to his allegiance by such agreeable provocations."[6]

A WITCHCRAFT TRIAL IN FRANCE

 Persecutions for witchcraft reached their high point in the sixteenth and seventeenth centuries, when tens of thousands of people were brought to trial. In this excerpt from the minutes of a trial in France in 1652, we can see why the accused witch stood little chance of exonerating herself.

The Trial of Suzanne Gaudry

28 May, 1652.... Interrogation of Suzanne Gaudry, prisoner at the court of Rieux.... During interrogations on May 28 and May 29, the prisoner confessed to a number of activities involving the devil.

Deliberation of the Court—June 3, 1652

The undersigned advocates of the Court have seen these interrogations and answers. They say that the aforementioned Suzanne Gaudry confesses that she is a witch, that she had given herself to the devil, that she had renounced God, Lent, and baptism, that she has been marked on the shoulder, that she has cohabited with the devil and that she has been to the dances, confessing only to have cast a spell upon and caused to die a beast of Philippe Cornié....

Third Interrogation, June 27

This prisoner being led into the chamber, she was examined to know if things were not as she had said and confessed at the beginning of her imprisonment.

—Answers no, and that what she has said was done so by force.

Pressed to say the truth, that otherwise she would be subjected to torture, having pointed out to her that her aunt was burned for this same subject.

—Answers that she is not a witch....

She was placed in the hands of the officer in charge of torture, throwing herself on her knees, struggling to cry, uttering several exclamations, without being able, nevertheless, to shed a tear. Saying at every moment that she is not a witch.

The Torture

On this same day, being at the place of torture.

This prisoner, before being strapped down, was admonished to maintain herself in her first confessions and to renounce her lover.

—Says that she denies everything she has said, and that she has no lover. Feeling herself being strapped down, says that she is not a witch, while struggling to cry... and upon being asked why she confessed to being one, said that she was forced to say it.

Told that she was not forced, that on the contrary she declared herself to be a witch without any threat.

—Says that she confessed it and that she is not a witch, and being a little stretched [on the rack] screams ceaselessly that she is not a witch.

Asked if she did not confess that she had been a witch for twenty-six years.

—Says that she said it, that she retracts it, crying that she is not a witch.

Asked if she did not make Philippe Cornié's horse die, as she confessed.

—Answers no, crying Jesus-Maria, that she is not a witch.

The mark having been probed by the officer, in the presence of Doctor Bouchain, it was adjudged by the aforesaid doctor and officer truly to be the mark of the devil.

Being more tightly stretched upon the torture rack, urged to maintain her confessions.

—Said that it was true that she is a witch and that she would maintain what she had said.

Asked how long she has been in subjugation to the devil.

—Answers that it was twenty years ago that the devil appeared to her, being in her lodgings in the form of a man dressed in a little cowhide and black breeches....

Verdict

July 9, 1652. In the light of the interrogations, answers, and investigations made into the charge against Suzanne Gaudry,... seeing by her own confessions that she is said to have made a pact with the devil, received the mark from him,... and that following this, she had renounced God, Lent, and baptism and had let herself be known carnally by him, in which she received satisfaction. Also, seeing that she is said to have been a part of nocturnal carols and dances.

For expiation of which the advice of the undersigned is that the office of Rieux can legitimately condemn the aforesaid Suzanne Gaudry to death, tying her to a gallows, and strangling her to death, then burning her body and burying it here in the environs of the woods.

Q *Why were women, particularly older women, especially vulnerable to accusations of witchcraft? What "proofs" are offered here that Suzanne Gaudry had consorted with the devil? What does this account tell us about the spread of witchcraft persecutions in the seventeenth century?*

By the mid-seventeenth century, the witchcraft hysteria had begun to subside. As governments grew stronger, fewer magistrates were willing to accept the unsettling and divisive conditions generated by the trials of witches. Moreover, by the beginning of the eighteenth century, more and more people were questioning altogether their old attitudes toward religion and found it especially contrary to reason to believe in the old view of a world haunted by evil spirits.

Economic Trends in the Seventeenth Century In the course of the seventeenth century, new economic trends also emerged. A set of economic ideas that historians call **mercantilism** came to dominate economic practices in the seventeenth century. According to the mercantilists, the prosperity of a nation depended on a plentiful supply of bullion (gold and silver). For this reason, it was desirable to achieve a favorable balance of trade in which goods exported were of greater value than those imported, promoting an influx of gold and silver payments that would increase the quantity of bullion. Furthermore, to encourage exports, the government should stimulate and protect export industries and trade by granting trade monopolies, encouraging investment in new industries through subsidies, importing foreign artisans, and improving transportation systems by building roads, bridges, and canals. By placing high tariffs on foreign goods, the government could reduce imports and prevent them from competing with domestic industries. Colonies were also deemed valuable as sources of raw materials and markets for finished goods.

Mercantilist theory on the role of colonies was matched in practice by Europe's overseas expansion. With the development of colonies and trading posts in the Americas and the East, Europeans embarked on an adventure in international commerce in the seventeenth century. Although some historians speak of a nascent world economy, we should remember that local, regional, and intra-European trade still predominated. At the end of the seventeenth century, for example, English imports totaled 360,000 tons, but only 5,000 tons came from the East Indies. What made the transoceanic trade rewarding, however, was not the volume of its goods but their value. Dutch, English, and French merchants were bringing back products that were still consumed largely by the wealthy but were beginning to make their way into the lives of artisans and merchants. Pepper and spices from the Indies, West Indian and Brazilian sugar, and Asian coffee and tea were becoming more readily available to European consumers.

The commercial expansion of the sixteenth and seventeenth centuries was made easier by new forms of commercial organization, especially the **joint-stock company.** Individuals bought shares in a company and received dividends on their investment while a board of directors ran the company and made the important business decisions. The return on investments could be spectacular. The joint-stock company made it easier to raise large amounts of capital for world trading ventures.

Despite the growth of commercial capitalism, most of the European economy still depended on an agricultural system that had experienced few changes since the thirteenth century. At least 80 percent of Europeans still worked on the land. Almost all of the peasants of western Europe were free of serfdom, although many still owed a variety of feudal dues to the nobility. Despite the expanding markets and rising prices, European peasants saw little or no improvement in their lot as they faced increased rents and fees and higher taxes imposed by the state.

Seventeenth-Century Crises: Revolution and War

During the first half of the seventeenth century, a series of rebellions and civil wars rocked the domestic stability of many European governments. A devastating war that affected much of Europe also added to the sense of crisis.

The Thirty Years' War (1618–1648) The Thirty Years' War began in 1618 in the Germanic lands of the Holy Roman Empire as a struggle between Catholic forces, led by the Habsburg Holy Roman Emperors, and Protestant—primarily Calvinist—nobles in Bohemia who rebelled against Habsburg authority (see Map 15.1). What began as a struggle over religious issues soon became a wider conflict perpetuated by political motivations as both minor and major European powers—Denmark, Sweden, France, and Spain—entered the war. The competition for European leadership between the Bourbon dynasty of France and the Habsburg dynasties of Spain and the Holy Roman Empire was an especially important factor. Nevertheless, most of the battles were fought on German soil (see the box on p. 375).

The war in Germany was officially ended in 1648 by the Peace of Westphalia, which proclaimed that all German states, including the Calvinist ones, were free to determine their own religion. The major contenders gained new territories, and France emerged as the dominant nation in Europe. The more than three hundred entities that made up the Holy Roman Empire were recognized as independent states, and each was given the power to conduct its own foreign policy; this brought an end to the Holy Roman Empire and ensured German disunity for another two hundred years. The Peace of Westphalia made it clear that political motives, not religious convictions, had become the guiding force in public affairs.

A Military Revolution? By the seventeenth century, war played an increasingly important role in European affairs.

MAP 15.1 Europe in the Seventeenth Century. This map shows Europe at the time of the Thirty Years' War (1618–1648). Although the struggle began in Bohemia and much of the fighting took place in the Germanic lands of the Holy Roman Empire, the conflict became a Europe-wide struggle.

Q Which countries engaged in the war were predominantly Protestant, which were Catholic, and which were mixed?

View an animated version of this map or related maps at www.cengage.com/history/ duikspiel/essentialworld6e

As military power was considered essential to a ruler's reputation and power, the pressure to build an effective military machine was intense. Some historians believe that the changes that occurred in the science of warfare between 1560 and 1650 warrant the title of military revolution.

These changes included increased use of firearms and cannons, greater flexibility and mobility in tactics, and better-disciplined and better-trained armies. These innovations necessitated standing armies, based partly on conscription, which grew ever larger and more expensive as the seventeenth century progressed. Such armies could be maintained only by levying heavier taxes, making war an economic burden and an ever more important part of the early modern European state. The creation of large bureaucracies to supervise the military resources of the state contributed to the growth in the power of governments.

THE FACE OF WAR IN THE SEVENTEENTH CENTURY

FAMILY & SOCIETY

We have a firsthand account of the face of war in Germany from a picaresque novel called *Simplicius Simplicissimus,* written by Jakob von Grimmelshausen. The author's experiences as a soldier in the Thirty Years' War give his descriptions of the effect of the war on ordinary people a certain vividness and reality. This selection describes the fate of a peasant farm, an experience all too familiar to thousands of German peasants between 1618 and 1648.

Jakob von Grimmelshausen, *Simplicius Simplicissimus*

The first thing these horsemen did in the nice back rooms of the house was to put in their horses. Then everyone took up a special job, one having to do with death and destruction. Although some began butchering, heating water, and rendering lard, as if to prepare for a banquet, others raced through the house, ransacking upstairs and down; not even the privy chamber was safe, as if the golden fleece of Jason might be hidden there. Still others bundled up big packs of cloth, household goods, and clothes, as if they wanted to hold a rummage sale somewhere. What they did not intend to take along they broke and spoiled. Some ran their swords into the hay and straw, as if there hadn't been hogs enough to stick. Some shook the feathers out of beds and put bacon slabs, hams, and other stuff in the ticking, as if they might sleep better on these. Others knocked down the hearth and broke the windows, as if announcing an ever-lasting summer. They flattened out copper and pewter dishes and baled the ruined goods. They burned up bedsteads, tables, chairs, and benches, though there were yards and yards of dry firewood outside the kitchen. Jars and crocks, pots and casseroles all were broken, either because they preferred their meat broiled or because they thought they'd eat only one meal with us. In the barn, the hired girl was handled so roughly that she was unable to walk away, I am ashamed to report. They stretched the hired man out flat on the ground, stuck a wooden wedge in his mouth to keep it open, and emptied a milk bucket full of stinking manure drippings down his throat; they called it a Swedish cocktail. He didn't relish it and made a very wry face. By this means they forced him to take a raiding party to some other place where they carried off men and cattle and brought them to our farm. Among those were my father, mother, and [sister] Ursula.

Then they used thumbscrews, which they cleverly made out of their pistols, to torture the peasants, as if they wanted to burn witches. Though he had confessed to nothing as yet, they put one of the captured hayseeds in the bake-oven and lighted a fire in it. They put a rope around someone else's head and tightened it like a tour-niquet until blood came out of his mouth, nose, and ears. In short, every soldier had his favorite method of making life miserable for peasants, and every peasant had his own misery. My father was, as I thought, particularly lucky because he confessed with a laugh what others were forced to say in pain and martyrdom. No doubt because he was the head of the household, he was shown special consider-ation; they put him close to a fire, tied him by his hands and legs, and rubbed damp salt on the bottoms of his feet. Our old nanny goat had to lick it off and this so tickled my father that he could have burst laughing. This seemed so clever and entertaining to me— I had never seen or heard my father laugh so long—that I joined him in laughter, to keep him company or perhaps to cover up my ignorance. In the midst of such glee he told them the whereabouts of hidden treasure much richer in gold, pearls, and jewelry than might have been expected on a farm.

I can't say much about the captured wives, hired girls, and daughters because the soldiers didn't let me watch their doings. But I do remember hearing pitiful screams from various dark corners and I guess that my mother and our Ursula had it no better than the rest.

Q *What does this document reveal about the effect of war on ordinary Europeans?*

Response to Crisis: The Practice of Absolutism

Q Focus Question: What was absolutism, and what were the main characteristics of the absolute monarchies that emerged in France, Prussia, Austria, and Russia?

Many people responded to the crises of the seventeenth century by searching for order. An increase in monar-chical power became an obvious means for achieving stability. The result was what historians have called **absolutism** or absolute monarchy. Absolutism meant that the sovereign power or ultimate authority in the state rested in the hands of a king who claimed to rule by divine right—the idea that kings received their power from God and were responsible to no one but God. Late-sixteenth-century political theorists believed that sover-eign power consisted of the authority to make laws, levy taxes, administer justice, control the state's administrative system, and determine foreign policy.

France Under Louis XIV

France during the reign of Louis XIV (1643–1715) has traditionally been regarded as the best example of the practice of absolute or divine-right monarchy in the

COMPARATIVE ILLUSTRATION

Sun Kings, West and East. At the end of the seventeenth century, two powerful rulers dominated their kingdoms. Both monarchs ruled states that dominated the affairs of the regions around them. And both rulers saw themselves as favored by divine authority—Louis XIV as a divine-right monarch and Kangxi as possessing the mandate of Heaven. Thus, both rulers saw themselves not as divine beings but as divinely ordained beings whose job was to govern organized societies. On the left, Louis XIV, who ruled France from 1643 to 1715, is seen in a portrait by Hyacinth Rigaud that captures the king's sense of royal dignity and grandeur. On the right, Kangxi, who ruled China from 1661 to 1722, is seen in a nineteenth-century portrait that shows the ruler seated in majesty on his imperial throne.

Q Considering that these rulers practiced very different religions, why did they justify their powers in such a similar fashion?

seventeenth century. French culture, language, and manners reached into all levels of European society. French diplomacy and wars overwhelmed the political affairs of western and central Europe. The court of Louis XIV seemed to be imitated everywhere in Europe (see the comparative illustration above).

Political Institutions One of the keys to Louis's power was his control of the central policy-making machinery of government, which he made part of his own court and household. The royal court located at Versailles served three purposes simultaneously: it was the personal household of the king, the location of central governmental machinery, and the place where powerful subjects came to seek favors and offices for themselves and their clients. The greatest danger to Louis's personal rule came from the very high nobles and princes of the blood (the royal princes), who considered it their natural role to

Interior of Versailles: The Hall of Mirrors. Pictured here is the exquisite Hall of Mirrors in King Louis XIV's palace at Versailles. Located on the second floor, the hall overlooks the park below. Hundreds of mirrors were placed on the wall opposite the windows to create an illusion of even greater width. Careful planning went into every detail of the interior decoration. Even the doorknobs were specially designed to reflect the magnificence of Versailles.

assert the policy-making role of royal ministers. Louis eliminated this threat by removing them from the royal council, the chief administrative body of the king, and enticing them to his court at Versailles, where he could keep them preoccupied with court life and out of politics. Instead of the high nobility and royal princes, Louis relied for his ministers on nobles who came from relatively new aristocratic families. His ministers were expected to be subservient: "I had no intention of sharing my authority with them," Louis said.

Louis's domination of his ministers and secretaries gave him control of the central policy-making machinery of government and thus authority over the traditional areas of monarchical power: the formulation of foreign policy, the making of war and peace, the assertion of the secular power of the crown against any religious authority, and the ability to levy taxes to fulfill these functions. Louis had considerably less success with the internal administration of the kingdom, however.

The Economy and the Military The cost of building palaces, maintaining his court, and pursuing his wars made finances a crucial issue for Louis XIV. He was most fortunate in having the services of Jean-Baptiste Colbert (1619–1683) as controller general of finances. Colbert sought to increase the wealth and power of France by general adherence to mercantilism, which focused on the role of the state and maintained that state intervention in the economy was desirable for the sake of the national good. To decrease imports and increase exports, Colbert granted subsidies to individuals who established new industries. To improve communications and the transportation of goods internally, he built roads and canals. To decrease imports directly, Colbert raised tariffs on foreign goods.

The increase in royal power that Louis pursued led the king to develop a professional army numbering 100,000 men in peacetime and 400,000 in time of war. To achieve the prestige and military glory befitting an absolute king as well as to ensure the domination of his Bourbon dynasty over European affairs, Louis waged four wars between 1667 and 1713. His ambitions roused much of Europe to form coalitions that were determined to prevent the certain destruction of the European balance of power by Bourbon hegemony. Although Louis added some territory to France's northeastern frontier and established a member of his own Bourbon dynasty on the throne of Spain, he also left France impoverished and surrounded by enemies.

Absolutism in Central and Eastern Europe

During the seventeenth century, a development of great importance for the modern Western world took place with the appearance in central and eastern Europe of three new powers: Prussia, Austria, and Russia.

Prussia Frederick William the Great Elector (1640–1688) laid the foundation for the Prussian state. Realizing that the land he had inherited, known as Brandenburg-Prussia, was a small, open territory with no natural frontiers for defense, Frederick William built an army of 40,000 men, the fourth largest in Europe. To sustain the army, Frederick William established the General War Commissariat to levy taxes for the army and oversee its growth. The Commissariat soon evolved into an agency for civil government as well. The new bureaucratic machine became the elector's chief instrument to govern the state. Many of its officials were members of the Prussian landed aristocracy, the Junkers, who also served as officers in the all-important army.

In 1701, Frederick William's son Frederick (1688–1713) officially gained the title of king. Elector Frederick III became King Frederick I, and Brandenburg-Prussia simply Prussia. In the eighteenth century, Prussia emerged as a great power in Europe.

Austria The Austrian Habsburgs had long played a significant role in European politics as Holy Roman Emperors, but by the end of the Thirty Years' War, their hopes of creating an empire in Germany had been dashed. In the seventeenth century, the house of Austria created a new empire in eastern and southeastern Europe.

The nucleus of the new Austrian Empire remained the traditional Austrian hereditary possessions: Lower and Upper Austria, Carinthia, Carniola, Styria, and Tyrol. To these had been added the kingdom of Bohemia and parts of northwestern Hungary. After the defeat of the Turks in 1687 (see Chapter 16), Austria took control of all of Hungary, Transylvania, Croatia, and Slovenia, thus establishing the Austrian Empire in southeastern Europe. By the beginning of the eighteenth century, the house of Austria had assembled an empire of considerable size.

The Austrian monarchy, however, never became a highly centralized, absolutist state, primarily because it contained so many different national groups. The Austrian Empire remained a collection of territories held together by the Habsburg emperor, who was archduke of Austria, king of Bohemia, and king of Hungary. Each of these regions had its own laws and political life.

From Muscovy to Russia A new Russian state had emerged in the fifteenth century under the leadership of the principality of Muscovy and its grand dukes. In the sixteenth century, Ivan IV (1533–1584) became the first ruler to take the title of *tsar* (the Russian word for *Caesar*). Ivan expanded the territories of Russia eastward and crushed the power of the Russian nobility. He was known as Ivan the Terrible because of his ruthless deeds, among them stabbing his son to death in a heated argument. When Ivan's dynasty came to an end in 1598, it was followed by a period of anarchy that did not end until the Zemsky Sobor (national assembly) chose Michael Romanov as the new tsar, establishing a dynasty that lasted until 1917. One of its most prominent members was Peter the Great.

Peter the Great (1689–1725) was an unusual character. A towering, strong man at 6 feet 9 inches tall, Peter enjoyed a low kind of humor—belching contests and crude jokes—and vicious punishments, including floggings, impalings, and roastings. Peter got a firsthand view of the West when he made a trip there in 1697–1698 and returned home with a firm determination to Westernize or Europeanize Russia. He was especially eager to borrow European technology in order to create the army and navy he needed to make Russia a great power.

As could be expected, one of his first priorities was the reorganization of the army and the creation of a navy. Employing both Russians and Europeans as officers, he conscripted peasants for twenty-five-year stints of service to build a standing army of 210,000 men. Peter has also been given credit for forming the first Russian navy.

To impose the rule of the central government more effectively throughout the land, Peter divided Russia into provinces. Although he hoped to create a "police state," by which he meant a well-ordered community governed in accordance with law, few of his bureaucrats shared his concept of duty to the state. Peter hoped for a sense of civic duty, but his own forceful personality created an atmosphere of fear that prevented it.

The object of Peter's domestic reforms was to make Russia into a great state and military power. His primary goal was to "open a window to the west," meaning an ice-free port easily accessible to Europe. This could only be achieved on the Baltic, but at that time, the Baltic coast was controlled by Sweden, the most important power in northern Europe. A long and hard-fought war with Sweden won Peter the lands he sought. In 1703, Peter began the construction of a new city, Saint Petersburg, his window to the west and a symbol that Russia was looking westward to Europe. Under Peter, Russia became a great military power and, by his death in 1725, an important European state.

England and Limited Monarchy

Q Focus Question: How and why did England avoid the path of absolutism?

Not all states were absolutist in the seventeenth century. One of the most prominent examples of resistance to absolute monarchy came in England, where king and Parliament struggled to determine the roles each should play in governing England.

Conflict Between King and Parliament

With the death of Queen Elizabeth I in 1603, the Tudor dynasty became extinct, and the Stuart line of rulers was inaugurated with the accession to the throne of Elizabeth's cousin, King James VI of Scotland, who became James I (1603–1625) of England. James espoused the divine right of kings, a viewpoint that alienated Parliament, which had grown accustomed under the Tudors to act on the premise that monarch and Parliament together ruled England as a "balanced polity." Then, too, the

Puritans—Protestants within the Anglican Church who, inspired by Calvinist theology, wished to eliminate every trace of Roman Catholicism from the Church of England—were alienated by the king's strong defense of the Anglican Church. Many of England's gentry, mostly well-to-do landowners, had become Puritans, and they formed an important and substantial part of the House of Commons, the lower house of Parliament. It was not wise to alienate these men.

The conflict that had begun during the reign of James came to a head during the reign of his son Charles I (1625–1649). Charles also believed in divine-right monarchy, and religious differences added to the hostility between Charles I and Parliament. The king's attempt to impose more ritual on the Anglican Church struck the Puritans as a return to Catholic practices. When Charles tried to force the Puritans to accept his religious policies, thousands of them went off to the "howling wildernesses" of America.

Civil War and Commonwealth

Grievances mounted until England finally slipped into a civil war (1642–1648) won by the parliamentary forces, due largely to the New Model Army of Oliver Cromwell, the only real military genius of the war. The New Model Army was composed primarily of more extreme Puritans known as the Independents, who, in typical Calvinist fashion, believed they were doing battle for God. As Cromwell wrote in one of his military reports, "Sir, this is none other but the hand of God; and to Him alone belongs the glory." We might give some credit to Cromwell; his soldiers were well trained in the new military tactics of the seventeenth century.

After the execution of Charles I on January 30, 1649, Parliament abolished the monarchy and the House of Lords and proclaimed England a republic or commonwealth. But Cromwell and his army, unable to work effectively with Parliament, dispersed it by force and established a military dictatorship. After Cromwell's death in 1658, the army decided that military rule was no longer feasible and restored the monarchy in the person of Charles II (1660–1685), the son of Charles I.

Restoration and a Glorious Revolution

Charles II was sympathetic to Catholicism, and Parliament's suspicions were aroused in 1672 when he took the audacious step of issuing the Declaration of Indulgence, which suspended the laws that Parliament had passed against Catholics and Puritans after the restoration of the monarchy. Parliament forced the king to suspend the declaration.

The accession of James II (1685–1688) to the crown virtually guaranteed a new constitutional crisis for

CHRONOLOGY Absolute and Limited Monarchy

France	
Louis XIV	1643–1715
Brandenburg-Prussia	
Frederick William the Great Elector	1640–1688
Elector Frederick III (King Frederick I)	1688–1713
Russia	
Ivan IV the Terrible	1533–1584
Peter the Great	1689–1725
First trip to the West	1697–1698
Construction of Saint Petersburg begins	1703
England	
Civil wars	1642–1648
Commonwealth	1649–1653
Charles II	1660–1685
Declaration of Indulgence	1672
James II	1685–1688
Glorious Revolution	1688
Bill of Rights	1689

England. An open and devout Catholic, his attempt to further Catholic interests made religion once more a primary cause of conflict between king and Parliament. James named Catholics to high positions in the government, army, navy, and universities. Parliamentary outcries against James's policies stopped short of rebellion because the members knew that he was an old man and that his successors were his Protestant daughters Mary and Anne, born to his first wife. But on June 10, 1688, a son was born to James II's second wife, also a Catholic. Suddenly, the specter of a Catholic hereditary monarchy loomed large. A group of prominent English noblemen invited the Dutch chief executive, William of Orange, husband of James's daughter Mary, to invade England. William and Mary raised an army and invaded England while James, his wife, and their infant son fled to France. With little bloodshed, England had undergone its "Glorious Revolution."

In January 1689, Parliament offered the throne to William and Mary, who accepted it along with the provisions of the Bill of Rights (see the box on p. 380). The Bill of Rights affirmed Parliament's right to make laws and levy taxes. The rights of citizens to keep arms and have a jury trial were also confirmed. By deposing one king and establishing another, Parliament had destroyed the divine-right theory of kingship (William was, after all, king by grace of Parliament, not God) and asserted its right to participate in the government. Parliament did not have

THE BILL OF RIGHTS

In 1688, the English experienced a bloodless revolution in which the Stuart king James II was replaced by Mary, James's daughter, and her husband, William of Orange. After William and Mary had assumed power, Parliament passed a Bill of Rights that specified the rights of Parliament and laid the foundation for a constitutional monarchy.

The Bill of Rights

Whereas the said late King James II having abdicated the government, and the throne being thereby vacant, his Highness the prince of Orange (whom it hath pleased Almighty God to make the glorious instrument of delivering this kingdom from popery and arbitrary power) did (by the device of the lords spiritual and temporal, and diverse principal persons of the Commons) cause letters to be written to the lords spiritual and temporal, being Protestants, and other letters to the several counties, cities, universities, boroughs, and Cinque Ports, for the choosing of such persons to represent them, as were of right to be sent to parliament, to meet and sit at Westminster upon the two and twentieth day of January, in this year 1689, in order to such an establishment as that their religion, laws, and liberties might not again be in danger of being subverted; upon which letters elections have been accordingly made.

And thereupon the said lords spiritual and temporal and Commons, pursuant to their respective letters and elections, being now assembled in a full and free representation of this nation, taking into their most serious consideration the best means for attaining the ends aforesaid, do in the first place (as their ancestors in like case have usually done), for the vindication and assertion of their ancient rights and liberties, declare:

1. That the pretended power of suspending laws, or the execution of laws, by regal authority, without consent of parliament is illegal.

2. That the pretended power of dispensing with the laws, or the execution of law by regal authority, as it hath been assumed and exercised of late, is illegal.

3. That the commission for erecting the late court of commissioners for ecclesiastical causes, and all other commissions and courts of like nature, are illegal and pernicious.

4. That levying money for or to the use of the crown by pretense of prerogative, without grant of parliament, for longer time or in other manner than the same is or shall be granted, is illegal.

5. That it is the right of the subjects to petition the king, and all commitments and prosecutions for such petitioning are illegal.

6. That the raising or keeping a standing army within the kingdom in time of peace, unless it be with consent of parliament, is against law.

7. That the subjects which are Protestants may have arms for their defense suitable to their conditions, and as allowed by law.

8. That election of members of parliament ought to be free.

9. That the freedom of speech, and debates or proceedings in parliament, ought not to be impeached or questioned in any court or place out of parliament.

10. That excessive bail ought not to be required, nor excessive fines imposed, nor cruel and unusual punishments inflicted.

11. That jurors ought to be duly impaneled and returned, and jurors which pass upon men in trials for high treason ought to be freeholders.

12. That all grants and promises of fines and forfeitures of particular persons before conviction are illegal and void.

13. And that for redress of all grievances, and for the amending, strengthening, and preserving of the laws, parliament ought to be held frequently.

Q *How did the Bill of Rights lay the foundation for a constitutional monarchy in England?*

complete control of the government, but it now had the right to participate in affairs of state. Over the next century, it would gradually prove to be the real authority in the English system of **limited (constitutional) monarchy.**

The Flourishing of European Culture

Q Focus Question: How did the artistic and literary achievements of this era reflect the political and economic developments of the period?

Despite religious wars and the growth of absolutism, European culture continued to flourish. The era was blessed with a number of prominent artists and writers.

Art: The Baroque

The artistic movement known as the **Baroque** dominated the Western artistic world for a century and a half. The Baroque began in Italy in the last quarter of the sixteenth century and spread to the rest of Europe and Latin America. Baroque artists sought to harmonize the Classical ideals of Renaissance art with the spiritual feelings of the sixteenth-century religious revival. In large part, Baroque art and architecture reflected the search for power that was characteristic of much of the seventeenth century. Baroque churches and palaces featured richly ornamented facades, sweeping staircases, and an overall splendor meant to impress people. Kings and princes wanted other kings and princes, as well as their own subjects, to be in awe of their power.

Peter Paul Rubens, *The Landing of Marie de' Medici at Marseilles.* The Flemish painter Peter Paul Rubens played a key role in spreading the Baroque style from Italy to other parts of Europe. In *The Landing of Marie de' Medici at Marseilles,* Rubens made dramatic use of light and color, bodies in motion, and luxurious nudes to heighten the emotional intensity of the scene. This was one of a cycle of twenty-one paintings dedicated to the queen mother of France.

Baroque painting was known for its use of dramatic effects to arouse the emotions, especially evident in the works of Peter Paul Rubens (1577–1640), a prolific artist and an important figure in the spread of the Baroque from Italy to other parts of Europe. In his artistic masterpieces, bodies in violent motion, heavily fleshed nudes, a dramatic use of light and shadow, and rich sensuous pigments converge to express intense emotions.

Art: Dutch Realism

The supremacy of Dutch commerce in the seventeenth century was paralleled by a brilliant flowering of Dutch painting. Wealthy patricians and burghers of Dutch urban society commissioned works of art for their guildhalls, town halls, and private dwellings. The interests of this burger society were reflected in the subject matter of many Dutch paintings: portraits of themselves, group portraits of their military companies and guilds, landscapes, seascapes, genre scenes, still lifes, and the interiors of their residences. Neither Classical nor Baroque, Dutch painters were primarily interested in the realistic portrayal of secular everyday life.

A Golden Age of Literature in England

In England, writing for the stage reached new heights between 1580 and 1640. The golden age of English literature is often called the Elizabethan Era because much of the English cultural flowering occurred during Elizabeth's reign. Elizbethan literature exhibits the exuberance and pride associated with English exploits under Queen Elizabeth. Of all the forms of Elizabethan literature, none expressed the energy and intellectual versatility of the era better than drama. And no dramatist is more famous or more accomplished than William Shakespeare (1564–1614).

Shakespeare was a "complete man of the theater." Although best known for writing plays, he was also an actor and a shareholder in the chief acting company of the time, the Lord Chamberlain's Company, which played in various London theaters. Shakespeare is to this day hailed as a genius. A master of the English language, he imbued its words with power and majesty. And his technical proficiency was matched by incredible insight into human psychology. Whether writing tragedies or comedies, Shakespeare exhibited a remarkable understanding of the human condition.

CONCLUSION

IN CHAPTER 14, WE OBSERVED how the movement of Europeans outside of Europe began to change the shape of world history. But what had made this development possible? After all, the religious division of Europe had led to almost a hundred years of religious warfare complicated by serious political, economic, and social issues—the worst series of wars and civil wars since the collapse of the western Roman Empire—before Europeans finally admitted that they would have to tolerate different ways to worship God.

At the same time, the concept of a united Christendom, held as an ideal since the Middle Ages, had been irrevocably destroyed by the religious wars, enabling a system of nation-states to emerge in which power politics took on increasing significance. Within those states slowly emerged some of the machinery that made possible a growing centralization of power. In absolutist states, strong monarchs with the assistance of their aristocracies took the lead in promoting greater centralization. In all the major European states, a growing concern for power led to larger armies and greater conflict, stronger economies, and more powerful governments. From a global point of view, Europeans—with their strong governments, prosperous economies, and strengthened

military forces—were beginning to dominate other parts of the world, leading to a growing belief in the superiority of their civilization.

Yet despite Europeans' increasing domination of global trade markets, they had not achieved their goal of diminishing the power of Islam, first pursued during the Crusades. In fact, as we shall see in the next chapter, in the midst of European expansion and exploration, three new and powerful Muslim empires were taking shape in the Middle East and South Asia.

TIMELINE

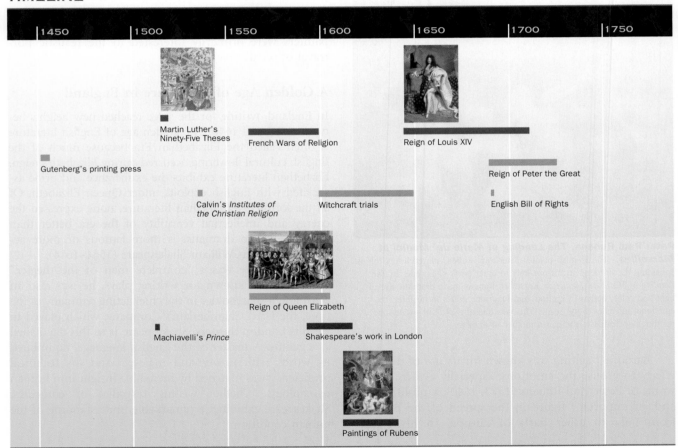

1450   1500   1550   1600   1650   1700   1750

Martin Luther's Ninety-Five Theses

French Wars of Religion

Reign of Louis XIV

Gutenberg's printing press

Reign of Peter the Great

Calvin's *Institutes of the Christian Religion*

Witchcraft trials

English Bill of Rights

Reign of Queen Elizabeth

Machiavelli's *Prince*

Shakespeare's work in London

Paintings of Rubens

SUGGESTED READING

The Reformation: General Works Basic surveys of the Reformation period include **H. J. Grimm,** *The Reformation Era, 1500–1650,* 2nd ed. (New York, 1973); **D. L. Jensen,** *Reformation Europe,* 2nd ed. (Lexington, Mass., 1990); and **D. MacCulloch,** *The Reformation* (New York, 2003). Also see the brief works by **U. Rublack,** *Reformation Europe* (Cambridge,

2005), and **P. Collison,** *The Reformation: A History* (New York, 2006).

The Protestant and Catholic Reformations The classic account of Martin Luther's life is **R. Bainton,** *Here I Stand: A Life of Martin Luther* (New York, 1950). More recent works include **H. A. Oberman,** *Luther: Man Between God and the Devil* (New York, 1992), and the brief biography by **M. Marty,** *Martin*

Luther (New York, 2004). On the role of Charles V, see **W. Maltby, *The Reign of Charles V*** (New York, 2002). The most comprehensive account of the various groups and individuals who are called Anabaptist is **G. H. Williams, *The Radical Reformation,*** 2nd ed. (Kirksville, Mo., 1992). A good survey of the English Reformation is **A. G. Dickens, *The English Reformation,*** 2nd ed. (New York, 1989). On John Calvin, see **W. G. Naphy, *Calvin and the Consolidation of the Genevan Reformation*** (Philadelphia, 2003). On the impact of the Reformation on the family, see **J. F. Harrington, *Reordering Marriage and Society in Reformation Germany*** (New York, 1995). A good introduction to the Catholic Reformation can be found in **R. P. Hsia, *The World of Catholic Renewal, 1540–1770*** (Cambridge, 1998).

Europe in Crisis, 1560–1650 On the French Wars of Religion, see **M. P. Holt, *The French Wars of Religion, 1562–1629*** (New York, 1995), and **R. J. Knecht, *The French Wars of Religion, 1559–1598,*** 2nd ed. (New York, 1996). A good biography of Philip II is **G. Parker, *Philip II,*** 3rd ed. (Chicago, 1995). Elizabeth's reign can be examined in **C. Haigh, *Elizabeth I,*** 2nd ed. (New York, 1998). On the Thirty Years' War, see **R. Bonney, *The Thirty Years' War, 1618–1648*** (Oxford, 2002). Witchcraft hysteria can be examined in **R. Briggs, *Witches and Neighbours: The Social and Cultural Context of European Witchcraft,*** 2nd ed. (Oxford, 2002).

Absolute and Limited Monarchy A solid and very readable biography of Louis XIV is **J. Levi, *Louis XIV*** (New York, 2004). For a brief study, see **P. R. Campbell, *Louis XIV, 1661–1715*** (London, 1993). On the creation of the Austrian state, see **P. S. Fichtner, *The Habsburg Monarchy, 1490–1848*** (New York, 2003). See **P. H. Wilson, *Absolutism in Central Europe*** (New York, 2000), on both Prussia and Austria. Works on Peter the Great include **P. Bushkovitz, *Peter the Great*** (Oxford, 2001), and **L. Hughes, *Russia in the Age of Peter the Great*** (New Haven, Conn., 1998). On the English Revolutions, see **M. A. Kishlansky, *A Monarchy Transformed*** (London, 1996), and **W. A. Speck, *The Revolution of 1688*** (Oxford, 1988).

European Culture For a general survey of Baroque culture, see **F. C. Marchetti et al., *Baroque, 1600–1770*** (New York, 2005). The literature on Shakespeare is enormous. For a biography, see **A. L. Rowse, *The Life of Shakespeare*** (New York, 1963).

WORLD HISTORY RESOURCES

Visit the website for *The Essential World History* **to access study aids such as Flashcards, Critical Thinking Exercises, and Chapter Quizzes:**
  www.cengage.com/history/duikspiel/essentialworld6e

DISCOVERY

GOVERNMENT AND SOCIETY Based on the following document, how did the Thirty Years' War affect the average peasant? How might the atrocities of war for a thirty-year period influence the average person's view of government? What might people seek in future governments? Do you see any parallels in the modern world? How were such wars related to European overseas expansion during this period? Do you see any connection between the wars in Europe and the rivalries of European nations overseas?

In thinking about this question, begin by breaking it down into the components shown below. A discussion of the significance of each component should appear in your answer.

POLITICS AND GOVERNMENT Look at the paintings of Elizabeth I (p. 371) and Louis XIV (p. 376). What were the artists attempting to portray about each ruler? What are the most prominent features of each painting? What might this say about how these monarchs wanted their people to view them? What are some similarities and differences between Elizabeth I and Louis XIV? How did kingship change between the reign of Elizabeth and the time of Louis XIV? How was European overseas expansion during this period related to the changes in kingship and political developments that occurred in Europe?

JAKOB VON GRIMMELSHAUSEN, *SIMPLICIUS SIMPLICISSIMUS*

The first thing these horsemen did in the nice back rooms of the house was to put in their horses. Then everyone took up a special job, one having to do with death and destruction. Although some began butchering, heating water, and rendering lard, as if to prepare for a banquet, others raced through the house, ransacking upstairs and down; not even the privy chamber was safe, as if the golden fleece of Jason might be hidden there. Still others bundled up big packs of cloth, household goods, and clothes, as if they wanted to hold a rummage sale somewhere. What they did not intend to take along they broke and spoiled. Some ran their swords into the hay and straw, as if there hadn't been hogs enough to stick. Some shook the feathers out of beds and put bacon slabs, hams, and other stuff in the ticking, as if they might sleep better on these. Others knocked down the hearth and broke the windows, as if announcing an everlasting summer. They flattened out copper and pewter dishes and baled the ruined goods. They burned up bedsteads, tables, chairs, and benches, though there were yards and yards of dry firewood outside the kitchen. Jars and crocks, pots and casseroles all were broken, either because they preferred their meat broiled or because they thought they'd eat only one meal with us. In the barn, the hired girl was handled so roughly that she was unable to walk away, I am ashamed to report. They stretched the hired man out flat on the ground, stuck a wooden wedge in his mouth to keep it open, and emptied a milk bucket full of stinking manure drippings down his throat; they called it a Swedish cocktail. He didn't relish it and made a very wry face. By this means they forced him to take a raiding party to some other place where they

carried off men and cattle and brought them to our farm. Among those were my father, mother, and [sister] Ursula.

Then they used thumbscrews, which they cleverly made out of their pistols, to torture the peasants, as if they wanted to burn witches. Though he had confessed to nothing as yet, they put one of the captured hayseeds in the bake-oven and lighted a fire in it. They put a rope around someone else's head and tightened it like a tourniquet until blood came out of his mouth, nose, and ears. In short, every soldier had his favorite method of making life miserable for peasants, and every peasant had his own misery. My father was, as I thought, particularly lucky because he confessed with a laugh what others were forced to say in pain and martyrdom. No doubt because he was the head of the household, he was shown special consideration; they put him close to a fire, tied him by his hands and legs, and rubbed damp salt on the bottoms of his feet. Our old nanny goat had to lick it off and this so tickled my father that he could have burst laughing. This seemed so clever and entertaining to me—I had never seen or heard my father laugh so long—that I joined him in laughter, to keep him company or perhaps to cover up my ignorance. In the midst of such glee he told them the whereabouts of hidden treasure much richer in gold, pearls, and jewelry than might have been expected on a farm.

I can't say much about the captured wives, hired girls, and daughters because the soldiers didn't let me watch their doings. But I do remember hearing pitiful screams from various dark corners and I guess that my mother and our Ursula had it no better than the rest.

CHAPTER OUTLINE AND FOCUS QUESTIONS

The Ottoman Empire

Q What was the ethnic composition of the Ottoman Empire, and how did the government of the sultan administer such a diverse population? How did Ottoman policy in this regard compare with the policies applied in Europe and Asia?

The Safavids

Q How did the Safavid Empire come into existence, and what led to its collapse?

The Grandeur of the Mughals

Q Although the Ottoman, Safavid, and Mughal Empires all adopted Islam as their state religion, their approach was often different. Describe the differences, and explain why they might have occurred.

CRITICAL THINKING

Q What were the main characteristics of each of the Muslim empires, and in what ways did they resemble each other? How were they distinct from their European counterparts?

Turks fight Christians at the Battle of Mohács.

© The Art Archive/Topkapi Museum, Istanbul/Gianni Dagli Orti

THE OTTOMAN ARMY, led by Sultan Suleyman the Magnificent, arrived at Mohács, on the plains of Hungary, on an August morning in 1526. The Turkish force numbered about 100,000 men, and in its baggage were three hundred new long-range cannons. Facing them was a somewhat larger European force, clothed in heavy armor but armed with only one hundred older cannons.

The battle began at noon and was over in two hours. The flower of the Hungarian cavalry had been destroyed, and 20,000 foot soldiers had drowned in a nearby swamp. The Ottomans had lost fewer than two hundred men. Two weeks later, they seized the Hungarian capital at Buda and prepared to lay siege to the nearby Austrian city of Vienna. Europe was in a panic. It was to be the high point of Turkish expansion in Europe.

In launching their Age of Exploration, European rulers had hoped that by controlling global markets, they could cripple the power of Islam and reduce its threat to the security of Europe. But the Christian nations' dream of expanding their influence around the globe at the expense of their great Muslim rival had not entirely been achieved. On the contrary, the Muslim world, which appeared to have entered a period of decline with the collapse of the Abbasid caliphate during the era of the Mongols, managed to revive in the shadow of Europe's Age of Exploration, a period that also saw the rise of three great Muslim empires. These powerful Muslim states—those of the Ottomans, the Safavids, and the Mughals—dominated the Middle East and the South Asian subcontinent and brought a measure of stability to a region that had been in turmoil for centuries. ❁

The Ottoman Empire

Q **Focus Questions:** What was the ethnic composition of the Ottoman Empire, and how did the government of the sultan administer such a diverse population? How did Ottoman policy in this regard compare with the policies applied in Europe and Asia?

The Ottoman Turks were among the various Turkic-speaking peoples who had spread westward from Central Asia in the ninth, tenth, and eleventh centuries. The first to appear were the Seljuk Turks, who initially attempted to revive the declining Abbasid caliphate in Baghdad. Later they established themselves in the Anatolian peninsula at the expense of the Byzantine Empire. Turks served as warriors or administrators, while the peasants who tilled the farmland were mainly Greek.

The Rise of the Ottoman Turks

In the late thirteenth century, a new group of Turks under the tribal leader Osman (1280–1326) began to consolidate their power in the northwestern corner of the Anatolian peninsula. At first, the Osman Turks were relatively peaceful and engaged in pastoral pursuits, but as the Seljuk Empire began to disintegrate in the early fourteenth century, they began to expand and founded the Osmanli (later to be known as Ottoman) dynasty, with its capital at Bursa.

The Ottomans gained a key advantage by seizing the Bosporus and the Dardanelles, between the Mediterranean and the Black seas. The Byzantine Empire, of course, had controlled the area for centuries, serving as a buffer between the Muslim Middle East and the Latin West. The Byzantines, however, had been severely weakened by the sack of Constantinople in the Fourth Crusade (in 1204) and the Western occupation of much of the empire for the next half century. In 1345, Ottoman forces under their leader Orkhan I (1326–1360) crossed the Bosporus for the first time to support a usurper against the Byzantine emperor in Constantinople. Setting up their first European base at Gallipoli at the Mediterranean entrance to the Dardanelles, Turkish forces expanded gradually into the Balkans and allied with fractious Serbian and Bulgar forces against the Byzantines. In these unstable conditions, the Ottomans gradually established permanent settlements throughout the area, where Turkish **beys** (provincial governors in the Ottoman Empire; from the Turkish *beg,* "knight") drove out the previous landlords and collected taxes from the local Slavic peasants. The Ottoman leader now began to claim the title of **sultan** or sovereign of his domain.

In 1360, Orkhan was succeeded by his son Murad I (1360–1389), who consolidated Ottoman power in the Balkans and gradually reduced the Byzantine emperor to a vassal. Murad now began to build up a strong military administration based on the recruitment of Christians into an elite guard. Called **Janissaries** (from the Turkish *yeni cheri,* "new troops"), they were recruited from the local Christian population in the Balkans and then converted to Islam and trained as foot soldiers or administrators. One of the major advantages of the Janissaries was that they were directly subordinated to the sultanate and therefore owed their loyalty to the person of the sultan. Other military forces were organized by the beys and were thus loyal to their local tribal leaders.

The Janissary corps also represented a response to changes in warfare. As the knowledge of firearms spread in the late fourteenth century, the Turks began to master the new technology, including siege cannons and muskets (see the comparative essay "The Changing Face of War" on p. 387). The traditional nomadic cavalry charge was now outmoded and was superseded by infantry forces armed with muskets. Thus, the Janissaries provided a well-armed infantry who served both as an elite guard to protect the palace and as a means of extending Turkish control in the Balkans. With his new forces, Murad defeated the Serbs at the famous Battle of Kosovo in 1389 and ended Serbian hegemony in the area.

Expansion of the Empire

Under Murad's successor, Bayazid I (1389–1402), the Ottomans advanced northward, annexed Bulgaria, and slaughtered the French cavalry at a major battle on the Danube. When Mehmet II (1451–1481) succeeded to the throne, he was determined to capture Constantinople. Already in control of the Dardanelles, he ordered the construction of a major fortress on the Bosporus just north of the city, which put the Turks in a position to strangle the Byzantines.

The Fall of Constantinople The last Byzantine emperor issued a desperate call for help from the Europeans, but only the Genoese came to his defense. With 80,000 troops ranged against only 7,000 defenders, Mehmet laid siege to Constantinople in 1453. In their attack on the city, the Turks made use of massive cannons with 26-foot barrels

COMPARATIVE ESSAY
THE CHANGING FACE OF WAR

SCIENCE & TECHNOLOGY

"War," as the renowned French historian Fernand Braudel once observed, "has always been a matter of arms and techniques. Improved techniques can radically alter the course of events." Braudel's remark was directed to the situation in the Mediterranean region during the sixteenth century, when the adoption of artillery changed the face of warfare and gave enormous advantages to the countries that stood at the head of the new technological revolution. But it could as easily have been applied to the present day, when potential adversaries possess weapons capable of reaching across oceans and continents.

One crucial aspect of military superiority, of course, lies in the nature of weaponry. From the invention of the bow and arrow to the advent of the atomic era, the possession of superior instruments of war has provided a distinct advantage against a poorly armed enemy. It was at least partly the possession of iron weapons, for example, that enabled the invading Hyksos to conquer Egypt during the second millennium B.C.E.

Mobility is another factor of vital importance. During the second millennium B.C.E., horse-drawn chariots revolutionized the art of war from the Mediterranean Sea to the Yellow River valley in northern China. Later, the invention of the stirrup enabled mounted warriors to shoot bows and arrows from horseback, a technique applied with great effect by the Mongols as they devastated civilizations across the Eurasian supercontinent.

To protect themselves from marauding warriors, settled societies began to erect massive walls around their cities and fortresses. That in turn led to the invention of siege weapons like the catapult and the battering ram. The Mongols allegedly even came up with an early form of chemical warfare, hurling human bodies infected with the plague into the bastions of their enemies.

The invention of explosives launched the next great revolution in warfare. First used as a weapon of war by the Tang dynasty in

A detail from the Great Altar of Pergamum showing Roman troops defeating Celtic warriors

China, explosives were brought to the West by the Turks, who used them with great effectiveness in the fifteenth century against the Byzantine Empire. But the Europeans quickly mastered the new technology and took it to new heights, inventing handheld firearms and mounting iron cannons on their warships. The latter represented a significant advantage to European fleets as they began to compete with rivals for control of the Indian and Pacific oceans.

The twentieth century saw revolutionary new developments in the art of warfare, from armored vehicles to airplanes to nuclear arms. But as weapons grow ever more fearsome, they are more risky to use, resulting in the paradox of the Vietnam War, when lightly armed Viet Cong guerrilla units were able to fight the world's mightiest army to a virtual standstill. As the Chinese military strategist Sun Tzu had long ago observed, victory in war often goes to the smartest, not the strongest.

Q *Why do you think it was the Europeans, rather than other peoples, who made use of firearms to expand their influence throughout the rest of the world?*

---

that could launch stone balls weighing up to 1,200 pounds each. The Byzantines stretched heavy chains across the Golden Horn, the inlet that forms the city's harbor, to prevent a naval attack from the north and prepared to make their final stand behind the 13-mile-long wall along the western edge of the city. But Mehmet's forces seized the tip of the peninsula north of the Golden

Horn and then dragged their ships overland across the peninsula from the Bosporus and put them into the water behind the chains. Finally, the walls were breached; the Byzantine emperor died in the final battle.

The Advance into Western Asia and Africa With their new capital at Constantinople, renamed Istanbul, the

The Turkish Conquest of Constantinople. Mehmet II put a stranglehold on the Byzantine capital of Constantinople with a surprise attack by Turkish ships, which were dragged overland and placed in the water behind the enemy's defense lines. In addition, the Turks made use of massive cannons that could launch stone balls weighing up to 1,200 pounds each. The heavy bombardment of the city walls presaged a new kind of warfare in Europe. Notice the fanciful Gothic interpretation of the city in this contemporary French miniature of the siege.

Ottoman Turks had become a dominant force in the Balkans and the Anatolian peninsula. They now began to advance to the east against the Shi'ite kingdom of the Safavids in Persia (see "The Safavids" later in this chapter), which had been promoting rebellion among the Anatolian tribal population and disrupting Turkish trade through the Middle East. After defeating the Safavids at a major battle in 1514, Emperor Selim I (1512–1520) consolidated Turkish control over the territory that had been ancient Mesopotamia and then turned his attention to the Mamluks in Egypt, who had failed to support the Ottomans in their struggle against the Safavids. The Mamluks were defeated in Syria in 1516; Cairo fell a year later. Now controlling several of the holy cities of Islam,

including Jerusalem, Mecca, and Medina, Selim declared himself to be the new caliph, or successor to Muhammad. During the next few years, Turkish armies and fleets advanced westward along the African coast, occupying Tripoli, Tunis, and Algeria and eventually penetrating almost to the Strait of Gibraltar (see Map 16.1).

The impact of Turkish rule on the peoples of North Africa was relatively light. Like their predecessors, the Turks were Muslims, and they preferred where possible to administer their conquered regions through local rulers. Direction by the central government was achieved through appointed pashas who collected taxes (and then paid a fixed percentage as tribute to the central government), maintained law and order, and were directly responsible to Istanbul. The Turks ruled from coastal cities like Algiers, Tunis, and Tripoli and made no attempt to control the interior beyond maintaining the trade routes through the Sahara to the trading centers along the Niger River. Meanwhile, local pirates along the Barbary Coast— the northern coast of Africa from Egypt to the Atlantic Ocean—competed with their Christian rivals in raiding the shipping that passed through the Mediterranean.

By the seventeenth century, the links between the imperial court in Istanbul and its appointed representatives in the Turkish regencies in North Africa had begun to decline. Some of the pashas were dethroned by local elites, while others, such as the bey of Tunis, became hereditary rulers. Even Egypt, whose agricultural wealth and control over the route to the Red Sea made it the most important country in the area to the Turks, gradually became autonomous under a new official class of Janissaries.

Turkish Expansion in Europe After their conquest of Constantinople in 1453, the Ottoman Turks tried to extend their territory in Europe. Under the leadership of Suleyman I the Magnificent (1520–1566), Turkish forces advanced up the Danube, seizing Belgrade in 1521 and winning a major victory over the Hungarians at the Battle of Mohács on the Danube in 1526. Subsequently, the Turks overran most of Hungary, moved into Austria, and advanced as far as Vienna, where they were finally repulsed in 1529. At the same time, they extended their power into the western Mediterranean and threatened to turn it into a Turkish lake until a large Turkish fleet was destroyed by the Spanish at Lepanto in 1571.

In the second half of the seventeenth century, the Ottoman Empire again took the offensive. By mid-1683, the Ottomans had marched through the Hungarian plain and laid siege to Vienna. Repulsed by a mixed army of Austrians, Poles, Bavarians, and Saxons, the Turks retreated and were pushed out of Hungary by a new European coalition. Although they retained the core of their

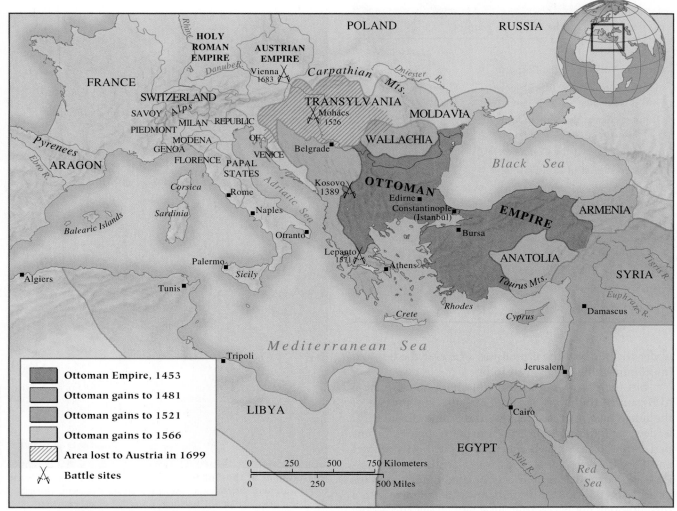

MAP 16.1 The Ottoman Empire. This map shows the territorial growth of the Ottoman Empire from the eve of the conquest of Constantinople in 1453 to the end of the seventeenth century, when a defeat at the hands of Austria led to the loss of a substantial portion of central Europe.

Q Where did the Ottomans come from?

View an animated version of this map or related maps at **www.cengage.com/history/ duikspiel/essentialworld6e**

empire, the Ottoman Turks would never again be a threat to Europe. The Turkish empire held together for the rest of the seventeenth and the eighteenth centuries, but it faced new challenges from the ever-growing Austrian Empire in southeastern Europe and the new Russian giant to the north.

The Nature of Turkish Rule

Like other Muslim empires in Persia and India, the Ottoman political system was the result of the evolution of tribal institutions into a sedentary empire. At the apex of the Ottoman system was the sultan, who was the supreme authority in both a political and a military sense. The origins of this system can be traced back to the bey, who was only a tribal leader, a first among equals, who could claim loyalty from his chiefs so long as he could provide booty and grazing lands for his subordinates. Disputes were settled by tribal law, while Muslim laws were secondary. Tribal leaders collected taxes—or booty—from areas under their control and sent one-fifth on to the bey. Both administrative and military power were centralized

CHRONOLOGY The Ottoman Empire

Reign of Osman I	1280–1326
Ottoman Turks cross the Bosporus	1345
Murad I consolidates Turkish power in the Balkans	1360
Ottomans defeat the Serbian army at Kosovo	1389
Rule of Mehmet II the Conqueror	1451–1481
Turkish conquest of Constantinople	1453
Turks defeat the Mamluks in Syria and seize Cairo	1516–1517
Reign of Suleyman I the Magnificent	1520–1566
Defeat of the Hungarians at Battle of Mohács	1526
Defeat of the Turks at Vienna	1529
Battle of Lepanto	1571
Second siege of Vienna	1683

Recruitment of the Children. The Ottoman Empire, like its Chinese counterpart, sought to recruit its officials on the basis of merit. Through the system called *devshirme* ("collection"), youthful candidates were selected from the non-Muslim population in villages throughout the empire. In this painting, an imperial officer is counting coins to pay for the children's travel expenses to Istanbul, where they will undergo extensive academic and military training. Note the concern of two of the mothers and a priest as they question the official, who undoubtedly underwent the process himself as a child. As they leave their family and friends, the children carry their worldly possessions in bags slung over their shoulders.

under the bey, and the capital was wherever the bey and his administration happened to be.

But the rise of empire brought about an adaptation to Byzantine traditions of rule. The status and prestige of the sultan now increased relative to the subordinate tribal leaders, and the position took on the trappings of imperial rule. Court rituals inherited from the Byzantines and Persians were adopted, as was a centralized administrative system that increasingly isolated the sultan in his palace. The position of the sultan was hereditary, with a son, although not necessarily the eldest, always succeeding the father. This practice led to chronic succession struggles upon the death of individual sultans, and the losers were often executed (strangled with a silk bowstring) or imprisoned. Heirs to the throne were assigned as provincial governors to provide them with experience.

The Harem The heart of the sultan's power was in the Topkapi Palace in the center of Istanbul. Topkapi (meaning "cannon gate") was constructed in 1459 by Mehmet II and served as an administrative center as well as the private residence of the sultan and his family. Eventually, it had a staff of 20,000 employees. The private domain of the sultan was called the **harem** ("sacred place"). Here he resided with his concubines. Normally, a sultan did not marry but chose several concubines as his favorites; they were accorded this status after they gave birth to sons. When a son became a sultan, his mother became known as the queen mother and served as adviser to the throne. This tradition, initiated by the influential wife of Suleyman the Magnificent, often resulted in considerable authority for the queen mother in the affairs of state.

Members of the harem, like the Janissaries, were often of slave origin and formed an elite element in Ottoman society. Since the enslavement of Muslims was forbidden, slaves were taken among non-Islamic peoples. Some concubines were prisoners selected for the position, while others were purchased or offered to the sultan as a gift. They were then trained and educated like the Janissaries in a system called *devshirme* ("collection"). *Devshirme* had originated in the practice of requiring local clan leaders to provide prisoners to the sultan as part of their tax

© The Bridgeman Art Library

obligation. Talented males were given special training for eventual placement in military or administrative positions, while their female counterparts were trained for service in the harem, with instruction in reading, the Qur'an, sewing and embroidery, and musical performance. They were ranked according to their status, and some were permitted to leave the harem to marry officials.

Unique to the Ottoman Empire from the fifteenth century onward was the exclusive use of slaves to reproduce its royal heirs. Contrary to myth, few of the women of the imperial harem were used for sexual purposes, as the majority were members of the sultan's extended family—sisters, daughters, widowed mothers, and in-laws, with their own personal slaves and entourage. Contemporary European observers compared the atmosphere in the Topkapi harem to a Christian nunnery, with its hierarchical organization, enforced chastity, and rule of silence.

Because of their proximity to the sultan, the women of the harem often wielded so much political power that the era has been called "the sultanate of women." Queen mothers administered the imperial household and engaged in diplomatic relations with other countries while controlling the marital alliances of their daughters with senior civilian and military officials or members of other royal families in the region. One princess was married seven separate times from the age of two after her previous husbands died either in battle or by execution.

Administration of the Government The sultan ruled through an imperial council that met four days a week and was chaired by the chief minister known as the **grand vezir** (*wazir,* sometimes rendered in English as *vizier*). The sultan often attended behind a screen, whence he could privately indicate his desires to the grand vezir. The latter presided over the imperial bureaucracy. Like the palace guard, the bureaucrats were not an exclusive group but were chosen at least partly by merit from a palace school for training officials. Most officials were Muslims by birth, but some talented Janissaries became senior members of the bureaucracy, and almost all the later grand vezirs came from the *devshirme* system.

Local administration during the imperial period was a product of Turkish tribal tradition and was similar in some respects to fief-holding in Europe. The empire was divided into provinces and districts governed by officials who, like their tribal predecessors, combined both civil and military functions. Senior officials were assigned land in fief by the sultan and were then responsible for collecting taxes and supplying armies to the empire. These lands were then farmed out to the local cavalry elite called the **sipahis,** who exacted a tax from all peasants in their fiefdoms for their salary.

Religion and Society in the Ottoman World

Like most Turkic-speaking peoples in the Anatolian peninsula and throughout the Middle East, the Ottoman ruling elites were Sunni Muslims. Ottoman sultans had claimed the title of caliph ("defender of the faith") since the early sixteenth century and thus theoretically were responsible for guiding the flock and maintaining Islamic law, the *Shari'a*. In practice, the sultan assigned these duties to a supreme religious authority, who administered the law and maintained a system of schools for educating Muslims.

Islamic law and customs were applied to all Muslims in the empire. Like their rulers, most Turkic-speaking people were Sunni Muslims, but some communities were attracted to Sufism (see Chapter 7) or other heterodox doctrines. The government tolerated such activities so long as their practitioners remained loyal to the empire, but in the early sixteenth century, unrest among these groups—some of whom converted to the Shi'ite version of Islamic doctrine—outraged the conservative *ulama* and eventually led to war against the Safavids (see "The Safavids" later in this chapter).

The Treatment of Minorities Non-Muslims—mostly Orthodox Christians (Greeks and Slavs), Jews, and Armenian Christians—formed a significant minority within the empire, which treated them with relative tolerance. Non-Muslims were compelled to pay a head tax (because of their exemption from military service), and they were permitted to practice their religion or convert to Islam, although Muslims were prohibited from adopting another faith. Most of the population in European areas of the empire remained Christian, but in some places, such as the territory now called Bosnia, substantial numbers converted to Islam.

Technically, women in the Ottoman Empire were subject to the same restrictions that afflicted their counterparts in other Muslim societies, but their position was ameliorated to some degree by various factors. In the first place, non-Muslims were subject to the laws and customs of their own religions; thus, Orthodox Christian, Jewish, and Armenian Christian women were spared some of the restrictions applied to their Muslim sisters. In the second place, Islamic laws as applied in the Ottoman Empire defined the legal position of women comparatively tolerantly. Women were permitted to own and inherit property, including their dowries. They could not be forced into marriage and in certain cases were permitted to seek a divorce. As we have seen, women often exercised considerable influence in the palace and in a few instances even served as senior officials, such as governors of provinces. The relatively tolerant attitude toward women in Ottoman-held territories has been ascribed by some to

A Turkish Discourse on Coffee

Coffee was first introduced to Turkey from the Arabian peninsula in the mid-sixteenth century and supposedly came to Europe during the Turkish siege of Vienna in 1529. The following account was written by Katib Chelebi, a seventeenth-century Turkish author who, among other things, compiled an extensive encyclopedia and bibliography. Here, in *The Balance of Truth,* he describes how coffee entered the empire and the problems it caused for public morality. (In the Muslim world, as in Europe and later in colonial America, the drinking of coffee was associated with coffeehouses, where rebellious elements often gathered to promote antigovernment activities.) Chelebi died in Istanbul in 1657, reportedly while drinking a cup of coffee.

Katib Chelebi, *The Balance of Truth*

[Coffee] originated in Yemen and has spread, like tobacco, over the world. Certain sheikhs, who lived with their dervishes in the mountains of Yemen, used to crush and eat the berries . . . of a certain tree. Some would roast them and drink their water. Coffee is a cold dry food, suited to the ascetic life and sedative of lust. . . .

It came to Asia Minor by sea, about 1543, and met with a hostile reception, fetwas [decrees] being delivered against it. For they said, Apart from its being roasted, the fact that it is drunk in gatherings, passed from hand to hand, is suggestive of loose living. It is related of Abul-Suud Efendi that he had holes bored in the ships that brought it, plunging their cargoes of coffee into the sea. But these strictures and prohibitions availed nothing. . . . One coffeehouse was opened after another, and men would gather together, with great eagerness and enthusiasm, to drink. Drug addicts in particular, finding it a life-giving thing, which increased their pleasure, were willing to die for a cup.

Storytellers and musicians diverted the people from their employments, and working for one's living fell into disfavor. Moreover the people, from prince to beggar, amused themselves with knifing one another. Toward the end of 1633, the late Ghazi Gultan Murad, becoming aware of the situation, promulgated an edict, out of regard and compassion for the people, to this effect: Coffeehouses throughout the Guarded Domains shall be dismantled and not opened hereafter. Since then, the coffeehouses of the capital have been as desolate as the heart of the ignorant. . . . But in cities and towns outside Istanbul, they are opened just as before. As has been said above, such things do not admit of a perpetual ban.

Q *Why do you think coffee became identified as a dangerous substance in the Ottoman Empire? Were the authorities successful in suppressing its consumption?*

Turkish tribal traditions, which took a more egalitarian view of gender roles than the sedentary societies of the region did.

The Ottomans in Decline

By the seventeenth century, signs of internal rot had begun to appear in the empire, although the first loss of imperial territory did not occur until 1699, when Transylvania and much of Hungary were ceded to Austria at the Treaty of Carlowitz. Apparently, a number of factors were involved. In the first place, the administrative system inherited from the tribal period began to break down. Although the *devshirme* system of training officials continued to function, *devshirme* graduates were now permitted to marry and inherit property and to enroll their sons in the palace corps. Thus, they were gradually transformed from a meritocratic administrative elite into a privileged and often degenerate hereditary caste. Local administrators were corrupted and taxes rose as the central bureaucracy lost its links with rural areas. The imperial treasury was depleted by constant wars, and transport and communications were neglected. Interest in science and technology, once a hallmark of the Arab Empire, was in decline. In addition, the empire was increasingly beset by economic difficulties caused by the diversion of trade routes away from the eastern Mediterranean and the price inflation brought about by the influx of cheap American silver.

Another sign of change within the empire was the increasing degree of material affluence and the impact of Western ideas and customs. Sophisticated officials and merchants began to mimic the habits and lifestyles of their European counterparts, dressing in the European fashion, purchasing Western furniture and art objects, and ignoring Muslim strictures against the consumption of alcohol and sexual activities outside marriage. During the sixteenth and early seventeenth centuries, coffee and tobacco were introduced into polite Ottoman society, and cafés for the consumption of both began to appear in the major cities (see the box above). One sultan in the early seventeenth century issued a decree prohibiting the consumption of both coffee and tobacco, arguing (correctly, no doubt) that many cafés were nests of antigovernment intrigue. He even began to wander incognito through the streets of Istanbul at night. Any of his subjects detected in immoral or illegal acts were summarily executed and their bodies left on the streets as an example to others.

There were also signs of a decline in competence within the ruling family. Whereas the first sultans reigned

The Suleymaniye Mosque, Istanbul. The magnificent mosques built under the patronage of Suleyman the Magnificent are a great legacy of the Ottoman Empire and a fitting supplement to Hagia Sophia, the cathedral built by the Byzantine emperor Justinian in the sixth century C.E. Towering under a central dome, these mosques seem to defy gravity and, like European Gothic cathedrals, convey a sense of weightlessness. The Suleymaniye Mosque is one of the most impressive and most graceful in Istanbul. A far cry from the seventh-century desert mosques constructed of palm trunks, the Ottoman mosques stand among the architectural wonders of the world. Under the massive dome, the interior of the Suleymaniye Mosque offers a quiet refuge for prayer and reflection, bathed in muted sunlight and the warmth of plush carpets, as shown in the inset photo.

twenty-seven years on average, later ones averaged only thirteen years, suggesting an increase in turmoil within the ruling cliques. The throne now went to the oldest surviving male, while his rivals were kept secluded in a latticed cage and thus had no governmental experience if they succeeded to rule. Later sultans also became less involved in government, and more power flowed to the office of the grand vezir (called the Sublime Porte) or to eunuchs and members of the harem. Palace intrigue increased as a result.

Ottoman Art

The Ottoman sultans were enthusiastic patrons of the arts and maintained large ateliers of artisans and artists, primarily at the Topkapi Palace in Istanbul but also in other important cities of the vast empire. The period from Mehmet II in the fifteenth century to the early eighteenth century witnessed the flourishing of pottery, rugs, silk and other textiles, jewelry, arms and armor, and calligraphy. All adorned the palaces of the rulers, testifying to their opulence and exquisite taste. The artists came from all parts of the realm and beyond.

Architecture By far the greatest contribution of the Ottoman Empire to world art was its architecture, especially the magnificent mosques of the second half of the sixteenth century. Traditionally, prayer halls in mosques were subdivided by numerous pillars that supported small individual domes, creating a private, forestlike atmosphere. The Turks, however, modeled their new mosques on the open floor plan of the Byzantine church of Hagia Sophia (completed in 537), which had been turned into a mosque by Mehmet II, and began to push the pillars toward the outer wall to create a prayer hall with an uninterrupted central area under one large dome. With this plan, large numbers of believers could worship in unison in accordance with Muslim preference. By the mid-sixteenth century, the greatest of all Ottoman architects, Sinan, began erecting the first of his eighty-one mosques with an uncluttered prayer area. Each was topped by an imposing dome, and often, as at Edirne, the entire building was framed with four towering narrow minarets. By emphasizing its vertical lines, the minarets camouflaged the massive stone bulk of the structure and gave it a feeling of incredible lightness. These four graceful minarets would find new expression sixty years later in India's white marble Taj Mahal (see "Mughal Culture" later in this chapter).

Earlier, in the thirteenth-century the Seljuk Turks of Anatolia had created beautiful tile decorations with two-color mosaics. Now Ottoman artists invented a new glazed tile art with painted flowers and geometrical designs in brilliant blue, green, yellow, and their own secret "tomato red." Entire walls, both interior and exterior, were covered with the painted tiles, which adorned palaces as well as mosques.

Textiles The sixteenth century also witnessed the flourishing of textiles and rugs. The Byzantine emperor Justinian had introduced the cultivation of silkworms to the West in the sixth century, and the silk industry resurfaced under the Ottomans. Perhaps even more famous than Turkish silks are the rugs. But whereas silks were produced under the patronage of the sultans, rugs were a peasant industry. Each village boasted its own distinctive design and color scheme for the rugs it produced.

The Safavids

Q Focus Question: How did the Safavid Empire come into existence, and what led to its collapse?

After the collapse of the empire of Tamerlane in the early fifteenth century, the area extending from Persia into Central Asia lapsed into anarchy. The Uzbeks, Turkic-speaking peoples from Central Asia, were the chief political and military force in the area. From their capital at

CHRONOLOGY	The Safavids	
Ismail seizes Iran and Iraq and becomes shah of Persia		1501
Ismail conquers Baghdad and defeats Uzbeks		1508
Reign of Shah Abbas I		1587–1629
Truce achieved between Ottomans and Safavids		1638
Collapse of the Safavid Empire		1723

Bokhara, east of the Caspian Sea, they maintained a semblance of control over the highly fluid tribal alignments until the emergence of the Safavid dynasty in Persia at the beginning of the sixteenth century.

The Safavid dynasty was founded by Shah Ismail (1487–1524), the descendant of a sheikh called Safi al-Din (thus the name *Safavid*), who traced his origins to Ali, the fourth imam of the Muslim faith. In the early fourteenth century, Safi had been the leader of a community of Turkic-speaking tribespeople in Azerbaijan, near the Caspian Sea. Safi's community was only one of many Sufi mystical religious groups throughout the area. In time, the doctrine spread among nomadic groups throughout the Middle East and was transformed into the more activist Shi'ite version of Islam. Its adherents were known as "red heads" because they wore a distinctive red cap with twelve folds, meant to symbolize allegiance to the twelve imams of the Shi'ite faith.

In 1501, after Ismail's forces seized much of Iran and Iraq, he proclaimed himself the shah of a new Persian state. Baghdad was subdued in 1508 and the Uzbeks and

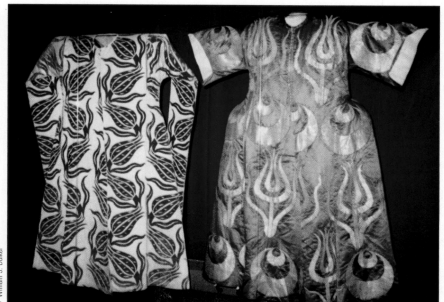

© William J. Duiker

Clothes Make the Man. Having traveled westward from China over the Silk Road, the production of silk got under way in the Ottoman Empire, from which it spread to Europe and imperial Russia. In the sixteenth and seventeenth centuries, stunning silk caftans such as those shown here radiated Ottoman splendor and power. Their voluminous size, vibrant colors, intricate designs, and sumptuous fabrics aggrandized the wearer—usually a courtier—in both physical and political stature. Magnificent bolts of silk were offered by sultans as diplomatic gifts to solidify political alliances, as well as to reward high officials for their loyalty to the dynasty. To show respect and allegiance during court rituals, officials had to kiss the hem of the sultan's caftan.

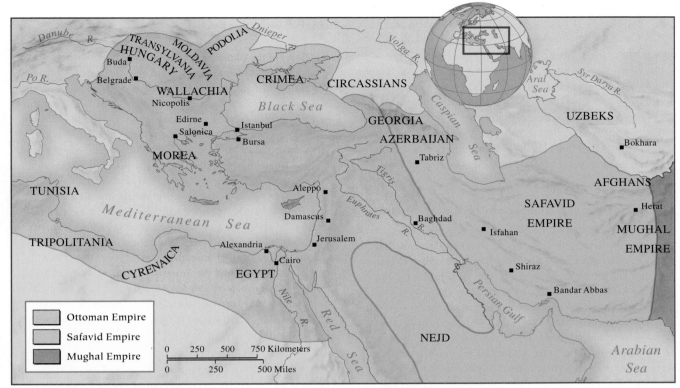

MAP 16.2 **The Ottoman and Safavid Empires, c. 1683.** During the seventeenth century, the Ottoman and Safavid Empires contested vigorously for hegemony in the eastern Mediterranean and the Middle East. This map shows the territories controlled by each state in the late seventeenth century.

Q Which states shared control over the ancient lands in the Tigris and Euphrates valleys? In which modern-day countries are those lands?

their capital at Bokhara shortly thereafter. Ismail now sent Shi'ite preachers into Anatolia to proselytize and promote rebellion among Turkish tribal peoples in the Ottoman Empire. In retaliation, the Ottoman sultan, Selim I, advanced against the Safavids in Iran and won a major battle near Tabriz in 1514. But Selim could not maintain control of the area, and Ismail regained Tabriz a few years later.

The Ottomans returned to the attack in the 1580s and forced the new Safavid shah, Abbas I the Great (1587–1629), to sign a punitive peace in which much territory was lost to his realm. The capital was subsequently moved from Tabriz in the northwest to Isfahan in the south. Still, it was under Shah Abbas that the Safavids reached the zenith of their glory. He established a system similar to the Janissaries in Turkey to train administrators to replace the traditional warrior elite. He also used the period of peace to strengthen his army, now armed with modern weapons, and in the early seventeenth century, he attempted to regain the lost territories. Although he had some initial success, war resumed in the 1620s, and a lasting peace was not achieved until 1638 (see Map 16.2).

Abbas the Great had managed to strengthen the dynasty significantly, and for a time after his death in 1629, it remained stable and vigorous. But succession conflicts plagued the dynasty. Partly as a result, the power of the more militant Shi'ites began to increase at court and in Safavid society at large. The intellectual freedom that had characterized the empire at its height was curtailed under the pressure of religious orthodoxy, and Iranian women, who had enjoyed considerable freedom and influence during the early empire, were forced to withdraw into seclusion and behind the veil. Meanwhile, attempts to suppress the religious beliefs of minorities led to increased popular unrest. In the early eighteenth century, Afghan warriors took advantage of local revolts to seize the capital of Isfahan, forcing the remnants of the Safavid ruling family to retreat to Azerbaijan, their original homeland. The Ottomans seized territories along the western border. Eventually, order was restored by the military adventurer Nadir Shah Afshar, who launched an extended series of campaigns that restored the country's borders and even

THE RELIGIOUS ZEAL OF SHAH ABBAS THE GREAT

RELIGION & PHILOSOPHY

Shah Abbas I, probably the greatest of the Safavid rulers, expanded the borders of his empire into areas of the southern Caucasus inhabited by Christians and other non-Muslim peoples. After Persian control was assured, he instructed that the local populations be urged to convert to Islam for their own protection and the glory of God. In this passage, his biographer, the Persian historian Eskander Beg Monshi, recounts the story of that effort.

The Conversion of a Number of Christians to Islam

This year the Shah decreed that those Armenians and other Christians who had been settled in [the southern Caucasus] and had been given agricultural land there should be invited to become Muslims. Life in this world is fraught with vicissitudes, and the Shah was concerned lest, in a period when the authority of the central government was weak, these Christians . . . might be subjected to attack by the neighboring Lor tribes (who are naturally given to causing injury and mischief), and their women and children carried off into captivity. In the areas in which these Christian groups resided, it was the Shah's purpose that the places of worship which they had built should become mosques, and the muezzin's call should be heard in them, so that these Christians might assume the guise of Muslims, and their future status accordingly be assured. . . .

Some of the Christians, guided by God's grace, embraced Islam voluntarily; others found it difficult to abandon their Christian faith and felt revulsion at the idea. They were encouraged by their monks and priests to remain steadfast in their faith. After a little pressure had been applied to the monks and priests, however, they desisted, and these Christians saw no alternative but to embrace Islam, though they did so with reluctance. The women and children embraced Islam with great enthusiasm, vying with one another in their eagerness to abandon their Christian faith and declare their belief in the unity of God. Some five thousand people embraced Islam. As each group made the Muslim declaration of faith, it received instruction in the Koran and the principles of the religious law of Islam, and all bibles and other Christian devotional material were collected and taken away from the priests.

In the same way, all the Armenian Christians who had been moved to [the area] were also forcibly converted to Islam. . . . Most people embraced Islam with sincerity, but some felt an aversion to making the Muslim profession of faith. True knowledge lies with God! May God reward the Shah for his action with long life and prosperity!

Q *How do the efforts to convert nonbelievers to Islam compare with similar programs by Muslim rulers in India, as described in Chapter 9? What is the author's point of view on the matter?*

---

occupied the Mughal capital of Delhi (see "Twilight of the Mughals" later in this chapter). After his death, the Zand dynasty ruled until the end of the eighteenth century.

Safavid Politics and Society

Like the Ottoman Empire, Iran under the Safavids was a mixed society. The Safavids had come to power with the support of nomadic Turkic-speaking tribal groups, and leading elements from those groups retained considerable influence within the empire. But the majority of the population were Iranian; most of them were farmers or townspeople, with attitudes inherited from the relatively sophisticated and urbanized culture of pre-Safavid Iran. Faced with the problem of integrating unruly Turkic-speaking tribal peoples with the sedentary Persian-speaking population of the urban areas, the Safavids used the Shi'ite faith as a unifying force (see the box above). The shah himself acquired an almost divine quality and claimed to be the spiritual leader of all Islam. Shi'ism was declared the state religion.

Although there was a landed aristocracy, aristocratic power and influence were firmly controlled by strong-minded shahs, who confiscated aristocratic estates when possible and brought them under the control of the crown. Appointment to senior positions in the bureaucracy was by merit rather than birth.

The Safavid shahs took a direct interest in the economy and actively engaged in commercial and manufacturing activities, although there was also a large and affluent urban bourgeoisie. Like the Ottoman sultan, one shah regularly traveled the city streets incognito to check on the honesty of his subjects. When he discovered that a baker and butcher were overcharging for their products, he had the baker cooked in his own oven and the butcher roasted on a spit.

At its height, Safavid Iran was a worthy successor to the great Persian empires of the past, although it was probably not as wealthy as its Mughal and Ottoman neighbors to the east and west. Hemmed in by the sea power of the Europeans to the south and by the land power of the Ottomans to the west, the early Safavids had no navy and were forced to divert overland trade with

Europe through southern Russia to avoid an Ottoman blockade. In the early seventeenth century, the situation improved when Iranian forces, in cooperation with the English, seized the island of Hormuz from Portugal and established a new seaport on the southern coast at Bandar Abbas. As a consequence, commercial ties with Europe began to increase.

Safavid Art and Literature

Persia witnessed an extraordinary flowering of the arts during the reign of Shah Abbas I. His new capital of Isfahan was a grandiose planned city with wide visual perspectives and a sense of order almost unique in the region. Shah Abbas ordered his architects to position his palaces, mosques, and bazaars around the Maydan-i-Shah, a massive rectangular polo ground. Much of the original city is still in good condition and remains the gem of modern Iran. The immense mosques are richly decorated with elaborate blue tiles. The palaces are delicate structures with unusual slender wooden columns. These architectural wonders of Isfahan epitomize the grandeur, delicacy, and color that defined the Safavid golden age. To adorn the splendid buildings, Safavid artisans created imaginative metalwork, tile decorations, and original and delicate glass vessels.

The greatest area of productivity, however, was in textiles. Silk weaving based on new techniques became a national industry. The silks depicted birds, animals, and flowers in a brilliant mass of color with silver and gold threads. Above all, carpet weaving flourished, stimulated by the great demand for Persian carpets in the West.

The long tradition of Persian painting continued in the Safavid era but changed from paintings to line drawings and from landscape scenes to portraits, mostly of young ladies, boys, lovers, or dervishes. Although some Persian artists studied in Rome, Safavid art was little influenced by the West. Riza-i-Abassi, the most famous artist of this period, created exquisite works on simple naturalistic subjects, such as an ox plowing, hunters, or lovers. Soft colors, delicacy, and flowing movement were the dominant characteristics of the painting of this era.

The Grandeur of the Mughals

Q Focus Question: Although the Ottoman, Safavid, and Mughal Empires all adopted Islam as their state religion, their approach was often different. Describe the differences, and explain why they might have occurred.

In retrospect, the period from the sixteenth to the eighteenth centuries can be viewed as a high point of traditional culture in India. The era began with the creation of one of the subcontinent's greatest empires—that of the Mughals. For the first time since the Mauryan dynasty, the entire subcontinent was united under a single government, with a common culture that inspired admiration and envy throughout the entire region.

The Mughal Empire reached its peak in the sixteenth century under the famed Emperor Akbar and maintained its vitality under a series of strong rulers for another century (see Map 16.3). Then the dynasty began to weaken, a process that was hastened by the increasingly insistent challenge of the foreigners arriving by sea. The Portuguese, who first arrived in 1498, were little more than an irritant. Two centuries later, however, Europeans began to seize control of regional trade routes and to meddle in the internal politics of the subcontinent. By the end of the eighteenth century, nothing remained of the empire but a shell. But some historians see the

The Royal Academy of Isfahan. Along with institutions such as libraries and hospitals, theological schools were often included in the mosque compound. One of the most sumptuous was the Royal Academy of Isfahan, built by the shah of Iran in the early eighteenth century. This view shows the large courtyard surrounded by arcades of student rooms, reminiscent of the arrangement of monks' cells in European cloisters. Note the similarities with the buildings in Tamerlane's capital at Samarkand, as shown on page 218.

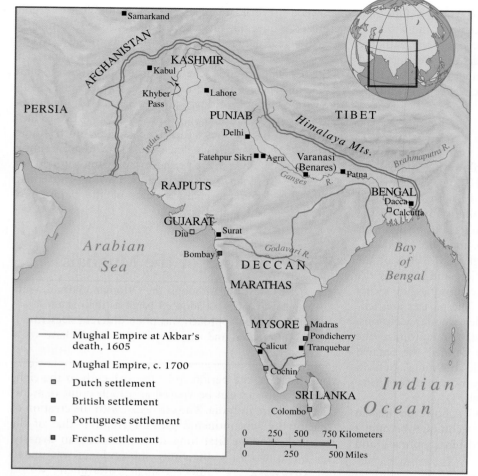

MAP 16.3 **The Mughal Empire.** This map shows the expansion of the Mughal Empire from the death of Akbar in 1605 to the rule of Aurangzeb at the end of the seventeenth century.

Q In which cities on the map were European settlements located? When did each group of Europeans arrive, and how did the settlements spread?

🌐 **View an animated version of this map or related maps at** www.cengage.com/history/ duikspiel/essentialworld6e

seeds of decay less in the challenge from abroad than in internal weakness—in the very nature of the empire itself, which was always more a heterogeneous collection of semiautonomous political forces than a centralized empire in the style of neighboring China.

The Founding of the Empire

When the Portuguese fleet led by Vasco da Gama arrived at the port of Calicut in the spring of 1498, the Indian subcontinent was still divided into a number of Hindu and Muslim kingdoms. But it was on the verge of a new era of unity that would be brought about by a foreign dynasty called the Mughals. Like so many recent rulers of northern India, the founders of the Mughal Empire were not natives of India but came from the mountainous region north of the Ganges River. The founder of the dynasty, known to history as Babur (1483–1530), had an illustrious pedigree. His father was descended from the great Asian conqueror Tamerlane, his mother from the Mongol conqueror Genghis Khan.

Babur had inherited a fragment of Tamerlane's empire in an upland valley of the Syr Darya River (see Map 16.2 on p. 395). Driven south by the rising power of the Uzbeks and then the Safavid dynasty in Persia, Babur and his warriors seized Kabul in 1504 and, thirteen years later, crossed the Khyber Pass to India.

Following a pattern that we have seen before, Babur began his rise to power by offering to help an ailing dynasty against its opponents. Although his own forces were far smaller than those of his adversaries, he possessed advanced weapons, including artillery, and used them to great effect. His use of mobile cavalry was particularly successful against the massed forces, supplemented by mounted elephants, of his enemy. In 1526, with only 12,000 troops against an enemy force nearly ten times that size, Babur captured Delhi and established his power in the plains of northern India. Over the next several years, he continued his conquests in northern India, until his early death in 1530 at the age of forty-seven.

Babur's success was due in part to his vigor and his charismatic personality, which earned him the undying loyalty of his followers. His son and successor Humayun (1530–1556) was, in the words of one British historian, "intelligent but lazy." In 1540, he was forced to flee to Persia, where he lived in exile for sixteen years. Finally, with the aid of the Safavid shah of Persia, he returned to India and reconquered Delhi in 1555 but died the following year in a household accident, reportedly from injuries suffered in a fall after smoking a pipeful of opium.

Humayun was succeeded by his son Akbar (1556–1605). Born while his father was living in exile, Akbar was only fourteen when he mounted the throne. Illiterate but highly intelligent and industrious, Akbar set out to extend his domain, then limited to Punjab and the upper Ganges River valley. "A monarch," he remarked, "should be ever intent on conquest, otherwise his neighbors rise in arms against him. The army should be exercised in warfare, lest from want of training they become self-indulgent."[1] By the end of his life, he had brought Mughal rule to most of the subcontinent, from the Himalaya Mountains to the Godavari River in central India and from Kashmir to the mouths of the Brahmaputra and the Ganges. In so doing, Akbar had created the greatest Indian empire since the Mauryan dynasty nearly two thousand years earlier. It was an empire that appeared highly centralized from the outside but was actually a collection of semiautonomous principalities ruled by provincial elites and linked together by the overarching majesty of the Mughal emperor.

Akbar and Indo-Muslim Civilization

Although Akbar was probably the greatest of the conquering Mughal monarchs, like his famous predecessor Asoka, he is best known for the humane character of his rule. Above all, he accepted the diversity of Indian society and took steps to reconcile his Muslim and Hindu subjects.

Religion Though raised an orthodox Muslim, Akbar had been exposed to other beliefs during his childhood and had little patience with the pedantic views of Muslim scholars at court. As emperor, he displayed a keen interest in other religions, not only tolerating Hindu practices in his own domains but also welcoming the expression of Christian views by his Jesuit advisers (the Jesuits first sent a mission to Agra in 1580). Akbar put his policy of religious tolerance into practice by taking a Hindu princess as one of his wives, and the success of this marriage may well have had an effect on his religious convictions. He patronized classical Indian arts and architecture and abolished many of the restrictions faced by Hindus in a Muslim-dominated society.

During his later years, Akbar became steadily more hostile to Islam. To the dismay of many Muslims at court, he sponsored a new form of worship called the Divine Faith (*Din-i-Ilahi*), which combined characteristics of several religions with a central belief in the infallibility of all decisions reached by the emperor. The new faith aroused deep hostility in Muslim circles and rapidly vanished after his death (see the box on p. 400).

Society and the Economy Akbar also extended his innovations to the empire's administration. Although the upper ranks of the government continued to be dominated by nonnative Muslims, a substantial proportion of lower-ranking officials were Hindus, and a few Hindus were appointed to positions of importance. At first, most officials were paid salaries, but later they were ordinarily assigned sections of agricultural land for their temporary use; they kept a portion of the taxes paid by the local peasants in lieu of a salary. These local officials, known as **zamindars,** were expected to forward the rest of the taxes from the lands under their control to the central government.

The same tolerance that marked Akbar's attitude toward religion and administration extended to the Mughal legal system. While Muslims were subject to the Islamic codes (the *Shari'a*), Hindu law applied to areas settled by Hindus, who after 1579 were no longer required to pay the unpopular *jizya,* or poll tax on non-Muslims. Punishments for crime were relatively mild, at least by the standards of the day, and justice was administered in a relatively impartial and efficient manner.

Overall, Akbar's reign was a time of peace and prosperity. Although all Indian peasants were required to pay about one-third of their annual harvest to the state through the *zamindars,* in general the system was applied fairly, and when drought struck in the 1590s, the taxes were reduced or even suspended altogether. Thanks to a long period of relative peace and political stability, commerce and manufacturing flourished. Foreign trade, in particular, thrived as Indian goods, notably textiles, tropical food products, spices, and precious stones, were exported in exchange for gold and silver. Tariffs on imports were low. Much of the foreign commerce was handled by Arab traders, since the Indians, like their Mughal rulers, did not care for travel by sea. Internal trade, however, was dominated by large merchant castes, who also were active in banking and handicrafts.

Empire in Crisis

Akbar died in 1605 and was succeeded by his son Jahangir (1605–1628). During the early years of his reign, Jahangir continued to strengthen central control over the vast empire. Eventually, however, his grip began to weaken (according to his memoirs, he "only wanted a bottle of wine and a piece of meat to make merry"), and the court fell under the influence of one of his wives, the Persian-born Nur Jahan. The empress took advantage of her position to enrich her own family and arranged for her niece Mumtaz Mahal to marry her husband's third son and ultimate successor, Shah Jahan. When Shah Jahan succeeded to the throne in 1628, he quickly demonstrated

A RELIGION FIT FOR A KING

RELIGION & PHILOSOPHY

Emperor Akbar's attempt to create a new form of religion, known as the "Divine Faith," was partly a product of his inquisitive mind. But it was also influenced by Akbar's long friendship with Abu'l Fazl Allami, a courtier who introduced the young emperor to the Shi'ite tradition that each generation produced an individual (*imam*) who possessed a "divine light" capable of interpreting the holy scriptures. One of the sources of this Muslim theory was the Greek philosopher Plato's idea of a "philosopher king," who in his wisdom could provide humanity with an infallible guide in affairs of religion, morality, and statecraft. Akbar, of course, found the idea appealing, since it provided support for his efforts to reform religious practices in the empire. Abu'l Fazl, however, made many enemies with his advice and was assassinated, probably at the order of Akbar's son and successor, Jahangir. The following excerpt is from Abu'l Fazl's writings on the subject.

Abu'l Fazl, *Institutes of Akbar*

Royalty is a light emanating from God, and a ray from the sun, the illuminator of the universe, the argument of the book of perfection, the receptacle of all virtues. Modern language calls this light the divine light, and the tongue of antiquity called it the sublime halo. It is communicated by God to kings without the intermediate assistance of anyone, and men, in the presence of it, bend the forehead of praise toward the ground of submission.

Again, many excellent qualities flow from the possession of this light:

1. *A paternal love toward the subjects.* Thousands find rest in the love of the king, and sectarian differences do not raise the dust of strife. In his wisdom, the king will understand the spirit of the age, and shape his plans accordingly.

2. *A large heart.* The sight of anything disagreeable does not unsettle him, nor is want of discrimination for him a source of disappointment. His courage steps in. His divine firmness gives him the power of requittal, nor does the high position of an offender interfere with it. The wishes of great and small are attended to, and their claims meet with no delay at his hands.

3. *A daily increasing trust in God.* When he performs an action, he considers God as the real doer of it [and himself as the medium] so that a conflict of motives can produce no disturbance.

4. *Prayer and devotion.* The success of his plans will not lead him to neglect, nor will adversity cause him to forget God and madly trust in man. He puts the reins of desire into the hands of reason; in the wide field of his desires he does not permit himself to be trodden down by restlessness; neither will he waste his precious time in seeking after that which is improper. He makes wrath, the tyrant, pay homage to wisdom, so that blind rage may not get the upper hand, and inconsiderateness overstep the proper limits. . . . He is forever searching after those who speak the truth and is not displeased with words that seem bitter but are, in reality, sweet. He considers the nature of the words and the rank of the speaker. He is not content with not committing violence, but he must see that no injustice is done within his realm.

Q *According to Abu'l Fazl, what role does the Mughal emperor play in promoting public morality? What tactics must he apply to ensure that his efforts will be successful?*

---

the single-minded quality of his grandfather (albeit in a much more brutal manner), ordering the assassination of all of his rivals in order to secure his position.

The Reign of Shah Jahan During a reign of three decades, Shah Jahan maintained the system established by his predecessors while expanding the boundaries of the empire by successful campaigns in the Deccan Plateau and against Samarkand, north of the Hindu Kush. But Shah Jahan's rule was marred by his failure to deal with the growing domestic problems. He had inherited a nearly empty treasury because of Empress Nur Jahan's penchant for luxury and ambitious charity projects. Though the majority of his subjects lived in grinding poverty, Shah Jahan's frequent military campaigns and expensive building projects put a heavy strain on the imperial finances and compelled him to raise taxes. At the same time, the government did little to improve rural conditions. In a country where transport was primitive (it often took three months to travel the 600 miles between Patna, in the middle of the Ganges River valley, and Delhi) and drought conditions frequent, the dynasty made few efforts to increase agricultural efficiency or to improve the roads or the irrigation network. A Dutch merchant in Gujarat described conditions during a famine in the mid-seventeenth century:

As the famine increased, men abandoned towns and villages and wandered helplessly. It was easy to recognize their condition: eyes sunk deep in head, lips pale and covered with slime, the skin hard, with the bones showing through, the belly nothing but a pouch hanging down empty, knuckles and kneecaps showing prominently. One would cry and howl for hunger, while another lay stretched on the ground dying in misery; wherever you went, you saw nothing but corpses.[2]

In 1648, Shah Jahan moved his capital from Agra to Delhi and built the famous Red Fort in his new capital city. But he is best known for the Taj Mahal in Agra, widely considered to be the most beautiful building in India, if not in the entire world. The story is a romantic one—that the Taj was built by the emperor in memory of his wife Mumtaz Mahal, who had died giving birth to her thirteenth child at the age of thirty-nine. But the reality has a less attractive side: the expense of the building, which employed 20,000 masons over twenty years, forced the government to raise agricultural taxes, further impoverishing many Indian peasants.

Rule of Aurangzeb Succession struggles returned to haunt the dynasty in the mid-1650s when Shah Jahan's illness led to a struggle for power between his sons Dara Shikoh and Aurangzeb. Dara Shikoh was described by his contemporaries as progressive and humane, but he apparently lacked political acumen and was outmaneuvered by Aurangzeb (1658–1707), who had Dara Shikoh put to death and then imprisoned his father in the fort at Agra.

Aurangzeb is one of the most controversial individuals in the history of India. A man of high principle, he attempted to eliminate many of what he considered to be India's social evils, prohibiting the immolation of widows on their husband's funeral pyre (*sati*), the castration of eunuchs, and the exaction of illegal taxes. With less success, he tried to forbid gambling, drinking, and prostitution. But Aurangzeb, a devout and somewhat doctrinaire Muslim, also adopted a number of measures that reversed the policies of religious tolerance established by his predecessors. The building of new Hindu temples was prohibited, and the Hindu poll tax was restored. Forced conversions to Islam were resumed, and non-Muslims were driven from the court. Aurangzeb's heavy-handed religious policies led to considerable domestic unrest and to a revival of Hindu fervor during the last years of his reign. A number of revolts also broke out against imperial authority.

Twilight of the Mughals During the eighteenth century, Mughal power was threatened from both within and without. Fueled by the growing power and autonomy of the local gentry and merchants, rebellious groups in provinces throughout the empire, from the Deccan to the Punjab, began to reassert local authority and reduce the power of the Mughal emperor to that of a "tinsel sovereign." Increasingly divided, India was vulnerable to attack from abroad. In 1739, Delhi was sacked by the Persians, who left it in ashes.

A number of obvious reasons for the virtual collapse of the Mughal Empire can be identified, including the draining of the imperial treasury and the decline in competence of the Mughal rulers. But it should also be noted that even at its height under Akbar, the empire was a loosely knit collection of heterogeneous principalities held together by the authority of the throne, which tried to combine Persian concepts of kingship with the Indian tradition of decentralized power. Decline set in when centrifugal forces gradually began to predominate over centripetal ones.

The Impact of Western Power in India

As we have seen, the first Europeans to arrive were the Portuguese. Although they established a virtual monopoly over regional trade in the Indian Ocean, they did not seek to penetrate the interior of the subcontinent but focused on establishing way stations en route to China and the Spice Islands. The situation changed at the end of the sixteenth century, when the English and the Dutch entered the scene. Soon both powers were in active competition with Portugal, and with each other, for trading privileges in the region (see the box on p. 402).

Penetration of the new market was not easy. When the first English fleet arrived at Surat, a thriving port on the northwestern coast of India, in 1608, their request for trading privileges was rejected by Emperor Jahangir. Needing lightweight Indian cloth to trade for spices in the East Indies, the English persisted, and in 1616, they were finally permitted to install their own ambassador at the imperial court in Agra. Three years later, the first English factory (trading station) was established at Surat.

During the next several decades, the English presence in India steadily increased while Mughal power gradually waned. By midcentury, additional English factories had been established at Fort William (now the great city of Calcutta) on the Hoogly River near the Bay of Bengal and in 1639 at Madras (Chennai) on the southeastern coast. From there, English ships carried Indian-made cotton goods to the East Indies, where they were bartered for spices, which were shipped back to England.

English success in India attracted rivals, including the Dutch and the French. The Dutch abandoned their interests to concentrate on the spice trade in the middle of the seventeenth century, but the French were more persistent and established factories of their own. For a brief period, under the ambitious empire builder Joseph François Dupleix, the French competed successfully with the British, even capturing Madras from a British garrison in 1746. But the military genius of Sir Robert Clive, an aggressive British administrator and empire builder who eventually became the chief representative of the East India Company in the subcontinent, and the refusal of the French government to provide financial support for

OPPOSING VIEWPOINTS
THE CAPTURE OF PORT HOOGLY

In 1632, the Mughal ruler, Shah Jahan, ordered an attack on the city of Hoogly, a fortified Portuguese trading post on the northeastern coast of India. For the Portuguese, who had profited from half a century of triangular trade between India, China, and various countries in the Middle East and Southeast Asia, the loss of Hoogly at the hands of the Mughals hastened the decline of their influence in the region. Presented here are two contemporary versions of the battle. The first, from the *Padshahnama* (Book of Kings), relates the course of events from the Mughal point of view. The second account is by John Cabral, a Jesuit missionary who was resident in Hoogly at the time.

The *Padshahnama*

During the reign of the Bengalis, a group of Frankish [European] merchants . . . settled in a place one *kos* from Satgaon . . . and, on the pretext that they needed a place for trading, they received permission from the Bengalis to construct a few edifices. Over time, due to the indifference of the governors of Bengal, many Franks gathered there and built dwellings of the utmost splendor and strength, fortified with cannons, guns, and other instruments of war. It was not long before it became a large settlement and was named Hoogly. . . . The Franks' ships trafficked at this port, and commerce was established, causing the market at the port of Satgaon to slump. . . . Of the peasants of those places, they converted some to Christianity by force and others through greed and sent them off to Europe in their ships. . . .

Since the improper actions of the Christians of Hoogly Port toward the Muslims were accurately reflected in the mirror of the mind of the Emperor before his accession to the throne, when the imperial banners cast their shadows over Bengal, and inasmuch as he was always inclined to propagate the true religion and eliminate infidelity, it was decided that when he gained control over this region he would eradicate the corruption of these abominators from the realm.

John Cabral, *Travels of Sebastian Manrique, 1629–1649*

Hugli continued at peace all the time of the great King Jahangir. For, as this Prince, by what he showed, was more attached to Christ than to Mohammad and was a Moor in name and dress only. . . . Sultan Khurram was in everything unlike his father, especially as regards the latter's leaning towards Christianity. . . . He declared himself the mortal enemy of the Christian name and the restorer of the law of Mohammad. . . . He sent a *firman* [order] to the Viceroy of Bengal, commanding him without reply or delay, to march upon the Bandel of Hugli and put it to fire and the sword. He added that, in doing so, he would render a signal service to God, to Mohammad, and to him. . . .

Consequently, on a Friday, September 24, 1632, . . . all the people [the Portuguese] embarked with the utmost secrecy. . . . Learning what was going on, and wishing to be able to boast that they had taken Hugli by storm, they [the imperialists] made a general attack on the Bandel by Saturday noon. They began by setting fire to a mine, but lost in it more men than we. Finally, however, they were masters of the Bandel.

Q *How do these two accounts of the Battle of Hoogly differ? Is there any way to reconcile the two accounts into a single narrative?*

Dupleix's efforts eventually left the French with only their fort at Pondicherry and a handful of small territories on the southeastern coast.

In the meantime, Clive began to consolidate British control in Bengal, where the local ruler had attacked Fort William and imprisoned the local British population in the infamous Black Hole of Calcutta (an underground prison for holding the prisoners, many of whom died in captivity). In 1757, a small British force numbering about three thousand defeated a Mughal-led army over ten times that size in the Battle of Plassey. As part of the spoils of victory, the British East India Company exacted from the now-decrepit Mughal court the authority to collect taxes from extensive lands in the area surrounding Calcutta. Less than ten years later, British forces seized the reigning Mughal emperor in a skirmish at Buxar, and the British began to consolidate their economic and administrative control over Indian territory through the surrogate power of the now powerless Mughal court (see Map 16.4 on p. 404).

To officials of the East India Company, the expansion of their authority into the interior of the subcontinent probably seemed like a simple commercial decision, a move designed to seek guaranteed revenues to pay for the increasingly expensive military operations in India. To historians, it marks a major step in the gradual transfer of all of the Indian subcontinent to the British East India Company and later, in 1858, to the British crown. The process was more haphazard than deliberate.

Economic Difficulties The company's takeover of vast landholdings, notably in the eastern Indian states of

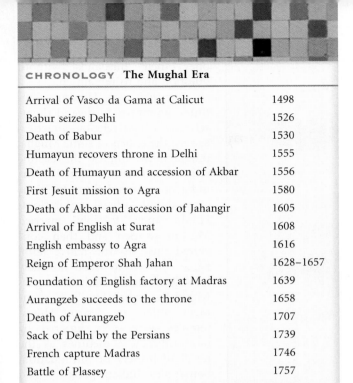

Orissa and Bengal, may have been a windfall for enterprising British officials, but it was a disaster for the Indian economy. In the first place, it resulted in the transfer of capital from the local Indian aristocracy to company officials, most of whom sent their profits back to Britain. Second, it hastened the destruction of once healthy local industries because British goods such as machine-made textiles were imported duty-free into India to compete against local products. Finally, British expansion hurt the peasants. As the British took over the administration of the land tax, they also applied British law, which allowed the lands of those unable to pay the tax to be confiscated. In the 1770s, a series of massive famines led to the death of an estimated one-third of the population in the areas under company administration. The British government attempted to resolve the problem by assigning tax lands to the local revenue collectors (*zamindars*) in the hope of transforming them into English-style rural gentry, but many collectors themselves fell into bankruptcy and sold their lands to absentee bankers while the now landless peasants remained in abject poverty. It was hardly an auspicious beginning to "civilized" British rule.

Resistance to the British   As a result of such problems, Britain's rise to power in India did not go unchallenged. Astute Indian commanders avoided pitched battles with the well-armed British troops but harassed and ambushed them in the manner of guerrillas in our time. Haidar Ali,

one of Britain's primary rivals for control in southern India, said:

> You will in time understand my mode of warfare. Shall I risk my cavalry which cost a thousand rupees each horse, against your cannon ball which cost two pice? No! I will march your troops until their legs swell to the size of their bodies. You shall not have a blade of grass, nor a drop of water. I will hear of you every time your drum beats, but you shall not know where I am once a month. I will give your army battle, but it must be when I please, and not when you choose.[3]

Unfortunately for India, not all its commanders were as astute as Haidar Ali. In the last years of the eighteenth century, the stage was set for the final consolidation of British rule over the subcontinent.

Society and Economy Under the Mughals

The Mughals were the last of the great traditional Indian dynasties. Like so many of their predecessors since the fall of the Guptas nearly a thousand years before, the Mughals were Muslims. But like the Ottoman Turks, the best Mughal rulers did not simply impose Islamic institutions and beliefs on a predominantly Hindu population; they combined Muslim with Hindu and even Persian concepts and cultural values in a unique social and cultural synthesis that still today seems to epitomize the greatness of Indian civilization.

The Position of Women   Whether Mughal rule had much effect on the lives of ordinary Indians seems somewhat problematic. The treatment of women is a good example. Women had traditionally played an active role in Mongol tribal society—many actually fought on the battlefield alongside the men—and Babur and his successors often relied on the women in their families for political advice. Women from aristocratic families were often awarded honorific titles, received salaries, and were permitted to own land and engage in business. Women at court sometimes received an education, and aristocratic women often expressed their creative talents by writing poetry, painting, or playing music. Women of all classes were adept at spinning thread, either for their own use or to sell to weavers to augment the family income. They sold simple cloth to local villages and fine cottons, silks, and wool to the Mughal court. By Akbar's rule, in fact, the textile manufacturing was of such high quality and so well established that India sold cloth to much of the world: Arabia, the coast of East Africa, Egypt, Southeast Asia, and Europe.

To a certain degree, these Mughal attitudes toward women may have had an impact on Indian society. Women were allowed to inherit land, and some even

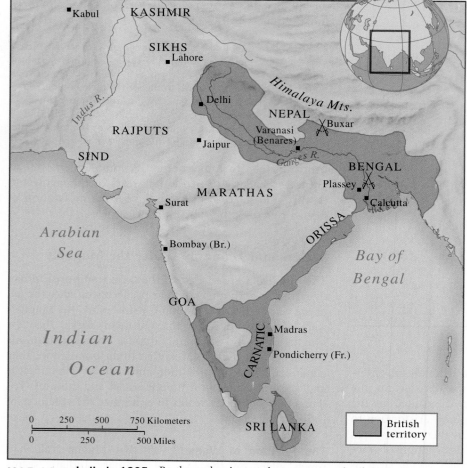

MAP 16.4 **India in 1805.** By the early nineteenth century, much of the Indian subcontinent had fallen under British domination.

Q Where was the capital of the Mughal Empire located?

View an animated version of this map or related maps at www.cengage.com/history/duikspiel/essentialworld6e

obey their husbands without question and to remain chaste.

For their part, Hindus sometimes attempted to defend themselves and their religious practices against the efforts of some Mughal monarchs to impose the Islamic religion and Islamic mores on the indigenous population. In some cases, despite official prohibitions, Hindu men forcibly married Muslim women and then converted them to the native faith, while converts to Islam normally lost all of their inheritance rights within the Indian family. Government orders to destroy Hindu temples were often ignored by local officials, sometimes as the result of bribery or intimidation. Sometimes Indian practices had an influence on the Mughal elites, as many Mughal chieftains married Indian women and adopted Indian forms of dress.

The Economy Long-term stability led to increasing commercialization and the spread of wealth to new groups within Indian society. The Mughal era saw the emergence of an affluent landed gentry and a prosperous merchant class. Members of prestigious castes from the pre-Mughal period reaped many of the benefits of the increasing wealth, but some of these changes transcended caste boundaries and led to the emergence of new groups who achieved status and wealth on the basis of economic achievement rather than traditional kinship ties. During the late eighteenth century, this economic prosperity was shaken by the decline of the Mughal Empire and the increasing European presence. But many prominent Indians reacted by establishing commercial relationships with the foreigners.

Mughal Culture

The era of the Mughals was one of synthesis in culture as well as in politics and religion. The Mughals combined Islamic themes with Persian and indigenous motifs to produce a unique style that enriched and embellished

possessed *zamindar* rights. Women from mercantile castes sometimes took an active role in business activities. At the same time, however, as Muslims, the Mughals subjected women to certain restrictions under Islamic law. On the whole, these Mughal practices coincided with and even accentuated existing tendencies in Indian society. The Muslim practice of isolating women and preventing them from associating with men outside the home (**purdah**) was adopted by many upper-class Hindus as a means of enhancing their status or protecting their women from unwelcome advances by Muslims in positions of authority. In other ways, Hindu practices were unaffected. The custom of *sati* continued to be practiced despite efforts by the Mughals to abolish it, and child marriage (most women were betrothed before the age of ten) remained common. Women were still instructed to

© Ian Bell

© William J. Duiker

ARTS & IDEAS

The Taj Mahal: Symbol of the Exotic East. The Taj Mahal, completed in 1653, was built by the Mughal emperor Shah Jahan as a tomb to glorify the memory of his beloved wife. Raised on a marble platform above the Jumna River, the Taj is dramatically framed by contrasting twin red sandstone mosques, magnificent gardens, and a long reflecting pool that mirrors and magnifies its beauty. The effect is one of monumental size, near blinding brilliance, and delicate lightness, a startling contrast to the heavier and more masculine Baroque style then popular in Europe. The Taj Mahal inspired many imitations, including the Royal Pavilion at Brighton, England (see the inset), constructed in 1815 to commemorate the British victory over Napoleon at Waterloo. The Pavilion is a good example of the way Europeans portrayed the "exotic" East.

Q How would you compare Mughal architecture, as exemplified by the Taj Majal, with the mosques erected by builders such as Sinan in the Ottoman Empire?

Indian art and culture. The Mughal emperors were zealous patrons of the arts and enticed painters, poets, and artisans from as far away as the Mediterranean. Apparently, the generosity of the Mughals made it difficult to refuse a trip to India. It was said that they would reward a poet with his weight in gold.

Architecture Undoubtedly, the Mughals' most visible achievement was in architecture. Here they integrated Persian and Indian styles in a new and sometimes breathtakingly beautiful form best symbolized by the Taj Mahal, built by the emperor Shah Jahan in the mid-seventeenth century (see the comparative illustration above). Although the human and economic cost of the Taj tarnishes the romantic legend of its construction, there is no denying the beauty of the building. It had evolved from a style that originated several decades earlier with the tomb of Humayun.

Humayun's mausoleum had combined Persian and Islamic motifs in a square building finished in red sandstone and topped with a dome. The Taj brought the style to perfection. Working with a model created by his Persian architect, Shah Jahan raised the dome and replaced the red sandstone with brilliant white marble. The entire exterior and interior surface is decorated with cut-stone geometrical patterns, delicate black stone tracery, or intricate inlay of colored precious stones in floral and Qur'anic arabesques. The technique of creating dazzling floral mosaics of lapis lazuli, malachite, carnelian, turquoise, and mother of pearl may have been introduced by Italian artists at the Mughal court. Shah Jahan spent his last years imprisoned in a room in the Red Fort at Agra; from his windows, he could see the beautiful memorial to his beloved wife.

The Taj was by no means the only magnificent building erected during the Mughal era. Akbar, who, in the words of a contemporary, "[dressed] the work of his mind and heart in the garment of stone and clay," was the first of the great Mughal builders. His first palace at Agra, the Red Fort, was begun in 1565. A few years later, he

Painting The other major artistic achievement of the Mughal period was painting. As in so many other areas of endeavor, painting in Mughal India resulted from the blending of two cultures. While living in exile, Emperor Humayun had learned to admire Persian miniatures. On his return to India in 1555, he invited two Persian masters to live in his palace and introduce the technique to his adopted land. His successor, Akbar, appreciated the new style and popularized it with his patronage. He established a state workshop at Fatehpur Sikri for two hundred artists, mostly Hindus, who worked under the guidance of the Persian masters to create the Mughal school of painting.

The "Akbar style" combined Persian with Indian motifs, such as the use of extended space and the portrayal of physical human action, characteristics not usually seen in Persian art. Akbar also apparently encouraged the imitation of European art forms, including the portrayal of Christian subjects, the use of perspective, lifelike portraits, and the shading of colors in the Renaissance style. The depiction of the human figure in Mughal painting outraged orthodox Muslims at court, but Akbar argued that the painter, "in sketching anything that has life . . . must come to feel that he cannot bestow individuality upon his work, and is thus forced to think of God, the Giver of Life, and will thus increase in knowledge."[4]

Jahangir the Magnificent. In 1615, the English ambassador to the Mughal court presented an official portrait of King James I to Shah Jahangir, who returned the favor with a portrait of himself. Thus was established a long tradition of exchanging paintings between the two empires. As it turned out, the practice altered the art of Mughal portraiture, which had previously shown the emperor in action poses, hunting, at official functions, or in battle. Henceforth, portraits of the ruler followed European practice by proclaiming the opulence and spiritual power of the empire. In this painting, Jahangir has chosen spiritual over earthly power by offering a book to a sheikh while ignoring the Ottoman sultan, King James I, and the Hindu artist who painted the picture. Even the cherubs, a European artifice, are dazzled by the shah's divine character, which is further demonstrated by an enormous halo.

ordered the construction of a new palace at Fatehpur Sikri, 26 miles west of Agra. The new palace was built in honor of a Sufi mystic who had correctly forecast the birth of a son to the emperor. In gratitude, Akbar decided to build a new capital city and palace on the site of the mystic's home in the village of Sikri. Over a period of fifteen years, from 1571 to 1586, a magnificent new city in red sandstone was constructed. Although the city was abandoned before completion and now stands almost untouched, it is a popular destination for tourists and pilgrims.

Literature The development of Indian literature was held back by the absence of printing, which was not introduced until the end of the Mughal era. Literary works were inscribed by calligraphers, and one historian has estimated that the library of Agra contained more than 24,000 volumes. Poetry, in particular, flourished under the Mughals, who established poet laureates at court. Poems were written in the Persian style and in the Persian language. In fact, Persian became the official language of the court until the sack of Delhi in 1739.

Another aspect of the long Mughal reign was a Hindu revival of devotional literature, much of it dedicated to Krishna and Rama. The retelling of the Ramayana in the vernacular culminated in the sixteenth-century Hindi version by the great poet Tulsidas (1532–1623). His *Ramcaritmanas* presents the devotional story with a deified Rama and Sita. Tulsidas's genius was in combining the conflicting cults of Vishnu and Shiva into a unified and overwhelming love for the divine, which he expressed in some of the most moving of all Indian poetry. The *Ramcaritmanas* has eclipsed its two-thousand-year-old Sanskrit ancestor in popularity and even became the basis of an Indian television series in the late 1980s.

TIMELINE

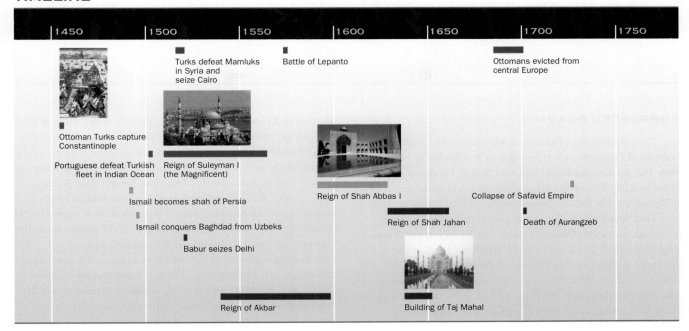

1450 1500 1550 1600 1650 1700 1750

Turks defeat Mamluks in Syria and seize Cairo

Battle of Lepanto

Ottomans evicted from central Europe

Ottoman Turks capture Constantinople

Portuguese defeat Turkish fleet in Indian Ocean

Reign of Suleyman I (the Magnificent)

Ismail becomes shah of Persia

Reign of Shah Abbas I

Collapse of Safavid Empire

Ismail conquers Baghdad from Uzbeks

Reign of Shah Jahan

Death of Aurangzeb

Babur seizes Delhi

Reign of Akbar

Building of Taj Mahal

CONCLUSION

THE THREE EMPIRES THAT we have discussed in this chapter exhibit a number of striking similarities. First of all, they were Muslim in their religious affiliation, although the Safavids were Shi'ite rather than Sunni, a distinction that often led to mutual tensions and conflict. More important, perhaps, they were all of nomadic origin, and the political and social institutions that they adopted carried the imprint of their preimperial past. Once they achieved imperial power, however, all three ruling dynasties displayed an impressive capacity to administer a large empire and brought a degree of stability to peoples who had all too often lived in conditions of internal division and war.

Another similarity is that the mastery of the techniques of modern warfare, including the use of firearms, played a central role in all three empires' ability to overcome their rivals and rise to regional hegemony. Some scholars have therefore labeled them "gunpowder empires" in the belief that technical prowess in the art of warfare was a key element in their success. Although that is undoubtedly true, we should not forget that other factors, such as dynamic leadership, political acumen, and the possession of an ardent following motivated by religious zeal, were equally if not more important in their drive to power and ability to retain it. Weapons by themselves do not an empire make.

The rise of these powerful Muslim states coincided with the opening period of European expansion at the end of the fifteenth century and the beginning of the sixteenth. The military and political talents of these empires helped protect much of the Muslim world from the resurgent forces of Christianity. To the contrary, the Ottoman Turks carried their empire into the heart of Christian Europe and briefly reached the gates of the great city of Vienna. By the end of the eighteenth century, however, the Safavid dynasty had imploded, and the powerful Mughal Empire was in a state of virtual collapse. Only the Ottoman Empire was still functioning. Yet it too had lost much of its early expansionistic vigor and was showing signs of internal decay.

The reasons for the decline of these empires have inspired considerable debate among historians. One factor was undoubtedly the expansion of European power into the Indian Ocean and the Middle East. But internal causes were probably more important in the long run. All three empires experienced growing factionalism within the ruling elite, incompetence within the palace, and the emergence of divisive forces in the empire at large—factors that have marked the passing of traditional empires since early times. Paradoxically, one of the greatest strengths of these empires—their mastery of gunpowder—may have simultaneously been a serious weakness in that it allowed them to develop a complacent sense of security. With little incentive to turn their attention to new developments in science and technology, they were increasingly vulnerable to attack by the advanced nations of the West. The weakening of the gunpowder empires created a political vacuum into which the dynamic and competitive forces of European capitalism were quick to enter.

The gunpowder empires, however, were not the only states in Asia that were able to resist the first outward thrust of European expansion. Farther to the east, the mature civilizations in China and Japan successfully faced a similar challenge from Western merchants and missionaries. Unlike their counterparts in South Asia and the Middle East, as the nineteenth century dawned, they continued to thrive.

SUGGESTED READING

Constantinople A dramatic recent account of the Muslim takeover of Constantinople is provided by **R. Crowley** in *1453: The Holy War for Constantinople and the Clash of Islam and the West* (New York, 2005). Crowley acknowledges his debt to the classic by **S. Runciman**, *The Fall of Constantinople, 1453* (Cambridge, 1965).

Ottoman Empire Two useful general surveys of Ottoman history are **C. Finkel**, *Osman's Dream: The History of the Ottoman Empire* (Jackson, Tenn., 2006), and **J. Goodwin**, *Lords of the Horizons: A History of the Ottoman Empire* (London, 2002). A highly readable, albeit less definitive, account is **Lord Kinross, The Ottoman Centuries: The Rise and Fall of the Ottoman Empire** (New York, 1977), which features a great many human-interest stories.

The life of Mehmet II is chronicled in **F. Babinger**, *Mehmed the Conqueror and His Time,* trans. **R. Manheim** (Princeton, N.J., 1979). On Suleyman the Magnificent, see **R. Merriman**, *Suleiman the Magnificent, 1520–1566* (Cambridge, 1944).

For the argument that the decline of the Ottoman Empire was not inevitable, see **E. Karsh et al.**, *Empires of the Sand: The Struggle for Mastery in the Middle East, 1789–1923* (Cambridge, Mass., 2001).

The Safavids On the Safavids, see **R. M. Savory**, *Iran Under the Safavids* (Cambridge, 1980), and **E. B. Monshi**, *History of Shah Abbas the Great,* 2 vols. (Boulder, Colo., 1978). For a thoughtful if scholarly account of the reasons for the rise of the Safavid Empire, see **R. J. Abisaab**, *Converting Persia: Shia Islam and the Safavid Empire, 1501–1736* (London, 2004).

The Mughals For an elegant overview of the Mughal Empire and its cultural achievements, see **A. Schimmel**, *The Empire of the Great Mughals: History, Art and Culture,* trans. **C. Attwood** (London, 2004). A dramatic account for the general reader is **W. Hansen**, *The Peacock Throne: The Drama of Mogul India* (New York, 1972).

There are a number of specialized works on various aspects of the period. For a treatment of the Mughal era in the context of Islamic rule in India, see **S. M. Ikram**, *Muslim Civilization in India* (New York, 1964). The concept of "gunpowder empires" is persuasively analyzed in **D. E. Streusand**, *The Formation of the Mughal Empire* (Delhi, 1989). Economic issues predominate in much recent scholarship. For example, **S. Subrahmanyan,**

The Political Economy of Commerce: Southern India, 1500–1650 (Cambridge, 1990), focuses on the interaction between internal and external trade in southern India during the early stages of the period. The Mughal Empire is analyzed in a broad Central Asian context in **R. C. Foltz, *Mughal India and Central Asia*** (Karachi, 1998). Finally, **K. N. Chaudhuri, *Trade and Civilization in the Indian Ocean: An Economic History from the Rise of Islam to 1750*** (Cambridge, 1985), views Indian commerce in the perspective of the regional trade network throughout the Indian Ocean.

For treatments of all three Muslim empires in a comparative context, see **J. J. Kissling et al., *The Last Great Muslim Empires*** (Princeton, N.J., 1996), and **M. G. S. Hodgson, *Rethinking World History: Essays on Europe, Islam, and World History*** (Cambridge, 1993).

Women of the Ottoman and Mughal Empires On the lives of women in the Ottoman and Mughal Empires, see **S. Hughes** and **B. Hughes**, *Women in World History,* vol. 2 (Armonk, N.Y., 1997). For a more detailed presentation of women in the imperial harem, consult **L. P. Peirce**, "Beyond Harem Walls: Ottoman Royal Women and the Exercise of Power," in *Gendered Domains: Rethinking Public and Private in Women's History,* ed. **D. O. Helly** and **S. M. Reverby** (Ithaca, N.Y., 1992), and **L. P. Peirce**, *The Imperial Harem: Women and Sovereignty in the Ottoman Empire* (Oxford, 1993). The fascinating story of the royal woman who played an important role behind the scenes is found in **E. B. Findly**, *Nur Jahan: Empress of Mughal India* (Oxford, 1993).

Art and Architecture On the art of this era, see **R. C. Craven**, *Indian Art: A Concise History,* rev. ed. (New York, 1997); **J. Bloom** and **S. Blair**, *Islamic Arts* (London, 1997); **M. C. Beach**, *The Imperial Image* (Washington, D.C., 1981); **M. C. Beach** and **E. Koch**, *King of the World: The Padshahnama* (London, 1997); and **M. Hattstein** and **P. Delius**, *Islam: Art and Architecture* (Königswinter, Germany, 2004).

WORLD HISTORY RESOURCES

Visit the website for *The Essential World History* to access study aids such as Flashcards, Critical Thinking Exercises, and Chapter Quizzes:

www.cengage.com/history/duikspiel/essentialworld6e

What were the main characteristics of each of the Muslim empires, and in what ways did they resemble each other? How were they distinct from their European counterparts?

In thinking about these questions, begin by breaking them down into the components shown below. A discussion of the significance of each component should appear in your answer.

POLITICS AND GOVERNMENT   Compare the size and scope of these Muslim empires over time. How did their size and populations affect the types of government that emerged and governmental policies toward the diverse ethnic groups within each empire?

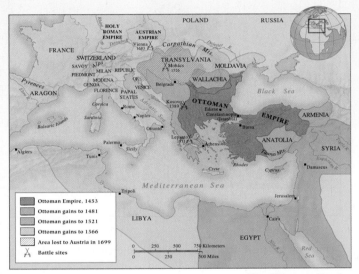

The Ottoman Empire

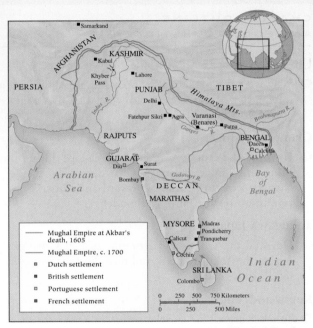

The Mughal Empire

The Ottoman and Safavid Empires, c. 1683

INTERACTION AND EXCHANGE   How was each of these empires eventually affected by Europeans? How does the decline of these empires correspond to the rise of European exploration?

CHAPTER 17
THE EAST ASIAN WORLD

Emperor Kangxi

CHAPTER OUTLINE
AND FOCUS QUESTIONS

China at Its Apex

Q Why were the Manchus so successful at establishing a foreign dynasty in China, and what were the main characteristics of Manchu rule?

Changing China

Q How did the economy and society change during the Ming and Qing eras, and to what degree did these changes seem to be leading toward an industrial revolution on the European model?

Tokugawa Japan

Q How did the society and economy of Japan change during the Tokugawa era, and how did Japanese culture reflect those changes?

Korea and Vietnam

Q To what degree did developments in Korea during this period reflect conditions in China and Japan? What were the most unique aspects of Vietnamese civilization?

CRITICAL THINKING

Q How did China and Japan respond to the coming of the Europeans, and what explains the differences in their approach? What impact did European contacts have on these two East Asian civilizations through the end of the eighteenth century?

IN DECEMBER 1717, Emperor Kangxi returned from a hunting trip north of the Great Wall and began to suffer from dizzy spells. Conscious of his approaching date with mortality—he was now nearly seventy years of age—the emperor called together his sons and leading government officials in the imperial palace and issued an edict summing up his ideas on the art of statecraft. Rulers, he declared, should be sincere in their reverence for Heaven's laws as the fundamental strategy for governing the country. Among those laws were the following: show concern for the welfare of the people, practice diligence, protect the state from its enemies, choose able advisers, and strike a careful balance between leniency and strictness, principle and expedience. That, he concluded, was all there was to it.[1]

Any potential successor to the throne would have been well advised to attend to the emperor's advice. Kangxi was not only one of the longest reigning of all Chinese rulers but also one of the wisest. His era was one of peace and prosperity, and after a half century of his rule, the empire was now at the zenith of its power and influence. As his life approached its end, Heaven must indeed have been pleased at the quality of his stewardship.

As for the emperor's edict, it clearly reflected the genius of Confucian teachings at their best and, with its emphasis on

 © Hu Weibiao/Panorama/The Image Works

prudence, compassion, and tolerance, has a timeless quality that applies to our age as well as to the golden age of the Qing dynasty (1644–1911).

Kangxi reigned during one of the most glorious eras in the long history of China. Under the Ming (1369–1644) and the early Qing dynasties, the empire expanded its borders to a degree not seen since the Han and the Tang. Chinese culture was the envy of its neighbors and earned the admiration of many European visitors, including Jesuit priests and Enlightenment philosophes.

On the surface, China appeared to be an unchanging society patterned after the Confucian vision of a "golden age" in the remote past. This indeed was the image presented by China's rulers, who referred constantly to tradition as a model for imperial institutions and cultural values. Although few observers could have been aware of it at the time, however, China was changing—and rather rapidly.

A similar process was under way in neighboring Japan. A vigorous new shogunate called the Tokugawa rose to power in the early seventeenth century and managed to revitalize the traditional system in a somewhat more centralized form that enabled it to survive for another 250 years. But major structural changes were taking place in Japanese society, and by the nineteenth century, tensions were growing as the gap between theory and reality widened.

One of the many factors involved in the quickening pace of change in both countries was contact with the West, which began with the arrival of Portuguese ships in Chinese and Japanese ports in the first half of the sixteenth century. The Ming and the Tokugawa initially opened their doors to European trade and missionary activity. Later, however, Chinese and Japanese rulers became concerned about the corrosive effects of Western ideas and practices and attempted to protect their traditional societies from external intrusion. But neither could forever resist the importunities of Western trading nations; nor were they able to inhibit the societal shifts that were taking place within their borders. When the doors to the West were finally reopened in the mid-nineteenth century, both societies were ripe for radical change. ❀

China at Its Apex

Q **Focus Question:** Why were the Manchus so successful at establishing a foreign dynasty in China, and what were the main characteristics of Manchu rule?

In 1514, a Portuguese fleet dropped anchor off the coast of China, just south of the Pearl River estuary and present-day Hong Kong. It was the first direct contact between the Chinese Empire and the West since the arrival of the Venetian adventurer Marco Polo two centuries earlier, and it opened an era that would eventually change the face of China and, indeed, all the world.

From the Ming to the Qing

Marco Polo had reported on the magnificence of China after visiting Beijing during the reign of Khubilai Khan, the great Mongol ruler. By the time the Portuguese fleet arrived off the coast of China, of course, the Mongol Empire had long since disappeared. It had gradually weakened after the death of Khubilai Khan and was finally overthrown in 1368 by a massive peasant rebellion under the leadership of Zhu Yuanzhang, who had declared himself the founding emperor of a new Ming (Bright) dynasty and assumed the reign title of Ming Hongwu (Ming Hung Wu, or Ming Martial Emperor).

As we have seen, the Ming inaugurated a period of territorial expansion westward into Central Asia and southward into Vietnam while consolidating control over China's vast heartland. At the same time, between 1405 and 1433 the dynasty sponsored a series of voyages under Admiral Zhenghe that spread Chinese influence far into the Indian Ocean. Then suddenly the voyages were discontinued, and the dynasty turned its attention to domestic concerns (see Chapter 10).

First Contacts with the West Despite the Ming's retreat from active participation in maritime trade, when the Portuguese arrived in 1514, China was in command of a vast empire that stretched from the steppes of Central Asia to the China Sea, from the Gobi Desert to the tropical rain forests of Southeast Asia. From the lofty perspective of the imperial throne in Beijing, the Europeans could only have seemed like an unusually exotic form of barbarian to be placed within the familiar framework of the tributary system, the hierarchical arrangement in which rulers of all other countries were regarded as "younger brothers" of the Son of Heaven. Indeed, the bellicose and uncultured behavior of the Portuguese so outraged Chinese officials that they expelled the Europeans, but after further negotiations, the Portuguese were permitted to occupy the tiny territory of Macao, a foothold they would retain until the end of the twentieth century.

Initially, the arrival of the Europeans did not have much impact on Chinese society. Direct trade between Europe and China was limited, and Portuguese ships became involved in the regional trade network, carrying silk from China to Japan in return for Japanese silver. Eventually, the Spanish also began to participate, using the Philippines as an anchor in the galleon trade between China and the great silver mines in the Americas.

More influential than trade, perhaps, were the ideas introduced by Christian missionaries. Among the most active and the most effective were highly educated Jesuits, who were familiar with European philosophical and

THE ART OF PRINTING

ARTS & IDEAS

Europeans obtained much of their early information about China from the Jesuits who served at the Ming court in the sixteenth and seventeenth centuries. Clerics such as the Italian Matteo Ricci (1552–1610), who arrived in China in 1601, found much to admire in Chinese civilization. Here Ricci expresses a keen interest in Chinese printing methods, which at that time were well in advance of the techniques used in the West. Later Christian missionaries expressed strong interest in Confucian philosophy and Chinese ideas of statecraft.

Matteo Ricci, *The Diary of Matthew Ricci*

The art of printing was practiced in China at a date somewhat earlier than that assigned to the beginning of printing in Europe, which was about 1405. It is quite certain that the Chinese knew the art of printing at least five centuries ago, and some of them assert that printing was known to their people before the beginning of the Christian era, about 50 B.C.E. Their method of printing differs widely from that employed in Europe, and our method would be quite impracticable for them because of the exceedingly large number of Chinese characters and symbols. . . .

Their method of making printed books is quite ingenious. The text is written in ink, with a brush made of very fine hair, on a sheet of paper which is inverted and pasted on a wooden tablet. When the paper has become thoroughly dry, its surface is scraped off quickly and with great skill, until nothing but a fine tissue bearing the characters remains on the wooden tablet. Then, with a steel graver, the workman cuts away the surface following the outlines of the characters until these alone stand out in low relief. From such a block a skilled printer can make copies with incredible speed, turning out as many as fifteen hundred copies in a single day. . . . This scheme of engraving wooden blocks is well adapted for the large and complex nature of the Chinese characters, but I do not think it would lend itself very aptly to our European type, which could hardly be engraved upon wood because of its small dimensions.

Their method of printing has one decided advantage, namely, that once these tablets are made, they can be preserved and used for making changes in the text as often as one wishes. Additions and subtractions can also be made as the tablets can be readily patched. . . . We have derived great benefit from this method of Chinese printing, as we employ the domestic help in our homes to strike off copies of the books on religious and scientific subjects which we translate into Chinese from the languages in which they were written originally. In truth, the whole method is so simple that one is tempted to try it for himself after once having watched the process. The simplicity of Chinese printing is what accounts for the exceedingly large numbers of books in circulation here and the ridiculously low prices at which they are sold.

Q *How did the Chinese method of printing differ from that used in Europe at that time? What were its advantages?*

---

scientific developments. Recognizing the Chinese pride in their own culture, the Jesuits attempted to draw parallels between Christian and Confucian concepts (for example, they identified the Western concept of God with the Chinese character for Heaven) and to show the similarities between Christian morality and Confucian ethics. European inventions such as the clock, the prism, and various astronomical and musical instruments impressed Chinese officials, hitherto deeply imbued with a sense of the superiority of Chinese civilization, and helped Western ideas win acceptance at court. An elderly Chinese scholar expressed his wonder at the miracle of eyeglasses:

> *White glass from across the Western Seas*
> *Is imported through Macao:*
> *Fashioned into lenses big as coins,*
> *They encompass the eyes in a double frame.*
> *I put them on—it suddenly becomes clear;*
> *I can see the very tips of things!*
> *And read fine print by the dim-lit window*
> *Just like in my youth.*[2]

For their part, the missionaries were much impressed with many aspects of Chinese civilization, and reports of their experiences heightened European curiosity about this great society on the other side of the world (see the box above). By the late seventeenth century, European philosophers and political thinkers had begun to praise Chinese civilization and to hold up Confucian institutions and values as a mirror to criticize their counterparts in the West.

The Ming Brought to Earth During the late sixteenth century, the Ming began to decline as a series of weak rulers led to an era of corruption, concentration of landownership, and ultimately peasant rebellions and tribal unrest along the northern frontier. The inflow of vast amounts of foreign silver resulted in an alarming increase in inflation. Then the arrival of the English and the Dutch, whose ships preyed on the Spanish galleon trade between Asia and the Americas, disrupted the silver trade; silver imports plummeted, severely straining the Chinese economy by raising the value of the metal relative to that of copper. Crop yields declined due to harsh weather, and the

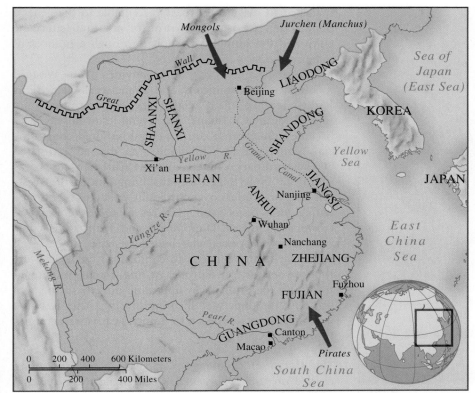

postal worker in central China who had been dismissed from his job as part of a cost-saving measure by the imperial court. In the 1630s, Li managed to extend the revolt throughout the country, and his forces finally occupied the capital of Beijing in 1644. The last Ming emperor committed suicide by hanging himself from a tree in the palace gardens.

But Li was unable to hold his conquest. The overthrow of the Ming dynasty presented a great temptation to the Manchus. With the assistance of many military commanders who had deserted from the Ming, they conquered Beijing on their own (see Map 17.1). Li Zicheng's army disintegrated, and the Manchus declared the creation of a new dynasty with the reign title of the Qing (Ch'ing, or Pure). Once again, China was under foreign rule.

MAP 17.1 China and Its Enemies During the Late Ming Era. During the seventeenth century, the Ming dynasty faced challenges on two fronts: from China's traditional adversaries, nomadic groups north of the Great Wall, and from new arrivals, European merchants who had begun to press for trading privileges along the southern coast.
Q How did these threats differ from those faced by previous dynasties in China?

The Greatness of the Qing

The accession of the Manchus to power in Beijing was not universally applauded. Some Ming loyalists fled to Southeast Asia, but others continued their resistance to the new rulers from inside the country. To make it easier to identify the rebels, the government ordered all Chinese to adopt Manchu dress and hairstyles. All Chinese males were to shave their foreheads and braid their hair into a queue; those who refused were to be executed. As a popular saying put it, "Lose your hair or lose your head."[3]

But the Manchus eventually proved to be more adept at adapting to Chinese conditions than their predecessors, the Mongols. Unlike the latter, who had tried to impose their own methods of ruling, the Manchus adopted the Chinese political system (although, as we shall see, they retained their distinct position within it) and were gradually accepted by most Chinese as the legitimate rulers of the country.

Like all of China's great dynasties, the Qing was blessed with a series of strong early rulers who pacified the country, rectified many of the most obvious social and economic inequities, and restored peace and prosperity. For the Ming dynasty, these strong emperors had been

resulting scarcity reduced the ability of the government to provide food in times of imminent starvation. High taxes, provoked in part by increased official corruption, led to rural unrest and worker violence in urban areas.

As always, internal problems were accompanied by unrest along the northern frontier. Following long precedent, the Ming had attempted to pacify the frontier tribes by forging alliances with them and granting trade privileges. One of the alliances was with the Manchus (also known as the Jurchen), the descendants of peoples who had briefly established a kingdom in northern China during the early thirteenth century. The Manchus, a mixed agricultural and hunting people, lived northeast of the Great Wall in the area known today as Manchuria.

At first, the Manchus were satisfied with consolidating their territory and made little effort to extend their rule south of the Great Wall. But during the first decades of the seventeenth century, a major epidemic devastated the population in many areas of the country. The suffering brought on by the epidemic helped spark a vast peasant revolt led by Li Zicheng (Li Tzu-ch'eng, 1604–1651), a

The Temple of Heaven. This temple, located in the capital city of Beijing, is one of the most important historical structures in China. Built in 1420 at the order of the Ming emperor Yongle, it served as the location for the emperor's annual ceremony appealing to Heaven for a good harvest. As a symbol of their efforts to continue the imperial traditions, the Manchu emperors embraced the practice as well. Yongle's temple burned to the ground in 1889 but was immediately rebuilt according to the original design.

managed to make the dynasty acceptable to the general population. As an active patron of arts and letters, he cultivated the support of scholars through a number of major projects.

During Kangxi's reign, the activities of the Western missionaries, Dominicans and Franciscans as well as Jesuits, reached their height. The emperor was quite tolerant of the Christians, and several Jesuit missionaries became influential at court. Several hundred court officials converted to Christianity, as did an estimated 300,000 ordinary Chinese. But the Christian effort was ultimately undermined by squabbling among the Western religious orders over the Jesuit policy of accommodating local beliefs and practices in order to facilitate conversion. Jealous Dominicans and Franciscans complained to the pope, who issued an edict ordering all missionaries and converts to conform to the official orthodoxy set forth in Europe. At first, Kangxi attempted to resolve the problem by appealing directly to the Vatican, but the pope was uncompromising. After Kangxi's death, his successor began to suppress Christian activities throughout China.

The Reign of Qianlong Kangxi's achievements were carried on by his successors, Yongzheng (Yung Cheng, 1722–1736) and Qianlong (1736–1795). Like Kangxi, Qianlong was known for his diligence, tolerance, and intellectual curiosity, and he too combined vigorous military action against the unruly tribes along the frontier with active efforts to promote economic prosperity, administrative efficiency, and scholarship and artistic excellence. The result was continued growth for the Manchu Empire throughout much of the eighteenth century.

But it was also under Qianlong that the first signs of the internal decay of the Manchu dynasty began to appear. The clues were familiar ones. Qing military campaigns along the frontier were expensive and placed heavy demands on the imperial treasury. As the emperor aged, he became less astute in selecting his subordinates and fell under the influence of corrupt elements at court.

Corruption at the center led inevitably to unrest in rural areas, where higher taxes, bureaucratic venality, and rising pressure on the land because of the growing population had produced economic hardship. The heart of the unrest was in central China, where discontented peasants who had recently been settled on infertile land launched a revolt known as the White Lotus Rebellion (1796–1804). The revolt was eventually suppressed but at great expense.

Qing Politics One reason for the success of the Manchus was their ability to adapt to their new environment.

Hongwu and Yongle; under the Qing, they would be Kangxi (K'ang Hsi) and Qianlong (Ch'ien Lung). The two Qing monarchs ruled China for well over a century, from the middle of the seventeenth century to the end of the eighteenth, and were responsible for much of the greatness of Manchu China.

The Reign of Kangxi Kangxi (1661–1722) was arguably the greatest ruler in Chinese history. Ascending to the throne at the age of seven, he was blessed with diligence, political astuteness, and a strong character and began to take charge of Qing administration while still an adolescent. During the six decades of his reign, Kangxi not only stabilized imperial rule by pacifying the restive peoples along the northern and western frontiers but also

The European Warehouses at Canton. Aggravated by the growing presence of foreigners in the eighteenth century, the Chinese court severely restricted the movement of European traders in China. They were permitted to live only in a compound near Canton during the months of the trading season and could go into the city only three times a month. In this painting, foreign flags (including, from the left, those of the United States, Sweden, Great Britain, and Holland), fly over the warehouses and residences of the foreign community, while Chinese sampans and junks sit anchored in the river.

They retained the Ming political system with relatively few changes. They also tried to establish their legitimacy as China's rightful rulers by stressing their devotion to the principles of Confucianism. Emperor Kangxi ostentatiously studied the sacred Confucian classics and issued a "sacred edict" that proclaimed to the entire empire the importance of the moral values established by the master (see the box on p. 427).

Still, the Manchus, like the Mongols, were ethnically, linguistically, and culturally distinct from their subject population. The Qing attempted to cope with this reality by adopting a two-pronged strategy. On the one hand, the Manchus, representing less than 2 percent of the entire population, were legally defined as distinct from everyone else in China. The Manchu nobles retained their aristocratic privileges, while their economic base was protected by extensive landholdings and revenues provided from the state treasury. Other Manchus were assigned farmland and organized into military units, called **banners,** which were stationed as separate units in

various strategic positions throughout China. These "bannermen" were the primary fighting force of the empire. Ethnic Chinese were prohibited from settling in Manchuria and were still compelled to wear their hair in a queue as a sign of submission to the ruling dynasty.

But while the Qing attempted to protect their distinct identity within an alien society, they also recognized the need to bring ethnic Chinese into the top ranks of imperial administration. Their solution was to create a system, known as **dyarchy,** in which all important administrative positions were shared equally by Chinese and Manchus. Meanwhile, the Manchus themselves, despite official efforts to preserve their separate language and culture, were increasingly assimilated into Chinese civilization.

China on the Eve of the Western Onslaught Unfortunately for China, the decline of the Qing dynasty occurred just as China's modest relationship with the West was about to give way to a new era of military

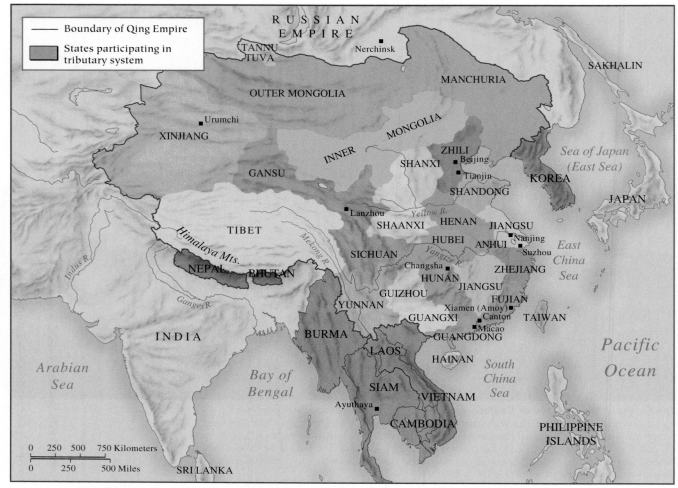

MAP 17.2 **The Qing Empire in the Eighteenth Century.** The boundaries of the Chinese Empire at the height of the Qing dynasty in the eighteenth century are shown on this map.

Q What areas were linked in tributary status to the Chinese Empire, and how did they benefit the empire?

View an animated version of this map or related maps at www.cengage.com/history/duikspiel/essentialworld6e

confrontation and increased pressure for trade. The first problems came in the north, where Russian traders seeking skins and furs began to penetrate the region between Siberian Russia and Manchuria. Earlier the Ming dynasty had attempted to deal with the Russians by the traditional method of placing them in a tributary relationship. But the tsar refused to play by Chinese rules. His envoys to Beijing ignored the tribute system and refused to perform the kowtow (the ritual of prostration and knocking the head on the ground performed by foreign emissaries before the emperor), the classic symbol of fealty demanded of all foreign ambassadors to the Chinese court. Formal diplomatic relations were finally established in 1689, when the Treaty of Nerchinsk settled the boundary dispute and provided for regular trade between the two countries. Through such arrangements, the Manchus were able not only to pacify the northern frontier but also to extend their rule over Xinjiang and Tibet to the west and southwest (see Map 17.2).

Dealing with the foreigners who arrived by sea was more difficult. By the end of the seventeenth century, the English had replaced the Portuguese as the dominant force in European trade. Operating through the

THE TRIBUTE SYSTEM IN ACTION

INTERACTION & EXCHANGE

In 1793, the British emissary Lord Macartney visited the Qing Empire to request the opening of formal diplomatic and trading relations between his country and China. Emperor Qianlong's reply, addressed to King George III of Britain, illustrates how the imperial court in Beijing viewed the world. King George could not have been pleased. The document provides a good example of the complacency with which the Celestial Empire viewed the world beyond its borders.

A Decree of Emperor Qianlong

An Imperial Edict to the King of England: You, O King, are so inclined toward our civilization that you have sent a special envoy across the seas to bring to our Court your memorial of congratulations on the occasion of my birthday and to present your native products as an expression of your thoughtfulness. On perusing your memorial, so simply worded and sincerely conceived, I am impressed by your genuine respectfulness and friendliness and greatly pleased.

As to the request made in your memorial, O King, to send one of your nationals to stay at the Celestial Court to take care of your country's trade with China, this is not in harmony with the state system of our dynasty and will definitely not be permitted. Traditionally people of the European nations who wished to render some service under the Celestial Court have been permitted to come to the capital. But after their arrival they are obliged to wear Chinese court costumes, are placed in a certain residence, and are never allowed to return to their own countries. This is the established rule of the Celestial Dynasty with which presumably you, O King, are familiar. Now you, O King, wish to send one of your nationals to live

in the capital, but he is not like the Europeans who come to Peking [Beijing] as Chinese employees, live there, and never return home again, nor can he be allowed to go and come and maintain any correspondence. This is indeed a useless undertaking.

Moreover the territory under the control of the Celestial Court is very large and wide. There are well-established regulations governing tributary envoys from the outer states to Peking, giving them provisions (of food and traveling expenses) by our post-houses and limiting their going and coming. There has never been a precedent for letting them do whatever they like. Now if you, O King, wish to have a representative in Peking, his language will be unintelligible and his dress different from the regulations; there is no place to accommodate him....

The Celestial Court has pacified and possessed the territory within the four seas. Its sole aim is to do its utmost to achieve good government and to manage political affairs, attaching no value to strange jewels and precious objects. The various articles presented by you, O King, this time are accepted by my special order to the office in charge of such functions in consideration of the offerings having come from a long distance with sincere good wishes. As a matter of fact, the virtue and prestige of the Celestial Dynasty having spread far and wide, the kings of the myriad nations come by land and sea with all sorts of precious things. Consequently there is nothing we lack, as your principal envoy and others have themselves observed. We have never set much store on strange or ingenious objects, nor do we need any more of your country's manufactures.

Q *What reasons did the emperor give for refusing Macartney's request to have a permanent British ambassador in Beijing? How did the tribute system differ from the principles of international relations as practiced in the West?*

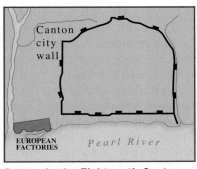

Canton in the Eighteenth Century

East India Company, which served as both a trading unit and the administrator of English territories in Asia, the English established their first trading post at Canton in 1699. Over the next decades, trade with China, notably the export of tea and silk to England, increased rapidly. To limit contact between Chinese and Europeans, the Qing licensed Chinese trading firms at Canton to be the exclusive conduit for trade with

the West. Eventually, the Qing confined the Europeans to a small island just outside the city wall and permitted them to reside there only from October through March.

For a while, the British tolerated this system, but by the end of the eighteenth century, the British government became restive at the uneven balance of trade between the two countries, which forced the British to ship vast amounts of silver bullion to China in exchange for its silks, porcelains, and teas. In 1793, a mission under Lord Macartney visited Beijing to press for liberalization of trade restrictions. A compromise was reached on the kowtow (Macartney was permitted to bend on one knee as was the British custom), but Qianlong expressed no interest in British manufactured products (see the box above). An exasperated Macartney compared the Chinese

Empire to "an old, crazy, first-rate man-of-war" that had once awed its neighbors "merely by her bulk and appearance" but was now destined under incompetent leadership to be "dashed to pieces on the shore."[4] With his contemptuous dismissal of the British request, the emperor had inadvertently sowed the seeds for a century of humiliation.

Changing China

Q **Focus Question:** How did the economy and society change during the Ming and Qing eras, and to what degree did these changes seem to be leading toward an industrial revolution on the European model?

During the Ming and Qing dynasties, China remained a predominantly agricultural society; nearly 85 percent of its people were farmers. But although most Chinese still lived in rural villages, the economy was undergoing a number of changes.

The Population Explosion

In the first place, the center of gravity was continuing to shift steadily from the north to the south. In the early centuries of Chinese civilization, the administrative and economic center of gravity was clearly in the north. By the early Qing, the economic breadbasket of China was located along the Yangtze River and regions to the south. One concrete indication of this shift occurred during the Ming dynasty, when Emperor Yongle ordered the renovation of the Grand Canal to facilitate the shipment of rice from the Yangtze delta to the food-starved north.

Moreover, the population was beginning to increase rapidly (see the comparative essay "Population Explosion" on p. 419). For centuries, China's population had remained within a range of 50 to 100 million, rising in times of peace and prosperity and falling in periods of foreign invasion and internal anarchy. During the Ming and the early Qing, however, the population increased from an estimated 70 to 80 million in 1390 to more than 300 million at the end of the eighteenth century. There were probably several reasons for this population increase: the relatively long period of peace and stability under the early Qing; the introduction of new crops from the Americas, including peanuts, sweet potatoes, and maize; and the planting of a new species of faster-growing rice from Southeast Asia.

Of course, this population increase meant much greater population pressure on the land, smaller farms, and a razor-thin margin of safety in case of climatic disaster. The imperial court attempted to deal with the problem through a variety of means, most notably by

CHRONOLOGY China During the Early Modern Era	
Rise of Ming dynasty	1369
Voyages of Zhenghe	1405–1433
Portuguese arrive in southern China	1514
Matteo Ricci arrives in China	1601
Li Zicheng occupies Beijing	1644
Manchus seize China	1644
Reign of Kangxi	1661–1722
Treaty of Nerchinsk	1689
First English trading post at Canton	1699
Reign of Qianlong	1736–1795
Lord Macartney's mission to China	1793
White Lotus Rebellion	1796–1804

preventing the concentration of land in the hands of wealthy landowners. Nevertheless, by the eighteenth century, almost all the land that could be irrigated was already under cultivation, and the problems of rural hunger and landlessness became increasingly serious.

Seeds of Industrialization

Another change that took place during the early modern period in China was the steady growth of manufacturing and commerce. Taking advantage of the long era of peace and prosperity, merchants and manufacturers began to expand their operations beyond their immediate provinces. Commercial networks began to operate on a regional and sometimes even a national basis, as trade in silk, metal and wood products, porcelain, cotton goods, and cash crops like cotton and tobacco developed rapidly. Foreign trade also expanded as Chinese merchants set up extensive contacts with countries in Southeast Asia.

Although this rise in industrial and commercial activity resembles the changes occurring in western Europe, China and Europe differed in several key ways. In the first place, members of the bourgeoisie in China were not as independent as their European counterparts. In China, trade and manufacturing remained under the firm control of the state. In addition, political and social prejudices against commercial activity remained strong. Reflecting an ancient preference for agriculture over manufacturing and trade, the state levied heavy taxes on manufacturing and commerce while attempting to keep agricultural taxes low.

One of the consequences of these differences was a growing technological gap between China and Europe. As we have seen, China had for long been at the

COMPARATIVE ESSAY
THE POPULATION EXPLOSION

EARTH & ENVIRONMENT

Between 1700 and 1800, Europe, China, and, to a lesser degree, India and the Ottoman Empire experienced a dramatic growth in population. In Europe, the population grew from 120 million people to almost 200 million by 1800; China, from less than 200 million to 300 million during the same period.

Four factors were important in causing this population explosion. First, better growing conditions, made possible by an improvement in climate, affected wide areas of the world and enabled people to produce more food. Summers in both China and Europe became warmer beginning in the early eighteenth century. Second, by the eighteenth century, people had begun to develop immunities to the epidemic diseases that had caused such widespread loss of life between 1500 and 1700. The movements of people by ship after 1500 had led to devastating epidemics. For example, the arrival of Europeans in Mexico introduced smallpox, measles, and chicken pox to a native population that had no immunities to European diseases. In 1500, between 11 and 20 million people lived in the area of Mexico; by 1650, only 1.5 million remained. Gradually, however, people developed immunities to these diseases.

A third factor in the population increase came from new food sources. As a result of the Columbian exchange (see the box on p. 344), American food crops—such as corn, potatoes, and sweet potatoes—were carried to other parts of the world, where they became important food sources. China had imported a new species of rice from Southeast Asia that had a shorter harvest cycle than that of existing varieties. These new foods provided additional sources of nutrition that enabled more people to live for a longer time. At the same time, land development and canal building in the eighteenth century also enabled government authorities to move food supplies to areas threatened with crop failure and famine.

Finally, the use of new weapons based on gunpowder allowed states to control larger territories and maintain a new degree of order. The early rulers of the Qing dynasty, for example, pacified the Chinese Empire and ensured a long period of peace and stability. Absolute monarchs achieved similar goals in a number of European states. Thus, deaths from violence were declining at the same time that an increase in food supplies and a decrease in deaths from diseases were occurring, thereby making possible in the eighteenth century the beginning of the world population explosion that persists to this day.

Q *What were the main reasons for the dramatic expansion in the world population during the early modern era?*

© British Museum/The Bridgeman Art Library

Festival of the Yam. The spread of a few major food crops made possible new sources of nutrition to feed more people. The importance of the yam to the Ashanti people of West Africa is evident in this celebration of a yam festival at harvest time in 1817.

---

forefront of the technological revolution that was beginning to transform the world in the early modern era, but its contribution to both practical and pure science failed to keep pace with Europe during the Qing dynasty, when, as the historian Benjamin Elman has noted, scholarly fashions turned back to antiquity as the prime source for knowledge of the world of natural and human events.

The Chinese reaction to European clockmaking techniques provides an example. In the early seventeenth century, the Jesuit Matteo Ricci introduced advanced European clocks driven by weights or springs. The emperor was fascinated and found the clocks more reliable than Chinese methods of keeping time. Over the next decades, European timepieces became a popular novelty at court, but the Chinese expressed little curiosity about the technology involved, provoking one European to remark that playthings like cuckoo clocks "will be received here with much greater interest than scientific instruments or *objets d'art*."[5]

Daily Life in Qing China

Daily life under the Ming and early Qing dynasties continued to follow traditional patterns. As in earlier periods, Chinese society was organized around the family. The ideal family unit in Qing China was the joint family, in which as many as three or even four generations lived under the same roof. When sons married, they brought their wives to live with them in the family homestead. Unmarried daughters would also remain in the house. Aging parents and grandparents remained under the same roof and were cared for by younger members of the household until they died. This ideal did not always correspond to reality, however, since many families did not possess sufficient land to support a large household.

The Family The family continued to be important in early Qing times for much the same reasons as in earlier times. As a labor-intensive society based primarily on the cultivation of rice, China needed large families to help with the harvest and to provide security for parents too old to work in the fields. Sons were particularly prized, not only because they had strong backs but also because they would raise their own families under the parental roof. With few opportunities for employment outside the family, sons had little choice but to remain with their parents and help on the land. Within the family, the oldest male was king, and his wishes theoretically had to be obeyed by all family members. Marriages were normally arranged for the benefit of the family, often by a go-between, and the groom and bride usually were not consulted. Frequently, they did not meet until the marriage ceremony. Under such conditions, love was clearly a secondary consideration. In fact, it was often viewed as detrimental since it inevitably distracted the attention of the husband and wife from their primary responsibility to the larger family unit.

Although this emphasis on filial piety might seem to represent a blatant disregard for individual rights, the obligations were not all on the side of the children. The father was expected to provide support for his wife and children and, like the ruler, was supposed to treat those in his care with respect and compassion. All too often, however, the male head of the family was able to exact his privileges without performing his responsibilities in return.

Beyond the joint family was the clan. Sometimes called a lineage, a clan was an extended kinship unit consisting of dozens or even hundreds of joint and nuclear families linked together by a clan council of elders and a variety of other common social and religious functions. The clan served a number of useful purposes. Some clans possessed lands that could be rented out to poorer families, or richer families within the clan might provide land for the poor. Since there was no general state-supported educational system, sons of poor families might be invited to study in a school established in the home of a more prosperous relative.

If the young man succeeded in becoming an official, he would be expected to provide favors and prestige for the clan as a whole.

The Role of Women In traditional China, the role of women had always been inferior to that of men. A sixteenth-century Spanish visitor to South China observed that Chinese women were "very secluded and virtuous, and it was a very rare thing for us to see a woman in the cities and large towns, unless it was an old crone." Women were more visible, he said, in rural areas, where they frequently could be seen working in the fields.[6]

The concept of female inferiority had deep roots in Chinese history. This view was embodied in the belief that only a male would carry on sacred family rituals and that men alone had the talent to govern others. Only males could aspire to a career in government or scholarship. Within the family system, the wife was clearly subordinated to the husband. Legally, she could not divorce her husband or inherit property. The husband, however, could divorce his wife if she did not produce male heirs, or he could take a second wife as well as a concubine for his pleasure. A widow suffered especially, because she had to either raise her children on a single income or fight off her former husband's greedy relatives, who would coerce her to remarry since, by law, they would then inherit all of her previous property and her original dowry.

Female children were less desirable because of their limited physical strength and because a girl's parents would have to pay a dowry to the parents of her future husband. Female children normally did not receive an education, and in times of scarcity when food was in short supply, daughters might even be put to death.

Though women were clearly inferior to men in theory, this was not always the case in practice. Capable women often compensated for their legal inferiority by playing a strong role within the family. Women were often in charge of educating the children and handled the family budget. Some privileged women also received training in the Confucian classics, although their schooling was generally for a shorter time and less rigorous than that of their male counterparts. A few produced significant works of art and poetry.

Cultural Developments

During the late Ming and the early Qing dynasties, traditional culture in China reached new heights of achievement. With the rise of a wealthy urban class, the demand for art, porcelain, textiles, and literature grew significantly.

The Imperial City in Beijing. During the fifteenth century, the Ming dynasty erected an immense imperial city on the remnants of the palace of Khubilai Khan in Beijing. Surrounded by 6½ miles of walls, the enclosed compound is divided into a maze of private apartments and offices; it also includes an imposing ceremonial quadrangle with stately halls for imperial audiences and banquets. Because it was off-limits to commoners, the compound was known as the Forbidden City. The fearsome lion shown in the inset, representing the omnipotence of the Chinese Empire, guards the entrance to the private apartments of the palace.

The Rise of the Chinese Novel During the Ming dynasty, a new form of literature appeared that eventually evolved into the modern Chinese novel. Although considered less respectable than poetry and nonfiction prose, these groundbreaking works (often written anonymously or under pseudonyms) were enormously popular, especially among well-to-do urban dwellers.

Written in a colloquial style, the new fiction was characterized by a realism that resulted in vivid portraits of Chinese society. Many of the stories sympathized with society's downtrodden—often helpless maidens—and dealt with such crucial issues as love, money, marriage, and power. Adding to the realism were sexually explicit passages that depicted the private side of Chinese life. Readers delighted in sensuous tales that, no matter how pornographic, always professed a moral lesson; the villains were punished and the virtuous rewarded.

The Dream of the Red Chamber is generally considered China's most distinguished popular novel. Published in 1791, it tells of the tragic love between two young people caught in the financial and moral disintegration of a powerful Chinese clan. The hero and the heroine, both sensitive and spoiled, represent the inevitable decline of the Chia family and come to an equally inevitable tragic end, she in death and he in an unhappy marriage to another.

The Art of the Ming and the Qing During the Ming and the early Qing, China produced its last outpouring of traditional artistic brilliance. Although most of the creative work was modeled on past examples, the art of this period is impressive for its technical perfection and breathtaking quantity.

In architecture, the most outstanding example is the Imperial City in Beijing. Building on the remnants of the palace of the Yuan dynasty, the Ming emperor Yongle ordered renovations when he returned the capital to Beijing in 1421. Succeeding emperors continued to add to the palace, but the basic design has not changed since the Ming era. Surrounded by high walls, the immense compound is divided into a maze of private apartments and offices and an imposing ceremonial

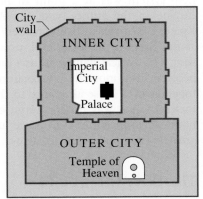

Beijing Under the Ming and the Manchus, 1400–1911

quadrangle with a series of stately halls for imperial audiences and banquets. The grandiose scale, richly carved marble, spacious gardens, and graceful upturned roofs also contribute to the splendor of the "Forbidden City."

The decorative arts flourished in this period, especially the intricately carved lacquerware and the boldly shaped and colored cloisonné, a type of enamelwork in which colored areas are separated by thin metal bands. Silk production reached its zenith, and the best-quality silks were highly prized in Europe, where chinoiserie, as Chinese art of all kinds was called, was in vogue. Perhaps the most famous of all the achievements of the Ming era was its blue-and-white porcelain, still prized by collectors throughout the world.

During the Qing dynasty, artists produced great quantities of paintings, mostly for home consumption. Inside the Forbidden City in Beijing, court painters worked alongside Jesuit artists and experimented with Western techniques. Most scholarly painters and the literati, however, totally rejected foreign techniques and became obsessed with traditional Chinese styles. As a result, Qing painting became progressively more repetitive and stale.

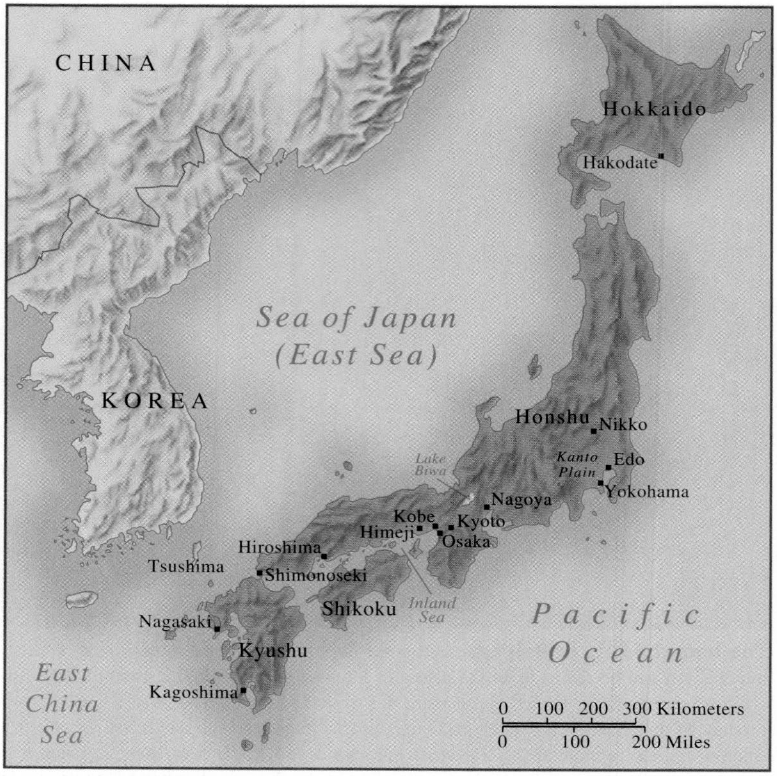

MAP 17.3 **Tokugawa Japan.** This map shows the Japanese islands during the long era of the Tokugawa shogunate. Key cities, including the shogun's capital of Edo, are shown.

Q Where was the imperial court located?

View an animated version of this map or related maps at www.cengage.com/history/duikspiel/essentialworld6e

Tokugawa Japan

Q Focus Question: How did the society and economy of Japan change during the Tokugawa era, and how did Japanese culture reflect those changes?

At the end of the fifteenth century, the traditional Japanese system was at a point of near anarchy. With the decline in the authority of the Ashikaga shogunate at Kyoto, clan rivalries had exploded into an era of warring states. Even at the local level, power was frequently diffuse. The typical daimyo (great lord) domain had often become little more than a coalition of fief-holders held together by a loose allegiance to the manor lord. Nevertheless, Japan was on the verge of an extended era of national unification and peace under the rule of its greatest shogunate—the Tokugawa.

The Three Great Unifiers

The process began in the mid-sixteenth century with the emergence of three very powerful political figures,

Oda Nobunaga (1568–1582), Toyotomi Hideyoshi (1582–1598), and Tokugawa Ieyasu (1598–1616). In 1568, Oda Nobunaga, the son of a samurai and a military commander under the Ashikaga shogunate, seized the imperial capital of Kyoto and placed the reigning shogun under his domination. During the next few years, the brutal and ambitious Nobunaga attempted to consolidate his rule throughout the central plains by defeating his rivals and suppressing the power of the Buddhist estates, but he was killed by one of his generals in 1582 before the process was complete. He was succeeded by Toyotomi Hideyoshi, a farmer's son who had worked his way up through the ranks to become a military commander. Hideyoshi located his capital at Osaka, where he built a castle to accommodate his headquarters, and gradually extended his power outward to the southern islands of Shikoku and Kyushu (see Map 17.3). By 1590, he had persuaded most of the daimyo on the Japanese islands to accept his authority and created a national currency. Then he invaded Korea

The Siege of Osaka Castle. In imitation of European castle architecture, the Japanese perfected a new type of fortress-palace in the early seventeenth century. Strategically placed high on a hilltop, constructed of heavy stone with tiny windows, and fortified by numerous watchtowers and massive walls, these strongholds were impregnable to arrows and catapults. They served as a residence for the local daimyo, while the castle compound also housed his army and contained the seat of the local government. Osaka Castle (on the right) was built by Hideyoshi essentially as a massive stage set to proclaim his power and grandeur. In 1615, the powerful warlord Tokugawa Ieyasu seized the castle, as shown in the screen painting above. The family's control over Japan lasted nearly 250 years. Note the presence of firearms, introduced by the Europeans half a century earlier.

in an abortive effort to export his rule to the Asian mainland.

Despite their efforts, however, neither Nobunaga nor Hideyoshi was able to eliminate the power of the local daimyo. Both were compelled to form alliances with some daimyo in order to destroy other more powerful rivals. At the conclusion of his conquests in 1590, Toyotomi Hideyoshi could claim to be the supreme proprietor of all registered lands in areas under his authority. But he then reassigned those lands as fiefs to the local daimyo, who declared their allegiance to him. The daimyo in turn began to pacify the countryside, carrying out extensive "sword hunts" to disarm the population and attracting samurai to their service. The Japanese tradition of decentralized rule had not yet been overcome.

After Hideyoshi's death in 1598, Tokugawa Ieyasu, the powerful daimyo of Edo (modern Tokyo), moved to fill the vacuum. Neither Hideyoshi nor Oda Nobunaga had claimed the title of shogun, but Ieyasu named himself shogun in 1603, initiating the most powerful and long-lasting of all Japanese shogunates. The Tokugawa rulers completed the restoration of central authority begun by Nobunaga and Hideyoshi and remained in power until 1868, when a war dismantled the entire system. As a contemporary phrased it, "Oda pounds the national rice cake, Hideyoshi kneads it, and in the end Ieyasu sits down and eats it."[7]

Opening to the West

The unification of Japan took place almost simultaneously with the coming of the Europeans. Portuguese traders sailing in a Chinese junk that may have been blown off course by a typhoon had landed on the islands in 1543. Within a few years, Portuguese ships were stopping at Japanese ports on a regular basis to take part in the regional trade between Japan, China, and Southeast Asia. The first Jesuit missionary, Francis Xavier, arrived in 1549.

Initially, the visitors were welcomed. The curious Japanese were fascinated by tobacco, clocks, spectacles, and other European goods, and local daimyo were interested in purchasing all types of European weapons and armaments. Oda Nobunaga and Toyotomi Hideyoshi found the new firearms helpful in defeating their enemies and unifying the islands. The effect on Japanese military architecture was particularly striking as local lords began to erect castles on the European model, many of which still exist today.

The missionaries also had some success in converting a number of local daimyo, some of whom may have been motivated in part by the desire for commercial profits. By the end of the sixteenth century, thousands of Japanese in the southernmost islands of Kyushu and Shikoku had become Christians. But papal claims to the loyalty of all Japanese Christians and the European habit of intervening

The Portuguese Arrive at Nagasaki. Portuguese traders landed in Japan by accident in 1543. In a few years, they arrived regularly, taking part in a regional trade network between Japan, China, and Southeast Asia. In these panels done in black lacquer and gold leaf, we see a late-sixteenth-century Japanese interpretation of the first Portuguese landing at Nagasaki.

in local politics soon began to arouse suspicion in official circles. Missionaries added to the problem by deliberately destroying local idols and shrines and turning some temples into Christian schools or churches.

The Christians Are Expelled   Inevitably, the local authorities reacted. In 1587, Toyotomi Hideyoshi issued an edict prohibiting further Christian activities within his domains. Japan, he declared, was "the land of the Gods," and the destruction of shrines by the foreigners was "something unheard of in previous ages."[8] The Jesuits were ordered to leave the country within twenty days. Hideyoshi was careful to distinguish missionary from trading activities, however, and merchants were permitted to continue their operations (see the box on p. 425).

The Jesuits protested the expulsion, and eventually Hideyoshi relented, permitting them to continue proselytizing so long as they were discreet. But he refused to repeal the edicts, and when the aggressive activities of newly arrived Spanish Franciscans aroused his ire, he ordered the execution of nine missionaries and a number of their Japanese converts. When the missionaries continued to interfere in local politics, Tokugawa Ieyasu ordered the eviction of all missionaries in 1612.

At first, Japanese authorities hoped to maintain commercial relations with European countries even while suppressing the Western religion, but eventually they decided to prohibit foreign trade altogether and closed the two major foreign factories on the island of Hirado and at Nagasaki. The sole remaining opening to the West was at Deshima Island in Nagasaki Harbor, where a small Dutch community was permitted to engage in limited trade with Japan (the Dutch, unlike the Portuguese and the Spanish, had not allowed missionary activities to interfere with their commercial interests). Dutch ships were permitted to dock at Nagasaki Harbor only once a year and, after close inspection, were allowed to remain for two or three months. Conditions on the island of Deshima itself were quite confining: the Dutch physician Engelbert Kaempfer complained that the Dutch lived in "almost perpetual imprisonment."[9] Nor were the Japanese free to engage in foreign trade. A small amount of commerce took place with China, but Japanese subjects of the shogunate were forbidden to leave the country on penalty of death.

Nagasaki and Hirado Island

The Tokugawa "Great Peace"

Once in power, the Tokugawa attempted to strengthen the system that had governed Japan for more than three

TOYOTOMI HIDEYOSHI EXPELS THE MISSIONARIES

RELIGION & PHILOSOPHY

When Christian missionaries in sixteenth-century Japan began to interfere in local politics and criticize traditional religious practices, Toyotomi Hideyoshi issued an edict calling for their expulsion. In this letter to the Portuguese viceroy in Asia, Hideyoshi explains his decision. Note his conviction that Buddhists, Confucianists, and followers of Shinto all believe in the same God and his criticism of Christianity for rejecting all other faiths.

Toyotomi Hideyoshi, Letter to the Viceroy of the Indies

Ours is the land of the Gods, and God is mind. Everything in nature comes into existence because of mind. Without God there can be no spirituality. Without God there can be no way. God rules in times of prosperity as in times of decline. God is positive and negative and unfathomable. Thus, God is the root and source of all existence. This God is spoken of by Buddhism in India, Confucianism in China, and Shinto in Japan. To know Shinto is to know Buddhism as well as Confucianism.

As long as man lives in this world, Humanity will be a basic principle. Were it not for Humanity and Righteousness, the sovereign would not be a sovereign, nor a minister of a state a minister. It is through the practice of Humanity and Righteousness that the foundations of our relationships between sovereign and minister, parent and child, and husband and wife are established. If you are interested in the profound philosophy of God and Buddha, request an explanation and it will be given to you. In your land one doctrine is taught to the exclusion of others, and you are not yet informed of the [Confucian] philosophy of Humanity and Righteousness. Thus there is no respect for God and Buddha and no distinction between sovereign and ministers. Through heresies you intend to destroy the righteous law. Hereafter, do not expound, in ignorance of right and wrong, unreasonable and wanton doctrines. A few years ago the so-called Fathers came to my country seeking to bewitch our men and women, both of the laity and clergy. At that time punishment was administered to them, and it will be repeated if they should return to our domain to propagate their faith. It will not matter what sect or denomination they represent—they shall be destroyed. It will then be too late to repent. If you entertain any desire of establishing amity with this land, the seas have been rid of the pirate menace, and merchants are permitted to come and go. Remember this.

Q *What reason did Hideyoshi give for prohibiting the practice of Christianity in Japan? How did his religious beliefs, as expressed in this document, differ from those of other religions such as Christianity and Islam?*

hundred years. They followed precedent in ruling through the *bakufu,* composed now of a coalition of daimyo, and a council of elders. But the system was more centralized than it had been previously. Now the shogunate government played a dual role. It set national policy on behalf of the emperor in Kyoto while simultaneously governing the shogun's own domain, which included about one-quarter of the national territory as well as the three great cities of Edo, Kyoto, and Osaka. As before, the state was divided into separate territories, called domains (**han**), which were ruled by a total of about 250 individual daimyo.

In theory, the daimyo were essentially autonomous in that they were able to support themselves from taxes on their lands (the shogunate received its own revenues from its extensive landholdings). In actuality, the shogunate was able to guarantee their loyalty by compelling the daimyo to maintain two residences, one in their own domains and the other at Edo, and to leave their families in Edo as hostages for the daimyo's good behavior. Keeping up two residences also put the Japanese nobility in a difficult economic position. Some were able to defray the high costs by concentrating on cash crops such as sugar, fish, and forestry products; but most were rice producers, and their revenues remained roughly the same throughout the period. The daimyo were also able to protect their economic interests by depriving their samurai retainers of their proprietary rights over the land and transforming them into salaried officials. The fief thus became a stipend, and the personal relationship between the daimyo and his retainers gradually gave way to a bureaucratic authority.

The Tokugawa also tinkered with the social system by limiting the size of the samurai class and reclassifying samurai who supported themselves by tilling the land as commoners. In fact, with the long period of peace brought about by Tokugawa rule, the samurai gradually ceased to be a warrior class and were required to live in the castle towns. As a gesture to their glorious past, samurai were still permitted to wear their two swords, and a rigid separation was maintained between persons of samurai status and the nonaristocratic segment of the population.

Seeds of Capitalism The long period of peace under the Tokugawa shogunate made possible a dramatic rise in commerce and manufacturing, especially in the growing cities of Edo, Kyoto, and Osaka. By the mid-eighteenth century, Edo, with a population of more than one million, was one of the largest cities in the world. The growth of trade and industry was stimulated by a rising standard of living—driven in part by technological advances in agriculture and an expansion of arable land—and the voracious appetites of the aristocrats for new products.

Most of this commercial expansion took place in the major cities and the castle towns, where the merchants and artisans lived along with the samurai, who were clustered in neighborhoods surrounding the daimyo's castle. Banking flourished, and paper money became the normal medium of exchange in commercial transactions. Merchants formed guilds not only to control market conditions but also to facilitate government control and the collection of taxes. Under the benign if somewhat contemptuous supervision of Japan's noble rulers, a Japanese merchant class gradually began to emerge from the shadows to play a significant role in the life of the Japanese nation. Some historians view the Tokugawa era as the first stage in the rise of an indigenous form of capitalism.

Eventually, the increased pace of industrial activity spread beyond the cities into rural areas. As in Great Britain, cotton was a major factor. Cotton had been introduced to China during the Song dynasty and had spread to Korea and Japan shortly thereafter. Traditionally, however, cotton cloth had been too expensive for the common people, who instead wore clothing made of hemp. Imports increased during the sixteenth century, however, when cotton cloth began to be used for uniforms, matchlock fuses, and sails. Eventually, technological advances reduced the cost, and specialized communities for producing cotton cloth began to appear in the countryside and were gradually transformed into towns. By the eighteenth century, cotton had firmly replaced hemp as the cloth of choice for most Japanese.

Not everyone benefited from the economic changes of the seventeenth and eighteenth centuries, however; the samurai were barred by tradition and prejudice from commercial activities. Most samurai still relied on their revenues from rice lands, which were often insufficient to cover their rising expenses; consequently, they fell heavily into debt. Others were released from servitude to their lord and became "masterless samurai." Occasionally, these unemployed warriors (known as *ronin,* or "wave men") revolted or plotted against the local authorities.

Land Problems The effects of economic developments on the rural population during the Tokugawa era are harder to estimate. Some farm families benefited by exploiting the growing demand for cash crops. But not all prospered. Most peasants continued to rely on rice cultivation and were whipsawed between declining profits and rising costs and taxes (as daimyo expenses increased, land taxes often took up to 50 percent of the annual harvest). Many were forced to become tenants or to work as wage laborers on the farms of wealthy neighbors or in village industries. When rural conditions in some areas became desperate, peasant revolts erupted. According to one estimate, nearly seven thousand disturbances took place during the Tokugawa era.

Some Japanese historians, influenced by a Marxist view of history, have interpreted such evidence as an indication that the Tokugawa economic system was highly exploitative, with feudal aristocrats oppressing powerless peasants. Recent scholars, however, have tended to adopt a more balanced view, maintaining that in addition to agriculture, manufacturing and commerce experienced extensive growth. Some point out that although the population doubled in the seventeenth century, a relatively low rate for the time period, so did the amount of cultivable land, while agricultural technology made significant advances.

The relatively low rate of population growth probably meant that Japanese peasants were spared the kind of land hunger that many of their counterparts in China faced. Recent evidence indicates that the primary reasons for the relatively low rate of population growth were late marriage, abortion, and infanticide.

Life in the Village

The changes that took place during the Tokugawa era had a major impact on the lives of ordinary Japanese. In some respects, the result was an increase in the power of

Some Confucian Commandments

FAMILY & SOCIETY

Although the Qing dynasty was of foreign origin, its rulers found Confucian maxims convenient for maintaining the social order. In 1670, the great emperor Kangxi issued the Sacred Edict to popularize Confucian values among the common people. The edict was read publicly at periodic intervals in every village in the country and set the standard for behavior throughout the empire. Like the Qing dynasty in China, the Tokugawa shoguns attempted to keep their subjects in line with decrees that carefully prescribed all kinds of behavior. As this decree, which was circulated in all Japanese villages, shows, the *bakufu* sought to be the moral instructor as well as the guardian and protector of the Japanese people.

Kangxi's Sacred Edict

1. Esteem most highly filial piety and brotherly submission, in order to give due importance to the social relations.
2. Behave with generosity toward your kindred, in order to illustrate harmony and benignity.
3. Cultivate peace and concord in your neighborhoods, in order to prevent quarrels and litigations.
4. Recognize the importance of husbandry and the culture of the mulberry tree, in order to ensure a sufficiency of clothing and food.
5. Show that you prize moderation and economy, in order to prevent the lavish waste of your means.
6. Give weight to colleges and schools, in order to make correct the practice of the scholar.
7. Extirpate strange principles, in order to exalt the correct doctrine.
8. Lecture on the laws, in order to warn the ignorant and obstinate.
9. Elucidate propriety and yielding courtesy, in order to make manners and customs good.
10. Labor diligently at your proper callings, in order to stabilize the will of the people.
11. Instruct sons and younger brothers, in order to prevent them from doing what is wrong.
12. Put a stop to false accusations, in order to preserve the honest and good.
13. Warn against sheltering deserters, in order to avoid being involved in their punishment.
14. Fully remit your taxes, in order to avoid being pressed for payment.
15. Unite in hundreds and tithing, in order to put an end to thefts and robbery.

16. Remove enmity and anger, in order to show the importance due to the person and life.

Maxims for Peasant Behavior

1. Young people are forbidden to congregate in great numbers.
2. Entertainments unsuited to peasants, such as playing the samisen or reciting ballad dramas, are forbidden.
3. Staging sumo matches is forbidden for the next five years.
4. The edict on frugality issued by the *han* at the end of last year must be observed.
5. Social relations in the village must be conducted harmoniously.
6. If a person has to leave the village for business or pleasure, that person must return by ten at night.
7. Father and son are forbidden to stay overnight at another person's house. An exception is to be made if it is to nurse a sick person.
8. Corvée [obligatory labor] assigned by the *han* must be performed faithfully.
9. Children who practice filial piety must be rewarded.
10. One must never get drunk and cause trouble for others.
11. Peasants who farm especially diligently must be rewarded.
12. Peasants who neglect farm work and cultivate their paddies and upland fields in a slovenly and careless fashion must be punished.
13. The boundary lines of paddy and upland fields must not be changed arbitrarily.
14. Recognition must be accorded to peasants who contribute greatly to village political affairs.
15. Fights and quarrels are forbidden in the village.
16. The deteriorating customs and morals of the village must be rectified.
17. Peasants who are suffering from poverty must be identified and helped.
18. This village has a proud history compared to other villages, but in recent years bad times have come upon us. Everyone must rise at six in the morning, cut grass, and work hard to revitalize the village.
19. The punishments to be meted out to violators of the village code and gifts to be awarded the deserving are to be decided during the last assembly meeting of the year.

Q *In what ways did Kangxi's set of commandments conform to the principles of State Confucianism? How do these standards compare with those applied in Japan, shown on the right?*

the central government at the village level. The shogunate increasingly relied on Confucian maxims advocating obedience and hierarchy to enhance its authority with the general population. Decrees from the *bakufu* instructed the peasants on all aspects of their lives, including their eating habits and their behavior (see the box above). At the same time, the increased power of the government led to more autonomy from the local daimyo for the peasants. Villages now had more control over their local affairs.

At the same time, the Tokugawa era saw the emergence of the nuclear family (ie) as the basic unit in Japanese society. In previous times, Japanese peasants had few legal rights. Most were too poor to keep their conjugal family unit intact or to pass property on to their children. Many lived at the manorial residence or worked as servants in the households of more affluent villagers. Now, with farm income on the rise, the nuclear family took on the same form as in China, although without the joint family concept. The Japanese system of inheritance was based on primogeniture. Family property was passed on to the eldest son, although younger sons often received land from their parents to set up their own families after marriage.

The Role of Women Another result of the changes under the Tokugawa was that women were somewhat more restricted than they had been previously. The rights of females were especially restricted in the samurai class, where Confucian values were highly influential. Male heads of households had broad authority over property, marriage, and divorce; wives were expected to obey their husbands on pain of death. Males often took concubines or homosexual partners, while females were expected to remain chaste. The male offspring of samurai parents studied the Confucian classics in schools established by the daimyo, while females were reared at home, where only the fortunate might receive a rudimentary training in reading and writing Chinese characters. Nevertheless, some women were able to become accomplished poets and painters since, in aristocratic circles, female literacy was prized for enhancing the refinement, social graces, and moral virtue of the home.

Women were similarly at a disadvantage among the common people. Marriages were arranged, and as in China, the new wife moved in with the family of her husband. A wife who did not meet the expectations of her spouse or his family was likely to be divorced. Still, gender relations were more egalitarian than among the nobility. Women were generally valued as childbearers and homemakers, and both men and women worked in the fields. Coeducational schools were established in villages and market towns, and about one-quarter of the students were female. Poor families, however, often put infant daughters to death or sold them into prostitution.

Such attitudes toward women operated within the context of the increasingly rigid stratification of Japanese society. Deeply conservative in their social policies, the Tokugawa rulers established strict legal distinctions between the four main classes in Japan (warriors, artisans, peasants, and merchants). Intermarriage between classes was forbidden in theory, although sometimes the prohibitions were ignored in practice. Below these classes were Japan's outcasts, the **eta.** Formerly, they were permitted to escape their status, at least in theory. The Tokugawa made their status hereditary and enacted severe discriminatory laws against them, regulating their place of residence, their dress, and even their hairstyles.

Tokugawa Culture

Under the Tokugawa, a vital new set of cultural values began to appear, especially in the cities. This innovative era witnessed the rise of popular literature written by and for the townspeople. With the development of woodblock printing in the early seventeenth century, literature became available to the common people, literacy levels rose, and lending libraries increased the accessibility of the printed word.

The Literature of the New Middle Class The best examples of this new urban fiction are the works of Saikaku (1642–1693), considered one of Japan's finest novelists. Saikaku's greatest novel, *Five Women Who Loved Love,* relates the amorous exploits of five women of the merchant class. Based partly on real-life experiences, it broke from the Confucian ethic of wifely fidelity to her husband and portrayed women who were willing to die for love— and all but one eventually did. Despite the tragic circumstances, the tone of the novel is upbeat and sometimes comic, and the author's wry comments prevent the reader from becoming emotionally involved with the heroines' misfortunes.

In the theater, the rise of *Kabuki* threatened the long dominance of the *No* play, replacing the somewhat restrained and elegant thematic and stylistic approach of the classical drama with a new emphasis on violence, music, and dramatic gestures. Significantly, the new drama emerged not from the rarefied world of the court but from the new world of entertainment and amusement (see the comparative illustration on p. 429). Its very commercial success, however, led to difficulties with the government, which periodically attempted to restrict or even suppress it. Early *Kabuki* was often performed by prostitutes, and shogunate officials, fearing that such activities could have a corrupting effect on the nation's morals, prohibited women from appearing on the stage; at the same time, they attempted to create a new professional class of male actors to impersonate female characters on stage.

In contrast to the popular literature of the Tokugawa period, poetry persevered in its more serious tradition. The most exquisite poetry was produced in the seventeenth century by the greatest of all Japanese poets, Basho (1644–1694). He was concerned with the search for the meaning of existence and the poetic expression of his experience.

COMPARATIVE ILLUSTRATION

Popular Culture: East and West. By the seventeenth century, a popular culture distinct from the elite culture of the nobility was beginning to emerge in the urban worlds of both the East and the West. On the left is a festival scene from the pleasure district of Kyoto known as the Gion. Spectators on a balcony are enjoying a colorful parade of floats and costumed performers. The festival originated as a celebration of the passing of a deadly epidemic in medieval Japan.

On the right is a scene from the celebration of Carnival on the Piazza Sante Croce in Florence, Italy. Carnival was a period of festivities before Lent, celebrated primarily in Roman Catholic countries. It became an occasion for indulgence in food, drink, games, and practical jokes as a prelude to the austerity of the forty-day Lenten season from Ash Wednesday to Easter.

Q Do festivals such as these still exist in our own day? What purpose might they serve?

With his love of Daoism and Zen Buddhism, Basho found answers to his quest for the meaning of life in nature, and his poems are grounded in seasonal imagery. The following are among his most famous poems:

> *The ancient pond*
> *A frog leaps in*
> *The sound of the water.*
> *On the withered branch*
> *A crow has alighted—*
> *The end of autumn.*

His last poem, dictated to a disciple only three days before his death, succinctly expressed his frustration with the unfinished business of life:

> *On a journey, ailing—*
> *my dreams roam about*
> *on a withered moor.*

Like all great artists, Basho made his poems seem effortless and simple. He speaks directly to everyone, everywhere.

(rotated caption on left) © The Newark Museum/Art Resource, NY

One of the Fifty-Three Stations of the Tokaido Road. This block print by the famous Japanese artist Ando Hiroshige shows the movement of goods along the main trunk road stretching from Kyoto to Edo in mid-nineteenth-century Japan. With gentle humor, Hiroshige portrayed in a series of color prints the customs of travelers passing through various post stations along the east coast road. These romantic and somewhat fanciful scenes, very popular at the time, evoke an idyllic past, filling today's viewer with nostalgia for the old Japan.

Tokugawa Art Art also reflected the dynamism and changes in Japanese culture under the Tokugawa regime. The shogun's order that all daimyo and their families live every other year in Edo set off a burst of building as provincial rulers competed to erect the most magnificent mansion. Furthermore, the shoguns themselves constructed splendid castles adorned with sumptuous, almost ostentatious decor and furnishings. And the prosperity of the newly rising merchant class added fuel to the fire. Japanese paintings, architecture, textiles, and ceramics all flourished during this affluent era.

Although Japan was isolated from the Western world during much of the Tokugawa era, Japanese art was enriched by ideas from other cultures. Japanese pottery makers borrowed both techniques and designs from Korea to produce handsome ceramics. The passion for "Dutch learning" inspired Japanese to study Western medicine, astronomy, and languages and also led to experimentation with oil painting and Western ideas of perspective and the interplay of light and dark. Europeans desired Japanese lacquerware and metalwork, inlaid with ivory and mother-of-pearl, and especially the ceramics, which were now as highly prized as those of the Chinese.

Perhaps the most famous of all Japanese art of the Tokugawa era is the woodblock print. Genre painting, or representations of daily life, began in the sixteenth century and found its new mass-produced form in the eighteenth-century woodblock print. The now literate mercantile class was eager for illustrated texts of the amusing and bawdy tales that had circulated in oral tradition. Some prints depict entire city blocks filled with people, trades, and festivals, while others show the interiors of houses; thus, they provide us with excellent visual documentation of the times. Others portray the "floating world" of the entertainment quarter, with scenes of carefree revelers enjoying the pleasures of life.

One of the most renowned of the numerous blockprint artists was Utamaro (1754–1806), who painted erotic and sardonic women in everyday poses, such as walking down the street, cooking, or drying their bodies after a bath. Hokusai (1760–1849) was famous for *Thirty-Six Views of Mount Fuji,* a new and bold interpretation of the Japanese landscape.

Korea and Vietnam

Q Focus Questions: To what degree did developments in Korea during this period reflect conditions in China and Japan? What were the most unique aspects of Vietnamese civilization?

While Japan was gradually moving away from its agrarian origins, the Yi dynasty in Korea was attempting to pattern its own society on the Chinese model. The dynasty had been founded by the military commander Yi Song Gye in the late fourteenth century and immediately set out to establish close political and cultural relations with the Ming dynasty. From their new capital at Seoul, located on the Han River in the center of the peninsula, the Yi rulers accepted a tributary relationship with their powerful neighbor and engaged in the wholesale adoption of Chinese institutions and values. As in China, the civil service examinations tested candidates on their knowledge of the Confucian classics, and success was viewed as an essential step toward upward mobility.

There were differences, however. As in Japan, the dynasty continued to restrict entry into the bureaucracy to members of the aristocratic class, known in Korea as the *yangban* (or "two groups," the civilian and military). At the same time, the peasantry remained in serflike conditions, working on government estates or on the manor holdings of the landed elite. A class of slaves (*chonmin*) labored on government plantations or served in certain occupations, such as butchers and entertainers, considered beneath the dignity of other groups in the population.

Eventually, Korean society began to show signs of independence from Chinese orthodoxy. In the fifteenth century, a phonetic alphabet for writing the Korean spoken language (*hangul*) was devised. Although it was initially held in contempt by the elites and used primarily as a teaching device, eventually it became the medium for private correspondence and the publishing of fiction for a popular audience. At the same time, changes were taking place in the economy, where rising agricultural production contributed to a population increase and the appearance of a small urban industrial and commercial sector, and in society, where the long domination of the *yangban* class began to weaken. As their numbers increased and their power and influence declined, some *yangban* became merchants or even moved into the ranks of the peasantry, further blurring the distinction between the aristocratic class and the common people.

In general, Korean rulers tried to keep the country isolated from the outside world, but they were not always successful. The Japanese invasion under Toyotomi Hideyoshi in the late sixteenth century had a disastrous impact on Korean society. A Manchu force invaded northern Korea in the 1630s and eventually compelled the Yi dynasty to declare allegiance to the new imperial government in Beijing. Korea was relatively untouched by the arrival of European merchants and missionaries, although information about Christianity was brought to the peninsula by Koreans returning from tribute missions to China, and a small Catholic community was established there in the late eighteenth century.

Vietnam: The Perils of Empire

Vietnam—or Dai Viet, as it was known at the time—had managed to avoid the fate of many of its neighbors during the seventeenth and eighteenth centuries. Isolated from the major maritime routes that passed through the region, the country was only peripherally involved in the spice trade with the West and had not suffered the humiliation of losing territory to European colonial powers. In fact, Dai Viet followed an imperialist path of its own, defeating the state of Champa to the south and imposing its suzerainty over the rump of the old Angkor empire—today known as Cambodia. The state of Dai Viet now extended from the Chinese border to the shores of the Gulf of Siam.

But expansion undermined the cultural integrity of traditional Vietnamese society, as those migrants who settled in the marshy Mekong River delta developed a "frontier spirit" far removed from the communal values long practiced in the old national heartland of the Red River valley. By the seventeenth century, a civil war had split Dai Viet into two squabbling territories, providing European powers with the opportunity to meddle in the country's internal affairs to their own benefit. In 1802, with the assistance of a French adventurer long active in the region, a member of the southern royal family managed to reunite the country under the new Nguyen dynasty, which lasted until 1945.

To placate China, the country was renamed Vietnam (South Viet), and the new imperial capital was established in the city of Hué, a small river port roughly equidistant from the two rich river valleys that provided the country with its chief sustenance, wet rice. The founder of the new dynasty, who took the reign title of Gia Long, fended off French efforts to promote Christianity among his subjects and sought to promote traditional Confucian values among an increasingly diverse populace.

CONCLUSION

WHEN CHRISTOPHER COLUMBUS sailed from southern Spain in his three ships in August 1492, he was seeking a route to China and Japan. He did not find it, but others soon did. In 1514, Portuguese ships arrived on the coast of southern China. Thirty years later, a small contingent of Portuguese merchants became the first Europeans to set foot on the islands of Japan.

At first, the new arrivals were welcomed, if only as curiosities. Eventually, several European nations established trade relations with China and Japan, and Christian missionaries of various religious orders were active in both countries and in Korea as well. But their success was short-lived. Europeans eventually began to be perceived as detrimental to law and order, and during the seventeenth century, the majority of the foreign merchants and missionaries were evicted from all three countries. From that time until the middle of the nineteenth century, China, Japan, and Korea were relatively little affected by events taking place beyond their borders.

That fact deluded many observers into the assumption that the societies of East Asia were essentially stagnant, characterized by agrarian institutions and values reminiscent of those of the feudal era in Europe. As we have seen, however, that picture is misleading, for all three countries were changing and by the early nineteenth century were quite different from what they had been three centuries earlier.

Ironically, these changes were especially marked in Tokugawa Japan, an allegedly "closed country," where traditional classes and institutions were under increasing strain, not only from the emergence of a new merchant class but also from the centralizing tendencies of the powerful Tokugawa shogunate. Some historians have seen strong parallels between Tokugawa Japan and early modern Europe, which gave birth to centralized empires and a strong merchant class during the same period. The image of the monarchy is reflected in a song sung at the shrine of Toyotomi Hideyoshi in Kyoto:

> Who's that
> Holding over four hundred provinces
> In the palm of his hand
> And entertaining at a tea-party?
> It's His Highness
> So mighty, so impressive![10]

By the beginning of the nineteenth century, then, powerful tensions, reflecting a growing gap between ideal and reality, were at work in both Chinese and Japanese society. Under these conditions, both countries were soon forced to face a new challenge from the aggressive power of an industrializing Europe.

TIMELINE

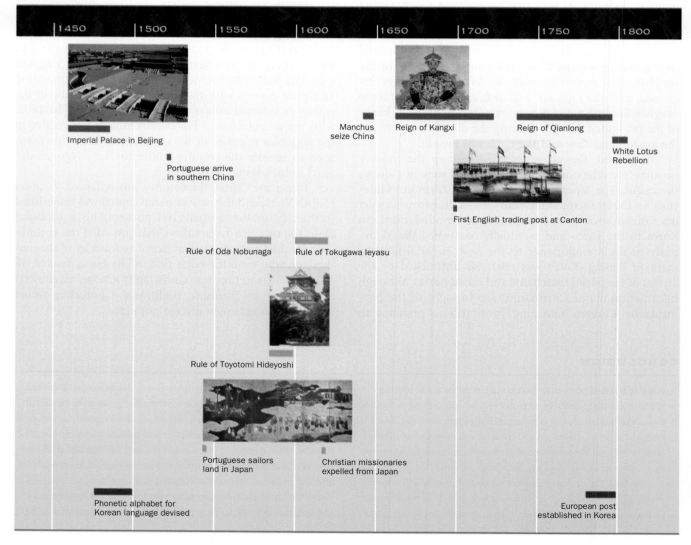

| 1450 | 1500 | 1550 | 1600 | 1650 | 1700 | 1750 | 1800 |

Imperial Palace in Beijing

Portuguese arrive in southern China

Manchus seize China

Reign of Kangxi

Reign of Qianlong

White Lotus Rebellion

First English trading post at Canton

Rule of Oda Nobunaga

Rule of Tokugawa Ieyasu

Rule of Toyotomi Hideyoshi

Portuguese sailors land in Japan

Christian missionaries expelled from Japan

Phonetic alphabet for Korean language devised

European post established in Korea

SUGGESTED READING

General For a general overview of this period in East Asian history, see volumes 8 and 9 of **F. W. Mote** and **D. Twitchett, eds., *The Cambridge History of China*** (Cambridge, 1976), and **J. W. Hall, ed., *The Cambridge History of Japan,*** vol. 4 (Cambridge, 1991).

Exploration and Science For information on Chinese voyages into the Indian Ocean, see **P. Snow, *The Star Raft: China's Encounter with Africa*** (Ithaca, N.Y., 1988). Also see **Ma Huan, *Ying-hai Sheng-lan: The Overall Survey of the Ocean's Shores*** (Bangkok, 1996), an ocean survey by a fifteenth-century Chinese cataloger. On Chinese science, see **B. Elman, *On Their Own Terms: Science in China, 1550–1900*** (Berkeley, Calif., 2005).

The Ming, Qing, and Kangxi Eras On the late Ming, see **J. D. Spence, *The Search for Modern China*** (New York, 1990), and **L. Struve, *The Southern Ming, 1644–1662*** (New Haven, Conn., 1984). On the rise of the Qing, see **F. Wakeman Jr., *The Great Enterprise: The Manchu Reconstruction of Imperial Order in Seventeenth-Century China*** (Berkeley, Calif., 1985). On Kangxi, see **J. D. Spence, *Emperor of China: Self-Portrait of K'ang Hsi*** (New York, 1974). Social issues are discussed in **S. Naquin** and **E. Rawski, *Chinese Society in the Eighteenth Century*** (New Haven, Conn., 1987). Also see **J. D. Spence** and **J. Wills, eds., *From Ming to Ch'ing*** (New Haven, Conn., 1979). For a recent account of Jesuit missionary experiences in China, see **L. Brockey, *Journey to the East: The Jesuit Mission to China, 1579–1724*** (Cambridge, 2007). For brief biographies of Ming and Qing luminaries such as Wang Yangming, Zheng Chenggong, and Emperor Qianlong, see **J. E. Wills Jr., *Mountains of Fame: Portraits in Chinese History*** (Princeton, N.J., 1994).

Chinese Literature and Art The best surveys of Chinese literature are **S. Owen, *An Anthology of Chinese Literature: Beginnings to 1911*** (New York, 1996), and **V. Mair, *The Columbia Anthology of Traditional Chinese Literature*** (New York, 1994). For a comprehensive introduction to the Chinese art of this period, see **M. Sullivan, *The Arts of China,*** 4th ed. (Berkeley, Calif., 1999), and **C. Clunas, *Art in China*** (Oxford, 1997). For the best introduction to the painting of this era, see **J. Cahill, *Chinese Painting*** (New York, 1977).

Japan On Japan before the rise of the Tokugawa, see **J. W. Hall et al., eds., *Japan Before Tokugawa: Political Consolidation and Economic Growth*** (Princeton, N.J., 1981), and **G. Elison** and **B. L. Smith, eds., *Warlords, Artists, and Commoners: Japan in the Sixteenth Century*** (Honolulu, 1981). See also **M. E. Berry, *Hideyoshi*** (Cambridge, Mass., 1982), the first biography of this fascinating figure in Japanese history. On early Christian activities, see **G. Elison, *Deus Destroyed: The Image of Christianity in Early Modern Japan*** (Cambridge, Mass., 1973). Buddhism is dealt with in **N. McMullin, *Buddhism and the State in Sixteenth-Century Japan*** (Princeton, N.J., 1984).

On the Tokugawa era, see **H. Bolitho, *Treasures Among Men: The Fudai Daimyo in Tokugawa Japan*** (New Haven, Conn., 1974), and **R. B. Toby, *State and Diplomacy in Early Modern Japan: Asia in the Development of the Tokugawa Bakufu*** (Princeton, N.J., 1984). The founder of the shogunate is portrayed in **C. Totman, *Tokugawa Ieyasu: Shogun*** (Torrance, Calif., 1983). See also **C. I. Mulhern, ed., *Heroic with Grace: Legendary Women of Japan*** (Armonk, N.Y., 1991). Three other worthwhile studies are **S. Vlastos, *Peasant Protests and Uprisings in Tokugawa Japan*** (Berkeley, Calif., 1986); **H. Ooms, *Tokugawa Ideology: Early Constructs, 1570–1680*** (Princeton, N.J., 1985); and **C. Nakane, ed., *Tokugawa Japan: The Social and Economic Antecedents of Modern Japan*** (Tokyo, 1990).

Women in China and Japan For a brief introduction to women in the Ming and Qing dynasties as well as the Tokugawa era, see **S. Hughes** and **B. Hughes, *Women in World History,*** vol. 2 (Armonk, N.Y., 1997), and **S. Mann** and **Y. Cheng, eds., *Under Confucian Eyes: Writings on Gender in Chinese History*** (Berkeley, Calif., 2001). Also see **D. Ko, J. K. Haboush,** and **J. R. Piggott, eds., *Women and Confucian Culture in Premodern China, Korea, and Japan*** (Berkeley, Calif., 2003). On women's literacy in seventeenth-century China, see **D. Ko, *Teachers of the Inner Chambers: Women and Culture in Seventeenth-Century China*** (Stanford, Calif., 1994). Most valuable is the collection of articles edited by **G. L. Bernstein, *Re-Creating Japanese Women, 1600–1945*** (Berkeley, Calif., 1991).

Japanese Literature and Art Of specific interest on Japanese literature of the Tokugawa era is **D. Keene, *World Within Walls: Japanese Literature of the Pre-Modern Era, 1600–1867*** (New York, 1976). For an introduction to Basho's life, poems, and criticism, consult the stimulating ***Basho and His Interpreters: Selected Hokku with Commentary*** (Stanford, Calif., 1991), by **M. Ueda.**

For the most comprehensive and accessible overview of Japanese art, see **P. Mason, *Japanese Art*** (New York, 1993). For a concise introduction to Japanese art of the Tokugawa era, see **J. Stanley-Baker, *Japanese Art*** (London, 1984).

WORLD HISTORY RESOURCES

Visit the website for *The Essential World History* **to access study aids such as Flashcards, Critical Thinking Exercises, and Chapter Quizzes:**

   www.cengage.com/history/duikspiel/essentialworld6e

DISCOVERY

How did China and Japan respond to the coming of the Europeans, and what explains the differences in their approach? What impact did European contacts have on these two East Asian civilizations through the end of the eighteenth century?

POLITICS AND GOVERNMENT Review Emperor Qianlong's response to King George III of Britain (document, p. 417) and Toyotomi Hideyoshi's letter explaining his decision to expel the Christian missionaries (document, p. 425). How do these documents reflect the views of China and Japan toward Europeans? What reasons does each leader give for his decision? Do you see any similarities between the views and actions of these leaders and those of Europeans toward non-Europeans that you have read about previously? How do you think the decisions of the Chinese and Japanese leaders may have influenced the future of both nations? What do you think are the advantages and disadvantages of having an open society as opposed to a closed one?

In thinking about these questions, begin by breaking them down into the components shown below. A discussion of the significance of each component should appear in your answer.

INTERACTION AND EXCHANGE Look at the paintings on pages 415 and 424. Both paintings depict economic interaction between Europeans and societies in East Asia. How do they differ? What do you see in the painting of Canton that is absent from the painting of Nagasaki? What does this tell you about how each government approached the idea of cultural and economic interaction? Which painting seems more "European," and why?

Why do you think that China and Japan (see the maps below) did not attempt to make inroads in Europe? Did either nation ever attempt exploration as the Europeans did? If so, why do you think they stopped? How might history have been different if they had undertaken such voyages?

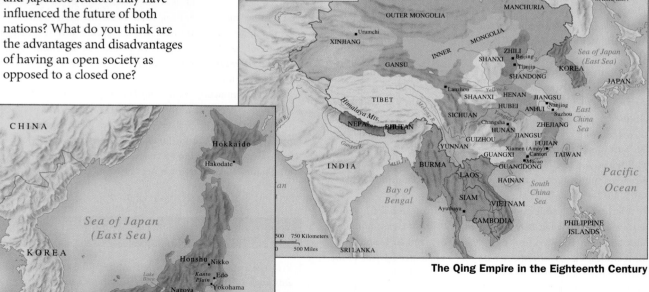

The Qing Empire in the Eighteenth Century

Tokugawa Japan

CHAPTER 18

THE WEST ON THE EVE OF A NEW WORLD ORDER

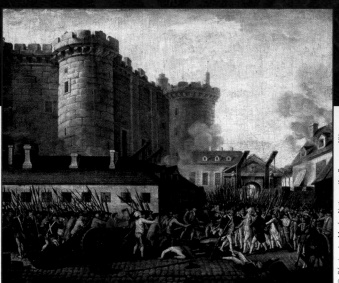

The storming of the Bastille

© Réunion des Musées Nationaux/Art Resource, NY

CHAPTER OUTLINE AND FOCUS QUESTIONS

Toward a New Heaven and a New Earth: An Intellectual Revolution in the West

Q Who were the leading figures of the Scientific Revolution and the Enlightenment, and what were their main contributions?

Economic Changes and the Social Order

Q What changes occurred in the European economy in the eighteenth century, and to what degree were these changes reflected in social patterns?

Colonial Empires and Revolution in the Western Hemisphere

Q How did Spain and Portugal administer their American colonies, and what were the main characteristics of Latin American society in the eighteenth century?

Toward a New Political Order and Global Conflict

Q What do historians mean by the term *enlightened absolutism,* and to what degree did eighteenth-century Prussia, Austria, and Russia exhibit its characteristics?

The French Revolution

Q What were the causes, the main events, and the results of the French Revolution?

The Age of Napoleon

Q Which aspects of the French Revolution did Napoleon preserve, and which did he destroy?

CRITICAL THINKING

Q In what ways were the American Revolution, the French Revolution, and the seventeenth-century English revolutions alike? In what ways were they different?

ON THE MORNING OF JULY 14, 1789, a Parisian mob of some eight thousand men and women in search of weapons streamed toward the Bastille, a royal armory filled with arms and ammunition. The Bastille was also a state prison, and although it held only seven prisoners at the time, in the eyes of these angry Parisians, it was a glaring symbol of the government's despotic policies. It was defended by the marquis de Launay and a small garrison of 114 men. The attack on the Bastille began in earnest in the early afternoon, and after three hours of fighting, de Launay and the garrison surrendered. Angered by the loss of ninety-eight protesters, the victors beat de Launay to death, cut off his head, and carried it aloft in triumph through the streets of Paris. When King Louis XVI was told the news of the fall of the Bastille by the duc de La Rochefoucauld-Liancourt, he exclaimed, "Why, this is a revolt." "No, Sire," replied the duke. "It is a revolution."

The French Revolution was a key factor in the emergence of a new world order. Historians have often portrayed the eighteenth century as the final phase of Europe's old order, before the violent upheaval and reordering of society associated with the French Revolution. The old order—still largely agrarian, dominated by kings and landed aristocrats, and grounded in privileges for nobles, clergy, towns, and provinces—seemed to continue a basic pattern that had prevailed in Europe since medieval times. But, just as a new intellectual order based on rationalism and secularism was emerging in Europe, demographic, economic, social, and political patterns were beginning to change in ways that proclaimed the emergence of a modern new order.

The French Revolution demolished the institutions of the old regime and established a new order based on individual rights, representative institutions, and a concept of loyalty to the nation rather than to the monarch. The revolutionary upheavals of the era, especially in France, created new liberal and national political ideals, summarized in the French revolutionary slogan, "Liberty, Equality, Fraternity," that transformed France and then spread to other European countries and the rest of the world. ✸

Toward a New Heaven and a New Earth: An Intellectual Revolution in the West

Q Focus Question: Who were the leading figures of the Scientific Revolution and the Enlightenment, and what were their main contributions?

In the seventeenth century, a group of scientists set the Western world on a new path known as the **Scientific Revolution,** which gave Europeans a new way of viewing the universe and their place in it. The Scientific Revolution affected only a small number of Europe's educated elite. But in the eighteenth century, this changed dramatically as a group of intellectuals popularized the ideas of the Scientific Revolution and used them to undertake a dramatic reexamination of all aspects of life. The widespread impact of these ideas on their society has caused historians ever since to call the eighteenth century in Europe the Age of Enlightenment.

The Scientific Revolution

The Scientific Revolution ultimately challenged conceptions and beliefs about the nature of the external world that had become dominant by the Late Middle Ages.

Toward a New Heaven: A Revolution in Astronomy

The philosophers of the Middle Ages had used the ideas of Aristotle, Ptolemy (the greatest astronomer of antiquity, who lived in the second century C.E.), and Christianity to form the Ptolemaic or **geocentric theory** of the universe. In this conception, the universe was seen as a series of concentric spheres with a fixed or motionless earth at its center. Composed of material substance, the earth was imperfect and constantly changing. The spheres that surrounded the earth were made of a crystalline, transparent substance and moved in circular orbits around the earth. The heavenly bodies, believed to number ten in 1500, were pure orbs of light, embedded in the moving, concentric spheres. Working outward from the earth, the first eight spheres contained the moon, Mercury, Venus, the sun, Mars, Jupiter, Saturn, and the fixed stars. The ninth sphere imparted to the eighth sphere of the fixed stars its daily motion, while the tenth sphere was frequently described as the prime mover that moved itself and imparted motion to the other spheres. Beyond the tenth sphere was the Empyrean Heaven—the location of God and all the saved souls. God and the saved souls were at one end of the universe, then, and humans were at the center. They had power over the earth, but their real purpose was to achieve salvation.

Nicolaus Copernicus (1473–1543), a native of Poland, was a mathematician who felt that Ptolemy's geocentric system failed to accord with the observed motions of the heavenly bodies and hoped that his **heliocentric (sun-centered) theory** would offer a more accurate explanation. Copernicus argued that the sun was motionless at the center of the universe. The planets revolved around the sun in the order of Mercury, Venus, the earth, Mars, Jupiter, and Saturn. The moon, however, revolved around the earth. Moreover, what appeared to be the movement of the sun around the earth was really explained by the daily rotation of the earth on its axis and the journey of the earth around the sun each year. But Copernicus did not reject the idea that the heavenly spheres moved in circular orbits.

The next step in destroying the geocentric conception and supporting the Copernican system was taken by Johannes Kepler (1571–1630). A brilliant German mathematician and astronomer, Kepler arrived at laws of planetary motion that confirmed Copernicus's heliocentric theory. In his first law, however, he revised Copernicus by showing that the orbits of the planets around the sun were not circular but elliptical, with the sun at one focus of the ellipse rather than at the center.

Kepler's work destroyed the basic structure of the Ptolemaic system. People could now think in new terms of the actual paths of planets revolving around the sun in elliptical orbits. But important questions remained unanswered. For example, what were the planets made of? An Italian scientist achieved the next important breakthrough to a new cosmology by answering that question.

Galileo Galilei (1564–1642) taught mathematics and was the first European to make systematic observations of the heavens by means of a telescope, inaugurating a new age in astronomy. Galileo turned his telescope to the skies and made a remarkable series of discoveries: mountains

Medieval Conception of the Universe. As this sixteenth-century illustration shows, the medieval cosmological view placed the earth at the center of the universe, surrounded by a series of concentric spheres. The earth was imperfect and constantly changing, while the heavenly bodies that surrounded it were perfect and incorruptible. Beyond the tenth and final sphere was heaven, where God and all the saved souls were located. (The circles read, from the center outward: 1. Moon, 2. Mercury, 3. Venus, 4. Sun, 5. Mars, 6. Jupiter, 7. Saturn, 8. Firmament of the Stars, 9. Crystalline Sphere, 10. Prime Mover, and at the end, Empyrean Heaven—Home of God and all the Elect, that is, saved souls.)

The Copernican System. The Copernican system was presented in *On the Revolutions of the Heavenly Spheres,* published shortly before Copernicus's death. As shown in this illustration from the first edition of the book, Copernicus maintained that the sun was the center of the universe while the planets, including the earth, revolved around it. Moreover, the earth rotated daily on its axis. (The circles read, from the outside in: 1. Immobile Sphere of the Fixed Stars, 2. Saturn, orbit of 30 years, 3. Jupiter, orbit of 12 years, 4. Mars, orbit of 2 years, 5. Earth, with the moon, orbit of one year, 6. Venus, 7. Mercury, orbit of 80 days, 8. Sun.)

on the moon, four moons revolving around Jupiter, and sunspots. Galileo's observations seemed to destroy yet another aspect of the traditional cosmology in that the universe seemed to be composed of material similar to that of earth rather than a perfect and unchanging substance.

Galileo's revelations, published in *The Starry Messenger* in 1610, made Europeans aware of a new picture of the universe. But the Catholic church condemned Copernicanism and ordered Galileo to abandon the Copernican thesis. The church attacked the Copernican system because it threatened not only Scripture but also an entire conception of the universe. The heavens were no longer a spiritual world but a world of matter.

By the 1630s and 1640s, most astronomers had come to accept the new heliocentric conception of the universe. Nevertheless, the problem of explaining motion in the universe and tying together the ideas of Copernicus, Galileo, and Kepler had not yet been done. This would be the work of an Englishman who has long been considered the greatest genius of the Scientific Revolution.

Isaac Newton (1642–1727) taught at Cambridge University, where he wrote his major work, *Mathematical Principles of Natural Philosophy,* known simply as the *Principia* by the first word of its Latin title. In the first book of the *Principia,* Newton defined the three laws of motion that govern the planetary bodies, as well as objects on earth. Crucial to his whole argument was the universal law of gravitation, which explained why the planetary bodies did not go off in straight lines but continued in elliptical orbits about the sun. In mathematical terms, Newton explained that every object in the universe is attracted to every other object by a force called gravity.

Newton had demonstrated that one mathematically proven universal law could explain all motion in the universe. At the same time, the Newtonian synthesis created a new cosmology in which the universe was seen as one huge, regulated machine that operated according to natural laws in absolute time, space, and motion. Newton's **world-machine** concept dominated the modern worldview until the twentieth century, when Albert

COMPARATIVE ESSAY
THE SCIENTIFIC REVOLUTION

SCIENCE & TECHNOLOGY

When Catholic missionaries began to arrive in China during the sixteenth century, they marveled at the sophistication of Chinese civilization and its many accomplishments, including woodblock printing and the civil service examination system. In turn, their hosts were impressed with European inventions such as the spring-driven clock and eyeglasses.

It is no surprise that the visitors from the West were impressed with what they saw in China, for that country had long been at the forefront of human achievement. From now on, however, Europe would take the lead in the advance of science and technology, a phenomenon that would ultimately result in bringing about the Industrial Revolution and beginning a transformation of human society that would lay the foundations of the modern world.

Why did Europe suddenly become the engine for rapid global change in the seventeenth and eighteenth centuries? One factor was the change in the European worldview, the shift from a metaphysical to a materialist perspective and the growing inclination among European intellectuals to question first principles. Whereas in China, for example, the "investigation of things" proposed by Song dynasty thinkers had been put to use analyzing and confirming principles first established by Confucius and his contemporaries, empirical scientists in early modern Europe rejected received religious ideas,

© The Print Collector/Alamy

The telescope—a European invention

developed a new conception of the universe, and sought ways to improve material conditions around them.

Why were European thinkers more interested in practical applications of their discoveries than their counterparts elsewhere? No doubt the literate mercantile and propertied elites of Europe were attracted to the new science because it offered new ways to exploit resources for profit. Some of the early scientists made it easier for these groups to accept the new ideas by showing how they could be applied directly to specific industrial and technological needs. Galileo, for example, consciously drew a connection between science and the material interests of the educated elite when he assured his listeners that the science of mechanics would be quite useful "when it becomes necessary to build bridges or other structures over water, something occurring mainly in affairs of great importance."

A final factor was the political changes that were beginning to take place in Europe during this period. Many European states enlarged their bureaucratic machinery and consolidated their governments in order to collect the revenues and amass the armies needed to compete militarily with rivals. Political leaders desperately sought ways to enhance their wealth and power and grasped eagerly at whatever tools were available to guarantee their survival and prosperity.

Q *Why did the Scientific Revolution emerge in Europe and not in China?*

Einstein's concept of relativity created a new picture of the universe.

Europe, China, and Scientific Revolutions An interesting question that arises is why the Scientific Revolution occurred in Europe and not in China. In the Middle Ages, China had been the most technologically advanced civilization in the world. After 1500, that distinction passed to the West (see the comparative essay "The Scientific Revolution" above). Historians are not sure why. Some have compared the sense of order in Chinese society to the competitive spirit existing in Europe. Others have emphasized China's ideological viewpoint that favored living in harmony with nature rather than trying to

dominate it. One historian has even suggested that China's civil service system drew the "best and the brightest" into government service, to the detriment of other occupations.

Background to the Enlightenment

The impetus for political and social change in the eighteenth century stemmed in part from the **Enlightenment.** The Enlightenment was a movement of intellectuals who were greatly impressed with the accomplishments of the Scientific Revolution. When they used the word *reason*—one of their favorite words—they were advocating the application of the scientific method to the understanding of all life. All institutions and all systems of thought were subject to the rational, scientific way of thinking if people would only free themselves from the shackles of past, worthless traditions, especially religious ones. If Isaac Newton could discover the natural laws regulating the world of nature, they too, by using reason, could find the laws that governed human society. This belief in turn led them to hope that they could make progress toward a better society than the one they had inherited. *Reason, natural law, hope, progress*—these were the buzzwords in the heady atmosphere of eighteenth-century Europe.

Major sources of inspiration for the Enlightenment were two Englishmen, Isaac Newton and John Locke (1632–1704). As mentioned earlier, Newton contended that the world and everything in it worked like a giant machine. Enchanted by the grand design of this world-machine, the intellectuals of the Enlightenment were convinced that by following Newton's rules of reasoning, they could discover the natural laws that governed politics, economics, justice, and religion.

John Locke's theory of knowledge also made a great impact. In his *Essay Concerning Human Understanding,* written in 1690, Locke denied the existence of innate ideas and argued instead that every person was born with a *tabula rasa,* a blank mind:

> Let us then suppose the mind to be, as we say, white paper, void of all characters, without any ideas. How comes it to be furnished? Whence comes it by that vast store which the busy and boundless fancy of man has painted on it with an almost endless variety? Whence has it all the materials of reason and knowledge? To this I answer, in one word, from experience.... Our observation, employed either about external sensible objects or about the internal operations of our minds perceived and reflected on by ourselves, is that which supplies our understanding with all the materials of thinking.[1]

By denying innate ideas, Locke's philosophy implied that people were molded by their environment, by whatever they perceived through their senses from their surrounding world. By changing the environment and subjecting people to proper influences, they could be changed and a new society created. And how should the environment be changed? Newton had paved the way: reason enabled enlightened people to discover the natural laws to which all institutions should conform.

The Philosophes and Their Ideas

The intellectuals of the Enlightenment were known by the French term *philosophes,* although they were not all French and few were philosophers in the strict sense of the term. The **philosophes** were literary people, professors, journalists, economists, political scientists, and, above all, social reformers. Although it was a truly international and cosmopolitan movement, the Enlightenment also enhanced the dominant role being played by French culture; Paris was its recognized capital. Most of the leaders of the Enlightenment were French. The French philosophes, in turn, affected intellectuals elsewhere and created a movement that touched the entire Western world, including the British and Spanish colonies in the Americas.

To the philosophes, the role of philosophy was not just to discuss the world but to change it. A spirit of rational criticism was to be applied to everything, including religion and politics. Spanning almost a century, the Enlightenment evolved with each succeeding generation, becoming more radical as new thinkers built on the contributions of their predecessors. A few individuals, however, dominated the landscape so completely that we can gain insight into the core ideas of the philosophes by focusing on the three French giants—Montesquieu, Voltaire, and Diderot.

Montesquieu Charles de Secondat, the baron de Montesquieu (1689–1755), came from the French nobility. His most famous work, *The Spirit of the Laws,* was published in 1748. In this comparative study of governments, Montesquieu attempted to apply the scientific method to the social and political arena to ascertain the "natural laws" governing the social and political relationships of human beings. Montesquieu distinguished three basic kinds of governments: republic, monarchy, and despotism.

Montesquieu used England as an example of monarchy, and it was his analysis of England's constitution that led to his most lasting contribution to political thought—the importance of checks and balances achieved by means of a **separation of powers.** He believed that England's system, with its separate executive, legislative, and judicial powers that served to limit and control each other, provided the greatest freedom and security for a state. The translation of his work into English two years after publication ensured that it would be read by American political leaders, who eventually incorporated its principles into the U.S. Constitution.

Voltaire The greatest figure of the Enlightenment was François-Marie Arouet, known simply as Voltaire (1694–1778). Son of a prosperous middle-class family from Paris, he studied law, although he achieved his first success as a playwright. Voltaire was a prolific author and wrote an almost endless stream of pamphlets, novels, plays, letters, philosophical essays, and histories.

Voltaire was especially well known for his criticism of traditional religion and his strong attachment to the ideal of religious toleration. As he grew older, Voltaire became ever more strident in his denunciations. "Crush the infamous thing," he thundered repeatedly—the infamous thing being religious fanaticism, intolerance, and superstition.

Throughout his life, Voltaire championed not only religious tolerance but also **deism,** a religious outlook shared by most other philosophes. Deism was built on the Newtonian world-machine, which implied the existence of a mechanic (God) who had created the universe. To Voltaire and most other philosophes, the universe was like a clock, and God was the clockmaker who had created it, set it in motion, and allowed it to run according to its own natural laws.

Diderot   Denis Diderot (1713–1784) was the son of a skilled craftsman from eastern France who became a writer so that he could be free to study and read in many subjects and languages. One of Diderot's favorite topics was Christianity, which he condemned as fanatical and unreasonable. Of all religions, Christianity, he averred, was the worst, "the most absurd and the most atrocious in its dogma."

Diderot's most famous contribution to the Enlightenment was the *Encyclopedia, or Classified Dictionary of the Sciences, Arts, and Trades,* a twenty-eight-volume compendium of knowledge that he edited and referred to as the "great work of his life." Its purpose, according to Diderot, was to "change the general way of thinking." It did precisely that in becoming a major weapon of the philosophes' crusade against the old French society. The contributors included many philosophes who attacked religious intolerance and advocated a program for social, legal, and political improvements that would lead to a society that was more cosmopolitan, more tolerant, more humane, and more reasonable. The *Encyclopedia* was sold to doctors, clergymen, teachers, lawyers, and even military officers, thus spreading the ideas of the Enlightenment.

Toward a New "Science of Man"   The Enlightenment belief that Newton's scientific methods could be used to discover the natural laws underlying all areas of human life led to the emergence in the eighteenth century of what the philosophes called a "science of man," or what we would call the social sciences. In a number of areas, such as economics, politics, and education, the philosophes arrived at natural laws that they believed governed human actions.

Adam Smith (1723–1790) has been viewed as one of the founders of the modern discipline of economics. Smith believed that individuals should be free to pursue their own economic self-interest. Through the actions of these individuals, all society would ultimately benefit. Consequently, the state should in no way interrupt the free play of natural economic forces by imposing government regulations on the economy but should leave it alone, a doctrine that subsequently became known as **laissez-faire** (French for "leave it alone").

Smith gave to government only three basic functions: it should protect society from invasion (army), defend its citizens from injustice (police), and keep up certain public works, such as roads and canals, that private individuals could not afford.

The Later Enlightenment   By the late 1760s, a new generation of philosophes who had grown up with the worldview of the Enlightenment began to move beyond their predecessors' beliefs. Most famous was Jean-Jacques Rousseau (1712–1778), whose political beliefs were presented in two major works. In his *Discourse on the Origins of the Inequality of Mankind,* Rousseau argued that people had adopted laws and governors in order to preserve their private property. In the process, they had become enslaved by government. What, then, should people do to regain their freedom? In his celebrated treatise *The Social Contract,* published in 1762, Rousseau found an answer in the concept of the social contract whereby an entire society agreed to be governed by its general will. Each individual might have a particular will contrary to the general will, but if the individual put his particular will (self-interest) above the general will, he should be forced to abide by the general will. "This means nothing less than that he will be forced to be free," said Rousseau, because the general will was not only political but also ethical; it represented what the entire community ought to do.

Another influential treatise by Rousseau was his novel *Émile,* one of the Enlightenment's most important works on education. Rousseau's fundamental concern was that education should foster, rather than restrict, children's natural instincts. Rousseau's own experiences had shown him the importance of the emotions. What he sought was a balance between heart and mind, between emotion and reason.

But Rousseau did not necessarily practice what he preached. His own children were sent to orphanages, where many children died at a young age. Rousseau also viewed women as "naturally" different from men. In Rousseau's *Émile,* Sophie, Émile's intended wife, was educated for her role as wife and mother by learning obedience and the nurturing skills that would enable her to provide loving care for her husband and children. Not everyone in the eighteenth century, however, agreed with Rousseau.

The "Woman Question" in the Enlightenment   For centuries, many male intellectuals had argued that the nature of women made them inferior to men and made male domination of women necessary and right. In the Scientific Revolution, however, some women had

THE RIGHTS OF WOMEN

FAMILY & SOCIETY

Mary Wollstonecraft responded to an unhappy childhood in a large family by seeking to lead an independent life. Few occupations were available for middle-class women in her day, but she survived by working as a teacher, chaperone, and governess to aristocratic children. All the while, she wrote and developed her ideas on the rights of women. This excerpt is taken from her *Vindication of the Rights of Woman,* written in 1792. This work established her reputation as the foremost British feminist thinker of the eighteenth century.

Mary Wollstonecraft, *Vindication of the Rights of Woman*

It is a melancholy truth—yet such is the blessed effect of civilization— the most respectable women are the most oppressed; and, unless they have understandings far superior to the common run of understandings, taking in both sexes, they must, from being treated like contemptible beings, become contemptible. How many women thus waste life away the prey of discontent, who might have practiced as physicians, regulated a farm, managed a shop, and stood erect, supported by their own industry, instead of hanging their heads surcharged with the dew of sensibility, that consumes the beauty to which it at first gave luster. . . .

Proud of their weakness, however, [women] must always be protected, guarded from care, and all the rough toils that dignify the mind. If this be the fiat of fate, if they will make themselves insignificant and contemptible, sweetly to waste "life away," let them not expect to be valued when their beauty fades, for it is the fate of the fairest flowers to be admired and pulled to pieces by the careless hand that plucked them. In how many ways do I wish, from the purest benevolence, to impress this truth on my sex; yet I fear that they will not listen to a truth that dear-bought experience has brought home to many an agitated bosom, nor willingly resign the privileges of rank and sex for the privileges of humanity, to which those have no claim who do not discharge its duties. . . .

Would men but generously snap our chains, and be content with rational fellowship instead of slavish obedience, they would find us more observant daughters, more affectionate sisters, more faithful wives, and more reasonable mothers—in a word, better citizens. We should then love them with true affection, because we should learn to respect ourselves; and the peace of mind of a worthy man would not be interrupted by the idle vanity of his wife.

Q *What picture does the author paint of the women of her day? Why are they in such a deplorable state? How does Wollstonecraft suggest that both women and men are at fault for the "slavish" situation of females?*

---

made notable contributions. Maria Winkelmann in Germany, for example, was an outstanding practicing astronomer. Nevertheless, when she applied for a position as assistant astronomer at the Berlin Academy, for which she was highly qualified, she was denied the post by the academy's members, who feared that hiring her would establish a precedent ("mouths would gape").

Female thinkers in the eighteenth century disagreed with this attitude and provided suggestions for improving the conditions of women. The strongest statement for the rights of women was advanced by the English writer Mary Wollstonecraft (1759–1797), viewed by many as the founder of modern European **feminism.**

In her *Vindication of the Rights of Woman,* written in 1792, Wollstonecraft pointed out two contradictions in the views of women held by such Enlightenment thinkers as Rousseau. To argue that women must obey men, she said, was contrary to the beliefs of the same individuals that a system based on the arbitrary power of monarchs over their subjects or slave owners over their slaves was wrong. The subjection of women to men was equally wrong. In addition, she argued that the Enlightenment was based on an ideal of reason innate in all human beings. If women have reason, then they too are entitled to the same rights that men have in education and in economic and political life (see the box above).

Culture in an Enlightened Age

Although the Baroque style that had dominated the seventeenth century continued to be popular, by the 1730s, a new style of decoration and architecture known as **Rococo** had spread throughout Europe. Unlike the Baroque, which stressed power, grandeur, and movement, Rococo emphasized grace, charm, and gentle action. Rococo rejected strict geometrical patterns and had a fondness for curves; it liked to follow the wandering lines of natural objects, such as seashells and flowers. It made much use of interlaced designs colored in gold with delicate contours and graceful arcs. Highly secular, its lightness and charm spoke of the pursuit of pleasure, happiness, and love.

Some of Rococo's appeal is evident already in the work of Antoine Watteau (1684–1721), whose lyrical views of aristocratic life, refined, sensual, and civilized, with gentlemen and ladies in elegant dress, revealed a world of upperclass pleasure and joy. Underneath that exterior, however, was an element of sadness as the artist revealed the fragility and transitory nature of pleasure, love, and life.

Antoine Watteau, *The Pilgrimage to Cythera*. Antoine Watteau was one of the most gifted painters in eighteenth-century France. His portrayal of aristocratic life reveals a world of elegance, wealth, and pleasure. In this painting, Watteau depicts a group of aristocratic pilgrims about to depart the island of Cythera, where they have paid homage to Venus, the goddess of love.

High Culture Historians have grown accustomed to distinguishing between a civilization's high culture and its popular culture. **High culture** is the literary and artistic culture of the educated and wealthy ruling classes; **popular culture** is the written and unwritten culture of the masses, most of which has traditionally been passed down orally.

By the eighteenth century, the two forms were beginning to blend, owing to the expansion of both the reading public and publishing. Whereas French publishers issued three hundred titles in 1750, about sixteen hundred were being published yearly in the 1780s. Although many of these titles were still aimed at small groups of the educated elite, many were also directed to the new reading public of the middle classes, which included women and even urban artisans.

Popular Culture The distinguishing characteristic of popular culture is its collective nature. Group activity was especially common in the *festival*, a broad name used to cover a variety of celebrations: community festivals in Catholic Europe that celebrated the feast day of the local patron saint; annual festivals, such as Christmas and Easter, that go back to medieval Christianity; and the ultimate festival, Carnival, which was celebrated in the Mediterranean world of Spain, Italy, and France and in Germany and Austria as well.

Carnival began after Christmas and lasted until the start of Lent, the forty-day period of fasting and purification leading up to Easter. Because during Lent people were expected to abstain from meat, sex, and most recreations, Carnival was a time of great indulgence when heavy consumption of food and drink was the norm. It was a time of intense sexual activity as well. Songs with double meanings that would ordinarily be considered offensive could be sung publicly at this time of year. A float of Florentine "keymakers," for example, sang this ditty to the ladies: "Our tools are fine, new and useful. We always carry them with us. They are good for anything. If you want to touch them, you can."[2]

Economic Changes and the Social Order

Q Focus Question: What changes occurred in the European economy in the eighteenth century, and to what degree were these changes reflected in social patterns?

The eighteenth century in Europe witnessed the beginning of economic changes that ultimately had a strong impact on the rest of the world.

New Economic Patterns

Europe's population began to grow around 1750 and continued to increase steadily. The total European population was probably around 120 million in 1700, 140 million in 1750, and 190 million in 1790. A falling death rate was perhaps the most important reason for this population growth. Of great significance in lowering death rates was the disappearance of bubonic plague, but so was diet. More plentiful food and better transportation of food supplies led to improved nutrition and relief from devastating famines.

More plentiful food was in part a result of improvements in agricultural practices and methods in the eighteenth century, especially in Britain, parts of France, and the Low Countries. Food production increased as more land was farmed, yields per acre increased, and climate improved. Also important to the increased yields was the cultivation of new vegetables, including two important American crops, the potato and maize (Indian corn). Both had been brought to Europe from the Americas in the sixteenth century.

In European industry in the eighteenth century, textiles were the most important product and were still mostly produced by master artisans in guild workshops. But in many areas textile production was shifting to the countryside through the "putting-out" or "domestic" system in which a merchant-capitalist entrepreneur bought the raw materials, mostly wool and flax, and "put them out" to rural workers who spun the raw material into yarn and then wove it into cloth on simple looms. Capitalist-entrepreneurs sold the finished product, made a profit, and used it to purchase materials to manufacture more. This system became known as the **cottage industry** because the spinners and weavers did their work on spinning wheels and looms in their own cottages.

Overseas trade boomed in the eighteenth century. Some historians speak of the emergence of a true global economy, pointing to the patterns of trade that interlocked Europe, Africa, the East, and the Americas (see Map 14.5 in Chapter 14). One such pattern involved the influx of gold and silver into Spain from its colonial American empire. Much of this gold and silver made its way to Britain, France, and the Netherlands in return for manufactured goods. British, Dutch, and French merchants in turn used their profits to buy tea, spices, silk, and cotton goods from China and India to sell in Europe. Another important source of trading activity involved the plantations of the Western Hemisphere. The plantations were worked by African slaves and produced tobacco, cotton, coffee, and sugar, all products in demand by Europeans.

Commercial capitalism created enormous prosperity for some European countries. By 1700, Spain, Portugal, and the Dutch Republic, which had earlier monopolized overseas trade, found themselves increasingly overshadowed by France and England, which built enormously profitable colonial empires in the course of the eighteenth century. After the French lost the Seven Years' War in 1763, Britain emerged as the world's strongest overseas trading nation, and London became the world's greatest port.

European Society in the Eighteenth Century

The pattern of Europe's social organization, first established in the Middle Ages, continued well into the eighteenth century. Society was still divided into the traditional "orders" or "estates" determined by heredity.

Because society was still mostly rural in the eighteenth century, the peasantry constituted the largest social group, about 85 percent of Europe's population. There were rather wide differences within this group, however, especially between free peasants and serfs. In eastern Germany, eastern Europe, and Russia, serfs remained tied to the lands of their noble landlords. In contrast, peasants in Britain, northern Italy, the Low Countries, Spain, most of France, and some areas of western Germany were largely free.

The nobles, who constituted only 2 to 3 percent of the European population, played a dominating role in society. Being born a noble automatically guaranteed a place at the top of the social order, with all its attendant privileges and rights. Nobles, for example, were exempt from many forms of taxation. Since medieval times, landed aristocrats had functioned as military officers, and eighteenth-century nobles held most of the important offices in the administrative machinery of state and controlled much of the life of their local districts.

Townspeople were still a distinct minority of the total population except in the Dutch Republic, Britain, and parts of Italy. At the end of the eighteenth century, about one-sixth of the French population lived in towns of two thousand people or more. The biggest city in Europe was London, with a million inhabitants; Paris was a little more than half that size.

Many cities in western and even central Europe had a long tradition of **patrician** oligarchies that continued to control their communities by dominating town and city councils. Just below the patricians stood an upper crust of the middle classes: nonnoble officeholders, financiers and bankers, merchants, wealthy *rentiers* who lived off their investments, and important professionals, including lawyers. Another large urban group consisted of the lower middle class, made up of master artisans, shopkeepers, and small traders. Below them were the laborers or working classes and a large group of unskilled workers who served as servants, maids, and cooks at pitifully low wages.

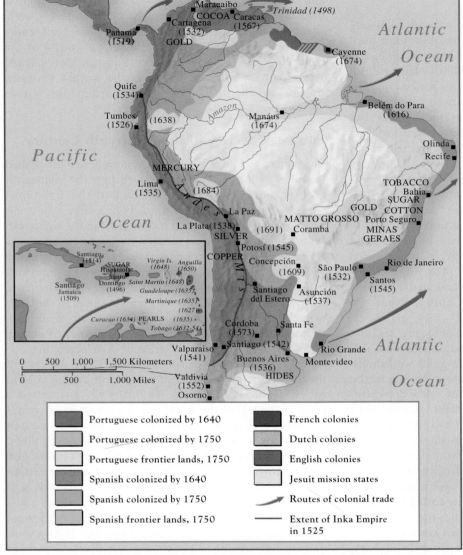

MAP 18.1 **Latin America in the Eighteenth Century.** In the eighteenth century, Latin America was largely the colonial preserve of the Spanish, although Portugal continued to dominate Brazil. The Latin American colonies supplied the Spanish and Portuguese with gold, silver, sugar, tobacco, cotton, and animal hides.

Q How do you explain the ability of Europeans to dominate such large areas of Latin America?

Colonial Empires and Revolution in the Western Hemisphere

Q Focus Question: How did Spain and Portugal administer their American colonies, and what were the main characteristics of Latin American society in the eighteenth century?

The colonial empires in the Western Hemisphere were an integral part of the European economy in the eighteenth century and became entangled in the conflicts of the European states. Nevertheless, the colonies of Latin America and British North America were developing along lines that sometimes differed significantly from those of Europe.

The Society of Latin America

In the sixteenth century, Portugal came to dominate Brazil while Spain established a colonial empire in the Western Hemisphere that included Central America, most of South America, and parts of North America. Within the lands of Central and South America, a new civilization arose that we have come to call Latin America (see Map 18.1).

Latin America was a multiracial society. Already by 1501, Spanish rulers allowed intermarriage between Europeans and native American Indians, whose offspring became known as **mestizos.** In addition, over a period of three centuries, possibly as many as 8 million African slaves were brought to Spanish and Portuguese America to work the plantations. **Mulattoes**—the offspring of Africans and whites—joined mestizos and descendants of whites, Africans, and native Indians to produce a unique multiracial society in Latin America.

The Economic Foundations Both the Portuguese and the Spanish sought to profit from their colonies in Latin America. One source of wealth came from the abundant supplies of gold and silver. The Spaniards were especially successful, finding supplies of gold in the Caribbean and New Granada (Colombia) and silver in Mexico and the viceroyalty of Peru. Most of the gold and silver was sent to Europe, and little remained in the Americas to benefit the people whose labor had produced it.

Although the pursuit of gold and silver offered prospects of fantastic wealth, agriculture proved to be a more abiding and more rewarding source of prosperity for Latin America. A noticeable feature of Latin American agriculture was the dominant role of the large landowner. Both Spanish and Portuguese landowners created immense estates, which left the Indians either to work as **peons**—native peasants permanently dependent on the landowners—on the estates or to subsist as poor farmers on marginal lands. This system of large landowners and dependent peasants has remained one of the persistent features of Latin American society. By the eighteenth century, both Spanish and Portuguese landowners were producing primarily for sale abroad.

Trade was another avenue for the economic exploitation of the American colonies. Latin American colonies became sources of raw materials for Spain and Portugal as gold, silver, sugar, tobacco, diamonds, animal hides, and a number of other natural products made their way to Europe. In turn, the mother countries supplied their colonists with manufactured goods.

The State and the Church in Colonial Latin America

Portuguese Brazil and Spanish America were colonial empires that lasted more than three hundred years. The difficulties of communication and travel between the Americas and Europe made it almost impossible for the Spanish and Portuguese monarchs to provide close regulation of their empires, so colonial officials in Latin America had considerable autonomy in implementing imperial policies. Nevertheless, the Iberians tried to keep the most important posts of colonial government in the hands of Europeans.

Starting in the mid-sixteenth century, the Portuguese monarchs began to assert control over Brazil by establishing the position of governor-general. To rule Spain's American empire, the Spanish kings appointed **viceroys,** the first of which was established for New Spain (Mexico) in 1535. Another viceroy was appointed for Peru in 1543. In the eighteenth century, two additional viceroyalties—New Granada and La Plata—were added. Viceroyalties were in turn subdivided into smaller units. All of the major government positions were held by Spaniards.

From the beginning of their conquest of lands in the Western Hemisphere, Spanish and Portuguese rulers were determined to convert the indigenous peoples to Christianity. This policy gave the Roman Catholic Church an important role to play in the Americas—one that added considerably to church power. Catholic missionaries fanned out to different parts of the Spanish Empire. To facilitate their efforts, missionaries brought Indians together into villages where the natives could be converted, taught trades, and encouraged to grow crops. The missions enabled the missionaries to control the lives of the Indians and keep them docile.

Sor Juana Inés de la Cruz. Nunneries in colonial Latin America gave women—especially upper-class women—some opportunity for intellectual activity. As a woman, Juana Inés de la Cruz was denied admission to the University of Mexico. Consequently, she entered a convent, where she wrote poetry and plays until her superiors forced her to focus on less worldly activities.

The Catholic church also built hospitals, orphanages, and schools that instructed Indian students in the rudiments of reading, writing, and arithmetic. The church also provided outlets for women other than marriage. Nunneries were places of prayer and quiet contemplation, but women in religious orders, many of them of aristocratic background, often lived well and operated outside their establishments by running schools and hospitals. Indeed, one of these nuns, Sor Juana Inés de la Cruz (1651–1695), was one of seventeenth-century Latin America's best-known literary figures. She wrote poetry and prose and urged that women be educated.

British North America

In the eighteenth century, Spanish power in the Western Hemisphere was increasingly challenged by the British.

FILM & HISTORY
THE MISSION (1986)

Directed by Roland Joffé, *The Mission* examines religion, politics, and colonialism in Europe and South America in the mid-eighteenth century. The movie begins with a flashback as Cardinal Altamirano (Ray McAnally) is dictating a letter to the pope to discuss the fate of the Jesuit missions in Paraguay. He begins by describing the establishment of a new Jesuit mission (San Carlos) in Spanish territory in the borderlands of Paraguay and Brazil. Father Gabriel (Jeremy Irons) has been able to win over the Guaraní Indians and create a community at San Carlos that is based on communal livelihood and property (private property is abolished). The mission includes dwellings and a church where the Guaraní can practice their new faith. This small community is joined by Rodrigo Mendozo (Robert De Niro), who had been a slave trader dealing in Indians and now seeks to atone for killing his brother in a fit of jealous rage by joining the mission at San Carlos. Won over to Father Gabriel's perspective, he also becomes a member of the Jesuit order.

The Jesuit missionary Father Gabriel (Jeremy Irons) with the Guaraní Indians of Paraguay before their slaughter by Portuguese troops

Soon, however, Cardinal Altamirano travels to South America, sent by a pope anxious to appease the Portuguese monarch who has been complaining about the activities of the Jesuits. Portuguese settlers in Brazil are eager to use the native people as slaves and to confiscate their communal lands and property. In 1750, when Spain agrees to turn over the Guaraní territory in Paraguay to Portugal, the settlers seize their opportunity. Although the cardinal visits a number of missions, including San Carlos, and obviously approves of their accomplishments, his hands are tied by the Portuguese king, who is threatening to disband the Jesuit order if the missions are not closed. The cardinal acquiesces, and Portuguese troops are sent to take over the missions. Although Rodrigo and the other Jesuits join the natives in fighting the Portuguese while Father Gabriel remains nonviolent, all are massacred. The cardinal returns to Europe, dismayed by the murderous activities of the Portuguese but hopeful that the Jesuit order will be spared. All is in vain, however, as the

Catholic monarchs of Europe expel the Jesuits from their countries and pressure Pope Clement XIV into disbanding the Jesuit order in 1773.

In its approach to the destruction of the Jesuit missions, *The Mission* clearly exalts the dedication of the Jesuits and their devotion to the welfare of the Indians. The movie ends with a small group of Guaraní children, all now orphans, picking up a few remnants of debris left in their destroyed mission and moving off down the river back into the wilderness to escape enslavement. The final words on the screen reinforce the movie's message about the activities of the Europeans who destroyed the native civilizations in their conquest of the Americas: "The Indians of South America are still engaged in a struggle to defend their land and their culture. Many of the priests who, inspired by faith and love, continue to support the rights of the Indians, do so with their lives," a reference to the ongoing struggle in Latin America against regimes that continue to oppress the landless masses.

(The United Kingdom of Great Britain came into existence in 1707, when the governments of England and Scotland were united; the term *British* came into use to refer to both English and Scots.) In eighteenth-century Britain, the king or queen and Parliament shared power, with Parliament gradually gaining the upper hand. The monarch chose ministers who were responsible to the crown and who set policy and guided Parliament. Parliament had the power to make laws, levy taxes, pass budgets, and indirectly influence the monarch's ministers.

The increase in trade and industry led to a growing middle class in Britain that favored expansion of trade and world empire. These people found a spokesman in William Pitt the Elder, who became prime minister in 1757 and expanded the British Empire by acquiring Canada and India in the Seven Years' War.

The American Revolution At the end of the Seven Years' War in 1763, Great Britain had become the world's greatest colonial power. In North America, Britain controlled

Canada and the lands east of the Mississippi. After the Seven Years' War, British policy makers sought to obtain new revenues from the colonies to pay for the British army's expenses in defending the colonists. An attempt to levy new taxes by the Stamp Act of 1765, however, led to riots and the law's quick repeal.

The Americans and the British had different conceptions of empire. The British envisioned a single empire with Parliament as the supreme authority throughout. The Americans, in contrast, had their own representative assemblies. They believed that neither king nor Parliament should interfere in their internal affairs and that no tax could be levied without the consent of their own assemblies.

Crisis followed crisis in the 1770s until 1776, when the colonists decided to declare their independence from Great Britain. On July 4, 1776, the Second Continental Congress approved a declaration of independence drafted by Thomas Jefferson. A stirring political document, the Declaration of Independence affirmed the Enlightenment's natural rights of "life, liberty, and the pursuit of happiness" and declared the colonies to be "free and independent states absolved from all allegiance to the British crown." The war for American independence had formally begun.

Of great importance to the colonies' cause was their support by foreign countries who were eager to gain revenge for earlier defeats at the hands of the British. French officers and soldiers served in the American Continental Army under George Washington as commander in chief. When the British army of General Cornwallis was forced to surrender to a combined American and French army and French fleet under Washington at Yorktown in 1781, the British decided to call it quits. The Treaty of Paris, signed in 1783, recognized the independence of the American colonies and granted the Americans control of the territory from the Appalachians to the Mississippi River.

Birth of a New Nation The thirteen American colonies had gained their independence, but a fear of concentrated power and concern for their own interests caused them to have little enthusiasm for establishing a united nation with a strong central government, and so the Articles of Confederation, ratified in 1781, did not create one. A movement for a different form of national government soon arose. In the summer of 1787, fifty-five delegates attended a convention in Philadelphia to revise the Articles of Confederation. The convention's delegates—wealthy, politically experienced, and well educated—rejected revision and decided instead to devise a new constitution.

The proposed United States Constitution established a central government distinct from and superior to governments of the individual states. The central or federal government was divided into three branches, each with some power to check the functioning of the others. A president would serve as the chief executive with the power to execute laws, veto the legislature's acts, supervise foreign affairs, and direct military forces. Legislative power was vested in the second branch of government, a bicameral legislature composed of the Senate, elected by the state legislatures, and the House of Representatives, elected directly by the people. A supreme court and other courts "as deemed necessary" by Congress provided the third branch of government. They would enforce the Constitution as the "supreme law of the land."

The Constitution was approved by the states—by a slim margin. Important to its success was a promise to add a bill of rights to the Constitution as the new government's first piece of business. Accordingly, in March 1789, the new Congress enacted the first ten amendments to the Constitution, ever since known as the Bill of Rights. These guaranteed freedom of religion, speech, press, petition, and assembly, as well as the right to bear arms, protection against unreasonable searches and arrests, trial by jury, due process of law, and protection of property rights. Many of these rights were derived from the **natural rights** philosophy of the eighteenth-century philosophes and the American colonists. Is it any wonder that many European intellectuals saw the American Revolution as the embodiment of the Enlightenment's political dreams?

Toward a New Political Order and Global Conflict

Q **Focus Question:** What do historians mean by the term *enlightened absolutism,* and to what degree did eighteenth-century Prussia, Austria, and Russia exhibit its characteristics?

There is no doubt that Enlightenment thought had some impact on the political development of European states in the eighteenth century. The philosophes believed in natural rights, which were thought to be privileges that ought not to be withheld from any person. These natural rights included equality before the law, freedom of religious worship, freedom of speech and press, and the rights to assemble, hold property, and pursue happiness.

But how were these natural rights to be established and preserved? Most philosophes believed that people needed to be ruled by an enlightened ruler. What, however, made rulers enlightened? They must allow religious toleration, freedom of speech and press, and the rights of private property. They must foster the arts, sciences, and education. Above all, they must obey the laws and enforce them fairly for all subjects. Only strong monarchs seemed capable of overcoming vested interests and effecting the reforms society needed. Reforms then should come from above (from absolute rulers) rather than from below (from the people).

Many historians once assumed that a new type of monarchy emerged in the later eighteenth century, which they called *enlightened despotism* or **enlightened absolutism.** Monarchs such as Frederick II of Prussia, Catherine the Great of Russia, and Joseph II of Austria supposedly followed the advice of the philosophes and ruled by enlightened principles. Recently, however, scholars have questioned the usefulness of the concept of enlightened absolutism. We can determine the extent to which it can be applied by examining the major "enlightened absolutists" of the late eighteenth century.

Prussia

Frederick II, known as Frederick the Great (1740–1786), was one of the best-educated and most cultured monarchs of the eighteenth century. He was well versed in Enlightenment thought and even invited Voltaire to live at his court for several years. A believer in the king as the "first servant of the state," Frederick the Great was a conscientious ruler who enlarged the Prussian army (to 200,000 men) and kept a strict watch over the bureaucracy.

For a time, Frederick seemed quite willing to make enlightened reforms. He abolished the use of torture except in treason and murder cases and also granted limited freedom of speech and press, as well as complete religious toleration. His efforts were limited, however, as he kept Prussia's rigid social structure and serfdom intact and avoided any additional reforms.

The Austrian Empire of the Habsburgs

The Austrian Empire had become one of the great European states by the beginning of the eighteenth century. Yet it was difficult to rule because it was a sprawling conglomerate of nationalities, languages, religions, and cultures (see Map 18.2).

Joseph II (1780–1790) believed in the need to sweep away anything standing in the path of reason. As he said, "I have made Philosophy the lawmaker of my empire; her logical applications are going to transform Austria." Joseph's reform program was far-reaching. He abolished serfdom, abrogated the death penalty, and established the principle of equality of all before the law. Joseph instituted drastic religious reforms as well, including complete religious toleration.

Joseph's reform program proved overwhelming for Austria, however. He alienated the nobility by freeing the serfs and alienated the church by his attacks on the monastic establishment. Joseph realized his failure when he wrote the epitaph for his own gravestone: "Here lies Joseph II, who was unfortunate in everything that he undertook." His successors undid many of his reforms.

Russia Under Catherine the Great

Catherine II the Great (1762–1796) was an intelligent woman who was familiar with the works of the philosophes and seemed to favor enlightened reforms. She invited the French philosophe Diderot to Russia and, when he arrived, urged him to speak frankly "as man to man." He did, outlining a far-reaching program of political and financial reform. But Catherine was skeptical about impractical theories, which, she said, "would have turned everything in my kingdom upside down." She did consider the idea of a new law code that would recognize the principle of the equality of all people in the eyes of the law. But in the end she did nothing, knowing that her success depended on the support of the Russian nobility. In 1785, she gave the nobles a charter that exempted them from taxes. Catherine's policy of favoring the landed nobility led to even worse conditions for the Russian peasants and sparked a rebellion, but it soon faltered and collapsed. Catherine responded with even harsher measures against the peasantry.

Above all, Catherine proved a worthy successor to Peter the Great in her policies of territorial expansion westward into Poland and southward to the Black Sea. Russia spread southward by defeating the Turks. Russian expansion westward occurred at the expense of neighboring Poland. In three partitions of Poland, Russia gained about 50 percent of Polish territory.

Enlightened Absolutism Reconsidered

Of the rulers we have discussed, only Joseph II sought truly radical changes based on Enlightenment ideas. Both Frederick II and Catherine II liked to talk about enlightened reforms, and they even attempted some. But neither ruler's policies seemed seriously affected by Enlightenment thought. Necessities of state and maintenance of the existing system took precedence over reform. Indeed, many historians maintain that Joseph, Frederick, and Catherine were all primarily guided by a concern for the power and well-being of their states. In the final analysis, heightened state power was used to create armies and wage wars to gain more power.

It would be foolish, however, to overlook the fact that the ability of enlightened rulers to make reforms was also

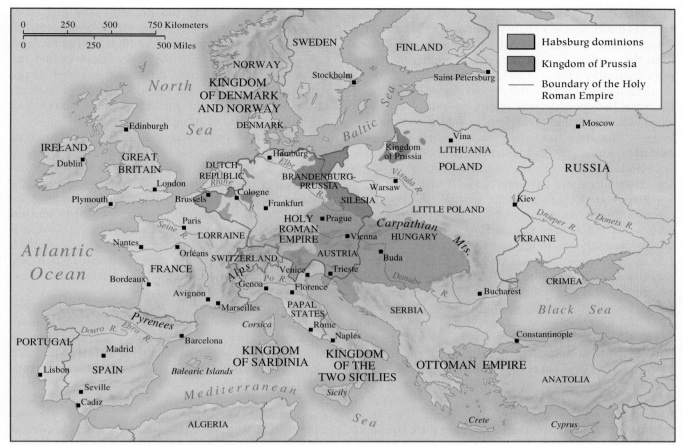

MAP 18.2 **Europe in 1763.** By the middle of the eighteenth century, five major powers dominated Europe—Prussia, Austria, Russia, Britain, and France. Each sought to enhance its power both domestically, through a bureaucracy that collected taxes and ran the military, and internationally, by capturing territory or preventing other powers from doing so.
Q Given the distribution of Prussian and Habsburg holdings, in what areas of Europe were they most likely to compete for land and power?
🖰 **View an animated version of this map or related maps at** www.cengage.com/history/duikspiel/essentialworld6e

limited by political and social realities. Everywhere in Europe, the hereditary aristocracy was still the most powerful class in society. As the chief beneficiaries of a system based on traditional rights and privileges for their class, the nobles were not willing to support a political ideology that trumpeted the principle of equal rights for all. The first serious challenge to their supremacy would come with the French Revolution, an event that blew open the door to the modern world of politics.

Changing Patterns of War: Global Confrontation

The philosophes condemned war as a foolish waste of life and resources in stupid quarrels of no value to humankind. Despite their criticisms, the rivalry among European states that led to costly struggles continued unabated. Eighteenth-century Europe consisted of a number of self-governing, individual states that were chiefly guided by the self-interest of the ruler. And as Frederick the Great of Prussia said, "The fundamental rule of governments is the principle of extending their territories."

By far the most dramatic confrontation occurred in the Seven Years' War. Although it began in Europe, it soon turned into a global conflict fought in Europe, India, and North America. In Europe, the British and Prussians fought the Austrians, Russians, and French. With his superb army and military skill, Frederick the Great of Prussia was able for some time to defeat the

Austrian, French, and Russian armies. Eventually, however, his forces were gradually worn down and faced utter defeat until a new Russian tsar withdrew Russia's troops from the conflict. A stalemate ensued, ending the European conflict in 1763.

The struggle between Britain and France in the rest of the world had more decisive results. In India, local rulers allied with British and French troops fought a number of battles. Ultimately, the British under Robert Clive won out, not because they had better forces but because they were more persistent. By the Treaty of Paris in 1763, the French withdrew and left India to the British.

The greatest conflicts of the Seven Years' War took place in North America, where it was known as the French and Indian War. French North America (Canada and Louisiana) was thinly populated and run by the French government as a vast trading area. British North America had come to consist of thirteen colonies on the eastern coast of the present United States. These were thickly populated, containing about 1.5 million people by 1750, and were also prosperous.

British and French rivalry finally led war. Despite initial French successes, the British went on to seize Montreal, the Great Lakes area, and the Ohio valley. The French were forced to make peace. By the Treaty of Paris, they ceded Canada and the lands east of the Mississippi to Britain. Their ally Spain transferred Spanish Florida to British control; in return, the French gave their Louisiana territory to the Spanish. By 1763, Great Britain had become the world's greatest colonial power. For France, the loss of its empire was soon followed by an even greater internal upheaval.

The French Revolution

Q Focus Question: What were the causes, the main events, and the results of the French Revolution?

The year 1789 witnessed two far-reaching events, the beginning of a new United States of America under its revamped Constitution and the eruption of the French Revolution. Compared with the American Revolution a decade earlier, the French Revolution was more complex, more violent, and far more radical in its attempt to construct both a new political and a new social order.

Background to the French Revolution

The root causes of the French Revolution must be sought in the condition of French society. Before the Revolution, France was a society grounded in privilege and inequality. Its population of 27 million was divided, as it had been since the Middle Ages, into three orders or estates.

Social Structure of the Old Regime The first estate consisted of the clergy and numbered about 130,000 people who owned approximately 10 percent of the land. Clergy were exempt from the *taille*, France's chief tax. Clergy were also radically divided: the higher clergy, stemming from aristocratic families, shared the interests of the nobility, while the parish priests were often poor and from the class of commoners.

The second estate was the nobility, composed of about 350,000 people who owned about 25 to 30 percent of the land. The nobility had continued to play an important and even crucial role in French society in the eighteenth century, holding many of the leading positions in the government, the military, the law courts, and the higher church offices. The nobles sought to expand their power at the expense of the monarchy and to maintain their control over positions in the military, church, and government. Common to all nobles were tax exemptions, especially from the *taille*.

The third estate, or the commoners of society, constituted the overwhelming majority of the French population. They were divided by vast differences in occupation, level of education, and wealth. The peasants, who alone constituted 75 to 80 percent of the total population, were by far the largest segment of the third estate. They owned about 35 to 40 percent of the land, although their landholdings varied from area to area and more than half had little or no land on which to survive. Serfdom no longer existed on any large scale in France, but French peasants still had obligations to their local landlords that they deeply resented. These "relics of feudalism," or aristocratic privileges, were obligations that survived from an earlier age and included the payment of fees for the use of village facilities, such as the flour mill, community oven, and winepress.

Another part of the third estate consisted of skilled craftspeople, shopkeepers, and other wage earners in the cities. In the eighteenth century, consumer prices had risen faster than wages, causing these urban groups to experience a noticeable decline in purchasing power. Engaged in a daily struggle for survival, many of these people would play an important role in the Revolution, especially in Paris.

About 8 percent of the population, or 2.3 million people, constituted the bourgeoisie or middle class, who owned about 20 to 25 percent of the land. This group included merchants, industrialists, and bankers who controlled the resources of trade, manufacturing, and finance and benefited from the economic prosperity after 1730. The bourgeoisie also included professional people—lawyers, holders of public offices, doctors, and writers. Many members of the bourgeoisie had their own set of grievances because they were often excluded from the social and political privileges monopolized by nobles.

Moreover, the new political ideas of the Enlightenment proved attractive to both the aristocracy and the bourgeoisie. Both elites, long accustomed to a new socioeconomic reality based on wealth and economic achievement, were increasingly frustrated by a monarchical system resting on privileges and on an old and rigid social order based on the concept of estates. The opposition of these elites to the **old order** led them ultimately to drastic action against the monarchical **old regime.** In a real sense, the Revolution had its origins in political grievances.

Other Problems Facing the French Monarchy The inability of the French monarchy to deal with new social realities was exacerbated by specific problems in the 1780s. Although France had enjoyed fifty years of economic expansion, bad harvests in 1787 and 1788 and the beginnings of a manufacturing depression resulted in food shortages, rising prices for food and other goods, and unemployment in the cities. The number of poor, estimated at almost one-third of the population, reached crisis proportions on the eve of the Revolution.

The immediate cause of the French Revolution was the near collapse of government finances. Costly wars and royal extravagance drove French governmental expenditures ever higher. On the verge of a complete financial collapse, the government of Louis XVI (1774–1792) was finally forced to call a meeting of the Estates-General, the French parliamentary body that had not met since 1614.

The Estates-General consisted of representatives from the three orders of French society. In the elections for the Estates-General, the government had ruled that the third estate should get double representation (it did, after all, constitute 97 percent of the population). Consequently, while both the first estate (the clergy) and the second estate (the nobility) had about three hundred delegates each, the third estate had almost six hundred representatives, most of whom were lawyers from French towns.

From Estates-General to National Assembly

The Estates-General opened at Versailles on May 5, 1789. It was troubled from the start with the question of whether voting should be by order or by head (each delegate having one vote). Traditionally, each order would vote as a group and have one vote. That meant that the first and second estates could outvote the third estate two to one. The third estate demanded that each deputy have one vote. With the assistance of liberal nobles and clerics, that would give the third estate a majority. When the first estate declared in favor of voting by order, the third estate

responded dramatically. On June 17, 1789, the third estate declared itself the "National Assembly" and decided to draw up a constitution. This was the first step in the French Revolution because the third estate had no legal right to act as the National Assembly. But this audacious act was soon in jeopardy, as the king sided with the first estate and threatened to dissolve the Estates-General. Louis XVI now prepared to use force.

The common people, however, saved the third estate from the king's forces. On July 14, a mob of Parisians stormed the Bastille, a royal armory, and proceeded to dismantle it, brick by brick. Louis XVI was soon informed that the royal troops were unreliable. Louis's acceptance of that reality signaled the collapse of royal authority; the king could no longer enforce his will.

At the same time, popular revolts broke out throughout France, both in the cities and in the countryside (see the comparative illustration on p. 452). Behind the popular uprising was a growing resentment of the entire landholding system, with its fees and obligations. The fall of the Bastille and the king's apparent capitulation to the demands of the third estate now led peasants to take matters into their own hands. The peasant rebellions that occurred throughout France had a great impact on the National Assembly meeting at Versailles.

Destruction of the Old Regime

One of the first acts of the National Assembly was to abolish the rights of landlords and the fiscal exemptions of nobles, clergy, towns, and provinces. Three weeks later, the National Assembly adopted the Declaration of the Rights of Man and the Citizen (see the box on p. 453). This charter of basic liberties proclaimed freedom and equal rights for all men and access to public office based on talent. All citizens were to have the right to take part in the legislative process. Freedom of speech and the press was coupled with the outlawing of arbitrary arrests.

The declaration also raised another important issue. Did its ideal of equal rights for "all men" also include women? Many deputies insisted that it did, provided that, as one said, "women do not hope to exercise political rights and functions." Olympe de Gouges, a playwright, refused to accept this exclusion of women from political rights. Echoing the words of the official declaration, she penned the Declaration of the Rights of Woman and the Female Citizen, in which she insisted that women should have all the same rights as men. The National Assembly ignored her demands.

Because the Catholic church was seen as an important pillar of the old order, it too was reformed. Most of the lands of the church were seized. The new Civil Constitution of the Clergy was put into effect. Both bishops and priests were to be elected by the people and paid by the state. The Catholic church, still an important institution in the life of the French people, now became an enemy of the Revolution.

By 1791, the National Assembly had finally completed a new constitution that established a limited constitutional monarchy. There was still a monarch (now called "king of the French"), but the new Legislative Assembly was to make the laws. The Legislative Assembly, in which sovereign power was vested, was to sit for two years and consist of 745 representatives chosen by an indirect system of election that preserved power in the hands of the more affluent members of society. A small group of 50,000 electors chose the deputies.

By 1791, the old order had been destroyed. Many people, however—including Catholic priests, nobles, lower classes hurt by a rise in the cost of living, peasants opposed to dues that had still not been eliminated, and political clubs like the Jacobins that offered more radical solutions to France's problems—opposed the new order. The king also made things difficult for the new government when he sought to flee France in June 1791 and almost succeeded before being recognized, captured, and brought back to Paris. In this unsettled situation, under a discredited and seemingly disloyal monarch, the new Legislative Assembly held its first session in October 1791. France's relations with the rest of Europe soon led to Louis's downfall.

On August 27, 1791, the monarchs of Austria and Prussia, fearing that revolution would spread to their countries, invited other European monarchs to use force to reestablish monarchical authority in France. The French fared badly in the initial fighting in the spring of 1792, and a frantic search for scapegoats began. As one observer noted, "Everywhere you hear the cry that the king is betraying us, the generals are betraying us, that nobody is to be trusted; . . . that Paris will be taken in six weeks by the Austrians. . . . We are on a volcano ready to spout flames."[3] Defeats in war coupled with economic shortages in the spring led to renewed political demonstrations, especially against the king. In August 1792, radical political groups in Paris took the king captive and forced the Legislative Assembly to suspend the monarchy and call for a national convention, chosen on the basis of universal male suffrage, to decide on the future form of government. The French Revolution was about to enter a more radical stage.

POLITICS & GOVERNMENT

COMPARATIVE ILLUSTRATION

Revolution and Revolt in France and China. Both France and China experienced revolutionary upheaval at the end of the eighteenth century and well into the nineteenth century. In both countries, common people often played an important role. At the right is a scene from the storming of the Bastille in 1789. This early success ultimately led to the overthrow of the French monarchy. At the top is a scene from one of the struggles during the Taiping Rebellion, a major peasant revolt in the mid-nineteenth century in China. An imperial Chinese army is shown recapturing the city of Nanjing from Taiping rebels in 1864.
Q What role did common people play in revolutionary upheavals in France and China in the eighteenth and nineteenth centuries?

DECLARATION OF THE RIGHTS OF MAN AND THE CITIZEN

POLITICS & GOVERNMENT

One of the important documents of the French Revolution, the Declaration of the Rights of Man and the Citizen was adopted in August 1789 by the National Assembly. The declaration affirmed that "men are born and remain free and equal in rights," that governments must protect these natural rights, and that political power is derived from the people.

Declaration of the Rights of Man and the Citizen

The representatives of the French people, organized as a national assembly, considering that ignorance, neglect, and scorn of the rights of man are the sole causes of public misfortunes and of corruption of governments, have resolved to display in a solemn declaration the natural, inalienable, and sacred rights of man, so that this declaration, constantly in the presence of all members of society, will continually remind them of their rights and their duties.... Consequently, the National Assembly recognizes and declares, in the presence and under the auspices of the Supreme Being, the following rights of man and citizen:

1. Men are born and remain free and equal in rights; social distinctions can be established only for the common benefit.
2. The aim of every political association is the conservation of the natural and imprescriptible rights of man; these rights are liberty, property, security, and resistance to oppression.
3. The source of all sovereignty is located in essence in the nation; no body, no individual can exercise authority which does not emanate from it expressly.
4. Liberty consists in being able to do anything that does not harm another person....

6. The law is the expression of the general will; all citizens have the right to concur personally or through their representatives in its formation; it must be the same for all, whether it protects or punishes. All citizens being equal in its eyes are equally admissible to all honors, positions, and public employments, according to their capabilities and without other distinctions than those of their virtues and talents.
7. No man can be accused, arrested, or detained except in cases determined by the law, and according to the forms which it has prescribed....
10. No one may be disturbed because of his opinions, even religious, provided that their public demonstration does not disturb the public order established by law.
11. The free communication of thoughts and opinions is one of the most precious rights of man: every citizen can therefore freely speak, write, and print....
14. Citizens have the right to determine for themselves or through their representatives the need for taxation of the public, to consent to it freely, to investigate its use, and to determine its rate, basis, collection, and duration....
16. Any society in which guarantees of rights are not assured nor the separation of powers determined has no constitution.

Q *What "natural rights" does this document proclaim? To what extent was the document influenced by the writings of the philosophes? What similarities exist between this French document and the American Declaration of Independence? Why do such parallels exist?*

The Radical Revolution

In September 1792, the newly elected National Convention began its sessions. Dominated by lawyers and other professionals, two-thirds of its deputies were under forty-five, and almost all had gained political experience as a result of the Revolution. Almost all distrusted the king. As a result, the convention's first step on September 21 was to abolish the monarchy and establish a republic. On January 21, 1793, the king was executed, and the destruction of the old regime was complete. But the execution of the king created new enemies for the Revolution both at home and abroad.

In Paris, the local government, known as the Commune, whose leaders came from the working classes, favored radical change and put constant pressure on the convention, pushing it to ever more radical positions. Moreover, peasants in the west and inhabitants of the major provincial cities refused to accept the authority of the convention.

A foreign crisis also loomed large. By the beginning of 1793, after the king had been executed, most of Europe—an informal coalition of Austria, Prussia, Spain, Portugal, Britain, the Dutch Republic, and even Russia—aligned militarily against France. Grossly overextended, the French armies began to experience reverses, and by late spring, France was threatened with invasion.

A Nation in Arms To meet these crises, the convention gave broad powers to an executive committee of twelve known as the Committee of Public Safety, which came to be dominated by Maximilien Robespierre. For a twelve-month period, from 1793 to 1794, the Committee of Public Safety took control of France. To save the Republic from its foreign foes, on August 23, 1793, the committee decreed a levy-in-mass, or universal mobilization of the nation:

> Young men will fight, young men are called to conquer. Married men will forge arms, transport military baggage and guns and will prepare food supplies. Women, who at long last are to take their rightful place in the revolution and follow their true destiny, will forget their futile tasks: their delicate hands will work at making clothes for soldiers; they will make tents and they will extend their tender care to shelters where the defenders of the *Patrie* [nation] will receive the help that their wounds require. Children will make lint of old cloth. It is for them that we are fighting: children, those beings destined to gather all the fruits of the revolution, will raise their pure hands toward the skies. And old men, performing their missions again, as of yore, will be guided to the public squares of the cities where they will kindle the courage of young warriors and preach the doctrines of hate for kings and the unity of the Republic.[4]

In less than a year, the French revolutionary government had raised an army of 650,000, and by 1795 it had pushed the allies back across the Rhine and even conquered the Austrian Netherlands.

The French revolutionary army was an important step in the creation of modern **nationalism.** Previously, wars had been fought between governments or ruling dynasties by relatively small armies of professional soldiers. The new French army was the creation of a "people's" government; its wars were now "people's" wars. The entire nation was to be involved in the war. But when dynastic wars became people's wars, warfare increased in ferocity and lack of restraint. The wars of the French revolutionary era opened the door to the total war of the modern world.

Reign of Terror   To meet the domestic crisis, the National Convention and the Committee of Public Safety launched the Reign of Terror. Revolutionary courts were instituted to protect the Republic from its internal enemies. In the course of nine months, 16,000 people were officially killed under the blade of the guillotine—a revolutionary device designed for the quick and efficient separation of heads from bodies.

Revolutionary armies were set up to bring recalcitrant cities and districts back under the control of the National Convention. The Committee of Public Safety decided to make an example of Lyons, which had defied the authority of the National Convention. By April 1794, some 1,880 citizens of Lyons had been executed. When the guillotine proved too slow, cannon fire was used to blow condemned men into open graves. A German observed:

> Whole ranges of houses, always the most handsome, burnt. The churches, convents, and all the dwellings of the former patricians were in ruins. When I came to the guillotine, the blood of those who had been executed a few hours beforehand was still running in the street.... I said to a group of [radicals] that it would be decent to clear away all this human blood. Why should it be cleared? one of them said to me. It's the blood of aristocrats and rebels. The dogs should lick it up.[5]

Equality and Slavery: Revolution in Haiti   Early in the French Revolution, the desire for equality led to a discussion of what to do about slavery. A club called Friends of the Blacks advocated the abolition of slavery, which was achieved in France in September 1791. But French planters in the West Indies, who profited greatly from the use of slaves on their sugar plantations, opposed the abolition of slavery in the French colonies. When the National Convention came to power, the issue was revisited, and on February 4, 1794, guided by ideals of equality, the government abolished slavery in the colonies.

In one French colony, slaves had already rebelled for their freedom. In 1791, black slaves in the French sugar colony of Saint-Domingue (the western third of the island of Hispaniola), inspired by the ideals of the revolution occurring in France, revolted against French plantation owners. Led by Toussaint L'Ouverture (1743–1803), a son of African slaves, more than 100,000 black slaves rose in revolt and seized control of all of Hispaniola. Later, an army sent by Napoleon captured L'Ouverture, who died in captivity in France. But the French soldiers, weakened by disease, soon succumbed to the slave forces. On January 1, 1804, the western part of Hispaniola, now called Haiti, announced its freedom and became the first independent state in Latin America. One of the French revolutionary ideals had triumphed abroad.

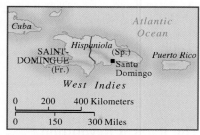

Revolt in Saint-Domingue

Reaction and the Directory

By the summer of 1794, the French had been successful on the battlefield against their foreign foes, making the Terror less necessary. But the Terror continued because Robespierre, who had come to dominate the Committee of Public Safety, became obsessed with purifying the body politic of all the corrupt. Many deputies in the National Convention began to fear that they were not safe while Robespierre was free to act and gathered enough votes to condemn him. Robespierre was guillotined on July 28, 1794.

Meeting of Estates-General	May 5, 1789
Formation of National Assembly	June 17, 1789
Fall of the Bastille	July 14, 1789
Declaration of the Rights of Man and the Citizen	August 26, 1789
Civil Constitution of the Clergy	July 12, 1790
Flight of the king	June 20–21, 1791
Attack on the royal palace	August 10, 1792
Abolition of the monarchy	September 21, 1792
Execution of the king	January 21, 1793
Levy-in-mass	August 23, 1793
Execution of Robespierre	July 28, 1794
Adoption of Constitution of 1795 and the Directory	August 22, 1795

After the death of Robespierre, a reaction set in as more moderate middle-class leaders took control. The Reign of Terror came to a halt, and the National Convention reduced the power of the Committee of Public Safety. In addition, a new constitution was drafted in August 1795 that reflected the desire for a stability that did not sacrifice the ideals of 1789. Five directors—the Directory—acted as the executive authority.

The period of the Revolution under the government of the Directory (1795–1799) was an era of stagnation and corruption. At the same time, the Directory faced political enemies from both the left and the right of the political spectrum. On the right, royalists who wanted to restore the monarchy continued their agitation. On the left, radical hopes of power were revived by continuing economic problems. Battered from both sides, unable to solve the country's economic problems, and still carrying on the wars inherited from the Committee of Public Safety, the Directory increasingly relied on the military to maintain its power. This led to a coup d'état in 1799 in which the popular military general Napoleon Bonaparte seized power.

The Age of Napoleon

Q Focus Question: Which aspects of the French Revolution did Napoleon preserve, and which did he destroy?

Napoleon dominated both French and European history from 1799 to 1815. He was born in Corsica in 1769 shortly after France had annexed the island. The young Napoleon Bonaparte was sent to France to study in one of the new military schools and was a lieutenant when the Revolution broke out in 1789. The Revolution and the European war that followed gave him new opportunities, and Napoleon rose quickly through the ranks. In 1794, at the age of only twenty-five, he was made a brigadier general by the Committee of Public Safety. Two years later, he commanded the French armies in Italy, where he won a series of victories and returned to France as a conquering hero (see the box on p. 456). After a disastrous expedition to Egypt, Napoleon returned to Paris, where he participated in the coup that gave him control of France. He was only thirty years old.

After the coup of 1799, a new form of the Republic—called the Consulate—was proclaimed in which Napoleon, as first consul, controlled the entire executive authority of government. He had overwhelming influence over the legislature, appointed members of the administrative bureaucracy, commanded the army, and conducted foreign affairs. In 1802, Napoleon was made consul for life, and in 1804, he returned France to monarchy when he became Emperor Napoleon I.

Domestic Policies

One of Napoleon's first domestic policies was to establish peace with the oldest and most implacable enemy of the Revolution, the Catholic church. In 1801, Napoleon arranged a concordat with the pope that recognized Catholicism as the religion of a majority of the French people. In return, the pope agreed not to raise the question of the church lands confiscated during the Revolution. As a result of the concordat, the Catholic church was no longer an enemy of the French government.

Napoleon's most enduring domestic achievement was his codification of the laws. Before the Revolution, France had some three hundred local legal systems. During the Revolution, efforts were made to prepare a single code of laws for the entire nation, but it remained for Napoleon to bring the work to completion in the famous Civil Code. This preserved most of the revolutionary gains by recognizing the principle of the equality of all citizens before the law, the abolition of serfdom and feudalism, and religious toleration. Property rights were also protected.

At the same time, the Civil Code strictly curtailed the rights of some people. During the radical phase of the French Revolution, new laws had made divorce an easy process for both husbands and wives and allowed sons and daughters to inherit property equally. Napoleon's Civil Code undid these laws. Divorce was still allowed but was made more difficult for women to obtain. Women

NAPOLEON AND PSYCHOLOGICAL WARFARE

POLITICS & GOVERNMENT

In 1796, at the age of twenty-seven, Napoleon Bonaparte was given command of the French army in Italy, where he won a series of stunning victories. His use of speed, deception, and surprise to overwhelm his opponents is well known. In this selection from a proclamation to his troops in Italy, Napoleon also appears as a master of psychological warfare.

Napoleon Bonaparte, Proclamation to French Troops in Italy (April 26, 1796)

Soldiers:

In a fortnight you have won six victories, taken twenty-one standards [flags of military units], fifty-five pieces of artillery, several strong positions, and conquered the richest part of Piedmont [in northern Italy]; you have captured 15,000 prisoners and killed or wounded more than 10,000 men. . . . You have won battles without cannon, crossed rivers without bridges, made forced marches without shoes, camped without brandy and often without bread. Soldiers of liberty, only republican troops could have endured what you have endured. Soldiers, you have our thanks! The grateful *Patrie* [nation] will owe its prosperity to you. . . .

The two armies which but recently attacked you with audacity are fleeing before you in terror; the wicked men who laughed at your misery and rejoiced at the thought of the triumphs of your enemies are confounded and trembling.

But, soldiers, as yet you have done nothing compared with what remains to be done. . . . Undoubtedly the greatest obstacles have been overcome; but you still have battles to fight, cities to capture, rivers to cross. Is there one among you whose courage is abating? No. . . . All of you are consumed with a desire to extend the glory of the French people; all of you long to humiliate those arrogant kings who dare to contemplate placing us in fetters; all of you desire to dictate a glorious peace, one which will indemnify the *Patrie* for the immense sacrifices it has made; all of you wish to be able to say with pride as you return to your villages, "I was with the victorious army of Italy!"

Q *What themes did Napoleon use to play on the emotions of his troops and inspire them to greater efforts? Do you think Napoleon believed these words? Why or why not?*

© Réunion des Musées Nationaux/Art Resource, NY

The Coronation of Napoleon. In 1804, Napoleon restored monarchy to France when he became Emperor Napoleon I. In the coronation scene painted by Jacques-Louis David, Napoleon is shown crowning his wife, the empress Josephine, while the pope looks on. The painting shows Napoleon's mother seated in the box in the background, even though she was not at the ceremony.

were now "less equal than men" in other ways as well. When they married, their property came under the control of their husbands.

Napoleon also developed a powerful, centralized administrative machine and worked hard to develop a bureaucracy of capable officials. Early on, the regime showed that it cared little whether the expertise of officials had been acquired in royal or revolutionary bureaucracies. Promotion, whether in civil or military offices, was to be based not on rank or birth but on ability only. This principle of a government career open to talent was, of course, what many bourgeois had wanted before the Revolution.

In his domestic policies, then, Napoleon both destroyed and preserved aspects of the Revolution. Although equality was preserved in the law code and the opening of careers to talent, the creation of a new aristocracy, the strong protection accorded to property rights, and the use of conscription for the military make it clear that much equality had been lost. Liberty was replaced by an initially benevolent despotism that grew increasingly arbitrary. Napoleon shut down sixty of France's seventy-three newspapers and insisted that all manuscripts be subjected to government scrutiny before they were published. Even the mail was opened by government police.

Napoleon's Empire

When Napoleon became consul in 1799, France was at war with a second European coalition of Russia, Great Britain, and Austria. Napoleon realized the need for a pause and made a peace treaty in 1802. But in 1803 war was renewed with Britain, which was soon joined by Austria, Russia, and Prussia in the Third Coalition. In a series of battles from 1805 to 1807, Napoleon's Grand Army defeated the Austrian, Prussian, and Russian armies, giving Napoleon the opportunity to create a new European order.

The Grand Empire From 1807 to 1812, Napoleon was the master of Europe. His Grand Empire was composed of three major parts: the French Empire, dependent states, and allied states (see Map 18.3). Dependent states were kingdoms under the rule of Napoleon's relatives; these came to include Spain, the Netherlands, the kingdom of Italy, the Swiss Republic, the Grand Duchy of Warsaw, and the Confederation of the Rhine (a union of all German states except Austria and Prussia). Allied states were those defeated by Napoleon and forced to join his struggle against Britain; these included Prussia, Austria, Russia, and Sweden.

Within his empire, Napoleon sought acceptance of certain revolutionary principles, including legal equality, religious toleration, and economic freedom. In the inner core and dependent states of his Grand Empire, Napoleon tried to destroy the old order. Nobility and clergy everywhere in these states lost their special privileges. He decreed equality of opportunity with offices open to talent, equality before the law, and religious toleration. This spread of French revolutionary principles was an important factor in the development of liberal traditions in these countries.

Napoleon hoped that his Grand Empire would last for centuries, but it collapsed almost as rapidly as it had been formed. As long as Britain ruled the waves, it was not subject to military attack. Napoleon hoped to invade Britain, but he could not overcome the British navy's decisive defeat of a combined French-Spanish fleet at Trafalgar in 1805. To defeat Britain, Napoleon turned to his **Continental System.** An alliance put into effect between 1806 and 1808, it attempted to prevent British goods from reaching the European continent in order to weaken Britain economically and destroy its capacity to wage war. But the Continental System failed. Allied states resented it; some began to cheat and others to resist.

Napoleon also encountered new sources of opposition. His conquests made the French hated oppressors and aroused the patriotism of the conquered people. A Spanish uprising against Napoleon's rule, aided by British support, kept a French force of 200,000 pinned down for years.

The Fall of Napoleon The beginning of Napoleon's downfall came in 1812 with his invasion of Russia. The refusal of the Russians to remain in the Continental System left Napoleon with little choice. Although aware of the risks in invading such a huge country, he also knew that if the Russians were allowed to challenge the Continental System unopposed, others would soon follow suit. In June 1812, he led his Grand Army of more than 600,000 men into Russia. Napoleon's hopes for victory depended on quickly defeating the Russian armies, but the Russian forces retreated and refused to give battle, torching their own villages and countryside to keep Napoleon's army from finding food. When the Russians did stop to fight at Borodino, Napoleon's forces won an indecisive and costly victory. When the remaining troops of the Grand Army arrived in Moscow, they found the city ablaze. Lacking food and supplies, Napoleon abandoned Moscow late in October and made a retreat across Russia in terrible winter conditions. Only 40,000 of the original 600,000 men managed to arrive back in Poland in January 1813.

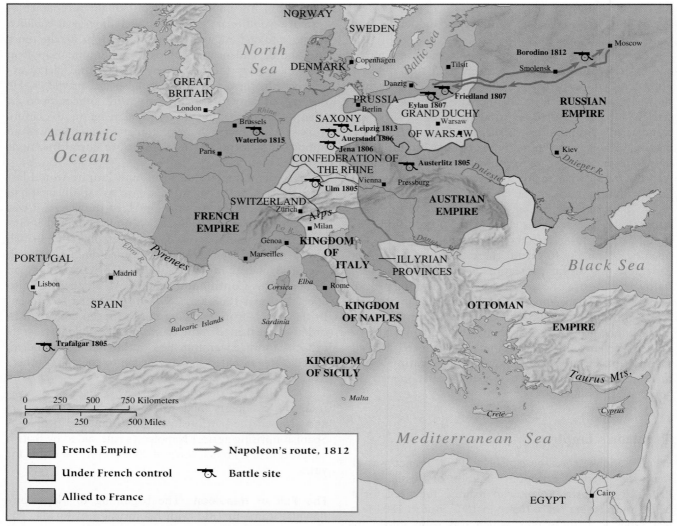

MAP 18.3 Napoleon's Grand Empire. Napoleon's Grand Army won a series of victories against Britain, Austria, Prussia, and Russia that gave the French emperor full or partial control over much of Europe by 1807.
Q On the Continent, what was the overall relationship between distance from France and degree of French control, and how can you account for this?

This military disaster led other European states to rise up and attack the crippled French army. Paris was captured in March 1814, and Napoleon was sent into exile on the island of Elba, off the coast of Italy. Meanwhile, the Bourbon monarchy was restored in the person of Louis XVIII, the count of Provence, brother of the executed king. (Louis XVII, son of Louis XVI, had died in prison at age ten.) Napoleon, bored on Elba, slipped back into France. When troops were sent to capture him, Napoleon opened his coat and addressed them: "Soldiers of the 5th regiment, I am your Emperor.... If there is a man among you would kill his Emperor, here I am!" No one fired a shot. Shouting "*Vive*

l'Empereur! Vive l'Empereur!" the troops went over to his side, and Napoleon entered Paris in triumph on March 20, 1815.

The powers that had defeated him pledged once more to fight him. Having decided to strike first at his enemies, Napoleon raised yet another army and moved to attack the allied forces stationed in what is now Belgium. At Waterloo on June 18, Napoleon met a combined British and Prussian army under the duke of Wellington and suffered a bloody defeat. This time, the victorious allies exiled him to Saint Helena, a small, forsaken island in the South Atlantic, off the coast of Africa. Only Napoleon's memory continued to haunt French political life.

TIMELINE

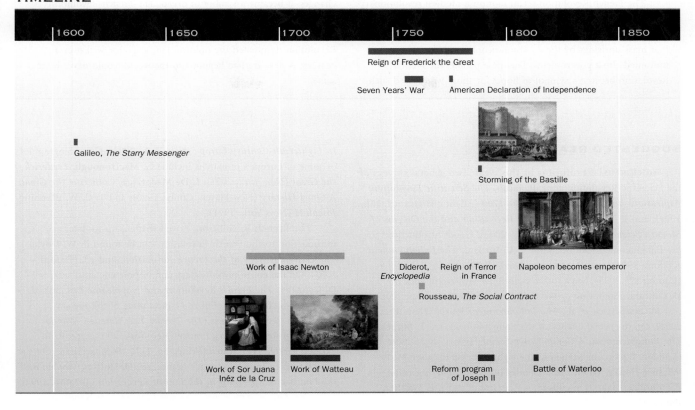

| | 1600 | 1650 | 1700 | 1750 | 1800 | 1850 |

Reign of Frederick the Great

Seven Years' War   American Declaration of Independence

Galileo, *The Starry Messenger*

Storming of the Bastille

Work of Isaac Newton   Diderot, *Encyclopedia*   Reign of Terror in France   Napoleon becomes emperor

Rousseau, *The Social Contract*

Work of Sor Juana Inéz de la Cruz   Work of Watteau   Reform program of Joseph II   Battle of Waterloo

CONCLUSION

THE SCIENTIFIC REVOLUTION was a major turning point in modern civilization. With a new conception of the universe came a new conception of humankind and the belief that by using reason alone people could understand and dominate the world of nature. In combination with the eighteenth-century Enlightenment, the Scientific Revolution gave the West an intellectual boost that contributed to the increased confidence of Western civilization. Europeans—with their strong governments, prosperous economies, and strengthened military forces—began to dominate other parts of the world, leading to a growing belief in the superiority of their civilization.

Everywhere in Europe at the beginning of the eighteenth century, the old order remained strong. Monarchs sought to enlarge their bureaucracies to raise taxes to support the large standing armies that had originated in the seventeenth century. The existence of five great powers, with two of them (France and Great Britain) embattled in the East and in the Western Hemisphere, ushered in a new scale of conflict; the Seven Years' War can legitimately be viewed as the first world war. Throughout Europe, increased demands for taxes to support these conflicts led to attacks on the privileged orders and a desire for change not met by the ruling monarchs. The inability of that old order to deal meaningfully with this desire for change led to a revolutionary outburst at the end of the eighteenth century that brought the old order to an end.

The revolutionary era of the late eighteenth century was a time of dramatic political transformations. Revolutionary upheavals, beginning in North America and continuing in France, spurred movements for political liberty and equality. The documents promulgated by these revolutions, the Declaration of Independence and the Declaration of the Rights of Man and the Citizen, embodied the fundamental ideas of the Enlightenment and created a liberal political agenda based on a belief in popular sovereignty—the people as the source of political power—and the principles of liberty and equality. Liberty meant, in theory, freedom from arbitrary power as well as the freedom to think, write, and worship as one chose. Equality meant equality in rights and equality of opportunity based on talent rather than wealth or status at birth. In practice, equality remained limited; property owners had greater opportunities for voting and office holding, and women were still not treated as the equals of men.

The French Revolution set in motion a modern revolutionary concept. No one had foreseen or consciously planned the upheaval that began in 1789, but thereafter, radicals and revolutionaries knew that mass uprisings by the common people could overthrow unwanted elitist governments. For these people, the French Revolution became a symbol of hope; for those who feared such changes, it became a symbol of dread. The French Revolution became the classic political and social model for revolution. At the same time, the liberal and national political ideals created by the Revolution dominated the political landscape for well over a century. A new era had begun, and the world would never be the same.

SUGGESTED READING

Intellectual Revolution in the West Two general surveys of the Scientific Revolution are **J. R. Jacob,** *The Scientific Revolution: Aspirations and Achievements, 1500–1700* (Atlantic Highlands, N.J., 1998), and **J. Henry,** *The Scientific Revolution and the Origins of Modern Science,* 2nd ed. (New York, 2002). Good introductions to the Enlightenment can be found in **U. Im Hof,** *The Enlightenment* (Oxford, 1994), and **D. Outram,** *The Enlightenment,* 2nd ed. (Cambridge, 2005). See also the beautifully illustrated work by **D. Outram,** *Panorama of the Enlightenment* (Los Angeles, 2006), and **M. Fitzpatrick et al.,** *The Enlightenment World* (New York, 2004). On the social history of the Enlightenment, see **T. Munck,** *The Enlightenment: A Comparative Social History, 1721–1794* (London, 2000). On women in the eighteenth century, see **M. E. Wiesner-Hanks,** *Women and Gender in Early Modern Europe* (Cambridge, 2000). On culture, see **E. Gesine** and **J. F. Walther,** *Rococo* (New York, 2007).

The Social Order On the European nobility in the eighteenth century, see **J. Dewald,** *The European Nobility, 1400–1800,* 2nd ed. (Cambridge, 2004). On European cities, see **J. de Vries,** *European Urbanization, 1500–1800* (Cambridge, Mass., 1984).

Colonial Empires For a brief survey of Latin America, see **E. B. Burns** and **J. A. Charlip,** *Latin America: An Interpretive History,* 8th ed. (Upper Saddle River, N.J., 2007). A more detailed work on colonial Latin American history is **J. Lockhardt** and **S. B. Schwartz,** *Early Latin America: A History of Colonial Spanish America and Brazil* (New York, 1983). A history of the revolutionary era in America can be found in **S. Conway,** *The War of American Independence, 1775–1783* (New York, 1995).

Enlightened Absolutism and Global Conflict On enlightened absolutism, see **D. Beales,** *Enlightenment and Reform in Eighteenth-Century Europe* (New York, 2005). Good biographies of some of Europe's monarchs include **G. MacDonough,** *Frederick the Great* (New York, 2001); **I. De Madariaga,** *Catherine the Great: A Short History* (New Haven, Conn., 1990); and **T. C. W. Blanning,** *Joseph II* (New York, 1994).

The French Revolution A well-written, up-to-date introduction to the French Revolution can be found in **W. Doyle,** *The Oxford History of the French Revolution,* 2nd ed. (Oxford, 2003). On the entire revolutionary and Napoleonic eras, see **O. Connelly,** *The French Revolution and Napoleonic Era,* 3rd ed. (Fort Worth, Tex., 2000). On the radical stage of the French Revolution, see **D. Andress,** *The Terror: The Merciless War for Freedom in Revolutionary France* (New York, 2005), and **R. R. Palmer,** *Twelve Who Ruled* (Princeton, N.J., 1965), a classic. On the role of women in revolutionary France, see **O. Hufton,** *Women and the Limits of Citizenship in the French Revolution* (Toronto, 1992).

The Age of Napoleon The best biography of Napoleon is **S. Englund,** *Napoleon: A Political Life* (New York, 2004). Also valuable are **G. J. Ellis,** *Napoleon* (New York, 1997); **M. Lyons,** *Napoleon Bonaparte and the Legacy of the French Revolution* (New York, 1994); and the massive biographies by **F. J. McLynn,** *Napoleon: A Biography* (London, 1997), and **A. Schom,** *Napoleon Bonaparte* (New York, 1997).

WORLD HISTORY RESOURCES

Visit the website for *The Essential World History* **to access study aids such as Flashcards, Critical Thinking Exercises, and Chapter Quizzes:**
www.cengage.com/history/duikspiel/essentialworld6e

In what ways were the American Revolution, the French Revolution, and the seventeenth-century English revolutions alike? In what ways were they different?

In thinking about these questions, begin by breaking them down into the components shown below. A discussion of the significance of each component should appear in your answer.

POLITICS AND GOVERNMENT Review the English Bill of Rights (below and on p. 380) and the French Declaration of the Rights of Man and the Citizen (at the right and on p. 453). What similarities and differences do you see in these two documents? How are these documents related to the American Declaration of Independence and the U.S. Constitution including the Bill of Rights? To what extent did each document reflect Enlightenment ideas? How did all of these documents reflect the concerns and ideals of those who led the revolutions? To what degree did these documents influence each other?

How might the spread of the ideas of the Scientific Revolution and the Enlightenment help to explain some of the differences between the English Bill of Rights of 1689 and the French and American declarations? To what extent did the Scientific Revolution and the Enlightenment create a new set of ideals that influenced both the American and the French revolutions? How did those ideals differ from those of the seventeenth-century English revolutions?

THE BILL OF RIGHTS

Whereas the said late King James II having abdicated the government, and the throne being thereby vacant, his Highness the prince of Orange (whom it hath pleased Almighty God to make the glorious instrument of delivering this kingdom from popery and arbitrary power) did (by the device of the lords spiritual and temporal, and diverse principal persons of the Commons) cause letters to be written to the lords spiritual and temporal, being Protestants, and other letters to the several counties, cities, universities, boroughs, and Cinque Ports, for the choosing of such persons to represent them, as were of right to be sent to parliament, to meet and sit at Westminster upon the two and twentieth day of January, in this year 1689, in order to such an establishment as that their religion, laws, and liberties might not again be in danger of being subverted; upon which letters elections have been accordingly made.

And thereupon the said lords spiritual and temporal and Commons, pursuant to their respective letters and elections, being now assembled in a full and free representation of this nation, taking into their most serious consideration the best means for attaining the ends aforesaid, do in the first place (as their ancestors in like case have usually done), for the vindication and assertion of their ancient rights and liberties, declare:

1. That the pretended power of suspending laws, or the execution of laws, by regal authority, without consent of parliament is illegal.
2. That the pretended power of dispensing with the laws, or the execution of law by regal authority, as it hath been assumed and exercised of late, is illegal.
3. That the commission for erecting the late court of commissioners for ecclesiastical causes, and all other commissions and courts of like nature, are illegal and pernicious.
4. That levying money for or to the use of the crown by pretense of prerogative, without grant of parliament, for longer time or in other manner than the same is or shall be granted, is illegal.
5. That it is the right of the subjects to petition the king, and all commitments and prosecutions for such petitioning are illegal.
6. That the raising or keeping a standing army within the kingdom in time of peace, unless it be with consent of parliament, is against law.
7. That the subjects which are Protestants may have arms for their defense suitable to their conditions, and as allowed by law.
8. That election of members of parliament ought to be free.
9. That the freedom of speech, and debates or proceedings in parliament, ought not to be impeached or questioned in any court or place out of parliament.
10. That excessive bail ought not to be required, nor excessive fines imposed, nor cruel and unusual punishments inflicted.
11. That jurors ought to be duly impaneled and returned, and jurors which pass upon men in trials for high treason ought to be freeholders.
12. That all grants and promises of fines and forfeitures of particular persons before conviction are illegal and void.
13. And that for redress of all grievances, and for the amending, strengthening, and preserving of the laws, parliament ought to be held frequently.

DECLARATION OF THE RIGHTS OF MAN AND THE CITIZEN

The representatives of the French people, organized as a national assembly, considering that ignorance, neglect, and scorn of the rights of man are the sole causes of public misfortunes and of corruption of governments, have resolved to display in a solemn declaration the natural, inalienable, and sacred rights of man, so that this declaration, constantly in the presence of all members of society, will continually remind them of their rights and their duties....Consequently, the National Assembly recognizes and declares, in the presence and under the auspices of the Supreme Being, the following rights of man and citizen:

1. Men are born and remain free and equal in rights; social distinctions can be established only for the common benefit.
2. The aim of every political association is the conservation of the natural and imprescriptible rights of man; these rights are liberty, property, security, and resistance to oppression.
3. The source of all sovereignty is located in essence in the nation; no body, no individual can exercise authority which does not emanate from it expressly.
4. Liberty consists in being able to do anything that does not harm another person....
6. The law is the expression of the general will; all citizens have the right to concur personally or through their representatives in its formation; it must be the same for all, whether it protects or punishes. All citizens being equal in its eyes are equally admissible to all honors, positions, and public employments, according to their capabilities and without other distinctions than those of their virtues and talents.
7. No man can be accused, arrested, or detained except in cases determined by the law, and according to the forms which it has prescribed....
10. No one may be disturbed because of his opinions, even religious, provided that their public demonstration does not disturb the public order established by law.
11. The free communication of thoughts and opinions is one of the most precious rights of man: every citizen can therefore freely speak, write, and print....
14. Citizens have the right to determine for themselves or through their representatives the need for taxation of the public, to consent to it freely, to investigate its use, and to determine its rate, basis, collection, and duration....
16. Any society in which guarantees of rights are not assured nor the separation of powers determined has no constitution.

MODERN PATTERNS
OF WORLD HISTORY (1800–1945)

THE PERIOD OF WORLD HISTORY from 1800 to 1945 was characterized by three major developments: the growth of industrialization, Western domination of the world, and the rise of nationalism. The three developments were, of course, interconnected. The Industrial Revolution became one of the major forces of change in the nineteenth century as it led Western civilization into the industrial era that has characterized the modern world. Beginning in Britain, it spread to the Continent and the Western Hemisphere in the course of the nineteenth century. At the same time, the Industrial Revolution created the technological means, including new weapons, by which the West achieved domination of much of the rest of the world by the end of the nineteenth century. Moreover, the existence of competitive European nation-states after 1870 was undoubtedly a major determinant in leading European states to embark on their intense scramble for overseas territory.

The advent of the industrial age had a number of lasting consequences for the world at large. On the one hand, the material wealth of the nations that successfully passed through the process increased significantly. In many cases, the creation of advanced industrial societies strengthened democratic institutions and led to a higher standard of living for the majority of the population. On the other hand, not all the consequences of the Industrial Revolution were beneficial. In the industrializing societies themselves, rapid economic change often led to widening disparities in the distribution of wealth and, with the decline in pervasiveness of religious belief, a sense of rootlessness and alienation among much of the population.

A second development that had a major impact on the era was the rise of nationalism. Like the Industrial Revolution, the idea of nationalism originated in eighteenth-century Europe, where it was a product of the secularization of the age and the experience of the French revolutionary and Napoleonic eras. Although the concept provided the basis for a new sense of community and the rise of the modern nation-state, it also gave birth to ethnic tensions and hatreds that resulted in bitter disputes and civil strife and contributed to the competition that eventually erupted into world war.

Industrialization and the rise of national consciousness also transformed the nature of war itself. New weapons of mass destruction created the potential for a new kind of warfare that reached beyond the battlefield into the very heartland of the enemy's territory, while the

concept of nationalism transformed war from the sport of kings to a matter of national honor and commitment. Since the French Revolution, governments had relied on mass conscription to defend the national cause, while their engines of destruction reached far into enemy territory to destroy the industrial base and undermine the will to fight. This trend was amply demonstrated in the two world wars of the twentieth century.

In the end, then, industrial power and the driving force of nationalism, the very factors that had created the conditions for European global dominance, contained the seeds for the decline of that dominance. These seeds germinated during the 1930s, when the Great Depression sharpened international competition and mutual antagonism, and then sprouted in the ensuing conflict, which for the first time spanned the entire globe. By the time World War II came to an end, the once powerful countries of Europe were exhausted, leaving the door ajar for the emergence of two new global superpowers, the United States and the Soviet Union, and for the collapse of the Europeans' colonial empires.

Europeans had begun to explore the world in the fifteenth century, but even as late as 1870, they had not yet completely penetrated North America, South America, Australia, or most of Africa. In Asia and Africa, with few exceptions, the Western presence was limited to trading posts. Between 1870 and 1914, Western civilization expanded into the rest of the Americas and Australia, while the bulk of Africa and Asia was divided into European colonies or spheres of influence. Two major events explain this remarkable expansion: the migration of many

Europeans to other parts of the world due to population growth and the revival of imperialism, which was made possible by the West's technological advances. Beginning in the 1880s, European states began an intense scramble for overseas territory. This revival of imperialism—the "new imperialism," some have called it—led Europeans to carve up Asia and Africa.

What was the overall economic effect of imperialism on the subject peoples? For most of the population in colonial areas, Western domination was rarely beneficial and often destructive. Although a limited number of merchants, large landowners, and traditional hereditary elites undoubtedly prospered under the umbrella of the expanding imperialistic economic order, the majority of colonial peoples, urban and rural alike, probably suffered considerable hardship as a result of the policies adopted by their foreign rulers.

Some historians point out, however, that for all the inequities of the colonial system, there was a positive side to the experience as well. The expansion of markets and the beginnings of a modern transportation and communications network, while bringing few immediate benefits to the colonial peoples, offered considerable promise for future economic growth. At the same time, colonial peoples soon learned the power of nationalism, and in the twentieth century, nationalism would become a powerful force in the rest of the world as nationalist revolutions moved through Asia, Africa, and the Middle East. Moreover, the exhaustive struggles of two world wars sapped the power of the European states, and the colonial powers no longer had the energy or the wealth to maintain their colonial empires after World War II. ❀

CHAPTER 19

THE BEGINNINGS OF MODERNIZATION: INDUSTRIALIZATION AND NATIONALISM IN THE NINETEENTH CENTURY

A meeting of the Congress of Vienna

© Scala/Art Resource, NY

IN SEPTEMBER 1814, hundreds of foreigners began to converge on Vienna, the capital city of the Austrian Empire. Many were members of European royalty—kings, archdukes, princes, and their wives—accompanied by their diplomatic advisers and scores of servants. Their congenial host was the Austrian emperor, Francis I, who never tired of regaling Vienna's guests with concerts, glittering balls, sumptuous feasts, and innumerable hunting parties. One participant remembered, "Eating, fireworks, public illuminations. For eight or ten days, I haven't been able to work at all. What a life!" Of course, not every waking hour was spent in pleasure during this gathering of notables, known to history as the Congress of Vienna. The guests were also representatives of all the states that had fought Napoleon, and their real business was to arrange a final peace settlement after almost a decade of war. On June 8, 1815, they finally completed their task.

The forces of upheaval unleashed during the French revolutionary and Napoleonic wars were temporarily quieted in 1815 as rulers sought to restore stability by reestablishing much of the old order to a Europe ravaged by war. But the Western world had been changed, and it would not readily go back to the old system. New ideologies of change, especially liberalism and nationalism, products of the upheaval initiated in France, had become too powerful to be contained.

The forces of change called forth revolts that periodically shook the West and culminated in a spate of revolutions in 1848. Some of the revolutions and revolutionaries were successful; most were not. And yet by 1870, many of the goals sought by the liberals and nationalists during the first half of the nineteenth century seemed to have been achieved. National unity became a reality in Italy and Germany, and many Western states developed parliamentary features. Between 1870 and 1914, these newly constituted states experienced a time of great tension. Europeans engaged in a race for colonies that intensified existing antagonisms among the European states, while the creation of huge conscript armies and enormous military establishments served to heighten tensions among the major powers.

During the late eighteenth and early nineteenth centuries, another revolution—an industrial one—transformed the economic and social structure of Europe and spawned the industrial era that has characterized modern world history. ❀

The Industrial Revolution and Its Impact

Q **Focus Question:** What were the basic features of the new industrial system created by the Industrial Revolution, and what effects did the new system have on urban life, social classes, family life, and standards of living?

During the Industrial Revolution, Europe shifted from an economy based on agriculture and handicrafts to an economy based on manufacturing by machines and automated factories. The Industrial Revolution triggered an enormous leap in industrial production that relied largely on coal and steam, which replaced wind and water as new sources of energy and power to drive laborsaving machines. In turn, these machines called for new ways of organizing human labor to maximize the benefits and profits from the new machines. As factories replaced shop and home workrooms, large numbers of people moved from the countryside to the cities to work in the new factories. The creation of a wealthy industrial middle class and a huge industrial working class (or proletariat) substantially transformed traditional social relationships.

The Industrial Revolution in Great Britain

The Industrial Revolution began in Britain in the 1780s. Improvements in agricultural practices in the eighteenth century led to a significant increase in food production. British agriculture could now feed more people at lower prices with less labor; even ordinary British families did not have to use most of their income to buy food, giving them the wherewithal to purchase manufactured goods. At the same time, rapid population growth in the second half of the eighteenth century provided a pool of surplus labor for the new factories of the emerging British industry.

A crucial factor in Britain's successful industrialization was the ability to produce cheaply the articles in greatest demand. The traditional methods of cottage industry could not keep up with the growing demand for cotton clothes throughout Britain and its vast colonial empire. Faced with this problem, British cloth manufacturers sought and accepted the new methods of manufacturing that a series of inventions provided. In so doing, these individuals ignited the Industrial Revolution.

Changes in Textile Production The invention of the flying shuttle enabled weavers to weave faster on a loom, thereby doubling their output. This created shortages of yarn until James Hargreaves's spinning jenny, perfected by 1768, allowed spinners to produce yarn in greater quantities. Edmund Cartwright's loom, powered by water and invented in 1787, allowed the weaving of cloth to catch up with the spinning of yarn. It was now more efficient to bring workers to the machines and organize their labor collectively in factories located next to rivers and streams, the sources of power for these early machines.

The invention of the steam engine pushed the cotton industry to even greater heights of productivity. In the 1760s, a Scottish engineer, James Watt (1736–1819), built an engine powered by steam that could pump water from mines three times as quickly as previous engines. In 1782, Watt developed a rotary engine that could turn a shaft and thus drive machinery. Steam power could now be applied to spinning and weaving cotton, and before long, cotton mills using steam engines were multiplying across Britain. Fired by coal, these steam engines could be located anywhere.

The boost given to cotton textile production by these technological changes was readily apparent. In 1760, Britain had imported 2.5 million pounds of raw cotton, which was farmed out to cottage industries. In 1787, the British imported 22 million pounds of cotton; most of it was spun on machines, some powered by water in large mills. By 1840, some 366 million pounds of cotton—now Britain's most important product in value—were being imported. By this time, British cotton goods were sold everywhere in the world.

Other Technological Changes The British iron industry was also radically transformed during the Industrial

Revolution. A better quality of iron came into being in the 1780s when Henry Cort developed a system called puddling, in which coke, derived from coal, was used to burn away impurities in pig iron (crude iron) and produce an iron of high quality. A boom then ensued in the British iron industry. By 1852, Britain produced almost 3 million tons of iron annually, more than the rest of the world combined.

The new high-quality wrought iron was in turn used to build new machines and ultimately new industries. In 1804, Richard Trevithick pioneered the first steam-powered locomotive on an industrial rail line in southern Wales. It pulled 10 tons of ore and seventy people at 5 miles per hour. Better locomotives soon followed. Engines built by George Stephenson and his son proved superior, and it was Stephenson's *Rocket* that was used on the first public railway line, which opened in 1830, extending 32 miles from Liverpool to Manchester. *Rocket* sped along at 16 miles per hour. Within twenty years, locomotives were traveling at 50 miles per hour. By 1840, Britain had almost 6,000 miles of railroads.

The railroad was an important contributor to the success and maturing of the Industrial Revolution. Railway construction created new job opportunities, especially for farm laborers and peasants who had long been accustomed to finding work outside their local villages. Perhaps most important, the proliferation of a cheaper and faster means of transportation had a ripple effect on the growth of the industrial economy. As the prices of goods fell, markets grew larger; increased sales meant more factories and more machinery, thereby reinforcing the self-sustaining aspect of the Industrial Revolution, a fundamental break with the traditional European economy. Continuous, self-sustaining economic growth came to be accepted as a fundamental characteristic of the new economy.

The Industrial Factory Another visible symbol of the Industrial Revolution was the factory (see the comparative illustration at the right). From its beginning, the factory created a new labor system. Factory owners wanted to use their new machines constantly. Workers were therefore obliged to work regular hours and in shifts to keep the machines producing at a steady rate. Early factory workers,

© CORBIS

© The Art Archive/Laurie Platt Winfrey

COMPARATIVE ILLUSTRATION

Textile Factories, West and East. The development of the factory changed the relationship between workers and employers as workers had to adjust to a new system of discipline that required them to work regular hours under close supervision. At the top is an 1851 illustration that shows women working in a British cotton factory. The factory system came later to the rest of the world than it did in Britain. Shown at the bottom is one of the earliest industrial factories in Japan, the Tomioka silk factory, built in the 1870s. Note that although women are doing the work in both factories, the managers are men.
Q What do you think were the major differences and similarities between British and Japanese factories (see also the box on p. 470)?

however, came from rural areas, where they were used to a different pace of life. Peasant farmers worked hard, especially at harvest time, but they were also used to periods of inactivity.

Early factory owners therefore had to institute a system of work discipline that required employees to became accustomed to working regular hours and doing the same work over and over. Of course, such work was boring, and factory owners resorted to tough methods to accomplish their goals. They issued minute and detailed factory regulations. Adult workers were fined for a wide variety of minor infractions, such as being a few minutes late for work, and dismissed for more serious misdoings, especially drunkenness, which set a bad example for younger workers and also courted disaster in the midst of dangerous machinery. Employers found that dismissals and fines worked well for adult employees; in a time when great population growth had produced large masses of unskilled labor, dismissal meant disaster. Children were less likely to understand the implications of dismissal, so they were sometimes disciplined more directly—often by beating. As the nineteenth century progressed, the second and third generations of workers came to view a regular workweek as a natural way of life.

By the mid-nineteenth century, Great Britain had become the world's first and richest industrial nation. Britain was the "workshop, banker, and trader of the world." It produced one-half of the world's coal and manufactured goods; in 1850, its cotton industry alone was equal in size to the industries of all other European countries combined.

The Spread of Industrialization

From Great Britain, industrialization spread to the continental countries of Europe and the United States at different times and speeds during the nineteenth century. First to be industrialized on the Continent were Belgium, France, and the German states. Their governments were especially active in encouraging the development of industrialization by, among other things, setting up technical schools to train engineers and mechanics and providing funds to build roads, canals, and railroads. By 1850, a network of iron rails had spread across Europe.

The Industrial Revolution also transformed the new nation in North America, the United States. In 1800, six out of every seven American workers were farmers, and there were no cities with more than 100,000 people. By 1860, however, the population had sextupled to 30 million people (larger than Great Britain), nine U.S. cities had populations over 100,000, and only 50 percent of American workers were farmers.

In sharp contrast to Britain, the United States was a large country. Thousands of miles of roads and canals were built linking east and west. The steamboat facilitated transportation on the Great Lakes, Atlantic coastal waters, and rivers. Most important in the development of an American transportation system was the railroad. Beginning with 100 miles in 1830, by 1860 there were more than 27,000 miles of railroad track covering the United States. This transportation revolution turned the United States into a single massive market for the manufactured goods of the Northeast, the early center of American industrialization.

Limiting the Spread of Industrialization to the Rest of the World

Before 1870, the industrialization that was transforming western and central Europe and the United States did not extend in any significant way to the rest of the world (see the comparative essay "The Industrial Revolution" on p. 468). Even in eastern Europe, industrialization lagged far behind. Russia, for example, was still largely rural and agricultural, ruled by an autocratic regime that preferred to keep the peasants in serfdom.

In other parts of the world where they had established control (see Chapter 21), newly industrialized European states pursued a deliberate policy of preventing the growth of mechanized industry. The experience of India is a good example. In the eighteenth century, India had become one of the world's greatest exporters of cotton cloth produced by hand labor. In the first half of the nineteenth century, much of India fell under the control of the British East India Company. With British control came inexpensive British factory-produced textiles, and soon thousands of Indian spinners and handloom weavers were unemployed. British policy encouraged Indians to export their raw materials while buying British-made goods.

The Social Impact of the Industrial Revolution

Eventually, the Industrial Revolution revolutionized the social life of Europe and the world. This change was already evident in the first half of the nineteenth century in the growth of cities and the emergence of new social classes.

Population Growth and Urbanization Population increases had already begun in the eighteenth century, but they became dramatic in the nineteenth century. In 1750, the total European population stood at an estimated 140 million; by 1850, it had almost doubled to 266 million. The key to the expansion of population was the decline in death rates throughout Europe. Wars and major epidemic diseases, such as plague and smallpox, became less frequent, which led to a drop in the number of deaths. Thanks to the increase in the food supply, more people were better fed and more resistant to disease.

Throughout Europe, cities and towns grew dramatically in the first half of the nineteenth century, a

COMPARATIVE ESSAY
THE INDUSTRIAL REVOLUTION

Why some societies were able to embark on the road to industrialization during the nineteenth century and others were not has long been debated. Some historians have found an answer in the cultural characteristics of individual societies, such as the Protestant work ethic in parts of Europe or the tradition of social discipline and class hierarchy in Japan. Others have placed more emphasis on practical reasons. To the historian Peter Stearns, for example, the availability of capital, natural resources, a network of trade relations, and navigable rivers all helped stimulate industrial growth in nineteenth-century Britain. By contrast, the lack of an urban market for agricultural goods (which reduced landowners' incentives to introduce mechanized farming) is sometimes cited as a reason for China's failure to set out on its own path toward industrialization.

The Steam Engine. Pictured here is an early steam engine developed by James Watt. The steam engine revolutionized the production of cotton goods and helped usher in the factory system.

To some observers, the ability of western European countries to exploit the wealth and resources of their colonies in Asia, Africa, and Latin America was crucial to their success in achieving industrial prowess. In their view, the Age of Exploration led to the creation of a new "world system" characterized by the emergence of global trade networks, propelled by the rising force of European capitalism in pursuit of precious metals, markets, and cheap raw materials.

These views are not mutually exclusive. In his recent book *The Great Divergence: China, Europe, and the Making of the Modern World Economy*, Kenneth Pomeranz argued that coal resources and access to the cheap raw materials of the Americas were both assets for Great Britain as it became the first to enter the industrial age.

Clearly, there is no single answer to this controversy. Whatever the case, the advent of the industrial age had a number of lasting consequences for the world at large. On the one hand, the material wealth of the nations that successfully passed through the process increased significantly. In many cases, the creation of advanced industrial societies strengthened democratic institutions and led to a higher standard of living for the majority of the population. It also helped reduce class barriers and bring about the emancipation of women from many of the legal and social restrictions that had characterized the previous era.

On the other hand, not all the consequences of the Industrial Revolution were beneficial. In the industrializing societies themselves, rapid economic change often led to widening disparities in the distribution of wealth and a sense of rootlessness and alienation among much of the population. Although some societies were able to manage these problems with a degree of success, others experienced a breakdown of social values and widespread political instability. In the meantime, the transformation of Europe into a giant factory sucking up raw materials and spewing manufactured goods out to the entire world had a wrenching impact on traditional societies whose own economic, social, and cultural foundations were forever changed by absorption into the new world order.

Q *What were the positive and negative consequences of the Industrial Revolution?*

---

phenomenon related to industrialization. By 1850, especially in Great Britain and Belgium, cities were rapidly becoming home to many industries. With the steam engine, factory owners could locate their manufacturing plants in urban centers where they had ready access to transportation facilities and large numbers of new arrivals from the country looking for work.

In 1800, Great Britain had one major city, London, with a population of one million, and six cities with populations between 50,000 and 100,000. Fifty years later, London's population had swelled to 2,363,000, and there were nine cities with populations over 100,000 and eighteen cities with populations between 50,000 and 100,000. More than 50 percent of the British population lived in towns and cities by 1850. Urban populations also grew on the Continent, but less dramatically.

The dramatic growth of cities in the first half of the nineteenth century produced miserable living conditions for many of the inhabitants. Located in the center of most industrial towns were the row houses of the industrial workers. Rooms were not large and were frequently overcrowded, as a government report of 1838 in Britain revealed: "There were 63 families where there were at least five persons to one bed; and there were some in which even six were packed in one bed, lying at the top and bottom—children and adults."[1]

Sanitary conditions in these towns were appalling; sewers and open drains were common on city streets: "In the centre of this street is a gutter, into which the refuse of animal and vegetable matters of all kinds, the dirty water from the washing of clothes and of the houses, are all poured, and there they stagnate and putrefy."[2] Unable to deal with human excrement, cities in the early industrial era smelled horrible and were extraordinarily unhealthy.

New Social Classes: The Industrial Middle Class   The rise of industrial capitalism produced a new middle-class group. The bourgeoisie or middle class was not new; it had existed since the emergence of cities in the Middle Ages. Originally, the bourgeois was a burgher or town dweller, active as a merchant, official, artisan, lawyer, or man of letters. As wealthy townspeople bought land, the original meaning of the word *bourgeois* became lost, and the term came to include people involved in commerce, industry, and banking as well as professionals such as teachers, physicians, and government officials.

The new industrial middle class was made up of the people who constructed the factories, purchased the machines, and figured out where the markets were (see the box on p. 470). Their qualities included resourcefulness, single-mindedness, resolution, initiative, vision, ambition, and often, of course, greed. As Jedediah Strutt, a cotton manufacturer said, "Getting of money . . . is the main business of the life of men."

Members of the industrial middle class sought to reduce the barriers between themselves and the landed elite, while at the same time trying to separate themselves from the laboring classes below them. The working class was actually a mixture of different groups in the first half of the nineteenth century, but in the course of the nineteenth century, factory workers would form an industrial **proletariat** that constituted a majority of the working class.

New Social Classes: The Industrial Working Class   Early industrial workers faced wretched working conditions. Work shifts ranged from twelve to sixteen hours a day, six days a week, with a half hour for lunch and dinner. There was no security of employment and no minimum wage. The worst conditions were in the cotton mills, where temperatures were especially debilitating. One report noted that "in the cotton-spinning work, these creatures are kept, fourteen hours in each day, locked up, summer and winter, in a heat of from eighty to eighty-four degrees." Mills were dirty, dusty, and unhealthy.

Conditions in the coal mines were also harsh. Although steam-powered engines were used to lift coal from the mines to the top, inside the mines, men still bore the burden of digging the coal out while horses, mules, women, and children hauled coal carts on rails to the lift. Dangerous conditions, including cave-ins, explosions, and gas fumes, were a way of life. The cramped conditions in the mines—tunnels were often only 3 or 4 feet high—and their constant dampness led to deformed bodies and ruined lungs.

Both children and women worked in large numbers in early factories and mines. Children had been an important part of the family economy in preindustrial times, working in the fields or carding and spinning wool at home. In the Industrial Revolution, however, child labor was exploited more than ever. The owners of cotton factories found child labor very helpful. Children had a particular delicate touch as spinners of cotton. Their smaller size made it easier for them to move under machines to gather loose cotton. Moreover, children were more easily trained to do factory work. Above all, children represented a cheap supply of labor. In 1821, about half of the British population was under twenty years of age. Hence children made up an abundant supply of labor, and they were paid only about one-sixth to one-third of what a man was paid. In the cotton factories in 1838, children under eighteen made up 29 percent of the total workforce; children as young as seven worked twelve to fifteen hours per day, six days a week, in cotton mills.

By 1830, women and children made up two-thirds of the cotton industry's labor. After the Factory Act of 1833, however, the number of children employed declined, and their places were taken by women, who came to dominate the labor forces of the early factories. Women made up 50 percent of the labor force in textile (cotton and woolen) factories before 1870. They were mostly unskilled laborers and were paid half or less of what men received.

The Growth of Industrial Prosperity

Q Focus Questions: What was the Second Industrial Revolution, and what effects did it have on economic and social life? What were the main ideas of Karl Marx, and what role did they play in politics and the union movement in the late nineteenth and early twentieth centuries?

After 1870, the Western world experienced a dynamic age of material prosperity. The new industries, new sources of energy, and new goods of the Second Industrial

INDUSTRIAL ATTITUDES IN BRITAIN AND JAPAN

SCIENCE & TECHNOLOGY

In the nineteenth century, a new industrial middle class in Great Britain took the lead in creating the Industrial Revolution. Japan did not begin to industrialize until after 1870 (see Chapter 22). There, too, an industrial middle class emerged, although there were also important differences in the attitudes of business leaders in Britain and Japan. Some of these differences can be seen in these documents. The first is an excerpt from *Self-Help,* a book first published in 1859, by Samuel Smiles, who espoused the belief that people succeed through "individual industry, energy, and uprightness." The two additional selections are by Shibuzawa Eiichi, a Japanese industrialist who supervised textile factories. Although his business career began in 1873, he did not write his autobiography, the source of his first excerpt, until 1927.

Samuel Smiles, *Self-Help*

"Heaven helps those who help themselves" is a well-worn maxim, embodying in a small compass the results of vast human experience. The spirit of self-help is the root of all genuine growth in the individual; and, exhibited in the lives of many, it constitutes the true source of national vigor and strength. Help from without is often enfeebling in its effects, but help from within invariably invigorates. Whatever is done for men or classes, to a certain extent takes away the stimulus and necessity of doing for themselves; and where men are subjected to overguidance and overgovernment, the inevitable tendency is to render them comparatively helpless....

National progress is the sum of individual industry, energy, and uprightness, as national decay is of individual idleness, selfishness, and vice.... If this view be correct, then it follows that the highest patriotism and philanthrophy consist, not so much in altering laws and modifying institutions as in helping and stimulating men to elevate and improve themselves by their own free and independent action as individuals....

Many popular books have been written for the purpose of communicating to the public the grand secret of making money. But there is no secret whatever about it, as the proverbs of every nation abundantly testify.... "A penny saved is a penny gained."—"Diligence is the mother of good-luck."—"No pains no gains."—"No sweat no sweet."—"Sloth, the key of poverty."—"Work, and thou shalt have."—"He who will not work, neither shall he eat."—"The world is his, who has patience and industry."

Shibuzawa Eiichi, *Autobiography*

I ... felt that it was necessary to raise the social standing of those who engaged in commerce and industry. By way of setting an example, I began studying and practicing the teachings of the *Analects of Confucius.* It contains teachings first enunciated more than twenty-four hundred years ago. Yet it supplies the ultimate in practical ethics for all of us to follow in our daily living. It has many golden rules for businessmen. For example, there is a saying: "Wealth and respect are what men desire, but unless a right way is followed, they cannot be obtained; poverty and lowly position are what men despise, but unless a right way is found, one cannot leave that status once reaching it." It shows very clearly how a businessman must act in this world.

Shibuzawa Eiichi on Progress

One must beware of the tendency of some to argue that it is through individualism or egoism that the State and society can progress most rapidly. They claim that under individualism, each individual competes with the others, and progress results from this competition. But this is to see merely the advantages and ignore the disadvantages, and I cannot support such a theory. Society exists, and a State has been founded. Although people desire to rise to positions of wealth and honor, the social order and the tranquility of the State will be disrupted if this is done egoistically. Men should not do battle in competition with their fellow men. Therefore, I believe that in order to get along together in society and serve the State, we must by all means abandon this idea of independence and self-reliance and reject egoism completely.

Q *What are the major similarities and differences between the business attitudes of Samuel Smiles and Shibuzawa Eiichi? How do you explain the differences?*

Revolution led people to believe that their material progress meant human progress.

New Products

The first major change in industrial development between 1870 and 1914 was the substitution of steel for iron. New methods for shaping steel made it useful in the construction of lighter, smaller, and faster machines and engines, as well as railways, ships, and armaments. In 1860, Great Britain, France, Germany, and Belgium produced 125,000 tons of steel; by 1913, the total was 32 million tons.

Electricity was a major new form of energy that could be easily converted into other forms of energy, such as heat, light, and motion, and moved relatively effortlessly through space by means of transmitting wires. In the 1870s, the first commercially practical generators of electrical current were developed, and by 1910, hydroelectric power stations and coal-fired steam-generating plants enabled homes and factories in whole neighborhoods to be tied into a single, common source of power.

An Age of Progress. Between 1871 and 1914, the Second Industrial Revolution led many Europeans to believe that they were living in an age of progress when most human problems would be solved by scientific achievements. This illustration is taken from a special issue of *The Illustrated London News* celebrating the Diamond Jubilee of Queen Victoria in 1897. On the left are scenes from 1837, when Victoria came to the British throne; on the right are scenes from 1897. The vivid contrast underscored the magazine's conclusion: "The most striking . . . evidence of progress during the reign is the ever increasing speed which the discoveries of physical science have forced into everyday life. Steam and electricity have conquered time and space to a greater extent during the last sixty years than all the preceding six hundred years witnessed."

Electricity spawned a number of inventions. The lightbulb, developed independently by the American Thomas Edison and the Briton Joseph Swan, permitted homes and cities to be illuminated by electric lights. By the 1880s, streetcars and subways powered by electricity had appeared in major European cities. Electricity also transformed the factory. Conveyor belts, cranes, machines, and machine tools could all be powered by electricity and located anywhere. Similarly, a revolution in communications began when Alexander Graham Bell invented the telephone in 1876 and Guglielmo Marconi sent the first radio waves across the Atlantic in 1901.

The development of the internal combustion engine, fired by oil and gasoline, provided a new source of power in transportation and gave rise to ocean liners as well as to the airplane and the automobile. In 1900, world production stood at 9,000 cars, but an American, Henry Ford, revolutionized the automotive industry with the mass production of the Model T. By 1916, Ford's factories were producing 735,000 cars a year. In 1903, at Kitty Hawk, North Carolina, brothers Orville and Wilbur Wright made the first flight in a fixed-wing airplane. In 1919, the first regular passenger air service was established.

New Patterns

Industrial production grew rapidly at this time because of the greatly increased sales of manufactured goods. An increase in real wages for workers after 1870, combined with lower prices for manufactured goods because of reduced transportation costs, made it easier for Europeans to buy consumer products. In the cities, the first department stores began to sell a whole new range of consumer goods made possible by the development of the steel and electrical industries. The desire to own sewing machines, clocks, bicycles, electric lights, and typewriters was rapidly generating a new consumer ethic that has been a crucial part of the modern economy.

Not all nations benefited from the Second Industrial Revolution. Between 1870 and 1914, Germany replaced Great Britain as the industrial leader of Europe. Moreover, by 1900, Europe was divided into two economic zones. Great Britain, Belgium, France, the Netherlands, Germany, the western part of the Austro-Hungarian Empire, and northern Italy constituted an advanced industrialized core that had a high standard of living, decent systems of transportation, and relatively healthy and educated peoples (see Map 19.1). Another part of Europe, the backward and little industrialized area to the south and east, consisting of southern Italy, most of Austria-Hungary, Spain, Portugal, the Balkan kingdoms, and Russia, was still largely agricultural and relegated by the industrial countries to the function of providing food and raw materials.

Toward a World Economy

The economic developments of the late nineteenth century, combined with the transportation revolution that saw the growth of marine transport and railroads, fostered a true world economy. By 1900, Europeans were receiving beef and wool from Argentina and Australia, coffee from Brazil, iron ore from Algeria, and sugar from Java. European capital was also invested abroad to develop railways, mines, electrical power plants, and banks. Of course, foreign countries also provided markets for the surplus manufactured goods of Europe. With its capital,

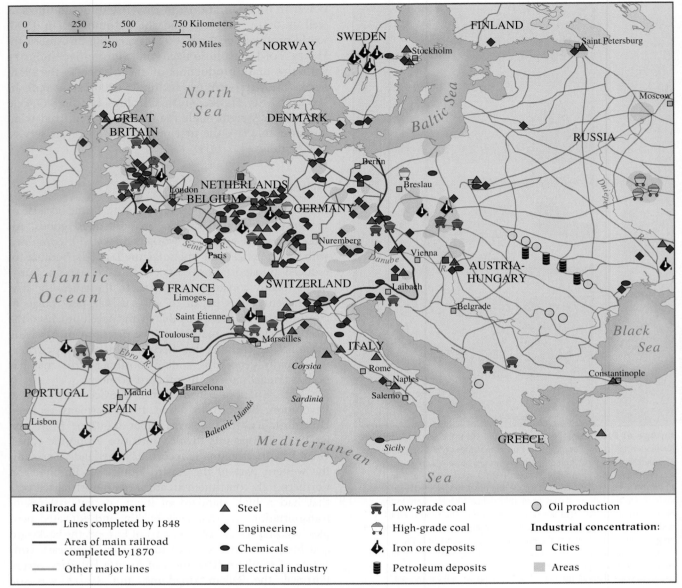

Railroad development
— Lines completed by 1848
— Area of main railroad completed by 1870
— Other major lines

▲ Steel
◆ Engineering
● Chemicals
■ Electrical industry

🛒 Low-grade coal
🛒 High-grade coal
⚗ Iron ore deposits
🛢 Petroleum deposits

⊙ Oil production

Industrial concentration:
▫ Cities
▨ Areas

MAP 19.1 The Industrial Regions of Europe at the End of the Nineteenth Century. By the end of the nineteenth century, the Second Industrial Revolution—in steelmaking, electricity, petroleum, and chemicals—had spurred substantial economic growth and prosperity in western and central Europe; it also sparked economic and political competition between Great Britain and Germany.

Q What correlation, if any, was there between industrial growth and political developments in the nineteenth century?

industries, and military might, Europe dominated the world economy by the beginning of the twentieth century.

The Spread of Industrialization

After 1870, industrialization began to spread beyond western and central Europe and North America. Especially

noticeable was its rapid development, fostered by governments, in Russia and Japan. A surge of industrialization began in Russia in the 1890s under the guiding hand of Sergei Witte, the minister of finance. Witte pushed the government toward a program of massive railroad construction. By 1900, 35,000 miles of track had been laid. Witte's program also made possible the rapid growth of a modern steel and coal industry, making Russia by 1900 the fourth-largest producer of steel, behind the United States, Germany, and Great Britain. At the same time, Russia was also turning out half of the world's oil production.

In Japan, the imperial government took the lead in promoting industry (see Chapter 22). The government financed industries, built railroads, brought foreign experts to train Japanese employees in new industrial techniques, and instituted a universal educational system based on applied science. By the end of the nineteenth century, Japan had developed key industries in tea, silk, armaments, and shipbuilding.

Women and Work: New Job Opportunities

During the course of the nineteenth century, working-class organizations upheld the belief that women should remain at home to bear and nurture children and not be allowed in the industrial workforce. Working-class men argued that keeping women out of industrial work would ensure the moral and physical well-being of families. In reality, however, when their husbands were unemployed, women had to do low-wage work at home or labor part-time in sweatshops to support their families.

The Second Industrial Revolution opened the door to new jobs for women. The development of larger industrial plants and the expansion of government services created a large number of service and white-collar jobs. The increased demand for white-collar workers at relatively low wages coupled with a shortage of male workers led employers to hire women. Big businesses and retail shops needed clerks, typists, secretaries, file clerks, and salesclerks. The expansion of government services opened opportunities for women to be secretaries and telephone operators and to take jobs in health care and social services. Compulsory education necessitated more teachers, and the development of modern hospital services opened the way for an increase in nurses.

Organizing the Working Classes

The desire to improve their working and living conditions led many industrial workers to form socialist political parties and socialist trade unions. These emerged after 1870, but the theory that made them possible had been developed more than two decades earlier in the work of Karl Marx. **Marxism** made its first appearance on the eve of the revolutions of 1848 with the publication of a short treatise titled *The Communist Manifesto*, written by two Germans, Karl Marx (1818–1883) and Friedrich Engels (1820–1895).

Marxist Theory Marx and Engels began their treatise with the statement that "the history of all hitherto existing society is the history of class struggles." Throughout history, then, oppressor and oppressed have "stood in constant opposition to one another."[3] One group of people—the oppressors—owned the means of production and thus had the power to control government and society. Indeed, government itself was but an instrument of the ruling class. The other group, which depended on the owners of the means of production, were the oppressed.

The **class struggle** continued in the industrialized societies of Marx's day. According to Marx, "Society as a whole is more and more splitting up into two great hostile camps, into two great classes directly facing each other: Bourgeoisie and Proletariat." Marx predicted that the struggle between the bourgeoisie and the proletariat would finally break into open revolution, "where the violent overthrow of the bourgeoisie lays the foundation

"Proletarians of the World, Unite." To improve their working and living conditions, many industrial workers, inspired by the ideas of Karl Marx, joined working-class or socialist parties. Pictured here is a socialist-sponsored poster that proclaims in German the closing words of *The Communist Manifesto*: "Proletarians of the World, Unite!"

THE CLASSLESS SOCIETY

FAMILY & SOCIETY

In *The Communist Manifesto,* Karl Marx and Friedrich Engels projected that the end product of the struggle between the bourgeoisie and the proletariat would be the creation of a classless society. In this selection, they discuss the steps by which that classless society would be reached.

Karl Marx and Friedrich Engels,
The Communist Manifesto

We have seen . . . , that the first step in the revolution by the working class is to raise the proletariat to the position of ruling class. . . . The proletariat will use its political supremacy to wrest, by degrees, all capital from the bourgeoisie, to centralize all instruments of production in the hands of the State, i.e., of the proletariat organized as the ruling class; and to increase the total of productive forces as rapidly as possible.

Of course, in the beginning, this cannot be effected except by means of despotic inroads on the rights of property, and on the conditions of bourgeois production; by means of measures, therefore, which appear economically insufficient and untenable, but which, in the course of the movement, outstrip themselves, necessitate further inroads upon the old social order, and are unavoidable as a means of entirely revolutionizing the mode of production.

These measures will of course be different in different countries.

Nevertheless, in the most advanced countries, the following will be pretty generally applicable:

1. Abolition of property in land and application of all rents of land to public purposes.
2. A heavy progressive or graduated income tax.
3. Abolition of all right of inheritance. . . .
5. Centralization of credit in the hands of the State, by means of a national bank with State capital and an exclusive monopoly.
6. Centralization of the means of communication and transport in the hands of the State.
7. Extension of factories and instruments of production owned by the State. . . .
8. Equal liability of all to labor. Establishment of industrial armies, especially for agriculture.
9. Combination of agriculture with manufacturing industries; gradual abolition of the distinction between town and country, by a more equable distribution of the population over the country.
10. Free education for all children in public schools. Abolition of children's factory labor in its present form. . . .

When, in the course of development, class distinctions have disappeared, and all production has been concentrated in the whole nation, the public power will lose its political character. Political power, properly so called, is merely the organized power of one class for oppressing another. If the proletariat during its contest with the bourgeoisie is compelled, by the force of circumstances, to organize itself as a class, if, by means of a revolution, it makes itself the ruling class, and, as such, sweeps away by force the old conditions of production, then it will, along with these conditions, have swept away the conditions for the existence of class antagonisms and of classes generally, and will thereby have abolished its own supremacy as a class.

In place of the old bourgeois society, with its classes and class antagonisms, we shall have an association, in which the free development of each is the condition for the free development of all.

Q *How did Marx and Engels define the proletariat? The bourgeoisie? Why did Marxists come to believe that this distinction was paramount for understanding history? For shaping the future?*

---

for the sway of the proletariat." Hence the fall of the bourgeoisie "and the victory of the proletariat are equally inevitable."[4] For a while, the proletariat would form a dictatorship in order to organize the means of production, but the end result would be a classless society, since classes themselves arose from the economic differences that would have been abolished. The state—itself an instrument of the bourgeois interests—would wither away (see the box above).

Socialist Parties In time, Marx's ideas were picked up by working-class leaders who formed socialist parties. Most important was the German Social Democratic Party (SPD), which emerged in 1875 and espoused revolutionary Marxist rhetoric while organizing itself as a mass political party competing in elections for the Reichstag (the lower house of parliament). Once in the Reichstag, SPD delegates worked to achieve legislation to improve the condition of the working class. When it received four million votes in the 1912 elections, the SPD became the largest single party in Germany.

Socialist parties also emerged in other European states. In 1889, leaders of the various socialist parties formed the Second International, an association of national socialist groups that would fight against capitalism worldwide. (The First International had failed in 1872.) The Second International took some coordinated actions—May Day (May 1), for example, was made an international labor holiday—but differences often wreaked havoc at the organization's congresses.

Marxist parties divided over the issue of **revisionism.** Pure Marxists believed in the imminent collapse of capitalism and the need for socialist ownership of the means of production. But others, called revisionists, rejected **revolutionary socialism** and argued that workers must organize mass political parties and work together with other progressive elements to gain reform. Evolution by democratic means, not revolution, would achieve the desired goal of socialism.

Another force working for evolutionary rather than revolutionary socialism was the development of trade unions. In Great Britain, unions won the right to strike in the 1870s. Soon after, the masses of workers in factories were organized into trade unions so that they could use the instrument of the strike. By 1900, there were two million workers in British trade unions; by 1914, there were almost four million union members. Trade unions in the rest of Europe had varying degrees of success, but by the outbreak of World War I, they had made considerable progress in bettering both the living and the working conditions of workers.

Reaction and Revolution: The Growth of Nationalism

Q Focus Questions: What were the major ideas associated with conservatism, liberalism, and nationalism, and what role did each ideology play in Europe between 1800 and 1850? What were the causes of the revolutions of 1848, and why did these revolutions fail?

Industrialization was a major force for change in the nineteenth century as it led the West into the machine-dependent modern world. Another major force for change was nationalism, which transformed the political map of Europe in the nineteenth century.

The Conservative Order

After the defeat of Napoleon, European rulers moved to restore much of the old order. This was the goal of the great powers—Great Britain, Austria, Prussia, and Russia—when they met at the Congress of Vienna in September 1814 to arrange a final settlement after the Napoleonic wars. The leader of the congress was the Austrian foreign minister, Prince Klemens von Metternich (1773–1859), who claimed that he was guided at Vienna by the **principle of legitimacy.** To reestablish peace and stability in Europe, he considered it necessary to restore the legitimate monarchs who would preserve traditional institutions. This had already been done in France with the restoration of the Bourbon monarchy and in a number of other states, but it did not stop the great powers from grabbing territory, often from the smaller, weaker states (see Map 19.2).

The peace arrangements of 1815 were but the beginning of a conservative reaction determined to contain the liberal and nationalist forces unleashed by the French Revolution. Metternich and his kind were representatives of the ideology known as **conservatism.** Most conservatives favored obedience to political authority, believed that organized religion was crucial to social order, hated revolutionary upheavals, and were unwilling to accept either the liberal demands for civil liberties and representative governments or the nationalistic aspirations generated by the French revolutionary era. After 1815, the political philosophy of conservatism was supported by hereditary monarchs, government bureaucracies, landowning aristocracies, and revived churches, both Protestant and Catholic. The conservative forces were dominant after 1815.

One method used by the great powers to maintain the new status quo they had constructed was the Concert of Europe, according to which Great Britain, Russia, Prussia, and Austria (and later France) agreed to meet periodically in conferences to take steps that would maintain the peace in Europe. Eventually, the great powers adopted a **principle of intervention,** asserting that they had the right to send armies into countries where there were revolutions to restore legitimate monarchs to their thrones.

Forces for Change

Between 1815 and 1830, conservative governments throughout Europe worked to maintain the old order. But, powerful forces for change—liberalism and nationalism—were also at work. **Liberalism** owed much to the Enlightenment of the eighteenth century and the American and French Revolutions at the end of that century; it was based on the idea that people should be as free from restraint as possible.

Liberals came to hold a common set of political beliefs. Chief among them was the protection of civil liberties, or the basic rights of all people, which included equality before the law; freedom of assembly, speech, and the press; and freedom from arbitrary arrest. All of these freedoms should be guaranteed by a written document, such as the American Bill of Rights. In addition to religious toleration for all, most liberals advocated separation of church and state. Liberals also demanded the right of peaceful opposition to the government in and out of parliament and the making of laws by a

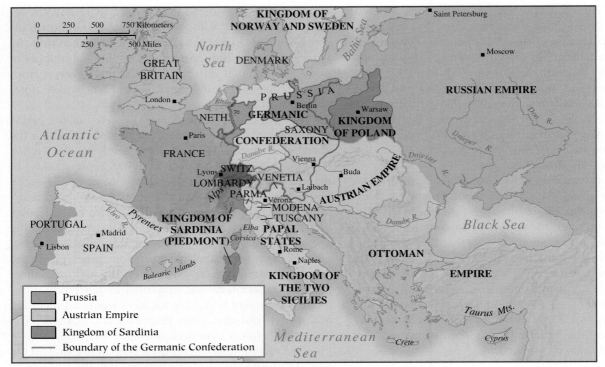

MAP 19.2 **Europe After the Congress of Vienna, 1815.** The Congress of Vienna imposed order on Europe based on the principles of monarchical government and a balance of power. Monarchs were restored in France, Spain, and other states recently under Napoleon's control, and much territory changed hands, often at the expense of small and weak states.

Q How did Europe's major powers manipulate territory to decrease the probability that France could again threaten the Continent's stability?

 View an animated version of this map or related maps at www.cengage.com/history/ duikspiel/essentialworld6e

representative assembly (legislature) elected by qualified voters. Thus, many liberals believed in a constitutional monarchy or constitutional state with limits on the powers of government to prevent despotism and in written constitutions that would guarantee these rights. Liberals were not democrats, however. They thought that the right to vote and hold office should be open only to men of property. As a political philosophy, liberalism was adopted by middle-class men, especially industrial middle-class men, who favored voting rights for themselves so that they could share power with the landowning classes.

Nationalism was an even more powerful ideology for change in the nineteenth century. Nationalism arose out of an awareness of being part of a community that has common institutions, traditions, language, and customs. This community is called a *nation,* and the primary political loyalty of individuals would be to the nation. Nationalism did not become a popular force for change until

the French Revolution. From then on, nationalists came to believe that each nationality should have its own government. Thus, the Germans, who were not united, wanted national unity in a German nation-state with one central government. Subject peoples, such as the Hungarians, wanted the right to establish their own autonomy rather than be subject to a German minority in the multinational Austrian Empire.

Nationalism, then, was a threat to the existing political order. A united Germany, for example, would upset the balance of power established at Vienna in 1815. Conservatives feared such change and tried hard to repress nationalism. The conservative order dominated much of Europe after 1815, but the forces of liberalism and nationalism, first generated by the French Revolution, continued to grow as that second great revolution, the Industrial Revolution, expanded and brought in new groups of people who wanted change. In 1848, these forces for change erupted.

The Revolutions of 1848

Revolution in France was the spark for revolution in other countries. Beginning in 1846, a severe industrial and agricultural depression in France brought untold hardship to the lower middle class, workers, and peasants, while the government's persistent refusal to lower the property qualification for voting angered the disenfranchised members of the middle class. When the government of King Louis-Philippe (1830–1848) refused to make changes, opposition grew and finally overthrew the monarchy on February 24, 1848. A group of moderate and radical republicans established a provisional government and called for the election by universal male suffrage of a "constituent assembly" that would draw up a new constitution.

The new constitution, ratified on November 4, 1848, established a republic (the Second Republic) with a single legislature elected to three-year terms by universal male suffrage and a president elected to a four-year term, also by universal male suffrage. In the elections for the presidency held in December 1848, Charles Louis Napoleon Bonaparte, the nephew of the famous French ruler, won a resounding victory.

News of the 1848 revolution in France led to upheaval in central Europe as well (see the box on p. 478). The Vienna settlement in 1815 had recognized the existence of thirty-eight sovereign states (called the Germanic Confederation) in what had once been the Holy Roman Empire. Austria and Prussia were the two great powers in terms of size and might; the other states varied considerably. In 1848, cries for change caused many German rulers to promise constitutions, a free press, jury trials, and other liberal reforms. In Prussia, King Frederick William IV (1840–1861) agreed to establish a new constitution and work for a united Germany.

The promise of unity reverberated throughout all the German states as governments allowed elections by universal male suffrage for deputies to an all-German parliament called the Frankfurt Assembly. Its purpose was to fulfill a liberal and nationalist dream—the preparation of a constitution for a new united Germany. But the Frankfurt Assembly failed to achieve its goal. The members had no real means of compelling the German rulers to accept the constitution they had drawn up. German unification was not achieved; the revolution had failed.

The Austrian Empire needed only the news of the revolution in Paris to erupt in flames in March 1848. The Austrian Empire was a multinational state, a collection of at least eleven ethnically distinct peoples, including Germans, Czechs, Magyars (Hungarians), Slovaks, Romanians, Serbians, and Italians, who had pledged their loyalty to the Habsburg emperor. The Germans, though only a quarter of the population, were economically dominant and played a leading role in governing Austria. In March, demonstrations in Buda, Prague, and Vienna led to the dismissal of Metternich, the Austrian foreign minister and the archsymbol of the conservative order, who fled abroad. In Vienna, revolutionary forces took control of the capital and demanded a liberal constitution. Hungary was given its own legislature and a separate national army.

Austrian officials had made concessions to appease the revolutionaries, but they were determined to reestablish firm control. As in the German states, they were increasingly encouraged by the divisions between radical and moderate revolutionaries. By the end of October 1848, Austrian military forces had crushed the radical rebels in Vienna, but it was only with the assistance of a Russian army of 140,000 men that the Hungarian revolution was finally put down in 1849. The revolutions in the Austrian Empire had failed.

So did revolutions in Italy. The Congress of Vienna had established nine states in Italy, including the Kingdom of Sardinia in the north, ruled by the house of Savoy; the Kingdom of the Two Sicilies (Naples and Sicily); the Papal

Austrian Students in the Revolutionary Civil Guard. In 1848, revolutionary fervor swept the European continent and toppled governments in France, central Europe, and Italy. In the Austrian Empire, students joined the revolutionary civil guard in taking control of Vienna and forcing the Austrian emperor to call a constituent assembly to draft a liberal constitution.

OPPOSING VIEWPOINTS
RESPONSE TO REVOLUTION: TWO PERSPECTIVES

Based on their political beliefs, Europeans responded differently to the specter of revolution that haunted Europe in the first half of the nineteenth century. The first excerpt is taken from a speech given by Thomas Babington Macaulay (1800–1859), a historian and a member of the British Parliament. Macaulay spoke in Parliament on behalf of the Reform Act of 1832, which extended the right to vote to the industrial middle classes of Britain. A revolution in France in 1830 that had resulted in some gains for the upper bourgeoisie had influenced his belief that it was better to reform than to have a political revolution.

The second excerpt is taken from the *Reminiscences* of Carl Schurz (1829–1906). Like many liberals and nationalists in Germany, Schurz received the news of the February Revolution of 1848 in France with much excitement and great expectations for revolutionary change in the German states. After the failure of the German revolution, Schurz made his way to the United States and eventually became a U.S. senator.

Thomas Babington Macaulay,
Speech of March 2, 1831

My hon[orable] friend the member of the University of Oxford tells us that, if we pass this law, England will soon be a Republic. The re-formed House of Commons will, according to him, before it has sat ten years, depose the King, and expel the Lords from their House. Sir, if my hon[orable] friend could prove this, he would have succeeded in bringing an argument for democracy infinitely stronger than any that is to be found in the works of [Thomas] Paine. His proposition is, in fact, this—that our monarchical and aristocratical institutions have no hold on the public mind of England; that these institutions are regarded with aversion by a decided majority of the middle class.... Now, sir, if I were convinced that the great body of the middle class in England look with aversion on monarchy and aristocracy, I should be forced, much against my will, to come to this conclusion, that monarchical and aristocratical institutions are unsuited to this country. Monarchy and aristocracy, valuable and useful as I think them, are still valuable and useful as means, and not as ends. The end of government is the happiness of the people; and I do not conceive that, in a country like this, the happiness of the people can be promoted by a form of government in which the middle classes place no confidence, and which exists only because the middle classes have no organ by which to make their sentiments known. But, sir, I am fully convinced that the middle classes sincerely wish to uphold the royal prerogatives, and the constitutional rights of the Peers....

But let us know our interest and our duty better. Turn where we may—within, around—the voice of great events is proclaiming to us, "Reform, that you may preserve." Now, therefore, while everything at home and abroad forebodes ruin to those who persist in a hopeless struggle against the spirit of the age; now,... take counsel, not of prejudice, not of party spirit... but of history, of reason, of the ages which are past, of the signs of this most portentous time.... Save property divided against itself. Save the multitude, endangered by their own ungovernable passions. Save the aristocracy, endangered by its own unpopular power. Save the greatest, and fairest, and most highly civilized community that ever existed, from calamities which may in a few days sweep away all the rich heritage of so many ages of wisdom and glory. The danger is terrible. The time is short. If this Bill should be rejected, I pray to God that none of those who concur in rejecting it may ever remember their votes with unavailing regret, amidst the wreck of laws, the confusion of ranks, the spoliation of property, and the dissolution of social order.

Carl Schurz, *Reminiscences*

One morning, toward the end of February, 1848, I sat quietly in my attic-chamber, working hard at my tragedy of "Ulrich von Hutten" [a sixteenth-century German knight], when suddenly a friend rushed breathlessly into the room, exclaiming: "What, you sitting here! Do you not know what has happened?"

"No; what?"

"The French have driven away Louis Philippe and proclaimed the republic."

I threw down my pen—and that was the end of "Ulrich von Hutten." I never touched the manuscript again. We tore down the stairs, into the street, to the market-square, the accustomed meeting-place for all the student societies after their midday dinner. Although it was still forenoon, the market was already crowded with young men talking excitedly. There was no shouting, no noise, only agitated conversation. What did we want there? This probably no one knew. But since the French had driven away Louis Philippe and proclaimed the republic, something of course must happen here, too....

The next morning there were the usual lectures to be attended. But how profitless! The voice of the professor sounded like a monotonous drone coming from far away. What he had to say did not seem to concern us. The pen that should have taken notes remained idle. At last we closed with a sigh the notebook and went away, impelled by a feeling that now we had something more important to do—to devote ourselves to the affairs of the fatherland. And this we did by seeking as quickly as possible again the company of our friends, in order to discuss what had happened and what was to come.

(continued)

(continued)

In these conversations, excited as they were, certain ideas and catchwords worked themselves to the surface, which expressed more or less the feelings of the people. Now had arrived in Germany the day for the establishment of "German Unity," and the founding of a great, powerful national German Empire. In the first line the convocation of a national parliament. Then the demands for civil rights and liberties, free speech, free press, the right of free assembly, equality before the law, a freely elected representation of the people with legislative power, responsibility of ministers, self-government of the communes, the right of the people to carry arms, the formation of a civic guard with elective officers, and so on—in short, that which was called a "constitutional form of government on a broad democratic basis." Republican ideas were at first only sparingly expressed. But the word *democracy* was soon on all tongues, and many, too, thought it a matter of course that if the princes should try to withhold from the people the rights and liberties demanded, force would take the place of mere petition. Of course the regeneration of the fatherland must, if possible, be accomplished by peaceable means.... Like many of my friends, I was dominated by the feeling that at last the great opportunity had arrived for giving to the German people the liberty which was their birthright and to the German fatherland its unity and greatness, and that it was now the first duty of every German to do and to sacrifice everything for this sacred object.

Q *What arguments did Macaulay use to support the Reform Bill of 1832? Was he correct? Why or why not? Why was Carl Schurz so excited when he heard the news about the revolution in France? Do you think being a university student helps explain his reaction? Why or why not? What differences do you see in the approaches of these two writers? What do these selections tell you about the development of politics in the German states and Britain in the nineteenth century?*

States; a handful of small duchies; and the important northern provinces of Lombardy and Venetia, which were now part of the Austrian Empire. Italy was largely under Austrian domination, but a new movement for Italian unity known as Young Italy led to initially successful revolts in 1848. By 1849, however, the Austrians had reestablished complete control over Lombardy and Venetia, and the old order also prevailed in the rest of Italy.

Throughout Europe in 1848–1849, moderate, middle-class liberals and radical workers soon divided over their aims, and the failure of the revolutionaries to stay united soon led to the reestablishment of authoritarian regimes. In other parts of the Western world, revolutions took somewhat different directions (see Chapter 20).

Nationalism in the Balkans: The Ottoman Empire and the Eastern Question

The Ottoman Empire had long been in control of much of the Balkans in southeastern Europe. By the beginning of the nineteenth century, however, the Ottoman Empire was in decline, and authority over its outlying territories in the Balkans waned. As a result, European governments, especially those of Russia and Austria, began to take an active interest in the disintegration of the empire, which they called the "sick man of Europe."

When the Russians invaded the Ottoman provinces of Moldavia and Wallachia, the Ottoman Turks declared war on Russia on October 4, 1853. In the following year, on March 28, Great Britain and France, fearful of Russian gains, declared war on Russia. The Crimean War, as the conflict came to be called, was poorly planned and poorly fought. Heavy losses caused the Russians to sue for peace.

By the Treaty of Paris, signed in March 1856, Russia agreed to allow Moldavia and Wallachia to be placed under the protection of all the great powers.

The Crimean War destroyed the Concert of Europe. Austria and Russia, the two chief powers maintaining the status quo in the first half of the nineteenth century, were now enemies because of Austria's unwillingness to support Russia in the war. Russia, defeated and humiliated by the obvious failure of its armies, withdrew from European affairs for the next two decades. Great Britain, disillusioned by its role in the war, also pulled back from continental affairs. Austria, paying the price for its neutrality, was now without friends among the great powers. This new international situation opened the door for the unification of Italy and Germany.

National Unification and the National State, 1848–1871

Q **Focus Question:** What actions did Cavour and Bismarck take to bring about unification in Italy and Germany, respectively, and what role did war play in their efforts?

The revolutions of 1848 had failed, but within twenty-five years, many of the goals sought by liberals and nationalists during the first half of the nineteenth century were achieved. Italy and Germany became nations, and many European states were led by constitutional monarchs.

The Unification of Italy

The Italians were the first people to benefit from the breakdown of the Concert of Europe. In 1850, Austria was still the dominant power on the Italian peninsula. After the failure of the revolution of 1848–1849, more and more Italians looked to the northern Italian state of Piedmont, ruled by the royal house of Savoy, as their best hope to achieve the unification of Italy. It was, however, doubtful that the little state could provide the leadership needed to unify Italy until King Victor Emmanuel II (1849–1878; 1861–1878 as king of Italy) named Count Camillo di Cavour (1810–1861) prime minister in 1852.

As prime minister, Cavour pursued a policy of economic expansion that increased government revenues and enabled Piedmont to equip a large army. Cavour, allied with the French emperor, Louis Napoleon, defeated the Austrians and gained control of Lombardy. Cavour's success caused nationalists in some northern Italian states (Parma, Modena, and Tuscany) to overthrow their governments and join Piedmont.

Meanwhile, in southern Italy, Giuseppe Garibaldi (1807–1882), a dedicated Italian patriot, raised an army of a thousand volunteers called Red Shirts because of the color of their uniforms. Garibaldi's forces swept through Sicily and then crossed over to the mainland and began a victorious march up the Italian peninsula. Naples, and with it the Kingdom of the Two Sicilies, fell in early September in 1860. Ever the patriot, Garibaldi chose to turn over his conquests to Cavour's Piedmontese forces. On March 17, 1861, the new kingdom of Italy was proclaimed under a centralized government subordinated to the control of Piedmont and King Victor Emmanuel II of the house of Savoy. The task of unification was not yet complete, however. Venetia in the north was taken from Austria in 1866. The Italian army annexed the city of Rome on September 20, 1870, and it became the new capital of the united Italian state.

The Unification of Italy

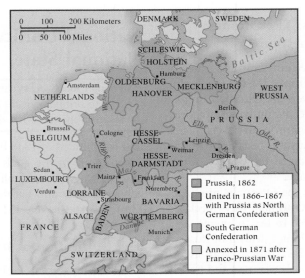

The Unification of Germany

The Unification of Germany

After the failure of the Frankfurt Assembly to achieve German unification in 1848–1849, more and more Germans looked to Prussia for leadership in the cause of German unification. Prussia had become a strong, prosperous, and authoritarian state, with the Prussian king in firm control of both the government and the army. In 1862, King William I (1861–1888) appointed a new prime minister, Count Otto von Bismarck (1815–1898). Bismarck has often been portrayed as the ultimate realist, the foremost nineteenth-century practitioner of *Realpolitik*—the "politics of reality." He said, "Not by speeches and majorities will the great questions of the day be decided—that was the mistake of 1848–1849—but by iron and blood."[5] Opposition to his domestic policy determined Bismarck on an active foreign policy, which led to war and German unification.

After defeating Denmark with Austrian help in 1864 and gaining control over the duchies of Schleswig and Holstein, Bismarck created friction with the Austrians and goaded them into a war on June 14, 1866.

Though the Austrians were barely defeated at Königgrätz on July 3, Prussia proceeded to organize the German states north of the Main River into the North German Confederation. The southern German states, largely Catholic, remained independent but signed military alliances with Prussia due to their fear of France, their western neighbor.

Prussia now dominated all of northern Germany, but problems with France soon arose. Bismarck realized that France would never be content with a strong German state to its east because of the potential threat to French security. Bismarck goaded the French into declaring war on Prussia on July 15, 1870. The Prussian armies advanced into France, and at Sedan, on September 2, 1870, they captured an entire French army and the French emperor Napoleon III himself. Paris capitulated on January 28, 1871. France had to give up the provinces of Alsace and Lorraine to the new German state, a loss that left the French burning for revenge.

Even before the war had ended, the southern German states had agreed to enter the North German

CHRONOLOGY	The Unification of Germany
King William I of Prussia	1861–1888
Danish War	1864
Austro-Prussian War	1866
Franco-Prussian War	1870–1871
German Empire is proclaimed	January 18, 1871

Confederation. On January 18, 1871, in the Hall of Mirrors in Louis XIV's palace at Versailles, William I was proclaimed kaiser (emperor) of the Second German Empire (the first was the medieval Holy Roman Empire). German unity had been achieved by the Prussian monarchy and the Prussian army. The Prussian leadership of German unification meant the triumph of authoritarian, militaristic values over liberal, constitutional sentiments in the development of the new German state. With its industrial resources and military might, the new state had become the strongest power on the Continent. A new European balance of power was at hand.

Nationalism and Reform: The European National State at Mid-Century

Unlike nations on the Continent, Great Britain managed to avoid the revolutionary upheavals of the first half of the nineteenth century. In the early part of the century, Great Britain was governed by the aristocratic landowning classes that dominated both houses of Parliament. But in 1832, to avoid turmoil like that on the Continent, Parliament passed a reform bill that increased the number of male voters, chiefly by adding members of the industrial middle class. By allowing the industrial middle class to join the landed interests in ruling Britain, Britain avoided revolution in 1848.

In the 1850s and 1860s, the British liberal parliamentary system made both social and political reforms that enabled the country to remain stable. One of the other reasons for Britain's stability was its continuing economic growth. After 1850, middle-class prosperity was at last coupled with some improvements for the working classes as real wages for laborers increased more than 25 percent between 1850 and 1870. The British sense of national pride was well reflected in Queen Victoria (1837–1901), whose sense of duty and moral respectability reflected the attitudes of her age, which has ever since been known as the Victorian Age.

Events in France after the revolution of 1848 moved toward the restoration of monarchy. Four years after his

© Bildarchiv Preussischer Kulturbesitz/Art Resource, NY

The Unification of Germany. Under Prussian leadership, a new German empire was proclaimed on January 18, 1871, in the Hall of Mirrors in the palace of Versailles. King William of Prussia became Emperor William I of the Second German Empire. Otto von Bismarck, the man who had been so instrumental in creating the new German state, is shown here, resplendently attired in his white uniform, standing at the foot of the throne.

election as president, Louis Napoleon restored an authoritarian empire. On December 2, 1852, Louis Napoleon assumed the title of Napoleon III (the first Napoleon had abdicated in favor of his son, Napoleon II, on April 6, 1814). The Second Empire had begun.

The first five years of Napoleon III's reign were a spectacular success. He took many steps to expand industrial growth. Government subsidies helped foster the rapid construction of railroads as well as harbors, roads, and canals. The major French railway lines were completed during Napoleon III's reign, and iron production tripled. In the midst of this economic expansion, Napoleon III also undertook a vast reconstruction of the city of Paris. The medieval Paris of narrow streets and old city walls was destroyed and replaced by a modern Paris of broad boulevards, spacious buildings, an underground sewage system, a new public water supply, and gaslights.

In the 1860s, as opposition to his rule began to mount, Napoleon III began to liberalize his regime. He gave the Legislative Corps more say in affairs of state, including debate over the budget. Liberalization policies worked initially; in a plebiscite in May 1870 on whether to accept a new constitution that might have inaugurated a parliamentary regime, the French people gave Napoleon III a resounding victory. This triumph was short-lived, however. War with Prussia in 1870 brought Napoleon III's ouster, and a republic was proclaimed.

Although nationalism was a major force in nineteenth-century Europe, one of the region's most powerful states, the Austrian Empire, managed to frustrate the desire of its numerous ethnic groups for self-determination. After the Habsburgs had crushed the revolutions of 1848–1849, they restored centralized, autocratic government to the empire. But Austria's defeat at the hands of the Prussians in 1866 forced the Austrians to deal with the fiercely nationalistic Hungarians.

The result was the negotiated *Ausgleich*, or Compromise, of 1867, which created the dual monarchy of Austria-Hungary. Each part of the empire now had its own constitution, its own legislature, its own governmental bureaucracy, and its own capital (Vienna for Austria and Budapest for Hungary). Holding the two states together were a single monarch—Francis Joseph (1848–1916) was emperor of Austria and king of Hungary—and a common army, foreign policy, and system of finances.

At the beginning of the nineteenth century, Russia was overwhelmingly rural, agricultural, and autocratic. The Russian imperial autocracy, based on soldiers, secret police, and repression, had withstood the revolutionary fervor of the first half of the nineteenth century.

Defeat in the Crimean War in 1856, however, led even staunch conservatives to realize that Russia was falling hopelessly behind the western European powers. Tsar Alexander II (1855–1881) decided to make serious reforms.

Serfdom was the most burdensome problem in tsarist Russia. On March 3, 1861, Alexander issued his emancipation edict (see the box on p. 483). Peasants were now free to own property and marry as they chose. But the system of land redistribution instituted after emancipation was not that favorable to them. The government provided land for the peasants by purchasing it from the landlords, but the landowners often chose to keep the best lands. The Russian peasants soon found that they had inadequate amounts of good arable land to support themselves.

Nor were the peasants completely free. The state compensated the landowners for the land given to the peasants, but the peasants were expected to repay the state in long-term installments. To ensure that the payments were made, peasants were subjected to the authority of their *mir* or village commune, which was collectively responsible for the land payments to the government. And since the village communes were responsible for the payments, they were reluctant to allow peasants to leave their land. Emancipation, then, led not to a free, landowning peasantry along the Western model but to an unhappy, land-starved peasantry that largely followed the old ways of agricultural production.

The European State, 1871–1914

Q Focus Questions: What general political trends were evident in the nations of western Europe in the late nineteenth and early twentieth centuries, and to what degree were those trends also apparent in the nations of central and eastern Europe? How did the growth of nationalism affect international affairs during the same period?

Throughout much of Europe by 1870, the national state had become the focus of people's loyalties. Only in Russia, eastern Europe, Austria-Hungary, and Ireland did national groups still struggle for independence.

Within the major European states, considerable progress was made in achieving such liberal practices as constitutions and parliaments, but it was largely in the western European states that **mass politics** became a reality. Reforms encouraged the expansion of political democracy through voting rights for men and the creation

EMANCIPATION: SERFS AND SLAVES

FAMILY & SOCIETY

Although overall their histories have been quite different, Russia and the United States shared a common feature in the 1860s. They were the only states in the Western world that still had large enslaved populations (the Russian serfs were virtually slaves). The leaders of both countries issued emancipation proclamations within two years of each other. The first excerpt is taken from the imperial decree of March 3, 1861, which freed the Russian serfs. The second excerpt is from Abraham Lincoln's Emancipation Proclamation, issued on January 1, 1863.

Alexander II's Imperial Decree, March 3, 1861

By the grace of God, we, Alexander II, Emperor and Autocrat of all the Russias, King of Poland, Grand Duke of Finland, etc., to all our faithful subjects, make known:

Called by Divine Providence and by the sacred right of inheritance to the throne of our ancestors, we took a vow in our innermost heart to respond to the mission which is intrusted to us as to surround with our affection and our Imperial solicitude all our faithful subjects of every rank and of every condition, from the warrior, who nobly bears arms for the defense of the country, to the humble artisan devoted to the works of industry; from the official in the career of the high offices of the State to the laborer whose plough furrows the soil. . . .

We thus came to the conviction that the work of a serious improvement of the condition of the peasants was a sacred inheritance bequeathed to us by our ancestors, a mission which, in the course of events, Divine Providence called upon us to fulfill. . . .

In virtue of the new dispositions above mentioned, the peasants attached to the soil will be invested within a term fixed by the law with all the rights of free cultivators. . . .

At the same time, they are granted the right of purchasing their close, and, with the consent of the proprietors, they may acquire in full property the arable lands and other appurtenances which are allotted to them as a permanent holding. By the acquisition in full property of the quantity of land fixed, the peasants are free from their obligations toward the proprietors for land thus purchased, and they enter definitely into the condition of free peasant-landholders.

Lincoln's Emancipation Proclamation, January 1, 1863

Now therefore, I, Abraham Lincoln, President of the United States, by virtue of the power in me vested as Commander-in-Chief of the Army and Navy of the United States in time of actual armed rebellion against the authority and government of the United States, and as a fit and necessary war measure for suppressing such rebellion, do, on this 1st day of January, A.D. 1863, and in accordance with my purpose to do so, . . . order and designate as the States and parts of States wherein the people thereof, respectively, are this day in rebellion against the United States the following, to wit:

Arkansas, Texas, Louisiana, . . . Mississippi, Alabama, Florida, Georgia, South Carolina, North Carolina, and Virginia. . . .

And by virtue of the power for the purpose aforesaid, I do order and declare that all persons held as slaves within said designated States and parts of States are, and henceforward shall be free; and that the Executive Government of the United States, including the military and naval authorities thereof, will recognize and maintain the freedom of said persons.

Q *What changes did Tsar Alexander II's emancipation of the serfs initiate in Russia? What effect did Lincoln's Emancipation Proclamation have on the southern "armed rebellion"? What reasons did each leader give for his action?*

of mass political parties. At the same time, however, similar reforms were strongly resisted in parts of Europe where the old political forces remained strong.

Western Europe: The Growth of Political Democracy

By 1871, Great Britain had a functioning two-party parliamentary system. For the next fifty years, Liberals and Conservatives alternated in power at regular intervals. Both parties were dominated by a ruling class composed of aristocratic landowners and upper-middle-class businesspeople. And both competed with each other in passing laws that expanded the right to vote. By 1918, all males over twenty-one and women over thirty could vote. Political democracy was soon accompanied by social welfare measures for the working class.

The growth of trade unions, which advocated more radical change of the economic system, and the emergence in 1900 of the Labour Party, which dedicated itself to the interests of the workers, caused the Liberals, who held the government from 1906 to 1914, to realize that they would have to create a program of social welfare or lose the support of the workers. Therefore, they voted for a series of social reforms. The National Insurance Act of 1911 provided benefits for workers in case of sickness and unemployment. Additional legislation provided a small pension for those over seventy.

In France, the confusion that ensued after the collapse of Louis Napoleon's Second Empire finally ended in 1875 when an improvised constitution established a republican form of government—the Third Republic—that lasted sixty-five years. France's parliamentary system was weak, however, because the existence of a dozen political parties forced the premier (or prime minister) to depend on a coalition of parties to stay in power. The Third Republic was notorious for its changes of government. Nevertheless, by 1914, the French Third Republic commanded the loyalty of most French people.

Central and Eastern Europe: Persistence of the Old Order

The constitution of the new imperial Germany begun by Chancellor Otto von Bismarck in 1871 provided for a bicameral legislature. The lower house of the German parliament, the Reichstag, was elected by universal male suffrage, but it did not have ministerial responsibility. Ministers of government, among whom the most important was the chancellor, were responsible to the emperor, not the parliament. The emperor also commanded the armed forces and controlled foreign policy and the government.

During the reign of Emperor William II (1888–1918), the new imperial Germany begun by Bismarck continued as an "authoritarian, conservative, military-bureaucratic power state." By the end of William's reign, Germany had become the strongest military and industrial power on the Continent, but the rapid change had also helped produce a society torn between modernization and traditionalism. With the expansion of industry and cities came demands for true democracy. Conservative forces, especially the landowning nobility and industrialists, two of the powerful ruling groups in imperial Germany, tried to block the movement for democracy by supporting William II's activist foreign policy. Expansion abroad, they believed, would divert people's attention from the yearning for democracy at home.

After the creation of the dual monarchy of Austria-Hungary in 1867, the Austrian part received a constitution that theoretically established a parliamentary system. In practice, however, Emperor Francis Joseph (1848–1916) largely ignored parliament, ruling by decree when parliament was not in session. The problem of the various nationalities also remained troublesome. The German minority that governed Austria felt increasingly threatened by the Czechs, Poles, and other Slavic groups within the empire. Their agitation in the parliament for autonomy led prime ministers after 1900 to ignore the parliament and rely increasingly on imperial decrees to govern.

CHRONOLOGY   The National State, 1870–1914

Great Britain	
Formation of Labour Party	1900
National Insurance Act	1911
France	
Republican constitution (Third Republic)	1875
Germany	
Bismarck as chancellor	1871–1890
Emperor William II	1888–1918
Austria-Hungary	
Emperor Francis Joseph	1848–1916
Russia	
Tsar Alexander III	1881–1894
Tsar Nicholas II	1894–1917
Russo-Japanese War	1904–1905
Revolution	1905

In Russia, the assassination of Alexander II in 1881 convinced his son and successor, Alexander III (1881–1894), that reform had been a mistake, and he lost no time in persecuting both reformers and revolutionaries. When Alexander III died, his weak son and successor, Nicholas II (1894–1917), began his rule with his father's conviction that the absolute power of the tsars should be preserved: "I shall maintain the principle of autocracy just as firmly and unflinchingly as did my unforgettable father."[6] But conditions were changing.

Industrialization progressed rapidly in Russia after 1890, and with industrialization came factories, an industrial working class, and the development of socialist parties, including the Marxist Social Democratic Party and the Social Revolutionaries. Although repression forced both parties to go underground, the growing opposition to the tsarist regime finally exploded into revolution in 1905.

The defeat of the Russians by the Japanese in 1904–1905 encouraged antigovernment groups to rebel against the tsarist regime. Nicholas II granted civil liberties and created a legislative assembly, the Duma, elected directly by a broad franchise. But real constitutional monarchy proved short-lived. By 1907, the tsar had curtailed the power of the Duma and relied again on the army and bureaucracy to rule Russia.

International Rivalries and the Winds of War

Bismarck had realized in 1871 that the emergence of a unified Germany as the most powerful state on the

MAP 19.3 **Europe in 1871.** German unification in 1871 upset the balance of power established at Vienna in 1815 and eventually led to a realignment of European alliances. By 1907, Europe was divided into two opposing camps: the Triple Entente of Great Britain, Russia, and France and the Triple Alliance of Germany, Austria-Hungary, and Italy.

Q How was Germany affected by the formation of the Triple Entente?

View an animated version of this map or related maps at www.cengage.com/history/ duikspiel/essentialworld6e

Continent (see Map 19.3) had upset the balance of power established at Vienna in 1815. Fearful of a possible anti-German alliance between France and Russia, and possibly even Austria, Bismarck made a defensive alliance with Austria in 1879. Three years later, this German-Austrian alliance was enlarged with the entrance of Italy, angry with the French over conflicting colonial ambitions in North Africa. The Triple Alliance of 1882—Germany, Austria-Hungary, and Italy—committed the three powers

to a defensive alliance against France. At the same time, Bismarck maintained a separate treaty with Russia.

When Emperor William II cashiered Bismarck in 1890 and took over direction of Germany's foreign policy, he embarked on an activist foreign policy dedicated to enhancing German power by finding, as he put it, Germany's rightful "place in the sun." One of his changes in Bismarck's foreign policy was to drop the treaty with Russia, which he viewed as being at odds with Germany's alliance with Austria. The ending of the alliance brought France and Russia together, and in 1894, the two powers concluded a military alliance. During the next ten years, German policies abroad caused the British to draw closer to France. By 1907, an alliance of Great Britain, France, and Russia—known as the Triple Entente—stood opposed to the Triple Alliance of Germany, Austria-Hungary, and Italy. Europe became divided into two opposing camps that became more and more inflexible and unwilling to compromise. A series of crises in the Balkans between 1908 and 1913 set the stage for World War I.

Crisis in the Balkans Over the course of the nineteenth century, the Balkan provinces of the Ottoman Empire had gradually gained their freedom, although the rivalry in the region between Austria and Russia complicated the process. By 1878, Greece, Serbia, and Romania had become independent states. Although freed from Ottoman rule, Montenegro was placed under an Austrian protectorate, while Bulgaria

The Balkans in 1913

achieved autonomous status under Russian protection. Bosnia and Herzegovina were placed under Austrian protection; Austria could occupy but not annex them.

Nevertheless, in 1908, Austria did annex the two Slavic-speaking territories. Serbia was outraged because the annexation dashed the Serbs' hopes of creating a large Serbian kingdom that would unite most of the southern Slavs. The Russians, as protectors of their fellow Slavs, supported the Serbs and opposed the Austrian action. Backed by the Russians, the Serbs prepared for war against Austria. At this point, William II intervened and demanded that the Russians accept Austria's annexation of Bosnia and Herzegovina or face war with Germany. Weakened from their defeat in the Russo-Japanese War in 1904–1905, the Russians backed down but vowed revenge. Two wars between the Balkan states in 1912–1913 further embittered the inhabitants of the region and generated more tensions among the great powers.

Serbia's desire to create a large Serbian kingdom remained unfulfilled. In their frustration, Serbian nationalists blamed the Austrians. Austria-Hungary was convinced that Serbia was a mortal threat to its empire and must at some point be crushed. As Serbia's chief supporters, the Russians were determined not to back down again in the event of a confrontation with Austria or Germany in the Balkans. The allies of Austria-Hungary and Russia were also determined to be more supportive of their respective allies in another crisis. By the beginning of 1914, two armed camps viewed each other with suspicion.

CONCLUSION

THE FORCES UNLEASHED between 1800 and 1870 by two revolutions—the French Revolution and the Industrial Revolution—led to Western global dominance by the end of the nineteenth century. The First and Second Industrial Revolutions seemed to prove to Europeans the underlying assumption of the Scientific Revolution of the seventeenth century—that human beings were capable of dominating nature. By rationally manipulating the material environment for human benefit, people could achieve new levels of material prosperity and produce machines hitherto not dreamed of in their wildest imaginings. Some of these new machines included weapons of war that enabled the Western world to devastate and dominate non-Western civilizations.

In 1815, a conservative order had been reestablished throughout Europe, but the revolutionary waves in Europe in the first half of the nineteenth century made it clear that the ideologies of liberalism and nationalism, unleashed by the French Revolution and now reinforced by the spread of industrialization, were still

alive and active. Between 1850 and 1871, the national state became the focus of people's loyalty. Wars, both foreign and civil, were fought to create unified nation-states, and both wars and changing political alignments served as catalysts for domestic reforms that made the nation-state the center of attention. Liberal nationalists had believed that unified nation-states would preserve individual rights and lead to a greater community of peoples. But the new nationalism of the late nineteenth century, loud and patriotic, did not unify peoples but divided them instead as the new national states became embroiled in bitter competition after 1871.

Between 1871 and 1914, the national state began to expand its functions beyond all previous limits. Fearful of the growth of socialism and trade unions, governments attempted to appease the working masses by adopting such **social insurance** measures as compensation for accidents, illness, and old age. These social welfare measures provided only limited benefits before 1914, but they signaled a new direction for state action to benefit all citizens.

This extension of state functions took place in an atmosphere of increased national loyalty. After 1871, nation-states increasingly sought to solidify the social order and win the active loyalty and support of their citizens by deliberately cultivating national feelings. Yet this policy contained potentially great dangers. Nations had discovered once again that imperialistic adventures and military successes could arouse nationalistic passions and smother domestic political unrest. But they also found—belatedly in 1914—that nationalistic feelings could also lead to intense international rivalries that made war almost inevitable.

TIMELINE

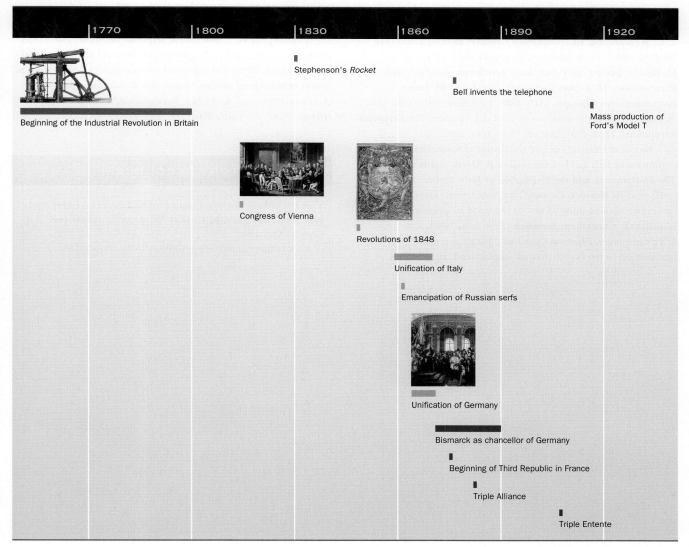

1770 1800 1830 1860 1890 1920

Beginning of the Industrial Revolution in Britain

Stephenson's *Rocket*

Bell invents the telephone

Mass production of Ford's Model T

Congress of Vienna

Revolutions of 1848

Unification of Italy

Emancipation of Russian serfs

Unification of Germany

Bismarck as chancellor of Germany

Beginning of Third Republic in France

Triple Alliance

Triple Entente

SUGGESTED READING

The Industrial Revolution and Its Impact Still a good introduction to the Industrial Revolution is the well-written work by **D. Landes,** *The Unbound Prometheus: Technological Change and Industrial Development in Western Europe from 1750 to the Present* (Cambridge, 1969). Also valuable is **J. Horn,** *The Industrial Revolution* (Westport, Conn., 2007). For a broader perspective, see

P. Stearns, *The Industrial Revolution in World History* (Boulder, Colo., 1993). On the role of the British, see **K. Morgan,** *The Birth of Industrial Britain: Social Change, 1750–1850* (New York, 2004). On the social impact of the Industrial Revolution, see **P. Pilbeam,** *The Middle Classes in Europe, 1789–1914* (Basingstoke, England, 1990), and **J. G. Williamson,** *Coping with City Growth During the British Industrial Revolution* (Cambridge, 2002).

The Growth of Industrial Prosperity The Second Industrial Revolution is well covered in **D. Landes, *The Unbound Prometheus.*** For a fundamental survey of European industrialization, see **A. S. Milward** and **S. B. Saul, *The Development of the Economies of Continental Europe, 1850–1914*** (Cambridge, Mass., 1977). On Marx, the standard work is **D. McLellan, *Karl Marx: His Life and Thought,*** 4th ed. (New York, 2006). See also **F. Wheen, *Karl Marx: A Life*** (New York, 2001).

The Growth of Nationalism, 1814–1848 For a good survey of the nineteenth century, see **R. Gildea, *Barricades and Borders: Europe, 1800–1914,*** 3rd ed. (Oxford, 2003). Also valuable is **T. C. W. Blanning, ed., *Nineteenth Century: Europe, 1789–1914*** (Oxford, 2000). For a survey of the period 1814–1848, see **M. Broers, *Europe After Napoleon: Revolution, Reaction, and Romanticism, 1814–1848*** (New York, 1996), and **M. Lyons, *Postrevolutionary Europe, 1815–1856*** (New York, 2006). The best introduction to the revolutions of 1848 is **J. Sperber, *The European Revolutions, 1848–1851,*** 2nd ed. (New York, 2005).

National Unification and the National State, 1848–1871 The unification of Italy can be examined in **B. Derek** and **E. F. Biagini, *The Risorgimento and the Unification of Italy,*** 2nd ed. (London, 2002), and **H. Hearder, *Cavour*** (New York, 1994). The unification of Germany can be pursued first in two good biographies of Bismarck, **E. Crankshaw, *Bismarck*** (New York, 1981), and **E. Feuchtwanger, *Bismarck*** (London, 2002). For a good introduction to the French Second Empire, see **J. F. McMillan,** *Napoleon III* (New York, 1991). On the Austrian Empire, see **R. Okey, *The Habsburg Monarchy*** (New York, 2001). Imperial Russia is covered in **T. Chapman, *Imperial Russia, 1801–1905*** (London, 2001). On Victorian Britain, see **W. L. Arnstein, *Queen Victoria*** (New York, 2005), and **I. Machlin, *Disraeli*** (London, 1995).

The European State, 1871–1914 On Britain, see **D. Read, *The Age of Urban Democracy: England, 1868–1914*** (New York, 1994). For a detailed examination of French history from 1871 to 1914, see **J.-M. Mayeur** and **M. Reberioux, *The Third Republic from Its Origins to the Great War, 1871–1914*** (Cambridge, 1984). On Germany, see **W. J. Mommsen, *Imperial Germany, 1867–1918*** (New York, 1995), and **E. Feuchtwanger, *Imperial Germany, 1850–1918*** (London, 2001). On aspects of Russian history, see **H. Rogger, *Russia in the Age of Modernization and Revolution, 1881–1917*** (London, 1983), and **A. Ascher, *Revolution of 1905: A Short History*** (Stanford, Calif., 2004).

In what ways was the development of industrialization related to the growth of nationalism?

In thinking about this question, begin by breaking it down into the components shown below. A discussion of the significance of each component should appear in your answer.

ARTS AND IDEAS Look at the painting of the proclamation of the Second German Empire (p. 481) and the painting of José de San Martín leading his troops in battle to liberate Chile from the Spaniards (on the left, p. 492). San Martín was one of the leaders of the South American independence movement in the nineteenth century—see Chapter 20. How do the two paintings reflect a sense of nationalism? What symbols are used to illustrate the power of these new nations? How can art help create a sense of national identity? Does nationalistic art need to be historically accurate? Do you think these depictions are historically accurate and give a realistic portrayal of the leaders? Can you think of any modern comparisons?

SCIENCE AND TECHNOLOGY Based on the comments of Samuel Smiles and Shibuzawa Eiichi (document, p. 470) and the comparative essay (p. 468), as well as the pictures in the comparative illustration (p. 466), comment on the differing views of industrialization in Eastern and Western societies. Did it serve the same purpose in both? Why did industrialization come much later to Eastern societies? How would this have affected the growth of nationalism?

POLITICS AND GOVERNMENT Looking at the maps below, consider whether there was any correlation between industrialization and nationalist movements in nineteenth-century Europe. Which regions in Europe were the first to industrialize? Which were the last? In which areas did nationalist movements succeed? Where did they fail? In which nations were liberal reforms implemented? Do you see any relationship between liberal reforms and industrialization?

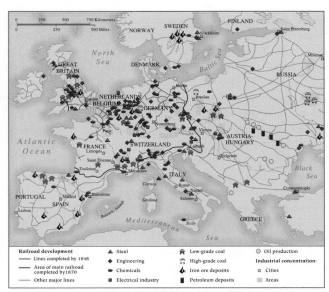

The Industrial Regions of Europe at the End of the Nineteenth Century

Europe in 1871

CHAPTER 20

THE AMERICAS AND SOCIETY AND CULTURE IN THE WEST

A portrait of Toussaint L'Ouverture, leader of the Haitian independence movement

© North Wind Picture Archives

CHAPTER OUTLINE AND FOCUS QUESTIONS

Latin America in the Nineteenth and Early Twentieth Centuries

Q What role did liberalism and nationalism play in Latin America between 1800 and 1870? What were the major economic, social, and political trends in Latin America in the late nineteenth and early twentieth centuries?

The North American Neighbors: The United States and Canada

Q What role did nationalism and liberalism play in the United States and Canada between 1800 and 1870? What economic, social, and political trends were evident in the United States and Canada between 1870 and 1914?

The Emergence of Mass Society

Q What is meant by the term *mass society,* and what were its main characteristics?

Cultural Life: Romanticism and Realism in the Western World

Q What were the main characteristics of Romanticism and Realism?

Toward the Modern Consciousness: Intellectual and Cultural Developments

Q What intellectual and cultural developments in the late nineteenth and early twentieth centuries "opened the way to a modern consciousness," and how did this consciousness differ from earlier worldviews?

CRITICAL THINKING

Q In what ways were the intellectual and cultural developments in the Western world between 1800 and 1914 related to the economic, social, and political developments?

NATIONALISM—one of the major forces for change in Europe in the nineteenth century—also affected Latin America as the colonial peoples there overthrew their Spanish and Portuguese masters and began the process of creating new national states. An unusual revolution in Haiti preceded the main independence movements. Pierre Dominique Toussaint L'Ouverture, the grandson of an African king, was born a slave in Saint-Domingue—the western third of the island of Hispaniola, a French sugar colony—in 1746. Educated by his godfather, Toussaint was able to amass a small private fortune through his own talents and the generosity of his French master. When black slaves in Saint-Domingue, inspired by news of the French Revolution, revolted in 1791, Toussaint became their leader. For years, Toussaint and his ragtag army struck at the French. By 1801, after his army had come to control Saint-Domingue, Toussaint assumed the role of ruler and issued a constitution that freed all slaves.

But Napoleon Bonaparte refused to accept Toussaint's control of France's richest colony and sent a French army of 23,000 men under General Leclerc, his brother-in-law, to crush the rebellion. Although yellow fever took its toll on the French, the superior size and weapons of their army enabled them to gain the upper hand. Toussaint was tricked into surrendering in 1802 with Leclerc's promise: "You will not find a more sincere friend than myself." What a friend! Toussaint was arrested, put in chains, and shipped to France, where he died a year later in a dungeon. The western part of Hispaniola, now called Haiti, however, became the first independent state in Latin America when Toussaint's lieutenants drove out the French forces in 1804. Haiti was only one of a number of places in the Americas where new nations were formed during the nineteenth century. Indeed, nation building was prominent in North America as the United States and Canada expanded.

As national states in both the Western Hemisphere and Europe were evolving in the nineteenth century, significant changes were occurring in society and culture. The rapid economic changes of the nineteenth century led to the emergence of mass society in the Western world, which meant improvements for the lower classes, who benefited from the extension of voting rights, a better standard of living, and universal education. The coming of mass society also created new roles for the governments of nation-states, which now fostered national loyalty, created mass armies by conscription, and took more responsibility for public health and housing measures in their cities. Cultural and intellectual changes paralleled these social developments, and after 1870, Western philosophers, writers, and artists began exploring modern cultural expressions that questioned traditional ideas and increasingly provoked a crisis of confidence. ❁

Latin America in the Nineteenth and Early Twentieth Centuries

Q **Focus Questions:** What role did liberalism and nationalism play in Latin America between 1800 and 1870? What were the major economic, social, and political trends in Latin America in the late nineteenth and early twentieth centuries?

The Spanish and Portuguese colonial empires in Latin America had been integrated into the traditional monarchical structure of Europe for centuries. When that structure was challenged, first by the ideas of the Enlightenment and then by the upheavals of the Napoleonic era, Latin America encountered the possibility of change. How it responded to that possibility, however, was determined in part by conditions unique to the region.

The Wars for Independence

By the end of the eighteenth century, the ideas of the Enlightenment and the new political ideals stemming from the successful revolution in North America were beginning to influence the creole elites (descendants of Europeans who became permanent inhabitants of Latin America). The principles of the equality of all people in the eyes of the law, free trade, and a free press proved very attractive. Sons of creoles, such as Simón Bolívar and José de San Martín, who became leaders of the independence movement, even went to European universities, where they imbibed the ideas of the Enlightenment.

Nationalistic Revolts in Latin America The creole elites soon began to use their new ideas to denounce the rule of the Iberian monarchs and the peninsulars (Spanish and Portuguese officials who resided in Latin America for political and economic gain). As Bolívar said in 1815, "It would be easier to have the two continents meet than to reconcile the spirits of Spain and America."[1] When Napoleon Bonaparte toppled the monarchies of Spain and Portugal, the authority of the Spaniards and Portuguese in their colonial empires was weakened, and between 1807 and 1825, a series of revolts enabled most of Latin America to become independent.

The first revolt was actually a successful slave rebellion. As we have seen, Toussaint L'Ouverture (1746–1803) led a revolt of more than 100,000 black slaves and seized control of all of Hispaniola. On January 1, 1804, the western part of the island, now called Haiti, announced its freedom and became the first independent postcolonial state in Latin America.

Beginning in 1810, Mexico, too, experienced a revolt, fueled initially by the desire of the creole elites to overthrow the rule of the peninsulars. The first real hero of Mexican independence was Miguel Hidalgo y Costilla, a parish priest in a small village about 100 miles from Mexico City. Hidalgo had studied the French Revolution and roused the local Indians and mestizos, many of whom were suffering from a major famine, to free themselves from the Spanish. On September 16, 1810, a crowd of Indians and mestizos, armed with clubs, machetes, and a few guns, quickly formed a mob army to attack the Spaniards, shouting, "Long live independence and death to the Spaniards." But Hidalgo was not a good organizer, and his forces were soon crushed. A military court sentenced Hidalgo to death, but his memory lived on. In fact, September 16, the first day of the uprising, is celebrated as Mexico's Independence Day.

The participation of Indians and mestizos in Mexico's revolt against Spanish control frightened both creoles and peninsulars. Fearful of the masses, they cooperated in defeating the popular revolutionary forces. The elites—both creoles and peninsulars—then decided to overthrow Spanish rule as a way of preserving their own power. They selected a creole military leader, Augustín de Iturbide, as their leader and the first emperor of Mexico in 1821. The new government fostered neither political nor economic changes, and it soon became apparent that Mexican independence had benefited primarily the creole elites.

The Liberators of South America. José de San Martín and Simón Bolívar are hailed as the leaders of the South American independence movement. In the painting on the left, by Theodore Géricault, a French Romantic painter, San Martín is shown leading his troops at the Battle of Chacabuco in Chile in 1817. The painting on the right shows Bolívar leading his troops across the Andes in 1823 to fight in Peru. This depiction of perfectly uniformed troops moving in neat formation through the snow of the Andes, by the Chilean artist Franco Gomez, is, of course, highly unrealistic.

Independence movements elsewhere in Latin America were likewise the work of elites—primarily creoles—who overthrew Spanish rule and set up new governments that they could dominate. José de San Martín (1778–1850) of Argentina and Simón Bolívar (1783–1830) of Venezuela, leaders of the independence movement, were both members of the creole elite, and both were hailed as the liberators of South America.

The Efforts of Bolívar and San Martín Simón Bolívar has long been regarded as the George Washington of Latin America. Born into a wealthy Venezuelan family, he was introduced as a young man to the ideas of the Enlightenment. While in Rome in 1805 to witness the coronation of Napoleon as king of Italy, he committed himself to free his people from Spanish control. He vowed, "I swear before the God of my fathers, by my fathers themselves, by my honor and by my country, that my arm shall not rest nor my mind be at peace until I have broken the chains that bind me by the will and power of Spain."[2] When he returned to South America, Bolívar began to lead the bitter struggle for independence in Venezuela as well as other parts of northern South America. Although he was acclaimed as the "liberator" of Venezuela in 1813 by the people, it was not until 1821 that he definitively defeated Spanish forces there. He went on to liberate Colombia, Ecuador, and Peru. Already in 1819, he had become president of Venezuela, at the time part of a federation that included Colombia and Ecuador. Bolívar was well aware of the difficulties in establishing stable republican governments in Latin America (see the box on p. 493).

While Bolívar was busy liberating northern South America from the Spanish, José de San Martín was concentrating his efforts on the southern part of the continent. Son of a Spanish army officer in Argentina, San Martín himself went to Spain and pursued a military career in the Spanish army. In 1811, after serving twenty-two years, he learned of the liberation movement in his native Argentina, abandoned his military career in Spain, and returned to his homeland in March 1812. Argentina had already been freed from Spanish control, but San Martín believed that the Spaniards must be removed from all of South America if any nation was to be free. In January 1817, he led his

Simón Bolívar on Government in Latin America

Simón Bolívar is acclaimed as the man who liberated Latin America from Spanish control. His interest in history and the ideas of the Enlightenment also led him to speculate on how Latin American nations would be governed after their freedom was obtained. This selection is taken from a letter written to the British governor of Jamaica.

Simón Bolívar, *The Jamaica Letter*

It is . . . difficult to foresee the future fate of the New World, to set down its political principles, or to prophesy what manner of government it will adopt. . . . We inhabit a world apart, separated by broad seas. We are young in the ways of almost all the arts and sciences, although in a certain manner, we are old in the ways of civilized society. . . . But we scarcely retain a vestige of what once was; we are, moreover, neither Indian nor European, but a species midway between the legitimate proprietors of this country and the Spanish usurpers. In short, though Americans by birth we derive our rights from Europe, and we have to assert these rights against the rights of the natives, and at the same time we must defend ourselves against the invaders. This places us in a most extraordinary and involved situation. . . .

The role of the inhabitants of the American hemisphere has for centuries been purely passive. Politically they were non-existent. We are still in a position lower than slavery, and therefore it is more difficult for us to rise to the enjoyment of freedom. . . . States are slaves because of either the nature or the misuse of their constitutions; a people is therefore enslaved when the government, by its nature or its vices, infringes on and usurps the rights of the citizen or subject. Applying these principles, we find that America

was denied not only its freedom but even an active and effective tyranny. . . .

It is harder, Montesquieu has written, to release a nation from servitude than to enslave a free nation. This truth is proven by the annals of all times, which reveal that most free nations have been put under the yoke, but very few enslaved nations have recovered their liberty. Despite the convictions of history, South Americans have made efforts to obtain liberal, even perfect, institutions, doubtless out of that instinct to aspire to the greatest possible happiness, which, common to all men, is bound to follow in civil societies founded on the principles of justice, liberty, and equality. But are we capable of maintaining in proper balance the difficult charge of a republic? Is it conceivable that a newly emancipated people can soar to the heights of liberty . . . ? Such a marvel is inconceivable and without precedent. There is no reasonable probability to bolster our hopes.

More than anyone, I desire to see America fashioned into the greatest nation in the world, greatest not so much by virtue of her area and wealth as by her freedom and glory. Although I seek perfection for the government of my country, I cannot persuade myself that the New World can, at the moment, be organized as a great republic. Since it is impossible, I dare not desire it; yet much less do I desire to have all America a monarchy because this plan is not only impracticable but also impossible. Wrongs now existing could not be righted, and our emancipation would be fruitless. The American states need the care of paternal governments to heal the sores and wounds of despotism and war.

Q *What problems did Bolívar foresee for Spanish America's political future? Do you think he believed in democracy? Why or why not?*

---

forces over the high Andes Mountains, an amazing feat in itself. Two-thirds of their pack mules and horses died during the difficult journey. Many of the soldiers suffered from lack of oxygen and severe cold while crossing mountain passes more than 2 miles above sea level. The arrival of San Martín's troops in Chile completely surprised the Spaniards, whose forces were routed at the Battle of Chacabuco on February 12, 1817.

In 1821, San Martín moved on to Lima, Peru, the center of Spanish authority. Convinced that he was unable to complete the liberation of all of Peru, San Martín welcomed the arrival of Bolívar and his forces. As he wrote to Bolívar, "For me it would have been the height of happiness to end the war of independence under the orders of a general to whom [South] America owes its freedom. Destiny orders it otherwise, and one must resign oneself to it."[3] Highly disappointed, San Martín left South America for Europe, where he remained until his death

in 1850. Meanwhile, Bolívar took on the task of crushing the last significant Spanish army at Ayacucho on December 9, 1824. By then, Peru, Uruguay, Paraguay, Colombia, Venezuela, Argentina, Bolivia, and Chile had all become free states (see Map 20.1). In 1823, the Central American states became independent and in 1838–1839 divided into five republics (Guatemala, El Salvador, Honduras, Costa Rica, and Nicaragua). Earlier, in 1822, the prince regent of Brazil had declared Brazil's independence from Portugal.

Independence and the Monroe Doctrine In the early 1820s, only one major threat remained to the newly won independence of the Latin American states. Reveling in their success in crushing rebellions in Spain and Italy, the victorious continental European powers favored the use of troops to restore Spanish control in Latin America. This time, Britain's opposition to intervention prevailed. Eager to gain access to an entire continent for investment

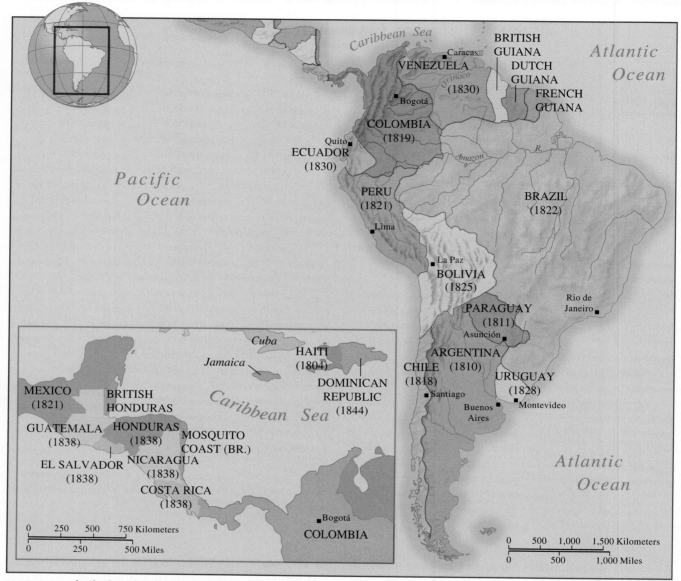

MAP 20.1 **Latin America in the First Half of the Nineteenth Century.** Latin American colonies took advantage of Spain's weakness during the Napoleonic wars to fight for independence, beginning with Argentina in 1810 and spreading throughout the region over the next decade with the help of leaders like Simón Bolívar and José de San Martín.
Q How many South American countries are sources of rivers that feed the Amazon, and roughly what percentage of the continent is contained within the Amazon's watershed?

and trade, the British proposed joint action with the United States against European interference in Latin America. Distrustful of British motives, President James Monroe acted alone in 1823, guaranteeing the independence of the new Latin American nations and warning against any further European intervention in the Americas under what is known as the Monroe Doctrine. Even more important to Latin American independence than American words was Britain's navy. All of the continental

European powers were reluctant to challenge British naval power, which stood between Latin America and any European invasion force.

The Difficulties of Nation Building

As Simón Bolívar had foreseen, the new Latin American nations, most of which began as republics, faced a number of serious problems between 1830 and 1870.

The wars for independence had themselves resulted in a staggering loss of population, property, and livestock. At the same time, disputes arose between nations over their precise boundaries.

Political Difficulties   The new nations of Latin America established republican governments, but they had had no experience in ruling themselves. Due to the insecurities prevalent after independence, strong leaders known as **caudillos** came to power. National caudillos were generally one of two types. One group, who supported the elites, consisted of autocrats who controlled (and often abused) state revenues, centralized power, and kept the new national states together. Sometimes they were also modernizers who built roads and canals, ports, and schools. These caudillos were usually supported by the Catholic church, the rural aristocracy, and the army, which emerged from the wars of independence as a powerful political force that often made and deposed governments. Many caudillos, in fact, were former army leaders.

In contrast, other caudillos were supported by the masses, became extremely popular, and served as instruments for radical change. Juan Manuel de Rosas, for example, who led Argentina from 1829 to 1852, became very popular by favoring Argentine interests against foreigners.

Economic Patterns   Although political independence brought economic independence, old patterns were quickly reestablished. Instead of Spain and Portugal, Great Britain now dominated the Latin American economy. Old trade patterns soon reemerged. Since Latin America served as a source of raw materials and foodstuffs for the industrializing nations of Europe and the United States, exports—especially wheat, tobacco, wool, sugar, coffee, and hides—to the North Atlantic countries increased noticeably. At the same time, finished consumer goods, especially textiles, were imported in increasing quantities, causing a decline in industrial production in Latin America.

Social Conditions   A fundamental underlying problem for all of the new Latin American nations was the persistent domination of society by the landed elites. Large estates remained an important aspect of Latin America's economic and social life. After independence, the size of these estates expanded even more. By 1848, the Sánchez Navarro family in Mexico owned seventeen haciendas (plantations) covering 16 million acres. Estates were often so large that they could not be farmed efficiently. As one Latin American newspaper put it, "The huge fortunes have the unfortunate tendency to grow even larger, and their owners possess vast

tracts of land, which lie fallow and abandoned. Their greed for land does not equal their ability to use it intelligently and actively."[4]

Land remained the basis of wealth, social prestige, and political power throughout the nineteenth century. The Latin American elites tended to identify with European standards of progress, which worked to their benefit, while the masses gained little. Landed elites ran governments, controlled courts, and maintained the system of debt peonage that provided large landowners with a supply of cheap labor. These landowners made enormous profits by concentrating on specialized crops for export, such as coffee, while the masses, left without land to grow basic food crops, lived in dire poverty.

Tradition and Change in the Latin American Economy and Society

After 1870, Latin America began to experience an era of rapid economic growth based to a large extent on the export of a few basic items, such as wheat and beef from Argentina, coffee from Brazil, nitrates from Chile, coffee and bananas from Central America, and sugar and silver from Peru. These foodstuffs and raw materials were exchanged for finished goods—textiles, machines, and luxury goods—from Europe and the United States. Despite their economic growth, Latin American nations remained economic colonies of Western nations.

Old patterns also still largely prevailed in society. Rural elites dominated their estates and their workers. Although slavery was abolished by 1888, former slaves and their descendants were at the bottom of their society. The Indians remained poverty-stricken.

One result of the new prosperity that came from increased exports was growth in the middle sectors of Latin American society—lawyers, merchants, shopkeepers, businesspeople, schoolteachers, professors, bureaucrats, and military officers. These middle sectors, which made up only 5 to 10 percent of the population, depending on the country, were hardly large enough in numbers to constitute a true middle class. Nevertheless, after 1900, the middle sectors continued to expand. They lived in the cities, sought education and decent incomes, and increasingly saw the United States as the model to emulate, especially in regard to industrialization and education.

As Latin American export economies boomed, the working class expanded, which in turn led to the growth of labor unions, especially after 1914. Radical unions often advocated the use of the general strike as an instrument for change. By and large, however, the governing elites succeeded in stifling the political influence of the working class by restricting workers' right to vote.

The need for industrial labor also led Latin American countries to encourage immigration from Europe. Between 1880 and 1914, three million Europeans, primarily Italians and Spaniards, settled in Argentina. More than 100,000 Europeans, mostly Italian, Portuguese, and Spanish, arrived in Brazil each year between 1891 and 1900.

As in Europe and the United States, industrialization led to urbanization, evident in both the emergence of new cities and the rapid growth of old ones. By 1900 Buenos Aires (the "Paris" of South America) had 750,000 inhabitants, and by 1914 it had two million—a fourth of Argentina's population.

Political Change in Latin America

Latin America also experienced a political transformation after 1870. Large landowners began to take a more direct interest in national politics and even in governing. In Argentina and Chile, for example, landholding elites controlled the governments, and although they produced constitutions similar to those of the United States and European nations, they ensured their power by regulating voting rights.

In some countries, large landowners supported dictators to ensure the interests of the ruling elite. Porfirio Díaz, who ruled Mexico from 1876 to 1910, created a conservative, centralized government with the support of the army, foreign capitalists, large landowners, and the Catholic church. Nevertheless, there were forces for change in Mexico that led to revolution in 1910.

During Díaz's dictatorial reign, 95 percent of the rural population owned no land at all, while about one thousand families owned almost all of Mexico. When a liberal landowner, Francisco Madero, forced Díaz from power, he opened the door to a wider revolution. Madero's ineffectiveness created a demand for agrarian reform led by Emiliano Zapata, who aroused the masses of landless peasants and began to seize the estates of the wealthy landholders. Between 1910 and 1920, the revolution caused untold destruction to the Mexican economy. Finally, in 1917 a new constitution established a strong presidency, implemented land reform policies, placed limits on foreign investors, and set an agenda for social welfare for workers.

By this time, a new power had begun to wield its influence over Latin America. By 1900, the United States, which had begun to emerge as a great world power, began to interfere in the affairs of its southern neighbors. As a result of the Spanish-American War (1898), Cuba became a U.S. protectorate, and Puerto Rico was annexed outright to the United States. American investments in Latin America soon followed; so did American resolve to protect these investments.

Between 1898 and 1934, American military forces were sent to Cuba, Mexico, Guatemala, Honduras, Nicaragua, Panama, Colombia, Haiti, and the Dominican Republic to protect American interests. At the same time, the United States became the chief foreign investor in Latin America.

© Snark/Art Resource, NY

Emiliano Zapata. The inability of Francisco Madero to carry out far-reaching reforms led to a more radical upheaval in the Mexican countryside. Emiliano Zapata led a band of Indians in a revolt against the large landowners of southern Mexico and issued his own demands for land reform.

The North American Neighbors: The United States and Canada

Q Focus Questions: What role did nationalism and liberalism play in the United States and Canada between 1800 and 1870? What economic, social, and political trends were evident in the United States and Canada between 1870 and 1914?

Colonial Latin America had distinctive features that differed from those found in the North American colonies. The North American colonies were a part of the British Empire, and although they gained their freedom from the British at different times, both the United States and Canada emerged as independent and prosperous nations whose political systems owed much to British political thought. In the nineteenth century, both the United States and Canada faced difficult obstacles in achieving national unity.

The Growth of the United States

The U.S. Constitution, ratified in 1789, committed the United States to two of the major influences of the first half of the nineteenth century, liberalism and nationalism. A strong force for national unity came from the Supreme Court while John Marshall (1755–1835) was chief justice from 1801 to 1835. Marshall made the Supreme Court into an important national institution by asserting the right of the Court to overrule an act of Congress if the Court found it to be in violation of the Constitution. Under Marshall, the Supreme Court contributed further to establishing the supremacy of the national government by curbing the actions of state courts and legislatures.

The election of Andrew Jackson (1767–1845) as president in 1828 opened a new era in American politics, the era of mass democracy. The electorate was expanded by dropping property qualifications; by the 1830s, suffrage had been extended to almost all adult white males. During the period from 1815 to 1850, the traditional liberal belief in the improvement of human beings was also given concrete expression through the establishment of detention schools for juvenile delinquents and new penal institutions, both motivated by the liberal belief that the right kind of environment would rehabilitate wayward individuals.

Slavery and the Coming of War

By the mid-nineteenth century, American national unity was increasingly threatened by the issue of slavery. Both North and South had grown dramatically during the first half of the nineteenth century, but in different ways. The cotton economy and social structure of the South were based on the exploitation of enslaved black Africans and their descendants. Although the importation of new slaves had been barred in 1808, there were four million slaves in the South by 1860—four times the number sixty years earlier. The cotton economy depended on plantation-based slavery, and the South was determined to maintain them. In the North, many people feared the spread of slavery into western territories.

As polarization over the issue of slavery intensified, compromise became less feasible. When Abraham Lincoln, the man who had said in a speech in Illinois in 1858 that "this government cannot endure permanently half slave and half free," was elected president in November 1860, the die was cast. Lincoln, the Republicans' second presidential candidate, carried only 2 of the 1,109 counties in the South; the Republican Party was not even on the ballot in ten southern states. On December 20, 1860, a South Carolina convention voted to repeal the state's ratification of the U.S. Constitution. In February 1861, six more southern states did the same, and a rival nation, the Confederate States of America, was formed. In April, fighting erupted between North and South.

The Civil War

The American Civil War (1861–1865) was an extraordinarily bloody struggle, a foretaste of the total war to come in the twentieth century. More than 600,000 soldiers died, either in battle or from deadly infectious diseases spawned by filthy camp conditions.

Over a period of four years, the Union states of the North mobilized their superior assets and gradually wore down the Confederate forces of the South. As the war dragged on, it had the effect of radicalizing public opinion in the North. What began as a war to save the Union became a war against slavery. On January 1, 1863, Lincoln issued his Emancipation Proclamation, declaring most of the nation's slaves "forever free" (see the box on p. 483 in Chapter 19). An increasingly effective Union blockade of the ports of the South, combined with a shortage of fighting men, made the Confederate cause desperate by the end of 1864. The final push of Union troops under General Ulysses S. Grant forced General Robert E. Lee's Confederate Army to surrender on April 9, 1865. Although problems lay ahead, the Union victory reunited the country and confirmed that the United States would thereafter again be "one nation, indivisible."

The Rise of the United States

Four years of bloody civil war had restored American national unity. The old South had been destroyed; one-fifth of its adult white male population had been killed, and four million black slaves had been freed. For a while

The Dead at Antietam. National unity in the United States dissolved over the issue of slavery and led to a bloody civil war that cost 600,000 American lives. This photograph shows the southern dead after the Battle of Antietam on September 17, 1862. The invention of photography in the 1830s made it possible to document the horrors of war in the most graphic manner.

© Peter Newark Military Pictures/The Bridgeman Art Library

In 1890, the richest 9 percent of Americans owned an incredible 71 percent of all the wealth. Labor unrest over unsafe working conditions, strict work discipline, and periodic cycles of devastating unemployment led workers to organize. By the turn of the century, one national organization, the American Federation of Labor, emerged as labor's dominant voice. Its lack of real power, however, was reflected in its membership figures. In 1900, it included only 8.4 percent of the American industrial labor force.

During the so-called Progressive Era after 1900, reform swept the United States. State governments enacted laws that governed hours, wages, and working conditions, especially for women and children. The realization that state laws were ineffective in dealing with nationwide problems, however, led to a Progressive movement at the national level. The Meat Inspection Act and Pure Food and Drug Act provided for a limited degree of federal regulation of industrial practices. The presidency of Woodrow Wilson (1913–1921) witnessed the enactment of a graduated federal income tax and the establishment of the Federal Reserve System, which permitted the national government to play a role in important economic decisions formerly made by bankers. Like European nations, the United States was slowly adopting policies that broadened the functions of the state.

at least, a program of radical change in the South was attempted. Slavery was formally abolished by the Thirteenth Amendment to the Constitution in 1865, and the Fourteenth and Fifteenth Amendments extended citizenship to blacks and gave black men the right to vote. Radical Reconstruction in the early 1870s tried to create a new South based on the principle of the equality of black and white people, but the changes were soon mostly undone. Militia organizations, such as the Ku Klux Klan, used violence to discourage blacks from voting. A new system of sharecropping made blacks once again economically dependent on white landowners. New state laws made it nearly impossible for blacks to exercise their right to vote. By the end of the 1870s, supporters of white supremacy were back in power everywhere in the South.

Prosperity and Progressivism   Between 1860 and 1914, the United States made the shift from an agrarian to a mighty industrial nation. American heavy industry stood unchallenged in 1900. In that year, the Carnegie Steel Company alone produced more steel than Great Britain's entire steel industry. Industrialization also led to urbanization. Whereas 20 percent of Americans lived in cities in 1860, more than 40 percent did in 1900.

The United States had become the world's richest nation and greatest industrial power. Yet serious questions remained about the quality of American life.

The United States as a World Power   At the end of the nineteenth century, the United States began to expand abroad. The Samoan Islands in the Pacific became the first important American colony; the Hawaiian Islands were next. By 1887, American settlers had gained control of the sugar industry on the Hawaiian Islands. As more Americans settled in Hawaii, they sought political power. When Queen Liliuokalani tried to strengthen the monarchy in order to keep the islands for the native peoples, the U.S. government sent Marines to "protect" American lives. The queen was deposed, and Hawaii was annexed by the United States in 1898.

The defeat of Spain in the Spanish-American War in 1898 expanded the American empire to include Cuba, Puerto Rico, Guam, and the Philippines. Although the

Filipinos appealed for independence, the Americans refused to grant it. As President William McKinley said, the United States had the duty "to educate the Filipinos and uplift and Christianize them," a remarkable statement in view of the fact that most of them had been Roman Catholics for centuries. It took three years and 60,000 troops to pacify the Philippines and establish U.S. control. By the beginning of the twentieth century, the United States had an empire.

The Making of Canada

North of the United States, the process of nation building was also making progress. Under the Treaty of Paris in 1763, Canada—or New France, as it was called—passed into the hands of the British. By 1800, most Canadians favored more autonomy, although the colonists disagreed on the form this autonomy should take. Upper Canada (now Ontario) was predominantly English speaking, whereas Lower Canada (now Quebec) was dominated by French Canadians.

In 1837, a number of Canadian groups rose in rebellion against British authority. Although the rebellions were crushed by the following year, the British government now began to seek ways to satisfy some of the Canadian demands. The U.S. Civil War proved to be a turning point. Fearful of American designs on Canada during the war, the British government finally capitulated to Canadian demands. In 1867, Parliament established the Dominion of Canada, with its own constitution. Canada now possessed a parliamentary system and ruled itself, although foreign affairs still remained under the control of the British government.

Canada faced problems of national unity between 1870 and 1914. At the beginning of 1870, the Dominion of Canada had only four provinces: Quebec, Ontario, Nova Scotia, and New Brunswick. With the addition of two more provinces in 1871—Manitoba and British Columbia—the Dominion now extended from the Atlantic Ocean to the Pacific. As the first prime minister, John Macdonald (1815–1891) moved to strengthen Canadian unity. He pushed for the construction of a transcontinental railroad, which was completed in 1885 and opened the western lands to industrial and commercial development. This also led to the incorporation of two more provinces—Alberta and Saskatchewan—in 1905 into the Dominion of Canada.

Real unity was difficult to achieve, however, because of the distrust between the English-speaking majority and the French-speaking

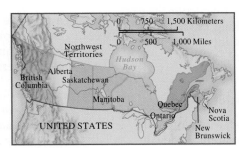

Canada, 1914

Canadians, living primarily in Quebec. Wilfred Laurier, who became the first French Canadian prime minister in 1896, was able to reconcile Canada's two major groups and resolve the issue of separate schools for French Canadians. During Laurier's administration, industrialization boomed, especially the production of textiles, furniture, and railway equipment. Hundreds of thousands of immigrants, primarily from central and eastern Europe, also flowed into Canada. Many settled on lands in the west, thus helping populate Canada's vast territories.

The Emergence of Mass Society

Q Focus Question: What is meant by the term *mass society*, and what were its main characteristics?

While new states were developing in the Western Hemisphere in the nineteenth century, a new kind of society—a **mass society**—was emerging in Europe, especially in the second half of the nineteenth century as a result of rapid economic and social changes. For the lower classes, mass society brought voting rights, an improved standard of living, and access to education. At the same time, however, mass society also made possible the development of organizations that manipulated the populations of the nation-states. To understand this mass society, we need to examine some aspects of its structure.

The New Urban Environment

One of the most important consequences of industrialization and the population explosion of the nineteenth century was urbanization. In the course of the nineteenth century, more and more people came to live in cities. In 1800, city dwellers constituted 40 percent of the population in Britain, 25 percent in France and Germany, and only 10 percent in eastern Europe. By 1914, urban residents had increased to 80 percent of the population in Britain, 45 percent in France, 60 percent in Germany, and 30 percent in eastern Europe. The size of cities also expanded dramatically, especially in industrialized countries. Between 1800 and 1900, London's population grew from 960,000 to 6.5 million and Berlin's from 172,000 to 2.7 million.

Urban populations grew faster than the general population primarily because of the vast migration from rural areas to cities. But cities also grew faster in the second half of the nineteenth century because health and the conditions of life in them were improving as urban reformers and city officials used new technology to ameliorate the urban landscape. Following the reformers' advice, city governments set up boards of health to improve the quality of housing and instituted regulations requiring all new buildings to have running water and internal drainage systems.

Middle-class reformers also focused on the housing needs of the working class. Overcrowded, disease-ridden slums were seen as dangerous not only to physical health but also to the political and moral health of the entire nation. V. A. Huber, a German housing reformer, wrote in 1861: "Certainly it would not be too much to say that the home is the communal embodiment of family life. Thus, the purity of the dwelling is almost as important for the family as is the cleanliness of the body for the individual."[5] To Huber, good housing was a prerequisite for stable family life, and without stable family life, society would fall apart.

Early efforts to attack the housing problem emphasized the middle-class, liberal belief in the power of private enterprise. By the 1880s, as the number and size of cities continued to mushroom, governments concluded that private enterprise could not solve the housing crisis. In 1890, a British law empowered local town councils to construct cheap housing for the working classes. More and more, governments were stepping into areas of activity that they would not have touched earlier.

The Social Structure of Mass Society

At the top of European society stood a wealthy elite, constituting but 5 percent of the population while controlling between 30 and 40 percent of its wealth. In the course of the nineteenth century, landed aristocrats had joined with the most successful industrialists, bankers, and merchants (the wealthy upper middle class) to form a new elite. In many cases, marriage united the two groups. Members of this elite, whether aristocratic or middle class in background, assumed leadership roles in government bureaucracies and military hierarchies.

The middle classes consisted of a variety of groups. Below the upper middle class was a group that included lawyers, doctors, and members of the civil service, as well as business managers, engineers, architects, accountants, and chemists benefiting from industrial expansion. Beneath this solid and comfortable middle group was a lower middle class of small shopkeepers, traders, manufacturers, and prosperous peasants.

Standing between the lower middle class and the lower classes were new groups of white-collar workers who were the product of the Second Industrial Revolution. They were the salespeople, bookkeepers, bank tellers, telephone operators, and secretaries. Though often paid little more than skilled laborers, these white-collar workers were committed to middle-class ideals of hard work, Christian morality, and propriety.

Below the middle classes on the social scale were the working classes, who constituted almost 80 percent of the European population. Many of them were landholding peasants, agricultural laborers, and sharecroppers, especially in eastern Europe. The urban working class included skilled artisans in traditional trades, such as cabinetmaking, printing, and jewelry making, and semiskilled laborers, such as carpenters, bricklayers, and many factory workers. At the bottom of the urban working class stood the largest group of workers, the unskilled laborers. They included day laborers, who worked irregularly for very low wages, and large numbers of domestic servants, most of whom were women.

The Experiences of Women

In 1800, women were largely defined by family and household roles. They remained legally inferior and economically dependent. Women struggled to change their status throughout the nineteenth century.

Marriage and the Family Many women in the nineteenth century aspired to the ideal of femininity popularized by writers and poets. Alfred Lord Tennyson's poem *The Princess* expressed it well:

> *Man for the field and woman for the hearth:*
> *Man for the sword and for the needle she:*
> *Man with the head and woman with the heart:*
> *Man to command and woman to obey;*
> *All else confusion.*

This traditional characterization of the sexes, based on gender-defined social roles, was virtually elevated to the status of universal male and female attributes in the nineteenth century. As the chief family wage earners, men worked outside the home for pay, while women were left with the care of the family, for which they were paid nothing. For most women throughout most of the nineteenth century, marriage was viewed as the only honorable and available career.

The most significant development in the modern family was the decline in the number of offspring born to the average woman. While some historians attribute increased birth control to more widespread use of coitus interruptus, or male withdrawal before ejaculation, others have emphasized female control of family size through abortion and even infanticide or abandonment. That a change in attitude occurred was apparent in the development of a movement to increase awareness of birth control methods. Europe's first birth control clinic opened in Amsterdam in 1882.

The family was the central institution of middle-class life. Men provided the family income while women focused on household and child care. The use of domestic servants in many middle-class homes, made possible by an abundant supply of cheap labor, reduced the amount of time middle-class women had to spend on household chores. At the same time, by reducing the number of children in the family, mothers could devote more time to child care and domestic leisure.

A Middle-Class Family. Nineteenth-century middle-class moralists considered the family the fundamental pillar of a healthy society. The family was a crucial institution in middle-class life, and togetherness constituted one of the important ideals of the middle-class family. This painting by William P. Frith, titled *Many Happy Returns of the Day*, shows a family birthday celebration for a little girl in which grandparents, parents, and children are taking part. The servant at the left holds the presents for the little girl.

The middle-class family fostered an ideal of togetherness. The Victorians devised the family Christmas with its Yule log, Christmas tree, songs, and exchange of gifts. In the United States, Fourth of July celebrations changed from drunken revels to family picnics by the 1850s.

Women in working-class families were more accustomed to hard work. Daughters in working-class families were expected to work until they married; even after marriage, they often did piecework at home to help support the family. For the children of the working classes, childhood was over by the age of nine or ten, when they became apprentices or were employed at odd jobs.

Between 1890 and 1914, however, family patterns among the working class began to change. High-paying jobs in heavy industry and improvements in the standard of living made it possible for working-class families to depend on the income of husbands and the wages of grown children. By the early twentieth century, some working-class mothers could afford to stay at home, following the pattern of middle-class women.

The Movement for Women's Rights   Modern European feminism, or the movement for women's rights, had its beginnings during the French Revolution, when some women advocated equality for women based on the doctrine of natural rights. In the 1830s, a number of women in the United States and Europe, who worked together in several reform movements, argued for the right of women to divorce and own property. These early efforts were not overly successful; women did not gain the right to their own property until 1870 in Britain, 1900 in Germany, and 1907 in France.

The fight for property rights was only a beginning for the women's movement, however. Some middle- and upper-middle-class women gained access to higher education, and others sought entry into occupations dominated by men. The first to fall was teaching. As medical training was largely closed to women, they sought alternatives in the development of nursing. Nursing pioneers included the British nurse Florence Nightingale, whose efforts during the Crimean War (1854–1856), along with those of Clara Barton in the American Civil War (1861–1865), transformed nursing into a profession of trained, middle-class "women in white."

By the 1840s and 1850s, the movement for women's rights had entered the political arena with the call for equal political rights. Many feminists believed that the right to vote was the key to all other reforms to improve the position of women. **Suffragists** had one basic aim, the right of women to full citizenship in the nation-state.

The British women's movement was the most vocal and active in Europe. Emmeline Pankhurst (1858–1928) and her daughters, Christabel and Sylvia, founded the Women's Social and Political Union in 1903, which enrolled mostly middle- and upper-class women. Pankhurst's organization realized the value of the media and used unusual publicity stunts to call attention to its demands. Derisively labeled "suffragettes" by male politicians, they pelted government officials with eggs, chained themselves to lampposts, smashed the windows of department stores on fashionable shopping streets, burned railroad cars, and went on hunger strikes in jail.

Before World War I, the demands for women's rights were being heard throughout Europe and the United States, although only in Norway and some American states did women receive the right to vote before 1914. It would take the dramatic upheaval of World War I before male-dominated governments capitulated on this basic issue. At the same time, at the turn of the twentieth century, a number of "new women" became prominent. These women rejected traditional feminine roles (see the box on p. 503) and sought new freedom outside the household and new roles other than those of wives and mothers.

Education in an Age of Mass Society

Education in the early nineteenth century was primarily for the elite or the wealthier middle class, but between 1870 and 1914, most Western governments began to offer at least primary education to both boys and girls between the ages of six and twelve. States also assumed responsibility for better training of teachers by establishing teacher-training schools. By the beginning of the twentieth century, many European states, especially in northern and western Europe, were providing state-financed primary schools, salaried and trained teachers, and free, compulsory elementary education.

Why did Western nations make this commitment to **mass education?** One reason was industrialization. The new firms of the Second Industrial Revolution demanded skilled labor. Both boys and girls with an elementary education had new possibilities of jobs beyond their villages or small towns, including white-collar jobs in railways and subways, post offices, banking and shipping firms, teaching, and nursing. Mass education furnished the trained workers industrialists needed.

The chief motive for mass education, however, was political. The expansion of suffrage created the need for a more educated electorate. Even more important, however, mass compulsory education instilled patriotism and nationalized the masses, providing an opportunity for even greater national integration. As people lost their ties to local regions and even to religion, nationalism supplied a new faith (see the comparative essay "The Rise of Nationalism" on p. 504).

Compulsory elementary education created a demand for teachers, and most of them were women. Many men viewed the teaching of children as an extension of women's "natural role" as nurturers of children. Moreover, females were paid lower salaries, in itself a considerable incentive for governments to encourage the establishment of teacher-training institutes for women. The first female colleges were really teacher-training schools. It was not until the beginning of the twentieth century that women were permitted to enter the male-dominated universities.

Leisure in an Age of Mass Society

With the Industrial Revolution came new forms of leisure. Work and leisure became opposites as leisure came to be viewed as what people do for fun after work. The new leisure hours created by the industrial system—evening hours after work, weekends, and later a week or two in the summer—largely determined the contours of the new **mass leisure.**

New technology created novel experiences for leisure, such as the Ferris wheel at amusement parks, while the subways and streetcars of the 1880s meant that even the working classes were no longer dependent on neighborhood facilities but could make their way to athletic games, amusement parks, and dance halls. Railroads could take people to the beaches on weekends.

By the late nineteenth century, team sports had also developed into another important form of mass leisure. Unlike the old rural games, they were no longer chaotic and spontaneous activities but became strictly organized with sets of rules and officials to enforce them. These rules were the products of organized athletic groups, such as the English Football Association (1863) and the American Bowling Congress (1895). The development of urban transportation systems made possible the construction of stadiums where thousands could attend, making mass spectator sports into a big business.

Cultural Life: Romanticism and Realism in the Western World

Q Focus Question: What were the main characteristics of Romanticism and Realism?

At the end of the eighteenth century, a new intellectual movement known as **Romanticism** emerged to challenge the ideas of the Enlightenment. The Enlightenment stressed reason as the chief means for discovering truth.

OPPOSING VIEWPOINTS
ADVICE TO WOMEN: TWO VIEWS

FAMILY & SOCIETY

Industrialization had a strong impact on middle-class women as strict gender-based social roles became the norm. Men worked outside the home to support the family, while women provided for the needs of their children and husband at home. In the first selection, *Woman in Her Social and Domestic Character* (1842), Elizabeth Poole Sanford gives advice to middle-class women on their proper role and behavior.

Although a majority of women probably followed the nineteenth-century middle-class ideal, an increasing number of women fought for women's rights. The second selection is taken from the third act of Henrik Ibsen's 1879 play *A Doll's House,* in which the character Nora Helmer declares her independence from her husband's control.

Elizabeth Poole Sanford, *Woman in Her Social and Domestic Character*

The changes wrought by Time are many....

It is thus that the sentiment for woman has undergone a change. The romantic passion which once almost deified her is on the decline; and it is by intrinsic qualities that she must now inspire respect. She is no longer the queen of song and the star of chivalry. But if there is less of enthusiasm entertained for her, the sentiment is more rational, and, perhaps, equally sincere; for it is in relation to happiness that she is chiefly appreciated.

And in this respect it is, we must confess, that she is most useful and most important. Domestic life is the chief source of her influence; and the greatest debt society can owe to her is domestic comfort.... A woman may make a man's home delightful, and may thus increase his motives for virtuous exertion. She may refine and tranquilize his mind—may turn away his anger or allay his grief. Her smile may be the happy influence to gladden his heart, and to disperse the cloud that gathers on his brow. And in proportion to her endeavors to make those around her happy, she will be esteemed and loved. She will secure by her excellence that interest and that regard which she might formerly claim as the privilege of her sex, and will really merit the deference which was then conceded to her as a matter of course....

Nothing is so likely to conciliate the affections of the other sex as a feeling that woman looks to them for support and guidance. In proportion as men are themselves superior, they are accessible to this appeal. On the contrary, they never feel interested in one who seems disposed rather to offer than to ask assistance. There is, indeed, something unfeminine in independence. It is contrary to nature, and therefore it offends. We do not like to see a woman affecting tremors, but still less do we like to see her acting the amazon. A really sensible woman feels her dependence. She does what she can; but she is conscious of inferiority, and therefore grateful for support. She knows that she is the weaker vessel, and that as such she should receive honor. In this view, her weakness is an attraction, not a blemish.

Henrik Ibsen, *A Doll's House*

NORA: Yes, it's true, Torvald. When I was living at home with Father, he told me his opinions and mine were the same. If I had different opinions, I said nothing about them, because he would not have liked it. He used to call me his doll-child and played with me as I played with my dolls. Then I came to live in your house.

HELMER: What a way to speak of our marriage!

NORA *(Undisturbed):* I mean that I passed from Father's hands into yours. You arranged everything to your taste and I got the same tastes as you; or pretended to—I don't know which—both, perhaps; sometimes one, sometimes the other. When I look back on it now, I seem to have been living here like a beggar, on handouts. I lived by performing tricks for you, Torvald.... I must stand quite alone if I am ever to know myself and my surroundings; so I cannot stay with you.

HELMER: You are mad! I shall not allow it! I forbid it!

NORA: It's no use your forbidding me anything now. I shall take with me only what belongs to me; from you I will accept nothing, either now or later....

HELMER: Forsake your home, your husband, your children! And you don't consider what the world will say.

NORA: I can't pay attention to that. I only know that I must do it.

HELMER: This is monstrous! Can you forsake your holiest duties?

NORA: What do you consider my holiest duties?

HELMER: Need I tell you that? Your duties to your husband and children.

NORA: I have other duties equally sacred.

HELMER: Impossible! What do you mean?

NORA: My duties toward myself.

HELMER: Before all else you are a wife and a mother.

NORA: That I no longer believe. Before all else I believe I am a human being just as much as you are—or at least that I should try to become one. I know that most people agree with you, Torvald, and that they say so in books. But I can no longer be satisfied with what most people say and what is in books. I must think things out for myself and try to get clear about them.

Q *According to Elizabeth Sanford, what is the proper role of women? What forces in nineteenth-century European society merged to shape Sanford's understanding of "proper" gender roles? In Ibsen's play, what challenges does Nora Helmer make to Sanford's view of the proper role and behavior of wives? Why is her husband so shocked? Why did Ibsen title this play* A Doll's House?

COMPARATIVE ESSAY
THE RISE OF NATIONALISM

POLITICS & GOVERNMENT

Like the Industrial Revolution, the concept of nationalism originated in eighteenth-century Europe, where it was the product of a variety of factors, including the spread of printing and the replacement of Latin with vernacular languages, the secularization of the age, and the experience of the French revolutionary and Napoleonic eras. The French were the first to show what a nation in arms could accomplish, but peoples conquered by Napoleon soon created their own national armies. At the beginning of the nineteenth century, peoples who had previously focused their identity on a locality or a region, on loyalty to a monarch or to a particular religious faith, now shifted their political allegiance to the idea of a nation, based on ethnic, linguistic, or cultural factors. The idea of the nation had explosive consequences: by the end of the first two decades of the twentieth century, the world's three largest multiethnic states—imperial Russia, Austria-Hungary, and the Ottoman Empire—had all given way to a number of individual nation-states.

The idea of establishing political boundaries on the basis of ethnicity, language, or culture had a broad appeal throughout Western civilization, but it had unintended consequences. Although the concept provided the basis for a new sense of community that was tied to liberal thought in the first half of the nineteenth century, it also gave birth to ethnic tensions and hatred in the second half of the century that resulted in bitter disputes and contributed to the competition between nation-states that eventually erupted into world war. Governments, following the lead of the radical government in Paris during the French Revolution, took full advantage of the rise of a strong national consciousness and transformed war into a demonstration of national honor and commitment. Universal schooling enabled states to arouse patriotic enthusiasm and create national unity. Most soldiers who joyfully went to war in 1914 were convinced that their nation's cause was just.

But if the concept of nationalism was initially the product of conditions in modern Europe, it soon spread to other parts of the world. Although a few societies, such as Vietnam, had already developed a strong sense of national identity, most of the peoples in Asia and Africa lived in multiethnic and multireligious communities and were not yet ripe for the spirit of nationalism. As we shall see, the first attempts to resist European colonial rule were thus often based on religious or ethnic identity, rather than on the concept of denied nationhood. But the imperialist powers, which at first benefited from the lack of political cohesion among their colonial subjects, eventually reaped what they had sowed. As the colonial peoples became familiar with Western concepts of democracy and self-determination, they too began to manifest a sense of common purpose that helped knit together the different elements in their societies to oppose colonial regimes and create the conditions for the emergence of future nations. For good or ill, the concept of nationalism had now achieved global proportions. We shall explore such issues, and their consequences, in greater detail in the chapters that follow.

© The Art Archive/Museo Civico, Modigliana, Italy/Alfredo Dagli Orti

Garibaldi. Giuseppe Garibaldi was a dedicated patriot and an outstanding example of the Italian nationalism that led to the unification of Italy by 1870.

Q *What is nationalism? How did it arise, and what impact did it have on the history of the nineteenth and twentieth centuries?*

Although the Romantics by no means disparaged reason, they tried to balance its use by stressing the importance of feeling, emotion, and imagination as sources of knowing.

The Characteristics of Romanticism

Many Romantics had a passionate interest in the past. They revived medieval Gothic architecture and left European countrysides adorned with pseudo-medieval castles and cities bedecked with grandiose neo-Gothic cathedrals, city halls, and parliamentary buildings. Literature, too, reflected this historical consciousness. The novels of Walter Scott (1771–1832) became European best-sellers in the first half of the nineteenth century. One of the most popular was *Ivanhoe,* in which Scott tried to evoke the clash between Saxon and Norman knights in medieval England.

GOTHIC LITERATURE: EDGAR ALLAN POE

ARTS & IDEAS

American writers and poets made significant contributions to the movement of Romanticism. Although Edgar Allan Poe (1809–1849) was influenced by the German Romantic school of mystery and horror, many literary historians give him the credit for pioneering the modern short story. This selection from the conclusion of "The Fall of the House of Usher" gives a feeling for the nature of so-called Gothic literature.

Edgar Allan Poe, "The Fall of the House of Usher"

No sooner had these syllables passed my lips, than—as if a shield of brass had indeed, at the moment, fallen heavily upon a floor of silver—I became aware of a distinct, hollow, metallic, and clangorous, yet apparently muffled, reverberation. Completely unnerved, I leaped to my feet; but the measured rocking movement of Usher was undisturbed. I rushed to the chair in which he sat. His eyes were bent fixedly before him, and throughout his whole countenance there reigned a stony rigidity. But, as I placed my hand upon his shoulder, there came a strong shudder over his whole person; a sickly smile quivered about his lips; and I saw that he spoke in a low, hurried, and gibbering murmur, as if unconscious of my presence. Bending closely over him, I at length drank in the hideous import of his words.

"Not hear it?—yes, I hear it, and have heard it. Long—long—long—many minutes, many hours, many days, have I heard it—yet I dared not—oh, pity me, miserable wretch that I am!—I dared not—I *dared* not speak! *We have put her living in the tomb!* Said I not that my senses were acute? I now tell you that I heard her first feeble movements in the hollow coffin. I heard them—many, many days ago—yet I dared not—*I dared not speak!* And now—to-night— . . . the rending of her coffin, and the grating of the iron hinges of her prison, and her struggles within the coppered archway of the vault! Oh whither shall I fly? Will she not be here anon? Is she not hurrying to upbraid me for my haste? Have I not heard her footstep on the stair? Do I not distinguish that heavy and horrible beating of her heart? MADMAN!"—here he sprang furiously to his feet, and shrieked out his syllables, as if in the effort he were giving up his soul—"MADMAN! I TELL YOU THAT SHE NOW STANDS WITHOUT THE DOOR!"

As if in the superhuman energy of his utterance there had been found the potency of a spell, the huge antique panels to which the speaker pointed threw slowly back, upon the instant, their ponderous and ebony jaws. It was the work of the rushing gust—but then without those doors there DID stand the lofty and enshrouded figure of the lady Madeline of Usher. There was blood upon her white robes, and the evidence of some bitter struggle upon every portion of her emaciated frame. For a moment she remained trembling and reeling to and fro upon the threshold, then, with a low moaning cry, fell heavily inward upon the person of her brother, and in her violent and now final death-agonies, bore him to the floor a corpse, and a victim to the terrors he had anticipated.

Q *What were the aesthetic aims of Gothic literature? How did it come to be called "Gothic"? How did its values relate to those of the Romantic movement as a whole?*

Many Romantics had a deep attraction to the exotic and unfamiliar. In an exaggerated form, this preoccupation gave rise to so-called **Gothic literature,** chillingly evident in Mary Shelley's *Frankenstein* and Edgar Allan Poe's short stories of horror (see the box above). Some Romantics even brought the unusual into their own lives by experimenting with cocaine, opium, and hashish in an attempt to find extraordinary experiences through drug-induced altered states of consciousness.

To the Romantics, poetry was the direct expression of the soul and therefore ranked above all other literary forms. Romantic poetry gave full expression to one of the most important characteristics of Romanticism: love of nature, especially evident in the poetry of William Wordsworth (1770–1850). His experience of nature was almost mystical as he claimed to receive "authentic tidings of invisible things":

> *One impulse from a vernal wood*
> *May teach you more of man,*

> *Of Moral Evil and of good,*
> *Than all the sages can.*[6]

Romantics believed that nature served as a mirror into which humans could look to learn about themselves.

Like the literary arts, the visual arts were also deeply affected by Romanticism. To Romantic artists, all artistic expression was a reflection of the artist's inner feelings; a painting should mirror the artist's vision of the world and be the instrument of his own imagination.

Eugène Delacroix (1798–1863) was one of the most famous French exponents of the Romantic school of painting. Delacroix visited North Africa in 1832 and was strongly impressed by its vibrant colors and the brilliant dress of the people. His paintings came to exhibit two primary characteristics, a fascination with the exotic and a passion for color. Both are apparent in his *Women of Algiers.* In Delacroix, theatricality and movement combined with a daring use of color. Many of his works reflect his own belief that "a painting should be a feast to the eye."

Eugène Delacroix, _Women of Algiers_. A characteristic of Romanticism was its love of the exotic and unfamiliar. In his _Women of Algiers,_ Delacroix reflected this fascination with the exotic. In this portrayal of harem concubines from North Africa, the clothes and jewelry of the women combine with their calm facial expressions to create an atmosphere of peaceful sensuality. At the same time, Delacroix's painting reflects his preoccupation with light and color.

A New Age of Science

With the Industrial Revolution came a renewed interest in basic scientific research. By the 1830s, new scientific discoveries led to many practical benefits that caused science to have an ever-greater impact on European life.

In biology, the Frenchman Louis Pasteur (1822–1895) discovered the germ theory of disease, which had enormous practical applications in the development of modern scientific medical practices. In chemistry, the Russian Dmitri Mendeleev (1834–1907) in the 1860s classified all the material elements then known on the basis of their atomic weights and provided the systematic foundation for the periodic law.

The popularity of scientific and technological achievement produced a widespread acceptance of the **scientific method** as the only path to objective truth and objective reality. This in turn undermined the faith of many people in religious revelation. It is no accident that the nineteenth century was an age of increasing **secularization,** evident in the belief that truth was to be found in the concrete material existence of human beings. No one did more to create a picture of humans as material beings

that were simply part of the natural world than Charles Darwin.

In 1859, Charles Darwin (1809–1882) published _On the Origin of Species by Means of Natural Selection._ The basic idea of this book was that all plants and animals had each evolved over a long period of time from earlier and simpler forms of life, a principle known as **organic evolution.** In every species, he argued, "many more individuals of each species are born than can possibly survive." This results in a "struggle for existence." Darwin believed that some organisms were more adaptable to the environment than others, a process that Darwin called **natural selection.** Those that were naturally selected for survival ("survival of the fit") reproduced and thrived. The unfit did not and became extinct. The fit who survived passed on small variations that enhanced their survival until, from Darwin's point of view, a new and separate species emerged. In _The Descent of Man,_ published in 1871, he argued for the animal origins of human beings. Humans were not an exception to the rule governing other species.

Realism in Literature and Art

The name **Realism** was first employed in 1850 to describe a new style of painting and soon spread to literature. The literary Realists of the mid-nineteenth century rejected Romanticism. They wanted to deal with ordinary characters from actual life rather than Romantic heroes in exotic settings.

The leading novelist of the 1850s and 1860s, the Frenchman Gustave Flaubert (1821–1880), perfected the Realist novel. His _Madame Bovary_ (1857) was a straightforward description of barren and sordid provincial life in France. Emma Bovary is trapped in a marriage to a drab provincial doctor. Impelled by the images of romantic love she has read about in novels, she seeks the same thing for herself in adulterous love affairs but is ultimately driven to suicide.

Gustave Courbet, *The Stonebreakers*. Realism, largely developed by French painters, aimed at a lifelike portrayal of the daily activities of ordinary people. Gustave Courbet was the most famous of the Realist artists. As is evident in *The Stonebreakers,* he sought to portray things as they really appear. He shows an old road builder and his young assistant in their tattered clothes, engrossed in their dreary work of breaking stones to construct a road.

Realism also made inroads into the Latin American literary scene by the second half of the nineteenth century. There, Realist novelists focused on the injustices of their society, evident in the work of Clorinda Matto de Turner (1852–1909). Her *Aves sin Nido* (*Birds without a Nest*) was a brutal revelation of the pitiful living conditions of the Indians in Peru. She especially blamed the Catholic church for much of their misery.

In art, too, Realism became dominant after 1850. Gustave Courbet (1819–1877), the most famous artist of the Realist school, reveled in realistic portrayals of everyday life. His subjects were factory workers, peasants, and the wives of saloonkeepers. "I have never seen either angels or goddesses, so I am not interested in painting them," he exclaimed. One of his famous works, *The Stonebreakers,* painted in 1849, shows two road workers engaged in the deadening work of breaking stones to build a road.

Toward the Modern Consciousness: Intellectual and Cultural Developments

Q Focus Question: What intellectual and cultural developments in the late nineteenth and early twentieth centuries "opened the way to a modern consciousness," and how did this consciousness differ from earlier worldviews?

Before 1914, many people in the Western world continued to believe in the values and ideals that had been generated by the Scientific Revolution and the Enlightenment. The idea that human beings could improve themselves and achieve a better society seemed to be proved by a rising standard of living, urban comforts, and mass education. It was easy to think that the human mind could make sense of the universe. Between 1870 and 1914, though, radically new ideas challenged these optimistic views and opened the way to a modern consciousness.

A New Physics

Science was one of the chief pillars underlying the optimistic and rationalistic view of the world that many Westerners shared in the nineteenth century. Supposedly based on hard facts and cold reason, science offered a certainty of belief in the orderliness of nature. The new physics dramatically altered that perspective.

Throughout much of the nineteenth century, Westerners adhered to the mechanical conception of the universe postulated by the classic physics of Isaac Newton. In this perspective, the universe was viewed as a giant machine in which time, space, and matter were objective realities that existed independently of the observers. Matter was thought to be composed of indivisible and solid material bodies called atoms.

Albert Einstein (1879–1955), a German-born patent officer working in Switzerland, questioned this view of the universe. In 1905, Einstein published his special theory of relativity, which stated that space and time are not absolute but relative to the observer. Neither space nor time had an existence independent of human experience. As Einstein later explained simply to a journalist: "It was formerly believed that if all material things disappeared out of the universe, time and space would be left. According to the **relativity theory,** however, time and space disappear

FREUD AND THE CONCEPT OF REPRESSION

RELIGION & PHILOSOPHY

Freud's psychoanalytical theories resulted from his attempt to understand the world of the unconscious. This excerpt is taken from a lecture given in 1909 in which Freud describes how he arrived at his theory of the role of repression.

Sigmund Freud, *Five Lectures on Psychoanalysis*

I did not abandon [the technique of encouraging patients to reveal forgotten experiences], however, before the observations I made during my use of it afforded me decisive evidence. I found confirmation of the fact that the forgotten memories were not lost. They were in the patient's possession and were ready to emerge in association to what was still known by him; but there was some force that prevented them from becoming conscious and compelled them to remain unconscious. The existence of this force could be assumed with certainty, since one became aware of an effort corresponding to it if, in opposition to it, one tried to introduce the unconscious memories into the patient's consciousness. The force which was maintaining the pathological condition became apparent in the form of resistance on the part of the patient.

It was on this idea of resistance, then, that I based my view of the course of psychical events in hysteria. In order to effect a recovery, it had proved necessary to remove these resistances. Starting out from the mechanism of cure, it now became possible to construct quite definite ideas of the origin of the illness. The same forces which, in the form of resistance, were now offering opposition to the forgotten material's being made conscious, must formerly have brought about the forgetting and must have pushed the pathogenic experiences in question out of consciousness. I gave the name of "repression" to this hypothetical process, and I considered that it was proved by the undeniable existence of resistance.

The further question could then be raised as to what these forces were and what the determinants were of the repression in which we now recognized the pathogenic mechanism of hysteria. A comparative study of the pathogenic situations which we had come to know through the cathartic procedure made it possible to answer this question. All these experiences had involved the emergence of a wishful impulse which was in sharp contrast to the subject's other wishes and which proved incompatible with the ethical and aesthetic standards of his personality. There had been a short conflict, and the end of this internal struggle was that the idea which had appeared before consciousness as the vehicle of this irreconcilable wish fell a victim to repression, was pushed out of consciousness with all its attached memories, and was forgotten. Thus, the incompatibility of the wish in question with the patient's ego was the motive for the repression; the subject's ethical and other standards were the repressing forces. An acceptance of the incompatible wishful impulse or a prolongation of the conflict would have produced a high degree of unpleasure; this unpleasure was avoided by means of repression, which was thus revealed as one of the devices serving to protect the mental personality.

Q *According to Freud, how did he discover the existence of repression? What function does repression perform?*

---

together with the things."[7] Einstein concluded that matter was nothing but another form of energy. His epochal formula $E = mc^2$—stating that each particle of matter is equivalent to its mass times the square of the velocity of light—was the key theory explaining the vast energies contained within the atom. It led to the atomic age.

Sigmund Freud and the Emergence of Psychoanalysis

At the turn of the twentieth century, Viennese physician Sigmund Freud (1856–1939) advanced a series of theories that undermined optimism about the rational nature of the human mind. Freud's thought, like the new physics, added to the uncertainties of the age. His major ideas were published in 1900 in *The Interpretation of Dreams.*

According to Freud, human behavior was strongly determined by the unconscious, by past experiences and internal forces of which people were largely oblivious.

For Freud, human behavior was no longer truly rational but rather instinctive or irrational. He argued that painful and unsettling experiences were blotted from conscious awareness but still continued to influence behavior since they had become part of the unconscious (see the box above). Repression began in childhood. Freud devised a method, known as **psychoanalysis,** by which a psychotherapist and patient could probe deeply into the memory in order to retrace the chain of repression all the way back to its childhood origins. By making the conscious mind aware of the unconscious and its repressed contents, the patient's psychic conflict was resolved.

The Impact of Darwin: Social Darwinism and Racism

In the second half of the nineteenth century, scientific theories were sometimes wrongly applied to achieve other ends. For example, Charles Darwin's principle of organic evolution was applied to the social order as **social**

© Erich Lessing/Art Resource, NY

© Christie's Images/SuperStock

COMPARATIVE ILLUSTRATION

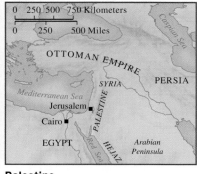
ARTS & IDEAS

Painting—West and East. Berthe Morisot, the first female painter to join the Impressionists, developed her own unique style. Her gentle colors and strong use of pastels are especially evident in *Young Girl by the Window,* seen at the left. The French Impressionist style also spread abroad. One of the most outstanding Japanese artists of the time was Kuroda Seiki (1866–1924), who returned from nine years in Paris to open a Western-style school of painting in Tokyo. Shown at the right is his *Under the Trees,* an excellent example of the fusion of contemporary French Impressionist painting with the Japanese tradition of courtesan prints.

Q What differences and similarities do you notice in these two paintings?

Darwinism, the belief that societies were organisms that evolved through time from a struggle with their environment. Such ideas were used in a radical way by rabid nationalists and racists. In their pursuit of national greatness, extreme nationalists insisted that nations, too, were engaged in a "struggle for existence" in which only the fittest survived.

Anti-Semitism Anti-Semitism had a long history in European civilization, but in the nineteenth century, as a result of the ideals of the Enlightenment and the French Revolution, Jews were increasingly granted legal equality in many European countries. Many Jews now left the ghetto and became assimilated into the cultures around them. Many became successful as bankers, lawyers, scientists, scholars, journalists, and stage performers.

These achievements represent only one side of the picture, however. In Germany and Austria during the 1880s and 1890s, conservatives founded right-wing anti-Jewish parties that used anti-Semitism to win the votes of

traditional lower-middle-class groups who felt threatened by the new economic forces of the times. The worst treatment of Jews at the turn of the century, however, occurred in eastern Europe, where 72 percent of the entire world Jewish population lived. Russian Jews were forced to live in certain regions of the country, and persecutions and pogroms were widespread. Hundreds of thousands of Jews decided to emigrate to escape the persecution.

Many Jews went to the United States, although some moved to Palestine, which soon became the focus of a Jewish nationalist movement called **Zionism.** For many Jews, Palestine, the land of ancient Israel, had

Palestine

long been the land of their dreams. Settlement in Palestine was difficult, however, because it was then part of the Ottoman Empire, which was opposed to Jewish immigration. Despite the problems, the First Zionist Congress, which met in Switzerland in 1897, proclaimed as its aim the creation of a "home in Palestine secured by public law" for the Jewish people. In 1900, around a thousand Jews migrated to Palestine, and the trickle rose to about three thousand a year between 1904 and 1914, keeping the Zionist dream alive.

The Culture of Modernity

The revolution in physics and psychology was paralleled by a revolution in literature and the arts. Before 1914, writers and artists were rebelling against the traditional literary and artistic styles that had dominated European cultural life since the Renaissance. The changes that they produced have since been called **Modernism.**

At the beginning of the twentieth century, a group of writers known as the Symbolists caused a literary revolution. Primarily interested in writing poetry and strongly influenced by the ideas of Freud, the Symbolists believed that an objective knowledge of the world was impossible. The external world was not real but only a collection of symbols that reflected the true reality of the individual human mind.

The period from 1870 to 1914 was one of the most fertile in the history of art. By the late nineteenth century, artists were seeking new forms of expression. The preamble to modern painting can be found in **Impressionism,** a movement that originated in France in the 1870s when a group of artists rejected the studios and museums and went out into the countryside to paint nature directly.

An important Impressionist painter was Berthe Morisot (1841–1895), who believed that women had a special vision that she described as "more delicate than that of men." She made use of lighter colors and flowing brushstrokes (see the comparative illustration on p. 509). Near the end of her life, she lamented the refusal of men to take her work seriously: "I don't think there has ever been a man who treated a woman as an equal, and that's all I would have asked, for I know I'm worth as much as they."[8]

In the 1880s, a new movement known as **Post-Impressionism** arose in France and soon spread to other European countries. A famous Post-Impressionist was the tortured and tragic figure Vincent van Gogh (1853–1890). For van Gogh, art was a spiritual experience. He was especially interested in color and believed that it could act as its own form of language.

By the beginning of the twentieth century, the belief that the task of art was to represent "reality" had lost

Pablo Picasso, *Les Demoiselles d'Avignon*.

Pablo Picasso, a major pioneer and activist of modern art, experimented with a remarkable variety of modern styles. *Les Demoiselles d'Avignon* was the first great example of Cubism, which one art historian called "the first style of this [twentieth] century to break radically with the past." Geometrical shapes replace traditional forms, forcing the viewer to re-create reality in his or her own mind. The head at the upper right of the painting reflects Picasso's attraction to aspects of African art, as is evident from the mask included at the left.

© Dr. Werner Muensterberger Collection/The Bridgeman Art Library

© 2008 Estate of Pablo Picasso/Artists Rights Society (ARS), New York/Digital Image © The Museum of Modern Art/Licensed by Scala/Art Resource, NY

much of its meaning. The growth of photography gave artists one reason to reject Realism. Invented in the 1830s, photography became popular and widespread after 1888 when George Eastman created the first Kodak camera for the mass market. What was the point of an artist's doing what the camera did better? Unlike the camera, which could only mirror reality, artists could create reality.

By 1905, one of the most important figures in modern art was just beginning his career. Pablo Picasso (1881–1973) was from Spain but settled in Paris in 1904. Picasso was extremely flexible and painted in a

remarkable variety of styles. He was instrumental in the development of a new style called **Cubism** that used geometrical designs as visual stimuli to re-create reality in the viewer's mind.

The modern artist's flight from "visual reality" reached a high point in 1910 with the beginning of **abstract painting.** A Russian who worked in Germany, Vasily Kandinsky (1866–1944) was one of its founders. Kandinsky sought to avoid representation altogether. He believed that art should speak directly to the soul. To do so, it must avoid any reference to visual reality and concentrate on line and color.

TIMELINE

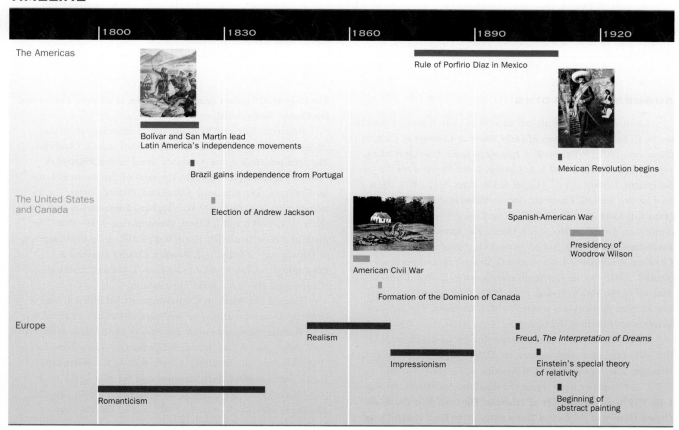

The Americas

Rule of Porfirio Diaz in Mexico

Bolívar and San Martín lead
Latin America's independence movements

Brazil gains independence from Portugal

Mexican Revolution begins

The United States
and Canada

Election of Andrew Jackson

Spanish-American War

Presidency of
Woodrow Wilson

American Civil War

Formation of the Dominion of Canada

Europe

Realism

Freud, *The Interpretation of Dreams*

Impressionism

Einstein's special theory
of relativity

Romanticism

Beginning of
abstract painting

1800   1830   1860   1890   1920

CONCLUSION

FROM THE SIXTEENTH CENTURY, much of the Western Hemisphere was under the control of Great Britain, Spain, and Portugal. But between 1776 and 1826, an age of revolution in the Atlantic world led to the creation of the United States and nine new nations in Latin America. Canada and other new nations in Latin America followed in the course of the nineteenth century. This age of revolution was an expression of the force of nationalism, which

had first emerged as a political ideology at the end of the eighteenth century. Influential, too, were the ideas of the Enlightenment that had made an impact on intellectuals and political leaders in both North and South America.

The new nations that emerged in the Western Hemisphere did not, however, develop without challenges to their national unity. Latin American nations often found it difficult to establish stable republics and resorted to strong leaders who used military force to govern. And although Latin American nations had achieved political independence, they found themselves economically dependent on Great Britain as well as their northern neighbor, the United States. The North American states had problems with national unity, too. The United States dissolved into four years of bloody civil war before reconciling, and Canada achieved only questionable unity owing to distrust between the English-speaking majority and the French-speaking minority.

By the second half of the nineteenth century, much of the Western world was experiencing a new mass society in which the lower classes in particular benefited from the right to vote, a higher standard of living, and new schools that provided them with some education. New forms of mass transportation, combined with new work patterns, enabled large numbers of people to enjoy weekend trips to "amusement" parks and seaside resorts, as well as to participate in new mass leisure activities.

By the end of the nineteenth century and the beginning of the twentieth century, a brilliant minority of intellectuals had created a modern consciousness in the West that questioned most Europeans' optimistic faith in reason, the rational structure of nature, and the certainty of progress. This cultural revolution also produced anxiety and created a degree of uncertainty that paralleled the anxiety and uncertainty generated by the European national rivalries that had grown stronger as a result of imperialistic expansion. At the same time, the Western condescending treatment of non-Western peoples, which we will examine in the next two chapters, caused educated, non-Western elites in these colonies to initiate movements for national independence. Before these movements could be successful, however, the power that Europeans had achieved through their mass armies and technological superiority had to be weakened. The Europeans soon inadvertently accomplished this task for their colonial subjects by demolishing their own civilization on the battlegrounds of World War I.

SUGGESTED READING

Latin America For general surveys of Latin American history, see M. C. Eakin, *The History of Latin America: Collision of Cultures* (New York, 2007); P. Bakewell, *A History of Latin America* (Oxford, 1997); and E. B. Burns and J. A. Charlip, *Latin America: An Interpretive History,* 8th ed. (Upper Saddle River, N.J., 2007). For a brief history, see J. C. Chasteen, *Born in Blood and Fire: A Concise History of Latin America,* 2nd ed. (New York, 2005). A standard work on the wars for independence is J. Lynch, *The Spanish American Revolutions, 1808–1826,* 2nd ed. (New York, 1986); but also see J. C. Chasteen, *Americanos: Latin America's Struggle for Independence* (Oxford, 2008). On the nineteenth century, see S. F. Voss, *Latin America in the Middle Period, 1750–1920* (Wilmington, Del., 2002). The Mexican Revolution is covered in M. J. Gonzales, *The Mexican Revolution, 1910–1940* (Albuquerque, N.M., 2002).

The United States and Canada On the United States in the first half of the nineteenth century, see D. W. Howe, *What God Hath Wrought: The Transformation of America, 1815–1848* (Oxford, 2007). The definitive one-volume history of the American Civil War is J. M. McPherson, *Battle Cry of Freedom: The Civil War Era in the Oxford History of the United States* series (New York, 2003). On the second half of the nineteenth century, see L. Gould, *America in the Progressive Era, 1890–1914* (New York, 2001). For a general history of Canada, see S. W. See, *History of Canada* (Westport, N.Y., 2001).

The Emergence of Mass Society in the West An interesting work on aristocratic life is D. Cannadine, *The Decline and Fall of the British Aristocracy* (New Haven, Conn., 1990). On the middle classes, see P. Pilbeam, *The Middle Classes in Europe, 1789–1914* (Basingstoke, England, 1990). On the working classes, see L. Berlanstein, *The Working People of Paris, 1871–1914* (Baltimore, 1984). The rise of feminism is examined in J. Rendall, *The Origins of Modern Feminism: Women in Britain, France and the United States* (London, 1985).

Romanticism and Realism For an introduction to the intellectual changes of the nineteenth century, see O. Chadwick, *The Secularization of the European Mind in the Nineteenth Century* (Cambridge, 1975). On the ideas of the Romantics, see M. Cranston, *The Romantic Movement* (Oxford, 1994). For an introduction to the arts, see W. Vaughan, *Romanticism and Art* (New York, 1994), and I. Ciseri, *Romanticism, 1780–1860: The Birth of a New Sensibility* (New York, 2003). A detailed biography of Darwin can be found in J. Bowlby, *Charles Darwin: A Biography* (London, 1990). On Realism, J. Malpas, *Realism* (Cambridge, 1997), is a good introduction.

Toward the Modern Consciousness: Intellectual and Cultural Developments Two well-regarded studies of Freud are P. D. Kramer, *Sigmund Freud: Inventor of the Modern Mind* (New York, 2006), and P. Gay, *Freud: A Life for Our Time* (New York, 1988). Modern anti-Semitism is covered in A. S. Lindemann, *Esau's Tears: Modern Anti-Semitism and the Rise of the Jews* (New York, 1997). Very valuable on modern art are G. Crepaldi, *The Impressionists* (New York, 2002), and B. Denvir, *Post-Impressionism* (New York, 1992).

WORLD HISTORY RESOURCES

Visit the website for *The Essential World History* to access study aids such as Flashcards, Critical Thinking Exercises, and Chapter Quizzes:

www.cengage.com/history/duikspiel/essentialworld6e

DISCOVERY

In what ways were the intellectual and cultural developments in the Western world between 1800 and 1914 related to the economic, social, and political developments?

In thinking about this question, begin by breaking it down into the components shown below. A discussion of the significance of each component should appear in your answer.

ARTS AND IDEAS In what ways did Romanticism represent a reaction to the Enlightenment, and how did Realism in turn represent a reaction against Romanticism? What inspired each movement? In what ways could both movements be considered a response to the social, economic, and political changes occurring during the nineteenth century?

Based on Picasso's *Les Demoiselles d'Avignon* (p. 510) and the excerpt from Freud's *Five Lectures on Psychoanalysis* (below and on p. 508), discuss how both Freud and Picasso moved away from using reality as a way to view and understand the world. Why were they interested in finding other ways to view the world? To what extent did artists and thinkers use the concepts of repression and irrationality in attempting to deal with the pressures created by industrialization and the political developments of the nineteenth century? How did these efforts lead to the further development of abstract art that completely avoids references to visual reality?

SCIENCE AND TECHNOLOGY Consider how scientific and technological developments affected intellectual and cultural life in the period from 1800 to 1914. How were these developments related to the economic, social, and political changes that occurred?

SIGMUND FREUD, *FIVE LECTURES ON PSYCHOANALYSIS*

I did not abandon [the technique of encouraging patients to reveal forgotten experiences], however, before the observations I made during my use of it afforded me decisive evidence. I found confirmation of the fact that the forgotten memories were not lost. They were in the patient's possession and were ready to emerge in association to what was still known by him; but there was some force that prevented them from becoming conscious and compelled them to remain unconscious. The existence of this force could be assumed with certainty, since one became aware of an effort corresponding to it if, in opposition to it, one tried to introduce the unconscious memories into the patient's consciousness. The force which was maintaining the pathological condition became apparent in the form of resistance on the part of the patient.

It was on this idea of resistance, then, that I based my view of the course of psychical events in hysteria. In order to effect a recovery, it had proved necessary to remove these resistances. Starting out from the mechanism of cure, it now became possible to construct quite definite ideas of the origin of the illness. The same forces which, in the form of resistance, were now offering opposition to the forgotten material's being made conscious, must formerly have brought about the forgetting and must have pushed the pathogenic experiences in question out of consciousness. I gave the name of "repression" to this hypothetical

process, and I considered that it was proved by the undeniable existence of resistance.

The further question could then be raised as to what these forces were and what the determinants were of the repression in which we now recognized the pathogenic mechanism of hysteria. A comparative study of the pathogenic situations which we had come to know through the cathartic procedure made it possible to answer this question. All these experiences had involved the emergence of a wishful impulse which was in sharp contrast to the subject's other wishes and which proved incompatible with the ethical and aesthetic standards of his personality. There had been a short conflict, and the end of this internal struggle was that the idea which had appeared before consciousness as the vehicle of this irreconcilable wish fell a victim to repression, was pushed out of consciousness with all its attached memories, and was forgotten. Thus, the incompatibility of the wish in question with the patient's ego was the motive for the repression; the subject's ethical and other standards were the repressing forces. An acceptance of the incompatible wishful impulse or a prolongation of the conflict would have produced a high degree of unpleasure; this unpleasure was avoided by means of repression, which was thus revealed as one of the devices serving to protect the mental personality.

CHAPTER 21
THE HIGH TIDE OF IMPERIALISM

Revere the conquering heroes: Establishing British rule in Africa

© Time & Life Pictures/Getty Images

IN 1877, THE YOUNG British empire builder Cecil Rhodes drew up his last will and testament. He bequeathed his fortune, achieved as a diamond magnate in South Africa, to two of his close friends and acquaintances. He also instructed them to use the inheritance to form a secret society with the aim of bringing about "the extension of British rule throughout the world, the perfecting of a system of emigration from the United Kingdom . . . especially the occupation by British settlers of the entire continent of Africa, the Holy Land, the valley of the Euphrates, the Islands of Cyprus and Candia [Crete], the whole of South America. . . . The ultimate recovery of the United States of America as an integral part of the British Empire . . . then finally the foundation of so great a power as to hereafter render wars impossible and promote the best interests of humanity."[1]

Preposterous as such ideas sound today, they serve as a graphic reminder of the hubris that characterized the worldview of Rhodes and many of his contemporaries during the age of imperialism, as well as the complex union of moral concern and vaulting ambition that motivated their actions on the world stage.

Through their efforts, Western colonialism spread throughout much of the non-Western world during the nineteenth and early twentieth centuries. Spurred by the demands of the Industrial

Revolution, a few powerful Western states—notably, Great Britain, France, Germany, Russia, and the United States—competed avariciously for consumer markets and raw materials for their expanding economies. By the end of the nineteenth century, virtually all of the traditional societies in Asia and Africa were under direct or indirect colonial rule. As the new century began, the Western imprint on Asian and African societies, for better or for worse, appeared to be a permanent feature of the political and cultural landscape. ⊛

The Spread of Colonial Rule

Q **Focus Question:** What were the causes of the new imperialism of the nineteenth century, and how did it differ from European expansion in earlier periods?

In the nineteenth century, a new phase of Western expansion into Asia and Africa began. Whereas European aims in the East before 1800 could be summed up in Vasco da Gama's famous phrase "Christians and spices," now a new relationship took shape as European nations began to view Asian and African societies as sources of industrial raw materials and as markets for Western manufactured goods. No longer were Western gold and silver exchanged for cloves, pepper, tea, silk, and porcelain. Now the prodigious output of European factories was sent to Africa and Asia in return for oil, tin, rubber, and the other resources needed to fuel the Western industrial machine.

The Motives

The reason for this change, of course, was the Industrial Revolution. Now industrializing countries in the West needed vital raw materials that were not available at home, as well as a reliable market for the goods produced in their factories. The latter factor became increasingly crucial as producers began to discover that their home markets could not always absorb domestic output and that they had to export their manufactures to make a profit.

As Western economic expansion into Asia and Africa gathered strength during the nineteenth century, it became fashionable to call the process **imperialism.** Although the term *imperialism* has many meanings, in this instance it referred to the efforts of capitalist states in the West to seize markets, cheap raw materials, and lucrative avenues for investment in the countries beyond Western civilization. In this interpretation, the primary motives behind the Western expansion were economic. Promoters of this view maintained that modern imperialism was a direct consequence of the modern industrial economy.

As in the earlier phase of Western expansion, however, the issue was not simply an economic one. Economic concerns were inevitably tinged with political overtones and with questions of national grandeur and moral purpose as well. In the minds of nineteenth-century Europeans, economic wealth, national status, and political power went hand in hand with the possession of a colonial empire. To global strategists, colonies brought tangible benefits in the world of balance-of-power politics as well as economic profits, and many nations became involved in the pursuit of colonies as much to gain advantage over their rivals as to acquire territory for its own sake.

The relationship between colonialism and national survival was expressed directly in a speech by the French politician Jules Ferry in 1885. A policy of "containment or abstinence," he warned, would set France on "the broad road to decadence" and initiate its decline into a "third- or fourth-rate power." British imperialists, convinced by the theory of social Darwinism that in the struggle between nations, only the fit are victorious and survive, agreed. As the British professor of mathematics Karl Pearson argued in 1900, "The path of progress is strewn with the wrecks of nations; traces are everywhere to be seen of the [slaughtered remains] of inferior races.... Yet these dead people are, in very truth, the stepping stones on which mankind has arisen to the higher intellectual and deeper emotional life of today."[2]

For some, colonialism had a moral purpose, whether to promote Christianity or to build a better world. The British colonial official Henry Curzon declared that the British Empire "was under Providence, the greatest instrument for good that the world has seen." To Cecil Rhodes, the most famous empire builder of his day, the extraction of material wealth from the colonies was only a secondary matter. "My ruling purpose," he remarked, "is the extension of the British Empire."[3] That British Empire, on which, as the saying went, "the sun never set," was the envy of its rivals and was viewed as the primary source of British global dominance during the second half of the nineteenth century.

The Tactics

With the change in European motives for colonization came a corresponding shift in tactics. Earlier, when their economic interests were more limited, European states had generally been satisfied to deal with existing independent states rather than attempting to establish direct control over vast territories. There had been exceptions where state power at the local level was at the point of collapse (as in India), where European economic interests were especially intense (as in Latin America and the East

Indies), or where there was no centralized authority (as in North America and the Philippines). But for the most part, the Western presence in Asia and Africa had been limited to controlling the regional trade network and establishing a few footholds where the foreigners could carry on trade and missionary activity.

After 1800, the demands of industrialization in Europe created a new set of dynamics. Maintaining access to industrial raw materials such as oil and rubber and setting up reliable markets for European manufactured products required more extensive control over colonial territories. As competition for colonies increased, the colonial powers sought to solidify their hold over their territories to protect them from attack by their rivals. During the last two decades of the nineteenth century, the quest for colonies became a scramble as all the major European states, now joined by the United States and Japan, engaged in a global land grab. In many cases, economic interests were secondary to security concerns or the requirements of national prestige. In Africa, for example, the British engaged in a struggle with their rivals to protect their interests in the Suez Canal and the Red Sea.

By 1900, almost all the societies of Africa and Asia were either under full colonial rule or, as in the case of China and the Ottoman Empire, at a point of virtual collapse. Only a handful of states, such as Japan in East

Asia, Thailand in Southeast Asia, Afghanistan and Iran in the Middle East, and mountainous Ethiopia in East Africa, managed to escape internal disintegration or subjection to colonial rule. For the most part, the exceptions were the result of good fortune rather than design. Thailand escaped subjugation primarily because officials in London and Paris found it more convenient to transform the country into a buffer state than to fight over it. Ethiopia and Afghanistan survived due to their remote location and mountainous terrain. Only Japan managed to avoid the common fate through a concerted strategy of political and economic reform.

The Colonial System

Q Focus Question: What types of administrative systems did the various colonial powers establish in their colonies, and how did these systems reflect the general philosophy of colonialism?

Now that they had control of most of the world, what did the colonial powers do with it? As we have seen, their primary objective was to exploit the natural resources of the subject areas and to open up markets for manufactured goods and capital investment from the mother country. In some cases, that goal could be realized in cooperation with local political elites, whose loyalty could be earned, or purchased, by economic rewards or by confirming them in their positions of authority and status in a new colonial setting. Sometimes, however, this policy of **indirect rule** was not feasible because local leaders refused to cooperate with their colonial masters or even actively resisted the foreign conquest. In such cases, the local elites were removed from power and replaced with a new set of officials recruited from the mother country.

In general, the societies most likely to actively resist colonial conquest were those with a long tradition of national cohesion and independence, such as Burma and Vietnam in Asia and the African Muslim states in northern Nigeria and Morocco.

The Company Resident and His Puppet. The British East India Company gradually replaced the sovereigns of the once-independent Indian states with puppet rulers who carried out the company's policies. Here we see the company's resident dominating a procession in Tanjore in 1825, while the Indian ruler, Sarabhoji, follows like an obedient shadow. As a boy, Sarabhoji had been educated by European tutors and had filled his life and home with English books and furnishings.

© Art Media, Victoria and Albert Museum, London/HIP/The Image Works

In those areas, the colonial powers tended to dispense with local collaborators and govern directly. In parts of Africa, the Indian subcontinent, and the Malay peninsula, where the local authorities, for whatever reason, were willing to collaborate with the imperialist powers, indirect rule was more common.

Overall, colonialism in India, Southeast Asia, and Africa exhibited many similarities but also some differences. Some of these variations can be traced to political or social differences among the colonial powers themselves. The French, for example, often tried to impose a centralized administrative system on their colonies that mirrored the system in use in France, while the British sometimes attempted to transform local aristocrats into the equivalent of the landed gentry at home in Britain. Other differences stemmed from conditions in the colonies themselves.

The Philosophy of Colonialism

To justify their rule, the colonial powers appealed in part to the time-honored maxim of "might makes right." By the end of the nineteenth century, that attitude received pseudoscientific validity from the concept of social Darwinism, which maintained that only societies that moved aggressively to adapt to changing circumstances would survive and prosper in a world governed by the Darwinian law of "survival of the fittest."

Some people, however, were uncomfortable with such a brutal view of the law of nature and sought a moral justification that appeared to benefit the victim. Here again, the concept of social Darwinism pointed the way. By bringing the benefits of Western democracy, capitalism, and Christianity to the tradition-ridden societies of Africa and Asia, the colonial powers were enabling primitive peoples to adapt to the challenges of the modern world. Buttressed by such comforting theories, sensitive Western minds could ignore the brutal aspects of colonialism and persuade themselves that in the long run, the results would be beneficial for both sides (see the box on p. 518). Few were as adept at describing the "civilizing mission" of colonialism as the French administrator and twice governor-general of French Indochina Albert Sarraut. While admitting that colonialism was originally an "act of force" undertaken for commercial profit, he insisted that by redistributing the wealth of the earth, the colonial process would result in a better life for all: "Is it just, is it legitimate that such [an uneven distribution of resources] should be indefinitely prolonged? . . . No! . . . Humanity is distributed throughout the globe. No race, no people has the right or power to isolate itself egotistically from the movements and necessities of universal life."[4]

But what about the possibility that historically and culturally the societies of Asia and Africa were fundamentally different from those of the West and could not, or would not, be persuaded to transform themselves along Western lines? In that case, a policy of cultural transformation could not be expected to succeed and could even lead to disaster.

Assimilation or Association? In fact, colonial theorists never decided this issue one way or the other. The French, who were most inclined to philosophize about the problem, adopted the terms **assimilation** (which implied an effort to transform colonial societies in the Western image) and **association** (implying collaboration with local elites while leaving local traditions alone) to describe the two alternatives and then proceeded to vacillate between them. French policy in Indochina, for example, began as one of association but switched to assimilation under pressure from those who felt that colonial powers owed a debt to their subject peoples. But assimilation (which in any case was never accepted as feasible or desirable by many colonial officials) aroused resentment among the local population, many of whom opposed the destruction of their native traditions. In the end, the French abandoned the attempt to justify their presence and fell back on a policy of ruling by force of arms.

Other colonial powers had little interest in the issue. The British, whether out of a sense of pragmatism or of racial superiority, refused to entertain the possibility of assimilation and treated their subject peoples as culturally and racially distinct.

India Under the British Raj

Q **Focus Question:** What were some of the major consequences of British rule in India, and how did they affect the Indian people?

By 1800, the once glorious empire of the Mughals had been reduced by British military power to a shadow of its former greatness. During the next few decades, the British sought to consolidate their control over the Indian subcontinent, expanding from their base areas along the coast into the interior. Some territories were taken over directly, first by the East India Company and later by the British crown; others were ruled indirectly through their local maharajas and rajas.

Colonial Reforms

Not all of the effects of British rule were bad. British governance over the subcontinent brought order and

OPPOSING VIEWPOINTS
WHITE MAN'S BURDEN, BLACK MAN'S SORROW

ARTS & IDEAS

One of the justifications for modern imperialism was the notion that the supposedly "more advanced" white peoples had a moral responsibility to raise "ignorant" native peoples to a higher level of civilization. Few captured this notion better than the British poet Rudyard Kipling (1865–1936) in his famous poem *The White Man's Burden*. His appeal, directed to the United States, became one of the most famous sets of verses in the English-speaking world.

That sense of moral responsibility, however, was often misplaced or, even worse, laced with hypocrisy. All too often, the consequences of imperial rule were detrimental to everyone living under colonial authority. Few observers described the destructive effects of Western imperialism on the African people as well as Edmund Morel, a British journalist whose book *The Black Man's Burden* pointed out some of the more harmful aspects of colonialism in the Belgian Congo.

Rudyard Kipling, *The White Man's Burden*

Take up the White Man's burden—
Send forth the best ye breed—
Go bind your sons to exile
To serve your captives' need;
To wait in heavy harness,
On fluttered folk and wild—
Your new-caught sullen peoples,
Half-devil and half-child.

Take up the White Man's burden—
In patience to abide,
To veil the threat of terror
And check the show of pride;
By open speech and simple,
An hundred times made plain
To seek another's profit,
And work another's gain.

Take up the White Man's burden—
The savage wars of peace—
Fill full the mouth of Famine
And bid the sickness cease;
And when your goal is nearest
The end for others sought,
Watch Sloth and heathen Folly
Bring all your hopes to nought.

Edmund Morel, *The Black Man's Burden*

It is [the Africans] who carry the "Black man's burden." They have not withered away before the white man's occupation. Indeed . . . Africa has ultimately absorbed within itself every Caucasian and, for that matter, every Semitic invader, too. In hewing out for himself a fixed abode in Africa, the white man has massacred the African in heaps. The African has survived, and it is well for the white settlers that he has. . . .

What the partial occupation of his soil by the white man has failed to do; what the mapping out of European political "spheres of influence" has failed to do; what the Maxim and the rifle, the slave gang, labour in the bowels of the earth and the lash, have failed to do; what imported measles, smallpox and syphilis have failed to do; whatever the overseas slave trade failed to do; the power of modern capitalistic exploitation, assisted by modern engines of destruction, may yet succeed in accomplishing.

For from the evils of the latter, scientifically applied and enforced, there is no escape for the African. Its destructive effects are not spasmodic; they are permanent. In its permanence resides its fatal consequences. It kills not the body merely, but the soul. It breaks the spirit. It attacks the African at every turn, from every point of vantage. It wrecks his polity, uproots him from the land, invades his family life, destroys his natural pursuits and occupations, claims his whole time, enslaves him in his own home.

Q *According to Kipling, why should Western nations take up the "white man's burden," as described in this poem? What was the "black man's burden," in the eyes of Edmund Morel?*

---

stability to a society that had been rent by civil war. By the early nineteenth century, British control had been consolidated and led to a relatively honest and efficient government that in many respects operated to the benefit of the average Indian. One of the benefits of the period was the heightened attention given to education. Through the efforts of the British administrator Thomas Babington Macaulay, a new school system was established to train the children of Indian elites, and the British civil service examination was introduced (see the box on p. 519).

The instruction of young girls also expanded, with the primary purpose of making them better wives and mothers for the educated male population. In 1875, a Madras medical college accepted its first female student.

British rule also brought an end to some of the more inhumane aspects of Indian tradition. The practice of *sati* was outlawed, and widows were legally permitted to remarry. The British also attempted to put an end to the endemic brigandage (known as *thuggee,* which gave rise to the English word *thug*) that had plagued travelers in

INDIAN IN BLOOD, ENGLISH IN TASTE AND INTELLECT

FAMILY & SOCIETY

Thomas Babington Macaulay (1800–1859) was named a member of the Supreme Council of India in the early 1830s. In that capacity, he was responsible for drawing up a new educational policy for British subjects in the area. In his *Minute on Education,* he considered the claims of English and various local languages to become the vehicle for educational training and decided in favor of the former. It is better, he argued, to teach Indian elites about Western civilization so as "to form a class who may be interpreters between us and the millions whom we govern; a class of persons, Indian in blood and color, but English in taste, in opinions, in morals, and in intellect." Later Macaulay became a prominent historian. The debate over the relative benefits of English and the various Indian languages continues today.

Thomas Babington Macaulay, *Minute on Education*

We have a fund to be employed as government shall direct for the intellectual improvement of the people of this country. The simple question is, what is the most useful way of employing it?

All parties seem to be agreed on one point, that the dialects commonly spoken among the natives of this part of India contain neither literary or scientific information, and are, moreover so poor and rude that, until they are enriched from some other quarter, it will not be easy to translate any valuable work into them....

What, then, shall the language [of education] be? One half of the Committee maintain that it should be the English. The other half strongly recommend the Arabic and Sanskrit. The whole question seems to me to be, which language is the best worth knowing?

I have no knowledge of either Sanskrit or Arabic—but I have done what I could to form a correct estimate of their value. I have read translations of the most celebrated Arabic and Sanskrit works. I have conversed both here and at home with men distinguished by their proficiency in the Eastern tongues. I am quite ready to take the Oriental learning at the valuation of the Orientalists themselves. I have never found one among them who could deny that a single shelf of a good European library was worth the whole native literature of India and Arabia.…

It is, I believe, no exaggeration to say, that all the historical information which has been collected from all the books written in the Sanskrit language is less valuable than what may be found in the most paltry abridgments used at preparatory schools in England. In every branch of physical or moral philosophy the relative position of the two nations is nearly the same.

Q *How did the author of this document justify the teaching of the English language in India? How might a critic have responded?*

India since time immemorial. Railroads, the telegraph, and the postal service were introduced to India shortly after they appeared in Great Britain itself. Work began on the main highway from Calcutta to Delhi in 1839 (see Map 21.1), and the first rail network in northern India was opened in 1853.

The Costs of Colonialism

But the Indian people paid a high price for the peace and stability brought by the British **raj** (from the Indian *raja,* or prince). Perhaps the most flagrant cost was economic. While British entrepreneurs and a small percentage of the Indian population attached to the imperial system reaped financial benefits from British rule, it brought hardship to millions of others in both the cities and the rural areas. The introduction of British textiles put thousands of Bengali women out of work and severely damaged the local textile industry.

In rural areas, the British introduced the *zamindar* system (see Chapter 16) in the misguided expectation that it would both facilitate the collection of agricultural taxes and create a new landed gentry, who could, as in

Britain, become the conservative foundation of imperial rule. But the local gentry took advantage of this new authority to increase taxes and force the less fortunate peasants to become tenants or lose their land entirely. British officials also made few efforts during the nineteenth century to introduce democratic institutions or values to the Indian people. As one senior political figure remarked in Parliament in 1898, democratic institutions "can no more be carried to India by Englishmen ... than they can carry ice in their luggage."[5]

British colonialism was also remiss in bringing the benefits of modern science and technology to India. Some limited forms of industrialization took place, notably in the manufacturing of textiles and jute (used in making rope). The first textile mill opened in 1856. Seventy years later, there were eighty mills in the city of Bombay (now Mumbai) alone. Nevertheless, the lack of local capital and the advantages given to British imports prevented the emergence of other vital new commercial and manufacturing operations.

Foreign rule also had a psychological effect on the Indian people. Although many British colonial officials sincerely tried to improve the lot of the people under their charge, British arrogance and contempt for native tradition cut deeply into the pride of many Indians, especially those of high caste, who were accustomed to a position of superior status in India. Educated Indians trained in the Anglo-Indian school system for a career in the civil service, as well as Eurasians born to mixed marriages, often imitated the behavior and dress of their rulers, speaking English, eating Western food, and taking up European leisure activities, but many rightfully wondered where their true cultural loyalties lay (see the comparative illustration on p. 521).

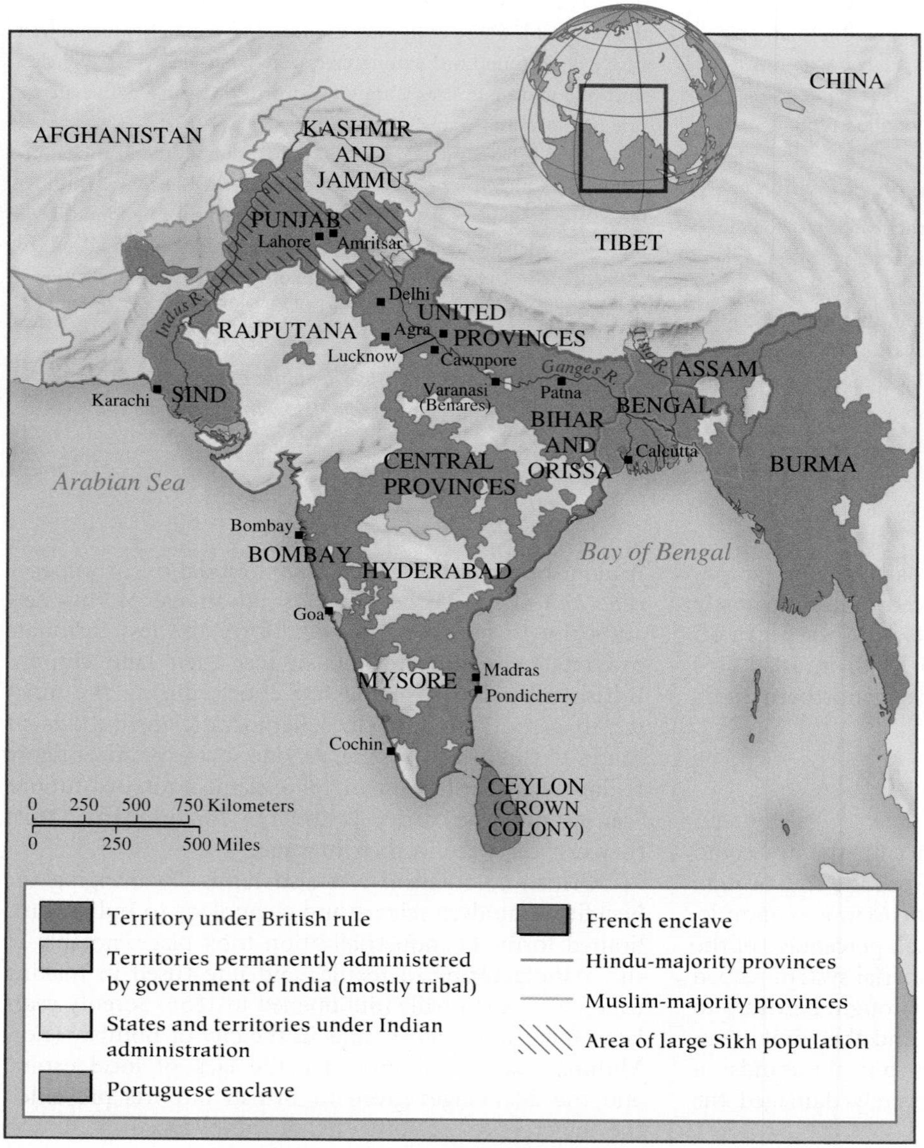

MAP 21.1 **India Under British Rule, 1805–1931.** This map shows the different forms of rule that the British applied in India under their control.

Q Where were the major cities of the subcontinent located, and under whose rule did they fall?

Colonial Regimes in Southeast Asia

Q **Focus Question:** Which Western countries were most active in seeking colonial possessions in Southeast Asia, and what were their motives in doing so?

In 1800, only two societies in Southeast Asia were under effective colonial rule: the Spanish Philippines and the Dutch East Indies. During the nineteenth century, however, European interest in Southeast Asia increased rapidly, and by 1900, virtually the entire area was under colonial rule (see Map 21.2 on p. 522).

"Opportunity in the Orient": The Colonial Takeover in Southeast Asia

The process began after the Napoleonic wars, when the British, by agreement with the Dutch, abandoned their claims to territorial possessions in the East Indies in return for a free hand in the Malay peninsula. In 1819, the colonial administrator Stamford Raffles founded a new British colony on the island of Singapore at the tip of the peninsula. Singapore became a major stopping point for traffic en route to and from China and other commercial centers in the region.

During the next few decades, the pace of European penetration into Southeast Asia accelerated. The British attacked lower Burma in 1826 and eventually established control over Burma, arousing fears in France that its British rival might soon aquire a monopoly of trade in South China. In 1857, the French government decided to compel the Vietnamese to accept French protection. A naval attack launched a year later was not a total success, but the French eventually forced the Nguyen dynasty in Vietnam to cede territories in the Mekong River delta.

INTERACTION & EXCHANGE

COMPARATIVE ILLUSTRATION

Cultural Influences—East and West. When Europeans moved into Asia in the nineteenth century, some Asians began to imitate European customs for prestige or social advancement. Seen at the left, for example, is a young Vietnamese during the 1920s dressed in Western sports clothes, learning to play tennis. Sometimes, however, the cultural influence went the other way. At the right, an English nabob, as European residents in India were often called, apes the manner of an Indian aristocrat, complete with harem and hookah, the Indian water pipe. The paintings on the wall, however, are in the European style.

Q Compare and contrast the styles used by the artists in these two paintings. What message do they send to the viewer?

Singapore and Malaya

A generation later, French rule was extended over the remainder of the country. By 1900, French seizure of neighboring Cambodia and Laos had led to the creation of the French-ruled Indochinese Union.

After the French conquest of Indochina, Thailand was the only remaining independent state on the Southeast Asian mainland. Under the astute leadership of two remarkable rulers, King Mongkut and his son, King Chulalongkorn, the Thai attempted to introduce Western learning and maintain relations with the major European powers without undermining internal stability or inviting an imperialist attack. In 1896, the British and the French agreed to preserve Thailand as an independent buffer zone between their possessions in Southeast Asia.

The final piece in the colonial edifice in Southeast Asia was put in place during the Spanish-American War in 1898 (see Chapter 20), when U.S. naval forces under Commodore George Dewey defeated the Spanish fleet in Manila Bay. President William McKinley agonized over the fate of the Philippines but ultimately decided that the moral thing to do was to turn the islands into an American colony to prevent them from falling into the hands of the Japanese. In fact, the Americans (like the Spanish before them) found the islands a convenient jumping-off point for the China trade (see Chapter 22). The mixture of moral idealism and the desire for profit was reflected in a speech given

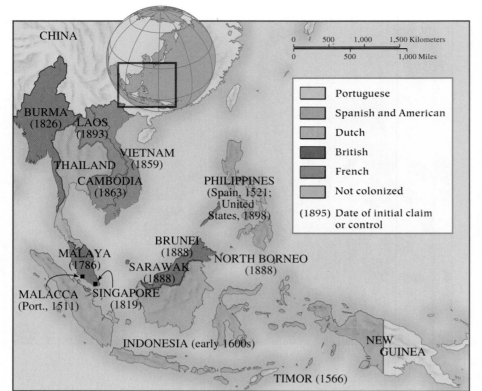

CHINA

BURMA
(1826)
LAOS
(1893)

VIETNAM
(1859)

THAILAND

CAMBODIA
(1863)

PHILIPPINES
(Spain, 1521;
United
States, 1898)

BRUNEI
(1888)

MALAYA
(1786)

SARAWAK
(1888)

NORTH BORNEO
(1888)

MALACCA
(Port., 1511)

SINGAPORE
(1819)

INDONESIA (early 1600s)

NEW
GUINEA

TIMOR (1566)

	Portuguese
	Spanish and American
	Dutch
	British
	French
	Not colonized

(1895) Date of initial claim
or control

0   500   1,000   1,500 Kilometers
0   500   1,000 Miles

MAP 21.2 Colonial Southeast Asia. This map shows the spread of European colonial rule into Southeast Asia from the sixteenth century to the end of the nineteenth. Malacca, initially seized by the Portuguese in 1511, was taken by the Dutch in the seventeenth century and then by the British one hundred years later.
Q What was the significance of Malacca?
View an animated version of this map or related maps at www.cengage.com/history/duikspiel/essentialworld6e

Government Hill in Singapore. After occupying the island of Singapore early in the nineteenth century, the British turned what was once a pirate lair at the entrance to the Strait of Malacca into one of the most important commercial seaports in Asia. By the end of the century, Singapore was home to a rich mixture of peoples, both European and Asian. This painting by a British artist in the mid-nineteenth century graphically displays the multiracial character of the colony as strollers of various ethnic backgrounds share space on Government Hill, with the busy harbor in the background. Almost all colonial port cities became melting pots of people from various parts of the world. Many of the immigrants served as merchants, urban laborers, and craftsmen in the new imperial marketplace.

in the U.S. Senate in January 1900 by Senator Albert Beveridge of Indiana:

> Mr. President, the times call for candor. The Philippines are ours forever, "territory belonging to the United States," as the Constitution calls them. And just beyond the Philippines are China's illimitable markets. We will not retreat from either. . . . We will not renounce our part in the mission of our race, trustee, under God, of the civilization of the world. And we will move forward to our work, not howling out regrets like slaves whipped to their burdens, but with gratitude for a task worthy of our strength, and thanksgiving to Almighty God that He has marked us as His chosen people, henceforth to lead in the regeneration of the world.[6]

Not all Filipinos agreed with Senator Beveridge's portrayal of the situation. Under the leadership of Emilio Aguinaldo, guerrilla forces fought bitterly against U.S. troops to establish their independence from both Spain and the United States. But America's first war against guerrilla forces in Asia was a success, and the bulk of the resistance collapsed in 1901. President McKinley had his stepping-stone to the rich markets of China.

The Nature of Colonial Rule

In Southeast Asia, economic profit was the immediate and primary aim of colonial enterprise. For that purpose, colonial powers tried wherever possible to work with local elites to facilitate the exploitation of natural resources. Indirect rule reduced the cost of training European administrators and had a less corrosive impact on the local culture. In the Dutch East Indies, for example, officials of the Dutch East India Company (VOC) entrusted local administration to the indigenous landed aristocracy, who maintained law and order and collected taxes in return for a payment from the VOC. The British followed a similar practice in Malaya. While establishing direct rule over the crucial commercial centers of Singapore and Malacca, the British allowed local Muslim rulers to maintain princely power in the interior of the peninsula.

Administration and Education Indirect rule, however convenient and inexpensive, was not always feasible. In some instances, local resistance to the colonial conquest made such a policy impossible. In Burma, the staunch opposition of the monarchy and other traditionalist forces caused the British to abolish the monarchy and administer the country directly through their colonial government in India. In Indochina, the French used both direct and indirect means. They imposed direct rule on the southern provinces in the Mekong delta but governed the north as a protectorate, with the emperor retaining titular authority from his palace in Huê. The French adopted a similar policy in Cambodia and Laos, where local rulers were left in charge with French advisers to counsel them.

Whatever method was used, colonial regimes in Southeast Asia, as elsewhere, were slow to create democratic institutions. The first legislative councils and assemblies were composed almost exclusively of European residents in the colony. The first representatives from the indigenous population were wealthy and conservative in their political views. When Southeast Asians complained, colonial officials gradually and reluctantly began to broaden the franchise. Albert Sarraut advised patience in awaiting the full benefits of colonial policy: "I will treat you like my younger brothers, but do not forget that I am the older brother. I will slowly give you the dignity of humanity."[7]

Colonial officials were also slow to adopt educational reforms. Although the introduction of Western education was one of the justifications of colonialism, colonial officials soon discovered that educating native elites could backfire. Often there were few jobs for highly trained lawyers, engineers, and architects in colonial societies, leading to the threat of an indigestible mass of unemployed intellectuals who would take out their frustrations on the colonial regime. As one French official noted in voicing his opposition to increasing the number of schools in Vietnam, educating the natives meant not "one coolie less, but one rebel more."

Economic Development Colonial powers were equally reluctant to take up the "white man's burden" in the area of economic development. As we have seen, their primary goals were to secure a source of cheap raw materials and to maintain markets for manufactured goods. Such objectives would be undermined by the emergence of advanced industrial economies. So colonial policy concentrated on the export of raw materials— teakwood from Burma; rubber and tin from Malaya; spices, tea and coffee, and palm oil from the East Indies; and sugar and copra (the meat of a coconut) from the Philippines.

A Rubber Plantation. Natural rubber was one of the most important cash crops in European colonies in Asia. Rubber trees, native to the Amazon River basin in Brazil, were eventually transplanted to Southeast Asia, where they became a major source of profit. Workers on the plantations received few benefits, however. Once the sap of the tree (known as latex and shown on the left) was extracted, it was hardened and pressed into sheets (shown on the right) and then sent to Europe for refining.

In some Southeast Asian colonial societies, a measure of industrial development did take place to meet the needs of the European population and local elites. Major manufacturing cities like Rangoon in lower Burma, Batavia on the island of Java, and Saigon in French Indochina grew rapidly. Although the local middle class benefited from the increased economic activity, most large industrial and commercial establishments were owned and managed by Europeans or, in some cases, by Indian or Chinese merchants.

Colonialism and the Countryside Despite the growth of an urban economy, the vast majority of people in the colonial societies continued to farm the land. Many continued to live by subsistence agriculture, but the colonial policy of emphasizing cash crops for export also led to the creation of a form of plantation agriculture in which peasants were recruited to work as wage laborers on rubber and tea plantations owned by Europeans. To maintain a competitive edge, the plantation owners kept the wages of their workers at poverty level. Many plantation workers were "shanghaied" (the English term originated from the practice of recruiting laborers, often from the docks and streets of Shanghai, by unscrupulous means such as the use of force, alcohol, or drugs) to work on plantations, where

conditions were often so inhumane that thousands died. High taxes, enacted by colonial governments to pay for administrative costs or improvements in the local infrastructure, were a heavy burden for poor peasants.

The situation was made even more difficult by the steady growth of the population. Peasants in Asia had always had large families on the assumption that a high proportion of their children would die in infancy. But improved sanitation and medical treatment resulted in lower rates of infant mortality and a staggering increase in population. The population of the island of Java, for example, increased from about a million in the precolonial era to about 40 million at the end of the nineteenth century. Under these conditions, the rural areas could no longer support the growing populations, and many young people fled to the cities to seek jobs in factories or shops. The migratory pattern gave rise to squatter settlements in the suburbs of the major cities.

As in India, colonial rule did bring some benefits to Southeast Asia. It led to the beginnings of a modern economic infrastructure and to what is sometimes called a "modernizing elite" dedicated to the creation of an advanced industrialized society. The development of an export market helped create an entrepreneurial class in rural areas. This happened, for example, on the outer islands of the Dutch East Indies (such as Borneo and Sumatra), where small growers of rubber trees, palm trees for oil, coffee, tea, and spices began to share in the profits of the colonial enterprise.

Empire Building in Africa

Q **Focus Question:** What factors were behind the "scramble for Africa," and what impact did it have on the continent?

Up to the beginning of the nineteenth century, the relatively limited nature of European economic interests in Africa had provided little temptation for the penetration of the interior or the political takeover of the coastal areas. The slave trade, the main source of European profit during the eighteenth century, could be carried on by using African rulers and merchants as intermediaries. Disease, political instability, the lack of transportation, and the generally unhealthy climate all deterred the Europeans from more extensive efforts in Africa.

The Growing European Presence in West Africa

As the new century dawned, the slave trade itself was in a state of decline. One reason was the growing sense of outrage among humanitarians in several European countries over the purchase, sale, and exploitation of human beings. Dutch merchants effectively ceased trafficking in slaves in 1795, and the Danes stopped in 1803. A few years later, the slave trade was declared illegal in both Great Britain and the United States. The British began to apply pressure on other nations to follow suit, and most did so after the end of the Napoleonic wars in 1815, leaving only Portugal and Spain as practitioners of the trade south of the equator. In the meantime, the demand for slaves began to decline in the Western Hemisphere. When slavery was abolished in the United States in 1863 and in Cuba and Brazil seventeen years later, the slave trade across the Atlantic was effectively brought to an end. It continued to exist, although at a reduced rate, along the Swahili coast in East Africa.

As the slave trade in the Atlantic declined during the first half of the nineteenth century, European interest in what was sometimes called "legitimate trade" in natural resources increased. Exports of peanuts, timber, hides, and palm oil from West Africa increased substantially during the first decades of the century, while imports of textile goods and other manufactured products rose.

Stimulated by growing commercial interests in the area, European governments began to push for a more permanent presence along the coast. During the first decades of the nineteenth century, the British established settlements along the Gold Coast and in Sierra Leone, where they set up agricultural plantations for freed slaves who had returned from the Western Hemisphere or had been liberated by British ships while en route to the Americas. A similar haven for ex-slaves was developed with the assistance of the United States in Liberia. The French occupied the area around the Senegal River near Cape Verde, where they attempted to develop peanut plantations.

The growing European presence in West Africa led to the emergence of a new class of Africans educated in Western culture and often employed by Europeans. Many became Christians, and some studied in European or American universities. At the same time, the European presence inevitably led to increasing tensions with African governments in the area. Most African states, especially those with a fairly high degree of political integration, were able to maintain their independence from this creeping European encroachment, called "informal empire" by some historians, but the prospects for the future were ominous. When local groups attempted to organize to protect their interests, the British stepped in and annexed the coastal states as the British colony of Gold Coast in 1874. At about the same time, the British extended an informal protectorate over warring ethnic groups in the Niger delta (see Map 21.3).

Imperialist Shadow over the Nile

A similar process was under way in the Nile valley. There had long been interest in shortening the trade route to the East by digging a canal across the low, swampy isthmus separating the Mediterranean from the Red Sea. At the end of the eighteenth century, Napoleon planned a military takeover of Egypt to cement French power in the eastern Mediterranean and open a faster route to India.

Napoleon's plan proved abortive. French troops landed in Egypt in 1798 and destroyed the ramshackle Mamluk regime in Cairo, but the British counterattacked, destroying the French fleet and eventually forcing the French to evacuate in disorder. The British restored the Mamluks to power, but in 1805, Muhammad Ali, an Ottoman army officer of either Turkish or Albanian extraction, seized control.

During the next three decades, Muhammad Ali introduced a series of reforms to bring Egypt into the modern world. He modernized the army, set up a public educational system (supplementing the traditional religious education provided in Muslim schools), and sponsored the creation of a small industrial sector producing refined sugar, textiles, munitions, and even ships. Muhammad Ali also extended Egyptian authority

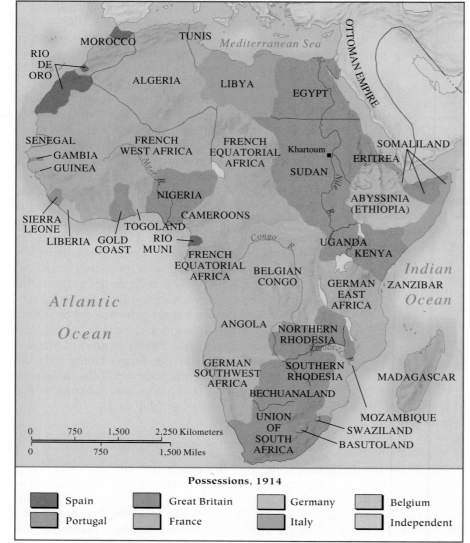

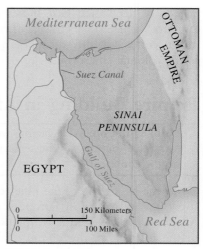

The Suez Canal

MAP 21.3 **Africa in 1914.** By the start of the twentieth century, virtually all of Africa was under some form of European rule. The territorial divisions established by colonial powers on the continent of Africa on the eve of World War I are shown here. **Q** Which European countries possessed the most colonies in Africa? Why did Ethiopia remain independent?

View an animated version of this map or related maps at www.cengage.com/history/duikspiel/essentialworld6e

Possessions, 1914

Spain	Great Britain	Germany	Belgium
Portugal	France	Italy	Independent

made the heretofore visionary plans for a Suez canal more urgent. In 1854, the French entrepreneur Ferdinand de Lesseps signed a contract to begin construction of the canal, and it was completed in 1869. The project brought little immediate benefit to Egypt, however. The construction not only cost thousands of lives but also left the Egyptian government deep in debt, forcing it to depend increasingly on foreign financial support. When an army revolt against growing foreign influence broke out in 1881, the British stepped in to protect their investment (they had bought Egypt's canal company shares in 1875) and establish an informal protectorate that would last until World War I.

Rising discontent in the Sudan added to Egypt's growing internal problems. In 1881, the Muslim cleric Muhammad Ahmad, known as the Mahdi (in Arabic, the "rightly guided one"), led a religious revolt that brought much of the upper Nile under his control. The famous British general Charles Gordon led a military force to Khartoum to restore Egyptian authority, but his besieged army was captured in 1885 by the Mahdi's troops, thirty-six hours before a British rescue mission reached Khartoum. Gordon himself died in the battle, which became one of the most dramatic news stories of the last quarter of the century.

southward into the Sudan and across the Sinai peninsula into Arabia, Syria, and northern Iraq and even briefly threatened to seize Istanbul itself. To prevent the possible collapse of the Ottoman Empire, the British and the French recognized Muhammad Ali as the hereditary **pasha** (later to be known as the *khedive*) of Egypt under the loose authority of the Ottoman government.

The growing economic importance of the Nile valley, along with the development of steam navigation,

The Opening of the Suez Canal. The Suez Canal, which connected the Mediterranean and the Red seas, was constructed under the direction of the French promoter Ferdinand de Lesseps. Still in use today, the canal is Egypt's greatest revenue producer. This sketch shows the ceremonial passage of the first ships through the canal in 1869. Note the combination of sail and steam power, reflecting the transition to coal-powered ships in the mid-nineteenth century.

Legacy of Shame. By the mid-nineteenth century, most European nations had prohibited the trade in African slaves, but slavery continued to exist in East Africa under the sponsorship of the sultan of Zanzibar. When the Scottish missionary David Livingstone witnessed a slave raid near Lake Tanganyika in 1871, he wrote, "It gave me the impression of being in Hell." Despite his efforts, the practice was not eradicated until well into the next century. Shown here are domestic slaves on the island of Zanzibar under the baton of a supervisor. The photograph was taken about 1890.

The weakening of Turkish rule in the Nile valley had a parallel farther to the west, where local viceroys in Tripoli, Tunis, and Algiers had begun to establish their autonomy. In 1830, the French, on the pretext of protecting European shipping in the Mediterranean from pirates, seized the area surrounding Algiers and integrated it into the French Empire. In 1881, the French imposed a protectorate on neighboring Tunisia. Only Tripoli and Cyrenaica (the Ottoman provinces that comprise modern Libya) remained under Turkish rule until the Italians took them in 1911–1912.

Arab Merchants and European Missionaries in East Africa

As always, events in East Africa followed their own distinctive pattern of development. Whereas the Atlantic slave trade was in decline, demand for slaves was increasing on the other side of the continent due to the growth of plantation agriculture in the region and on the islands off the coast. The French introduced sugar to the island of Réunion early in the century, and plantations of cloves (introduced from the Moluccas in the eighteenth century) were established under Omani Arab ownership on the island of Zanzibar. Zanzibar itself became the major shipping port along the entire east coast during the early nineteenth century, and the sultan of Oman, who had reasserted Arab suzerainty over the region in the aftermath of the collapse of Portuguese authority, established his capital at Zanzibar in 1840.

The tenacity of the slave trade in East Africa—Zanzibar had now become the largest slave market in Africa—was undoubtedly a major reason for the rise of Western interest and Christian missionary activity in the region during the middle of the century. The most renowned missionary was the Scottish doctor David Livingstone, who arrived in Africa in 1841. Because Livingstone

FILM & HISTORY
KHARTOUM (1966)

The mission of General Charles "Chinese" Gordon to Khartoum in 1884 was one of the most dramatic news stories of the late nineteenth century. Gordon had already become renowned in his native Great Britain for his successful efforts to bring an end to the practice of slavery in North Africa. He had also attracted attention—and acquired his nickname—for helping the Manchu Empire suppress the Taiping Rebellion in China in the 1860s (see Chapter 22). But the Khartoum affair not only marked the tragic culmination of his storied career but also symbolized in broader terms the epic struggle in Britain between advocates and opponents of imperial expansion. The battle for Khartoum thus became an object lesson in modern British history.

Proponents of British imperial expansion argued that the country must project its power in the Nile River valley to protect the Suez Canal as its main trade route to the East. Critics argued that imperial overreach would inevitably entangle the country in unwinnable wars in far-off places. The film *Khartoum*, produced in London in 1966, dramatically captures the ferocity of the battle for the Nile as well as its significance for the future of the British Empire. General Gordon, stoically played by the American actor Charlton Heston, is a devout Christian who has devoted his life to carrying out the moral imperative of imperialism in the continent of Africa. When peace in the Sudan (then a British protectorate in the upper Nile River valley) is threatened by the forces of radical Islam led by the Muslim mystic Muhammad Ahmad—known as the Mahdi—Gordon leads a mission to Khartoum under orders to prevent catastrophe there. But Prime Minister William Ewart Gladstone, admirably portrayed by the consummate British actor Ralph Richardson, fears that Gordon's messianic desire to save the Sudan will entrap his government in an

General Charles Gordon (Charlton Heston) astride his camel in Khartoum, Sudan

unwinnable war; he thus orders Gordon to lead an evacuation of the city. The most fascinating character in the film is the Mahdi himself (played brilliantly by Sir Laurence Olivier), who firmly believes that he has a sacred mandate to carry the Prophet's words to the global Muslim community.

The conclusion of the film, set in the breathtaking beauty of the Nile River valley, takes place as the clash of wills reaches a climax in the battle for control of Khartoum. Although the film's portrayal of a face-to-face meeting between Gordon and the Mahdi is not based on fact, the narrative serves as an object lesson on the dangers of imperial overreach and as an eerie foretaste of the clash between Islam and Christendom in our own day.

spent much of his time exploring the interior of the continent, discovering Victoria Falls in the process, he was occasionally criticized for being more explorer than missionary. But Livingstone was convinced that it was his divinely appointed task to bring Christianity to the far reaches of the continent, and his passionate opposition to slavery did far more to win public support for the abolitionist cause than did the efforts of any other figure of his generation. Public outcries provoked the British to redouble their efforts to bring the slave trade in East Africa to an end, and in 1873, the slave market at Zanzibar was finally closed as the result of pressure from London. Shortly before, Livingstone had died of illness in Central Africa, but some of his followers brought his body to the coast for burial.

Bantus, Boers, and British in the South

Nowhere in Africa did the European presence grow more rapidly than in the south. During the eighteenth century, the Boers, Afrikaans-speaking farmers descended from the original Dutch settlers of the Cape Colony, began to migrate eastward. After the British seized control of the cape from the Dutch during the Napoleonic wars, the Boers' eastward migration intensified, culminating in the Great Trek of the mid-1830s. In part, the Boers' departure was provoked by the different attitude of the British toward the native population. Slavery was abolished in the British Empire in 1834, and the British government was generally more sympathetic to the rights of the local African population than were the Afrikaners, many of whom believed

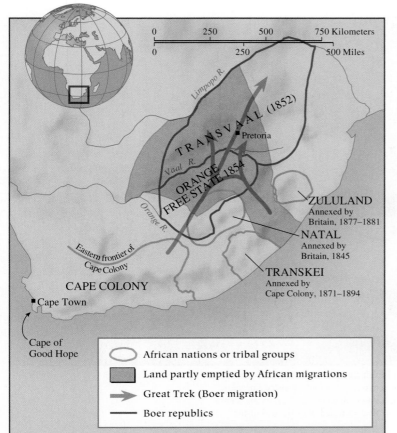

MAP 21.4 **The Struggle for Southern Africa.** European settlers from the Cape Colony expanded into adjacent areas of southern Africa during the nineteenth century. The arrows indicate the routes taken by the Afrikaans-speaking Boers.

Q Who were the Boers, and why did they migrate eastward?

that white superiority was ordained by God and fled from British rule to control their own destiny. Eventually, the Boers formed their own independent republics—the Orange Free State and the South African Republic (usually called the Transvaal; see Map 21.4).

Although the Boer occupation of the eastern territory was initially facilitated by internecine warfare among the local inhabitants of the region, the new settlers met some resistance. In the early nineteenth century, the Zulus, a Bantu people led by a talented ruler named Shaka, engaged in a series of wars with the Europeans that ended only when Shaka was overthrown.

The Scramble for Africa

At the beginning of the 1880s, most of Africa was still independent. European rule was limited to the fringes of the continent, such as Algeria, the Gold Coast, and South Africa. Other areas like Egypt, lower Nigeria,

Senegal, and Mozambique were under various forms of loose protectorate. But the pace of European penetration was accelerating, and the constraints that had limited European rapaciousness were fast disappearing.

The scramble began in the mid-1880s, when several European states, including Belgium, France, Germany, Great Britain, and Portugal, engaged in a feeding frenzy to seize a piece of African territory before the carcass had been picked clean. By 1900, virtually all of the continent had been placed under some form of European rule. The British had consolidated their authority over the Nile valley and seized additional territories in East Africa (see Map 21.3 on p. 526). The French retaliated by advancing eastward from Senegal into the central Sahara. They also occupied the island of Madagascar and other territories in West and Central Africa. In between, the Germans claimed the hinterland opposite Zanzibar, as well as coastal strips in West and Southwest Africa north of the cape, and King Leopold II of Belgium claimed the Congo. Eventually, Italy entered the contest and seized modern Libya and some of the Somali coast.

What had happened to spark the sudden imperialist hysteria that brought an end to African independence? Clearly, the level of trade between Europe and Africa was not sufficient to justify the risks and the expense of conquest. More important than economic interests were the intensified rivalries among the European states that led them to engage in imperialist takeovers out of fear that if they did not, another state might do so, leaving them at a disadvantage. In the most famous example, the British solidified their control over the entire Nile valley to protect the Suez Canal from seizure by the French.

Another consideration might be called the "missionary factor," as European missionary interests lobbied with their governments for colonial takeovers to facilitate their efforts to convert the African population to Christianity. The concept of social Darwinism and the "white man's burden" persuaded many that it was in the interests of the African people, as well as those of their conquerors, to be introduced more rapidly to the benefits of Western civilization. Even David Livingstone had become convinced that missionary work and economic development had to go hand in hand, pleading to his fellow Europeans to introduce the "three Cs" (Christianity, commerce, and civilization) to the continent. How much easier such a task would be if African peoples were under benevolent European rule!

The Sunday Battle. When Boer "trekkers" seeking to escape British rule arrived in the Transvaal in the 1830s and 1840s, they were bitterly opposed by the Zulus, a Bantu-speaking people who resisted European encroachments on their territory for decades. In this 1847 lithograph, thousands of Zulu warriors are shown engaged in battle with their European rivals. Zulu resistance was not finally quelled until the end of the nineteenth century.

There were more prosaic reasons as well. Advances in Western technology and European superiority in firearms made it easier than ever for a small European force to defeat superior numbers. Furthermore, life expectancy for Europeans living in Africa had improved. With the discovery that quinine (extracted from the bark of the cinchona tree) could provide partial immunity from the ravages of malaria, the mortality rate for Europeans living in Africa dropped dramatically in the 1840s. By the end of the century, European residents in tropical Africa faced only slightly higher risks of death by disease than individuals living in Europe.

Under these circumstances, King Leopold of Belgium used missionary activities as an excuse to claim vast territories in the Congo River basin (Belgium, he said, as "a small country, with a small people," needed a colony to enhance its image).[8] This set off a desperate race among European nations to stake claims throughout sub-Saharan Africa. Leopold ended up with the territories south of the Congo River, while France occupied areas to the north (Leopold bequeathed the Congo to Belgium on his death). Meanwhile, on the eastern side of the continent, Germany annexed the colony of Tanganyika. To avert the possibility of violent clashes among the great powers, the German chancellor, Otto von Bismarck, convened a conference in Berlin in 1884 to set ground rules for future annexations of African territory by European nations. Like the famous Open Door Notes fifteen years later (see Chapter 22), the conference combined high-minded resolutions with a hardheaded recognition of practical interests. The delegates called for free commerce in the Congo and along the Niger River as well as for further efforts to end the slave trade. At the same time, the participants recognized the inevitability of the imperialist dynamic, agreeing only that future annexations of African territory should not be given international recognition until effective occupation had been demonstrated. No African delegates were present at the conference.

The Berlin Conference had been convened to avert war and reduce tensions among European nations competing for the spoils of Africa. During the next few years, African territories were annexed without provoking a major confrontation between the Western powers, but in the late 1890s, Britain and France reached the brink of conflict at Fashoda, a small town on the Nile River in the Sudan. The French had been advancing eastward across the Sahara with the transparent objective of controlling

Dutch abolish slave trade in Africa	1795
Napoleon invades Egypt	1798
Slave trade declared illegal in Great Britain	1808
French seize Algeria	1830
Boers' Great Trek in southern Africa	1830s
Sultan of Oman establishes capital at Zanzibar	1840
David Livingstone arrives in Africa	1841
Slavery abolished in the United States	1863
Suez Canal completed	1869
Zanzibar slave market closed	1873
British establish Gold Coast colony	1874
British establish informal protectorate over Egypt	1881
Berlin Conference on Africa	1884
Charles Gordon killed at Khartoum	1885
Confrontation at Fashoda	1898
Boer War	1899–1902
Union of South Africa established	1910

the regions around the upper Nile. In 1898, British and Egyptian troops seized the Sudan from successors of the Mahdi and then marched southward to head off the French. After a tense face-off at Fashoda, the French government backed down, and British authority over the area was secured.

Colonialism in Africa

Having seized Africa in what could almost be described as a fit of hysteria, the European powers had to decide what to do with it. With economic concerns relatively limited except for isolated areas like the gold mines in the Transvaal and copper deposits in the Belgian Congo, interest in Africa declined, and most European governments settled down to govern their new territories with the least effort and expense possible. In many cases, this meant a form of indirect rule similar to what the British used in the princely states in India. The British with their tradition of decentralized government at home were especially prone to adopt this approach.

Indirect Rule in West Africa In the minds of British administrators, the stated goal of indirect rule was to preserve African political traditions. The desire to limit cost and inconvenience was one reason for this approach, but it may also have been due to the conviction that Africans were inherently inferior to the white race and thus incapable of adopting European customs and institutions.

In any event, indirect rule entailed relying to the greatest extent possible on existing political elites and institutions. Initially, in some areas, the British simply asked a local ruler to formally accept British authority and to fly the Union Jack over official buildings. Sometimes it was the Africans who did the bidding, as in the case of the African leaders in Cameroons who wrote to Queen Victoria:

> We *wish* to have your laws in our towns. We want to have every *fashion* altered; also we will do according to your Consul's *word*. Plenty wars here in our country. Plenty murder and plenty idol worshippers. Perhaps these *lines* of our writing will look to you as an *idle* tale.
> We have *spoken* to the English consul plenty times about having an English *government* here. We never have answer from you, so we wish to write you *ourselves*.[9]

Nigeria offers a typical example of British indirect rule. British officials maintained the central administration, but local authority was assigned to native chiefs, with British district officers serving as intermediaries with the central administration. Where a local aristocracy did not exist, the British assigned administrative responsibility to clan heads from communities in the vicinity. The local authorities were expected to maintain law and order and to collect taxes from the native population. As a general rule, indigenous customs were left undisturbed, although the institution of slavery was abolished. A dual legal system was instituted that applied African laws to Africans and European laws to foreigners.

One advantage of such an administrative system was that it did not severely disrupt local customs and institutions. Nevertheless, it had several undesirable consequences. In the first place, it was essentially a fraud, since all major decisions were made by the British administrators while the native authorities served primarily as the means of enforcing decisions. Moreover, indirect rule served to perpetuate the autocratic system often in use prior to colonial takeover.

The British in East Africa The situation was somewhat different in East Africa, especially in Kenya, which had a relatively large European population attracted by the temperate climate in the central highlands. The local government had encouraged white settlers to migrate to the area as a means of promoting economic development and encouraging financial self-sufficiency. To attract Europeans, fertile farmlands in the central highlands were reserved for European settlement, while specified reserve lands were set aside for Africans. The presence of a substantial European minority (although, in fact, they represented only about 1 percent of the entire population) had an impact on Kenya's political development. The white settlers actively sought self-government and dominion status similar to that granted to such former British possessions as Canada and Australia. The British government, however, was not willing to run the risk of provoking racial tensions with the African majority and agreed only to establish separate government organs for the European and African populations.

British Rule in South Africa   The British used a different system in southern Africa, where there was a high percentage of European settlers. The situation was further complicated by a growing division between English-speaking and Afrikaner elements within the European population. The discovery of gold and diamonds in the Boer republic of the Transvaal was the source of the problem. Clashes between the Afrikaner population and foreign (mainly British) miners and developers led to an attempt by Cecil Rhodes, prime minister of the Cape Colony and a prominent entrepreneur in the area, to subvert the Transvaal and bring it under British rule. In 1899, the so-called Boer War broke out between Britain and the Transvaal, which was backed by its fellow republic, the Orange Free State. Guerrilla resistance by the Boers was fierce, but the vastly superior forces of the British were able to prevail by 1902. To compensate the defeated Afrikaner population for the loss of independence, the British government agreed that only whites would vote in the now essentially self-governing colony. The Boers were placated, but the brutalities committed during the war (the British introduced an institution later to be known as the concentration camp) created bitterness on both sides that continued to fester through future decades.

In 1910, the British agreed to the creation of the independent Union of South Africa, which combined the old Cape Colony and Natal with the Boer republics. The new union adopted a representative government, but only for the European population, while the African reserves of Basutoland (now Lesotho), Bechuanaland (now Botswana), and Swaziland were subordinated directly to the crown. The union was now free to manage its own domestic affairs and possessed considerable autonomy in foreign relations. Formal British rule was also extended to the remaining lands south of the Zambezi River, which were eventually divided into the territories of Northern and Southern Rhodesia. Southern Rhodesia attracted many British immigrants, and in 1922, after a popular referendum, it became a crown colony.

Direct Rule   Most other European nations governed their African possessions through a form of direct rule. The prototype was the French system, which reflected the centralized administrative system introduced in France itself by Napoleon. As in the British colonies, at the top of the pyramid was a French official, usually known as the governor-general, who was appointed from Paris and governed with the aid of a bureaucracy in the capital city. At the provincial level, French commissioners were assigned to deal with local administrators, but the latter were required to be conversant in French and could be transferred to a new position at the needs of the central government.

Moreover, the French ideal was to assimilate their African subjects into French culture rather than preserving their native traditions. Africans were eligible to run for office and to serve in the French National Assembly, and a few were appointed to high positions in the colonial administration. Such policies reflected the relative absence of racist attitudes in French society, as well as the conviction among the French of the superiority of Gallic culture and their revolutionary belief in the universality of human nature.

After World War I, European colonial policy in Africa entered a new and more formal phase. The colonial administrative network was extended to a greater degree into outlying areas, where it was represented by a district official and defended by a small native army under European command. Greater attention was given to improving social services, including education, medicine and sanitation, and communications. The colonial system was now viewed more formally as a moral and social responsibility, a "sacred trust" to be maintained by the civilized countries until the Africans became capable of self-government. More emphasis was placed on economic development and on the exploitation of natural resources to provide the colonies with the means of achieving self-sufficiency. More Africans were now serving in colonial administrations, although relatively few held positions of responsibility. At the same time, race consciousness probably increased during this period. Segregated clubs, schools, and churches were established as more European officials brought their wives and began to raise families in the colonies. European feelings of superiority to their African subjects led to countless examples of cruelty similar to Western practices in Asia. Although the institution of slavery was discouraged, African workers were often subjected to unbelievably harsh conditions as they were put to use in promoting the cause of imperialism.

Women in Colonial Africa   The establishment of colonial rule had a mixed impact on the rights and status of women in Africa. Sexual relationships changed profoundly during the colonial era, sometimes in ways that could justly be described as beneficial. Colonial governments attempted to bring an end to forced marriage, bodily mutilation such as clitoridectomy, and polygamy. Missionaries introduced women to Western education and encouraged them to organize themselves to defend their interests.

But the colonial system had some unfavorable consequences as well. African women had traditionally benefited from the prestige of matrilineal systems and were empowered by their traditional role as the primary agricultural producers in their community. Under colonialism, European settlers not only took the best land for themselves but also, in introducing new agricultural techniques, tended to deal exclusively with males, encouraging them to develop lucrative cash crops, while women were restricted to traditional farming methods. Whereas African men applied chemical fertilizer to the fields, women used manure. While men began to use bicycles, and eventually trucks, to transport goods, women still carried their goods on their heads, a practice that continues today. In British colonies, Victorian attitudes of female subordination led to restrictions on women's freedom, and positions in government that they had formerly held were now closed to them.

The Emergence of Anticolonialism

Q Focus Question: How did the subject peoples respond to colonialism, and what role did nationalism play in their response?

Thus far we have looked at the colonial experience primarily from the point of view of the colonial powers. Equally important is the way the subject peoples reacted to the experience. From the perspective of the more than half a century of independence movements since World War II, it seems clear that their primary response was to turn to nationalism as a means of preserving their ethnic, cultural, or religious identity.

Stirrings of Nationhood

As we have seen, nationalism refers to a state of mind rising out of an awareness of being part of a community that possesses common institutions, traditions, language, and customs (see the comparative essay "The Rise of Nationalism" on p. 504 in Chapter 20). Few nations in the world today meet such criteria. Most modern states contain a variety of ethnic, religious, and linguistic communities, each with its own sense of cultural and national identity. Should Canada, for example, which includes peoples of French, English, and Native American heritage, be considered a nation? Another question is how nationalism differs from other forms of tribal, religious, or linguistic affiliation. Should every group that resists assimilation into a larger cultural unity be called nationalist?

Such questions complicate the study of nationalism even in Europe and North America and make agreement on a definition elusive. They create even greater

dilemmas in discussing Asia and Africa, where most societies are deeply divided by ethnic, linguistic, and religious differences and the very term *nationalism* is a foreign phenomenon imported from the West (see the box on p. 534). Prior to the colonial era, most traditional societies in Africa and Asia were formed on the basis of religious beliefs, tribal loyalties, or devotion to hereditary monarchies.

The advent of European colonialism brought the consciousness of modern nationhood to many of the societies of Asia and Africa. The creation of European colonies with defined borders and a powerful central government led to the weakening of tribal and village ties and a significant reorientation in the individual's sense of political identity. The introduction of Western ideas of citizenship and representative government produced a new sense of participation in the affairs of government. At the same time, the appearance of a new elite class based not on hereditary privilege or religious sanction but on alleged racial or cultural superiority aroused a shared sense of resentment among the subject peoples who felt a common commitment to the creation of an independent society. By the first quarter of the twentieth century, political movements dedicated to the overthrow of colonial rule had arisen throughout much of the non-Western world.

Traditional Resistance: A Precursor to Nationalism

The beginnings of modern nationalism can be found in the initial resistance by the indigenous peoples to the colonial conquest. Although, strictly speaking, such resistance was not "nationalist" because it was essentially motivated by the desire to defend traditional institutions, it did reflect a primitive concept of nationhood in that it aimed at protecting the homeland from the invader; later patriotic groups have often hailed early resistance movements as the precursors of twentieth-century nationalist movements. Thus, traditional resistance to colonial conquest may logically be viewed as the first stage in the development of modern nationalism.

Such resistance took various forms. For the most part, it was led by the existing ruling class. In the Ashanti kingdom in Africa and in Burma and Vietnam in Southeast Asia, resistance to Western domination was initially directed by the imperial courts. In South Africa, as we have seen, the Zulus engaged in a bitter war of resistance to Boer colonists arriving from the Cape Colony. In some cases, traditionalists continued to oppose foreign conquest even after resistance had collapsed at the center. After the decrepit monarchy in Vietnam had bowed to French pressure, a number of civilian and military officials set up an

THE CIVILIZING MISSION IN EGYPT

FAMILY & SOCIETY

In many parts of the colonial world, European occupation served to sharpen class divisions in traditional societies. Such was the case in Egypt, where the British protectorate, established in the early 1880s, benefited many elites, who profited from the introduction of Western culture. Ordinary Egyptians, less inclined to adopt foreign ways, seldom profited from the European presence. In response, British administrators showed little patience for their subjects who failed to recognize the superiority of Western civilization. This view found expression in the words of the governor-general, Lord Cromer, who remarked in exasperation, "The mind of the Oriental, . . . like his picturesque streets, is eminently wanting in symmetry. His reasoning is of the most slipshod description." Cromer was especially irritated at the local treatment of women, arguing that the seclusion of women and the wearing of the veil were the chief causes of Islamic backwardness.

Such views were echoed by some Egyptian elites, who were utterly seduced by Western culture and embraced the colonialists' condemnation of native ways. The French-educated lawyer Qassim Amin was one example. His book *The Liberation of Women,* published in 1899 and excerpted here, precipitated a heated debate between those who considered Western nations the liberators of Islam and those who reviled them as oppressors.

Qassim Amin, *The Liberation of Women*

European civilization advances with the speed of steam and electricity, and has even overspilled to every part of the globe so that there is not an inch that he [European man] has not trodden underfoot. Any place he goes he takes control of its resources . . . and turns them into profit . . . and if he does harm to the original inhabitants, it is only that he pursues happiness in this world and seeks it wherever he may find it. . . . For the most part he uses his intellect, but when circumstances require it, he deploys force. He does not seek glory from his possessions and colonies, for he has enough of this through his intellectual achievements and scientific inventions. What drives the Englishman to dwell in India and the French in Algeria . . . is profit and the desire to acquire resources in countries where the inhabitants do not know their value or how to profit from them.

When they encounter savages they eliminate them or drive them from the land, as happened in America . . . and is happening now in Africa. . . . When they encounter a nation like ours, with a degree of civilization, with a past, and a religion . . . and customs and . . . institutions . . . they deal with its inhabitants kindly. But they do soon acquire its most valuable resources, because they have greater wealth and intellect and knowledge and force. . . . [The veil constituted] a huge barrier between woman and her elevation, and consequently a barrier between the nation and its advance.

Q *Why did the author believe that Western culture would be beneficial to Egyptian society? How might a critic of colonialism have responded?*

---

organization called Can Vuong (literally "save the king") and continued their resistance without imperial sanction (see the box on p. 535).

The first stirrings of nationalism in India took place in the early nineteenth century with the search for a renewed sense of cultural identity. In 1828, Ram Mohan Roy, a *brahmin* from Bengal, founded the Brahmo Samaj (Society of Brahma). Roy probably had no intention of promoting Indian national independence but created the new organization as a means of helping his fellow religionists defend the Hindu religion against verbal attacks by their British acquaintances.

Sometimes traditional resistance to Western penetration went beyond elite circles. Most commonly, it appeared in the form of peasant revolts. Rural rebellions were not uncommon in traditional Asian societies as a means of expressing peasant discontent with high taxes, official corruption, rising rural debt, and famine in the countryside. Under colonialism, rural conditions often deteriorated as population density increased and peasants were driven off the land to make way for plantation agriculture. Angry peasants then vented their frustration at the foreign invaders. For example, in Burma, the Buddhist monk Saya San led a peasant uprising against the British many years after they had completed their takeover.

The Sepoy Rebellion Sometimes the resentment had a religious basis, as in the Sudan, where the revolt led by the Mahdi had strong Islamic overtones, although it was initially provoked by Turkish misrule in Egypt. More significant than Roy's Brahmo Samaj in its impact on British policy was the famous Sepoy Rebellion of 1857 in India. The sepoys (derived from *sipahi,* a Turkish word meaning horseman or soldier) were native troops hired by the East India Company to protect British interests in the region. Unrest within Indian units of the colonial army had been common since early in the century, when it had been sparked by economic issues, religious sensitivities, or nascent anticolonial sentiment. In 1857, tension erupted when the British adopted the new Enfield rifle for use by sepoy infantrymen. The new weapon was a muzzle loader that used paper cartridges covered with animal fat and

OPPOSING VIEWPOINTS
TO RESIST OR NOT TO RESIST

INTERACTION & EXCHANGE

How to respond to the imposition of colonial rule was sometimes an excruciating problem for political elites in many Asian countries. Not only did resistance often seem futile but it could even add to the suffering of the indigenous population. Hoang Cao Khai and Phan Dinh Phung were members of the Confucian scholar-gentry from the same village in Vietnam. Yet they reacted in dramatically different ways to the French conquest of their country. Their exchange of letters, reproduced here, illustrates the dilemmas they faced.

Hoang Cao Khai's Letter to Phan Dinh Phung

Soon, it will be seventeen years since we ventured upon different paths of life. How sweet was our friendship when we both lived in our village.... At the time when the capital was lost and after the royal carriage had departed, you courageously answered the appeals of the King by raising the banner of righteousness. It was certainly the only thing to do in those circumstances. No one will question that.

But now the situation has changed and even those without intelligence or education have concluded that nothing remains to be saved. How is it that you, a man of vast understanding, do not realize this? ... You are determined to do whatever you deem righteous.... But though you have no thoughts for your own person or for your own fate, you should at least attend to the sufferings of the population of a whole region....

Until now your actions have undoubtedly accorded with your loyalty. May I ask however what sin our people have committed to deserve so much hardship? I would understand your resistance, did you involve but your family for the benefit of a large number. As of now, hundreds of families are subject to grief; how do you have the heart to fight on? I venture to predict that, should you pursue your struggle, not only will the population of our village be destroyed but our entire country will be transformed into a sea of blood and a mountain of bones. It is my hope that men of your superior morality and honesty will pause a while to appraise the situation.

Reply of Phan Dinh Phung to Hoang Cao Khai

In your letter, you revealed to me the causes of calamities and of happiness. You showed me clearly where advantages and disadvantages lie. All of which sufficed to indicate that your anxious concern was not only for my own security but also for the peace and order of our entire region. I understood plainly your sincere arguments.

I have concluded that if our country has survived these past thousand years when its territory was not large, its army not strong, its wealth not great, it was because the relationships between king and subjects, fathers and children, have always been regulated by the five moral obligations. In the past, the Han, the Sung, the Yuan, the Ming time and again dreamt of annexing our country and of dividing it up into prefectures and districts within the Chinese administrative system. But never were they able to realize their dream. Ah! if even China, which shares a common border with our territory, and is a thousand times more powerful than Vietnam, could not rely upon her strength to swallow us, it was surely because the destiny of our country had been willed by Heaven itself.

The French, separated from our country until the present day by I do not know how many thousand miles, have crossed the oceans to come to our country. Wherever they came, they acted like a storm, so much so that the Emperor had to flee. The whole country was cast into disorder. Our rivers and our mountains have been annexed by them at a stroke and turned into a foreign territory.

Moreover, if our region has suffered to such an extent, it was not only from the misfortunes of war. You must realize that wherever the French go, there flock around them groups of petty men who offer plans and tricks to gain the enemy's confidence.... They use every expedient to squeeze the people out of their possessions. That is how hundreds of misdeeds, thousands of offenses have been perpetrated. How can the French not be aware of all the suffering that the rural population has had to endure? Under these circumstances, is it surprising that families should be disrupted and the people scattered?

My friend, if you are troubled about our people, then I advise you to place yourself in my position and to think about the circumstances in which I live. You will understand naturally and see clearly that I do not need to add anything else.

Q *Explain briefly the reasons advanced by each writer to justify his actions. Which argument do you think would have earned more support from contemporaries? Why?*

---

lard; because the cartridge had to be bitten off, it broke strictures against high-class Hindus' eating animal products and Muslim prohibitions against eating pork. Protests among sepoy units in northern India turned into a full-scale mutiny, supported by uprisings in rural districts in various parts of the country. But the revolt lacked clear goals, and rivalries between Hindus and Muslims and discord among the leaders within each community prevented coordination of operations. Although Indian troops often fought bravely and outnumbered the British six to one, they were poorly organized, and the British forces (supplemented in many cases by sepoy troops) suppressed the rebellion. Still, the revolt frightened the British, who introduced a number of reforms and suppressed the final

COMPARATIVE ESSAY
IMPERIALISM: THE BALANCE SHEET

Few periods of history are as controversial among scholars and casual observers as the era of imperialism. To defenders of the colonial enterprise like the poet Rudyard Kipling, imperialism was the "white man's burden," a disagreeable but necessary phase in the evolution of human society, lifting up the toiling races from tradition to modernity and bringing an end to poverty, famine, and disease (see the box on p. 518).

Critics took exception to such views, portraying imperialism as a tragedy of major proportions. The insatiable drive of the advanced economic powers for access to raw materials and markets created an exploitative environment that transformed the vast majority of colonial peoples into a permanent underclass, while restricting the benefits of modern technology to a privileged few. Kipling's "white man's burden" was dismissed as a hypocritical gesture to hoodwink the naive and salve the guilty feelings of those who recognized imperialism for what it was—a savage act of rape.

Defenders of the colonial experiment sometimes concede that there were gross inequities in the colonial system but point out that there was a positive side to the experience as well. The expansion of markets and the beginnings of a modern transportation and communications network, while bringing few immediate benefits to the colonial peoples, laid the groundwork for future economic growth. At the same time, the introduction of new ways of looking at human freedom, the relationship between the individual and society, and democratic principles set the stage for the adoption of such ideas after the restoration of independence following World War II. Finally, the colonial experience offered a new approach to the traditional relationship between men and women. Although colonial rule was by no means uniformly beneficial to the position of women in African and Asian societies, growing awareness of the struggle for equality by women in the West offered their counterparts in the colonial territories a weapon to fight against the long-standing barriers of custom and legal discrimination.

How, then, are we to draw up a final balance sheet on the era of Western imperialism? Both sides have good points to make, but

Gateway to India. Built in the Roman imperial style by the British to commemorate the visit to India of King George V and Queen Mary in 1911, the Gateway to India was erected at the water's edge in the harbor of Bombay (now Mumbai), India's greatest port city. For thousands of British citizens arriving in India, the Gateway to India was the first view of their new home and a symbol of the power and majesty of the British raj.

perhaps the critics have the best of the argument. Although the colonial authorities sometimes did provide the beginnings of an infrastructure that could eventually serve as the foundation of an advanced industrial society, all too often they sought to prevent the rise of industrial and commercial sectors in their colonies that might provide competition to producers in the home country. Sophisticated, age-old societies that could have been left to respond to the technological revolution in their own way were thus squeezed dry of precious national resources under the false guise of a "civilizing mission." As the sociologist Clifford Geertz remarked in his book *Agricultural Involution: The Processes of Ecological Change in Indonesia*, the tragedy is not that the colonial peoples suffered through the colonial era but that they suffered for nothing.

Q *Based on the information available to you, do you think the imperialistic practices of the nineteenth and twentieth centuries can be justified on moral or political grounds?*

---

remnants of the Mughal dynasty, which had supported the mutiny; responsibility for governing the subcontinent was then turned over to the crown.

Like the Sepoy Rebellion, traditional resistance movements usually met with little success. Peasants armed with pikes and spears were no match for Western armies possessing the most terrifying weapons then known to human society. In a few cases, such as the revolt of the Mahdi at Khartoum, the natives were able to defeat the invaders temporarily. But such successes were rare, and the late nineteenth century witnessed the seemingly inexorable march of the Western powers, armed with the Gatling gun (the first rapid-fire weapon and the precursor of the modern machine gun), to mastery of the globe.

© William J. Duiker

TIMELINE

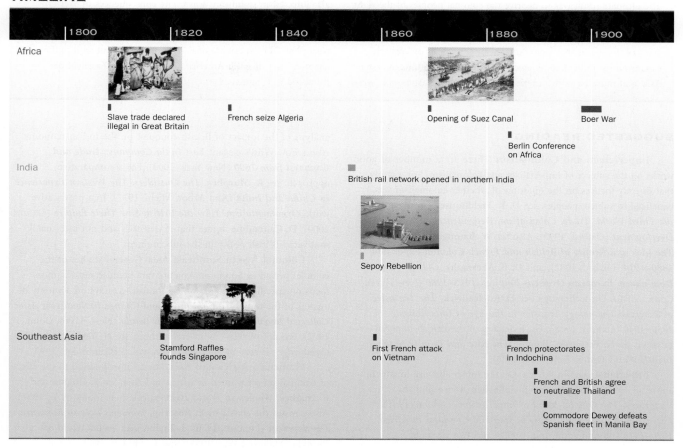

Africa

1800   1820   1840   1860   1880   1900

Slave trade declared illegal in Great Britain

French seize Algeria

Opening of Suez Canal

Boer War

Berlin Conference on Africa

India

British rail network opened in northern India

Sepoy Rebellion

Southeast Asia

Stamford Raffles founds Singapore

First French attack on Vietnam

French protectorates in Indochina

French and British agree to neutralize Thailand

Commodore Dewey defeats Spanish fleet in Manila Bay

CONCLUSION

BY THE FIRST QUARTER of the twentieth century, virtually all of Africa and a good part of South and Southeast Asia were under some form of colonial rule. With the advent of the age of imperialism, a global economy was finally established, and the domination of Western civilization over those of Africa and Asia appeared to be complete.

Defenders of colonialism argue that the system was a necessary if painful stage in the evolution of human societies. Critics, however, charge that the Western colonial powers were driven by an insatiable lust for profits (see the comparative essay "Imperialism: The Balance Sheet" on p. 536). They dismiss the Western civilizing mission as a fig leaf to cover naked greed and reject the notion that imperialism played a salutary role in hastening the adjustment of traditional societies to the demands of industrial civilization. In the blunt words of two Western critics of imperialism: "Why is Africa (or for that matter Latin America and much of Asia) so poor? . . . The answer is very brief: we have made it poor."[10]

Between these two irreconcilable views, where does the truth lie? This chapter has contended that neither extreme position is justified. Although colonialism did introduce the peoples of Asia and Africa to new technology and the expanding economic marketplace, it was unnecessarily brutal in its application and all too often failed to realize the exalted claims and objectives of its promoters. Existing economic networks—often potentially valuable as a foundation for later economic development—were ruthlessly swept aside in the interests of providing markets for Western manufactured goods. Potential sources of native industrialization were nipped in the bud to avoid competition for factories in Amsterdam, London, Pittsburgh, or Manchester. Training in Western democratic ideals and practices was ignored out of fear that the recipients might use them as weapons against the ruling authorities.

The fundamental weakness of colonialism, then, was that it was ultimately based on the self-interests of the citizens of the colonial powers. Where those interests collided with the needs of the colonial peoples, those of the former always triumphed.

The ultimate result was to deprive the colonial peoples of the right to make their own choices about their own destiny.

The continent of Africa and southern Asia were not the only areas of the world that were buffeted by the winds of Western expansionism in the late nineteenth century. The nations of eastern Asia, and those of Latin America and the Middle East as well, were also affected in significant ways. The consequences of Western political, economic, and military penetration varied substantially from one region to another, however, and therefore require separate treatment. The experience of East Asia will be dealt with in the next chapter. That of Latin America and the Middle East will be discussed in Chapter 24.

SUGGESTED READING

Imperialism and Colonialism There are a number of good works on the subject of imperialism and colonialism. For a study that directly focuses on the question of whether colonialism was beneficial to subject peoples, see **D. K. Fieldhouse, *The West and the Third World: Trade, Colonialism, Dependence, and Development*** (Oxford, 1999). Also see **W. Baumgart, *Imperialism: The Idea and Reality of British and French Colonial Expansion, 1880–1914*** (Oxford, 1982), and **D. B. Abernathy, *Global Dominance: European Overseas Empires, 1415–1980*** (New Haven, Conn., 2000). On technology, see **D. R. Headrick, *The Tentacles of Progress: Technology Transfer in the Age of Imperialism, 1850–1940*** (Oxford, 1988). For a defense of the British imperial mission, see **N. Ferguson, *Empire: The Rise and Demise of the British World Order*** (New York, 2003).

Imperialist Age in Africa On the imperialist age in Africa, above all see **R. Robinson** and **J. Gallagher, *Africa and the Victorians: The Official Mind of Imperialism*** (London, 1961). Also see **B. Vandervoort, *Wars of Imperial Conquest in Africa, 1830–1914*** (Bloomington, Ind., 1998), and two works by **T. Pakenham, *The Scramble for Africa*** (New York, 1991) and ***The Boer War*** (London, 1979). On southern Africa, see **J. Guy, *The Destruction of the Zulu Kingdom*** (London, 1979), and **D. Nenoon** and **B. Nyeko, *Southern Africa Since 1800*** (London, 1984). Also informative is **R. O. Collins, ed., *Historical Problems of Imperial Africa*** (Princeton, N.J., 1994).

India For an overview of the British takeover and administration of India, see **S. Wolpert, *A New History of India*,** 8th ed. (New York, 2008). **C. A. Bayly, *Indian Society and the Making of the British Empire*** (Cambridge, 1988), is a scholarly analysis of the impact of British conquest on the Indian economy. Also see **A. Wild's** elegant ***East India Company: Trade and Conquest from 1600*** (New York, 2000). For a comparative approach, see **R. Murphey, *The Outsiders: The Western Experience in China and India*** (Ann Arbor, Mich., 1977). In a provocative work, ***Ornamentalism: How the British Saw Their Empire*** (Oxford, 2000), **D. Cannadine** argues that it was class and not race that motivated British policy in the subcontinent.

Colonial Age in Southeast Asia General studies of the colonial period in Southeast Asia are rare because most authors focus on specific areas. For some stimulating essays on a variety of aspects of the topic, see ***Continuity and Change in Southeast Asia: Collected Journal Articles of Harry J. Benda*** (New Haven, Conn., 1972). For an overview by several authors, see **N. Tarling, ed., *The Cambridge History of Southeast Asia,*** vol. 3 (Cambridge, 1992).

Women in Africa and Asia For an introduction to the effects of colonialism on women in Africa and Asia, see **S. Hughes** and **B. Hughes, *Women in World History,*** vol. 2 (Armonk, N.Y., 1997). Also consult the classic by **E. Boserup, *Women's Role in Economic Development*** (London, 1970); **J. Taylor, *The Social World of Batavia*** (Madison, Wis., 1983); and **L. Ahmed, *Women and Gender in Islam*** (New Haven, Conn., 1992).

WORLD HISTORY RESOURCES

Visit the website for *The Essential World History* **to access study aids such as Flashcards, Critical Thinking Exercises, and Chapter Quizzes:**
  www.cengage.com/history/duikspiel/essentialworld6e

DISCOVERY

What were the consequences of the new imperialism of the nineteenth century for the colonies and the colonial powers? How do you feel the imperialist countries should be evaluated in terms of their motives and stated objectives?

In thinking about these questions, begin by breaking them down into the components shown below. A discussion of the significance of each component should appear in your answer.

POLITICS AND GOVERNMENT Why did European nations want more colonies in the nineteenth century? What role may nationalism have played in the rush to acquire colonies? Looking at the map of Africa, think about why France would have benefited from its geographically concentrated colonies.

Review Kipling's poem and the excerpt from Morel (below and on p. 518). What did Kipling mean by the "white man's burden"? Do you think the "civilizing missions" portrayed in the poem are examples of nationalism? Do you think the imperialists were sincere when they talked about "civilizing missions," or were they being hypocritical? What did Morel mean when he said "It kills not the body merely, but the soul"? Do you agree with him?

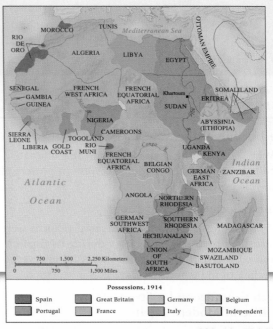

Africa in 1914

WHITE MAN'S BURDEN, BLACK MAN'S SORROW

Rudyard Kipling, *The White Man's Burden*

Take up the White Man's burden—
Send forth the best ye breed—
Go bind your sons to exile
To serve your captives' need;
To wait in heavy harness,
On fluttered folk and wild—
Your new-caught sullen peoples,
Half-devil and half-child.

Take up the White Man's burden—
In patience to abide,
To veil the threat of terror
And check the show of pride;
By open speech and simple,
An hundred times made plain
To seek another's profit,
And work another's gain.
Take up the White Man's burden—
The savage wars of peace—
Fill full the mouth of Famine
And bid the sickness cease;
And when your goal is nearest
The end for others sought,
Watch Sloth and heathen Folly
Bring all your hopes to nought.

Edmund Morel, *The Black Man's Burden*

It is [the Africans] who carry the "Black man's burden." They have not withered away before the white man's occupation. Indee... Africa has ultimately absorbed within itself every Caucasian and, for that matter, every Semitic invader, too. In hewing out for himself a fixed abode in Africa, the white man has massacred the African in heaps. The African has survived, and it is well for the white settlers that he has....

What the partial occupation of his soil by the white man has failed to do; what the mapping out of European political "spheres of influence" has failed to do; what the Maxim and the rifle, the slave gang, labour in the bowels of the earth and the lash, have failed to do; what imported measles, smallpox and syphilis have failed to do; whatever the overseas slave trade failed to do; the power of modern capitalistic exploitation, assisted by modern engines of destruction, may yet succeed in accomplishing.

For from the evils of the latter, scientifically applied and enforced, there is no escape for the African. Its destructive effects are not spasmodic; they are permanent. In its permanence resides its fatal consequences. It kills not the body merely, but the soul. It breaks the spirit. It attacks the African at every turn, from every point of vantage. It wrecks his polity, uproots him from the land, invades his family life, destroys his natural pursuits and occupations, claims his whole time, enslaves him in his own home.

CHAPTER 22
SHADOWS OVER THE PACIFIC: EAST ASIA UNDER CHALLENGE

The Macartney mission to China, 1793

The Art Archive/Eileen Tweedy

CHAPTER OUTLINE AND FOCUS QUESTIONS

The Decline of the Manchus

Q Why did the Qing dynasty decline and ultimately collapse, and what role did the Western powers play in this process?

Chinese Society in Transition

Q What political, economic, and social reforms were instituted by the Qing dynasty during its final decades, and why were they not more successful in reversing the decline of Manchu rule?

A Rich Country and a Strong State: The Rise of Modern Japan

Q To what degree was the Meiji Restoration a "revolution," and to what degree did it succeed in transforming Japan?

CRITICAL THINKING

Q How did China and Japan each respond to Western pressures in the nineteenth century, and what implication did their different responses have for each nation's history?

THE BRITISH EMISSARY Lord Macartney had arrived in Beijing in 1793 with a caravan loaded with six hundred cases of gifts for the emperor. Flags and banners provided by the Chinese proclaimed in Chinese characters that the visitor was an "ambassador bearing tribute from the country of England." But the tribute was in vain, for Macartney's request for an increase in trade between the two countries was flatly rejected, and he left Beijing in October with nothing to show for his efforts. Not until half a century later would the Qing dynasty—at the point of a gun—agree to the British demand for an expansion of commercial ties.

In fact, the Chinese emperor Qianlong had responded to the requests of his visitor with polite but poorly disguised condescension. To Macartney's proposal that a British ambassador be stationed in the capital of Beijing, the emperor replied that such a request was "not in harmony with the state system of our dynasty and will definitely not be permitted." As for the British envoy's suggestion that regular trade relations be established between the two countries, that proposal was also rejected. We receive all sorts of precious things, replied the Celestial Emperor, as gifts from the myriad nations. "Consequently," he added, "there is nothing we lack, as your principal envoy and others have themselves observed. We have never set much store on strange or ingenious objects, nor do we need more of your country's manufactures."

Historians have often viewed the failure of the Macartney mission as a reflection of the disdain of Chinese rulers toward their counterparts in other countries and their serene confidence in the superiority of Chinese civilization in a world inhabited by barbarians. If that was the case, Qianlong's confidence was misplaced, for as the eighteenth century came to an end, the country faced a growing challenge not only from the escalating power and ambitions of the West, but from its own growing internal weakness as well. When insistent British demands for the right to carry out trade and missionary activities in China were rejected, Britain resorted to force and in the Opium War, which broke out in 1839, gave Manchu troops a sound thrashing. A humiliated China was finally forced to open its doors. ❀

The Decline of the Manchus

Q **Focus Question:** Why did the Qing dynasty decline and ultimately collapse, and what role did the Western powers play in this process?

In 1800, the Qing (Ch'ing) or Manchu dynasty was at the height of its power. China had experienced a long period of peace and prosperity under the rule of two great emperors, Kangxi and Qianlong. Its borders were secure, and its culture and intellectual achievements were the envy of the world. Its rulers, hidden behind the walls of the Forbidden City in Beijing, had every reason to describe their patrimony as the "Central Kingdom." But a little over a century later, humiliated and harassed by the black ships and big guns of the Western powers, the Qing dynasty, the last in a series that had endured for more than two thousand years, collapsed in the dust (see Map 22.1).

Historians once assumed that the primary reason for the rapid decline and fall of the Manchu dynasty was the intense pressure applied to a proud but somewhat complacent traditional society by the modern West. Now, however, most historians believe that internal changes played a major role in the dynasty's collapse and point out that at least some of the problems suffered by the Manchus during the nineteenth century were self-inflicted.

Both explanations have some validity. Like so many of its predecessors, after an extended period of growth, the Qing dynasty began to suffer from the familiar dynastic ills of official corruption, peasant unrest, and incompetence at court. Such weaknesses were probably exacerbated by the rapid growth in population. The long era of peace and stability, the introduction of new crops from the Americas, and the cultivation of new, fast-ripening strains of rice enabled the Chinese population to double between 1550 and 1800. The population

continued to grow, reaching the unprecedented level of 400 million by the end of the nineteenth century. Even without the irritating presence of the Western powers, the Manchus were probably destined to repeat the fate of their imperial predecessors. The ships, guns, and ideas of the foreigners simply highlighted the growing weakness of the Manchu dynasty and likely hastened its demise. In doing so, Western imperialism still exerted an indelible impact on the history of modern China—but as a contributing, not a causal, factor.

Opium and Rebellion

By 1800, Westerners had been in contact with China for more than two hundred years, but after an initial period of flourishing relations, Western traders had been limited to a small commercial outlet at Canton. This arrangement was not acceptable to the British, however. Not only did they chafe at being restricted to a tiny enclave, but the growing British appetite for Chinese tea created a severe balance-of-payments problem. After the failure of the Macartney mission in 1793, another mission, led by Lord Amherst, arrived in China in 1816. But it too achieved little except to worsen the already strained relations between the two countries. The British solution was opium. A product more addictive than tea, opium was grown in northeastern India and then shipped to China. Opium had been grown in southwestern China for several hundred years but had been used primarily for medicinal purposes. Now, as imports increased, popular demand for the product in southern China became insatiable despite an official prohibition on its use. Soon bullion was flowing out of the Chinese imperial treasury into the pockets of British merchants.

The Chinese became concerned and tried to negotiate. In 1839, Lin Zexu (Lin Tse-hsu; 1785–1850), a Chinese official appointed by the court to curtail the opium trade, appealed to Queen Victoria on both moral and practical grounds and threatened to prohibit the sale of rhubarb (widely used as a laxative in nineteenth-century Europe) to Great Britain if she did not respond (see the box on p. 543). But moral principles, then as now, paled before the lure of commercial profits, and the British continued to promote the opium trade, arguing that if the Chinese did not want the opium, they did not have to buy it. Lin Zexu attacked on three fronts, imposing penalties on smokers, arresting dealers, and seizing supplies from importers as they attempted to smuggle the drug into China. The last tactic caused his downfall. When he blockaded the foreign factory area in Canton to force traders to hand over their remaining chests of opium, the British government, claiming that it could not permit British subjects "to be exposed to insult and injustice,"

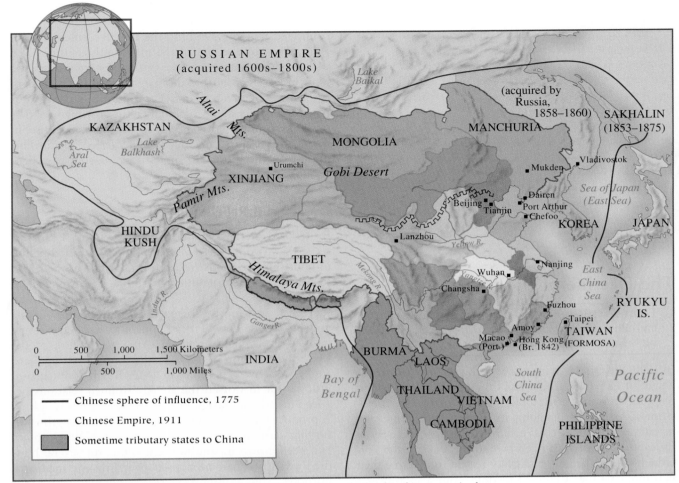

RUSSIAN EMPIRE
(acquired 1600s–1800s)

(acquired by
Russia,
1858–1860) SAKHALIN
(1853–1875)

- Chinese sphere of influence, 1775
- Chinese Empire, 1911
- Sometime tributary states to China

MAP 22.1 **The Qing Empire.** Shown here is the Qing Empire at the height of its power in the late eighteenth century, together with its shrunken boundaries at the moment of dissolution in 1911. **Q** How do China's tributary states on this map differ from those in Map 17.2? Which of them fell under the influence of foreign powers during the nineteenth century? ● **View an animated version of this map or related maps at** www.cengage.com/history/duikspiel/essentialworld6e

launched a naval expedition to punish the Manchus and force the court to open China to foreign trade.[1]

The Opium War The Opium War (1839–1842) lasted three years and demonstrated the superiority of British firepower and military tactics (including the use of a shallow-draft steamboat that effectively harassed Chinese coastal defenses). British warships destroyed Chinese coastal and river forts and seized the offshore island of Chusan, not far from the mouth of the Yangtze River. When a British fleet sailed virtually unopposed up the Yangtze to Nanjing and cut off the supply of "tribute grain" from southern to northern China, the Qing finally agreed to British terms. In the Treaty of Nanjing in 1842, the Chinese agreed to open five coastal ports to British

trade, limit tariffs on imported British goods, grant extraterritorial rights to British citizens in China, and pay a substantial indemnity to cover the costs of the war. China also agreed to cede the island of Hong Kong (dismissed by a senior British official as a "barren rock") to Great Britain. Nothing was said in the treaty about the opium trade, which continued unabated until it was brought under control through Chinese government efforts in the early twentieth century.

Although the Opium War has traditionally been considered the beginning of modern Chinese history, it is unlikely that many Chinese at the time would have seen it that way. This was not the first time that a ruling dynasty had been forced to make concessions to foreigners, and the opening of five coastal ports to the British hardly

A LETTER OF ADVICE TO THE QUEEN

Lin Zexu was the Chinese imperial commissioner in Canton at the time of the Opium War. Prior to the conflict, he attempted to use reason and the threat of retaliation to persuade the British to cease importing opium illegally into southern China. The following excerpt is from a letter that he wrote to Queen Victoria. In it, he appeals to her conscience while showing the condescension that the Chinese traditionally displayed to the rulers of other countries.

Lin Zexu, Letter to Queen Victoria

The kings of your honorable country by a tradition handed down from generation to generation have always been noted for their politeness and submissiveness.... Privately we are delighted with the way in which the honorable rulers of your country deeply understand the grand principles and are grateful for the Celestial grace.... The profit from trade has been enjoyed by them continuously for two hundred years. This is the source from which your country has become known for its wealth.

But after a long period of commercial intercourse, there appear among the crowd of barbarians both good persons and bad, unevenly. Consequently there are those who smuggle opium to seduce the Chinese people and so cause the spread of the poison to all provinces....

The wealth of China is used to profit the barbarians. That is to say, the great profit made by barbarians is all taken from the rightful share of China. By what right do they then in return use

the poisonous drug to injure the Chinese people?... Let us ask, where is your conscience? I have heard that the smoking of opium is very strictly forbidden by your country; that is because the harm caused by opium is clearly understood. Since it is not permitted to do harm to your own country, then even less should you let it be passed on to the harm of other countries—how much less to China! Of all that China exports to foreign countries, there is not a single thing which is not beneficial to people.... Is there a single article from China which has done any harm to foreign countries? Take tea and rhubarb, for example; the foreign countries cannot get along for a single day without them.... On the other hand, articles coming from the outside to China can only be used as toys. We can take them or get along without them. Nevertheless our Celestial Court lets tea, silk, and other goods be shipped without limit and circulated everywhere without begrudging it in the slightest. This is for no other reason but to share the benefit with the people of the whole world....

May you, O King, check your wicked and sift your vicious people before they come to China, in order to guarantee the peace of your nation, to show further the sincerity of your politeness and submissiveness, and to let the two countries enjoy together the blessings of peace.... After receiving this dispatch will you immediately give us a prompt reply regarding the details and circumstances of your cutting off the opium traffic. Be sure not to put this off.

Q *How did the imperial commissioner seek to persuade Queen Victoria to prohibit the sale of opium in China? To what degree are his arguments persuasive?*

The Opium War. The Opium War, waged between China and Great Britain between 1839 and 1842, was China's first conflict with a European power. Lacking modern military technology, the Chinese suffered a humiliating defeat. In this painting, heavily armed British steamships destroy unwieldy Chinese junks along the Chinese coast. China's humiliation at sea was a legacy of its rulers' lack of interest in maritime matters since the middle of the fifteenth century, when Chinese junks were among the most advanced sailing ships in the world.

constituted a serious threat to the security of the empire. Although a few concerned Chinese argued that the court should learn more about European civilization, others contended that China had nothing to learn from the barbarians and that borrowing foreign ways would undercut the purity of Confucian civilization.

For the time being, the Manchus attempted to deal with the problem in the traditional way of playing the foreigners off against each other. Concessions granted to the British were offered to other Western nations, including the United States, and soon thriving foreign concession areas were operating in treaty ports along the southern Chinese coast from Canton to Shanghai.

The Taiping Rebellion In the meantime, the Qing court's failure to deal with pressing internal economic problems led to a major peasant revolt that shook the foundations of the empire. On the surface, the Taiping (T'ai p'ing) Rebellion owed something to the Western incursion; the leader of the uprising, Hong Xiuquan (Hung Hsiu-ch'uan), a failed examination candidate, was a Christian convert who viewed himself as a younger brother of Jesus and hoped to establish what he referred to as a "Heavenly Kingdom of Supreme Peace" in China. But there were many local causes as well. The rapid increase in population forced millions of peasants to eke out a living as sharecroppers or landless laborers. Official corruption and incompetence led to the whipsaw of increased taxes and a decline in government services; even the Grand Canal was allowed to silt up, hindering the shipment of grain. In 1853, the rebels seized the old Ming capital of Nanjing, but that proved to be the rebellion's high-water mark. Plagued by factionalism, the rebellion gradually lost momentum until it was finally suppressed in 1864.

One reason for the dynasty's failure to deal effectively with the internal unrest was its continuing difficulties with the Western imperialists. In 1856,

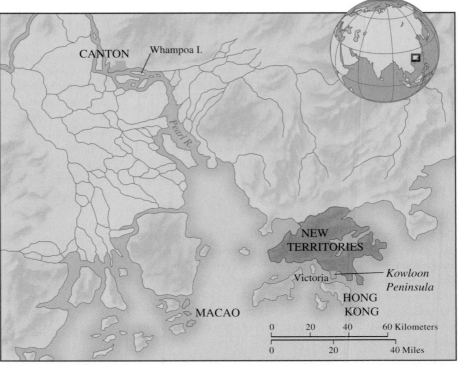

MAP 22.2 **Canton and Hong Kong.** This map shows the estuary of the Pearl River in southern China, an important area of early contact between China and Europe.
Q What was the importance of Canton? What were the New Territories, and when were they annexed by the British?

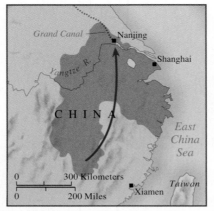

The Taiping Rebellion

the British and the French, still smarting from trade restrictions and limitations on their missionary activities, launched a new series of attacks against China and seized Beijing in 1860. As punishment, British troops destroyed the imperial summer palace just outside the city. In the ensuing Treaty of Tianjin (Tientsin), the Qing agreed to humiliating new concessions: the legalization of the opium trade, the opening of additional ports to foreign trade, and the cession of the peninsula of Kowloon (opposite the island of Hong Kong) to the British (see Map 22.2). Additional territories in the north were ceded to Russia.

Efforts at Reform

By the late 1870s, the old dynasty was well on the road to internal disintegration. In fending off the Taiping Rebellion, the Manchus had been compelled to rely for support on armed forces under regional command. After quelling the revolt, many of these regional commanders refused to disband their units and, with the support of the local gentry, continued to collect local taxes for their own use. The dreaded pattern of imperial breakdown, so familiar in Chinese history, was beginning to appear once again.

In its weakened state, the court finally began to listen to the appeals of reform-minded officials, who called for a new policy of **"self-strengthening,"** in which Western technology would be adopted while Confucian principles and institutions were maintained intact. This policy, popularly known by its slogan "East for Essence, West for Practical Use," remained the guiding standard for Chinese foreign and domestic policy for nearly a quarter of a century. Some even called for reforms in education and in China's hallowed political institutions. Pointing to the power and prosperity of Great Britain, the journalist Wang Tao (Wang T'ao, 1828–1897) remarked, "The real strength of England . . . lies in the fact that there is a sympathetic understanding between the governing and the governed, a close relationship between the ruler and the people. . . . My observation is that the daily domestic political life of England actually embodies the traditional ideals of our ancient Golden Age."[2] Such democratic ideas were too radical for most moderate reformers, however. One of the leading court officials of the day, Zhang Zhidong (Chang Chih-tung), countered:

> The doctrine of people's rights will bring us not a single benefit but a hundred evils. Are we going to establish a parliament? . . . Even supposing the confused and clamorous people are assembled in one house, for every one of them who is clear-sighted, there will be a hundred others whose vision is beclouded; they will converse at random and talk as if in a dream—what use will it be?[3]

The Climax of Imperialism For the time being, Zhang Zhidong's arguments won the day. During the last quarter of the century, the Manchus attempted to modernize their military establishment and build up an industrial base without disturbing the essential elements of traditional Chinese civilization. Railroads, weapons arsenals, and shipyards were built, but the value system remained essentially unchanged.

In the end, the results spoke for themselves. During the last two decades of the nineteenth century, the European penetration of China, both political and military, intensified. Rapacious imperialists began to bite off the outer edges of the Qing Empire. The Gobi Desert north of the Great Wall, Central Asia, and Tibet, all inhabited by non-Chinese peoples and never fully assimilated into the Chinese Empire, were gradually lost. In the north and northwest, the main beneficiary was Russia, which took advantage of the dynasty's weakness to force the cession of territories north of the Amur River in Siberia. In Tibet, competition between Russia and Great Britain prevented

either power from seizing the territory outright but at the same time enabled Tibetan authorities to revive local autonomy never recognized by the Chinese. In the south, British and French advances in mainland Southeast Asia removed Burma and Vietnam from their traditional vassal relationship to the Manchu court. Even more ominous were the foreign spheres of influence in the Chinese heartland, where local commanders were willing to sell exclusive commercial, railroad-building, or mining privileges.

The breakup of the Manchu dynasty accelerated at the end of the nineteenth century. In 1894, the Qing went to war with Japan over Japanese incursions into the Korean peninsula, which threatened China's long-held suzerainty over the area (see "Joining the Imperialist Club" later in this chapter). To the surprise of many observers, the Chinese were roundly defeated, confirming to some critics the devastating failure of the policy of self-strengthening by halfway measures. The disintegration of China accelerated in 1897, when Germany, a new entry in the race for spoils in East Asia, used the pretext of the murder of two German missionaries by Chinese rioters to demand the cession of territories in the Shandong (Shantung) peninsula. The imperial court approved the demand, setting off a scramble for territory by other interested powers (see Map 22.3). Russia now demanded the Liaodong peninsula with its ice-free port at Port Arthur, and Great Britain weighed in with a request for a coaling station in northern China.

The government responded to the challenge with yet another effort at reform. In the spring of 1898, an outspoken advocate of change, the progressive Confucian scholar Kang Youwei (K'ang Yu-wei), won the support of the young Guangxu (Kuang Hsu) emperor for a comprehensive reform program patterned after recent measures in Japan. Without change, Kang argued, China would perish. During the next several weeks, the emperor issued edicts calling for major political, administrative, and educational reforms. Not surprisingly, Kang's proposals were opposed by many conservatives, who saw little advantage and much risk in copying the West. More important, the new program was opposed by the emperor's aunt, the Empress Dowager Cixi (Tz'u Hsi), the real power at court (see the comparative illustration on p. 547). Cixi had begun her political career as a concubine to an earlier emperor. After his death, she became a dominant force at court and in 1878 placed her infant nephew, the future Guangxu emperor, on the throne. For two decades, she ruled in his name as regent. With the aid of conservatives in the army, she arrested and executed several of the reformers and had the emperor incarcerated in the palace. With Cixi's palace coup, the so-called One Hundred Days of reform came to an end.

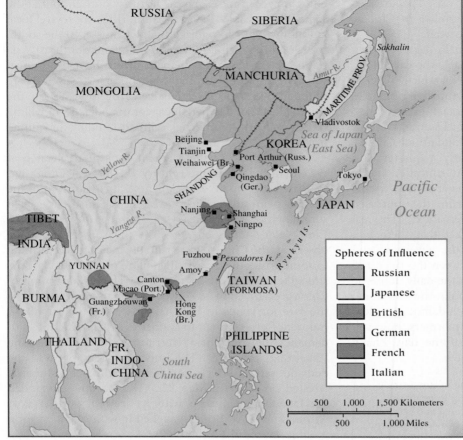

MAP 22.3 **Foreign Possessions and Spheres of Influence About 1900.** At the end of the nineteenth century, China was being carved up like a melon by foreign imperialist powers.

Q Which of the areas marked on the map were removed from Chinese control during the nineteenth century?

🔊 **View an animated version of this map or related maps at** www.cengage.com/history/duikspiel/essentialworld6e

Opening the Door to China During the next two years, foreign pressure on the dynasty intensified. With encouragement from the British, who hoped to avert a total collapse of the Manchu Empire, U.S. Secretary of State John Hay presented the other imperialist powers with a proposal to ensure equal economic access to the China market for all states. Hay also suggested that all powers join together to guarantee the territorial and administrative integrity of the Chinese Empire. Though probably motivated more by the United States' preference

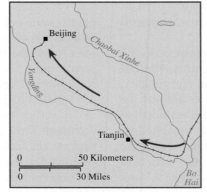

The International Expeditionary Force Advances to Beijing to Suppress the Boxers

for open markets than by a benevolent wish to protect China, the so-called **Open Door Notes** did have the practical effect of reducing the imperialist hysteria over access to the China market. The "gentlemen's agreement" about the Open Door (it was not a treaty, but merely a pious and nonbinding expression of intent) served to deflate fears in Britain, France, Germany, and Russia that other powers would take advantage of China's weakness to dominate the China market.

In the long run, then, the Open Door was a positive step that brought a measure of sanity to imperialist meddling in East Asia. Unfortunately, it came too late to stop the domestic explosion known as the Boxer Rebellion. The Boxers, so-called because of the physical exercises they performed (which closely resembled the more martial forms of tai chi), were members of a secret society operating primarily in rural areas in northern China. Provoked by a damaging drought and high unemployment caused in part by foreign economic activity (the introduction of railroads and steamships, for example, undercut the livelihood of barge workers on the rivers and canals), the Boxers attacked foreign residents and besieged the foreign legation quarter in Beijing until the foreigners were rescued by an international expeditionary force in the late summer of 1900. As punishment, the foreign troops destroyed a number of temples in the capital suburbs, and the Chinese government was compelled to pay a heavy indemnity to the foreign governments involved in suppressing the uprising.

The Collapse of the Old Order

During the next few years, the old dynasty tried desperately to reform itself. The empress dowager, who had long

COMPARATIVE ILLUSTRATION

Female Rulers—East and West. The prominent female rulers in the late nineteenth century were Empress Dowager Cixi of China and Queen Victoria of Great Britain. Cixi, shown at the left, was the most powerful figure in late-nineteenth-century China. Originally a concubine at the imperial court, she later placed her young nephew on the throne and dominated the political scene for a quarter of a century until her death in 1908. Conservative in her views, she staunchly resisted her advisers' suggestions for changes to help China face the challenge posed by the West. Queen Victoria, shown at the right, had the longest reign in British history (1837–1901). During this time, the British Empire reached the height of its power, but by the turn of the twentieth century, the monarchy was increasingly less relevant in Britain's liberal parliamentary system of government. Nevertheless, Victoria's sense of duty and moral responsibility reflected the attitudes of her age, which has ever since been known as the Victorian Age.

Q What other examples of influential female rulers can you recall from previous chapters in this book? What is distinctive about the two shown here?

resisted change, now embraced a number of reforms. The venerable civil service examination system was replaced by a new educational system based on the Western model. In 1905, a commission was formed to study constitutional changes; over the next few years, legislative assemblies were established at the provincial level, and elections for a national assembly were held in 1910.

Such moves helped shore up the dynasty temporarily, but history shows that the most dangerous period for an authoritarian system is when it begins to reform itself, because change breeds instability and performance rarely matches rising expectations. Such was the case in China. The emerging new provincial elite, composed of merchants, professionals, and reform-minded gentry, soon

PROGRAM FOR A NEW CHINA

POLITICS & GOVERNMENT

In 1905, Sun Yat-sen united a number of anti-Manchu groups into a single patriotic organization called the Revolutionary Alliance (Tongmenghui). The new organization eventually formed the core of his Guomindang, or Nationalist Party. This excerpt is from the organization's manifesto, published in 1905 in Tokyo. Note that Sun believed that the Chinese people were not ready for democracy and required a period of tutelage to prepare them for the final era of constitutional government. This was a formula that would be adopted by many other political leaders in Asia and Africa after World War II.

Sun Yat-sen, *Manifesto for the Tongmenghui*

By order of the Military Government, . . . the Commander-in-Chief of the Chinese National Army proclaims the purposes and platform of the Military Government to the people of the nation:

Therefore we proclaim to the world in utmost sincerity the outline of the present revolution and the fundamental plan for the future administration of the nation.

1. *Drive out the Tartars:* The Manchus of today were originally the eastern barbarians beyond the Great Wall. They frequently caused border troubles during the Ming dynasty; then when China was in a disturbed state they came inside Shanhaikuan, conquered China, and enslaved our Chinese people. . . . The extreme cruelties and tyrannies of the Manchu government have now reached their limit. With the righteous army poised against them, we will overthrow that government, and restore our sovereign rights.

2. *Restore China:* China is the China of the Chinese. The government of China should be in the hands of the Chinese. After driving out the Tartars we must restore our national state. . . .

3. *Establish the Republic:* Now our revolution is based on equality, in order to establish a republican government. All our people are equal and all enjoy political rights. . . .

4. *Equalize land ownership:* The good fortune of civilization is to be shared equally by all the people of the nation. We should improve our social and economic organization, and assess the value of all the land in the country. Its present price shall be received by the owner, but all increases in value resulting from reform and social improvements after the revolution shall belong to the state, to be shared by all the people, in order to create a socialist state, where each family within the empire can be well supported, each person satisfied, and no one fail to secure employment. . . .

The above four points will be carried out in three steps in due order. The first period is government by military law. When the righteous army has arisen, various places will join the cause. . . . Evils like the oppression of the government, the greed and graft of officials, . . . the cruelty of tortures and penalties, the tyranny of tax collections, the humiliation of the queue [the requirement that all Chinese males braid their hair]—shall all be exterminated together with the Manchu rule. Evils in social customs, such as the keeping of slaves, the cruelty of foot binding, the spread of the poison of opium, should also all be prohibited. . . .

The second period is that of government by a provisional constitution. When military law is lifted in each *hsien* [district], the Military Government shall return the right of self-government to the local people. . . .

The third period will be government under the constitution. Six years after the provisional constitution has been enforced a constitution shall be made. The military and administrative powers of the Military Government shall be annulled; the people shall elect the president, and elect the members of parliament to organize the parliament.

Q *What were Sun Yat-sen's key proposals to transform China into a modern, technologically based society? How does his program compare with the so-called Meiji reforms in Japan, discussed later in this chapter?*

---

became impatient with the slow pace of political change and were disillusioned to find that the new assemblies were intended to be primarily advisory rather than legislative. The government also alienated influential elements by financing railway development projects through foreign firms rather than local investors. The reforms also had little meaning for peasants, artisans, miners, and transportation workers, whose living conditions were being eroded by rising taxes and official venality. Rising rural unrest was an ominous sign of deep-seated resentment to which the dynasty would not, or could not, respond.

The Rise of Sun Yat-sen The first physical manifestations of future revolution appeared during the last decade of the nineteenth century with the formation of the Revive China Society by the young radical Sun Yat-sen (1866–1925). Born in a village south of Canton, Sun was educated in Hawaii and returned to China to practice medicine. Soon he turned his full attention to the ills of Chinese society.

At first, Sun's efforts yielded few positive results, but in a convention in Tokyo in 1905, he managed to unite radical groups from across China in the so-called Revolutionary Alliance (Tongmenghui, or T'ung Meng Hui). The new organization's program was based on Sun's "three people's principles" of nationalism (meaning primarily the elimination of Manchu rule over China), democracy, and people's livelihood. It called for a three-stage process beginning with a military takeover and ending with a constitutional democracy (see the box above). Although the new

FILM & HISTORY
THE LAST EMPEROR (1987)

On November 14, 1908, the Chinese emperor Guangxu died in Beijing. One day later, Empress Dowager Cixi—the real power behind the throne—passed away as well. A three-year-old boy, to be known in history as Henry Puyi, ascended the throne. Three years later, the Qing dynasty collapsed, and the deposed monarch lived out the remainder of his life in a China lashed by political turmoil and violence. He finally died in 1967 at the height of the Great Proletarian Cultural Revolution.

The Last Emperor (1987), directed by the Italian filmmaker Bernardo Bertolucci, is a brilliant portrayal of the experience of one hapless individual in a nation caught up in the throes of a seemingly endless revolution. The film evokes the fading majesty of the last days of imperial China but also the chaos of the warlord era and the terrors of the Maoist period, when the last shreds of the former emperor's personality were shattered under the pressure of Communist brainwashing techniques. The main character, who never appears to grasp what is happening to his country, lives and dies a nonentity.

Three-year-old Puyi (Richard Vuu), the last emperor of China, watches an emissary approach at the Imperial Palace.

The film, based on Puyi's autobiography, benefits from having been filmed partly onsite in the Imperial City. The only major Western actor to appear in the movie is the veteran film star Peter O'Toole, who plays Puyi's tutor when he was an adolescent.

organization was small and relatively inexperienced, it benefited from rising popular discontent.

The Revolution of 1911   In October 1911, Sun's followers launched an uprising in the industrial center of Wuhan, in central China. With Sun traveling in the United States, the insurrection lacked leadership, but the decrepit government's inability to react quickly encouraged political forces at the provincial level to take measures into their own hands. The dynasty was now in a state of virtual collapse: the empress dowager had died in 1908, one day after her nephew; the throne was now occupied by China's "last emperor," the infant Puyi (P'u Yi). Sun's party had neither the military strength nor the political base necessary to seize the initiative, however, and was forced to turn to a representative of the old order, General Yuan Shikai (Yuan Shih-k'ai). A prominent figure in military circles since the beginning of the century, Yuan had been placed in charge of the imperial forces sent to suppress the rebellion, but now he abandoned the Manchus and acted on his own behalf. In negotiations with

representatives of Sun Yat-sen's party (Sun himself had arrived in China in January 1912), he agreed to serve as president of a new Chinese republic. The old dynasty and the age-old system that it had attempted to preserve were no more.

Although the dynasty was gone, Sun and his followers were unable to consolidate their gains. The program of the Revolutionary Alliance was based on Western liberal democratic principles aimed at the urban middle class, but the middle class in China was too small to form the basis for a new political order. The vast majority of the Chinese people still lived on the land. Sun had hoped to win their support with a land reform program, but few peasants had participated in the 1911 revolution. In failing to create new institutions and values to provide a framework for a changing society, the events of 1911 were less a revolution than a collapse of the old order. Weakened by imperialism and its own internal weaknesses, the old dynasty had come to an abrupt end before new political and social forces were ready to fill the vacuum.

Lord Macartney's mission to China	1793
Opium War	1839–1842
Taiping rebels seize Nanjing	1853
Taiping Rebellion suppressed	1864
Cixi becomes regent for nephew, the Guangxu emperor	1878
Sino-Japanese War	1894–1895
One Hundred Days reform	1898
Open Door policy	1899
Boxer Rebellion	1900
Commission to study constitution formed	1905
Deaths of Cixi and the Guangxu emperor	1908
Revolution in China	1911

What China had experienced was part of a historical process that was bringing down traditional empires across the globe, both in regions threatened by Western imperialism and in Europe itself, where tsarist Russia, the Austro-Hungarian Empire, and the Ottoman Empire all came to an end within a few years after the collapse of the Qing. The circumstances of their demise were not all the same. The Austro-Hungarian Empire, for example, was dismembered by the victorious allies after World War I, and the fate of tsarist Russia was directly linked to that conflict. Still, all four regimes shared the responsibility for their common fate in that they had failed to meet the challenges posed by the times. All had responded to the forces of industrialization and popular participation in the political process with hesitation and reluctance, and their attempts at reform were too little and too late. All paid the supreme price for their folly.

Chinese Society in Transition

Q **Focus Question:** What political, economic, and social reforms were instituted by the Qing dynasty during its final decades, and why were they not more successful in reversing the decline of Manchu rule?

The growing Western presence in China during the late nineteenth and early twentieth centuries obviously had a major impact on Chinese society; hence many historians have traditionally asserted that the arrival of the Europeans shook China out of centuries of slumber and launched it on the road to revolutionary change. In fact, when the European economic penetration began to accelerate in the mid-nineteenth century, Chinese society was already in a state of transition. The growth of industry and trade was particularly noticeable in the cities, where a national market for such commodities as oil, copper, salt, tea, and porcelain had developed. The foundation of an infrastructure more conducive to the rise of a money economy appeared to be in place. In the countryside, new crops introduced from abroad significantly increased food production and aided population growth. The Chinese economy had never been more productive or more complex.

Obstacles to Industrialization

Whether these changes by themselves would eventually have led to an industrial revolution and the rise of a capitalist society on the Western model in the absence of Western intervention is a question that historians cannot answer. Certainly, a number of obstacles would have made it difficult for China to embark on the Western path if it had wished to do so.

Although industrial production was on the rise, it was still based almost entirely on traditional methods. There was no uniform system of weights and measures, and the banking system was still primitive by European standards. The use of paper money, invented by the Chinese centuries earlier, was still relatively limited. The transportation system, which had been neglected since the end of the Yuan dynasty, was increasingly chaotic. There were few paved roads, and the Grand Canal, long the most efficient means of carrying goods from north to south, was silting up. As a result, merchants had to rely more and more on the coastal route, where they faced increasing competition from foreign shipping.

Although foreign concession areas in the coastal cities provided a conduit for the importation of Western technology and modern manufacturing methods, the Chinese borrowed less than they might have. Foreign manufacturing enterprises could not legally operate in China until the last decade of the nineteenth century, and their methods had little influence beyond the concession areas. Chinese efforts to imitate Western methods, notably in shipbuilding and weapons manufacture, were dominated by the government and often suffered from mismanagement.

Equally serious problems persisted in the countryside. The rapid increase in population had led to smaller plots and burgeoning numbers of tenant farmers. Whether per capita consumption of food was on the decline is not clear from the available evidence, but apparently rice as a staple of the diet was increasingly being replaced by less nutritious foods. Some farmers benefited from switching to commercial agriculture to supply the markets of the growing coastal cities, but the shift entailed a sizable investment. Many farmers went so deeply into debt that they eventually lost their land.

Most important, perhaps, was that the Qing dynasty was still locked into a traditional mind-set that discouraged commercial activities and prized the time-honored virtues of agrarian society. China also lacked the European tradition of a vigorous and self-confident merchant class based in cities that were autonomous.

The Impact of Imperialism In any event, the advent of the imperialist era in the second half of the nineteenth century made such questions academic; imperialism created serious distortions in the local economy that resulted in massive changes in Chinese society during the twentieth century. Whether the Western intrusion was beneficial or harmful is debated to this day. The Western presence undoubtedly accelerated the development of the Chinese economy in some ways: the introduction of modern means of production, transport, and communications; the creation of an export market; and the steady integration of the Chinese market into the nineteenth-century global economy. To many Westerners at the time, it was self-evident that such changes would ultimately benefit the Chinese people (see the comparative essay "Imperialism and the Global Environment" on p. 552). In their view, Western civilization represented the most advanced stage of human development. By supplying (in the catch phrase of the day) "oil for the lamps of China," it was providing a backward society with an opportunity to move up a notch or two on the ladder of human evolution.

Not everyone agreed. The Russian Marxist Vladimir Lenin contended that Western imperialism actually hindered the process of structural change in preindustrial societies because it thwarted the rise of a local industrial and commercial sector in order to maintain colonies and semicolonies as a market for Western manufactured goods and a source of cheap labor and materials. Fellow Marxists in China such as Mao Zedong (see Chapter 24) later took up Lenin's charge and asserted that if the West had not intervened, China would have found its own road to capitalism and thence to socialism and communism.

Many historians today would say that the answer is too complex for such simplistic explanations. By shaking China out of its traditional mind-set, imperialism accelerated the process of change that had begun in the late Ming and early Qing periods and forced the Chinese to adopt new ways of thinking and acting. At the same time, China paid a heavy price in the destruction of its local industry while many of the profits flowed abroad. Although industrial revolution is a painful process whenever and wherever it occurs, the Chinese found the experience doubly painful because it was foisted on China from the outside.

Daily Life

At the beginning of the nineteenth century, daily life for most Chinese was not substantially different from what it had been centuries earlier. Most were farmers, living in millions of villages in rice fields and on hillsides throughout the countryside. Their lives were governed by the harvest cycle, village custom, and family ritual. Their roles in society were firmly fixed by the time-honored principles of Confucian social ethics. Male children, at least the more fortunate ones, were educated in the Confucian classics, while females remained in the home or in the fields. All children were expected to obey their parents, and all wives to submit to their husbands.

A visitor to China a hundred years later would have seen a very different society, although one still recognizably Chinese. Change was most striking in the coastal cities, where the educated and affluent had been visibly affected by the growing Western cultural presence. Confucian social institutions and behavioral norms were declining rapidly in influence, while those of Europe and North America were on the ascendant. Change was much less noticeable in the countryside, but even there, the customary bonds had been dangerously frayed by the rapidly changing times.

Some of the change can be traced to the educational system. During the nineteenth century, the importance of a Confucian education steadily declined as up to half of the degree holders had purchased their degrees. After 1906, when the government abolished the civil service examinations, a Confucian education ceased to be the key to a successful career, and Western-style education became more desirable. The old dynasty attempted to modernize by establishing an educational system on the Western model with universal education at the elementary level. Such plans had some effect in the cities, where public schools, missionary schools, and other private institutions educated a new generation of Chinese with little knowledge of or respect for the past.

The Status of Women The status of women was also in transition. During the mid-Qing era, women were still expected to remain in the home. Their status as useless sex objects was painfully symbolized by the practice of foot binding, a custom that had probably originated among court entertainers in the Tang dynasty and spread to the common people by the Song. By the mid-nineteenth century, more than half of all adult women probably had bound feet.

COMPARATIVE ESSAY
IMPERIALISM AND THE GLOBAL ENVIRONMENT

EARTH & ENVIRONMENT

As we have seen, beginning in the 1870s, European states engaged in an intense scramble for overseas territory. This "new imperialism" led Europeans to carve up Asia and Africa and create colonial empires. Within these empires, European states exercised complete political control over the indigenous societies and redrew political boundaries to meet their needs. In Africa, for example, in drawing the boundaries that separated one colony from another (boundaries that often became the boundaries of the modern countries of Africa), Europeans paid no attention to the existing political divisions; they often divided cohesive communities between colonies or incorporated two communities that were hostile to each other into the same colony.

In similar fashion, Europeans paid little or no heed to the economic needs of their colonial subjects but instead arranged the economies of their empires to meet their own needs in the world market. In the process, Europeans often dramatically altered the global environment, a transformation that was made visible in a variety of ways. Westerners built railways and ports, erected telegraph lines, drilled for oil, and mined for gold, tin, iron ore, and copper. All of these projects transformed and often scarred the natural landscape.

Landscapes, however, were even more dramatically altered by Europe's demand for cash food crops. Throughout vast regions of Africa and Asia, tropical forests were felled to make way for plantations that cultivated crops that could be exported for sale. In Ceylon (modern Sri Lanka) and India, the British cut down vast tropical forests to plant row upon row of tea bushes. The Dutch razed forests in the East Indies to plant cinchona trees imported from Peru. (Quinine, derived from the trees' bark, dramatically reduced the death rate from malaria and made it possible for Europeans to live more securely in the tropical regions of Africa and Asia.) In Indochina, the French replaced extensive forests with sugar and coffee plantations. Native workers, who were usually paid pitiful wages by their European overseers, provided the labor for all of these vast plantations.

In many areas, precious farmland was turned over to the cultivation of cash crops. In the Dutch East Indies, farmers were forced to plow up some of their rice fields to make way for the cultivation

Picking Tea Leaves in Ceylon. In this 1900 photograph, women on a plantation in Ceylon (Sri Lanka) pick tea leaves for shipment abroad. The British cut down vast stands of tropical forests in Ceylon and India to grow tea to satisfy demand back home.

of sugar. In West Africa, overplanting of cash crops damaged fragile grasslands and turned parts of the Sahel into a wasteland.

European states, however, greatly profited from this transformed environment. In *Agriculture in the Tropics: An Elementary Treatise*, written in 1909, the British botanist John Christopher Willis expressed his thoughts on this European policy:

> Whether planting in the tropics will always continue to be under European management is another question, but the northern powers will not permit that the rich and as yet comparatively undeveloped countries of the tropics should be entirely wasted by being devoted merely to the supply of the food and clothing wants of their own people, when they can also supply the wants of the colder zones in so many indispensable products.

In Willis's eyes, the imperialist transformation of the environments of Asia and Africa to serve European needs was entirely justified.

Q *How would you compare the effects of imperialism on the environment in colonial countries with the impact of the Industrial Revolution in Europe and North America?*

During the second half of the nineteenth century, signs of change began to appear. Women began to seek employment in factories—notably in cotton mills and in the silk industry, established in Shanghai in the 1890s. Some women were active in dissident activities, such as the Taiping Rebellion and the Boxer movement, and a few fought beside men in the 1911 revolution. Qiu Jin, a well-known female revolutionary, wrote a manifesto calling for women's liberation and then organized a revolt against the Manchu government, only to be captured and executed at the age of thirty-two in 1907.

Women with Bound Feet. To provide the best possible marriage for their daughters, upper-class families began to perform foot binding during the Song dynasty. Eventually, the practice spread to all social classes in China. Although small feet were supposed to denote a woman of leisure, most Chinese women with bound feet contributed to the labor force, working mainly in textiles and handicrafts to supplement the family income.

By the end of the century, educational opportunities for women began to appear for the first time. Christian missionaries opened some girls' schools, mainly in the foreign concession areas. Although only a relatively small number of women were educated in these schools, they had a significant impact on Chinese society as progressive intellectuals began to argue that ignorant women produced ignorant children. In 1905, the court announced its intention to open public schools for girls, but few such schools ever materialized. The government also began to take steps to discourage the practice of foot binding, initially with only minimal success.

A Rich Country and a Strong State: The Rise of Modern Japan

Q **Focus Question:** To what degree was the Meiji Restoration a "revolution," and to what degree did it succeed in transforming Japan?

By the beginning of the nineteenth century, the Tokugawa shogunate had ruled the Japanese islands for two hundred years. It had revitalized the old governmental system, which had virtually disintegrated under its predecessors. It had driven out the foreign traders and missionaries and isolated the country from almost all contacts with the outside world. The Tokugawa maintained formal relations only with Korea, although informal trading links with Dutch and Chinese merchants continued at Nagasaki. Isolation, however, did not mean stagnation. Although the vast majority of Japanese still depended on agriculture for their livelihood, a vigorous manufacturing and commercial sector had begun to emerge during the long period of peace and prosperity. As a result, Japanese society had begun to undergo deep-seated changes, and traditional class distinctions were becoming blurred. Eventually, these changes would end Tokugawa rule and destroy the traditional feudal system.

Some historians speculate that the Tokugawa system was beginning to come apart, just as the medieval order in Europe had started to disintegrate at the beginning of the Renaissance. Factionalism and corruption plagued the central bureaucracy, while rural unrest, provoked by a series of poor harvests brought about by bad weather, swept the countryside. Farmers fled to the towns, where anger was already rising as a result of declining agricultural incomes and shrinking stipends for the samurai. Many of the samurai lashed out at the perceived incompetence and corruption of the government. In response, the *bakufu* became increasingly rigid, persecuting its critics and attempting to force fleeing peasants to return to their lands. The government also intensified its efforts to maintain the nation's isolation from the outside world, driving away foreign ships that were beginning to prowl along the Japanese coast in increasing numbers.

An End to Isolation

To the Western powers, the continued isolation of Japanese society was an affront and a challenge. Driven by the growing rivalry among themselves and convinced that the expansion of trade on a global basis would benefit all nations, Western nations began to approach Japan in the hope of opening up the hermit kingdom to foreign economic interests.

The first to succeed was the United States. American steamships crossing the northern Pacific needed a fueling station before going on to China and other ports in the area. In the summer of 1853, an American fleet of four warships under Commodore Matthew C. Perry arrived in Edo Bay (now Tokyo Bay) with a letter from President Millard Fillmore asking for the opening of foreign relations between the two countries. A few months later, Perry returned with a larger fleet for an answer. In his absence, Japanese officials had hotly debated the issue. Some argued that contacts with the West would be both politically and morally disadvantageous to Japan, while others pointed to U.S. military superiority and recommended

A Gift for the Emperor. When Commodore Perry arrived in Tokyo Bay with a small fleet of U.S. warships in July 1853, the size, speed, and armaments of the "black ships" frightened Japanese onlookers and undoubtedly contributed to the willingness of the Tokugawa shogunate to seek a compromise with the foreigners. One Japanese artist recorded his impression of the visitors, who on a later occasion offered their hosts the gift of a steam locomotive.

concessions. For the shogunate in Edo, the black guns of Perry's ships proved decisive, and Japan agreed to the Treaty of Kanagawa, which provided for the return of shipwrecked American sailors, the opening of two ports, and the establishment of a U.S. consulate on Japanese soil. In 1858, U.S. Consul Townsend Harris negotiated a more elaborate commercial treaty calling for the opening of several ports to U.S. trade and residence, the exchange of ministers, and the granting of extraterritorial privileges for U.S. residents in Japan. Similar treaties were soon signed with several European nations.

The decision to open relations with the Western barbarians was highly unpopular in some quarters, particularly in regions distant from the shogunate headquarters in Edo. Resistance was especially strong in two of the key outside daimyo territories in the south, Satsuma and Choshu, both of which had strong military traditions. In 1863, the "Sat-Cho" alliance forced the hapless shogun to promise to end relations with the West. The shogun eventually reneged on the agreement, but the rebellious groups soon disclosed their own weakness. When Choshu troops fired on Western ships in the Strait of Shimonoseki, the Westerners fired back and destroyed the Choshu fortifications. The incident convinced the rebellious samurai of the need to strengthen their own military and intensified their unwillingness to give in to the West. Having strengthened their influence at the

imperial court in Kyoto, they demanded the shogun's resignation and the restoration of the emperor's power. In January 1868, rebel armies attacked the shogun's palace in Kyoto and proclaimed the restored authority of the emperor. After a few weeks, resistance collapsed, and the venerable shogunate system was brought to an end.

The Meiji Restoration

Although the victory of the Sat-Cho faction had appeared on the surface to be a triumph of tradition over change, the new leaders soon realized that Japan must change to survive. Accordingly, they embarked on a policy of comprehensive reform that would lay the foundations of a modern industrial nation within a generation.

The symbol of the new era was the young emperor himself, who had taken the reign name Meiji ("enlightened rule") on ascending the throne after the death of his father in 1867. Although the post-Tokugawa period was termed a "restoration," the Meiji ruler, who shared the Sat-Cho group's newly adopted modernist outlook, was controlled by the new leadership just as the shogun had controlled his predecessors. In tacit recognition of the real source of political power, the new capital was located at Edo (now renamed Tokyo, "eastern capital"), and the imperial court was moved to the shogun's palace in the center of the city.

PROGRAM FOR REFORM IN JAPAN

POLITICS & GOVERNMENT

In the spring of 1868, the reformers drew up a program for transforming Japanese society along Western lines in the post-Tokugawa era. Though vague in its essentials, the Charter Oath is a good indication of the plans that were carried out during the Meiji Restoration.

The Charter Oath of Emperor Meiji

By this oath we set up as our aim the establishment of the national weal on a broad basis and the framing of a constitution and laws.

1. Deliberative assemblies shall be widely established and all matters decided by public discussion.
2. All classes, high and low, shall unite in vigorously carrying out the administration of affairs of state.
3. The common people, no less than the civil and military officials, shall each be allowed to pursue his own calling so that there may be no discontent.
4. Evil customs of the past shall be broken off and everything based upon the just laws of Nature.
5. Knowledge shall be sought throughout the world so as to strengthen the foundations of imperial rule.

Q *Compare this program with the Declaration of the Rights of Man and the Citizen drafted during the French Revolution and discussed in Chapter 18. To what extent do these principles conform to the concepts of liberal democracy as practiced in Western societies? To what degree were they implemented in Japan?*

The Transformation of Japanese Politics   Once in power, the new leaders launched a comprehensive reform of Japanese political, social, economic, and cultural institutions and values. They moved first to abolish the remnants of the old order and strengthen executive power in their hands. To undercut the power of the daimyo, hereditary privileges were abolished in 1871, and the great lords lost title to their lands. As compensation, they were given government bonds and were named governors of the territories formerly under their control. The samurai, comprising about 8 percent of the total population, received a lump-sum payment to replace their traditional stipends, but they were forbidden to wear the sword, the symbol of their hereditary status.

The Meiji modernizers also set out to create a modern political system on the Western model. In the Charter Oath of 1868, the new leaders promised to create a new deliberative assembly within the framework of continued imperial rule (see the box above). Although senior positions in the new government were given to the daimyo, the key posts were dominated by modernizing samurai, eventually to be known as the **genro,** or elder statesmen, from the Sat-Cho clique.

During the next two decades, the Meiji government undertook a systematic study of Western political systems. A constitutional commission under Ito Hirobumi traveled to several Western countries, including Great Britain, Germany, Russia, and the United States, to study their political systems. As the process evolved, a number of factions appeared, each representing different political ideas. The most prominent were the Liberal Party and the Progressive Party. The Liberal Party favored political reform on the Western liberal democratic model with supreme authority vested in the parliament as the representative of the people. The Progressive Party called for the distribution of power between the legislative and executive branches, with a slight nod to the latter.

The Constitution of 1890   During the 1870s and 1880s, these factions competed for preeminence. In the end, the Progressives emerged victorious. The Meiji Constitution, which was adopted in 1890, was based on the Bismarckian model with authority vested in the executive branch; the imperialist faction was pacified by the statement that the constitution was the gift of the emperor. Members of the cabinet were to be handpicked by the Meiji oligarchs. The upper house of parliament was to be appointed and have equal legislative powers with the lower house, called the Diet, whose members would be elected. The core ideology of the state was called the *kokutai* (national polity), which embodied (although in very imprecise form) the concept of the uniqueness of the Japanese system based on the supreme authority of the emperor.

The result was a system that was democratic in form but despotic in practice, modern in appearance but still traditional in that power remained in the hands of a ruling oligarchy. The system permitted the traditional ruling class to retain its influence and economic power while acquiescing in the emergence of new institutions and values.

Meiji Economics   With the end of the daimyo domains, the government needed to establish a new system of landownership that would transform the mass of the rural population from indentured serfs into citizens. To do so,

The Emperor Inspects His Domain. A crucial challenge for the Japanese government during the Meiji era was to provide for the food needs of the country by increasing the productivity of agricultural workers. In this painting, Emperor Meiji inspects farmers planting rice seedlings in a flooded field. The practice of showing the imperial face in public was an innovation introduced by Emperor Meiji that earned him the affection of his subjects.

stimulus to Japan's industrial revolution. The government provided financial subsidies to needy industries, training, foreign advisers, improved transport and communications, and a universal educational system emphasizing applied science. In contrast to China, Japan was able to achieve results with minimum reliance on foreign capital.

During the late Meiji era, Japan's industrial sector began to grow. Besides tea and silk, other key industries were weaponry, shipbuilding, and sake (fermented rice wine). From the start, the distinctive feature of the Meiji model was the intimate relationship between government and private business in terms of operations and regulations. Once an individual enterprise or industry was on its feet (or, sometimes, when it had ceased to make a profit), it was turned over entirely to private ownership, although the government often continued to play some role even after its direct involvement in management was terminated. One historian has explained the process:

[The Meiji government] pioneered many industrial fields and sponsored the development of others, attempting to cajole businessmen into new and risky kinds of endeavor, helping assemble the necessary capital, forcing weak companies to merge into stronger units, and providing private entrepreneurs with aid and privileges of a sort that would be corrupt favoritism today. All this was in keeping with Tokugawa traditions that business operated under the tolerance and patronage of government. Some of the political leaders even played a dual role in politics and business.[4]

it enacted a land reform program that redefined the domain lands as the private property of the tillers while compensating the previous owner with government bonds. One reason for the new policy was that the government needed operating revenues. To remedy the problem, the Meiji leaders added a new agriculture tax, which was set at an annual rate of 3 percent of the estimated value of the land. The new tax proved to be a lucrative and dependable source of income for the government, but it was onerous for the farmers, who had previously paid a fixed percentage of their harvest to the landowner. As a result, in bad years, many taxpaying peasants were unable to pay their taxes and were forced to sell their lands to wealthy neighbors. Eventually, the government reduced the tax to 2.5 percent of the land value. Still, by the end of the century, about 40 percent of all farmers were tenants.

With its budget needs secured, the government turned to the promotion of industry with the basic objective of guaranteeing Japan's survival against the challenge of Western imperialism. Building on the small but growing industrial economy that already existed under the Tokugawa, the Meiji reformers provided a massive

From the workers' perspective, the Meiji reforms had a less attractive side. As we have seen, the new land tax provided the funds to subsidize the growth of the industrial sector, but it imposed severe hardships on the rural population, many of whom abandoned their farms and fled to the cities, where they provided an abundant source of cheap labor for Japanese industry. As in Europe during the early decades of the Industrial Revolution, workers toiled for long hours in the coal mines and textile mills, often under horrendous conditions. Reportedly, coal miners employed on a small island in Nagasaki Harbor worked naked in temperatures up to 130 degrees Fahrenheit. If they tried to escape, they were shot.

Building a Modern Social Structure By the late Tokugawa era, the rigidly hierarchical social order was showing signs of disintegration. Rich merchants were buying their way into the ranks of the samurai, and Japanese of all classes were beginning to abandon their rice fields and move into the growing cities. Nevertheless, community and hierarchy still formed the basis of Japanese society. The lives of all Japanese were determined by their membership in various social organizations—the family, the village, and their social class. Membership in a particular social class determined a person's occupation and social relationships with others. Women in particular were constrained by the "three obediences" imposed on their gender: child to father, wife to husband, and widow to son. Husbands could easily obtain a divorce, but wives could not (one regulation allegedly decreed that a husband could divorce his spouse if she drank too much tea or talked too much). Marriages were arranged, and the average age at marriage for females was sixteen years. Females did not share inheritance rights with males, and few received any education outside the family.

The Meiji reformers destroyed much of the traditional social system in Japan. With the abolition of hereditary rights in 1871, the legal restrictions of the past were brought to an end with a single stroke. Special privileges for the aristocracy were abolished, as were the legal restrictions on the *eta*, the traditional slave class (numbering about 400,000 in the 1870s). Another key focus of the reformers was the army. The Sat-Cho reformers had been struck by the weakness of the Japanese forces in clashes with Western powers and embarked on a major program to create a military force that could compete in the modern world. The old feudal army based on the traditional warrior class was abolished, and an imperial army based on universal conscription was formed in 1871.

Education also underwent major changes. The Meiji leaders recognized the need for universal education including technical subjects, and after a few years of experimenting, they adopted the American model of a three-tiered system culminating in a series of universities and specialized institutes. In the meantime, they sent bright students to study abroad and brought foreign scholars to Japan to teach in the new schools, where much of the content was inspired by Western models. In another break with tradition, women for the first time were given an opportunity to get an education.

Western influence was evident elsewhere as well. Western fashions became the rage in elite circles, and the ministers of the first Meiji government were known as the "dancing cabinet" because of their addiction to Western-style ballroom dancing. Young people, increasingly exposed to Western culture and values, began to imitate the clothing styles, eating habits, and social practices of their European and American counterparts. They even took up American sports when baseball was introduced.

Traditional Values and Women's Rights The self-proclaimed transformation of Japan into a "modern society," however, by no means detached the country entirely from its traditional moorings. Although an educational order in 1872 increased the percentage of Japanese women exposed to public education, conservatives soon began to impose restrictions and bring about a return to more traditional social relationships. Traditional values were given a firm legal basis in the Constitution of 1890, which restricted the franchise to males and defined individual liberties as "subject to the limitations imposed by law," and by the Civil Code of 1898, which de-emphasized individual rights and essentially placed women within the context of their role in the family (see the box on p. 558).

By the end of the nineteenth century, however, changes were under way as women began to play a crucial role in their nation's effort to modernize. Urged by their parents to augment the family income, as well as by the government to fulfill their patriotic duty, young girls were sent en masse to work in textile mills. From 1894 to 1912, women represented 60 percent of the Japanese labor force. Thanks to them, by 1914, Japan was the world's leading exporter of silk and dominated cotton manufacturing. If it had not been for the export revenues earned from textile exports, Japan might not have been able to develop its heavy industry and military prowess without an infusion of foreign capital.

Japanese women received few rewards for their contribution to the nation, however. In 1900, new regulations prohibited women from joining political organizations or attending public meetings. Beginning in 1905, a group of independent-minded women petitioned the Japanese parliament to rescind this restriction, but it was not repealed until 1922.

Joining the Imperialist Club

Traditionally, Japan had not been an expansionist country. Now, however, the Japanese did not just imitate the domestic policies of their Western mentors; they also emulated the Western approach to foreign affairs. This is perhaps not surprising. The Japanese regarded themselves as particularly vulnerable in the world economic arena. Their territory was small, lacking in resources, and densely populated, and they had no natural outlet for expansion. To observant Japanese, the lessons of history were clear. Western nations had amassed wealth and power not only because of their democratic systems and high level of education but also because of their colonies.

The Japanese began their program of territorial expansion close to home (see Map 22.4). In 1874, after a brief conflict with China, Japan was able to claim

THE RULES OF GOOD CITIZENSHIP IN JAPAN

FAMILY & SOCIETY

After seizing power from the Tokugawa shogunate in 1868, the new Japanese leaders turned their attention to the creation of a new political system that would bring the country into the modern world. After exploring various systems in use in the West, a constitutional commission decided to adopt the system used in imperial Germany because of its paternalistic character. To promote civic virtue and obedience among the citizenry, the government then drafted an imperial rescript that was to be taught to every schoolchild in the country. The rescript instructed all children to obey their sovereign and place the interests of the community and the state above their own personal desires.

Imperial Rescript on Education, 1890

Know ye, Our subjects:

Our Imperial Ancestors have founded Our Empire on a basis broad and everlasting, and have deeply and firmly implanted virtue. Our subjects ever united in loyalty and filial piety have from generation to generation illustrated the beauty thereof. This is the glory of the fundamental character of Our Empire, and herein also lies the source of Our education. Ye, Our subjects, be filial to your parents, affectionate to your brothers and sisters, as husbands and wives be harmonious, as friends true; bear yourselves in modesty and moderation; extend your benevolence to all; pursue learning and cultivate arts, and thereby develop intellectual faculties and perfect moral powers; furthermore, advance public good and promote common interests; always respect the Constitution and observe the laws; should emergency arise, offer yourselves to the State; and thus guard and maintain the prosperity of Our Imperial Throne coeval with heaven and earth. So shall ye not only be Our good and faithful subjects, but render illustrious the best traditions of your forefathers.

Q *What, according to this document, was the primary purpose of education in Meiji Japan? How did these goals compare with those in China and the West?*

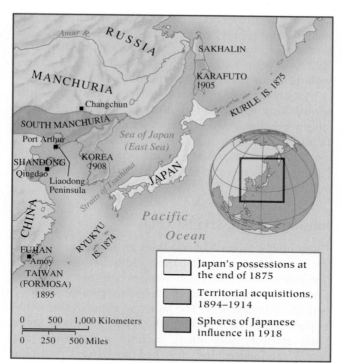

MAP 22.4 Japanese Overseas Expansion During the Meiji Era. Beginning in the late nineteenth century, Japan ventured beyond its home islands and became an imperialist power. The extent of Japanese colonial expansion through World War I is shown here.
Q Which parts of imperial China came under Japanese influence?

suzerainty over the Ryukyu Islands, long tributary to the Chinese Empire. Two years later, Japanese naval pressure forced Korea to open three ports to Japanese commerce.

During the early decades of the nineteenth century, Korea had followed Japan's example and attempted to isolate itself from outside contact except for periodic tribute missions to China. Christian missionaries, mostly Chinese or French, were vigorously persecuted. But Korea's problems were basically internal. In the early 1860s, a peasant revolt, inspired in part by the Taiping Rebellion in China, caused considerable devastation before being crushed in 1864. In succeeding years, the Yi dynasty sought to strengthen the country by returning to traditional values and fending off outside intrusion, but rural poverty and official corruption remained rampant. A U.S. fleet, following the example of Commodore Perry in Japan, sought to open the country in 1871 but was driven off with considerable loss of life.

Korea's most persistent suitor, however, was Japan, which was determined to bring an end to Korea's dependency status with China and modernize it along Japanese lines. In 1876, the two countries signed an agreement opening three treaty ports to Japanese commerce in return for Japanese recognition of Korean independence. During the 1880s, Sino-Japanese rivalry over Korea intensified. When a new peasant rebellion broke out in Korea in 1894, China and Japan intervened on opposite sides (see the box on p. 559). During the war, the Japanese navy destroyed the Chinese fleet and seized the Manchurian city of Port Arthur. In the Treaty of

OPPOSING VIEWPOINTS
TWO VIEWS OF THE WORLD

During the nineteenth century, China's hierarchical way of looking at the outside world came under severe challenge, not only from European countries avid for new territories in Asia but also from the rising power of Japan, which accepted the Western view that a colonial empire was the key to national greatness. Japan's first objective was Korea, long a dependency of China, and in 1894, the competition between China and Japan in the Korean peninsula led to war. The following declarations of war by the rulers of the two countries are revealing. Note the Chinese use of the derogatory term *Wojen* ("dwarf people") in referring to the Japanese.

Declaration of War Against China

Korea is an independent state. She was first introduced into the family of nations by the advice and guidance of Japan. It has, however, been China's habit to designate Korea as her dependency, and both openly and secretly to interfere with her domestic affairs. At the time of the recent insurrection in Korea, China despatched troops thither, alleging that her purpose was to afford a succor to her dependent state. We, in virtue of the treaty concluded with Korea in 1882, and looking to possible emergencies, caused a military force to be sent to that country.

Wishing to procure for Korea freedom from the calamity of perpetual disturbance, and thereby to maintain the peace of the East in general, Japan invited China's cooperation for the accomplishment of the object. But China, advancing various pretexts, declined Japan's proposal.... Such conduct on the part of China is not only a direct injury to the rights and interests of this Empire, but also a menace to the permanent peace and tranquility of the Orient.... In this situation,... we find it impossible to avoid a formal declaration of war against China.

Declaration of War Against Japan

Korea has been our tributary for the past two hundred odd years. She has given us tribute all this time, which is a matter known to the world. For the past dozen years or so Korea has been troubled by repeated insurrections and we, in sympathy with our small tributary, have as repeatedly sent succor to her aid.... This year another rebellion was begun in Korea, and the King repeatedly asked again for aid from us to put down the rebellion. We then ordered Li Hung-chang to send troops to Korea; and they having barely reached Yashan the rebels immediately scattered. But the *Wojen*, without any cause whatever, suddenly sent their troops to Korea, and entered Seoul, the capital of Korea, reinforcing them constantly until they have exceeded ten thousand men. In the meantime the Japanese forced the Korean king to change his system of government, showing a disposition every way of bullying the Koreans....

As Japan has violated the treaties and not observed international laws, and is now running rampant with her false and treacherous actions commencing hostilities herself, and laying herself open to condemnation by the various powers at large, we therefore desire to make it known to the world that we have always followed the paths of philanthropy and perfect justice throughout the whole complications, while the *Wojen*, on the other hand, have broken all the laws of nations and treaties which it passes our patience to bear with. Hence we commanded Li Hung-chang to give strict orders to our various armies to hasten with all speed to root the *Wojen* out of their lairs.

Q *Compare the worldviews of China and Japan at the end of the nineteenth century as reflected in these two declarations. Which point of view do you find more persuasive?*

Shimonoseki, the Chinese were forced to recognize the independence of Korea and cede Taiwan and the Liaodong peninsula with its strategic naval base at Port Arthur to Japan.

Shortly thereafter, under pressure from the European powers, the Japanese returned the Liaodong peninsula to China, but in the early twentieth century, they went back on the offensive. Rivalry with Russia over influence in Korea led to increasingly strained relations between the two countries. In 1904, Japan launched a surprise attack on the Russian naval base at Port Arthur, which Russia had taken from China in 1898. The Japanese armed forces were weaker, but Russia faced difficult logistical problems along its new Trans-Siberian Railway and severe political instability at home. In 1905, after Japanese warships sank almost the entire Russian fleet off the coast of Korea, the Russians agreed to a humiliating peace, ceding the strategically located Liaodong peninsula back to Japan, as well as southern Sakhalin and the Kurile Islands. Russia also agreed to abandon its political and economic influence in Korea and southern Manchuria, which now came increasingly under Japanese control. The Japanese victory stunned the world, including the colonial peoples of Southeast Asia, who now began to realize that the white race was not necessarily invincible.

During the next few years, the Japanese consolidated their position in northeastern Asia, annexing Korea in 1908 as an integral part of Japan. When the Koreans protested the seizure, Japanese reprisals resulted in thousands of deaths. The United States was the first nation to recognize the annexation in return for Tokyo's declaration of respect for U.S. authority in the Philippines. In 1908, the United States recognized Japanese interests in the region in return for Japanese acceptance of the principles of the Open Door. But mutual suspicion between the two countries was growing, sparked in part by U.S. efforts to restrict immigration from all Asian countries.

Japanese Culture in Transition

The wave of Western technology and ideas that entered Japan in the second half of the nineteenth century greatly altered the shape of traditional Japanese culture. Literature in particular was affected as European models eclipsed the repetitive and frivolous tales of the Tokugawa era. Dazzled by this "new" literature, Japanese authors began translating and imitating the imported models. Experimenting with Western verse, Japanese poets were at first influenced primarily by the British but eventually adopted such French styles as Symbolism, Dadaism, and Surrealism, although some traditional poetry was still composed.

As the Japanese invited technicians, engineers, architects, and artists from Europe and the United States to teach their "modern" skills to a generation of eager students, the Meiji era became a time of massive consumption of Western artistic techniques and styles. Japanese architects and artists created huge buildings of steel and reinforced concrete adorned with Greek columns and cupolas, oil paintings reflecting the European concern with depth perception and shading, and bronze sculptures of secular subjects.

Cultural exchange also went the other way as Japanese arts and crafts, porcelains, textiles, fans, folding screens, and woodblock prints became the vogue in Europe and North America. Japanese art influenced

Total Humiliation. Whereas China had persevered in hiding behind the grandeur of its past, Japan had embraced the West, modernizing itself politically, militarily, and culturally. China's humiliation at the hands of its newly imperialist neighbor is evident in this scene, where the differences in dress and body posture of the officials negotiating the treaty after the war reflect China's disastrous defeat by the Japanese in 1895.

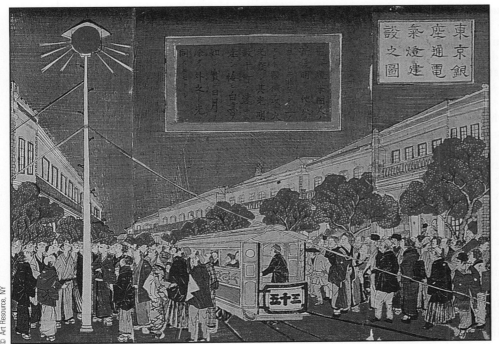

The Ginza in Downtown Tokyo. This 1877 woodblock print shows the Ginza, a major commercial thoroughfare in downtown Tokyo, with modern brick buildings, rickshaws, and a horse-drawn streetcar. The centerpiece and focus of public attention is a new electric streetlight. In combining traditional form with modern content, this print symbolizes the unique ability of the Japanese to borrow ideas from abroad while preserving much of the essence of their traditional culture.

Western painters such as Vincent van Gogh, Edgar Degas, and James Whistler, who experimented with flatter compositional perspectives and unusual poses. Japanese gardens, with their exquisite attention to the positioning of rocks and falling water, also became especially popular.

After the initial period of mass absorption of Western art, a national reaction occurred at the end of the nineteenth century as many artists returned to pre-Meiji techniques. In 1889, the Tokyo School of Fine Arts (today the Tokyo National University of Fine Arts and Music) was founded to promote traditional Japanese art. Over the next several decades, Japanese art underwent a dynamic resurgence, reflecting the nation's emergence as a prosperous and powerful state. While some Japanese artists attempted to synthesize native and foreign techniques, others returned to past artistic traditions for inspiration.

The Meiji Restoration: A Revolution from Above

Japan's transformation from a feudal, agrarian society to an industrializing, technologically advanced society in little more than half a century has frequently been described by outside observers (if not by the Japanese themselves) in almost miraculous terms. Some historians have questioned this characterization, pointing out that the achievements of the Meiji leaders were spotty. In *Japan's Emergence as a Modern State,* the Canadian historian E. H. Norman lamented that the Meiji Restoration was an "incomplete revolution" because it had not ended the economic and social inequities of feudal society or enabled the common people to participate fully in the governing process. Although the *genro* were enlightened in many respects, they were also despotic and elitist, and the distribution of wealth remained as unequal as it had been under the old system.[5]

These criticisms are persuasive, although they could also be applied to most other societies going through the early stages of industrialization. In any event, from an economic perspective, the Meiji Restoration was certainly one of the great success stories of modern times. Not only did the Meiji leaders put Japan firmly on the path to economic and political development, but they also managed to remove the unequal treaty provisions that had been imposed at mid-century. Japanese achievements are especially impressive when compared with the difficulties experienced by China, which was not only unable to realize significant changes in its traditional society but had not even reached a consensus on the need for doing so. Japan's achievements more closely resemble those of Europe, but whereas the West needed a century and a half to achieve a significant level of industrial development, the Japanese realized it in forty years.

One of the distinctive features of Japan's transition from a traditional to a modern society during the Meiji era was that it took place for the most part without violence or the kind of social or political revolution that occurred in so many other countries. The Meiji Restoration, which began the process, has been called a "revolution from above," a comprehensive restructuring of Japanese society by its own ruling group.

Sources of Japanese Uniqueness The differences between the Japanese response to the West and that of China and many other nations in the region have sparked considerable debate among students of comparative history, and a number of explanations have been offered. Some have argued that Japan's success was partly due to good fortune. Lacking abundant natural resources, it was exposed to less pressure from the West than many of its neighbors. That argument is problematic, however, and would probably not have been accepted by Japanese observers at the time. Nor does it explain why nations under considerably less pressure, such as Laos and Nepal, did not advance even more quickly. All in all, the luck hypothesis is not very persuasive.

Some explanations have already been suggested in this book. Japan's unique geographic position in Asia was certainly a factor. China, a continental nation with a heterogeneous ethnic composition, was distinguished from its neighbors by its Confucian culture. By contrast, Japan was an island nation, ethnically and linguistically homogeneous, and had never been conquered. Unlike the Chinese or many other peoples in the region, the Japanese had little to fear from cultural change in terms of its effect on their national identity. If Confucian culture, with all its accouterments, was what defined the Chinese gentleman, his Japanese counterpart, in the familiar image, could discard his sword and kimono and don a modern military uniform or a Western business suit and still feel comfortable in both worlds.

Fusing East and West The final product was an amalgam of old and new, native and foreign, forming a new civilization that was still uniquely Japanese. There were some undesirable consequences, however. Because Meiji politics was essentially despotic, Japanese leaders were able to fuse key traditional elements such as the warrior ethic and the concept of feudal loyalty with the dynamics of modern industrial capitalism to create a state totally dedicated to the possession of material wealth and national power. This combination of *kokutai* and capitalism was highly effective but explosive in its international manifestation. Like modern Germany, which also entered the industrial age directly from feudalism, Japan eventually engaged in a policy of repression at home and expansion abroad in order to achieve its national objectives (see the comparative essay "Paths to Modernization" on p. 634 in Chapter 25). In Japan, as in Germany, it took defeat in war to disconnect the drive for national development from the feudal ethic and bring about the transformation to a pluralistic society dedicated to living in peace and cooperation with its neighbors.

CONCLUSION

FEW AREAS OF THE WORLD resisted the Western incursion as stubbornly and effectively as East Asia. Although military, political, and economic pressure by the European powers was relatively intense during this era, two of the main states in the area were able to retain their independence (although China admittedly was reduced to the status of a near colony during the first quarter of the twentieth century) while the third—Korea—was temporarily absorbed by one of its larger neighbors. Why the Chinese and the Japanese were able to prevent a total political and military takeover by foreign powers is an interesting question. One key reason was that both had a long history as well-defined states with a strong sense of national community and territorial cohesion. Although China had frequently been conquered, it had retained its sense of unique culture and identity. Geography, too, was in its favor. As a continental nation, China was able to survive partly because of its sheer size. Japan possessed the advantage of an island location.

Even more striking, however, is the different way in which the two states attempted to deal with the challenge. While the Japanese chose to face the problem in a pragmatic manner, borrowing foreign ideas and institutions that appeared to be of value and at the same time were not in conflict with traditional attitudes and customs, China agonized over the issue for half a century while conservative elements fought a desperate battle to retain a maximum of the traditional heritage intact.

This chapter has discussed some of the possible reasons for those differences. In retrospect, it is difficult to avoid the conclusion that the Japanese approach was the more effective one. Whereas the Meiji leaders were able to set in motion an orderly transition from a traditional to an advanced society, in China the old system collapsed in disorder, leaving chaotic conditions that were still not rectified a generation later. China would pay a heavy price for its failure to respond coherently to the challenge.

But the Japanese "revolution from above" was by no means an unalloyed success. Ambitious efforts by Japanese leaders to carve out a share in the spoils of empire led to escalating conflict with China as well as with rival Western powers and in the early 1940s to global war. We will deal with that issue in Chapter 25. Meanwhile, in Europe, a combination of old rivalries and the effects of the Industrial Revolution were leading to a bitter regional conflict that eventually engulfed the entire world.

TIMELINE

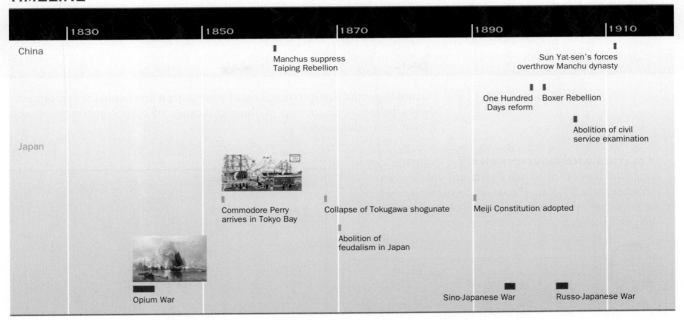

| | 1830 | 1850 | 1870 | 1890 | 1910 |

China

Manchus suppress Taiping Rebellion

Sun Yat-sen's forces overthrow Manchu dynasty

One Hundred Days reform   Boxer Rebellion

Abolition of civil service examination

Japan

Commodore Perry arrives in Tokyo Bay

Collapse of Tokugawa shogunate

Meiji Constitution adopted

Abolition of feudalism in Japan

Opium War

Sino-Japanese War   Russo-Japanese War

SUGGESTED READING

China For a general overview of modern Chinese history, see **I. C. Y. Hsu**, *The Rise of Modern China*, 6th ed. (Oxford, 2000). Also see **J. Spence's** stimulating work *The Search for Modern China* (New York, 1990).

On the Taiping Rebellion, **J. Spence**, *God's Chinese Son: The Taiping Heavenly Kingdom of Hong Xiuquan* (New York, 1996), has become a classic. Social issues are dealt with in **E. S. Rawski**, *The Last Emperors: A Social History of Qing Imperial Institutions* (Berkeley, Calif., 1998). On the Manchus' attitude toward modernization, see **D. Pong**, *Shen Pao-chen and China's Modernization in the Nineteenth Century* (New York, 1994). For a series of stimulating essays on various aspects of China's transition to modernity, see **Wenhsin Yeh, ed.**, *Becoming Chinese: Passages to Modernity and Beyond* (Berkeley, Calif., 2000).

Sun Yat-sen's career is explored in **M. C. Bergère**, *Sun Yat-sen*, trans. **J. Lloyd** (Stanford, Calif., 2000). **S. Seagraves's** *Dragon Lady: The Life and Legend of the Last Empress of China* (New York, 1992) is a revisionist treatment of Empress Dowager Cixi. On the Boxer Rebellion, the definitive work is **J. Esherick**, *The Origins of the Boxer Uprising* (Berkeley, Calif., 1987). Also see **D. Preston**, *The Boxer Rebellion: The Dramatic Story of China's War on Foreigners That Shook the World in the Summer of 1900* (Berkeley, Calif., 2001).

Japan The Meiji period of modern Japan is covered in **M. B. Jansen, ed.**, *The Emergence of Meiji Japan* (Cambridge, 1995).

Also see **D. Keene**, *Emperor of Japan: Meiji and His World, 1852–1912* (New York, 2000). See also **C. Gluck**, *Japan's Modern Myths: Ideology in the Late Meiji Period* (Princeton, N.J., 1985). On the economy, see **R. Smethurst**, *Agricultural Development and Tenancy Disputes in Japan, 1870–1940* (Princeton, N.J., 1986), and **M. Hane**, *Peasants, Rebels, and Outcastes: The Underside of Modern Japan* (New York, 1982). To understand the role of the samurai in the Meiji Revolution, see **E. Ikegami**, *The Taming of the Samurai: Honorific Individualism and the Making of Modern Japan* (Cambridge, 1995).

On the international scene, **W. Lafeber**, *The Clash: U.S.-Japanese Relations Throughout History* (New York, 1997), is slow reading but a good source of information. Also see **M. Peattie** and **R. Myers**, *The Japanese Colonial Empire, 1895–1945* (Princeton, N.J., 1984). The best introduction to Japanese art is **P. Mason**, *History of Japanese Art* (New York, 1993). See also **J. S. Baker's** concise *Japanese Art* (London, 1984).

WORLD HISTORY RESOURCES

Visit the website for *The Essential World History* **to access study aids such as Flashcards, Critical Thinking Exercises, and Chapter Quizzes:**

www.cengage.com/history/duikspiel/essentialworld6e

DISCOVERY

How did China and Japan each respond to Western pressures in the nineteenth century, and what implication did their different responses have for each nation's history?

In thinking about this question, begin by breaking it down into the components shown below. A discussion of the significance of each component should appear in your answer.

POLITICS AND GOVERNMENT Using the maps, trace the process by which China not only lost its tributary states but was "reduced to the status of a near colony." How and why were European nations able to gain such influence in China?

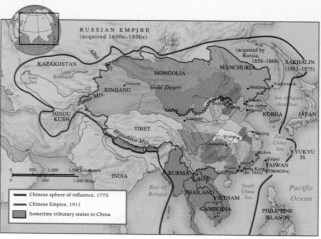

The Qing Empire

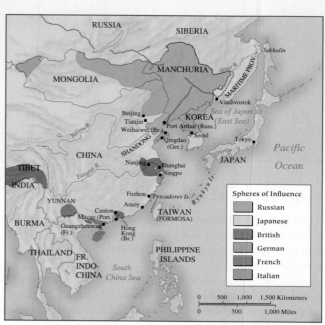

Foreign Possessions and Spheres of Influence About 1900

INTERACTION AND EXCHANGE Looking at the map at the right and considering the Japanese print showing the negotiations after the Sino-Japanese War (p. 560), compare the changes in Japanese and Chinese influence in East Asia in the late nineteenth and early twentieth centuries. What enabled the Japanese to become an imperialist power, whereas China did not? How would Japanese expansion affect future relations between the two nations? Which of these two nations adapted more effectively to Western ideas? Was this a positive development?

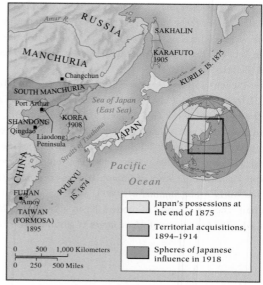

Japanese Overseas Expansion During the Meiji Era

CHAPTER 23
THE BEGINNING OF THE TWENTIETH-CENTURY CRISIS: WAR AND REVOLUTION

© Archives Charmet/The Bridgeman Art Library

British troops wait for the signal to attack.

ON JULY 1, 1916, BRITISH and French infantry forces attacked German defensive lines along a 25-mile front near the Somme River in France. Each soldier carried almost 70 pounds of equipment, making it "impossible to move much quicker than a slow walk." German machine guns soon opened fire: "We were able to see our comrades move forward in an attempt to cross No-Man's Land, only to be mown down like meadow grass," recalled one British soldier. "I felt sick at the sight of this carnage and remember weeping." In one day, more than 21,000 British soldiers died. After six months of fighting, the British had advanced 5 miles; one million British, French, and German soldiers had been killed or wounded.

Philip Gibbs, an English war correspondent, described what he saw in the German trenches that the British forces overran: "Victory!... Some of the German dead were young boys, too young to be killed for old men's crimes, and others might have been old or young. One could not tell because they had no faces, and were just masses of raw flesh in rags of uniforms. Legs and arms lay separate without any bodies thereabout."

World War I (1914–1918) was the defining event of the twentieth century. Overwhelmed by the size of its battles, the extent of its casualties, and its impact on all facets of life, contemporaries referred to it simply as the "Great War." The Great War was all the more disturbing to Europeans because it came after a period that many believed to have been an age of progress. Material prosperity and a fervid belief in scientific and technological advancement had convinced many people that the world stood on the verge of creating the utopia that humans had dreamed of for centuries. The historian Arnold Toynbee expressed what the pre–World War I era had meant to his generation:

> [We had expected] that life throughout the world would become more rational, more humane, and more democratic and that, slowly, but surely, political democracy would produce greater social justice. We had also expected that the progress of science and technology would make mankind richer, and that this increasing wealth would gradually spread from a minority to a majority. We had expected that all this would happen peacefully. In fact we thought that mankind's course was set for an earthly paradise.[1]

After 1918, it was no longer possible to maintain naive illusions about the progress of Western civilization. As World War I was followed by revolutionary upheavals, the mass murder machines of totalitarian regimes, and the destructiveness of World War II, it became all too apparent that instead of a utopia, Western civilization had become a nightmare. World War I and the revolutions it spawned can properly be seen as the first stage in the crisis of the twentieth century. ✺

The Road to World War I

Q Focus Question: What were the long-range and immediate causes of World War I?

On June 28, 1914, the heir to the Austrian throne, Archduke Francis Ferdinand, was assassinated in the Bosnian city of Sarajevo. Although this event precipitated the confrontation between Austria and Serbia that led to World War I, underlying forces had been propelling Europeans toward armed conflict for a long time.

Nationalism and Internal Dissent

The system of nation-states that had emerged in Europe in the second half of the nineteenth century (see Map 23.1) had led to severe competition. Rivalries over colonies and trade intensified during an era of frenzied imperialist expansion, while the division of Europe's great powers into two loose alliances (Germany, Austria, and Italy on one side and France, Great Britain, and Russia on the other) only added to the tensions. The series of crises that tested these alliances in the 1900s and early 1910s had left European states embittered, eager for revenge, and willing to go to war to preserve the power of their national states.

The growth of nationalism in the nineteenth century had yet another serious consequence. Not all ethnic groups had achieved the goal of nationhood. Slavic minorities in the Balkans and the multiethnic Habsburg Empire, for example, still dreamed of creating their own national states. So did the Irish in the British Empire and the Poles in the Russian Empire.

National aspirations, however, were not the only source of internal strife at the beginning of the twentieth century. Socialist labor movements had grown more powerful and were increasingly inclined to use strikes, even violent ones, to achieve their goals. Some conservative leaders, alarmed at the increase in labor strife and class division, even feared that European nations were on the verge of revolution. Did these statesmen opt for war in 1914 because they believed that "prosecuting an active foreign policy," as some Austrian leaders expressed it, would smother "internal troubles"? Some historians have argued that the desire to suppress internal disorder may have encouraged some leaders to take the plunge into war in 1914.

Militarism

The growth of large mass armies after 1900 not only heightened the existing tensions in Europe but also made it inevitable that if war did come, it would be highly destructive. **Conscription**—obligatory military service—had been established as a regular practice in most Western countries before 1914 (the United States and Britain were major exceptions). European military machines had doubled in size between 1890 and 1914. The Russian army was the largest, with 1.3 million men, and the French and Germans were not far behind, with 900,000 each. The British, Italian, and Austrian armies numbered between 250,000 and 500,000 soldiers.

Militarism, however, involved more than just large armies. As armies grew, so did the influence of military leaders, who drew up vast and complex plans for quickly mobilizing millions of men and enormous quantities of supplies in the event of war. Fearful that changes in these plans would cause chaos in the armed forces, military leaders insisted that their plans could not be altered. In the crises during the summer of 1914, the generals' lack of flexibility forced European political leaders to make decisions for military instead of political reasons.

The Outbreak of War: Summer 1914

Militarism, nationalism, and the desire to stifle internal dissent may all have played a role in the coming of World

MAP 23.1 **Europe in 1914.** By 1914, two alliances dominated Europe: the Triple Entente of Britain, France, and Russia and the Triple Alliance of Germany, Austria-Hungary, and Italy. Russia sought to bolster fellow Slavs in Serbia, whereas Austria-Hungary was intent on increasing its power in the Balkans and thwarting Serbia's ambitions. Thus, the Balkans became the flash point for World War I.

Q Which nonaligned nations were positioned between the two alliances?

View an animated version of this map or related maps at www.cengage.com/history/duikspiel/essentialworld6e

The British ambassador to Vienna wrote in 1913:

> Serbia will some day set Europe by the ears, and bring about a universal war on the Continent.... I cannot tell you how exasperated people are getting here at the continual worry which that little country causes to Austria under encouragement from Russia.... It will be lucky if Europe succeeds in avoiding war as a result of the present crisis. The next time a Serbian crisis arises..., I feel sure that Austria-Hungary will refuse to admit of any Russian interference in the dispute and that she will proceed to settle her differences with her little neighbor by herself.[2]

It was against this backdrop of mutual distrust and hatred that the events of the summer of 1914 were played out.

Assassination of Francis Ferdinand
The assassination of the Austrian Archduke Francis Ferdinand and his wife, Sophia, on June 28, 1914, was carried out by a Bosnian activist who worked for the Black Hand, a Serbian terrorist organization dedicated to the creation of a pan-Slavic kingdom. The Austrian government saw an opportunity to "render Serbia innocuous once and for all by a display of force," as the Austrian foreign minister put it. Fearful of Russian intervention on Serbia's behalf, Austrian leaders sought the backing of their German allies. Emperor William II and his chancellor gave their assurance that Austria-Hungary could rely on Germany's "full support," even if "matters went to the length of a war between Austria-Hungary and Russia."

Strengthened by German support, Austrian leaders issued an ultimatum to Serbia on July 23 in which they made such extreme demands that Serbia had little choice but to reject some of them in order to preserve its sovereignty. Austria then declared war on Serbia on July 28. But Russia was determined to support Serbia's cause, and on July 28, Tsar Nicholas II ordered partial mobilization of the Russian army against Austria. The Russian general staff informed the tsar that their mobilization plans were based on a war against both Germany and Austria

War I, but the decisions made by European leaders in the summer of 1914 directly precipitated the conflict. It was another crisis in the Balkans that forced this predicament on European statesmen.

As we have seen, states in southeastern Europe had struggled to free themselves from Ottoman rule in the course of the nineteenth and early twentieth centuries. But the rivalry between Austria-Hungary and Russia for domination of these new states created serious tensions in the region. By 1914, Serbia, supported by Russia, was determined to create a large, independent Slavic state in the Balkans, while Austria-Hungary, which had its own Slavic minorities to contend with, was equally set on preventing that possibility. Many Europeans perceived the inherent dangers in this explosive situation.

simultaneously. They could not execute partial mobilization without creating chaos in the army. Consequently, the Russian government ordered full mobilization of the Russian army on July 29, knowing that the Germans would consider this an act of war against them. Germany reacted quickly. It issued an ultimatum that Russia must halt its mobilization within twelve hours. When the Russians ignored it, Germany declared war on Russia on August 1.

Impact of the Schlieffen Plan At this stage of the conflict, German war plans determined whether France would become involved in the war. Under the guidance of General Alfred von Schlieffen, chief of staff from 1891 to 1905, the German general staff had devised a military plan based on the assumption of a two-front war with France and Russia, because the two powers had formed a military alliance in 1894. The Schlieffen Plan called for a small holding action against Russia while most of the German army would make a rapid invasion of France before Russia could become effective in the east or before the British could cross the English Channel to help France. This meant invading France by advancing along the level coastal area in neutral Belgium where the army could move faster than on the rougher terrain to the southeast. After the planned quick defeat of the French, the German army expected to redeploy to the east against Russia. Under the Schlieffen Plan, Germany could not mobilize its troops solely against Russia and therefore declared war on France on August 3 after it had issued an ultimatum to Belgium on August 2 demanding the right of German troops to pass through Belgian territory. On August 4, Great Britain declared war on Germany, officially over this violation of Belgian neutrality but in fact over the British desire to maintain its world power. As one British diplomat argued, if Germany and Austria would win the war, "what would be the position of a friendless England?" By August 4, all the great powers of Europe were at war.

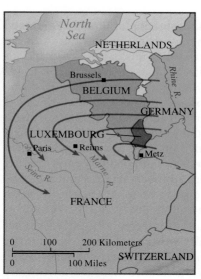

The Schlieffen Plan

The Great War

Q Focus Questions: Why did the course of World War I turn out to be so different from what the belligerents had expected? How did World War I affect the belligerents' governmental and political institutions, economic affairs, and social life?

Before 1914, many political leaders had become convinced that war involved so many political and economic risks that it was not worth fighting. Others had believed that "rational" diplomats could control any situation and prevent the outbreak of war. At the beginning of August 1914, both of these prewar illusions were shattered, but the new illusions that replaced them soon proved to be equally foolish.

1914–1915: Illusions and Stalemate

Europeans went to war in 1914 with great enthusiasm (see the box on p. 569). Government propaganda had been successful in stirring up national antagonisms before the war. Now in August 1914, the urgent pleas of governments for defense against aggressors fell on receptive ears in every belligerent nation. A new set of illusions also fed the enthusiasm for war. Almost everyone in August 1914 believed that the war would be over in a few weeks. People were reminded that all European wars since 1815 had, in fact, ended in a matter of weeks. Both the soldiers who exuberantly boarded the trains for the war front in August 1914 and the jubilant citizens who bombarded them with flowers when they departed believed that the warriors would be home by Christmas.

German hopes for a quick end to the war rested on a military gamble. The Schlieffen Plan had called for the German army to make a vast circling movement through Belgium into northern France and then sweep around Paris and surround most of the French army (see Map 23.2). But the German advance was halted only 20 miles from Paris at the First Battle of the Marne (September 6–10). The war quickly turned into a stalemate as neither the Germans nor the French could dislodge each other from the trenches they had begun to dig for shelter.

In contrast to the Western Front, the war in the east was marked by much more mobility, although the cost in lives was equally enormous. At the beginning of the war, the Russian army moved into eastern Germany but was decisively defeated at the Battle of Tannenberg on August 30 and the Battle of the Masurian Lakes on September 15. The Russians were no longer a threat to German territory.

The Austrians, Germany's allies, fared less well initially. They had been defeated by the Russians in Galicia and thrown out of Serbia as well. To make matters worse,

THE EXCITEMENT OF WAR

The incredible outpouring of patriotic enthusiasm that greeted the declaration of war at the beginning of August 1914 demonstrated the power that nationalistic feeling had attained at the beginning of the twentieth century. Many Europeans seemingly believed that the war had given them a higher purpose, a renewed dedication to the greatness of their nations. These selections are taken from three sources: the autobiography of Stefan Zweig, an Austrian writer; the memoirs of Robert Graves, a British writer; and a letter by a German soldier, Walter Limmer, to his parents.

Stefan Zweig, *The World of Yesterday*

The next morning I was in Austria. In every station placards had been put up announcing general mobilization. The trains were filled with fresh recruits, banners were flying, music sounded, and in Vienna I found the entire city in a tumult.... There were parades in the street, flags, ribbons, and music burst forth everywhere, young recruits were marching triumphantly, their faces lighting up at the cheering....

And to be truthful, I must acknowledge that there was a majestic, rapturous, and even seductive something in this first outbreak of the people from which one could escape only with difficulty. And in spite of all my hatred and aversion for war, I should not like to have missed the memory of those days. As never before, thousands and hundreds of thousands felt what they should have felt in peace time, that they belonged together. A city of two million, a country of nearly fifty million, in that hour felt that they were participating in world history, in a moment which would never recur, and that each one was called upon to cast his infinitesimal self into the glowing mass, there to be purified of all selfishness. All differences of class, rank, and language were flooded over at that moment by the rushing feeling of fraternity....

What did the great mass know of war in 1914, after nearly half a century of peace? They did not know war, they had hardly given it a thought. It had become legendary, and distance had made it seem romantic and heroic. They still saw it in the perspective of their school readers and of paintings in museums; brilliant cavalry attacks in glittering uniforms, the fatal shot always straight through the heart, the entire campaign a resounding march of victory—"We'll be home at Christmas," the recruits shouted laughingly to their mothers in August of 1914.... A rapid excursion into the romantic, a wild, manly adventure—that is how the war of 1914 was painted in the imagination of the simple man, and the younger people were honestly afraid that they might miss this most wonderful and exciting experience of their lives; that is why they hurried and thronged to the colors, and that is why they shouted and sang in the trains that carried them to the slaughter; wildly and feverishly the red wave of blood coursed through the veins of the entire nation.

Robert Graves, *Goodbye to All That*

I had just finished with Charterhouse and gone up to Harlech, when England declared war on Germany. A day or two later I decided to enlist. In the first place, though the papers predicted only a very short war—over by Christmas at the outside—I hoped that it might last long enough to delay my going to Oxford in October, which I dreaded. Nor did I work out the possibilities of getting actively engaged in the fighting, expecting garrison service at home, while the regular forces were away. In the second place, I was outraged to read of the Germans' cynical violation of Belgian neutrality. Though I discounted perhaps twenty per cent of the atrocity details as wartime exaggeration, that was not, of course, sufficient.

Walter Limmer, Letter to His Parents

In any case I mean to go into this business.... That is the simple duty of every one of us. And this feeling is universal among the soldiers, especially since the night when England's declaration of war was announced in the barracks. We none of us got to sleep till three o'clock in the morning, we were so full of excitement, fury, and enthusiasm. It is a joy to go to the Front with such comrades. We are bound to be victorious! Nothing else is possible in the face of such determination to win.

Q *After reading these three selections, what do you think it is about war that creates such feelings of patriotism and enthusiasm? Why do you think peace was a less effective unifier of countries? Is this still true today?*

---

the Italians betrayed the Germans and Austrians and entered the war on the Allied side by attacking Austria in May 1915. (France, Great Britain, and Russia were called the Allied Powers, or Allies.) By this time, the Germans had come to the aid of the Austrians. A German-Austrian army routed the Russian army in Galicia and pushed the Russians back 300 miles into their own territory. Russian casualties stood at 2.5 million killed, captured, or wounded; the Russians had almost been knocked out of the war. Buoyed by their success, the Germans and Austrians, joined by the Bulgarians in September 1915, attacked Serbia and eliminated it from the war.

1916–1917: The Great Slaughter

The successes in the east enabled the Germans to move back to the offensive in the west. The early trenches dug in 1914, stretching from the English Channel to the frontiers of Switzerland, had by now become elaborate systems of defense. Both lines of trenches were protected

MAP 23.2 **World War I, 1914–1918.** This map shows how greatly the Western and Eastern Fronts of World War I differed. After initial German gains in the west, the war became bogged down in trench warfare, with little change in the battle lines between 1914 and 1918. The Eastern Front was marked by considerable mobility, with battle lines shifting by hundreds of miles.

Q How do you explain the difference in the two fronts?

🐚 **View an animated version of this map or related maps at** www.cengage.com/history/ duikspiel/essentialworld6e

by barbed-wire entanglements 3 to 5 feet high and 30 yards wide, concrete machine-gun nests, and mortar batteries, supported farther back by heavy artillery. Troops lived in holes in the ground, separated from each other by a "no-man's land."

The development of **trench warfare** on the Western Front baffled military leaders, who had been trained to fight wars of movement and maneuver. Periodically, the high command on either side would order an offensive that would begin with an artillery barrage to flatten the enemy's barbed wire and leave the enemy in a state of shock. After "softening up" the enemy in this fashion, a mass of soldiers would climb out of their trenches with fixed bayonets and hope to work their way toward the enemy trenches. The attacks rarely worked, as the machine gun put hordes of men advancing unprotected across open fields at a severe disadvantage. In 1916 and 1917, millions of young men were sacrificed in the search

THE REALITY OF WAR: TRENCH WARFARE

The romantic illusions about the excitement and adventure of war that filled the minds of so many young men as they marched off to battle quickly disintegrated after a short time in the trenches on the Western Front. This description of trench warfare is taken from the most famous novel that emerged from World War I, Erich Maria Remarque's *All Quiet on the Western Front,* published in 1929. Remarque had fought in the trenches in France.

Erich Maria Remarque, *All Quiet on the Western Front*

We wake up in the middle of the night. The earth booms. Heavy fire is falling on us. We crouch into corners. We distinguish shells of every calibre.

Each man lays hold of his things and looks again every minute to reassure himself that they are still there. The dugout heaves, the night roars and flashes. We look at each other in the momentary flashes of light, and with pale faces and pressed lips shake our heads.

Every man is aware of the heavy shells tearing down the parapet, rooting up the embankment and demolishing the upper layers of concrete.... Already by morning a few of the recruits are green and vomiting. They are too inexperienced....

The bombardment does not diminish. It is falling in the rear too. As far as one can see it spouts fountains of mud and iron. A wide belt is being raked.

The attack does not come, but the bombardment continues. Slowly we become mute. Hardly a man speaks. We cannot make ourselves understood.

Our trench is almost gone. At many places it is only eighteen inches high; it is broken by holes, and craters, and mountains of earth. A shell lands square in front of our post. At once it is dark. We are buried and must dig ourselves out....

Towards morning, while it is still dark, there is some excitement. Through the entrance rushes in a swarm of fleeing rats that try to storm the walls. Torches light up the confusion. Everyone yells and curses and slaughters. The madness and despair of many hours unloads itself in this outburst. Faces are distorted, arms strike out, the beasts scream; we just stop in time to avoid attacking one another....

Suddenly it howls and flashes terrifically, the dugout cracks in all its joints under a direct hit, fortunately only a light one that the concrete blocks are able to withstand. It rings metallically; the walls reel; rifles, helmets, earth, mud, and dust fly everywhere. Sulfur fumes pour in.... The recruit starts to rave again and two others follow suit. One jumps up and rushes out, we have trouble with the other two. I start after the one who escapes and wonder whether to shoot him in the leg—then it shrieks again; I fling myself down and when I stand up the wall of the trench is plastered with smoking splinters, lumps of flesh, and bits of uniform. I scramble back.

The first recruit seems actually to have gone insane. He butts his head against the wall like a goat. We must try tonight to take him to the rear. Meanwhile we bind him, but so that in case of attack he can be released.

Suddenly the nearer explosions cease. The shelling continues but it has lifted and falls behind us; our trench is free. We seize the hand grenades, pitch them out in front of the dugout, and jump after them. The bombardment has stopped and a heavy barrage now falls behind us. The attack has come.

No one would believe that in this howling waste there could still be men; but steel helmets now appear on all sides out of the trench, and fifty yards from us a machine gun is already in position and barking.

The wire entanglements are torn to pieces. Yet they offer some obstacle. We see the storm troops coming. Our artillery opens fire. Machine guns rattle, rifles crack. The charge works its way across. Haie and Kropp begin with the hand grenades. They throw as fast as they can; others pass them, the handles with the strings already pulled. Haie throws seventy-five yards, Kropp sixty; it has been measured; the distance is important. The enemy as they run cannot do much before they are within forty yards.

We recognize the distorted faces, the smooth helmets: they are French. They have already suffered heavily when they reach the remnants of the barbed-wire entanglements. A whole line has gone down before our machine guns; then we have a lot of stoppages and they come nearer.

I see one of them, his face upturned, fall into a wire cradle. His body collapses, his hands remain suspended as though he were praying. Then his body drops clean away and only his hands with the stumps of his arms, shot off, now hang in the wire.

Q *What is causing the "madness and despair" Remarque describes in the trenches? Why does the recruit in this scene apparently go insane?*

for the elusive breakthrough. In ten months at Verdun, 700,000 men lost their lives over a few miles of terrain.

Warfare in the trenches of the Western Front produced unimaginable horrors (see the box above). Battlefields were hellish landscapes of barbed wire, shell holes, mud, and injured and dying men. The introduction of poison gas in 1915 produced new forms of injuries. As one British writer described them:

> I wish those people who write so glibly about this being a holy war could see a case of mustard gas ... could see the poor things burnt and blistered all over with great

mustard-coloured suppurating blisters with blind eyes all sticky . . . and stuck together, and always fighting for breath, with voices a mere whisper, saying that their throats are closing and they know they will choke.[3]

Soldiers in the trenches also lived with the persistent presence of death. Since combat went on for months, soldiers had to carry on in the midst of countless bodies of dead men or the remains of men dismembered by artillery barrages. Many soldiers remembered the stench of decomposing bodies and the swarms of rats that grew fat in the trenches.

The Widening of the War

As another response to the stalemate on the Western Front, both sides sought to gain new allies that might provide a winning advantage. The Ottoman Empire had already come into the war on Germany's side in August 1914. Russia, Great Britain, and France declared war on the Ottoman Empire in November. Although the Allies attempted to open a Balkan front by landing forces at Gallipoli, southwest of Constantinople, in April 1915, the entry of Bulgaria into the war on the side of the Central Powers (as Germany, Austria-Hungary, and the Ottoman Empire were called) and a disastrous campaign at Gallipoli caused them to withdraw.

A Global Conflict The war that originated in Europe rapidly became a world conflict (see the comparative illustration at the right). In the Middle East, a British officer who came to be known as Lawrence of Arabia (1888–1935) incited Arab princes to revolt against their Ottoman overlords in 1917. In 1918, British forces from Egypt destroyed the rest of the Ottoman Empire in the Middle East. For their Middle East campaigns, the British mobilized forces from India, Australia, and New Zealand.

In 1914, Germany possessed four colonies in Africa: Togoland, Cameroons, South West Africa, and German East Africa. British and French forces quickly occupied Togoland in West Africa, but Cameroons was not taken until 1916. British and white African forces invaded South West Africa in 1914 and forced the Germans to surrender in July 1915. The Allied campaign in East Africa proved more difficult and costly, and it was not until 1918 that the German forces surrendered there.

© Bettmann/Corbis

© Getty Images

COMPARATIVE ILLUSTRATION

POLITICS & GOVERNMENT

Soldiers from Around the World. Although World War I began in Europe, it soon became a global conflict fought in different areas of the world and with soldiers from all parts of the world. France, especially, recruited troops from its African colonies to fight in Europe. The photo at the top shows French African troops fighting in the trenches on the Western Front. About 80,000 Africans were killed or injured in Europe. The photo at the bottom shows a group of German soldiers in their machine-gun nest on the Western Front.

Q What do these photographs reveal about the nature of World War I and the role of African troops in the conflict?

In these battles, Allied governments drew mainly on African soldiers, but some states, especially France, also recruited African troops to fight in Europe. The French drafted more than 170,000 West African soldiers. While some served as garrison forces in North Africa, many of the West African troops fought in the trenches on the Western Front. About 80,000 Africans were killed or injured in Europe.

Hundreds of thousands of Africans were also used for labor, especially for carrying supplies and building roads and bridges. In East Africa, both sides drafted African laborers as carriers for their armies. More than 100,000 of these laborers died from disease and starvation resulting from neglect. In East Asia, thousands of Chinese and Indochinese also worked as laborers in European factories.

In East Asia and the Pacific, Japan joined the Allies on August 23, 1914, primarily to seize control of German territories in Asia. The Japanese took possession of German territories in China, as well as the German-occupied Marshall, Mariana, and Caroline Islands. The decision to reward Japan for its cooperation eventually created difficulties in China (see Chapter 24).

Entry of the United States   Most important to the Allied cause was the entry of the United States into the war. American involvement grew out of the naval conflict between Germany and Great Britain. Britain used its superior naval power to maximum effect by setting up a naval blockade of Germany. Germany retaliated by imposing a counterblockade enforced by the use of unrestricted submarine warfare. Strong American protests over the German sinking of passenger liners, especially the British ship *Lusitania* on May 7, 1915, when more than a hundred Americans lost their lives, forced the German government to suspend unrestricted submarine warfare in September 1915.

In January 1917, however, eager to break the deadlock in the war, the Germans decided on another military gamble by returning to unrestricted submarine warfare. German naval officers convinced Emperor William II that the use of unrestricted submarine warfare could starve the British into submission within five months, certainly before the Americans could act. The return to unrestricted submarine warfare brought the United States into the war on April 6, 1917. Although U.S. troops did not arrive in Europe in large numbers until the following year, the entry of the United States into the war gave the Allied Powers a psychological boost when they needed it.

The year 1917 had not been a good year for them. Allied offensives on the Western Front were disastrously defeated. The Italian armies were smashed in October, and in November, the Bolshevik Revolution in Russia (see "The Russian Revolution" later in this chapter) led to Russia's withdrawal from the war, leaving Germany free to concentrate entirely on the Western Front. The cause of the Central Powers looked favorable, although war weariness in the Ottoman Empire, Bulgaria, Austria-Hungary, and Germany was beginning to take its toll.

The home front was rapidly becoming a cause for as much concern as the war front.

The Home Front: The Impact of Total War

The prolongation of World War I made it a **total war** that affected the lives of all citizens, however remote they might be from the battlefields. The need to organize masses of men and matériel for years of combat (Germany alone had 5.5 million men in active units in 1916) led to increased centralization of government powers, economic regimentation, and manipulation of public opinion to keep the war effort going.

Political Centralization and Economic Regimentation
Because the war was expected to be short, little thought had been given to long-term wartime needs. Governments had to respond quickly, however, when the war machines failed to achieve their knockout blows and made ever greater demands for men and matériel. To meet these needs, governments expanded their powers. Countries drafted tens of millions of young men for that elusive breakthrough to victory.

Throughout Europe, wartime governments also expanded their powers over their economies. Free market capitalistic systems were temporarily shelved as governments experimented with price, wage, and rent controls; rationed food supplies and materials; and nationalized transportation systems and industries. Under total war mobilization, the distinction between soldiers at war and civilians at home was narrowed. In the view of political leaders, all citizens constituted a national army.

Control of Public Opinion   As the Great War dragged on and casualties grew worse, the patriotic enthusiasm that had marked the early days of the conflict waned. By 1916, there were numerous signs that civilian morale was beginning to crack under the pressure of total war. Governments took strenuous measures to fight the growing opposition to the war. Even parliamentary regimes resorted to an expansion of police powers to stifle internal dissent. The British Parliament, for example, passed the Defence of the Realm Act (DORA), which allowed the public authorities to arrest dissenters and charge them as traitors. Newspapers were censored, and sometimes their publication was even suspended.

Wartime governments also made active use of propaganda to arouse enthusiasm for the war. At first, public officials needed to do little to achieve this goal. The British and French, for example, exaggerated German atrocities in Belgium and found that their citizens were only too willing to believe these accounts. But as the war dragged on and morale sagged, governments

WOMEN OF BRITAIN SAY — "GO!"

© The Art Archive/Gianni Dagli Orti

British Recruiting Poster. As the conflict persisted month after month, governments resorted to active propaganda campaigns to generate enthusiasm for the war. In this British recruiting poster, the government tried to pressure men into volunteering for military service. By 1916, the British were forced to adopt compulsory military service.

were forced to devise new techniques for stimulating declining enthusiasm.

Women in the War Effort   World War I opened up new roles for women. Because so many men went off to fight at the front, women were called on to take over jobs and responsibilities that had not been available to them before, including jobs that had been considered beyond the "capacity of women." These included such occupations as chimney sweeps, truck drivers, farm laborers, and factory workers in heavy industry (see the box on p. 575). Thirty-eight percent of the workers in the Krupp Armaments works in Germany in 1918 were women. Nevertheless, despite government regulations that brought about a noticeable increase in women's wages, women working in industry never earned as much as men at any time during the war.

Even worse, women's place in the workforce was far from secure. Both men and women seemed to think that many of the new jobs for women were only temporary, an expectation quite evident in the British poem "War Girls," written in 1916:

> There's the girl who clips your ticket for the train,
> And the girl who speeds the lift from floor to floor,
> There's the girl who does a milk-round in the rain,
> And the girl who calls for orders at your door.
> Strong, sensible, and fit,
> They're out to show their grit,
> And tackle jobs with energy and knack.
> No longer caged and penned up,
> They're going to keep their end up
> Till the khaki soldier boys come marching back.[4]

At the end of the war, governments moved quickly to remove women from the jobs they had been encouraged to take earlier, and wages for women who remained employed were lowered.

Nevertheless, in some countries, the role played by women in the wartime economies did have a positive impact on the women's movement for political emancipation. The most obvious gain was the right to vote, granted to women in Britain in January 1918 and in Germany and Austria immediately after the war. Contemporary media, however, tended to focus on the more noticeable yet in some ways more superficial social emancipation of upper- and middle-class women. In ever larger numbers, these young women took jobs, had their own apartments, and showed their new independence by smoking in public, wearing shorter dresses, and adopting radical new hairstyles.

Crisis in Russia and the End of the War

Q **Focus Question:** What were the causes of the Russian Revolution of 1917, and why did the Bolsheviks prevail in the civil war and gain control of Russia?

By 1917, total war was creating serious domestic turmoil in all of the European belligerent states. Only one, however, experienced the kind of complete collapse that others were predicting might happen throughout Europe. Out of Russia's collapse came the Russian Revolution.

The Russian Revolution

Tsar Nicholas II was an autocratic ruler who relied on the army and the bureaucracy to uphold his regime.

WOMEN IN THE FACTORIES

During World War I, women were called on to assume new job responsibilities, including factory work. In this selection, Naomi Loughnan, a young, upper-middle-class woman, describes the experiences in a munitions plant that considerably broadened her perspective on life.

Naomi Loughnan, "Munition Work"

We little thought when we first put on our overalls and caps and enlisted in the Munition Army how much more inspiring our life was to be than we had dared to hope. Though we munition workers sacrifice our ease, we gain a life worth living. Our long days are filled with interest, and with the zest of doing work for our country in the grand cause of Freedom. As we handle the weapons of war we are learning great lessons of life. In the busy, noisy workshops we come face to face with every kind of class, and each one of these classes has something to learn from the others....

Engineering mankind is possessed of the unshakable opinion that no woman can have the mechanical sense. If one of us asks humbly why such and such an alteration is not made to prevent this or that drawback to a machine, she is told, with a superior smile, that a man has worked her machine before her for years, and that therefore if there were any improvement possible it would have been made. As long as we do exactly what we are told and do not attempt to use our brains, we give entire satisfaction, and are treated as nice, good children. Any swerving from the easy path prepared for us by our males arouses the most scathing contempt in their manly bosoms.... Women have, however, proved that their entry into the munition world has increased the output. Employers who forget things personal in their patriotic desire for large results are enthusiastic over the success of women in the shops. But their workmen have to be handled with the utmost tenderness and caution lest they should actually imagine it was being suggested that women could do their work equally well, given equal conditions of training—at least where muscle is not the driving force....

The coming of the mixed classes of women into the factory is slowly but surely having an educative effect upon the men. "Language" is almost unconsciously becoming subdued. There are fiery exceptions, who make our hair stand up on end under our close-fitting caps, but a sharp rebuke or a look of horror will often straighten out the most savage.... It is grievous to hear the girls also swearing and using disgusting language. Shoulder to shoulder with the children of the slums, the upper classes are having their eyes opened at last to the awful conditions among which their sisters have dwelt. Foul language, immorality, and many other evils are but the natural outcome of overcrowding and bitter poverty.... Sometimes disgust will overcome us, but we are learning with painful clarity that the fault is not theirs whose actions disgust us, but must be placed to the discredit of those other classes who have allowed the continued existence of conditions which generate the things from which we shrink appalled.

Q *The two groups Naomi Loughnan observes closely in this passage are men and lower-class women. What did she learn about these groups while working in the munitions factory? What did she learn about herself?*

But World War I magnified Russia's problems and severely challenged the tsarist government. Russian industry was unable to produce the weapons needed for the army. Many soldiers were sent to the front without rifles and told to pick one up from a dead comrade. Ill-led and ill-armed, Russian armies suffered incredible losses. Between 1914 and 1916, two million soldiers were killed, and another four to six million were wounded or captured.

In the meantime, Tsar Nicholas II was increasingly insulated from events by his German-born wife, Alexandra, a well-educated woman who had fallen under the sway of Rasputin, a Siberian peasant whom she regarded as a holy man because he alone seemed able to stop the bleeding of her hemophiliac son. Rasputin's influence with the tsarina made him a power behind the throne, and he did not hesitate to interfere in government affairs. As the leadership at the top experienced a series of military and economic disasters, the middle class, aristocrats, peasants, soldiers, and workers grew more and more disenchanted with the tsarist regime. Even aristocrats who supported the monarchy felt the need to do something to reverse the deteriorating situation. For a start, they assassinated Rasputin in December 1916. But by then, it was too late to save the monarchy.

The March Revolution At the beginning of 1917, a series of strikes led by working-class women broke out in the capital city of Petrograd (formerly Saint Petersburg). A few weeks earlier, the government had introduced bread rationing in the capital city after the price of bread had skyrocketed. Many of the women who stood in the lines waiting for bread were also factory workers who had put in twelve-hour days. The Russian government soon became aware of the volatile situation in the capital. One police report stated: "Mothers of families, exhausted by endless standing in line at stores, distraught over their half-starving and sick children, are today perhaps closer to revolution than [the liberal opposition leaders] and of course they are a great deal more dangerous because they are the combustible material for which only a single spark is needed to burst into flame."[5] On March 8, a day celebrated since 1910 as International Women's Day, about 10,000 women marched through Petrograd demanding "peace and bread." Soon the women were joined by other workers, and together they called for a general strike that succeeded in shutting down all the factories in the city on March 10. Nicholas ordered his troops to disperse the crowds by shooting them if necessary, but large numbers of the soldiers soon joined the demonstrators. The Duma (legislature), which the tsar had tried to dissolve, met anyway and on March 12 declared that it was assuming governmental responsibility. It established a provisional government on March 15; the tsar abdicated the same day.

The Provisional Government, which came to be led in July by Alexander Kerensky, decided to carry on the war to preserve Russia's honor—a major blunder because it satisfied neither the workers nor the peasants, who wanted more than anything an end to the war. The Provisional Government also faced another authority, the **soviets,** or councils of workers' and soldiers' deputies. The soviet of Petrograd had been formed in March 1917; at the same time, soviets sprang up spontaneously in army units, factory towns, and rural areas. The soviets represented the more radical interests of the lower classes and were largely composed of socialists of various kinds. One group—the Bolsheviks—came to play a crucial role.

Lenin and the Bolshevik Revolution The Bolsheviks were a small faction of Russian Social Democrats who had come under the leadership of Vladimir Ulianov, known to the world as V. I. Lenin (1870–1924). Under Lenin's direction, the Bolsheviks became a party dedicated to violent revolution. He believed that only a revolution could destroy the capitalist system and that a "vanguard" of activists must form a small party of well-disciplined professional revolutionaries to accomplish this task. Between 1900 and 1917, Lenin spent most of his time in exile in Switzerland. When the Provisional Government was set up in March 1917, he believed that an opportunity for the Bolsheviks to seize power had come. A month later, with the connivance of the German High Command, which hoped to create disorder in Russia, Lenin was shipped to Russia in a "sealed train" by way of Finland.

Lenin believed that the Bolsheviks must work toward gaining control of the soviets of soldiers, workers, and peasants and then use them to overthrow the Provisional Government. At the same time, the Bolsheviks sought mass support through promises geared to the needs of the people: an end to the war, redistribution of all land to the peasants, the transfer of factories and industries from capitalists to committees of workers, and the relegation of

government power from the Provisional Government to the soviets. Three simple slogans summed up the Bolshevik program: "Peace, Land, Bread," "Worker Control of Production," and "All Power to the Soviets."

By the end of October, the Bolsheviks had achieved a slight majority in the Petrograd and Moscow soviets. The number of party members had also grown from 50,000 to 240,000. With Leon Trotsky (1877–1940), a fervid revolutionary, as chairman of the Petrograd soviet, Lenin and the Bolsheviks were in a position to seize power in the name of the soviets. During the night of November 6, pro-soviet and pro-Bolshevik forces took control of Petrograd. The Provisional Government quickly collapsed, with little bloodshed. The following night, the All-Russian Congress of Soviets, representing local soviets from all over the country, affirmed the transfer of power. At the second session, on the night of November 8, Lenin announced the new Soviet government, the Council of People's Commissars, with himself as its head.

But the Bolsheviks, soon renamed the Communists, still faced enormous obstacles. For one thing, Lenin had promised peace, and that, he realized, was not an easy promise to fulfill because of the humiliating losses of Russian territory that it would entail. There was no real choice, however. On March 3, 1918, Lenin signed the Treaty of Brest-Litovsk with Germany and gave up eastern Poland, Ukraine, and the Baltic provinces. He had promised peace to the Russian people; but real peace did not come, for the country soon sank into civil war.

Civil War There was great opposition to the new Communist regime, not only from groups loyal to the tsar but also from bourgeois and aristocratic liberals and anti-Leninist socialists. In addition, thousands of Allied troops were eventually sent to different parts of Russia.

Between 1918 and 1921, the Communist (Red) Army was forced to fight on many fronts. The first serious threat to the Communists came from Siberia, where a White (anti-Communist) force attacked westward and advanced almost to the Volga River. Attacks also came from the Ukrainians in the southwest and from the Baltic regions. In mid-1919, White forces swept through Ukraine and advanced almost to Moscow before being pushed back. By 1920, the major White forces had been defeated, and Ukraine had been retaken. The next year, the Communist regime regained control over the independent nationalist governments in the Caucasus: Georgia, Russian Armenia, and Azerbaijan.

How had Lenin and the Bolsheviks triumphed over what seemed at one time to be overwhelming forces? For one thing, the Red Army became a well-disciplined fighting force, largely due to the organizational genius of Leon Trotsky. As commissar of war, Trotsky reinstated the

Lenin and Trotsky. Vladimir Lenin and Leon Trotsky were important figures in the Bolsheviks' successful seizure of power in Russia. On the left, Lenin is seen addressing a rally in Moscow in 1917. On the right, Trotsky, who became commissar of war in the new regime, is shown haranguing his troops.

draft and insisted on rigid discipline; soldiers who deserted or refused to obey orders were summarily executed.

In addition, the disunity of the anti-Communist forces seriously weakened the efforts of the Whites. Political differences created distrust among the Whites and prevented them from cooperating effectively. It was difficult enough to achieve military cooperation; political differences made it virtually impossible. The lack of a common goal on the part of the Whites was in sharp contrast to the single-minded sense of purpose of the Communists.

The Communists also succeeded in translating their revolutionary faith into practical instruments of power. A policy of **"war communism,"** for example, was used to ensure regular supplies for the Red Army. "War communism" included the nationalization of banks and most industries, the forcible requisition of grain from peasants, and the centralization of state power under Bolshevik control. Another Bolshevik instrument was "revolutionary terror." A new Red secret police—known as the Cheka—instituted the Red Terror, aimed at nothing less than the destruction of all who opposed the new regime.

Finally, the intervention of foreign armies enabled the Communists to appeal to the powerful force of Russian patriotism. Appalled by the takeover of power in Russia by the radical Communists, the Allied Powers intervened. At one point, more than 100,000 foreign troops—mostly Japanese, British, American, and French—were stationed on Russian soil. This intervention by the Allies enabled the Communist government to appeal to patriotic Russians to fight the attempts of foreigners to control their country.

By 1921, the Communists were in control of Russia. In the course of the civil war, the Communist regime had also transformed Russia into a bureaucratically centralized state dominated by a single party. It was also a state that was largely hostile to the Allied Powers that had sought to assist the Communists' enemies in the civil war.

The Last Year of the War

For Germany, the withdrawal of the Russians in March 1918 offered renewed hope for a favorable end to the war. The victory over Russia persuaded Erich von Ludendorff (1865–1937), who guided German military operations, and most German leaders to make one final military gamble—a grand offensive in the west to break the military stalemate. The German attack was launched in March and

	1914
Battle of Tannenberg	August 26–30
First Battle of the Marne	September 6–10
Battle of Masurian Lakes	September 15
	1915
Battle of Gallipoli begins	April 25
Italy declares war on Austria-Hungary	May 23
	1916
Battle of Verdun	February 21–December 18
	1917
United States enters the war	April 6
	1918
Last German offensive	March 21–July 18
Second Battle of the Marne	July 18
Allied counteroffensive	July 18–November 10
Armistice between Allies and Germany	November 11

lasted into July, but an Allied counterattack, supported by the arrival of 140,000 fresh American troops, defeated the Germans at the Second Battle of the Marne on July 18. Ludendorff's gamble had failed.

On September 29, 1918, General Ludendorff informed German leaders that the war was lost and insisted that the government sue for peace at once. When German officials discovered, however, that the Allies were unwilling to make peace with the autocratic imperial government, reforms were instituted to create a liberal government. Meanwhile, popular demonstrations broke out throughout Germany. William II capitulated to public pressure and abdicated on November 9, and the Socialists under Friedrich Ebert (1871–1925) announced the establishment of a republic. Two days later, on November 11, 1918, the new German government agreed to an armistice. The war was over.

The Casualties of the War World War I devastated European civilization. Between 8 and 9 million soldiers died on the battlefields; another 22 million were wounded. Many of the survivors died later from war injuries or lived on without arms or legs or with other forms of mutilation. The birthrate in many European countries declined noticeably as a result of the death or maiming of so many young men. World War I also created a lost generation of war veterans who had become accustomed

to violence and who would later band together in support of Mussolini and Hitler in their bids for power.

Nor did the killing affect only soldiers. Untold numbers of civilians died from war injuries or starvation. In 1915, after an Armenian uprising against the Ottoman government, the government retaliated with fury by killing Armenian men and expelling women and children. Within seven months, 600,000 Armenians had been killed, and 500,000 had been deported. Of the latter, 400,000 died while marching through the deserts and swamps of Syria and Mesopotamia. By September 1915, an estimated one million Armenians were dead, the victims of genocide.

The Peace Settlement

In January 1919, the delegations of twenty-seven victorious Allied nations gathered in Paris to conclude a final settlement of the Great War. Over a period of years, the reasons for fighting World War I had been transformed from selfish national interests to idealistic principles. No one expressed the latter better than the U.S. president Woodrow Wilson (1856–1924). Wilson's proposals for a truly just and lasting peace included "open covenants of peace, openly arrived at" instead of secret diplomacy; the reduction of national armaments to a "point consistent with domestic safety"; and the self-determination of people so that "all well-defined national aspirations shall be accorded the utmost satisfaction." As the spokesman for a new world order based on democracy and international cooperation, Wilson was enthusiastically cheered by many Europeans when he arrived in Europe for the peace conference.

Wilson soon found, however, that more practical motives guided other states at the Paris Peace Conference. The secret treaties and agreements that had been made before the war could not be totally ignored, even if they did conflict with the principle of self-determination enunciated by Wilson. National interests also complicated the deliberations of the Paris Peace Conference. David Lloyd George (1863–1945), prime minister of Great Britain, had won a decisive electoral victory in December 1918 on a platform of making the Germans pay for this dreadful war.

France's approach to peace was primarily determined by considerations of national security. To Georges Clemenceau (1841–1929), the feisty premier of France who had led his country to victory, the French people had borne the brunt of German aggression. They deserved revenge and security against future German aggression.

The most important decisions at the Paris Peace Conference were made by Wilson, Clemenceau, and Lloyd George. In the end, only compromise made it possible to achieve a peace settlement. Wilson's wish that

MAP 23.3 **Territorial Changes in Europe and the Middle East After World War I.** The victorious Allies met in Paris to determine the shape and nature of postwar Europe. At the urging of U.S. President Woodrow Wilson, many nationalist aspirations of former imperial subjects were realized with the creation of several new countries from the prewar territory of Austria-Hungary, Germany, Russia, and the Ottoman Empire.

Q What new countries emerged in Europe and the Middle East?

View an animated version of this map or related maps at www.cengage.com/history/ duikspiel/essentialworld6e

the creation of an international peacekeeping organization be the first order of business was granted, and already on January 25, 1919, the conference adopted the principle of the League of Nations. In return, Wilson agreed to make compromises on territorial arrangements to guarantee the establishment of the League, believing that a functioning League could later rectify bad arrangements.

The Treaty of Versailles The final peace settlement consisted of five separate treaties with the defeated nations—Germany, Austria, Hungary, Bulgaria, and Turkey. The Treaty of Versailles with Germany, signed on June 28, 1919, was by far the most important. The Germans considered it a harsh peace and were particularly unhappy with Article 231, the so-called **War Guilt Clause,** which declared Germany (and Austria) responsible for starting the war and ordered Germany to pay **reparations** for all the damage to which the Allied governments and their people were subjected as a result of the war.

The military and territorial provisions of the treaty also rankled Germans. Germany had to reduce its army to 100,000 men, cut back its navy, and eliminate its air force. German territorial losses included the return of Alsace and Lorraine to France and sections of Prussia to the new Polish state (see Map 23.3). German land west and as far as 30 miles east of the Rhine was established as a demilitarized zone and stripped of all armaments or fortifications to serve as a barrier to any future German military moves westward against France. Outraged by the "dictated peace," the new German government complained but accepted the treaty.

The Other Peace Treaties The separate peace treaties made with the other Central Powers extensively redrew the map of eastern Europe. Many of these changes merely ratified what the war had already accomplished. Both the German and Russian Empires lost considerable territory in eastern Europe, and the Austro-Hungarian Empire disappeared altogether. New nation-states emerged from the lands of these three empires: Finland, Latvia, Estonia, Lithuania, Poland, Czechoslovakia, Austria, and Hungary. Territorial rearrangements were also made in the Balkans. Serbia formed the nucleus of a new southern Slavic state, called Yugoslavia, which combined Serbs, Croats, and Slovenes.

Although the Paris Peace Conference was supposedly guided by the principle of self-determination, the mixtures of peoples in eastern Europe made it impossible to draw boundaries along neat ethnic lines. As a result of compromises, virtually every eastern European state was left with a minorities problem that could lead to future conflicts. Germans in Poland; Hungarians, Poles, and Germans in Czechoslovakia; Hungarians in Romania; and the combination of Serbs, Croats, Slovenes, Macedonians, and Albanians in Yugoslavia all became sources of later conflict.

Yet another centuries-old empire, the Ottoman Empire, was dismembered by the peace settlement after the war. To gain Arab support against the Ottoman Turks during the war, the Western Allies had promised to recognize the independence of Arab states in the Middle Eastern lands of the Ottoman Empire. But the imperialist habits of Western nations died hard. After the war, France was given control of Lebanon and Syria, while Britain received Iraq and Palestine. Officially, both acquisitions were called **mandates,** a system whereby a nation officially administered a territory on behalf of the League of Nations. The system of mandates could not hide the fact that the principle of national self-determination at the Paris Peace Conference was largely for Europeans.

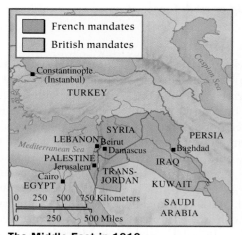

French mandates

British mandates

The Middle East in 1919

An Uncertain Peace

Q Focus Question: What problems did Europe and the United States face in the 1920s?

Four years of devastating war had left many Europeans with a profound sense of despair and disillusionment. The Great War indicated to many people that something was dreadfully wrong with Western values. In *The Decline of the West,* the German writer Oswald Spengler (1880–1936) reflected this disillusionment when he emphasized the decadence of Western civilization and posited its collapse.

The Search for Security

The peace settlement at the end of World War I had tried to fulfill the nineteenth-century dream of nationalism by creating new boundaries and new states. From its inception, however, this peace settlement had left nations unhappy and only too eager to revise it.

U.S. President Woodrow Wilson had recognized that the peace treaties contained unwise provisions that could serve as new causes for conflicts, and he had placed many of his hopes for the future in the League of Nations. The League, however, was not particularly effective in maintaining the peace. The failure of the United States to join the League in a backlash of isolationist sentiment undermined its effectiveness from the beginning. Moreover, the League could use only economic sanctions to halt aggression.

France's search for security between 1919 and 1924 was founded primarily on a strict enforcement of the Treaty of Versailles. This tough policy toward Germany began with the issue of reparations, the payments that the Germans were supposed to make to compensate for war damage. In April 1921, the Allied Reparations Commission settled on a sum of 132 billion marks ($33 billion) for German reparations, payable in annual installments of 2.5 billion (gold) marks. The new German republic made its first payment in 1921, but by the following year, facing financial problems, the German government announced that it was unable to pay more. Outraged, the French government sent troops to occupy the Ruhr valley, Germany's chief industrial and mining center. If the Germans would not pay reparations, the French would collect reparations in kind by operating and using the Ruhr mines and factories.

Both Germany and France suffered from the French occupation of the Ruhr. The German government adopted a policy of passive resistance to French occupation that was largely financed by printing more paper money. This only intensified the inflationary pressures that had already begun in Germany by the end of the war. The German mark became worthless, and economic disaster fueled political upheavals. All the nations, including France, were happy to cooperate with the American suggestion for a new conference of experts to reassess the reparations problem.

In August 1924, an international commission produced a new plan for reparations. The Dawes Plan, named after the American banker who chaired the commission, reduced the reparations and stabilized Germany's payments on the basis of its ability to pay. The Dawes Plan also granted an initial $200 million loan for German recovery, which opened the door to heavy American investments in Europe that helped create a new era of European prosperity between 1924 and 1929.

With prosperity came a new age of European diplomacy. A spirit of cooperation was fostered by the foreign ministers of Germany and France, Gustav Stresemann and Aristide Briand, who concluded the Treaty of Locarno in 1925. This guaranteed Germany's new western borders with France and Belgium. Although Germany's new eastern borders with Poland were conspicuously absent from the agreement, the Locarno pact was viewed by many as the beginning of a new era of European peace.

The spirit of Locarno was based on little real substance, however. Germany lacked the military power to alter its western borders even if it wanted to. And the issue of disarmament soon proved that even the spirit of Locarno could not bring nations to cut back on their weapons. Germany, of course, had been disarmed with the expectation that other states would do likewise. Numerous disarmament conferences, however, failed to achieve anything substantial as states were unwilling to trust their security to anyone but their own military forces.

The Great Depression

Almost as devastating as the two world wars in the first half of the twentieth century was the economic collapse that ravaged the world in the 1930s. Two events set the stage for the Great Depression: a downturn in domestic economic activities and an international financial crisis precipitated by the collapse of the American stock market in 1929.

Already in the mid-1920s, prices for agricultural goods were beginning to decline rapidly due to overproduction of basic commodities, such as wheat. In addition to domestic economic troubles, much of the European prosperity between 1924 and 1929 had been built on American bank loans to Germany. The crash of the U.S. stock market in October 1929 led panicky American investors to withdraw many of their funds from Germany and other European markets. The withdrawal of funds seriously weakened the banks of Germany and other central European states. By 1931, trade was slowing down, industrialists were cutting back production, and unemployment was increasing as the effects of international bank failures had a devastating impact on domestic economies.

Economic depression was by no means a new phenomenon in European history, but the depth of the economic downturn after 1929 fully justifies the label Great Depression. During 1932, the worst year of the depression, one British worker in four was unemployed; in Germany, six million people, 40 percent of the labor force, were out of work. The unemployed and homeless filled the streets of the cities of the advanced industrial countries (see the box on p. 582).

Great Depression: Bread Lines in Paris. The Great Depression devastated the European economy and had serious political repercussions. Because of its more balanced economy, France did not feel the effects of the depression as quickly as other European countries. By 1931, however, even France was experiencing lines of unemployed people at free-food centers.

THE GREAT DEPRESSION: UNEMPLOYED AND HOMELESS IN GERMANY

FAMILY & SOCIETY

In 1932, Germany had six million unemployed workers, many of them wandering aimlessly about the country, begging for food and seeking shelter in city lodging houses for the homeless. The Great Depression was an important factor in the rise to power of Adolf Hitler and the Nazis. This selection presents a description of the unemployed homeless in 1932.

Heinrich Hauser, "With Germany's Unemployed"

An almost unbroken chain of homeless men extends the whole length of the great Hamburg-Berlin highway.... All the highways in Germany over which I have traveled this year presented the same aspect....

Most of the hikers paid no attention to me. They walked separately or in small groups, with their eyes on the ground. And they had the queer, stumbling gait of barefooted people, for their shoes were slung over their shoulders. Some of them were guild members—carpenters ... milkmen ... and bricklayers ... but they were in a minority. Far more numerous were those whom one could assign to no special profession or craft—unskilled young people, for the most part, who had been unable to find a place for themselves in any city or town in Germany, and who had never had a job and never expected to have one. There was something else that had never been seen before—whole families that had piled all their goods into baby carriages and wheelbarrows that they were pushing along as they plodded forward in dumb despair. It was a whole nation on the march.

I saw them—and this was the strongest impression that the year 1932 left with me—I saw them, gathered into groups of fifty or a hundred men, attacking fields of potatoes. I saw them digging up the potatoes and throwing them into sacks while the farmer who owned the field watched them in despair and the local policeman looked on gloomily from the distance. I saw them staggering toward the lights of the city as night fell, with their sacks on their backs. What did it remind me of? Of the War, of the worst periods of starvation in 1917 and 1918, but even then people paid for the potatoes....

I saw that the individual can know what is happening only by personal experience. I know what it is to be a tramp. I know what cold and hunger are.... But there are two things that I have only recently experienced—begging and spending the night in a municipal lodging house.

I entered the huge Berlin municipal lodging house in a northern quarter of the city....

Distribution of spoons, distribution of enameled-ware bowls with the words "Property of the City of Berlin" written on their sides. Then the meal itself. A big kettle is carried in. Men with yellow smocks have brought it in, and men with yellow smocks ladle out the food. These men, too, are homeless and they have been expressly picked by the establishment and given free food and lodging and a little pocket money in exchange for their work about the house.

Where have I seen this kind of food distribution before? In a prison that I once helped to guard in the winter of 1919 during the German civil war. There was the same hunger then, the same trembling, anxious expectation of rations. Now the men are standing in a long row, dressed in their plain nightshirts that reach to the ground, and the noise of their shuffling feet is like the noise of big wild animals walking up and down the stone floor of their cages before feeding time. The men lean far over the kettle so that the warm steam from the food envelops them, and they hold out their bowls as if begging and whisper to the attendant, "Give me a real helping. Give me a little more." A piece of bread is handed out with every bowl.

My next recollection is sitting at table in another room on a crowded bench that is like a seat in a fourth-class railway carriage. Hundreds of hungry mouths make an enormous noise eating their food. The men sit bent over their food like animals who feel that someone is going to take it away from them. They hold their bowl with their left arm partway around it, so that nobody can take it away, and they also protect it with their other elbow and with their head and mouth, while they move the spoon as fast as they can between their mouth and the bowl.

Q *Why did Hauser compare the scene he describes from 1932 with the experiences of 1917 and 1918? Why did he compare the hungry men to animals?*

Governments seemed powerless to deal with the crisis. The classic liberal remedy for depression, a deflationary policy of balanced budgets, which involved cutting costs by lowering wages and raising tariffs to exclude other countries' goods from home markets, only served to worsen the economic crisis and cause even greater mass discontent. This in turn led to serious political repercussions. Increased government activity in the economy was one reaction.

Another effect was a renewed interest in Marxist doctrines. Hadn't Marx predicted that capitalism would destroy itself through overproduction? Communism took on new popularity, especially with workers and intellectuals. Finally, the Great Depression increased the attractiveness of facile dictatorial solutions, especially from a new movement known as fascism. Everywhere, democracy seemed on the defensive in the 1930s.

The Democratic States

After World War I, Great Britain went through a period of serious economic difficulties. During the war, Britain had lost many of the markets for its industrial products, especially to the United States and Japan. The postwar decline of such staple industries as coal, steel, and textiles led to a rise in unemployment, which reached the two million mark in 1921. But Britain soon rebounded and from 1925 to 1929 experienced an era of renewed prosperity.

By 1929, however, Britain faced the growing effects of the Great Depression. A national government (a coalition of Liberals and Conservatives) claimed credit for bringing Britain out of the worst stages of the depression, primarily by using the traditional policies of balanced budgets and protective tariffs. British politicians had largely ignored the new ideas of a Cambridge economist, John Maynard Keynes (1883–1946), who published his *General Theory of Employment, Interest and Money* in 1936. He condemned the traditional view that in a free economy, depressions should be left to work themselves out. Keynes argued that unemployment stemmed not from overproduction but from a decline in demand and maintained that demand could be increased by putting people back to work building highways and public structures, even if governments had to go into debt to pay for these works, a concept known as **deficit spending.**

After the defeat of Germany, France had become the strongest power on the European continent, but between 1921 and 1926, no French government seemed capable of solving the country's financial problems. Like other European countries, though, France did experience a period of relative prosperity between 1926 and 1929.

Because it had a more balanced economy than other nations, France did not begin to feel the full effects of the Great Depression until 1932. Then economic instability soon had political repercussions. During a nineteen-month period in 1932 and 1933, six different cabinets were formed as France faced political chaos. Finally, in June 1936, a coalition of leftist parties—Communists, Socialists, and Radicals—formed a new government, the Popular Front, but its policies failed to solve the problems of the depression. By 1938, the French were experiencing a serious decline of confidence in their political system.

After the imperial Germany of William II had come to an end in 1918 with Germany's defeat in World War I, a German democratic state known as the Weimar Republic was established. From its beginnings, the Weimar Republic was plagued by a series of problems. The republic had no truly outstanding political leaders and faced serious economic difficulties. Germany experienced runaway inflation in 1922 and 1923; widows, orphans, the retired elderly, army officers, teachers, civil servants, and others who lived on fixed incomes all watched their monthly stipends become worthless and their lifetime savings disappear. Their economic losses increasingly pushed the middle class to the rightist parties that were hostile to the republic. To make matters worse, after a period of prosperity from 1924 to 1929, Germany faced the Great Depression. Unemployment increased to 3 million in March 1930 and 4.4 million by December of the same year. The depression paved the way for the rise of extremist parties.

After Germany, no Western nation was more affected by the Great Depression than the United States. By 1932, U.S. industrial production fell to 50 percent of what it had been in 1929. By 1933, there were 15 million unemployed. Under these circumstances, the Democrat Franklin Delano Roosevelt (1882–1945) was able to win a landslide electoral victory in 1932. He and his advisers pursued a policy of active government intervention in the economy that came to be known as the New Deal. Economic intervention included a stepped-up program of public works, such as the Works Progress Administration (WPA), which was established in 1935 and employed between two and three million people who worked at building bridges, roads, post offices, and airports. In 1935, the Social Security Act created a system of old-age pensions and unemployment insurance.

The New Deal provided some social reform measures, but it did not solve the unemployment problems of the Great Depression. In May 1937, during what was considered a period of full recovery, American unemployment still stood at seven million.

Socialism in Soviet Russia

The civil war in Russia had taken an enormous toll of life. Lenin had pursued a policy of war communism, but once the war was over, peasants began to sabotage the program by hoarding food. Added to this problem was drought, which caused a famine between 1920 and 1922 that claimed as many as five million lives. Industrial collapse paralleled the agricultural disaster. By 1921, industrial output was only 20 percent of its 1913 levels. Russia was exhausted. A peasant banner proclaimed, "Down with Lenin and horseflesh, Bring back the Tsar and pork." As Leon Trotsky said, "The country, and the government with it, were at the very edge of the abyss."[6]

In March 1921, Lenin pulled Russia back from the abyss by adopting his **New Economic Policy** (NEP), a modified version of the old capitalist system. Peasants were now allowed to sell their produce openly. Retail stores as well as small industries that employed fewer than twenty employees could now operate under private ownership, although heavy industry, banking, and mines remained in the hands of the government.

In 1922, Lenin and the Communists formally created a new state called the Union of Soviet Socialist Republics, known as the USSR by its initials or the Soviet Union by its shortened form. Already by that year, a revived market and a good harvest had brought the famine to an end; Soviet agricultural production climbed to 75 percent of its prewar level.

Lenin's death in 1924 inaugurated a struggle for power among the seven members of the Politburo, the institution that had become the leading organ of the party. The Politburo was divided over the future direction of Soviet Russia. The Left, led by Leon Trotsky, wanted to end the NEP, launch Russia on the path of rapid industrialization, and spread the revolution abroad. Another group in the Politburo, called the Right, rejected the cause of world revolution and wanted instead to concentrate on constructing a socialist state in Russia. This group also favored a continuation of Lenin's NEP.

These ideological divisions were underscored by an intense personal rivalry between Leon Trotsky and Joseph Stalin (1879–1953). In 1924, Trotsky held the post of commissar of war and was the leading spokesman for the Left in the Politburo. Stalin was content to hold the dull bureaucratic job of party general secretary while other Politburo members held party positions that enabled them to display their brilliant oratorical abilities. Stalin was skillful in avoiding allegiance to either the Left or Right factions in the Politburo. He was also a good organizer (his fellow Bolsheviks called him "Comrade Index-Card") and used his post as party general secretary to gain complete control of the Communist Party. Trotsky was expelled from the party in 1927. By 1929, Stalin had succeeded in eliminating the Bolsheviks of the revolutionary era from the Politburo and establishing a dictatorship.

In Pursuit of a New Reality: Cultural and Intellectual Trends

Q Focus Question: How did the cultural and intellectual trends of the interwar years reflect the crises of those years as well as the experience of World War I?

In the aftermath of the Great War, as they tried to rebuild their lives, Europeans wondered what had gone wrong with Western civilization. For many, their faith in progress had been shattered. The Great Depression only added to the despair lingering from World War I.

The political and economic uncertainties were paralleled by social innovations. The Great War had served to break down many traditional middle-class attitudes, especially toward sexuality. In the 1920s, women's physical appearance changed dramatically. Short skirts, short hair, the use of cosmetics that were once thought to be the preserve of prostitutes, and the new practice of suntanning gave women a new image. This change in physical appearance, which stressed more exposure of a woman's body, was also accompanied by frank discussions of sexual matters. In 1926, the Dutch physician Theodor van de Velde published *Ideal Marriage: Its Physiology and Technique,* which became an international best-seller. Van de Velde described female and male anatomy and glorified sexual pleasure in marriage.

Nightmares and New Visions

Uncertainty also pervaded the cultural and intellectual achievements of the interwar years. Postwar artistic trends were largely a working out of the implications of prewar developments. Abstract painting, for example, became ever more popular (see the comparative essay "A Revolution in the Arts" on p. 585). In addition, prewar fascination with the absurd and the unconscious content of the mind seemed even more appropriate after the nightmare landscapes of World War I battlefronts. This gave rise to both the Dada movement and Surrealism.

Dadaism enshrined the purposelessness of life; revolted by the insanity of life, the Dadaists tried to give it expression by creating "anti-art." The 1918 Berlin Dada Manifesto maintained that "Dada is the international expression of our times, the great rebellion of artistic movements." Many Dadaists assembled pieces of junk (wire, string, rags, scraps of newspaper, nails, washers) into collages, believing that they were transforming the refuse of their culture into art. In the hands of Hannah Höch (1889–1978), Dada became an instrument to comment on women's roles in the new mass culture (see the illustration on p. 585).

Perhaps more important as an artistic movement was **Surrealism,** which sought a reality beyond the material, sensible world and found it in the world of the unconscious through the portrayal of fantasies, dreams, or nightmares. The Spaniard Salvador Dalí (1904–1989) became the high priest of Surrealism and in his

COMPARATIVE ESSAY
A REVOLUTION IN THE ARTS

ARTS & IDEAS

The period between 1880 and 1930 witnessed a revolution in the arts throughout Western civilization. Fueled in part by developments in physics and psychology, artists and writers rebelled against the traditional belief that the task of art was to represent "reality" and experimented with innovative new techniques in order to approach reality from a totally fresh perspective.

From Impressionism and Expressionism to Cubism, abstract art, Dadaism, and Surrealism, painters seemed intoxicated with the belief that their canvases would help reveal the radically changing world. Especially after the cataclysm of World War I, which shattered the image of a rational society, artists sought an absolute freedom of expression, confident that art could redefine humanity in the midst of chaos. Other arts soon followed their lead: James Joyce turned prose on its head by focusing on his characters' innermost thoughts, and Arnold Schönberg created atonal music by using a scale composed of twelve notes independent of any tonal key.

This revolutionary spirit is exemplified by Pablo Picasso's canvas *Les Demoiselles d'Avignon,* painted in 1907 (see the illustration on p. 510). Picasso used geometrical designs to create a new reality and appropriated other cultural resources, including African masks, in his effort to revitalize Western art.

Another example of the revolutionary approach to art was the decision by the French artist Marcel Duchamp to enter a porcelain urinal in a 1917 art exhibit held in New York City. By signing it and giving it the title "Fountain," Duchamp proclaimed that he had transformed the urinal into a work of art. His "ready-mades" (as such art would henceforth be labeled) declared that art was whatever the artist proclaimed as art.

Such intentionally irreverent acts demystified the nearly sacred reverence that had traditionally been attached to works of art. Essentially, Duchamp and others claimed that anything under the sun could be selected as a work of art because the mental choice itself equaled the act of artistic creation. Therefore, art need not be a manual construct; it need only be a mental conceptualization. This liberating concept opened the floodgates of the art world, allowing the new century to swim in this free-flowing, exploratory torrent.

Hannah Höch, *Cut with the Kitchen Knife Dada Through the Last Weimar Beer Belly Cultural Epoch of Germany.* Hannah Höch, a prominent figure in the postwar Dada movement, used photomontage to create images that reflected on women's issues. In *Cut with the Kitchen Knife,* she combined pictures of German political leaders with sports stars, Dada artists, and scenes from urban life. One major theme emerged: the confrontation between the anti-Dada world of German political leaders and the Dada world of revolutionary ideals. Höch associated women with Dada and the new world.

Q *How was the revolution in the arts between 1880 and 1930 related to the political, economic, and social developments of the same period?*

mature phase became a master of representational Surrealism. Dalí portrayed recognizable objects entirely divorced from their normal context. By placing objects into unrecognizable relationships, Dalí created a disturbing world in which the irrational had become tangible.

Probing the Unconscious

Interest in the unconscious, evident in Surrealism, was also apparent in the development of new literary techniques that emerged in the 1920s. One of its most apparent manifestations was in the "stream of consciousness"

Salvador Dalí, *The Persistence of Memory*. Surrealism was an important artistic movement in the 1920s. Influenced by the theories of Freudian psychology, Surrealists sought to reveal the world of the unconscious, or the "greater reality" that they believed existed beyond the world of physical appearances. As is evident in this painting, Salvador Dalí sought to portray the world of dreams by painting recognizable objects in unrecognizable relationships.

The German writer Hermann Hesse (1877–1962) dealt with the unconscious in a different fashion. His novels reflected the influence of new psychological theories and Eastern religions and focused on, among other things, the spiritual loneliness of modern human beings in a mechanized urban society. Hesse's novels made a large impact on German youth in the 1920s. He won the Nobel Prize for Literature in 1946.

For much of the Western world, the best way to find (or escape) reality was through mass entertainment. The 1930s was the heyday of the Hollywood studio system, which in the single year of 1937 turned out nearly six hundred feature films. Supplementing the movies were cheap paperbacks and radio, which brought sports, soap operas, and popular music to the depression-weary masses.

The increased size of audiences and the ability of radio and cinema, unlike the printed word, to provide an immediate mass experience added new dimensions to mass culture. Favorite film actors and actresses became stars, whose lives then became subject to public adoration and scrutiny. Sensuous actresses such as Marlene Dietrich, whose appearance in the early sound film *The Blue Angel* catapulted her to fame, popularized new images of women's sexuality.

technique in which the writer presented an interior monologue or a report of the innermost thoughts of each character. The most famous example of this genre was written by the Irish exile James Joyce (1882–1941). His *Ulysses,* published in 1922, told the story of one day in the life of ordinary people in Dublin by following the flow of their inner dialogue.

CONCLUSION

WORLD WAR I SHATTERED the society of late nineteenth- and early twentieth-century Europe. The incredible destruction and the deaths of almost 10 million people undermined the whole idea of progress. New propaganda techniques had manipulated entire populations into sustaining their involvement in a meaningless slaughter.

World War I was a total war that involved a mobilization of resources and populations and increased government centralization of power over the lives of its citizens. Civil liberties, such as freedom of the press, speech, assembly, and movement, were circumscribed in the name of national security. The war made the practice of strong central authority a way of life.

The turmoil wrought by the Great War seemed to lead to even greater insecurity. Revolutions dismembered old empires

and created new states that fostered unexpected problems. Expectations that Europe and the world would return to normalcy were soon dashed by the failure to achieve a lasting peace, economic collapse, and the rise of authoritarian governments that not only restricted individual freedoms but also sought even greater control over the lives of their subjects in order to guide them to achieve the goals of their totalitarian regimes.

Finally, World War I was the beginning of the end of European hegemony over world affairs. By weakening their own civilization on the battlegrounds of Europe, Europeans inadvertently encouraged the subject peoples of their vast colonial empires to initiate movements for national independence. In the next chapter, we examine some of those movements.

TIMELINE

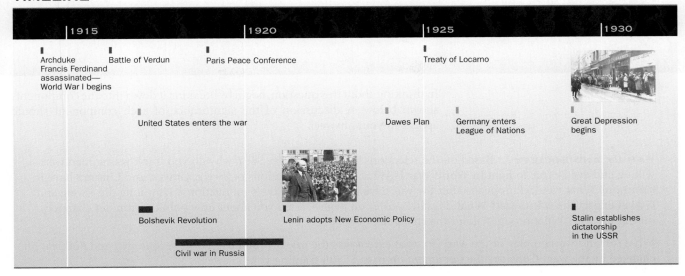

| 1915 | 1920 | 1925 | 1930 |

Archduke Francis Ferdinand assassinated—World War I begins

Battle of Verdun

Paris Peace Conference

Treaty of Locarno

United States enters the war

Dawes Plan

Germany enters League of Nations

Great Depression begins

Bolshevik Revolution

Lenin adopts New Economic Policy

Stalin establishes dictatorship in the USSR

Civil war in Russia

SUGGESTED READING

General Works on Twentieth-Century Europe A number of general works on European history in the twentieth century provide a context for understanding both World War I and the Russian Revolution. Especially valuable is **N. Ferguson,** *The War of the World: Twentieth-Century Conflict and the Descent of the West* (New York, 2006). See also **R. Paxton,** *Europe in the Twentieth Century,* 4th ed. (New York, 2004), and **E. D. Brose,** *History of Europe in the Twentieth Century* (Oxford, 2004).

Causes of World War I The historical literature on the causes of World War I is vast. Good starting points are the works by **J. Joll** and **G. Martel,** *The Origins of the First World War,* 3rd ed. (London, 2006), and **A. Mombauer,** *The Origins of the First World War: Controversies and Consensus* (London, 2002). On the events leading to war, see **D. Fromkin,** *Europe's Last Summer: Who Started the Great War in 1914?* (New York, 2004).

World War I The best brief account of World War I is **H. Strachan,** *The First World War* (New York, 2004). See also **J. Keegan,** *An Illustrated History of the First World War* (New York, 2001), and **S. Audoin-Rouzeau** and **A. Becker,** *14–18: Understanding the Great War* (New York, 2002). On the global nature of World War I, see **M. S. Neiberg,** *Fighting the Great War: A Global History* (Cambridge, Mass., 2005), and **J. H. Morrow Jr.,** *The Great War: An Imperial History* (London, 2004). On the role of women in World War I, see **S. Grayzel,** *Women and the First World War* (London, 2002), and **G. Braybon** and **P. Summerfield,** *Women's Experiences in Two World Wars* (London, 1987). On the Paris Peace Conference, see **M. MacMillan,** *Paris, 1919: Six Months That Changed the World* (New York, 2002).

The Russian Revolution A good introduction to the Russian Revolution can be found in **R. A. Wade,** *The Russian Revolution, 1917,* 2nd ed. (Cambridge, 2005), and **S. Fitzpatrick,** *The Russian Revolution, 1917–1932,* 2nd ed. (New York, 2001). For a study that puts the Russian Revolution into the context of World War I, see **P. Holquist,** *Making War, Forging Revolution* (Cambridge, Mass., 2002). On Lenin, see **R. Service,** *Lenin: A Biography* (Cambridge, Mass., 2000). On social reforms, see **W. Goldman,** *Women, the State, and Revolution* (Cambridge, 1993). A comprehensive study of the Russian civil war is **W. B. Lincoln,** *Red Victory: A History of the Russian Civil War* (New York, 1989).

The 1920s For a general introduction to the post–World War I period, see **M. Kitchen,** *Europe Between the Wars,* 2nd ed. (London, 2006). On European security issues after the Peace of Paris, see **S. Marks,** *The Illusion of Peace: Europe's International Relations, 1918–1933,* 2nd ed. (New York, 2003). On the Great Depression, see **C. P. Kindleberger,** *The World in Depression, 1929–39,* rev. ed. (Berkeley, Calif., 1986). On Great Britain, see **B. B. Gilbert,** *Britain, 1914–1945* (London, 1996). France is covered in **A. P. Adamthwaite,** *Grandeur and Misery: France's Bid for Power in Europe, 1914–1940* (London, 1995). On Weimar Germany, see **P. Bookbinder,** *Weimar Germany* (New York, 1996).

WORLD HISTORY RESOURCES

Visit the website for *The Essential World History* **to access study aids such as Flashcards, Critical Thinking Exercises, and Chapter Quizzes:**

www.cengage.com/history/duikspiel/essentialworld6e

DISCOVERY

What conclusions can you draw about the impact of World War I on European political institutions and social structures?

In thinking about this question, begin by breaking it down into the components shown below. A discussion of the significance of each component should appear in your answer.

FAMILY AND SOCIETY   Based on the selections below (also on p. 569), why do you think young men were willing and even eager to fight in World War I? What did the motivations of Zweig, Graves, and Limmer have in common? What would Europeans after the war have thought about their motivations? How long did Zweig and Graves expect the war to last? What does the poster on page 574 tell you about how public sentiment changed during the war? What brought about the change?

What role did women play in the war? To what extent was the role of women in social, economic, and political life changed by the war? Consider the document on page 575 in framing your answer.

THE EXCITEMENT OF WAR

Stefan Zweig, *The World of Yesterday*

The next morning I was in Austria. In every station placards had been put up announcing general mobilization. The trains were filled with fresh recruits, banners were flying, music sounded, and in Vienna I found the entire city in a tumult.... There were parades in the street, flags, ribbons, and music burst forth everywhere, young recruits were marching triumphantly, their faces lighting up at the cheering....

And to be truthful, I must acknowledge that there was a majestic, rapturous, and even seductive something in this first outbreak of the people from which one could escape only with difficulty. And in spite of all my hatred and aversion for war, I should not like to have missed the memory of those days. As never before, thousands and hundreds of thousands felt what they should have felt in peace time, that they belonged together. A city of two million, a country of nearly fifty million, in that hour felt that they were participating in world history, in a moment which would never recur, and that each one was called upon to cast his infinitesimal self into the glowing mass, there to be purified of all selfishness. All differences of class, rank, and language were flooded over at that moment by the rushing feeling of fraternity....

What did the great mass know of war in 1914, after nearly half a century of peace? They did not know war, they had hardly given it a thought. It had become legendary, and distance had made it seem romantic and heroic. They still saw it in the perspective of their school readers and of paintings in museums; brilliant cavalry attacks in glittering uniforms, the fatal shot always straight through the heart, the entire campaign a resounding march of victory— "We'll be home at Christmas," the recruits shouted laughingly to their mothers in August of 1914.... A rapid excursion into the romantic, a wild, manly adventure—that is how the war of 1914 was painted in the imagination of the simple man, and the younger people were honestly afraid that they might miss this most wonderful and exciting experience of their lives; that is why they hurried and thronged to the colors, and that is why they shouted and sang in the trains that carried them to the slaughter; wildly and feverishly the red wave of blood coursed through the veins of the entire nation.

Robert Graves, *Goodbye to All That*

I had just finished with Charterhouse and gone up to Harlech, when England declared war on Germany. A day or two later I decided to enlist. In the first place, though the papers predicted only a very short war—over by Christmas at the outside—I hoped that it might last long enough to delay my going to Oxford in October, which I dreaded. Nor did I work out the possibilities of getting actively engaged in the fighting, expecting garrison service at home, while the regular forces were away. In the second place, I was outraged to read of the Germans' cynical violation of Belgian neutrality. Though I discounted perhaps twenty per cent of the atrocity details as wartime exaggeration, that was not, of course, sufficient.

Walter Limmer, Letter to His Parents

In any case I mean to go into this business.... That is the simple duty of every one of us. And this feeling is universal among the soldiers, especially since the night when England's declaration of war was announced in the barracks. We none of us got to sleep till three o'clock in the morning, we were so full of excitement, fury, and enthusiasm. It is a joy to go to the Front with such comrades. We are bound to be victorious! Nothing else is possible in the face of such determination to win.

CHAPTER 24
NATIONALISM, REVOLUTION, AND DICTATORSHIP: ASIA, THE MIDDLE EAST, AND LATIN AMERICA FROM 1919 TO 1939

Mohandas "Mahatma" Gandhi, the "Soul of India"

IN 1930, MOHANDAS GANDHI, the sixty-one-year-old leader of the nonviolent movement for Indian independence from British rule, began a march to the sea with seventy-eight followers. Their destination was Dandi, a little coastal town some 240 miles away. The group covered about 12 miles a day. As they went, Gandhi preached his doctrine of nonviolent resistance to British rule in every village he passed through: "Civil disobedience is the inherent right of a citizen. He dare not give it up without ceasing to be a man." By the time he reached Dandi, twenty-four days later, his small group had become a nonviolent army of thousands. When they arrived at Dandi, Gandhi picked up a pinch of salt from the sand. All along the coast, thousands did likewise, openly breaking British laws that prohibited Indians from making their own salt. The British had long profited from their monopoly on the making and sale of salt, an item much in demand in a tropical country. By their simple acts of disobedience, Gandhi and the Indian people had taken a bold step on their long march to independence.

The salt march was but one of many nonviolent activities that Mohandas Gandhi undertook between World War I and World War II to win India's goal of national independence from British rule. World War I had not only deeply affected the lives of Europeans but had also undermined the prestige of Western

589

civilization in the minds of many observers in the rest of the world. When Europeans devastated their own civilization on the battlefields of Europe, the subject peoples of their vast colonial empires were quick to understand what it meant. In Africa and Asia, where initial efforts to fend off Western encroachment in the late nineteenth century had failed, movements for national independence began to take shape. Some were inspired by the nationalist and liberal movements of the West, while others began to look toward the new Marxist model provided by the victory of the Communists in Soviet Russia, who soon worked to spread their revolutionary vision to African and Asian societies. In the Middle East, World War I ended the rule of the Ottoman Empire and led to the creation of new states, many of which soon fell under European domination. Latin American countries, although not fully subjected to colonial rule, watched with wary eyes the growing U.S. and European influence over their own national economies. ❀

The Rise of Nationalism

Q **Focus Question:** What were the various stages in the rise of nationalist movements in Asia and the Middle East, and what problems did they face?

Although the West had emerged from World War I relatively intact, its political and social foundations and its self-confidence had been severely undermined. Within Europe, doubts about the future viability of Western civilization were widespread, especially among the intellectual elite. These doubts were quick to reach the attention of perceptive observers in Asia and Africa and contributed to a rising tide of unrest against Western political domination throughout the colonial and semicolonial world. That unrest took a variety of forms but was most notably displayed in increasing worker activism, rural protest, and a rising sense of national fervor among anticolonialist intellectuals. In areas of Asia, Africa, and Latin America where independent states had successfully resisted the Western onslaught, the discontent fostered by the war and later by the Great Depression led to a loss of confidence in democratic institutions and the rise of political dictatorships.

Modern Nationalism

The first stage of resistance to the West in Asia and Africa (see Chapters 21 and 22) had met with humiliation and failure and must have confirmed many Westerners' conviction that colonial peoples lacked both the strength and the know-how to create modern states and govern their own destinies. In fact, the process was just beginning. The next phase—the rise of modern nationalism—began to take shape at the beginning of the twentieth century and was the product of the convergence of several factors. The primary source of anticolonialist sentiment was a new urban middle class of Westernized intellectuals. In many cases, these merchants, petty functionaries, clerks, students, and professionals had been educated in Western-style schools. A few had spent time in the West. Many spoke Western languages, wore Western clothes, and worked in occupations connected with the colonial regime. Some even wrote in the languages of their colonial masters.

The results were paradoxical. On the one hand, this "new class" admired Western culture and sometimes harbored a deep sense of contempt for traditional ways. On the other hand, many strongly resented the foreigners and their arrogant contempt for colonial peoples. Though eager to introduce Western ideas and institutions into their own society, these intellectuals were dismayed at the gap between ideal and reality, theory and practice, in colonial policy. Although Western political thought exalted democracy, equality, and individual freedom, democratic institutions were primitive or nonexistent in the colonies.

Equality in economic opportunity and social life was also noticeably lacking. Normally, the middle classes did not suffer in the same manner as impoverished peasants or menial workers on sugar or rubber plantations, but they, too, had complaints. They were usually relegated to low-level jobs in the government or business and paid less than Europeans in similar positions. The superiority of the Europeans was expressed in a variety of ways, including "whites only" clubs and the use of the familiar form of the language (normally used by adults to children) when addressing the natives.

Under these conditions, many of the new urban educated class were very ambivalent toward their colonial masters and the civilization that they represented. Out of this mixture of hopes and resentments emerged the first stirrings of modern nationalism in Asia and Africa. During the first quarter of the century, in colonial and semicolonial societies from the Suez Canal to the shores of the Pacific Ocean, educated native peoples began to organize political parties and movements seeking reforms or the end of foreign rule and the restoration of independence.

Religion and Nationalism At first, many of the leaders of these movements did not focus clearly on the idea of nationhood but tried to defend native economic interests or religious beliefs. In Burma, for example, the first expression of modern nationalism came from students at the University of Rangoon, who protested against official persecution of the Buddhist religion and British lack of respect for local religious traditions. Adopting the name Thakin (a polite term in the Burmese language meaning "lord" or "master," thus emphasizing their demand for the right to rule themselves), they protested against British arrogance and failure to observe local customs in Buddhist temples (such as failing to remove their footwear). Only in the 1930s did the Thakins begin to focus specifically on national independence.

In the Dutch East Indies, the Sarekat Islam (Islamic Association) began as a self-help society among Muslim merchants to fight against domination of the local economy by Chinese interests. Eventually, activist elements began to realize that the source of the problem was not the Chinese merchants but the colonial presence, and in the 1920s, Sarekat Islam was transformed into a new organization, the Nationalist Party of Indonesia (PNI), that focused on national independence. Like the Thakins in Burma, this party would eventually lead the country to independence after World War II.

The Nationalist Quandary: Independence or Modernization?   Building a new nation, however, requires more than a shared sense of grievances against the foreign invader. A host of other issues also had to be resolved. Soon patriots throughout the colonial world were engaged in a lively and sometimes acrimonious debate over such questions as whether independence or modernization should be their primary objective. The answer depended in part on how the colonial regime was perceived. If it was viewed as a source of needed reforms in a traditional society, a gradualist approach made sense. But if it was seen primarily as an impediment to change, the first priority, in the minds of many, was to bring it to an end. The vast majority of patriotic individuals were convinced that to survive, their societies must adopt much of the Western way of life; yet many were equally determined that the local culture would not, and should not, become a carbon copy of the West. What was the national identity, after all, if it did not incorporate some elements from the traditional way of life?

Another reason for using traditional values was to provide ideological symbols that the common people could understand and would rally around. Though aware that they needed to enlist the mass of the population in the common struggle, most urban intellectuals had difficulty communicating with the teeming population in the countryside who did not understand such complicated and unfamiliar concepts as democracy and nationhood. As the Indonesian intellectual Sutan Sjahrir lamented, many Westernized intellectuals had more in common with their colonial rulers than with the native population in the rural villages (see the box on p. 592). As one French colonial official remarked in some surprise to

a French-educated Vietnamese reformist, "Why, Monsieur, you are more French than I am!"

Gandhi and the Indian National Congress

Nowhere in the colonial world were these issues debated more vigorously than in India. Before the Sepoy Rebellion (see Chapter 21), Indian consciousness had focused mainly on the question of religious identity. But in the latter half of the nineteenth century, a stronger sense of national consciousness began to arise, provoked by the conservative policies and racial arrogance of the British colonial authorities.

The first Indian nationalists were almost invariably upper class and educated. Many of them were from urban areas such as Bombay (Mumbai), Madras (Chennai), and Calcutta. Some were trained in law and were members of the civil service. At first, many tended to prefer reform to revolution and believed that India needed modernization before it could handle the problems of independence. Such reformists did have some effect. In the 1880s, the government introduced a measure of self-government for the first time. All too often, however, such efforts were sabotaged by local British officials.

The slow pace of reform convinced many Indian nationalists that relying on British benevolence was futile. In 1885, a small group of Indians, with some British participation, met in Bombay to form the Indian National Congress (INC). They hoped to speak for all India, but most were high-class English-trained Hindus. Like their reformist predecessors, members of the INC did not demand immediate independence and accepted the need for reforms to end traditional abuses like child marriage and *sati*. At the same time, they called for an Indian share in the governing process and more spending on economic development and less on military campaigns along the frontier. The British responded with a few concessions, but change was glacially slow.

The INC also had difficulty reconciling religious differences within its ranks. The stated goal of the INC was to seek self-determination for all Indians regardless of class or religious affiliation, but many of its leaders were Hindu and inevitably reflected Hindu concerns. In the first decade of the twentieth century, the separate Muslim League was created to represent the interests of the millions of Muslims in Indian society.

Nonviolent Resistance   In 1915, a young Hindu lawyer returned from South Africa to become active in the INC. He transformed the movement and galvanized India's struggle for independence and identity. Mohandas Gandhi was born in 1869 in Gujarat, in western India, the son of a government minister. In the late nineteenth century,

THE DILEMMA OF THE INTELLECTUAL

Sutan Sjahrir (1909–1966) was a prominent leader of the Indonesian nationalist movement who briefly served as prime minister of the Republic of Indonesia in the 1950s. Like many Western-educated Asian intellectuals, he was tortured by the realization that by education and outlook he was closer to his colonial masters—in his case, the Dutch—than to his own people. He wrote the following passage in a letter to his wife in 1935 and later included it in his book *Out of Exile.*

Sutan Sjahrir, *Out of Exile*

Am I perhaps estranged from my people? . . . Why are the things that contain beauty for them and arouse their gentler emotions only senseless and displeasing for me? In reality, the spiritual gap between my people and me is certainly no greater than that between an intellectual in Holland . . . and the undeveloped people of Holland. . . . The difference is rather . . . that the intellectual in Holland does not feel this gap because there is a portion—even a fairly large portion—of his own people on approximately the same intellectual level as himself. . . .

This is what we lack here. Not only is the number of intellectuals in this country smaller in proportion to the total population—in fact, very much smaller—but in addition, the few who are here do not constitute any single entity in spiritual outlook, or in any spiritual life or single culture whatsoever. . . . It is for them so much more difficult than for the intellectuals in Holland. In Holland

they build—both consciously and unconsciously—on what is already there. . . . Even if they oppose it, they do so as a method of application or as a starting point.

In our country this is not the case. Here there has been no spiritual or cultural life, and no intellectual progress for centuries. There are the much-praised Eastern art forms but what are these except bare rudiments from a feudal culture that cannot possibly provide a dynamic fulcrum for people of the twentieth century? . . . Our spiritual needs are needs of the twentieth century; our problems and our views are of the twentieth century. Our inclination is no longer toward the mystical, but toward reality, clarity, and objectivity. . . .

We intellectuals here are much closer to Europe or America than we are to the Borobudur or Mahabharata or to the primitive Islamic culture of Java and Sumatra. . . .

So, it seems, the problem stands in principle. It is seldom put forth by us in this light, and instead most of us search unconsciously for a synthesis that will leave us internally tranquil. We want to have both Western science and Eastern philosophy, the Eastern "spirit," in the culture. But what is this Eastern spirit? It is, they say, the sense of the higher, of spirituality, of the eternal and religious, as opposed to the materialism of the West. I have heard this countless times, but it has never convinced me.

Q *Why does the author feel estranged from his native culture? What is his answer to the challenges faced by his country in coming to terms with the modern world?*

---

he studied in London and became a lawyer. In 1893, he went to South Africa to work in a law firm serving Indian émigrés working as laborers there. He soon became aware of the racial prejudice and exploitation experienced by Indians living in the territory and tried to organize them to protect their interests.

On his return to India, Gandhi immediately became active in the independence movement, setting up a movement based on nonviolent resistance (the Hindi term was **satyagraha,** "hold fast to the truth") to try to force the British to improve the lot of the poor and grant independence to India. His goal was twofold: to convert the British to his views while simultaneously strengthening the unity and sense of self-respect of his compatriots. When the British attempted to suppress dissent, he called on his followers to refuse to obey British regulations.

British India Between the Wars

He began to manufacture his own clothes (Gandhi now dressed in a simple *dhoti* made of coarse homespun cotton) and adopted the spinning wheel as a symbol of Indian resistance to imports of British textiles.

Gandhi, now increasingly known as India's "Great Soul" (*Mahatma*), organized mass protests to achieve his aims, but in 1919, they got out of hand and led to violence and British reprisals. British troops killed hundreds of unarmed protesters in the enclosed square in the city of Amritsar in northwestern India. When the protests spread, Gandhi was horrified at the violence and briefly retreated from active politics. Nevertheless, he was arrested for his role in the protests and spent several years in prison.

Gandhi combined his anticolonial activities with an appeal to the spiritual instincts of all Indians.

FILM & HISTORY
GANDHI (1982)

To many of his contemporaries, Mohandas Gandhi—usually referred to as the Mahatma, or "great soul"—was the conscience of India. Son of a senior Indian official from the state of Gujarat and trained as a lawyer at University College in London, Gandhi first encountered racial discrimination when he sought to provide legal assistance to Indian laborers living under the apartheid regime in South Africa. On his return to India in 1915, he rapidly emerged as a fierce critic of British colonial rule over his country. His message of *satyagraha* ("hold fast to the truth")—embodying the idea of a steadfast but nonviolent resistance to the injustice and inhumanity inherent in the colonial enterprise—inspired millions of his compatriots in their long struggle for national independence. It also earned the admiration and praise of sympathetic observers around the world. His death by assassination at the hands of a Hindu fanatic in 1948 shocked the world.

Time, however, has somewhat dimmed his message. Gandhi's vision of a future India was symbolized by the spinning wheel—he rejected the industrial age and material pursuits in favor of the simple pleasures of the traditional Indian village. Since achieving independence, however, India has followed the path of national wealth and power laid out by Jawaharlal Nehru, Gandhi's friend and colleague. Gandhi's appeal for religious tolerance and mutual respect at home gave way rapidly to the reality of a bloody conflict between Hindus and Muslims that has not yet been eradicated in our own day. On the global stage, his vision of world peace and brotherly love has been similarly ignored, first during the Cold War and more recently by the "clash of civilizations" between Western countries and the forces of militant Islam.

Jawaharlal Nehru (Roshan Seth), Mahatma Gandhi (Ben Kingsley), and Muhammad Ali Jinnah (Alyque Padamsee) confer before the partition of India into Hindu and Muslim states.

It was at least partly in an effort to revive and perpetuate the message of the Mahatma that the British filmmaker Richard Attenborough directed the film *Gandhi* (1982). Epic in its length and scope, the film seeks to present a faithful rendition of the life of its subject, from his introduction to apartheid in South Africa at the turn of the century to his tragic death after World War II. Actor Ben Kingsley, son of an Indian father and an English mother, plays the title role with intensity and conviction. The film was widely praised and earned eight Academy Awards. Kingsley received an Oscar in the Best Actor category.

Though he had been born and raised a Hindu, his universalist approach to the idea of God transcended individual religion, although it was shaped by the historical themes of Hindu belief. At a speech given in London in September 1931, he expressed his view of the nature of God as "an indefinable mysterious power that pervades everything . . . , an unseen power which makes itself felt and yet defies all proof."[1]

While Gandhi was in prison, the political situation continued to evolve. In 1921, the British passed the Government of India Act, transforming the heretofore advisory Legislative Council into a bicameral parliament, two-thirds of whose members would be elected. Similar bodies were created at the provincial level. In a stroke, five million Indians were enfranchised. But such reforms were no longer enough for many members of the INC, who wanted to push aggressively for full independence. The British exacerbated the situation by increasing the salt tax and prohibiting the Indian people from manufacturing or harvesting their own salt. Gandhi, now released from prison, returned to his earlier policy of **civil disobedience** by openly joining several dozen supporters in a 240-mile walk to the sea, where he picked up a lump of salt and urged Indians to ignore the law. Gandhi and many other members of the INC were arrested.

Organizations to promote women's rights in India had been established shortly after 1900, and Indian women now played an active role in the movement. Women accounted for about 20,000, or nearly 10 percent, of all those arrested and jailed for taking part in demonstrations

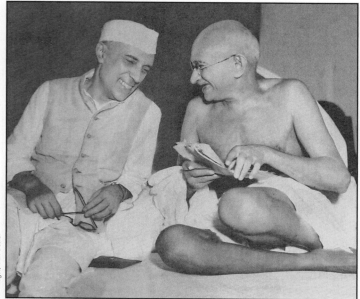

POLITICS & GOVERNMENT

COMPARATIVE ILLUSTRATION

Masters and Disciples. When the founders of nationalist movements passed leadership over to their successors, the result was often a change in the strategy and tactics of the organizations. When Jawaharlal Nehru (left photo, on the left) replaced Mahatma Gandhi (wearing a simple Indian *dhoti* rather than the Western dress favored by his colleagues) as leader of the Indian National Congress, the movement adopted a more secular posture. In China, Chiang Kai-shek (right photo, standing) took Sun Yat-sen's Nationalist Party in a more conservative direction after Sun's death in 1925.

Q How would you compare the roles played by these four leaders in furthering political change in their respective countries?

during the interwar period. Women marched, picketed foreign shops, and promoted the spinning and wearing of homemade cloth. By the 1930s, women's associations were also actively involved in promoting social reforms, including women's education, the introduction of birth control devices, the abolition of child marriage, and universal suffrage. In 1929, the Sarda Act raised the minimum age of marriage to fourteen.

New Leaders and New Problems In the 1930s, a new figure entered the movement in the person of Jawaharlal Nehru (1889–1964), son of an earlier INC leader. Educated in the law in Great Britain and a *brahmin* by birth, Nehru personified the new Anglo-Indian politician: secular, rational, upper class, and intellectual. In fact, he appeared to be everything that Gandhi was not. With his emergence, the independence movement embarked on two paths, religious and secular, native and Western, traditional and modern. The dual character of the INC

leadership may well have strengthened the movement by bringing together the two primary impulses behind the desire for independence: elite nationalism and the primal force of Indian traditionalism. But it portended trouble for the nation's new leadership in defining India's future path in the contemporary world. In the meantime, Muslim discontent with Hindu dominance over the INC was increasing. In 1940, the Muslim League called for the creation of a separate Muslim state of Pakistan ("land of the pure") in the northwest. As communal strife between Hindus and Muslims increased, many Indians came to realize with sorrow (and some British colonialists with satisfaction) that British rule was all that stood between peace and civil war.

The Nationalist Revolt in the Middle East

In the Middle East, as in Europe, World War I hastened the collapse of old empires. The Ottoman Empire, which had dominated the eastern Mediterranean since the seizure of Constantinople in 1453, had been growing steadily weaker since the end of the eighteenth century, troubled by rising governmental corruption, a decline in the effectiveness of the sultans, and the loss of considerable territory in the Balkans and southwestern Russia. In North Africa, Ottoman authority, tenuous at best, had disintegrated in the nineteenth century, enabling the French to seize Algeria and Tunisia and the British to establish a protectorate over the Nile River valley.

Decline of the Ottoman Empire Reformist elements in Istanbul, to be sure, had tried from time to time to resist the trend, but military defeats continued: Greece declared its independence, and Ottoman power declined steadily in the Middle East. A rising sense of nationality among Serbs, Armenians, and other minority peoples threatened the internal stability and cohesion of the empire. In the 1870s, a new generation of Ottoman reformers seized power in Istanbul and pushed through a constitution aimed at creating a legislative assembly that would represent all the peoples in the state. But the sultan they placed on the throne suspended the new charter and attempted to rule by traditional authoritarian means.

By the end of the nineteenth century, the defunct 1876 constitution had become a symbol of change for reformist elements, now grouped together under the common name **Young Turks.** They found support in the Ottoman army and administration and among Turks living in exile. In 1908, the Young Turks forced the sultan to restore the constitution, and he was removed from power the following year.

But the Young Turks had appeared at a moment of crisis for the empire. Internal rebellions, combined with Austrian annexations of Ottoman territories in the Balkans, undermined support for the new government and provoked the army to step in. With most minorities from the old empire now removed from Istanbul's authority, many ethnic Turks began to embrace a new concept of a Turkish state based on all those of Turkish nationality.

The final blow to the old empire came in World War I, when the Ottoman government allied with Germany in the hope of driving the British from Egypt and restoring Ottoman rule over the Nile valley. In response, the British declared an official protectorate over Egypt and, aided by the efforts of the dashing if eccentric British adventurer T. E. Lawrence (popularly known as Lawrence of Arabia), sought to undermine Ottoman rule in the Arabian peninsula by encouraging Arab nationalists there. In 1916, the local governor of Mecca declared Arabia independent from Ottoman rule, while British troops, advancing from Egypt, seized Palestine (see the spot map on p. 580 in Chapter 23). In October 1918, having suffered more than

300,000 casualties during the war, the Ottoman Empire negotiated an armistice with the Allied Powers.

Mustafa Kemal and the Modernization of Turkey
During the next few years, the tottering empire began to fall apart as the British and the French made plans to divide up Ottoman territories in the Middle East and the Greeks won Allied approval to seize the western parts of the Anatolian peninsula for their dream of re-creating the substance of the old Byzantine Empire. The impending collapse energized key elements in Turkey under the leadership of a war hero, Colonel Mustafa Kemal (1881–1938), who had commanded Turkish forces in their successful defense of the Dardanelles against a British invasion during World War I. Now he resigned from the army and convoked a national congress that called for the creation of an elected government and the preservation of the remaining territories of the old empire in a new republic of Turkey. Establishing his new capital at Ankara, Kemal's forces drove the Greeks from the Anatolian peninsula and persuaded the British to agree to a new treaty. In 1923, the last of the Ottoman sultans fled the country, which was now declared a Turkish republic. The Ottoman Empire had come to an end.

AP Images

Mustafa Kemal Atatürk. The war hero Mustafa Kemal took the initiative in creating the republic of Turkey. As president of the new republic, Atatürk ("Father Turk," as he came to be called) worked hard to transform Turkey into a modern secular state by restructuring the economy, adopting Western dress, and breaking the powerful hold of Islamic traditions. He is now reviled by Muslim fundamentalists for his opposition to an Islamic state. In this illustration, Atatürk (in civilian clothes) hosts the Shah of Persia during the latter's visit to Turkey in July 1934.

During the next few years, President Mustafa Kemal (now popularly known as Atatürk, or "Father Turk") attempted to transform Turkey into a modern secular republic. The trappings of a democratic system were put in place, centered on an elected Grand National Assembly, but the president was relatively intolerant of opposition and harshly suppressed critics of his rule. Turkish nationalism was emphasized, and the Turkish language, now written in the Roman alphabet, was shorn of many of its Arabic elements. Popular education was emphasized, old aristocratic titles like *pasha* and *bey* were abolished, and all Turkish citizens were given family names in the European style.

Atatürk also took steps to modernize the economy, overseeing the establishment of a light industrial sector producing textiles, glass, paper, and cement and instituting a five-year plan on the Soviet model to provide for state direction over the economy. Atatürk was no admirer of Soviet communism, however, and the Turkish economy can be better described as a form of state capitalism. He also encouraged the modernization of the agricultural sector through the establishment of training institutions and model farms, but such reforms had relatively little effect on the nation's predominantly conservative peasantry.

Perhaps the most significant aspect of Atatürk's reform program was his attempt to break the power of the Islamic clerics and transform Turkey into a secular state. The caliphate was formally abolished in 1924 (see the box on p. 597), and *Shari'a* (Islamic law) was replaced by a revised version of the Swiss law code. The fez (the brimless cap worn by Turkish Muslims) was abolished as a form of headdress, and women were discouraged from wearing the veil in the traditional Islamic custom. Women received the right to vote in 1934 and were legally guaranteed equal rights with men in all aspects of marriage and inheritance. Education and the professions were now open to citizens of both genders, and some women even began to participate in politics. All citizens were given the right to convert to another religion at will.

The legacy of Mustafa Kemal Atatürk was enormous. Although not all of his reforms were widely accepted in practice, especially by devout Muslims, most of the changes he introduced were retained after his death in 1938. In virtually every respect, the Turkish republic was the product of his determined efforts to create a modern Turkish nation.

Iran Under the Pahlavi Dynasty

Modernization in Iran In the meantime, a similar process was under way in Persia. Under the Qajar dynasty (1794–1925), the country had not been very successful in resisting Russian advances in the Caucasus or resolving its domestic problems. To secure themselves from foreign influence, the Qajars moved the capital from Tabriz to Tehran, in a mountainous area just south of the Caspian Sea. During the mid-nineteenth century, one modernizing shah attempted to introduce political and economic reforms but was impeded by resistance from tribal and religious—predominantly Shi'ite—forces. To buttress its rule, the dynasty turned increasingly to Russia and Great Britain to protect itself from its own people.

Eventually, the growing foreign presence led to the rise of a native Persian nationalist movement. Supported actively by Shi'ite religious leaders, opposition to the regime rose steadily among both peasants and merchants in the cities, and in 1906, popular pressures forced the reigning shah to grant a constitution on the Western model.

As in the Ottoman Empire and Manchu China, however, the modernizers had moved too soon, before their power base was secure. With the support of the Russians and the British, the shah was able to regain control, while the two foreign powers began to divide the country into separate spheres of influence. One reason for the growing foreign presence in Persia was the discovery of oil reserves in the southern part of the country in 1908. Within a few years, oil exports increased rapidly, with the bulk of the profits going into the pockets of British investors.

In 1921, an officer in the Persian army by the name of Reza Khan (1878–1944) led a mutiny and seized power in Tehran. The new ruler's original intention had been to establish a republic; but resistance from traditional forces impeded his efforts, and in 1925, the new Pahlavi dynasty, with Reza Khan as shah, replaced the now defunct Qajar dynasty. During the next few years, Reza Khan attempted to follow the example of Atatürk in Turkey, introducing a number of reforms to strengthen the central government, modernize the civilian and military bureaucracy, and establish a modern economic infrastructure. He also officially changed the name of the nation to Iran.

Unlike Atatürk, Reza Khan did not attempt to destroy the power of Islamic beliefs, but he did encourage the establishment of a Western-style educational system and forbade women to wear the veil

OPPOSING VIEWPOINTS
ISLAM IN THE MODERN WORLD: TWO VIEWS

As part of his plan to transform Turkey into a modern society, Mustafa Kemal Atatürk sought to free his country from what he considered to be outdated practices imposed by traditional beliefs. The first excerpt is from a speech in which he proposed bringing an end to the caliphate, which had been in the hands of Ottoman sultans since the formation of the empire. But not all Muslims wished to move in the direction of a more secular society. Mohammed Iqbal, a well-known Muslim poet in colonial India, was also a prominent advocate of the creation of a separate state for Muslims in South Asia. The second selection is from an address he presented to the All-India Muslim League in December 1930, explaining the rationale for his proposal.

Atatürk, Speech to the Assembly (October 1924)

The sovereign entitled Caliph was to maintain justice among the three hundred million Muslims on the terrestrial globe, to safeguard the rights of these peoples, to prevent any event that could encroach upon order and security, and confront every attack which the Muslims would be called upon to encounter from the side of other nations. It was to be part of his attributes to preserve by all means the welfare and spiritual development of Islam....

If the Caliph and Caliphate, as they maintained, were to be invested with a dignity embracing the whole of Islam, ought they not to have realized in all justice that a crushing burden would be imposed on Turkey, on her existence; her entire resources and all her forces would be placed at the disposal of the Caliph?...

For centuries our nation was guided under the influence of these erroneous ideas. But what has been the result of it? Everywhere they have lost millions of men. "Do you know," I asked, "how many sons of Anatolia have perished in the scorching deserts of the Yemen? Do you know the losses we have suffered in holding Syria and Egypt and in maintaining our position in Africa? And do you see what has come out of it? Do you know?

"Those who favor the idea of placing the means at the disposal of the Caliph to brave the whole world and the power to administer the affairs of the whole of Islam must not appeal to the population of Anatolia alone but to the great Muslim agglomerations which are eight or ten times as rich in men.

"New Turkey, the people of New Turkey, have no reason to think of anything else but their own existence and their own welfare. She has nothing more to give away to others."

Mohammed Iqbal, Speech to the All-India Muslim League (1930)

It cannot be denied that Islam, regarded as an ethical ideal plus a certain kind of polity—by which expression I mean a social structure regulated by a legal system and animated by a specific ethical ideal—has been the chief formative factor in the life history of the Muslims of India. It has furnished those basic emotions and loyalties which gradually unify scattered individuals and groups and finally transform them into a well-defined people. Indeed it is no exaggeration to say that India is perhaps the only country in the world where Islam, as a people-building force, has worked at its best. In India, as elsewhere, the structure of Islam as a society is almost entirely due to the working of Islam as a culture inspired by a specific ethical ideal. What I mean to say is that Muslim society, with its remarkable homogeneity and inner unity, has grown to be what it is under the pressure of the laws and institutions associated with the culture of Islam.

Communalism in its higher aspect, then, is indispensable to the formation of a harmonious whole in a country like India. The units of Indian society are not territorial as in European countries. India is a continent of human groups belonging to different religions. Their behavior is not at all determined by a common race consciousness. Even the Hindus do not form a homogeneous group. The principle of European democracy cannot be applied to India without recognizing the fact of communal groups. The Muslim demand for the creation of a Muslim India within India is, therefore, perfectly justified....

I therefore demand the formation of a consolidated Muslim State in the best interests of India and Islam. For India it means security and peace resulting from an internal balance of power; for Islam an opportunity to rid itself of the stamp that Arabian imperialism was forced to give it, to mobilize its law, its education, its culture, and to bring them into closer contact with its own original spirit and with the spirit of modern times.

Q *Why did Mustafa Kemal believe that the caliphate no longer met the needs of the Turkish people? Why did Mohammed Iqbal believe that a separate state for Muslims in India would be required? How did he attempt to persuade non-Muslims that this would be to their benefit as well?*

in public. Women continued to be exploited, however; it was their intensive labor in the carpet industry that provided major export earnings—second only to oil—in the interwar period. To strengthen the sense of Persian nationalism and reduce the power of Islam, Reza Khan attempted to popularize the symbols and beliefs of pre-Islamic times. Like his Qajar predecessors, however, he was hindered by strong foreign influence. When the

Soviet Union and Great Britain decided to send troops into the country during World War II, he resigned in protest and died three years later.

Nation Building in Iraq   One other consequence of the collapse of the Ottoman Empire was the emergence of a new political entity along the Tigris and Euphrates rivers, once the heartland of ancient empires. Lacking defensible borders and sharply divided along ethnic and religious lines—a Shi'ite majority in rural areas was balanced by a vocal Sunni minority in the cities and a largely Kurdish population in the northern mountains—the region had been under Ottoman rule since the seventeenth century. With the advent of World War I, British forces occupied the lowland area from Baghdad southward to the Persian Gulf in order to protect the oil-producing regions in neighboring Iran from a German takeover.

Although the British claimed to have arrived as liberators, in 1920 the League of Nations placed the country under British control as the mandate of Iraq. Civil unrest and growing anti-Western sentiment rapidly dispelled any plans for the possible emergence of an independent government, and in 1921, after the suppression of resistance forces, the country was placed under the titular authority of King Faisal of Syria, a descendant of the Prophet Muhammad. Faisal relied for support primarily on the politically more sophisticated urban Sunni population, although they represented less than a quarter of the population. The discovery of oil near Kirkuk in 1927 increased the value of the area to the British, who granted formal independence to Iraq in 1932, although British advisers retained a strong influence over the fragile government.

The Rise of Arab Nationalism and the Issue of Palestine   Unrest against Ottoman rule had existed in the Arabian peninsula since the eighteenth century, when the Wahhabi revolt attempted to drive out the outside influences and cleanse Islam of corrupt practices that had developed in past centuries. The revolt was eventually suppressed, but Wahhabi influence persisted.

World War I offered an opportunity for the Arabs to throw off the shackles of Ottoman rule—but what would replace them? The Arabs were not a nation but an idea, and disagreement over what constitutes an Arab plagued generations of political leaders who sought unsuccessfully to knit together the disparate peoples of the region into a single Arab nation.

When the Arab leaders in Mecca declared their independence from Ottoman rule in 1916, they had hoped for British support, but they were to be sorely disappointed. As mentioned earlier, at the close of the war, the British and French agreed to create a number of mandates

in the area under the general supervision of the League of Nations. Iraq was assigned to the British; Syria and Lebanon (the two areas were separated so that Christian peoples in Lebanon could be placed under Christian administration) were given to the French.

The land of Palestine—once the home of the Jews but now inhabited primarily by Muslim Palestinians and a few thousand Christians—became a separate mandate. According to the Balfour Declaration, issued by the British foreign secretary, Lord Balfour, in November 1917, Palestine was to be a national home for the Jews. The declaration, later confirmed by the League of Nations, was ambiguous on the legal status of the territory and promised that the decision would not undermine the rights of the non-Jewish peoples currently living in the area. But Arab nationalists were incensed. How could a national home for the Jewish people be established in a territory where the majority of the population was Muslim?

In the early 1920s, a leader of the Wahhabi movement, Ibn Saud (1880–1953), united Arab tribes in the northern part of the Arabian peninsula and drove out the remnants of Ottoman rule. Ibn Saud was a descendant of the family that had led the Wahhabi revolt in the eighteenth century. Devout and gifted, he won broad support among Arab tribal peoples and established the kingdom of Saudi Arabia throughout much of the peninsula in 1932.

At first, his new kingdom, consisting essentially of the vast wastes of central Arabia, was desperately poor. But during the 1930s, American companies began to explore for oil, and in 1938, Standard Oil made a successful strike at Dhahran, on the Persian Gulf. Soon an Arabian-American oil conglomerate, popularly called Aramco, was established, and the isolated kingdom was suddenly inundated by Western oilmen and untold wealth.

In the meantime, Jewish immigrants began to arrive in Palestine in response to the promises made in the Balfour Declaration. As tensions between the new arrivals and existing Muslim residents began to escalate, the British tried to restrict Jewish immigration into the

European Jewish Refugees. After the 1917 Balfour Declaration promised a Jewish homeland in Palestine, increasing numbers of European Jews emigrated there. Their goal was to build a new life in a Jewish land. Like the refugees aboard this ship, they celebrated as they reached their new homeland. The sign reads "Keep the gates open, we are not the last"—a reference to British efforts to slow the pace of Jewish immigration in response to protests by Muslim residents.

little appeal to many patriotic intellectuals in the non-Western world. Marx believed that nationhood and religion were essentially false ideas that diverted the attention of the oppressed masses from the critical issues of class struggle. Instead, Marx stressed an "internationalist" outlook based on class consciousness and the eventual creation of a classless society with no artificial divisions based on culture, nation, or religion.

Lenin and the East The situation began to change after the Russian Revolution in 1917. The rise to power of Lenin's Bolsheviks demonstrated that a revolutionary party espousing Marxist principles could overturn a corrupt, outdated system and launch a new experiment dedicated to ending human inequality and achieving a paradise on earth. In 1920, Lenin proposed a new revolutionary strategy designed to relate Marxist doctrine and practice to non-Western societies. His reasons were not entirely altruistic. Soviet Russia, surrounded by capitalist powers, desperately needed allies in its struggle to survive in a hostile world. To Lenin, the anticolonial movements emerging in North Africa, Asia, and the Middle East after World War I were natural allies of the beleaguered new regime in Moscow. Lenin was convinced that only the ability of the imperialist powers to find markets, raw materials, and sources of capital investment in the non-Western world kept capitalism alive. If the tentacles of capitalist influence in Asia and Africa could be severed, imperialism would weaken and collapse.

territory, while Arab voices rejected the concept of a separate state. In a bid to relieve Arab sensitivities, Britain created a separate emirate of Trans-Jordan out of the eastern section of Palestine. After World War II, it would become the independent kingdom of Jordan. The stage was set for the conflicts that would take place in the region after World War II.

Nationalism and Revolution in Asia and Africa

Before the Russian Revolution, to most intellectuals in Asia and Africa, "Westernization" referred to the capitalist democratic civilization of western Europe and the United States, not the doctrine of social revolution developed by Karl Marx. Until 1917, Marxism was regarded as a utopian idea rather than a concrete system of government. Moreover, to many intellectuals, Marxism appeared to have little relevance to conditions in Asia and Africa. Marxist doctrine, after all, declared that a communist society would arise only from the ashes of an advanced capitalism that had already passed through an industrial revolution. From the perspective of Marxist historical analysis, most societies in Asia and Africa were still at the feudal stage of development; they lacked the economic conditions and political awareness to achieve a socialist revolution that would bring the working class to power. Finally, the Marxist view of nationalism and religion had

Establishing such an alliance was not easy, however. Most nationalist leaders in colonial countries belonged to the urban middle class, and many abhorred the idea of a comprehensive revolution to create a totally egalitarian society. In addition, many still adhered to traditional religious beliefs and were opposed to the atheistic principles of classic Marxism.

Since it was unrealistic to expect bourgeois nationalist support for social revolution, Lenin sought a compromise by which Communist parties could be organized among the working classes in the preindustrial societies of Asia and Africa. These parties would then forge informal alliances with existing middle-class parties to struggle against the traditional ruling class and Western imperialism. Such an alliance, of course, could not be permanent because many bourgeois nationalists in Asia and Africa would reject an egalitarian, classless society. Once the imperialists had been overthrown, therefore, the Communist parties would turn against their erstwhile nationalist partners to seize power on their own and carry out the socialist revolution.

Lenin's strategy became a major element in Soviet foreign policy in the 1920s. Soviet agents fanned out across the world to carry Marxism beyond the boundaries of industrial Europe. The primary instrument of this effort was the **Communist International,** or **Comintern** for short. Formed in 1919 at Lenin's prodding, the Comintern was a worldwide organization of Communist parties dedicated to the advancement of world revolution. At its headquarters in Moscow, agents from around the world were trained in the precepts of world communism and then sent back to their countries to form Marxist parties and promote the cause of social revolution. By the end of the 1920s, almost every colonial or semicolonial society in Asia had a party based on Marxist principles. The Soviets had less success in the Middle East, where Marxist ideology appealed mainly to minorities such as Jews and Armenians in the cities, and in black Africa, where Soviet strategists in any case felt that conditions were not sufficiently advanced for the creation of Communist organizations.

ideology, dealing not with the hereafter but with the here and now or, indeed, with a remote future when the state would wither away and the "classless society" would replace the lost truth of traditional faiths.

Of course, the new doctrine's appeal was not the same in all non-Western societies. In Confucian societies such as China and Vietnam, where traditional belief systems had been badly discredited by their failure to counter the Western challenge, communism had an immediate impact and rapidly became a major factor in the anticolonial movement. In Buddhist and Muslim societies, where traditional religion remained strong and actually became a cohesive factor in the resistance movement, communism had less success. To maximize their appeal and minimize potential conflict with traditional ideas, Communist parties frequently attempted to adapt Marxist doctrine to indigenous values and institutions. In the Middle East, for example, the Ba'ath Party in Syria adopted a hybrid socialism combining Marxism with Arab nationalism. In Africa, radical intellectuals talked vaguely of a uniquely "African road to socialism."

The degree to which these parties were successful in establishing alliances with nationalist parties and building a solid base of support among the mass of the population also varied from place to place. In some instances, the

The Appeal of Communism According to Marxist doctrine, the rank and file of Communist parties should be urban factory workers alienated from capitalist society by inhuman working conditions. In practice, many of the leaders even in European Communist parties tended to be urban intellectuals or members of the lower middle class. That phenomenon was even more true in the non-Western world, where most early Marxists were rootless intellectuals. Some were probably drawn into the movement for patriotic reasons and saw Marxist doctrine as a new, more effective means of modernizing their societies and removing the colonial exploiters. Others were attracted by the message of egalitarian communism and the utopian dream of a classless society. For those who had lost their faith in traditional religion, communism often served as a new secular

Nguyen the Patriot at Tours. At a meeting held on Christmas Day in 1920, the French progressive movement split into two separate organizations, the French Socialist Party (FSP) and the French Communist Party (FCP). One participant at the congress—held in the French industrial city of Tours—was a young Vietnamese radical who took the pseudonym Nguyen Ai Quoc (Nguyen the Patriot). In this photo, Nguyen announces his decision to join the new FCP on the grounds that it alone could help bring about the liberation of the oppressed peoples of Asia and Africa from colonial rule. A quarter of a century later, Nguyen would resurface as the Comintern agent and Vietnamese revolutionary leader Ho Chi Minh.

Communists were briefly able to establish a cooperative relationship with the bourgeois parties. The most famous example was the alliance between the Chinese Communist Party and Sun Yat-sen's Nationalist Party (discussed in the next section). These efforts were abandoned in 1928 when the Comintern, reacting to Chiang Kai-shek's betrayal of the alliance with the Chinese Communist Party, declared that Communist parties should restrict their recruiting efforts to the most revolutionary elements in society—notably, the urban intellectuals and the working class. Harassed by colonial authorities and saddled with strategic directions from Moscow that often had little relevance to local conditions, Communist parties in most colonial societies had little success in the 1930s and failed to build a secure base of support among the mass of the population.

Revolution in China

Q **Focus Question:** What problems did China encounter between the two world wars, and what solutions did the Nationalists and the Communists propose to solve them?

Overall, revolutionary Marxism had its greatest impact in China, where a group of young radicals founded the Chinese Communist Party (CCP) in 1921. The rise of the CCP was a consequence of the failed revolution of 1911. When political forces are too weak or too divided to consolidate their power during a period of instability, the military usually steps in to fill the vacuum. In China, Sun Yat-sen and his colleagues had accepted General Yuan Shikai (Yuan Shih-k'ai) as president of the new Chinese republic in 1911 because they lacked the military force to compete with his control over the army. But some had misgivings about Yuan's intentions. As one remarked in a letter to a friend, "We don't know whether he will be a George Washington or a Napoleon."

As it turned out, he was neither. Showing little comprehension of the new ideas sweeping into China from the West, Yuan ruled in a traditional manner, reviving Confucian rituals and institutions and eventually trying to found a new imperial dynasty. Yuan's dictatorial inclinations rapidly led to clashes with Sun's party, now renamed the *Guomindang* (*Kuomintang*), or Nationalist Party. When Yuan dissolved the new parliament, the Nationalists launched a rebellion. When it failed, Sun Yat-sen fled to Japan.

Yuan was strong enough to brush off the challenge from the revolutionary forces but not to turn back the clock of history. He died in 1916 and was succeeded by one of his military subordinates. For the next several

CHRONOLOGY Revolution in China

May Fourth demonstrations	1919
Formation of Chinese Communist Party	1921
Death of Sun Yat-sen	1925
Northern Expedition	1926–1928
Establishment of Nanjing republic	1928
Long March	1934–1935

years, China slipped into semianarchy as the power of the central government disintegrated and military warlords seized power in the provinces.

Mr. Science and Mr. Democracy: The New Culture Movement

In the meantime, discontent with existing conditions continued to rise in various sectors of Chinese society. The most vocal protests came from radical intellectuals, who opposed Yuan Shikai's conservative rule but were now convinced that political change could not take place until the Chinese people were more familiar with trends in the outside world. Braving the displeasure of Yuan and his successors, progressive intellectuals at Peking University launched the **New Culture Movement,** aimed at abolishing the remnants of the old system and introducing Western values and institutions into China. Using the classrooms of China's most prestigious university as well as the pages of newly established progressive magazines and newspapers, the intellectuals introduced a bewildering mix of new ideas, from the philosophy of Friedrich Nietzsche to the feminist plays of Henrik Ibsen. As such ideas flooded into China, they stirred up a new generation of educated Chinese youth, who chanted "Down with Confucius and sons" and talked of a new era dominated by "Mr. Sai" (Mr. Science) and "Mr. De" (Mr. Democracy). No one was a greater defender of free thought and speech than the chancellor of Peking University, Cai Yuanpei (Ts'ai Yüan-p'ei): "Regardless of what school of thought a person may adhere to, so long as that person's ideas are justified and conform to reason and have not been passed by through the process of natural selection, although there may be controversy, such ideas have a right to be presented."[2] Not surprisingly, such views earned the distrust of conservative military officers, one of whom threatened to lob artillery shells into Peking University to destroy the poisonous new ideas and eliminate their advocates.

Discontent among intellectuals, however, was soon joined by the rising chorus of public protest against

Japan's efforts to expand its influence on the mainland. During the first decade of the twentieth century, Japan had taken advantage of the Qing's decline to extend its domination over Manchuria and Korea (see Chapter 22). In 1915, the Japanese government insisted that Yuan Shikai accept a series of twenty-one demands that would have given Japan a virtual protectorate over the Chinese government and economy. Yuan was able to fend off the most far-reaching Japanese demands by arousing popular outrage in China, but at the Paris Peace Conference four years later, Japan received Germany's sphere of influence in Shandong Province as a reward for its support of the Allied cause in World War I. On hearing that the Chinese government had accepted the decision, on May 4, 1919, patriotic students, supported by other sectors of the urban population, demonstrated in Beijing and other major cities of the country. Although this May Fourth Movement did not lead to the restoration of Shandong, it did alert a substantial part of the politically literate population to the threat to national survival and the incompetence of the warlord government.

The Nationalist-Communist Alliance

By 1920, central authority had almost ceased to exist in China. Two competing political forces now began to emerge from the chaos. One was Sun Yat-sen's Nationalist Party. From Canton, Sun sought international assistance to carry out his national revolution. The other was the CCP. Following Lenin's strategy, Comintern agents soon advised the new party to link up with the more experienced Nationalists. Sun Yat-sen needed the expertise and the diplomatic support that Soviet Russia could provide because his anti-imperialist rhetoric had alienated many Western powers. In 1923, the two parties formed an alliance to oppose the warlords and drive the imperialist powers out of China.

For three years, with the assistance of a Comintern mission in Canton, the two parties submerged their mutual suspicions and mobilized and trained a revolutionary army to march north and seize control over China. The so-called Northern Expedition began in the summer of 1926 (see Map 24.1). By the following spring, revolutionary forces were in control of all Chinese territory south of the Yangtze River, including the major river ports of Wuhan and Shanghai. But tensions between the two parties now surfaced. Sun Yat-sen had died of cancer in 1925 and was succeeded as head of the

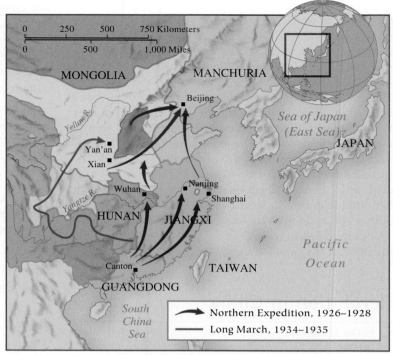

MAP 24.1 **The Northern Expedition and the Long March.** This map shows the routes taken by the combined Nationalist-Communist forces during the Northern Expedition of 1926–1928. The blue arrow indicates the route taken by Communist units during the Long March led by Mao Zedong.

Q Where did Mao establish his new headquarters?

⚫ **View an animated version of this map or related maps at** www.cengage.com/history/duikspiel/essentialworld6e

Nationalist Party by his military subordinate, Chiang Kai-shek (see the comparative illustration on p. 594). Chiang feigned support for the alliance with the Communists but actually planned to destroy them. In April 1927, he struck against the Communists and their supporters in Shanghai, killing thousands. After the massacre, most of the Communist leaders went into hiding in the city, where they attempted to revive the movement in its traditional base among the urban working class. Some party members, however, led by the young Communist organizer Mao Zedong (Mao Tse-tung), fled to the hilly areas south of the Yangtze River.

Unlike most CCP leaders, Mao was convinced that the Chinese revolution must be based not on workers in the big cities but on the impoverished peasants in the countryside. The son of a prosperous farmer, Mao served as an agitator in rural villages in his native province of Hunan during the Northern Expedition in the fall of 1926. At that time, he wrote a famous report to the party leadership suggesting that the CCP support peasant

A CALL FOR REVOLT

 POLITICS & GOVERNMENT

In the fall of 1926, Nationalist and Communist forces moved north from Canton on their Northern Expedition in an effort to defeat the warlords.

The young Communist Mao Zedong accompanied revolutionary troops into his home province of Hunan, where he submitted a report to the CCP Central Committee calling for a massive peasant revolt against the ruling order. The report shows his confidence that peasants could play an active role in the Chinese revolution despite the skepticism of many of his colleagues.

Mao Zedong, "The Peasant Movement in Hunan"

During my recent visit to Hunan I made a firsthand investigation of conditions.... In a very short time, ... several hundred million peasants will rise like a mighty storm, ... a force so swift and violent that no power, however great, will be able to hold it back. They will smash all the trammels that bind them and rush forward along the road to liberation. They will sweep all the imperialists, warlords, corrupt officials, local tyrants, and evil gentry into their graves. Every revolutionary party and every revolutionary comrade will be put to the test, to be accepted or rejected as they decide. There are three alternatives. To march at their head and lead them? To trail behind them, gesticulating and criticizing? Or to stand in their way and oppose them? Every Chinese is free to choose, but events will force you to make the choice quickly.

The main targets of attack by the peasants are the local tyrants, the evil gentry and the lawless landlords, but in passing they also hit out against patriarchal ideas and institutions, against the corrupt officials in the cities and against bad practices and customs in the rural areas.... As a result, the privileges which the feudal landlords enjoyed for thousands of years are being shattered to pieces.... With the collapse of the power of the landlords, the peasant associations have now become the sole organs of authority, and the popular slogan "All power to the peasant associations" has become a reality.

The peasants' revolt disturbed the gentry's sweet dreams. When the news from the countryside reached the cities, it caused immediate uproar among the gentry.... From the middle social strata upwards to the Kuomintang right-wingers, there was not a single person who did not sum up the whole business in the phrase, "It's terrible!" ... Even quite progressive people said, "Though terrible, it is inevitable in a revolution." In short, nobody could altogether deny the word "terrible." But ... the fact is that the great peasant masses have risen to fulfill their historic mission.... What the peasants are doing is absolutely right; what they are doing is fine! "It's fine!" is the theory of the peasants and of all other revolutionaries. Every revolutionary comrade should know that the national revolution requires a great change in the countryside. The Revolution of 1911 did not bring about this change, hence its failure. This change is now taking place, and it is an important factor for the completion of the revolution. Every revolutionary comrade must support it, or he will be taking the stand of counterrevolution.

Q *Why did Mao Zedong believe that rural peasants could help bring about a social revolution in China? How does his vision compare with the reality of the Bolshevik Revolution in Russia?*

---

demands for a land revolution (see the box above). But his superiors refused, fearing that such radical policies would destroy the alliance with the Nationalists.

The Nanjing Republic

In 1928, Chiang Kai-shek founded a new Chinese republic at Nanjing, and over the next three years, he sought to reunify China by a combination of military operations and inducements to various northern warlords to join his movement. He also attempted to put an end to the Communists, rooting them out of their urban base in Shanghai and their rural redoubt in the rugged hills of Jiangxi (Kiangsi) Province. He succeeded in the latter task in 1931, when most party leaders were forced to flee Shanghai for Mao's base in southern China. Three years later, using their superior military strength, Chiang's troops surrounded the Communist base in Jiangxi, inducing Mao's young People's Liberation Army (PLA) to abandon its guerrilla lair and embark on the famous Long March, an arduous journey of thousands of miles on foot through mountains, marshes, and deserts to the small provincial town of Yan'an (Yenan) 200 miles north of the city of Xian in the dusty hills of northern China (see Map 24.1).

Meanwhile, Chiang was trying to build a new nation. When the Nanjing republic was established in 1928, Chiang publicly declared his commitment to Sun Yat-sen's Three People's Principles. In a program announced in 1918, Sun had written about the all-important second stage of "political tutelage":

China ... needs a republican government just as a boy needs school. As a schoolboy must have good teachers and helpful friends, so the Chinese people, being for the first time under republican rule, must have a farsighted revolutionary government for their training. This calls for the period of political tutelage, which is a necessary transitional stage from monarchy to republicanism. Without this, disorder will be unavoidable.[3]

Mao Zedong on the Long March. In 1934, the Communist leader Mao Zedong led his bedraggled forces on the famous Long March from southern China to a new location at Yan'an, in the hills just south of the Gobi Desert. The epic journey has ever since been celebrated as a symbol of the party's willingness to sacrifice for the revolutionary cause. In the photo shown here, Mao sits astride a white horse as he accompanies his followers on the march. Reportedly, he was the only participant allowed to ride a horse en route to Yan'an.

In keeping with Sun's program, Chiang announced a period of political indoctrination to prepare the Chinese people for a final stage of constitutional government. In the meantime, the Nationalists would use their dictatorial power to carry out a land reform program and modernize the urban industrial sector.

But it would take more than paper plans to create a new China. Years of neglect and civil war had severely frayed the political, economic, and social fabric of the nation. There were faint signs of an impending industrial revolution in the major urban centers, but most of the people in the countryside, drained by warlord exactions and civil strife, were still grindingly poor and overwhelmingly illiterate. A westernized middle class had begun to emerge in the cities and formed much of the natural constituency of the Nanjing government. But this new westernized elite, preoccupied with bourgeois values of individual advancement and material accumulation, had few links with the peasants in the countryside or the rickshaw drivers "running in this world of suffering," in the poignant words of a Chinese poet. In an expressive phrase, some critics dismissed Chiang and his chief followers as "banana Chinese"—yellow on the outside, white on the inside.

The Best of East and West Chiang was aware of the difficulty of introducing exotic foreign ideas into a society still culturally conservative. While building a modern industrial sector, he attempted to synthesize modern Western ideas with traditional Confucian values of hard work, obedience, and moral integrity. In the officially

promoted New Life Movement, sponsored by his Wellesley-educated wife, Mei-ling Soong, Chiang sought to propagate traditional Confucian social ethics such as integrity, propriety, and righteousness, while rejecting what he considered the excessive individualism and material greed of Western capitalism.

Unfortunately for Chiang, Confucian ideas—at least in their institutional form—had been widely discredited by the failure of the traditional system to solve China's growing problems. With only a tenuous hold over the Chinese provinces, a growing Japanese threat in the north, and a world suffering from the Great Depression, Chiang made little progress with his program. Chiang repressed all opposition and censored free expression, thereby alienating many intellectuals and political moderates. A land reform program was enacted in 1930 but had little effect.

Chiang Kai-shek's government had little more success in promoting industrial development. During the decade of precarious peace following the Northern Expedition, industrial growth averaged only about 1 percent annually. Much of the national wealth was in the hands of senior officials and close subordinates of the ruling elite. Military expenses consumed half the budget, and distressingly little was devoted to social and economic development.

The new government, then, had little success in dealing with China's deep-seated economic and social problems. The deadly combination of internal disintegration and foreign pressure now began to coincide with the virtual collapse of the global economic order during the Great Depression and the rise of militant political forces in Japan determined to extend Japanese influence and power in an unstable Asia. These forces and the turmoil they unleashed will be examined in the next chapter.

"Down with Confucius and Sons": Economic, Social, and Cultural Change in Republican China

The transformation of the old order that had commenced at the end of the Qing era continued into the period of the early Chinese republic. The industrial sector continued to grow, albeit slowly. Although about 75 percent of all industrial production was still craft-produced in the early 1930s, mechanization was gradually beginning to replace manual labor in a number of traditional industries, notably in the manufacture of textile goods. Traditional Chinese exports, such as silk and tea, were hard-hit by the Great Depression, however, and manufacturing suffered a decline during the 1930s. It is difficult to gauge conditions in the countryside during the early republican era, but there is no doubt that farmers were often victimized by high taxes imposed by local warlords and the endemic political and social conflict.

Social Changes   Social changes followed shifts in the economy and the political culture. By 1915, the assault on the old system and values by educated youth was intense. The main focus of the attack was the Confucian concept of the family—in particular, filial piety and the subordination of women. Young people insisted on the right to choose their own mates and their own careers. Women began to demand rights and opportunities equal to those enjoyed by men (see the box on p. 606). More broadly, progressives called for an end to the concept of duty to the community and praised the Western individualist ethos. The popular short story writer Lu Xun (Lu Hsun) criticized the Confucian concept of family as a "man-eating" system that degraded humanity. In a famous short story titled "Diary of a Madman," the protagonist remarks:

> I remember when I was four or five years old, sitting in the cool of the hall, my brother told me that if a man's parents were ill, he should cut off a piece of his flesh and boil it for them if he wanted to be considered a good son. I have only just realized that I have been living all these years in a place where for four thousand years they have been eating human flesh.[4]

Such criticisms did have some beneficial results. During the early republic, the tyranny of the old family system began to decline, at least in urban areas, under the impact of economic changes and the urgings of the New Culture intellectuals. Women began to escape their cloistered existence and seek education and employment alongside their male contemporaries. Free choice in marriage and a more relaxed attitude toward sex became commonplace among affluent families in the cities, where the teenage children of Westernized elites aped the clothing, social habits, and even the musical tastes of their contemporaries in Europe and the United States.

But as a rule, the new individualism and women's rights did not penetrate to the textile factories, where more than a million women worked in conditions resembling slave labor, or to the villages, where traditional attitudes and customs still held sway (see the comparative essay "Out of the Doll's House" on p. 607). Arranged marriages continued to be the rule rather than the exception, and concubinage remained common. According to a survey taken in the 1930s, well over two-thirds of the marriages even among urban couples had been arranged by their parents.

A New Culture   Nowhere was the struggle between traditional and modern more visible than in the field of culture. Beginning with the New Culture era, radical reformists criticized traditional culture as the symbol and instrument of feudal oppression that must be entirely eradicated before a new China could stand with dignity in the modern world. During the 1920s and 1930s, Western literature and art became highly popular, especially among the urban middle class. Traditional culture continued to prevail among more conservative elements, and some intellectuals argued for a new art that would synthesize the best of Chinese and foreign culture. But the most creative artists were interested in imitating foreign trends, while traditionalists were more concerned with preservation.

Literature in particular was influenced by foreign ideas as Western genres like the novel and the short story attracted a growing audience. Although most Chinese novels written after World War I dealt with Chinese subjects, they reflected the Western tendency toward social realism and often dealt with the new Westernized middle class (Mao Dun's *Midnight,* for example, describes the changing mores of Shanghai's urban elites) or the disintegration of the traditional Confucian family (Ba Jin's famous novel *Family* is an example). Most of China's modern authors displayed a clear contempt for the past.

Japan Between the Wars

Q **Focus Question:** How did Japan address the problems of nation building in the first decades of the twentieth century, and why did democratic institutions not take hold more effectively?

During the first two decades of the twentieth century, Japan made remarkable progress toward the creation of an advanced society on the Western model. The political

AN ARRANGED MARRIAGE

Under Western influence, Chinese social customs changed dramatically for many urban elites in the interwar years. A vocal women's movement, inspired in part by translations of Henrik Ibsen's play *A Doll's House,* campaigned aggressively for universal suffrage and an end to sexual discrimination. Some progressives called for free choice in marriage and divorce and even for free love. By the 1930s, the government had taken some steps to free women from patriarchal marriage constraints and realize sexual equality. But life was generally unaffected in the villages, where traditional patterns held sway. This often created severe tensions between older and younger generations, as this passage by the popular twentieth-century novelist Ba Jin shows.

Ba Jin, *Family*

Brought up with loving care, after studying with a private tutor for a number of years, Chueh-hsin entered middle school. One of the school's best students, he graduated four years later at the top of his class. He was very interested in physics and chemistry and hoped to study abroad, in Germany. His mind was full of beautiful dreams. At that time he was the envy of his classmates.

In his fourth year at middle school, he lost his mother. His father later married again, this time to a younger woman who had been his mother's cousin. Chueh-hsin was aware of his loss, for he knew full well that nothing could replace the love of a mother. But her death left no irreparable wound in his heart; he was able to console himself with rosy dreams of his future. Moreover, he had someone who understood him and could comfort him—his pretty cousin Mei, "mei" for "plum blossom."

But then, one day, his dreams were shattered, cruelly and bitterly shattered. The evening he returned home carrying his diploma, the plaudits of his teachers and friends still ringing in his ears, his father called him into his room and said:

"Now that you've graduated, I want to arrange your marriage. Your grandfather is looking forward to having a great-grandson, and I, too, would like to be able to hold a grandson in my arms. You're old enough to be married; I won't feel easy until I fulfill my obligation to find you a wife. Although I didn't accumulate much money in my years away from home as an official, still I've put by enough for us to get along on. My health isn't what it used to be; I'm thinking of spending my time at home and having you help me run the household affairs. All the more reason you'll be needing a wife. I've already arranged a match with the Li family. The thirteenth of next month is a good day. We'll announce the engagement then. You can be married within the year...."

Chueh-hsin did not utter a word of protest, nor did such a thought ever occur to him. He merely nodded to indicate his compliance with his father's wishes. But after he returned to his own room, and shut the door, he threw himself down on his bed, covered his head with the quilt and wept. He wept for his broken dreams.

He was deeply in love with Mei, but now his father had chosen another, a girl he had never seen, and said that he must marry within the year. What's more, his hopes of continuing his studies had burst like a bubble. It was a terrible shock to Chueh-hsin. His future was finished, his beautiful dreams shattered.

He cried his disappointment and bitterness. But the door was closed and Chueh-hsin's head was beneath the bedding. No one knew. He did not fight back, he never thought of resisting. He only bemoaned his fate. But he accepted it. He complied with his father's will without a trace of resentment. But in his heart he wept for himself, wept for the girl he adored—Mei, his "plum blossom."

Q *Why does Chueh-hsin comply with the wishes of his father in the matter of his marriage? Why were arranged marriages so prevalent in traditional China?*

---

system based on the Meiji Constitution of 1890 began to evolve along Western pluralistic lines, and a multiparty system took shape. The economic and social reforms launched during the Meiji era led to increasing prosperity and the development of a modern industrial and commercial sector.

Experiment in Democracy

During the first quarter of the twentieth century, Japanese political parties expanded their popular following and became increasingly competitive. Individual pressure groups began to appear in Japanese society, along with an independent press and a bill of rights. The influence of

the old ruling oligarchy, the *genro,* had not yet been significantly challenged, however, nor had that of its ideological foundation, the *kokutai.*

These fragile democratic institutions were able to survive throughout the 1920s. During that period, the military budget was reduced, and a suffrage bill enacted in 1925 granted the vote to all Japanese males, thus continuing the process of democratization begun earlier in the century. Women remained disenfranchised; but women's associations gained increasing visibility during the 1920s, and many women were active in the labor movement and in campaigning for various social reforms.

But the era was also marked by growing social turmoil, and two opposing forces within the system were

COMPARATIVE ESSAY
OUT OF THE DOLL'S HOUSE

In Henrik Ibsen's play *A Doll's House,* published in 1879 and excerpted on page 503, Nora Helmer informs her husband, Torvald, that she will no longer accept his control over her life and announces her intention to leave home to start her life anew. When the outraged Torvald cites her sacred duties as wife and mother, Nora replies that she has other duties just as sacred, those to herself. "I can no longer content myself with what most people say," she declares. "I must think over things for myself and get to understand them."

To Ibsen's contemporaries, such remarks were revolutionary. In nineteenth-century Europe, the traditional characterization of the sexes, based on gender-defined social roles, had been elevated to the status of a universal law. As the family wage earners, men were expected to go off to work, while women were assigned the responsibility of caring for home and family. Women were advised to accept their lot and play their role as effectively and as gracefully as possible. In other parts of the world, women generally had even fewer rights in comparison with their male counterparts. Often, as in traditional China, they were viewed as a sex object.

The ideal, however, did not always match reality. With the advent of the Industrial Revolution, many women, especially those from the lower classes, were driven by the need for supplemental income to seek employment outside the home, often in the form of menial labor. Some women, inspired by the ideals of human dignity and freedom expressed during the Enlightenment and the French Revolution, began to protest against a tradition of female inferiority that had long kept them in a "doll's house" of male domination and to claim equal rights before the law.

© The Art Archive/Marc Charmet

The Chinese "Doll's House." A woman in traditional China binding her feet

The movement to liberate women from the iron cage of legal and social inferiority first began to gain ground in English-speaking countries such as Great Britain and the United States, but it gradually spread to the continent of Europe and then to colonial areas in Africa and Asia. By the first decades of the twentieth century, women's liberation movements were under way in parts of North Africa, the Middle East, and East Asia, voicing a growing demand for access to education, equal treatment before the law, and the right to vote. Nowhere was this more the case than in China, where a small minority of educated women began to agitate for equal rights with men.

Progress, however, was often agonizingly slow, especially in societies where age-old traditional values had not yet been undermined by the corrosive force of the Industrial Revolution. In many colonial societies, the effort to improve the condition of women was subordinated to the goal of gaining national independence. In some instances, women's liberation movements were led by educated elites who failed to include the concerns of working-class women in their agendas. Colonialism, too, was a double-edged sword, as the sexist bias of European officials combined with indigenous traditions of male superiority to marginalize women even further. As men moved to the cities to exploit opportunities provided by the new colonial administration, women were left to cope with their traditional responsibilities in the villages, often without the safety net of male support that had sustained them during the precolonial era.

Q *From the information available to you, do you believe that the imperialist policies applied in colonial territories served to benefit the cause of women's rights or not?*

gearing up to challenge the prevailing wisdom. On the left, a Marxist labor movement began to take shape in the early 1920s in response to growing economic difficulties. On the right, ultranationalist groups called for a rejection of Western models of development and a more militant approach to realizing national objectives.

This cultural conflict between old and new, native and foreign, was reflected in literature. Japanese self-confidence had been restored after the victories over China and Russia and launched an age of cultural creativity in the early twentieth century. Fascination with Western literature gave birth to a striking new genre

The Great Tokyo Earthquake. On September 1, 1923, a massive earthquake struck the central Japanese island of Honshu, causing more than 130,000 deaths and virtually demolishing the capital city of Tokyo. Though the quake was a national tragedy, it also came to symbolize the ingenuity of the Japanese people, whose efforts led to a rapid reconstruction of the city in a new and more modern style. That unity of national purpose would be demonstrated again a quarter of a century later in Japan's swift recovery from the devastation of World War II.

© Getty Images

called the "I novel." Defying traditional Japanese reticence, some authors reveled in self-exposure with confessions of their innermost thoughts. Others found release in the "proletarian literature" movement of the early 1920s. Inspired by Soviet literary examples, these authors wanted literature to serve socialist goals in order to improve the lives of the working class. Finally, some Japanese writers blended Western psychology with Japanese sensibility in exquisite novels reeking with nostalgia for the old Japan. One well-known example is Junichiro Tanizaki's *Some Prefer Nettles,* published in 1929, which delicately juxtaposed the positive aspects of both traditional and modern Japan. By the 1930s, however, military censorship increasingly inhibited free literary expression.

A *Zaibatsu* Economy

Japan also continued to make impressive progress in economic development. Spurred by rising domestic demand as well as continued government investment in the economy, the production of raw materials tripled between 1900 and 1930, and industrial production increased more than twelvefold. Much of the increase went into exports, and Western manufacturers began to complain about increasing competition from the Japanese.

As often happens, rapid industrialization was accompanied by some hardship and rising social tensions. In the Meiji model, various manufacturing processes were concentrated in a single enterprise, the **zaibatsu,** or financial clique. Some of these firms were existing merchant companies that had the capital and the foresight to

move into new areas of opportunity. Others were formed by enterprising samurai, who used their status and experience in management to good account in a new environment. Whatever their origins, these firms, often with official encouragement, gradually developed into large conglomerates that controlled a major segment of the Japanese economy. By 1937, the four largest *zaibatsu* (Mitsui, Mitsubishi, Sumitomo, and Yasuda) controlled 21 percent of the banking industry, 26 percent of mining, 35 percent of shipbuilding, 38 percent of commercial shipping, and more than 60 percent of paper manufacturing and insurance.

This concentration of power and wealth in a few major industrial combines created problems in Japanese society. In the first place, it resulted in the emergence of a dual economy: on the one hand, a modern industry characterized by up-to-date methods and massive government subsidies, and on the other, a traditional manufacturing sector characterized by conservative methods and small-scale production techniques.

Concentration of wealth also led to growing economic inequalities. As we have seen, economic growth had been achieved at the expense of the peasants, many of whom fled to the cities to escape rural poverty. That labor surplus benefited the industrial sector, but the urban proletariat was still poorly paid and ill-housed. A rapid increase in population (the total population of the Japanese islands increased from an estimated 43 million in 1900 to 73 million in 1940) led to food shortages and the threat of rising unemployment. In the meantime, those left on the farm continued to suffer. As late as the beginning of World War II, an estimated one-half of all Japanese farmers were tenants.

Shidehara Diplomacy

A final problem for Japanese leaders in the post-Meiji era was the familiar dilemma of finding sources of raw materials and foreign markets for the nation's manufactured goods. Until World War I, Japan had dealt with the problem by seizing territories such as Taiwan, Korea, and southern Manchuria and transforming them into colonies or protectorates of the growing Japanese empire. That policy had begun to arouse the concern, and in some cases the hostility, of the Western nations. China was also becoming apprehensive; as we have seen, Japanese demands for Shandong Province at the Paris Peace Conference in 1919 aroused massive protests in major Chinese cities.

The United States was especially concerned about Japanese aggressiveness. Although the United States had been less active than some European states in pursuing colonies in the Pacific, it had a strong interest in keeping the area open for U.S. commercial activities. In 1922, in Washington, D.C., the United States convened a major conference of nations with interests in the Pacific to discuss problems of regional security. The Washington Conference led to agreements on several issues, but the major accomplishment was a nine-power treaty recognizing the territorial integrity of China and the Open Door. The other participants induced Japan to accept these provisions by accepting its special position in Manchuria.

During the remainder of the 1920s, Japanese governments attempted to play by the rules laid down at the Washington Conference. Known as Shidehara diplomacy, after the foreign minister (and later prime minister) who attempted to carry it out, this policy sought to use diplomatic and economic means to realize Japanese interests in Asia. But this approach came under severe pressure as Japanese industrialists began to move into new areas, such as heavy industry, chemicals, mining, and the manufacturing of appliances and automobiles. Because such industries desperately needed resources not found in abundance locally, the Japanese government came under increasing pressure to find new sources abroad.

In the early 1930s, with the onset of the Great Depression and growing tensions in the international arena, nationalist forces rose to dominance in the government. Whereas party leaders during the 1920s had attempted to realize Japanese aspirations within the existing global political and economic framework, the dominant elements in the government in the 1930s, a mixture of military officers and ultranationalist politicians, were convinced that the diplomacy of the 1920s had failed; they advocated a more aggressive approach to protecting national interests in a brutal and competitive world. (see Chapter 25).

Nationalism and Dictatorship in Latin America

Q Focus Questions: What problems did the nations of Latin America face in the interwar years? To what degree were they a consequence of foreign influence?

Although the nations of Latin America played little role in World War I, that conflict nevertheless exerted an impact on the region, especially on its economy. By the end of the 1920s, the region was also strongly influenced by another event of global proportions—the Great Depression.

A Changing Economy

At the beginning of the twentieth century, virtually all of Latin America, except for the three Guianas, British Honduras, and some of the Caribbean islands, had achieved independence (see Map 24.2). The economy of the region was based largely on the export of foodstuffs and raw materials. Some countries relied on exports of only one or two products. Argentina, for example, exported primarily beef and wheat; Chile, nitrates and copper; Brazil and the Caribbean nations, sugar; and the Central American states, bananas. A few reaped large profits from these exports, but for the majority of the population, the returns were meager.

The Role of the Yankee Dollar World War I led to a decline in European investment in Latin America and a rise in the U.S. role in the local economies. By the late 1920s, the United States had replaced Great Britain as the foremost source of investment in Latin America. Unlike the British, however, U.S. investors put their funds directly into production enterprises, causing large segments of the area's export industries to fall into American hands. A number of Central American states, for example, were popularly labeled "banana republics" because of the power and influence of the U.S.-owned United Fruit Company. American firms also dominated the copper mining industry in Chile and Peru and the oil industry in Mexico, Peru, and Bolivia.

The Effects of Dependence

During the late nineteenth century, most governments in Latin America had been increasingly dominated by

MAP 24.2 **Latin America in the First Half of the Twentieth Century.** Shown here are the boundaries dividing the countries of Latin America after the independence movements of the nineteenth century.

Q Which areas remained under European rule?

together possessed more than half of the land and wealth of Latin America.

Argentina The political domination of Argentina by an elite minority often had disastrous effects. The Argentine government, controlled by landowners who had benefited from the export of beef and wheat, was slow to recognize the growing importance of establishing a local industrial base. In 1916, Hipólito Irigoyen (1852–1933), head of the Radical Party, was elected president on a program to improve conditions for the middle and lower classes. Little was achieved, however, as the party became increasingly corrupt and drew closer to the large landowners. In 1930, the army overthrew Irigoyen's government and reestablished the power of the landed class. But their efforts to return to the previous export economy and suppress the growing influence of the labor unions failed.

Brazil Brazil followed a similar path. In 1889, the army overthrew the Brazilian monarchy, installed by Portugal years before, and established a republic. But it was dominated by landed elites, many of whom had grown wealthy through their ownership of coffee plantations. By 1900, three-quarters of the world's coffee was grown in Brazil. As in Argentina, the ruling oligarchy ignored the importance of establishing an urban industrial base. When the Great Depression ravaged profits from coffee exports, a wealthy rancher, Getúlio Vargas (1883–1954), seized power and ruled the country as president from 1930 to 1945. At first, Vargas sought to appease workers by declaring an eight-hour workday and a minimum wage, but, influenced by the apparent success of fascist regimes in Europe, he ruled by increasingly autocratic means and relied on a police force that used torture to silence his opponents.

landed or military elites, who controlled the mass of the population—mostly impoverished peasants—by the blatant use of military force. This trend toward authoritarianism increased during the 1930s as domestic instability caused by the effects of the Great Depression led to the creation of dictatorships throughout the region. This trend was especially evident in Argentina and Brazil and to a lesser degree in Mexico—three countries that

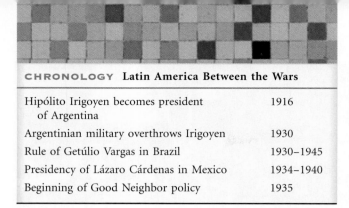

His industrial policy was relatively enlightened, however, and by the end of World War II, Brazil had become Latin America's major industrial power. In 1945, the army, fearing that Vargas might prolong his power illegally after calling for new elections, forced him to resign.

Mexico   Mexico, in the early years of the new century, was in a state of turbulence. Under the rule of dictator Porfirio Díaz (see Chapter 20), the real wages of the working class had declined. Moreover, 95 percent of the rural population owned no land, and about a thousand families ruled almost all of Mexico. When a liberal landowner, Francisco Madero, forced Díaz from power in 1910, he opened the door to a wider revolution. Madero's ineffectiveness triggered a demand for agrarian reform led by Emiliano Zapata (1879–1919), who aroused the masses of landless peasants in southern Mexico and began to seize the haciendas of wealthy landholders.

For the next several years, Zapata and rebel leader Pancho Villa (1878–1923), who operated in the northern state of Chihuahua, became an important political force in the country by publicly advocating efforts to redress the economic grievances of the poor. But neither had a broad grasp of the challenges facing the country, and power eventually gravitated to a more moderate group of reformists around the Constitutionalist Party. The latter were intent on breaking the power of the great landed families and U.S. corporations, but without engaging in radical land reform or the nationalization of property. After a bloody conflict that cost the lives of thousands, the moderates consolidated power, and in 1917, they promulgated a new constitution that established a strong presidency, initiated land reform policies, established limits on foreign investment, and set an agenda for social welfare programs.

In 1920, Constitutionalist leader Alvaro Obregón assumed the presidency and began to carry out his reform program. But real change did not take place until the presidency of General Lázaro Cárdenas (1895–1970)

in 1934. Cárdenas won wide popularity with the peasants by ordering the redistribution of 44 million acres of land controlled by landed elites. He also seized control of the oil industry, which had hitherto been dominated by major U.S. oil companies. Alluding to the Good Neighbor policy, President Roosevelt refused to intervene, and eventually Mexico agreed to compensate U.S. oil companies for their lost property. It then set up PEMEX, a governmental organization, to run the oil industry.

Latin American Culture

The first half of the twentieth century witnessed a dramatic increase in literary activity in Latin America, a result in part of its ambivalent relationship with Europe and the United States. Many authors, while experimenting with imported modernist styles, felt compelled to proclaim Latin America's unique identity through the adoption of native themes and social issues. In *The Underdogs* (1915), for example, Mariano Azuela (1873–1952) presented a sympathetic but not uncritical portrait of the Mexican Revolution as his country entered an era of unsettling change.

In their determination to commend Latin America's distinctive characteristics, some writers extolled the promise of the region's vast virgin lands and the diversity of its peoples. In *Don Segundo Sombra,* published in 1926, Ricardo Guiraldes (1886–1927) celebrated the life of the ideal gaucho (cowboy), defining Argentina's hope and strength through the enlightened management of its fertile earth. Likewise, in *Dona Barbara,* Rómulo Gallegos (1884–1969) wrote in a similar vein about his native Venezuela. Other authors pursued the theme of solitude and detachment, a product of the region's physical separation from the rest of the world.

Latin American artists followed their literary counterparts in joining the Modernist movement in Europe, yet they too were eager to promote the emergence of a new regional and national essence. In Mexico, where the government provided financial support for painting murals on public buildings, the artist Diego Rivera (1886–1957) began to produce a monumental style of mural art that served two purposes: to illustrate the national past by portraying Aztec legends and folk customs and to popularize a political message in favor of realizing the social goals of the Mexican Revolution. His wife, Frida Kahlo (1907–1954), incorporated Surrealist whimsy in her own paintings, many of which were portraits of herself and her family.

Struggle for the Banner. Like Diego Rivera, David Alfaro Siqueiros (1896–1974) adorned public buildings with large murals that celebrated the Mexican Revolution and the workers' and peasants' struggle for freedom. Beginning in the 1930s, Siqueiros expressed sympathy for the exploited and downtrodden peoples of Mexico in dramatic frescoes such as this one. He painted similar murals in Uruguay, Argentina, and Brazil and was once expelled from the United States, where his political art and views were considered too radical.

CONCLUSION

THE TURMOIL BROUGHT about by World War I not only resulted in the destruction of several of the major Western empires and a redrawing of the map of Europe but also opened the door to political and social upheavals elsewhere in the world. In the Middle East, the decline and fall of the Ottoman Empire led to the creation of the secular republic of Turkey. The state of Saudi Arabia emerged in the Arabian peninsula, and Palestine became a source of tension between newly arrived Jewish immigrants and longtime Muslim residents.

Other parts of Asia and Africa also witnessed the rise of movements for national independence. In Africa, these movements were spearheaded by native leaders educated in Europe or the United States. In India, Gandhi and his campaign of civil disobedience played a crucial role in his country's bid to be free of British rule. Communist movements also began to emerge in Asian societies as radical elements sought new methods of bringing about the overthrow of Western imperialism. Japan continued to follow its own path to modernization, which, although successful from an economic point of view, took a menacing turn during the 1930s.

Between 1919 and 1939, China experienced a dramatic struggle to establish a modern nation. Two dynamic political organizations—the Nationalists and the Communists—competed for legitimacy as the rightful heirs of the old order. At first, they formed an alliance in an effort to defeat their common adversaries, but cooperation ultimately turned to conflict. The Nationalists under Chiang Kai-shek emerged supreme, but Chiang found it difficult to control the remnants of the warlord regime in China, while the Great Depression undermined his efforts to build an industrial nation.

During the interwar years, the nations of Latin America faced severe economic problems because of their dependence on exports. Increasing U.S. investments in Latin America contributed to growing hostility toward the powerful neighbor to the north. The Great Depression forced the region to begin developing new industries, but it also led to the rise of authoritarian governments, some of them modeled after the fascist regimes of Italy and Germany.

By demolishing the remnants of their old civilization on the battlefields of World War I, Europeans had inadvertently encouraged the subject peoples of their vast colonial empires to begin their own movements for national independence.

The process was by no means completed in the two decades following the Treaty of Versailles, but the bonds of imperial rule had been severely strained. Once Europeans began to weaken themselves in the even more destructive conflict of World War II, the hopes of African and Asian peoples for national independence and freedom could at last be realized. It is to that devastating world conflict that we now turn.

TIMELINE

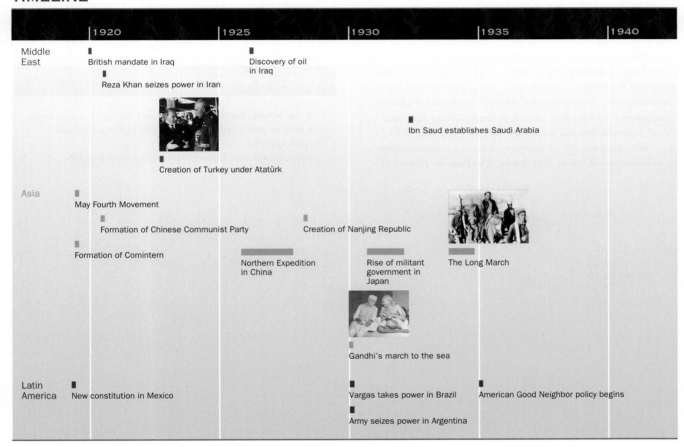

	1920	1925	1930	1935	1940
Middle East	British mandate in Iraq / Reza Khan seizes power in Iran / Creation of Turkey under Atatürk	Discovery of oil in Iraq	Ibn Saud establishes Saudi Arabia		
Asia	May Fourth Movement / Formation of Chinese Communist Party / Formation of Comintern	Northern Expedition in China	Creation of Nanjing Republic / Rise of militant government in Japan / Gandhi's march to the sea	The Long March	
Latin America	New constitution in Mexico		Vargas takes power in Brazil / Army seizes power in Argentina	American Good Neighbor policy begins	

SUGGESTED READING

Nationalism The classic study of nationalism in the non-Western world is **R. Emerson, *From Empire to Nation*** (Boston, 1960). For a more recent approach, see **B. Anderson, *Imagined Communities: Reflections on the Origin and Spread of Nationalism*** (London, 1983). On nationalism in India, see **S. Wolpert, *Congress and Indian Nationalism: The Pre-Independence Phase*** (New York, 1988). Also see **P. Chatterjee, *The Nation and Its Fragments: Colonial and Postcolonial Histories*** (Princeton, N.J., 1993), and **E. Gellner, *Nations and Nationalism*** (Ithaca, N.Y., 1994).

Gandhi There have been a number of studies of Mahatma Gandhi and his ideas. See, for example, **S. Wolpert, *Gandhi's Passion: The Life and Legacy of Mahatma Gandhi*** (Oxford, 1999), and **D. Dalton, *Mahatma Gandhi: Nonviolent Power in Action*** (New York, 1995). For a study of Nehru, see **J. M. Brown, *Nehru*** (New York, 2000).

Middle East For a general survey of events in the Middle East in the interwar era, see **E. Bogle, *The Modern Middle East: From Imperialism to Freedom*** (Upper Saddle River, N.J., 1996). For more specialized studies, see **I. Gershoni et al., *Egypt, Islam, and the***

Arabs: The Search for Egyptian Nationhood (Oxford, 1993), and
W. Laqueur, A History of Zionism: From the French Revolution to
the Establishment of the State of Israel (New York, 1996). The role
of Atatürk is examined in A. Mango, Atatürk: The Biography of the
Founder of Modern Turkey (New York, 2000). The Palestinian issue
is dealt with in B. Morris, Righteous Victims: The Palestinian
Conflict, 1880–2000 (New York, 2001). On the founding of Iraq, see
S. Mackey, The Reckoning: Iraq and the Legacy of Saddam Hussein
(New York, 2002). Nascent nationalist movements in Africa are
discussed in R. Collins, Historical Problems of Imperial Africa
(Princeton, N.J., 1994). For a penetrating account of the fall of the
Ottoman Empire and its consequences for the postwar era, see
D. Fromkin, A Peace to End All Peace: The Fall of the Ottoman
Empire and the Creation of the Modern Middle East
(New York, 2001).

China On the early Chinese republic, a good study is
J. Fitzgerald, Awakening China: Politics, Culture, and Class in the
Nationalist Revolution (Stanford, Calif., 1996). The rise of the Chinese
Communist Party is discussed in A. Dirlik, The Origins of Chinese
Communism (Oxford, 1989). Also see J. Fenby, Chiang Kai-shek:
China's Generalissimo and the Nation He Lost (New York, 2003).

Latin America For an overview of Latin American history in
the interwar period, see E. Williamson, The Penguin History of
Latin America (Harmondsworth, England, 1992). Also see
J. Franco, The Modern Culture of Latin America: Society and
the Artist (Harmondsworth, England, 1970).

Women For a general introduction to the women's movement
during this era, consult C. Johnson-Odim and M. Strobel, eds.,
Restoring Women to History (Bloomington, Ind., 1999). For
collections of essays concerning African women, see C. Robertson
and I. Berger, Women and Class in Africa (New York, 1986), and
S. Stichter and J. I. Parparti, eds., Patriarchy and Class: African
Women in the Home and Workforce (Boulder, Colo., 1988). To
follow the women's movement in India, see S. Tharu and K. Lalita,
Women Writing in India, vol. 2 (New York, 1993). For Japan,
see S. Sievers, Flowers in Salt: The Beginnings of Feminist
Consciousness in Modern Japan (Stanford, Calif., 1983).

WORLD HISTORY RESOURCES

Visit the website for *The Essential World History* to access study
aids such as Flashcards, Critical Thinking Exercises, and
Chapter Quizzes:
   www.cengage.com/history/duikspiel/essentialworld6e

DISCOVERY

How did the societies discussed in this chapter deal with the political, economic, and social challenges that they faced after World War I, and how did these challenges differ from one region to another?

In thinking about this question, begin by breaking it down into the components shown below. A discussion of the significance of each component should appear in your answer.

POLITICS AND GOVERNMENT   The text points out that when the leadership of nationalist movements passes from the founders to their successors, there is often a change in strategies and tactics. How do the four leaders shown in the photos on page 594 illustrate this point? Compare their goals and the strategies and tactics they used to try to achieve their goals. How did each of them attempt to solve the problems that his country faced?

Considering the speeches by Mustafa Kemal and Mohammed Iqbal (below and on p. 597), discuss the relationship between Western values and traditional religion and culture in India and in the countries that were formed from the Ottoman Empire. What tensions existed between them? Why did such tensions pose difficulties for nationalist leaders? How did developments in Turkey, Iraq, and India differ during the interwar years? Can you see any connection between these differences and the current political situation in each nation? Do you think that having a leader who had been a military officer such as Mustafa Kemal creates any problems for a nation?

ISLAM IN THE MODERN WORLD: TWO VIEWS

Atatürk, Speech to the Assembly (October 1924)

The sovereign entitled Caliph was to maintain justice among the three hundred million Muslims on the terrestrial globe, to safeguard the rights of these peoples, to prevent any event that could encroach upon order and security, and confront every attack which the Muslims would be called upon to encounter from the side of other nations. It was to be part of his attributes to preserve by all means the welfare and spiritual development of Islam. …

If the Caliph and Caliphate, as they maintained, were to be invested with a dignity embracing the whole of Islam, ought they not to have realized in all justice that a crushing burden would be imposed on Turkey, on her existence; her entire resources and all her forces would be placed at the disposal of the Caliph?…

For centuries our nation was guided under the influence of these erroneous ideas. But what has been the result of it? Everywhere they have lost millions of men. "Do you know," I asked, "how many sons of Anatolia have perished in the scorching deserts of the Yemen? Do you know the losses we have suffered in holding Syria and Egypt and in maintaining our position in Africa? And do you see what has come out of it? Do you know?

"Those who favor the idea of placing the means at the disposal of the Caliph to brave the whole world and the power to administer the affairs of the whole of Islam must not appeal to the population of Anatolia alone but to the great Muslim agglomerations which are eight or ten times as rich in men.

"New Turkey, the people of New Turkey, have no reason to think of anything else but their own existence and their own welfare. She has nothing more to give away to others."

Mohammed Iqbal, Speech to the All-India Muslim League (1930)

It cannot be denied that Islam, regarded as an ethical ideal plus a certain kind of polity—by which expression I mean a social structure regulated by a legal system and animated by a specific ethical ideal—has been the chief formative factor in the life history of the Muslims of India. It has furnished those basic emotions and loyalties which gradually unify scattered individuals and groups and finally transform them into a well-defined people. Indeed it is no exaggeration to say that India is perhaps the only country in the world where Islam, as a people-building force, has worked at its best. In India, as elsewhere, the structure of Islam as a society is almost entirely due to the working of Islam as a culture inspired by a specific ethical ideal. What I mean to say is that Muslim society, with its remarkable homogeneity and inner unity, has grown to be what it is under the pressure of the laws and institutions associated with the culture of Islam.

Communalism in its higher aspect, then, is indispensable to the formation of a harmonious whole in a country like India. The units of Indian society are not territorial as in European countries. India is a continent of human groups belonging to different religions. Their behavior is not at all determined by a common race consciousness. Even the Hindus do not form a homogeneous group. The principle of European democracy cannot be applied to India without recognizing the fact of communal groups. The Muslim demand for the creation of a Muslim India within India is, therefore, perfectly justified.…

I therefore demand the formation of a consolidated Muslim State in the best interests of India and Islam. For India it means security and peace resulting from an internal balance of power; for Islam an opportunity to rid itself of the stamp that Arabian imperialism was forced to give it, to mobilize its law, its education, its culture, and to bring them into closer contact with its own original spirit and with the spirit of modern times.

CHAPTER 25

THE CRISIS DEEPENS: WORLD WAR II

Adolf Hitler salutes military leaders and soldiers during a military rally.

© Hugo Jaeger/Time Life Pictures/Getty Images

CHAPTER OUTLINE AND FOCUS QUESTIONS

Retreat from Democracy: Dictatorial Regimes

Q What are the characteristics of totalitarian states, and to what degree were these characteristics present in Fascist Italy, Nazi Germany, and Stalinist Russia? To what extent, if any, was Japan a totalitarian state?

The Path to War

Q What were the underlying causes of World War II, and what specific steps taken by Nazi Germany and Japan led to war?

World War II

Q What were the main events of World War II in Europe and Asia?

The New Order

Q What was the nature of the new orders that Germany and Japan attempted to establish in the territories they occupied?

The Home Front

Q What were conditions like on the home front for the major belligerents in World War II?

Aftermath of the War

Q What were the costs of World War II? How did the Allies' visions of the postwar differ, and how did these differences contribute to the emergence of the Cold War?

CRITICAL THINKING

Q What was the relationship between World War I and World War II, and what were the differences in the ways the wars were fought?

ON FEBRUARY 3, 1933, three days after he had been appointed chancellor of Germany, Adolf Hitler met secretly with Germany's leading generals. He revealed to them his desire to remove the "cancer of democracy," create a new authoritarian leadership, and forge a new domestic unity. All Germans would need to realize that "only a struggle [could save them] and that everything else must be subordinated to this idea." Since Germany's living space was too small for its people, Hitler said, Germany must rearm and prepare for "the conquest of new living space in the east and its ruthless Germanization." Even before he had consolidated his power, Adolf Hitler had a clear vision of his goals, and their implementation meant another war in Europe. World War II in Europe was Hitler's war. Other countries may have contributed by not resisting Hitler earlier, but Nazi Germany's actions alone made World War II inevitable.

It became far more than just Hitler's war, however. World War II was really two conflicts: one provoked by the ambitions of Germany in Europe, the other by the ambitions of Japan in Asia. When the United States and major European nations raised their tariff rates against Japanese imports in the early 1930s in a desperate effort to protect local businesses and jobs, militant groups in Tokyo began to argue that Japan must obtain by violent action what it could not secure by peaceful means. By 1941, with the United States embroiled in both wars, the two had merged into a single global conflict.

Although World War I had been described as a total war, World War II was even more so and was fought on a scale unique in history. Almost everyone in the warring countries was involved in one way or another—as soldiers; as workers in wartime industries; as ordinary citizens subject to invading armies, military occupation, or bombing raids; as refugees; or as victims of mass extermination. The world had never witnessed such widespread death and destruction at the hands of humans. ✱

Retreat from Democracy: Dictatorial Regimes

Q Focus Questions: What are the characteristics of totalitarian states, and to what degree were these characteristics present in Fascist Italy, Nazi Germany, and Stalinist Russia? To what extent, if any, was Japan a totalitarian state?

The rise of dictatorial regimes in the 1930s had a great deal to do with the coming of World War II. By 1939, only two major states in Europe, France and Great Britain, remained democratic. Italy and Germany had succumbed to the political movement called **fascism,** and Soviet Russia under Stalin moved toward repressive totalitarianism. A host of other European states and Latin American countries adopted authoritarian structures of different kinds, while a militarist regime in Japan moved that country down the path to war.

The dictatorial regimes between the wars assumed both old and new forms. Dictatorship was not new, but the modern **totalitarian state** was. The totalitarian regimes, best exemplified by Stalinist Russia and Nazi Germany, greatly extended the functions and power of the central state. The new "total states" expected the active loyalty and commitment of citizens to the regime's goal, whether it be war, a socialist society, or a thousand-year Reich. They used modern mass propaganda techniques and high-speed communications to conquer the minds and hearts of their subjects. The total state sought to control not only the economic, political, and social aspects of life but the intellectual and cultural aspects as well.

The modern totalitarian state was to be led by a single leader and a single party. It ruthlessly rejected the liberal ideal of limited government power and constitutional guarantees of individual freedoms. Indeed, individual freedom was to be subordinated to the collective will of the masses, organized and determined for them by the leader or leaders. Modern technology also gave total states unprecedented police controls to enforce their wishes on their subjects.

The Birth of Fascism

In the early 1920s, Benito Mussolini (1883–1945) burst on the Italian scene with the first successful fascist movement in Europe. In 1919, Mussolini, a veteran of World War I, had established a new political group, the *Fascio di Combattimento* (League of Combat), which won support from middle-class industrialists fearful of working-class agitation and large landowners who objected to agricultural strikes. The movement gained momentum as Mussolini's nationalist rhetoric and the middle-class fear of socialism, Communist revolution, and disorder made the Fascists seem more and more attractive. On October 29, 1922, after Mussolini and the Fascists threatened to march on Rome if they were not given power, King Victor Emmanuel (1900–1946) capitulated and made Mussolini prime minister of Italy.

By 1926, Mussolini had established the institutional framework for a Fascist dictatorship. The prime minister was made "head of government" with the power to legislate by decree. The police were empowered to arrest and confine anybody for both nonpolitical and political crimes without due process of law. The government was given the power to dissolve political and cultural associations. In 1926, all anti-Fascist parties were outlawed, and a secret police force was established. By the end of the year, Mussolini ruled Italy as *Il Duce,* the leader.

Mussolini conceived of the Fascist state as totalitarian: "Fascism is totalitarian, and the Fascist State, the synthesis and unity of all values, interprets, develops and gives strength to the whole life of the people."[1] Mussolini did try to create a police state, but it was not very effective. Neither was the Italian Fascists' attempt to exercise control over all forms of mass media, including newspapers, radio, and cinema, in order to use propaganda as a means of integrating the masses into the state. Most commonly, Fascist propaganda was disseminated through simple slogans, such as "Mussolini is always right," plastered on walls all over Italy.

The Fascists portrayed the family as the pillar of the state and women as the basic foundation of the family. "Woman into the home" became the Fascist slogan. Women were to be homemakers and baby producers, "their natural and fundamental mission in life," according to Mussolini, for population growth was viewed as an indicator of national strength. Employment outside the home might distract women from conception: "It forms an independence and consequent physical and moral habits contrary to child bearing."[2]

Despite the instruments of repression, the use of propaganda, and the creation of numerous Fascist organizations, Mussolini never achieved the degree of totalitarian control attained in Hitler's Germany or Stalin's Soviet Union. Mussolini and the Fascist Party never completely destroyed the old power structure, and they were soon overshadowed by a much more powerful fascist movement to the north.

Hitler and Nazi Germany

In 1923, a small rightist party led by an obscure Austrian rabble-rouser named Adolf Hitler (1889–1945) attempted to seize power in southern Germany in the notorious Beer Hall Putsch. Although the effort failed, the attempted putsch brought Hitler and the Nazis to national prominence.

Hitler's Rise to Power, 1919–1933 At the end of World War I, after four years of service on the Western Front, Hitler went to Munich and decided to enter politics. In 1919, he joined the obscure German Workers' Party, one of a number of right-wing extreme nationalist parties. By the summer of 1921, Hitler had assumed control of the party, which he renamed the National Socialist German Workers' Party, or Nazi Party for short. In two years, membership reached 55,000, including 15,000 in the party militia, the SA (for *Sturmabteilung*, or Storm Troops).

The overconfident Hitler staged an armed uprising against the government in Munich in November 1923, the Beer Hall Putsch. The putsch was quickly crushed, and Hitler was sentenced to prison. During his brief stay in jail, he wrote *Mein Kampf* (My Struggle), an autobiographical account of his movement and its underlying ideology—extreme German nationalism, virulent anti-Semitism, and anticommunism linked together by a social Darwinian theory of struggle that stresses the right of superior nations to *Lebensraum* (living space) through expansion and the right of superior individuals to secure authoritarian leadership over the masses.

During his imprisonment, Hitler also came to the realization that the Nazis would have to come to power by constitutional means, not by overthrowing the Weimar Republic. After his release from prison, Hitler reorganized the Nazi Party and competed for votes with the other political parties. By 1929, the Nazis had a national party organization.

Three years later, the Nazi Party had 800,000 members and had become the largest party in the Reichstag. No doubt Germany's economic difficulties were a crucial factor in the Nazis' rise to power. Unemployment rose dramatically, from 4.35 million in 1931 to 6 million by the winter of 1932. Claiming to stand above all differences, Hitler promised that he would create a new Germany free of class differences and party infighting. His appeal to national pride, national honor, and traditional militarism struck receptive chords in his listeners. After attending one of Hitler's rallies, a schoolteacher in Hamburg said: "When the speech was over, there was roaring enthusiasm and applause. . . . Then he went—How many look up to him with touching faith as their savior, their deliverer from unbearable distress."[3]

Increasingly, the right-wing elites of Germany—the industrial magnates, landed aristocrats, military establishment, and higher bureaucrats—came to see Hitler as the man who had the mass support to establish a right-wing, authoritarian regime that would save Germany and their privileged positions from a Communist takeover. Under pressure, President Paul von Hindenburg agreed to allow Hitler to become chancellor (on January 30, 1933) and form a new government.

Within two months, Hitler laid the foundations for the Nazis' complete takeover of Germany. The crowning step of Hitler's "legal seizure" of power came on March 23, when the Reichstag, by a two-thirds vote, passed the Enabling Act, which empowered the government to dispense with constitutional forms for four years while it issued laws to deal with the country's problems.

With their new source of power, the Nazis acted quickly to bring all institutions under their control. The civil service was purged of Jews and democratic elements, concentration camps were established for opponents of the new regime, trade unions were dissolved, and all political parties except the Nazis were abolished. By the end of the summer of 1933, Hitler and the Nazis had established the foundations for a totalitarian state. When Hindenburg died on August 2, 1934, the office of Reich president was abolished, and Hitler became *der Führer* (the leader)—sole ruler of Germany.

The Nazi State, 1933–1939 Having smashed the parliamentary state, Hitler now felt the real task was at hand: to develop the "total state." Hitler's goal was the development of an Aryan racial state that would dominate Europe and possibly the world for generations to come. Hitler stated:

> We must develop organizations in which an individual's entire life can take place. Then every activity and every need of every individual will be regulated by the collectivity represented by the party. There is no longer any arbitrary will, there are no longer any free realms in which the individual belongs to himself. . . . The time of personal happiness is over.[4]

The Nazis pursued the realization of this totalitarian ideal in a variety of ways.

The Nazi Mass Spectacle. Hitler and the Nazis made clever use of mass spectacles to rally the German people behind the Nazi regime. These mass demonstrations evoked intense enthusiasm, as is evident in this photograph of Hitler arriving at the Bückeberg near Hamelin for the Harvest Festival in 1937. Almost one million people were present for the celebration.

Mass demonstrations and spectacles were orchestrated to draw the German nation into a collective fellowship and to mobilize it as an instrument for Hitler's policies. These mass demonstrations, especially the party rallies that were held in Nuremberg every September, combined the symbolism of a religious service with the merriment of a popular amusement and usually evoked mass enthusiasm and excitement.

Despite the symbolism and Hitler's goal of establishing an all-powerful government that would maintain absolute control and order, in actuality, Nazi Germany was the scene of almost constant personal and institutional conflict, which resulted in administrative chaos. Struggle characterized relationships within the party, within the state, and between party and state. Hitler, of course, remained the ultimate decision maker and absolute ruler.

In the economic sphere, Hitler and the Nazis also worked to establish control. Although the regime used public works projects and "pump-priming" grants to private construction firms to foster employment and end the depression, there is little doubt that rearmament did far more to solve the unemployment problem. Unemployment, which had stood at 6 million in 1932, dropped to 2.6 million in 1934 and less than 500,000 in 1937. This was an important factor in convincing many Germans to accept the new regime despite its excesses.

For those who needed coercion, the Nazi total state had its instruments of terror and repression. Especially important were the *Schutzstaffeln* (guard squadrons), known simply as the SS. The SS, under the direction of Heinrich Himmler (1900–1945), came to control all of the regular and secret police forces. Himmler and the SS functioned on the basis of two principles: terror and ideology. Terror included the instruments of repression and murder: secret police, criminal police, concentration camps, and later execution squads and death camps for the extermination of the Jews. For Himmler, the primary goal of the SS was to further the Aryan "master race."

The Nazi total state was intended to be an Aryan racial state. From its beginning, the Nazi Party reflected the strong anti-Semitic beliefs of Adolf Hitler. Women were to play a crucial role in the Aryan racial state as bearers of the children who would bring about the triumph of the Aryan race. To the Nazis, the differences between men and women were natural: men were destined to be warriors and political leaders; women were to be wives and mothers.

Once in power, the Nazis translated anti-Semitic ideas into anti-Semitic policies. In September 1935, at the annual party rally in Nuremberg, the Nazis announced new racial laws, which excluded German Jews from German citizenship and forbade marriages and extramarital relations between Jews and German citizens.

A more violent phase of anti-Jewish activity took place in 1938 and 1939, initiated on November 9–10, 1938, by the infamous *Kristallnacht*, the "night of shattered glass." The assassination of a third secretary in the German embassy in Paris became the excuse for a Nazi-led destructive rampage against the Jews in which synagogues were burned, seven thousand Jewish businesses were destroyed, and at least one hundred Jews were killed. Jews were barred from all public buildings and prohibited from owning or working in any retail store.

The Stalinist Era in the Soviet Union

Joseph Stalin made a significant shift in economic policy in 1928 when he launched his first five-year plan. Its real goal was nothing less than the transformation of the agrarian Soviet Union into an industrial country virtually overnight. Instead of producing consumer goods, the first five-year plan emphasized production of capital goods and armaments and succeeded in quadrupling the production of heavy machinery and doubling oil production. Between 1928 and 1937, during the first two five-year plans, steel production increased from 4 million to 18 million tons per year.

Rapid industrialization was accompanied by an equally rapid collectivization of agriculture. Its goal was to eliminate private farms and push people into collective farms. Strong resistance to Stalin's plans from peasants who hoarded crops and killed livestock only caused him to step up the program. By 1934, Russia's 26 million family farms had been collectivized into 250,000 units, though at a tremendous cost, since the hoarding of food and the slaughter of livestock produced widespread famine. Perhaps 10 million peasants died in the artificially created famines of 1932 and 1933. The only concession Stalin made to the peasants was to allow each collective farm worker to have one tiny privately owned garden plot.

To achieve his goals, Stalin strengthened the party bureaucracy under his control. Those who resisted were sent into forced labor camps in Siberia. Stalin's desire for sole control of decision making also led to purges of the Old Bolsheviks. Between 1936 and 1938, the most prominent Old Bolsheviks were put on trial and condemned to death. During this same time, Stalin undertook a purge of army officers, diplomats, union officials, party members, intellectuals, and numerous ordinary citizens. Estimates are that eight million Russians were arrested; millions were sent to forced labor camps in Siberia from which they never returned.

The Stalinist era also reversed much of the permissive social legislation of the early 1920s. Advocating complete equality of rights for women, the Communists had made divorce and abortion easy to obtain while also encouraging women to work outside the home and to set their own moral standards. After Stalin came to power, the family was praised as a miniature collective in which parents were responsible for inculcating values of duty, discipline, and hard work. Abortion was outlawed, and divorced fathers who failed to support their children were fined heavily.

The Rise of Militarism in Japan

The rise of militant forces in Japan resulted not from a seizure of power by a new political party but from the growing influence of militant elements at the top of the political hierarchy. In the early 1930s, confrontations with China in Manchuria, combined with the onset of the Great Depression, brought an end to the fragile stability of the immediate postwar years.

The depression had a disastrous effect on Japan, as many European countries, along with the United States, raised stiff tariff walls against cheap Japanese imports in order to protect their struggling domestic industries. The ensuing economic slowdown imposed a heavy burden on the fragile democracy in Japan. Although civilian cabinets tried desperately to cope with the economic challenges presented by the world depression, the political parties were no longer able to stem the growing influence of militant nationalist elements. Extremist patriotic organizations began to terrorize Japanese society by assassinating businessmen and public figures identified with the policy of conciliation toward the outside world. Some argued that Western-style political institutions should be replaced by a new system that would return to traditional Japanese values and imperial authority. Their message of "Asia for the Asians" became increasingly popular as the Great Depression convinced many Japanese that capitalism was unsuitable for Japan.

During the mid-1930s, the influence of the military and extreme nationalists over the government steadily increased. National elections continued to take place, but cabinets were dominated by the military or advocates of Japanese expansionism. In February 1936, junior army officers led a coup, briefly occupying the Diet building and other key government installations in Tokyo and assassinating several members of the cabinet. The ringleaders were quickly tried and convicted of treason, but under conditions that further strengthened the influence of the military.

The Path to War

Q **Focus Question:** What were the underlying causes of World War II, and what specific steps taken by Nazi Germany and Japan led to war?

Only twenty years after the "war to end war," the world plunged back into the nightmare. The efforts at collective security in the 1920s proved meaningless in view of the growth of Nazi Germany and the rise of militant Japan.

The Path to War in Europe

World War II in Europe had its beginnings in the ideas of Adolf Hitler, who believed that only the Aryans were capable of building a great civilization. To Hitler, Germany needed more land to support a larger population and be a great power. Already in the 1920s, in the second volume of *Mein Kampf*, Hitler had indicated that a National Socialist regime would find this land to the east—in Russia.

On March 9, 1935, in defiance of the Treaty of Versailles, Hitler announced the creation of an air force and one week later the introduction of a military draft that

OPPOSING VIEWPOINTS
THE MUNICH CONFERENCE

At the Munich Conference, the leaders of France and Great Britain capitulated to Hitler's demands on Czechoslovakia. Although the British prime minister, Neville Chamberlain, defended his actions at Munich as necessary for peace, another British statesman, Winston Churchill, characterized the settlement at Munich as "a disaster of the first magnitude."

Winston Churchill, Speech to the House of Commons, October 5, 1938

I will begin by saying what everybody would like to ignore or forget but which must nevertheless be stated, namely, that we have sustained a total and unmitigated defeat, and that France has suffered even more than we have.... The utmost my right honorable Friend the Prime Minister ... has been able to gain for Czechoslovakia and in the matters which were in dispute has been that the German dictator, instead of snatching his victuals from the table, has been content to have them served to him course by course.... And I will say this, that I believe the Czechs, left to themselves and told they were going to get no help from the Western Powers, would have been able to make better terms than they have got....

We are in the presence of a disaster of the first magnitude which has befallen Great Britain and France. Do not let us blind ourselves to that....

And do not suppose that this is the end. This is only the beginning of the reckoning. This is only the first sip, the first foretaste of a bitter cup which will be proffered to us year by year unless by a

supreme recovery of moral health and martial vigor, we arise again and take our stand for freedom as in the olden time.

Neville Chamberlain, Speech to the House of Commons, October 6, 1938

That is my answer to those who say that we should have told Germany weeks ago that, if her army crossed the border of Czechoslovakia, we should be at war with her. We had no treaty obligations and no legal obligations to Czechoslovakia. When we were convinced, as we became convinced, that nothing any longer would keep the Sudetenland within the Czechoslovakian State, we urged the Czech Government as strongly as we could to agree to the cession of territory, and to agree promptly.... It was a hard decision for anyone who loved his country to take, but to accuse us of having by that advice betrayed the Czechoslovakian State is simply preposterous. What we did was to save her from annihilation and give her a chance of new life as a new State, which involves the loss of territory and fortifications, but may perhaps enable her to enjoy in the future and develop a national existence under a neutrality and security comparable to that which we see in Switzerland today. Therefore, I think the Government deserve the approval of this House for their conduct of affairs in this recent crisis which has saved Czechoslovakia from destruction and Europe from Armageddon.

Q *What were the opposing views of Churchill and Chamberlain on the Munich Conference? Why did they disagree so much? With whom do you agree? Why?*

---

would expand Germany's army from 100,000 to 550,000 troops. Hitler's unilateral repudiation of the Versailles treaty brought a swift reaction as France, Great Britain, and Italy condemned Germany's action and warned against future aggressive steps. But nothing concrete was done.

Meanwhile Hitler gained new allies. In October 1935, Benito Mussolini had committed Fascist Italy to imperial expansion by invading Ethiopia. Mussolini welcomed Hitler's support and began to draw closer to the German dictator. In October 1936, Hitler and Mussolini concluded an agreement that recognized their common interests, and one month later, Mussolini referred publicly to the new Rome-Berlin Axis. Also in November, Germany and Japan (the rising military power in the Far East) concluded the Anti-Comintern Pact and agreed to maintain a common front against communism.

By 1937, Germany was once more a "world power," as Hitler proclaimed. Hitler was convinced that neither the French nor the British would provide much opposition to

his plans and decided in 1938 to move to achieve one of his longtime goals: *Anschluss* (union) with Austria. By threatening Austria with invasion, Hitler coerced the Austrian chancellor into putting Austrian Nazis in charge of the government. The new government promptly invited German troops to enter Austria and assist in maintaining law and order. One day later, on March 13, 1938, after his triumphal return to his native land, Hitler formally annexed Austria to Germany.

Hitler's next objective was the destruction of Czechoslovakia, and he believed that France and Britain would not use force to defend that nation. He was right again. On September 15, 1938, Hitler demanded the cession of the Sudetenland, in northern Czechoslovakia, to Germany and expressed his willingness to risk "world war" to achieve his objective. Instead of objecting, the British, French, Germans, and Italians—at a hastily arranged conference at Munich—reached an agreement that met all of Hitler's demands (see the box above).

German troops were allowed to occupy the Sudetenland. Increasingly, Hitler was convinced of his own infallibility, and he had by no means been satisfied at Munich. In March 1939, Hitler occupied all the Czech lands (Bohemia and Moravia), while the Slovaks, with Hitler's encouragement, declared their independence of the Czechs and became a puppet state (Slovakia) of Nazi Germany. On the evening of March 15, 1939, Hitler triumphantly declared in Prague that he would be known as the greatest German of them all.

At last, the Western states reacted to Hitler's threat. When Hitler began to demand the return of Danzig (which had been made a free city by the Treaty of Versailles to serve as a seaport for Poland) to Germany, Britain offered to protect Poland in the event of war. At the same time, both France and Britain realized that only the Soviet Union was powerful enough to help contain Nazi aggression and began political and military negotiations with Stalin and the Soviets.

Meanwhile, Hitler pressed on. To preclude an alliance between the West and the Soviet Union, which would open the danger of a two-front war, Hitler negotiated his own nonaggression pact with Stalin and shocked the world with its announcement on August 23, 1939. The treaty with the Soviet Union gave Hitler the freedom to attack Poland. He told his generals: "Now Poland is in the position in which I wanted her.... I am only afraid that at the last moment some swine or other will yet submit to me a plan for mediation."[5] He need not have worried. On September 1, German forces invaded Poland; two days later, Britain and France declared war on Germany. Europe was again at war.

The Path to War in Asia

During the mid-1920s, Japan had maintained a strong military and economic presence in Manchuria, an area in northeastern China controlled by the Chinese warlord Zhang Zuolin. But in 1928, the latter formed an alliance with Chiang Kai-shek, whose new Nanjing government was seeking to extend its sway northward from the Yangtze valley. Threatened with the loss of Manchuria's

A Japanese Victory in China. After consolidating its authority over Manchuria, Japan began to expand into northern China. Direct hostilities between Japanese and Chinese forces began in 1937. This photograph shows victorious Japanese forces in January 1938 riding under the arched Chungshan Gate in Nanjing after they had conquered the Chinese capital city. By 1939, Japan had conquered most of eastern China.

© Keystone/Getty Images

rich natural resources, in September 1931 Japanese military officers stationed in the area launched a coup to bring about a complete Japanese takeover of the region. Despite worldwide protests from the League of Nations, which eventually condemned the seizure, Japan steadily strengthened its control over Manchuria (now renamed Manchukuo) and began to expand its military presence south of the Great Wall in North China.

For the moment, Chiang Kai-shek attempted to avoid a direct confrontation with Japan so that he could deal with what he considered the greater threat from the Chinese Communists, still holed up in their mountain base at Yan'an. When clashes between Chinese and Japanese troops broke out, he sought to appease Tokyo by granting Japan the authority to administer areas in North China. But as Japan moved steadily southward, popular protests in Chinese cities against Japanese aggression intensified. In December 1936, Chiang ended his military efforts against the Communists in Yan'an and formed a new united front against the Japanese. When Chinese and Japanese forces clashed at the Marco Polo Bridge, south of Beijing, in July 1937, China refused to apologize, and hostilities spread.

A Monroe Doctrine for Asia To avoid provoking the United States, Japan did not declare war on China. Nevertheless, neither side would compromise, and the

JAPAN'S JUSTIFICATION FOR EXPANSION

 POLITICS & GOVERNMENT

Advocates of Japanese expansion justified their proposals by claiming both economic necessity and moral imperatives. Note the familiar combination of motives in this passage written by an extremist military leader in the late 1930s.

Hashimoto Kingoro on the Need for Emigration and Expansion

We have already said that there are only three ways left to Japan to escape from the pressure of surplus population. We are like a great crowd of people packed into a small and narrow room, and there are only three doors through which we might escape, namely emigration, advance into world markets, and expansion of territory. The first door, emigration, has been barred to us by the anti-Japanese immigration policies of other countries. The second door, advance into world markets, is being pushed shut by tariff barriers and the abrogation of commercial treaties. What should Japan do when two of the three doors have been closed against her?

It is quite natural that Japan should rush upon the last remaining door.

It may sound dangerous when we speak of territorial expansion, but the territorial expansion of which we speak does not in any sense of the word involve the occupation of the possessions of other countries, the planting of the Japanese flag thereon, and the declaration of their annexation to Japan. It is just that since the Powers have suppressed the circulation of Japanese materials and merchandise abroad, we are looking for some place overseas where Japanese capital, Japanese skills and Japanese labor can have free play, free from the oppression of the white race.

We would be satisfied with just this much. What moral right do the world powers who have themselves closed to us the two doors of emigration and advance into world markets have to criticize Japan's attempt to rush out of the third and last door?

If they do not approve of this, they should open the doors which they have closed against us and permit the free movement overseas of Japanese emigrants and merchandise....

At the time of the Manchurian incident, the entire world joined in criticism of Japan. They said that Japan was an untrustworthy nation. They said that she had recklessly brought cannon and machine guns into Manchuria, which was the territory of another country, flown airplanes over it, and finally occupied it. But the military action taken by Japan was not in the least a selfish one. Moreover, we do not recall ever having taken so much as an inch of territory belonging to another nation. The result of this incident was the establishment of the splendid new nation of Manchuria. The Powers are still discussing whether or not to recognize this new nation, but regardless of whether or not other nations recognize her, the Manchurian empire has already been established, and now, seven years after its creation, the empire is further consolidating its foundations with the aid of its friend, Japan.

And if it is still protested that our actions in Manchuria were excessively violent, we may wish to ask the white race just which country it was that sent warships and troops to India, South Africa, and Australia and slaughtered innocent natives, bound their hands and feet with iron chains, lashed their backs with iron whips, proclaimed these territories as their own, and still continues to hold them to this very day.

Q *What arguments did Hashimoto Kingoro make in favor of Japanese territorial expansion? What was his reaction to the condemnation of Japan by Western nations?*

"China incident" of 1937 eventually turned into a major conflict. Japan advanced up the Yangtze River and seized the Chinese capital of Nanjing in December, but Chiang Kai-shek refused to capitulate and moved his government upriver to Hankou. When the Japanese seized that city, he retreated to Changqing, in remote Sichuan province, and kept his capital there for the remainder of the war.

Japanese strategists had hoped to force Chiang to agree to join a Japanese-dominated "New Order in East Asia," comprising Japan, Manchuria, and China, but when he refused to cooperate, Tokyo turned to the dissident politician Wang Jingwei, who agreed to form a pro-Japanese puppet government in Nanjing. The "New Order" was part of a larger Japanese plan to seize Soviet Siberia, with its rich resources, and create a new "Monroe Doctrine for Asia," with Japan guiding its Asian neighbors on the path to development and prosperity (see the box above).

During the late 1930s, Japan had begun to cooperate with Nazi Germany on the assumption that the two countries would ultimately launch a joint attack on the Soviet Union and divide up its resources between them. But when Berlin suddenly surprised the world by signing a nonaggression pact with Moscow in August 1939, Japanese strategists were compelled to reevaluate their long-term objectives. Japan was not strong enough to defeat the Soviet Union alone and so began to shift its eyes southward, to the vast resources of Southeast Asia—the oil of the Dutch East Indies, the rubber and tin of Malaya, and the rice of Burma and Indochina.

A move southward, of course, would risk war with the European colonial powers and the United States. Japan's attack on China in the summer of 1937 had already aroused strong criticism abroad, particularly in the United States. When Japan demanded the right to occupy airfields and exploit economic resources in French Indochina in the summer of 1940, the United States warned the Japanese that it would cut off the sale of oil and scrap iron unless Japan withdrew from the area and returned to its borders of 1931.

In Tokyo, the American threat of retaliation was viewed as a threat to Japan's long-term objectives. It badly needed oil and scrap iron from the United States. Should they be cut off, Japan would have to find them elsewhere. Japan was thus caught in a dilemma. To obtain guaranteed access to natural resources that would be necessary to fuel the Japanese military machine, Japan must risk being cut off from its current source of raw materials that would be needed in the event of a conflict. After much debate, Japan decided to launch a surprise attack on American and European colonies in Southeast Asia in the hope of a quick victory that would evict the United States from the region.

World War II

Q Focus Question: What were the main events of World War II in Europe and Asia?

Hitler stunned Europe with the speed and efficiency of the German blitzkrieg, or "lightning war." Armored columns or panzer divisions (a panzer division was a strike force of about three hundred tanks and accompanying forces and supplies) supported by airplanes broke quickly through Polish lines and encircled the bewildered Polish troops. Conventional infantry units then moved in to hold the newly conquered territory. Within four weeks, Poland had surrendered. On September 28, 1939, Germany and the Soviet Union officially divided Poland between them.

Europe at War

After a winter of waiting, Hitler resumed the war on April 9, 1940, with another blitzkrieg against Denmark and Norway (see Map 25.1). One month later, on May 10, the Germans launched their attack on the Netherlands, Belgium, and France. The main assault through Luxembourg and the Ardennes forest was completely unexpected by the French and British forces. German panzer divisions were able to break through the weak French defensive positions there and race across northern France, splitting the Allied armies and trapping French troops and the entire British army on the beaches of Dunkirk. Only by heroic efforts did the British achieve a gigantic evacuation of 330,000 Allied troops. The French capitulated on June 22. German armies occupied

about three-fifths of France while the French hero of World War I, Marshal Henri Pétain, established an authoritarian regime (known as Vichy France) over the remainder. Germany was now in control of western and central Europe, but Britain still had not been defeated.

As Hitler realized, an amphibious invasion of Britain would be possible only if Germany gained control of the air. At the beginning of August 1940, the Luftwaffe (the German air force) launched a major offensive against British air and naval bases, harbors, communication centers, and war industries. The British fought back doggedly, supported by an effective radar system that gave them early warning of German attacks. Nevertheless the British air force suffered critical losses by the end of August and was probably saved by Hitler's change of strategy. In September, in retaliation for a British attack on Berlin, Hitler ordered a shift from military targets to massive bombing of British cities to break British morale. The British rebuilt their air strength quickly and were soon inflicting major losses on Luftwaffe bombers. By the end of September, Germany had to postpone the invasion of Britain.

Although he had no desire for a two-front war, Hitler became convinced that Britain was remaining in the war only because it expected Soviet support. If the Soviet Union were smashed, Britain's last hope would be eliminated. Although the invasion of the Soviet Union was scheduled for spring 1941, the attack was delayed because of problems in the Balkans. Hitler had already obtained the political cooperation of Hungary, Bulgaria, and Romania, but Mussolini's disastrous invasion of Greece in October 1940 exposed Hitler's southern flank to British air bases in Greece. To secure his Balkan flank, German troops seized both Yugoslavia and Greece in April. Now reassured, Hitler turned to the east and invaded the Soviet Union on June 22, 1941.

The massive attack stretched out along a 1,800-mile front. German troops advanced rapidly, capturing two million Soviet soldiers. By November, one German army group had swept through Ukraine, while a second was besieging Leningrad; a third approached within 25 miles of Moscow, the Soviet capital. An early winter and unexpected Soviet resistance, however, brought a halt to the German advance. For the first time in the war, German armies had been stopped. A Soviet counterattack in December 1941 came as an ominous ending to the year for the Germans. By that time, another of Hitler's decisions—the declaration of war on the United States—turned another European conflict into a global war.

Japan at War

On December 7, 1941, Japanese aircraft attacked the U.S. naval base at Pearl Harbor in the Hawaiian Islands. The same day, other units launched additional assaults on

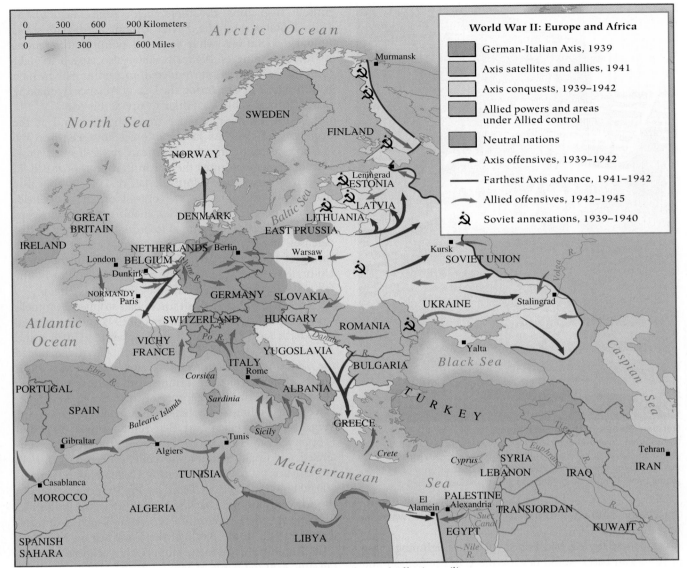

MAP 25.1 World War II in Europe and North Africa. With its fast and effective military, Germany quickly overwhelmed much of western Europe. Hitler overestimated his country's capabilities, however, and underestimated those of his opponents. By late 1942, his invasion of the Soviet Union was failing, and the United States had become a major factor in the war. The Allies successfully invaded Italy in 1943 and France in 1944.

Q Which countries were neutral, and how did geography help make their neutrality an option?

🔊 **View an animated version of this map or related maps at** www.cengage.com/history/

duikspiel/essentialworld6e

the Philippines and began advancing toward the British colony of Malaya (see Map 25.2). Shortly after this, Japanese forces invaded the Dutch East Indies and occupied a number of islands in the Pacific Ocean. By the spring of 1942, almost all of Southeast Asia and much of the western Pacific had fallen to the Japanese. Japan

declared the establishment of the Greater East Asia Co-Prosperity Sphere, encompassing the entire region under Japanese tutelage, and announced its intention to liberate the colonial areas of Southeast Asia from Western colonial rule. For the moment, however, Japan needed the resources of the region for its war machine and

German Troops in the Soviet Union. At first, the German attack on the Soviet Union was enormously successful, leading one German general to remark in his diary, "It is probably no overstatement to say that the Russian campaign has been won in the space of two weeks." This picture shows German troops firing on Soviet positions.

placed the countries under its own rule on a wartime basis.

Japanese leaders had hoped that their lightning strike at American bases would destroy the U.S. Pacific fleet and persuade President Franklin D. Roosevelt to accept Japanese domination of the Pacific. But Japan had miscalculated. The attack on Pearl Harbor galvanized American opinion and won broad support for Roosevelt's war policy. The United States now joined with European nations and Nationalist China in a combined effort to defeat Japan and end its hegemony in the Pacific. Believing that American involvement in the Pacific would render the United States ineffective in the European theater of war, Hitler declared war on the United States four days after Pearl Harbor.

The Turning Point of the War, 1942–1943

The entry of the United States into the war created a coalition (the Grand Alliance) that ultimately defeated the Axis Powers (Germany, Italy, and Japan). To overcome mutual suspicions, the three major Allies, Britain, the United States, and the Soviet Union, agreed to stress military operations while ignoring political differences. At the beginning of 1943, the Allies also agreed to fight until the Axis Powers surrendered unconditionally, which had the effect of cementing the Grand Alliance by making it nearly impossible for Hitler to divide his foes.

Defeat, however, was far from Hitler's mind at the beginning of 1942. As Japanese forces advanced into the Pacific after crippling the American naval fleet at Pearl Harbor, Hitler continued the war in Europe against Britain and the Soviet Union. Until the fall of 1942, it appeared that the Germans might still prevail on the battlefield. Reinforcements in North Africa enabled the Afrika Korps under General Erwin Rommel to break through the British defenses in Egypt and advance toward Alexandria. In the spring of 1942, a renewed German offensive in the Soviet Union led to the capture of the entire Crimea. But by the fall of 1942, the war had turned against the Germans.

In North Africa, British forces had stopped Rommel's troops at El Alamein in the summer of 1942 and then forced them back across the desert. In November 1942, British and American forces invaded French North Africa and forced the German and Italian troops to surrender in May 1943. On the Eastern Front, the turning point of the war occurred at Stalingrad. After the capture of the Crimea, Hitler decided that Stalingrad, a major industrial center on the Volga, should be taken next. Between November 1942 and February 1943, German troops were stopped, then encircled, and finally forced to surrender on February 2, 1943 (see the box on p. 628). The entire German Sixth Army of 300,000 men was lost. By February 1943, German forces in the Soviet Union were back to their positions of June 1942.

The tide of battle in the Far East also turned dramatically in 1942. In the Battle of the Coral Sea on May 7–8, 1942, American naval forces stopped the Japanese advance. On June 4, at the Battle of Midway Island, American planes destroyed all four of the attacking Japanese aircraft carriers and established American naval superiority in the Pacific. By the fall of 1942, Allied forces were beginning to gather for offensive operations: into South China from Burma, through the East Indies by a process of "island hopping" by troops commanded by the U.S. general Douglas MacArthur, and across the Pacific with a combination of U.S. Army, Marine, and Navy attacks on Japanese-held islands. After a series of bitter engagements in the waters of the Solomon Islands from August to November 1942, Japanese fortunes began to fade.

The Last Years of the War

By the beginning of 1943, the tide of battle had turned against Germany, Italy, and Japan. After the Axis forces had

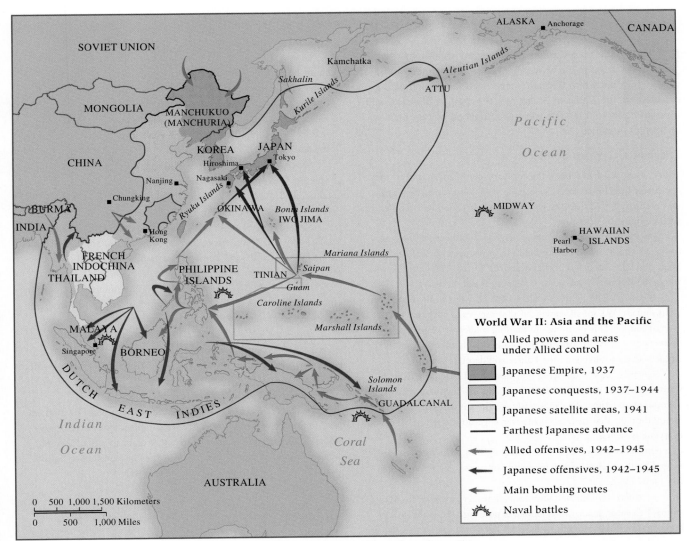

MAP 25.2 **World War II in Asia and the Pacific.** In 1937, Japan invaded northern China, beginning its effort to create a "Great East Asia Co-Prosperity Sphere." Further expansion led the United States to end iron and oil sales to Japan. Deciding that war with the United States was inevitable, Japan engineered a surprise attack on Pearl Harbor.

Q Why was control of the islands in the western Pacific of great importance both to the Japanese and to the Allies?

🦅 **View an animated version of this map or related maps at** www.cengage.com/history/ duikspiel/essentialworld6e

surrendered in Tunisia on May 13, 1943, the Allies crossed the Mediterranean and carried the war to Italy. After taking Sicily, Allied troops began the invasion of mainland Italy in September. In the meantime, after the ouster and arrest of Benito Mussolini, a new Italian government offered to surrender to Allied forces. But Mussolini was liberated by the Germans in a daring raid and then set up as the head of a puppet German state in northern Italy while German troops moved in and occupied much of Italy. The new

defensive lines established by the Germans in the hills south of Rome were so effective that the Allied advance up the Italian peninsula was a painstaking affair accompanied by heavy casualties. Rome did not fall to the Allies until June 4, 1944. By that time, the Italian war had assumed a secondary role anyway as the Allies opened their long-awaited "second front" in western Europe.

Under the direction of the American general Dwight D. Eisenhower (1890–1969), the Allies landed five assault

A German Soldier at Stalingrad

POLITICS & GOVERNMENT

The Soviet victory at Stalingrad was a major turning point in World War II. This excerpt comes from the diary of a German soldier who fought and died in the Battle of Stalingrad. His dreams of victory and a return home with medals were soon dashed by the realities of Soviet resistance.

Diary of a German Soldier

Today, after we'd had a bath, the company commander told us that if our future operations are as successful, we'll soon reach the Volga, take Stalingrad, and then the war will inevitably soon be over. Perhaps we'll be home by Christmas.

July 29. The company commander says the Russian troops are completely broken, and cannot hold out any longer. To reach the Volga and take Stalingrad is not so difficult for us. The Führer knows where the Russians' weak point is. Victory is not far away....

August 10. The Führer's orders were read out to us. He expects victory of us. We are all convinced that they can't stop us.

August 12. This morning outstanding soldiers were presented with decorations.... Will I really go back to Elsa without a decoration? I believe that for Stalingrad the Führer will decorate even me....

September 4. We are being sent northward along the front toward Stalingrad. We marched all night and by dawn had reached Voroponovo Station. We can already see the smoking town. It's a happy thought that the end of the war is getting nearer. That's what everyone is saying....

September 8. Two days of nonstop fighting. The Russians are defending themselves with insane stubbornness. Our regiment has lost many men....

September 16. Our battalion, plus tanks, is attacking the [grain storage] elevator, from which smoke is pouring—the grain in it is burning; the Russians seem to have set light to it themselves. Barbarism. The battalion is suffering heavy losses....

October 10. The Russians are so close to us that our planes cannot bomb them. We are preparing for a decisive attack. The Führer has ordered the whole of Stalingrad to be taken as rapidly as possible....

October 22. Our regiment has failed to break into the factory. We have lost many men; every time you move you have to jump over bodies....

November 10. A letter from Elsa today. Everyone expects us home for Christmas. In Germany everyone believes we already hold Stalingrad. How wrong they are. If they could only see what Stalingrad has done to our army....

November 21. The Russians have gone over to the offensive along the whole front. Fierce fighting is going on. So, there it is—the Volga, victory, and soon home to our families! We shall obviously be seeing them next in the other world.

November 29. We are encircled. It was announced this morning that the Führer has said: "The army can trust me to do everything necessary to ensure supplies and rapidly break the encirclement."

December 3. We are on hunger rations and waiting for the rescue that the Führer promised....

December 14. Everybody is racked with hunger. Frozen potatoes are the best meal, but to get them out of the ice-covered ground under fire from Russian bullets is not so easy....

December 26. The horses have already been eaten. I would eat a cat; they say its meat is also tasty. The soldiers look like corpses or lunatics, looking for something to put in their mouths. They no longer take cover from Russian shells; they haven't the strength to walk, run away, and hide. A curse on this war!

Q *What did this soldier believe about the Führer? Why? What was the source of his information? Why is the battle for Stalingrad considered a major turning point in World War II?*

---

divisions on the beaches of Normandy on June 6 in history's greatest naval invasion. An initially indecisive German response enabled the Allied forces to establish a beachhead. Within three months, they had landed two million men and a half-million vehicles that pushed inland and broke through German defensive lines.

After the breakout, Allied troops moved south and east and liberated Paris by the end of August. By March 1945, they had crossed the Rhine River and advanced deep into Germany. At the end of April 1945, Allied armies in northern Germany moved toward the Elbe River, where they finally linked up with the Soviets. The Soviets had come a long way since the Battle of Stalingrad in 1943. In the summer of 1943, German forces were soundly defeated by the Soviets at the Battle of Kursk

(July 5–12), the greatest tank battle of World War II. Soviet forces now began a relentless advance westward. The Soviets had reoccupied Ukraine by the end of 1943 and lifted the siege of Leningrad and moved into the Baltic states by the beginning of 1944. Advancing along a northern front, Soviet troops occupied Warsaw in January 1945 and entered Berlin in April. Meanwhile, Soviet troops along a southern front swept through Hungary, Romania, and Bulgaria.

In January 1945, Hitler had moved into a bunker 55 feet under Berlin to direct the final stages of the war. In his final political testament, Hitler, consistent to the end in his rabid anti-Semitism, blamed the Jews for the war. Hitler committed suicide on April 30, two days after Mussolini had been shot by partisan Italian forces.

Germany and the Soviet Union divide Poland	September 28, 1939
Blitzkrieg against Denmark and Norway	April 1940
Blitzkrieg against Belgium, Netherlands, and France	May 1940
France surrenders	June 22, 1940
Battle of Britain	Fall 1940
Nazi seizure of Yugoslavia and Greece	April 1941
Germany invades the Soviet Union	June 22, 1941
Japanese attack on Pearl Harbor	December 7, 1941
Battle of the Coral Sea	May 7–8, 1942
Battle of Midway Island	June 4, 1942
Allied invasion of North Africa	November 1942
German surrender at Stalingrad	February 2, 1943
Axis forces surrender in North Africa	May 1943
Battle of Kursk	July 5–12, 1943
Invasion of mainland Italy	September 1943
Allied invasion of France	June 6, 1944
Hitler commits suicide	April 30, 1945
Germany surrenders	May 7, 1945
Atomic bomb dropped on Hiroshima	August 6, 1945
Japan surrenders	August 14, 1945

On May 7, German commanders surrendered. The war in Europe was over.

Allied war plans for Asia had originally called for a massive military advance on the Japanese home islands through China, making full use of the latent strength of Chiang Kai-shek's armed forces. By 1943, however, President Roosevelt had lost confidence in the ability of Chiang Kai-shek's government to play a positive role in Allied operations and had turned to a "Pacific strategy" based on a gradual advance by U.S. military forces across the Pacific Ocean. Beginning in 1943, American forces had gone on the offensive and proceeded, slowly at times, across the Pacific. The Americans took an increasing toll of enemy resources, especially at sea and in the air. As Allied military power drew inexorably closer to the main Japanese islands in the first months of 1945, President Harry Truman, who had succeeded to the presidency on the death of Franklin Roosevelt in April, decided to use atomic weapons to bring the war to an end without the necessity of an Allied invasion of the Japanese homeland. The first bomb was dropped on the city of Hiroshima on August 6. Three days later, a second bomb was dropped on Nagasaki. Japan surrendered unconditionally on August 14. World War II was finally over.

The New Order

Q **Focus Question:** What was the nature of the new orders that Germany and Japan attempted to establish in the territories they occupied?

The initial victories of the Germans and the Japanese had given them the opportunity to restructure society in Europe and Asia. Both followed policies of ruthless domination of their subject peoples.

The New Order in Europe

In 1942, the Nazi empire stretched across continental Europe from the English Channel in the west to the outskirts of Moscow in the east. Nazi-occupied Europe was largely organized in one of two ways. Some areas, such as western Poland, were directly annexed by Nazi Germany and made into German provinces. Most of occupied Europe was administered by German military or civilian officials, combined with different degrees of indirect control from collaborationist regimes.

Because the conquered lands in the east contained the living space for German expansion and were, in Nazi eyes, populated by racially inferior Slavic peoples, Nazi administration there was considerably more ruthless. Soon after the conquest of Poland, Heinrich Himmler, the leader of the SS, was put in charge of German resettlement plans in the east. Himmler's task was to evacuate the inferior Slavic peoples and replace them with Germans, a policy first applied to the new German provinces created from the lands of western Poland. One million Poles were uprooted and dumped in southern Poland. Hundreds of thousands of ethnic Germans (descendants of Germans who had migrated years earlier from Germany to different parts of southern and eastern Europe) were encouraged to colonize the designated areas in Poland. By 1942, two million ethnic Germans had been settled in Poland.

Labor shortages in Germany led to a policy of ruthless mobilization of foreign labor for Germany. In 1942, a special office was created to recruit labor for German farms and industries. By the summer of 1944, seven million foreign workers were laboring in Germany where they constituted 20 percent of the labor force. At the same time, another seven million workers were supplying forced labor in their own countries on farms, in industries, and even in military camps. The brutality of Germany's recruitment policies often led more and more people to resist the Nazi occupation forces.

The Holocaust

No aspect of the Nazi new order was more terrifying than the deliberate attempt to exterminate the Jews of Europe.

The Holocaust: Activities of the *Einsatzgruppen*. The mobile killing units known as the *Einsatzgruppen* were active during the first phase of mass killings of the Holocaust. This picture shows the execution of a Jew by a member of one of these SS killing squads. Onlookers include members of the German army, the German Labor Service, and even Hitler Youth. When it became apparent that this method of killing was inefficient, it was replaced by the death camps.

Racial struggle was a key element in Hitler's ideology and meant to him a clearly defined conflict of opposites: the Aryans, creators of human cultural development, against the Jews, parasites who were trying to destroy the Aryans. Himmler and the SS organization closely shared Hitler's racial ideology. The SS was given responsibility for what the Nazis called their **Final Solution** to the "Jewish problem"— annihilation of the Jews. After the defeat of Poland, the SS ordered special strike forces (***Einsatzgruppen***) to round up all Polish Jews and concentrate them in ghettos established in a number of Polish cities.

In June 1941, the *Einsatzgruppen* were given new responsibilities as mobile killing units. These SS death squads followed the regular army's advance into Russia. Their job was to round up Jews in their villages, execute them, and bury them in mass graves, often giant pits dug by the victims themselves before they were shot. But the constant killing led to morale problems among the SS executioners. During a visit to Minsk in the Soviet Union, Himmler tried to build morale by pointing out that he "would not like it if Germans did such a thing gladly. But their conscience was in no way impaired, for they were soldiers who had to carry out every order unconditionally. He alone had responsibility before God and Hitler for everything that was happening."[6]

Although it has been estimated that as many as one million Jews were killed by the *Einsatzgruppen,* this approach to solving the Jewish problem was soon perceived as inadequate. Instead, the Nazis opted for the systematic annihilation of the European Jewish population in specially built death camps. Jews from countries occupied by Germany (or sympathetic to Germany) were rounded up, packed like cattle into freight trains, and shipped to Poland, where six extermination centers were built to dispose of them. The largest and most famous was Auschwitz-Birkenau. Medical technicians chose Zyklon B (the commercial name for hydrogen cyanide) as the most effective gas for quickly killing large numbers of people in gas chambers designed to look like "shower rooms" to facilitate the cooperation of the victims. After gassing, the corpses were burned in specially built crematoria.

The death camps were in operation by the spring of 1942; by the summer, Jews were also being shipped from France, Belgium, and the Netherlands. Even as the Allies were making significant advances in 1944, Jews were being shipped from Greece and Hungary. A harrowing experience awaited the Jews when they arrived at one of the six death camps. Rudolf Höss, commandant at Auschwitz-Birkenau, described it:

> We had two SS doctors on duty at Auschwitz to examine the incoming transports of prisoners. The prisoners would be marched by one of the doctors who would make spot decisions as they walked by. Those who were fit for work were sent into the camp. Others were sent immediately to the extermination plants. Children of tender years were invariably exterminated since by reason of their youth they were unable to work.... At Auschwitz we endeavored to fool the victims into thinking that they were to go through a delousing process. Of course, frequently they realized our true intentions and we sometimes had riots and difficulties due to that fact.[7]

About 30 percent of the arrivals at Auschwitz were sent to a labor camp; the remainder went to the gas chambers (see the box on p. 633). After they had been gassed, the bodies were burned in the crematoria. The victims' goods and even their bodies were used for economic gain. Female hair was cut off, collected, and turned into cloth or used to stuff mattresses. The Germans killed between five and six million Jews, more than three million of them in the death camps. Virtually 90 percent of the Jewish populations of Poland, the Baltic countries, and Germany were exterminated.

The Nazis were also responsible for another **Holocaust,** the death by shooting, starvation, or overwork of at least another 9 to 10 million people. Because the Nazis considered the Gypsies of Europe a race containing alien blood (like the Jews), they were systematically rounded up for extermination. About 40 percent of Europe's one million Gypsies were killed in the death camps. The leading elements of the "subhuman" Slavic peoples—the clergy, intelligentsia, civil leaders, judges, and lawyers—were arrested and deliberately killed. Probably an additional four million Poles, Ukrainians, and Byelorussians lost their lives as slave laborers for Nazi Germany. Finally, at least three million Soviet prisoners of war, and probably more, were killed in captivity.

The New Order in Asia

Once Japan's takeover was completed, Japanese war policy in the occupied areas in Asia became essentially defensive, as Japan hoped to use its new possessions to meet its needs for raw materials, such as tin, oil, and rubber, as well as to serve as an outlet for Japanese manufactured goods. To provide a structure for the arrangement, Japanese leaders set up the Greater East Asia Co-Prosperity Sphere as a self-sufficient community designed to provide mutual benefits to the occupied areas and the home country.

The Japanese conquest of Southeast Asia had been accomplished under the slogan "Asia for the Asians." Japanese officials in occupied territories quickly promised that independent governments would be established under Japanese tutelage. Such governments were eventually established in Burma, the Dutch East Indies, Vietnam, and the Philippines.

In fact, however, real power rested with the Japanese military authorities in each territory, and the local Japanese military command was directly subordinated to the army general staff in Tokyo. The economic resources of the colonies were exploited for the benefit of the Japanese war machine, while natives were recruited to serve in local military units or conscripted to work on public works projects. In some cases, the people living in the occupied areas were subjected to severe hardships. In Indochina, for example, forced requisitions of rice by the local Japanese authorities for shipment abroad created a food shortage that caused the starvation of more than a million Vietnamese in 1944 and 1945.

At first, many Southeast Asian nationalists took Japanese promises at face value and agreed to cooperate with their new masters. But as the exploitative nature of Japanese occupation policies became clear, sentiment turned against the new order. Japanese officials sometimes unwittingly provoked such attitudes by their arrogance and contempt for local customs.

Japanese military planners had little respect for their subject peoples and viewed the Geneva Convention on the laws of war as little more than a fabrication of Western countries to tie the hands of their adversaries. In conquering northern and central China, the Japanese freely used poison gas and biological weapons, which caused the deaths of millions of Chinese citizens. The Japanese occupation of the onetime Chinese capital of Nanjing was especially brutal. In the notorious "Nanjing Incident," they spent several days killing, raping, and looting the local population.

Japanese soldiers also treated Koreans savagely. Almost 800,000 Koreans were sent overseas, most of them as forced laborers, to Japan. Tens of thousands of women from Korea and the Philippines were forced to be "comfort women" (prostitutes) for Japanese troops. In construction projects to help their war effort, the Japanese also made extensive use of labor forces composed of both prisoners of war and local peoples. In building the Burma-Thailand railway in 1943, for example, the Japanese used 61,000 Australian, British, and Dutch prisoners of war and almost 300,000 workers from Burma, Malaya, Thailand, and the Dutch East Indies. By the time the railway was completed, 12,000 Allied prisoners of war and 90,000 native workers had died as a result of the inadequate diet and appalling work conditions in an unhealthy climate.

The Home Front

Q **Focus Question:** What were conditions like on the home front for the major belligerents in World War II?

World War II was even more of a total war than World War I. Fighting was much more widespread and covered most of the world. The number of civilians killed was far higher.

Mobilizing the People: Three Examples

The initial defeats of the Soviet Union led to drastic emergency mobilization measures that affected the civilian population. Leningrad, for example, experienced nine hundred days of siege, during which its inhabitants became so desperate for food that they ate dogs, cats, and mice.

FILM & HISTORY
Europa, Europa (1990)

Directed by Agnieszka Holland, *Europa, Europa* (known as *Hitler-junge Salomon* [Hitler Youth Salomon] in Germany) is the harrowing story of one Jewish boy's escape from the horrors of Nazi persecution. It is based on the memoirs of Salomon Perel, a German Jew of Polish background who survived by pretending to be a pure Aryan. The film begins in 1938 during *Kristallnacht* when the family of Solly (Perel's nickname) is attacked in their hometown of Peine, Germany. Solly's sister is killed, and the family moves back to Poland. When the Nazis invade Poland, Solly (Marco Hofschneider) and his brother are sent east, but the brothers become separated and Solly is placed in a Soviet orphanage in Grodno in the eastern part of Poland occupied by the Soviets.

For two years, Solly becomes a dedicated Communist youth, but when the Germans invade in 1941, he falls into their hands and quickly assumes a new identity in order to survive. He becomes Josef "Jupp" Peters, supposedly the son of German parents from Latvia. Fluent in both Russian and German, Solly/Jupp becomes a translator for the German forces. After an unintended act of bravado, he is rewarded by being sent to a Hitler Youth school where he lives in fear of being exposed as a Jew because of his circumcised penis. He manages to survive the downfall of Nazi Germany and at the end of the war makes his way with his brother, who has also survived, to Palestine. Throughout much of the movie, Solly/Jupp lives in constant fear that his true identity as a Jew will be recognized, but his luck, charm, and resourcefulness enable him to survive a series of extraordinary events.

Although there is no way of knowing if each detail of this movie is historically accurate (and some are clearly inaccurate, such as a bombing run by a plane that was not developed until after the war), overall the story has the ring of truth. The fanaticism of both the Soviet and the Nazi officials who indoctrinate young people seems real. The scene in the Hitler Youth school on how to identify a Jew is realistic, even when it is made ironic by the instructor's choice of Solly/Jupp to demonstrate the characteristics of a true Aryan. The movie also realistically portrays the fearful world in which Jews had to live under the Nazis before the war and the horrible conditions of the Jewish ghettos in Polish cities during the war. The film shows how people had to fight for their survival in a world

Salomon Perel/Josef Peters (Marco Hofschneider) as a Hitler Youth member

Les Films Du Losange/CCC Filmkunst/The Kobal Collection

of ideological madness, when Jews were killed simply for being Jews. The attitudes of the German soldiers also seem real. Many are shown following orders and killing Jews based on the beliefs in which they have been indoctrinated. But the movie also portrays some German soldiers whose humanity did not allow them to kill Jews. One homosexual soldier discovers that Solly/Jupp is a Jew when he tries—unsuccessfully—to have sex with him. The soldier then becomes the boy's protector until he himself is killed in battle.

Many movies have been made about the horrible experiences of Jews during World War II, but this one is quite different from most of them. It might never have been made except for the fact that Salomon Perel, who was told by his brother not to tell his story because no one would believe it, was inspired to write his memoirs after a 1985 reunion with his former Hitler Youth group leader. This passionate and intelligent film is ultimately a result of that encounter.

As the German army made its rapid advance into Soviet territory, the factories in the western part of the Soviet Union were dismantled and shipped to the interior—to the Urals, western Siberia, and the Volga region. Machines were set down on the bare earth, and walls went up around them as workers began their work.

Stalin called the widespread military and industrial mobilization of the nation a "battle of machines," and the Soviets won, producing 78,000 tanks and 98,000 artillery pieces. In 1943, fully 55 percent of Soviet national income went for war matériel, compared to 15 percent in 1940 (see the comparative essay "Paths to Modernization" on p. 634).

Soviet women played a major role in the war effort. Women and girls were enlisted for work in industries, mines, and railroads. Overall the number of women

THE HOLOCAUST: THE CAMP COMMANDANT AND THE CAMP VICTIMS

FAMILY & SOCIETY

The systematic annihilation of millions of men, women, and children in extermination camps makes the Holocaust one of the most horrifying events in history. The first document is taken from an account by Rudolf Höss, commandant of the extermination camp at Auschwitz-Birkenau. In the second document, a French doctor explains what happened at one of the crematoria described by Höss.

Commandant Höss Describes the Equipment

The two large crematoria, Nos. I and II, were built during the winter of 1942–43.... Each ... could cremate c. 2,000 corpses within twenty-four hours.... Crematoria I and II both had underground undressing and gassing rooms which could be completely ventilated. The corpses were brought up to the ovens on the floor above by lift. The gas chambers could hold c. 3,000 people.

The firm of Topf had calculated that the two smaller crematoria, III and IV, would each be able to cremate 1,500 corpses within twenty-four hours. However, owing to the wartime shortage of materials, the builders were obliged to economize, and so the undressing rooms and gassing rooms were built above ground and the ovens were of a less solid construction. But it soon became apparent that the flimsy construction of these two four-retort ovens was not up to the demands made on it. No. III ceased operating altogether after a short time and later was no longer used. No. IV had to be repeatedly shut down since after a short period in operation of 4–6 weeks, the ovens and chimneys had burnt out. The victims of the gassing were mainly burnt in pits behind crematorium IV.

The largest number of people gassed and cremated within twenty-four hours was somewhat over 9,000.

A French Doctor Describes the Victims

It is mid-day, when a long line of women, children, and old people enter the yard. The senior official in charge ... climbs on a bench to tell them that they are going to have a bath and that afterward they will get a drink of hot coffee. They all undress in the yard.... The doors are opened and an indescribable jostling begins. The first people to enter the gas chamber begin to draw back. They sense the death which awaits them. The SS men put an end to this pushing and shoving with blows from their rifle butts beating the heads of the horrified women who are desperately hugging their children. The massive oak double doors are shut. For two endless minutes one can hear banging on the walls and screams which are no longer human. And then—not a sound. Five minutes later the doors are opened. The corpses, squashed together and distorted, fall out like a waterfall.... The bodies, which are still warm, pass through the hands of the hairdresser, who cuts their hair, and the dentist, who pulls out their gold teeth.... One more transport has just been processed through No. IV crematorium.

Q *What "equipment" does Höss describe? What process does the French doctor describe? Is there any sympathy for the victims in either account? Why or why not? How could such a horrifying process have been allowed to occur? Who was held responsible after the war? Was this sufficient?*

---

working in industry increased almost 60 percent. Soviet women were also expected to dig antitank ditches and work as air raid wardens. In addition, the Soviet Union was the only country in World War II to use women as combatants. Soviet women functioned as snipers and as crews in bomber squadrons.

In August 1914, Germans had enthusiastically cheered their soldiers marching off to war; in September 1939, the streets were quiet. Many Germans were apathetic or, even worse for the Nazi regime, had a foreboding of disaster. Hitler was very aware of the importance of the home front. He believed that the collapse of the home front in World War I had caused Germany's defeat. To avoid a repetition of that experience, he adopted economic policies that may indeed have cost Germany the war.

To maintain the morale of the home front during the first two years of the war, Hitler refused to cut production of consumer goods or increase the production of armaments. After German defeats on the Russian front and the American entry into the war, however, the situation changed. Early in 1942, Hitler finally ordered a massive increase in armaments production and the size of the army. Hitler's architect, Albert Speer, was made minister for armaments and munitions in 1942. By eliminating waste and rationalizing procedures. Speer was able to triple the production of armaments between 1942 and 1943, despite the intense Allied air raids. Speer's urgent plea for a total mobilization of resources for the war effort went unheeded, however. Hitler, fearful of civilian morale problems that would undermine the home front, refused any dramatic cuts in the production of consumer goods. A total mobilization of the economy was not implemented until 1944, but by that time, it was too late.

The war produced a reversal in Nazi attitudes toward women. Nazi resistance to female employment declined as the war progressed and more and more men were

COMPARATIVE ESSAY
PATHS TO MODERNIZATION

To the casual observer, the most important feature of the first half of the twentieth century was the rise of a virulent form of competitive nationalism that began in Europe and ultimately descended into the cauldron of two destructive world wars. Behind the scenes, however, the leading countries were also engaging in another form of competition over the most effective path to modernization.

The traditional approach, fostered by an independent urban merchant class, had been adopted by Great Britain, France, and the United States and led to the emergence of democratic societies on the capitalist model. A second approach, adopted in the late nineteenth century by imperial Germany and Meiji Japan, was carried out by traditional elites in the absence of a strong independent bourgeois class. They relied on strong government intervention to promote the growth of national wealth and power and led ultimately to the formation of fascist and militarist regimes during the depression years of the early 1930s.

The third approach, selected by Vladimir Lenin after the Bolshevik Revolution in 1917, was designed to carry out an industrial revolution without going through an intermediate capitalist stage. Guided by the Communist Party in the almost total absence of an urban middle class, this approach envisaged the creation of an advanced industrial society by destroying the concept of private property. Although Lenin's plans ultimately called for the "withering of the state," the party adopted totalitarian methods to eliminate enemies of the revolution and carry out the changes needed to create a future classless utopia.

How did these various approaches contribute to the series of crises that afflicted the world during the first half of the twentieth century? The democratic-capitalist approach proved to be a considerable success in an economic sense, leading to the creation of advanced economies that could produce manufactured goods at a rate never seen before. Societies just beginning to undergo their own industrial revolutions tried to imitate the success of the capitalist nations by carrying out their own "revolutions from above" in Germany and Japan. But the Great Depression and competition over resources and markets soon led to an intense rivalry between the

The Soviet Path to Modernization. One aspect of the Soviet effort to create an advanced industrial society was to collectivize agriculture, which included a rapid mechanization of food production. Seen here are peasants watching a new tractor at work.

established capitalist states and their ambitious late arrivals, a rivalry that ultimately erupted into global conflict.

In the first decade of the twentieth century, imperial Russia appeared ready to launch its own bid to join the ranks of the industrialized nations. But that effort was derailed by its entry into World War I, and before that conflict had come to an end, the Bolsheviks were in power. Isolated from the capitalist marketplace by mutual consent, the Soviet Union was able to avoid being dragged into the Great Depression but, despite Stalin's efforts, was unsuccessful in staying out of the "battle of imperialists" that followed at the end of the 1930s. As World War II came to an end, the stage was set for a battle of the victors—the United States and the Soviet Union—over political and ideological supremacy.

Q *What were the three major paths to modernization in the first half of the twentieth century, and why did they lead to conflict?*

---

called up for military service. Nazi magazines now proclaimed, "We see the woman as the eternal mother of our people, but also as the working and fighting comrade of the man."[8] But the number of women working in industry, agriculture, commerce, and domestic service increased only slightly. The total number of employed women in September 1944 was 14.9 million, compared

with 14.6 million in May 1939. Many women, especially those of the middle class, resisted regular employment, particularly in factories.

Wartime Japan was a highly mobilized society. To guarantee its control over all national resources, the government set up a planning board to control prices, wages, the utilization of labor, and the allocation of resources.

Traditional habits of obedience and hierarchy, buttressed by the concept of imperial divinity, were emphasized to encourage citizens to sacrifice their resources, and sometimes their lives, for the national cause. The system culminated in the final years of the war, when young Japanese were encouraged to volunteer en masse to serve as pilots in the suicide missions (known as *kamikaze*, "divine wind") against U.S. battleships.

Women's rights too were to be sacrificed to the greater national cause. Already by 1937, Japanese women were being exhorted to fulfill their patriotic duty by bearing more children and by espousing the slogans of the Greater Japanese Women's Association. Japan was extremely reluctant to mobilize women on behalf of the war effort, however. General Hideki Tojo, prime minister from 1941 to 1944, opposed female employment, arguing that "the weakening of the family system would be the weakening of the nation.... We are able to do our duties only because we have wives and mothers at home."[9] Female employment increased during the war, but only in areas where women traditionally worked, such as the textile industry and farming. Instead of using women to meet labor shortages, the Japanese government brought in Korean and Chinese laborers.

The Frontline Civilians: The Bombing of Cities

Bombing was used in World War II against a variety of targets, including military targets, enemy troops, and civilian populations. The bombing of civilians made World War II as devastating for civilians as for frontline soldiers. A small number of bombing raids in the last year of World War I had given rise to the argument that public outcry over the bombing of civilian populations would be an effective way to coerce governments into making peace. Consequently, European air forces began to develop long-range bombers in the 1930s.

The first sustained use of civilian bombing contradicted the theory. Beginning in early September 1940, the German Luftwaffe subjected London and many other British cities and towns to nightly air raids, making the Blitz (as the British called the German air raids) a national experience. Londoners took the first heavy blows but kept up their morale, setting the standard for the rest of the British population (see the comparative illustration on p. 636).

The British failed to learn from their own experience, however; Prime Minister Winston Churchill and his advisers believed that destroying German communities would break civilian morale and bring victory. Major bombing raids began in 1942. On May 31, 1942, Cologne became the first German city to be subjected to an attack by a thousand bombers. Bombing raids added an element of terror to circumstances already made difficult by growing shortages of food, clothing, and fuel. Germans especially feared incendiary bombs, which ignited firestorms that swept destructive paths through the cities. The ferocious bombing of Dresden from February 13 to 15, 1945, set off a firestorm that may have killed as many as 35,000 inhabitants and refugees.

Germany suffered enormously from the Allied bombing raids. Millions of buildings were destroyed, and possibly half a million civilians died from the raids. Nevertheless, it is highly unlikely that Allied bombing sapped the morale of the German people. Instead Germans, whether pro-Nazi or anti-Nazi, fought on stubbornly, often driven simply by a desire to live. Nor did the bombing destroy Germany's industrial capacity. The Allied strategic bombing survey revealed that the production of war matériel actually increased between 1942 and 1944.

In Japan, the bombing of civilians reached a horrendous new level with the use of the first atomic bomb. Attacks on Japanese cities by the new American B-29 Superfortresses, the biggest bombers of the war, had begun on November 24, 1944. By the summer of 1945, many of Japan's industries had been destroyed, along with one-fourth of its dwellings. After the Japanese government decreed the mobilization of all people between the ages of thirteen and sixty into the so-called People's Volunteer Corps, President Truman and his advisers decided that Japanese fanaticism might mean a million American casualties, and Truman decided to drop the newly developed atomic bomb on Hiroshima and Nagasaki. The destruction was incredible. Of 76,000 buildings near the hypocenter of the explosion in Hiroshima, 70,000 were flattened, and 140,000 of the city's 400,000 inhabitants had died by the end of 1945. Over the next five years, another 50,000 perished from the effects of radiation. The dropping of the atomic bomb on Hiroshima on August 6, 1945, announced the dawn of the nuclear age.

Aftermath of the War

Q **Focus Questions:** What were the costs of World War II? How did the Allies' visions of the postwar differ, and how did these differences contribute to the emergence of the Cold War?

World War II was the most destructive war in history. Much had been at stake. Nazi Germany followed a worldview based on racial extermination and the

COMPARATIVE ILLUSTRATION

FAMILY & SOCIETY

The Bombing of Civilians—East and West. World War II was the most destructive war in world history, not only for frontline soldiers but for civilians at home as well. The most devastating bombing of civilians came near the end of World War II when the United States dropped atomic bombs on the Japanese cities of Hiroshima and Nagasaki. At the left is a view of Hiroshima after the bombing that shows the incredible devastation produced by the atomic bomb. The picture at the right shows a street in Clydebank, near Glasgow in Scotland, the day after the city was bombed by the Germans in March 1941. Only 7 of the city's 12,000 houses were left undamaged; 35,000 of the 47,000 inhabitants became homeless overnight.

Q What was the rationale for bombing civilian populations? Did such bombing achieve its goal?

enslavement of millions in order to create an Aryan racial empire. The Japanese, fueled by extreme nationalist ideals, also pursued dreams of empire in Asia that led to mass murder and untold devastation. Fighting the Axis Powers in World War II required the mobilization of millions of ordinary men and women in the Allied countries who struggled to preserve a different way of life. As Winston Churchill once put it, "War is horrible, but slavery is worse."

The Costs of World War II

The costs of World War II were enormous. At least 21 million soldiers died. Civilian deaths were even greater and are now estimated at around 40 million. Of these, more than 28 million were Russian and Chinese. The Soviet Union experienced the greatest losses: 10 million soldiers and 19 million civilians. In 1945, millions of

people around the world faced starvation: in Europe, 100 million people depended on food relief of some kind.

Millions of people had also been uprooted by the war and became "displaced persons." Europe alone may have had 30 million displaced persons, many of whom found it hard to return home. In Asia, millions of Japanese were returned from the former Japanese empire to Japan, while thousands of Korean forced laborers returned to Korea.

Everywhere cities lay in ruins. In Europe, the physical devastation was especially bad in eastern and southeastern Europe as well as in the cities of western and central Europe. In Asia, China had experienced extensive devastation from eight years of conflict. So too had the Philippines, while large sections of the major cities in Japan had been destroyed in air raids. The total monetary cost of the war has been estimated at $4 trillion.

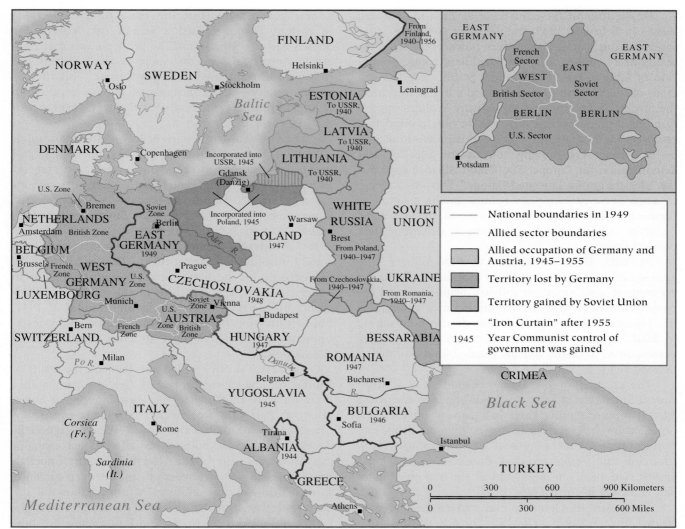

MAP 25.3 Territorial Changes in Europe After World War II. In the last months of World War II, the Red Army occupied much of eastern Europe. Stalin sought pro-Soviet satellite states in the region as a buffer against future invasions from western Europe, whereas Britain and the United States wanted democratically elected governments. Soviet military control of the territory settled the question.

Q Which country gained the greatest territory at the expense of Germany?

View an animated version of this map or related maps at www.cengage.com/history/
duikspiel/essentialworld6e

The economies of most belligerents, with the exception of the United States, were left on the brink of disaster.

The Allied War Conferences

Stalin, Roosevelt, and Churchill, the leaders of the Big Three of the Grand Alliance, met at Tehran, the capital of Iran, in November 1943 to decide the future course of the war. Stalin and Roosevelt argued successfully for an American-British invasion of the Continent through France, which they scheduled for the spring of 1944. This meant that Soviet and British-American forces would meet in defeated Germany along a north-south dividing line and that Soviet forces would liberate eastern Europe. The Allies also agreed to a partition of postwar Germany.

By the time of the conference at Yalta in southern Russia in February 1945, the defeat of Germany was a foregone conclusion. The Western powers now faced the reality of 11 million Red Army soldiers taking possession of large portions of Europe. Stalin, deeply suspicious of the Western powers, desired a buffer to protect the Soviet Union from possible future Western aggression but at the same time was eager to obtain important resources and strategic military positions. Roosevelt by this time was moving toward the idea of self-determination for Europe. The Grand Alliance approved the "Declaration on Liberated Europe." This was a pledge to assist liberated European nations in the creation of "democratic institutions of their own choice." Liberated countries were to hold free elections to determine their political systems.

At Yalta, Roosevelt sought Russian military help against Japan. Development of the atomic bomb was not yet assured, and American military planners feared the possible loss of as many as one million men in invading the Japanese home islands. Roosevelt therefore agreed to Stalin's price for military assistance against Japan: possession of Sakhalin and the Kurile Islands, as well as railroad rights in Manchuria.

The creation of the United Nations was a major American concern at Yalta. Roosevelt hoped to ensure the participation of the Big Three in a postwar international organization before difficult issues divided them into hostile camps. After a number of compromises, both Churchill and Stalin accepted Roosevelt's plans for a United Nations organization and set the first meeting for San Francisco in April 1945.

The issues of Germany and eastern Europe were treated less decisively. The Big Three reaffirmed that Germany must surrender unconditionally and created four occupation zones (see Map 25.3 on p. 637). A compromise was also worked out in regard to Poland. Stalin agreed to free elections in the future to determine a new government. But the issue of free elections in eastern Europe caused a serious rift between the Soviets and the Americans. The principle was that eastern European governments would be freely elected, but they were also supposed to be pro-Russian. This attempt to reconcile two irreconcilable goals was doomed to failure, as soon became evident at the next conference of the Big Three.

The Potsdam conference of July 1945 began under a cloud of mistrust. Roosevelt had died on April 12 and had been succeeded as president by Harry Truman. At Potsdam, Truman demanded free elections throughout eastern Europe. Stalin responded, "A freely elected government in any of these East European countries would be anti-Soviet, and that we cannot allow."[10] After a bitterly fought and devastating war, Stalin sought absolute military security. To him, it could be gained only by the presence of Communist states in eastern Europe. Free elections might result in governments hostile to the Soviets. By the middle of 1945, only an invasion by Western forces could undo developments in eastern Europe, and few people favored such a policy.

As the war slowly receded into the past, the reality of conflicting ideologies reappeared (see the comparative essay on p. 634). Many in the West interpreted Soviet policy as part of a worldwide Communist conspiracy. The Soviets, for their part, viewed Western—especially American—policy as nothing less than global capitalist expansionism or, in Leninist terms, economic imperialism. In March 1946, in a speech to an American audience, former British prime minister Winston Churchill declared that "an iron curtain" had "descended across the continent," dividing Germany and Europe into two hostile camps. Stalin branded Churchill's speech a "call to war with the Soviet Union." Only months after the world's most devastating conflict had ended, the world seemed once again to be bitterly divided.

CONCLUSION

WORLD WAR II was the most devastating total war in human history. Germany, Italy, and Japan had been utterly defeated. Perhaps as many as 60 million people—combatants and civilians—had been killed in only six years. In Asia and Europe, cities had been reduced to rubble, and millions of people faced starvation as once fertile lands stood neglected or wasted.

What were the underlying causes of the war? One direct cause was the effort by two rising powers, Germany and Japan, to make up for their relatively late arrival on the scene to carve out global empires. Key elements in both countries had resented the agreements reached after the end of World War I, which divided the world in a manner favorable to their rivals, and hoped to overturn them at the earliest opportunity. In Germany and Japan, the legacy of a past marked by a strong military tradition still wielded strong influence over the political system and the mindset of the entire population. It is no surprise that under the impact of the Great Depression, which had severe effects in both countries, militant forces determined to enhance national wealth and power soon overwhelmed fragile democratic institutions.

Whatever the causes of World War II, the consequences were soon evident. European hegemony over the world was at an end, and two new superpowers had emerged on the fringes of Western civilization to take its place. Even before the last battles had been fought, the United States and the Soviet Union had arrived at different visions of the postwar world, and their differences soon led to the new and potentially even more devastating conflict known as the Cold War. And even though Europeans seemed merely pawns in the struggle between the two superpowers, they managed to stage a remarkable recovery of their own civilization. In Asia, defeated Japan made a miraculous economic recovery, while the era of European domination finally came to an end.

TIMELINE

	1925	1930	1935	1940	1945

Europe

Mussolini creates Fascist dictatorship in Italy

Hitler and Nazis come to power in Germany

Fall of France

German defeat at Stalingrad

Kristallnacht

The Holocaust

Stalin's first five-year plan begins

Conferences at Yalta and Potsdam

Asia

Japanese takeover of Manchuria

Japanese attack on Pearl Harbor

Japanese create Ministry for Great East Asia

Atomic bomb dropped on Hiroshima

SUGGESTED READING

The Dictatorial Regimes For a general study of fascism, see **S. G. Payne, *A History of Fascism*** (Madison, Wis., 1996), and **R. O. Paxton, *The Anatomy of Fascism*** (New York, 2004). The best biography of Mussolini is **R. J. B. Bosworth, *Mussolini*** (London, 2002). On Fascist Italy, see **R. J. B. Bosworth, *Mussolini's Italy: Life Under the Fascist Dictatorship*** (New York, 2006).

Two brief but sound surveys of Nazi Germany are **J. J. Spielvogel, *Hitler and Nazi Germany: A History,*** 5th ed. (Upper Saddle River, N.J., 2005), and **W. Benz, *A Concise History of the Third Reich,*** trans **T. Dunlap** (Berkeley, Calif., 2006). The best biography of Hitler is **I. Kershaw, *Hitler, 1889–1936: Hubris*** (New York, 1999), and ***Hitler: Nemesis*** (New York, 2000). On the rise of the Nazis to power, see **R. J. Evans, *The Coming of the Third Reich*** (New York, 2004), and ***The Third Reich in Power, 1933–1939*** (New York, 2005).

The collectivization of agriculture in the Soviet Union is examined in **S. Fitzpatrick, *Stalin's Peasants: Resistance and Survival in the Russian Village After Collectivization*** (New York, 1995). Industrialization is covered in **H. Kuromiya, *Stalin's Industrial Revolution: Politics and Workers, 1928–1932*** (New York, 1988). On Stalin himself, see **R. Service, *Stalin: A Biography*** (Cambridge, Mass., 2006), and **R. W. Thurston, *Life and Terror in Stalin's Russia, 1934–1941*** (New Haven, Conn., 1996).

The Path to War On the causes of World War II, see **A. J. Crozier, *Causes of the Second World War*** (Oxford, 1997).

On the origins of the war in the Pacific, see **A. Iriye, *The Origins of the Second World War in Asia and the Pacific*** (London, 1987).

World War II General works on World War II include the comprehensive study by **G. Weinberg, *A World at Arms: A Global History of World War II,*** 2nd ed. (Cambridge, 2005), and **J. Campbell, *The Experience of World War II*** (New York, 1989). For briefer histories, see **J. Plowright, *Causes, Course, and Outcomes of World War II*** (New York, 2007), and **M. J. Lyon, *World War II: A Short History,*** 4th ed. (Upper Saddle River, N.J., 2004).

The Holocaust Excellent studies of the Holocaust include **R. Hilberg, *The Destruction of the European Jews,*** rev. ed., 3 vols. (New York, 1985); **S. Friedländer, *The Years of Extermination: Nazi Germany and the Jews, 1939–1945*** (New York, 2007); and **L. Yahil, *The Holocaust*** (New York, 1990). For brief studies, see **J. Fischel, *The Holocaust*** (Westport, Conn., 1998), and **D. Dwork** and **R. J. van Pelt, *Holocaust: A History*** (New York, 2002).

The Home Front On the home front in Germany, see **M. Kitchen, *Nazi Germany at War*** (New York, 1995). The Soviet Union during the war is examined in **M. Harrison, *Soviet Planning in Peace and War, 1938–1945*** (Cambridge, 1985). The Japanese home front is examined in **T. R. H. Havens, *The Valley of Darkness: The Japanese People and World War Two*** (New York, 1978).

On the Allied bombing campaign against Germany, see **R. Neillands, *The Bomber War: The Allied Air Offensive Against Nazi Germany*** (New York, 2005), and **J. Friedrich, *The Fire: The Bombing of Germany,*** trans. **A. Brown** (New York, 2006). On the use of the atomic bomb in Japan, see **M. Gordin, *Five Days in August: How World War II Became a Nuclear War*** (Princeton, N.J., 2006).

Emergence of the Cold War On the emergence of the Cold War, see **L. Gaddis, *The Cold War: A New History*** (New York, 2005); **J. W. Langdon, *A Hard and Bitter Peace: A Global History of the Cold War*** (Englewood Cliffs, N.J., 1995); and **J. Smith, *The Cold War, 1945–1991*** (Oxford, 1998).

WORLD HISTORY RESOURCES

Visit the website for *The Essential World History* to access study aids such as Flashcards, Critical Thinking Exercises, and Chapter Quizzes:

www.cengage.com/history/duikspiel/essentialworld6e

What was the relationship between World War I and World War II, and what were the differences in the ways the wars were fought?

In thinking about this question, begin by breaking it down into the components shown below. A discussion of the significance of each component should appear in your answer.

FAMILY AND SOCIETY Considering the material under the heading "The Home Front" (p. 631) and the photos on page 636, discuss how World War II affected civilians. What differences do you see from World War I? What steps did governments take to mobilize their populations during both wars? What roles did civilians play on the home front during both wars? Why did civilians become military targets during World War II? How did military attacks against civilians become a common tactic in modern warfare? Based on this chapter and Chapter 23, which war was more deadly for civilians?

In what way can the Holocaust be considered another example of attacks on civilians during war?

During World War II, the Allies agreed to go on fighting until the Axis Powers surrendered unconditionally. What effect do you think this decision had on the course of the war and on the treatment of civilians during the war?

POLITICS AND GOVERNMENT Considering the maps below and Map 23.2 (p. 570), discuss the differences in the way the wars were fought. In framing your answer, consider not only the geographic aspects of the wars but also differences in weapons, tactics, and strategies. Consider also the description of trench warfare in Chapter 23 (document, p. 571) and the account of the siege of Stalingrad (document, p. 628). Do you find any similarities between the wars?

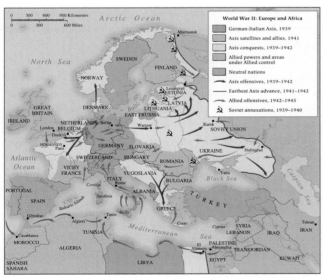

World War II in Europe and North Africa

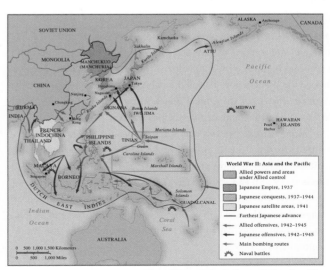

World War II in Asia and the Pacific

TOWARD A GLOBAL CIVILIZATION?
THE WORLD SINCE 1945

AS WORLD WAR II came to an end, the survivors of that bloody struggle could afford to face the future with a cautious optimism. Europeans might hope that the bitter rivalry that had marked relations among the Western powers would finally be put to an end and that the wartime alliance of the United States, Great Britain, and the Soviet Union could be maintained into the postwar era.

More than sixty years later, these hopes have been only partly realized. In the decades following the war, the Western capitalist nations managed to recover from the economic depression that had led into World War II and advanced to a level of economic prosperity never seen before. The bloody conflicts that had erupted among European nations during the first half of the twentieth century came to an end, and Germany and Japan were fully integrated into the world community.

At the same time, the prospects for a stable, peaceful world and an end to balance-of-power politics were hampered by the emergence of a grueling and sometimes tense ideological struggle between the socialist and capitalist camps, a competition headed by the only remaining great powers, the Soviet Union and the United States.

In the shadow of this rivalry, the Western European states made a remarkable economic recovery and reached untold levels of prosperity. In Eastern Europe, Soviet domination, both politically and economically, seemed so complete that many doubted it could ever be undone. But communism had never developed deep roots in Eastern Europe, and in the late 1980s, when Soviet leader Mikhail Gorbachev indicated that his government would no longer pursue military intervention, Eastern European states acted quickly to establish their freedom and adopt new economic structures based on Western models.

Outside the West, the peoples of Africa and Asia had their own reasons for optimism as World War II came to a close. In the Atlantic Charter, Franklin Roosevelt and Winston Churchill had set forth a joint declaration of their peace aims calling for the self-determination of all peoples and self-government and sovereign rights for all nations that had been deprived of them.

As it turned out, some colonial powers were reluctant to divest themselves of their colonies. Still, World War II had severely undermined the stability of the colonial order, and by the end of the 1940s, most colonies in Asia had received their independence. Africa followed a decade or two later.

Broadly speaking, the leaders of these newly liberated countries set forth three goals at the outset of independence. They wanted to throw off the shackles of Western economic domination and ensure material prosperity for all of their citizens. They wanted to introduce new political institutions that would enhance the right of self-determination of their peoples. And they wanted to develop a sense of common nationhood within the population and establish secure territorial boundaries. Most opted to follow a capitalist or a moderately socialist path toward economic development. In a few cases—most notably in China and Vietnam—revolutionary leaders opted for the Communist mode of development.

Regardless of the path chosen, the results were often disappointing. Much of Africa and Asia remained economically dependent on the

© William J. Duiker

advanced industrial nations. Some societies faced severe problems of urban and rural poverty.

What had happened to tarnish the bright dream of economic affluence? During the late 1950s and early 1960s, one school of thought was dominant among scholars and government officials in the United States. Known as modernization theory, this school took the view that the problems faced by the newly independent countries were a consequence of the difficult transition from a traditional to a modern society. Modernization theorists were convinced that agrarian countries were destined to follow the path of the West toward the creation of modern industrial societies but would need time as well as substantial amounts of economic and technological assistance from the West to complete the journey.

Eventually, modernization theory began to come under attack from a new generation of younger scholars. In their view, the responsibility for continued economic underdevelopment in the developing world lay not with the countries themselves but with their continued domination by the ex-colonial powers. In this view, known as dependency theory, the countries of Asia, Africa, and Latin America were the victims of the international marketplace, which charged high prices for the manufactured goods of the West while dooming preindustrial countries to low prices for their own raw material exports. Efforts by such countries to build up their own industrial sectors and move into the stage of self-sustaining growth were hampered by foreign control—through European- and American-owned corporations—over many of their resources. To end this "neocolonial" relationship, the dependency theory advocates argued, developing societies should reduce their economic ties with the West and practice a policy of economic self-reliance, thereby taking control over their own destinies.

Leaders of African and Asian countries also encountered problems creating new political cultures responsive to the needs of their citizens. At first, most accepted the concept of democracy as the defining theme of that culture. Within a decade, however, democratic systems throughout the developing world were replaced by military dictatorships or one-party governments that redefined the concept of democracy to fit their own preferences. It was clear that the difficulties in building democratic political institutions in developing societies had been underestimated.

The problem of establishing a common national identity has in some ways been the most daunting of all the challenges facing the new nations of Asia and Africa. Many of these new states were a composite of a wide variety of ethnic, religious, and linguistic groups who found it difficult to agree on common symbols of nationalism. Problems of establishing an official language and delineating territorial boundaries left over from the colonial era created difficulties in many countries. Internal conflicts spawned by deep-rooted historical and ethnic hatreds have proliferated throughout the world, leading to a vast new movement of people across state boundaries equal to any that has occurred since the great population migrations of the thirteenth and fourteenth centuries.

The introduction of Western cultural values and customs has also had a destabilizing effect in many areas. Although such ideas are welcomed by some groups, they are firmly resisted by others. Where Western influence has the effect of undermining traditional customs and religious beliefs, it often provokes violent hostility and sparks tension and even conflict within individual societies. Much of the anger recently directed at the United States in Muslim countries has undoubtedly been generated by such feelings.

Nonetheless, social and political attitudes are changing rapidly in many Asian and African countries as new economic circumstances have led to a more secular worldview, a decline in traditional hierarchical relations, and a more open attitude toward sexual practices. In part, these changes have been a consequence of the influence of Western music, movies, and television. But they are also a product of the growth of an affluent middle class in many societies of Asia and Africa.

Today we live not only in a world economy but in a world society, where a revolution in the Middle East can cause a rise in the price of oil in the United States and a change in social behavior in Malaysia and Indonesia, where the collapse of an empire in Asia can send shock waves as far as Hanoi and Havana, and where a terrorist attack in New York City or London can disrupt financial markets around the world. ❀

EAST AND WEST IN THE GRIP OF THE COLD WAR

Churchill, Roosevelt, and Stalin at Yalta

© The Art Archive/Imperial War Museum, London, UK

"OUR MEETING HERE in the Crimea has reaffirmed our common determination to maintain and strengthen in the peace to come that unity of purpose and of action which has made victory possible and certain for the United Nations in this war. We believe that this is a sacred obligation which our Governments owe to our peoples and to all the peoples of the world."[1]

With these ringing words, drafted at the Yalta Conference in February 1945, U.S. President Franklin D. Roosevelt, Soviet leader Joseph Stalin, and British Prime Minister Winston Churchill affirmed their common hope that the Grand Alliance that had been victorious in World War II could be sustained into the postwar era. Only through continuing and growing cooperation and understanding among the three Allies, the statement asserted, could a secure and lasting peace be realized that, in the words of the Atlantic Charter, would "afford assurance that all the men in all the lands may live out their lives in freedom from fear and want."

Roosevelt hoped that the decisions reached at Yalta would provide the basis for a stable peace in the postwar era. Allied occupation forces—American, British, and French in the west and Soviet in the east—were to bring about the end of Axis administration and to organize the free election of democratic governments throughout

Europe. To foster mutual trust and an end to the suspicions that had marked relations between the capitalist world and the Soviet Union prior to the war, Roosevelt tried to reassure Stalin that Moscow's legitimate territorial aspirations and genuine security needs would be adequately met in a durable peace settlement.

It was not to be. Within months after the German surrender, the mutual trust among the Allies—if it had ever truly existed—rapidly disintegrated, and the dream of a stable peace was replaced by the specter of a potential nuclear holocaust. The United Nations, envisioned by its founders as a mechanism for adjudicating international disputes, became mired in partisan bickering. As the Cold War between Moscow and Washington intensified, Europe was divided into two armed camps, while the two superpowers, glaring at each other across a deep ideological divide, held the survival of the entire world in their hands. ❀

The Collapse of the Grand Alliance

Q **Focus Question:** Why were the United States and the Soviet Union suspicious of each other after World War II, and what events between 1945 and 1949 heightened the tensions between the two nations?

The problems started in Europe. At the end of the war, Soviet military forces occupied all of Eastern Europe and the Balkans (except Greece, Albania, and Yugoslavia), while U.S. and other Allied forces secured the western part of the Continent. Roosevelt had assumed that free elections, administered promptly by "democratic and peace-loving forces," would lead to democratic governments responsive to the local population. But it soon became clear that the Soviet Union interpreted the Yalta agreement differently. When Soviet occupation authorities began forming a new Polish government, Stalin refused to accept the Polish government-in-exile—headquartered in London during the war and composed primarily of landed aristocrats who harbored a deep distrust of the Soviet Union—and instead set up a government composed of Communists who had spent the war in Moscow. Roosevelt complained to Stalin but eventually agreed to a compromise whereby two members of the London government were included in the new Communist regime. A week later, Roosevelt was dead of a cerebral hemorrhage, emboldening Stalin to do pretty much as he pleased.

Soviet Domination of Eastern Europe

Similar developments took place in all of the states occupied by Soviet troops. Coalitions of all political parties (except fascist or right-wing parties) were formed to run the government, but within a year or two, the Communist Party in each coalition had assumed the lion's share of power. It was then a short step to the establishment of one-party Communist governments. Between 1945 and 1947, Communist governments became firmly entrenched in East Germany, Bulgaria, Romania, Poland, and Hungary. In Czechoslovakia, with its strong tradition of democratic institutions, the Communists did not achieve their goals until 1948. After the Czech elections of 1946, the Communist Party shared control of the government with the non-Communist parties. When it appeared that the latter might win new elections early in 1948, the Communists seized control of the government on February 25. All other parties were dissolved, and the Communist leader Klement Gottwald became the new president of Czechoslovakia.

Yugoslavia was a notable exception to the pattern of Soviet dominance in Eastern Europe. The Communist Party there had led resistance to the Nazis during the war and easily assumed power when the war ended. Josip Broz, known as Tito (1892–1980), the leader of the Communist resistance movement, appeared to be a loyal Stalinist. After the war, however, he moved to establish an independent Communist state. Stalin hoped to take control of Yugoslavia, but Tito refused to capitulate to Stalin's demands and gained the support of the people (and some sympathy in the West) by portraying the struggle as one of Yugoslav national freedom. In 1958, the Yugoslav party congress asserted that Yugoslav Communists did not see themselves as deviating from communism, only from Stalinism. They considered their more decentralized system, in which workers managed themselves and local communes exercised some political power, closer to the Marxist-Leninist ideal.

To Stalin (who had once boasted, "I will shake my little finger, and there will be no more Tito"), the creation of pliant pro-Soviet regimes throughout Eastern Europe may simply have represented his interpretation of the Yalta peace agreement and a reward for sacrifices suffered during the war, satisfying Moscow's aspirations for a buffer zone against the capitalist West. If the Soviet leader had any intention of promoting future Communist revolutions in Western Europe—and there is some indication that he did—such developments would have to await the appearance of a new capitalist crisis a decade or more into the future. As Stalin undoubtedly recalled, Lenin had always maintained that revolutions come in waves.

Descent of the Iron Curtain

To the United States, however, the Soviet takeover of Eastern Europe represented an ominous development that threatened Roosevelt's vision of a durable peace. Public suspicion of Soviet intentions grew rapidly, especially among the millions of Americans who still had relatives living in Eastern Europe. Winston Churchill was quick to put such fears into words. In a highly publicized speech at Westminster College in Fulton, Missouri, in March 1946, the former British prime minister declared that an "iron curtain" had "descended across the Continent," dividing Germany and Europe itself into two hostile camps. Stalin responded by branding Churchill's speech a "call to war with the Soviet Union." But he need not have worried. Although public opinion in the United States placed increasing pressure on Roosevelt's successor, Harry Truman (1884–1972), to devise an effective strategy to counter Soviet advances abroad, the American people were in no mood for another war.

The first threat of a U.S.-Soviet confrontation took place in the Middle East. During World War II,

Eastern Europe in 1948

British and Soviet troops had been stationed in Iran to prevent Axis occupation of the rich oil fields in that country. Both nations had promised to withdraw their forces after the war, but at the end of 1945, there were ominous signs that Moscow might attempt to use its troops as a bargaining chip to annex Iran's northern territories—known as Azerbaijan—into the Soviet Union. When the government of Iran, with strong U.S. support, threatened to take the issue to the United Nations, the Soviets backed down and removed their forces from that country in the spring of 1946.

The Truman Doctrine

A civil war in Greece created another potential arena for confrontation between the superpowers and an opportunity for the Truman administration to take a stand. Communist guerrilla forces supported by Tito's Yugoslavia had taken up arms against the pro-Western government in Athens. Great Britain had initially assumed primary responsibility for promoting postwar reconstruction in the eastern Mediterranean, but in 1947, continuing economic problems caused the British to withdraw from the active role they had been playing in both Greece and Turkey. President Truman, alarmed by British weakness and the possibility of Soviet expansion into the eastern Mediterranean, responded with the Truman Doctrine, which said in essence that the United States would provide money to countries that claimed they were threatened by Communist expansion. If the Soviets were not stopped in Greece, the Truman argument ran, then the United States would have to face the spread of communism throughout the free world. As Dean Acheson, the U.S. secretary of state, explained, "Like apples in a barrel infected by disease, the corruption of Greece would infect Iran and all the East . . . likewise Africa . . . Italy . . . France. . . . Not since Rome and Carthage has there been such a polarization of power on this earth."[2]

The U.S. suspicion that Moscow was actively supporting the insurgent movement in Greece turned out to be unfounded. Stalin was apparently unhappy with Tito's promoting the conflict, not only because he suspected that the latter was attempting to create his own sphere of influence in the Balkans but also because it risked provoking a direct confrontation with the United States. But the Truman Doctrine had its intended effect in the United States, where public concern about the future intentions of the Soviet Union rose to new heights.

A Call to Arms. Within five years of the end of World War II, the Grand Alliance that had brought victory over the Axis Powers was in tatters. In March 1946, former British Prime Minister Winston Churchill, in an address given at Westminster College in Fulton, Missouri, declared that Soviet occupation of Eastern Europe had divided the Continent into two conflicting halves, separated by an "iron curtain." The speech is often credited with launching the first salvo in the Cold War.

The Marshall Plan

The proclamation of the Truman Doctrine was followed in June 1947 by the European Recovery Program, better known as the Marshall Plan, which provided $13 billion for the economic recovery of war-torn Europe. Underlying the program was the belief that Communist aggression fed off economic turmoil. As General George C. Marshall observed in a speech at Harvard University, "Our policy is not directed against any country or doctrine but against hunger, poverty, desperation, and chaos."[3]

From the Soviet perspective, the Marshall Plan was capitalist imperialism, a thinly veiled attempt to buy the support of the smaller European countries "in return for the relinquishing . . . of their economic and later also their political independence."[4] A Soviet spokesperson described the United States as the "main force in the imperialist camp," whose ultimate goal was "the strengthening of imperialism, preparation for a new imperialist war, a struggle against socialism and democracy, and the support of reactionary and antidemocratic, pro-fascist regimes and movements." Although the Marshall Plan was open to the Soviet Union and its Eastern European satellite states, they refused to participate. The Soviets were in no position to compete financially with the United States, however, and could do little to counter the Marshall Plan except tighten their control in Eastern Europe.

Europe Divided

By 1947, the split in Europe between East and West had become a fact of life. At the end of World War II, the United States had favored a quick end to its commitments in Europe. But American fears of Soviet aims caused the United States to play an increasingly important role in European affairs. In an article in *Foreign Affairs* in July 1947, George Kennan, a well-known U.S. diplomat with much knowledge of Soviet affairs, advocated a policy of **containment** against further aggressive Soviet moves. Kennan favored the "adroit and vigilant application of counter-force at a series of constantly shifting geographical and political points, corresponding to the shifts and maneuvers of Soviet policy." When the Soviets blockaded Berlin in 1948, containment of the Soviet Union became formal U.S. policy (see the box on p. 648).

The Berlin Blockade The fate of Germany had become a source of heated contention between East and West. Aside from **denazification** and the partitioning of

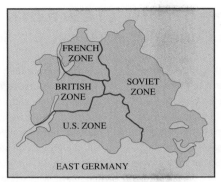

Berlin at the Start of the Cold War

Germany (and Berlin) into four occupied zones, the Allied powers had agreed on little with regard to the conquered nation. Even denazification proceeded differently in the various zones of occupation. The Americans and British proceeded methodically—the British had tried two million cases by 1948—while the Soviets (and French) went after major criminals and allowed lesser officials to go free. The Soviet Union, hardest hit by the war, took reparations from Germany by pillaging German industry. The technology-starved Soviets dismantled and removed to Russia 380 factories from the western zones of Berlin before transferring their control to the Western powers. By the summer of 1946, two hundred chemical, paper, and textile factories in the East German zone had likewise been shipped to the Soviet Union. At the same time, the German Communist Party was reestablished, under the control of Walter Ulbricht (1893–1973), and was soon in charge of the political reconstruction of the Soviet zone in eastern Germany.

Although the foreign ministers of the four occupying powers kept meeting in an attempt to arrive at a final peace treaty with Germany, they moved further and further apart. At the same time, the British, French, and Americans gradually began to merge their zones economically and by February 1948 were making plans for unification of these sectors and the formation of a national government. In an effort to secure all of Berlin and to halt the creation of a West German government, the Soviet Union imposed a blockade of West Berlin that prevented all traffic from entering the city's western zones through Soviet-controlled territory in East Germany.

The Western powers faced a dilemma. Direct military confrontation seemed dangerous, and no one wished to risk World War III. Therefore, an attempt to break through the blockade with tanks and trucks was ruled out. The solution was to deliver supplies for the city's inhabitants by plane. At its peak, the Berlin Airlift flew 13,000 tons of supplies daily into Berlin. The Soviets, also not wanting war, did not interfere and finally lifted the blockade in May 1949. The blockade of Berlin had severely increased tensions between the United States and the Soviet Union and brought the separation of Germany into two states. The Federal Republic of Germany was formally created from the three Western zones in September 1949, and a month later, the separate German Democratic Republic (GDR) was established in East Germany. Berlin remained a divided city and the source of much contention between East and West.

OPPOSING VIEWPOINTS

WHO STARTED THE COLD WAR? AMERICAN AND SOVIET PERSPECTIVES

Although the United States and the Soviet Union had cooperated during World War II to defeat the Germans and Japanese, differences began to appear as soon as victory became certain. The year 1946 was an especially important turning point in the relationship between the two new superpowers. George Kennan, an American diplomat regarded as an expert on Soviet affairs, was asked to write an analysis of one of Stalin's speeches. His U.S. Foreign Service dispatch, which came to be known as the Long Telegram, was sent to U.S. embassies, U.S. State Department officials, and military leaders. The Long Telegram gave a highly critical view of Soviet intentions. A response to Kennan's position was written by Nikolai Novikov, a former Soviet ambassador to the United States. His response was read by Vyacheslav Molotov, the Soviet foreign minister, but historians are not sure if Stalin or other officials also read it and were influenced by it.

George Kennan, The Long Telegram, February 1946

At the bottom of [the Soviet] neurotic view of world affairs is a traditional and instinctive Russian sense of insecurity. Originally, this was the insecurity of a peaceful agricultural people trying to live on a vast exposed plain in the neighborhood of fierce nomadic peoples. To this was added, as Russia came into contact with the economically advanced West, the fear of more competent, more powerful, more highly organized societies.... For this reason [the Russians] have always feared foreign penetration, feared direct contact between the Western world and their own.... And they have learned to seek security only in patient but deadly struggle for total destruction of rival power, never in compacts and compromises with it....

In summary, we have here a political force committed fanatically to the belief that with the United States there can be no permanent modus vivendi, that it is desirable and necessary [that] the internal harmony of our society be disrupted, our traditional way of life be destroyed, the international authority of our state be broken, if Soviet power is to be secure.... In addition it has an elaborate and far-flung apparatus for exertion of its influence in other countries, an apparatus of amazing flexibility and versatility, managed by people whose experience and skill in underground methods are presumably without parallel in history. Finally, it is seemingly inaccessible to considerations of reality in its basic reactions.... This is admittedly not a pleasant picture.... But I would like to record my

conviction that the problem is within our power to solve—and that without recourse to any general conflict.... I think we may approach calmly and with good heart the problem of how to deal with Russia ... [but] we must have the courage and self-confidence to cling to our own methods and conceptions of human society. After all, the greatest danger that can befall us in coping with this problem of Soviet communism is that we shall allow ourselves to become like those with whom we are coping.

Nikolai Novikov, Telegram, September 27, 1946

One of the stages in the achievement of dominance over the world by the United States is its understanding with England concerning the partial division of the world on the basis of mutual concessions. The basic lines of the secret agreement between the United States and England regarding the division of the world consist, as shown by facts, in their agreement on the inclusion of Japan and China in the sphere of influence of the United States in the Far East.... The American policy in China is striving for the complete economic and political submission of China to the control of American monopolistic capital.

Obvious indications of the U.S. effort to establish world dominance are also to be found in the increase in military potential in peacetime and in the establishment of a large number of naval and air bases both in the United States and beyond its borders.

Careful note should be taken of the fact that the preparation by the United States for a future war is being conducted with the prospect of war against the Soviet Union, which in the eyes of American imperialists is the main obstacle in the path of the United States to world domination. This is indicated by facts such as the tactical training of the American army for war with the Soviet Union as the future opponent, the placing of American strategic bases in regions from which it is possible to launch strikes on Soviet territory, intensified training and strengthening of Arctic regions as close approaches to the USSR, and attempts to prepare Germany and Japan to use those countries in a war against the USSR.

Q *In Kennan's view, what was the Soviet policy after World War II? What did he believe determined that policy, and how did he think the United States should respond? In Novikov's view, what was the goal of U.S. foreign policy, and how did he believe the Americans planned to achieve it? Why was it so difficult to achieve a common ground between the two positions?*

NATO and the Warsaw Pact The search for security in the new world of the Cold War also led to the formation of military alliances. The North Atlantic Treaty Organization (NATO) was formed in April 1949 when Belgium, Denmark, France, Great Britain, Iceland, Italy, Luxembourg, the Netherlands, Norway, and Portugal signed a

treaty with the United States and Canada. All the powers agreed to provide mutual assistance if any one of them was attacked. A few years later, Greece, Turkey, and West Germany joined NATO.

The Eastern European states soon followed suit. In 1949, they formed the Council for Mutual Economic

© Keystone/Getty Images

A City Divided. In 1948, U.S. planes airlifted supplies into Berlin to break the blockade that Soviet troops had imposed to isolate the city. Shown here is "Checkpoint Charlie," located at the boundary between the U.S. and Soviet zones of Berlin, just as Soviet roadblocks are about to be removed. The banner at the entrance to the Soviet sector reads, ironically, "The sector of freedom greets the fighters for freedom and right of the Western sectors."

Assistance (COMECON) for economic cooperation. Then, in 1955, Albania, Bulgaria, Czechoslovakia, East Germany, Hungary, Poland, Romania, and the Soviet Union organized a formal military alliance, the Warsaw Pact. Once again, Europe was tragically divided into hostile alliance systems (see Map 26.1).

Who Started the Cold War? There has been considerable historical debate over who bears responsibility for starting the Cold War. In the 1950s, most scholars in the West assumed that the bulk of the blame must fall on the shoulders of Stalin, whose determination to impose Soviet rule on Eastern Europe snuffed out hopes for freedom and self-determination there and aroused justifiable fears of Communist expansion in the West. During the next decade, however, revisionist historians—influenced in part by aggressive U.S. policies in Southeast Asia—began to argue that the fault lay primarily in Washington, where Truman and his anti-Communist advisers abandoned the precepts of Yalta and sought to encircle the Soviet Union with a tier of pliant U.S. client states.

More recently, many historians have adopted a more nuanced view, observing that both the United States and the Soviet Union took some unwise steps at the end of World War II. Both nations, however, were working within a framework conditioned by the past. The rivalry between the two superpowers ultimately stemmed from their different historical perspectives and their irreconcilable political ambitions. Intense competition for political and military supremacy had long been a regular feature of Western civilization. The United States and the Soviet Union were the heirs of that European tradition of power politics, and it should not surprise us that two such different systems would seek to extend their way of life to the rest of the world. Because of its need to secure its western border, the Soviet Union was not prepared to give up the advantages it had gained in Eastern Europe from Germany's defeat. But neither were Western leaders prepared to accept without protest the establishment of a system of Soviet satellites that not only threatened the security of Western Europe but also deeply offended Western sensibilities because of its blatant disregard of the Western concept of human rights.

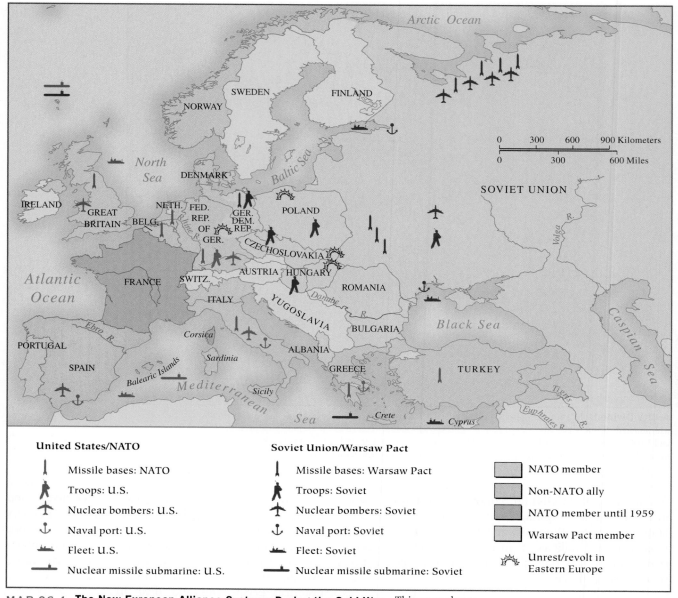

MAP 26.1 The New European Alliance Systems During the Cold War. This map shows postwar Europe as it was divided during the Cold War into two contending power blocs, the NATO alliance and the Warsaw Pact. Major military and naval bases are indicated by symbols on the map.

Q Where on the map was the so-called iron curtain?

View an animated version of this map or related maps at www.cengage.com/history/duikspiel/essentialworld6e

This does not necessarily mean that both sides bear equal responsibility for starting the Cold War. Some revisionist historians have claimed that the U.S. doctrine of containment was a provocative action that aroused Stalin's suspicions and drove Moscow into a position of hostility toward the West. This charge lacks credibility. As

information from the Soviet archives and other sources has become available, it is increasingly clear that Stalin's suspicions of the West were rooted in his Marxist-Leninist worldview and long predated Washington's enunciation of the doctrine of containment. As his foreign minister, Vyacheslav Molotov, once remarked, Soviet policy was inherently aggressive and would be triggered whenever the opportunity offered. Although Stalin apparently had no master plan to advance Soviet power into Western Europe, he was probably prepared to make every effort to do so once the next revolutionary wave arrived. Western leaders were fully justified in reacting to this possibility by strengthening their own lines of defense. On the other hand, a case can be made that in deciding to respond to the Soviet challenge in a primarily military manner, Western leaders overreacted to the situation and virtually guaranteed that the Cold War would be transformed into an arms race that could conceivably result in a new and uniquely destructive war.

Cold War in Asia

Q Focus Question: How and why did Mao Zedong and the Communists come to power in China, and what were the Cold War implications of their triumph?

The Cold War was somewhat slower to make its appearance in Asia. At Yalta, Stalin formally agreed to enter the Pacific War against Japan three months after the close of the conflict with Germany. As a reward for Soviet participation in the struggle against Japan, Roosevelt promised that Moscow would be granted "preeminent interests" in Manchuria (interests reminiscent of those possessed by imperial Russia prior to its defeat at the hands of Japan in 1904–1905) and the establishment of a Soviet naval base at Port Arthur. In return, Stalin promised to sign a treaty of alliance with the Republic of China, thus implicitly committing the Soviet Union not to provide the Chinese Communists with support in a possible future civil war. Although many observers would later question Stalin's sincerity in making such a commitment to the vocally anti-Communist Chiang Kai-shek, in Moscow the decision probably had a logic of its own. Stalin had no particular liking for the independent-minded Mao Zedong and indeed did not anticipate a Communist victory in any civil war in China. Only an agreement with Chiang could provide the Soviet Union with a strategically vital economic and political presence in northern China.

The Truman administration was equally reluctant to get embroiled in a confrontation with Moscow over the unfolding events in East Asia. Suspicion of Chiang Kai-shek ran high in Washington, and as we shall see, many key U.S. policymakers hoped to avoid a deeper involvement in China by brokering a compromise agreement between Chiang and his Communist rival, Mao.

Despite these commitments, the Allied agreements soon broke down, and East Asia was sucked into the vortex of the Cold War by the end of the 1940s. The root of the problem lay in the underlying weakness of Chiang's regime, which threatened to create a political vacuum in East Asia that both Moscow and Washington would be tempted to fill.

The Chinese Civil War

As World War II came to an end in the Pacific, relations between the government of Chiang Kai-shek in China and its powerful U.S. ally had become frayed. Although Roosevelt had hoped that Republican China would be the keystone of his plan for peace and stability in Asia after the war, U.S. officials became disillusioned with the corruption of Chiang's government and his unwillingness to risk his forces against the Japanese (he hoped to save them for use against the Communists after the war in the Pacific ended), and China was no longer the focus of Washington's close attention as the war came to a close. Nevertheless, U.S. military and economic aid to China had been substantial, and at war's end, the new Truman administration still hoped that it could rely on Chiang to support U.S. postwar goals in the region.

While Chiang Kai-shek wrestled with Japanese aggression and problems of national development, the Communists were building up their strength in northern China. To enlarge their political base, they carried out a "mass line" policy (from the masses to the masses), reducing land rents and confiscating the lands of wealthy landlords. By the end of World War II, 20 to 30 million Chinese were living under the administration of the Communists, and their People's Liberation Army (PLA) included nearly one million troops.

As the war came to an end, world attention began to focus on the prospects for renewed civil strife in China. Members of a U.S. liaison team stationed in Yan'an were impressed by the performance of the Communists, and some recommended that the United States should support them or at least remain neutral in a possible conflict between Communists and Nationalists for control of China. The Truman administration, though skeptical of Chiang's ability to forge a strong and prosperous country, was increasingly concerned about the spread of communism in Europe and tried to find a peaceful solution through the formation of a coalition government of all parties in China.

The Communist Triumph   The effort failed. By 1946, full-scale war between the Nationalist government, now re-installed in Nanjing, and the Communists resumed. Now Chiang Kai-shek's errors came home to roost. In the countryside, millions of peasants, attracted to the Communists by promises of land and social justice, flocked to serve in Mao Zedong's PLA. In the cities, middle-class Chinese, normally hostile to communism, were alienated by

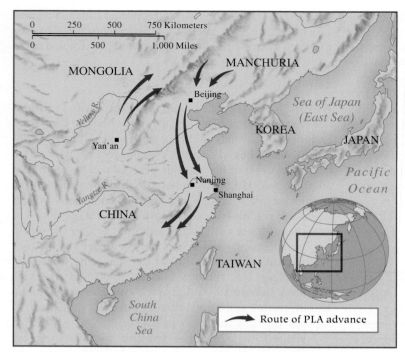

MAP 26.2 **The Chinese Civil War.** After the close of the Pacific War in 1945, the Nationalist Chinese government and the Chinese Communists fought a bitter civil war that ended with a victory by the latter in 1949. The path of the Communist advance is displayed on the map.

Q Where did Chiang Kai-shek's government retreat to after its defeat?

Chiang's brutal suppression of all dissent and his government's inability to slow the ruinous rate of inflation or solve the economic problems it caused. With morale dropping in the cities, Chiang's troops began to defect to the Communists. Sometimes whole divisions, officers as well as ordinary soldiers, changed sides. By 1948, the PLA was advancing south out of Manchuria and had encircled Beijing. Communist troops took the old imperial capital, crossed the Yangtze the following spring, and occupied the commercial hub of Shanghai (see Map 26.2). During the next few months, Chiang's government and two million of his followers fled to Taiwan, which the Japanese had returned to Chinese control after World War II.

The Truman administration reacted to the spread of Communist power in China with acute discomfort. Washington had no desire to see a Communist government on the mainland, but it had little confidence in Chiang Kai-shek's ability to realize Roosevelt's dream of a strong, united, and prosperous China. In December 1945, President Truman sent General George C. Marshall to China in a last-ditch effort to bring about a peaceful settlement, but anti-Communist elements in the Republic of China resisted U.S. pressure to create a coalition government with the Chinese Communist Party (CCP). During the next two years, the United States gave limited military support to Chiang's regime but refused to commit U.S. power to guarantee its survival. The administration's hands-off policy deeply angered many members of Congress, who charged that the White House was "soft on communism" and declared further that Roosevelt had betrayed Chiang Kai-shek at Yalta by granting privileges in Manchuria to the Soviet Union. In their view, Soviet troops had hindered the dispatch of Chiang's forces to the area and provided the PLA with weapons to use against its rivals.

Mao Zedong and Chiang Kai-shek Exchange a Toast. After World War II, the United States sent General George C. Marshall to China in an effort to prevent civil war between Chiang Kai-shek's government and Mao Zedong's Communists. Marshall's initial success was symbolized by this toast between Mao (at the left) and Chiang. But suspicion ran too deep, and soon conflict ensued, leading to a Communist victory in 1949. Chiang's government retreated to the island of Taiwan.

WHO LOST CHINA?

 In 1949, with China about to fall under the control of the Communists, President Truman instructed the State Department to prepare a White Paper explaining why the U.S. policy of seeking to avoid a Communist victory in China had failed. The authors of the paper concluded that responsibility lay at the door of Nationalist Chinese leader Chiang Kai-shek and that there was nothing the United States could have done to alter the result. Most China observers today would accept that assessment, but it did little at the time to deflect criticism of the administration for selling out the interests of our ally in China.

U.S. State Department White Paper on China, 1949

When peace came the United States was confronted with three possible alternatives in China: (1) it could have pulled out lock, stock, and barrel; (2) it could have intervened militarily on a major scale to assist the Nationalists to destroy the Communists; (3) it could, while assisting the Nationalists to assert their authority over as much of China as possible, endeavor to avoid a civil war by working for a compromise between the two sides.

The first alternative would, and I believe American public opinion at the time so felt, have represented an abandonment of our international responsibilities and of our traditional policy of friendship for China before we had made a determined effort to be of assistance. The second alternative policy, while it may look attractive theoretically, in retrospect, was wholly impracticable. The Nationalists had been unable to destroy the Communists during the ten years before the war. Now after the war the Nationalists were . . . weakened, demoralized, and unpopular. They had quickly dissipated their popular support and prestige in the areas liberated from the Japanese by the conduct of their civil and military officials.

The Communists on the other hand were much stronger than they had ever been and were in control of most of North China. Because of the ineffectiveness of the Nationalist forces, which was later to be tragically demonstrated, the Communists probably could have been dislodged only by American arms. It is obvious that the American people would not have sanctioned such a colossal commitment of our armies in 1945 or later. We therefore came to the third alternative policy whereunder we faced the facts of the situation and attempted to assist in working out a modus vivendi which would avert civil war but nevertheless preserve and even increase the influence of the National Government. . . .

The distrust of the leaders of both the Nationalist and Communist Parties for each other proved too deep-seated to permit final agreement, notwithstanding temporary truces and apparently promising negotiations. The Nationalists, furthermore, embarked in 1946 on an overambitious military campaign in the face of warnings by General Marshall that it not only would fail but would plunge China into economic chaos and eventually destroy the National Government. . . .

The unfortunate but inescapable fact is that the ominous result of the civil war in China was beyond the control of the government of the United States. Nothing that this country did or could have done within the reasonable limits of its capabilities could have changed that result; nothing that was left undone by this country has contributed to it. It was the product of internal Chinese forces, forces which this country tried to influence but could not. A decision was arrived at within China, if only a decision by default.

Q *How did the authors of the White Paper explain the Communist victory in China? According to this argument, what actions might have prevented it?*

In later years, sources in both Moscow and Beijing indicated that the Soviet Union gave little assistance to the CCP in its struggle against the Nanjing regime. In fact, Stalin periodically advised Mao against undertaking the effort. Although Communist forces undoubtedly received some assistance from Soviet occupation troops in Manchuria, their victory ultimately stemmed from conditions inside China, not from the intervention of outside powers. So indeed argued the Truman administration in 1949, when it issued a White Paper that placed most of the blame for the debacle at the feet of Chiang Kai-shek's regime (see the box above).

Many Americans, however, did not agree. With the Communist victory, Asia became a theater of the Cold War and an integral element of American politics. During the spring of 1950, under pressure from Congress and

public opinion to define U.S. interests in Asia, the Truman administration adopted a new national security policy, known as NSC-68, that implied that the United States would take whatever steps were necessary to stem the further expansion of communism in the region. Containment had come to East Asia.

The New China

Communist leaders in China, from their new capital of Beijing, probably hoped that their accession to power in 1949 would bring about an era of peace in the region and permit their new government to concentrate on domestic goals. But the desire for peace was tempered by their determination to erase a century of humiliation at the hands of imperialist powers and to restore the traditional

A Pledge of Eternal Friendship. After the Communist victory in the Chinese civil war, Chairman Mao Zedong traveled to Moscow, where in 1950 he negotiated a treaty of friendship and cooperation with the Soviet Union. The poster shown here trumpets the results of the meeting: "Long live and strengthen the unbreakable friendship and cooperation of the Soviet and Chinese peoples!" The two leaders, however, did not get along. Mao reportedly complained to colleagues that obtaining assistance from Stalin was "like taking meat from a tiger's mouth."

outer frontiers of the empire. In addition to recovering territories that had been part of the Manchu Empire, such as Manchuria, Taiwan, and Tibet, the Chinese leaders also hoped to restore Chinese influence in former tributary areas such as Korea and Vietnam.

It soon became clear that these two goals were not always compatible. Negotiations between Mao and Stalin, held in Moscow in January 1950, led to Soviet recognition of Chinese sovereignty over Manchuria and Xinjiang (the desolate lands north of Tibet that were known as Chinese Turkestan because many of the peoples in the area were of Turkic origin), although the Soviets retained a measure of economic influence in both areas. Chinese troops occupied Tibet in 1950 and brought it under Chinese administration for the first time in more than a century. But in Korea and Taiwan, China's efforts to re-create the imperial buffer zone provoked new conflicts with foreign powers.

The problem of Taiwan was a consequence of the Cold War. As the civil war in China came to an end, the Truman administration appeared determined to avoid entanglement in China's internal affairs and indicated

that it would not seek to prevent a Communist takeover of the island, now occupied by Chiang Kai-shek's Republic of China. But as tensions between the United States and the new Chinese government escalated during the winter of 1949–1950, influential figures in the United States began to argue that Taiwan was crucial to U.S. defense strategy in the Pacific.

The Korean War

The outbreak of war in Korea also helped bring the Cold War to East Asia. After the Sino-Japanese War in 1894–1895, Korea, long a Chinese tributary, had fallen increasingly under the rival influences of Japan and Russia. After the Japanese defeated the Russians in 1905, Korea became an integral part of the Japanese Empire and remained so until 1945. The removal of Korea from Japanese control had been one of the stated objectives of the Allies in World War II, and on the eve of Japanese surrender in August 1945, the Soviet Union and the United States agreed to divide the country into two separate occupation zones at the 38th parallel. They originally planned to hold national elections after the restoration of peace to reunify Korea under an independent government. But as U.S.-Soviet relations deteriorated, two separate governments emerged in Korea, a Communist one in the north and an anti-Communist one in the south.

Tensions between the two governments ran high along the dividing line, and on June 25, 1950, with the apparent approval of Stalin, North Korean troops invaded the south. The Truman administration immediately ordered U.S. naval and air forces to support South Korea, and the United Nations Security Council (with the Soviet delegate absent to protest the UN's refusal to assign China's seat to the new government in Beijing) passed a resolution calling on member nations to jointly resist the invasion, in line with the security provisions of the United Nations Charter. By September, UN forces under the command of U.S. General Douglas MacArthur marched northward across the 38th parallel with the aim of unifying Korea under a single, non-Communist government.

President Truman worried that by approaching the Chinese border at the Yalu River, the UN troops could trigger Chinese intervention, but MacArthur assured him that China would not respond. In November, however, Chinese "volunteer" forces intervened in force on the side of North Korea and drove the UN troops southward in disarray. A static defense line was eventually established near the original dividing line at the 38th parallel (see Map 26.3), although the war continued.

To many Americans, the Chinese intervention in Korea was clear evidence that China intended to promote

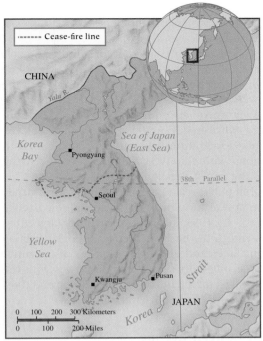

MAP 26.3 **The Korean Peninsula.** In June 1950, North Korean forces crossed the 38th parallel in a sudden invasion of the south. Shown here is the cease-fire line that brought an end to the war in 1953.

Q What is the importance of the Yalu River?

communism throughout Asia, and recent evidence suggests that Mao was convinced that a revolutionary wave was on the rise in Asia. In fact, however, China's decision to enter the war was probably motivated in large part by the fear that hostile U.S. forces might be stationed on the Chinese frontier and perhaps even launch an attack across the border. MacArthur intensified such fears by calling publicly for air attacks on Manchurian cities in preparation for an attack on Communist China.

In any case, the outbreak of the Korean War was particularly unfortunate for China. Immediately after the invasion, President Truman dispatched the U.S. Seventh Fleet to the Taiwan Strait to prevent a possible Chinese invasion of Taiwan. Even more unfortunate, the invasion hardened Western attitudes against the new Chinese government and led to China's isolation from the major capitalist powers for two decades. The United States continued to support the Nationalist government in Taiwan as the only legal representative of the Chinese people and supported its occupation of China's seat on the UN Security Council. As a result, China was cut off from all forms of economic and technological assistance and was forced to rely almost entirely on the Soviet Union, with which it had signed a pact of friendship and cooperation in early 1950.

Conflict in Indochina

During the mid-1950s, China sought to build contacts with the nonsocialist world. A cease-fire agreement brought the Korean War to an end in July 1953, and China signaled its desire to live in peaceful coexistence with other independent countries in the region. But a relatively minor conflict now began to intensify on China's southern flank, in French Indochina. The struggle had begun after World War II, when the Indochinese Communist Party led by Ho Chi Minh (1890–1969), at the head of a multiparty nationalist alliance called the Vietminh Front, seized power in northern and central Vietnam after the surrender of imperial Japan. After abortive negotiations between Ho's government and the returning French, war broke out in December 1946. French forces occupied the cities and the densely populated lowlands, while the Vietminh took refuge in the mountains.

For three years, the Vietminh waged a "people's war" of national liberation from colonial rule, gradually increasing in size and effectiveness. At the time, however, the conflict in Indochina attracted relatively little attention from world leaders, who viewed the events there as only one aspect of the transition to independence of colonialized territories in postwar Asia. The Truman administration was uneasy about Ho's longstanding credentials as a Soviet agent but was equally reluctant to anger anticolonialist elements in the area by intervening on behalf of the French. Moscow had even less interest in the region. Stalin—still hoping to see the Communist Party come to power in Paris—ignored Ho's request for recognition of his movement as the legitimate representative of the national interests of the Vietnamese people.

But what had begun as an anticolonial struggle by the Vietminh Front against the French became entangled in the Cold War after the CCP came to power in China. In early 1950, Beijing began to provide military assistance to the Vietminh to burnish its revolutionary credentials and protect its own borders from hostile forces. The Truman administration, increasingly concerned that a revolutionary "Red tide" was sweeping through the region, decided to provide financial and technical assistance to the French while pressuring them to prepare for an eventual transition to independent non-Communist governments in Vietnam, Laos, and Cambodia.

With casualties mounting and the French public tired of fighting the "dirty war" in Indochina, the French agreed to a peace settlement with the Vietminh at the Geneva Conference in 1954. Vietnam was temporarily divided into a northern Communist half (known as the Democratic Republic of Vietnam, or DRV) and a non-Communist southern half based in Saigon (eventually to

Indochina After 1954

be known as the Republic of Vietnam). A demilitarized zone separated the two at the 17th parallel. Elections were to be held in two years to create a unified government. Cambodia and Laos were both declared independent under neutral governments. French forces, which had suffered a major defeat at the hands of Vietminh troops at the Battle of Dien Bien Phu in the spring of 1954, were withdrawn from all three countries.

China had played an active role in bringing about the settlement and clearly hoped that it would reduce tensions in the area, but subsequent efforts to improve relations between China and the United States foundered on the issue of Taiwan. In the fall of 1954, the United States signed a mutual security treaty with the Republic of China guaranteeing U.S. military support in case of an invasion of Taiwan. When Beijing demanded U.S. withdrawal from Taiwan as the price for improved relations, diplomatic talks between the two countries collapsed.

From Confrontation to Coexistence

Q Focus Question: What events led to the era of coexistence in the 1960s, and to what degree did each side contribute to the reduction in international tensions?

The decade of the 1950s opened with the world teetering on the edge of a nuclear holocaust. The Soviet Union had detonated its first nuclear device in 1949, and the two blocs—capitalist and socialist—viewed each other across an ideological divide that grew increasingly bitter with each passing year. Yet as the decade drew to a close, a measure of sanity crept into the Cold War, and the leaders of the major world powers began to seek ways to coexist in a peaceful and stable world.

The first clear sign of change occurred after Stalin's death in early 1953. His successor, Georgy Malenkov (1902–1988), openly hoped to improve relations with the Western powers in order to reduce defense expenditures and shift government spending to growing consumer needs. Nikita Khrushchev (1894–1971), who replaced Malenkov in 1955, continued his predecessor's efforts to reduce tensions with the West and improve the living standards of the Soviet people.

In an adroit public relations touch, in 1956 Khrushchev promoted an appeal for a policy of **peaceful coexistence** with the West. In 1955, he had surprisingly agreed to negotiate an end to the postwar occupation of Austria by the victorious allies and allow the creation of a neutral country with strong cultural and economic ties with the West. He also called for a reduction in defense expenditures and reduced the size of the Soviet armed forces.

Ferment in Eastern Europe

At first, Western leaders were suspicious of Khrushchev's motives, especially in light of events that were taking place in Eastern Europe. The key to security along the western frontier of the Soviet Union was the string of Eastern European satellite states that had been assembled in the aftermath of World War II (see Map 26.1). Once Communist domination had been assured, a series of "little Stalins" put into power by Moscow instituted Soviet-type five-year plans that emphasized heavy industry rather than consumer goods, the collectivization of agriculture, and the nationalization of industry. They also appropriated the political tactics that Stalin had perfected in the Soviet Union, eliminating all non-Communist parties and establishing the classical institutions of repression—the secret police and military forces. Dissidents were tracked down and thrown into prison, and "national Communists" who resisted total subservience to the Soviet Union were charged with treason in mass show trials and executed.

Despite these repressive efforts, discontent became increasingly evident in several Eastern European countries. Hungary, Poland, and Romania harbored bitter memories of past Russian domination and suspected that Stalin, under the guise of proletarian internationalism, was seeking to revive the empire of the tsars. For the vast majority of peoples in Eastern Europe, the imposition of the so-called people's democracies (a term invented by Moscow to define a society in the early stage of socialist transition) resulted in economic hardship and severe threats to the most basic political liberties. The first indications of unrest appeared in East Berlin, where popular riots broke out against Communist rule in 1953. The riots eventually subsided, but the virus had spread to neighboring countries.

In Poland, public demonstrations against an increase in food prices in 1956 escalated into widespread protests against the regime's economic policies, restrictions on the freedom of Catholics to practice their religion, and the continued presence of Soviet troops (as called for by the Warsaw Pact) on Polish soil. In a desperate effort to defuse the unrest, the party leader stepped down and was replaced by Wladyslaw Gomulka (1905–1982), a popular figure who had previously been demoted for his "nationalist" tendencies. When Gomulka took steps to ease the crisis, Khrushchev flew to Warsaw to warn him against adopting policies that could undermine the political dominance of the party and weaken security links with the Soviet Union. After a tense confrontation, Poland agreed to remain in the Warsaw Pact and to maintain the sanctity of party rule; in return, Gomulka was authorized to adopt domestic reforms, such as easing restrictions on religious practice and ending the policy of forced collectivization in rural areas.

The Hungarian Revolution   The developments in Poland sent shock waves throughout the region. The impact was strongest in neighboring Hungary, where the methods of the local "little Stalin," Matyas Rakosi, were so brutal that he had been summoned to Moscow for a lecture. In late October 1956, student-led popular riots broke out in the capital of Budapest and soon spread to other towns and villages throughout the country. Rakosi was forced to resign and was replaced by Imre Nagy (1896–1958), a national Communist who attempted to satisfy popular demands without arousing the anger of Moscow. Unlike Gomulka, however, Nagy was unable to contain the zeal of leading members of the protest movement, who sought major political reforms and the withdrawal of Hungary from the Warsaw Pact. On November 1, Nagy promised free elections, which, given the mood of the country, would probably have brought an end to Communist rule. After a brief moment of uncertainty, Moscow decided on firm action. Soviet troops, recently withdrawn at Nagy's request, returned to Budapest and installed a new government under the more pliant party leader János Kádár (1912–1989). While Kádár rescinded many of Nagy's measures, Nagy sought refuge in the Yugoslav embassy. A few weeks later, he left the embassy under the promise of safety but was quickly arrested, convicted of treason, and executed.

Different Roads to Socialism   The dramatic events in Poland and Hungary graphically demonstrated the vul-

How the Mighty Have Fallen.   In the fall of 1956, Hungarian freedom fighters rose up against Communist domination of their country in the short-lived Hungarian revolution. Their actions threatened Soviet hegemony in Eastern Europe, however, and in late October, Soviet leader Nikita Khrushchev dispatched troops to quell the uprising. In the meantime, the Hungarian people had demonstrated their discontent by toppling a gigantic statue of Joseph Stalin in the capital of Budapest. Statues of the Soviet dictator had been erected in all the Soviet satellites after World War II. ("W.C." identifies a public toilet in European countries.)

nerability of the Soviet satellite system in Eastern Europe, and many observers throughout the world anticipated that the United States would intervene on behalf of the freedom fighters in Hungary. After all, the Eisenhower administration had promised that it would "roll back" communism, and radio broadcasts by the U.S.-sponsored Radio Liberty and Radio Free Europe had encouraged the peoples of Eastern Europe to rise up against Soviet domination. In reality, Washington was well aware that U.S. intervention could lead to nuclear war and limited itself to protests against Soviet brutality in crushing the uprising.

The year of discontent was not without consequences, however. Soviet leaders now recognized that Moscow could maintain control over its satellites in Eastern Europe only by granting them the leeway to adopt domestic policies appropriate to local conditions. Khrushchev had already embarked on this path in 1955 when he assured Tito that there were "different roads to socialism." Some Eastern European Communist leaders now took Khrushchev at his word and adopted reform programs to make socialism more palatable to their subject populations. Even Kádár, derisively labeled the "butcher of Budapest," managed to preserve many of Nagy's reforms to allow a measure of capitalist incentive and freedom of expression in Hungary.

Crisis over Berlin   But in the late 1950s, a new crisis erupted over the status of Berlin. The Soviet Union had

Rivalry in the Third World

Yet Khrushchev could rarely avoid the temptation to gain an advantage over the United States in the competition for influence throughout the world, a posture that exacerbated the unstable relationship between the two global superpowers. Unlike Stalin, who had exhibited a profound distrust of all political figures who did not slavishly follow his lead, Khrushchev viewed the dismantling of colonial regimes in Asia, Africa, and Latin America as a potential advantage for the Soviet Union. When neutralist leaders like Nehru in India, Tito in Yugoslavia, and Sukarno in Indonesia founded the **Nonaligned Movement** in 1955 as a means of providing an alternative to the two major power blocs, Khrushchev took every opportunity to promote Soviet interests in the Third World

The Kitchen Debate. During the late 1950s, the United States and the Soviet Union sought to defuse Cold War tensions by encouraging cultural exchanges between the two countries. On one occasion, U.S. Vice President Richard M. Nixon visited Moscow in conjunction with the arrival of an exhibit to introduce U.S. culture and society to the Soviet people. Here Nixon lectures Soviet Communist Party chief Nikita Khrushchev on the technology of the U.S. kitchen. On the other side of Nixon, at the far right, is future Soviet president Leonid Brezhnev.

launched its first intercontinental ballistic missile (ICBM) in August 1957, arousing U.S. fears of a missile gap between the United States and the Soviet Union. Khrushchev attempted to take advantage of the U.S. frenzy over missiles to solve the problem of West Berlin, which had remained a "Western island" of prosperity inside the relatively poverty-stricken state of East Germany. Many East Germans sought to escape to West Germany by fleeing through West Berlin, a serious blot on the credibility of the GDR and a potential source of instability in East-West relations. In November 1958, Khrushchev announced that unless the West removed its forces from West Berlin within six months, he would turn over control of the access routes to the East Germans. Unwilling to accept an ultimatum that would have abandoned West Berlin to the Communists, U.S. President Dwight D. Eisenhower and the West stood firm, and Khrushchev eventually backed down.

Despite such periodic crises in East-West relations, there were tantalizing signs that an era of true peaceful coexistence between the two power blocs could be achieved. In the late 1950s, the United States and the Soviet Union initiated a cultural exchange program. While Leningrad's Kirov Ballet appeared at theaters in the United States, Benny Goodman and the film *West Side Story* played in Moscow. In 1958, Khrushchev visited the United States and had a brief but friendly encounter with President Eisenhower at the presidential retreat in northern Maryland.

(as the nonaligned countries of Asia, Africa, and Latin America were now popularly called). Khrushchev openly sought alliances with strategically important neutralist countries like India, Indonesia, and Egypt, while Washington's ability to influence events at the United Nations began to wane.

In January 1961, just as John F. Kennedy (1917–1963) assumed the U.S. presidency, Khrushchev unnerved the new president at an informal summit meeting in Vienna by declaring that the Soviet Union would provide active support to national liberation movements throughout the world. There were rising fears in Washington of Soviet meddling in such sensitive trouble spots as Southeast Asia, where insurgent activities in Indochina continued to simmer; in Central Africa, where the pro-Soviet tendencies of radical leader Patrice Lumumba aroused deep suspicion in Washington; and in the Caribbean, where a little-known Cuban revolutionary named Fidel Castro threatened to transform his country into an advanced base for Soviet expansion in the Americas.

The Cuban Missile Crisis and the Move Toward Détente

In 1959, a left-wing revolutionary named Fidel Castro (b. 1927) overthrew the Cuban dictator Fulgencio Batista and established a Soviet-supported totalitarian regime. As tensions increased between the new government in Havana

FILM & HISTORY
THE MISSILES OF OCTOBER (1973)

Never has the world been closer to nuclear holocaust than in the month of October 1962, when U.S. and Soviet leaders found themselves in direct confrontation over Nikita Khrushchev's decision to introduce Soviet missiles into Cuba, just 90 miles from the coast of the United States. When President John F. Kennedy announced that U.S. warships would intercept Soviet freighters destined for Cuban ports, the two countries teetered on the verge of war. Only after protracted and delicate negotiations was the threat defused. The confrontation sobered leaders on both sides of the "iron curtain" and led to the signing of the first test ban treaty, as well as the opening of a hotline between Moscow and Washington.

The Missiles of October, a made-for-TV film produced in 1973, is a tense political drama that is all the more riveting because it is based on fact. Although it is less well known than the more recent *Thirteen Days,* released in 2000, it is in many ways more persuasive, and the acting is demonstrably superior. The film stars William Devane as John F. Kennedy and Martin Sheen as his younger

John Kennedy (William Devane, seated) and Robert Kennedy (Martin Sheen) confer with advisers.

© Everett Collection

brother, Robert. Based in part on Robert Kennedy's *Thirteen Days* (New York, 1969), a personal account of the crisis that was published shortly after his assassination in 1968, the film traces the tense discussions that took place in the White House as the president's key advisers debated how to respond to the Soviet challenge. President Kennedy remains cool as he reins in his more bellicose advisers to bring about a compromise solution that successfully avoids the seemingly virtual certainty of a nuclear confrontation with Moscow.

Because the film is based on the recollections of Robert F. Kennedy, it presents a favorable portrait of his brother's handling of the crisis, as might be expected, and the somewhat triumphalist attitude at the end of the film is perhaps a bit exaggerated. But Khrushchev's colleagues in the Kremlin and his Cuban ally, Fidel Castro, viewed the U.S.-Soviet agreement as a humiliation for Moscow that nevertheless set the two global superpowers on the road to a more durable and peaceful relationship. It was one Cold War story that had a happy ending.

---

and the United States, the Eisenhower administration broke relations with Cuba and drafted plans to overthrow Castro, who reacted by drawing closer to Moscow.

Soon after taking office in early 1961, Kennedy approved a plan to support an invasion of Cuba by anti-Castro exiles. But the attempted landing at the Bay of Pigs in southern Cuba was an utter failure. At Castro's invitation, the Soviet Union then began to station nuclear missiles in Cuba, within striking distance of the American mainland. (That the United States had placed nuclear weapons in Turkey within easy range of the Soviet Union was a fact that Khrushchev was quick to point out.) When U.S. intelligence discovered that a Soviet fleet carrying more missiles was heading to Cuba, Kennedy decided to dispatch U.S. warships into the Atlantic to prevent the fleet from reaching its destination.

This approach to the problem was risky but had the benefit of delaying confrontation and giving the two sides time to find a peaceful solution. After a tense standoff

during which the two countries came frighteningly close to a direct nuclear confrontation (the Soviet missiles already in Cuba were launch-ready), Khrushchev finally sent a conciliatory letter to Kennedy agreeing to turn back the fleet if Kennedy pledged not to invade Cuba. In a secret concession not revealed until many years later, the president also promised to dismantle U.S. missiles in Turkey. To the world, however (and to an angry Castro), it appeared that Kennedy had bested Khrushchev. "We were eyeball to eyeball," noted U.S. Secretary of State Dean Rusk, "and they blinked."

The ghastly realization that the world might have faced annihilation in a matter of days had a profound effect on both sides. A communication hotline between Moscow and Washington was installed in 1963 to expedite rapid communication between the two superpowers in time of crisis. In the same year, the two powers agreed to ban nuclear tests in the atmosphere, a step that served to lessen the tensions between the two nations.

The Sino-Soviet Dispute

Nikita Khrushchev had launched his slogan of peaceful coexistence as a means of improving relations with the capitalist powers; ironically, one result of the campaign was to undermine Moscow's ties with its close ally China. During Stalin's lifetime, Beijing had accepted the Soviet Union as the acknowledged leader of the socialist camp. After Stalin's death, however, relations began to deteriorate. Part of the reason may have been Mao Zedong's contention that he, as the most experienced Marxist leader, should now be acknowledged as the most authoritative voice within the socialist community. But another determining factor was that just as Soviet policies were moving toward moderation, China's were becoming more radical.

Several other issues were involved, including territorial disputes along the Sino-Soviet border and China's unhappiness with limited Soviet economic assistance. But the key sources of disagreement involved ideology and the Cold War. Chinese leaders were convinced that the successes of the Soviet space program confirmed that the socialists were now technologically superior to the capitalists (the East Wind, trumpeted the Chinese official press, had now triumphed over the West Wind), and they urged Khrushchev to go on the offensive to promote world revolution. Specifically, China wanted Soviet assistance in retaking Taiwan from Chiang Kai-shek. But Khrushchev was trying to improve relations with the West and rejected Chinese demands for support against Taiwan.

By the end of the 1950s, the Soviet Union had begun to remove its advisers from China, and in 1961, the dispute broke into the open. Increasingly isolated, China voiced its hostility to what Mao described as the "urban industrialized countries" (which included the Soviet Union) and portrayed itself as the leader of the "rural underdeveloped countries" of Asia, Africa, and Latin America in a global struggle against imperialist oppression. In effect, China had applied Mao Zedong's concept of people's war in an international framework (see the box on p. 661).

The Second Indochina War

China's radicalism was intensified in the early 1960s by the outbreak of renewed war in Indochina. The Eisenhower administration had opposed the peace settlement at Geneva in 1954, which divided Vietnam temporarily into two separate regroupment zones, specifically because the provision for future national elections opened up the possibility that the entire country would come under Communist rule. But Eisenhower had been unwilling to send U.S. military forces to continue the conflict without the full support of the British and the French, who preferred to seek a negotiated settlement. In the end, Washington promised not to break the provisions of the agreement but refused to commit itself to the results.

During the next several months, the United States began to provide aid to the new government in South Vietnam. Under the leadership of the anti-Communist politician Ngo Dinh Diem, the government began to root out dissidents. With the tacit approval of the United States, Diem refused to hold the national elections called for by the Geneva Accords. It was widely anticipated, even in Washington, that the Communists would win such elections. In 1959, Ho Chi Minh, despairing of the peaceful unification of the country under Communist rule, decided to return to a policy of revolutionary war in the south.

Late the following year, a political organization that was designed to win the support of a wide spectrum of the population was founded in an isolated part of South Vietnam. Known as the National Liberation Front (NLF), it was under the secret but firm leadership of high-ranking Communists in North Vietnam (the Democratic Republic of Vietnam).

By 1963, South Vietnam was on the verge of collapse. Diem's autocratic methods and inattention to severe economic inequality had alienated much of the population, and revolutionary forces, popularly known as the Viet Cong (Vietnamese Communists) and supported by the Communist government in the North, expanded their influence throughout much of the country. In the fall of 1963, with the approval of the Kennedy administration, senior military officers overthrew the Diem regime. But factionalism kept the new military leadership from reinvigorating the struggle against the insurgent forces, and the situation in South Vietnam grew worse. By early 1965, the Viet Cong, their ranks now swelled by military units infiltrating from North Vietnam, were on the verge of seizing control of the entire country. In March, President Lyndon Johnson decided to send U.S. combat troops to South Vietnam to prevent a total defeat for the anti-Communist government in Saigon. Over the next three years, U.S. troop levels steadily increased as the White House counted on U.S. firepower to persuade Ho Chi Minh to abandon his quest to unify Vietnam under Communist leadership.

The Role of China Chinese leaders observed the gradual escalation of the conflict in South Vietnam with mixed feelings. They were undoubtedly pleased to have a firm Communist ally—one that had in many ways followed the path of Mao Zedong—just beyond their southern frontier. Yet they were concerned that bloodshed in South Vietnam might enmesh China in a new conflict with the

OPPOSING VIEWPOINTS
PEACEFUL COEXISTENCE OR PEOPLE'S WAR?

INTERACTION & EXCHANGE

The Soviet leader Vladimir Lenin had contended that war between the socialist and imperialist camps was inevitable because the imperialists would never give up without a fight. That assumption had probably guided the thoughts of Joseph Stalin, who told colleagues shortly after World War II that a new war would break out in fifteen to twenty years. But Stalin's successor, Nikita Khrushchev, feared that a new world conflict could result in a nuclear holocaust and contended that the two sides must learn to coexist, although peaceful competition would continue. In this speech given in Beijing in 1959, Khrushchev attempted to persuade the Chinese to accept his views. But Chinese leaders argued that the "imperialist nature" of the United States would never change and countered that the crucial area of competition was in the Third World, where "people's wars" would bring down the structure of imperialism. That argument was presented in 1966 by Marshall Lin Biao of China, at that time one of Mao Zedong's closest allies.

Khrushchev's Speech to the Chinese, 1959

Comrades! Socialism brings to the people peace—that greatest blessing. The greater the strength of the camp of socialism grows, the greater will be its possibilities for successfully defending the cause of peace on this earth. The forces of socialism are already so great that real possibilities are being created for excluding war as a means of solving international disputes. . . .

When I spoke with President Eisenhower—and I have just returned from the United States of America—I got the impression that the President of the U.S.A.—and not a few people support him—understands the need to relax international tension. . . .

There is only one way of preserving peace—that is the road of peaceful coexistence of states with different social systems. The question stands thus: either peaceful coexistence or war with its catastrophic consequences. Now, with the present relation of forces between socialism and capitalism being in favor of socialism, he who would continue the "cold war" is moving towards his own destruction. . . .

It is not at all because capitalism is still strong that the socialist countries speak out against war, and for peaceful coexistence. No, we have no need of war at all. If the people do not want it, even such a noble and progressive system as socialism cannot be imposed by force of arms. The socialist countries therefore, while carrying through a consistently peace-loving policy, concentrate their efforts on peaceful construction; they fire the hearts of men by the force of their example in building socialism, and thus lead them to follow in their footsteps. The question of when this or that country will take

the path to socialism is decided by its own people. This, for us, is the holy of holies.

Lin Biao, "Long Live the Victory of People's War"

Many countries and peoples in Asia, Africa, and Latin America are now being subjected to aggression and enslavement on a serious scale by the imperialists headed by the United States and their lackeys. . . . As in China, the peasant question is extremely important in these regions. The peasants constitute the main force of the national-democratic revolution against the imperialists and their lackeys. In committing aggression against these countries, the imperialists usually begin by seizing the big cities and the main lines of communication. But they are unable to bring the vast countryside completely under their control. . . . The countryside, and the countryside alone, can provide the revolutionary basis from which the revolutionaries can go forward to final victory. Precisely for this reason, Mao Tse-tung's theory of establishing revolutionary base areas in the rural districts and encircling the cities from the countryside is attracting more and more attention among the people in these regions.

Taking the entire globe, if North America and Western Europe can be called "the cities of the world," then Asia, Africa, and Latin America constitute "the rural areas of the world." Since World War II, the proletarian revolutionary movement has for various reasons been temporarily held back in the North American and West European capitalist countries, while the people's revolutionary movement in Asia, Africa, and Latin America has been growing vigorously. In a sense, the contemporary world revolution also presents a picture of the encirclement of cities by the rural areas. In the final analysis, the whole cause of world revolution hinges on the revolutionary struggles of the Asian, African, and Latin American peoples, who make up the overwhelming majority of the world's population. The socialist countries should regard it as their internationalist duty to support the people's revolutionary struggles in Asia, Africa, and Latin America. . . .

Ours is the epoch in which world capitalism and imperialism are heading for their doom and communism is marching to victory. Comrade Mao Tse-tung's theory of people's war is not only a product of the Chinese revolution, but has also the characteristic of our epoch. The new experience gained in the people's revolutionary struggles in various countries since World War II has provided continuous evidence that Mao Tse-tung's thought is a common asset of the revolutionary people of the whole world.

Q *Why did Nikita Khrushchev feel that, contrary to Lenin's prediction, conflict between the socialist and capitalist camps was no longer inevitable? How did Lin Biao respond?*

United States. Nor did they welcome the specter of a powerful and ambitious united Vietnam, which might wish to extend its influence throughout mainland Southeast Asia, an area that Beijing considered its own backyard.

Chinese leaders therefore tiptoed delicately through the minefield of the Indochina conflict. As the war escalated in 1964 and 1965, Beijing publicly announced that the Chinese people fully supported their comrades seeking national liberation but privately assured Washington that China would not directly enter the conflict unless U.S. forces threatened its southern border. Beijing also refused to cooperate fully with Moscow in shipping Soviet goods to North Vietnam through Chinese territory.

Despite its dismay at the lack of full support from China, the Communist government in North Vietnam responded to U.S. escalation by infiltrating more of its own regular troops into the South, and by 1968, the war had reached a stalemate (see the comparative illustration at the right). The Communists were not strong enough to overthrow the government in Saigon, whose weakness was shielded by the presence of half a million U.S. troops, but President Johnson was reluctant to engage in all-out war on North Vietnam for fear of provoking a global nuclear conflict. In the fall, after the Communist-led Tet offensive undermined claims of progress in Washington and aroused intense antiwar protests in the United States, peace negotiations began in Paris.

Quest for Peace Richard Nixon came into the White House in 1969 on a pledge to bring an honorable end to the Vietnam War. With U.S. public opinion sharply divided on the issue, he began to withdraw U.S. troops while continuing to hold peace talks in Paris. But the centerpiece of his strategy was to improve relations with China and thus undercut Chinese support for the North Vietnamese war effort. During the 1960s, relations between Moscow and Beijing had reached a point of extreme tension, and thousands of troops were

AP Images

© Three Lions/Getty Images

POLITICS & GOVERNMENT

COMPARATIVE ILLUSTRATION

War in the Rice Paddies. The first stage of the Vietnam War consisted primarily of guerrilla conflict, as Viet Cong insurgents relied on guerrilla tactics in their effort to bring down the U.S.-supported government in Saigon. In 1965, however, President Lyndon Johnson ordered U.S. combat troops into South Vietnam (top photo) in a desperate bid to prevent a Communist victory in that beleaguered country. The Communist government in Hanoi, North Vietnam, responded in kind, sending its own regular forces down the Ho Chi Minh Trail to confront U.S. troops on the battlefield. In the photo on the bottom, North Vietnamese troops storm the U.S. Marine base at Khe Sanh, near the demilitarized zone, in 1968, the most violent year of the war. U.S. military commanders viewed the use of helicopters as a key factor in defeating the insurgent forces in Vietnam. This conflict, however, was one instance when technological superiority did not produce a victory on the battlefield.

Q How do you think helicopters were used to assist U.S. operations in South Vietnam? Why didn't they produce a favorable result?

stationed on both sides of their long common frontier. To intimidate their Communist rivals, Soviet sources hinted that they might launch a preemptive strike to destroy Chinese nuclear facilities in Xinjiang. Sensing an opportunity to split the two onetime allies, Nixon sent his emissary, Henry Kissinger, on a secret trip to China. Responding to assurances that the United States was determined to withdraw from Indochina and hoped to improve relations with the mainland regime, Chinese leaders invited President Nixon to visit China in early 1972. Nixon accepted, and the two sides agreed to set aside their differences over Taiwan to pursue a better mutual relationship.

The Fall of Saigon   Incensed at the apparent betrayal by their close allies, North Vietnamese leaders decided to seek a peaceful settlement of the war in the south. In January 1973, a peace treaty was signed in Paris calling for the removal of all U.S. forces from South Vietnam. In return, the Communists agreed to halt military operations and to engage in negotiations to resolve their differences with the Saigon regime. But negotiations between north and south over the political settlement soon broke down, and in early 1975, the Communists resumed the offensive. At the end of April, under a massive assault by North Vietnamese military forces, the South Vietnamese government surrendered. A year later, the country was unified under Communist rule.

The Communist victory in Vietnam was a severe humiliation for the United States, but its strategic impact was limited because of the new relationship with China. During the next decade, Sino-American relations continued to improve. In 1979, diplomatic ties were established between the two countries under an arrangement whereby the United States renounced its mutual security treaty with the Republic of China in return for a pledge from China to seek reunification with Taiwan by peaceful means. By the end of the 1970s, China and the United States had forged a "strategic relationship" in which they would cooperate against the common threat of Soviet hegemony in Asia.

Why had the United States failed to achieve its objective of preventing a Communist victory in Vietnam? One leading member of the Johnson administration later commented that Washington had underestimated the determination of its adversary in Hanoi and overestimated the patience of the American people. Deeper reflection suggests, however, that another factor was equally important: the United States had overestimated the ability of its client state in South Vietnam to defend itself against a disciplined adversary. In subsequent years, it became a crucial lesson to the Americans on the perils of nation building.

An Era of Equivalence

Q **Focus Question:** Why did the Cold War briefly flare up again in the 1980s, and why did it come to a definitive end at the end of the decade?

When the Johnson administration sent U.S. combat troops to South Vietnam in 1965, Washington's main concern was with Beijing, not Moscow. By the mid-1960s, U.S. officials viewed the Soviet Union as an essentially conservative power, more concerned with protecting its vast empire than with expanding its borders. In fact, U.S. policy makers periodically sought Soviet assistance in seeking a peaceful settlement of the Vietnam War. As long as Khrushchev was in power, they found a receptive ear in Moscow. Khrushchev was firmly dedicated to promoting peaceful coexistence (at least on his terms) and sternly advised the North Vietnamese against a resumption of revolutionary war in South Vietnam.

After October 1964, when Khrushchev was replaced by a new leadership headed by party chief Leonid Brezhnev (1906–1982) and Prime Minister Alexei Kosygin (1904–1980), Soviet attitudes about Vietnam became more ambivalent. On the one hand, the new Soviet leaders had no desire to see the Vietnam conflict poison relations between the great powers. On the other hand, Moscow was eager to demonstrate its support for the North Vietnamese to deflect Chinese charges that the Soviet Union had betrayed the interests of the oppressed peoples of the world. As a result, Soviet officials publicly voiced sympathy for the U.S. predicament in Vietnam but put no pressure on their allies to bring an end to the war. Indeed, the Soviet Union became Hanoi's main supplier of advanced military equipment in the final years of the war.

The Brezhnev Doctrine

In the meantime, new Cold War tensions were brewing in Eastern Europe, where discontent with Stalinist policies began to emerge in Czechoslovakia. The latter had not shared in the thaw of the mid-1950s and remained under the rule of the hard-liner Antonin Novotny (1904–1975), who had been installed in power by Stalin himself. By the late 1960s, however, Novotny's policies had led to widespread popular alienation, and in 1968, with the support of intellectuals and reformist party members, Alexander Dubček (1921–1992) was elected first secretary of the Communist Party. He immediately attempted to create what was popularly called "socialism with a human face," relaxing restrictions on freedom of speech and the press and the right to travel abroad. Economic reforms were announced, and party control over all aspects of society

THE BREZHNEV DOCTRINE

POLITICS & GOVERNMENT

In the summer of 1968, when the new Communist Party leaders in Czechoslovakia were seriously considering proposals for reforming the totalitarian system there, the Warsaw Pact nations met under the leadership of Soviet party chief Leonid Brezhnev to assess the threat to the socialist camp. Shortly after, military forces of several Soviet bloc nations entered Czechoslovakia and imposed a new government subservient to Moscow. The move was justified by the spirit of "proletarian internationalism" and was widely viewed as a warning to China and other socialist states not to stray too far from Marxist-Leninist orthodoxy, as interpreted by the Soviet Union. But Moscow's actions also raised tensions in the Cold War.

A Letter to the Central Committee of the Communist Party of Czechoslovakia

Dear comrades!

On behalf of the Central Committees of the Communist and Workers' Parties of Bulgaria, Hungary, the German Democratic Republic, Poland, and the Soviet Union, we address ourselves to you with this letter, prompted by a feeling of sincere friendship based on the principles of Marxism-Leninism and proletarian internationalism and by the concern of our common affairs for strengthening the positions of socialism and the security of the socialist community of nations.

The development of events in your country evokes in us deep anxiety. It is our firm conviction that the offensive of the reactionary forces, backed by imperialists, against your Party and the foundations of the social system in the Czechoslovak Socialist Republic, threatens to push your country off the road of socialism and that consequently it jeopardizes the interests of the entire socialist system. . . .

We neither had nor have any intention of interfering in such affairs as are strictly the internal business of your Party and your state, nor of violating the principles of respect, independence, and equality in the relations among the Communist Parties and socialist countries. . . .

At the same time we cannot agree to have hostile forces push your country from the road of socialism and create a threat of severing Czechoslovakia from the socialist community. . . . This is the common cause of our countries, which have joined in the Warsaw Treaty to ensure independence, peace, and security in Europe, and to set up an insurmountable barrier against the intrigues of the imperialist forces, against aggression and revenge. . . . We shall never agree to have imperialism, using peaceful or nonpeaceful methods, making a gap from the inside or from the outside in the socialist system, and changing in imperialism's favor the correlation of forces in Europe. . . .

That is why we believe that a decisive rebuff of the anti-Communist forces, and decisive efforts for the preservation of the socialist system in Czechoslovakia are not only your task but ours as well. . . .

We express the conviction that the Communist Party of Czechoslovakia, conscious of its responsibility, will take the necessary steps to block the path of reaction. In this struggle you can count on the solidarity and all-round assistance of the fraternal socialist countries.

Warsaw, July 15, 1968.

Q *How did Leonid Brezhnev justify the Soviet decision to invade Czechoslovakia? To what degree do you find his arguments persuasive?*

---

was reduced. A period of euphoria erupted that came to be known as the "Prague Spring."

It proved to be short-lived. Encouraged by Dubček's actions, some Czechs called for more far-reaching reforms, including neutrality and withdrawal from the Soviet bloc. To forestall the spread of this "spring fever," the Soviet Red Army, supported by troops from other Warsaw Pact states, invaded Czechoslovakia in August 1968 and crushed the reform movement. Gustav Husák (1913–1991), a committed Stalinist, replaced Dubček and restored the old order, while Moscow attempted to justify its action by issuing the so-called Brezhnev Doctrine (see the box above).

In East Germany as well, Stalinist policies continued to hold sway. The ruling Communist government in East Germany, led by Walter Ulbricht, had consolidated its position in the early 1950s and became a faithful Soviet satellite. Industry was nationalized and agriculture collectivized. After the 1953 workers' revolt was crushed by Soviet tanks, a steady flight of East Germans to West

Germany ensued, primarily through the city of Berlin. This exodus of mostly skilled laborers ("Soon only party chief Ulbricht will be left," remarked one Soviet observer sardonically) created economic problems and in 1961 led the East German government to erect a wall separating East Berlin from West Berlin, as well as even more fearsome barriers along the entire border with West Germany.

After building the Berlin Wall, East Germany succeeded in developing the strongest economy among the Soviet Union's Eastern European satellites. In 1971, Ulbricht was succeeded by Erich Honecker (1912–1994), a party hard-liner. Propaganda increased, and the use of the Stasi, the secret police, became a hallmark of Honecker's virtual dictatorship. Honecker ruled unchallenged for the next eighteen years.

An Era of Détente

Still, under Brezhnev and Kosygin, the Soviet Union continued to pursue peaceful coexistence with the West and adopted a generally cautious posture in foreign affairs. By the early 1970s, a new age in Soviet-American relations had emerged, often referred to by the French term *détente*, meaning a reduction of tensions between the two sides. One symbol of **détente** was the Anti-Ballistic Missile (ABM) Treaty, often called SALT I (for Strategic Arms Limitation Talks), signed in 1972, in which the two nations agreed to limit the size of their ABM systems.

Washington's objective in pursuing the treaty was to make it unlikely that either superpower could win a nuclear exchange by launching a preemptive strike against the other. U.S. officials believed that a policy of "equivalence," in which the two sides had roughly equal power, was the best way to avoid a nuclear confrontation. Détente was pursued in other ways as well. When President Nixon took office in 1969, he sought to increase trade and cultural contacts with the Soviet Union. His purpose was to set up a series of "linkages" in U.S.-Soviet relations that would persuade Moscow of the economic and social benefits of maintaining good relations with the West.

A symbol of that new relationship was the Helsinki Accords. Signed in 1975 by the United States, Canada, and all European nations on both sides of the iron curtain, these accords recognized all borders in Europe that had been established since the end of World War II, thereby formally acknowledging for the first time the Soviet sphere of influence in Eastern Europe. The Helsinki Accords also committed the signatories to recognize and protect the human rights of their citizens, a clear effort by the Western states to improve the performance of the Soviet Union and its allies in that arena.

Renewed Tensions in the Third World

Protection of human rights became one of the major foreign policy goals of the next U.S. president, Jimmy Carter (b. 1924). Ironically, just at the point when U.S. involvement in Vietnam came to an end and relations with China began to improve, U.S.-Soviet relations began to sour, for several reasons. Some Americans had become increasingly concerned about aggressive new tendencies in Soviet foreign policy. The first indication came in Africa. Soviet influence was on the rise in Somalia, across the Red Sea from South Yemen, and later in neighboring Ethiopia. In Angola, once a colony of Portugal, an insurgent movement supported by Cuban troops came to power. In 1979, Soviet troops were sent across the border into Afghanistan to protect a newly installed Marxist regime facing internal resistance from fundamentalist Muslims. Some observers suspected that the ultimate objective of the Soviet advance into hitherto neutral Afghanistan was to extend Soviet power into the oil fields of the Persian Gulf. To deter such a possibility, the White House

promulgated the Carter Doctrine, which stated that the United States would use its military power, if necessary, to safeguard Western access to the oil reserves in the Middle East. In fact, sources in Moscow later disclosed that the Soviet advance had little to do with the oil of the Persian Gulf but was an effort to increase Soviet influence in a region increasingly beset by Islamic fervor. Soviet officials feared that Islamic activism could spread to the Muslim populations in the Soviet republics in Central Asia and were confident that the United States was too distracted by the **"Vietnam syndrome"** (the public fear of U.S. involvement in another Vietnam-type conflict) to respond.

Another reason for the growing suspicion of the Soviet Union in the United States was that some U.S. defense analysts began to charge that the Soviet Union had rejected the policy of equivalence and was seeking strategic superiority in nuclear weapons. Accordingly, they argued for a substantial increase in U.S. defense spending. Such charges, combined with evidence of Soviet efforts in Africa and the Middle East and reports of the persecution of Jews and dissidents in the Soviet Union, helped undermine public support for détente in the United States. These changing attitudes were reflected in the failure of the Carter administration to obtain congressional approval of a new arms limitation agreement (SALT II), signed with the Soviet Union in 1979.

Countering the Evil Empire

The early years of the administration of President Ronald Reagan (1911–2004) witnessed a return to the harsh rhetoric, if not all of the harsh practices, of the Cold War. President Reagan's anti-Communist credentials were well known. In a speech given shortly after his election in 1980, he referred to the Soviet Union as an "evil empire" and frequently voiced his suspicion of Soviet motives in foreign affairs. In an effort to eliminate perceived Soviet advantages in strategic weaponry, the White House began a military buildup that stimulated a renewed arms race. In 1982, the Reagan administration introduced the nuclear-tipped cruise missile, whose ability to fly at low altitudes made it difficult to detect by enemy radar. Reagan also became an ardent exponent of the Strategic Defense Initiative (SDI), nicknamed **"Star Wars."** The intent behind this proposed defense system was not only to create a space shield that could destroy incoming missiles but also to force Moscow into an arms race that it could not hope to win.

The Reagan administration also adopted a more activist, if not confrontational, stance in the Third World. That attitude was most directly demonstrated in Central America, where the revolutionary Sandinista regime had been established in Nicaragua after the overthrow of the Somoza dictatorship in 1979. Charging that the Sandinista regime was supporting a guerrilla insurgency movement in nearby El Salvador, the Reagan administration began to provide material aid to the government in El Salvador while simultaneously supporting an anti-Communist guerrilla movement (the **Contras**) in Nicaragua. Though the administration insisted that it was countering the spread of communism in the Western Hemisphere, its Central American policy aroused considerable controversy in Congress, where some members charged that growing U.S. involvement could lead to a repeat of the nation's bitter experience in Vietnam.

Northern Central America

The Reagan administration also took the offensive in other areas. By providing military support to the anti-Soviet insurgents in Afghanistan, the White House helped maintain a Vietnam-like war in Afghanistan that entangled the Soviet Union in its own quagmire. Like the Vietnam War, the conflict in Afghanistan resulted in heavy casualties and demonstrated that the influence of a superpower was limited in the face of strong nationalist, guerrilla-type opposition.

Toward a New World Order

In 1985, Mikhail Gorbachev was elected secretary of the Communist Party of the Soviet Union. During Brezhnev's last years and the brief tenures of his two successors (see Chapter 27), the Soviet Union had entered an era of serious economic decline, and the dynamic new party chief was well aware that drastic changes would be needed to rekindle the dreams that had inspired the Bolshevik Revolution. During the next few years, he launched a program of restructuring (*perestroika*) to revitalize the Soviet system. As part of that program, he set out to improve relations with the United States and the rest of the capitalist world. When he met with President Reagan in Reykjavik, the capital of Iceland, the two leaders agreed to set aside their ideological differences.

Gorbachev's desperate effort to rescue the Soviet Union from collapse was too little and too late. As 1991 drew to a close, the Soviet Union, so long an apparently permanent fixture on the global scene, suddenly disintegrated; in its place arose fifteen new nations. That same year, the string of Soviet satellites in Eastern Europe broke loose from Moscow's grip and declared their independence from Communist rule. The Cold War was over.

The end of the Cold War lulled many observers into the seductive vision of a new world order that would be characterized by peaceful cooperation and increasing prosperity. Sadly, such hopes have not been realized (see the comparative essay "Global Village or Clash of Civilizations?" on p. 667). A bitter civil war in the Balkans in the mid-1990s graphically demonstrated that old fault lines of national and ethnic hostility still divided the post–Cold War world. Elsewhere, bloody ethnic and religious disputes broke out in Africa and the Middle East. Then, on September 11, 2001, the world entered a dangerous new era when terrorists attacked the nerve centers of U.S. power in New York City and Washington, D.C., inaugurating a new round of tension between the West and the forces of militant Islam. These events will be discussed in greater detail in the chapters that follow.

In the meantime, other issues beyond the headlines clamor for attention. Environmental problems and the threat of global warming, the growing gap between rich and poor nations, and tensions caused by migrations of peoples all present a growing threat to political stability and the pursuit of happiness. As the twenty-first century progresses, the task of guaranteeing the survival of the human race appears to be just as challenging, and even more complex, than it was during the Cold War.

COMPARATIVE ESSAY
GLOBAL VILLAGE OR CLASH OF CIVILIZATIONS?

As the Cold War came to an end in 1991, statesmen, scholars, and political pundits began to forecast the emergence of a "new world order." One hypothesis was that the decline of communism signaled that the industrial capitalist democracies of the West had triumphed in the world of ideas and were now poised to remake the rest of the world in their own image.

Not all agreed with this optimistic view of the world situation. In *The Clash of Civilizations and the Remaking of the World Order,* the historian Samuel P. Huntington suggested that the post–Cold War era, far from marking the triumph of Western ideals, would be characterized by increased global fragmentation and a "clash of civilizations" based on ethnic, cultural, or religious differences. According to Huntington, the twenty-first century would be dominated by disputatious cultural blocs in East Asia, Western Europe and the United States, Eurasia, and the Middle East. The dream of a universal order—a global village—dominated by Western values, he concluded, is a fantasy.

Recent events have lent some support to Huntington's hypothesis. The collapse of the Soviet Union led to the emergence of an atmosphere of conflict and tension all along the perimeter of the old Soviet Empire. More recently, the terrorist attack on the United States in September 2001 set the advanced nations of the West and much of the Muslim world on a collision course. As for the new economic order—now enshrined as official policy in Western capitals—public anger at the impact of globalization and the recent worldwide financial crisis has reached disturbing levels in many countries, leading to a growing demand for self-protection and group identity in an impersonal and rapidly changing world.

Are we then headed toward Huntington's prediction of multiple power blocs divided by religion and culture? His thesis is indeed a useful corrective to the complacent tendency of many observers to view Western civilization as the zenith of human achievement. On the other hand, by dividing the world into competing cultural blocs, Huntington has underestimated the centrifugal forces at work in the

Ronald McDonald in Indonesia. This giant statue welcomes young Indonesians to a McDonald's restaurant in Jakarta, the capital city. McDonald's food chain symbolizes the globalization of today's world civilization.

various regions of the world. As the industrial and technological revolutions spread across the face of the earth, their impact is measurably stronger in some societies than in others, thus intensifying historical rivalries in a given region while establishing links between individual societies and counterparts in other parts of the world. In recent years, for example, Japan has had more in common with the United States than with its traditional neighbors, China and Korea.

The most likely scenario for the next few decades, then, is more complex than either the global village hypothesis or its rival, the clash of civilizations. The twenty-first century will be characterized by simultaneous trends toward globalization and fragmentation as the thrust of technology and information transforms societies and gives rise to counterreactions among societies seeking to preserve a group identity and sense of meaning and purpose in a confusing world.

Q *In the next decade, do you believe that the forces of globalization or of fragmentation will be the stronger?*

CONCLUSION

AT THE END OF WORLD WAR II, a new conflict appeared in Europe as the two superpowers, the United States and the Soviet Union, began to compete for political domination. This ideological division soon spread to the rest of the world as the United States fought in Korea and Vietnam to prevent the spread of communism, promoted by the new Maoist government in China, while the Soviet Union used its influence to prop up pro-Soviet regimes in Asia, Africa, and Latin America.

What had begun, then, as a confrontation across the great divide of the "iron curtain" in Europe eventually took on global significance,

much as the major European powers had jostled for position and advantage in Africa and eastern Asia prior to World War I. As a result, both Moscow and Washington became entangled in areas that in themselves had little importance in terms of real national security interests.

As the twentieth century entered its last two decades, however, there were tantalizing signs of a thaw in the Cold War. In 1979, China and the United States decided to establish mutual diplomatic relations, a consequence of Beijing's decision to focus on domestic reform and stop supporting wars of national liberation in Asia. Six years later, the ascent of Mikhail Gorbachev to leadership in the Soviet Union, culminating in the collapse of the Soviet Union in 1991, brought a final end to almost half a century of bitter rivalry between the world's two superpowers.

The Cold War thus ended without the horrifying vision of a mushroom cloud. Unlike the earlier rivalries that had resulted in two world wars, this time the antagonists had gradually come to realize that the struggle for supremacy could be carried out in the political and economic arena rather than on the battlefield. And in the final analysis, it was not military superiority, but political, economic, and cultural factors that brought about the triumph of Western civilization over the Marxist vision of a classless utopia. The world's statesmen could now shift their focus to other problems of mutual concern.

TIMELINE

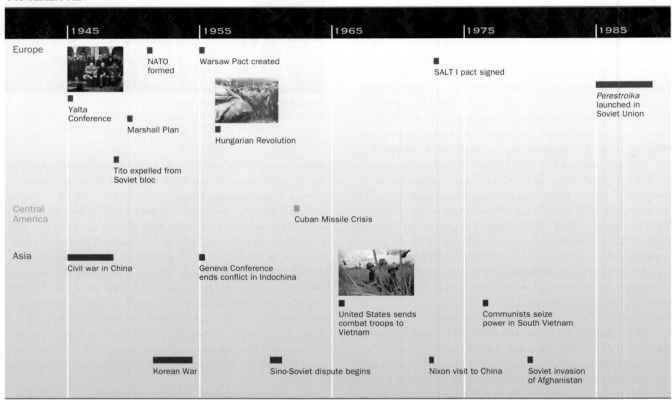

SUGGESTED READING

Cold War Literature on the Cold War is abundant. Two general accounts are **R. B. Levering, *The Cold War, 1945–1972*** (Arlington Heights, Ill., 1982), and **B. A. Weisberger, *Cold War, Cold Peace: The United States and Russia Since 1945*** (New York, 1984). Two works that maintain that the Soviet Union was chiefly responsible for the Cold War are **H. Feis, *From Trust to Terror: The Onset of the Cold War, 1945–1950*** (New York, 1970), and **A. Ulam, *The Rivals: America and Russia Since World War II*** (New York, 1971). Revisionist studies on the Cold War have emphasized U.S. responsibility for the Cold War, especially its global aspects. These works include **J. Kolko** and **G. Kolko, *The Limits of Power: The World and United States Foreign Policy, 1945–1954*** (New York,

1972); **W. La Feber, *America, Russia, and the Cold War, 1945–1966,*** 8th ed. (New York, 2002); and **M. Sherwin, *A World Destroyed: The Atomic Bomb and the Grand Alliance*** (New York, 1975). For a highly competent retrospective analysis of the Cold War era, see **J. L. Gaddis, *We Now Know: Rethinking Cold War History*** (Oxford, 1997). Also see his more general work ***The Cold War: A New History*** (New York, 2005). For the perspective of a veteran journalist, see **M. Frankel, *High Noon in the Cold War: Kennedy, Khrushchev, and the Cuban Missile Crisis*** (New York, 2004).

A number of studies of the early stages of the Cold War have been based on documents unavailable until the late 1980s or early 1990s. See, for example, **O. A. Westad, *Cold War and Revolution: Soviet-American Rivalry and the Origins of the Chinese Civil War***

(New York, 1993); **D. A. Mayers, *Cracking the Monolith: U.S. Policy Against the Sino-Soviet Alliance, 1949–1955*** (Baton Rouge, La., 1986); and **Chen Jian, *China's Road to the Korean War: The Making of the Sino-American Confrontation*** (New York, 1994). **S. Goncharov, J. W. Lewis,** and **Xue Litai, *Uncertain Partners: Stalin, Mao, and the Korean War*** (Stanford, Calif., 1993), provides a fascinating view of the war from several perspectives.

For important studies of Soviet foreign policy, see **A. B. Ulam, *Dangerous Relations: The Soviet Union in World Politics, 1970–1982*** (New York, 1983). The effects of the Cold War on Germany are examined in **J. H. Backer, *The Decision to Divide Germany: American Foreign Policy in Transition*** (Durham, N.C., 1978). On atomic diplomacy in the Cold War, see **G. F. Herken, *The Winning Weapon: The Atomic Bomb in the Cold War, 1945–1950*** (New York, 1981). For a good introduction to the arms race, see **E. M. Bottome, *The Balance of Terror: A Guide to the Arms Race,*** rev. ed. (Boston, 1986).

China There are several informative surveys of Chinese foreign policy since the Communist rise to power. A particularly insightful account is **Chen Jian, *Mao's China and the Cold War*** (Chapel Hill,

N.C., 2001). On Sino-U.S. relations, see **H. Harding, *A Fragile Relationship: The United States and China Since 1972*** (Washington, D.C., 1992), and W. Burr, ed., ***The Kissinger Transcripts: The Top-Secret Talks with Beijing and Moscow*** (New York, 1998). On Chinese policy in Korea, see **Shu Guang Zhang, *Mao's Military Romanticism: China and the Korean War*** (Lawrence, Kans., 2001), and **Xiaobing Li et al., *Mao's Generals Remember Korea*** (Lawrence, Kans., 2001). On Sino-Vietnamese relations, see **Ang Cheng Guan, *Vietnamese Communists' Relations with China and the Second Indochina Conflict*** (Jefferson, N.C., 1997).

How have historians answered the question of whether the United States or the Soviet Union bears the primary responsibility for the Cold War, and what evidence can be presented on each side of the issue?

In thinking about this question, begin by breaking it down into the components shown below. A discussion of the significance of each component should appear in your answer.

INTERACTION AND EXCHANGE   In framing your answers to the following questions, consider the chapter material especially the discussion under the heading "Who Started the Cold War?" (p. 649) and the views of George Kennan and Nikolai Novikov (document, p. 648). Who coined the term *iron curtain* and why? What evidence of an "iron curtain" do you see on the accompanying maps? What were Soviet goals in Eastern Europe? How did the United States and the Soviet Union differ in their views of postwar Germany and Eastern Europe? How did the use of language heighten tensions? How would Kennan and Novikov answer the question of who bears the primary responsibility for the Cold War?

Were the post–World War II struggles in Third World nations really a part of the Cold War, or just regional conflicts or even civil wars? How did the United States view them, and how did this view determine American reactions? Was there such a thing as "monolithic communism," whereby all Communist actions around the world were orchestrated by Moscow? In what ways did the policy of containment commit the United States to involvement around the world? How is the current "war on terrorism" similar to the Cold War?

Eastern Europe in 1948

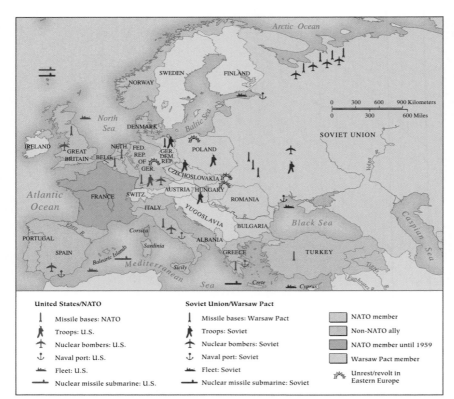

United States/NATO	Soviet Union/Warsaw Pact	
Missile bases: NATO	Missile bases: Warsaw Pact	NATO member
Troops: U.S.	Troops: Soviet	Non-NATO ally
Nuclear bombers: U.S.	Nuclear bombers: Soviet	NATO member until 1959
Naval port: U.S.	Naval port: Soviet	Warsaw Pact member
Fleet: U.S.	Fleet: Soviet	Unrest/revolt in Eastern Europe
Nuclear missile submarine: U.S.	Nuclear missile submarine: Soviet	

The New European Alliance Systems During the Cold War

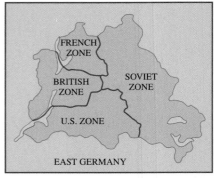

Berlin at the Start of the Cold War

CHAPTER 27
BRAVE NEW WORLD: COMMUNISM ON TRIAL

CHAPTER OUTLINE
AND FOCUS QUESTIONS

The Postwar Soviet Union

Q How did Nikita Khrushchev change the system that the Soviet dictator Joseph Stalin had put in place before his death in 1953? To what degree did his successors continue Khrushchev's policies?

The Disintegration of the Soviet Empire

Q What were the key components of *perestroika,* which Mikhail Gorbachev espoused during the 1980s? Why were they unsuccessful in preventing the collapse of the Soviet Union?

The East Is Red: China Under Communism

Q What were Mao Zedong's chief goals for China, and what policies did he institute to try to achieve them?

"Serve the People": Chinese Society Under Communism

Q What significant political, economic, and social changes have taken place in China since the death of Mao Zedong? Have they been successful?

CRITICAL THINKING

Q Why has communism survived in China when it failed in Eastern Europe and Russia? Compare conditions in China today with those in countries elsewhere in the world that have abandoned the Communist system. Are Chinese leaders justified in claiming that without party leadership, the country would fall into chaos?

© William J. Duiker

Shopping in Moscow

ACCORDING TO KARL MARX, capitalism is a system that involves the exploitation of man by man; under socialism, it is the other way around. That wry joke was typical of popular humor in post–World War II Moscow, where the dreams of a future utopia had faded in the grim reality of life in the Soviet Union.

For the average Soviet citizen after World War II, few images better symbolized the shortcomings of the Soviet system than a long line of people queuing up outside an official state store selling consumer goods. Because the command economy was so inefficient, items of daily use were chronically in such short supply that when a particular item became available, people often lined up immediately to buy several for themselves and their friends. Sometimes, when people saw a line forming, they would automatically join the queue without even knowing what item was available for purchase!

Despite the evident weaknesses of the centralized Soviet economy, the Communist monopoly on power seemed secure, as did Moscow's hold over its client states in Eastern Europe. In fact, for three decades after the end of World War II, the Soviet Empire appeared to be a permanent feature of the international landscape. But by the early 1980s, it was clear that there were cracks in the Kremlin wall. The Soviet economy was stagnant, the minority nationalities were restive, and Eastern European leaders were

671

increasingly emboldened to test the waters of the global capitalist marketplace. In the United States, the newly elected president, Ronald Reagan, boldly predicted the imminent collapse of the "evil empire."

Within a period of less than three years (1989–1991), the Soviet Union ceased to exist as a nation. Russia and other former Soviet republics declared their separate independence, Communist regimes in Eastern Europe were toppled, and the long-standing division of postwar Europe came to an end. Although Communist parties survived the demise of the system and showed signs of renewed vigor in some countries in the region, their monopoly is gone, and they must now compete with other parties for power.

The fate of communism in China has been quite different. Despite some turbulence, communism has survived in China, even as that nation takes giant strides toward becoming an economic superpower. Yet, as China's leaders struggle to bring the nation into the twenty-first century, many of the essential principles of Marxist-Leninist dogma have been tacitly abandoned. ❁

The Postwar Soviet Union

Q **Focus Questions:** How did Nikita Khrushchev change the system that the Soviet dictator Joseph Stalin had put in place before his death in 1953? To what degree did his successors continue Khrushchev's policies?

World War II had left the Soviet Union as one of the world's two superpowers and its leader, Joseph Stalin, in a position of strength. He and his Soviet colleagues were now in control of a vast empire that included Eastern Europe, much of the Balkans, and new territory gained from Japan in East Asia.

From Stalin to Khrushchev

At the same time, World War II had devastated the Soviet Union. Nearly 30 million citizens lost their lives, and cities such as Kiev, Kharkov, and Leningrad suffered enormous physical destruction. As the lands that had been occupied by the German forces were liberated, the Soviet government turned its attention to restoring their economic structures. Nevertheless, in 1945, agricultural production was only 60 percent and steel output only 50 percent of prewar levels. The Soviet people faced incredibly difficult conditions: ill-housed and poorly clothed, they worked longer hours and ate less they than before the war.

Stalinism in Action In the immediate postwar years, the Soviet Union removed goods and materials from occupied Germany and extorted valuable raw materials

from its satellite states in Eastern Europe (see Map 27.1). More important, however, to create a new industrial base, Stalin returned to the method he had used in the 1930s—the extraction of development capital from Soviet labor. Working hard for little pay and for precious few consumer goods, Soviet laborers were expected to produce goods for export with little in return for themselves. The incoming capital from abroad could then be used to purchase machinery and Western technology. The loss of millions of men in the war meant that much of this tremendous workload fell upon Soviet women, who performed almost 40 percent of the heavy manual labor.

The pace of economic recovery in the postwar Soviet Union was impressive. By 1947, industrial production had attained 1939 levels. New power plants, canals, and giant factories were built, and industrial enterprises and oil fields were established in Siberia and Soviet Central Asia.

Although Stalin's economic recovery policy was successful in promoting growth in heavy industry, primarily for the benefit of the military, consumer goods remained scarce as long-suffering Soviet citizens were still being asked to suffer for a better tomorrow. Heavy industry grew at a rate three times that of personal consumption. Moreover, the housing shortage was acute, with living conditions especially difficult in the overcrowded cities.

When World War II ended in 1945, Stalin had been in power for more than fifteen years. Political terror enforced by several hundred thousand secret police ensured that he would remain in power. By the late 1940s, an estimated nine million Soviet citizens were in Siberian concentration camps.

Increasingly distrustful of competitors, Stalin exercised sole authority and pitted his subordinates against each other. His morbid suspicions extended to even his closest colleagues, causing his associates to become completely cowed. As he remarked mockingly on one occasion, "When I die, the imperialists will strangle all of you like a litter of kittens."[1]

The Rise and Fall of Khrushchev Stalin died—presumably of natural causes—in 1953 and, after some bitter infighting within the party leadership, was succeeded by Georgy Malenkov, a veteran administrator and ambitious member of the Politburo (the party's governing body). But Malenkov's reform goals did not necessarily appeal to key groups, including the army, the Communist Party, the managerial elite, and the security services (now known as the Committee on Government Security, or KGB). In 1953, Malenkov was removed from his position as party leader, and by 1955 power had shifted to his rival, the new party general secretary, Nikita Khrushchev.

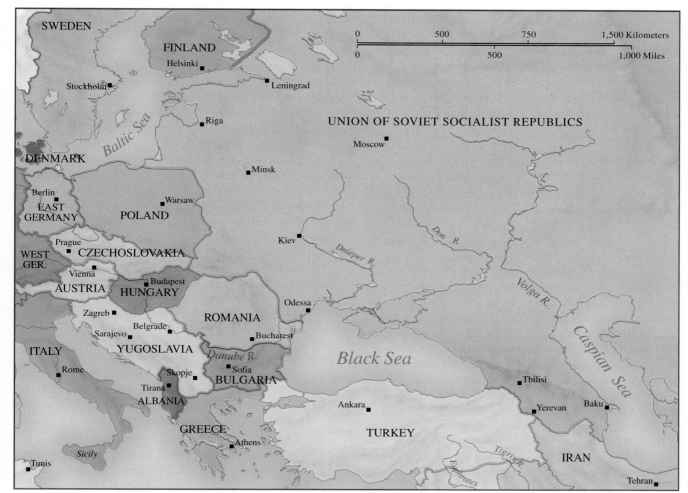

MAP 27.1 **Eastern Europe Under Soviet Rule.** After World War II, the boundaries of Eastern Europe were redrawn as a result of Allied agreements reached at the Tehran and Yalta conferences. This map shows the new boundaries that were established throughout the region, placing Soviet power at the center of Europe.

Q How had the boundaries changed from the prewar era?

Once in power, Khrushchev moved vigorously to boost the performance of the Soviet economy and revitalize Soviet society. In an attempt to release the stranglehold of the central bureaucracy over the national economy, he abolished dozens of government ministries and split up the party and government apparatus. Khrushchev also attempted to rejuvenate the stagnant agricultural sector. He attempted to spur production by increasing profit incentives and opened "virgin lands" in Soviet Kazakhstan to bring thousands of acres of new land under cultivation.

An innovator by nature, Khrushchev had to overcome the inherently conservative instincts of the Soviet bureaucracy, as well as those of the mass of the Soviet population. His plan to remove the "dead hand" of the state, however laudable in intent, alienated much of the Soviet official class, and his effort to split the party angered those who saw it as the central force in the Soviet system. Khrushchev's agricultural schemes inspired similar opposition. His effort to persuade Russians to eat more corn (an idea he had apparently picked up during a visit to the United States) earned him the mocking nickname "Cornman." The industrial growth rate, which had soared in the early 1950s, now declined dramatically, from 13 percent in 1953 to 7.5 percent in 1964.

Khrushchev was probably best known for his policy of **destalinization.** Khrushchev had risen in the party hierarchy as a Stalin protégé, but he had been deeply disturbed by his mentor's excesses and, once in a position

KHRUSHCHEV DENOUNCES STALIN

Three years after Stalin's death, the new Soviet premier, Nikita Khrushchev, addressed the Twentieth Congress of the Communist Party and denounced the former Soviet dictator for his crimes. This denunciation was the beginning of a policy of destalinization.

Khrushchev Addresses the Twentieth Party Congress, February 1956

Comrades,... quite a lot has been said about the cult of the individual and about its harmful consequences.... The cult of the person of Stalin... became at a certain specific stage the source of a whole series of exceedingly serious and grave perversions of Party principles, of Party democracy, of revolutionary legality.

Stalin absolutely did not tolerate collegiality in leadership and in work and... practiced brutal violence, not only toward everything which opposed him, but also toward that which seemed to his capricious and despotic character, contrary to his concepts.

Stalin abandoned the method of ideological struggle for that of administrative violence, mass repressions and terror.... Arbitrary behavior by one person encouraged and permitted arbitrariness in others. Mass arrests and deportations of many thousands of people, execution without trial and without normal investigation created conditions of insecurity, fear, and even desperation.

Stalin showed in a whole series of cases his intolerance, his brutality, and his abuse of power.... He often chose the path of repression and annihilation, not only against actual enemies, but also against individuals who had not committed any crimes against the Party and the Soviet government....

Many Party, Soviet, and economic activists who were branded in 1937–8 as "enemies" were actually never enemies, spies, wreckers, and so on, but were always honest communists; they were only so stigmatized, and often, no longer able to bear barbaric tortures, they charged themselves (at the order of the investigative judges-falsifiers) with all kinds of grave and unlikely crimes.

This was the result of the abuse of power by Stalin, who began to use mass terror against the Party cadres.... Stalin put the Party and the NKVD [the Soviet police agency] up to the use of mass terror when the exploiting classes had been liquidated in our country and when there were no serious reasons for the use of extraordinary mass terror. The terror was directed... against the honest workers of the Party and the Soviet state....

Stalin was a very distrustful man, sickly, suspicious.... Everywhere and in everything he saw "enemies," "two-facers," and "spies." Possessing unlimited power, he indulged in great willfulness and choked a person morally and physically. A situation was created where one could not express one's own will. When Stalin said that one or another would be arrested, it was necessary to accept on faith that he was an "enemy of the people." What proofs were offered? The confession of the arrested.... How is it possible that a person confesses to crimes that he had not committed? Only in one way—because of application of physical methods of pressuring him, tortures, bringing him to a state of unconsciousness, deprivation of his judgment, taking away of his human dignity.

Q *What were the key charges that Khrushchev made against his predecessor? Can it be said that Khrushchev corrected these problems?*

of authority, moved to excise the Stalinist legacy from Soviet society. The campaign began at the Twentieth National Congress of the Communist Party in February 1956, when Khrushchev gave a long speech in private criticizing some of Stalin's major shortcomings. The speech had apparently not been intended for public distribution, but it was quickly leaked to the Western press and created a sensation throughout the world (see the box above). Under Khrushchev's instructions, thousands of prisoners were released from concentration camps.

Khrushchev's personality, however, did not endear him to higher Soviet officials, who frowned at his tendency to crack jokes and play the clown. Foreign policy failures further damaged Khrushchev's reputation among his colleagues (see Chapter 26). While he was away on vacation in 1964, a special meeting of the Soviet Politburo voted him out of office (because of "deteriorating health") and forced him into retirement.

The Brezhnev Years (1964–1982)

The ouster of Nikita Khrushchev in October 1964 vividly demonstrated the challenges that would be encountered by any leader sufficiently bold to try to reform the Soviet system. Leonid Brezhnev (1906–1982), the new party chief, was undoubtedly aware of these realities of Soviet politics, and his long tenure in power was marked, above all, by the desire to avoid changes that might provoke instability, either at home or abroad. Brezhnev was himself a product of the Soviet system. He had entered the ranks of the party leadership under Stalin, and although he was not a particularly avid believer in party ideology, he was no partisan of reform.

Still, Brezhnev sought stability in the domestic arena. He and his prime minister, Alexei Kosygin (1904–1980), undertook what might be described as a program of "de-Khrushchevization," returning the responsibility for

Behind the Kremlin Walls. A historic walled city in the heart of Moscow, the Kremlin long served as the home of the tsars during the imperial era. After the Bolshevik Revolution, it was occupied by Stalin and his successors. Its physical appearance reflects its varied history, as forbidding structures like the Communist Party headquarters (below) were balanced by the fairy-tale domes and cupolas of Russian Orthodox churches (right)—relics of a faith that came under harsh attacks during the many decades of Soviet rule.

© William J. Duiker

© William J. Duiker

long-term planning to the central ministries and reuniting the Communist Party apparatus. Despite some cautious attempts to stimulate the stagnant farm sector, there was no effort to revise the basic collective system. In the industrial sector, the regime launched a series of reforms designed to give factory managers (themselves employees of the state) more responsibility for setting prices, wages, and production quotas. These **"Kosygin reforms"** had little effect, however, because they were stubbornly resisted by the bureaucracy.

A Controlled Society Brezhnev also initiated a significant retreat from Khrushchev's policy of destalinization. Criticism of the "Great Leader" had angered conservatives both within the party hierarchy and among the public at large, many of whom still revered Stalin as a hero and a defender of Russia against Nazi Germany. Early in Brezhnev's reign, Stalin's reputation began to revive. Although his alleged shortcomings were not totally ignored, he was now described in the official press as "an outstanding party leader" who had been primarily responsible for the successes achieved by the Soviet Union.

The regime also adopted a more restrictive policy toward dissidents in Soviet society. Critics of the Soviet system, such as the physicist Andrei Sakharov (1921–1989), were harassed and arrested or, like the famous writer Alexander Solzhenitsyn, forced to leave the country. Free expression was also restricted. The media were controlled by the state and presented only what the state wanted people to hear. The government made strenuous efforts to prevent the Soviet people from being exposed to harmful foreign ideas, especially modern art, literature, and contemporary Western rock music. When the Summer Olympic Games were held in Moscow in 1980, Soviet newspapers advised citizens to keep their children indoors to keep them from being polluted with "bourgeois" ideas passed on by foreign visitors.

A Stagnant Economy Soviet leaders also failed to achieve their objective of revitalizing the national economy. Whereas growth rates during the early Khrushchev era had been impressive (prompting Khrushchev during a reception at the Kremlin in the 1950s to chortle to an American guest, "We will bury you," referring to the United States), under Brezhnev industrial growth declined to an annual rate of less than 4 percent in the early 1970s and less than 3 percent in the period from 1975 to 1980. Successes in the agricultural sector were equally meager.

One of the primary problems with the Soviet economy was the absence of incentives. Salary structures offered little reward for hard labor and extraordinary achievement. Pay differentials operated in a much narrower range than in most Western societies, and there was little danger of being dismissed. According to the Soviet constitution, every Soviet citizen was guaranteed an opportunity to work.

There were, of course, some exceptions to the general rule. Athletic achievement was highly prized, and a gymnast of Olympic stature would receive great rewards in the form of prestige and lifestyle. Senior officials did not receive high salaries but were provided with countless perquisites, such as access to foreign goods, official automobiles with a chauffeur, and entry into prestigious institutions of higher learning for their children.

An Aging Leadership Brezhnev died in November 1982 and was succeeded by Yuri Andropov (1914–1984), a party veteran and head of the Soviet secret services. During his brief tenure as party chief, Andropov was a vocal advocate of reform, but when he died after only a few months in office, little had been done to change the system. He was succeeded, in turn, by a mediocre party stalwart, the elderly Konstantin Chernenko (1911–1985). With the Soviet system in crisis, Moscow seemed stuck in a time warp.

Cultural Expression in the Soviet Bloc

In his occasional musings about the future Communist utopia, Karl Marx had predicted that a new, classless society would replace the exploitative and hierarchical systems of feudalism and capitalism. In their free time, workers would produce a new, advanced culture, proletarian in character and egalitarian in content.

The reality in the post–World War II Soviet Union and Eastern Europe was somewhat different. Under Stalin, a series of government decrees made all forms of literary and scientific expression dependent on the state. All Soviet culture was expected to follow the party line. Historians, philosophers, and social scientists all grew accustomed to quoting Marx, Lenin, and, above all, Stalin as their chief authorities. Novels and plays, too, were supposed to portray Communist heroes and their efforts to create a better society. No criticism of existing social conditions was permitted. Some areas of intellectual activity were virtually abolished; the science of genetics

disappeared, and few movies were made during Stalin's final years.

Stalin's death brought a modest respite from cultural repression. Writers and artists banned during the Stalin years were again allowed to publish. Still, Soviet authorities, including Khrushchev, were reluctant to allow cultural freedom to move far beyond official Soviet ideology.

These restrictions, however, did not prevent the emergence of some significant Soviet literature, although authors paid a heavy price if they alienated the Soviet authorities. Boris Pasternak (1890–1960), who began his literary career as a poet, won the Nobel Prize in 1958 for his celebrated novel *Doctor Zhivago*, written between 1945 and 1956 and published in Italy in 1957. But the Soviet government condemned Pasternak's anti-Soviet tendencies, banned the novel, and would not allow him to accept the prize. The author had alienated the authorities by describing a society scarred by the excesses of Bolshevik revolutionary zeal.

Alexander Solzhenitsyn (1918–2008) created an even greater furor than Pasternak. Solzhenitsyn had spent eight years in forced labor camps for criticizing Stalin, and his *One Day in the Life of Ivan Denisovich*, which won him the Nobel Prize in 1970, was an account of life in those camps. Khrushchev allowed the book's publication as part of his destalinization campaign. Solzhenitsyn then wrote *The Gulag Archipelago*, a detailed indictment of the whole system of Soviet oppression. Soviet authorities expelled Solzhenitsyn from the Soviet Union in 1973.

In the Eastern European satellites, cultural freedom varied considerably from country to country. In Poland, intellectuals had access to Western publications as well as greater freedom to travel to the West. Hungarian and Yugoslav Communists, too, tolerated a certain level of intellectual activity that was not liked but at least was not prohibited. Elsewhere intellectuals were forced to conform to the regime's demands. After the Soviet invasion of Czechoslovakia in 1968, Czech Communists pursued a policy of strict cultural control.

Social Changes According to Marxist doctrine, state control of industry and the elimination of private property were supposed to lead to a classless society. Although that ideal was never achieved, it did have important social consequences. The desire to create a classless society, for example, led to noticeable changes in education. In some countries, laws mandated quota systems based on class. As education became crucial for obtaining new jobs in the Communist system, enrollments rose in both secondary schools and universities.

The new managers of society, regardless of their class background, realized the importance of higher education

"It's So Difficult to Be a Woman Here"

FAMILY & SOCIETY

One of the major problems that Soviet women faced was the need to balance work and family roles, a problem conspicuously ignored by authorities. This excerpt is taken from a series of interviews of thirteen women in Moscow conducted in the late 1970s by Swedish investigators. As is evident in this interview with Anna, a young wife and mother, these Soviet women took pride in their achievements but were also frustrated with their lives. It is hardly surprising that the conflicting pressures on women caught between the demands of the family and the state's push for industrialization would result in a drop in birthrates and a change in family structure.

Moscow Women: Interview with Anna

[Anna is twenty-one and married, has a three-month-old daughter, and lives with her husband and daughter in a one-room apartment with a balcony and a large bathroom. Anna works as a hairdresser; her husband is an unemployed writer.]

Are there other kinds of jobs dominated by women?
Of course! Preschool teachers are exclusively women. Also beauticians. But I guess that's about all. Here women work in every profession, from tractor drivers to engineers. But I think there ought to be more jobs specifically for women so that there are some differences. In this century women have to be equal to men. Now women wear pants, have short hair, and hold important jobs, just like men. There are almost no differences left. Except in the home.

Do women and men have the same goal in life?
Of course. Women want to get out of the house and have careers, just the same as men do. It gives women a lot of advantages, higher wages, and so on. In that sense we have the same goal, but socially I don't think so. The family is, after all, more important for a woman. A man can live without a family; all he needs is for a woman to come from time to time to clean for him and do his laundry. He sleeps with her if he feels like it. Of course, a woman can adopt this lifestyle, but I still think that most women want their own home, family, children. From time immemorial, women's instincts have been rooted in taking care of their families, tending to their husbands, sewing, washing—all the household chores. Men are supposed to provide for the family; women should keep the home fires burning. This is so deeply ingrained in women that there's no way of changing it.

Whose career do you think is the most important?
The man's, naturally. The family is often broken up because women don't follow their men when they move where they can get a job. That was the case of my in-laws. They don't live together any longer because my father-in-law worked for a long time as far away as Smolensk. He lived alone, without his family, and then, of course, it was only natural that things turned out the way they did. It's hard for a man to live without his family when he's used to being taken care of all the time. Of course there are men who can endure, who continue to be faithful, etc., but for most men it isn't easy. For that reason I think a woman ought to go where her husband does....

That's the way it is. Women have certain obligations, men others. One has to understand that at an early age. Girls have to learn to take care of a household and help at home. Boys too, but not as much as girls. Boys ought to be with their fathers and learn how to do masculine chores....

It's so difficult to be a woman here. With emancipation, we lead such abnormal, twisted lives, because women have to work the same as men do. As a result, women have very little time for themselves to work on their femininity.

Q *What does this interview reveal about the role of women in the Soviet Union? In what sense was that role different from that of women in the West?*

---

and used their power to gain special privileges for their children. By 1971, 60 percent of the children of white-collar workers attended university, but only 36 percent of the children of blue-collar families did so, although these families constituted 60 percent of the population.

Ideals of equality also did not include women. Men dominated the leadership positions of the Communist parties. Women did have greater opportunities in the workforce and even in the professions, however. In the Soviet Union, women comprised 51 percent of the labor force in 1980; by the mid-1980s, they constituted 50 percent of the engineers, 80 percent of the doctors, and 75 percent of the teachers and teachers' aides. But many of these were low-paying jobs; most female doctors, for example, worked in primary care and were paid less than skilled machinists. The chief administrators in hospitals and schools were still men.

Moreover, although women made up nearly half of the workforce, they were never freed from their traditional roles in the home (see the box above). Most women had to work what came to be known as the "double shift." After working eight hours in their jobs, they came home to do the housework and care for the children. They might also spend two hours a day in long lines at a number of stores waiting to buy food and clothes. Because of the housing shortage, a number of families would share a kitchen, making even meal preparation a complicated task.

Nearly three-quarters of a century after the Bolshevik Revolution, then, the Marxist dream of an advanced, egalitarian society was as far away as ever. Although in some respects, conditions in the socialist camp were a distinct improvement over those before World War II, many problems and inequities were as intransigent as ever.

The Disintegration of the Soviet Empire

Q **Focus Questions:** What were the key components of *perestroika*, which Mikhail Gorbachev espoused during the 1980s? Why were they unsuccessful in preventing the collapse of the Soviet Union?

On the death of Konstantin Chernenko in 1985, party leaders selected the talented and vigorous Soviet official Mikhail Gorbachev to succeed him. The new Soviet leader had shown early signs of promise. Born into a peasant family in 1931, Gorbachev combined farmwork with school and received the Order of the Red Banner for his agricultural efforts. This award and his good school record enabled him to study law at the University of Moscow. After receiving his law degree in 1955, he returned to his native southern Russia, where he eventually became first secretary of the Communist Party in the city of Stavropol. In 1978, he was made a member of the party's Central Committee in Moscow. Two years later, he became a full member of the ruling Politburo and secretary of the Central Committee.

During the early 1980s, Gorbachev began to realize the immensity of Soviet problems and the crucial need for massive reform to transform the system. During a visit to Canada in 1983, he discovered to his astonishment that Canadian farmers worked hard on their own initiative. "We'll never have this for fifty years," he reportedly remarked.[2] On his return to Moscow, he set in motion a series of committees to evaluate the situation and recommend measures to improve the system.

The Gorbachev Era

With his election as party general secretary in 1985, Gorbachev seemed intent on taking earlier reforms to their logical conclusions. The cornerstone of his program was **perestroika,** or "restructuring." At first, it meant only a reordering of economic policy, as Gorbachev called for the beginning of a market economy with limited free enterprise and some private property (see the comparative illustration on p. 679). But Gorbachev soon perceived

CHRONOLOGY The Soviet Bloc and Its Demise

Death of Joseph Stalin	1953
Rise of Nikita Khrushchev	1955
Khrushchev's destalinization speech	1956
Removal of Khrushchev	1964
The Brezhnev era	1964–1982
Rule of Andropov and Chernenko	1982–1985
Gorbachev comes to power in Soviet Union	1985
Collapse of Communist governments in Eastern Europe	1989
Disintegration of Soviet Union	1991

that in the Soviet system, the economic sphere was intimately tied to the social and political spheres. Any efforts to reform the economy without political or social reform would be doomed to failure. One of the most important instruments of *perestroika* was **glasnost,** or "openness." Soviet citizens and officials were encouraged to discuss openly the strengths and weaknesses of the Soviet Union. The arts also benefited from the new policy as previously banned works were now published and motion pictures were allowed to depict negative aspects of Soviet life. Music based on Western styles, such as jazz and rock, could now be performed openly. Religious activities, long banned by the authorities, were once again tolerated.

Political reforms were equally revolutionary. In June 1987, the principle of two-candidate elections was introduced; previously, voters had been presented with only one candidate. At the Communist Party conference in 1988, Gorbachev called for the creation of a new Soviet parliament, the Congress of People's Deputies, whose members were to be chosen in competitive elections. It convened in 1989, the first such meeting in the nation since 1918. Early in 1990, Gorbachev legalized the formation of other political parties and struck out Article 6 of the Soviet constitution, which guaranteed the "leading role" of the Communist Party. Hitherto, the position of first secretary of the party was the most important post in the Soviet Union, but as the Communist Party became less closely associated with the state, the powers of this office diminished. Gorbachev attempted to consolidate his power by creating a new state presidency, and in March 1990 he became the Soviet Union's first president.

The Beginning of the End One of Gorbachev's most serious problems stemmed from the character of the Soviet Union. The Union of Soviet Socialist Republics was a truly multiethnic country, containing 92 nationalities

COMPARATIVE ILLUSTRATION

Sideline Industries: Creeping Capitalism in a Socialist Paradise. In the late 1980s, Communist leaders in both the Soviet Union and China began to encourage their citizens to engage in private commercial activities as a means of reviving moribund economies. In the photo on the left, a Soviet farmworker displays fruits and vegetables for sale on a street corner in Odessa, a seaport on the Black Sea. On the right, a Chinese cobbler sets up shop on a busy thoroughfare in the commercial hub of Shanghai. As it turns out, the Chinese took up the challenge of entrepreneurship with much greater success and enthusiasm than their Soviet counterparts did.

Q Why do you think Chinese citizens adopted capitalist reforms in the countryside more enthusiastically than their Soviet counterparts?

and 112 recognized languages. Previously, the iron hand of the Communist Party, centered in Moscow, had kept a lid on the centuries-old ethnic tensions that had periodically erupted throughout the history of this region. As Gorbachev released this iron grip, ethnic groups throughout the Soviet Union began to call for sovereignty of the republics and independence from Russian-based rule centered in Moscow. Such movements sprang up first in Georgia in late 1988 and then in Latvia, Estonia, Moldova, Uzbekistan, Azerbaijan, and Lithuania.

In December 1989, the Communist Party of Lithuania declared itself independent of the Communist Party of the Soviet Union. Despite pleas from Gorbachev, who supported self-determination but not secession, other Soviet republics eventually followed suit. Ukraine voted for independence on December 1, 1991. A week later, the leaders of Russia, Ukraine, and Belarus announced that the Soviet Union had "ceased to exist" and would be replaced by a "commonwealth of independent states." Gorbachev resigned on December 25, 1991, and turned over his responsibilities as commander in chief to Boris Yeltsin (1931–2007), the president of Russia. By the end of 1991, one of the largest empires in world history had

come to an end, and a new era had begun in its lands (see Map 27.2 and Chapter 28).

Eastern Europe: From Satellites to Sovereign Nations

The disintegration of the Soviet Union had an immediate impact on its neighbors to the west. First to respond, as in 1956, was Poland, where popular protests at high food prices had erupted in the early 1980s, leading to the rise of an independent labor movement called Solidarity. Led by Lech Walesa (b. 1943), Solidarity rapidly became an influential force for change and a threat to the government's monopoly of power. In 1988, the Communist government bowed to the inevitable and permitted free national elections to take place, resulting in the election of Walesa as president of Poland in December 1990. When Moscow took no action to reverse the verdict in Warsaw, Poland entered the post-Communist era.

In Hungary, as in Poland, the process of transition had begun many years previously. After crushing the Hungarian revolution of 1956, the Communist government of János Kádár had tried to assuage popular

MAP 27.2 **Eastern Europe and the Former Soviet Union.** After the disintegration of the Soviet Union in 1991, several onetime Soviet republics declared their independence. This map shows the new configuration of the states that emerged in the 1990s from the former Soviet Union. The breakaway region of Chechnya is indicated on the map.

Q What new nations have appeared from the old Soviet Union since the end of the Cold War?

opinion by enacting a series of far-reaching economic reforms (labeled "communism with a capitalist face-lift"). But as the 1980s progressed, the economy sagged, and in 1989, the regime permitted the formation of opposition political parties, leading eventually to the formation of a non-Communist coalition government in elections held in March 1990.

The transition in Czechoslovakia was more abrupt. After Soviet troops crushed the Prague Spring in 1968, hard-line Communists under Gustav Husák followed a policy of massive repression to maintain their power. In 1977, dissident intellectuals formed an organization called Charter 77 as a vehicle for protest against violations of human rights. Dissident activities increased during the 1980s, and when massive demonstrations broke out in several major cities in 1989, President Husák's government, lacking any real popular support, collapsed. At the end of December, he was replaced by Václav Havel (b. 1936), a dissident playwright who had been a leading figure in Charter 77.

But the most dramatic events took place in East Germany, where a persistent economic slump and the ongoing oppressiveness of the regime of Erich Honecker led to a flight of refugees and mass demonstrations against the regime in the summer and fall of 1989.

Capitulating to popular pressure, the Communist government opened its entire border with the West. The Berlin Wall, the most tangible symbol of the Cold War, became the site of a massive celebration, and most of it was dismantled by joyful Germans from both sides of the border. In March 1990, free elections led to the formation of a non-Communist government that rapidly carried out a program of political and economic reunification with West Germany (see Chapter 28).

The East Is Red: China Under Communism

Q Focus Question: What were Mao Zedong's chief goals for China, and what policies did he institute to try to achieve them?

In the fall of 1949, China was at peace for the first time in twelve years. The newly victorious Communist Party, under the leadership of its chairman, Mao Zedong, turned its attention to consolidating its power base and healing the wounds of war. Its long-term goal was to construct a socialist society, but its leaders realized that popular support for the revolution was based on the party's platform of honest government, land reform, social justice, and peace rather than on the utopian goal of a classless society. Accordingly, the new regime adopted a moderate program of political and economic recovery known as New Democracy.

New Democracy

With **New Democracy**—patterned roughly after Lenin's New Economic Policy in Soviet Russia in the 1920s (see Chapter 23)—the new Chinese leadership tacitly recognized that time and extensive indoctrination would be needed to convince the Chinese people of the superiority of socialism. In the meantime, the party would rely on capitalist profit incentives to spur productivity. Manufacturing and commercial firms were permitted to remain under private ownership, although with stringent government regulations. To win the support of the poorer peasants, who made up the majority of the population, a land redistribution program was adopted, but the collectivization of agriculture was postponed.

In a number of key respects, New Democracy was a success. About two-thirds of the peasant households in the country received land and thus had reason to be grateful to the new regime. Spurred by official tolerance for capitalist activities and the end of internal conflict, the national economy began to rebound, although agricultural production still lagged behind both official targets and the growing population, which was increasing at an annual rate of more than 2 percent.

The Transition to Socialism

In 1953, party leaders launched the nation's first five-year plan (patterned after similar Soviet plans), which called for substantial increases in industrial output. Lenin had believed that mechanization would induce Russian peasants to join collective farms, which, because of their greater size and efficiency, could better afford to purchase expensive farm machinery. But the difficulty of providing tractors and reapers for millions of rural villages eventually convinced Mao that it would take years, if not decades, for China's infant industrial base to meet the needs of a modernizing agricultural sector. He therefore decided to begin collectivization immediately, in the hope that collective farms would increase food production and release land, labor, and capital for the industrial sector. Accordingly, beginning in 1955, virtually all private farmland was collectivized (although peasant families were allowed to retain small private plots), and most businesses and industries were nationalized.

Collectivization was achieved without provoking the massive peasant unrest that had taken place in the Soviet Union during the 1930s, but the hoped-for production increases did not materialize; in 1958, at Mao's insistent urging, party leaders approved a more radical program known as the **Great Leap Forward.** Existing rural collectives, normally the size of a traditional village, were combined into vast "people's communes," each containing more than 30,000 people. These communes were to be responsible for all administrative and economic tasks at the local level. The party's official slogan promised "Hard work for a few years, happiness for a thousand."[3]

The communes were a disaster. Administrative bottlenecks, bad weather, and peasant resistance to the new system (which, among other things, attempted to eliminate work incentives and destroy the traditional family as the basic unit of Chinese society) combined to drive food production downward, and over the next few years, as many as 15 million people may have died of starvation. In 1960, the experiment was essentially abandoned. Although the commune structure was retained, ownership and management were returned to the collective level. Mao was severely criticized by some of his more pragmatic colleagues.

The Great Proletarian Cultural Revolution

But Mao was not yet ready to abandon either his power or his dream of a totally egalitarian society. In 1966, he returned to the attack, mobilizing discontented youth and disgruntled party members into revolutionary units known as Red Guards, who were urged to take to the streets to cleanse Chinese society—from local schools and factories to government ministries in Beijing—of impure elements who (in Mao's mind, at least) were guilty of "taking the capitalist road." Supported by his wife, Jiang Qing, and other radical party figures, Mao launched China on a new forced march toward communism.

The so-called **Great Proletarian Cultural Revolution** lasted for ten years, from 1966 to 1976. Some Western observers interpreted it as a simple power struggle between Mao Zedong and some of his key rivals such as Liu Shaoqi (Liu Shao-ch'i), Mao's designated successor, and Deng Xiaoping (Teng Hsiao-p'ing), the party's general secretary. Both were removed from their positions, and Liu later died, allegedly of torture, in a Chinese prison. But real policy disagreements were involved. Mao and his supporters feared that capitalist values and the remnants of "feudalist" Confucian ideas would undermine ideological fervor and betray the revolutionary cause. He was convinced that only an atmosphere of **"uninterrupted revolution"** could enable the Chinese to overcome the lethargy of the past and achieve the final stage of utopian communism.

the "four olds" (old thought, old culture, old customs, and old habits). They destroyed temples and religious sculptures; they tore down street signs and replaced them with new ones carrying revolutionary names. At one point, the city of Shanghai even ordered that the significance of colors in stoplights be changed so that red (the revolutionary color) would indicate that traffic could move.

But a mood of revolutionary ferment and enthusiasm is difficult to sustain. Key groups, including bureaucrats, urban professionals, and many military officers, did not share Mao's belief in the benefits of "uninterrupted revolution" and constant turmoil. Inevitably, the sense of anarchy and uncertainty caused popular support for the movement to erode, and when the end came in 1976, the vast majority of the population may well have welcomed its demise.

The Red Sun in Our Hearts. During the Great Proletarian Cultural Revolution, Chinese art was restricted to topics that promoted revolution and the thoughts of Chairman Mao Zedong. All the knowledge that the true revolutionary required was to be found in Mao's *Little Red Book*, a collection of his sayings on proper revolutionary behavior. In this painting, Chairman Mao's portrait hovers above a crowd of his admirers, who wave copies of the book as a symbol of their total devotion to him and his vision of a future China.

Mao's opponents argued for a more pragmatic strategy that gave priority to nation building over the ultimate Communist goal of spiritual transformation. (Deng Xiaoping reportedly once remarked, "Black cat, white cat, what does it matter so long as it catches the mice?"). But with Mao's supporters now in power, the party carried out vast economic and educational reforms that virtually eliminated any remaining profit incentives, established a new school system that emphasized "Mao Zedong thought," and stressed practical education at the elementary level at the expense of specialized training in science and the humanities in the universities. School learning was discouraged as a legacy of capitalism, and Mao's famous *Little Red Book* (officially, *Quotations of Chairman Mao Zedong,* a slim volume of Maoist aphorisms to encourage good behavior and revolutionary zeal) was hailed as the most important source of knowledge in all areas (see the illustration above).

The radicals' efforts to destroy all vestiges of traditional society were reminiscent of the Reign of Terror in revolutionary France, when the Jacobins sought to destroy organized religion and even created a new revolutionary calendar (see the box on p. 683). Red Guards rampaged through the country, attempting to eradicate

From Mao to Deng

Mao Zedong died in September 1976 at the age of eighty-three. After a short but bitter succession struggle, the pragmatists led by Deng Xiaoping (1904–1997) seized power from the radicals and formally brought the Cultural Revolution to an end. The egalitarian policies of the previous decade were reversed, and a new program emphasizing economic modernization was introduced.

Under the leadership of Deng Xiaoping, who placed his supporters in key positions throughout the party and the government, attention focused on what were called the **Four Modernizations:** industry, agriculture, technology, and national defense. Many of the restrictions against private activities and profit incentives were eliminated, and people were encouraged to work hard to benefit themselves and Chinese society. The familiar slogan "Serve the people" was replaced by a new one repugnant to the tenets of Mao Zedong thought: "Create wealth for the people."

By adopting this pragmatic approach (in the Chinese aphorism, "cross the river by feeling the stones") in the years after 1976, China made great strides in ending its

MAKE REVOLUTION!

POLITICS & GOVERNMENT

In 1966, Mao Zedong unleashed the power of revolution on China. Rebellious youth in the form of Red Guards rampaged through all levels of society, exposing anti-Maoist elements, suspected "capitalist roaders," and those identified with the previous ruling class. In this poignant excerpt, Nien Cheng, the widow of an official of Chiang Kai-shek's regime, describes a visit by Red Guards to her home during the height of the Cultural Revolution.

Nien Cheng, *Life and Death in Shanghai*

Suddenly the doorbell began to ring incessantly. At the same time, there was furious pounding of many fists on my front gate, accompanied by the confused sound of hysterical voices shouting slogans. The cacophony told me that the time of waiting was over and that I must face the threat of the Red Guards and the destruction of my home....

Outside, the sound of voices became louder. "Open the gate! Open the gate! Are you all dead? Whey don't you open the gate?" Someone was swearing and kicking the wooden gate. The horn of the truck was blasting too....

I stood up to put the book on the shelf. A copy of the Constitution of the People's Republic caught my eye. Taking it in my hand and picking up the bunch of keys I had ready on my desk, I went downstairs.

At the same moment, the Red Guards pushed open the front door and entered the house. There were thirty or forty senior high school students, aged between fifteen and twenty, led by two men and one woman much older.

The leading Red Guard, a gangling youth with angry eyes, stepped forward and said to me, "We are the Red Guards. We have come to take revolutionary action against you!"

Though I knew it was futile, I held up the copy of the Constitution and said calmly, "It's against the Constitution of the People's Republic of China to enter a private house without a search warrant."

The young man snatched the document out of my hand and threw it on the floor. With his eyes blazing, he said, "The Constitution is abolished. It was a document written by the Revisionists within the Communist Party. We recognize only the teachings of our Great Leader Chairman Mao."...

Another young man used a stick to smash the mirror hanging over the blackwood chest facing the front door.

Mounting the stairs, I was astonished to see several Red Guards taking pieces of my porcelain collection out of their padded boxes. One young man had arranged a set of four Kangxi wine cups in a row on the floor and was stepping on them. I was just in time to hear the crunch of delicate porcelain under the sole of his shoe. The sound pierced my heart. Impulsively I leapt forward and caught his leg just as he raised his foot to crush the next cup. He toppled. We fell in a heap together.... The other Red Guards dropped what they were doing and gathered around us, shouting at me angrily for interfering in their revolutionary activities.

The young man whose revolutionary work of destruction I had interrupted said angrily, "You shut up! These things belong to the old culture. They are the useless toys of the feudal emperors and the modern capitalist class and have no significance to us, the proletarian class. They cannot be compared to cameras and binoculars, which are useful for our struggle in time of war. Our Great Leader Chairman Mao taught us, 'If we do not destroy, we cannot establish.' The old culture must be destroyed to make way for the new socialist culture."

Q *What were the Red Guards trying to accomplish in this excerpt? To what degree did they succeed in remaking Chinese society and changing the character of the Chinese people?*

---

chronic problems of poverty and underdevelopment. Per capita income roughly doubled during the 1980s; housing, education, and sanitation improved; and both agricultural and industrial output skyrocketed.

But critics, both Chinese and foreign, complained that Deng Xiaoping's program had failed to achieve a "fifth modernization": democracy. In the late 1970s, ordinary citizens pasted "big character posters" criticizing the abuses of the past on the so-called Democracy Wall near Tiananmen Square in downtown Beijing. But it soon became clear that the new leaders would not tolerate any direct criticism of the Communist Party or of Marxist-Leninist ideology. Dissidents were suppressed, and some were sentenced to long prison terms.

Incident at Tiananmen Square

As long as economic conditions for the majority of Chinese were improving, the government was able to isolate dissidents from other elements in society. But in the late 1980s, an overheated economy led to rising inflation and growing discontent among salaried workers, especially in the cities. At the same time, corruption, nepotism, and favored treatment for senior officials and party members were provoking increasing criticism. In May 1989, student protesters carried placards demanding "Science and Democracy," an end to official corruption, and the resignation of China's aging party leadership. These demands received widespread support from the urban population (although notably less in rural areas) and led to massive demonstrations in Tiananmen Square.

Deng Xiaoping and other aging party leaders turned to the army to protect their base of power and suppress what they described as "counterrevolutionary elements." Deng was undoubtedly counting on the fact that many Chinese, particularly in rural areas, feared a recurrence of the disorder of the Cultural Revolution and craved economic prosperity more than political reform. In the months after troops and tanks rolled into Tiananmen Square to crush the demonstrations, the government issued new regulations requiring courses on Marxist-Leninist ideology in the schools, suppressed dissidents within the intellectual community, and made it clear that while economic reforms would continue, the Chinese Communist Party (CCP) would not be allowed to lose its monopoly on power. Harsh punishments were imposed on those accused of undermining the Communist system and supporting its enemies abroad.

A Return to Confucius?

In the 1990s, the government began to cultivate urban support by reducing the rate of inflation and guaranteeing the availability of consumer goods in great demand among the rising middle class. Under Deng Xiaoping's successor, Jiang Zemin (b. 1926), who occupied the positions of both party chief and president of China, the government promoted rapid economic growth while cracking down harshly on political dissent. That policy paid dividends in bringing about a perceptible decline in alienation among the urban populations. Industrial production continued to increase rapidly, leading to predictions that China would become one of the economic superpowers of the twenty-first century. But discontent in rural areas began to increase, as lagging farm incomes, high taxes, and official corruption sparked resentment in the countryside.

Partly out of fear that such developments could undermine the socialist system and the rule of the CCP, conservative leaders attempted to curb Western influence and restore faith in Marxism-Leninism. In what may have been a tacit recognition that Marxist exhortations were no longer an effective means of enforcing social discipline, the party turned to Confucianism as an antidote. Ceremonies celebrating the birth of Confucius now received official sanction, and the virtues promoted by the master, such as righteousness, propriety, and filial piety, were widely cited as an antidote to the tide of antisocial behavior. An article in the official newspaper *People's Daily* asserted that the spiritual crisis in contemporary Western culture stemmed from the incompatibility between science and the Christian religion. The solution, the author maintained, was Confucianism, "a nonreligious humanism that can provide the basis for morals and the value of life." Because a culture combining science and Confucianism was taking shape in East Asia, he asserted, "it will thrive particularly well in the next century and will replace modern and contemporary Western culture."[4]

In the world arena, China now relies on the spirit of nationalism to achieve its goals, conducting an independent foreign policy and playing an increasingly active role in the region. To some of its neighbors, including Japan, India, and Russia, China's new posture is cause for disquiet and gives rise to suspicions that it is once again preparing to flex its muscle as in the imperial era. The first example of this new attitude took place as early as 1979, when Chinese forces briefly invaded Vietnam as punishment for the Vietnamese occupation of neighboring Cambodia. In the 1990s, China aroused concern in the region by claiming sole ownership over the Spratly Islands in the South China Sea and over Diaoyu Island (also claimed by Japan) near Taiwan (see Map 27.3).

The Potala Palace in Tibet. Tibet was a distant and reluctant appendage of the Chinese Empire during the Qing dynasty. Since the rise to power of the Communist Party in 1949, the regime in Beijing has consistently sought to integrate the region into the People's Republic of China. Resistance to Chinese rule, however, has been widespread. In recent years, the Dalai Lama, the leading religious figure in Tibetan Buddhism, has attempted without success to persuade Chinese leaders to allow a measure of autonomy for the Tibetan people. In 2008, massive riots by frustrated Tibetans took place in the capital city of Lhasa just prior to the opening of the Olympic Games in Beijing. The Potala Palace, symbol of Tibetan identity, was constructed in the seventeenth century in Lhasa and serves today as the foremost symbol of the national and cultural aspirations of the Tibetan people.

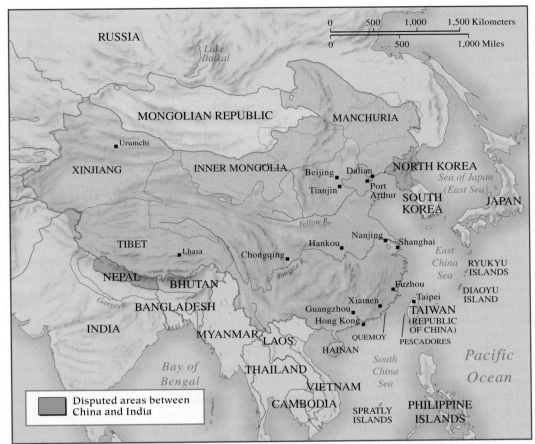

MAP 27.3 The People's Republic of China. This map shows China's current boundaries. Major regions are indicated in capital letters.

Q In which regions are there movements against Chinese rule?

To Chinese leaders, however, such actions simply represent legitimate efforts to resume China's rightful role in the affairs of the region. After a century of humiliation at the hands of the Western powers and neighboring Japan, the nation, in Mao's famous words of 1949, "has stood up" and no one will be permitted to humiliate it again. For the moment, at least, a fervent patriotism seems to be on the rise in China, actively promoted by the party as a means of holding the country together. Pride in the achievement of national sports teams is intense, and two young authors recently achieved wide acclaim with the publication of their book *The China That Can Say No*, a response to criticism of the country in the United States and Europe. The decision by the International Olympic Committee to award the 2008 Summer Games to Beijing led to widespread celebration throughout the country.

Pumping up the spirit of patriotism is not a solution to all problems, however. Unrest is growing among China's national minorities: in Xinjiang, where restless Muslim peoples are observing with curiosity the emergence of independent Islamic states in Central Asia, and in Tibet, where the official policy of quelling separatist sentiment has led to the violent suppression of Tibetan culture and an influx of thousands of ethnic Chinese immigrants. In the meantime, the Falun Gong religious movement, which the government has attempted to suppress as a potentially serious threat to its authority, is an additional indication that with the disintegration of the old Maoist utopia, the Chinese people will need more than a pallid version of Marxism-Leninism or a revived Confucianism to fill the gap.

Whether the current leadership will be able to prevent further erosion of the party's power and prestige is unclear. In the short term, efforts to slow the process of change may succeed because many Chinese are understandably fearful of punishment and concerned for their careers. And high economic growth rates can sometimes obscure a multitude of problems as many individuals will opt to chase the fruits of materialism rather than the less tangible benefits of personal freedom. But in the long run, the party leadership must resolve the contradiction between political authoritarianism and economic prosperity. One is reminded of Chiang Kai-shek's failed attempt during the 1930s to revive Confucian ethics as a standard of behavior for modern China: dead ideologies cannot be revived by decree.

New leaders installed in 2002 and 2003 have indicated that they are aware of the magnitude of the problem. Hu Jintao (b. 1942), who replaced Jiang Zemin as CCP general secretary and head of state, has called for further reforms to open up Chinese society and bridge the yawning gap between rich and poor. In recent years, the government has shown a growing tolerance for the public exchange of ideas, which has surfaced with the proliferation of bookstores, avant-garde theater, experimental art exhibits, and the Internet. In 2005, an estimated 27 percent of all Chinese citizens possessed a cell phone. Today, despite the government's efforts to restrict access to certain websites, more people are "surfing the Net" in China than in any other country except the United States. The Internet is wildly popular with those under thirty, who use it for online games, downloading videos and music, and instant messaging. The challenges, however, continue to be daunting. At the CCP's Seventeenth National Congress, held in October 2007, President Hu emphasized the importance of adopting a "scientific view of development," a vague concept calling for social harmony, improved material prosperity, and a reduction in the growing income gap between rich and poor in Chinese society. But he insisted that the Communist Party must remain the sole political force in charge of carrying out the revolution. Ever fearful of chaos, party leaders are convinced that only a firm hand at the tiller can keep the ship of state from crashing onto the rocks.

In the fall of 2008, an economic crisis struck the financial sector in the United States and then spread rapidly around the globe. Although China's rapid economic growth over the last two decades had shielded it from previous economic downturns, this recession threatened to have a more lasting impact as global demand for Chinese goods dropped significantly. By the end of 2008, massive layoffs in Chinese factories specializing in the export trade raised the specter of rising social unrest and presented a new challenge to the CCP's leadership.

"Serve the People": Chinese Society Under Communism

Q Focus Questions: What significant political, economic, and social changes have taken place in China since the death of Mao Zedong? Have they been successful?

When the Communist Party came to power in 1949, Chinese leaders made it clear that their policies would differ from the Soviet model in one key respect. Whereas the Bolsheviks had distrusted nonrevolutionary elements in Russia and relied almost exclusively on the use of force to achieve their objectives, the CCP sought to win support from the mass of the population by carrying out reforms that could win popular support. This "mass line" policy, as it was called, worked fairly well until the late 1950s, when Mao and his radical allies adopted policies such as the Great Leap Forward that began to alienate much of the population. Ideological purity was valued over expertise in building an advanced and prosperous society.

Economics in Command

When he came to power in the late 1970s, Deng Xiaoping recognized the need to restore credibility to a system on the verge of breakdown and hoped that rapid economic growth would satisfy the Chinese people and prevent them from demanding political reforms. The post-Mao leaders clearly emphasized economic performance over ideological purity. To stimulate the stagnant industrial sector, which had been under state control since the end of the New Democracy era, they reduced bureaucratic controls over state industries and allowed local managers to have more say over prices, salaries, and quality control. Productivity was encouraged by permitting bonuses for extra effort, a policy that had been discouraged during the Cultural Revolution. The regime also tolerated the emergence of a small private sector. Unemployed youths were encouraged to set up restaurants, bicycle or radio repair shops, and handicraft shops on their own initiative (see the comparative illustration on p. 679).

Finally, the regime opened up the country to foreign investment and technology. Special economic zones were established in urban centers near the coast (ironically, many were located in the old nineteenth-century treaty ports), where lucrative concessions were offered to encourage foreign firms to build factories. The tourist industry was encouraged, and students were sent abroad to study.

The new leaders especially stressed educational reform. The system adopted during the Cultural Revolution, emphasizing practical education and ideology at the expense of higher education and modern science, was rapidly abandoned (the *Little Red Book* was even withdrawn from circulation and could no longer be found on bookshelves), and a new system based generally on the Western model was instituted. Admission to higher education was based on success in merit examinations, and courses in science and mathematics received high priority.

Agricultural Reform No economic reform program could succeed unless it included the countryside. Three decades of socialism had done little to increase food production or to lay the basis for a modern agricultural sector. China, with a population numbering one billion, could still barely feed itself. Peasants had little incentive to work and few opportunities to increase production through mechanization, the use of fertilizer, or better irrigation.

Under Deng Xiaoping, agricultural policy made a rapid about-face. Under the new **rural responsibility system,** adopted shortly after Deng had consolidated his authority, collectives leased land to peasant families, who paid a quota in the form of rent to the collective. Anything produced on the land above that payment could be sold on the private market or consumed. To soak up excess labor in the villages, the government encouraged the formation of so-called sideline industries, a modern equivalent of the traditional cottage industries in premodern China. Peasants raised fish or shrimp, made consumer goods, and even assembled living room furniture and appliances for sale to their newly affluent compatriots.

The reform program had a striking effect on rural production. Grain production increased rapidly, and farm income doubled during the 1980s. Yet it also created problems. In the first place, income at the village level became more unequal as some enterprising farmers (known locally as "ten-thousand-dollar households") earned profits several times those realized by their less fortunate or less industrious neighbors. When some farmers discovered that they could earn more by growing cash crops or other specialized commodities, they devoted less land to rice and other grain crops, thereby threatening to reduce the supply of China's most crucial staple. Finally, the agricultural policy threatened to undermine the government's population control program, which party leaders viewed as crucial to the success of the Four Modernizations.

Since a misguided period in the mid-1950s when Mao Zedong had argued that more labor would result in higher productivity, China had been attempting to limit its population growth. By 1970, the government had launched a stringent family planning program—including education, incentives, and penalties for noncompliance—to persuade the Chinese people to limit themselves to one child per family. The program has had some success, and population growth was reduced drastically in the early 1980s. The rural responsibility system, however, undermined the program because it encouraged farm families to pay the penalties for having additional children in the belief that their labor would increase family income and provide the parents with a form of social security for their old age. Today, China's population has surpassed 1.3 billion.

CHRONOLOGY China Under Communist Rule

New Democracy	1949–1955
Era of collectivization	1955–1958
Great Leap Forward	1958–1960
Great Proletarian Cultural Revolution	1966–1976
Death of Mao Zedong	1976
Era of Deng Xiaoping	1978–1997
Tiananmen Square incident	1989
Presidency of Jiang Zemin	1993–2002
Hu Jintao becomes president	2002

Evaluating the Four Modernizations Still, the overall effects of the modernization program were impressive. The standard of living improved for the majority of the population. Whereas a decade earlier, the average Chinese had struggled to earn enough to buy a bicycle, radio, watch, or washing machine, by the late 1980s, many were beginning to purchase videocassette recorders, refrigerators, and color television sets. Yet the rapid growth of the economy created its own problems: inflationary pressures, greed, envy, increased corruption, and—most dangerous of all for the regime—rising expectations. Young people in particular resented restrictions on employment (many young people in China are still required to accept the jobs that are offered to them by the government or school officials) and opportunities to study abroad. Disillusionment ran high, especially in the cities, where lavish living by officials and rising prices for goods aroused widespread alienation and cynicism.

During the 1990s, growth rates in the industrial sector continued to be high as domestic capital became increasingly available to compete with the growing presence of foreign enterprises. The government finally recognized the need to close down inefficient state enterprises, and by the end of the decade, the private sector, with official encouragement, accounted for more than 10 percent of the gross domestic product. A stock market opened, and China's prowess in the international marketplace improved dramatically.

As a result of these developments, China now possesses a large and increasingly affluent middle class and a burgeoning domestic market for consumer goods. More than 80 percent of all urban Chinese now own a color television set, a refrigerator, and a washing machine. One-third own their homes, and nearly as many have an air conditioner. For the more affluent, a private automobile is increasingly a possibility. Like their counterparts elsewhere in Asia, urban Chinese are increasingly brand-name conscious, a characteristic that provides a considerable challenge to local manufacturers.

became too expensive). China's entry into the World Trade Organization (WTO) in 2001 was greeted with great optimism but has been of little benefit to farmers facing the challenges of cheap foreign imports. Taxes and local corruption add to their complaints, and land seizures by the government or by local officials are a major source of anger in rural communities. In desperation, millions of rural Chinese have left for the big cities, where many of them are unable to find steady employment and are forced to live in squalid conditions in crowded tenements or in the sprawling suburbs. Millions of others remain on the farm but attempt to maximize their income by producing for the market or increasing the size of their families. Although China's population control program continues to limit rural couples to two children, such regulations are widely flouted despite stringent penalties.

Another factor hindering China's rush to economic advancement is the impact on the environment. With the rising population, fertile land is in increasingly short supply (China, with twice the population, now has only two-thirds as much irrigable land as it had in 1950). Soil erosion is a major problem, especially in the north, where the desert is encroaching on farmlands. Water is also a problem. A massive dam project now under way in the Yangtze River valley has sparked protests from environmentalists, as well

Silk Workers of the World, Unite! In recent years, many critics have charged that Chinese goods can be marketed at cheap prices abroad only because factories pay low wages to workers, who must often labor in abysmal working conditions. The silk industry, which represents one of China's key high-end export products, is a case in point. At this factory in Wuxi, women spend ten hours a day with their hands immersed in boiling water as they unwind filaments from cocoons onto a spool of silk yarn. Their blistered red hands testify to the difficulty of their painful task.

But as Chinese leaders have discovered, rapid economic change never comes without cost. The closing of state-run factories has led to the dismissal of millions of workers each year, and the private sector, although growing at more than 20 percent annually, has struggled to absorb them. Poor working conditions and low salaries are frequent complaints in Chinese factories, resulting in periodic outbreaks of labor unrest. Demographic conditions, however, are changing. The reduction in birthrates since the 1980s will eventually lead to a labor shortage, resulting in an upward pressure on workers' salaries and inflation in the marketplace.

Discontent has been increasing in the countryside as well, where farmers earn only about half the salary of their urban counterparts (the government tried to increase the official purchase price for grain but rescinded the order when it

Tourism and the Environment: The Sand Dunes of Dunhuang. For centuries, the Central Asian commercial hub of Dunhuang was an important stop on the Silk Road. Today, it remains a major tourist attraction, not only because of the Buddhist relics located in nearby caves, but also for the strikingly beautiful sand dunes located just outside the modern city. Yet these massive mountains of sand are also a visual example of China's growing environmental problem, as the dunes are rapidly encroaching on nearby pasture lands because of the widespread practice of overgrazing. Soil erosion and the loss of farm and pasture lands are a major problem for China, as its population continues its rapid increase.

VIEWS ON MARRIAGE

FAMILY & SOCIETY

One of the major goals of the Communist government in China was to reform the tradition of marriage and place it on a new egalitarian basis. In the following excerpt, a writer with the magazine *China Youth Daily* describes the ideal marriage and explains how socialist marriage differs from its capitalist counterpart.

The Correct Viewpoint Toward Marriage

Now then, what is our viewpoint? Is it different from that of the exploiting bourgeois class?

For one thing, our basic concept on marriage is and must be that we build our happiness upon the premise that happiness should be shared by all. We advocate equal rights for man and woman, equal rights for husband and wife. We oppose the idea that man is superior to woman or that the husband has special prerogatives over his wife. We also oppose any discrimination against or ill treatment of the wife.

We believe that marriage should be based solely upon mutual consent. We oppose the so-called arranged marriage, or the use of any deceitful or compulsory method by one of the parties in this matter. We uphold the system of monogamy. Husband and wife ought to have true and exclusive love toward each other, and concubinage is not permitted.

We believe that the very basic foundations for love between man and woman are common political understanding, comradeship in work, mutual help, and mutual respect. Money, position, or the so-called prettiness should not be taken into consideration for a right marriage, because they are not reliable foundations for love.

We also believe that solemnity and fidelity are important elements for a correct relationship between husband and wife, and for a happy family life. To abandon one's partner by any improper means is to be opposed. In our society, those who intend to pursue their happiness at the expense of others run contradictory to the moral principle of Communism and will never be happy.

For the exploiting class, the concept about marriage is just the opposite. The landlord class believes in pursuing happiness by making other people suffer. They subscribe to such biased viewpoints as "man is superior to woman," "man is more important than woman," "man should dominate woman," etc. Under this type of ideology, women are merely slaves and properties of men and marriage is nothing but a process of buying and selling with compulsion. In the bourgeois society the whole matrimonial relationship is built upon money, and becomes simply a "monetary relationship." In economic relationships women belong to men. Love is nothing but a merchandise; women trade their flesh for men's money. This concept about marriage is indeed reactionary and it shall meet with our firm opposition.

Among our young worker comrades there are still a few whose thinking is still under the influence of the exploiting class. They cannot do away with the thinking that man is superior to woman; they look down upon their own wives, especially those who have lower education and those who come from rural areas. When they look for lovers, what concerns the man most is whether the woman is pretty or not; what concerns the woman most is whether the man is earning high wages and has a high position. They disregard all the other elements for a good match.

Some of them even use deception to steal love or to force the other party to marry them. Their attitude toward love and marriage is most revolting. They love the new ones and forsake the old, get themselves involved in multi-angle romance, or even seek excuses as grounds for divorce. All this sort of thinking and behavior is certainly contradictory to the moral quality of the working class and Communism, and contradictory to the socialist concept and system of marriage. Therefore those who have formed such a wrong concept about marriage ought to adopt a correct one in accordance with the moral principle of Communism. Only then will there be possibility for true love and happy family life.

Q *How, according to this document, will socialist marriage differ from its capitalist counterpart? What changes in traditional Chinese practices will take place?*

---

as from local peoples forced to migrate from the area. The rate of air pollution is ten times the level in the United States, contributing to growing health concerns. To add to the challenge, more than 400,000 new cars and trucks appear on the country's roads each year. Chinese leaders now face the uncomfortable reality that the pains of industrialization are not exclusive to capitalist countries.

Social Problems

At the root of Marxist-Leninist ideology is the idea of building a new citizen free from the prejudices, ignorance, and superstition of the "feudal" era and the capitalist desire for self-gratification. This new citizen would be characterized not only by a sense of racial and sexual equality but also by the selfless desire to contribute his or her utmost for the good of all.

Women and the Family From the very start, the Chinese Communist government intended to bring an end to the Confucian legacy in modern China. Women were given the vote and encouraged to become active in the political process. At the local level, an increasing number of women became active in the CCP and in collective organizations. In 1950, a new marriage law guaranteed women equal rights with men (see the box above).

Most important, perhaps, it permitted women for the first time to initiate divorce proceedings against their husbands. Within a year, nearly one million divorces had been granted.

The regime also undertook to destroy the influence of the traditional family system. To the Communists, loyalty to the family, a crucial element in the Confucian social order, undercut loyalty to the state and to the dictatorship of the proletariat.

At first, however, the new government moved carefully to avoid alienating its supporters in the countryside unnecessarily. When collective farms were established in the mid-1950s, payment for hours worked in the form of ration coupons was made not to the individual but to the family head, thus maintaining the traditionally dominant position of the patriarch. When people's communes were established in the late 1950s, payments went to the individual.

During the political radicalism of the Great Leap Forward, children were encouraged to report to the authorities any comments by their parents that criticized the system. Such practices continued during the Cultural Revolution, when children were expected to tell on their parents, students on their teachers, and employees on their superiors. Some have suggested that Mao deliberately encouraged such practices to bring an end to the traditional "politics of dependency." According to this theory, historically the famous "five relationships" forced individuals to swallow their anger and frustration and accept the hierarchical norms established by Confucian ethics (known in Chinese as "to eat bitterness"). By encouraging the oppressed elements in society—the young, the female, and the poor—to voice their bitterness, Mao was hoping to break the tradition of dependency. Such denunciations had been issued against landlords and other "local tyrants" in the land reform tribunals of the late 1940s and early 1950s. Later, during the Cultural Revolution, they were applied to other authority figures in Chinese society.

Lifestyle Changes The post-Mao era brought a decisive shift away from revolutionary utopianism and back toward the pragmatic approach to nation building. For most people, it meant improved living conditions and a qualified return to family traditions. For the first time, millions of Chinese saw the prospect of a house or an urban apartment with a washing machine, television set, and indoor plumbing. Young people whose parents had given them patriotic names such as Build the Country, Protect Mao Zedong, and Assist Korea began to choose more elegant and cosmopolitan names for their own children. Some names, such as Surplus Grain or Bring a Younger Brother, expressed hope for the future.

The new attitudes were also reflected in physical appearance. For a generation after the civil war, clothing had been restricted to the traditional baggy "Mao suit" in olive drab or dark blue, but by the 1980s, young people craved such fashionable Western items as designer jeans, trendy sneakers, and sweat suits (or reasonable facsimiles). Cosmetic surgery to create a more buxom figure or a more Western facial look became increasingly common among affluent young women in the cities. Many had the epicanthic fold over their eyelids removed or their noses enlarged—a curious decision in view of the tradition of referring derogatorily to foreigners as "big noses."

Religious practices and beliefs also changed. As the government became more tolerant, some Chinese began to return to the traditional Buddhist faith or to folk religions, and Buddhist and Taoist temples were once again crowded with worshipers. Despite official efforts to suppress its more evangelical forms, Christianity became increasingly popular; like the "rice Christians" (persons who supposedly converted for economic reasons) of the past, many viewed it as a symbol of success and cosmopolitanism.

As with all social changes, China's reintegration into the outside world has had a price. Arranged marriages, nepotism, and mistreatment of females (for example, under the one-child rule, parents reportedly killed female infants to regain the possibility of having a son) have come back, although such behavior likely survived under the cloak of revolutionary purity for a generation. Materialistic attitudes are prevalent among young people, along with a corresponding cynicism about politics and the CCP (see the comparative essay "Family and Society in an Era of Change" on p. 691). Expensive weddings are now increasingly common, and bribery and favoritism are all too frequent. Crime of all types, including an apparently growing incidence of prostitution and sex crimes against women, appears to be on the rise. To discourage sexual abuse, the government now seeks to provide free legal services for women living in rural areas.

There is also a price to pay for the trend toward privatization. Under the Maoist system, the elderly and the sick were provided with retirement benefits and health care by the state or by the collective organizations. Under current conditions, with the latter no longer playing such a social role and more workers operating in the private sector, the safety net has been removed. The government recently attempted to fill the gap by enacting a social security law, but because of lack of funds, eligibility is limited primarily to individuals in the urban sector of the economy. Those living in the countryside—who still represent 60 percent of the population—are essentially left to their own devices.

COMPARATIVE ESSAY
FAMILY AND SOCIETY IN AN ERA OF CHANGE

It is one of the paradoxes of the modern world that at a time of political stability and economic prosperity for many people in the advanced capitalist societies, public cynicism about the system is increasingly widespread. Alienation and drug use are at dangerously high levels, and the rate of criminal activities in most areas remains much higher than in the immediate postwar era.

Although the reasons advanced to explain this paradox vary widely, many observers place the responsibility for many contemporary social problems on the decline of the traditional family system. There has been a steady rise in the percentage of illegitimate births and single-parent families in countries throughout the Western world. In the United States, approximately half of all marriages end in divorce. Even in two-parent families, more and more parents work full time, leaving the children to fend for themselves on their return from school. In many countries in Europe, the birthrate has dropped to alarming levels, leading to a severe labor shortage that is attracting a rising number of immigrants from other parts of the world.

Observers point to several factors as an explanation for these conditions: the growing emphasis in advanced capitalist states on an individualistic lifestyle devoted to instant gratification, a phenomenon promoted vigorously by the advertising media; the rise of the feminist movement, which has freed women from the servitude imposed on their predecessors, but at the expense of

removing them from full-time responsibility for the care of the next generation; and the increasing mobility of contemporary life, which disrupts traditional family ties and creates a sense of rootlessness and impersonality in the individual's relationship to the surrounding environment.

This phenomenon is not unique to Western civilization. The traditional nuclear family is also under attack in many societies around the world. Even in East Asia, where the Confucian tradition of family solidarity has been endlessly touted as a major factor in the region's economic success, the incidence of divorce and illegitimate births is on the rise, as is the percentage of women in the workforce. Older citizens frequently complain that the Asian youth of today are too materialistic, faddish, and steeped in the individualistic values of the West. Such criticisms are now voiced in mainland China as well as in the capitalist societies around its perimeter (see Chapter 30).

In societies less exposed to the individualist lifestyle portrayed so prominently in Western culture, traditional attitudes about the family continue to hold sway. In the Middle East, governmental and religious figures seek to prevent the Western media from undermining accepted mores. Success is sometimes elusive, however, as the situation in Iran demonstrates. Despite the zealous guardians of Islamic morality, many young Iranians are clamoring for the individual freedoms that have been denied to them since the Islamic Revolution took place more than three decades ago (see Chapter 29).

China's "Little Emperors." To curtail population growth, Chinese leaders launched a massive family planning program that restricted urban families to a single child. Under these circumstances, in conformity with tradition, sons are especially prized, and some Chinese complain that many parents overindulge their children, turning them into spoiled "little emperors."

© William J. Duiker

Q *Do you see indications that young people in China are becoming more like their counterparts in the West?*

China's Changing Culture

The rise to power of the Communists in 1949 added a new dimension to the debate over the future of culture in China. The new leaders rejected the Western attitude of "art for art's sake" and, like their Soviet counterparts, viewed culture as an important instrument of indoctrination. The standard would no longer be aesthetic quality or the personal preference of the artist but "art for life's sake," whereby culture would serve the interests of socialism.

At first, the new emphasis on socialist realism did not entirely extinguish the influence of traditional culture. Mao and his colleagues tolerated—and even encouraged—efforts by artists to synthesize traditional ideas with socialist concepts and Western techniques. During the Cultural Revolution, however, all forms of traditional

Downtown Beijing. Deng Xiaoping's policy of Four Modernizations had a dramatic visual effect on the capital city of Beijing, as evidenced by this photo of skyscrapers thrusting up beyond the walls of the fifteenth-century Imperial City. Many of these buildings are apartment houses for the capital city's growing population, most of them migrants from the countryside looking for employment. The transformation of Beijing visually highlights the country's abandonment of traditional styles in favor of the contemporary global culture.

culture came to be viewed as reactionary. Socialist realism became the only acceptable standard in literature, art, and music. All forms of traditional expression were forbidden.

Nowhere were the dilemmas of the new order more challenging than in literature. In the heady afterglow of the Communist victory, many progressive writers supported the new regime and enthusiastically embraced Mao's exhortation to create a new Chinese literature for the edification of the masses. But in the harsher climate of the 1960s, many writers were criticized by the party for their excessive individualism and admiration for Western culture. Such writers either toed the new line and suppressed their doubts or were jailed and silenced, as was Ding Ling, the most prominent woman writer in China during the twentieth century. Born in 1904, she joined the CCP during the early 1930s and settled in Yan'an, where she wrote her most famous novel, *The Sun Shines over the Sangan River,* which praised the land reform program. After the Communist victory in 1949, however, she was criticized for her individualism and outspoken views. During the Cultural Revolution, she was sentenced to hard labor. She died in 1981.

After Mao's death, Chinese culture was finally released from the shackles of socialist realism. In painting, where for a decade the only acceptable standard for excellence was praise for the party and its policies, the new permissiveness

led to a revival of interest in both traditional and Western forms. Although some painters continued to blend Eastern and Western styles, others imitated trends from abroad, experimenting with a wide range of previously prohibited art styles, including Cubism and abstract painting.

In the late 1980s, two avant-garde art exhibits shocked the Chinese public and provoked the wrath of the party. An exhibition of nude paintings, the first ever held in China, attracted many viewers but reportedly offended the modesty of many Chinese. The second was an exhibit presenting the works of various schools of Modern and Postmodern art. The event resulted in considerable commentary and some expressions of public hostility. After a Communist critic lambasted the works as promiscuous and ideologically reactionary, the government declared that henceforth it would regulate all art exhibits.

The limits of freedom of expression were most apparent in literature. During the early 1980s, party leaders encouraged Chinese writers to express their views on the mistakes of the past, and a new "literature of the wounded" began to describe the brutal and arbitrary character of the Cultural Revolution. One of the most prominent writers was Bai Hua, whose film script *Bitter Love* described the life of a young Chinese painter who joined the revolutionary movement during the 1940s but was destroyed during the Cultural Revolution when his work was condemned as counterrevolutionary. The film depicts the condemnation through a view of a street in Beijing "full of people waving the *Quotations of Chairman Mao,* all those devout and artless faces fired by a feverish fanaticism." Driven from his home for posting a portrait of a third-century B.C.E. defender of human freedom on a Beijing wall, the artist flees the city. At the end of the film, he dies in a snowy field, where his corpse and a semicircle made by his footprints form a giant question mark.

In criticizing the excesses of the Cultural Revolution, Bai Hua was only responding to Deng Xiaoping's appeal for intellectuals to speak out, but he was soon criticized for failing to point out the essentially beneficial role of the CCP in recent Chinese history, and his film was withdrawn from circulation in 1981. Bai Hua was compelled to recant his errors and to state that the great ideas of Mao Zedong on art and literature were "still of universal guiding significance today."[5]

As the attack on Bai Hua illustrates, many party leaders remained suspicious of the impact that "decadent" bourgeois culture could have on the socialist foundations of Chinese society, and the official press periodically warned that China should adopt only the "positive" aspects of Western culture (notably, its technology and its work ethic) and not the "negative" elements such as drug use, pornography, and hedonism. Conservatives were especially incensed by the tendency of many writers to dwell on the shortcomings of the socialist system and to come uncomfortably close to direct criticism of the role of the CCP. One such example is the author Mo Yan (b. 1955), whose novels *The Garlic Ballads* (1988) and *The Republic of Wine* (2000) expose the rampant corruption of contemporary Chinese society, the roots of which he attributes to one-party rule.

Another author whose writings fell under the harsh glare of official disapproval is Zhang Xinxin (b. 1953).

Her controversial novellas and short stories, which explored Chinese women's alienation and spiritual malaise, were viewed by many as a negative portrayal of contemporary society, provoking the government in 1984 to prohibit her from publishing for a year. Determined and resourceful, Zhang turned to reporting. With a colleague, she interviewed one hundred "ordinary" people to record their views on all aspects of everyday life.

One of the chief targets of China's recent "spiritual civilization" campaign is author Wang Shuo (b. 1958), whose writings have been banned for exhibiting a sense of "moral decay." In his novels *Playing for Thrills* (1989) and *Please Don't Call Me Human* (2000), Wang highlighted the seamier side of contemporary urban society, peopled with hustlers, ex-convicts, and other assorted hooligans. Spiritually depleted, hedonistic, and amoral in their approach to life, his characters represent the polar opposite of the socialist ideal.

CONCLUSION

FOR FOUR DECADES after the end of World War II, the world's two superpowers competed for global hegemony. The Cold War became the dominant feature on the international scene and determined the internal politics of many countries around the world as well.

By the early 1980s, some of the tension had gone out of the conflict as it appeared that both Moscow and Washington had learned to tolerate the other's existence. Skeptical minds even suspected that both countries drew benefits from their mutual rivalry and saw it as an advantage in carrying on their relations with friends and allies. Few suspected that the Cold War, which had long seemed a permanent feature of world politics, was about to come to an end.

What brought about the collapse of the Soviet Empire? Some observers argue that the ambitious defense policies adopted by the Reagan administration forced Moscow into an arms race it could not afford, which ultimately led to a collapse of the Soviet economy. Others suggest that Soviet problems were more deep-rooted and would have ended in the disintegration of the Soviet Union even without outside stimulation. Both arguments have some validity, but the latter is surely closer to the mark. For years, if not decades, leaders in the Kremlin had disguised or ignored the massive inefficiencies of the Soviet system. In the 1980s, the perceptive Mikhail Gorbachev tried to save the system by instituting radical reforms. By then, however, it was too late.

Why has communism survived in China, albeit in a substantially altered form, when it failed in Eastern Europe and the Soviet Union? One of the primary factors is probably cultural. Although the doctrine of Marxism-Leninism originated in Europe, many of its main precepts, such as the primacy of the community over the individual and the denial of the concept of private property, run counter to trends in Western civilization. This inherent conflict is especially evident in the societies of central Europe, which were strongly influenced by Enlightenment philosophy and the Industrial Revolution. These forces were weaker in the countries farther to the east, but both had begun to penetrate tsarist Russia by the end of the nineteenth century.

By contrast, Marxism-Leninism found a more receptive climate in China and other countries in the region influenced by Confucian tradition. In its political culture, the Communist system exhibits many of the same characteristics as traditional Confucianism—a single truth, an elite governing class, and an emphasis on obedience to the community and its governing representatives—while feudal attitudes regarding female inferiority, loyalty to the family, and bureaucratic arrogance are hard to break. On the surface, China today bears a number of uncanny similarities to the China of the past.

Yet these similarities should not blind us to the real changes that are taking place in Chinese society today. Although the youthful protesters in Tiananmen Square were comparable in some respects to the reformist elements of the early republic, the China of today is fundamentally different from that of the early twentieth century. Literacy rates and the standard of living are far higher, the pressures of outside powers are less threatening, and China has entered its own industrial and technological revolution. For many Chinese, independent talk radio and the Internet are a greater source of news and views than are the official media. Where Sun Yat-sen, Chiang Kai-shek, and even Mao Zedong broke their lances on the rocks of centuries of tradition, poverty, and ignorance, China's present leaders rule a country much more aware of the world and its place in it.

TIMELINE

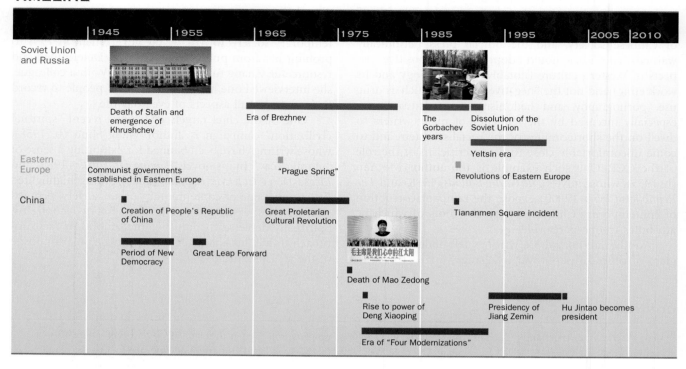

	1945	1955	1965	1975	1985	1995	2005	2010

Soviet Union and Russia

Death of Stalin and emergence of Khrushchev

Era of Brezhnev

The Gorbachev years

Dissolution of the Soviet Union

Yeltsin era

Eastern Europe

Communist governments established in Eastern Europe

"Prague Spring"

Revolutions of Eastern Europe

China

Creation of People's Republic of China

Great Proletarian Cultural Revolution

Tiananmen Square incident

Period of New Democracy

Great Leap Forward

Death of Mao Zedong

Rise to power of Deng Xiaoping

Presidency of Jiang Zemin

Hu Jintao becomes president

Era of "Four Modernizations"

SUGGESTED READING

Russia and the Soviet Union For a general view of modern Russia, see **M. Malia, *Russia Under Western Eyes*** (Cambridge, Mass., 1999), and **M. T. Poe, *The Russian Moment in World History*** (Princeton, N.J., 2003). On the Khrushchev years, see **W. Taubman, *Khrushchev: The Man and His Era*** (New York, 2004). For an overview of the Soviet era, see **R. J. Hill, *The Soviet Union: Politics, Economics, and Society,*** 2nd ed. (London, 1989); **M. Lewin, *The Gorbachev Phenomenon*** (Berkeley, Calif., 1988); **G. Hosking, *The Awakening of the Soviet Union*** (London, 1990); and **S. White, *Gorbachev and After*** (Cambridge, 1991). For an inquiry into the reasons for the Soviet collapse, see **R. Conquest, *Reflections on a Ravaged Century*** (New York, 1999), and **R. Strayer, *Why Did the Soviet Union Collapse? Understanding Historical Change*** (New York, 1998).

Soviet Satellites For a general study of the Soviet satellites in Eastern Europe, see **S. Fischer-Galati, *Eastern Europe in the 1980s*** (London, 1981). Additional studies on the recent history of these countries include **T. G. Ash, *The Polish Revolution: Solidarity*** (New York, 1984); **B. Kovrig, *Communism in Hungary from Kun to Kádár*** (Stanford, Calif., 1979); **T. G. Ash, *The Magic Lantern: The Revolution of '89 Witnessed in Warsaw, Budapest, Berlin, and Prague*** (New York, 1990); and **S. Ramet, *Nationalism and Federalism in Yugoslavia*** (Bloomington, Ind., 1992).

China After World War II A number of useful surveys deal with China after World War II. The most comprehensive treatment of the Communist period is **M. Meisner, *Mao's China and After: A History of the People's Republic*** (New York, 1999). Also see **R. Macfarquhar, ed., *The Politics of China: The Eras of Mao and Deng*** (Cambridge, 1997). Interesting documents can be found in **M. Selden, ed., *The People's Republic of China: A Documentary History of Revolutionary Change*** (New York, 1978).

Communist China There are countless specialized studies on various aspects of the Communist period in China. The Cultural Revolution is treated dramatically in **S. Karnow, *Mao and China: Inside China's Cultural Revolution*** (New York, 1972). For individual accounts of the impact of the revolution on people's lives, see the celebrated book by **Nien Cheng, *Life and Death in Shanghai*** (New York, 1986). A recent critical biography of China's "Great Helmsman" is **J. Chang** and **J. Halliday, *Mao: The Unknown Story*** (New York, 2005).

Post-Mao China On the early post-Mao period, see **O. Schell, *To Get Rich Is Glorious*** (New York, 1986), and the sequel, ***Discos and Democracy: China in the Throes of Reform*** (New York, 1988). The 1989 demonstrations and their aftermath are chronicled in **L. Feigon's** eyewitness account, ***China Rising: The Meaning of Tiananmen*** (Chicago, 1990), and **D. Morrison, *Massacre in Beijing*** (New York, 1989). Documentary materials relating to the events of 1989 are chronicled in **A. J. Nathan** and **P. Link, eds.,** *The Tiananmen Papers* (New York, 2001). Subsequent events are analyzed in **J. Fewsmith,** *China Since Tiananmen: The Politics of Transition* (Cambridge, 2001). On China's challenge from the process of democratization, see **J. Gittings,** *The Changing Face of China: From Mao to Market* (Oxford, 2005). Also see **T. Saich,** *Governance and Politics in China* (New York, 2002). China's evolving role in the world is traced in **S. Shirk,** *China: Fragile Superpower* (Oxford, 2007).

Chinese Literature and Art For a comprehensive introduction to twentieth-century Chinese literature, consult **E. Widmer** and **D. Der-Wei Wang, eds.,** *From May Fourth to June Fourth: Fiction and Film in Twentieth-Century China* (Cambridge, Mass., 1993), and **J. Lau** and **H. Goldblatt,** *The Columbia Anthology of Modern Chinese Literature* (New York, 1995). To witness daily life in the mid-1980s, see **Z. Xinxin** and **S. Ye,** *Chinese Lives: An Oral History of Contemporary China* (New York, 1987). For the most comprehensive analysis of twentieth-century Chinese

art, consult **M. Sullivan,** *Arts and Artists of Twentieth-Century China* (Berkeley, Calif., 1996).

Women in China For a discussion of the women's movement in China during the postwar period, see **J. Stacey,** *Patriarchy and Socialist Revolution in China* (Berkeley, Calif., 1983), and **M. Wolf,** *Revolution Postponed: Women in Contemporary China* (Stamford, Conn., 1985). Gender issues are treated in **B. Entwistle** and **G. E. Henderson, eds.,** *Redrawing Boundaries: Work, Households, and Gender in China* (Berkeley, Calif., 2000).

Why has communism survived in China when it failed in Eastern Europe and Russia? Compare conditions in China today with those in countries elsewhere in the world that have abandoned the Communist system. Are Chinese leaders justified in claiming that without party leadership, the country would fall into chaos?

In thinking about these questions, begin by breaking them down into the components shown below. A discussion of the significance of each component should appear in your answer.

POLITICS AND GOVERNMENT Review this chapter's timeline below and also look back at the events related to Russia and the Soviet Union in the timelines for Chapters 23, 25, and 26 (pp. 587, 639, 668). What are the key events in the history of Communist China? What are the key events in Soviet history? Which nation seemed to place more emphasis on the role of individual leaders in carrying out the revolutionary program? Why?

How do the timelines reveal a basic difference between the Chinese and Soviet approaches to dealing with problems? Do you think this difference may help in part to explain why communism has survived in China? How have the Chinese differed from the Soviets in their approach to communism?

TIMELINE

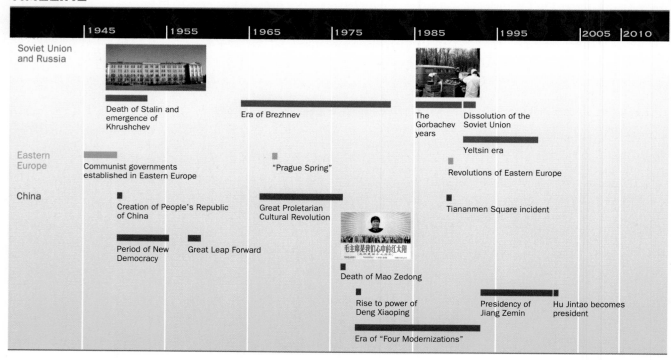

| | 1945 | 1955 | 1965 | 1975 | 1985 | 1995 | 2005 | 2010 |

Soviet Union and Russia
Death of Stalin and emergence of Khrushchev
Era of Brezhnev
The Gorbachev years
Dissolution of the Soviet Union
Yeltsin era

Eastern Europe
Communist governments established in Eastern Europe
"Prague Spring"
Revolutions of Eastern Europe

China
Creation of People's Republic of China
Great Proletarian Cultural Revolution
Tiananmen Square incident
Period of New Democracy
Great Leap Forward
Death of Mao Zedong
Rise to power of Deng Xiaoping
Presidency of Jiang Zemin
Hu Jintao becomes president
Era of "Four Modernizations"

CHAPTER 28
EUROPE AND THE WESTERN HEMISPHERE SINCE 1945

Children play amid the ruins of Warsaw, Poland, at the end of World War II.

CHAPTER OUTLINE AND FOCUS QUESTIONS

Recovery and Renewal in Europe

Q What problems have the nations of Western Europe faced since 1945, and what steps have they taken to try to solve these problems? What problems have Eastern European nations faced since 1989?

Emergence of the Superpower: The United States

Q What political, social, and economic changes has the United States experienced since 1945?

The Development of Canada

Q What political, social, and economic developments has Canada experienced since 1945?

Latin America Since 1945

Q What problems have the nations of Latin America faced since 1945, and what role has Marxist ideology played in their efforts to solve these problems?

Society and Culture in the Western World

Q What major social, cultural, and intellectual developments have occurred in Western Europe and North America since 1945?

CRITICAL THINKING

Q What are the similarities and differences between the major political, economic, and social developments in the first half of the twentieth century and those in the second half of the century?

THE END OF WORLD WAR II in Europe had been met with great joy. One visitor in Moscow reported, "I looked out of the window [at 2 A.M.], almost everywhere there were lights in the windows—people were staying awake. Everyone embraced everyone else, someone sobbed aloud." But after the victory parades and celebrations, Europeans awoke to a devastating realization: their civilization was in ruins. Almost 40 million people (both soldiers and civilians) had been killed over the last six years. Massive air raids and artillery bombardments had reduced many of the great cities of Europe to heaps of rubble. The Polish capital of Warsaw had been almost completely obliterated. An American general described Berlin: "Wherever we looked, we saw desolation. It was like a city of the dead. Suffering and shock were visible in every face. Dead bodies still remained in canals and lakes and were being dug out from under bomb debris." Many Europeans were homeless.

Between 1945 and 1970, Europe not only recovered from the devastating effects of World War II but also experienced an economic resurgence that seemed nothing less than miraculous. Economic growth and virtually full employment continued so long that the first postwar recession, in 1973, came as a shock to Western Europe. It was short-lived, however, and economic growth returned. After the collapse of Communist governments in the revolutions

697

of 1989, a number of Eastern European states sought to create market economies and join the military and economic unions first formed by Western European states.

The most significant factor after 1945 was the emergence of the United States as the world's richest and most powerful nation. American prosperity reached new heights in the two decades after World War II, but a series of economic and social problems—including racial division and staggering budget deficits—have given the nation plenty of internal matters to grapple with over the past half century.

To the south of the United States lay the vast world of Latin America, with its own unique heritage. Although some Latin Americans in the nineteenth century had looked to the United States as a model for their own development, in the twentieth century, many attacked the United States for its military and economic domination of Central and South America. At the same time, many Latin American countries struggled with economic and political instability.

In addition to the transformation from Cold War to post–Cold War realities, other changes were shaping the Western outlook. The demographic face of European countries changed as massive numbers of immigrants created more ethnically diverse populations. New artistic and intellectual currents, the continued advance of science and technology, the effort to come to grips with environmental problems, the surge of the women's liberation movement—all spoke of a vibrant, ever-changing world. At the same time, a devastating terrorist attack in the United States in 2001 made the Western world vividly aware of its vulnerability to international terrorism. A global financial collapse in 2008 also presented new challenges to both Western and world economic stability. ✿

Recovery and Renewal in Europe

Q **Focus Questions:** What problems have the nations of Western Europe faced since 1945, and what steps have they taken to try to solve these problems? What problems have Eastern European nations faced since 1989?

All the nations of Europe faced similar problems at the end of World War II. Above all, they needed to rebuild their shattered economies. Yet, within a few years after the defeat of Germany and Italy, an incredible economic revival brought renewed growth to Western Europe.

Western Europe: The Triumph of Democracy

With the economic aid of the Marshall Plan, the countries of Western Europe recovered relatively rapidly from the devastation of World War II. Between the early 1950s and late 1970s, industrial production surpassed all previous records, and Western Europe experienced virtually full employment.

France: From de Gaulle to New Uncertainties The history of France for nearly a quarter century after the war was dominated by one man—Charles de Gaulle (1890–1970). Initially, he had withdrawn from politics, but in 1958, frightened by the bitter divisions within France caused by the Algerian crisis (see Chapter 29), the panic-stricken leaders of the Fourth Republic offered to let de Gaulle take over the government and revise the constitution.

De Gaulle's constitution for the Fifth Republic greatly enhanced the power of the office of president, who now had the right to choose the prime minister, dissolve parliament, and supervise both defense and foreign policy. As the new president, de Gaulle sought to return France to a position of great power. With that goal in mind, he invested heavily in the nuclear arms race. France exploded its first nuclear bomb in 1960. Despite his successes, de Gaulle did not really achieve his ambitious goals; in truth, France was too small for such global ambitions.

During de Gaulle's presidency, France became a major industrial producer and exporter, but problems remained. The expansion of traditional industries, such as coal, steel, and railroads, which had all been nationalized, led to large government deficits. The cost of living increased faster than in the rest of Europe. Increased dissatisfaction led in May 1968 to a series of student protests, followed by a general strike by the labor unions. Although he restored order, de Gaulle resigned from office in April 1969 and died the next year.

The worsening of France's economic situation in the 1970s brought a shift to the left politically. By 1981, the Socialists had become the dominant party in the National Assembly, and the Socialist leader, François Mitterrand (1916–1995), was elected president. Mitterrand passed a number of measures to aid workers: an increased minimum wage, expanded social benefits, a mandatory fifth week of paid vacation for salaried workers, and a thirty-nine-hour workweek. The victory of the Socialists led them to enact some of their more radical reforms: the government nationalized the major banks, the space and electronics industries, and important insurance firms.

The Socialist policies, however, largely failed, and within three years, a decline in support caused the Mitterrand government to return some of the economy to private enterprise. But France's economic decline continued, and in 1993, a coalition of conservative parties won 80 percent of the seats. The move to the right was strengthened when the conservative mayor of Paris, Jacques Chirac (b. 1932), was elected president in May 1995 and reelected in 2002. Resentment against foreign-born residents led many French voters to call for restrictions on all new immigration. Chirac himself pursued a plan of sending illegal immigrants back to their home countries.

In the fall of 2005, however, antiforeign sentiment provoked a backlash of its own, as young Muslims in the crowded suburbs of Paris rioted against dismal living conditions and the lack of employment opportunities for foreign residents in France. Tensions between the Muslim community and the remainder of the French population became a chronic source of social unrest throughout the country—an unrest that Nicolas Sarkozy (b. 1955), elected as president in 2007, promised to address.

From West Germany to Germany   Under the pressures of the Cold War, the three western zones of Germany were unified as the Federal Republic of Germany in 1949. Konrad Adenauer (1876–1967), the leader of the Christian Democratic Union (CDU), served as chancellor from 1949 to 1963 and became the Federal Republic's "founding hero."

Adenauer's chancellorship is largely associated with the resurrection of the West German economy, often referred to as the "economic miracle." It was largely guided by the minister of finance, Ludwig Erhard. Although West Germany had only 52 percent of the territory of prewar Germany, by 1955 the West German gross domestic product exceeded that of prewar Germany. Unemployment fell from 8 percent in 1950 to 0.4 percent in 1965.

After the Adenauer era, German voters moved politically from the center-right of the Christian Democrats to the center-left: in 1969, the Social Democrats became the leading party. The first Social Democratic chancellor was Willy Brandt (1913–1992), who was especially successful with his "opening toward the east" (known as *Ostpolitik*), for which he received the Nobel Peace Prize in 1972. On March 19, 1971, Brandt worked out the details of a treaty with East Germany (the former Russian zone) that led to greater cultural, personal, and economic contacts between West and East Germany.

In 1982, the Christian Democratic Union of Helmut Kohl (b. 1930) formed a new center-right government. Kohl was a clever politician who benefited greatly from an economic boom in the mid-1980s and the 1989 revolution in East Germany, which led to the reunification of the two Germanies, making the new Germany, with its 79 million people, the leading power in Europe. Reunification brought immediate political dividends to the Christian Democrats, but all too soon, the realization set in that the revitalization of eastern Germany would take far more money than was originally thought. Kohl's government soon faced the politically undesirable prospect of raising taxes substantially. Moreover, the virtual collapse of the economy in eastern Germany led to extremely high unemployment and severe discontent. One response was the return to power of the Social Democrats under the leadership of Gerhard Schroeder (b. 1944) in

elections in 1998. But Schroeder failed to cure Germany's economic woes, and, as a result of elections in 2005, Angela Merkel (b. 1954), leader of the Christian Democrats, became the first female chancellor in German history.

The Decline of Great Britain   The end of World War II left Britain with massive economic problems. In elections held immediately after the war, the Labour Party overwhelmingly defeated Winston Churchill's Conservatives. Labour had promised far-reaching reforms, particularly in the area of social welfare, and in a country with a tremendous shortage of consumer goods and housing, its platform was quite appealing. The new Labour government under Clement Attlee (1883–1967) proceeded to turn Britain into a modern **welfare state.**

The process began with the nationalization of the Bank of England, the coal and steel industries, public transportation, and public utilities, such as electricity and gas. In 1946, the new government established a comprehensive **social security** program and nationalized medical insurance, thereby enabling the state to subsidize the unemployed, the sick, and the aged. A health act established a system of socialized medicine that forced doctors and dentists to work with state hospitals, although private practice could be maintained. The British welfare state became the norm for most European nations after the war.

Continuing economic problems, however, brought the Conservatives back into power from 1951 to 1964. Although they favored private enterprise, the Conservatives accepted the welfare state. By now the British economy had recovered from the war, but the slow rate of its recovery reflected a long-term economic decline. At the same time, as the influence of the United States and the Soviet Union continued to rise, Britain's ability to play the role of a world power declined substantially. Between 1964 and 1979, Conservatives and Labour alternated in power, but neither party was able to deal with Britain's ailing economy.

In 1979, the Conservatives returned to power under Margaret Thatcher (b. 1925), who became the first woman to serve as prime minister in British history (see the box on p. 700). The "Iron Lady," as she was called, broke the power of the labor unions, but she was not able to eliminate the basic components of the social welfare system. "Thatcherism," as her economic policy was termed, improved the British economic situation, but at a price. The south of England, for example, prospered, but the old industrial areas of the Midlands and north declined and were beset by high unemployment and poverty.

Margaret Thatcher dominated British politics in the 1980s. But in 1990, Labour's fortunes revived when Thatcher's government attempted to replace local property

MARGARET THATCHER: ENTERING A MAN'S WORLD

POLITICS & GOVERNMENT

In 1979, Margaret Thatcher became the first woman to serve as Britain's prime minister and went on to be its longest-serving prime minister as well. In this excerpt from her autobiography, Thatcher describes how she was interviewed by Conservative Party officials when they first considered her as a possible candidate for Parliament as a representative from Dartford. Thatcher ran for Parliament for the first time in 1950; she lost but did increase the Conservative vote total in the district by 50 percent over the previous election.

Margaret Thatcher, *The Path to Power*

And they did [consider her]. I was invited to have lunch with John Miller and his wife, Phee, and the Dartford Woman's Chairman, Mrs. Fletcher, on the Saturday on Llandudno Pier. Presumably, and in spite of any reservations about the suitability of a woman candidate for their seat, they liked what they saw. I certainly got on well with them. The Millers were to become close friends and I quickly developed a healthy respect for the dignified Mrs. Fletcher. After lunch we walked back along the pier to the Conference Hall in good time for a place to hear Winston Churchill give the Party Leader's speech. It was the first we had seen of him that week, because in those days the Leader did not attend the Conference itself, appearing only at a final rally on the Saturday. Foreign affairs naturally dominated his speech—it was the time of the Berlin blockade and the Western airlift—and his message was somber, telling us that only American nuclear weapons stood between Europe and communist tyranny and warning of "what seems a remorselessly approaching third world war."

I did not hear from Dartford until December, when I was asked to attend an interview at Palace Chambers, Bridge Street—then housing Conservative Central Office—not far from Parliament itself. With a large number of other hopefuls I turned up on the evening of Thursday 30 December for my first Selection Committee. Very few outside the political arena know just how nerve-racking such occasions are. The interviewee who is not nervous and tense is very likely to perform badly: for, as any chemist will tell you, the adrenaline needs to flow if one is to perform at one's best. I was lucky in that at Dartford there were some friendly faces around the table, and it has to be said that on such occasions there are advantages as well as disadvantages to being a young woman making her way in the political world.

I found myself short-listed, and was asked to go to Dartford itself for a further interview. Finally, I was invited to the Bull Hotel in Dartford on Monday 31 January 1949 to address the Association's Executive Committee of about fifty people. As one of five would-be candidates, I had to give a fifteen-minute speech and answer questions for a further ten minutes.

It was the questions which were more likely to cause me trouble. There was a good deal of suspicion of woman candidates, particularly in what was regarded as a tough industrial seat like Dartford. This was quite definitely a man's world into which not just angels feared to tread. There was, of course, little hope of winning it for the Conservatives, though this is never a point that the prospective candidate even in a Labour seat as safe as Ebbw Vale would be advised to make. The Labour majority was an all but unscalable 20,000. But perhaps this unspoken fact turned to my favour. Why not take the risk of adopting the young Margaret Roberts? There was not much to lose, and some good publicity for the Party to gain.

The most reliable sign that a political occasion has gone well is that you have enjoyed it. I enjoyed that evening at Dartford, and the outcome justified my confidence. I was selected.

Q *In this account, is Margaret Thatcher's being a woman more important to her or to others? Why would this disparity exist?*

---

taxes with a flat-rate tax payable by every adult. Many British subjects argued that this was nothing more than a poll tax that would allow the rich to get away with paying the same rate as the poor. In 1990, Thatcher resigned, and later, in new elections in 1997, the Labour Party won a landslide victory. The new prime minister, Tony Blair (b. 1953), was a moderate whose youthful energy immediately instilled new vigor on the political scene. Blair was one of the prominent leaders in forming an international coalition against terrorism after the terrorist attack on the United States in 2001. Four years later, however, his support of the U.S. war in Iraq, when a majority of Britons opposed it, caused his popularity to plummet. In the summer of 2007, he stepped down and allowed the new Labour Party leader Gordon Brown (b. 1951) to become prime minister.

Eastern Europe After Communism

The fall of Communist governments in Eastern Europe during the revolutions of 1989 brought a wave of euphoria to Europe. The new structures meant an end to a postwar European order that had been imposed on unwilling peoples by the victorious forces of the Soviet Union (see Chapter 26). In 1989 and 1990, new governments throughout Eastern Europe worked diligently to scrap the remnants of the old system and introduce the democratic procedures and market systems they believed would revitalize their scarred lands. But this process proved to be neither simple nor easy. Nevertheless, by the beginning of the twenty-first century, many of these states, especially Poland and the Czech Republic, were

Margaret Thatcher. Great Britain's first female prime minister, Margaret Thatcher was a strong leader who dominated British politics in the 1980s and served in the post longer than any man. This picture of Thatcher was taken during a meeting with French president François Mitterrand in 1986.

making a successful transition to both free markets and democracy.

The revival of the post–Cold War Eastern European states was evident in their desire to join both the North Atlantic Treaty Organization (NATO) and the European Union (EU), the two major Cold War institutions of Western European unity. In 1997, Poland, the Czech Republic, and Hungary became full members of NATO. In 2004, ten nations—including Hungary, Poland, the Czech Republic, Slovenia, Estonia, Latvia, and Lithuania—joined the EU, and Romania and Bulgaria joined in 2007.

Yet not all are convinced that inclusion in European integration is a good thing. Eastern Europeans fear that their countries will be dominated by investment from their prosperous neighbors. The global economic crisis of 2008–2009 has been particularly troublesome for many Eastern European nations.

The Disintegration of Yugoslavia From its beginning in 1919, Yugoslavia had been an artificial creation. After World War II, the dictatorial Marshal Tito had managed to hold together the six republics and two autonomous provinces that constituted Yugoslavia. After his death in 1980, no strong leader emerged, and at the end of the 1980s, Yugoslavia was caught up in the reform movements sweeping through Eastern Europe.

After negotiations among the six republics failed, Slovenia and Croatia declared their independence in June 1991. This action was opposed by Slobodan Milošević (1941–2006), the leader of the province of Serbia. He asserted that these republics could only be independent if new border arrangements were made to accommodate the Serb minorities in those republics who did not want to live outside the boundaries of Serbia. Serbian forces attacked both new states and, although unsuccessful against Slovenia, captured one-third of Croatia's territory.

The international recognition of independent Slovenia and Croatia in 1992 and of Macedonia and Bosnia and Herzegovina soon thereafter did not deter the Serbs, who now turned their guns on Bosnia. By mid-1993, Serbian forces had acquired 70 percent of Bosnian territory. The Serbian policy of **ethnic cleansing**—killing or forcibly removing Bosnian Muslims from their lands—revived memories of Nazi atrocities in World War II. This account by one Muslim survivor from the town of Srebrenica is eerily reminiscent of the activities of the Nazi *Einsatzgruppen* (see Chapter 25):

> When the truck stopped, they told us to get off in groups of five. We immediately heard shooting next to the trucks.... About ten Serbs with automatic rifles told us to lie down on the ground face first. As we were getting down, they started to shoot, and I fell into a pile of corpses. I felt hot liquid

running down my face. I realized that I was only grazed. As they continued to shoot more groups, I kept on squeezing myself in between dead bodies.[1]

As the fighting spread, European nations and the United States began to intervene to stop the bloodshed, and in the fall of 1995, a fragile cease-fire agreement was reached. An international peacekeeping force was stationed in the area to prevent further hostilities.

Peace in Bosnia, however, did not bring peace to Yugoslavia. A new war erupted in 1999 over Kosovo, an autonomous province within the Serbian republic. Kosovo's inhabitants were mainly ethnic Albanians, but the province was also home to a Serbian minority. In 1989, Yugoslav president Milošević stripped Kosovo of its autonomous status. Four years later, some groups of ethnic Albanians founded the Kosovo Liberation Army (KLA) and began a campaign against Serbian rule in Kosovo. When Serb forces began to massacre ethnic Albanians in an effort to crush the KLA, the United States and its NATO allies mounted a bombing campaign that forced Milošević to stop. In the fall elections of 2000, Milošević himself was ousted from power, and he was later put on trial by an international tribunal for war crimes against humanity for his ethnic cleansing policies throughout Yugoslavia's disintegration. He died in 2006 during that trial.

The fate of Bosnia and Kosovo has not yet been finally determined. NATO troops remain in Bosnia, trying to keep the peace, while other NATO military forces maintain an uneasy peace in Kosovo.

The last political vestige of Yugoslavia ceased to exist in 2004 when the new national government officially renamed the truncated country Serbia and Montenegro. Two years later, Montenegrins voted in favor of independence. Thus, by 2006, all six republics cobbled together to form Yugoslavia in 1918 were once again independent nations.

The New Russia: From Empire to Nation

Soon after the disintegration of the Soviet Union in 1991, a new era began in Russia with the presidency of Boris Yeltsin. A new constitution created a two-chamber parliament and established a strong presidency. During the mid-1990s, Yeltsin was able to maintain a precarious grip on power while seeking to implement reforms that would set Russia on a firm course toward a pluralistic political system and a market economy. But the new post-Communist Russia remained as fragile as ever. Burgeoning economic inequality and rampant corruption aroused widespread criticism and shook the confidence of the Russian people in the superiority of the capitalist system over the one that existed under Communist rule.

A nagging war in the Caucasus—where the people of Chechnya resolutely sought national independence from Russia—drained the government budget and exposed the decrepit state of the once vaunted Red Army. In presidential elections held in 1996, Yeltsin was reelected, but his precarious health raised serious questions about the future of the country.

The Putin Era At the end of 1999, Yeltsin suddenly resigned his office and was replaced by Vladimir Putin (b. 1952), a former member of the KGB. Putin vowed to bring an end to the rampant corruption and inexperience that permeated Russian political culture and to strengthen the role of the central government in managing the affairs of state.

Putin also vowed to bring the breakaway state of Chechnya back under Russian authority and to assume a more assertive role in international affairs. The new president took advantage of growing public anger at Western plans to expand the NATO alliance into Eastern Europe to restore Russia's position as an influential force in the world.

Putin attempted to deal with the chronic problems in Russian society by centralizing his control over the system and by silencing critics—notably in the Russian media. Such moves aroused unease among many observers in the West. But there was widespread concern in Russia about the decline of the social order—marked by increases in alcoholism, sexual promiscuity, and criminal activities and the disintegration of the traditional family system—and many of Putin's compatriots supported his attempt to restore a sense of pride and discipline in Russian society.

Putin's popularity among the Russian people was also strengthened by Russia's growing prosperity at the beginning of the twenty-first century. During his presidency, Putin made significant economic reforms while rising oil prices strengthened the Russian economy, which grew dramatically until the 2008–2009 global economic crisis.

After serving two terms as president, Putin was unable to run for a third term because the Russian constitution mandates term limits. After the victory of his chosen successor, Dmitry Medvedev, in the 2008 presidential elections, however, Putin was appointed as prime minister, a position that enables him to continue to exercise considerable power.

The Unification of Europe

As we saw in Chapter 26, the divisions created by the Cold War led the nations of Western Europe to seek military security by forming NATO in 1949. The destructiveness of two world wars, however, caused many thoughtful Europeans to consider the need for some additional form of unity.

In 1957, France, West Germany, the Benelux countries (Belgium, the Netherlands, and Luxembourg), and Italy signed the Treaty of Rome, which created the European Economic Community (EEC). The EEC eliminated customs barriers for the six member nations and created a large free-trade area protected from the rest of the world by a common external tariff. All the member nations benefited economically. In 1973, Great Britain, Ireland, and Denmark gained membership in what now was called the European Community (EC). Greece joined in 1981, followed by Spain and Portugal in 1986. In 1995, Austria, Finland, and Sweden also became members of the EC.

The European Union The European Community was an economic union, not a political one. By 2000, the EC contained 370 million people and constituted the world's largest single trading entity, transacting one-fourth of the world's commerce. In the 1980s and 1990s, the EC moved toward even greater economic integration. The Treaty on European Union, which went into effect on January 1, 1994, turned the European Community into the European Union, a true economic and monetary union. One of its first goals was achieved in 1999 with the introduction of a common currency, the euro. On January 1, 2002, the euro officially replaced twelve national currencies; by 2010, it had been officially adopted by four additional nations.

In addition to having a single internal market and a common currency for those sixteen members, the EU has also established a common agricultural policy, which provides subsidies to farmers to enable them to sell their goods competitively on the world market. The end of national passports has given millions of Europeans greater flexibility in travel. The EU has been less successful in setting common foreign policy goals, primarily because individual nations still see foreign policy as a national priority and are reluctant to give up this power to a single overriding institution.

Toward a United Europe At the beginning of the twenty-first century, the EU established a new goal: to incorporate into the union the states of eastern and southeastern Europe. Many of these states were considerably poorer than the current members, which raised the possibility that adding these nations might weaken the EU itself. To lessen that danger, EU members established a set of qualifications requiring applicants to demonstrate their commitment both to market capitalism and to democracy and to exhibit respect for minorities and human

rights as well as for the rule of law. In May 2004, the EU took the plunge and added ten new members: Cyprus, the Czech Republic, Estonia, Hungary, Latvia, Lithuania, Malta, Poland, Slovakia, and Slovenia, thereby enlarging the population of the EU to 455 million people. In January 2007, the EU expanded again as Bulgaria and Romania joined the union (see Map 28.1).

Emergence of the Superpower: The United States

Q Focus Question: What political, social, and economic changes has the United States experienced since 1945?

At the end of World War II, the United States emerged as one of the world's two superpowers. As its Cold War confrontation with the Soviet Union intensified, the United States directed much of its energy toward combating the spread of communism throughout the world. With the collapse of the Soviet Union at the beginning of the 1990s, the United States became the world's foremost military power.

American Politics and Society Through the Vietnam Era

Franklin Roosevelt's New Deal of the 1930s initiated a basic transformation of American society that continued between 1945 and 1970. It included a dramatic increase in the role and power of the federal government, the rise of organized labor as a significant force in the economy and politics, a commitment to the welfare state, and a grudging acceptance of minority problems. The New Deal in American politics was bolstered by the election of Democratic presidents—Harry Truman in 1948, John F. Kennedy in 1960, and Lyndon B. Johnson in 1964. Even the election of a Republican president, Dwight D. Eisenhower, in 1952 and 1956 did not significantly alter the fundamental direction of the New Deal.

The economic boom after World War II fueled confidence in the American way of life. A shortage of consumer goods during the war left Americans with both surplus income and the desire to purchase these goods after the war. Then, too, the growing influence of organized labor enabled more and more workers to get the wage increases that spurred the growth of the domestic market. Between 1945 and 1973, real wages grew an average of 3 percent a year, the most prolonged advance in U.S. history.

Starting in the 1960s, however, problems that had been glossed over earlier came to the fore. The decade began on a youthful and optimistic note when John F. Kennedy

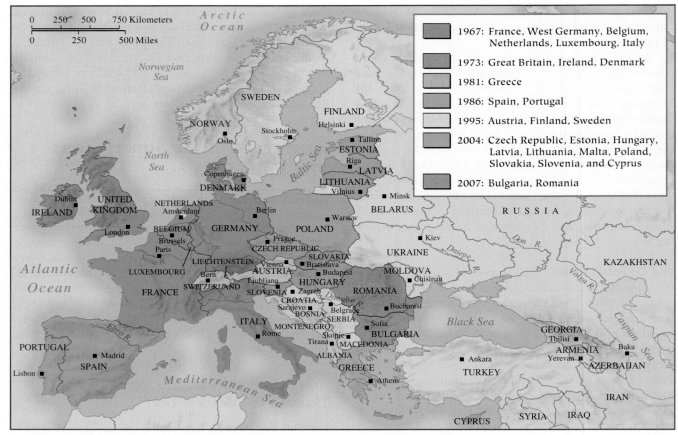

MAP 28.1 European Union, 2009. Beginning in 1957 as the European Economic Community, also known as the Common Market, the union of European states seeking to integrate their economies has gradually grown from six members to twenty-seven. By 2002, the European Union had achieved two major goals—the creation of a single internal market and a common currency—although it has been less successful at working toward common political and foreign policy goals.

Q What additional nations do you think will eventually join the European Union?

Legend in map:

- 1967: France, West Germany, Belgium, Netherlands, Luxembourg, Italy
- 1973: Great Britain, Ireland, Denmark
- 1981: Greece
- 1986: Spain, Portugal
- 1995: Austria, Finland, Sweden
- 2004: Czech Republic, Estonia, Hungary, Latvia, Lithuania, Malta, Poland, Slovakia, Slovenia, and Cyprus
- 2007: Bulgaria, Romania

(1917–1963), at age forty-three, became the youngest elected president in the history of the United States and the first born in the twentieth century. His own administration, cut short by an assassin's bullet on November 22, 1963, focused primarily on foreign affairs. Kennedy's successor, Lyndon B. Johnson (1908–1973), who won a new term as president in a landslide in 1964, used his stunning mandate to pursue the growth of the welfare state, first begun in the New Deal. Johnson's programs included health care for the elderly and the War on Poverty, to be fought with food stamps and the Job Corps.

Johnson's other domestic passion was achieving equal rights for black Americans. In August 1963, the eloquent Reverend Martin Luther King Jr. (1929–1968) led the March on Washington for Jobs and Freedom to dramatize blacks' desire for freedom. This march and King's

impassioned plea for racial equality had an electrifying effect on the American people. President Johnson pursued the cause of civil rights. As a result of his initiative, Congress enacted the Civil Rights Act of 1964, which created the machinery to end segregation and discrimination in the workplace and all public accommodations. The Voting Rights Act the following year eliminated obstacles to black participation in elections in southern states. But laws alone could not guarantee the Great Society that Johnson envisioned, and soon the administration faced bitter social unrest.

In the North and the West, blacks had had voting rights for many years, but local patterns of segregation resulted in considerably higher unemployment rates for blacks (and Hispanics) than for whites and left blacks segregated in huge urban ghettos. In the summer of 1965, race riots erupted in the Watts district of Los Angeles that led to thirty-four deaths and the destruction of over one thousand buildings. After King was assassinated in 1968, more than one hundred cities erupted in rioting, including Washington, D.C., the nation's capital. The riots led to a "white backlash" and a severe racial division of America.

Antiwar protests also divided the American people after President Johnson committed American troops to a costly war in Vietnam (see Chapter 26). The killing of four student protesters at Kent State University in 1970 by the Ohio National Guard shocked both activists and ordinary Americans, and thereafter the vehemence of the antiwar movement began to subside. But the combination of antiwar demonstrations and riots in the cities caused many people to call for "law and order," an appeal used by Richard Nixon (1913–1994), the Republican presidential candidate in 1968. With Nixon's election in 1968, a shift to the right in American politics had begun.

The Shift Rightward After 1973

Nixon eventually ended American involvement in Vietnam by gradually withdrawing American troops. Politically, he pursued a "southern strategy," carefully calculating that "law and order" issues would appeal to southern whites. The Republican strategy, however, also gained support among white Democrats in northern cities, where court-mandated busing to achieve racial integration had provoked a white backlash.

As president, Nixon was paranoid about conspiracies and resorted to subversive methods of gaining political intelligence on his political opponents. Nixon's zeal led to the Watergate scandal—a botched attempt to bug the Democratic National Headquarters and the ensuing cover-up. Although Nixon repeatedly denied involvement in the affair, secret tapes he made of his own conversations in the White House revealed otherwise. On August 9, 1974, Nixon resigned in disgrace, an act that saved him from almost certain impeachment and conviction.

After Watergate, American domestic politics focused on economic issues. Gerald Ford (1913–2006) became president when Nixon resigned, only to lose in the 1976 election to the former governor of Georgia, Jimmy Carter (b. 1924). By 1980, the Carter administration faced two devastating problems. High inflation and a decline in average weekly earnings were causing a perceptible drop in American living standards. At the same time, a crisis abroad had erupted when fifty-three Americans were taken hostage by the Iranian government of Ayatollah Khomeini and held for nearly fifteen months (see Chapter 29). Carter's inability to gain the release of the American hostages led to perceptions at home that he was a weak president. His overwhelming loss to Ronald Reagan (1911–2004) in

the election of 1980 brought forward the chief exponent of right-wing Republican policies.

The Reagan Revolution, as it has been called, sent U.S. policy in a number of new directions. Reversing decades of changes, Reagan cut back on the welfare state by decreasing spending on food stamps, school lunch programs, and job programs. At the same time, his administration fostered the largest peacetime military buildup in American history. Total federal spending rose from $631 billion in 1981 to more than $1 trillion by 1986. The administration's spending policies produced record government deficits, which loomed as an obstacle to long-term growth. In the 1970s, the total national debt was $420 billion; under Reagan it reached three times that amount.

The inability of Reagan's successor, George H. W. Bush (b. 1924), to deal with the deficit problem, coupled with an economic downturn, led to the election of a Democrat, Bill Clinton (b. 1946), in November 1992. The new president was a southerner who claimed to be a new Democrat—one who favored a number of the Republican policies of the 1980s. This was a clear indication that the rightward drift in American politics was by no means ended by this Democratic victory.

President Clinton's political fortunes were aided considerably by a lengthy economic revival. A steady reduction in the annual government budget deficit strengthened confidence in the performance of the national economy. Much of Clinton's second term, however, was overshadowed by charges of misconduct stemming from the president's affair with a White House intern. After a bitter partisan struggle, the U.S. Senate acquitted the president on two articles of impeachment brought by the House of Representatives. But Clinton's problems helped the Republican candidate, George W. Bush (b. 1946), to win the presidential election in 2000.

The first four years of Bush's administration were largely occupied with the war on terrorism and the U.S.-led war on Iraq (see Chapter 29). The Department of Homeland Security was established after the 2001 terrorist assaults to help protect the country from future terrorist acts. At the same time, Bush pushed tax cuts through Congress that mainly favored the wealthy and helped produce record deficits reminiscent of the Reagan years. Environmentalists were especially disturbed by the Bush administration's efforts to weaken environmental laws and regulations to benefit American corporations. During his second term, Bush's popularity plummeted drastically as discontent grew over the Iraq War, financial corruption in the Republican Party, and the administration's poor handling of relief efforts after Hurricane Katrina. The many failures of the Bush administration led to the lowest approval ratings for a modern president and opened the door for a dramatic change in American politics.

A new and often inspiring voice—that of Barack Obama (b. 1961)—who campaigned on a platform of change "we can believe in" and ending the war in Iraq led to an overwhelming Democratic victory in the elections of 2008. The dramatic collapse of the American financial system in the fall of 2008 also favored the Democrats. Obama moved quickly at the beginning of 2009 to deal with the economic recession that some called the worst since the Great Depression. At the same time, Obama emphasized the need to deal quickly with the health care crisis, global warming, the decline in the educational system, and failed economic policies.

The Development of Canada

Q Focus Question: What political, social, and economic developments has Canada experienced since 1945?

For twenty-five years after World War II, Canada realized extraordinary economic prosperity as it set out on a new path of industrial development, including electronic, aircraft, nuclear, and chemical engineering industries. Much of the Canadian growth, however, was financed by capital from the United States, which resulted in American ownership of Canadian businesses. While many Canadians welcomed the economic growth, others feared American economic domination of Canada.

After 1945, the Liberal Party continued to dominate Canadian politics. Under Lester Pearson (1897–1972), the Liberals created Canada's welfare state by enacting a national social security system (the Canada Pension Plan) and a national health insurance program. The most prominent Liberal government, however, was that of Pierre Trudeau (1919–2000), who came to power in 1968.

Trudeau's government pushed a vigorous program of industrialization, but inflation and Trudeau's efforts to impose the will of the federal government on the powerful provincial governments alienated voters and weakened his government. Economic recession in the early 1980s brought Brian Mulroney (b. 1939), leader of the Progressive Conservative Party, to power in 1984. Mulroney's government sought greater privatization of Canada's state-run corporations and negotiated a free-trade agreement with the United States. Bitterly resented by many Canadians, the agreement cost Mulroney's government much of its popularity. In 1993, the ruling Conservatives were overwhelmingly defeated, and the Liberal leader, Jean Chrétien (b. 1934), became prime minister. Chrétien's conservative fiscal policies, combined with strong economic growth, enabled his government to have a budgetary surplus by the late 1990s and led to another Liberal victory in the elections of 1997. Charges of widespread financial corruption

in the government, however, led to a Conservative victory early in 2006, and Stephen Harper (b. 1959) became the new prime minister.

Latin America Since 1945

Q Focus Question: What problems have the nations of Latin America faced since 1945, and what role has Marxist ideology played in their efforts to solve these problems?

The Great Depression of the 1930s had led to political instability in many Latin American countries that resulted in military coups and militaristic regimes (see Chapter 24). But the depression also provided the impetus for Latin America to move from a traditional to a modern economic structure. Since the nineteenth century, Latin Americans had exported raw materials, especially minerals and foodstuffs, while buying the manufactured goods of the industrialized countries in Europe and the United States. As a result of the depression, however, exports were cut in half, and the revenues available to buy manufactured goods declined. This encouraged many Latin American countries to develop industries to produce goods that were formerly imported. Due to a shortage of capital in the private sector, governments often invested in the new industries, thus leading, for example, to government-run steel industries in Chile and Brazil and oil industries in Argentina and Mexico.

By the 1960s, however, Latin American countries still found themselves dependent on the United States, Europe, and now Japan, especially for the advanced technology needed for modern industries. Because of the great poverty in many Latin American countries, domestic markets were limited in size, and many Latin American countries often failed to find markets abroad for their products. These failures led to instability and a new reliance on military regimes, especially to curb the power of the new industrial middle class and working classes, which had increased in size and power as a result of industrialization. In the 1960s, repressive military regimes in Chile, Brazil, and Argentina abolished political parties and often returned to export-import economies financed by foreigners.

In the 1970s, Latin American regimes grew even more dependent on borrowing from abroad, especially from banks in Europe and the United States, to maintain their failing economies. Between 1970 and 1982, debt to foreigners increased from $27 billion to $315.3 billion. By 1982, a number of governments announced that they could no longer pay interest on their debts to foreign banks, and their economies began to crumble.

In the 1980s, the debt crisis was paralleled by a movement toward democracy. Many people realized that military power without popular consent was incapable of providing a strong state. Then, too, there was a swelling of popular support for basic rights and free and fair elections. By the 1980s and early 1990s, democratic regimes were in place everywhere except Cuba, some of the Central American states, Chile, and Paraguay. At the end of the twentieth century and beginning of the twenty-first, a noticeable political trend in Latin America has been the election of left-wing governments, evident in the election of Hugo Chávez (b. 1954) in Venezuela in 1998, Luiz Inácio Lula de Silva (b. 1945) in Brazil in 2002, Michelle Bachelet (b. 1951) in Chile in 2006, and Daniel Ortega (b. 1945) in Nicaragua in 2007.

South America

The United States has also played an important role in Latin America since 1945. As mentioned earlier, beginning in the 1920s, the United States replaced Britain as the foremost investor in Latin America. Unlike the British, however, American investors put funds directly into production enterprises, with the result that large segments of Latin America's export industries fell into American hands. The American-owned United Fruit Company turned a number of Central American nations into "banana republics," while American companies gained control of the copper-mining industry in Chile and Peru and the oil industry in Mexico, Peru, and Bolivia. The control of these industries by American investors reinforced a growing nationalist consciousness against America as a neo-imperialist power.

But the United States also tried to pursue a new relationship with Latin America. In 1948, the nations of the Western Hemisphere formed the Organization of American States (OAS), which was intended to eliminate unilateral interference by one state in the internal or external affairs of any other state. But as the Cold War between the United States and the Soviet Union intensified, American policy makers grew anxious about the possibility of Communist regimes arising in Central America and the Caribbean and returned to a policy of unilateral action when they believed that Soviet agents were attempting to establish Communist governments. Especially after the success of Castro in Cuba (see the next section), the desire of the United States to prevent "another Cuba" largely determined American policy toward Latin America until the end of the Cold War in

the 1990s. The United States provided massive military aid to anti-Communist regimes, regardless of their nature.

The Threat of Marxist Revolutions: The Example of Cuba

Since 1934, Cuba had been ruled by a dictatorship, headed by Fulgencio Batista (1901–1973) and closely tied economically to American investors. During the early 1950s, a strong opposition movement to Batista's government developed, led by Fidel Castro (b. 1926). Castro maintained that only armed force could overthrow Batista, but when their initial assaults on Batista's regime met with little success, Castro's forces, based in the Sierra Maestra, went over to guerrilla warfare (see the box on p. 708). As the rebels gained more support, Batista's regime responded with such brutality that he alienated his own supporters. The dictator fled in December 1958, and Castro's revolutionaries seized Havana on January 1, 1959.

Relations between Cuba and the United States quickly deteriorated early in 1960 when the Soviet Union agreed to buy Cuban sugar and provide $100 million in credits. In October 1960, the United States imposed a trade embargo on Cuba, thus driving Castro closer to the Soviet Union.

On January 3, 1961, the United States broke diplomatic relations with Cuba. The new American president, John F. Kennedy, supported a coup attempt against Castro's government, but the landing of fourteen hundred CIA-assisted Cuban exiles in Cuba at the Bay of Pigs on April 17, 1961, turned into a total military disaster. The Soviets were now encouraged to make an even greater commitment to Cuban independence by installing nuclear missiles in the country, an act that led to a showdown with the United States (see Chapter 26 on the Cuban Missile Crisis). As its part of the bargain to defuse the crisis, the United States agreed not to invade Cuba.

In Cuba, Castro's socialist revolution proceeded, with mixed results. The Cuban revolution did secure some social gains for its people, especially in health care and education. The regime provided free medical services for all citizens, and the population's health improved noticeably. Illiteracy was wiped out by developing new schools and establishing teacher-training institutes that tripled the number of teachers within ten years.

CASTRO'S REVOLUTIONARY IDEALS

POLITICS & GOVERNMENT On July 26, 1953, Fidel Castro and a small group of supporters launched an ill-fated attack on the Moncada Barracks in Santiago de Cuba. Castro was arrested and put on trial. This excerpt is taken from the speech he presented in his defense, in which he discussed the goals of the revolutionaries.

Fidel Castro, "History Will Absolve Me"

I stated that the second consideration on which we based our chances for success was one of social order because we were assured of the people's support. When we speak of the people we do not mean the comfortable ones, the conservative elements of the nation, who welcome any regime of oppression, any dictatorship, and despotism, prostrating themselves before the master of the moment until they grind their foreheads into the ground. When we speak of struggle, the people means the vast unredeemed masses, to whom all make promises and whom all deceive; we mean the people who yearn for a better, more dignified, and more just nation. . . .

In the brief of this cause there must be recorded the five revolutionary laws that would have been proclaimed immediately after the capture of the Moncada barracks and would have been broadcast to the nation by radio. . . .

The First Revolutionary Law would have returned power to the people and proclaimed the Constitution of 1940 the supreme Law of the land, until such time as the people should decide to modify or change it. . . .

The Second Revolutionary Law would have granted property, not mortgageable and not transferable, to all planters, subplanters, lessees, partners, and squatters who hold parcels of five or less *caballerias* [tracts of land, about 33 acres] of land, and the state would indemnify the former owners on the basis of the rental which they would have received for these parcels over a period of ten years.

The Third Revolutionary Law would have granted workers and employees the right to share 30 percent of the profits of all the large industrial, mercantile, and mining enterprises, including the sugar mills. . . .

The Fourth Revolutionary Law would have granted all planters the right to share 55 percent of the sugar production and a minimum quota of forty thousand *arrobas* [25 pounds] for all small planters who have been established for three or more years.

The Fifth Revolutionay Law would have ordered the confiscation of all holdings and ill-gotten gains of those who had committed frauds during previous regimes, as well as the holdings and ill-gotten gains of all their legatees and heirs.

Q *What did Fidel Castro intend to accomplish by his revolution in Cuba? On whose behalf did he fight this revolution?*

Eschewing rapid industrialization, Castro encouraged agricultural diversification. But the Cuban economy continued to rely on the production and sale of sugar. Economic problems forced Castro's regime to depend on Soviet subsidies and the purchase of Cuban sugar by Soviet bloc countries. After the collapse of these Communist regimes in 1989, Cuba lost their support. Although economic conditions continued to decline, Fidel Castro remained in power until 2008 when illness forced him to resign the presidency; his brother, Raúl Castro (b. 1931), succeeded him.

Nationalism and the Military: The Example of Argentina

The military became the power brokers of many twentieth-century Latin American nations. Fearful of the forces unleashed by the development of industry, the military intervened in Argentinean politics in 1930 and propped up the cattle and wheat oligarchy that had controlled the reins of power since the beginning of the twentieth century. An organization of restless military officers overthrew the civilian oligarchy in June 1943. But the new military regime was unsure about how to deal with the working classes. One member, Juan Perón (1895–1974), used his position as labor secretary in the military government to curry favor with the workers. In 1944, Perón became vice president of the military government and made sure that people knew he was responsible for social welfare measures. But as Perón grew more popular, other army officers grew fearful of his power and arrested him. An uprising by workers forced the officers to back down, and in 1946, Perón was elected president.

Perón pursued a policy of increased industrialization in order to please his chief supporters—labor and the urban middle class. At the same time, he sought to free Argentina from foreign investors. The government bought the railways; took over the banking, insurance, shipping, and communications industries; and assumed regulation of imports and exports. But Perón's regime was also authoritarian. His wife, Eva Perón, founded women's organizations to support the government while Perón organized fascist gangs, modeled after Hitler's Brown Shirts, who used violence to intimidate his opponents. But growing corruption in Perón's government and the alienation of more and more people by the regime's excesses encouraged the military to overthrow him in September 1955. Perón went into exile in Spain.

Juan and Eva Perón. Elected president of Argentina in 1946, Juan Perón soon established an authoritarian regime that nationalized some of Argentina's basic industries and organized fascist gangs to overwhelm its opponents. He is shown here with his wife, Eva, during the inauguration ceremonies initiating his second term as president in 1952.

Overwhelmed by problems, however, military leaders decided to allow Perón to come back from exile in Spain. Reelected as president in September 1973, Perón died one year later. In 1976, the military installed a new regime and used the occasion to kill more than six thousand leftists. But economic problems persisted, and the regime tried to divert people's attention by invading the Falkland Islands in April 1982. Great Britain, which had controlled the islands since the nineteenth century, decisively defeated the Argentinean forces. The loss discredited the military and opened the door to civilian rule. In 1983, Raúl Alfonsín (1927–2009) was elected president and sought to reestablish democratic practices. In elections in 1989, the Peronist Carlos Saúl Menem (b. 1930) won. This peaceful transfer of power gave hope that Argentina was moving on a democratic path. Despite problems of foreign debt and inflation, the government of President Néstor Kirchner (b. 1950) witnessed economic growth after he took office in 2003. He was succeeded in 2007 by his wife, Cristina Fernández (b. 1953), who became the first elected female president of Argentina.

The Mexican Way

During the 1950s and 1960s, Mexico's ruling party (known as the Institutional Revolutionary Party, or PRI) focused on a balanced program of industrial policy. Fifteen years of steady economic growth combined with low inflation and real gains in wages for more and more people made those years seem a golden age in Mexico's economic development. At the end of the 1960s, students began to protest Mexico's one-party system. On October 2, 1968, a demonstration of university students in Tlatelolco Square in Mexico City was met by police, who opened fire, killing hundreds of students. Leaders of the PRI became concerned about the need for change in the system.

During the 1970s, the next two presidents, Luis Echeverría (b. 1922) and José López Portillo (1920–2004), introduced political reforms. Rules for the registration of political parties were eased, thus making their growth more likely, and greater freedom of debate in the press and at universities was allowed. But economic problems continued to trouble Mexico. In the late 1970s, vast new reserves of oil were discovered in Mexico, making the government even more dependent on oil revenues. When world oil prices dropped in the mid-1980s, Mexico was no longer able to make payments on its foreign debt, which had reached $80 billion in 1982.

The debt crisis and rising unemployment increased dissatisfaction with the government, which was especially evident in the 1988 election, when the PRI's choice for president, Carlos Salinas (b. 1948), who would be expected to win in a landslide, won by only a 50.3 percent majority. Increasing dissatisfaction with the government's economic policies finally led to the unthinkable: in 2000, Vicente Fox (b. 1942) defeated the PRI candidate for the presidency. Despite high hopes, Fox's adminstration failed to deal with police corruption and bureaucratic inefficiency in the government. His successor, Felipe Calderón (b. 1963), made immigration reform a major priority, although with little success. His attempt to wage a massive war on Mexico's drug cartels has led to an ongoing conflict.

Society and Culture in the Western World

Q Focus Question: What major social, cultural, and intellectual developments have occurred in Western Europe and North America since 1945?

Socially, culturally, and intellectually, the Western world since 1945 has been marked by much diversity.

The Emergence of a New Society

During the postwar era, such products of new technologies as computers, television, jet planes, contraceptive devices, and new surgical techniques all dramatically altered the nature of human life. The rapid changes in postwar society were fueled by scientific advances and rapid economic growth. Called a technocratic society by some observers and the **consumer society** by others, postwar Western society was marked by a fluid social structure and new movements for change.

Especially noticeable in European society after 1945 were the changes in the middle class. Such traditional middle-class groups as businesspeople and professionals in law, medicine, and the universities were greatly augmented by a new group of managers and technicians as large companies and government agencies employed increasing numbers of white-collar supervisory and administrative personnel.

Changes also occurred among the traditional lower classes. Especially notable was the dramatic shift of people from rural to urban areas. The number of people in agriculture declined drastically. But the size of the industrial working class did not expand. In West Germany, industrial workers made up 48 percent of the labor force throughout the 1950s and 1960s. Thereafter the number of industrial workers began to dwindle as the number of white-collar service employees increased. At the same time, a substantial increase in real wages enabled the working classes to aspire to the consumption patterns of the middle class. Buying on the installment plan became widespread in the 1950s and gave workers a chance to imitate the middle class by buying such products as televisions, washing machines, refrigerators, vacuum cleaners, record players, and automobiles.

Rising incomes, combined with shorter working hours, created an even greater market for mass leisure activities. Between 1900 and 1980, the workweek was reduced from sixty hours to around forty hours, and the number of paid holidays increased. All aspects of popular culture—music, sports, media—became commercialized and opened opportunities for leisure activities.

Social change was also evident in both educational patterns and student attitudes. Before World War II, higher education had largely remained the preserve of Europe's wealthier classes. After the war, European states began to foster greater equality of opportunity in higher education by eliminating fees, and universities experienced an influx of students from the middle and lower classes. Enrollments grew dramatically; in France, 4.5 percent of young people went to a university in 1950. By 1965, the figure had increased to 14.5 percent.

But there were problems. Overcrowded classrooms, professors who paid little attention to students, administrators who acted in an authoritarian fashion, and an education that to many seemed irrelevant to the realities of the modern age led to an outburst of student revolts in the late 1960s. In part, these were an extension of the anti–Vietnam War protests in American universities in the mid-1960s. Perhaps the most famous student revolt occurred in France in 1968. It erupted at the University of Nanterre outside Paris but soon spread to the Sorbonne, the main campus of the University of Paris. French students demanded a greater voice in the administration of the university, took over buildings, and then expanded the scale of their protests by inviting workers to support them. Half of France's workforce went on strike in May 1968. After the Gaullist government instituted a hefty wage hike, the workers returned to work and the police repressed the remaining student protesters.

There were several reasons for the student radicalism. Some students were genuinely motivated by the desire to reform the university. Others were protesting the Vietnam War, which they viewed as a product of Western imperialism. They also attacked other aspects of Western society, such as its materialism, and expressed concern about becoming cogs in the large and impersonal bureaucratic mechanisms of the modern world.

The Permissive Society

Some critics referred to the new society of postwar Europe as the **permissive society.** Sweden took the lead in the propagation of the so-called sexual revolution of the 1960s, and the rest of Europe and the United States soon followed. Sex education in the schools and the decriminalization of homosexuality were but two aspects of Sweden's liberal approach. The introduction of the birth control pill, which became widely available by the mid-1960s, gave people more freedom in sexual behavior. Meanwhile, sexually explicit movies, plays, and books broke new ground in the treatment of once-hidden subjects.

The new standards were evident in the breakdown of the traditional family. Divorce rates increased dramatically, especially in the 1960s, while premarital and extramarital sexual experiences also rose substantially. A survey in the Netherlands in 1968 revealed that 78 percent of men and 86 percent of women had participated in extramarital sex.

The 1960s also saw the emergence of the drug culture. Marijuana, though illegal, was widely used by college and university students. For young people more interested in higher levels of consciousness, Timothy Leary, who had done research at Harvard on the psychedelic (perception-altering) effects of lysergic acid diethylamide (LSD), became the high priest of hallucinogenic experiences.

© Henry Diltz/CORBIS

The "Love-In." In the 1960s, a number of outdoor public festivals for young people combined music, drugs, and sex. Flamboyant dress, face painting, free-form dancing, and drugs were vital ingredients in creating an atmosphere dedicated to "love and peace." Shown here are "hippies" dancing around a decorated bus at a "love-in" during 1967's Summer of Love.

The trend toward smaller families contributed to changes in women's employment in both Europe and the United States, primarily because women now needed to devote far fewer years to rearing children. That led to a large increase in the number of married women in the workforce. At the beginning of the twentieth century, even working-class wives tended to stay at home if they could afford to do so. In the postwar period, this was no longer the case. In the United States, for example, in 1900, married women made up about 15 percent of the female labor force; by 1970, their number had increased to 62 percent.

But the increased number of women in the workforce did not change some old patterns. Working-class women in particular still earned salaries lower than those of men for equal work. In the 1960s, women earned only 60 percent of men's wages in Britain, 50 percent in France, and 63 percent in West Germany. In addition, women still tended to enter traditionally female jobs. Many European women also still faced the double burden of earning income on the one hand and raising a family and maintaining the household on the other. Such inequalities led increasing numbers of women to rebel.

New attitudes toward sex and the use of drugs were only two manifestations of a growing youth movement in the 1960s that questioned authority and fostered rebellion against the older generation. Spurred on by opposition to the Vietnam War and a growing political consciousness, the youth rebellion became a youth protest movement by the second half of the 1960s (see the box on p. 712).

Women in the Postwar World

Despite their enormous contributions to the war effort, women at the end of World War II were removed from the workforce so that there would be jobs for the soldiers returning home. After the horrors of war, people seemed willing for a while to return to traditional family practices. Female participation in the workforce declined, and birthrates began to rise, creating a "baby boom." This increase in the birthrate, however, did not last, and the size of families began to decline by the mid-1960s. Largely responsible for this decline was the widespread practice of birth control. The condom, invented in the nineteenth century, was already in wide use, but the development in the 1960s of oral contraceptives, known as birth control pills or simply "the pill," provided a convenient and reliable means of birth control that quickly spread to all Western countries.

The Feminist Movement: The Search for Liberation

Women's wartime participation helped them achieve one of the major aims of the nineteenth-century feminist movement—the right to vote. After World War I, many governments acknowledged the contributions of women to the war effort by granting them suffrage. Sweden, Great Britain, Germany, Poland, Hungary, Austria, and Czechoslovakia did so in 1918, followed by the United States in 1920. Women in France and Italy did not obtain the right to vote until 1945. After World War II, little was heard of feminist concerns, but by the 1960s, women began to assert their rights again and speak as feminists. Along with the student upheavals of the late 1960s came renewed interest in **feminism,** or the **women's liberation movement,** as it was now called.

Of great importance to the emergence of the postwar women's liberation movement was the work of Simone de

"THE TIMES THEY ARE A-CHANGIN'": THE MUSIC OF YOUTHFUL PROTEST

In the 1960s, the lyrics of rock music reflected the rebellious mood of many young people. Bob Dylan (b. 1941), who became a vastly influential performer and recording artist, expressed the feelings of the younger generation. His song "The Times They Are a-Changin'," released in 1964, has been called an "anthem for the protest movement."

Bob Dylan, "The Times They Are a-Changin'"

Come gather 'round people
Wherever you roam
And admit that the waters
Around you have grown
And accept it that soon
You'll be drenched to the bone
If your time to you
Is worth savin'
Then you better start swimmin'
Or you'll sink like a stone
For the times they are a-changin'

Come writers and critics
Who prophesize with your pen
And keep your eyes wide
The chance won't come again
And don't speak too soon
For the wheel's still in spin
And there's no tellin' who
That it's namin'
For the loser now
Will be later to win
For the times they are a-changin'

Come senators, congressmen
Please heed the call
Don't stand in the doorway

Don't block up the hall
For he that gets hurt
Will be he who has stalled
There's a battle outside
And it is ragin'
It'll soon shake your windows
And rattle your walls
For the times they are a-changin'

Come mothers and fathers
Throughout the land
And don't criticize
What you can't understand
Your sons and your daughters
Are beyond your command
Your old road
Is rapidly agin'
Please get out of the new one
If you can't lend your hand
For the times they are a-changin'

The line it is drawn
The curse it is cast
The slow one now
Will later be fast
As the present now
Will later be past
The order is
Rapidly fadin'
And the first one now
Will later be last
For the times they are a-changin'

Q *What caused the student campus revolts of the 1960s? What and whom does Dylan identify as the problem in this song?*

Beauvoir (1908–1986), who supported herself as a teacher and later as a novelist and writer. De Beauvoir believed that she lived a "liberated" life for a twentieth-century European woman, but for all her freedom, she still came to perceive that as a woman, she faced limits that men did not. In 1949, she published her highly influential work *The Second Sex,* in which she argued that as a result of male-dominated societies, women had been defined by their differences from men and consequently received second-class status: "What particularly signalizes the situation of woman is that she—a free autonomous being like all human creatures—nevertheless finds herself in a world where men compel her to assume the status of the Other."[2] De Beauvoir took an active role in the French women's movement of the 1970s, and her book was a major influence on both sides of the Atlantic.

Transformation in Women's Lives To ensure natural replacement of a country's population, women need to produce an average of 2.1 children each. Many European countries fall far short of this mark; their populations stopped growing in the 1960s, and the trend has continued ever since. By the 1990s, among the nations of the European Union, the average number of children per mother was 1.4. Spain's rate, 1.15 in 2002, was among the lowest in the world.

At the same time, the number of women in the workforce has continued to rise. In Britain, for example, women accounted for 32 percent of the labor force in 1970 but 44 percent in 1990. Moreover, women have entered new employment areas. Greater access to universities and professional schools has enabled women to take jobs in law, medicine, government, business, and education. In the Soviet Union, for example, about 70 percent of doctors and teachers were women. Nevertheless, economic inequality still often prevails; women receive lower wages than men for comparable work and receive fewer promotions to management positions.

Feminists in the women's liberation movement came to believe that women themselves must transform the fundamental conditions of their lives. Women sought and gained a measure of control over their own bodies by seeking to legalize both contraception and abortion. In the 1960s and 1970s, hundreds of thousands of European women worked to repeal laws that outlawed contraception and abortion and began to meet with success. Even in Catholic countries, where the church remained opposed to abortion, legislation allowing contraception and abortion was passed in the 1970s and 1980s.

As more women have become activists, they have also become involved in new issues. Some women began to try to affect the political environment by allying with the anti-nuclear movement. In 1981, a group of women protested American nuclear missiles in Britain by chaining themselves to the fence of an American military base. Thousands more joined in creating a peace camp around the military compound. Enthusiasm ran high; one participant said, "I'll never forget that feeling; it'll live with me for ever. . . . As we walked round, and we clasped hands. . . . It was for women; it was for peace; it was for the world."[3]

Women in the West have also reached out to work with women from the rest of the world in international conferences to change the conditions of their lives. Between 1975 and 1995, the United Nations held conferences on women's issues in Mexico City, Copenhagen, Nairobi, and Beijing. These meetings made clear the differences between women from Western and non-Western countries. Whereas women from Western countries spoke about political, economic, cultural, and sexual rights, women from developing countries in Latin America, Africa, and Asia focused their attention on bringing an end to the violence, hunger, and disease that haunt their lives.

The Growth of Terrorism

Acts of terror by individuals and groups opposed to governments became a frightening aspect of modern Western society. During the late 1970s and early 1980s, small bands of terrorists used assassination, indiscriminate killing of civilians, the taking of hostages, and the hijacking of airplanes to draw attention to their demands or to destabilize governments in the hope of achieving their political goals. Terrorist acts garnered considerable media attention.

Motivations for terrorist acts varied considerably. Left- and right-wing terrorist groups flourished in the late 1970s and early 1980s, but terrorist acts also stemmed from militant nationalists who wished to create separatist states. Most prominent was the Irish Republican Army (IRA), which resorted to vicious attacks against the ruling government and innocent civilians in Northern Ireland.

Although left- and right-wing terrorist activities declined in Europe in the 1980s, international terrorism continued. Angered over the loss of their territory to Israel, some militant Palestinians responded with a policy of terrorist attacks against Israel's supporters. Palestinian terrorists operated throughout European countries, attacking both Europeans and American tourists; Palestinian terrorists massacred vacationers at airports in Rome and Vienna in 1985. State-sponsored terrorism was often an integral part of international terrorism. Militant governments, especially in Iran, Libya, and Syria, assisted terrorist organizations that carried out attacks on Europeans and Americans. On December 21, 1988, Pan American flight 103 from Frankfurt to New York exploded over Lockerbie, Scotland, killing all 259 passengers and crew members. A massive investigation finally revealed that the bomb responsible for the explosion had been planted by two Libyan terrorists.

Terrorist Attack on the United States One of the most destructive acts of terrorism occurred on September 11, 2001, in the United States. Four groups of terrorists hijacked four commercial jet airplanes after takeoff from Boston, Newark, and Washington, D.C. The hijackers flew two of the airplanes directly into the towers of the World Trade Center in New York City, causing these buildings, as well as a number of surrounding buildings, to collapse. A third hijacked plane slammed into the Pentagon near Washington, D.C. The fourth plane, apparently headed for Washington, crashed instead in an isolated area of Pennsylvania. In total, more than three thousand people were killed, including everyone aboard the four airliners.

These coordinated acts of terror were carried out by hijackers connected to the international terrorist organization known as al-Qaeda (see the comparative illustration on p. 714), run by the mysterious Osama bin Laden. A native of Saudi Arabia of Yemeni extraction, bin Laden used an inherited fortune to set up terrorist training

AP Images/Carmen Taylor

AP Images

**POLITICS &
GOVERNMENT**

COMPARATIVE ILLUSTRATION

International Terrorism. The first decade of the twenty-first century has seen a
number of acts of international terrorism. At the left is a picture of a hijacked
U.S. airliner about to hit one of the twin towers of the World Trade Center in
New York City while smoke billows from the site of the first such attack on September 11,
2001. This devastating plot was carried out by the international terrorist group known as
al-Qaeda. At the right is a scene from another al-Qaeda attack, the bombing of two nightclubs
in Bali, a popular resort in Indonesia, on October 12, 2002. Almost two hundred people,
including Indonesians, Australians, Canadians, French, and Britons, were killed, and more
than one hundred others were injured.

camps in Afghanistan, under the protection of that nation's militant fundamentalist Islamic rulers known as the
Taliban.

U.S. president George W. Bush vowed to wage a
lengthy and thorough war on terrorism and worked to
create a coalition of nations to assist in ridding the world
of al-Qaeda and other terrorist groups. Within weeks of
the attack on America, U.S. and NATO air forces began
bombing Taliban-controlled command centers, airfields,
and al-Qaeda hiding places in Afghanistan. On the
ground, Afghan forces, assisted by U.S. special forces,
pushed the Taliban out and gained control of the country
by the end of November. A democratic multiethnic government was installed but continues to face problems
from revived Taliban activity (see Chapter 29).

The Environment and the Green Movements

Beginning in the 1970s, environmentalism became an
important item on the European political agenda. By that
time, serious ecological problems had become all too
apparent. Air pollution, produced by nitrogen oxide and
sulfur dioxide emissions from road vehicles, power plants,

and industrial factories, was causing respiratory illnesses
and having corrosive effects on buildings and monuments. Many rivers, lakes, and seas had become so polluted that they posed serious health risks. Dying forests
and disappearing wildlife alarmed more and more people.
The opening of Eastern Europe after the revolutions of
1989 brought to the world's attention the incredible environmental destruction of that region caused by unfettered industrial pollution.

Environmental concerns forced the major political
parties in Europe to advocate new regulations for the
protection of the environment. A disastrous accident at
the Soviet nuclear power plant at Chernobyl, Ukraine, in
1986 made Europeans even more aware of potential environmental hazards, and 1987 was touted as the "year of
the environment."

Growing ecological awareness also gave rise to Green
movements and Green parties throughout Europe in the
1970s. Most visible was the Green Party in Germany,
which was officially organized in 1979 and by 1987
had elected forty-two delegates to the West German
parliament. Green parties also competed successfully in
Sweden, Austria, and Switzerland.

Western Culture Since 1945

Intellectually and culturally, the Western world since World War II has been notable for innovation as well as diversity. Especially since 1970, new directions have led some observers to speak of a Postmodern cultural world.

Postwar Literature   The most significant new trend in postwar literature was known as the Theater of the Absurd. Its most famous proponent was the Irishman Samuel Beckett (1906–1990), who lived in France. In Beckett's *Waiting for Godot* (1952), the action on the stage is transparently unrealistic. Two men wait around for the appearance of someone, with whom they may or may not have an appointment. During the course of the play, nothing seems to be happening. The audience is never told if the action in front of them is real or imagined. Suspense is maintained not by having the audience wonder "What is going to happen next?" but simply "What is happening now?"

The Theater of the Absurd reflected its time. The postwar period was one of disillusionment with fixed ideological beliefs in politics or religion. The same disillusionment that underscored the bleak worldview of absurdist drama and literature also inspired the **existentialism** of writers Albert Camus (1913–1960) and Jean-Paul Sartre (1905–1980), with its sense of the world's meaninglessness. The beginning point of the existentialism of Sartre and Camus was the absence of God in the universe. Although the death of God was tragic, it also meant that humans had no preordained destiny and were utterly alone in the universe with no future and no hope. As Camus expressed it:

> A world that can be explained even with bad reasons is a familiar world. But, on the other hand, in a universe suddenly divested of illusions and lights, man feels an alien, a stranger. His exile is without remedy since he is deprived of the memory of a lost home or the hope of a promised land. This divorce between man and his life, the actor and his setting, is properly the feeling of absurdity.[4]

According to Camus, then, the world was absurd and without meaning; humans, too, are without meaning and purpose. Reduced to despair and depression, humans have but one source of hope—themselves.

Postmodernism   The term *Postmodern* covers a variety of intellectual and artistic styles and ways of thinking that have been prominent since the 1970s. In the broadest sense, **Postmodernism** rejects the modern Western belief in an objective truth and instead focuses on the relative nature of reality and knowledge.

While existentialists wrestled with notions of meaning and existence, a group of French philosophers in the 1960s attempted to understand how meaning and knowledge operate through the study of language and signs. **Poststructuralism** or **deconstruction,** formulated by Jacques Derrida (1930–2004), holds that culture is created and can therefore be analyzed in a variety of ways, according to the manner in which people create their own meaning. Hence there is no fixed truth or universal meaning.

Michel Foucault (1926–1984) drew on Derrida to explore relationships of power. Believing that "power is exercised, rather than possessed," Foucault argued that the diffusion of power and oppression marks all relationships. For example, any act of teaching entails components of assertion and submission, as the student adopts the ideas of the person in power. Therefore, all norms are culturally produced and entail some degree of power struggle.

Postmodernism was also evident in literature. One center of Postmodernism was in Central and Eastern Europe, especially in the work of Milan Kundera (b. 1929) of Czechoslovakia. Kundera blended fantasy with realism, using fantasy to examine moral issues while remaining optimistic about the human condition. Indeed, in his first novel, *The Unbearable Lightness of Being,* published in 1984, Kundera does not despair because of the political repression that he so aptly describes in his native Czechoslovakia but allows his characters to use love as a way to a better life. The human spirit can be lessened but not destroyed.

Trends in Art

Following the war, the United States dominated the art world, much as it did the world of popular culture. New York City replaced Paris as the artistic center of the West. The Guggenheim Museum, the Museum of Modern Art, and the Whitney Museum of Modern Art, together with New York's numerous art galleries, promoted modern art and helped determine artistic tastes throughout much of the world. One of the styles that became synonymous with the emergence of the New York art scene was **Abstract Expressionism.**

Dubbed "action painting" by one critic, Abstract Expressionism was energetic and spontaneous, qualities evident in the enormous canvases of Jackson Pollock (1912–1956). In such works as *Lavender Mist* (1950) paint seems to explode, enveloping the viewer with emotion and movement. Pollock's swirling forms and seemingly chaotic patterns broke all conventions of form and structure. His drip paintings, with their total abstraction, were extremely influential with other artists, and he eventually became a celebrity. Inspired by Native American sand painters, Pollock painted with the canvas on the floor. He explained, "On the floor I am more at ease.

Jackson Pollock at Work. One of the best-known practitioners of Abstract Expressionism, which remained at the center of the artistic mainstream after World War II, was the American Jackson Pollock, who achieved his ideal of total abstraction in his drip paintings. He is shown here at work at his Long Island studio. Pollock found it easier to cover his large canvases with exploding patterns of color when he put them on the floor.

I feel nearer, more a part of the painting, since this way I can walk around it, work from four sides and be literally in the painting. When I am in the painting, I am not aware of what I am doing. There is pure harmony."

Postmodernism's eclectic commingling of past tradition with Modernist innovation became increasingly evident in architecture. Robert Venturi argued that architects should look as much to the commercial strips of Las Vegas as to the historical styles of the past for inspiration. One example is provided by Charles Moore. His *Piazza d'Italia* (1976–1980) in New Orleans is an outdoor plaza that combines Classical Roman columns with stainless steel and neon lights. This blending of modern-day materials with historical references distinguished the Postmodern architecture of the late 1970s and 1980s from the Modernist glass box.

Throughout the 1980s and 1990s, the art and music industries increasingly adopted the techniques of marketing and advertising. With large sums of money invested in painters and musicians, pressure mounted to achieve critical and commercial success. Negotiating the distinction between art and popular culture was essential since many equated merit with sales or economic value.

In the art world, Neo-Expressionism reached its zenith in the mid-1980s. Neo-Expressionist artists like Anselm Kiefer became increasingly popular as the art market soared. Born in Germany in 1945, Kiefer combines aspects of Abstract Expressionism, collage, and German Expressionism to create works that are stark and haunting. His *Departure from Egypt* (1984) is a meditation on Jewish history and its descent into the horrors of Nazism. Kiefer hoped that a portrayal of Germany's atrocities could free Germans from their past and bring some good out of evil.

The World of Science and Technology

Many of the scientific and technological achievements since World War II have revolutionized people's lives. During World War II, university scientists were recruited to work for their governments and develop new weapons and practical instruments of war. British physicists played a crucial role in the development of an improved radar system that helped defeat the German air force in the Battle of Britain in 1940. German scientists created self-propelled rockets as well as jet airplanes to keep Hitler's hopes alive for a miraculous turnaround in the war. The computer, too, was a wartime creation. The British mathematician Alan Turing designed a primitive computer to assist British intelligence in breaking the secret codes of German ciphering machines. The most famous product of wartime scientific research was the atomic bomb, created by a team of American and European scientists under the guidance of the physicist J. Robert Oppenheimer. Although most wartime devices were created for destructive purposes, they could easily be adapted for peacetime uses.

The postwar alliance of science and technology led to an accelerated rate of change that became a fact of life in Western society (see the comparative essay "From the Industrial Age to the Technological Age" on p. 717). One product of this alliance—the computer—may yet prove to be the most revolutionary of all the technological inventions of the twentieth century. Early computers, which required thousands of vacuum tubes to function, were large and hot and took up considerable space. The development of the transistor and then the silicon chip

COMPARATIVE ESSAY
FROM THE INDUSTRIAL AGE TO THE TECHNOLOGICAL AGE

SCIENCE & TECHNOLOGY

As many observers have noted, a key aspect of the world economy is that it is in the process of transition to what has been called a "postindustrial age," characterized by a system that is not only increasingly global in scope but also increasingly technology-intensive in character. Since World War II, a stunning array of technological changes—especially in transportation, communications, space exploration, medicine, and agriculture—have transformed the world in which we live. Technological changes have also raised new questions and concerns as well as producing some unexpected results. Some scientists have worried that genetic engineering might accidentally result in new strains of deadly bacteria that cannot be controlled outside the laboratory. Some doctors have recently warned that the overuse of antibiotics has created supergerms that are resistant to antibiotic treatment. The Technological Revolution has also led to the development of more advanced methods of destruction. Most frightening have been nuclear weapons.

The transition to a technology-intensive postindustrial world, which the futurologist Alvin Toffler has dubbed the Third Wave (the first two being the Agricultural and Industrial Revolutions), has produced difficulties for people in many walks of life—for blue-collar workers, whose high wages price them out of the market as firms begin to move their factories abroad; for the poor and uneducated, who lack the technical skills to handle complex tasks in the contemporary economy; and

© Adastra/Getty Images

The Technological Age. A communication satellite is seen orbiting above the earth.

even for some members of the middle class, who have been fired or forced into retirement as their employers seek to reduce payrolls or outsource jobs to compete in the global marketplace.

It is now increasingly clear that the Technological Revolution, like the Industrial Revolution that preceded it, will entail enormous consequences and may ultimately give birth to a new era of social and political instability. The success of advanced capitalist states in the post–World War II era has been built on a broad consensus on the importance of two propositions: (1) the need for high levels of government investment in education, communications, and transportation as a means of meeting the challenges of continued economic growth and technological innovation and (2) the desirability of cooperative efforts in the international arena as a means of maintaining open markets for the free exchange of goods.

In the twenty-first century, these assumptions are increasingly under attack as citizens refuse to vote for the tax increases required to support education and oppose the formation of trading alliances to promote the free movement of goods and labor across national borders. The breakdown of the public consensus that brought modern capitalism to a pinnacle of achievement raises serious questions about the likelihood that the coming challenges of the Third Wave can be successfully met without a growing measure of political and social tension.

Q *What is implied by the term* Third Wave, *and what challenges does the Third Wave present to humanity?*

---

produced a revolutionary new approach to computer design. With the invention in 1971 of the microprocessor, a machine that combines the equivalent of thousands of transistors on a single, tiny silicon chip, the road was open for the development of the personal computer. By the 1990s, the personal computer had become a regular fixture in businesses, schools, and homes. The Internet—the world's largest computer network—provides people around the world with quick access to immense quantities of information, as well as rapid communication and commercial transactions. As of 2010, estimates are that more than a billion people worldwide are using the Internet.

Despite the marvels produced by science and technology, some people have come to question their underlying assumption—that scientific knowledge gives human beings the ability to manipulate the environment for their benefit. They maintain that some technological advances have far-reaching side effects that are damaging to the environment. Chemical fertilizers, for example, once touted for producing larger crops, have wreaked havoc with the ecological balance of streams, rivers, and woodlands. *Small Is Beautiful*, written by the British economist E. F. Schumacher (1911–1977), is a fundamental critique of the dangers of the new science and technology (see the box on p. 718).

SMALL IS BEAUTIFUL: THE LIMITS OF MODERN TECHNOLOGY

SCIENCE & TECHNOLOGY

Although science and technology have produced an amazing array of achievements in the postwar world, some voices have been raised in criticism of their sometimes destructive aspects. In 1975, in a book titled *Small Is Beautiful,* the British economist E. F. Schumacher examined the effects modern industrial technology has had on the earth's resources.

E. F. Schumacher, *Small Is Beautiful*

Is it not evident that our current methods of production are already eating into the very substance of industrial man? To many people this is not at all evident. Now that we have solved the problem of production, they say, have we ever had it so good? Are we not better fed, better clothed, and better housed than ever before—and better educated? Of course we are: most, but by no means all, of us: in the rich countries. But this is not what I mean by "substance." The substance of mankind cannot be measured by Gross National Product. Perhaps it cannot be measured at all, except for certain symptoms of loss. However, this is not the place to go into the statistics of these symptoms, such as crime, drug addiction, vandalism, mental breakdown, rebellion, and so forth. Statistics never prove anything.

I started by saying that one of the most fateful errors of our age is the belief that the problem of production has been solved. This illusion, I suggested, is mainly due to our inability to recognize that the modern industrial system, with all its intellectual sophistication, consumes the very basis on which it has been erected. To use the language of the economist, it lives on irreplaceable capital which it cheerfully treats as income. I specified three categories of such capital:

fossil fuels, the tolerance margins of nature, and the human substance. Even if some readers should refuse to accept all three parts of my argument, I suggest that any one of them suffices to make my case.

And what is my case? Simply that our most important task is to get off our present collision course. And who is there to tackle such a task? I think every one of us.... To talk about the future is useful only if it leads to action now. And what can we do now, while we are still in the position of "never having had it so good"? To say the least... we must thoroughly understand the problem and begin to see the possibility of evolving a new lifestyle, with new methods of production and new patterns of consumption: a lifestyle designed for permanence. To give only three preliminary examples: in agriculture and horticulture, we can interest ourselves in the perfection of production methods which are biologically sound, build up soil fertility, and produce health, beauty, and permanence. Productivity will then look after itself. In industry, we can interest ourselves in the evolution of small-scale technology, relatively nonviolent technology, "technology with a human face," so that people have a chance to enjoy themselves while they are working, instead of working solely for their pay packet and hoping, usually forlornly, for enjoyment solely during their leisure time.

Q *According to Schumacher, under what illusion are modern humans living? What three irreplaceable things does he suggest people are consuming without noticing? What is "technology with a human face"? How does the author suggest this might transform modern life? Are Schumacher's ideas Postmodern? Why or why not?*

The Explosion of Popular Culture

Popular culture since 1900, and especially since World War II, has played an important role in helping Western people define themselves. It also reflects the economic system that supports it, for this system manufactures, distributes, and sells the images that people consume as popular culture. Modern popular culture is therefore inextricably tied to the mass consumer society in which it has emerged.

The United States has been the most influential force in shaping popular culture in the West and, to a lesser degree, the entire world. Through movies, music, advertising, and television, the United States has spread its particular form of consumerism and the American dream to millions around the world. In 1923, the *New York Morning Post* noted that "the film is to America what the flag was once to Britain. By its means Uncle Sam may hope some day... to Americanize the world."[5] That day has already come.

Motion pictures were the primary vehicle for the diffusion of American popular culture in the years immediately following World War I and continued to find ever wider markets as the century rolled on. Television, developed in the 1930s, did not become readily available until the late 1940s, but by 1954, there were 32 million sets in the United States as television became the centerpiece of middle-class life. In the 1960s, as television spread around the world, American networks unloaded their products on Europe and the Third World at extraordinarily low prices.

The United States has also dominated popular music since the end of World War II. Jazz, blues, rhythm and blues, rap, and rock and roll have been by far the most popular music forms in the Western world—and much of the non-Western world—during this time. All of them originated in the United States, and all are rooted in African American musical innovations. These forms later spread to the rest of the world, inspiring local artists, who then transformed the music in their own ways.

The introduction of the video music channel MTV in the early 1980s radically changed the music scene by making image as important as sound in the selling of records. Artists like Michael Jackson and Madonna became superstars by treating the music video as an art form. Rather than merely a recorded performance, many videos were short films with elaborate staging and special effects set to music. The music of the 1980s was also affected by technological advances, especially the advent of the synthesizer, an electronic piano that produced computerized sounds.

In the postwar years, sports have become a major product of both popular culture and the leisure industry. The development of satellite television and various electronic breakthroughs have helped make sports a global phenomenon. Olympic Games can now be broadcast around the globe from anywhere in the world. Sports have become a cheap form of entertainment, as fans do not have to leave their homes to enjoy athletic competitions. As sports television revenues have escalated, many sports now receive the bulk of their yearly revenue from television contracts.

CONCLUSION

WESTERN EUROPE BECAME a new community in the 1950s and 1960s as a remarkable economic recovery fostered a new optimism. Western European states became accustomed to political democracy, and with the development of the European Community, many of them began to move toward economic unity. But nagging economic problems, new ethnic divisions, environmental degradation, and the inability to work together to stop a civil war in their own backyard have all indicated that what had been seen as a glorious new path for Europe in the 1950s and 1960s had become laden with pitfalls in the 1990s and early 2000s.

In the Western Hemisphere, the two North American countries—the United States and Canada—built prosperous economies and relatively stable communities in the 1950s, but there too, new problems, including ethnic, racial, and linguistic differences as well as persistent economic difficulties, dampened the optimism of the earlier decade. Though some Latin American nations shared in the economic growth of the 1950s and 1960s, it was not matched by any real political stability. Only in the 1980s did democratic governments begin to replace oppressive military regimes.

Western societies after 1945 were also participants in an era of rapidly changing international relationships. While Latin American countries struggled to find a new relationship with the colossus to the north, European states reluctantly let go of their colonial empires. Between 1947 and 1962, virtually every colony achieved independence and statehood. Decolonization was a difficult and even bitter process, but as we shall see in the next chapters, it created a new world as the non-Western states ended the long ascendancy of the Western nations.

TIMELINE

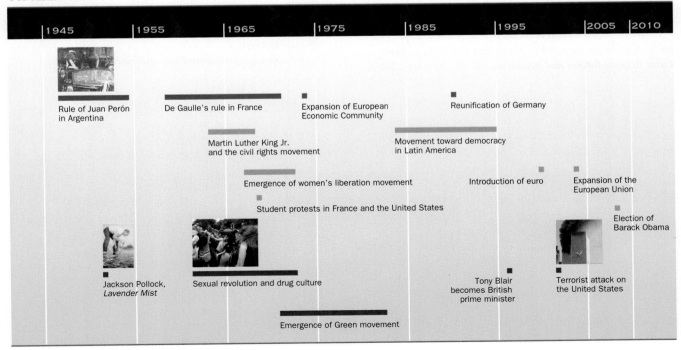

| 1945 | 1955 | 1965 | 1975 | 1985 | 1995 | 2005 | 2010 |

Rule of Juan Perón in Argentina

De Gaulle's rule in France

Expansion of European Economic Community

Reunification of Germany

Martin Luther King Jr. and the civil rights movement

Movement toward democracy in Latin America

Emergence of women's liberation movement

Introduction of euro

Expansion of the European Union

Student protests in France and the United States

Election of Barack Obama

Jackson Pollock, Lavender Mist

Sexual revolution and drug culture

Tony Blair becomes British prime minister

Terrorist attack on the United States

Emergence of Green movement

SUGGESTED READING

Europe Since 1945 For a well-written survey on Europe since 1945, see **T. Judt, *Postwar: A History of Europe Since 1945*** (New York, 2005). See also **W. I. Hitchcock, *The Struggle for Europe: The Turbulent History of a Divided Continent, 1945–2002*** (New York, 2002). On the building of common institutions in Western Europe, see **S. Henig, *The Uniting of Europe: From Discord to Concord*** (London, 1997). For a survey of West Germany, see **H. A. Turner, *Germany from Partition to Reunification*** (New Haven, Conn., 1992). France under de Gaulle is examined in **J. Jackson, *Charles de Gaulle*** (London, 2003). On Britain, see **K. O. Morgan, *The People's Peace: British History, 1945–1990*** (Oxford, 1992). On the recent history of these countries, see **E. J. Evans, *Thatcher and Thatcherism*** (New York, 1997); **M. Temple, *Blair*** (London, 2006); **D. S. Bell, *François Mitterrand*** (Cambridge, 2005); and **P. O'Dochartaigh, *Germany Since 1945*** (New York, 2004). On Eastern Europe, see **P. Kenney, *The Burden of Freedom: Eastern Europe Since 1989*** (London, 2006).

The United States and Canada For a general survey of U.S. history since 1945, see **W. H. Chafe, *Unfinished Journey: America Since World War II*** (Oxford, 2006). More detailed accounts can be found in two volumes by **J. T. Patterson** in the Oxford History of the United States series: ***Grand Expectations: The United States, 1945–1974*** (Oxford, 1997) and ***Restless Giant: The United States from Watergate to Bush v. Gore*** (Oxford, 2005). Information on Canada can be found in **S. W. See, *History of Canada*** (Westport, N.Y., 2001), and **C. Brown, ed., *The Illustrated History of Canada***, 4th ed. (Toronto, 2003).

Latin America For general surveys of Latin American history, see **M. C. Eakin, *The History of Latin America: Collision of Cultures*** (New York, 2007), and **E. Bradford Burns** and **J. A. Charlip, *Latin America: An Interpretive History,*** 8th ed. (Upper Saddle River, N.J., 2007). The twentieth century is the focus of **T. E. Skidmore** and **P. H. Smith, *Modern Latin America,*** 6th ed. (Oxford, 2004). Works on other countries examined in this chapter include **L. A. Pérez, *Cuba: Between Reform and Revolution,*** 3rd ed. (New York, 2005);

J. A. Page, *Perón: A Biography* (New York, 1983); **L. A. Romero, *History of Argentina in the Twentieth Century,*** trans. **J. P. Brennan** (University Park, Pa., 2002); and **M. C. Meyer** and **W. L. Sherman, *The Course of Mexican History,*** 8th ed. (New York, 2006).

Society in the Western World On the sexual revolution of the 1960s, see **D. Allyn, *Make Love, Not War: The Sexual Revolution—An Unfettered History*** (New York, 2000). On the women's liberation movement, see **C. Duchen, *Women's Rights and Women's Lives in France, 1944–1968*** (New York, 1994); **D. Meyer, *The Rise of Women in America, Russia, Sweden, and Italy,*** 2nd ed. (Middletown, Conn., 1989); and **K. C. Berkeley, *The Women's Liberation Movement in America*** (Westport, Conn., 1999). The changing role of women is examined in **R. Rosen, *The World Split Open: How the Modern Women's Movement Changed America*** (New York, 2001). On terrorism, see **W. Laqueur, *History of Terrorism*** (New York, 2001), and **C. E. Simonsen** and **J. R. Spendlove, *Terrorism Today: The Past, the Players, the Future,*** 3rd ed. (Upper Saddle River, N.J., 2006). On the development of Green Parties, see **M. O'Neill, *Green Parties and Political Change in Contemporary Europe*** (Aldershot, England, 1997).

Western Culture Since 1945 For a general view of postwar thought and culture, see **J. A. Winders, *European Culture Since 1848: From Modern to Postmodern and Beyond,*** rev. ed. (New York, 2001). On existentialism, see **T. Flynn, *Existentialism: A Very Short History,*** 5th ed. (Oxford, 2006). On Postmodernism, see **C. Butler, *Postmodernism: A Very Short Introduction*** (Oxford, 2002). On the arts, see **A. Marwick, *Arts in the West Since 1945*** (Oxford, 2002).

What are the similarities and differences between the major political, economic, and social developments in the first half of the twentieth century and those in the second half of the century?

In thinking about this question, begin by breaking it down into the components shown below. A discussion of the significance of each component should appear in your answer.

POLITICS AND GOVERNMENT Examine the map of Europe in 2009 and the maps of the aftermaths of World War I and World War II shown here and on page 637. What changes do you see? Considering all of these maps and the material in this chapter, what evidence can you find that for the first time in many centuries, "Europe" exists entirely on the European continent? Why is this?

European Union, 2009

Latin America in the First Half of the Nineteenth Century

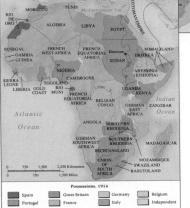
Africa in 1914

Territorial Changes in Europe and the Middle East After World War I

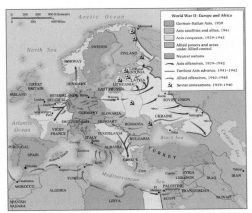
World War II in Europe and North Africa

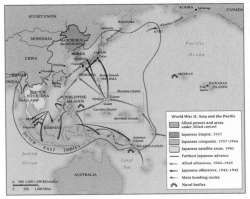
World War II in Asia and the Pacific

721

CHAPTER 29
CHALLENGES OF NATION BUILDING
IN AFRICA AND THE MIDDLE EAST

The African community, soul of a continent

© William J. Duiker

AT THE END OF WORLD WAR II, many societies in Asia and Africa had already been exposed to over half a century of colonial rule. Although Europeans complacently assumed that colonialism was a necessary evil in the process of introducing civilization to backward peoples around the globe, many Asians and Africans disagreed. Some even argued that the Western drive for political hegemony and economic profit, far from being a panacea for the world's ills, was a plague that threatened ultimately to destroy human civilization.

One aspect of Western civilization that many observers in Asia and Africa rejected was the concept of the nation-state as the natural unit of communal identity in the modern world. In their view, nationalism was at the root of many of the evils of the twentieth century and should be rejected as a model for development in the postwar period. In Africa, some intellectuals pointed to the traditional village community as a unique symbol of the humanistic and spiritual qualities of the African people and promoted the concept of "blackness" (*négritude*) as a common bond that could knit all the peoples of the continent into a cohesive community. A similar rejection of the nation-state was prevalent in the Middle East, where many Muslims viewed Western materialist culture as a threat to the fundamental principles of Islam. To fend off the new threat from an old adversary, some dreamed of resurrecting the concept of a global caliphate (see Chapter 7) to unify all Muslim peoples in realizing their common destiny throughout the Islamic world.

Time has not been kind to such dreams of transnational solidarity and cooperation in the postwar world. Although the peoples of Africa and the Middle East were gradually liberated from the formal trappings of European authority, the legacy of colonialism in the form of political inexperience and continued European economic domination has frustrated the efforts of the leaders of the emerging new states to achieve political stability. At the same time, arbitrary boundaries imposed by the colonial powers, combined with ethnic and religious divisions, have led to bitter conflicts that have posed a severe obstacle to the dream of solidarity and cooperation in forging a common destiny. Today, these two regions, although blessed with enormous potential, are among the most volatile and conflict-ridden areas in the world. ✸

Uhuru: The Struggle for Independence in Africa

Q **Focus Question:** What role did nationalist movements play in the transition to independence in Africa, and how did such movements differ from their counterparts elsewhere?

In the three decades following the end of World War II, the peoples of Africa were gradually liberated from the formal trappings of European colonialism.

The Colonial Legacy

As in Asia, colonial rule had a mixed impact on the societies and peoples of Africa (see Chapter 21). The Western presence brought a number of short-term and long-term benefits to Africa, such as improved transportation and communication facilities, and in a few areas laid the foundation for a modern industrial and commercial sector. Improved sanitation and medical care increased life expectancy. The introduction of selective elements of Western political systems after World War II laid the basis for the gradual creation of democratic societies.

Yet the benefits of Westernization were distributed very unequally, and the vast majority of Africans found their lives little improved, if at all. Only South Africa and French-held Algeria, for example, developed modern industrial sectors, extensive railroad networks, and modern communications systems. In both countries, European settlers were numerous, most investment capital for industrial ventures was European, and whites constituted almost the entire professional and managerial class.

Members of the native population were generally restricted to unskilled or semiskilled jobs at wages less than one-fifth those enjoyed by Europeans.

Many colonies concentrated on export crops—peanuts in Senegal and Gambia, cotton in Egypt and Uganda, coffee in Kenya, and palm oil and cocoa products in the Gold Coast. Here the benefits of development were somewhat more widespread. In some cases, the crops were grown on plantations, which were usually owned by Europeans. But plantation agriculture was not always suitable in Africa (sometimes the cultivation of cash crops eroded the fragile soil base and turned farmland into desert), and much farming was done by free or tenant farmers. In some areas, where landownership was traditionally vested in the community, the land was owned and leased by the corporate village. The vast majority of the profits from the exports, however, accrued to Europeans or to merchants from other foreign countries, such as India and the Arab emirates. The vast majority of Africans continued to be subsistence farmers growing food for their own consumption.

The Rise of Nationalism

Political organizations for African rights did not arise until after World War I, and then only in a few areas, such as British-ruled Kenya and the Gold Coast. After World War II, following the example of independence movements elsewhere, groups organized political parties with independence as their objective. In the Gold Coast, Kwame Nkrumah (1909–1972) led the Convention People's Party, the first formal political party in black Africa. In the late 1940s, Jomo Kenyatta (1894–1978) founded the Kenya African National Union (KANU), which focused on economic issues but had an implied political agenda as well.

For the most part, these political activities were basically nonviolent and were led by Western-educated African intellectuals. Their constituents were primarily urban professionals, merchants, and members of labor unions. But the demand for independence was not entirely restricted to the cities. In Kenya, for example, the widely publicized Mau Mau movement among the Kikuyu people used terrorism as an essential element of its program to achieve *uhuru* (Swahili for "freedom") from the British. Although most of the violence was directed against other Africans, the specter of Mau Mau terrorism alarmed the European population and convinced the British government in 1959 to promise eventual independence.

In areas such as South Africa and Algeria, where the political system was dominated by European settlers, the transition to independence was more complicated.

In South Africa, political activity by local Africans began with the formation of the African National Congress (ANC) in 1912. Initially, the ANC was dominated by Western-oriented intellectuals and had little mass support. Its goal was to achieve economic and political reforms, including full equality for educated Africans, within the framework of the existing system. But the ANC's efforts met with little success, while conservative white parties managed to stiffen the segregation laws. In response, the ANC became increasingly radicalized, and by the 1950s, the prospects for a violent confrontation were growing.

In Algeria, resistance to French rule by Berbers and Arabs in rural areas had never ceased. After World War II, urban agitation intensified, leading to a widespread rebellion against colonial rule in the mid-1950s. At first, the French government tried to maintain its authority in Algeria. But when Charles de Gaulle became president in 1958, he reversed French policy, and Algeria became independent under President Ahmad Ben Bella (1918–2004) in 1962. The armed struggle in Algeria hastened the transition to statehood in its neighbors as well. Tunisia won its independence in 1956 after some urban agitation and rural unrest but retained close ties with Paris. The French attempted to suppress the nationalist movement in Morocco by sending Sultan Muhammad V into exile, but the effort failed; in 1956, he returned as the ruler of the independent state of Morocco.

Most black African nations achieved their independence in the late 1950s and 1960s, beginning with the Gold Coast, now renamed Ghana, in 1957 (see Map 29.1). Nigeria, the Belgian Congo (renamed Zaire and then the Democratic Republic of the Congo), Kenya, Tanganyika (later, when joined with Zanzibar, renamed Tanzania), and several other countries soon followed. Most of the French colonies agreed to accept independence within the framework of de Gaulle's French Community. By the late 1960s, only parts of southern

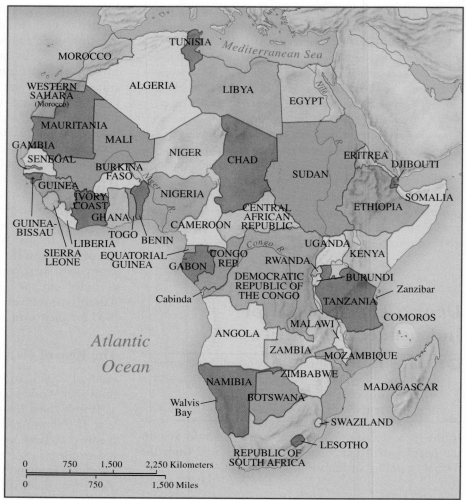

MAP 29.1 Modern Africa. This map shows the division of independent states in Africa today.

Q Why was unity so difficult to achieve in African regions?

Africa and the Portuguese possessions of Mozambique and Angola remained under European rule.

Independence thus came later to Africa than to most of Asia. Several factors help explain the delay. For one thing, colonialism was established in Africa somewhat later than in most areas of Asia, and the inevitable reaction from the local population was consequently delayed. Furthermore, with the exception of a few areas in West Africa and along the Mediterranean, coherent states with a strong sense of cultural, ethnic, and linguistic unity did not exist in most of Africa. Most traditional states, such as Ashanti in West Africa, Songhai in the southern Sahara, and Bakongo in the Congo basin, were collections of heterogeneous peoples with little sense of national or cultural identity. It is hardly surprising that when opposition to colonial rule emerged, unity was difficult to achieve.

The Era of Independence

Q Focus Question: How have dreams clashed with realities in the independent nations of Africa, and how have African governments sought to meet these challenges?

The newly independent African states faced intimidating challenges. Although Western political institutions, values, and technology had been introduced, at least in the cities, the exposure to European civilization had been superficial at best for most Africans and tragic for many. At the outset of independence, most African societies were still primarily agrarian and traditional, and their modern sectors depended mainly on imports from the West.

Pan-Africanism and Nationalism: The Destiny of Africa

Like the leaders of new states in South and Southeast Asia, most African leaders came from the urban middle class. They had studied in either Europe or the United States and spoke and read European languages. Although most were profoundly critical of colonial policies, they appeared to accept the relevance of the Western model to Africa and gave at least lip service to Western democratic values.

Their views on economics were somewhat more diverse. Some, like Jomo Kenyatta of Kenya and General Mobutu Sese Seko (1930–1997) of Zaire, were advocates of Western-style capitalism. Others, like Julius Nyerere (1922–1999) of Tanzania, Kwame Nkrumah of Ghana, and Sékou Touré (1922–1984) of Guinea, preferred an "African form of socialism," which bore slight resemblance to the Marxist-Leninist socialism practiced in the Soviet Union. According to its advocates, it was descended from traditional communal practices in precolonial Africa.

At first, most of the new African leaders accepted the national boundaries established during the colonial era. But as we have seen, these boundaries were artificial creations of the colonial powers. Virtually all of the new states included widely diverse ethnic, linguistic, and territorial groups. Zaire, for example, was composed of more than two hundred territorial groups speaking seventy-five different languages. Such conditions posed a severe challenge to the task of forming cohesive nation-states.

A number of leaders—including Nkrumah of Ghana, Touré of Guinea, and Kenyatta of Kenya—were enticed by the dream of **pan-Africanism,** a concept of continental unity that transcended national boundaries. Nkrumah in particular hoped a pan-African union could be established that would unite all of the new countries of the continent in a broader community. His dream achieved concrete manifestation in the Organization of African Unity (OAU), which was founded in 1963 (see the box on p. 726).

Pan-Africanism originated among French-educated African intellectuals during the first half of the twentieth century. A basic element was the concept of *négritude* (blackness), which held that there was a distinctive "African personality" that owed nothing to Western materialism and provided a common sense of destiny for all black African peoples. Whereas Western civilization prized rational thought and material achievement, African culture emphasized emotional expression and a common sense of humanity.

Dream and Reality: Political and Economic Conditions in Independent Africa

The program of the OAU called for an Africa based on freedom, equality, justice, and dignity and on the unity, solidarity, prosperity, and territorial integrity of African states. It did not take long for reality to set in. Vast disparities in education and wealth made it hard to establish material prosperity in much of Africa. Expectations that independence would lead to stable political structures based on "one person, one vote" were soon disappointed as the initial phase of pluralistic governments gave way to a series of military regimes and one-party states. Between 1957 and 1982, more than seventy leaders of African countries were overthrown by violence, and the pace has not abated in recent years.

The Problem of Neocolonialism Part of the problem could be (and was) ascribed to the lingering effects of colonialism. Most new countries in Africa were dependent on the export of a single crop or natural resource. When prices fluctuated or dropped, these countries were at the mercy of the vagaries of the international market. In several cases, the resources were still controlled by foreigners, leading to the charge that colonialism had been succeeded by **neocolonialism,** in which Western domination was maintained by economic rather than by political or military means.

World trade policies often exacerbated these problems. While advanced countries took aggressive action to reduce tariff barriers on the worldwide flow of industrial goods, at the same time they provided massive subsidies to protect domestic producers of agricultural goods, thus preventing poor countries in Africa and Asia from improving their economic conditions through agricultural exports. To make matters worse, most African states had to import technology and manufactured goods from the

TOWARD AFRICAN UNITY

POLITICS & GOVERNMENT

In May 1963, the leaders of thirty-two African states met in Addis Ababa, the capital of Ethiopia, to discuss the creation of an organization that would represent the interests of all the newly independent countries of Africa. The result was the Organization of African Unity. An excerpt from its charter is presented here. Although the organization did not realize all of the aspirations of its founders, it provided a useful forum for the discussion and resolution of its members' common problems. In 2001, it was replaced by the new African Union, which was designed to bring about increased cooperation among the states on the continent.

Charter of the Organization of African Unity

We, the Heads of African States and Governments assembled in the City of Addis Ababa, Ethiopia;

CONVINCED that it is the inalienable right of all people to control their own destiny;

CONSCIOUS of the fact that freedom, equality, justice, and dignity are essential objectives for the achievement of the legitimate aspirations of the African peoples;

CONSCIOUS of our responsibility to harness the natural and human resources of our continent for the total advancement of our peoples in spheres of human endeavor;

INSPIRED by a common determination to promote understanding among our peoples and cooperation among our States in response to the aspirations of our peoples for brotherhood and solidarity, in a larger unity transcending ethnic and national differences;

CONVINCED that, in order to translate this determination into a dynamic force in the cause of human progress, conditions for peace and security must be established and maintained;

DETERMINED to safeguard and consolidate the hard-won independence as well as the sovereignty and territorial integrity of our States, and to fight against neocolonialism in all its forms;

DEDICATED to the general progress of Africa; . . .

DESIROUS that all African States should henceforth unite so that the welfare and well-being of their peoples can be assured;

RESOLVED to reinforce the links between our states by establishing and strengthening common institutions;

HAVE agreed to the present Charter.

Q *What are the key objectives expressed in this charter? To what degree have they been achieved?*

West, and the prices of those goods rose more rapidly than those of the export products.

The new states contributed to their own problems. Scarce national resources were squandered on military equipment or expensive consumer goods rather than on building up their infrastructure to provide the foundation for an industrial economy. Corruption, a painful reality throughout the modern world, became almost a way of life in Africa as bribery became necessary to obtain even the most basic services.

Africa in the Cold War   Many of the problems encountered by the new nations of Africa have also been ascribed to the fact that independence has not ended Western interference in Africa's political affairs. Many African leaders were angered when Western powers led by the United States conspired to overthrow the radical politician Patrice Lumumba (1925–1961) in Zaire in the early 1960s. Lumumba, who had been educated in the Soviet Union, aroused fears in Washington that he might promote Soviet influence in Central Africa (see Chapter 26).

The episode reinforced the desire of African leaders to form the OAU as a means of reducing Western influence on the continent, but the strategy achieved few results. Although many African leaders agreed to adopt a neutral stance in the Cold War, competition between

Moscow and Washington throughout the region was fierce, often undermining the efforts of fragile governments to build stable new nations. As a result, African states have had difficulty achieving a united position on many issues, and their disagreements have left the region vulnerable to external influence and conflict. Border disputes festered in many areas of the continent, and in some cases—as with Morocco and a rebel movement in Western Sahara and between Kenya and Uganda—flared into outright war.

Even within many African nations, the concept of nationhood has been undermined by the renascent force of regionalism or tribalism. Nigeria, with the largest population on the continent, was rent by civil strife during the late 1960s when dissident Ibo groups in the southeast attempted unsuccessfully to form the independent state of Biafra. Another force undermining nationalism in Africa has been pan-Islamism. Its prime exponent in Africa was the Egyptian president Gamal Abdul Nasser (see "Nasser and Pan-Arabism" later in this chapter). After Nasser's death in 1970, the torch of Islamic unity in Africa was carried by the Libyan president Muammar Qadhafi (b. 1942), whose ambitions to create a greater Muslim nation in the Sahara under his authority led to conflict with neighboring Chad. The Islamic resurgence also surfaced in Ethiopia, where Muslim tribespeople in Eritrea rebelled against the Marxist regime of Colonel Mengistu in Addis Ababa. More recently, it has flared up in Nigeria and other nations of West Africa, where divisions between Muslims and Christians have erupted into violence.

The Population Bomb   Finally, rapid population growth crippled efforts to create modern economies. By the 1980s, annual population growth averaged nearly 3 percent throughout Africa, the highest rate of any continent. Drought conditions and the inexorable spread of the Sahara (usually known as *desertification,* caused partly by overcultivation of the land) led to widespread hunger and starvation, first in West African countries such as Niger and Mali and then in Ethiopia, Somalia, and Sudan.

Predictions are that the population of Africa will increase by at least 200 million over the next ten years, but that estimate does not take into account the prevalence of AIDS, which has reached epidemic proportions in Africa. According to one estimate, one-third of the entire population of sub-Saharan Africa is infected with the virus, including a high percentage of the urban middle class. More than 75 percent of the AIDS cases reported around the world are on the continent of Africa. In some countries, AIDS is transmitted via the tradition that requires a widow to have sexual relations with one of her deceased husband's male relatives. Some observers estimate that without measures to curtail the effects of the disease, it will have a significant impact on several African countries by reducing population growth.

Poverty is endemic in Africa, particularly among the three-quarters of the population still living off the land. Urban areas have grown tremendously, but as in much of Asia, most are surrounded by massive squatter settlements of rural peoples who had fled to the cities in search of a better life. The expansion of the cities has overwhelmed fragile transportation and sanitation systems and led to rising pollution and perpetual traffic jams, while millions are forced to live without running water and electricity. Meanwhile, the fortunate few (all too often government officials on the take) live the high life and emulate the consumerism of the West (in a particularly expressive phrase, the rich in many East African countries are known as *wabenzi,* or "Mercedes-Benz people").

The Search for Solutions

While the problems of nation building mentioned so far have to one degree or another afflicted all of the emerging states of Africa, each has sought to deal with the challenge in its own way, and sometimes, as we shall see, with strikingly different consequences. Despite all its shared difficulties, Africa today remains one of the most diverse regions on the globe.

Tanzania: An African Route to Socialism   Concern over the dangers of economic inequality inspired a number of African leaders to restrict foreign investment and nationalize the major industries and utilities while promoting democratic ideals and values. Julius Nyerere of Tanzania was the most consistent, promoting the ideals of socialism and self-reliance through his Arusha Declaration of 1967, which set forth the principles for building a socialist society in Africa. Nyerere did not seek to establish a Leninist-style dictatorship of the proletariat in Tanzania, but neither was he a proponent of a multiparty democracy, which in his view would be divisive under the conditions prevailing in Africa:

> Where there is one party—provided it is identified with the nation as a whole—the foundations of democracy can be firmer, and the people can have more opportunity to exercise a real choice, than when you have two or more parties.

To import the Western parliamentary system into Africa, he argued, could lead to violence, since the opposition parties would be viewed as traitors by the majority of the population.[1]

Taking advantage of his powerful political influence, Nyerere placed limitations on income and established village collectives to avoid the corrosive effects of economic inequality and government corruption. Sympathetic foreign countries provided considerable economic aid to assist the experiment, and many observers noted that levels of corruption, political instability, and ethnic strife were lower in Tanzania than in many other African countries. Nyerere's vision was not shared by all of his compatriots, however. Political elements on the island of Zanzibar, citing the stagnation brought by two decades of socialism, agitated for autonomy or even total separation from the mainland. Tanzania also has poor soil, inadequate rainfall, and limited resources, all of which have contributed to its slow growth and continuing rural and urban poverty.

In 1985, Nyerere voluntarily retired from the presidency. In his farewell speech, he confessed that he had failed to achieve many of his ambitious goals to create a socialist society in Africa. In particular, he admitted that his plan to collectivize the traditional private farm (*shamba*) had run into strong resistance from conservative peasants. "You can socialize what is not traditional," he remarked. "The *shamba* can't be socialized." But Nyerere insisted that many of his policies had succeeded in improving social and economic conditions, and he argued that the only real solution was to consolidate the multitude of small countries in the region into a larger East African Federation.

Kenya: The Perils of Capitalism   The countries that opted for capitalism faced their own dilemmas. Neighboring Kenya, blessed with better soil in the highlands, a local tradition of aggressive commerce, and a residue of European settlers, welcomed foreign investment and profit incentives. The results have been mixed. Kenya has a strong current of indigenous African capitalism and a substantial middle class, mostly based in the capital, Nairobi. But landlessness, unemployment, and income inequities are high, even by African standards (almost one-fifth of the country's nearly 40 million people are squatters, and unemployment is currently estimated at 45 percent). The rate of population growth—more than 3 percent annually—is one of the highest in the world. Eighty percent of the population remains rural, and 40 percent of the people live below the poverty line. The result has been widespread unrest in a country formerly admired for its successful development.

Kenya's problems have been exacerbated by chronic disputes between disparate ethnic groups and simmering tensions between farmers and pastoralists. For many years, the country maintained a fragile political stability under the dictatorial rule of President Daniel arap Moi (b. 1924), one of the most authoritarian of African leaders. Plagued by charges of corruption, Moi finally agreed to retire in 2002, but under his successor, Mwai Kibaki (b. 1931), the twin problems of political instability and widespread poverty continue to afflict the country. When presidential elections held in January 2008 led to a victory for Kibaki's party, opposition elements—angered by the government's perceived favoritism to Kibaki's Kikuyu constituency—launched numerous protests, resulting in violent riots throughout the country. A fragile truce was eventually put in place.

South Africa: An End to Apartheid Perhaps Africa's greatest success story is in South Africa, where the white government—which long maintained a policy of racial segregation (**apartheid**) and restricted black sovereignty to a series of small "Bantustans" in relatively infertile areas of the country—finally accepted the inevitability of African involvement in the political process and the national economy. In 1990, the government of President Frederik W. de Klerk (b. 1936) released African National Congress leader Nelson Mandela (b. 1918) from prison, where he had been held since 1964. In 1993, the two leaders agreed to hold democratic national elections the following spring. In the meantime, ANC representatives agreed to take part in a transitional coalition government with de Klerk's National Party. Those elections resulted in a substantial majority for the ANC, and Mandela became president.

In May 1996, a new constitution was approved, calling for a multiracial state. The National Party immediately went into opposition, claiming that the new charter did not adequately provide for joint decision making by members of the coalition.

In 1999, a major step toward political stability was taken when Nelson Mandela stepped down from the presidency, to be replaced by his long-time disciple Thabo Mbeki (b. 1942). The new president faced a number of intimidating problems, including rising unemployment, widespread lawlessness, chronic corruption, and an ominous flight of capital and professional personnel from the country. Mbeki's conservative economic policies earned the support of some white voters and the country's new black elite but provoked criticism from labor union groups, who contended that the benefits of the new black leadership were not seeping down to the poor. The government's promises to carry out an extensive land reform program—aimed at providing farmland to the nation's

Cape Town: A Tale of Two Cities. First settled by the Dutch in the seventeenth century, Cape Town is the most modern city in Africa, as well as one of its most beautiful. Situated at the foot of scenic Table Mountain, its business and financial center has long been dominated by Europeans (see the left photo). Despite the abolition of apartheid in the 1990s, much of Cape Town's black population still resides in the crowded "townships" located along the fringes of the city, as shown in the right photo.

40 million black farmers—were not fulfilled, provoking some squatters to seize unused private lands near Johannesburg. In 2008, disgruntled ANC members forced Mbeki out of office.

Still, South Africa remains the wealthiest and most industrialized state in Africa and the best hope that a multiracial society can succeed on the continent. The country's black elite now number nearly one-quarter of its wealthiest households, compared with only 9 percent in 1991.

Nigeria: A Nation Divided If the situation in South Africa provides grounds for modest optimism, the situation in Nigeria provides reason for serious concern. Africa's largest country in terms of population and one of its wealthiest because of substantial oil reserves, Nigeria was for many years in the grip of military strongmen. During his rule, General Sani Abacha (1943–1998) ruthlessly suppressed all opposition and in late 1995 ordered the execution of a writer despite widespread protests from human rights groups abroad. Ken Saro-Wiwa had criticized environmental damage caused by foreign interests in southern Nigeria, but the regime's major concern was his support for separatist activities in the area that had launched the Biafran insurrection in the late 1960s. When Abacha died in 1998 under mysterious circumstances, national elections led to the creation of a civilian government under Olusegun Obasanjo (b. 1937).

Civilian leadership has not been a panacea for Nigeria's problems, however. Although Obasanjo promised reforms to bring an end to the corruption and favoritism that had long plagued Nigerian politics, the results were disappointing (the state power company—known as NEPA—was so inefficient that Nigerians joked that the initials stood for "never expect power again"). When presidential elections held in 2007 led to the election of Umaru Yar'Adua (b. 1951), an obscure member of Obasanjo's ruling political party, opposition forces and neutral observers complained that the vote had been seriously flawed.

One of the most critical problems facing the Nigerian government in recent years has been rooted in religious disputes. In early 2000, riots between Christians and Muslims broke out in several northern cities as a result of the decision by Muslim provincial officials to apply *Shari'a* throughout their jurisdictions. The violence has abated as local officials managed to craft compromise policies that limit the application of some of the harsher aspects of Muslim law, but the dispute continues to threaten the fragile unity of Africa's most populous country.

Tensions in the Desert A similar rift has been at the root of the lengthy civil war that has been raging in Sudan. Conflict between Muslim pastoralists—supported

CHRONOLOGY Modern Africa

Ghana gains independence from Great Britain	1957
Algeria gains independence from France	1962
Formation of the Organization of African Unity	1963
Biafra Revolt in Nigeria	1966–1970
Arusha Declaration in Tanzania	1967
Nelson Mandela released from prison	1990
Nelson Mandela elected president of South Africa	1994
Genocide in Central Africa	1996–2000
Olusegun Obasanjo elected president of Nigeria	1999
Creation of the African Union	2001
Civil war breaks out in Sudan	2004
Ethnic riots in Kenya	2008

by the central government in Khartoum—and predominantly Christian black farmers in the southern part of the country was finally brought to an end in 2004, but new outbreaks of violence have erupted in western Darfur province, leading to reports of widespread starvation among the local villagers. The United Nations, joined by other African countries, has sought to bring an end to the bloodshed. The violence continues, however, and now threatens to overflow into neighboring Chad.

The dispute between Muslims and Christians in the southern Sahara is a contemporary variant of the traditional tensions that have existed between farmers and pastoralists throughout recorded history. Muslim cattle herders, migrating southward to escape the increasing desiccation of the grasslands south of the Sahara, compete for precious land with indigenous—primarily Christian—farmers. As a result of the religious revival now under way throughout the continent, the confrontation often leads to outbreaks of violence with strong religious and ethnic overtones (see the comparative essay "Religion and Society" on p. 730).

Central Africa: Cauldron of Conflict The most tragic situation is in the Central African states of Rwanda and Burundi, where a chronic conflict between the minority Tutsis and the Hutu majority has led to a bitter civil war, with thousands of refugees fleeing to the neighboring Congo. In another classic example of conflict between pastoral and farming peoples, the nomadic Tutsis, supported by the colonial Belgian government, had long dominated the sedentary Hutu population. It was the

COMPARATIVE ESSAY
RELIGION AND SOCIETY

RELIGION & PHILOSOPHY

The nineteenth and twentieth centuries witnessed a steady trend toward the secularization of society as people increasingly turned from religion to science for explanations of natural phenomena and for answers to the challenges of everyday life.

In recent years, however, the trend has reversed as religious faith in all its guises appears to be reviving in much of the world. Although the percentage of people attending religious services on a regular basis or professing firm religious convictions has been dropping steadily in many countries, the intensity of religious belief appears to be growing among the faithful. This phenomenon has been widely publicized in the United States, where the evangelical movement has become a significant force in politics and an influential factor in defining many social issues. But it has also occurred in Latin America, where a drop in membership in the Roman Catholic Church has been offset by significant increases in the popularity of evangelical Protestant sects. In the Muslim world, the influence of traditional Islam has been steadily on the rise, not only in the Middle East but also in non-Arab countries like Malaysia and Indonesia (see Chapter 30). In Africa, as we observe in this chapter, the appeal of both Christianity and Islam appears to be on the rise. Even in Russia and China, where half a century of Communist government sought to eradicate religion as the "opiate of the people," the popularity of religion is growing.

One major reason for the increasing popularity of religion in contemporary life is the desire to counter the widespread sense of malaise brought on by the absence of any sense of meaning and purpose in life—a purpose that religious faith provides. For many evangelical Christians in the United States, for example, the adoption of a Christian lifestyle is seen as a necessary prerequisite for resolving problems of crime, drugs, and social alienation. It is likely that a similar phenomenon is present with other religions and in other parts of the world.

Historical evidence suggests, however, that although religious fervor may serve to enhance the sense of community and commitment among believers, it can have a highly divisive impact on society as a whole, as the examples of Northern Ireland, Yugoslavia, Africa, and the Middle East vividly attest. Even where the effect is less dramatic, as in the United States and Latin America, religion divides as well as unites, and it will be a continuing task for religious leaders of all faiths to promote tolerance for peoples of other persuasions.

Another challenge for contemporary religion is to find ways to coexist with expanding scientific knowledge. Influential figures in the evangelical movement in the United States, for example, not only support a conservative social agenda but also express a growing suspicion of the role of technology and science in the contemporary world. Similar views are often expressed by significant factions in other world religions. Although fear of the impact of science on contemporary life is widespread, efforts to turn the clock back to a mythical golden age are not likely to succeed in the face of powerful forces for change set in motion by advances in scientific knowledge.

© William J. Duiker

Carrying Food to the Temple. Bali is the only island in Indonesia where the local population adheres to the Hindu faith. Here worshipers carry food to the local temple to be blessed before being consumed.

Q *What do you think are the chief causes behind the increasing visibility of religion in contemporary society?*

---

attempt of the Bantu-speaking Hutus to bring an end to Tutsi domination that initiated the most recent conflicts, marked by massacres on both sides. In the meantime, the presence of large numbers of foreign troops and refugees intensified centrifugal forces inside Zaire, where General Mobutu Sese Seko (1939–2001) had long ruled with an iron hand. In 1997, military forces led by Mobutu's longtime opponent Laurent Kabila managed to topple the general's corrupt government. Once in power, Kabila renamed the country the Democratic Republic of the Congo and promised a return to democratic practices.

The new government systematically suppressed political dissent, however, and in January 2001, Kabila was assassinated, to be succeeded by his son. Peace talks to end the conflict began that fall, but the fighting has continued.

Sowing the Seeds of Democracy

Not all the news in Africa has been bad. Stagnant economies have led to the collapse of one-party regimes and the emergence of fragile democracies in several countries. Dictatorships were brought to an end in Ethiopia, Liberia, and Somalia, although in each case the fall of the regime was later followed by political instability or civil war. In Senegal, national elections held in the summer of 2000 brought an end to four decades of rule by the once-dominant Socialist Party. The new president, Abdoulaye Wade (b. 1926), was a staunch advocate of promoting development throughout Africa on the capitalist model. Perhaps the most notorious dictator was Idi Amin (c. 1925–2003) of Uganda, who led a military coup against Prime Minister Milton Obote in 1971. After ruling by terror and brutal repression of dissident elements, he was finally deposed in 1979, and in May 1996, Uganda held its first presidential election in more than fifteen years.

Significantly, most Africans are not about to despair. In a survey of African opinion in 2007, the majority of respondents were optimistic about the future and confident that they would be economically better off in five years.

The African Union: A Glimmer of Hope It is clear that African societies have not yet begun to surmount the challenges they have faced since independence. Most African states are still poor and their populations illiterate. Moreover, African concerns continue to carry little weight in the international community. A recent agreement by the World Trade Organization (WTO) on the need to reduce agricultural subsidies in the advanced nations has been widely ignored. In 2000, the General Assembly of the United Nations (UN) passed the Millennium Declaration, which called for a dramatic reduction in the incidence of poverty, hunger, and illiteracy worldwide by the year 2015. So far, however, little has been done to realize these ambitious goals. At a conference on the subject in September 2005, the participants squabbled over how to fund the effort. Some delegations, including that of the United States, argued that external assistance cannot succeed unless the nations of Africa adopt measures to bring about good government and sound economic policies.

Certainly, part of the solution to the continent's multiple problems must come from within. Although there are gratifying signs of progress toward political stability in some countries, including Senegal and South Africa, other nations, especially Sudan, Somalia, and Zimbabwe, are still racked by civil war or ruled by brutal dictatorships. Conflicts between Muslims and Christians in West Africa threaten to spread throughout the region. To alleviate such problems, UN peacekeeping forces have been sent to several African countries, including the Democratic Republic of the Congo, Eritrea, the Ivory Coast, and Sierra Leone.

A significant part of the problem is that the nation-state system is not well suited to the African continent. Africans must find better ways to cooperate with one another and to protect and promote their own interests. A first step in that direction was taken in 1991, when the OAU agreed to establish the African Economic Community (AEC). In 2001, the OAU was replaced by the African Union, which is intended to provide greater political and economic integration throughout the continent on the pattern of the European Union (see Chapter 28). The new organization has already sought to mediate several of the conflicts in the region.

As Africa evolves, it is useful to remember that economic and political change is often an agonizingly slow and painful process. Introduced to industrialization and concepts of Western democracy only a century ago, African societies are still groping for ways to graft Western political institutions and economic practices onto a native structure still significantly influenced by traditional values and attitudes.

Continuity and Change in Modern African Societies

> **Q** **Focus Questions:** How did the rise of independent states affect the lives and the role of women in African societies? How does that role compare with other parts of the contemporary world?

In general, the impact of the West has been greater on urban and educated Africans and more limited on their rural and illiterate compatriots. After all, the colonial presence was first and most firmly established in the cities. Many cities, including Dakar, Lagos, Johannesburg, Cape Town, Brazzaville, and Nairobi, are direct products of the colonial experience. Most African cities today look like their counterparts elsewhere in the world. They have high-rise buildings, blocks of residential apartments, wide boulevards, neon lights, movie theaters, and traffic jams.

Education

The educational system has been the primary means of introducing Western values and culture. In the precolonial era, formal schools did not really exist in Africa except for parochial schools in Christian Ethiopia and academies to train young males in Islamic doctrine and law in Muslim societies in North and West Africa. For the average African, education took place at home or in the village courtyard and stressed socialization and vocational training. Traditional education in Africa was not necessarily inferior to that in Europe. Social values and customs were transmitted to the young by storytellers, often village elders, who could gain considerable prestige through their performance.

Learning the ABCs in Niger. Educating the young is one of the most crucial problems for many African societies today. Few governments are able to allocate the funds necessary to meet the challenge, so religious organizations—Muslim or Christian—often take up the slack. In this photo, students at a *madrasa*—a Muslim school designed to teach the Qur'an—are learning how to read Arabic, the language of Islam's holy scripture. *Madrasas* are one of the most prominent forms of schooling in Muslim societies in West Africa today.

Europeans introduced modern Western education into Africa in the nineteenth century. At first, the schools concentrated on vocational training, with some instruction in European languages and Western civilization. Eventually, pressure from Africans led to the introduction of professional training, and the first institutes of higher learning were established in the early twentieth century.

With independence, African countries established their own state-run schools. The emphasis was on the primary level, but high schools and universities were established in major cities. The basic objectives have been to introduce vocational training and improve literacy rates. Unfortunately, both funding and trained teachers are scarce in most countries, and few rural areas have schools. As a result, illiteracy remains high, estimated at about 70 percent of the population across the continent. There has been a perceptible shift toward education in the vernacular languages. In West Africa, only about one in four adults is conversant in a Western language.

Rural Life

Outside the major cities, where about three-quarters of the continent's inhabitants live, Western influence has had less of an impact. Millions of people throughout Africa (as in Asia) live much as their ancestors did, in thatched huts without modern plumbing and electricity (see the comparative illustration on p. 733); they farm or hunt by traditional methods, practice time-honored family rituals, and believe in the traditional deities. Even here, however, change is taking place. Slavery has been eliminated, for the most part, although there have been persistent reports of raids by slave traders on defenseless villages in the southern Sudan. Economic need, though, has brought about massive migrations as some leave to work on plantations, others move to the cities, and still others flee to refugee camps to escape starvation.

African Women

One of the consequences of colonialism and independence has been a change in the relationship between men and women. In precolonial Africa, as in traditional societies in Asia, men and women had distinctly different roles. Women in sub-Saharan Africa, however, generally did not live under the severe legal and social disabilities that we have seen in such societies as China and India. Their role, it has been said, was "complementary rather than subordinate to that of men."[2] As we have seen, however, the role of women changed in a number of ways in colonial Africa, and not for the better (see Chapter 21).

The Impact of Independence Independence has had a significant impact on gender roles in African society. Almost without exception, the new governments established the principle of sexual equality and permitted women to vote and run for political office. Yet as elsewhere, women continue to operate at a disability in a world dominated by males. Politics remains a male preserve, and although a few professions, such as teaching, child care, and clerical work, are dominated by women, most African women are employed in menial positions such as agricultural labor, factory work, and retail trade or as domestics. Education is open to all at the elementary level, but women comprise less than 20 percent of students at the upper levels in most African societies today.

Not surprisingly, women have made the greatest strides in the cities. Most urban women, like men, now marry on the basis of personal choice, although a significant minority are still willing to accept their parents' choice. After marriage, African women appear to occupy a more equal position than their counterparts in most

COMPARATIVE ILLUSTRATION

Traditional Patterns in the Countryside. In various parts of the world, many people continue to follow patterns of living that are centuries old. In Africa, houses in the countryside are often constructed with a wooden frame woven from poles and branches, known as wattle, daubed with mud, and then covered with a thatched roof. At the left is a scene from a Kenyan village not far from the Indian Ocean, where a young man is applying mud to the wall of his future house. The photo at the right shows a village in India, where housing styles and village customs have changed little since they were first described by Portuguese travelers in the sixteenth century. Note that the houses have thatched roofs and mud-and-straw walls plastered with dung reminiscent of those found in Africa.

Q What are the presumed advantages and disadvantages of the mud-and-thatch houses for rural peoples in contemporary Africa and Asia?

Asian countries. Each marriage partner tends to maintain a separate income, and women often have the right to possess property separate from their husbands. While many wives still defer to their husbands in the traditional manner, others are like the woman in Abioseh Nicol's story "A Truly Married Woman," who, after years of living as a common law wife with her husband, is finally able to provide the price and finalize the marriage. After the wedding, she declares, "For twelve years I have got up every morning at five to make tea for you and breakfast. Now I am a truly married woman [and] you must treat me with a little more respect. You are now my husband and not a lover. Get up and make yourself a cup of tea."[3]

In rural areas, where traditional attitudes continue to exert a strong influence, individuals may still be subordinated to communalism. In some societies, female genital mutilation, the traditional rite of passage for a young girl's transit to womanhood, is still widely practiced. Polygamy is also not uncommon, and arranged marriages are still the rule rather than the exception.

The dichotomy between rural and urban values can lead to acute tensions. Many African villagers regard the cities as the fount of evil, decadence, and corruption. Women in particular have suffered from the tension between the pull of the city and the village (see the box on p. 735). As men are drawn to the cities in search of employment and excitement, their wives and girlfriends are left behind, both literally and figuratively, in the native village.

African Culture

Inevitably, the tension between traditional and modern, native and foreign, and individual and communal that has permeated contemporary African society has spilled over into culture. In general, in the visual arts and music, utility and ritual have given way to pleasure and decoration. In the process, Africans have been affected to a certain extent by foreign influences but have retained their distinctive characteristics. Wood carving, metalwork, painting, and sculpture, for example, have preserved their traditional forms but are now increasingly

Salt of the Earth. During the precolonial era, many West African societies were forced to import salt from Mediterranean countries in exchange for tropical products and gold. Today the people of Senegal satisfy their domestic needs by mining salt deposits contained in lakes like this one in the interior of the country. These lakes are the remnants of vast seas that covered the region of the Sahara in prehistoric times. Note that women are doing much of the heavy labor: men occupy the managerial positions.

adapted to serve the tourist industry and the export market.

Literature No area of African culture has been so strongly affected by political and social events as literature. Except for Muslim areas in North and East Africa, precolonial Africans did not have a written literature, although their tradition of oral storytelling served as a rich repository of history, custom, and folk culture. The first written literature in the vernacular or in European languages emerged during the nineteenth century in the form of novels, poetry, and drama.

Angry at the negative portrayal of Africa in Western literature, African authors initially wrote primarily for a European audience as a means of establishing black dignity and purpose. Embracing the ideals of *négritude,* many glorified the emotional and communal aspects of the traditional African experience. The Nigerian Chinua Achebe (b. 1930) is considered the first major African novelist to write in the English language. In his writings, he attempted to interpret African history from a native perspective and to forge a new sense of African identity. In his trailblazing novel *Things Fall Apart* (1958), he recounted the story of a Nigerian who refused to submit to

the new British order and eventually committed suicide. Criticizing his contemporaries who accepted foreign rule, the protagonist lamented that the white man "has put a knife on the things that held us together and we have fallen apart."

In recent decades, the African novel has taken a dramatic turn, shifting its focus from the brutality of the foreign oppressor to the shortcomings of the new native leadership. Having gained independence, African politicians were portrayed as mimicking and even outdoing the injustices committed by their colonial predecessors. A prominent example of this genre is the work of the Kenyan Ngugi Wa Thiong'o (b. 1938). His first novel, *A Grain of Wheat,* takes place on the eve of *uhuru,* or independence. Although it mocks the racism, snobbishness, and superficiality of local British society, its chief interest lies in its unsentimental and even unflattering portrayal of ordinary Kenyans in their daily struggle for survival.

Many of Ngugi's contemporaries have followed his lead and focused their frustration on the failure of the continent's new leadership to carry out the goals of independence (see the box on p. 736). One of the most outstanding is the Nigerian Wole Soyinka (b. 1934). His

OPPOSING VIEWPOINTS
AN AFRICAN LAMENT

Like many other areas, Africa faces the challenge of adopting the technological civilization of the West while remaining true to its own cultural heritage. Often this challenge poses terrible personal dilemmas in terms of individual career choices and lifestyles. Few have expressed this dilemma more poignantly than the Ugandan writer Okot p'Bitek (1931–1982). In the following excerpts from two of his prose poems, Lawino laments that her husband is abandoning his African roots in a vain search for modernity. Ocol replies bitterly that African tradition is nothing but rotting buffalo and native villages in ruins. In these short poems, the author has highlighted one of the key dilemmas faced by many Africans today.

Okot p'Bitek, *Song of Lawino*

All I ask
Is that my husband should stop the insults,
My husband should refrain
From heaping abuses on my head.
Listen Ocol, my old friend,
The ways of your ancestors
Are good,
Their customs are solid
And not hollow
They are not thin, not easily breakable
They cannot be blown away
By the winds
Because their roots reach deep into the soil.

I do not understand
The ways of foreigners
But I do not despise their customs.
Why should you despise yours?
Listen, my husband,
You are the son of a Chief.

The pumpkin in the old homestead
Must not be uprooted!

Otok p'Bitek, *Song of Ocol*

Your song
Is rotting buffalo
Left behind by
Fleeing poachers, . . .

All the valley,
Make compost of the Pumpkins
And the other native vegetables,
The fence dividing
Family holdings
Will be torn down,
We will uproot
The trees demarcating
The land of clan from clan.

We will obliterate
Tribal boundaries
And throttle native tongues
To dumb death. . . .

Houseboy, Listen . . .
Help the woman
Pack her things,
Then sweep the house clean
And wash the floor,
I am off to Town
To fetch the painter.

Q *What, in essence, is the nature of Lawino's plea to her husband? How does he respond? How do these verses relate to the debate over pan-Africanism?*

---

novel *The Interpreters* (1965) lambasted the corruption and hypocrisy of Nigerian politics. Succeeding novels and plays have continued that tradition, resulting in a Nobel Prize for Literature in 1986. In 1994, however, Soyinka barely managed to escape arrest, and he lived abroad for several years until the military regime ended.

A number of Africa's most prominent writers today are women. Traditionally, African women were valued for their talents as storytellers, but writing was strongly discouraged by both traditional and colonial authorities on the grounds that women should occupy themselves with their domestic obligations. In recent years,

however, a number of women have emerged as prominent writers of African fiction. Two examples are Buchi Emecheta (b. 1940) of Nigeria and Ama Ata Aidoo (b. 1942) of Ghana. Beginning with *Second Class Citizen* (1975), which chronicled the breakdown of her own marriage, Emecheta has published numerous works exploring the role of women in contemporary African society and decrying the practice of polygamy. Ama Ata Aidoo has focused on the identity of today's African women and the changing relations between men and women in society. In her novel *Changes: A Love Story* (1991), she chronicles the lives of three women, none

OPPOSING VIEWPOINTS
AFRICA: DARK CONTINENT OR RADIANT LAND?

 Colonialism camouflaged its economic objectives under the cloak of a "civilizing mission," which in Africa was aimed at illuminating the so-called Dark Continent with Europe's brilliant civilization. In 1899, the Polish-born English author Joseph Conrad (1857–1924) fictionalized his harrowing journey up the Congo River in the novella *Heart of Darkness*. Conrad's protagonist, Marlow, travels upriver to locate a Belgian trader who has mysteriously disappeared. The novella describes Marlow's gradual recognition of the egregious excesses of colonial rule, as well as his realization that such evil lurks in everyone's heart. The story concludes with a cry: "The horror! The horror!" Voicing views that expressed his Victorian perspective, Conrad described an Africa that was incomprehensible, sensual, and primitive.

Over the years, Conrad's work has provoked much debate. Author Chinua Achebe, for one, lambasted *Heart of Darkness* as a radical diatribe. Since independence, many African writers have been prompted to counter Conrad's portrayal by reaffirming the dignity and purpose of the African people. One of the first to do so was the Guinean author Camara Laye (1928–1980), who in 1954 composed a brilliant novel, *The Radiance of the King,* which can be viewed as the mirror image of Conrad's *Heart of Darkness*. In Laye's work, Clarence, another European protagonist, undertakes a journey into the impenetrable heart of Africa. This time, however, he is enlightened by the process, thereby obtaining self-knowledge and ultimately salvation.

Joseph Conrad, *Heart of Darkness*

We penetrated deeper and deeper into the heart of darkness. It was very quiet there. At night sometimes the roll of drums behind the curtain of trees would run up the river and remain sustained faintly, as if hovering in the air high over our heads, till the first break of day. Whether it meant war, peace, or prayer we could not tell.... But suddenly, as we struggled round a bend, there would be a glimpse of rush walls, of peaked grass-roofs, a burst of yells, a whirl of black limbs, a mass of hands clapping, of feet stamping, of bodies swaying, of eyes rolling, under the droop of heavy and motionless foliage. The steamer toiled along slowly on the edge of a black and incomprehensible frenzy. The prehistoric man was cursing us, praying to us, welcoming us—who could tell? We were cut off from the comprehension of our surroundings; we glided past like phantoms, wondering and secretly appalled, as sane men would be before an enthusiastic outbreak in a madhouse....

Camara Laye, *The Radiance of the King*

At that very moment the king turned his head, turned it imperceptibly, and his glance fell upon Clarence....

"Yes, no one is as base as I, as naked as I," he thought. "And you, lord, you are willing to rest your eyes upon me!" Or was it because of his very nakedness? ... "Because of your very nakedness!" the look seemed to say. "That terrifying void that is within you and which opens to receive me; your hunger which calls to my hunger; your very baseness which did not exist until I gave it leave; and the great shame you feel...."

When he had come before the king, when he stood in the great radiance of the king, still ravaged by the tongue of fire, but alive still, and living only through the touch of that fire, Clarence fell upon his knees, for it seemed to him that he was finally at the end of his seeking, and at the end of all seekings.

Q *Compare the depictions of the continent of Africa in these two passages. Is Laye making a response to Conrad? If so, what is it?*

---

presented as a victim but all caught up in the struggle for survival and happiness.

The Destiny of Africa

Nowhere in the developing world is the dilemma of continuity and change more agonizing than in Africa. Mesmerized by the spectacle of Western affluence yet repulsed by the bloody trail from slavery to World War II and the atomic bombs over Hiroshima and Nagasaki, African intellectuals have been torn between the dual images of Western materialism and African exceptionalism.

What is the destiny of Africa? Some Africans still yearn for the dreams embodied in the program of the OAU. Novelist Ngugi Wa Thiong'o calls for "an internationalization of all the democratic and social struggles for human equality, justice, peace, and progress."[4] Some African political leaders, however, have discarded the democratic ideal and turned their attention to systems based on the subordination of the individual to the community as the guiding principle of national development (see Chapter 30). Whether African political culture today is well placed to imitate the strategy adopted by the fast-growing nations of East Asia—which in any event are now encountering problems of their own—is questionable. Like all peoples, Africans must ultimately find their own solutions within the context of their own traditions, not by seeking to imitate the example of others.

Crescent of Conflict

Q **Focus Question:** What problems have the nations of the Middle East faced since the end of World War II, and to what degree have they managed to resolve those problems?

"We Muslims are of one family even though we live under different governments and in various regions."[5] So said Ayatollah Ruholla Khomeini, the Islamic religious figure and leader of the 1979 revolution that overthrew the shah in Iran. The ayatollah's remark was dismissed by some as just a pious wish by a religious mystic. In fact, however, it illustrates a crucial aspect of the political dynamics in the region.

If the concept of "blackness" represents an alternative to the system of nation-states in Africa, the forces of militant Islam have played a similar role in the Middle East. In both regions, a yearning for a sense of community beyond national borders tugs at the emotions and intellect of their inhabitants.

A dramatic example of the powerful force of pan-Islamic sentiment took place on September 11, 2001, when Muslim militants hijacked four U.S. airliners and turned them into missiles aimed at the center of world capitalism. The headquarters of the terrorist network that carried out the attack—known as al-Qaeda and led by Osama bin Laden (see Chapter 28)—was located in Afghanistan, but the militants themselves came from several different Muslim states. Although moderate Muslims throughout the world condemned the attack, it was clear that bin Laden and his cohorts had tapped into a well-spring of hostility and resentment directed at much of the Western world.

What were the sources of Muslim anger? In a speech released on videotape shortly after the attack, bin Laden declared that the attacks were a response to the "humiliation and disgrace" that have afflicted the Islamic world for more than eighty years, a period dating back to the end of World War I. For the Middle East, the period between the two world wars was an era of transition. With the fall of the Ottoman and Persian Empires, new modernizing regimes emerged in Turkey and Iran, and a more traditionalist but fiercely independent government was established in Saudi Arabia. Elsewhere, European influence continued to be strong; the British and French had mandates in Syria, Lebanon, Jordan, and Palestine, and British influence persisted in Iraq, southern Arabia, and throughout the Nile valley.

During World War II, the Middle East became the cockpit of European rivalries, as it had been during World War I. The region was more significant to the warring powers than previously because of the growing importance of oil and the Suez Canal's position as a vital sea route.

The Question of Palestine

As in other areas of Asia, the end of World War II led to the emergence of a number of independent states. Jordan, Lebanon, and Syria, all European mandates before the war, became independent. Egypt, Iran, and Iraq, though still under a degree of Western influence, became increasingly autonomous. Sympathy for the idea of Arab unity led to the formation of the Arab League in 1945, but different points of view among its members prevented it from achieving anything of substance.

The one issue on which all Muslim states in the area could agree was the question of Palestine. As tensions between Jews and Arabs in that mandate intensified during the 1930s, the British attempted to limit Jewish immigration into the area and firmly rejected proposals for independence, despite the promise made in the 1917 Balfour Declaration (see Chapter 24).

After World War II ended, the situation drifted rapidly toward crisis, as thousands of Jewish refugees, many of them from displaced persons camps in Europe, sought to migrate to Palestine despite British efforts to prevent their arrival. As violence between Muslims and Jews intensified in the fall of 1947, the issue was taken up in the UN General Assembly. After an intense debate, the assembly voted to approve the partition of Palestine into two separate states, one for the Jews and one for the Arabs. The city of Jerusalem was to be placed under international control. A UN commission was established to iron out the details and determine the future boundaries.

During the next several months, growing hostility between Jewish and Arab forces—the latter increasingly supported by neighboring Muslim states—provoked the British to announce their decision to withdraw their own peacekeeping forces by May 15, 1948. Shortly after the stroke of midnight, as the British mandate formally came to a close, the Zionist leader David Ben-Gurion (1886–1973) announced the independence of the state of Israel. Later that same day, the new state was formally recognized by the United States, while military forces from several neighboring Muslim states—all of which had vigorously opposed the formation of a Jewish state in the region—entered Israeli territory but were beaten back. Thousands of Arab residents of the new state fled. Internal dissonance among the Arabs, combined with the strength of Jewish resistance groups, contributed to the failure of the invasion, but the bitterness between the two sides did not subside, and the Muslim states refused to recognize the new state of Israel, which became a member of the United Nations, legitimizing it in the eyes of the rest of the world. The stage for future conflict was set.

The exodus of thousands of Palestinian refugees into neighboring Muslim states had repercussions that are still felt today. Jordan, which had become an independent kingdom under its Hashemite ruler, was flooded by the arrival of one million urban Palestinians, overwhelming its own half million people, most of whom were Bedouins. To the north, the state of Lebanon had been created to provide the local Christian community with a country of their own, but the arrival of the Palestinian refugees upset the delicate balance between Christians and Muslims. Moreover, the creation of Lebanon had angered the Syrians, who had lost that land as well as other territories to Turkey as a result of European decisions before and after the war.

Nasser and Pan-Arabism

The dispute over Palestine placed Egypt in an uncomfortable position. Technically, Egypt was not an Arab state. King Farouk, who had acceded to power in 1936, had frequently declared support for the Arab cause, but the Egyptian people were not Bedouins and shared little of the culture of the peoples across the Red Sea. In 1952, King Farouk, whose corrupt habits had severely eroded his early popularity, was overthrown by a military coup engineered by young military officers who abolished the monarchy and established a republic.

In 1954, one of those officers, Colonel Gamal Abdul Nasser (1918–1970), seized power in his own right and immediately instituted a land reform program. He also adopted a policy of neutrality in foreign affairs and expressed sympathy for the Arab cause. The British presence had rankled many Egyptians for years, for even after granting Egypt independence, Britain had retained control over the Suez Canal to protect its route to the Indian Ocean. In 1956, Nasser suddenly nationalized the Suez Canal Company, which had been under British and French administration. Seeing a threat to their route to the Indian Ocean, the British and the French launched a joint attack on Egypt to protect their investment. They were joined by Israel, whose leaders had grown exasperated at sporadic Arab commando raids on Israeli territory and now decided to strike back. But the Eisenhower administration in the United States, concerned that the attack smacked of a revival of colonialism, supported Nasser and brought about the withdrawal of foreign forces from Egypt and of Israeli troops from the Sinai peninsula.

The United Arab Republic   Nasser now turned to pan-Arabism. In 1958, Egypt united with Syria as the United Arab Republic (UAR). The union had been proposed by the Ba'ath Party, which advocated the unity of all Arab states in a new socialist society. In 1957, the Ba'ath Party assumed power in Syria and opened talks with Egypt on a union between the two countries, which took place in March 1958 following a plebiscite. Nasser was named president of the new state.

Egypt and Syria hoped that the union would eventually include all Arab states, but other Arab leaders, including young King Hussein (1935–1999) of Jordan and the kings of Iraq and Saudi Arabia, were suspicious. The latter two in particular feared pan-Arabism on the reasonable assumption that they would be asked to share their vast oil revenues with the poorer states of the Middle East. Indeed, in Nasser's view, through Arab unity, this wealth could be used to improve the standard of living in the area.

In the end, Nasser's plans brought an end to the UAR. When the government announced the nationalization of a large number of industries and utilities in 1961, a military coup overthrew the Ba'ath leaders in Damascus, and the new authorities declared that Syria would end its relationship with Egypt.

The breakup of the UAR did not end the dream of pan-Arabism. During the mid-1960s, Egypt took the lead in promoting Arab unity against Israel. At a meeting of Arab leaders held in Jerusalem in 1964, the Palestine Liberation Organization (PLO) was set up under Egyptian sponsorship to represent the interests of the Palestinians. According to the charter of the PLO, only the Palestinian people (and thus not Jewish immigrants from abroad) had the right to form a state in the old British mandate. A guerrilla movement called al-Fatah, led by the dissident PLO figure Yasir Arafat (1929–2004), began to launch terrorist attacks on Israeli territory.

The Arab-Israeli Dispute

Growing Arab hostility was a constant threat to the security of Israel, whose leaders dedicated themselves to creating a Jewish homeland. The government attempted to build a democratic and modern state that would be a magnet for Jews throughout the world and a symbol of Jewish achievement.

Ensuring the survival of the tiny state surrounded by antagonistic Arab neighbors was a considerable challenge, made more difficult by divisions within the Israeli population. Some were immigrants from Europe, while others came from other states in the Middle East. Some were secular and even socialist in their views, while others were politically and religiously conservative. The state was also home to Christians as well as Muslim Palestinians who had not fled to other countries. To balance these diverse interests, Israel established a parliament, called the Knesset,

Formation of the state of Israel	1948
Founding of the Palestine Liberation Organization	1964
Six-Day War between Arab states and Israel	1967
Yom Kippur War between Arab states and Israel	1973
Camp David accords	1978
Peace talks between Israel and Syria begin	1999
Election of Ariel Sharon as prime minister of Israel	2000
Withdrawal of Israeli settlers from Gaza	2005
Resumption of hostilities in Gaza	2008

on the European model, with proportional representation based on the number of votes each party received in the general election. The parties were so numerous that none ever received a majority of votes, and all governments had to be formed from a coalition of several parties. As a result, moderate secular leaders such as longtime prime minister David Ben-Gurion had to cater to more marginal parties composed of conservative religious groups.

The Six-Day War By the spring of 1967, relations between Israel and its Arab neighbors had deteriorated as Nasser attempted to improve his standing in the Arab world by imposing a blockade against Israeli commerce through the Gulf of Aqaba. Concerned that it might be isolated, and lacking firm support from Western powers (which had originally guaranteed Israel the freedom to use the Gulf of Aqaba), in June 1967, Israel suddenly launched air strikes against Egypt and several of its Arab neighbors. Israeli armies then broke the blockade at the head of the Gulf of Aqaba and occupied the Sinai peninsula. Other Israeli forces attacked Jordanian territory on the West Bank of the Jordan River (Jordan's King Hussein had recently signed an alliance with Egypt and placed his army under Egyptian command), occupied the whole of Jerusalem, and seized Syrian military positions in the Golan Heights, along the Israeli-Syrian border (see Map 29.2). Israel's brief, six-day war had tripled the size of its territory but aroused even more bitter hostility among the Arabs; one million Palestinians were added inside its borders, most of them on the West Bank of the Jordan River.

During the next few years, the focus of the Arab-Israeli dispute shifted as Arab states demanded the return of the territories lost in the 1967 war. Nasser died in 1970 and was succeeded by his vice president, ex-general Anwar al-Sadat (1918–1981). Sadat attempted to renew

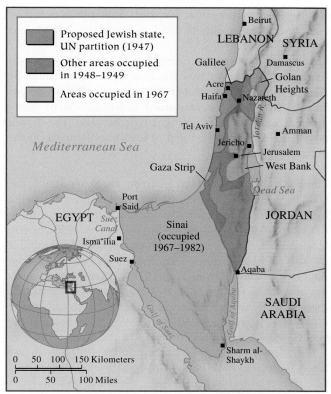

MAP 29.2 Israel and Its Neighbors. This map shows the evolution of the state of Israel since its founding in 1948. Areas occupied by Israel after the Six-Day War in 1967 are indicated in green.

Q What is the significance of the West Bank?

Arab unity through a new confrontation with Israel. In 1973, on Yom Kippur (the Jewish Day of Atonement), an Israeli national holiday, Egyptian forces suddenly launched an air and artillery attack on Israeli positions in the Sinai just east of the Suez Canal. Syrian armies attacked Israeli positions in the Golan Heights. After early Arab successes, the Israelis managed to recoup some of their losses on both fronts. As a superpower confrontation between the United States and the Soviet Union loomed, a cease-fire was finally reached.

The Camp David Agreement After his election as U.S. president in 1976, Jimmy Carter began to press for a compromise peace based on Israel's return of territories occupied during the 1967 war and Arab recognition of the state of Israel. By now, Sadat was anxious to reduce his military expenses and announced his willingness to seek peace. In September 1978, he and Israeli prime minister Menachem Begin (1913–1992) met with Carter at Camp David, the presidential retreat in Maryland. In the first treaty signed with a Muslim state, Israel agreed to withdraw from the Sinai but not from other occupied territories unless other Muslim countries recognized Israel.

The promise of the Camp David agreement was not fulfilled. One reason was the assassination of Sadat by Islamic militants in October 1981. But there were deeper causes, including the continued unwillingness of many Arab governments to recognize Israel and the Israeli government's encouragement of Jewish settlements on the occupied West Bank.

The PLO and the *Intifada* During the early 1980s, the militancy of the Palestinians increased, leading to rising unrest, popularly labeled the ***intifada*** (uprising), among PLO supporters living inside Israel. As the 1990s began, U.S.-sponsored peace talks opened between Israel and a number of its neighbors, but progress was slow. Terrorist attacks by Palestinian militants resulted in heavy casualties and shook the confidence of many Jewish citizens that their security needs had been adequately protected. At the same time, Jewish residents of the West Bank resisted the extension of Palestinian authority in the area.

A new Labour government under Prime Minister Ehud Barak (b. 1942) sought to revitalize the peace process. Negotiations resumed with the PLO and also got under way with Syria over a peace settlement in Lebanon and the possible return of the Golan Heights. But in late 2000, peace talks broke down over the future of the city of Jerusalem, leading to massive riots by Palestinians and the election of a more hard-line Israeli prime minister, former defense minister Ariel Sharon (b. 1928). Sharon's ascent

to leadership was accompanied by a rash of suicide attacks by Palestinians against Israeli targets, an intensive Israeli military crackdown on suspected terrorist sites inside Palestinian territory, and a dramatic increase in bloodshed on both sides. The death of Yasi Arafat in 2004 and his replacement by Palestinian moderate Mahmoud Abbas (b. 1935), as well as the withdrawal of Israeli settlers from Gaza in 2005, raised modest hopes for progress in peace talks, but key issues remain unresolved, including the future status of Jerusalem and Jewish settlements in the occupied territories. In 2006, radical Muslim forces operating in southern Lebanon launched massive attacks on Israeli cities. In response, Israeli troops crossed the border in an effort to wipe out the source of the assault. Two years later, militants in the Gaza Strip launched their own rocket attacks on sites in southern Israel. The latter responded forcefully, thereby raising the specter of a wider conflict. As attitudes hardened, national elections in early 2009 led to the return to office of former Israeli prime minister Benjamin Netanyahu (b. 1949).

Revolution in Iran

In the late 1970s, another crisis arose in Iran, one of the key oil-exporting countries in the region. Under the leadership of Shah Mohammad Reza Pahlavi (1919–1980), who had taken over from his father in 1941, Iran had become one of the richest countries in the Middle East. During the 1950s and 1960s, Iran became a prime U.S. ally in the Middle East. With encouragement from the United States, which hoped that Iran could become

The Temple Mount at Jerusalem. The Temple Mount is one of the most sacred sites in the city of Jerusalem. Originally, it was the site of a temple built during the reign of Solomon, king of the Jews, about 1000 B.C.E. The western wall of the temple is shown in the foreground. Beyond the wall is the Dome of the Rock complex, built on the place from which Muslims believe that Muhammad ascended to heaven. Sacred to both religions, the Temple Mount is now a major bone of contention between Muslims and Jews and a prime obstacle to a final settlement of the Arab-Israeli dispute.

© William J. Duiker

a force for stability in the Persian Gulf, the shah attempted to carry through a series of social and economic reforms to transform the country into the most advanced in the region. Per capita income increased dramatically, literacy rates improved, a modern communications infrastructure took shape, and an affluent middle class emerged in the capital of Tehran.

Under the surface, however, trouble was brewing. Despite an ambitious land reform program, many peasants were still landless, unemployment among intellectuals was dangerously high, and the urban middle class was squeezed by high inflation. Some of the unrest took the form of religious discontent as millions of devout Muslims looked with distaste at a new Iranian civilization based on greed, sexual license, and material accumulation.

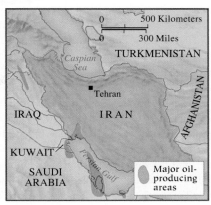

Iran

The Fall of the Shah Leading the opposition was Ayatollah Ruholla Khomeini (1900–1989), an austere Shi'ite cleric who had been exiled to Iraq and then to France because of his outspoken opposition to the shah's regime. From Paris, Khomeini continued his attacks in print, on television, and in radio broadcasts. By the late 1970s, large numbers of Iranians began to respond to Khomeini's diatribes against the "satanic regime," and demonstrations by his supporters were repressed with ferocity by the police. But workers' strikes grew in intensity. In 1979, the government collapsed and was replaced by a hastily formed Islamic republic. The new government, dominated by Shi'ite clergy under the guidance of Ayatollah Khomeini, immediately began to introduce traditional Islamic law. A new reign of terror ensued as supporters of the shah were rounded up and executed.

Though much of the outside world focused on the U.S. embassy in Tehran, where militants held a number of foreign hostages, the Iranian Revolution involved much more. In the eyes of the ayatollah and his followers, the United States was "the great Satan," the powerful protector of Israel, and the enemy of Muslim peoples everywhere. Furthermore, it was responsible for the corruption of Iranian society under the shah. With economic conditions in Iran rapidly deteriorating, the Islamic revolutionary government finally agreed to free the hostages in return for the release of Iranian assets in the United States.

During the next few years, the intensity of the Iranian Revolution moderated slightly as the government displayed a modest tolerance for loosening clerical control over freedom of expression and social activities. But rising criticism of rampant official corruption and a high rate of inflation sparked a new wave of government repression in the mid-1990s; newspapers were censored, the universities were purged of disloyal or "un-Islamic" elements, and religious militants raided private homes in search of blasphemous activities.

In 1997, the moderate Muslim cleric Mohammad Khatemi was elected president of Iran. Khatemi, whose victory reflected a growing desire among many Iranians for a more pluralistic society open to the outside world, promoted a number of reforms, including an easing of press censorship, which led to the emergence of several reformist newspapers and magazines, as well as a relaxation of dress codes and restrictions on women's activities. After his reelection in August 2001, he immediately vowed to continue his reformist efforts. In the days following the terrorist attacks on the United States on September 11, he declared publicly that Muslims must reject terrorism as a tool in promoting Islam. But conservative clerics, anxious to contain the longing for personal freedom that is increasing among younger Iranians, struck back by curtailing freedom of the press and defying parliamentary legislation that they considered destructive of the purity of the Islamic state. Although student protests erupted into the streets in 2003, hard-liners continued to reject proposals to expand civil rights and limit the power of the clerics.

In 2004, presidential elections brought a new leader, Mahmoud Ahmadinejad (b. 1956), to power in Tehran. He immediately inflamed the situation by calling publicly for the destruction of the state of Israel, while his government aroused unease throughout the world by indicating its determination to develop a nuclear energy program, ostensibly for peaceful purposes. Iran has also provided support for the Hezbollah organization in Lebanon and other terrorist groups in the region. Despite worsening conditions at home that eroded the government's popularity, Ahmadinejad was reelected in June 2009, although opponents claimed that numerous irregularities had occurred during the elections.

Crisis in the Gulf

Although much of the Iranians' anger was directed against the United States during the early phases of the revolution, Iran had equally hated enemies closer to

FILM & HISTORY
PERSEPOLIS (2007)

The Iranian author Marjane Satrapi (b. 1969) has re-created *Persepolis,* her autobiographical graphic novel, as an enthralling animated film of the same name. Using simple black-and-white animation, the movie recounts key stages in the turbulent history of modern Iran as seen through the eyes of a spirited young girl, also named Marjane. The dialogue is in French with English subtitles (a version dubbed in English is also available), and the voices of the characters are rendered beautifully by Danielle Darrieux, Catherine Deneuve, Chiara Mastroianni, and other European film stars.

In the film, Marjane is the daughter of middle-class left-wing intellectuals who abhor the dictatorship of the shah and actively participate in his overthrow in 1979. After the revolution, however, the severity of the ayatollah's Islamic rule arouses their secularist and democratic impulses. Encouraged by her loving grandmother, who reinforces her modernist and feminist instincts, Marjane resents having to wear a head scarf and the educational restrictions imposed by the puritanical new Islamic regime, but to little avail. Emotionally exhausted and fearful of political retribution from the authorities, her family finally sends her to study in Vienna.

Study abroad, however, is not a solution to Marjane's problems. She is distressed by the nihilism and emotional shallowness of her new Austrian school friends, who seem oblivious to the contrast between their privileged lives and her own experience of living under the shadow of a tyrannical regime. Disillusioned by the loneliness of exile and several failed love affairs, she descends into a deep depression and then decides to return to Tehran. When she discovers that her family is still suffering from political persecution, however, she decides to leave the country permanently and settles in Paris.

Observing the events, first through the eyes of a child and then through the perceptions of an innocent schoolgirl, the viewer of the film is forced to fill in the blanks, as Marjane initially cannot comprehend the meaning of the adult conversations swirling around her. As Marjane passes through adolescence into adulthood, the realization of the folly of human intransigence and superstition becomes painfully clear, both to her and to the audience. Although animated films have long been a staple in the cinema, thanks in part to Walt Disney, both the novel and the film *Persepolis* demonstrate how graphic design can depict a momentous event in history with clarity and compassion.

---

home. To the north, the immense power of the Soviet Union, driven by atheistic communism, was viewed as a modern version of the Russian threat of previous centuries. To the west was a militant and hostile Iraq, now under the leadership of the ambitious Saddam Hussein (1937–2006). Iraq had just passed through a turbulent period. The monarchy had been overthrown by a military coup in 1958, but conflicts within the ruling military junta led to chronic instability, and in 1979 Colonel Saddam Hussein, a prominent member of the local Ba'athist Party, seized power on his own.

The Vision of Saddam Hussein Saddam Hussein was a fervent believer in the Ba'athist vision of a single Arab state in the Middle East and soon began to persecute non-Arab elements in Iraq, including Persians and Kurds. He then turned his sights to territorial expansion to the east.

Iraq and Iran had long had an uneasy relationship, fueled by religious differences (Iranian Islam is predominantly Shi'ite, while the ruling caste in Iraq was Sunni) and a perennial dispute over borderlands adjacent to the Persian Gulf, the vital waterway for the export of oil from both countries. Like several of its neighbors, Iraq had long dreamed of unifying the Arabs

but had been hindered by internal factions and suspicion among its neighbors.

During the mid-1970s, Iran gave some support to a Kurdish rebellion in the mountains of Iraq. In 1975, the government of the shah agreed to stop aiding the rebels in return for territorial concessions at the head of the Gulf. Five years later, however, the Kurdish revolt had been suppressed.

Saddam Hussein now saw his opportunity; accusing Iran of violating the territorial agreement, he launched an attack on his neighbor in 1980. The war was a bloody one and lasted for nearly ten years. Poison gas was used against civilians, and children were employed to clear minefields. Finally, with both sides virtually exhausted, a cease-fire was arranged in the fall of 1988.

The bitter conflict with Iran had not slaked Saddam Hussein's appetite for territorial expansion. In early August 1990, Iraqi military forces suddenly moved across the border and occupied the small neighboring country of Kuwait at the head of the Gulf. The immediate pretext was the claim that Kuwait was pumping oil from fields inside Iraqi territory. Baghdad was also angry over the Kuwaiti government's demand for repayment of loans it had made to Iraq during the war with Iran. But the underlying reason was Iraq's contention that Kuwait was legally a part of Iraq. Kuwait had been part of the Ottoman Empire until the beginning of the twentieth century, when the local prince had agreed to place his patrimony under British protection. When Iraq became independent in 1932, it claimed the area on the grounds that the state of Kuwait had been created by British imperialism, but opposition from major Western powers and other countries in the region, which feared the consequences of a "greater Iraq," prevented an Iraqi takeover.

Operation Desert Storm The Iraqi invasion of Kuwait in 1990 sparked an international outcry, and the United States assembled a multinational coalition that under the name Operation Desert Storm liberated the country and destroyed a substantial part of Iraq's armed forces. President George H. W. Bush had promised the American people that U.S. troops would not fight with one hand tied behind their backs (a clear reference to the Vietnam War), but the allied forces did not occupy Baghdad at the end of the war out of fear that doing so would cause a breakup of the country, an eventuality that would operate to the benefit of Iran. The allies hoped instead that Saddam's regime would be ousted by an internal revolt. In the meantime, harsh economic sanctions were imposed on the Iraqi government as the condition for peace. The anticipated overthrow of Saddam Hussein did not materialize, however, and his tireless efforts to evade the conditions of the cease-fire continued to bedevil the next U.S. president, Bill Clinton, and his successor, George W. Bush.

Conflicts in Afghanistan and Iraq

The terrorist attacks launched against U.S. cities in September 2001 added a new dimension to the Middle Eastern equation. After the failure of the Soviet Union to quell the rebellion in Afghanistan during the 1980s, a fundamentalist Muslim group known as the Taliban, supported covertly by the United States, seized power in Kabul and ruled the country with a fanaticism reminiscent of the Cultural Revolution in China. Backed by conservative religious forces in Pakistan, the Taliban provided a base of operations for Osama bin Laden's al-Qaeda terrorist network. After the attacks of September 11, a coalition of forces led by the United States overthrew the Taliban and attempted to build a new and moderate government.

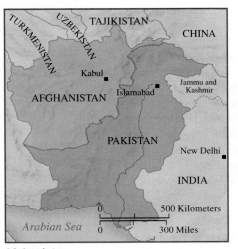

Afghanistan

But the country's history of bitter internecine warfare among various tribal groups presents a severe challenge to those efforts, and Taliban forces, operating in the mountainous regions adjacent to the border with neighboring Pakistan, have managed to regroup and now pose a serious challenge to the government in Kabul.

In the meantime, the George W. Bush administration, charging that Iraqi dictator Saddam Hussein not only had provided support to bin Laden's terrorist organization but also sought to develop weapons of mass destruction, threatened to invade Iraq and remove him from power. The plan, widely debated in the media and opposed by many of the United States' traditional allies, disquieted Arab leaders and fanned anti-American sentiment throughout the Muslim world. Nevertheless, in March 2003, American-led forces attacked Iraq and overthrew Saddam Hussein's regime. In the months that followed, occupation forces sought to restore stability to the country while setting forth plans to lay the foundations of a future democratic society. But although Saddam Hussein was captured by U.S. troops and later executed, armed resistance by militant Muslim elements continues although the level of violence has gradually subsided.

Iraq

Efforts are under way to train an Iraqi military force capable of defeating the insurgents, and a provisional government has been formed, the embryo of a future pro-Western state that could serve as an emblem of democracy in the Middle East. Squabbling among Sunni, Shi'ite, and Kurdish elements within the country, however, is a vivid reminder that a similar effort by the British eighty years earlier ended without success.

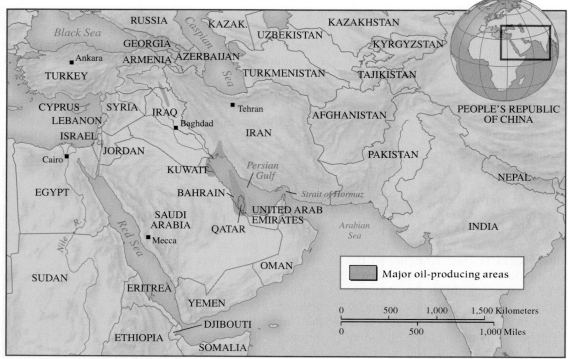

MAP 29.3 The Modern Middle East. Shown here are the boundaries of the independent states in the contemporary Middle East.

Q Which are the major oil-producing countries?

Society and Culture in the Contemporary Middle East

Q Focus Question: How have religious issues affected economic, social, and cultural conditions in the Middle East in recent decades?

To many seasoned observers, such plans seem unrealistic, as democratic values have laid down few roots in the region. In some cases—notably on the Arabian peninsula—feudal rulers remain in power. The kings of Saudi Arabia, for example, continue to rule by traditional precepts and, citing the distinctive character of Muslim political institutions, have been reluctant to establish representative political institutions. In general, these rulers maintain and even enforce the strict observance of traditional customs. Religious police in Saudi Arabia are responsible for enforcing the Muslim dress code, maintaining the prohibition against alcohol, and making sure businesses close during the time for prayer.

Varieties of Government

In other societies, traditional authority has been replaced by charismatic one-party rule or military dictatorships. Nasser's regime in Egypt is a good example of a single-party state where the leader won political power by the force of his presence or personality. Ayatollah Khomeini in Iran, Muammar Qadhafi in Libya, and Saddam Hussein in Iraq are other examples. Although their personal characteristics and images differed, they all owed much of their power to their personal appeal.

In other instances, charismatic rule has given way to modernizing bureaucratic regimes. Examples include the governments of Syria, Yemen, Turkey, and Egypt since Nasser, where Anwar al-Sadat and his successor, Hosni Mubarak (b. 1929), focused their regimes on performance (see Map 29.3). Sometimes the authoritarian character of the regimes has been modified by some democratic tendencies, especially in Turkey, where free elections and the sharing of power have become more prevalent in recent years. A few Arab nations, such as Bahrain, Kuwait, and Jordan, have also engaged in limited forms of democratic experimentation.

Only in Israel, however, are democratic institutions firmly established. The Israeli system suffers from the proliferation of minor parties, some of which are able to dictate policy because their support is essential to keeping a government in power. Nevertheless, the government generally reflects the popular will, and power is transferred by peaceful and constitutional means.

The Economics of the Middle East: Oil and Other Factors

Few areas exhibit a greater disparity of individual and national wealth than the Middle East. While millions live in abject poverty, a fortunate few rank among the wealthiest people in the world. The primary reason for this disparity is oil. Unfortunately for most of the peoples of the region, oil reserves are distributed unevenly and all too often are located in areas where the population density is low. Egypt and Turkey, with more than 75 million inhabitants apiece, have almost no oil reserves. The combined population of oil-rich Kuwait, the United Arab Emirates, and Saudi Arabia is less than 30 million people.

Economics and Islam Not surprisingly, considering their different resources and political systems, the states of the Middle East have adopted diverse approaches to the problem of developing strong and stable economies. Some, like Nasser in Egypt and the leaders of the Ba'ath Party in Syria, attempted to create a form of Arab socialism, favoring a high level of government involvement in the economy to relieve the inequities of the free enterprise system. Others turned to the Western capitalist model to maximize growth while using taxes or development projects to build a modern infrastructure, redistribute wealth, and maintain political stability and economic opportunity for all.

Socialist theories of economic development such as Nasser's were often suggested as a way to promote economic growth while meeting the requirements of Islamic doctrine. Although the Qur'an has little to say about economics and can be variously interpreted as capitalist or socialist, it is clear in its opposition to charging interest and in its concern for the material welfare of the Muslim community, the *umma*. According to socialist theories, state intervention in the economic sector would bring about rapid development, while land redistribution and the nationalization or regulation of industry would minimize the harsh inequities of the marketplace. In general, however, the socialist approach has had little success, and most governments, including those of Egypt and Syria, have shifted to a more free enterprise approach while encouraging foreign investment to compensate for a lack of capital or technology.

Agricultural Policies Although the amount of arable land is relatively small, most countries in the Middle East rely on farming to supply food for their growing populations. Much of the fertile land was owned by wealthy absentee landlords, but land reform programs in several countries have attempted to alleviate this problem. The most comprehensive was instituted in Egypt, where Nasser and his successors managed to reassign nearly a

CHRONOLOGY The Modern Middle East

King Farouk overthrown in Egypt	1952
Egypt nationalizes the Suez Canal	1956
Formation of the United Arab Republic	1958
Iranian Revolution	1979
Iran-Iraq War begins	1980
Iraqi invasion of Kuwait	1990
Persian Gulf War (Operation Desert Storm)	1991
Al-Qaeda terrorist attack on the United States	2001
U.S.-led forces invade Iraq	2003
Ahmadinejad elected president of Iran	2004

See also the chronology of the Arab-Israeli conflict on p. 739

quarter of all cultivable lands by limiting the amount a single individual could hold. Similar programs in Iran, Iraq, Libya, and Syria generally had less effect.

Agricultural productivity throughout the region has been plagued by the lack of water. With populations growing at more than 2 percent annually on average in the Middle East (more than 3 percent in some countries), several governments have tried to increase the amount of water available for irrigation. Many attempts have been sabotaged by government ineptitude, political disagreements, and territorial conflicts, however. Today, the dearth of water in the region is reaching crisis proportions.

Migratory Workers Another way governments have attempted to deal with rapid population growth is to encourage emigration. Oil-producing states with small populations, such as Saudi Arabia and the United Arab Emirates, have imported labor from other countries in the region, mostly to work in the oil fields. Since the mid-1980s, the majority of the population in the smallest states has been composed of foreign nationals, who often send the bulk of their salaries back to their families in their home countries. When oil revenues declined in the late 1980s, and 1990s, however, several governments took measures to stabilize or reduce the migrant population.

Obstacles to Democracy What explains the failure of democratic institutions and values to take root in the contemporary Middle East? Some observers attribute the cause to the willingness of Western governments to coddle dictatorships as a means of preserving their access to the vast oil reserves located on the Arabian peninsula. Others ascribe it to deep-seated factors embedded in the history and culture of the region or in the religion of Islam itself. Whatever the cause, critics charge that the

ISLAM AND DEMOCRACY

RELIGION & PHILOSOPHY

One of George W. Bush's key objectives in launching the invasion of Iraq in 2003 was to promote the emergence of democratic states throughout the Middle East. According to U.S. officials, one of the ultimate causes of the formation of terrorist movements in Muslim societies is the prevalence in such countries of dictatorial governments that do not serve the interests of their citizens. According to the Pakistani author of this editorial, the problem lies as much with the actions of Western countries as it does with political attitudes in the Muslim world.

M. J. Akbar, "Linking Islam to Dictatorship"

Let us examine a central canard, that Islam and democracy are incompatible. This is an absurdity. There is nothing Islamic or un-Islamic about democracy. Democracy is the outcome of a political process, not a religious process.

It is glibly suggested that "every" Muslim country is a dictatorship, but the four largest Muslim populations of the world—in Indonesia, India, Bangladesh, and Turkey—vote to change governments. Pakistan could easily have been on this list.

Voting does not make these Muslims less or more religious. There are dictators among Muslims just as there are dictators among Christians, Buddhists, and Hindus (check out Nepal).... Christian Latin America has seen ugly forms of dictatorship, as has Christian Africa.

What is unique to the Muslim world is not the absence of democracy but the fact that in 1918, after the defeat of the Ottoman Empire, every single Muslim in the world lived under foreign subjugation.

Every single one, from Indonesia to Morocco via Turkey. The Turks threw out their invaders within a few years under the great leadership of Kemal Atatürk, but the transition to self-rule in other Muslim countries was slow, uncertain, and full of traps planted by the world's preeminent powers.

The West, in the shape of Britain, France, or America, was never interested in democracy when a helpful dictator or king

would serve. When people got a chance to express their wish, it was only logical that they would ask for popular rule. It was the street that brought Mossadegh to power in Iran and drove the shah of Iran to tearful exile in Rome. Who brought the shah of Iran and autocracy back to Iran? The CIA.

If Iranian democracy had been permitted a chance in 1953, there would have been no uprising led by Ayatollah Khomeini in 1979. In other countries, where the struggle for independence was long and brutal, as in Algeria and Indonesia, the militias who had fought the war institutionalized army authority. In other instances, civilian heroes confused their own well-being with national health. They became regressive dictators. Once again, there was nothing Islamic about it.

Muslim countries will become democracies, too, because it is the finest form of modern governance. But it will be a process interrupted by bloody experience as the street wrenches power from usurpers.

Democracy has happened in Turkey. It has happened in Bangladesh. It is happening in Indonesia. It almost happened in Pakistan, and the opportunity will return. Democracy takes time in the most encouraging environments.

Democracy has become the latest rationale for the occupation of Iraq.... Granted, democracy is always preferable to tyranny no matter how it comes. But Iraqis are not dupes. They will take democracy and place it at the service of nationalism. A decade ago, America was careless about the definition of victory. Today it is careless about the definition of democracy.

There is uncertainty and apprehension across the Muslim nations: uncertainty about where they stand, and apprehension about both American power and the repugnant use of terrorism that in turn invites the exercise of American power. There is also anger that a legitimate cause like that of Palestine can get buried in the debris of confusion. Muslims do not see Palestinians as terrorists.

Q *How does the author answer the charge that democracy and Islam are incompatible? To what degree is the West responsible for the problems of the Middle East?*

lack of personal freedom has aroused a level of popular discontent that local governments seek to deflect—often with great success—onto the West (see the box above). For their part, Middle Eastern political leaders undoubtedly fear that greater popular participation in the affairs of state could disrupt the precarious stability of many states in the region.

The Islamic Revival

In recent years, many developments in the Middle East have been described in terms of a resurgence of

traditional values and customs in response to Western influence. Indeed, some conservative religious forces in the area have consciously attempted to replace foreign culture and values with allegedly "pure" Islamic forms of belief and behavior.

But the Islamic revival is not a simple dichotomy between traditional and modern, native and foreign, or irrational and rational. In the first place, many Muslims in the Middle East still believe that Islamic values and modern ways are not incompatible and may even be mutually reinforcing. Second, the resurgence of what are sometimes called "fundamentalist" Islamic groups may, in

The Quiet Spirit of a Mosque. For Muslims, the mosque is a revered oasis for worship, reflection, and the reading of the Qur'an. Required to pray five times a day—at dawn, noon, midafternoon, sunset, and early evening—a Muslim, after ritual ablutions, prostrates himself facing Mecca to proclaim "There is no god but Allah, and Muhammad is his prophet." But the mosque is also a place for quiet devotion, a refuge from the bustle of daily life. The artwork in a mosque should reflect motifs from the Qur'an. In this photo, two of the faithful pray in a mosque under iron lamps on plush layers of carpets decorated with Qur'anic symbols.

© William J. Duiker

a Middle Eastern context, appear to be a rational and practical response to self-destructive practices, such as corruption and hedonism, drunkenness, prostitution, and the use of drugs. Finally, the reassertion of Islamic values is seen as a means of establishing a cultural identity and fighting off the overwhelming impact of Western ideas (see the comparative essay on p. 730).

Modernist Islam Initially, many Muslim intellectuals responded to Western influence by trying to create a "modernized" set of Islamic beliefs and practices that would not clash with the demands of the twentieth century. This process took place in most Islamic societies, but it was especially prevalent in Turkey, Egypt, and Iran, all of which attempted to make use of Islamic values while asserting the primacy of other issues such as political and economic development.

These secularizing trends were particularly noticeable among the political, intellectual, and economic elites in urban areas. They had less influence in the countryside, among the poor, and among devout elements within the clergy. Many of the clerics believed that Western influence in the cities had given birth to political and economic corruption, sexual promiscuity, hedonism, individualism, and the prevalence of alcohol, pornography, and drugs. Although such practices had long existed in the Middle East, they were now far more visible and socially acceptable.

Return to Tradition The movement to return to traditional practices strengthened after World War II and reached its zenith in Iran under Ayatollah Khomeini. It is not surprising that Iran took the lead, in light of its long tradition of ideological purity within the Shi'ite sect as well as the uncompromisingly secular character of the shah's reforms in the postwar era. In Iran today, traditional Islamic beliefs are all-pervasive and extend into education, clothing styles, social practices, and the legal system.

The cultural and social effects of the Iranian Revolution were profound as Iranian ideas spread throughout the area. In Algeria, the political influence of fundamentalist Islamic groups grew substantially and enabled them to win a stunning victory in the national elections in 1992. When the military stepped in to cancel the second round of elections and crack down on the militants, the latter responded with a campaign of terrorism against moderates that has claimed thousands of lives.

A similar trend emerged in Egypt, where militant groups such as the Muslim Brotherhood engaged in terrorism, including the assassination of Sadat and attacks on foreign tourists, who are considered carriers of corrupt Western influence.

Even in Turkey, generally considered the most secular of Islamic societies, a militant political group known as the Islamic Welfare Party took power in a coalition government formed in 1996. Worried moderates voiced their concern that the secular legacy of Kemal Atatürk was being eroded, and eventually the new prime minister Necmettin Erbakan, agreed to resign under heavy pressure from the military. Frustrated with delays in its application for membership in the European Union and uncomfortable with the militancy of its Arab neighbors, Turkey has established a security relationship with Israel and seeks close ties with the United States. But religious and economic discontent lies just beneath the surface.

Women and Islam

Nowhere have the fault lines between tradition and modernity within Muslim societies in the Middle East been so

Iranian Women Practicing Soccer. Despite the rule that they must cover their bodies in public, young Iranian women play soccer and other sports, attend schools and universities, and partake in other activities of the modern world. Here we see a young woman playing soccer in her black-hooded garment. Although they rarely did so before the Islamic Revolution, today about two million Iranian women take part in sports.

instructed to wear the veil and to dress modestly in public. Films produced in postrevolutionary Iran rarely featured women, and when they did, physical contact between men and women was prohibited. The events in Iran had repercussions in secular Muslim societies such as Egypt, Turkey, and far-off Malaysia, where women began to dress more modestly in public, and criticism of open sexuality in the media became increasingly frequent.

The most conservative nation by far is still Saudi Arabia, where women are not only segregated and expected to wear the veil in public but are also restricted in education and forbidden to drive automobiles. Still, women's rights have been extended in a few countries. In 1999, women obtained the right to vote in Kuwait, while they have been granted an equal right with their husbands to seek a divorce in Egypt. Even in Iran, women have many freedoms that they lacked before the twentieth century; for example, they can attend a university, receive military training, vote, practice birth control, and publish fiction.

Literature and Art

As in other areas of Asia and Africa, the encounter with the West in the nineteenth and twentieth centuries stimulated a cultural renaissance in the Middle East. Muslim authors translated Western works into Arabic and Persian and began to experiment with new literary forms.

Literature Iran has produced one of the most prominent national literatures in the contemporary Middle East. Since World War II, Iranian literature has been hampered somewhat by political considerations, since it has been expected to serve first the Pahlavi monarchy and then the Islamic republic. Nevertheless, Iranian writers are among the most prolific in the region and often write in prose, which has finally been accepted as the equal of poetry.

Despite the male-oriented character of Iranian society, many of the new writers have been women. Since the revolution, the veil and the *chador,* an all-enveloping cloak, have become the central metaphor in Iranian women's writing. Those who favor the veil and *chador* praise them as the last bastion of defense against Western cultural imperialism. Behind the veil, the Islamic woman can breathe freely, unpolluted by foreign exploitation and moral corruption. Other Iranian women, however, consider the *chador* a "mobile prison" or an oppressive anachronism from the Dark Ages. As one writer, Sousan Azadi, expressed it, "As I pulled the *chador* over me, I felt a heaviness descending over me. I was hidden and in hiding.

sharp as in the ongoing debate over the role of women. At the beginning of the twentieth century, women's place in Middle Eastern society had changed little since the death of the prophet Muhammad. Women were secluded in their homes and had few legal, political, or social rights.

During the first decades of the twentieth century, advocates of modernist views began to contend that Islamic doctrine was not inherently opposed to women's rights. To modernists, Islamic traditions such as female seclusion, wearing the veil, and even polygamy were actually pre-Islamic folk traditions that had been tolerated in the early Islamic era and continued to be practiced in later centuries. Such views had considerable impact on a number of Middle Eastern societies, including Turkey and Iran. As we have seen, greater rights for women were a crucial element in the social revolution promoted by Kemal Atatürk in Turkey. In Iran, Shah Reza Khan and his son granted female suffrage and encouraged the education of women.

In recent years, a more traditional view of women's role has tended to prevail in many Middle Eastern countries. Attacks by religious conservatives on the growing role of women contributed to the emotions underlying the Iranian Revolution of 1979. Iranian women were

There was nothing visible left of Sousan Azadi."[6] Whether or not they accept the veil and *chador,* women writers are a vital part of contemporary Iranian literature and are addressing all aspects of social issues.

Like Iran, Egypt in the twentieth century has experienced a flowering of literature accelerated by the establishment of the Egyptian republic in the early 1950s. The most illustrious contemporary Egyptian writer was Naguib Mahfouz (1911–2006), who won the Nobel Prize for Literature in 1988. His *Cairo Trilogy* (1952) chronicles three generations of a merchant family in Cairo during the tumultuous years between the world wars. Mahfouz was particularly adept at blending panoramic historical events with the intimate lives of ordinary human beings.

Unlike many other modern writers, his message was essentially optimistic and reflected his hope that religion and science can work together for the overall betterment of humankind.

Art Like literature, the art of the modern Middle East has been profoundly influenced by its exposure to Western culture. At first, artists tended to imitate Western models, but later they began to experiment with national styles, returning to earlier forms for inspiration. Some emulated the writers in returning to the village to depict peasants and shepherds, but others followed international trends and attempted to express the alienation and disillusionment that characterize so much of modern life.

TIMELINE

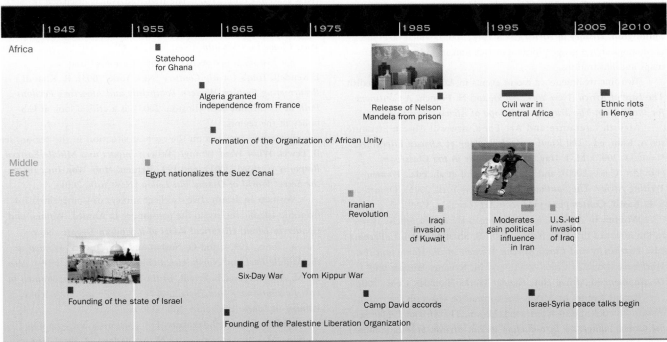

| | 1945 | 1955 | 1965 | 1975 | 1985 | 1995 | 2005 | 2010 |

Africa

Statehood for Ghana

Algeria granted independence from France

Formation of the Organization of African Unity

Release of Nelson Mandela from prison

Civil war in Central Africa

Ethnic riots in Kenya

Middle East

Egypt nationalizes the Suez Canal

Iranian Revolution

Iraqi invasion of Kuwait

Moderates gain political influence in Iran

U.S.-led invasion of Iraq

Six-Day War   Yom Kippur War

Founding of the state of Israel

Camp David accords

Israel-Syria peace talks begin

Founding of the Palestine Liberation Organization

CONCLUSION

THE MIDDLE EAST, like the continent of Africa, is one of the most unstable regions in the the world today. In part, this turbulence is due to the continued interference of outsiders attracted by the massive oil reserves under the parched wastes of the Arabian peninsula and in the vicinity of the Persian Gulf. Oil is indeed both a blessing and a curse to the peoples of the region.

Another factor contributing to the volatility of the Middle East is the tug-of-war between the sense of ethnic identity in the form of nationalism and the intense longing to be part of a broader Islamic community, a dream that dates back to the time of the prophet

Muhammad. The desire to create that community—a vision threatened by the presence of the alien state of Israel—inspired Gamal Abdul Nasser in the 1950s and Ayatollah Khomeini in the 1970s and 1980s and probably has motivated many of the actions of Saddam Hussein and Osama bin Laden.

A final reason for the turmoil currently affecting the Middle East is the intense debate over the role of religion in civil society. Although efforts in various Muslim countries to return to an allegedly purer form of Islam appear harsh and even repugnant to many observers, it is important to note that Muslim societies are not alone in deploring the sense of moral decline that is now allegedly taking place in societies throughout the world. Nor are they alone in advocating a restoration of traditional religious values as a means of reversing the trend. Not infrequently, members of such groups turn to violence as a means of making their point.

Whatever the reasons, it is clear that a deep-seated sense of anger is surging through much of the Islamic world today, an anger that transcends specific issues like the situation in Iraq or the Arab-Israeli dispute. Although economic privation and political oppression are undoubtedly important factors, the roots of Muslim resentment, as historian Bernard Lewis has pointed out, lie in a historical sense of humiliation at the hands of a Western colonialism that first emerged centuries ago, when the Arab hegemony in the Mediterranean region was replaced by European domination, and culminated early in the twentieth century, when much of the Middle East was occupied by Western colonial regimes. Today, the world is reaping the harvest of that long-cultivated bitterness, and the consequences cannot be foreseen.

SUGGESTED READING

Africa: General For a general survey of contemporary African history, see **R. Oliver, *The African Experience*** (New York, 2000), which contains interesting essays on a variety of themes, and **K. Shillington, *History of Africa*** (New York, 2005), which takes a chronological and geographical approach and includes excellent maps and illustrations.

Two fine treatments of recent events in Africa are **M. Meredith, *The Fate of Africa*** (New York, 2005), and **H. French, *A Continent for the Taking: The Tragedy and Hope of Africa*** (New York, 2004).

African Literature and Art For a survey of African literature, see **A. Kalu, ed., *The Rienner Anthropology of African Literatures*** (London, 2007); **M. J. Hay, *African Novels in the Classroom*** (Boulder, Colo., 2000); and **M. J. Daymond et al., eds., *Women Writing Africa: The Southern Region*** (New York, 2003). On art, see **S. L. Kasfir, *Contemporary African Art*** (London, 1999).

Women in Africa For interesting analyses of women's issues in the Africa of this time frame, see **S. B. Stichter** and **J. L. Parpart** eds., ***Patriarchy and Class: African Women in the Home and the Workforce*** (Boulder, Colo., 1988), and **M. Kevane, *Women and Development in Africa: How Gender Works*** (Boulder, Colo., 2004).

Recent Events in Africa For contrasting views on the reasons for Africa's current difficulties, see **J. Marah, *The African People in the Global Village: An Introduction to Pan-African Studies*** (Lanham, Md., 1998), and **G. Ayittey, *Africa in Chaos*** (New York, 1998).

The Middle East Good general surveys of the modern Middle East include **A. Goldschmidt Jr., *A Concise History of the Middle East*** (Boulder, Colo., 2005), and **G. E. Perry, *The Middle East: Fourteen Islamic Centuries*** (Elizabeth, N.J., 1992). On Israel and the Palestinian question, see **D. Ross, *The Missing Peace: The Inside Story of the Fight for Middle East Peace*** (New York, 2004). On Jerusalem, see **B. Wasserstein, *Divided Jerusalem: The Struggle for the Holy City*** (New Haven, Conn., 2000). The issue of oil is examined in **D. Yergin et al., *The Prize: The Epic Quest for Oil, Money, and Power*** (New York, 1993). Also see **M. H. Kerr** and **E. S. Yassin, eds., *Rich and Poor States in the Middle East: Egypt and the New Arab Order*** (Boulder, Colo., 1985).

Iran and Iraq On the Iranian Revolution, see **S. Bakash, *The Reign of the Ayatollahs*** (New York, 1984). Iran's role in Middle Eastern politics and diplomacy is analyzed in **T. Parsi, *Treacherous Alliance: The Secret Dealings of Israel, Iran, and the United States*** (New Haven, Conn., 2007). The Iran-Iraq War is discussed in **C. Davies, ed., *After the War: Iran, Iraq and the Arab Gulf*** (Chichester, England, 1990), and **S. C. Pelletiere, *The Iran-Iraq War: Chaos in a Vacuum*** (New York, 1992).

For historical perspective on the invasion of Iraq, see **J. Kendell, *Iraq's Unruly Century*** (New York, 2003). **R. Khalidi, *Resurrecting Empire: Western Footprints and America's Perilous Path in the Middle East*** (Boston, 2003), is a critical look at U.S. policy in the region.

For expert analysis on the current situation in the region, see **B. Lewis, *What Went Wrong? Western Impact and Middle Eastern Response*** (Oxford, 2001), and **P. L. Bergen, *Holy War, Inc.: Inside the Secret World of Osama bin Laden*** (New York, 2001).

Women in Islam Two excellent surveys of women in Islam from pre-Islamic society to the present are **L. Ahmed, *Women and Gender in Islam: Historical Roots of a Modern Debate*** (New Haven, Conn., 1993), and **G. Nashat** and **J. E. Tucker, *Women in the Middle East and North Africa*** (Bloomington, Ind., 1999). Also see **M. Afkhami** and **E. Friedl, *In the Eye of the Storm: Women in Post-Revolutionary Iran*** (Syracuse, N.Y., 1994), and **W. Wiebke, *Women in Islam*** (Princeton, N.J., 1995).

Middle Eastern Literature For a scholarly but accessible overview of Arabic literature, see **M. M. Badawi, *A Short History of Modern Arab Literature*** (Oxford, 1993). On Iranian literature, see **S. Sullivan** and **F. Milani, *Stories by Iranian Women Since the Revolution*** (Austin, Tex., 1991), and **M. M. Khorrami** and **S. Vatanabadi, eds., *A Feast in the Mirror: Short Stories by Contemporary Iranian Women*** (Boulder, Colo., 2000).

WORLD HISTORY RESOURCES

Visit the website for *The Essential World History* to access study aids such as Flashcards, Critical Thinking Exercises, and Chapter Quizzes:

www.cengage.com/history/duikspiel/essentialworld6e

What factors can be advanced to explain the chronic instability and internal conflict that have characterized conditions in Africa and the Middle East since World War II?

In thinking about this question, begin by breaking it down into the components shown below. A discussion of the significance of each component should appear in your answer.

INTERACTION AND EXCHANGE   Look at the map of the Middle East. Which nations in the Middle East are major oil producers? What types of governments do these nations have? To what extent have Western nations been involved in the affairs of these nations? How have oil revenues or the lack thereof affected political and economic developments in countries throughout the region? Which nations are democracies, and which are dictatorships or monarchies?

According to M. J. Akbar (document, p. 746), what role has the West played in promoting nondemocratic governments? What was the Western nations' rationale for this? Do you think that nondemocratic governments in Muslim countries are related to Islam, or should the lack of democracy be attributed to other factors such as economic conditions? How have the divisions within Islam, as shown in the map of Iraq, contributed to political instability in that country? In what ways has the West contributed to the problems of the Middle East? To the problems of Africa?

Iraq

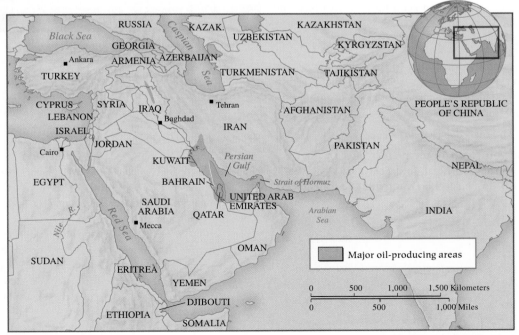

The Modern Middle East

CHAPTER 30
TOWARD THE PACIFIC CENTURY?

The Petronas Towers in Kuala Lumpur, Malaysia

© Angelo Cavalli/Getty Images

FIRST-TIME VISITORS to the Malaysian capital of Kuala Lumpur are astonished to observe a pair of twin towers thrusting up above the surrounding buildings into the clouds. The Petronas Towers rise 1,483 feet from ground level; they were the world's tallest buildings at the time of their completion in 1998. (They have since been surpassed by Taipei 101, in Taiwan; the Shanghai World Financial Center; and Burj Khalifa, in Dubai.)

Beyond their status as an architectural achievement, the Petronas Towers announced the emergence of Southeast Asia as a major player on the international scene. It is no accident that the foundations were laid on the site of the Selangor Cricket Club, symbol of British colonial hegemony in Southeast Asia. "These towers," commented one local official, "will do wonders for Asia's self-esteem and confidence, which I think is very important, and which I think at this moment are at the point of takeoff."[1]

The sky-piercing towers in Kuala Lumpur and Taipei are not alone in signaling Asia's new prominence on the world stage in the century now unfolding. Several other cities in the region, including Hong Kong, Singapore, Tokyo, and Shanghai, have become major capitals of finance and monuments of economic prowess, rivaling the traditional centers of New York, London, Berlin, and Paris.

That the nations of the Pacific Rim would become a driving force in global development was all but unimaginable after World War II, when the Communist triumph in China ushered in an era of intense competition between the capitalist and socialist camps. Bitter conflicts in Korea and Vietnam were visible manifestations of a region in turmoil. Yet today, many of the nations of eastern Asia have become models of successful nation building, characterized by economic prosperity and political stability. They have heralded the opening of what has been called the "Pacific Century." ❀

South Asia

Q Focus Question: How did Gandhi's and Nehru's goals for India differ, and what role did each leader's views play in shaping modern India?

In 1947, nearly two centuries of British colonial rule came to an end when two new independent nations, India and Pakistan, came into being.

The End of the British Raj

During the 1930s, the nationalist movement in India was severely shaken by factional disagreements between Hindus and Muslims. The outbreak of World War II subdued these sectarian clashes, but they erupted again after the war ended in 1945. Battles between Hindus and Muslims broke out in several cities, and Muhammad Ali Jinnah (1876–1948), leader of the Muslim League, demanded the creation of a separate state for each. Meanwhile, the Labour Party, which had long been critical of the British colonial legacy on both moral and economic grounds, had come to power in Britain, and the new prime minister, Clement Attlee, announced that power would be transferred to "responsible Indian hands" by June 1948.

But the imminence of independence did not dampen communal strife. As riots escalated, the British reluctantly accepted the inevitability of partition and declared that on August 15, 1947, two independent nations—Hindu India and Muslim Pakistan—would be established. Pakistan would be divided between the main area of Muslim habitation in the Indus River valley in the west and a separate territory in east Bengal 2,000 miles to the east. Although Mahatma Gandhi warned that partition would provoke "an orgy of blood,"[2] he was increasingly regarded as a figure of the past, and his views were ignored.

The British instructed the rulers in the princely states to choose which state they would join by August 15, but problems arose in predominantly Hindu Hyderabad, where the nawab (viceroy) was a Muslim, and mountainous Kashmir, where a Hindu prince ruled over a Muslim population. After independence was declared, the flight of millions of Hindus and Muslims across the borders led to violence and the deaths of more than a million people. One of the casualties was Gandhi, who was assassinated on January 30, 1948, as he was going to morning prayer. The assassin, a Hindu militant, was apparently motivated by Gandhi's opposition to a Hindu India.

Independent India

With independence, the Indian National Congress, now renamed the Congress Party, moved from opposition to the responsibility of power under Jawaharlal Nehru, the new prime minister. The prospect must have been intimidating. The vast majority of India's 400 million people were poor and illiterate. The new nation encompassed a significant number of ethnic groups and fourteen major languages. Although Congress Party leaders spoke bravely of building a new nation, Indian society still bore the scars of past wars and divisions.

The government's first problem was to resolve disputes left over from the transition period. The rulers of Hyderabad and Kashmir had both followed their own preferences rather than the wishes of their subject populations. Nehru was determined to include both states within India. In 1948, Indian troops invaded Hyderabad and annexed the area. India was also able to seize most of Kashmir, but at the cost of creating an intractable problem that has poisoned relations with Pakistan down to the present day.

An Experiment in Democratic Socialism Under Nehru's leadership, India adopted a political system on the British model, with a figurehead president and a parliamentary form of government. A number of political parties operated legally, but the Congress Party, with its enormous prestige and charismatic leadership, was dominant at both the central and the local levels.

Nehru had been influenced by British socialism and patterned his economic policy roughly after the program of the British Labour Party. The state took over ownership of the major industries and resources, transportation, and utilities, while private enterprise was permitted at the local and retail levels. Farmland remained in private hands, but rural cooperatives were officially encouraged.

In other respects, Nehru was a devotee of Western materialism. He was convinced that to succeed, India must industrialize. In advocating industrialization, Nehru

Although Jawaharlal Nehru and Mohandas Gandhi agreed on their desire for an independent India, their visions of the future of their homeland were dramatically different. Nehru favored industrialization to build material prosperity, whereas Gandhi praised the simple virtues of manual labor. The first excerpt is from a speech by Nehru; the second is from a letter written by Gandhi to Nehru.

Nehru's Socialist Creed

I am convinced that the only key to the solution of the world's problems and of India's problems lies in socialism, and when I use this word I do so not in a vague humanitarian way but in the scientific economic sense.... I see no way of ending the poverty, the vast unemployment, the degradation and the subjection of the Indian people except through socialism. That involves vast and revolutionary changes in our political and social structure, the ending of vested interests in land and industry, as well as the feudal and autocratic Indian states system. That means the ending of private property, except in a restricted sense, and the replacement of the present profit system by a higher ideal of cooperative service.... In short, it means a new civilization, radically different from the present capitalist order. Some glimpse we can have of this new civilization in the territories of the U.S.S.R. Much has happened there which has pained me greatly and with which I disagree, but I look upon that great and fascinating unfolding of a new order and a new civilization as the most promising feature of our dismal age.

A Letter to Jawaharlal Nehru

I believe that if India, and through India the world, is to achieve real freedom, then sooner or later we shall have to go and live in the villages—in huts, not in palaces. Millions of people can never live in cities and palaces in comfort and peace. Nor can they do so by killing one another, that is, by resorting to violence and untruth.... We can have the vision of... truth and nonviolence only in the simplicity of the villages. That simplicity resides in the spinning wheel and what is implied by the spinning wheel....

You will not be able to understand me if you think that I am talking about the villages of today. My ideal village still exists only in my imagination.... In this village of my dreams the villager will not be dull—he will be all awareness. He will not live like an animal in filth and darkness. Men and women will live in freedom, prepared to face the whole world. There will be no plague, no cholera, and no smallpox. Nobody will be allowed to be idle or to wallow in luxury. Everyone will have to do body labor. Granting all this, I can still envisage a number of things that will have to be organized on a large scale. Perhaps there will even be railways and also post and telegraph offices. I do not know what things there will be or will not be. Nor am I bothered about it. If I can make sure of the essential thing, other things will follow in due course. But if I give up the essential thing, I give up everything.

Q *What are the key differences between these two views on the future of India? Why do you think Nehru's proposals triumphed over those of Mahatma Gandhi?*

---

departed sharply from Gandhi, who believed that materialism was morally corrupting and that only simplicity and nonviolence (as represented by the traditional Indian village and the symbolic spinning wheel) could save India, and the world itself, from self-destruction (see the box above).

The primary themes of Nehru's foreign policy were anticolonialism and antiracism. Under his guidance, India took a neutral stance in the Cold War and sought to provide leadership to all newly independent nations in Asia, Africa, and Latin America. India's neutrality put it at odds with the United States, which during the 1950s was trying to mobilize all nations against what it viewed as the menace of international communism.

Relations with Pakistan continued to be troubled. India refused to consider Pakistan's claim to Kashmir, even though the majority of the population there was Muslim. Tension between the two countries persisted, erupting into war in 1965. In 1971, when riots against the Pakistani government broke out in East Pakistan, India

intervened on the side of East Pakistan, which declared its independence as the new nation of Bangladesh (see Map 30.1).

The Post-Nehru Era Nehru's death in 1964 aroused concern that Indian democracy was dependent on the Nehru mystique. When his successor, a Congress Party veteran, died in 1966, party leaders selected Nehru's daughter, Indira Gandhi (no relation to Mahatma Gandhi), as the new prime minister. Gandhi (1917–1984) was inexperienced in politics, but she quickly showed the steely determination of her father.

Like Nehru, Gandhi embraced democratic socialism and a policy of neutrality in foreign affairs, but she was more activist in promoting her objectives than her father. To combat rural poverty, she nationalized banks, provided loans to peasants on easy terms, built low-cost housing, distributed land to the landless, and introduced electoral reforms to enfranchise the poor.

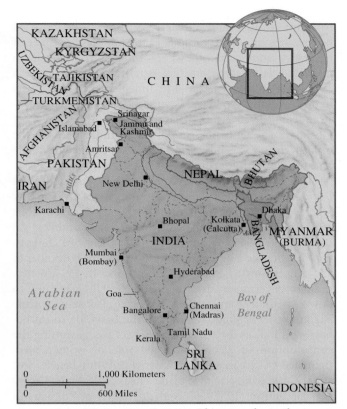

MAP 30.1 **Modern South Asia.** This map shows the boundaries of all the states in contemporary South Asia. **Q** Which of the countries on this map have a Muslim majority?

Gandhi was especially worried by India's growing population and, in an effort to curb the growth rate, adopted a policy of forced sterilization. This policy proved unpopular, however, and, along with growing official corruption and Gandhi's authoritarian tactics, led to her defeat in the general election of 1975, the first time the Congress Party had failed to win a majority at the national level.

A minority government of procapitalist parties was formed, but within two years, Gandhi was back in power. She now faced a new challenge, however, in the rise of religious strife. The most dangerous situation was in the Punjab, where militant Sikhs were demanding autonomy or even independence from India. Gandhi did not shrink from a confrontation and attacked Sikh rebels hiding in their Golden Temple in the city of Amritsar. The incident aroused widespread anger among the Sikh community, and in 1984, Sikh members of Gandhi's personal body-guard assassinated her.

By now, Congress Party politicians were convinced that the party could not remain in power without a member of the Nehru family at the helm. Gandhi's son Rajiv (1944–1991), a commercial airline pilot with little interest in politics, was persuaded to replace his mother as prime minister. Rajiv lacked the strong ideological and political convictions of his mother and grandfather and allowed a greater role for private enterprise. But his government was criticized for cronyism, inefficiency, and corruption.

Rajiv Gandhi also sought to play a role in regional affairs, mediating a dispute between the government in Sri Lanka and Tamil rebels (known as the "Elam tigers") who were ethnically related to the majority population in southern India. The decision cost him his life: while campaigning for reelection in 1991, he was assassinated by a member of the Tiger organization. India faced the future without a member of the Nehru family as prime minister.

During the early 1990s, the Congress Party remained the leading party, but the powerful hold it once had on the Indian electorate was gone. New parties, such as the militantly Hindu Bharatiya Janata Party (BJP), actively vied with the Congress Party for control of the central and state governments. Growing political instability at the center was accompanied by rising tensions between Hindus and Muslims.

When a coalition government formed under Congress leadership collapsed, the BJP, under Prime Minister A. B. Vajpayee, ascended to power and played on Hindu sensibilities to build its political base. The new government based its success on an aggressive program of privatization in the industrial and commercial sectors and made a major effort to promote the nation's small but growing technological base. But BJP leaders had underestimated the discontent of India's less affluent citizens (an estimated 350 million Indians earn less than one U.S. dollar a day), and in the spring of 2004, a stunning defeat in national elections forced the Vajpayee government to resign. The Congress Party returned to power at the head of a coalition government based on a commitment to maintain economic growth while carrying out reforms in rural areas, including public works projects and hot lunch programs for all primary school children. But sectarian strife between Hindus and Muslims, as well as pervasive official corruption, continued to bedevil the government. In the fall of 2008, a terrorist attack in the city of Mumbai left nearly 200 dead and raised serious questions about the effectiveness of Indian security procedures. Indian officials charged that the inspiration for the attack came from Pakistan.

The Land of the Pure: Pakistan Since Independence

When Pakistan achieved independence in August 1947, it was, unlike its neighbor India, in all respects a new nation, based on religious conviction rather than historical or ethnic tradition. The unique state consisted of two separate territories 2,000 miles apart. West Pakistan, including the Indus River basin and the West Punjab, was perennially short of water and was populated by dry crop farmers and peoples of the steppe. East Pakistan was made up of the marshy deltas of the Ganges and Brahmaputra rivers. Densely populated with rice farmers, it was the home of the artistic and intellectual Bengalis.

The peoples of West Pakistan were especially diverse and included, among others, Pushtuns, Baluchis, and Punjabis. The Pushtuns are organized on a tribal basis and have kinship ties with the majority population across the border in neighboring Afghanistan. Many are nomadic and cross the border on a regular basis with their flocks. The Baluchis straddle the border with Iran, while the region of Punjab was divided between Pakistan and India at the moment of independence.

Even though the new state was an essentially Muslim society, its first years were marked by intense internal conflicts over religious, linguistic, and regional issues. Muhammad Ali Jinnah's vision of a democratic state that would assure freedom of religion and equal treatment for all was opposed by those who advocated a state based on Islamic principles.

Even more dangerous was the division between east and west. Many in East Pakistan felt that the government, based in the west, ignored their needs. In 1952, riots erupted in East Pakistan over the government's decision to adopt Urdu, a language derived from Hindi and used by Muslims in northern India, as the national language of the entire country. Most East Pakistanis spoke Bengali, an unrelated language. Tensions persisted, and in March 1971, East Pakistan declared its independence as the new nation of Bangladesh. Pakistani troops attempted to restore central government authority in the capital of Dhaka, but rebel forces supported by India went on the offensive, and the government bowed to the inevitable and recognized independent Bangladesh.

The breakup of the union between East and West Pakistan undermined the fragile authority of the military regime that had ruled Pakistan since 1958 and led to its replacement by a civilian government under Zulfikar Ali Bhutto (1928–1979). But now religious tensions came to the fore, despite a new constitution that made a number of key concessions to conservative Muslims. In 1977, a new military government under General Zia Ul Ha'q came to power with a commitment to make Pakistan a truly Islamic state. Islamic law became the basis for social behavior as well as for the legal system. Laws governing the consumption of alcohol and the role of women were tightened in accordance with strict Muslim beliefs. But after Zia was killed in a plane crash, Pakistanis elected Benazir Bhutto (1953–2007), the daughter of Zulfikar Ali Bhutto and a supporter of secularism who had been educated in the United States. She too was removed from power by a military regime, in 1990, on charges of incompetence and corruption. Reelected in 1993, she attempted to crack down on opposition forces but was removed once again in 1997 amid renewed charges of official corruption. Her successor soon came under fire for the same reason and in 1999 was ousted by a military coup led by General Pervez Musharraf (b. 1943), who promised to restore political stability and honest government.

In September 2001, Pakistan became the focus of international attention when a coalition of forces arrived in Afghanistan to overthrow the Taliban regime and destroy the al-Qaeda terrorist network. Despite considerable support for the Taliban among the local population, President Musharraf pledged his help in bringing terrorists to justice. He also promised to return his country to the secular principles espoused by Muhammad Ali Jinnah. His situation was complicated by renewed tensions with India over Kashmir and a series of violent clashes between Muslims and Hindus in India. In 2003, however, relations began to improve as both sides promised to seek a peaceful solution to the Kashmir dispute.

By then, however, problems had begun to escalate on the domestic front. As Musharraf sought to fend off challenges from radical Muslim groups—some of them allied with Taliban forces in neighboring Afghanistan— secular opposition figures criticized the authoritarian nature of his regime. When Benazir Bhutto returned from exile to present herself as a candidate in presidential elections to be held early in 2008, she was assassinated, leading to widespread suspicions of official involvement. In September 2008, amid growing political turmoil, Benazir Bhutto's widower, Asif Ali Zardari (b. 1955), was elected president of Pakistan.

The new civilian government, which is composed of an uneasy coalition of several political parties, faces a number of challenges in coping with the multitude of problems affecting the country today. Half of the entire population of 150 million lives in poverty, and illiteracy is widespread. In a nation where much of the rural population still professes loyalty to traditional tribal leaders, the sense of nationalism remains fragile, while military elites, who have long played a central role in Pakistani politics, continue to press their own agenda. Official sources indicate that the new regime hopes to shift its strategy from suppression by force to diplomacy, offering limited autonomy to tribal regions in return for their cooperation in operations against rebel forces along the border with Afghanistan. The future stability of the state of Pakistan hangs in the balance.

Poverty and Pluralism in South Asia

The leaders of the new states that emerged in South Asia after World War II faced a number of problems. The peoples of South Asia were still overwhelmingly poor and illiterate, while the sectarian, ethnic, and cultural divisions that had plagued Indian society for centuries had not dissipated.

The Politics of Communalism Perhaps the most sincere effort to create democratic instititutions was in India, where the new constitution called for social justice, liberty, equality of status and opportunity, and fraternity. All citizens were guaranteed protection from discrimination based on religious belief, race, caste, gender, or place of birth.

In theory, then, India became a full-fledged democracy on the British parliamentary model. In actuality, a number of distinctive characteristics made the system less than fully democratic in the Western sense but may also have enabled it to survive. As we have seen, India became in essence a one-party state. By leading the independence movement, the Congress Party had amassed massive public support, which enabled it to retain its preeminent position in Indian politics for three decades. After Nehru's death in 1964, however, problems emerged that had been disguised by his adept maneuvering. Part of the problem was the familiar one of a party too long in power. Party officials became complacent and all too easily fell prey to the temptations of corruption and pork-barrel politics.

Another problem was **communalism.** Beneath the surface unity of the new republic lay age-old ethnic, linguistic, and religious divisions. Because of India's vast size and complex history, no national language had ever emerged. Hindi was the most prevalent, but it was the native language of less than one-third of the population. During the colonial period, English had served as the official language of government, but it was spoken only by the educated elite and represented an affront to national pride. Eventually, India recognized fourteen official tongues, making the parliament sometimes sound like the Tower of Babel.

Divisiveness increased after Nehru's death, and under his successors, official corruption grew. Only the lack of appeal of its rivals and the Nehru family charisma carried on by his daughter Indira Gandhi kept the Congress Party in power. But she was unable to prevent the progressive disintegration of the party's power base at the state level, where regional or ideological parties won the allegiance of voters by exploiting ethnic or social revolutionary themes.

During the 1980s, religious tensions began to intensify. As we have seen, Gandhi's uncompromising approach to Sikh separatism led to her assassination in 1984. In 1992, at Ayodhya, in northern India, Hindu militants destroyed a mosque allegedly built on the site of King Rama's birthplace, where a Hindu temple had once existed, and erected a temporary temple at the site. Their actions provoked clashes between Hindus and Muslims throughout India, and sparked protests in neighboring Pakistan where rioters destroyed a number of Hindu shrines.

In recent years, communal divisions have intensified, as militant Hindu groups agitate for a state that caters to the Hindu majority, now numbering more than 800 million people. In the spring of 2002, violence between Hindus and Muslims flared up again over plans by Hindu activists to build a permanent temple to Rama at the site of the destroyed mosque at Ayodhya. In the summer of 2006, unknown terrorists killed dozens of Indians in a series of bombings on commuter trains in Mumbai. In the eastern state of Orissa, pitched battles have recently broken out between Hindus and Christians over efforts by the latter to win converts to their faith.

The Economy Nehru's answer to the social and economic inequality that had long afflicted the subcontinent was socialism. He instituted a series of five-year plans, which led to the creation of a relatively large and reasonably efficient state-run industrial sector, centered on steel, vehicles, and textiles. Industrial production almost tripled between 1950 and 1965, and per capita income rose by 50 percent between 1950 and 1980, although it was still less than $300 (in U.S. dollars). By the 1970s, however, industrial growth had slowed. The lack of modern infrastructure was a problem, as was the rising price of oil, most of which had to be imported.

India's major economic weakness, however, was in agriculture. At independence, mechanization was almost unknown, fertilizer was rarely used, and most farms were small and uneconomical because of the Hindu tradition of dividing the land equally among all male children. As a result, the vast majority of the Indian people lived in conditions of abject poverty. Landless laborers outnumbered landowners by almost two to one. The government attempted to relieve the problem by redistributing land to the poor, limiting the size of landholdings, and encouraging farmers to form voluntary cooperatives. But all three programs ran into widespread opposition.

Another problem was overpopulation. Even before independence, the country had had difficulty supporting its people. In the 1950s and 1960s, the population grew by more than 2 percent annually, twice the nineteenth-century rate. Beginning in the 1960s, the Indian government sought to curb population growth. Indira Gandhi instituted a program combining monetary rewards and compulsory sterilization. Males who had fathered too many children were sometimes forced to undergo a vasectomy. Popular resistance undermined the program, however, and the goals were scaled back in the 1970s. As a result, India has made little progress in holding down its burgeoning population, now estimated at more than one billion. Nevertheless, as a result of media popularization and better government programs, the trend today, even in poor rural villages, is toward smaller families. The average number of children a woman bears has declined from six in 1950 to three today.

After the death of Indira Gandhi in 1984, her son Rajiv proved more receptive to foreign investment and a greater role for the private sector in the economy. India began to export more manufactured goods, including computer software. The pace of change has accelerated under Rajiv Gandhi's successors, who have continued to transfer state-run industries to private hands. These policies have stimulated the growth of a prosperous new middle class, now estimated at more than 100 million. Consumerism has soared, and sales of television sets, automobiles, DVD players, and cell phones have increased dramatically. Equally important, Western imports are being replaced by new products manufactured in India with Indian brand names (see the box on p. 759).

One consequence of India's entrance into the industrial age is the emergence of a small but vibrant technological sector that provides many important services to the world's advanced nations. The city of Bangalore in South India has become an important technological center, benefiting from low wages and the presence of skilled labor with proficiency in the English language. It has also become a symbol of the "outsourcing" of jobs from the United States and Europe, a practice that has led to an increase in middle-class unemployment throughout the Western world.

As in the industrialized countries of the West, economic growth in India has been accompanied by environmental damage. Water and air pollution has led to illness and death for many people, and an environmental movement has emerged. Some critics, reflecting the traditional anti-imperialist attitude of Indian intellectuals, blame Western capitalist corporations for the problem, as in the highly publicized case of leakage from a foreign-owned chemical plant at Bhopal. Much of the problem, however, comes from state-owned factories erected with Soviet aid. And not all the environmental damage can be ascribed to industrialization. The Ganges River is so polluted by human overuse that it is risky for Hindu believers to bathe in it.

Moreover, many Indians have not benefited from the new prosperity. Nearly one-third of the population lives below the national poverty line. Millions continue to live in urban slums, such as the famous "City of Joy" in Kolkata (Calcutta), and most farm families remain desperately poor. Despite the socialist rhetoric of India's leaders, the inequality of wealth in India is as pronounced as it is in capitalist nations in the West. Indeed, India has been described as two nations: an educated urban India of 100 million people surrounded by more than nine times that many impoverished peasants in the countryside (see the comparative illustration on p. 760).

Caste, Class, and Gender Although the constitution of 1950 guaranteed equal treatment and opportunity for all, regardless of caste, and prohibited discrimination based on untouchability, prejudice is hard to eliminate. Untouchability persists, particularly in the villages, where *harijans,* now called **dalits,** still perform menial tasks and are often denied fundamental human rights.

After independence, India's leaders also sought to equalize treatment of the sexes. The constitution expressly forbade discrimination based on gender and called for equal pay for equal work. Laws prohibited child marriage, *sati,* and the payment of a dowry by the bride's family. Women were encouraged to attend school and enter the labor market.

Such laws, along with the dynamics of economic and social change, have had a major impact on the lives of many Indian women. Middle-class women in urban areas are much more likely to seek employment outside the home, and many hold managerial and professional positions. Some Indian women, however, choose to play a dual role—a modern one in their work and in the marketplace and a more submissive, traditional one at home.

SAY NO TO McDONALD'S AND KFC!

One of the consequences of Rajiv Gandhi's decision to deregulate the Indian economy has been an increase in the presence of foreign corporations, including U.S. fast-food restaurant chains. Their arrival set off a storm of protest in India: from environmentalists concerned that raising grain for chickens is an inefficient use of land, from religious activists angry at the killing of animals for food, and from nationalists anxious to protect the domestic market from foreign competition. Fast-food restaurants now represent a growing niche in Indian society, but most cater to local tastes, avoiding beef products and offering many vegetarian dishes, such as the Veg Pizza McPuff. The author of this piece, which appeared in the *Hindustan Times,* was Maneka Gandhi, a daughter-in-law of Indira Gandhi and a one-time minister of the environment who has emerged as a prominent rival of Congress Party president Sonia Gandhi.

Why India Doesn't Need Fast Food

India's decision to allow Pepsi Foods Ltd. to open 60 restaurants in India—30 each of Pizza Hut and Kentucky Fried Chicken—marks the first entry of multinational, meat-based junk-food chains into India. If this is allowed to happen, at least a dozen other similar chains will very quickly arrive, including the infamous McDonald's.

The implications of allowing junk-food chains into India are quite stark. As the name denotes, the foods served at Kentucky Fried Chicken (KFC) are chicken-based and fried. This is the worst combination possible for the body and can create a host of health problems, including obesity, high cholesterol, heart ailments, and

many kinds of cancer. Pizza Hut products are a combination of white flour, cheese, and meat—again, a combination likely to cause disease. . . .

Then there is the issue of the environmental impact of junk-food chains. Modern meat production involves misuse of crops, water, energy, and grazing areas. In addition, animal agriculture produces surprisingly large amounts of air and water pollution.

KFC and Pizza Hut insist that their chickens be fed corn and soybeans. Consider the diversion of grain for this purpose. As the outlets of KFC and Pizza Hut increase in number, the poultry industry will buy up more and more corn to feed the chickens, which means that the corn will quickly disappear from the villages, and its increased price will place it out of reach for the common man. Turning corn into junk chicken is like turning gold into mud. . . .

It is already shameful that, in a country plagued by famine and flood, we divert 37 percent of our arable land to growing animal fodder. Were all of that grain to be consumed directly by humans, it would nourish five times as many people as it does after being converted into meat, milk, and eggs. . . .

Of course, it is not just the KFC and Pizza Hut chains of Pepsi Foods Ltd. that will cause all of this damage. Once we open India up by allowing these chains, dozens more will be eagerly waiting to come in. Each city in America has an average of 5,000 junk-food restaurants. Is that what we want for India?

Q *Why does the author of this article oppose the introduction of fast-food restaurants in India? Do you think her complaints apply in the United States as well?*

Like other aspects of life, the role of women has changed much less in rural areas. In the early 1960s, many villagers still practiced the institution of *purdah.* Female children are still much less likely to receive an education. The overall literacy rate in India today is about 60 percent, but it is undoubtedly much lower among women. Laws relating to dowry, child marriage, and inheritance are routinely ignored in the countryside. There have been a few highly publicized cases of *sati,* although undoubtedly more women die of mistreatment at the hands of their husband or of other members of his family.

South Asian Art and Literature Since Independence

Recent decades have witnessed a prodigious outpouring of literature in India. Because of the vast quantity of works published (India is currently the third-largest publisher of English-language books in the world), only a few of the most prominent fiction writers can be

mentioned here. Anita Desai (b. 1937) was one of the first prominent female writers in contemporary India. Her writing focuses on the struggle of Indian women to achieve a degree of independence. In her first novel, *Cry, the Peacock,* the heroine finally seeks liberation by murdering her husband, preferring freedom at any cost to remaining a captive of traditional society.

The most controversial writer from India today is Salman Rushdie (b. 1947). In *Midnight's Children,* published in 1980, the author linked his protagonist, born on the night of independence, to the history of modern India, its achievements and its frustrations. Rushdie's later novels have tackled such problems as religious intolerance, political tyranny, social injustice, and greed and corruption. His attack on Islamic fundamentalism in *The Satanic Verses* (1988) won plaudits from literary critics but provoked widespread criticism among Muslims, including a death sentence by Ayatollah Khomeini in Iran.

Like Chinese and Japanese artists, Indian artists have agonized over how best to paint with a modern yet

COMPARATIVE ILLUSTRATION

EARTH & ENVIRONMENT

Two Indias. Contemporary India is a study in contrasts. In the photo on the right, middle-class students learn to use computers, symbolizing their country's recent drive to join the global technological marketplace. Yet India today remains, above all, a nation of villages. On the left, women in colorful saris fill their pails of water at the village well. As in many developing countries, the scarcity of water is one of India's most crucial problems.

Q Do such stark contrasts between wealth and poverty in Indian society define conditions in all other countries in Asia?

indigenous mode of expression. During the colonial period, Indian art went in several directions at once. One school of painters favored traditional themes; another experimented with a colorful primitivism founded on folk art. Many Indian artists painted representational social art extolling the suffering and silent dignity of India's impoverished millions.

After 1960, however, most Indian artists adopted abstract art as their medium. Surrealism in particular, with its emphasis on spontaneity and the unconscious, appeared closer to the Hindu tradition of favoring intuition over reason. Yet Indian artists are still struggling to find the ideal way to be both modern and Indian.

Young Hindu Bride in Gold Bangles. Awaiting the marriage ceremony, a young bride sits with her female relatives at the Meenakshi Hindu temple, one of the largest in southern India. Although child marriage is illegal, Indian girls are still married at a young age. With the marital union arranged by the parents, this young bride may not have met her groom. Bedecked in gold jewelry and rich silks—part of her dowry—she nervously waits the priest's blessing before she moves to her husband's home. There she will begin a life of servitude to her in-laws' family.

Southeast Asia

Q Focus Question: What kinds of problems have the nations of Southeast Asia faced since 1945, and how have they attempted to solve these problems?

As we have seen (see Chapter 25), Japanese wartime occupation had a great impact on attitudes among the peoples of Southeast Asia. It demonstrated the vulnerability of colonial rule in the region and showed that an Asian power could defeat Europeans. The Allied governments themselves also contributed—sometimes unwittingly—to rising aspirations for independence by promising self-determination for all peoples at the end of the war.

Some followed through on their promise. In July 1946, the United States granted total independence to the Philippines. The Americans maintained a military presence on the islands, however, and U.S. citizens retained economic and commercial interests in the new country.

The British, too, were willing to bring an end to a century of imperialism in the region. In 1948, the Union of Burma received its independence. Malaya's turn came in 1957, after a Communist guerrilla movement had been suppressed.

The French and the Dutch, however, both regarded their colonies in the region as economic necessities as well as symbols of national grandeur and refused to turn them over to nationalist movements at the end of the war. The Dutch attempted to suppress a rebellion in the East Indies led by Sukarno (1901–1970), leader of the Indonesian Nationalist Party. But the United States, which feared a Communist victory there, pressured the Dutch to grant independence to Sukarno and his non-Communist forces, and in 1950, the Dutch finally agreed to recognize the new Republic of Indonesia.

The situation was somewhat different in Vietnam, where the Communists seized power throughout most of the country. After the French refused to recognize the new government and reimposed their rule, war broke out in December 1946. At the time, it was only an anticolonial war, but it would soon become much more (see Chapter 26).

In the Shadow of the Cold War

Many of the leaders of the newly independent states in Southeast Asia (see Map 30.2) admired Western political institutions and hoped to adapt them to their own countries. New constitutions were patterned on Western democratic models, and multiparty political systems quickly sprang into operation.

The Search for a New Political Culture   By the 1960s, most of these budding experiments in pluralist democracy had been abandoned or were under serious threat. Some had

been replaced by military or one-party autocratic regimes. In Burma, a moderate government based on the British parliamentary system and dedicated to Buddhism and nonviolent Marxism had given way to a military regime. In Thailand, too, the military now ruled. In the Philippines, President Ferdinand Marcos (1917–1989) discarded democratic restraints and established his own centralized control. In South Vietnam, under pressure from Communist-led insurgents, Ngo Dinh Diem and his successors paid lip service to the Western democratic model but ruled by authoritarian means.

One problem faced by most of these states was that independence had not brought material prosperity or ended economic inequality and the domination of the local economies by foreign interests. Most economies in the region were still characterized by tiny industrial sectors; they lacked technology, educational resources, and capital investment.

The presence of widespread ethnic, linguistic, cultural, and economic differences also made the transition to Western-style democracy difficult. In Malaya, for example, the majority Malays—most of whom were farmers—feared economic and political domination by the local Chinese minority, who were much more experienced in industry and commerce. In 1961, the Federation of Malaya, whose ruling party was dominated by Malays, integrated former British possessions on the island of Borneo into the new Union of Malaysia in a move to increase the non-Chinese proportion of the country's population.

The most prominent example of a failed experiment in democracy was in Indonesia. In 1950, the new leaders drew up a constitution creating a parliamentary system under a titular presidency. Sukarno was elected the first president. A spellbinding orator, Sukarno played a major role in creating a sense of national identity among the disparate peoples of the Indonesian archipelago.

In the late 1950s, Sukarno, exasperated at the incessant maneuvering among devout Muslims, Communists, and the army, dissolved the constitution and attempted to rule on his own through what he called guided democracy. As he described it, **guided democracy** was closer to Indonesian traditions and superior to the Western variety. Highly suspicious of the West, Sukarno nationalized foreign-owned enterprises and sought economic aid from China and the Soviet Union while relying for domestic support on the Indonesian Communist Party.

The army and many devout Muslims resented Sukarno's increasing reliance on the Communists, and Muslims were further upset by his refusal to consider a state based on Islamic principles. In 1965, military officers launched a coup d'état that provoked a mass popular uprising, which resulted in the slaughter of several hundred thousand suspected Communists, many of whom were overseas Chinese, long distrusted by the Muslim majority. In 1967, a military government under General Suharto (1921–2008) was installed.

MAP 30.2 **Modern Southeast Asia.** Shown here are the countries that comprise contemporary Southeast Asia. The names of major islands are indicated in italics.

Q Which of the countries in Southeast Asia have democratic governments?

The new government made no pretensions of reverting to democratic rule, but it did restore good relations with the West and sought foreign investment to repair the country's ravaged economy. But it also found it difficult to placate Muslim demands for an Islamic state.

The one country in Southeast Asia that explicitly rejected the Western model was North Vietnam. Ho Chi Minh and his colleagues opted for the Stalinist pattern of national development, based on Communist Party rule and socialist forms of ownership. In 1958, stimulated by the success of collectivization in neighboring China, the government launched a three-year plan to lay the foundation for a socialist society. Collective farms were established, and all industry and commerce above the family level were nationalized.

Recent Trends: On the Path to Development

With the end of the Vietnam War and the gradual rapprochement between China and the United States in the late 1970s, the ferment and uncertainty that had marked the first three decades of independence in Southeast Asia gradually gave way to an era of greater political stability and material prosperity. In the Philippines, the dictatorial Marcos regime was overthrown by a massive public uprising in 1986 and replaced by a democratically elected government under President Corazon Aquino (1933–2009), the widow of a popular politician assassinated a few years earlier. Aquino was unable to resolve many of the country's chronic economic and social difficulties, however, and political stability remains elusive; one of her successors, ex-actor Joseph Estrada, was forced

FILM & HISTORY
THE YEAR OF LIVING DANGEROUSLY (1982)

President Sukarno of Indonesia was one of the most prominent figures in Southeast Asia in the first two decades after World War II. A key figure in the nationalist movement while the country was under Dutch colonial rule, he became the elected president of the new republic when it was granted formal independence in 1950. The charismatic Sukarno initially won broad popular support for his efforts to end colonial dependency and improve living conditions for the impoverished local population. But the government's economic achievements failed to match his fiery oratory, and when political unrest began to spread through Indonesian society in the early 1960s, Sukarno dismantled the parliamentary system that had been installed at independence and began to crack down on dissidents.

These conditions provide the setting for the Australian film *The Year of Living Dangerously* (1982). Based on a novel of the same name by Christian Koch, the movie takes place in the summer of 1965, at a time when popular unrest against the dictatorial government had reached a crescendo and the country appeared about to descend into civil war. The newly arrived Australian reporter Guy Hamilton (Mel Gibson) is befriended by a diminutive Chinese-Indonesian journalist named Billy Kwan, effectively played by Linda Hunt, who won an Academy Award for her performance. Kwan, who has become increasingly disenchanted with Sukarno's failure to live up his promises, introduces Hamilton to the seamy underside of Indonesian society, as well as to radical elements connected to the Communist Party who are planning a coup to seize power in Jakarta.

The movie reaches a climax as Hamilton—a quintessentially ambitious reporter out to get a scoop on the big story—inadvertently becomes involved in the Communist plot and arouses the suspicions of government authorities. As Indonesia appears ready to descend into chaos, Hamilton finally recognizes the extent of the danger and manages to board the last plane from Jakarta. Others are not so

Photographer Billy Kwan (Linda Hunt) and reporter Guy Hamilton (Mel Gibson) film a political protest.

MGM/UA/The Kobal Collection

fortunate, as Sukarno's security police crack down forcefully on critics of his regime.

The Year of Living Dangerously (the title comes from a remark made by Sukarno during his presidential address in August 1964) is an important if underrated film that dramatically portrays a crucial incident in a volatile region caught in the throes of the global Cold War. The beautiful scenery (the movie was shot in the Philippines because the story was banned in Indonesia) and a haunting film score help create a mood of tension spreading through a tropical paradise.

---

to resign on the charge of corruption. At the same time, Muslims in the southern island of Mindanao have mounted a terrorist campaign in an effort to obtain autonomy or independence.

In other nations, the trends have been modestly favorable. Malaysia is a practicing democracy, although tensions persist between Malays and Chinese as well as between secular and orthodox Muslims who seek to create an Islamic state. In neighboring Thailand, the military has found it expedient to hold national elections for civilian governments, but the danger of a military takeover is never far beneath the surface. In the fall of 2008, massive protests against the existing government threatened to throw Thai society into a state of paralysis.

The Fall of the Suharto Regime   In Indonesia, difficult economic conditions caused by the financial crisis of 1997 (see the later section), combined with popular anger against the Suharto government (several members of his family had reportedly used their positions to amass considerable wealth), led to demands for his resignation and violent riots as Muslims and students took to the streets. Forced to step down in the spring of 1998, Suharto was replaced by his deputy, B. J. Habibie, who called for the establishment of a national assembly to select a new government based on popular aspirations. The assembly selected a moderate Muslim leader as president, but he was charged with corruption and incompetence and was replaced in 2001 by his vice president, Sukarno's daughter Megawati Sukarnoputri (b. 1947).

Soccer, a Global Obsession. Professional soccer has become the most popular sport in the world. It offers a diversion from daily drudgery and promotes intense patriotism as each nation supports its team. Moreover, children the world over enjoy playing soccer, even when there are no playing fields in the vicinity. Shown here is an informal match held in an ancestral Chinese temple in Hoi An, a town in central Vietnam that once served as a major entry point for European, Chinese, and Japanese merchants who took part in the regional trade network. Today, Vietnam is once again opening its doors to the outside world.

Vietnam and Burma Elsewhere in the region, progress toward democracy has been mixed. In Vietnam, the trend has been toward a greater popular role in the governing process. Elections for the unicameral parliament are more open than in the past. The government remains suspicious of Western-style democracy, however, and represses any opposition to the Communist Party's guiding role over the state.

Only in Burma (now renamed Myanmar), where the military has been in complete control since the early 1960s, have the forces of greater popular participation been virtually silenced. Even there, however, the power of the ruling regime of General Ne Win (1911–2002) and his successors, known as SLORC, has been vocally challenged by Aung San Suu Kyi (b. 1945), the admired daughter of one of the heroes of the country's struggle for national liberation after World War II. Massive flooding after a powerful typhoon in 2008 laid bare the regime's incompetence in dealing with a humanitarian crisis.

The new government faced a severe challenge, not only from the economic crisis but also from dissident elements seeking autonomy or even separation from the republic. Under pressure from the international community, Indonesia agreed to grant independence to the onetime Portuguese colony of East Timor, where the majority of the people are Roman Catholics. But violence provoked by pro-Indonesian militia units forced many refugees to flee the new country. Religious tensions have also erupted between Muslims and Christians elsewhere in the archipelago, and Muslim rebels in western Sumatra continue to agitate for a political system based on strict adherence to fundamentalist Islam.

In direct elections held in 2004, General Susilo Yudhoyono defeated Megawati Sukarnoputri and ascended to the presidency. The new chief executive promised a new era of political stability, honest government, and economic reform but faces a number of severe challenges. Concerned about high wages and the risk of terrorism, a number of foreign firms have relocated their factories elsewhere in Asia, forcing thousands of workers to return to the countryside. Pressure from traditional Muslims to abandon the nation's secular tradition and move toward the creation of an Islamic state continues to grow. That the country was able to hold democratic elections in the midst of such tensions holds some promise for the future.

Crisis and Recovery The trend toward more representative systems of government has been due in part to increasing prosperity and the growth of an affluent and educated middle class. Although Indonesia, Burma, and the three Indochinese states are still overwhelmingly agrarian, Malaysia and Thailand have been undergoing relatively rapid economic development.

In the late summer of 1997, however, these economic gains were threatened and popular faith in the ultimate benefits of globalization was shaken as a financial crisis swept through the region. The crisis was triggered by a number of problems, including growing budget deficits caused by excessive government expenditures on ambitious development projects, irresponsible lending and investment practices by financial institutions, and an overvaluation of local currencies relative to the U.S. dollar. An underlying cause of these problems was the prevalence of backroom deals between politicians and business leaders that temporarily enriched both groups at the cost of eventual economic dislocation.

As local currencies plummeted in value, the International Monetary Fund agreed to provide assistance, but only on the condition that the governments concerned

© William J. Duiker

permit greater transparency in their economic systems and allow market forces to operate more freely, even at the price of bankruptcies and the loss of jobs. By the early 2000s, there were signs that the economies in the region had weathered the crisis and were beginning to recover. But the massive tsunami that struck in December 2004 was another setback to economic growth, as well as a human tragedy of enormous proportions.

Regional Conflict and Cooperation: The Rise of ASEAN

In addition to their continuing internal challenges, Southeast Asian states have been hampered by serious tensions among themselves. Some of these tensions were a consequence of historical rivalries and territorial disputes that had been submerged during the long era of colonial rule. Cambodia, for example, has bickered with both of its neighbors, Thailand and Vietnam, over mutual frontiers drawn up originally by the French for their own convenience.

After the fall of Saigon and the reunification of Vietnam under Communist rule in 1975, the lingering border dispute between Cambodia and Vietnam erupted again. In April 1975, a brutal revolutionary regime under the leadership of the Khmer Rouge dictator Pol Pot (c. 1928–1998) came to power in Cambodia and proceeded to carry out the massacre of more than one million Cambodians. Then, claiming that vast territories in the Mekong delta had been seized from Cambodia by the Vietnamese in previous centuries, the Khmer Rouge regime launched attacks across the common border. In response, Vietnamese forces invaded Cambodia in December 1978 and installed a pro-Hanoi regime in Phnom Penh. Fearful of Vietnam's increasing power in the region, China launched a brief attack on Vietnam to demonstrate its displeasure.

The outbreak of war among the erstwhile Communist allies aroused the concern of other countries in the neighborhood. In 1967, several non-Communist countries had established the Association of Southeast Asian Nations (ASEAN). Composed of Indonesia, Malaysia, Thailand, Singapore, and the Philippines, ASEAN at first concentrated on cooperative social and economic endeavors, but after the end of the Vietnam War, it cooperated with other states in an effort to force the Vietnamese to withdraw from Cambodia. In 1991, the Vietnamese finally withdrew, and a new government was formed in Phnom Penh.

The growth of ASEAN from a weak collection of diverse states into a stronger organization whose members cooperate militarily and politically has helped provide the nations of Southeast Asia with a more cohesive voice to represent their interests on the world stage. That Vietnam was admitted into ASEAN in 1996 should provide both Hanoi and its neighbors with greater leverage in dealing with China—their powerful neighbor to the north.

Daily Life: Town and Country in Contemporary Southeast Asia

The urban-rural dichotomy observed in India also is found in Southeast Asia, where the cities resemble those in the West while the countryside often appears little changed from precolonial days. In cities such as Bangkok, Manila, and Jakarta, broad boulevards lined with skyscrapers alternate with muddy lanes passing through neighborhoods packed with wooden shacks topped by thatch or rusty tin roofs. Nevertheless, in recent decades, millions of Southeast Asians have fled to these urban slums. Although most available jobs are menial, the pay is better than in the villages.

Traditional Customs, Modern Values The urban migrants change not only their physical surroundings but their attitudes and values as well. Sometimes the move leads to a decline in traditional beliefs. Nevertheless, Buddhist, Muslim, and Confucian beliefs remain strong, even in cosmopolitan cities such as Bangkok, Jakarta, and Singapore. This preference for the traditional also shows up in lifestyle. Native dress—or an eclectic blend of Asian and Western dress—is still common. Traditional music, art, theater, and dance remain popular, although Western rock music has

Holocaust in Cambodia. When the Khmer Rouge seized power in Cambodia in April 1975, they immediately emptied the capital of Phnom Penh and systematically began to eliminate opposition elements throughout the country. Thousands were tortured in the infamous Tuol Sleng prison and then marched out to the countryside, where they were massacred. Their bodies were thrown into massive pits. The succeeding government disinterred the remains, which are now displayed at an outdoor museum on the site. Today, a measure of political and economic stability has begun to return to the country. The commandant of the prison, Comrade Deuch, is currently on trial in Phnom Penh.

become fashionable among the young, and Indonesian filmmakers complain that Western films are beginning to dominate the market.

Changing Roles for Women One of the most significant changes that has taken place in Southeast Asia in recent decades is in the role of women in society. In general, women in the region have historically faced fewer restrictions on their activities and enjoyed a higher status than women elsewhere in Asia. Nevertheless, they were not the equal of men in every respect. With independence, Southeast Asian women gained new rights. Virtually all of the constitutions adopted by the newly independent states granted women full legal and political rights, including the right to work. Today, women have increased opportunities for education and have entered careers previously reserved for men. Women have become more active in politics, and as we have seen, some have served as heads of state.

Yet women are not truly equal to men in any country in Southeast Asia. In Vietnam, women are legally equal to men, yet until recently no women had served in the Communist Party's ruling politburo. In Thailand, Malaysia, and Indonesia, women rarely hold senior positions in government service or in the boardrooms of major corporations.

A Region in Flux

Today, the Western image of a Southeast Asia mired in the Vietnam conflict and the tensions of the Cold War has become a memory. In ASEAN, the states in the region have created the framework for a regional organization that can serve their common political, economic, technological, and security interests. A few members of ASEAN are already on the road to advanced development.

To be sure, there are continuing signs of trouble. The financial crisis of the late 1990s aroused serious political

One World, One Fashion. One of the negative aspects of tourism is the eroding of distinctive ethnic cultures, even in previously less traveled areas. Nevertheless, fashions from other lands often seem exotic and enticing. This village chief from Flores, a remote island in the Indonesian archipelago, seems very proud of his designer sunglasses.

unrest in Indonesia, and the region's economies, though recovering, still bear the scars of the crisis. There are disquieting signs that al-Qaeda has established a presence in the region. Myanmar remains isolated and appears mired in a state of chronic underdevelopment and brutal military rule. The three states of Indochina remain potentially unstable and have not yet been fully integrated into the region as a whole. All things considered, however, the situation is more promising today than would have seemed possible a generation ago. Unlike the case in Africa and the Middle East, the nations of Southeast Asia have put aside the bitter legacy of the colonial era to embrace the wave of globalization that has been sweeping the world in the post–World War II era.

Japan: Asian Giant

Q **Focus Question:** How did the Allied occupation after World War II change Japan's political and economic institutions, and what remained unchanged?

In August 1945, Japan was in ruins, its cities destroyed, its vast Asian empire in ashes, its land occupied by a foreign army. Half a century later, Japan had emerged as the second-greatest industrial power in the world, democratic in form and content and a source of stability throughout the region. Japan's achievement spawned a number of Asian imitators.

The Transformation of Modern Japan

For five years after the end of the war in the Pacific, Japan was governed by an Allied administration under the command of U.S. general Douglas MacArthur. As commander of the occupation administration, MacArthur was responsible for demilitarizing Japanese society, destroying the Japanese war machine, trying Japanese civilian and military officials charged with war crimes, and laying the foundations of postwar Japanese society.

One of the sturdy pillars of Japanese militarism had been the giant business cartels, known as *zaibatsu*. Allied policy was designed to break up the *zaibatsu* into smaller units in the belief that corporate concentration not only hindered competition but was inherently undemocratic and conducive to political authoritarianism. Occupation planners also intended to promote the formation of independent labor unions in order to lessen the power of the state over the economy and provide a mouthpiece for downtrodden Japanese workers. Economic inequality in rural areas was to be reduced by a comprehensive land reform program that would turn the land over to those who farmed it. Finally, the educational system was to be remodeled along American lines so that it would turn out

independent individuals rather than automatons subject to manipulation by the state.

The Allied program was an ambitious and even audacious plan to remake Japanese society and has been justly praised for its clear-sighted vision and altruistic motives. Parts of the program, such as the constitution, the land reforms, and the educational system, succeeded brilliantly. But as other concerns began to intervene, changes or compromises were made that were not always successful. In particular, with the rise of Cold War sentiment in the United States in the late 1940s, the goal of decentralizing the Japanese economy gave way to the desire to make Japan a key partner in the effort to defend East Asia against international communism. Convinced of the need to promote economic recovery in Japan, U.S. policy makers began to show more tolerance for the *zaibatsu*. Concerned about growing radicalism within the new labor movement, U.S. occupation authorities placed less emphasis on the independence of the labor unions.

The Cold War also affected U.S. foreign relations with Japan. On September 8, 1951, the United States and other former belligerent nations signed a peace treaty restoring Japanese independence. In turn, Japan renounced any claim to such former colonies or territories as Taiwan, Korea, and southern Sakhalin and the Kurile Islands (see Map 30.3). On the same day, Japan and the United States signed a defensive alliance and agreed that the latter could maintain military bases on the Japanese islands. Japan was now formally independent but in a new dependency relationship with the United States. A provision in the new constitution renounced war as an instrument of national policy and prohibited the raising of an army.

Politics and Government The Allied occupation administrators started with the conviction that Japanese expansionism was directly linked to the institutional and ideological foundations of the Meiji Constitution. Accordingly, they set out to change Japanese politics into something closer to the pluralistic model used in most Western nations. Yet a number of characteristics of the postwar Japanese political system reflected the tenacity of the traditional political culture. Although Japan had a multiparty system with two major parties, the Liberal Democrats and the Socialists, in practice there was a "government party" and a permanent opposition—the Liberal Democrats were not voted out of office for thirty years.

That tradition changed suddenly in 1993, when the ruling Liberal Democrats, shaken by persistent reports of corruption and cronyism between politicians and business interests, failed to win a majority of seats in parliamentary elections. The new coalition government, however, quickly split into feuding factions, and in 1995, the Liberal Democrats returned to power.

Successive prime ministers proved unable to carry out promised reforms, and in 2001, Junichiro Koizumi (b. 1942), a former minister of health and welfare, was elected prime minister. His personal charisma raised expectations that he might be able to bring about significant changes, but bureaucratic resistance to reform and chronic factionalism within the Liberal Democratic Party thwarted his efforts, and since he left office in 2006, the desire for change has remained largely unrealized.

Japan, Inc. The challenges for future Japanese leaders include not only curbing persistent political corruption but also reducing the government's involvement in the economy. Since the Meiji period, the government has played an active role in mediating management-labor disputes, establishing price and wage policies, and subsidizing vital industries and enterprises producing goods for export. This government intervention in the economy was once cited as a key reason for the efficiency of Japanese industry and the emergence of the country as an industrial giant. In recent years, however, as the economy remained mired in recession, the government's actions have increasingly come under fire. Japanese firms now argue that deregulation is needed to enable them to innovate to keep up with the competition. Such reforms, however, have been resisted by powerful government ministries.

Atoning for the Past Lingering social problems also need to be addressed. Minorities such as the *eta* (now known as the **Burakumin**) and Korean residents in Japan continue to be subjected to legal and social discrimination. For years, official sources were reluctant to divulge growing evidence that thousands of Korean women were conscripted to serve as prostitutes (euphemistically called "comfort women") for Japanese soldiers during the war, and many Koreans living in Japan contend that such prejudicial attitudes continue to exist. Representatives of the "comfort women" have demanded both financial

MAP 30.3 Modern Japan. Shown here are the four main islands that comprise the contemporary state of Japan.

Q Which is the largest?

compensation and a formal letter of apology from the Japanese government for the treatment they received during the Pacific War. Negotiations over the issue have been under way for several years.

Japan's behavior during World War II has been an especially sensitive issue. During the early 1990s, critics at home and abroad charged that textbooks printed under the guidance of the Ministry of Education did not adequately discuss the atrocities committed by the Japanese government and armed forces during World War II. Other Asian governments were particularly incensed at Tokyo's failure to accept responsibility for such behavior and demanded a formal apology. The government expressed remorse, but only in the context of the aggressive actions of all colonial powers during the imperialist era.

The Economy Nowhere are the changes in postwar Japan so visible as in the economic sector, where Japan developed into a major industrial and technological power in the space of a century, surpassing such advanced Western societies as Germany, France, and Great Britain.

Although this "Japanese miracle" has often been described as beginning after the war as a result of the Allied reforms, Japanese economic growth in fact began much earlier, with the Meiji reforms, which helped transform Japan from an autocratic society based on semifeudal institutions into an advanced capitalist democracy.

As noted, the officials of the Allied occupation identified the Meiji economic system with centralized power and the rise of Japanese militarism. But with the rise of Cold War tensions, the policy of breaking up the *zaibatsu* was scaled back. Looser ties between companies were still allowed, and a new type of informal relationship, sometimes called the **keiretsu,** or "interlocking arrangement," began to take shape. Through such arrangements among suppliers, wholesalers, retailers, and financial institutions, the *zaibatsu* system was reconstituted under a new name.

The occupation administration had more success with its program to reform the agricultural system. Half of the population still lived on farms, and half of all farmers were still tenants. Under the land reform program, all lands owned by absentee landlords and all cultivated landholdings over an established maximum were sold on easy credit terms to the tenants. The program created a strong class of yeoman farmers, and tenants declined to about 10 percent of the rural population.

During the next fifty years, Japan re-created the stunning results of the Meiji era. In 1950, the Japanese gross domestic product was about one-third that of Great Britain or France. Today, it is larger than both put together and well over half that of the United States. Japan is one of the greatest exporting nations in the world, and its per capita income equals or surpasses that of most advanced Western states.

In the last decades, however, the Japanese economy has run into serious difficulties, raising the question of whether the Japanese model is as appealing as many observers earlier declared. A rise in the value of the yen hurt exports and burst the bubble of investment by Japanese banks that had taken place under the umbrella of government protection. Lacking a domestic market equivalent in size to the United States, in the 1990s the Japanese economy slipped into a recession that has not yet abated. Economic conditions worsened in 2008 and 2009 as Japanese exports declined significantly as a consequence of the global economic downturn.

These economic difficulties have placed heavy pressure on some of the vaunted features of the Japanese economy. The tradition of lifetime employment created a bloated white-collar workforce and has made downsizing difficult. Today, job security is on the decline as increasing numbers of workers are being laid off. A disproportionate burden has fallen on women, who lack seniority and continue to suffer from various forms of discrimination in the workplace.

A final change is that slowly but inexorably, the Japanese market is beginning to open up to international competition. Greater exposure to foreign competition may improve the performance of Japanese manufacturers. In recent years, Japanese consumers have become increasingly critical of the quality of some domestic products, provoking one cabinet minister to complain about "sloppiness and complacency" among Japanese firms. One apparent reason for the country's recent quality problems is the cost-cutting measures adopted by Japanese companies to meet the challenges from abroad.

A Society in Transition

During the occupation, Allied planners set out to change social characteristics that they believed had contributed to Japanese aggressiveness before and during World War II. The new educational system removed all references to filial piety, patriotism, and loyalty to the emperor while emphasizing the individualistic values of Western civilization. The new constitution and a revised civil code eliminated remaining legal restrictions on women's rights to obtain a divorce, hold a job, or change their domicile. Women were guaranteed the right to vote and were encouraged to enter politics.

Such efforts to remake Japanese behavior through legislation were only partially successful. During the past sixty years, Japan has unquestionably become a more individualistic and egalitarian society. At the same time, many of the distinctive characteristics of traditional Japanese society have persisted to the present day, although in somewhat altered form. The emphasis on loyalty to the group and community relationships, for example, is reflected in the strength of corporate loyalties in contemporary Japan.

Emphasis on the work ethic also remains strong. The tradition of hard work is taught at a young age. The Japanese school year runs for 240 days a year, compared with 180 days in the United States, and work assignments outside class tend to be more extensive. The results are impressive: Japanese schoolchildren consistently earn higher scores on achievement tests than children in other advanced countries. At the same time, this devotion to success has often been accompanied by bullying by teachers and what Americans might consider an oppressive sense of conformity (see the box on p. 771).

By all accounts, independent thinking is on the increase in Japan. In some cases, it leads to antisocial behavior, such as crime or membership in a teenage gang. Usually, it is expressed in more indirect ways, such as the recent fashion among young people of dyeing their hair brown (known in Japanese as "tea hair"). Because the practice is banned in many schools and generally frowned on by the older generation (one police chief dumped a pitcher of beer on a student with brown hair whom he noticed in a bar), many young Japanese dye their hair as a gesture of independence. When seeking employment or getting married, however, they often return their hair to its natural color.

One of the more tenacious legacies of the past in Japanese society is sexual inequality. Although women are now legally protected against discrimination in employment, very few have reached senior levels in business, education, or politics. Women now constitute nearly 50 percent of the workforce; but most are in retail or

From Conformity to Counterculture. Traditionally, schoolchildren in Japan have worn uniforms to promote conformity with the country's communitarian social mores. In the left photo, young students dressed in identical uniforms are on a field trip to Kyoto's Nijo Castle, built in 1603 by Tokugawa Ieyasu. Recently, however, a youth counterculture has emerged in Japan. On the right, fashion-conscious teenagers with "tea hair"—heirs of Japan's long era of affluence—revel in their expensive hip-hop outfits, platform shoes, and layered dresses. Such dress habits symbolize the growing revolt against conformity in contemporary Japan.

service occupations, and their average salary is only about half that of men. There is a feminist movement in Japan, but it has none of the vigor and mass support of its counterpart in the United States.

Religion and Culture When Japan was opened to the West in the nineteenth century, many Japanese became convinced of the superiority of foreign ideas and institutions and were especially interested in Western religion and culture. Although Christian converts were few, numbering less than 1 percent of the population, the influence of Christianity was out of proportion to the size of the community.

Today, Japan includes almost 1.5 million Christians, along with 93 million Buddhists. Many Japanese also follow Shinto, no longer identified with reverence for the emperor and the state. As in the West, increasing urbanization has led to a decline in the practice of organized religion, although evangelical sects have proliferated in recent years. The largest and best-known sect is Soka Gakkai, a lay Buddhist organization that has attracted millions of followers and formed its own political party, the Komeito. Zen Buddhism retains its popularity, and some businesspeople seek to use Zen techniques to learn how to focus on willpower as a means of outwitting a competitor.

Western literature, art, and music have also had a major impact on Japanese society. After World War II, many of the writers who had been active before the war resurfaced, but now their writing reflected demoralization.

Many were attracted to existentialism, and some turned to hedonism and nihilism. For these disillusioned authors, defeat was compounded by fear of the Americanization of postwar Japan. One of the best examples of this attitude was the novelist Yukio Mishima (1925–1970), who led a crusade to stem the tide of what he described as America's "universal and uniform 'Coca-Colonization'" of the world in general and Japan in particular.[3] Mishima's ritual suicide in 1970 was the subject of widespread speculation and transformed him into a cult figure.

One of Japan's most serious-minded contemporary authors is Kenzaburo Oe (b. 1935). His work, rewarded with a Nobel Prize for Literature in 1994, focuses on Japan's ongoing quest for modern identity and purpose. His characters reflect the spiritual anguish precipitated by the collapse of the imperial Japanese tradition and the subsequent adoption of Western culture—a trend that Oe contends has culminated in unabashed materialism, cultural decline, and a moral void. Yet unlike Mishima, Oe does not wish to reinstill the imperial traditions of the past but rather seeks to regain spiritual meaning by retrieving the sense of communality and innocence found in rural Japan.

Other aspects of Japanese culture have also been influenced by Western ideas. Western music is very popular in Japan, and scores of Japanese classical musicians have succeeded in the West. Even rap music has gained a foothold among Japanese youth, although without the association with sex, drugs, and violence that

GROWING UP IN JAPAN

FAMILY & SOCIETY

Japanese schoolchildren grow up in a much more regimented environment than U.S. children experience. Most Japanese schoolchildren, for example, wear black-and-white uniforms to school. These regulations are examples of rules adopted by middle school systems in various parts of Japan. The Ministry of Education in Tokyo concluded that these regulations were excessive, but they are probably typical.

School Regulations, Japanese Style

1. Boys' hair should not touch the eyebrows, the ears, or the top of the collar.
2. No one should have a permanent wave, or dye his or her hair. Girls should not wear ribbons or accessories in their hair. Hair dryers should not be used.
3. School uniform skirts should be ___ centimeters above the ground, no more and no less (differs by school and region).
4. Keep your uniform clean and pressed at all times. Girls' middy blouses should have two buttons on the back collar. Boys' pant cuffs should be of the prescribed width. No more than 12 eyelets should be on shoes. The number of buttons on a shirt and tucks in a shirt are also prescribed.
5. Wear your school badge at all times. It should be positioned exactly.
6. Going to school in the morning, wear your book bag strap on the right shoulder; in the afternoon on the way home, wear it on the left shoulder. Your book case thickness, filled and unfilled, is also prescribed.
7. Girls should wear only regulation white underpants of 100% cotton.
8. When you raise your hand to be called on, your arm should extend forward and up at the angle prescribed in your handbook.
9. Your own route to and from school is marked in your student rule handbook; carefully observe which side of each street you are to use on the way to and from school.
10. After school you are to go directly home, unless your parent has written a note permitting you to go to another location. Permission will not be granted by the school unless this other location is a suitable one. You must not go to coffee shops. You must be home by ___ o'clock.
11. It is not permitted to drive or ride a motorcycle, or to have a license to drive one.
12. Before and after school, no matter where you are, you represent our school, so you should behave in ways we can all be proud of.

Q *What is the apparent purpose of these regulations? Why does Japan appear to place more restrictions on students' behavior than most Western countries do?*

---

it has in the United States. As one singer remarked, "We've been very fortunate, and we don't want to bother our Moms and Dads. So we don't sing songs that would disturb parents."[4]

The Little Tigers

Q **Focus Questions:** What factors have contributed to the economic success achieved by the Little Tigers? To what degree have they applied the Japanese model in forging their developmental strategies?

The success of postwar Japan in meeting the challenge from the capitalist West soon caught the eye of other Asian nations. By the 1980s, several smaller states in the region—known collectively as the "Little Tigers"—had successively followed the Japanese example.

South Korea: A Peninsula Divided

In 1953, the Korean peninsula was exhausted from three years of bitter fraternal war, a conflict that took the lives of an estimated four million Koreans on both sides of the 38th parallel. Although a cease-fire was signed in July 1953, it was a fragile peace that left two heavily armed and mutually hostile countries facing each other suspiciously.

North of the truce line was the People's Republic of Korea (PRK), a police state under the dictatorial rule of the Communist leader Kim Il Sung (1912–1994). To the south was the Republic of Korea, under the equally autocratic President Syngman Rhee (1875–1965), a fierce anti-Communist who had led the resistance to the northern invasion. After

The Korean Peninsula Since 1953

several years of harsh rule in the Republic of Korea, marked by government corruption, fraudulent elections, and police brutality, demonstrations broke out in the capital city of Seoul in the spring of 1960 and forced Rhee into retirement.

In 1961, a coup d'état in South Korea placed General Chung Hee Park (1917–1979) in power. The new regime promulgated a new constitution, and in 1963, Park was elected president of a civilian government. He set out to foster recovery of the economy from decades of foreign occupation and civil war. Because the private sector had been relatively weak under Japanese rule, the government played an active role in the process by instituting a series of five-year plans that targeted specific industries for development, promoted exports, and funded infrastructure development.

The program was a solid success. Benefiting from the Confucian principles of thrift, respect for education, and hard work, as well as from Japanese capital and technology, Korea gradually emerged as a major industrial power in East Asia. The largest corporations—including Samsung, Daewoo, and Hyundai—were transformed into massive conglomerates called *chaebol,* the Korean equivalent of the *zaibatsu* of prewar Japan. Korean businesses began to compete actively with the Japanese for export markets in Asia and throughout the world.

But like many other countries in the region, South Korea was slow to develop democratic principles. Although his government functioned with the trappings of democracy, Park continued to rule by autocratic means and suppressed all forms of dissidence. In 1979, Park was assassinated. But after a brief interregnum of democratic rule, in 1980 a new military government under General Chun Doo Hwan (b. 1931) seized power. The new regime was as authoritarian as its predecessors, but after student riots in 1987, by the end of the decade opposition to autocratic rule had spread to much of the urban population.

National elections were finally held in 1989, and South Korea reverted to civilian rule. Successive presidents sought to rein in corruption while cracking down on the *chaebols* and initiating contacts with the Communist regime in the PRK on possible steps toward eventual reunification of the peninsula. After the Asian financial crisis in 1997, economic conditions temporarily worsened, but they have since recovered, and the country is increasingly competitive in world markets today. Symbolic of South Korea's growing self-confidence is the nation's new president, Lee Myung-bak (b. 1941), elected in 2007. An ex-mayor of Seoul, he is noted for his rigorous efforts to beautify the city and improve the quality of life of his compatriots, including the installation of a new five-day workweek. His most serious challenge, however, is to protect the national economy, which is heavily dependent on exports, from the ravages of the recent economic crisis.

In the meantime, relations with North Korea, now under the dictatorial rule of Kim Il Sung's son Kim Jong Il (b. 1941) and on the verge of becoming a nuclear power, remain tense. Multinational efforts to persuade the regime to suspend its nuclear program continue, although North Korea claimed to have successfully conducted a nuclear test in 2009.

Taiwan: The Other China

After retreating to Taiwan following their defeat by the Communists, Chiang Kai-shek's government, which continued to refer to itself as the Republic of China (ROC), contended that it remained the legitimate representative of the Chinese people and would eventually return in triumph to the mainland.

Modern Taiwan

The Nationalists had much more success on Taiwan than they had achieved on the mainland. In the relatively secure environment provided by a security treaty with the United States, signed in 1954, the ROC was able to concentrate on economic growth without worrying about a Communist invasion.

The government moved rapidly to create a solid agricultural base. A land reform program led to the reduction of rents, and landholdings over 3 acres were purchased by the government and resold to the tenants at reasonable prices. At the same time, local manufacturing and commerce were strongly encouraged. By the 1970s, Taiwan had become one of the most dynamic industrial economies in East Asia.

In contrast to the Communist regime in the People's Republic of China (PRC), the ROC actively maintained Chinese tradition, promoting respect for Confucius and the ethical principles of the past, such as hard work, frugality, and filial piety. Although there was some corruption in both the government and the private sector, income differentials between the wealthy and the poor were generally less than elsewhere in the region, and the overall standard of living increased substantially. Health and sanitation improved, literacy rates were quite high, and an active family planning program reduced the rate of population growth.

The Chiang Kai-shek Memorial in Taipei. While the Chinese government on the mainland attempted to destroy all vestiges of traditional culture, the Republic of China on Taiwan sought to preserve the cultural heritage as a link between past and present. This policy is graphically displayed in the mausoleum for Chiang Kai-shek in downtown Taipei, shown in this photograph. The mausoleum, with its massive entrance gate, not only glorifies the nations's leader but recalls the grandeur of old China.

Singapore and Hong Kong: The Littlest Tigers

The smallest but by no means the least successful of the Little Tigers are Singapore and Hong Kong. Both contain large populations densely packed into small territories. Singapore, once a British colony and briefly a part of the state of Malaysia, is now an independent nation. Hong Kong was a British colony until it was returned to PRC control in 1997. In recent years, both have emerged as industrial powerhouses, with standards of living well above those of their neighbors.

The success of Singapore must be ascribed in good measure to the will and energy of its political leaders. When it became independent in August 1965, Singapore's longtime position as an entrepôt for trade between the Indian Ocean and the South China Sea was on the wane.

Within a decade, Singapore's role and reputation had dramatically changed. Under the leadership of Prime Minister Lee Kuan-yew (b. 1923), the government cultivated an attractive business climate while engaging in public works projects to feed, house, and educate its two million citizens. The major components of success have been shipbuilding, oil refineries, tourism, electronics, and finance—the city-state has become the banking hub of the entire region.

As in the other Little Tigers, an authoritarian political system has guaranteed a stable environment for economic growth. Until his retirement in 1990, Lee Kuan-yew and his People's Action Party dominated Singapore politics, and opposition elements were intimidated into silence or arrested. The prime minister openly declared that the Western model of pluralist democracy was not appropriate for Singapore. Confucian values of thrift, hard work, and obedience to authority were promoted as the ideology of the state (see the box on p. 774).

After the death of Chiang Kai-shek in 1975, the ROC slowly began to move toward a more representative form of government, including elections and legal opposition parties. A national election in 1992 resulted in a bare majority for the Nationalists over strong opposition from the Democratic Progressive Party (DPP). But political liberalization had its dangers; some members of the DPP began to agitate for an independent Republic of Taiwan, a possibility that aroused concern within the Nationalist government in Taipei and frenzied hostility in the PRC. The election of DPP leader Chen Shui-bian (b. 1950) as ROC president in March 2000 angered Beijing, which threatened to invade Taiwan should the island continue to delay unification with the mainland. The return to power of the Nationalist Party in 2008 has at least for the time being eased relations with mainland China.

The United States continues to provide defensive military assistance to the Taiwanese armed forces and has made it clear that it supports self-determination for the people of Taiwan and that it expects the final resolution of the Chinese civil war to be by peaceful means. In the meantime, economic and cultural contacts between Taiwan and the mainland are steadily increasing. Nevertheless, the Taiwanese have shown no inclination to accept the PRC's offer of "one country, two systems," under which the ROC would accept the PRC as the legitimate government of China in return for autonomous control over the affairs of Taiwan.

The Republic of Singapore

To Those Living in Glass Houses

INTERACTION & EXCHANGE

Kishore Mahbubani was permanent secretary in the Ministry of Foreign Affairs in Singapore from 1993 to 1998. Previously, he served as his country's ambassador to the United Nations. In this 1994 article, adapted from a piece in the *Washington Quarterly,* the author advises his audience to stop lecturing Asian societies on the issue of human rights and focus attention instead on problems in the United States. In his view, today the countries of the West have much to learn from their counterparts in East Asia. This viewpoint is shared by many other observers, political leaders, and foreign affairs specialists in the region.

Kishore Mahbubani, "Go East, Young Man"

In a major reversal of a pattern lasting centuries, many Western societies, including the U.S., are doing some major things fundamentally wrong, while a growing number of East Asian societies are doing the same things right. The results are most evident in the economic sphere. In purchasing power parity terms, East Asia's gross domestic product is already larger than that of either the U.S. or European community. Such economic prosperity, contrary to American belief, results not just from free-market arrangements but also from the right social and political choices....

In most Asian eyes, the evidence of real social decay in the U.S. is clear and palpable. Since 1960, the U.S. population has grown by 41%. In the same period, there has been a 560% increase in violent crimes, a 419% increase in illegitimate births, a 400% increase in divorce rates, a 300% increase in children living in single-parent homes, a more than 200% increase in teenage suicide rates, and a drop of almost 80 points in [SAT] scores. A clear American paradox is that a society that places such a high premium on freedom has effectively reduced the physical freedom of most Americans, especially those who live in large cities. They live in heavily fortified homes, think twice before taking an evening stroll around their neighborhoods, and feel increasingly threatened by random violence when they are outside.

To any Asian, it is obvious that the breakdown of the family and social order in the U.S. owes itself to a mindless ideology that maintains that the freedom of a small number of individuals who are known to pose a threat to society (criminals, terrorists, street gang members, drug dealers) should not be constrained (for example, through detention without trial), even if to do so would enhance the freedom of the majority.... This belief is purely and simply a gross violation of common sense.

My hope is that Americans will come to visit East Asia in greater numbers. When they do, they will come to realize that their society has swung much too much in one direction: liberating the individual while imprisoning society. The relatively strong and stable family and social institutions of East Asia will appear more appealing. And as Americans experience the freedom of walking on city streets in Asia, they may begin to understand that freedom can also result from greater social order and discipline. Perhaps the best advice to give to a young American is: "Go East, Young Man."

Q *What are the author's criticisms of Western civilization? How does he justify the "Asian" approach to politics and society?*

But economic success has begun to undermine the authoritarian foundations of the system as a more sophisticated citizenry voices aspirations for more political freedoms and an end to government paternalism. Lee Kuan-yew's successor, Goh Chok Tong (b. 1950), promised a "kinder, gentler" Singapore, and political restrictions on individual behavior were gradually relaxed. In 2004, Lee Hsien-luong (b. 1952), the son of Lee Kaun-yew, became prime minister, arousing optimism that the trend toward a more pluralistic political system would continue.

The future of Hong Kong is not so clear-cut. As in Singapore, sensible government policies and the hard work of its people have enabled Hong Kong to thrive. At first, the prosperity of the colony depended on a plentiful supply of cheap labor. Inundated with refugees from the mainland during the 1950s and 1960s, the population of Hong Kong burgeoned to more than six million. More recently, Hong Kong has benefited from increased tourism, manufacturing, and the growing economic prosperity of neighboring Guangdong province, the most prosperous region of the PRC. Unlike the other societies discussed in this chapter, Hong Kong has relied on an unbridled free market system rather than active state intervention in the economy. At the same time, by allocating substantial funds for transportation, sanitation, education, and public housing, the government has created favorable conditions for economic development.

When Britain's ninety-nine-year lease on the New Territories, the foodbasket of the colony, expired on July 1, 1997, Hong Kong returned to mainland authority. Although the

Hong Kong

Chinese promised the British that for fifty years, the people of Hong Kong would live under a capitalist system and be essentially self-governing, recent statements by Chinese leaders have raised questions about the degree of autonomy Hong Kong will continue to receive under Chinese rule.

The China Factor

One of the primary reasons for the growing preeminence of East Asia on the economic scene is the emergence of mainland China as a major player in the global marketplace. A quarter of a century ago, China was a predominantly rural nation with an archaic state-run industrial sector. Today, with a predominantly market-driven economy and an industrious low-wage workforce, it has become an economic powerhouse, taking over the role previously played by Japan in leading the resurgence of East Asia in world affairs (see Chapter 27).

What effect this will have on future developments in the region is still unclear. For the moment, the new China is both a blessing and a curse to its neighbors: a major importer of raw materials from other countries in Asia, but a dangerous competitor in the export market. A period of political instability in China, of course, would dramatically change the equation. Barring unforseen circumstances, however, the emergence of China represents a significant step in transforming the vision of the Pacific Century into a reality.

On the Margins of Asia: Postwar Australia and New Zealand

Technically, Australia and New Zealand are not part of Asia, and throughout their short history, both countries have identified culturally and politically with the West rather than with their Asian neighbors. Their political institutions and values are derived from Europe, and their economies resemble those of the advanced countries of the world rather than the preindustrial societies of much of Southeast Asia. Both are currently members of the British Commonwealth and of the U.S.-led ANZUS (Australia, New Zealand, and the United States) alliance.

Yet trends in recent years have been drawing both states, especially Australia, closer to Asia. In the first place, immigration from East and Southeast Asia has increased rapidly. More than one-half of current immigrants into Australia come from East Asia, and by early this century, about 7 percent of the population of about 18 million people will be of Asian descent. In New Zealand, residents of Asian descent represent only about 3 percent of the population of 3.5 million, but about 12 percent of the population are Maoris, Polynesian peoples who settled on the islands about a thousand years ago. Second, trade relations with Asia are increasing rapidly. About 60 percent of Australia's export markets today are in East Asia, and the region is the source of about one-half of its imports. Asian trade with New Zealand is also on the increase.

Whether Australia and New Zealand will ever become an integral part of the Asia-Pacific region is uncertain. Cultural differences stemming from the European origins of the majority of the population in both countries hinder mutual understanding on both sides of the divide. But economic and geographic realities act as a powerful force, and should the Pacific region continue on its current course toward economic prosperity and political stability, the role of Australia and New Zealand will assume greater significance.

COMPARATIVE ESSAY
ONE WORLD, ONE ENVIRONMENT

EARTH & ENVIRONMENT

A crucial factor affecting the evolution of society and the global economy in the early twenty-first century is the growing concern over the impact of industrialization on the earth's environment. Humans have always caused some harm to their natural surroundings, but never has the danger of significant ecological damage been as extensive as during the past century. The effects of chemicals introduced into the atmosphere or into rivers, lakes, and oceans have increasingly threatened the health and well-being of all living species.

For many years, the main focus of environmental concern was in the developed countries of the West, where industrial effluents, automobile exhaust, and the use of artificial fertilizers and insecticides led to urban smog, extensive damage to crops and wildlife, and a major reduction of the ozone layer in the upper atmosphere. In recent years, the problem has spread elsewhere. China's headlong rush to industrialization has resulted in major ecological damage in that country. Industrial smog has created almost unlivable conditions in many cities in Asia, while hillsides denuded of their forests have caused severe problems of erosion that have destroyed farmlands. Destruction of the rain forest is a growing problem in many parts of the world, notably in Brazil and Indonesia. With the forest cover throughout the earth rapidly disappearing, there is less plant life to perform the crucial process of reducing carbon dioxide levels in the atmosphere.

One of the few beneficial consequences of such incidents has been a growing international consensus that environmental concerns have taken on a truly global character. Although the danger of global warming—caused by the release, as a result of industrialization, of

© Judyth Platt/Ecoscene/CORBIS

hothouse gases into the atmosphere—has not yet been definitively proved, it has become a source of sufficient concern to bring about an international conference on the subject in Kyoto, Japan, in December 1997. If, as many scientists predict, worldwide temperatures continue to increase, the rise in sea levels could pose a significant threat to low-lying islands and coastal areas throughout the world, while climatic change could lead to severe droughts or excessive rainfall in cultivated areas.

It is one thing to recognize a problem, however, and another to solve it. So far, cooperative efforts among nations to alleviate environmental problems have all too often been hindered by economic forces or by political, ethnic, and religious disputes. The 1997 conference on global warming, for example, was marked by bitter disagreement over the degree to which developing countries should share the burden of cleaning up the environment. The fact is, few nations have been willing to take unilateral action that might pose an obstacle to economic development plans or lead to a rise in unemployment. In 2001, President George W. Bush refused to sign the Kyoto Agreement on the grounds that it discriminated against advanced Western countries.

At the end of 2009, another international conference on global warming, held in Copenhagen, Denmark, also was marked by disagreements between the developed and developing nations. As a result, it achieved few concrete results, despite a more active role by the United States.

Q *What are the major reasons why progress in cleaning up the environment has been so difficult to achieve?*

Destruction of the Environment. This stunted tree has been killed by acid rain, a combination of sulfuric and nitric acids mixed with moisture in the air. Entire forests of trees killed by acid rain are becoming common sights in Canada, the United States, and northern Europe.

CONCLUSION

THE RISE OF ASIA as a crucial factor in the global economic order has sparked widespread debate, and sometimes concern, in major world capitals. Some observers see major Asian states like China, Japan, and even India as future competitors with advanced Western nations (see the comparative essay "Global Village or Clash of Civilizations?" in Chapter 26), an observation made more ominous in recent years by the outsourcing of jobs to the region.

To some observers, the economic achievements of the nations of the western Pacific have come at a high price, in the form of political authoritarianism and a lack of attention to human rights. Until recently, government repression of opposition has been common in many of these nations. In addition, the rights of national minorities and women are often still limited in comparison with the advanced nations of the West. Developments such as the financial crisis of 1997 and the long economic downturn in Japan have also somewhat tarnished the image of the "Asian miracle," raising concern that some of the factors that contributed to economic success in prior years are now making it difficult for governments to develop open and accountable financial systems.

Rapid economic development in eastern and southern Asia has also exacted an environmental price. Industrial pollution in China and India and the burning of forests in Indonesia and other Southeast Asian nations increasingly threaten the fragile ecosystem and create friction among nations within the region (see the comparative essay "One World, One Environment" on p. 776). Unless the region's nations learn to cooperate effectively to deal with the problem in future years, it will ultimately begin to undermine the dramatic economic and social progress that has taken place.

Still, it should be kept in mind that progress has not always been easy to achieve in the West and even now frequently fails to match expectations. A look at the historical record suggests that political pluralism is often a by-product of economic growth and that political values and institutions evolve in response to changing social conditions. A rising standard of living and increased social mobility should go far toward enhancing political freedom and promoting social justice in the countries bordering the western Pacific.

The efforts of these nations to find a way to accommodate traditional and modern, native and foreign, raise a final question. As we have seen, Mahatma Gandhi believed that materialism is ultimately a dead end. In light of contemporary concerns about the emptiness of life in the West and the self-destructiveness of material culture, can his message be ignored?

TIMELINE

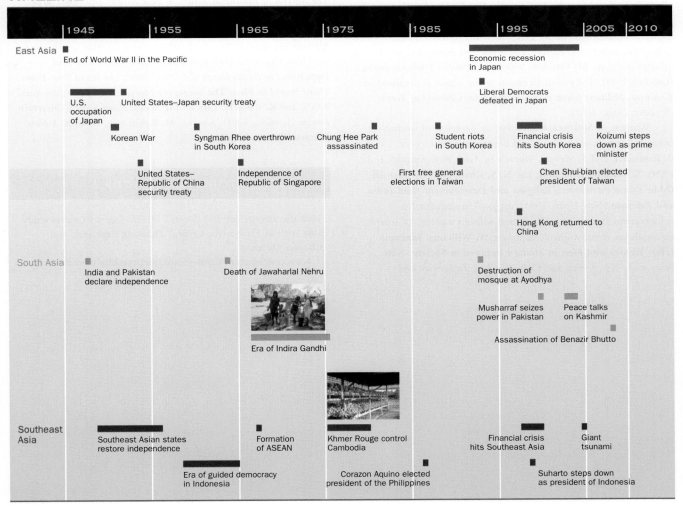

| | 1945 | 1955 | 1965 | 1975 | 1985 | 1995 | 2005 | 2010 |

East Asia — End of World War II in the Pacific

Economic recession in Japan

U.S. occupation of Japan — United States–Japan security treaty

Liberal Democrats defeated in Japan

Korean War — Syngman Rhee overthrown in South Korea — Chung Hee Park assassinated — Student riots in South Korea — Financial crisis hits South Korea — Koizumi steps down as prime minister

United States–Republic of China security treaty — Independence of Republic of Singapore — First free general elections in Taiwan — Chen Shui-bian elected president of Taiwan

Hong Kong returned to China

South Asia — India and Pakistan declare independence — Death of Jawaharlal Nehru — Destruction of mosque at Ayodhya

Era of Indira Gandhi

Musharraf seizes power in Pakistan — Peace talks on Kashmir

Assassination of Benazir Bhutto

Southeast Asia — Southeast Asian states restore independence — Formation of ASEAN — Khmer Rouge control Cambodia — Financial crisis hits Southeast Asia — Giant tsunami

Era of guided democracy in Indonesia — Corazon Aquino elected president of the Philippines — Suharto steps down as president of Indonesia

SUGGESTED READING

The Indian Subcontinent Since 1945 For a survey of postwar Indian history, see **P. Brass, *The New Cambridge History of India: The Politics of Independence*** (Cambridge, 1990), and **S. Tharoor, *India: From Midnight to the Millennium*** (New York, 1997). On India's founding father, see **J. Brown, *Nehru: A Political Life*** (New Haven, Conn., 2003). The life and career of Indira Gandhi have been well chronicled. Two fine biographies are **T. Ali, *An Indian Dynasty: The Story of the Nehru-Gandhi Family*** (New York, 1985), and **K. Frank, *Indira: The Life of Indira Nehru Gandhi*** (New York, 2000). On Pakistan, see **O. B. Jones, *Pakistan: Eye of the Storm*** (New Haven, Conn., 2002). Also of interest is **C. Baxter, *Bangladesh: From a Nation to a State*** (Boulder, Colo., 1997).

Indian Literature On Indian literature, see **D. Ray** and **A. Singh, eds., *India: An Anthology of Contemporary Writing*** (Athens, Ohio, 1983). See also **S. Tharu** and **K. Lalita, eds., *Women Writing in India,*** vol. 2 (New York, 1993).

Southeast Asia Since 1945 There are a number of standard surveys of the history of modern Southeast Asia. One is **N. Tarling, *Southeast Asia: A Modern History*** (Oxford, 2002). For a more scholarly approach, see **N. Tarling, ed., *The Cambridge History of Southeast Asia,*** vol. 4 (Cambridge, 1999). **T. Friend, *Indonesian Destinies*** (Cambridge, Mass., 2003), is a fine introduction to Indonesian society and culture. For a political perspective on the Suharto years, see **M. Vatiokis, *Indonesian Politics Under Suharto*** (London, 1993). The rise of terrorism in the region is discussed in **Z. Abuza, *Militant Islam in Southeast Asia: Crucible of Terror*** (Boulder, Colo., 2003).

Women in Southeast Asia For an overview of women's issues in contemporary South and Southeast Asia, consult **B. Ramusack** and **S. Sievers, *Women in Asia*** (Bloomington, Ind., 1999). **K. Bhasin, R. Menon**, and **N. S. Khan, eds., *Against All Odds: Essays on Women, Religion and Development from India and Pakistan*** (New Delhi, 1994), explores fundamentalist conservatism among both Hindu and Muslim women. Of interest on Southeast Asian women's issues are **W. Williams, *Japanese Lives: Women and Men in Modern Indonesian Society*** (New Brunswick, N.J., 1991), and **C. B. N. Chin, *In Service and Servitude: Foreign Female Domestic Workers and the Malaysian "Modernity" Project*** (New York, 1998).

Japan Since 1945 For a balanced treatment of all issues relating to postwar Japan, see **J. McLain, *Japan: A Modern History*** (New York, 2001). **I. Buruma, *Inventing Japan*** (New York, 2002), offers a more journalistic approach that raises questions about the future of democracy in Japan. For a topical treatment with a strong emphasis on economic and social matters, **J. E. Hunter, *The Emergence of Modern Japan: An Introductory History Since 1853*** (London, 1989), is excellent. For an extensive analysis of Japan's adjustment to the Allied occupation, see **J. W. Dower, *Embracing Defeat: Japan in the Wake of World War II*** (New York, 1999). **T. Heymann, *On an Average Day in Japan*** (New York, 1992), provides an interesting statistical comparison of Japanese and American society. On the role of women in modern Japan, see **D. Robins-Mowry, *The Hidden Sun: Women of Modern Japan*** (Boulder, Colo., 1983), and **N. Bornoff, *Pink Samurai: Love, Marriage, and Sex in Contemporary Japan*** (New York, 1991).

The Little Tigers On the four Little Tigers and their economic development, see **E. F. Vogel, *The Four Little Dragons: The Spread of Industrialization in East Asia*** (Cambridge, Mass., 1991); **J. W. Morley, ed., *Driven by Growth: Political Change in the Asia-Pacific Region*** (Armonk, N.Y., 1992); and **J. Woronoff, *Asia's Miracle Economies*** (New York, 1986). For individual treatments of the Little Tigers, see **Hak-kyu Sohn, *Authoritarianism and Opposition in South Korea*** (London, 1989); **Lee Kuan Yew, *From Third World to First: The Singapore Story, 1965–2000*** (New York, 2000); and **K. Rafferty, *City on the Rocks: Hong Kong's Uncertain Future*** (London, 1991). Also see **M. Rubinstein, *Taiwan: A New History*** (New York, 2001).

DISCOVERY

How would you compare the performance of the nations of South, Southeast, and East Asia since World War II? What do you feel accounts for the differences?

In thinking about these questions, begin by breaking them down into the components shown below. A discussion of the significance of each component should appear in your answer.

POLITICS AND GOVERNMENT   What are the key differences in Nehru's and Gandhi's views on the future of India (see the document below and on p. 754)? Why do you think Nehru's ideas triumphed over those of Gandhi? What has India gained by moving from a village to a modern urban culture? What might some people say it has lost? What role did Hinduism play in the development of a modern India? How does India's performance compare with that of the other countries of the region?

TWO VISIONS FOR INDIA

Nehru's Socialist Creed

I am convinced that the only key to the solution of the world's problems and of India's problems lies in socialism, and when I use this word I do so not in a vague humanitarian way but in the scientific economic sense.... I see no way of ending the poverty, the vast unemployment, the degradation and the subjection of the Indian people except through socialism. That involves vast and revolutionary changes in our political and social structure, the ending of vested interests in land and industry, as well as the feudal and autocratic Indian states system. That means the ending of private property, except in a restricted sense, and the replacement of the present profit system by a higher ideal of cooperative service.... In short, it means a new civilization, radically different from the present capitalist order. Some glimpse we can have of this new civilization in the territories of the U.S.S.R. Much has happened there which has pained me greatly and with which I disagree, but I look upon that great and fascinating unfolding of a new order and a new civilization as the most promising feature of our dismal age.

A Letter to Jawaharlal Nehru

I believe that if India, and through India the world, is to achieve real freedom, then sooner or later we shall have to go and live in the villages—in huts, not in palaces. Millions of people can never live in cities and palaces in comfort and peace. Nor can they do so by killing one another, that is, by resorting to violence and untruth.... We can have the vision of... truth and nonviolence only in the simplicity of the villages. That simplicity resides in the spinning wheel and what is implied by the spinning wheel....

You will not be able to understand me if you think that I am talking about the villages of today. My ideal village still exists only in my imagination.... In this village of my dreams the villager will not be dull—he will be all awareness. He will not live like an animal in filth and darkness. Men and women will live in freedom, prepared to face the whole world. There will be no plague, no cholera, and no smallpox. Nobody will be allowed to be idle or to wallow in luxury. Everyone will have to do body labor. Granting all this, I can still envisage a number of things that will have to be organized on a large scale. Perhaps there will even be railways and also post and telegraph offices. I do not know what things there will be or will not be. Nor am I bothered about it. If I can make sure of the essential thing, other things will follow in due course. But if I give up the essential thing, I give up everything.

FAMILY AND SOCIETY   What is the apparent purpose of Japanese school regulations like those listed on page 771? Do you think Indian families and schools impose similar rules on schoolchildren? Why or why not? Why does Japan appear to place more restrictions on students' behavior than most Western countries do? Which of these regulations make the most sense to you? The least sense? What biases do you think inform your answers? What relationship do you think may exist between rules like these and a modern capitalist society? Review the views of Kishore Mahbubani (p. 774). What do you think he would say about such rules?

From Conformity to Counterculture

779

ON A VISIT TO NUREMBERG, Germany, with his family in 2000, Jackson Spielvogel, one of the authors of this textbook, was startled to find that the main railroad station, where he had once arrived as a Fulbright student, was now ostentatiously adorned with McDonald's Golden Arches. McDonald's was the brainstorm of two brothers who opened a cheap burger restaurant in California in 1940. When they expanded their operations to Arizona, they began to use two yellow arches to make their building visible from blocks away. After Ray Kroc, an enterprising businessman, bought the burgeoning business from the brothers, McDonald's arches rapidly spread all over the United States. And they didn't stop there. The fast-food industry, which now relied on computers to maximize the automated processing of its food, found an international market. McDonald's spread to Japan in 1971 and to Russia and China in 1990; by 1995, more than half of all McDonald's restaurants were located outside the United States. By 2000, McDonald's was serving 50 million people throughout the world every day.

McDonald's is but one of numerous U.S. companies that use the latest technology and actively seek global markets. Indeed, sociologists have coined the term *McDonaldization* to refer to "the process whereby the principles of the fast-food restaurant are coming to dominate more and more sectors of American society as well as the rest of the world."[1] Multinational corporations like McDonald's have brought about a worldwide homogenization of societies and made us aware of the political, economic, and social interdependence of the world's nations and the global nature of our contemporary problems. An important part of this global awareness is the technological dimension. The growth of new technology has made possible levels of world communication that simply did not exist before. At the same time that Osama bin Laden and al-Qaeda were denouncing the forces of modernization, they were promoting their message by using advanced telecommunication systems that have only recently been developed. The Technological Revolution has tied peoples and nations closely together and contributed to **globalization,** the term that is frequently used today to describe the process by which peoples and nations have become more interdependent.

McDonald's in India. McDonald's has become an important symbol of U.S. cultural influence throughout the world. Seen here is a McDonald's located in a traditional building in New Delhi, India. The children outside are trying to make some money by selling balloons to other children who can afford to buy fast food.

The Global Economy

Especially since the 1970s, the world has developed a **global economy** in which the production, distribution, and sale of goods are accomplished on a worldwide scale. Several international institutions have contributed to the rise of the global economy. Soon after the end of World War II, the United States and other nations established the World Bank and the International Monetary Fund (IMF) as a means of expanding global markets and avoiding dramatic economic crises such as the Great Depression of the 1930s. The World Bank is actually a group of five international organizations, largely controlled by developed countries, which provides grants, loans, and advice for economic development to developing countries. The goal of the IMF is to oversee the global financial system by supervising exchange rates and offering financial and technical assistance to developing nations. Today, 186 countries are members of the IMF. Critics have argued, however, that both the World Bank and the IMF sometimes push non-Western nations to adopt inappropriate Western economic practices that only aggravate the poverty and debt of developing nations.

Another reflection of the new global economic order is the **multinational corporation** or **transnational corporation** (a company that has divisions in more than two countries). Prominent examples of multinational corporations include Siemens, Coca-Cola, ExxonMobil, Mitsubishi, and Sony. These companies are among the two hundred largest multinational corporations, which are responsible for more than half of the world's industrial production. In 2000, some 71 percent of these corporations were headquartered in just three countries—the United States, Japan, and Germany. In addition, these supercorporations dominate much of the world's investment capital, technology, and markets. A recent comparison of corporate sales and national gross domestic product disclosed that only forty-nine of the world's hundred largest economic entities are nations; the remaining fifty-one are corporations. For this reason, some observers believe that economic globalization is more appropriately labeled "corporate globalization."

Another important component of economic globalization is free trade. In 1947, talks led to the creation of the General Agreement on Tariffs and Trade (GATT), a global trade organization that was replaced in 1995 by the World Trade Organization (WTO). Made up of more than 150 member nations, the WTO arranges trade agreements and settles trade disputes. The goal of the WTO is to open up world markets and maximize global production. But the WTO also has its critics. Some charge that it has harmed small and developing countries, contributing to the ever growing gap between rich and poor nations. Others contend that it has ignored environmental and health problems that have arisen as manufacturing jobs have been transferred from developed countries like the United States to developing countries with fewer protections for workers and the environment.

The extent of globalization became especially evident in 2008 when a collapse of the largely unregulated financial markets in the United States quickly led to a worldwide recession. Manufacturing plunged, unemployment rose, and banks faltered as countries around the world faced new and daunting economic challenges. The IMF estimated that global output would fall by 1.3 percent in 2009, the first decline in sixty years. Although there were some signs of recovery by May, most economists believed that the worst global slump since the Great Depression of the 1930s was far from over.

Global Culture and the Digital Age

Since the invention of the microprocessor in 1971, the capabilities of computers have expanded by leaps and bounds, resulting in today's information age or digital age. Beginning in the 1980s, computer companies like Apple and Microsoft competed to create more powerful computers. By the 1990s, the booming technology industry had made Microsoft founder Bill Gates the richest man in the world. Much of this success was due to several innovations involving computers that made them indispensable devices for communication, information, and entertainment.

The Technological World

The advent of electronic mail, or e-mail, transformed communication in the mid-1990s. As the capacity of computers to transmit data increased, e-mail messages could be accompanied by document and image attachments, making them a workable and speedier alternative to conventional postal mail and other delivery methods. At the same time, the Internet, especially its World Wide Web, was becoming an information exchange for people around the world. A network of smaller, interlinking Web pages, the Internet provides access to sites devoted to news, commerce, entertainment, and academic scholarship. As computer processors have become more powerful, these websites now possess video and music capabilities in addition to text-based documents.

Advances in telecommunications led to cellular or mobile phones. Though cellular phones existed in the 1970s and 1980s, it was not until the digital components of these devices were reduced in size in the 1990s that cell phones became truly portable. Cell phones have since become enormously important, and not only for communication. Indeed, many nations have become financially dependent on their sales for economic growth. The ubiquity of cell phones and their ability to transfer data electronically have made text messaging a global communications craze. Text and instant messaging have revolutionized written language, as shorthand script has replaced complete sentences for the purposes of relaying brief messages.

In 2001, Apple introduced the iPod, a portable digital music player. The pocket-sized device has since revolutionized the music industry, as downloading music electronically from the Internet has surpassed the purchasing of records (CDs, tapes, and other physical forms) in stores. In fact, CD sales declined by nearly 25 percent from 2000 to 2006.

Reality in the Digital Age

Advances in communication and information during the digital age have led many people to suggest that world cultures are becoming increasingly interdependent and homogenized. Many contemporary artists have questioned the effects of the computer age on identity and material reality. According to some, the era of virtual reality, or what the French philosopher Jean Baudrillard has termed "hyperreality," has displaced cultural uniqueness and bodily presence.

The Body and Identity in Contemporary Art   By focusing on bodily experience and cultural norms, contemporary artists have attempted to restore what has been lost in the digital age. Kiki Smith (b. 1954), an American artist born in Germany, creates sculptures of the human body that often focus on anatomical processes. These works, commonly made of wax or plaster, question the politics surrounding the body, including AIDS and domestic abuse, while reconnecting to bodily experiences.

Contemporary artists also continue to explore the interaction between the Western and non-Western world, particularly with the **multiculturalism** generated by global migrations (see "The Social Challenges of Globalization" later in this Epilogue). For example, the art of Yinka Shonibare (b. 1962), who was born in London to Nigerian parents, grew up in Nigeria, and now resides in England, investigates the notion of hybrid identity as he creates clothing and tableaux that fuse European designs with African traditions. The success of Shonibare's work indicates how, in the digital age, Western peoples remain interested in other cultures and traditions. This emergence of a global culture has become part of the new globalism at the beginning of the twenty-first century.

Globalization and the Environmental Crisis

Taking a global perspective at the beginning of the twenty-first century has led many people to realize that everywhere on the planet, human beings are interdependent in regard to the air they breathe, the water they drink, the food they consume, and the climate that affects their lives. At the same time, however, human activities are creating environmental challenges that threaten the very foundation of human existence on earth (see the box on p. 783).

One problem is population growth. As of December 2009, the world population was estimated at more than 6.8 billion people, only twenty-one years after passing the 5 billion mark. At its current rate of growth, the world population could reach 12.8 billion by 2050, according to the United Nations' long-range population projections. The result has been an increased demand for food and other resources that has put great pressure on the earth's ecosystems. At the same time, the failure to grow enough food for more and more people, a problem exacerbated by drought conditions beginning to appear on several continents, has created a severe problem, as an estimated 1 billion people worldwide today suffer from hunger. Every year, more than 8 million people die of hunger, many of them young children.

Another problem is the pattern of consumption as the wealthy nations of the Northern Hemisphere consume vast quantities of the planet's natural resources. The United States, for example, which has 6 percent of the planet's people, consumes 30 to 40 percent of its resources. The spread of these consumption patterns to other parts of the world raises serious questions about the ability of the planet to sustain itself and its population. As a result of the economic slowdown in 2008 and 2009, for example, more automobiles are now sold in China than in the United States.

Yet another threat to the environment is **global warming,** which has the potential to create a worldwide crisis. Virtually all of the world's scientists agree that the **greenhouse effect,** the warming of the earth because of the buildup of carbon dioxide in the atmosphere, is contributing to devastating droughts and storms, the melting of the polar ice caps, and rising sea levels that could inundate coastal regions in the second half of the twenty-first century. Also alarming is the potential loss of biodiversity. Seven out of ten biologists believe the planet is now experiencing an alarming extinction of both plant and animal species.

The Social Challenges of Globalization

Since 1945, tens of millions of people have migrated from one part of the world to another. These migrations have occurred for many reasons. Persecution for political reasons caused many people from Pakistan, Bangladesh, Sri Lanka, and eastern Europe to seek refuge in western European countries, while brutal civil wars in Asia, Africa, the Middle East, and Europe led millions of refugees to seek safety in neighboring countries. Most people who have migrated, however, have done so to find jobs. Latin Americans seeking a better life have migrated to the

A Warning to Humanity

EARTH & ENVIRONMENT

As human threats to the environment grew, world scientists began to organize and respond to the crisis. One group, founded in 1969, was the Union of Concerned Scientists, a nonprofit organization of professional scientists and private citizens, now with more than 200,000 members. In November 1992, the Union of Concerned Scientists published an appeal from 1,700 of the world's leading scientists. The first selection is taken from this "Warning to Humanity."

Earlier, in 1988, in response to the threat of global warming, the United Nations established the Intergovernmental Panel on Climate Change (IPCC) to study the latest scientific information on global warming and climate change. In 2007, more than 2,500 scientists from more than 130 countries contributed to the group's most recent report, "Climate Change, 2007: The Fourth Assessment Report," released in November 2007. The second selection is taken from the Web page that summarizes the basic findings of the 2007 report.

"World Scientists' Warning to Humanity," 1992

Human beings and the natural world are on a collision course. Human activities inflict harsh and often irreversible damage on the environment and on critical resources. If not checked, many of our current practices put at serious risk the future that we wish for human society and the plant and animal kingdoms, and may so alter the living world that it will be unable to sustain life in the manner that we know. Fundamental changes are urgent if we are to avoid the collision our present course will bring about. The environment is suffering critical stress:

The Atmosphere

Stratospheric ozone depletion threatens us with enhanced ultraviolet radiation at the earth's surface, which can be damaging or lethal to many life forms. Air pollution near ground level, and acid precipitation, are already causing widespread injury to humans, forests, and crops.

Water Resources

Heedless exploitation of depletable ground water supplies endangers food production and other essential human systems. Heavy demands on the world's surface waters have resulted in serious shortages in some 80 countries, containing 40% of the world's population. Pollution of rivers, lakes, and ground water further limits the supply.

Oceans

Destructive pressure on the oceans is severe, particularly in the coastal regions which produce most of the world's food fish. The total marine catch is now at or above the estimated maximum sustainable yield. Some fisheries have already shown signs of collapse.

Soil

Loss of soil productivity, which is causing extensive land abandonment, is a widespread by-product of current practices in agriculture and animal husbandry. Since 1945, 11% of the earth's vegetated surface has been degraded—an area larger than India and China combined—and per capita food production in many parts of the world is decreasing.

Forests

Tropical rain forests, as well as tropical and temperate dry forests, are being destroyed rapidly. At present rates, some critical forest types will be gone in a few years, and most of the tropical rain forest will be gone before the end of the next century. With them will go large numbers of plant and animal species.

Living Species

The irreversible loss of species, which by 2100 may reach one-third of all species now living, is especially serious. . . . Much of this damage is irreversible on a scale of centuries, or permanent. Other processes appear to pose additional threats. Increasing levels of gases in the atmosphere from human activities, including carbon dioxide released from fossil fuel burning and from deforestation, may alter climate on a global scale.

Warning

We the undersigned, senior members of the world's scientific community, hereby warn all humanity of what lies ahead. A great change in our stewardship of the earth and the life on it is required, if vast human misery is to be avoided and our global home on this planet is not to be irretrievably mutilated.

"Findings of the IPCC Fourth Assessment Report," 2007

Human Responsibility for Climate Change

The report finds that it is "very likely" that emissions of heat-trapping gases from human activities have caused "most of the observed increase in globally averaged temperatures since the mid-20th century." Evidence that human activities are the major cause of recent climate change is even stronger than in prior assessments.

(continued)

(continued)

Warming Is Unequivocal

The report concludes that it is "unequivocal" that Earth's climate is warming, "as is now evident from observations of increases in global average air and ocean temperatures, widespread melting of snow and ice, and rising global mean sea level." The report also confirms that the current atmospheric concentration of carbon dioxide and methane, two important heat-trapping gases, "exceeds by far the natural range over the last 650,000 years."

Additional IPCC Findings on Recent Climate Change

Rising Temperatures

- Eleven of the last 12 years rank among the 12 hottest years on record (since 1850, when sufficient worldwide temperature measurements began).
- Over the last 50 years, "cold days, cold nights, and frost have become less frequent, while hot days, hot nights, and heat waves have become more frequent."

Increasingly Severe Weather (storms, precipitation, drought)

- The intensity of tropical cyclones (hurricanes) in the North Atlantic has increased over the past 30 years, which correlates with increases in tropical sea surface temperatures.
- Storms with heavy precipitation have increased in frequency over most land areas. Between 1900 and 2005, long-term trends show significantly increased precipitation in eastern parts of North and South America, northern Europe, and northern and central Asia.
- Droughts have become longer and more intense, and have affected larger areas since the 1970s, especially in the tropics and subtropics.

Q *What problems and challenges do these two reports present? What do these two reports have in common? How do they differ?*

United States, while guest workers from Turkey, southern and eastern Europe, North Africa, India, and Pakistan have migrated to more prosperous western European countries. In 2005, nearly 200 million people, about 3 percent of the world's population, lived outside the country where they were born.

The migration of millions of people has also provoked a social backlash in many countries. Foreign workers have often become scapegoats when countries face economic problems. Political parties in France and Norway, for example, have called for the removal of blacks, Muslims, and Arabs in order to protect the ethnic or cultural purity of their nations, while in Asian countries, there is animosity against other Asian ethnic groups.

Another challenge of globalization is the wide gap between rich and poor nations. The rich nations, or **developed nations,** are located mainly in the Northern Hemisphere. They include the United States, Canada, Germany, and Japan, which have well-organized industrial and agricultural systems, advanced technologies, and effective educational systems. The poor nations, or **developing nations,** include many nations in Africa, Asia, and Latin America, which often have primarily agricultural economies with little technology. A serious problem in many developing nations is explosive population growth, which has led to severe food shortages often caused by poor soil but also by economic factors. Growing crops for export to developed countries, for example, may lead to enormous profits for large landowners but leaves many small farmers with little land on which to grow food.

Civil wars have also created food shortages. War not only disrupts normal farming operations, but warring groups try to limit access to food to weaken or kill their enemies. In Sudan, 1.3 million people starved when combatants of a civil war in the 1980s prevented food from reaching them. As unrest continued during the early 2000s in Sudan's Darfur region, families were forced to leave their farms. As a result, an estimated 70,000 people starved by mid-2004.

Global Movements and New Hopes

As people have become aware that the problems humans face are not just national or regional but global in scope, they have responded to this challenge in different ways. One approach has been to develop grassroots social movements, including ones devoted to environmental concerns, women's and men's liberation, human potential, appropriate technology, and nonviolence. "Think globally, act locally" is frequently the slogan of these grassroots groups. Related to the emergence of these social movements is the growth of **nongovernmental organizations (NGOs).** According to one analyst, NGOs are an important instrument in the cultivation of global perspectives: "Since NGOs by definition are identified with interests that transcend national boundaries, we expect all NGOs to define problems in global terms, to take account of human interests and needs as they are found in all parts of the planet."[2] NGOs are often represented at the United Nations and include professional, business, and cooperative organizations; foundations; religious, peace, and disarmament groups; youth and women's organizations; environmental and human rights groups; and research institutes. The number of international NGOs increased from 176 in 1910 to 40,000 in 2006.

And yet hopes for global approaches to global problems have also been hindered by political, ethnic, and religious differences. Pollution of the Rhine River by factories along its banks provokes angry disputes among European nations, and the United States and Canada have argued about the effects of acid rain on Canadian forests. The collapse of the Soviet Union and its satellite system seemed to provide an enormous boost to the potential for international cooperation on global issues, but it has had almost the opposite effect. The bloody conflict in the former Yugoslavia indicates the dangers inherent in the rise of nationalist sentiment among various ethnic and religious groups in eastern Europe. The widening gap between wealthy nations and poor, developing nations threatens global economic stability. Many conflicts begin with regional issues and then develop into international concerns. International terrorist groups seek to wreak havoc around the world.

Thus, even as the world becomes more global in culture and interdependent in its mutual relations, centrifugal forces are still at work attempting to redefine the political, cultural, and ethnic ways in which the world is divided. Such efforts are often disruptive and can sometimes work against measures to enhance our human destiny. But they also represent an integral part of human character and human history and cannot be suppressed in the relentless drive to create a world society.

There are already initial signs that as the common dangers posed by environmental damage, overpopulation, and scarcity of resources become even more apparent, societies around the world will find ample reason to turn their attention from cultural differences to the demands of global interdependence. The greatest challenge of the twenty-first century may be to reconcile the drive for individual and group identity with the common needs of the human community.

SUGGESTED READING

Useful books on different facets of the new global civilization include **M. B. Steger,** *Globalization: A Very Short Introduction* (New York, 2003); **J. H. Mittelman,** *The Globalization Syndrome* (Princeton, N.J., 2000); **M. Waters,** *Globalization,* 2nd ed. (London, 2001); **P. O'Meara et al., eds.,** *Globalization and the Challenges of the New Century* (Bloomington, Ind., 2000); and **H. French,** *Vanishing Borders* (New York, 2000). For a comprehensive examination of the digital age, see **M. Castells,** *The Information Age,* 3 vols. (Oxford, 1996–1998).

THEMES FOR UNDERSTANDING WORLD HISTORY

AS THEY PURSUE their craft, historians often organize their material on the basis of themes that enable them to ask and try to answer basic questions about the past. Such is our intention here. In preparing the sixth edition of this book, we have selected several major themes that we believe are especially important in understanding the course of world history. These themes transcend the boundaries of time and space and have relevance to all cultures since the beginning of the human experience.

In the chapters that follow, we will refer to these themes frequently as we advance from the prehistoric era to the present. Where appropriate, we shall make comparisons across cultural boundaries, or across different time periods. To facilitate this process, we have included a comparative essay in each chapter that focuses on a particular theme within the specific time period dealt with in that section of the book. For example, the comparative essays in Chapters 1 and 6 deal with the human impact on the natural environment during the premodern era, while those in Chapters 21 and 25 discuss the issue during the age of imperialism and in the contemporary world. Each comparative essay is identified with a particular theme, although it will be noted that many essays deal with several themes at the same time.

We have sought to illustrate these themes through the use of comparative illustrations in each chapter. These illustrations are comparative in nature and seek to encourage the reader to think about thematic issues in cross-cultural terms, while not losing sight of the unique characteristics of individual societies. Our seven themes, each divided into two subtopics, are listed below.

1. *Politics and Government* The study of politics seeks to answer certain basic questions that historians have about the structure of a society: How were people governed? What was the relationship between the ruler and the ruled? What people or groups of people (the political elites) held political power? What actions did people take to guarantee their security or change their form of government?

2. *Arts and Ideas* We cannot understand a society without looking at its culture, or the common ideas, beliefs, and patterns of behavior that are passed on from one generation to the next. Culture includes both high culture and popular culture. High culture consists of the writings of a society's thinkers and the works of its artists. A society's popular culture is the world of ideas and experiences of ordinary people. Today, the media have embraced the term *popular culture* to describe the current trends and fashionable styles.

3. *Religion and Philosophy* Throughout history, people have sought to find a deeper meaning to human life. How have the world's great religions, such as Hinduism, Buddhism, Judaism, Christianity, and Islam, influenced people's lives? How have they spread to create new patterns of culture in other parts of the world?

4. *Family and Society* The most basic social unit in human society has always been the family. From a study of family and social patterns, we learn about the different social classes that make up a society and their relationships with one another. We also learn about the role of gender in individual societies. What different roles did men and women play in their societies? How and why were those roles different?

5. *Science and Technology* For thousands of years, people around the world have made scientific discoveries and technological innovations that have changed our world. From the creation of stone tools that made farming easier to advanced computers that guide our airplanes, science and technology have altered how humans have related to their world.

6. *Earth and the Environment* Throughout history, peoples and societies have been affected by the physical world in which they live. Climatic changes alone have been an important factor in human history. Through their economic activities, peoples and societies, in turn, have also made an impact on their world. Human activities have affected the physical environment and even endangered the very existence of entire societies and species.

7. *Interaction and Exchange* Many world historians believe that the exchange of ideas and innovations is the driving force behind the evolution of human societies. The introduction of agriculture, writing and printing, metal working, and navigational techniques, for example, spread gradually from one part of the world to other regions and eventually changed the face of the entire globe. The process of cultural and technological exchange took place in various ways, including trade, conquest, and the migration of peoples.

ONE OF THE MOST difficult challenges in studying world history is coming to grips with the multitude of names, words, and phrases in unfamiliar languages. Unfortunately, this problem has no easy solution. We have tried to alleviate the difficulty, where possible, by providing an English-language translation of foreign words or phrases, a glossary, and a pronunciation guide. The issue is especially complicated in the case of Chinese because two separate systems are commonly used to transliterate the spoken Chinese language into the Roman alphabet. The Wade-Giles system, invented in the nineteenth century, was the most frequently used until recent years, when the pinyin system was adopted by the People's Republic of China as its own official form of transliteration. We have opted to use the latter, as it appears to be gaining acceptance in the United States, but the initial use of a Chinese word is accompanied by its Wade-Giles equivalent in parentheses for the benefit of those who may encounter the term in their outside reading.

In our examination of world history, we also need to be aware of the dating of time. In recording the past, historians try to determine the exact time when events occurred. World War II in Europe, for example, began on September 1, 1939, when Adolf Hitler sent German troops into Poland, and ended on May 7, 1945, when Germany surrendered. By using dates, historians can place events in order and try to determine the development of patterns over periods of time.

If someone asked you when you were born, you would reply with a number, such as 1991. In the United States, we would all accept that number without question, because it is part of the dating system followed in the Western world (Europe and the Western Hemisphere). In this system, events are dated by counting backward or forward from the birth of Christ (assumed to be the year 1). An event that took place 400 years before the birth of Christ would most commonly be dated 400 B.C. (before Christ). Dates after the birth of Christ are labeled as A.D. These letters stand for the Latin words *anno domini,* which mean "in the year of the Lord" (or the year of the birth of Christ). Thus, an event that took place 250 years after the birth of Christ is written A.D. 250, or in the year of the Lord 250. It can also be written as 250, just as you would not give your birth year as A.D. 1991, but simply 1991.

Some historians now prefer to use the abbreviations B.C.E. ("before the common era") and C.E. ("common era") instead of B.C. and A.D. This is especially true of world historians who prefer to use symbols that are not so Western or Christian oriented. The dates, of course, remain the same. Thus, 1950 B.C.E. and 1950 B.C. would be the same year, as would A.D. 40 and 40 C.E. In keeping with the current usage by many world historians, this book will use the terms B.C.E. and C.E.

Historians also make use of other terms to refer to time. A decade is 10 years; a century is 100 years; and a millennium is 1,000 years. The phrase fourth century B.C.E. refers to the fourth period of 100 years counting backward from 1, the assumed date of the birth of Christ. Since the first century B.C.E would be the years 100 B.C.E. to 1 B.C.E., the fourth century B.C.E would be the years 400 B.C.E. to 301 B.C.E. We could say, then, that an event in 350 B.C.E. took place in the fourth century B.C.E.

The phrase fourth century C.E. refers to the fourth period of 100 years after the birth of Christ. Since the first period of 100 years would be the years 1 to 100, the fourth period or fourth century would be the years 301 to 400. We could say, then, for example, that an event in 350 took place in the fourth century. Likewise, the first millennium B.C.E refers to the years 1000 B.C.E to 1 B.C.E; the second millennium C.E refers to the years 1001 to 2000.

The dating of events can also vary from people to people. Most people in the Western world use the Western calendar, also known as the Gregorian calendar after Pope Gregory XIII who refined it in 1582. The Hebrew calendar, on the other hand, uses a different system in which the year 1 is the equivalent of the Western year 3760 B.C.E., considered by Jews to be the date of the creation of the world. Thus, the Western year 2010 is the year 5770 on the Jewish calendar. The Islamic calendar begins year 1 on the day Muhammad fled Mecca, which is the year 622 on the Western calendar.

GLOSSARY

absolutism   a form of government where the sovereign power or ultimate authority rested in the hands of a monarch who claimed to rule by divine right and was therefore responsible only to God.

Abstract Expressionism   a post–World War II artistic movement that broke with all conventions of form and structure in favor of total abstraction.

Agricultural (Neolithic) Revolution   the shift from hunting animals and gathering plants for sustenance to producing food by systematic agriculture that occurred gradually between 10,000 and 4000 B.C.E. (the Neolithic or "New Stone" Age).

agricultural revolution   the application of new agricultural techniques that allowed for a large increase in productivity in the eighteenth century.

Amerindian   earliest inhabitants of North and South America. Original theories suggested migration from Siberia across the Bering Land Bridge; more recent evidence suggests migration also occurred by sea from regions of the South Pacific to South America.

anarchism   a political theory that holds that all governments and existing social institutions are unnecessary and advocates a society based on voluntary cooperation.

ANC   the African National Congress. Founded in 1912, it was the beginning of political activity by South African blacks. Banned by politically dominant European whites in 1960, it was not officially "unbanned" until 1990. It is now the official majority party of the South African government.

Analects   the body of writing containing conversations between Confucius and his disciples that preserves his worldly wisdom and pragmatic philosophies.

anti-Semitism   hostility toward or discrimination against Jews.

apartheid   the system of racial segregation practiced in the Republic of South Africa until the 1990s, which involved political, legal, and economic discrimination against nonwhites.

appeasement   the policy, followed by the European nations in the 1930s, of accepting Hitler's annexation of Austria and Czechoslovakia in the belief that meeting his demands would assure peace and stability.

Aramaic   a Semitic language dominant in the Middle East in the first century B.C.E.; still in use in small regions of the Middle East and southern Asia.

Arianism   a Christian heresy that taught that Jesus was inferior to God. Though condemned by the Council of Nicaea in 325, Arianism was adopted by many of the Germanic peoples who entered the Roman Empire over the next centuries.

aristocracy   a class of hereditary nobility in medieval Europe; a warrior class who shared a distinctive lifestyle based on the institution of knighthood, although there were social divisions within the group based on extremes of wealth.

Arthasastra   an early Indian political treatise that sets forth many fundamental aspects of the relationship of rulers and their subjects. It has been compared to Machiavelli's well-known book, *The Prince*, and has provided principles upon which many aspects of social organization have developed in the region.

Aryans   Indo-European-speaking nomads who entered India from the Central Asian steppes between 1500 and 1000 B.C.E. and greatly affected Indian society, notably by establishing the caste system. The term was later adopted by German Nazis to describe their racial ideal.

asceticism   a lifestyle involving the denial of worldly pleasures. Predominantly associated with Hindu, Buddhist, or Christian religions, adherents perceive their practices as a path to greater spituality.

ASEAN   the Association for the Southeast Asian Nations formed in 1967 to promote the prosperity and political stability of its member nations. Currently Brunei, Indonesia, Laos, Malaysia, Myanmar, the Philippines, Singapore, Thailand, and Vietnam are members. Other countries in the region participate as "observer" members.

Ausgleich   the "Compromise" of 1867 that created the dual monarchy of Austria-Hungary. Austria and Hungary each had its own capital, constitution, and legislative assembly, but were united under one monarch.

authoritarian state   a state that has a dictatorial government and some other trappings of a totalitarian state, but does not demand that the masses be actively involved in the regime's goals as totalitarian states do.

auxiliaries   troops enlisted from the subject peoples of the Roman Empire to supplement the regular legions composed of Roman citizens.

bakufu   the centralized government set up in Japan in the twelfth century. See shogunate system.

balance of power   a distribution of power among several states such that no single nation can dominate or interfere with the interests of another.

Banners   Originally established in 1639 by the Qing empire, the Eight Banners were administrative divisions into which all Manchu families were placed. Banners quickly evolved into the basis of Manchu military organization with each required to raise and support a prescribed number of troops.

Bao-jia **system**   the Chinese practice, reportedly originated by the Qin dynasty in the third century B.C.E., of organizing families into groups of five or ten to exercise mutual control and surveillance and reduce loyalty to the family.

Baroque   a style that dominated Western painting, sculpture, architecture and music from about 1580 to 1730, generally characterized by elaborate ornamentation and dramatic effects. Important practitioners included Bernini, Rubens, Handel, and Bach.

Bedouins   nomadic tribes originally from northern Arabia, who became important traders after the domestication of the camel during the first millennium B.C.E. Early converts to Islam, their values and practices deeply affected Muhammad.

benefice   in the Christian church, a position, such as a bishopric, that consisted of both a sacred office and the right of the holder to the annual revenues from the position.

Berbers   an ethnic group indigenous to western North Africa.

bey   a provincial governor in the Ottoman Empire.

bhakti in Hinduism, devotion as a means of religious observance open to all persons regardless of class.

bicameral legislature a legislature with two houses.

Black Death the outbreak of plague (mostly bubonic) in the mid-fourteenth century that killed from 25 to 50 percent of Europe's population.

blitzkrieg "lightning war." A war conducted with great speed and force, as in Germany's advance at the beginning of World War II.

bodhi Wisdom. Sometimes described as complete awareness of the true nature of the universe.

bodhisattvas in some schools of Buddhism, individuals who have achieved enlightenment but, because of their great compassion, have chosen to renounce Nirvana and to remain on earth in spirit form to help all human beings achieve release from reincarnation.

Bolsheviks a small faction of the Russian Social Democratic Party who were led by Lenin and dedicated to violent revolution; seized power in Russia in 1917 and were subsequently renamed the Communists.

bonsai originating in China in the first millenium B.C.E. and known there as *penzai*, it was imported to Japan between 700–900 C.E. *Bonsai* combines patience and artistry in the cultivation of stunted trees and shrubs to create exquisite nature scenes in miniature.

boyars the Russian nobility.

Brahman the Hindu word roughly equivalent to God; the Divine basis of all being; regarded as the source and sum of the cosmos.

brahmin A member of the Hindu priestly caste or class; literally "one who has realized or attempts to realize Brahman." Traditionally, duties of a *brahmin* include studying Hindu religious scriptures and transmitting them to others orally. The priests of Hindu temples are *brahmin*.

Brezhnev Doctrine the doctrine, enunciated by Leonid Brezhnev, that the Soviet Union had a right to intervene if socialism was threatened in another socialist state; used to justify the use of Soviet troops in Czechoslovakia in 1968.

Buddhism a religion and philosophy based on the teachings of Siddhartha Gautama in about 500 B.C.E. Principally practiced in China, India, and other parts of Asia, Buddhism has 360 million followers and is considered a major world releigion.

Burakumin A Japanese minority similar to *dalits* (or untouchables) in Indian culture. Past and current discrimination has resulted in lower educational attainment and socioeconomic status for members of this group. Movements with objectives ranging from "liberation" to integration have tried over the years to change this situation.

Bushido the code of conduct observed by samurai warriors; comparable to the European concept of chilvalry.

caliph the secular leader of the Islamic community.

calpulli in Aztec society, a kinship group, often of a thousand or more, which served as an intermediary with the central government, providing taxes and conscript labor to the state.

capital material wealth used or available for use in the production of more wealth.

caste system a system of rigid social hierarchy in which all members of that society are assigned by birth to specific "ranks," and inherit specific roles and privileges.

cartel a combination of independent commercial enterprises that work together to control prices and limit competition.

Cartesian dualism Descartes's principle of the separation of mind and matter (and mind and body) that enabled scientists to view matter as something separate from themselves that could be investigated by reason.

caudillos strong leaders in nineteenth-century Latin America, who were usually supported by the landed elites and ruled chiefly by

military force, though some were popular; they included both modernizers and destructive dictators.

censorate one of the three primary Chinese ministries, originally established in the Qin dynasty, whose inspectors surveyed the efficiency of officials throughout the system.

chaebol a South Korean business structure similar to the Japanese keiretsu.

Chan Buddhism a Chinese sect (Zen in Japanese) influenced by Daoist ideas, which called for mind training and a strict regimen as a means of seeking enlightenment.

chansons de geste a form of vernacular literature in the High Middle Ages that consisted of heroic epics focusing on the deeds of warriors.

chinampas in Mesoamerica, artifical islands crisscrossed by canals that provided water for crops and easy transportation to local markets.

chivalry the ideal of civilized behavior that emerged among the nobility in the eleventh and twelfth centuries under the influence of the church; a code of ethics knights were expected to uphold.

Christian (northern) humanism an intellectual movement in northern Europe in the late fifteenth and early sixteenth centuries that combined the interest in the classics of the Italian Renaissance with an interest in the sources of early Christianity, including the New Testament and the writings of the church fathers.

civic humanism an intellectual movement of the Italian Renaissance that saw Cicero, who was both an intellectual and a statesman, as the ideal and held that humanists should be involved in government and use their rhetorical training in the service of the state.

civil rights the basic rights of citizens including equality before the law, freedom of speech and press, and freedom from arbitrary arrest.

civil service examination an elaborate Chinese system of selecting bureaucrats on merit, first introduced in 165 C.E., developed by the Tang dynasty in the seventh century C.E. and refined under the Song dynasty; later adopted in Vietnam and with less success in Japan and Korea. It contributed to efficient government, upward mobility, and cultural uniformity.

class struggle the basis of the Marxist analysis of history, which says that the owners of the means of production have always oppressed the workers and predicts an inevitable revolution. See Marxism.

Cold War the ideological conflict between the Soviet Union and the United States after World War II.

collective farms large farms created in the Soviet Union by Stalin by combining many small holdings into one large farm worked by the peasants under government supervision.

collective security the use of an international army raised by an association of nations to deter aggression and keep the peace.

coloni free tenant farmers who worked as sharecroppers on the large estates of the Roman Empire (singular: *colonus*).

Comintern a worldwide organization of Communist parties, founded by Lenin in 1919, dedicated to the advancement of world revolution; also known as the Third International.

common law law common to the entire kingdom of England; imposed by the king's courts beginning in the twelfth century to replace the customary law used in county and feudal courts that varied from place to place.

communalism in South Asia, the tendency of people to band together in mutually antagonistic social sub-groups; elsewhere used to describe unifying trends in the larger community.

commune in medieval Europe, an association of townspeople bound together by a sworn oath for the purpose of obtaining basic liberties from the lord of the territory in which the town was located; also, the self-governing town after receiving its liberties.

conciliarism a movement in fourteenth- and fifteenth-century Europe that held that final authority in spiritual matters resided with a general church council, not the pope; emerged in response to the Avignon papacy and the Great Schism and used to justify the summoning of the Council of Constance (1414–1418).

condottieri leaders of bands of mercenary soldiers in Renaissance Italy who sold their services to the highest bidder.

Confucianism a system of thought based on the teachings of Confucius (551–479 B.C.E.) that developed into the ruling ideology of the Chinese state. See neo-Confucianism.

conquistadors "conquerors." Leaders in the Spanish conquests in the Americas, especially Mexico and Peru, in the sixteenth century.

conscription a military draft.

conservatism an ideology based on tradition and social stability that favored the maintenance of established institutions, organized religion, and obedience to authority and resisted change, especially abrupt change.

consuls the chief executive officers of the Roman Republic. Two were chosen annually to administer the government and lead the army in battle.

consumer society a term applied to Western society after World War II as the working classes adopted the consumption patterns of the middle class and installment plans, credit cards, and easy credit made consumer goods such as appliances and automobiles widely available.

containment a policy adopted by the United States in the Cold War. Its goal was to use whatever means, short of all-out war, to limit Soviet expansion.

Continental System Napoleon's effort to bar British goods from the Continent in the hope of weakening Britain's economy and destroying its capacity to wage war.

Contras in Nicaragua in the 1980s, an anti-Sandinista guerrilla movement supported by the U.S. Reagan administration.

Coptic a form of Christianity, originally Egyptian, that has thrived in Ethiopia since the fourth century C.E.

cosmopolitanism the quality of being sophisticated and having wide international experience.

cottage industry a system of textile manufacturing in which spinners and weavers worked at home in their cottages using raw materials supplied to them by capitalist entrepreneurs.

Crusade in the Middle Ages, a military campaign in defense of Christendom.

cultural relativism the belief that no culture is superior to another because culture is a matter of custom, not reason, and derives its meaning from the group holding it.

cuneiform "wedge-shaped." A system of writing developed by the Sumerians that consisted of wedge-shaped impressions made by a reed stylus on clay tablets.

daimyo prominent Japanese families who provided allegiance to the local shogun in exchange for protection; similar to vassals in Europe.

dalits commonly referred to as untouchables; the lowest level of Indian society, technically outside the caste system and considered less than human; renamed *harijans* ("children of God") by Gandhi, they remain the object of discrimination despite affirmative action programs.

Dao a Chinese philosophical concept, literally "The Way," central to both Confucianism and Daoism, that describes the behavior proper to each member of society; somewhat similar to the Indian concept of *dharma*.

Daoism a Chinese philosophy traditionally ascribed to the perhaps legendary Lao Tzu, which holds that acceptance and spontaneity are the keys to harmonious interaction with the universal order; an alternative to Confucianism.

decolonization the process of becoming free of colonial status and achieving statehood; occurred in most of the world's colonies between 1947 and 1962.

deficit spending the concept, developed by John Maynard Keynes in the 1930s, that in times of economic depression governments should stimulate demand by hiring people to do public works, such as building highways, even if this increased public debt.

deism belief in God as the creator of the universe who, after setting it in motion, ceased to have any direct involvement in it and allowed it to run according to its own natural laws.

demesne the part of a manor retained under the direct control of the lord and worked by the serfs as part of their labor services.

denazification after World War II, the Allied policy of rooting out any traces of Nazism in German society by bringing prominent Nazis to trial for war crimes and purging any known Nazis from political office.

depression a very severe, protracted economic downturn with high levels of unemployment.

destalinization the policy of denouncing and undoing the most repressive aspects of Stalin's regime; begun by Nikita Khrushchev in 1956.

détente the relaxation of tension between the Soviet Union and the United States that occurred in the 1970s.

devshirme in the Ottoman Empire, a system (literally, "collection") of training talented children to be administrators or members of the sultan's harem; originally meritocratic, by the seventeenth century, it degenerated into a hereditary caste.

dharma in Hinduism and Buddhism, the law that governs the universe, and specifically human behavior.

dialectic logic, one of the seven liberal arts that made up the medieval curriculum. In Marxist thought, the process by which all change occurs through the clash of antagonistic elements.

Diaspora the scattering of Jews throughout the ancient world after the Babylonian captivity in the sixth century B.C.E.

dictator in the Roman Republic, an official granted unlimited power to run the state for a short period of time, usually six months, during an emergency.

diocese the area under the jurisdiction of a Christian bishop; based originally on Roman administrative districts.

direct representation a system of choosing delegates to a representative assembly in which citizens vote directly for the delegates who will represent them.

divination the practice of seeking to foretell future events by interpreting divine signs, which could appear in various forms, such as in entrails of animals, in patterns in smoke, or in dreams.

divine-right monarchy a monarchy based on the belief that monarchs receive their power directly from God and are responsible to no one except God.

domino theory the belief that if the Communists succeeded in Vietnam, other countries in Southeast and East Asia would also fall (like dominoes) to communism; a justification for the U.S. intervention in Vietnam.

dualism the belief that the universe is dominated by two opposing forces, one good and the other evil.

dyarchy during the Qing dynasty in China, a system in which all important national and provincial admininstrative positions were shared equally by Chinese and Manchus, which helped to consolidate both Manchu rule and their assimilation.

dynastic state a state where the maintenance and expansion of the interests of the ruling family is the primary consideration.

economic imperialism   the process in which banks and corporations from developed nations invest in underdeveloped regions and establish a major presence there in the hope of making high profits; not necessarily the same as colonial expansion in that businesses invest where they can make a profit, which may not be in their own nation's colonies.

El Niño   periodic changes in water temperature at the surface of the Pacific Ocean, which can lead to major environmental changes and may have led to the collapse of the Moche civilization in what is now Peru.

emir   "commander" (Arabic), used by Muslim rulers in southern Spain and elsewhere.

empiricism   the practice of relying on observation and experiment.

enclosure movement   in the eighteenth century, the fencing in of the old open fields, combining many small holdings into larger units that could be farmed more efficiently.

encomienda   a grant from the Spanish monarch to colonial conquistadors; see *encomienda* system.

encomienda **system**   the system by which Spain first governed its American colonies. Holders of an *encomienda* were supposed to protect the Indians as well as using them as laborers and collecting tribute but in practice exploited them.

encyclical   a letter from the pope to all the bishops of the Roman Catholic Church.

enlightened absolutism   an absolute monarchy where the ruler follows the principles of the Enlightenment by introducing reforms for the improvement of society, allowing freedom of speech and the press, permitting religious toleration, expanding education, and ruling in accordance with the laws.

Enlightenment   an eighteenth-century intellectual movement, led by the philosophes, that stressed the application of reason and the scientific method to all aspects of life.

entrepreneur   one who organizes, operates, and assumes the risk in a business venture in the expectation of making a profit.

Epicureanism   a philosophy founded by Epicurus in the fourth century B.C.E. that taught that happiness (freedom from emotional turmoil) could be achieved through the pursuit of pleasure (intellectual rather than sensual pleasure).

equestrians   a group of extremely wealthy men in the late Roman Republic who were effectively barred from high office, but sought political power commensurate with their wealth; called equestrians because many had gotten their start as cavalry officers (*equites*).

eta   in feudal Japan, a class of hereditary slaves who were responsible for what were considered degrading occupations, such as curing leather and burying the dead.

ethnic cleansing   the policy of killing or forcibly removing people of another ethnic group; used by the Serbs against Bosnian Muslims in the 1990s.

eucharist   a Christian sacrament in which consecrated bread and wine are consumed in celebration of Jesus' Last Supper; also called the Lord's Supper or communion.

eunuch   a man whose testicles have been removed; a standard feature of the Chinese imperial system, the Ottoman Empire, and the Mughal dynasty, among others.

evolutionary socialism   a socialist doctrine espoused by Eduard Bernstein who argued that socialists should stress cooperation and evolution to attain power by democratic means rather than by conflict and revolution.

fascism   an ideology or movement that exalts the nation above the individual and calls for a centralized government with a dictatorial leader, economic and social regimentation, and forcible suppression of opposition; in particular, the ideology of Mussolini's Fascist regime in Italy.

feminism   the belief in the social, political, and economic equality of the sexes; also, organized activity to advance women's rights.

fief   a landed estate granted to a vassal in exchange for military services.

filial piety   in traditional China, in particular, a hierarchical system in which every family member has his or her place, subordinate to a patriarch who has in turn reciprocal responsibilities.

Final Solution   the physical extermination of the Jewish people by the Nazis during World War II.

five pillars of Islam   the core requirements of the faith, observation of which would lead to paradise: belief in Allah and his Prophet Muhammad; prescribed prayers; observation of Ramadan; pilgrimage to Mecca; and giving alms to the poor.

five relationships   in traditional China, the hierarchical interpersonal associations considered crucial to social order, within the family, between friends, and with the king.

folk culture   the traditional arts and crafts, literature, music, and other customs of the people; something that people make, as opposed to modern popular culture, which is something people buy.

foot binding   an extremely painful process, common in China throughout the second millenium C.E., that compressed girls' feet to half their natural size, representing submissiveness and self-discipline, which were considered necessary attributes for an ideal wife.

four modernizations   the slogan for radical reforms of Chinese industry, agriculture, technology, and national defense, instituted by Deng Xiaoping after his accession to power in the late 1970s.

free trade   the unrestricted international exchange of goods with low or no tariffs.

fundamentalism   a movement that emphasizes rigid adherence to basic religious principles; often used to describe evangelical Christianity, it also characterizes the practices of Islamic conservatives.

general strike   a strike by all or most workers in an economy; espoused by Georges Sorel as the heroic action that could be used to inspire the workers to destroy capitalist society.

genin   landless laborers in feudal Japan, who were effectively slaves.

gentry   well-to-do English landowners below the level of the nobility; played an important role in the English Civil War of the seventeenth century.

geocentric theory   the idea that the earth is at the center of the universe and that the sun and other celestial objects revolve around the earth.

glasnost   "openness." Mikhail Gorbachev's policy of encouraging Soviet citizens to openly discuss the strengths and weaknesses of the Soviet Union.

Gleichschaltung   the coordination of all government institutions under Nazi control in Germany from 1933.

global civilization   human society considered as a single worldwide entity, in which local differences are less important than overall similarities.

good emperors   the five emperors who ruled from 96 to 180 (Nerva, Trajan, Hadrian, Antoninus Pius, and Marcus Aurelius), a period of peace and prosperity for the Roman Empire.

Grand Council   the top of the government hierarchy in the Song dynasty in China.

grand *vezir*   (also, *vizier*) the chief executive in the Ottoman Empire, under the sultan.

Great Leap Forward   a short-lived, radical experiment in China, started in 1958, which created vast rural communes and attempted to replace the family as the fundamental social unit.

Great Proletarian Cultural Revolution   an attempt to destroy all vestiges of tradition in China, in order to create a totally egalitarian society; launched by Mao Zedong in 1966, it became virtually anarchic and lasted only until Mao's death in 1976.

Great Schism   the crisis in the late medieval church when there were first two and then three popes; ended by the Council of Constance (1414–1418).

green revolution   the introduction of technological agriculture, especially in India in the 1960s, which increased food production substantially but also exacerbated rural inequality because only the wealthier farmers could afford fertilizer.

guest workers   foreign workers working temporarily in European countries.

guided democracy   the name given by President Sukarno of Indonesia in the late 1950s to his style of government, which theoretically operated by consensus.

guild   an association of people with common interests and concerns, especially people working in the same craft. In medieval Europe, guilds came to control much of the production process and to restrict entry into various trades.

guru   teacher, especially in the Hindu, Buddhist and Sikh religious traditions, where it is an important honorific.

gymnasium   in Classical Greece, a place for athletics; in the Hellenistic Age, a secondary school with a curriculum centered on music, physical exercise, and literature.

Hadith   a collection of the sayings of the Prophet Muhammad, used to supplement the revelations contained in the Qur'an.

Hanseatic League   a commercial and military alliance of north German coastal towns, increasingly powerful in the fifteenth century C.E.

harem   the private domain of a ruler such as the sultan in the Ottoman Empire or the caliph of Baghdad, generally large and mostly inhabited by the extended family.

Hegira   the flight of Muhammad from Mecca to Medina in 622, which marks the first date on the official calendar of Islam.

heliocentric theory   the idea that the sun (not the earth) is at the center of the universe.

Hellenistic   literally, "to imitate the Greeks"; the era after the death of Alexander the Great when Greek culture spread into the Near East and blended with the culture of that region.

helots   serfs in ancient Sparta, who were permanently bound to the land that they worked for their Spartan masters.

heresy   the holding of religious doctrines different from the official teachings of the church.

Hermeticism   an intellectual movement beginning in the fifteenth century that taught that divinity is embodied in all aspects of nature; included works on alchemy and magic as well as theology and philosophy. The tradition continued into the seventeenth century and influenced many of the leading figures of the Scientific Revolution.

hetairai   highly sophisticated courtesans in ancient Athens who offered intellectual and musical entertainment as well as sex.

hieroglyphics   a highly pictorial system of writing most often associated with ancient Egypt. Also used (with different "pictographs") by other ancient peoples such as the Mayans.

high culture   the literary and artistic culture of the educated and wealthy ruling classes.

Hinayana   the scornful name for Theravada Buddhism ("lesser vehicle") used by devotees of Mahayana Buddhism.

Hinduism   the main religion in India, it emphasizes reincarnation, based on the results of the previous life, and the desirability of escaping this cycle. Its various forms feature both asceticism and the pleasures of ordinary life, and encompass a multitude of gods as different manifestations of one ultimate reality.

Holocaust   the mass slaughter of European Jews by the Nazis during World War II.

Hopewell culture   a Native American society that flourished from about 200 B.C.E. to 400 C.E., noted for large burial mounds and extensive manufacture. Largely based in Ohio, its traders ranged as far as the Gulf of Mexico.

hoplites   heavily armed infantry soldiers used in ancient Greece in a phalanx formation.

Huguenots   French Calvinists.

humanism   an intellectual movement in Renaissance Italy based upon the study of the Greek and Roman classics.

Hundred Schools   (of philosophy) in China around the third century B.C.E., a wide-ranging debate over the nature of human beings, society, and the universe. The Schools included Legalism and Daoism, as well as Confucianism.

hydraulic society   a society organized around a large irrigation system.

iconoclasm   an eighth-century Byzantine movement against the use of icons (pictures of sacred figures), which was condemned as idolatry.

ideology   a political philosophy such as conservatism or liberalism.

imam   an Islamic religious leader; some traditions say there is only one per generation, others use the term more broadly.

imperialism   the policy of extending one nation's power either by conquest or by establishing direct or indirect economic or cultural authority over another. Generally driven by economic self-interest, it can also be motivated by a sincere (if often misguided) sense of moral obligation.

imperium   "the right to command." In the Roman Republic, the chief executive officers (consuls and praetors) possessed the *imperium;* a military commander was an *imperator.* In the Roman Empire, the title *imperator,* or emperor, came to be used for the ruler.

indirect representation   a system of choosing delegates to a representative assembly in which citizens do not choose the delegates directly but instead vote for electors who choose the delegates.

indirect rule   a colonial policy of foreign rule in cooperation with local political elites; implemented in much of India and Malaya, and parts of Africa, it was not feasible where resistance was greater.

individualism   emphasis on and interest in the unique traits of each person.

indulgence   the remission of part or all of the temporal punishment in purgatory due to sin; granted for charitable contributions and other good deeds. Indulgences became a regular practice of the Christian church in the High Middle Ages, and their abuse was instrumental in sparking Luther's reform movement in the sixteenth century.

infanticide   the practice of killing infants.

inflation   a sustained rise in the price level.

intifada   the "uprising" of Palestinians living under Israeli control, especially in the 1980s and 1990s.

intendants   royal officials in seventeenth-century France who were sent into the provinces to execute the orders of the central government.

intervention, principle of   the idea, after the Congress of Vienna, that the great powers of Europe had the right to send armies into countries experiencing revolution to restore legitimate monarchs to their thrones.

Islam   the religion derived from the revelations of Muhammad, the Prophet of Allah; literally, "submission" (to the will of Allah); also the culture and civilization based upon the faith.

isolationism   a foreign policy in which a nation refrains from making alliances or engaging actively in international affairs.

Jainism   an Indian religion, founded in the fifth century B.C.E., which stresses extreme simplicity.

Janissaries   an elite core of eight thousand troops personally loyal to the sultan of the Ottoman Empire.

jati   a kinship group, the basic social organization of traditional Indian society, to some extent specialized by occupation.

jihad   in Islam, "striving in the way of the Lord." The term is ambiguous and has been subject to varying interpretations, from the practice of conducting raids against local neighbors to the conduct of "holy war" against unbelievers.

joint-stock company   a company or association that raises capital by selling shares to individuals who receive dividends on their investment while a board of directors runs the company.

joint-stock investment bank   a bank created by selling shares of stock to investors. Such banks potentially have access to much more capital than do private banks owned by one or a few individuals.

Jomon   the earliest known Neolithic inhabitants of Japan, named for the cord pattern of their pottery.

justification by faith   the primary doctrine of the Protestant Reformation; taught that humans are saved not through good works, but by the grace of God, bestowed freely through the sacrifice of Jesus.

Kabuki   a form of Japanese theater that developed in the seventeenth century C.E.; originally disreputable, it became a highly stylized art form.

kami   spirits who were worshiped in early Japan, and resided in trees, rivers and streams. See Shinto.

karma   a fundamental concept in Hindu (and later Buddhist, Jain, and Sikh) philosophy, that rebirth in a future life is determined by actions in this or other lives; the word refers to the entire process, to the individual's actions, and also to the cumulative result of those actions, for instance a store of good or bad *karma.*

keiretsu   a type of powerful industrial or financial conglomerate that emerged in post–World War II Japan following the abolition of *zaibatsu.*

khanates   Mongol kingdoms, in particular the subdivisions of Genghis Khan's empire ruled by his heirs.

kokutai   the core ideology of the Japanese state, particularly during the Meiji Restoration, stressing the uniqueness of the Japanese system and the supreme authority of the emperor.

kolkhoz   a collective farm in the Soviet Union, in which the great bulk of the land was held and worked communally. Between 1928 and 1934, 250,000 kolkhozes replaced 26 million family farms.

kshatriya   originally, the warrior class of Aryan society in India; ranked below (sometimes equal to) *brahmins,* in modern times often government workers or soldiers.

laissez-faire   "to let alone." An economic doctrine that holds that an economy is best served when the government does not interfere but allows the economy to self-regulate according to the forces of supply and demand.

latifundia   large landed estates in the Roman Empire (singular: *latifundium*).

lay investiture   the practice in which a layperson chose a bishop and invested him with the symbols of both his temporal office and his spiritual office; led to the Investiture Controversy, which was ended by compromise in the Concordat of Worms in 1122.

Lebensraum   "living space." The doctrine, adopted by Hitler, that a nation's power depends on the amount of land it occupies; thus, a nation must expand to be strong.

Legalism   a Chinese philosophy that argued that human beings were by nature evil and would follow the correct path only if coerced by harsh laws and stiff punishments. Adopted as official ideology by the Qin dynasty, it was later rejected but remained influential.

legitimacy, principle of   the idea that after the Napoleonic wars peace could best be reestablished in Europe by restoring legitimate monarchs who would preserve traditional institutions; guided Metternich at the Congress of Vienna.

Leninism   Lenin's revision of Marxism that held that Russia need not experience a bourgeois revolution before it could move toward socialism.

liberal arts   the seven areas of study that formed the basis of education in medieval and early modern Europe. Following Boethius and other late Roman authors, they consisted of grammar, rhetoric, and dialectic or logic (the *trivium*) and arithmetic, geometry, astronomy, and music (the *quadrivium*).

liberalism   an ideology based on the belief that people should be as free from restraint as possible. Economic liberalism is the idea that the government should not interfere in the workings of the economy. Political liberalism is the idea that there should be restraints on the exercise of power so that people can enjoy basic civil rights in a constitutional state with a representative assembly.

limited liability   the principle that shareholders in a joint-stock corporation can be held responsible for the corporation's debts only up to the amount they have invested.

limited (constitutional) monarchy   a system of government in which the monarch is limited by a representative assembly and by the duty to rule in accordance with the laws of the land.

lineage group   the descendants of a common ancestor; relatives, often as opposed to immediate family.

Longshan   a Neolithic society from near the Yellow River in China, sometimes identified by its black pottery.

maharaja   originally, a king in the Aryan society of early India (a great raja); later used more generally to denote an important ruler.

Mahayana   a school of Buddhism that promotes the idea of universal salvation through the intercession of *bodhisattvas;* predominant in north Asia.

majlis   a council of elders among the Bedouins of the Roman era.

mandate of Heaven   the justification for the rule of the Zhou dynasty in China; the king was charged to maintain order as a representative of Heaven, which was viewed as an impersonal law of nature.

mandates   a system established after World War I whereby a nation officially administered a territory (mandate) on behalf of the League of Nations. Thus, France administered Lebanon and Syria as mandates, and Britain administered Iraq and Palestine.

Manichaeanism   an offshoot of the ancient Zorastrian religion, influenced by Christianity; became popular in central Asia in the eighth century C.E.

manor   an agricultural estate operated by a lord and worked by peasants who performed labor services and paid various rents and fees to the lord in exchange for protection and sustenance.

Marshall Plan   the European Recovery Program, under which the United States provided financial aid to European countries to help them rebuild after World War II.

Marxism   the political, economic, and social theories of Karl Marx, which included the idea that history is the story of class struggle and that ultimately the proletariat will overthrow the bourgeoisie and establish a dictatorship en route to a classless society.

mass education   a state-run educational system, usually free and compulsory, that aims to ensure that all children in society have at least a basic education.

mass leisure   forms of leisure that appeal to large numbers of people in a society including the working classes; emerged at the end of the nineteenth century to provide workers with amusements after work and on weekends; used during the twentieth century by totalitarian states to control their populations.

mass politics   a political order characterized by mass political parties and universal male and (eventually) female suffrage.

mass society   a society in which the concerns of the majority—the lower classes—play a prominent role; characterized by extension of voting rights, an improved standard of living for the lower classes, and mass education.

materialism   the belief that everything mental, spiritual, or ideal is an outgrowth of physical forces and that truth is found in concrete material existence, not through feeling or intuition.

matrilinear   passing through the female line, for example from a father to his sister's son rather than his own, as practiced in some African societies; not necessarily, or even usually, combined with matriarchy, in which women rule.

megaliths   large stones, widely used in Europe from around 4000 to 1500 B.C.E. to create monuments, including sophisticated astronomical observatories.

Meiji Restoration   the period during the late 19th and early 20th century in which fundamental economic and cultural changes occured in Japan, tranforming it from a feudal and agrarian society to an industrial and technological society.

mercantilism   an economic theory that held that a nation's prosperity depended on its supply of gold and silver and that the total volume of trade is unchangeable; therefore, advocated that the government play an active role in the economy by encouraging exports and discouraging imports, especially through the use of tariffs.

Mesoamerica   the region stretching roughly from modern central Mexico to Honduras, in which the Olmec, Mayan, Aztec and other civilizations developed.

Mesolithic Age   the period from 10,000 to 7000 B.C.E., characterized by a gradual transition from a food-gathering/hunting economy to a food-producing economy.

mestizos   the offspring of intermarriage between Europeans, originally Spaniards, and native American Indians.

metics   resident foreigners in ancient Athens; not permitted full rights of citizenship but did receive the protection of the laws.

Middle Passage   the journey of slaves from Africa to the Americas as the middle leg of the triangular trade.

Middle Path   a central concept of Buddhism, which advocates avoiding extremes of both materialism and asceticism; also known as the Eightfold Way.

mihrab   the niche in a mosque's wall that indicates the direction of Mecca, usually containing an ornately decorated panel representing Allah.

militarism   a policy of aggressive military preparedness; in particular, the large armies based on mass conscription and complex, inflexible plans for mobilization that most European nations had before World War I.

millet   an administrative unit in the Ottoman empire used to organize religious groups.

ministerial responsibility   a tenet of nineteenth-century liberalism that held that ministers of the monarch should be responsible to the legislative assembly rather than to the monarch.

Modernism   the new artistic and literary styles that emerged in the decades before 1914 as artists rebelled against traditional efforts to portray reality as accurately as possible (leading to Impressionism and Cubism) and writers explored new forms.

monotheistic/monotheism   having only one god; the doctrine or belief that there is only one god.

muezzin   the man who calls Muslims to prayer at the appointed times; nowadays often a tape-recorded message played over loudspeakers.

mulattoes   the offspring of Africans and Europeans, particularly in Latin America.

Munich syndrome   a term used to criticize efforts to appease an aggressor, as in the Munich agreement of 1938, on the grounds that they only encourage his appetite for conquest.

mutual deterrence   the belief that nuclear war could best be prevented if both the United States and the Soviet Union had sufficient nuclear weapons so that even if one nation launched a preemptive first strike, the other could respond and devastate the attacker.

mystery religions   religions that involve initiation into secret rites that promise intense emotional involvement with spiritual forces and a greater chance of individual immortality.

nationalism   a sense of national consciousness based on awareness of being part of a community—a "nation"—that has common institutions, traditions, language, and customs and that becomes the focus of the individual's primary political loyalty.

nationalities problem   the dilemma faced by the Austro-Hungarian Empire in trying to unite a wide variety of ethnic groups including, among others, Austrians, Hungarians, Poles, Croats, Czechs, Serbs, Slovaks, and Slovenes in an era when nationalism and calls for self-determination were coming to the fore.

nationalization   the process of converting a business or industry from private ownership to government control and ownership.

nation in arms   the people's army raised by universal mobilization to repel the foreign enemies of the French Revolution.

nation-state   a form of political organization in which a relatively homogeneous people inhabits a sovereign state, as opposed to a state containing people of several nationalities.

NATO   the North Atlantic Treaty Organization; a military alliance formed in 1949 in which the signatories (Belgium, Canada, Denmark, France, Great Britain, Iceland, Italy, Luxembourg, the Netherlands, Norway, Portugal, and the United States) agreed to provide mutual assistance if any one of them was attacked; later expanded to include other nations, including former members of the Warsaw Pact—Poland, the Czech Republic, and Hungary.

natural laws   a body of laws or specific principles held to be derived from nature and binding upon all human society even in the absence of positive laws.

natural rights   certain inalienable rights to which all people are entitled; include the right to life, liberty, and property, freedom of speech and religion, and equality before the law.

natural selection   Darwin's idea that organisms that are most adaptable to their environment survive and pass on the variations that enabled them to survive, while other, less adaptable organisms become extinct; "survival of the fittest."

Nazi New Order   the Nazis' plan for their conquered territories; included the extermination of Jews and others considered inferior, ruthless exploitation of resources, German colonization in the east, and the use of Poles, Russians, and Ukrainians as slave labor.

négritude   a philosophy shared among African blacks that there exists a distinctive "African personality" that owes nothing to Western values and provides a common sense of purpose and destiny for black Africans.

neo-Confucianism   the dominant ideology of China during the second millennium C.E., it combined the metaphysical speculations of Buddhism and Daoism with the pragmatic Confucian approach to society, maintaining that the world is real, not illusory, and that fulfillment comes from participation, not withdrawal.

It encouraged an intellectual environment that valued continuity over change and tradition over innovation.

neocolonialism   the use of economic rather than political or military means to maintain Western domination of developing nations.

Neolithic Revolution   the development of agriculture, including the planting of food crops and the domestication of farm animals, around 10,000 B.C.E.

Neoplatonism   a revival of Platonic philosophy; in the third century C.E., a revival associated with Plotinus; in the Italian Renaissance, a revival associated with Marsilio Ficino who attempted to synthesize Christianity and Platonism.

New Course   a short-lived, liberalizing change in Soviet policy to its Eastern European allies instituted after the death of Stalin in 1953.

New Culture Movement   a protest launched at Peking University after the failure of the 1911 revolution, aimed at abolishing the remnants of the old system and introducing Western values and institutions into China.

New Deal   the reform program implemented by President Franklin Roosevelt in the 1930s, which included large public works projects and the introduction of Social Security.

New Democracy   the initial program of the Chinese Communist government, from 1949 to 1955, focusing on honest government, land reform, social justice, and peace rather than on the utopian goal of a classless society.

New Economic Policy   a modified version of the old capitalist system introduced in the Soviet Union by Lenin in 1921 to revive the economy after the ravages of the civil war and war communism.

new imperialism   the revival of imperialism after 1880 in which European nations established colonies throughout much of Asia and Africa.

new monarchies   the governments of France, England, and Spain at the end of the fifteenth century, where the rulers were successful in reestablishing or extending centralized royal authority, suppressing the nobility, controlling the church, and insisting upon the loyalty of all peoples living in their territories.

Nirvana   in Buddhist thought, enlightenment, the ultimate transcendence from the illusion of the material world; release from the wheel of life.

nobiles   "nobles." The small group of families from both patrician and plebeian origins who produced most of the men who were elected to office in the late Roman Republic.

Nok culture   in northern Nigeria, one of the most active early iron-working societies in Africa, artifacts from which date back as far as 500 B.C.E.

nuclear family   a family group consisting only of father, mother, and children.

nun   female religious monk.

old regime/old order   the political and social system of France in the eighteenth century before the Revolution.

oligarchy   rule by a few.

Open Door notes   a series of letters sent in 1899 by U.S. Secretary of State John Hay to Great Britain, France, Germany, Italy, Japan, and Russia, calling for equal economic access to the China market for all states and for the maintenance of the territorial and administrative integrity of the Chinese Empire.

optimates   "best men." Aristocratic leaders in the late Roman Republic who generally came from senatorial families and wished to retain their oligarchical privileges.

opium trade   the sale of the addictive product of the poppy, specifically by British traders to China in the 1830s. Chinese attempts to prevent it led to the Opium War of 1839–1842, which resulted in British access to Chinese ports and has traditionally been considered the beginning of modern Chinese history.

orders/estates   the traditional tripartite division of European society based on heredity and quality rather than wealth or economic standing, first established in the Middle Ages and continuing into the eighteenth century; traditionally consisted of those who pray (the clergy), those who fight (the nobility), and those who work (all the rest).

organic evolution   Darwin's principle that all plants and animals have evolved over a long period of time from earlier and simpler forms of life.

Organization of African Unity   founded in Addis Ababa in 1963, it was intended to represent the interests of all the newly independent countries of Africa and provided a forum for the discussion of common problems until 2001, when it was replaced by the African Union.

Paleolithic Age   the period of human history when humans used simple stone tools (c. 2,500,000–10,000 B.C.E.).

pan-Africanism   the concept of African continental unity and solidarity in which the common interests of African countries transcend regional boundaries.

pantheism   a doctrine that equates God with the universe and all that is in it.

pariahs   members of the lowest level of traditional Indian society, technically outside the class system itself; also known as untouchables.

pasha   an administrative official of the Ottoman Empire, responsible for collecting taxes and maintaining order in the provinces; later, some became hereditary rulers.

paterfamilias   the dominant male in a Roman family whose powers over his wife and children were theoretically unlimited, though they were sometimes circumvented in practice.

patriarchal/patriarchy   a society in which the father is supreme in the clan or family; more generally, a society dominated by men.

patriarchal family   a family in which the husband/father dominates his wife and children.

patricians   great landowners who became the ruling class in the Roman Republic.

patrilinear   passing through the male line, from father to son; often combined with patriarchy.

patronage   the practice of awarding titles and making appointments to government and other positions to gain political support.

Pax Romana   "Roman peace." A term used to refer to the stability and prosperity that Roman rule brought to the Mediterranean world and much of western Europe during the first and second centuries C.E.

peaceful coexistence   the policy adopted by the Soviet Union under Khrushchev in 1955, and continued by his successors, that called for economic and ideological rivalry with the West rather than nuclear war.

Pentateuch   the first five books of the Hebrew Bible (Genesis, Exodus, Leviticus, Numbers, and Deuteronomy).

peoples' democracies   a term invented by the Soviet Union to define a society in the early stage of socialist transition, applied to Eastern European countries in the 1950s.

perestroika   "restructuring." A term applied to Mikhail Gorbachev's economic, political, and social reforms in the Soviet Union.

permissive society   a term applied to Western society after World War II to reflect the new sexual freedom and the emergence of a drug culture.

Petrine supremacy   the doctrine that the bishop of Rome—the pope—as the successor of Saint Peter (traditionally considered the first bishop of Rome) should hold a preeminent position in the church.

phalanx a rectangular formation of tightly massed infantry soldiers.

philosophes intellectuals of the eighteenth-century Enlightenment who believed in applying a spirit of rational criticism to all things, including religion and politics, and who focused on improving and enjoying this world, rather than on the afterlife.

plebeians the class of Roman citizens who included nonpatrician landowners, craftspeople, merchants, and small farmers in the Roman Republic. Their struggle for equal rights with the patricians dominated much of the Republic's history.

pluralism the practice in which one person holds several church offices simultaneously; a problem of the late medieval church.

pogroms organized massacres of Jews.

polis an ancient Greek city-state encompassing both an urban area and its surrounding countryside; a small but autonomous political unit where all major political and social activities were carried out in a central location.

political democracy a form of government characterized by universal suffrage and mass political parties.

politiques a group who emerged during the French Wars of Religion in the sixteenth century; placed politics above religion and believed that no religious truth was worth the ravages of civil war.

polygyny the practice of having more than one wife at a time.

polytheistic/polytheism having many gods; belief in or the worship of more than one god.

popular culture as opposed to high culture, the unofficial, written and unwritten culture of the masses, much of which was passed down orally; centers on public and group activities such as festivals. In the twentieth century, refers to the entertainment, recreation, and pleasures that people purchase as part of mass consumer society.

populares "favoring the people." Aristocratic leaders in the late Roman Republic who tended to use the people's assemblies in an effort to break the stranglehold of the *nobiles* on political offices.

popular sovereignty the doctrine that government is created by and subject to the will of the people, who are the source of all political power.

portolani charts of landmasses and coastlines made by navigators and mathematicians in the thirteenth and fourteenth centuries.

Poststructuralism a theory formulated by Jacques Derrida in the 1960s, holding that there is no fixed, universal truth since culture is created and can therefore be analyzed in various ways.

praetorian guard the military unit that served as the personal bodyguard of the Roman emperors.

praetors the two senior Roman judges, who had executive authority when the consuls were away from the city and could also lead armies.

Prakrit an ancient Indian language, a simplified form of Sanskrit.

predestination the belief, associated with Calvinism, that God, as a consequence of his foreknowledge of all events, has predetermined those who will be saved (the elect) and those who will be damned.

price revolution the dramatic rise in prices (inflation) that occurred throughout Europe in the sixteenth and early seventeenth centuries.

primogeniture an inheritance practice in which the eldest son receives all or the largest share of the parents' estate.

principate the form of government established by Augustus for the Roman Empire; continued the constitutional forms of the Republic and consisted of the *princeps* ("first citizen") and the senate, although the *princeps* was clearly the dominant partner.

proletariat the industrial working class. In Marxism, the class who will ultimately overthrow the bourgeoisie.

Protestant Reformation the western European religious reform movement in the sixteenth century C.E. that divided Christianity into Catholic and Protestant groups.

purdah the Indian term for the practice among Muslims and some Hindus of isolating women and preventing them from associating with men outside the home.

Pure Land a Buddhist sect, originally Chinese but later popular in Japan, which taught that devotion alone could lead to enlightenment and release.

Puritans English Protestants inspired by Calvinist theology who wished to remove all traces of Catholicism from the Church of England.

querelles des femmes "arguments about women." A centuries-old debate about the nature of women that continued during the Scientific Revolution as those who argued for the inferiority of women found additional support in the new anatomy and medicine.

quipu an Inka record-keeping system that used knotted strings rather than writing.

raj common name for the British colonial regime in India.

raja originally, a chieftain in the Aryan society of early India, a representative of the gods; later used more generally to denote a ruler.

Ramadan the holy month of Islam, during which believers fast from dawn to sunset; since the Islamic calendar is lunar, Ramadan migrates through the seasons.

rationalism a system of thought based on the belief that human reason and experience are the chief sources of knowledge.

realism in medieval Europe, the school of thought that, following Plato, held that the individual objects we perceive are not real but merely manifestations of universal ideas existing in the mind of God. In the nineteenth century, a school of painting that emphasized the everyday life of ordinary people, depicted with photographic realism.

Realpolitik "politics of reality." Politics based on practical concerns rather than theory or ethics.

real wages/income/prices wages/income/prices that have been adjusted for inflation.

reason of state the principle that a nation should act on the basis of its long-term interests and not merely to further the dynastic interests of its ruling family.

reincarnation the idea that the individual soul is reborn in a different form after death; in Hindu and Buddhist thought, release from this cycle is the objective of all living souls.

relativity theory Einstein's theory that holds, among other things, that (1) space and time are not absolute but are relative to the observer and interwoven into a four-dimensional space-time continuum and (2) matter is a form of energy ($E = mc^2$).

Renaissance the "rebirth" of Classical culture that occurred in Italy between c. 1350 and c. 1550; also, the earlier revivals of Classical culture that occurred under Charlemagne and in the twelfth century.

rentier a person who lives on income from property and is not personally involved in its operation.

reparations payments made by a defeated nation after a war to compensate another nation for damage sustained as a result of the war; required from Germany after World War I.

revisionism a socialist doctrine that rejected Marx's emphasis on class struggle and revolution and argued instead that workers should work through political parties to bring about gradual change.

revolution a fundamental change in the political and social organization of a state.

revolutionary socialism the socialist doctrine espoused by Georges Sorel who held that violent action was the only way to achieve the goals of socialism.

rhetoric the art of persuasive speaking; in the Middle Ages, one of the seven liberal arts.

Rococo a style, especially of decoration and architecture, that developed from the Baroque and spread throughout Europe by the 1730s. While still elaborate, it emphasized curves, lightness, and charm in the pursuit of pleasure, happiness, and love.

ronin Japanese warriors made unemployed by developments in the early modern era, since samurai were forbidden by tradition to engage in commerce.

rural responsibility system post-Maoist land reform in China, under which collectives leased land to peasant families, who could consume or sell their surplus production and keep the profits.

sacraments rites considered imperative for a Christian's salvation. By the thirteenth century consisted of the eucharist or Lord's Supper, baptism, marriage, penance, extreme unction, holy orders, and confirmation of children; Protestant reformers of the sixteenth century generally recognized only two—baptism and communion (the Lord's Supper).

samurai literally "retainer"; similar to European knights. Usually in service to a particular shogun, these Japanese warriors lived by a strict code of ethics and duty.

Sanskrit an early Indo-European language, in which the Vedas were composed, beginning in the second millenium B.C.E. It survived as the language of literature and the bureaucracy for centuries after its decline as a spoken tongue.

sans-culottes the common people who did not wear the fine clothes of the upper classes (*sans-culottes* means "without breeches") and played an important role in the radical phase of the French Revolution.

sati the Hindu ritual requiring a wife to throw herself upon her deceased husband's funeral pyre.

satori enlightenment, in the Japanese, especially Zen, Buddhist tradition.

satrap/satrapy a governor with both civil and military duties in the ancient Persian Empire, which was divided into satrapies, or provinces, each administered by a satrap.

satyagraha the Hindi term for the practice of nonviolent resistance, as advocated by Mohandas Gandhi; literally, "hold fast to the truth".

scholar-gentry in Song dynasty China, candidates who passed the civil service examinations and whose families were non-aristocratic landowners; eventually, a majority of the bureaucracy.

scholasticism the philosophical and theological system of the medieval schools, which emphasized rigorous analysis of contradictory authorities; often used to try to reconcile faith and reason.

School of Mind a philosophy espoused by Wang Yangming during the mid-Ming era of China, which argued that mind and the universe were a single unit and knowledge was therefore obtained through internal self-searching rather than through investigation of the outside world; for a while, a significant but unofficial rival to neo-Confucianism.

scientific method a method of seeking knowledge through inductive principles; uses experiments and observations to develop generalizations.

Scientific Revolution the transition from the medieval worldview to a largely secular, rational, and materialistic perspective; began in the seventeenth century and was popularized in the eighteenth.

secularization the process of becoming more concerned with material, worldly, temporal things and less with spiritual and religious things.

self-determination the doctrine that the people of a given territory or a particular nationality should have the right to determine their own government and political future.

self-strengthening a late-nineteenth-century Chinese policy, by which Western technology would be adopted while Confucian principles and institutions were maintained intact.

senate/senators the leading council of the Roman Republic; composed of about 300 men (senators) who served for life and dominated much of the political life of the Republic.

sepoys native troops hired by the East India Company to protect British interests in south Asia, who formed the basis of the British Indian Army.

serf a peasant who is bound to the land and obliged to provide labor services and pay various rents and fees to the lord; considered unfree but not a slave because serfs could not be bought and sold.

Shari'a a law code, originally drawn up by Muslim scholars shortly after the death of Muhammad, that provides believers with a set of prescriptions to regulate their daily lives.

sheikh originally, the ruler of a Bedouin tribe; later, also used as a more general honorific.

Shi'ite the second largest tradition of Islam, which split from the majority Sunni soon after the death of Muhammad, in a disagreement over the succession; especially significant in Iran and Iraq.

Shinto a kind of state religion in Japan, derived from beliefs in nature spirits and until recently linked with belief in the divinity of the emperor and the sacredness of the Japanese nation.

shogun a powerful Japanese leader, originally military, who ruled under the titular authority of the emperor.

shogunate system the system of government in Japan in which the emperor exercised only titular authority while the shogun (regional military dictators) exercised actual political power.

Sikhism a religion, founded in the early sixteenth century in the Punjab, which began as an attempt to reconcile the Hindu and Muslim traditions and developed into a significant alternative to both.

sipahis in the Ottoman Empire, local cavalry elites, who held fiefdoms and collected taxes.

skepticism a doubtful or questioning attitude, especially about religion.

Social Darwinism the application of Darwin's principle of organic evolution to the social order; led to the belief that progress comes from the struggle for survival as the fittest advance and the weak decline.

socialism an ideology that calls for collective or government ownership of the means of production and the distribution of goods.

social security/social insurance government programs that provide social welfare measures such as old age pensions and sickness, accident, and disability insurance.

Socratic method a form of teaching that uses a question-and-answer format to enable students to reach conclusions by using their own reasoning.

Sophists wandering scholars and professional teachers in ancient Greece who stressed the importance of rhetoric and tended toward skepticism and relativism.

soviets councils of workers' and soldiers' deputies formed throughout Russia in 1917; played an important role in the Bolshevik Revolution.

sphere of influence a territory or region over which an outside nation exercises political or economic influence.

Star Wars nickname of the Strategic Defense Initiative, proposed by President Reagan, which was intended to provide a shield that would destroy any incoming missiles; named after a popular science-fiction movie series.

stateless societies the pre-Columbian communities in much of the Americas who developed substantial cultures without formal states.

State Confucianism   the integration of Confucian doctrine with Legalist practice under the Han dynasty in China, which became the basis of Chinese political thought until the modern era.

Stoicism   a philosophy founded by Zeno in the fourth century B.C.E. that taught that happiness could be obtained by accepting one's lot and living in harmony with the will of God, thereby achieving inner peace.

stupa   originally a stone tower holding relics of the Buddha, more generally a place for devotion, often architecturally impressive and surmounted with a spire.

subinfeudation   the practice in which a lord's greatest vassals subdivided their fiefs and had vassals of their own, and those vassals, in turn, subdivided their fiefs and so on down to simple knights whose fiefs were too small to subdivide.

Sublime Porte   the office of the grand *vezir* in the Ottoman Empire.

sudras   the classes that represented the great bulk of the Indian population from ancient time, mostly peasants, artisans or manual laborers; ranked below *brahmins, kshatriyas,* and *vaisyas,* but above the pariahs.

suffrage   the right to vote.

suffragists   those who advocate the extension of the right to vote (suffrage), especially to women.

Sufism   a mystical school of Islam, noted for its music, dance, and poetry, which became prominent in about the thirteenth century.

sultan   "holder of power," a title commonly used by Muslim rulers in the Ottoman Empire, Egypt, and elsewhere; still in use in parts of Asia, sometimes for regional authorities.

Sunni   the largest tradition of Islam, from which the Shi'ites split soon after the death of Muhammad, in a disagreement over the succession.

Supreme Ultimate   according to Neo-Confucianists, a transcendent world, distinct from the material world in which humans live, but to which humans may aspire; a set of abstract principles, roughly equivalent to the Dao.

surplus value   in Marxism, the difference between a product's real value and the wages of the worker who produced the product.

Swahili   a mixed African-Arabian culture that developed by the twelfth century along the east coast of Africa; also, the national language of Kenya and Tanzania.

syncretism   the combining of different forms of belief or practice, as, for example, when two gods are regarded as different forms of the same underlying divine force and are fused together.

Taika reforms   the seventh-century "great change" reforms that established the centralized Japanese state.

taille   a French tax on land or property, developed by King Louis XI in the fifteenth century as the financial basis of the monarchy. It was largely paid by the peasantry; the nobility and the clergy were exempt.

Tantrism   a mystical Buddhist sect, which emphasized the importance of magical symbols and ritual in seeking a path to enlightenment.

tariffs   duties (taxes) imposed on imported goods; usually imposed both to raise revenue and to discourage imports and protect domestic industries.

tetrarchy   rule by four; the system of government established by Diocletian (284–305) in which the Roman Empire was divided into two parts, each ruled by an "Augustus" assisted by a "Caesar."

theocracy   a government based on a divine authority.

Theravada   a school of Buddhism that stresses personal behavior and the quest for understanding as a means of release from the wheel of life, rather than the intercession of bodhisattvas; predominant in Sri Lanka and Southeast Asia.

three-field system   in medieval agriculture, the practice of dividing the arable land into three fields so that one could lie fallow while the others were planted in winter grains and spring crops.

three kingdoms   Koguryo, Paekche, and Silla, rivals but all under varying degrees of Chinese influence, which together controlled virtually all of Korea from the fourth to the seventh centuries.

three obediences   the traditional duties of Japanese women, in permanent subservience: child to father, wife to husband, and widow to son.

tithe   a tenth of one's harvest or income; paid by medieval peasants to the village church.

Tongmenghui   the political organization—"Revolutionary Alliance"— formed by Sun Yat-sen in 1905, which united various revolutionary factions and ultimately toppled the Manchu dynasty.

Torah   the body of law in Hebrew Scripture, contained in the Pentateuch (the first five books of the Hebrew Bible).

totalitarian state   a state characterized by government control over all aspects of economic, social, political, cultural, and intellectual life, the subordination of the individual to the state, and insistence that the masses be actively involved in the regime's goals.

total war   warfare in which all of a nation's resources, including civilians at home as well as soldiers in the field, are mobilized for the war effort.

trade union   an association of workers in the same trade, formed to help members secure better wages, benefits, and working conditions.

transubstantiation   a doctrine of the Roman Catholic Church that teaches that during the eucharist the substance of the bread and wine is miraculously transformed into the body and blood of Jesus.

trench warfare   warfare in which the opposing forces attack and counterattack from a relatively permanent system of trenches protected by barbed wire; characteristic of World War I.

tribunes of the plebs   beginning in 494 B.C.E., Roman officials who were given the power to protect plebeians against arrest by patrician magistrates.

tribute system   an important element of Chinese foreign policy, by which neighboring states paid for the privilege of access to Chinese markets, received legitimation and agreed not to harbor enemies of the Chinese Empire.

Truman Doctrine   the doctrine, enunciated by Harry Truman in 1947, that the United States would provide economic aid to countries that said they were threatened by Communist expansion.

twice-born   the males of the higher castes in traditional Indian society, who underwent an initiation ceremony at puberty.

tyrant/tyranny   in an ancient Greek *polis* (or an Italian city-state during the Renaissance), a ruler who came to power in an unconstitutional way and ruled without being subject to the law.

uhuru   "freedom" (Swahili), and so a key slogan in the African independence movements, especially in Kenya.

uji   a clan in early Japanese tribal society.

ulama   a convocation of leading Muslim scholars, the earliest of which shortly after the death of Muhammad drew up a law code, called the *Shari'a,* based largely on the Qur'an and the sayings of the Prophet, to provide believers with a set of prescriptions to regulate their daily lives.

umma   the Muslim community, as a whole.

uncertainty principle   a principle in quantum mechanics, posited by Heisenberg, that holds that one cannot determine the path of an electron because the very act of observing the electron would affect its location.

unconditional surrender   complete, unqualified surrender of a nation.

uninterrupted revolution   the goal of the Great Proletarian Cultural Revolution launched by Mao Zedong in 1966.

utopian socialists intellectuals and theorists in the early nineteenth century who favored equality in social and economic conditions and wished to replace private property and competition with collective ownership and cooperation; deemed impractical and "utopian" by later socialists.

vaisya the third-ranked class in traditional Indian society, usually merchants.

varna Indian classes, or castes. See caste system.

vassal a person granted a fief, or landed estate, in exchange for providing military services to the lord and fulfilling certain other obligations such as appearing at the lord's court when summoned and making a payment on the knighting of the lord's eldest son.

veneration of ancestors the extension of filial piety to include care for the deceased, for instance by burning replicas of useful objects to accompany them on their journey to the next world.

vernacular the everyday language of a region, as distinguished from a language used for special purposes. For example, in medieval Paris, French was the vernacular, but Latin was used for academic writing and for classes at the University of Paris.

Vietnam syndrome the presumption, from the 1970s on, that the U.S. public would object to a protracted military entanglement abroad, such as another Vietnam-type conflict.

vizier (also, *vezir*) the prime minister in the Abbasid caliphate and elsewhere, a chief executive.

volkish thought the belief that German culture is superior and that the German people have a universal mission to save Western civilization from inferior races.

war communism Lenin's policy of nationalizing industrial and other facilities and requisitioning the peasants' produce during the civil war in Russia.

War Guilt Clause the clause in the Treaty of Versailles that declared that Germany (and Austria) were responsible for starting World War I and ordered Germany to pay reparations for the damage the Allies had suffered as a result of the war.

Warsaw Pact a military alliance, formed in 1955, in which Albania, Bulgaria, Czechoslovakia, East Germany, Hungary, Poland, Romania, and the Soviet Union agreed to provide mutual assistance. Dissolved in 1991, most former members eventually joined NATO.

welfare state a social/political system in which the government assumes the primary responsibility for the social welfare of its citizens by providing such things as social security, unemployment benefits, and health care.

well field system the theoretical pattern of land ownership in early China, named for the appearance of the Chinese character for "well," in which farmland was divided into nine segments and a peasant family would cultivate one for their own use and cooperate with seven others to cultivate the ninth for the landlord.

wergeld "money for a man." In early Germanic law, a person's value in monetary terms, which was paid by a wrongdoer to the family of the person who had been injured or killed.

White Lotus a Chinese Buddhist sect, founded in 1133 C.E., that sought political reform; in 1796–1804, a Chinese peasant revolt.

women's liberation movement the struggle for equal rights for women, which has deep roots in history but achieved new prominence under this name in the 1960s, building on the work of, among others, Simone de Beauvoir and Betty Friedan.

world-machine Newton's conception of the universe as one huge, regulated, and uniform machine that operated according to natural laws in absolute time, space, and motion.

Yangshao a Neolithic society from near the Yellow River in China, sometimes identified by its painted pottery.

Young Turks a successful Turkish reformist group in the late nineteenth and early twentieth centuries.

zaibatsu powerful business cartels formed in Japan during the Meiji era and outlawed following World War II.

zamindars Indian tax collectors, who were assigned land, from which they kept part of the revenue; the British revived the system in a misguided attempt to create a landed gentry.

Zen Buddhism (in Chinese, Chan or Ch'an) a school of Buddhism particularly important in Japan, some of whose adherents stress that enlightenment (satori) can be achieved suddenly, though others emphasize lengthy meditation.

ziggurat a massive stepped tower upon which a temple dedicated to the chief god or goddess of a Sumerian city was built.

Zionism an international movement that called for the establishment of a Jewish state or a refuge for Jews in Palestine.

Zoroastrianism a religion founded by the Persian Zoroaster in the seventh century B.C.E.; characterized by worship of a supreme god Ahuramazda who represents the good against the evil spirit, identified as Ahriman.

Abbasid uh-BAH-sid or AB-uh-sid
Abd al-Rahman ub-duh-rahkh-MAHN
Abu al-Abbas uh-BOOL-uh-BUSS
Abu Bakr uh-boo-BAHK-ur
Achebe, Chinua ah-CHAY-bay, CHIN-wah
Achilles uh-KIL-eez
Adenauer, Konrad AD-uh-now-ur
aediles EE-dylz
Aegospotami ee-guh-SPOT-uh-mee
Aeolians ee-OH-lee-unz
Aequi EE-kwy
Aeschylus ESS-kuh-luss
Aetius ay-EE-shuss
Afrikaners ah-fri-KAH-nurz
Agesilaus uh-jess-uh-LAY-uss
Agincourt AH-zhen-koor
Aguinaldo, Emilio ah-gwee-NAHL-doh, ay-MEEL-yoh
Ahlwardt, Hermann AHL-vart, hayr-MAHN
Ahuramazda uh-hoor-uh-MAHZ-duh
Aix-la-Chapelle ex-lah-shah-PELL
Ajanta uh-JUHN-tuh
Akhenaten ah-khuh-NAH-tun
Akhetaten ah-khuh-TAH-tun
Akkadians uh-KAY-dee-unz
Alaric AL-uh-rik
Alberti, Leon Battista al-BAYR-tee, LAY-un buh-TEESS-tuh
Albigensians al-buh-JEN-see-unz
Albuquerque, Afonso de AL-buh-kur-kee, ah-FAHN-soh day
Alcibiades al-suh-BY-uh-deez
Alcuin AL-kwin
Alemanni al-uh-MAH-nee
al-Fatah al-FAH-tuh
al-Hakim al-hah-KEEM
Alia, Ramiz AH-lee-uh, rah-MEEZ
al-Khwarizmi al-KHWAR-iz-mee
Allah AH-lah
al-Ma'mun al-muh-MOON
Almeida, Francesco da ahl-MAY-duh, frahn-CHAYSS-koh
al-Sadat, Anwar ah-sah-DAHT, ahn-WAHR
Aidoo, Ama Ata ah-EE-doo, AH-mah AH-tah
Amaterasu ah-muh-teh-RAH-suh
Amenhotep ah-mun-HOH-tep
Anasazi ah-nuh-SAH-zee
Andreotti, Giulio ahn-dray-AH-tee, JOOL-yoh
Andropov, Yuri ahn-DRAHP-awf, YOOR-ee

Anjou AHN-zhoo
Antigonid an-TIG-uh-nid
Antigonus Gonatus an-TIG-oh-nuss guh-NAH-tuss
Antiochus an-TY-uh-kuss
Antonescu, Ion an-tuh-NESS-koo, YON
Antoninus Pius an-tuh-NY-nuss PY-uss
Anyang ahn-YAHNG
apella uh-PELL-uh
Apollonius ap-uh-LOH-nee-uss
Aquinas, Thomas uh-KWY-nuss
Arafat, Yasir ah-ruh-FAHT, yah-SEER
aratrum uh-RAH-trum
Arawak AR-uh-wahk
Archimedes ahr-kuh-MEE-deez
Argonautica ahr-guh-NAWT-uh-kuh
Aristarchus ar-iss-TAR-kus
Aristotle AR-iss-tot-ul
Arjuna ahr-JOO-nuh
Arsinoë ahr-SIN-oh-ee
artium baccalarius ar-TEE-um bak-uh-LAR-ee-uss
artium magister ar-TEE-um muh-GISS-ter
Aryan AR-ee-un
Ashikaga ah-shee-KAH-guh
Ashkenazic ash-kuh-NAH-zik
Ashoka uh-SHOH-kuh
Ashurbanipal ah-shur-BAH-nuh-pahl
Ashurnasirpal ah-shur-NAH-zur-pahl
asiento ah-SYEN-toh
assignat ah-see-NYAH
Assyrians uh-SEER-ee-unz
Astell, Mary AST-ul
Atahualpa ah-tuh-WAHL-puh
Attalid AT-uh-lid
audiencias ow-dee-en-SEE-uss
Auerstadt OW-urr-shtaht
augur AW-gurr
Augustine AW-guh-steen
Aum Shinri Kyo awm-shin-ree-KYO
Aung San Suu Kyi AWNG-sawn-soo-chee
Aurelian aw-REEL-yun
Auschwitz-Birkenau OW-shvitz-BEER-kuh-now
Ausgleich OWSS-glykh
auspices AWSS-puh-sizz
Austerlitz AWSS-tur-litz
Australopithecines aw-stray-loh-PITH-uh-synz
Austrasia awss-TRAY-zhuh
Autun oh-TUNH

Avalokitesvara uh-VAH-loh-kee-TESH-vuh-ruh
Avicenna av-i-SENN-uh
Avignon ah-veen-YOHNH
Ayacucho ah-ya-KOO-choh
Ayodhya ah-YOHD-hyah
Ayuthaya ah-yoo-TY-yuh
Azerbaijan az-ur-by-JAN
Ba'ath BAHTH
Baader-Meinhof BAH-durr-MYN-huff
Babeuf, Gracchus bah-BUFF, GRAK-uss
Babur BAH-burr
Bach, Johann Sebastian BAKH, yoh-HAHN suh-BASS-chun
Baden-Powell, Robert BAD-un-POW-ul
Bai Hua by HWA
bakufu buh-KOO-foo or Japanese bah-KOO-fuh
Bakunin, Michael buh-KOON-yun
Balboa, Vasco Nuñez de bal-BOH-uh, BAHS-koh NOON-yez day
Ballin, Albert BAH-leen
Bandaranaike, Sirimavo bahn-dur-uh-NY-uh-kuh, see-ree-MAH-voh
Banque de Belgique BAHNK duh bel-ZHEEK
Ban Zhao bahn ZHOW
Bao-jia BOW-jah
Barbarossa bar-buh-ROH-suh
Baroque buh-ROHK
Barth, Karl BAHRT
Basho BAH-shoh
Bastille bass-STEEL
Basutoland buh-SOO-toh-land
Batista, Fulgencio bah-TEES-tuh, full-JEN-see-oh
Bauhaus BOW-howss
Bayazid by-uh-ZEED
Bayle, Pierre BELL, PYAYR
Beauharnais, Josephine de boh-ar-NAY, zhoh-seff-FEEN duh
Beauvoir, Simone de boh-VWAR, see-MUHN duh
Bebel, August BAY-bul, ow-GOOST
Beccaria, Cesare buh-KAH-ree-uh, CHAY-zuh-ray
Bechuanaland bech-WAH-nuh-land
Bede BEED
Begin, Menachem BAY-gin, muh-NAH-khum
Beguines bay-GEENZ
Beiderbecke, Bix BY-der-bek, BIKS
Beijing bay-ZHING

Belarus   bell-uh-ROOSS

Belgioioso, Cristina   bell-joh-YOH-soh

Belisarius   bell-uh-SAH-ree-uss

benefice   BEN-uh-fiss

Benin   bay-NEEN

Bergson, Henri   BAYRK-suhn, ahn-REE

Berlioz, Hector   BAYR-lee-ohz, hek-TOR

Berlusconi, Silvio   bayr-loo-SKOH-nee,
   SEEL-vee-oh

Bernhardi, Friedrich von   bayrn-HAR-dee,
   FREED-reekh fun

Bernini, Gian Lorenzo   bur-NEE-nee, JAHN
   loh-RENT-zoh

Bernstein, Eduard   BAYRN-shtyn, AY-doo-art

Bethman-Hollweg, Theobald von   BET-mun-
   HOHL-vek, TAY-oh-bahlt fun

Bhagavad Gita   bah-guh-vahd-GEE-tuh

Bharatiya Janata   BAR-ruh-tuh JAH-nuh-tuh

Bhutto, Zulfikar Ali   BOO-toh, ZOOL-fee-kahr
   ah-LEE

Bismarck, Otto von   BIZ-mark, OH-toh fun

Blanc, Louis   BLAHNH, LWEE

Blitzkrieg   BLITZ-kreeg

Blum, Léon   BLOOM, LAY-ohnh

Boccaccio, Giovanni   boh-KAH-choh,
   joe-VAH-nee

Bodichon, Barbara   boh-di-SHOHNH

Boer   BOOR or BOR

Boethius   boh-EE-thee-uss

Boleyn, Anne   BUH-lin or buh-LIN

Bolívar, Simón   boh-LEE-var, see-MOHN

Bologna   boh-LOHN-yuh

Bolsheviks   BOHL-shuh-viks

Bora, Katherina von   BOH-rah, kat-uh-REE-
   nuh fun

Borobudur   boh-roh-buh-DOOR

Bosnia   BAHZ-nee-uh

Bosporus   BAHSS-pruss

Bossuet, Jacques   baw-SWAY, ZHAHK

Botswana   baht-SWAH-nuh

Botta, Giuseppe   BOH-tah, joo-ZEP-pay

Botticelli, Sandro   bot-i-CHELL-ee,
   SAHN-droh

Boulanger, Georges   boo-lahnh-ZHAY,
   ZHORZH

boule   BOOL

Bracciolini, Poggio   braht-choh-LEE-nee,
   POH-djoh

Brahe, Tycho   BRAH, TY-koh

Brahmo Samaj   BRAH-moh suh-MAHJ

Bramante, Donato   brah-MAHN-tay,
   doh-NAH-toh

Brandt, Willy   BRAHNT, VIL-ee

Brasidas   BRASS-i-duss

Brest-Litovsk   BREST-li-TUFFSK

Brétigny   bray-tee-NYEE

Brezhnev, Leonid   BREZH-neff, lyee-oh-NYEET

Briand, Aristide   bree-AHNH, ah-ruh-STEED

Broz, Josip   BRAWZ, yaw-SEEP

Brunelleschi, Filippo   BROO-nuh-LESS-kee,
   fee-LEE-poh

Brüning, Heinrich   BRUR-ning, HYN-rikh

Bückeberg   BURK-uh-bayrk

Bulganin, Nicolai   bool-GAN-yin, nyik-uh-LY

Bund Deutscher Mädel   BOONT DOIT-chur
   MAY-dul

Bundesrat   BOON-duss-raht

Burckhardt, Jacob   BOORK-hart, YAK-ub

Burschenschaften   BOOR-shun-shahf-tun

Bushido   BOO-shee-doh

Cabral, Pedro   kuh-BRAL, PAY-droh

cahiers de doléances   ka-YAY duh doh-lay-
   AHNSS

Cai Yuanpei   TSY yoo-wan-PAY

Calais   ka-LAY

Calas, Jean   ka-LAH, ZHAHNH

Caligula   kuh-LIG-yuh-luh

caliph   KAY-liff

caliphate   KAY-luh-fayt

Callicrates   kuh-LIK-ruh-teez

Calonne, Charles de   ka-LUNN, SHAHRL duh

Cambyses   kam-BY-seez

Camus, Albert   ka-MOO, ahl-BAYR

Can Vuong   kahn VWAHNG

Canaanites   KAY-nuh-nytss

Cannae   KAH-nee

Cao Cao   TSOW-tsow

Capet, Hugh   ka-PAY, YOO

Capetian   kuh-PEE-shun

Caracalla   kuh-RAK-uh-luh

Caraffa, Gian Pietro   kuh-RAH-fuh, JAHN
   PYAY-troh

carbonari   kar-buh-NAH-ree

Cárdenas, Lázaro   KAHR-day-nahss,
   LAH-zah-roh

Carolingian   kar-uh-LIN-jun

carruca   kuh-ROO-kuh

Carthage   KAHR-thij

Carthaginian   kahr-thuh-JIN-ee-un

Cartier, Jacques   kahr-TYAY, ZHAK

Casa de Contratación   KAH-sah day KOHN-
   trah-tahk-SYOHN

Cassiodorus   kass-ee-uh-DOR-uss

Castiglione, Baldassare   ka-steel-YOH-nay,
   bal-duh-SAH-ray

Castro, Fidel   KASS-troh, fee-DELL

Çatal Hüyük   chaht-ul-hoo-YOOK

Catharism   KATH-uh-riz-um

Catullus   kuh-TULL-uss

Cavendish, Margaret   KAV-un-dish

Cavour, Camillo di   kuh-VOOR, kuh-MEEL-
   oh dee

Ceaușescu, Nicolae   chow-SHES-koo, nee-
   koh-LY

celibacy   SELL-uh-buh-see

cenobitic   sen-oh-BIT-ik

Cereta, Laura   say-RAY-tuh, LOW-ruh

Cerularius, Michael   sayr-yuh-LAR-ee-uss

Cézanne, Paul   say-ZAHN, POHL

Chacabuco   chahk-ah-BOO-koh

Chaeronea   ker-uh-NEE-uh

Chaldean   kal-DEE-un

Chamorro, Violeta Barrios de   chah-MOH-roh,
   vee-oh-LET-uh bah-REE-ohss day

Champlain, Samuel de   shonh-PLENH or sham-
   PLAYN, sahm-WEL duh

Chandragupta Maurya   chun-druh-GOOP-tuh
   MOWR-yuh

Chang'an   CHENG-AHN

chanson de geste   shahn-SONH duh ZHEST

Chao Phraya   chow-PRY-uh

Charlemagne   SHAR-luh-mayn

Chateaubriand, François-René de   shah-TOH-
   bree-AHNH, frahnh-SWAH-ruh-NAY duh

Châtelet, marquise du   shat-LAY, mahr-KEEZ
   duh

Chauvet   shoh-VAY

Chavín de Huántar   chah-VEEN day HWAHN-
   tahr

Chechnya   CHECH-nyuh

Cheka   CHEK-uh

Chennai   CHEN-ny

Chen Shuibian   CHEN-shwee-BYAHN

Chiang Kai-shek   CHANG ky-SHEK

Chichén Itzá   chee-CHEN-eet-SAH

Chimor   chee-MAWR

Chirac, Jacques   shee-RAK, ZHAHK

Chongqing   chung-CHING

Chrétien de Troyes   kray-TYEN duh TRWAH

Chrétien, Jean   kray-TYEN, ZHAHNH

Chrysoloras, Manuel   kriss-uh-LAWR-uss,
   man-WEL

Cicero   SIS-uh-roh

Cincinnatus   sin-suh-NAT-uss

ciompi   CHAHM-pee

Cistercians   sis-TUR-shunz

Cixi   TSEE-chee

Clairvaux   klayr-VOH

Claudius   KLAW-dee-uss

Cleisthenes   KLYSS-thuh-neez

Clemenceau, Georges   kluh-mahn-SOH,
   ZHORZH

Clovis   KLOH-viss

Codreanu, Corneliu   kaw-dree-AH-noo,
   kor-NELL-yoo

Colbert, Jean-Baptiste   kohl-BAYR, ZHAHN-
   bap-TEEST

Colonia Agrippinensis   kuh-LOH-nee-uh
   uh-grip-uh-NEN-suss

colonus   kuh-LOH-nuss

Columbanus   kah-lum-BAY-nuss

comitia centuriata   kuh-MISH-ee-uh sen-choo-
   ree-AH-tuh

Commodus   KAHM-uh-duss

Comnenus   kahm-NEE-nuss

Comte, Auguste   KOHNT, ow-GOOST

concilium plebis   kahn-SILL-ee-um PLEE-biss

Concordat of Worms kun-KOR-dat uv WURMZ or VORMPS

Condorcet, Marie-Jean de konh-dor-SAY, muh-REE-ZHAHNH duh

condottieri kahn-duh-TYAY-ree

Confucius kun-FYOO-shuss

conquistador kahn-KEESS-tuh-dor

consul KAHN-sull

Contarini, Gasparo kahn-tuh-REE-nee, GAHS-puh-roh

conversos kohn-VAYR-sohz

Copán koh-PAHN

Copernicus, Nicolaus kuh-PURR-nuh-kuss, NEE-koh-lowss

Córdoba KOR-duh-buh

Corinth KOR-inth

Corpus Hermeticum KOR-pus hur-MET-i-koom

Corpus Iuris Civilis KOR-pus YOOR-iss SIV-i-liss

corregidores kuhr-reg-uh-DOR-ayss

Cortés, Hernán kor-TAYSS or kor-TEZ, hayr-NAHN

Corvinus, Matthias kor-VY-nuss, muh-THY-uss

Courbet, Gustave koor-BAY, goo-STAHV

Crassus KRASS-uss

Crécy kray-SEE

Credit Anstalt KRAY-deet AHN-shtahlt

Crédit Mobilier kray-DEE moh-bee-LYAY

Croatia kroh-AY-shuh

Croesus KREE-suss

cum manu koom MAH-noo

Curie, Marie kyoo-REE

Cypselus SIP-suh-luss

Cyrenaica seer-uh-NAY-uh-kuh

Dadaism DAH-duh-iz-um

Daimler, Gottlieb DYM-lur, GUHT-leeb

daimyo DYM-yoh

Dai Viet dy VYET

d'Albret, Jeanne dahl-BRAY, ZHAHN

Dalí, Salvador dah-LEE, sahl-vah-DOR

Dandin DUN-din

Danton, Georges dahn-TONH, ZHORZH

Dao de Jing DOW-deh-JING

Darius duh-RY-uss

Darmstadt DARM-shtaht

dauphin DAW-fin

David, Jacques-Louis dah-VEED, ZHAHK-LWEE

de Gaulle, Charles duh GOHL, SHAHRL

De Rerum Novarum day RAY-rum noh-VAR-um

Debelleyme, Louis-Maurice duh-buh-LAYM, LWEE-moh-REESS

Debussy, Claude duh-byoo-SEE, KLOHD

décades day-KAD

Decameron dee-KAM-uh-run

decarchies DEK-ar-keez

decemviri duh-SEM-vuh-ree

Deffand, marquise du duh-FAHNH, mar-KEEZ doo

Dei-Anang DAY-ah-NAHNG

Deir el Bahri dayr-ahl-BAH-ree

Delacroix, Eugène duh-lah-KRWAH, oo-ZHEN

Démar, Claire DAY-mar

Demosthenes duh-MAHSS-thuh-neez

Deng Xiaoping DENG-show-PING

Denikin, Anton dyin-YEE-kin, ahn-TOHN

Desai, Anita dess-SY

descamisados dayss-kah-mee-SAH-dohss

Descartes, René day-KART, ruh-NAY

Dessau DESS-ow

d'Este, Isabella DESS-tay, ee-suh-BELL-uh

détente day-TAHNT

devshirme dev-SHEER-may

dharma DAR-muh

d'Holbach, Paul dohl-BAHK, POHL

dhoti DOH-tee

Diaghilev, Sergei DYAHG-yuh-lif, syir-GAY

Dias, Bartholomeu DEE-ush, bar-toh-loh-MAY-oo

Diaspora dy-ASS-pur-uh

Diderot, Denis dee-DROH, duh-NEE

Ding Ling DING LING

Diocletian dy-uh-KLEE-shun

Disraeli, Benjamin diz-RAY-lee

Djibouti juh-BOO-tee

Djoser ZHOH-sur

Dollfuss, Engelbert DAWL-fooss, ENG-ul-bayrt

Domesday Book DOOMZ-day book

Domitian doh-MISH-un

Donatello, Donato di doh-nuh-TELL-oh, doh-NAH-toh dee

Donatist DOH-nuh-tist

Donatus duh-NAY-tus

Dopolavoro duh-puh-LAH-vuh-roh

Dorians DOR-ee-unz

Doryphoros doh-RIF-uh-rohss

Dostoevsky, Fyodor dus-tuh-YEF-skee, FYUD-ur

Douhet, Giulio doo-AY, JOOL-yoh

Dreyfus, Alfred DRY-fuss

Du Bois, W. E. B. doo-BOISS

Dubček, Alexander DOOB-chek

Dufay, Guillaume doo-FAY, gee-YOHM

Duma DOO-muh

Duong Thu Huong ZHWAHNG too HWAHNG

Dupleix, Joseph-François doo-PLEKS

Dürer, Albrecht DOO-rur, AHL-brekht

Dzerzhinksy, Felix djur-ZHIN-skee

Ebert, Friedrich AY-bayrt, FREE-drikh

ecclesia ek-KLEE-zee-uh

Eckhart, Meister EK-hart, MY-stur

Einsatzgruppen YN-zahtz-groop-un

Einstein, Albert YN-styn

Ekaterinburg i-kat-tuh-RIN-burk

Emecheta, Buchi ay-muh-CHAY-tuh, BOO-chee

encomienda en-koh-MYEN-duh

Engels, Friedrich ENG-ulz, FREE-drikh

Enki EN-kee

Enlil EN-lil

Entente Cordiale ahn-TAHNT kor-DYAHL

entrepôt ahn-truh-POH

Epaminondas i-PAM-uh-NAHN-duss

Ephesus EFF-uh-suss

ephor EFF-ur

Epicureanism ep-i-kyoo-REE-uh-ni-zum

Epicurus ep-i-KYOOR-uss

episcopos i-PIS-kuh-puss

equestrians i-KWES-tree-unz

equites EK-wuh-teez

Erasistratus er-uh-SIS-truh-tuss

Erasmus, Desiderius i-RAZZ-mus, dez-i-DEER-ee-uss

Eratosthenes er-uh-TAHSS-thuh-neez

eremitical er-uh-MIT-i-kul

Erhard, Ludwig AYR-hart, LOOD-vik

Estonia ess-TOH-nee-uh

Etruscans i-TRUSS-kunz

Euclid YOO-klid

Euripides yoo-RIP-uh-deez

exchequer EKS-chek-ur

Execrabilis ek-suh-KRAB-uh-liss

Eylau Y-low

Falange fuh-LANJ

Fang Lizhu FAHNG lee-ZHOO

fasces FASS-eez

Fascio di Combattimento FASH-ee-oh dee com-bat-ee-MEN-toh

Fatimid FAT-i-mid

Fedele, Cassandra FAY-duh-lee

Feltre, Vittorino da FELL-tray, vee-tor-EE-noh dah

Ficino, Marsilio fee-CHEE-noh, mar-SIL-yoh

Fischer, Joschka FISH-ur, YUSH-kah

Flaubert, Gustave floh-BAYR, goo-STAHV

Fleury, Cardinal floo-REE

fluyt FLYT

Foch, Ferdinand FUSH, fayr-di-NAWNH

Fontainebleau FAWNH-ten-bloh

Fontenelle, Bernard de fawnt-NELL, bayr-NAHR duh

Fouquet, Nicolas foo-KAY, nee-koh-LAH

Fourier, Charles foo-RYAY, SHAHRL

Francesca, Piero della frahn-CHESS-kuh, PYAY-roh del-luh

Freud, Sigmund FROID, SIG-mund or ZIG-munt

Friedan, Betty free-DAN

Friedland FREET-lahnt

Friedrich, Caspar David FREED-rikh, kass-PAR dah-VEET

Froissart, Jean frwah-SAR, ZHAHNH

Fronde FROHND

Fu Xi foo SHEE

Fu Xuan foo SHWAHN

fueros FWYA-rohss

Führerprinzip FYOOR-ur-prin-TSEEP

Fujiwara foo-jee-WAH-rah

gabelle gah-BELL

Gaiseric GY-zuh-rik

Galba GAHL-buh

Galilei, Galileo GAL-li-lay, gal-li-LAY-oh

Gama, Vasco da GAHM-uh, VAHSH-koh dah

Gandhi, Mohandas (Mahatma) GAHN-dee, moh-HAHN-dus (mah-HAHT-muh)

Garibaldi, Giuseppe gar-uh-BAHL-dee, joo-ZEP-pay

Gasperi, Alcide de GAHSS-puh-ree, ahl-SEE-day day

Gatti de Gamond, Zoé gah-TEE duh gah-MOHNH, zoh-AY

Gaugamela gaw-guh-MEE-luh

Gelasius juh-LAY-shuss

Genghis Khan JING-uss or GENG-uss KAHN

genin gay-NIN

Gentileschi, Artemisia jen-tuh-LESS-kee, ar-tuh-MEE-zhuh

Geoffrin, Marie-Thérèse de zhoh-FRENH, ma-REE-tay-RAYZ duh

gerousia juh-ROO-see-uh

Gesamtkunstwerk guh-ZAHMT-koonst-vayrk

Gierek, Edward GYER-ek, ED-vahrt

Gilgamesh GILL-guh-mesh

Giolitti, Giovanni joh-LEE-tee, joe-VAHN-nee

Giotto JOH-toh

Girondins juh-RAHN-dinz

glasnost GLAHZ-nohst

Gleichschaltung glykh-SHAHL-toonk

Goebbels, Joseph GUR-bulz

Goethe, Johann Wolfgang von GUR-tuh, yoh-HAHN VULF-gahnk fun

Gokhale, Gopal GOH-ku-lay, goh-PAHL

Gömbös, Julius GUM-buhsh

Gomulka, Wladyslaw goh-MOOL-kuh, vlah-DIS-lahf

gonfaloniere gun-fah-loh-NYAY-ray

Gonzaga, Gian Francesco gun-DZAH-gah, JAHN frahn-CHES-koh

Gorbachev, Mikhail GOR-buh-chof, meek-HAYL

Göring, Hermann GUR-ing, hayr-MAHN

Gottwald, Clement GAWT-valt, klay-MENT

Gouges, Olympe GOOZH, oh-LAMP

Gracchus, Tiberius and Gaius GRAK-us, ty-BEER-ee-uss *and* GY-uss

grandi GRAHN-dee

Grieg, Edvard GREEG, ED-vart

Groote, Gerard GROH-tuh

Gropius, Walter GROH-pee-uss, VAHL-tuh

Grossdeutsch GROHS-doich

Groza, Petra GRO-zhuh, PET-ruh

Guan Yin gwahn-YIN

Guangdong gwahng-DUNG

Guangxu gwahng-SHOO

Guangzhou gwahng-JOH

Guaraní gwahr-uh-NEE

Guicciardini, Francesco gwee-char-DEE-nee, frahn-CHESS-koh

Guindorf, Reine GWIN-dorf, RY-nuh

Guise GEEZ

Guizot, François gee-ZOH, frahnh-SWAH

Gujarat goo-juh-RAHT

Guomindang gwoh-min-DAHNG

Gustavus Adolphus goo-STAY-vus uh-DAHL-fuss

Gutenberg, Johannes GOO-ten-bayrk, yoh-HAH-nuss

Guzman, Gaspar de goos-MAHN, gahs-PAR day

Habsburg HAPS-burg

Hadith huh-DEETH

Hadrian HAY-dree-un

Hagia Sophia HAG-ee-uh soh-FEE-uh

hajj HAJ

Hammurabi hahm-uh-RAH-bee

Han Gaozu HAHN gow-DZOO

Han Wudi HAHN woo-DEE

Handel, George Friedrich HAN-dul

Hankou HAHN-kow

Hannibal HAN-uh-bul

Hanukkah HAH-nuh-kuh

Harappa huh-RAP-uh

Hardenberg, Karl von HAR-den-bayrk, KARL fun

Harun al-Rashid huh-ROON ah-rah-SHEED

Hassan ben Sabbah khah-SAHN ben shah-BAH

Hatshepsut hat-SHEP-soot

Haushofer, Karl HOWSS-hoh-fuh

Haussmann, Baron HOWSS-mun

Havel, Vaclav HAH-vul, VAHT-slahf

Haydn, Franz Joseph HY-dun, FRAHNTS YO-zef

Hedayat, Sadeq hay-DY-yaht, sah-DEK

hegemon HEJ-uh-mun

Hegira hee-JY-ruh

Heian hay-AHN

Heisenberg, Werner HY-zun-bayrk, VAYR-nur

heliaea HEE-lee-ee

Hellenistic hel-uh-NIS-tik

helots HEL-uts

Heraclius he-ruh-KLY-uss or huh-RAK-lee-uss

Herculaneum hur-kyuh-LAY-nee-um

Herodotus huh-ROD-uh-tuss

Herophilus huh-ROF-uh-luss

Herzegovina HAYRT-suh-guh-VEE-nuh

Herzen, Alexander HAYRT-sun

Herzl, Theodor HAYRT-sul, TAY-oh-dor

Heshen HEH-shen

Hesiod HEE-see-ud

Hesse, Hermann HESS-uh, hayr-MAHN

hetairai huh-TY-ry

Heydrich, Reinhard HY-drikh, RYN-hart

Hideyoshi, Toyotomi hee-day-YOH-shee, toh-yoh-TOH-mee

hieroglyph HY-uh-roh-glif

Hildegard of Bingen HIL-duh-gard uv BING-un

Hindenburg, Paul von HIN-den-boork, POWL fun

Hiroshima hee-roh-SHEE-muh

Hisauchi, Michio hee-sah-OO-chee, mee-CHEE-OH

Hitler Jugend HIT-luh YOO-gunt

Ho Chi Minh HOH CHEE MIN

Höch, Hannah HURKH

Hohenstaufen hoh-en-SHTOW-fen

Hohenzollern hoh-en-TSULL-urn

Hohenzollern-Sigmaringen hoh-en-TSULL-urn-zig-mah-RING-un

Hokkaido hoh-KY-doh

Hokusai HOH-kuh-sy

Holtzendorf HOHLT-sen-dorf

Homo sapiens HOH-moh SAY-pee-unz

Honecker, Erich HOH-nek-uh, AY-reekh

Hong Xiuquan HOONG shee-oo-CHWAHN

Honorius hoh-NOR-ee-uss

hoplites HAHP-lyts

Horace HOR-uss

Horthy, Miklós HOR-tee, MIK-lohsh

Hosokawa, Mirohiro hoh-soh-KAH-wah, mee-roh-HEE-roh

Höss, Rudolf HURSS

Hoxha, Enver HAW-jah, EN-vayr

Huang Di hwahng-DEE

Huayna Inca WY-nuh INK-uh

Huê HWAY

Huguenots HYOO-guh-nots

Huitzilopochtli WEET-see-loh-POHCHT-lee

Humayun hoo-MY-yoon

Husák, Gustav HOO-sahk, goo-STAHV

Ibn Saud ib-un-sah-OOD

Ibn Sina ib-un SEE-nuh

iconoclasm y-KAHN-uh-claz-um

Ictinus ik-TY-nuss

Ife EE-fay

Ignatius of Loyola ig-NAY-shuss uv loi-OH-luh

Il Duce eel DOO-chay

Île-de-France EEL-duh-fronhss

illustrés ee-loo-STRAY

illustrissimi ee-loo-STREE-see-mee

imperator im-puh-RAH-tur

imperium im-PEER-ee-um

intendant anh-tahnh-DAHNH or in-TEN-dunt

Irigoyen, Hipólito ee-ree-GOH-yen, ee-POH-lee-toh

Isis Y-sis

Issus ISS-uss

Iturbide, Agustín de ee-tur-BEE-day, ah-goo-STEEN dat

Itzamna eet-SAHM-nuh

ius civile YOOSS see-VEE-lay

ius gentium YOOSS GEN-tee-um

ius naturale   YOOSS nah-too-RAH-lay

Izanagi   ee-zah-NAH-gee

Izanami   ee-zah-NAH-mee

Izvestia   iz-VESS-tee-uh

Jacobin   JAK-uh-bin

Jacquerie   zhak-REE

Jadwiga   yahd-VEE-guh

Jagiello   yahg-YEL-oh

Jahn, Friedrich Ludwig   YAHN, FREED-rikh LOOD-vik

jati   JAH-tee

Jaufré Rudel   zhoh-FRAY roo-DEL

Jaurès, Jean   zhaw-RESS, ZHAHNH

Jena   YAY-nuh

Jiang Qing   jahng-CHING

Jiang Zemin   JAHNG zuh-MIN

Jiangxi   JAHNG-shee

jihad   jee-HAHD

Jinnah, Muhammad Ali   JIN-uh, moh-HAM-ed ah-LEE

Joffre, Joseph   ZHUFF-ruh, zhoh-ZEFF

Journal des Savants   zhoor-NAHL day sah-VAHNH

Juana Inés de la Cruz, Sor   HWAH-nuh ee-NAYSS day lah KROOZ, SAWR

Judaea   joo-DEE-uh

Judas Maccabaeus   JOO-dus mak-uh-BEE-uss

Jung, Carl   YOONG

Junkers   YOONG-kurz

Jupiter Optimus Maximus   JOO-puh-tur AHP-tuh-muss MAK-suh-muss

Jurchen   roor-ZHEN

Justinian   juh-STIN-ee-un

Juvenal   JOO-vuh-nul

Ka'aba   KAH-buh

Kádár, János   KAH-dahr, YAH-nush

Kalidasa   kah-lee-DAH-suh

kamikaze   kah-mi-KAH-zee

Kanagawa   kah-nah-GAH-wah

Kanchipuram   kahn-CHEE-poo-rum

Kandinsky, Vasily   kan-DIN-skee, vus-YEEL-yee

Kang Youwei   KAHNG yow-WAY

Kangxi   GANG-zhee

Kanishka   kuh-NISH-kuh

Kant, Immanuel   KAHNT, i-MAHN-yoo-el

Karisma Kapoor   kuh-RIZ-muh kuh-POOR

Karlowitz   KARL-oh-vits

Karlsbad   KARLSS-baht

Kaunitz, Wenzel von   KOW-nits, VENT-sul fun

Kautilya   kow-TIL-yuh

Kazakhstan   ka-zak-STAN or kuh-zahk-STAHN

Kemal Atatürk, Mustafa   kuh-MAHL ah-tah-TIRK, moos-tah-FAH

Kenyatta, Jomo   ken-YAHT-uh, JOH-moh

Kerensky, Alexander   kuh-REN-skee

Keynes, John Maynard   KAYNZ

Khadija   kaha-DEE-jah

Khajuraho   khah-joo-RAH-hoh

Khanbaliq   khahn-bah-LEEK

Khomeini, Ayatollah Ruholla   khoh-MAY-nee, ah-yah-TUL-uh roo-HUL-uh

Khrushchev, Nikita   KHROOSH-chawf, nuh-KEE-tuh

Khubilai Khan   KOO-bluh KAHN

Kikuya   ki-KOO-yuh

Kilwa   KIL-wuh

Kim Dae Jung   kim day JOONG

Kim Il Sung   kim il SOONG

Kirghiz   keer-GEEZ

Kleindeutsch   KLYN-doich

Knesset   kuh-NESS-it

Koguryo   koh-GOOR-yoh

Kohl, Helmut   KOHL, HEL-moot

koiné   koi-NAY

Koizumi, Junichero   koh-ee-ZOO-mee, joo-nee-CHAY-roh

kokutai   koh-kuh-TY

Kolchak, Alexander   kul-CHAHK

Kollantai, Alexandra   kul-lun-TY

Kongxi   koong-SHEE

Königgrätz   kur-nig-GRETS

Kornilov, Lavr   kor-NYEE-luff, LAH-vur

Koryo   KAWR-yoh

Kosciuszko, Thaddeus   kaw-SHOOS-koh, tah-DAY-oosh

Kosovo   KAWSS-suh-voh

Kossuth, Louis   KAWSS-uth or KAW-shoot

Kostunica, Vojislav   kuh-STOO-nit-suh, VOH-yee-slav

Kosygin, Alexei   kuh-SEE-gun, uh-LEK-say

kouros   KOO-rohss

Koyaanisqatsi   koh-YAH-niss-kaht-see

Kraft durch Freude   KRAHFT doorkh FROI-duh

Kreditanstalt   kray-deet-AHN-shtalt

Krishna   KRISH-nuh

Kristallnacht   kri-STAHL-nahkht

Krupp, Alfred   KROOP

Kuchuk-Kainarji   koo-CHOOK-ky-NAR-jee

Kukulcan   koo-kul-KAHN

kulaks   KOO-lahks

Kulturkampf   kool-TOOR-kahmpf

Kun, Béla   KOON, BAY-luh

Kundera, Milan   koon-DAYR-uh, MEE-lahn

Kursk   KOORSK

Kushanas   koo-SHAH-nuz

Kwasniewski, Aleksander   kwahsh-NYEF-skee

Kyangyi   kyang-YEE

Kyoto   KYOH-toh

Kyushu   KYOO-shoo

la belle époque   lah BEL ay-PUK

Lafayette, marquis de   lah-fay-ET, mar-KEE duh

laissez-faire   less-ay-FAYR

Lamarck, Jean-Baptiste   lah-MARK, ZHAHNH-bah-TEEST

Lancaster   LAN-kas-tur

Lao Tzu   LOW-dzuh

La Rochefoucauld-Liancourt, duc de   lah-RUSH-foo-koh-lee-ahnh-KOOR, dook duh

Las Navas de Tolosa   lahss nah-vahss day toh-LOH-suh

latifundia   lat-i-FOON-dee-uh

Latium   LAY-shum

Latvia   LAT-vee-uh

Launay, marquis de   loh-NAY, mar-KEE duh

Laurier, Wilfred   LOR-ee-ay

Lavoisier, Antoine   lah-vwah-ZYAY, an-TWAHN

Lazar   lah-ZAR

Le Tellier, François Michel   luh tel-YAY, frahnh-SWAH mee-SHEL

Lebensraum   LAY-benz-rowm

Lee Kuan-yew   LEE-kwahn-YOO

Les Demoiselles d'Avignon   lay dem-wah-ZEL dah-vee-NYOHNH

Lespinasse, Julie de   less-pee-NAHSS, zhoo-LEE duh

Lévesque, René   lay-VEK, ruh-NAY

Leviathan   luh-VY-uh-thun

Leyster, Judith   LESS-tur

Liège   lee-EZH

Li Su   lee SOO

Li Yuan   lee YWAHN

Li Zicheng   lee zee-CHENG

Liaodong   LYOW-doong

Licinius   ly-SIN-ee-uss

Liebenfels, Lanz von   LEE-bun-felss, LAHNTS fun

Liebknecht, Karl   LEEP-knekht

Liebknecht, Wilhelm   LEEP-knekht, VIL-helm

Liliuokalani   LIL-ee-uh-woh-kuh-LAH-nee

Lin Zexu   LIN dzeh-SHOO

Lindisfarne   LIN-dis-farn

Lionne, Hugues de   LYUN, OOG duh

List, Friedrich   LIST, FREED-rikh

Liszt, Franz   LIST, FRAHNTS

Lithuania   lith-WAY-nee-uh

Liu Bang   lyoo BAHNG

Liu Ling   lyoo LING

Liu Shaoqi   lyoo show-CHEE

Livy   LIV-ee

Longshan   loong-SHAHN

L'Ouverture, Toussaint   loo-vayr-TOOR, too-SANH

Louvois   loo-VWAH

Lu Xun   loo SHUN

Lucretius   loo-KREE-shus

Luddites   LUD-yts

Ludendorff, Erich   LOO-dun-dorf

Lueger, Karl   LOO-gur

Luftwaffe   LOOFT-vahf-uh

l'uomo universale   LWOH-moh OO-nee-vayr-SAH-lay

Luoyang   LWOH-yahng

Lützen   LURT-sun

Luxemburg, Rosa   LOOK-sum-boork

Lyons LYOHNH

Maastricht MAHSS-trikht

Ma'at MAH-ut

Macao muh-KOW

Machiavelli, Niccolò mahk-ee-uh-VEL-ee, nee-koh-LOH

Maginot Line MA-zhi-noh lyn

Magna Graecia MAG-nuh GREE-shuh

Magyars MAG-yarz

Mahabharata muh-hahb-huh-RAH-tuh

maharaja mah-huh-RAH-juh

Mahavira mah-hah-VEE-ruh

Mahayana mah-huh-YAH-nuh

Mahfouz, Naguib mahkh-FOOZ, nah-GEEB

Mahmud of Ghazni MAHKH-mood uv GAHZ-nee

Maimonides my-MAH-nuh-deez

Maistre, Joseph de MESS-truh, zhoh-ZEF duh

maius imperium MY-yoos im-PEE-ree-um

Malaysia muh-LAY-zhuh

Malaya muh-LAY-uh

Malenkov, Georgy muh-LEN-kuf, gyee-OR-gyee

Mallarmé, Stéphane mah-lahr-MAY, stay-FAHN

Malleus Maleficarum mal-EE-uss mal-uh-FIK-uh-rum

Malthus, Thomas MAWL-thuss

Mamallapuram muh-MAH-luh-poor-um

Manchukuo man-CHOO-kwoh

Manetho MAN-uh-thoh

Mao Dun mow DOON

Mao Zedong mow zee-DOONG

Marconi, Guglielmo mahr-KOH-nee, gool-YEL-moh

Marcus Aurelius MAR-kuss aw-REE-lee-uss

Marcuse, Herbert mar-KOO-zuh

Marie Antoinette muh-REE an-twuh-NET

Marius MAR-ee-uss

Marquez, Gabriel Garcia mar-KEZ

Marseilles mar-SAY

Marsiglio of Padua mar-SIL-yoh uv PAD-juh-wuh

Masaccio muh-ZAH-choh

Masaryk, Thomas MAS-uh-rik

Mästlin, Michael MEST-lin

Matteotti, Giacomo mat-tay-AHT-tee, JAHK-uh-moh

Maxentius mak-SEN-shuss

Maximian mak-SIM-ee-un

Maya MY-uh

Mazarin maz-uh-RANH

Mazzini, Giuseppe maht-SEE-nee, joo-ZEP-pay

Megasthenes muh-GAS-thuh-neez

Mehmet meh-MET

Meiji MAY-jee

Mein Kampf myn KAHMPF

Meir, Golda may-EER

Melanchthon, Philip muh-LANK-tun

Menander muh-NAN-dur

Mencius MEN-shuss

Mendeleyev, Dmitri men-duh-LAY-ef, di-MEE-tree

Mensheviks MENS-shuh-viks

Mercator, Gerardus mur-KAY-tur, juh-RAHR-dus

Merian, Maria Sibylla MAY-ree-un

Merovingian meh-ruh-VIN-jee-un

Mesopotamia mess-uh-puh-TAY-mee-uh

Messiaen, Olivier meh-SYANH, oh-lee-VYAY

mestizos mess-TEE-zohz

Metaxas, John muh-tahk-SAHSS

Metternich, Klemens von MET-ayr-nikh, KLAY-menss fun

Mexica meh-SHEE-kuh

Michel, Louise mee-SHEL

Michelangelo my-kuh-LAN-juh-loh

Mieszko MYESH-koh

millet mi-LET

Millet, Jean-François mi-YEH, ZHAHNH-frahnh-SWAH

Milošević, Slobodan mi-LOH-suh-vich, sluh-BOH-dahn

Miltiades mil-TY-uh-deez

Minamoto Yoritomo mee-nah-MOH-toh, yoh-ree-TOH-moh

Minseito MEEN-say-toh

Mirandola, Pico della mee-RAN-doh-lah, PEE-koh DELL-uh

Mishima, Yukio mi-SHEE-muh, yoo-KEE-oh

missi dominici MISS-ee doh-MIN-i-chee

Mitterrand, François MEE-tayr-rahnh, frahnh-SWAH

Moche moh-CHAY

Moctezuma mahk-tuh-ZOO-muh

Mogadishu moh-guh-DEE-shoo

Mohács MOH-hach

Mohenjo-Daro mo-HEN-jo-DAH-roh

Moldavia mohl-DAY-vee-uh

Moldova mohl-DOH-vuh

Molière, Jean-Baptiste mohl-YAYR, ZHAHNH-bah-TEEST

Molotov, Vyacheslav MAHL-uh-tawf, vyich-chiss-SLAHF

Mombasa mahm-BAH-suh

Monet, Claude moh-NEH, KLOHD

Mongkut MAWNG-koot

Montaigne, Michel de mahn-TAYN, mee-SHEL duh

Montefeltro, Federigo da mahn-tuh-FELL-troh, fay-day-REE-goh dah

Montesquieu MOHN-tess-kyoo

Montessori, Maria mahn-tuh-SOR-ee

Morisot, Berthe mor-ee-ZOH, BAYRT

Mozambique moh-zam-BEEK

Mozart, Wolfgang Amadeus MOH-tsart, VULF-gahng ah-muh-DAY-uss

Muawiya moo-AH-wee-yah

Mudejares moo-theh-KHAH-rayss

Mughal MOO-gul

Muhammad moh-HAM-ud or moh-HAHM-ud

Mühlberg MURL-bayrk

Mukden MOOK-dun

mulattoes muh-LAH-tohz

Mumbai MUM-by

Müntzer, Thomas MURN-tsur

Murad moo-RAHD

Musharraf, Pervaiz moo-SHAHR-uf, pur-VEZ

Muslim MUZ-lum

Mutsuhito moo-tsoo-HEE-toh

Myanmar MYAN-mahr

Mycenaean my-suh-NEE-un

Nabonidas nab-uh-NY-duss

Nabopolassar nab-uh-puh-LASS-ur

Nagasaki nah-gah-SAH-kee

Nagy, Imry NAHJ, IM-ray

Nanjing nan-JING

Nantes NAHNT

Nara NAH-rah

Nasrin, Taslima naz-REEN, tah-SLEE-muh

Nasser, Gamal Abdul NAH-sur, juh-MAHL ahb-DOOL

Navarre nuh-VAHR

Nebuchadnezzar neb-uh-kud-NEZZ-ur

Nehru, Jawaharlal NAY-roo, juh-WAH-hur-lahl

Nero NEE-roh

Nerva NUR-vuh

Netanyahu, Benjamin net-ahn-YAH-hoo

Neumann, Balthasar NOI-mahn, BAHL-tuh-zahr

Neumann, Solomon NOI-mahn

Neustria NOO-stree-uh

Nevsky, Alexander NYEF-skee

Newcomen, Thomas NYOO-kuh-mun or nyoo-KUM-mun

Ngo Dinh Diem GOH din DYEM

Nguyen NGWEN

Nicias NISS-ee-uss

Nietzsche, Friedrich NEE-chuh, FREED-rikh

Nimwegen NIM-vay-gun

Ninhursaga nin-HUR-sah-guh

Nkrumah, Kwame en-KROO-muh, KWAH-may

nobiles no-BEE-layz

Nobunaga, Oda noh-buh-NAH-guh, OH-dah

Nogarola, Isotta noh-guh-ROH-luh, ee-ZAHT-uh

Novalis, Friedrich noh-VAH-lis, FREED-rikh

Novotny, Antonin noh-VAHT-nee, AHN-toh-nyeen

novus homo NOH-vuss HOH-moh

nuoc mam NWAHK MAHM

Nyame NYAH-may

Nystadt NEE-shtaht

Oaxaca wah-HAH-kuh

Octavian ahk-TAY-vee-un

Odoacer oh-doh-AY-sur

Odysseus oh-DISS-ee-uss

Oe, Kenzaburo   OH-ay, ken-zuh-BOO-roh

Olivares   oh-lee-BAH-rayss

Olmec   AHL-mek or OHL-mek

Omar Khayyam   OH-mar ky-YAHM

Ometeotl   oh-met-tee-AH-tul

optimates   ahp-tuh-MAH-tayz

Oresteia   uh-res-TY-uh

Orkhan   or-KHAHN

Osaka   oh-SAH-kuh

Osama bin Laden   oh-SAH-muh bin LAH-dun

Osiris   oh-SY-russ

Ostara   oh-STAH-ruh

Ostpolitik   OHST-poh-lee-teek

ostrakon   AHSS-truh-kahn

Ostrogoths   AHSS-truh-gahthss

Ovid   OH-vid

Oxenstierna, Axel   OOK-sen-shur-nah, AHK-sul

Pacal   pa-KAL

Pachakuti   pah-chah-KOO-tee

Paekche   bayk-JEE

Pagan   puh-GAHN

Paleologus   pay-lee-AWL-uh-guss

Panaetius   puh-NEE-shuss

Pankhurst, Emmeline   PANK-hurst

papal curia   PAY-pul KYOOR-ee-uh

Papen, Franz von   PAH-pun, FRAHNTS fun

Paracelsus   par-uh-SELL-suss

Parlement   par-luh-MAHNH

Parti Québécois   par-TEE kay-bek-KWAH

Pascal, Blaise   pass-KAHL, BLEZ

Pasternak, Boris   PASS-tur-nak, buh-REESS

Pasteur, Louis   pass-TOOR, LWEE

Pataliputra   pah-tah-lee-POO-truh

paterfamilias   pay-tur-fuh-MEEL-yus

Pensées   pahnh-SAY

Pentateuch   PEN-tuh-took

Pepin   PEP-in or pay-PANH

perestroika   per-uh-STROI-kuh

Pergamum   PUR-guh-mum

Pericles   PER-i-kleez

perioeci   per-ee-EE-see

Perpetua   pur-PET-choo-uh

Pétain, Henri   pay-TANH, AHN-ree

Petite Roquette   puh-TEET raw-KET

Petrarch   PEE-trark or PET-trark

Petronius   pi-TROH-nee-uss

phalansteries   fuh-LAN-stuh-reez

philosophe   fee-loh-ZAWF

Phintys   FIN-tiss

Phoenicians   fuh-NEE-shunz

Photius   FOH-shuss

Picasso, Pablo   pi-KAH-soh

Pietism   PY-uh-tiz-um

Pilsudski, Joseph   peel-SOOT-skee

Piscator, Erwin   PIS-kuh-tor, AYR-vin

Pisistratus   puh-SIS-truh-tuss

Pissarro, Camille   pee-SAH-roh, kah-MEEL

Pizan, Christine de   pee-ZAHN, kris-TEEN duh

Pizarro, Francesco   puh-ZAHR-oh, frahn-CHESS-koh

Planck, Max   PLAHNK

Plantagenet   plan-TAJ-uh-net

Plassey   PLASS-ee

Plato   PLAY-toh

Plautus   PLAW-tuss

plebiscita   pleb-i-SEE-tuh

Poincaré, Raymond   pwanh-kah-RAY, ray-MOHNH

polis   POH-liss

politiques   puh-lee-TEEKS

Pollaiuolo, Antonio   pohl-ly-WOH-loh

Poltava   pul-TAH-vuh

Polybius   puh-LIB-ee-uss

Pombal, marquis de   pum-BAHL, mar-KEE duh

Pompadour, madame de   POM-puh-door, mah-DAHM duh

Pompeii   pahm-PAY

Pompey   PAHM-pee

pontifex maximus   PAHN-ti-feks MAK-si-muss

Popul Vuh   puh-PUL VOO

populares   PAWP-oo-lahr-ayss

populo grasso   PAWP-oo-loh GRAH-soh

Postumus   PAHS-choo-muss

Potosí   poh-toh-SEE

Potsdam   PAHTS-dam

Poussin, Nicholas   poo-SANH, NEE-koh-lah

Praecepter Germaniae   PREE-sep-tur gayr-MAHN-ee-ee

praetor   PREE-tur

Prakrit   PRAH-krit

Pravda   PRAHV-duh

Primo de Rivera   PREE-moh day ri-VAY-ruh

primogeniture   pree-moh-JEN-i-chur

princeps   PRIN-seps

Principia   prin-SIP-ee-uh

Procopius   pruh-KOH-pee-uss

procurator   PROK-yuh-ray-tur

Ptolemaic   tahl-uh-MAY-ik

Ptolemy   TAHL-uh-mee

Pugachev, Emelyan   poo-guh-CHAWF, yim-yil-YAHN

Punic   PYOO-nik

Putin, Vladimir   POO-tin

Pyongyang   pyawng-YANG

Pyrrhic   PEER-ik

Pyrrhus   PEER-uss

Pythagoras   puh-THAG-uh-russ

Qajar   kuh-JAHR

Qianlong   CHAN-loong

Qin   CHIN

Qin Shi Huangdi   chin shee hwang-DEE

Qing   CHING

Qiu Jin   chee-oo-JIN

Qu   CHOO

quadrivium   kwah-DRIV-ee-um

quaestors   KWES-turs

querelle des femmes   keh-REL day FAHM

Quesnay, François   keh-NAY, frahnn-SWAH

Quetzalcoatl   KWET-sul-koh-AHT-ul

Quraishi   koo-RY-shee

Qur'an   kuh-RAN or kuh-RAHN

Rabe'a of Qozdar   rah-BAY-uh uv kuz-DAHR

Racine, Jean-Baptiste   ra-SEEN, ZHAHNH-buh-TEEST

Rahner, Karl   RAH-nur

Rajput   RAHJ-poot

Rama   RAH-mah

Ramayana   rah-mah-YAH-nah

Ramcaritmanas   RAM-kah-rit-MAH-nuz

Rameses   RAM-uh-seez

Raphael   RAFF-ee-ul

Rasputin   rass-PYOO-tin

Rathenau, Walter   RAH-tuh-now, VAHL-tuh

Realpolitik   ray-AHL-poh-lee-teek

Realschule   ray-AHL-shoo-luh

Reichsrat   RYKHSS-raht

Reichstag   RYKHSS-tahk

Rembrandt van Rijn   REM-brant vahn RYN

Rémy, Nicholas   ray-MEE, nee-koh-LAH

Renan, Ernst   re-NAHNH

Rhee, Syngman   REE, SING-mun

Ricci, Matteo   REE-chee, ma-TAY-oh

Richelieu   REESH-uh-lyuh

Ricimer   RISS-uh-mur

Rig Veda   RIK-vee-duh

Rikstag   RIKS-tahk

Rilke, Rainer Maria   RILL-kuh, RY-nuh mah-REE-uh

Rimbaud, Arthur   ram-BOH, ar-TOOR

risorgimento   ree-SOR-jee-men-toh

Riza-i-Abassi   ree-ZAH-yah-BAH-see

Robespierre, Maximilien   ROHBZ-pyayr, mak-see-meel-YENH

Rococo   ruh-KOH-koh

Rocroi   roh-KRWAH

Röhm, Ernst   RURM

Rommel, Erwin   RAHM-ul

Romulus Augustulus   RAHM-yuh-luss ow-GOOS-chuh-luss

Rossbach   RAWSS-bahkh

Rousseau, Jean-Jacques   roo-SOH, ZHAHNH-ZHAHK

Rurik   ROO-rik

Ryswick   RYZ-wik

Sacrosancta   sak-roh-SANK-tuh

Saikaku   sy-KAH-koo

Saint-Just   sanh-ZHOOST

Saint-Simon, Henri de   sanh-see-MOHNH, ahnh-REE duh

Sakharov, Andrei   SAH-kuh-rawf, ahn-DRAY

Saladin   SAL-uh-din

Salazar, Antonio   SAL-uh-zahr

Sallust   SAL-ust

Samnite   SAM-nyt
Samudragupta   suh-mood-ruh-GOOP-tuh
samurai   SAM-uh-ry
San Martín, José de   san mar-TEEN, hoh-SAY day
Sandinista   san-duh-NEES-tuh
sans-culottes   sahnh-koo-LUT or sanz-koo-LAHTSS
Sarraut, Albert   sah-ROH, ahl-BAYR
Sartre, Jean-Paul   SAR-truh, ZHAHNH-POHL
Sassanid   suh-SAN-id
sati   suh-TEE
satrap   SAY-trap
satrapy   SAY-truh-pee
Satyricon   sa-TEER-uh-kahn
Schaumburg-Lippe   SHOWM-boorkh-LEE-puh
Schleswig-Holstein   SHLESS-vik-HOHL-shtyn
Schlieffen, Alfred von   SHLEE-fun, AHL-fret fun
Schliemann, Heinrich   SHLEE-mahn, HYN-rikh
Schmidt, Helmut   SHMIT, HEL-moot
Schönberg, Arnold   SHURN-bayrk, AR-nawlt
Schönborn   SHURN-bawn
Schönerer, Georg von   SHURN-uh-ruh, GAY-ork fun
Schröder, Gerhard   SHRUR-duh, GAYR-hahrt
Schuschnigg, Karl von   SHOOSH-nik, KAHRL fun
Schutzmannschaft   SHOOTS-mahn-shahft
Scipio Aemilianus   SEE-pee-oh ee-mil-YAY-nuss
Scipio Africanus   SEE-pee-oh af-ree-KAY-nuss
scriptoria   skrip-TOR-ee-uh
Ségur   say-GOO-uh
Sejm   SAYM
Seleucid   suh-LOO-sid
Seleucus   suh-LOO-kuss
Seljuk   SEL-jook
Seneca   SEN-uh-kuh
Sephardic   suh-FAHR-dik
Septimius Severus   sep-TIM-ee-uss se-VEER-uss
serjents   sayr-ZHAHNH
Sforza, Ludovico   SFORT-sah, loo-doh-VEE-koh
Shakuntala   shah-koon-TAH-lah
Shalmaneser   shal-muh-NEE-zur
Shandong   SHAHN-doong
Shang   SHAHNG
Shari'a   shah-REE-uh
Shen Nong   shun-NOONG
Shi'ite   SHEE-YT
Shidehara   shee-de-HAH-rah
Shiga Naoya   SHEE-gah NOW-yah
Shikoku   shee-KOH-koo
Shimonoseki   shee-moh-noh-SEK-ee
Shiva   SHIV-uh
Shotoku Taishi   shoh-TOH-koo ty-EE-shee
Sichuan   SEECH-wahn
Siddhartha Gautama   si-DAR-tuh GAW-tuh-muh

Sieveking, Amalie   SEE-vuh-king, uh-MAHL-yuh
Sieyès, Abbé   syay-YESS, ab-BAY
Sigiriya   see-gee-REE-uh
signoria   seen-YOR-ee-uh
Silla   SIL-uh
Silva, Luis Inácio Lula de   LWEES ee-NAH-syoh LOO-luh duh-SEEL-vuh
Sima Qian   SEE-mah chee-AHN
sine manu   sy-nee-MAY-noo
sipahis   suh-PAH-heez
Sita   SEE-tuh
Slovenia   sloh-VEE-nee-uh
Société Générale   soh-see-ay-TAY zhay-nay-RAHL
Socrates   SAHK-ruh-teez
Solon   SOH-lun
Solzhenitsyn, Alexander   sohl-zhuh-NEET-sin
Somme   SUM
Song Taizu   SOONG ty-DZOO
Soong, Mei-ling   SOONG, may-LING
Sophocles   SAHF-uh-kleez
Sorel, Georges   soh-RELL, ZHORZH
Spartacus   SPAR-tuh-kuss
Spartiates   spar-tee-AH-teez
Speer, Albert   SHPAYR
Speransky, Michael   spyuh-RAHN-skee
Spinoza, Benedict de   spi-NOH-zuh
squadristi   skwah-DREES-tee
Srebrenica   sreb-bruh-NEET-suh
stadholder   STAD-hohl-dur
Staël, Germaine de   STAHL, zhayr-MEN duh
Stakhanov, Alexei   stuh-KHAH-nuf, uh-LEK-say
Stasi   SHTAH-see
Stauffenberg, Claus von   SHTOW-fen-berk, KLOWSS fun
Stein, Heinrich von   SHTYN, HYN-rikh fun
Stilicho   STIL-i-koh
Stoicism   STOH-i-siz-um
Stolypin, Peter   stuh-LIP-yin
strategoi   strah-tay-GOH-ee
Stravinsky, Igor   struh-VIN-skee, EE-gor
Stresemann, Gustav   SHTRAY-zuh-mahn, GOOS-tahf
Strozzi, Alessandra   STRAWT-see
Struensee, John Frederick   SHTROO-un-zay
Sturmabteilung   SHTOORM-ap-ty-loonk
Sudetenland   soo-DAY-tun-land
sudra   SOO-druh or SHOO-druh
Suger   soo-ZHAYR
Suharto   soo-HAHR-toh
Sui Wendi   SWEE wen-DEE
Sui Yangdi   SWEE yahng-DEE
Sukarno   soo-KAHR-noh
Sukarnoputri, Megawati   soo-kahr-noh-POO-tree, meg-uh-WAH-tee
Suleiman   SOO-lay-mahn
Suleymaniye   soo-lay-MAHN-ee-eh

Sulla   SUL-uh
Sumerians   soo-MER-ee-unz or soo-MEER-ee-unz
Summa Theologica   SOO-muh tay-oh-LAH-jee-kuh
Sun Yat-sen   SOON yaht-SEN
Suppiluliumas   suh-PIL-oo-LEE-uh-muss
Suttner, Bertha von   ZOOT-nuh, BAYR-tuh fun
Swaziland   SWAH-zee-land
Symphonie Fantastique   SANH-foh-nee fahn-tas-TEEK
Taaffe, Edward von   TAH-fuh, ED-vahrt fun
Taban lo Liyong   tuh-BAN loh-lee-YAWNG
Tacitus   TASS-i-tuss
Tahuantinsuyu   tuh-HWAHN-tin-SOO-yoo
Taika   TY-kuh
taille   TY
Taiping   ty-PING
Talleyrand, Prince   tah-lay-RAHNH
Tanganyika   tang-an-YEE-kuh
Tanizaki, Junichiro   tan-i-ZAH-kee, jun-i-CHEE-roh
Tanzania   tan-zuh-NEE-uh
Temuchin   TEM-yuh-jin
Tenochtitlán   tay-nawch-teet-LAHN
Teotihuacán   tay-noh-tee-hwa-KAHN
Tertullian   tur-TUL-yun
Texcoco   tess-KOH-koh
Thales   THAY-leez
Theocritus   thee-AHK-ruh-tuss
Theodora   thee-uh-DOR-uh
Theodoric   thee-AHD-uh-rik
Theodosius   thee-uh-DOH-shuss
Theognis   thee-AHG-nuss
Theravada   thay-ruh-VAH-duh
Thermopylae   thur-MAHP-uh-lee
Thiers, Adolphe   TYAYR, a-DAWLF
Thucydides   thoo-SID-uh-deez
Thutmosis   thoot-MOH-suss
Tiananmen   TYAHN-ahn-men
Tianjin   TYAHN-jin
Tiberius   ty-BEER-ee-uss
Tiglath-pileser   TIG-lath-py-LEE-zur
Tikal   tee-KAHL
Tirpitz, Admiral von   TEER-pits
Tisza, István   TISS-ah, ISHT-vun
Tito   TEE-toh
Titus   TY-tuss
Tlaloc   tuh-lah-LOHK
Tlaltelolco   tuh-lahl-teh-LOH-koh
Tlaxcala   tuh-lah-SKAH-lah
Toer, Pramoedya   TOOR, pra-MOO-dyah
Tojo, Hideki   TOH-joh, hee-DEK-ee
Tokugawa Ieyasu   toh-koo-GAH-wah ee-yeh-YAH-soo
Tolstoy, Leo   TOHL-stoy
Tongmenghui   toong-meng-HWEE
Topa Inca   TOH-puh INK-uh

Topkapi   tawp-KAH-pee
Torah   TOR-uh
Tordesillas   tor-day-SEE-yass
Touré, Sékou   too-RAY, say-KOO
Trajan   TRAY-jun
Trevithick, Richard   TREV-uh-thik
Tristan, Flora   TRISS-tun
trivium   TRIV-ee-um
Trotsky, Leon   TRAHT-skee
Troyes   TRWAH
Trudeau, Pierre   troo-DOH, PYAYR
Trufaut, François   troo-FOH, frahnh-SWAH
Tsara, Tristan   TSAHR-rah, TRISS-tun
Tübingen   TUR-bing-un
Tughluq   tug-LUK
Tulsidas   tool-see-DAHSS
Tutankhamun   too-tang-KAH-mun
Tyche   TY-kee
Uccello, Paolo   oo-CHEL-oh, POW-loh
uhuru   oo-HOO-roo
uji   OO-jee
Ulbricht, Walter   OOL-brikht, VAHL-tuh
Ulianov, Vladimir   ool-YA-nuf
Umayyads   oo-MY-adz
Unam Sanctam   OO-nahm **SAHNK-tahm**
universitas   yoo-nee-VAYR-see-tahss
Utamaro   OO-tah-mah-roh
Uzbekistan   ooz-BEK-i-stan
vaisya   VISH-yuh
Vajpayee, Atal Behari   VAHJ-py-ee, AH-tahl
   bi-HAH-ree
Valens   VAY-linz
Valentinian   val-en-TIN-ee-un
Valéry, Paul   vah-lay-REE, POHL
Valois   val-WAH
Van de Velde, Theodore   vahn duh VEL-duh,
   TAY-oh-dor
van Eyck, Jan   vahn YK or van AYK, YAHN
van Gogh, Vincent   van GOH
Vasa, Gustavus   VAH-suh, GUSS-tuh-vuss
Vega, Lope de   VAY-guh, LOH-pay day
Velde, Theodor van de   VEL-duh, tay-oh-DOR
   vahn duh
Vendée   vahnh-DAY
Venetia   vuh-NEE-shuh
Verdun   vur-DUN
Vergerio, Pietro Paolo   vur-JEER-ee-oh, PYAY-
   troh POW-loh

Versailles   vayr-SY
Vesalius, Andreas   vuh-SAY-lee-uss, ahn-
   DRAY-uss
Vespasian   vess-PAY-zhun
Vespucci, Amerigo   vess-POO-chee, ahm-ay-
   REE-goh
Vesuvius   vuh-SOO-vee-uss
Vichy   VISH-ee
Vierzehnheiligen   feer-tsayn-HY-li-gen
Virchow, Rudolf   FEER-khoh, ROO-dulf
Virgil   VUR-jul
Visconti, Giangaleazzo   vees-KOHN-tee,
   jahn-gah-lay-AH-tsoh
Vishnu   VISH-noo
Visigoths   VIZ-uh-gathz
Voilquin, Suzanne   vwahl-KANH,
   soo-ZAHN
Volk   FULK
Volkschulen   FULK-shoo-lun
Voltaire   vohl-TAYR
Wafd   WAHFT
Wagner, Richard   VAG-nur, RIKH-art
Walesa, Lech   vah-WENT-sah, LEK
Wallachia   wah-LAY-kee-uh
Wallenstein, Albrecht von   VAHL-en-shtyn,
   AWL-brekht
Wang Anshi   WAHNG ahn-SHEE
Wang Shuo   wahng-SHWOH
Wang Tao   wahng-TOW
Wannsee   VAHN-zay
Watteau, Antoine   wah-TOH, AHN-twahn
Weill, Kurt   VYL
Weizsäcker, Richard von   VYTS-zek-ur,
   RIKH-art
wergeld   WUR-geld
Windischgrätz, Alfred   VIN-dish-grets
Winkelmann, Maria   VINK-ul-mahn
Witte, Sergei   VIT-uh, syir-GYAY
Wittenberg   VIT-ten-bayrk
Wojtyla, Karol   voy-TEE-wah, KAH-rul
Wollstonecraft, Mary   WULL-stun-kraft
Wu Zhao   woo-ZHOW
Würzburg   VURTS-boork
Wyclif, John   WIK-lif
Xavier, Francis   ZAY-vee-ur
Xerxes   ZURK-seez
Xhosa   KHOH-suh
Xia   SHEE-ah

Xian   SHEE-ahn
Xiangyang   SHYAHNG-yahng
Ximenes   khee-MAY-ness
Xinjiang   SHIN-jyahng
Xiongnu   SHYAHNG-noo
Xui Tong   shwee-TOONG
Yahweh   YAH-way
Yan'an   yuh-NAHN
Yang Guifei   yahng gwee-FAY
Yangshao   yahng-SHOW
Yangtze   YANG-tsee
Yayoi   yah-YO-ee
Yeats, William Butler   YAYTS
Yeltsin, Boris   YELT-sun
Yi Jing   yee-JING
Yi Song-gye   YEE song-YEE
yishuv   YISH-uv
Yuan Shikai   yoo-AHN shee-KY
Yudhoyono, Susilo   yood-hoh-YOH-noh,
   soo-SEE-loh
Yue   yoo-EH
zaibatsu   zy-BAHT-soo *or Japanese*
   DZY-bahtss
Zanj   ZANJ
Zanzibar   ZAN-zi-bar
Zasulich, Vera   tsah-SOO-likh
Zemsky Sobor   ZEM-skee suh-BOR
zemstvos   ZEMPST-vohz
Zeno   ZEE-noh
Zenobia   zuh-NOH-bee-uh
zeppelin   ZEP-puh-lin
Zeus   ZOOSS
Zhang Zhidong   JANG jee-DOONG
Zhao Ziyang   JOW dzee-YAHNG
Zhenotdel   zhen-ut-DEL
Zhivkov, Todor   ZHIV-kuff, toh-DOR
Zia ul-Haq, Mohammad   ZEE-uh ool-HAHK
ziggurat   ZIG-uh-rat
Zimmermann, Dominikus   TSIM-ur-mahn,
   doh-MEE-nee-kooss
Zinzendorf, Nikolaus von   TSIN-sin-dorf, NEE-
   koh-LOWSS fun
Zola, Émile   ZOH-lah, ay-MEEL
zollverein   TSOHL-fuh-ryn
Zoroaster   ZOR-oh-ass-tur
Zuanzong   zwahn-ZOONG
Zuni   ZOO-nee
Zwingli, Ulrich   TSFING-lee, OOL-rikh

DOCUMENTS

Continued from page xii

MAP CREDITS

The authors wish to acknowledge their use of the following books as references in preparing the maps listed here:

MAP 14.1 Geoffrey Barraclough, ed., *Times Atlas of World History* (Maplewood, N.J.: Hammond Inc., 1978), p. 160.

MAP 16.3 Geoffrey Barraclough, ed., *Times Atlas of World History* (Maplewood, N.J.: Hammond, Inc., 1978), p. 173.

MAP 17.1 Jonathan Spence, *The Search for Modern China* (New York: W. W. Norton, 1990), p. 19.

MAP 17.2 Conrad Schirokauer, A *Brief History of Chinese and Japanese Civilizations,* 2nd ed. (San Diego: Harcourt Brace Jovanovich, 1989), p. 330.

MAP 17.3 John K. Fairbank, Edwin O. Reischauer, and Albert M. Craig, *East Asia: Tradition and Transformation* (Boston: Houghton Mifflin, 1973), pp. 402–403.

MAP 21.1 Geoffrey Barraclough, ed., *Times Atlas of World History* (Maplewood, N.J.: Hammond, Inc., 1978), p. 235.

MAP 22.2 John K. Fairbank, Edwin O. Reischauer, and Albert M. Craig, *East Asia: Tradition and Transformation* (Boston: Houghton Mifflin, 1973), p. 451.

MAP 22.4 Geoffrey Barraclough, ed., *Times Atlas of World History* (Maplewood, N.J.: Hammond, Inc., 1978), p. 243.

CHAPTER NOTES

CHAPTER 14

1. From *A Journal of the First Voyage of Vasco da Gama* (London, 1898), cited in J. H. Parry, *The European Reconnaissance: Selected Documents* (New York, 1968), p. 82.
2. H. J. Benda and J. A. Larkin, eds., *The World of Southeast Asia: Selected Historical Readings* (New York, 1967), p. 13.
3. Parry, *European Reconnaissance,* quoting from A. Cortesão, *The Summa Oriental of Tomé Pires,* vol. 2 (London, 1944), pp. 283, 287.
4. Quoted in J. H. Parry, *The Age of Reconnaissance: Discovery, Exploration, and Settlement, 1450 to 1650* (New York, 1963), p. 33.
5. Quoted in R. B. Reed, "The Expansion of Europe," in R. DeMolen, ed., *The Meaning of the Renaissance and Reformation* (Boston, 1974), p. 308.
6. K. N. Chaudhuri, *Trade and Civilization in the Indian Ocean: An Economic History from the Rise of Islam to 1750* (Cambridge, 1985), p. 65.
7. Quoted in M. Leon-Portilla, ed., *The Broken Spears: The Aztec Account of the Conquest of Mexico* (Boston, 1969), p. 51.
8. Quoted in Parry, *Age of Reconnaissance,* pp. 176–177.
9. Quoted in B. Davidson, *Africa in History: Themes and Outlines* (London, 1968), p. 137.

CHAPTER 15

1. N. Machiavelli, *The Prince,* trans. D. Wootton (Indianapolis, Ind., 1995), p. 48.
2. Quoted in R. Bainton, *Here I Stand: A Life of Martin Luther* (New York, 1950), p. 144.
3. J. Calvin, *Institutes of the Christian Religion,* trans. J. Allen (Philadelphia, 1936), vol. 1, p. 228; vol. 2, p. 181.
4. Quoted in B. S. Anderson and J. P. Zinsser, *A History of Their Own: Women in Europe from Prehistory to the Present,* vol. 1 (New York, 1988), p. 259.
5. Quoted in J. O'Malley, *The First Jesuits* (Cambridge, Mass., 1993), p. 76.
6. Quoted in J. Klaits, *Servants of Satan: The Age of Witch Hunts* (Bloomington, Ind., 1985), p. 68.

CHAPTER 16

1. Vincent A. Smith, *The Oxford History of India* (Oxford, 1967), p. 341.
2. Quoted in Michael Edwardes, *A History of India: From the Earliest Times to the Present Day* (London, 1961), p. 188.
3. Quoted in Edwardes, *History of India,* p. 220.
4. Quoted in Roy C. Craven, *Indian Art: A Concise History* (New York, 1976), p. 205.

CHAPTER 17

1. From Jonathan D. Spence, *Emperor of China: Self-Portrait of K'ang Hsi* (New York, 1974), pp. 143–144.
2. Richard Strassberg, *The World of K'ang Shang-jen: A Man of Letters in Early Ch'ing China* (New York, 1983), p. 275.
3. Lynn Struve, *The Southern Ming, 1644–1662* (New Haven, Conn., 1984), p. 61.
4. J. L. Cranmer-Byng, *An Embassy to China: Lord Macartney's Journal, 1793–1794* (London, 1912), p. 340.

5. Daniel J. Boorstin, *The Discoverers: A History of Man's Search to Know His World and Himself* (New York, 1983), p. 63.
6. C. R. Boxer, ed., *South China in the Sixteenth Century* (London, 1953), p. 265.
7. Chie Nakane and Sinzaburo Oishi, eds., *Tokugawa Japan* (Tokyo, 1990), p. 14.
8. Quoted in Jurgis Elisonas, "Christianity and the Daimyo," in John Whitney Hall, ed., *The Cambridge History of Japan,* vol. 4 (Cambridge, 1991), p. 360.
9. Engelbert Kaempfer, *The History of Japan: Together with a Description of the Kingdom of Siam, 1690–1692,* vol. 2 (Glasgow, 1906), pp. 173–174.
10. Quoted in Ryusaku Tsunda et al., *Sources of Japanese Tradition* (New York, 1964), p. 313.

CHAPTER 18

1. J. Locke, *An Essay Concerning Human Understanding* (New York, 1964), pp. 89–90.
2. Quoted in P. Burke, *Popular Culture in Early Modern Europe,* rev. ed. (New York, 1994), p. 186.
3. Quoted in W. Doyle, *The Oxford History of the French Revolution* (Oxford, 1989), p. 184.
4. Quoted in L. Gershoy, *The Era of the French Revolution* (Princeton, N.J., 1957), p. 157.
5. Quoted in Doyle, *The Oxford History of the French Revolution,* p. 254.

CHAPTER 19

1. Quoted in E. Royston Pike, *Human Documents of the Industrial Revolution in Britain* (London, 1966), p. 343.
2. Ibid., p. 315.
3. Karl Marx and Friedrich Engels, *The Communist Manifesto* (Harmondsworth, England, 1967), p. 80. Originally published in 1848.
4. Ibid., pp. 91, 94.
5. Quoted in Louis L. Snyder, ed., *Documents of German History* (New Brunswick, N.J., 1958), p. 202.
6. Quoted in Shmuel Galai, *The Liberation Movement in Russia, 1900–1905* (Cambridge, 1973), p. 26.

CHAPTER 20

1. Quoted in J. C. Chasteen, *Americanos: Latin America's Struggle for Independence* (Oxford, 2008), p. 122.
2. Quoted in P. Bakewell, *A History of Latin America* (Oxford, 1997), p. 367.
3. Quoted in M. C. Eakin, *The History of Latin America: Collision of Cultures* (New York, 2007), p. 188.
4. Quoted in E. B. Burns, *Latin America: A Concise Interpretive History,* 4th ed. (Englewood Cliffs, N.J., 1986), p. 116.
5. Quoted in N. Bullock and J. Read, *The Movement for Housing Reform in Germany and France, 1840–1914* (Cambridge, 1985), p. 42.
6. W. Wordsworth, "The Tables Turned," *Poems of Wordsworth,* ed. M. Arnold (London, 1963), p. 138.
7. Quoted in A. E. E. McKenzie, *The Major Achievements of Science,* vol. 1 (New York, 1960), p. 310.

8. Quoted in A. Higonnet, *Berthe Morisot's Images of Women* (Cambridge, Mass., 1992), p. 19.

CHAPTER 21

1. Quoted in J. G. Lockhart and C. M. Wodehouse, *Rhodes* (London, 1963), pp. 69–70.
2. K. Pearson, *National Life from the Standpoint of Science* (London, 1905), p. 184.
3. Quoted in H. Braunschwig, *French Colonialism, 1871–1914* (London, 1961), p. 80.
4. Quoted in G. Garros, *Forceries Humaines* (Paris, 1926), p. 21.
5. Cited in B. Schwartz's review of D. Cannadine's *Ornamentalism: How the British Saw Their Empire, Atlantic,* November 2001, p. 135.
6. Quoted in R. Bartlett, ed., *The Record of American Diplomacy: Documents and Readings in the History of American Foreign Relations* (New York, 1952), p. 385.
7. Quoted in L. Roubaud, *Vietnam: La Tragédie Indochinoise* (Paris, 1926), p. 80.
8. Quoted in T. Pakenham, *The Scramble for Africa* (New York, 1991), p. 13.
9. Quoted in Pakenham, *Scramble for Africa,* p. 182, citing a letter to Queen Victoria dated August 7, 1879.
10. Quoted in P. C. W. Gutkind and I. Wallerstein, eds., *The Political Economy of Contemporary Africa* (Beverly Hills, Calif., 1976), p. 14.

CHAPTER 22

1. Hosea Ballou Morse, *The International Relations of the Chinese Empire,* vol. 2 (London, 1910–1918), p. 622.
2. Quoted in Ssu-yu Teng and John K. Fairbank, eds., *China's Response to the West: A Documentary Survey, 1839–1923* (New York, 1970), p. 140.
3. Ibid., p. 167.
4. John K. Fairbank, Albert M. Craig, and Edwin O. Reischauer, *East Asia: Tradition and Transformation* (Boston, 1973), p. 514.
5. Quoted in John W. Dower, ed., *The Origins of the Modern Japanese State: Selected Writings of E. H. Norman* (New York, 1975), p. 13.

CHAPTER 23

1. Arnold Toynbee, *Surviving the Future* (New York, 1971), pp. 106–107.
2. Quoted in Joachim Remak, "1914—The Third Balkan War: Origins Reconsidered," *Journal of Modern History* 43 (1971): 364–365.
3. Quoted in J. M. Winter, *The Experience of World War I* (New York, 1989), p. 142.
4. Quoted in Catherine W. Reilly, ed., *Scars upon My Heart: Women's Poetry and Verse of the First World War* (London, 1981), p. 90.
5. Quoted in William M. Mandel, *Soviet Women* (Garden City, N.Y., 1975), p. 43.
6. Quoted in Irving Howe, ed., *The Basic Writings of Trotsky* (London, 1963), p. 162.

CHAPTER 24

1. Speech by Mahatma Gandhi, delivered in London in September 1931 during his visit for the first Roundtable Conference.
2. Ts'ai Yuan-p'ei, "Ta Lin Ch'in-nan Han," in *Ts'ai Yuan-p'ei Hsien-sheng Ch'uan-chi* [Collected Works of Mr. Ts'ai Yuan-p'ei] (Taipei, 1968), pp. 1057–1058.
3. Quoted in William Theodore de Bary et al., eds., *Sources of Chinese Tradition* (New York, 1963), p. 783.
4. Lu Xun, "Diary of a Madman," in *Selected Works of Lu Hsun,* vol. 1 (Peking, 1957), p. 20.

CHAPTER 25

1. Benito Mussolini, "The Doctrine of Fascism," in Adrian Lyttleton, ed., *Italian Fascisms* (London, 1973), p. 42.

2. Quoted in Alexander De Grand, "Women Under Italian Fascism," *Historical Journal* 19 (1976), pp. 958–959.
3. Quoted in Jackson J. Spielvogel, *Hitler and Nazi Germany: A History,* 5th ed. (Upper Saddle River, N.J., 2005), p. 60.
4. Quoted in Joachim Fest, *Hitler,* trans. Richard Winston and Clara Winston (New York, 1974), p. 418.
5. *Documents on German Foreign Policy,* ser. D, vol. 7 (London, 1956), p. 204.
6. Quoted in Raul Hilberg, *The Destruction of the European Jews,* vol. 1, rev. ed. (New York, 1985), pp. 332–333.
7. *Nazi Conspiracy and Aggression,* vol. 6 (Washington, D.C., 1946), p. 789.
8. Quoted in Claudia Koonz, "Mothers in the Fatherland: Women in Nazi Germany," in Renate Bridenthal and Claudia Koonz, eds., *Becoming Visible: Women in European History* (Boston, 1977), p. 466.
9. Quoted in John Campbell, *The Experience of World War II* (New York, 1989), p. 143.
10. Quoted in Norman Graebner, *Cold War Diplomacy, 1945–1960* (Princeton, N.J., 1962), p. 117.

CHAPTER 26

1. Quoted in *Department of State Bulletin,* February 11, 1945, pp. 213–216.
2. Quoted in J. M. Jones, *The Fifteen Weeks (February 21–June 5, 1947),* 2nd ed. (New York, 1964), pp. 140–141.
3. Quoted in W. Laqueur, *Europe in Our Time* (New York, 1992), p. 111.
4. Quoted in W. Loth, *The Division of the World, 1941–1955* (New York, 1988), pp. 160–161.

CHAPTER 27

1. Quoted in V. Zubok and C. Pleshakov, *Inside the Kremlin's Cold War: From Stalin to Khrushchev* (Cambridge, Mass., 1996), p. 166.
2. Quoted in H. Smith, *The New Russians* (New York, 1990), p. 74.
3. Quoted in S. Karnow, *Mao and China: Inside China's Cultural Revolution* (New York, 1972), p. 95.
4. Quoted in F. Ching, "Confucius, the New Saviour," *Far Eastern Economic Review,* November 10, 1994, p. 37.
5. Quoted in J. Spence, *Chinese Roundabout: Essays in History and Culture* (New York, 1992), p. 285.

CHAPTER 28

1. Quoted in W. I. Hitchcock, *The Struggle for Europe: The Turbulent History of a Divided Continent, 1945–2002* (New York, 2003), pp. 399–400.
2. Simone de Beauvoir, *The Second Sex,* trans. H. M. Parshley (New York, 1961), p. xxviii.
3. Quoted in Renate Bridenthal, "Women in the New Europe," in Renate Bridenthal, Susan Mosher Stuard, and Merry E. Wiesner, eds., *Becoming Visible: Women in European History,* 3rd ed. (Boston, 1998), pp. 564–565.
4. Quoted in Henry Grosshans, *The Search for Modern Europe* (Boston, 1970), p. 421.
5. Quoted in Richard Maltby, ed., *Passing Parade: A History of Popular Culture in the Twentieth Century* (New York, 1989), p. 11.

CHAPTER 29

1. Cited in M. Meredith, *The Fate of Africa* (New York, 2005), p. 168.
2. K. Little, *African Women in Towns: An Aspect of Africa's Social Revolution* (Cambridge, 1973), p. 6.
3. A. Nicol, *A Truly Married Woman and Other Stories* (London, 1965), p. 12.
4. Ngugi Wa Thiong'o, *Decolonizing the Mind: The Politics of Language in African Literature* (Portsmouth, N.H., 1986), p. 103.

5. Quoted in R. R. Andersen, R. F. Seibert, and J. G. Wagner, *Politics and Change in the Middle East: Sources of Conflict and Accommodation,* 4th ed. (Englewood Cliffs, N.J., 1982), p. 51.
6. S. Azadi, with A. Ferrante, *Out of Iran* (London, 1987), p. 223.

CHAPTER 30

1. *New York Times,* May 2, 1996.
2. Quoted in L. Collins and D. Lapierre, *Freedom at Midnight* (New York, 1975), p. 252.

3. Y. Mishima and G. Bownas, eds., *New Writing in Japan* (Harmondsworth, England, 1972), p. 16.
4. *New York Times,* January 29, 1996.

EPILOGUE

1. Quoted in J. N. Pieterse, *Globalization and Culture* (Lanham, Md., 2004), p. 49.
2. E. Boulding, *Women in the Twentieth Century World* (New York, 1977), pp. 187–188.

INDEX

Italicized page numbers show the locations of illustrations.

Bharatiya Janata Party (BJP, India), 755
Bhopal, chemical leak in, 758
Bhutto family (Pakistan): Benazir, 756, 757;
  Zulfikar Ali, 756
Biafra, 726, 729
Bible, 363, 364
Big Three: World War II and, 637–638
Bill of Rights: in England, 379, 380; in
  U.S., 447
Bin Laden, Osama, 713–714, 737, 743
Biological weapons, 631
Birth control, 501, 711, 713. *See also* Family
  planning
Birthrate, 501; in China, 687, 688; in Europe,
  578, 712–713; after World War I, 578
Bishops (Christian), 451–452
Bismarck, Otto von, 480–481, *481,*
  484–485, 530
Bitter Love (Chinese film), 692
Black Hand (Serbian organization), 567
Black Hole of Calcutta, 402
Blackness (négritude): concept of, 722
Blacks: in South Africa, 728–729. *See also*
  African Americans
Blair, Tony, 700
Blitz, 635
Blitzkrieg (lightning war), 624
Blockade: of Berlin, 647
Blues (music), 718
Boers, 346, 528–529, *530,* 532, 533
Boer War, 532
Bohemia, 364, 373, 378
Bokhara, 394, 395
Boleyn, Anne, 367
Bolívar, Simón, 491, 492, *492,* 493
Bolivia, 493, 707
Bolshevik Revolution (1917), 573, 576
Bolsheviks (Soviet Union), 576–577, 599
Bombay. *See* Mumbai (Bombay)
Bombings: of Japan, 629, 635, *636;* in
  World War II, 629, 635, *636*
Books: in China, 412; printing of, 363
Borders: of China, 416, 416 (map), 660; of
  post–World War I Germany, 579–580, 579
  (map), 581. *See also* Boundaries;
  Frontiers
Borneo, 336, 525, 761
Borodino, battle at, 457
Bosnia, 391, 486, 566, 567, 701, 702
Bosnian Muslims, 701–702
Bosporus, 386
Botswana. *See* Bechuanaland (Botswana)
Boundaries: in Africa, 724 (map), 725; in
  Middle East, 744 (map). *See also* Borders;
  Frontiers
Bourbon dynasty (France), 370, 373, 377,
  458, 475
Bourgeois/bourgeoisie, 469, 473–474; in France,
  450–451, 457
Boxer Rebellion (China), 546, 546 (map)
Brahmaputra River region, 399
Brahmo Samaj (India), 534
Brandenburg-Prussia, 377–378

Brandt, Willy, 699
Braudel, Fernand, 387
Brazil, 341, 445, 471, 609, 610–611, 706, 707;
  African slaves in, 346–347; Portuguese
  government of, 345
Brest-Litovsk, Treaty of, 576
Brezhnev, Leonid, *658,* 663, 674–676
Brezhnev Doctrine, 663–664
Briand, Aristide, 581
Britain. *See* Battle of Britain; England
  (Britain)
British, use of term, 446
British Columbia, 499
British East India Company, 345, 401, 402, 417,
  516, 517
British Empire, 447, 515–516, 723, 753. *See also*
  Colonies and colonization; Independence;
  specific locations
British Honduras, 609
Brown, Gordon, 700
Brown Shirts, in Nazi Germany, 708
Broz, Josip. *See* Tito (Yugoslavia)
Bubonic plague, 443
Buda, 477
Budapest, 482
Buddhism, *355;* in China, 690; in Japan, 770;
  kingship in, 353
Buenos Aires, 496
Buffers: after World War II, 638
Building. *See also* Housing
Bulgaria, 569, 572, 573, 628, 703; Nazi Germany
  and, 624; Soviet Union and, 645
Bulgars, 386
Bullion (gold and silver), 373
Burakumin (Japanese minority), 768. *See also*
  Eta (Japanese class)
Bureaucracy: in China, 686; in Europe, 374; in
  France, 457; in Korea, 431; in Middle East
  regimes, 744
Burghers, 363
Burj Dubai, 752
Burma (Myanmar), 351, 353, *355;* colonialism
  and, 516, 520, 523; democracy and, 764;
  development in, 764; England and, 545;
  Japan and, 623, 631; manufacturing in, 524;
  nationalism in, 590–591
Burundi: Rwanda and, 729–730
Bush, George H. W., 705, 743
Bush, George W., 705; Iraq War and, 743;
  Kyoto Agreement and, 776; terrorism
  and, 714
Business: in Japan, 556, 767, 768; in South
  Korea, 772; women in, 404
Buxar: battle at, 402
Byelorussians, 631. *See also* Belarus
Byzantine Empire: decline and fall of, 386–387,
  388

Cabot, John, 340 (map), 341
Cabral, John, 402
Cabral, Pedro, 341
Cacao (kakaw), 343

Cairo, 388
Cairo Trilogy (Mahfouz), 749
Cai Yuanpei, 601
Calcutta (Kolkata), 401, 402
Calderón, Felipe, 709
Calicut (Kozhikode, India), 334, *334,* 339
Caliphs and caliphate: in Ottoman Empire, 388,
  391; in Turkey, 596
Calligraphy: Mughal, 406
Calvin, John, and Calvinism, 365–367
Cambodia, 351, 353, 765; France and, 521,
  523, 655, 656; Khmer Rouge and, 765, *766;*
  Vietnam and, 431
Cameroons, 531, 572
Camp David Agreement (1978), 739–740
Camus, Albert, 715
Canada, 446, 450, 499, 499 (map), 533, 706
Canals: Suez, 525, 526, 526 (map), *527*
Cane sugar. *See* Sugar industry
Cannon, 386–387
Canton, *415, 417,* 544 (map)
Cape Colony, 529 (map), 532
Cape Horn, 343 (map)
Cape of Good Hope, 339, 344, 346
Cape Town, *728*
Cape Verde, 350, 525
Capitalism: in Africa, 727–728; American trade
  and, 343; China and, 687, 691; commercial,
  373, 443; European expansionism and, 337; in
  Japan, 425–426, 562; Lenin on, 599; Marx on,
  671; modernization and, 634; in Soviet Union
  and China, *679*
Caravels, *338*
Cárdenas, Lázaro, 611
Caribbean region, 341, 342, 345; Cuba and, 658;
  independence and, 609
Carlowitz, Treaty of, 392
Carnegie Steel Company, 498
Carnival, 442
Caroline Islands, 573
Carpini, John Plano, 337
Cars. *See* Automobiles
Cartels: in Japan, 767
Carter, Jimmy, 665, 705, 739–740
Carter Doctrine, 665
Cartwright, Edmund, 465
Castes: in India, 404, 758
Castles: in Japan, *423*
Castro, Fidel, 658, 707–708
Castro, Raúl, 708
Casualties: in World War I, 565, 569, 573, 575,
  578; in World War II, 636. *See also* specific
  battles and wars
Catherine of Aragon, 367
Catherine the Great (Russia), 448
Catholicism. *See* Roman Catholicism
Catholic Reformation, 367–369
Caucasus region, 702
Caudillos (leaders), 495
Cavalry: in India, 398
Cavour, Camillo di, 480
Cebu, Philippines, 344
Celibate clergy, 367

Frith, William P., *501*
Frontiers: of Thailand and Vietnam, 765
Fundamentalism: Islamic, 746–747

Galicia, 568, 569
Galilei, Galileo, 436–437
Gallegos, Rómulo, 611
Gallipoli, 386, 572
Gandhi, Mohandas (Mahatma), *589,* 589–590, 591–594, *593, 594,* 753, 754, 777
Gandhi family (India): Indira, 754, 757, 758; Maneka, 759; Rajiv, 755, 758; Sonia, 759
Ganges River region, 399
Gao, 350
Garibaldi, Giuseppe, 480, 504
Garlic Ballads, The (Mo Yan), 693
Gateway to India, *536*
Gatling gun, 536
Gaucho, 611
Gaudry, Suzanne, witchcraft trial of, 372
Gaullist movement, 710
Gautama Buddha. *See* Buddhism
Gays and lesbians. *See* Homosexuality
Gaza Strip, 740
Gdavari River region, 399
Geertz, Clifford, 536
Gender: in Africa, 732–733; in India, 758–759. *See also* Men; Women
General Theory of Employment, Interest, and Money (Keynes), 583
Genetic engineering, 717
Geneva, Calvin in, 367
Geneva Accords, 660
Geneva Conference (1954), 660
Geneva Convention: on laws of war, 631
Genital mutilation, 532, 733
Genocide, against Armenians, 578
Genro (Japan), 555, 561
Gentry: in India, 519
Geocentric theory, 436
Geography: of Japan, 562
George V (England): in India, *536*
Georgia (nation), 576, 679
Géricault, Theodore, *492*
German Democratic Republic (GDR). *See* East Germany
German East Africa, 572
Germanic Confederation, 477
German Labor Service: in World War II, *630*
German people: in Austria, 484; ethnic Germans after World War II, 629
German Social Democratic Party (SPD), 474
Germany: African colonies of, 572; alliances of, 485–486; Allied bombings of, 635; anti-Semitism in, 509; economy in, 583, 619, 699; Great Depression in, 582; Green Party in, 714–715; imperialism by, 529, 545; industrialization and, 467, 471; Luther in, 364; military in, 566; nationalism and, 476; in 1918, 578; occupation of, 638; old order in, 484; partition of, 637; reparations and, 579, 580–581; reunification of, 680, 699; submarine

warfare by, 573; Thirty Years' War and, 373; unification of, 477, 480–481, 480 (map); Versailles Treaty and, 579–580; women in, 574; after World War I, 579–581. *See also* East Germany; Nazi Germany; West Germany; World War I; World War II
Ghana, 724, 725
Ghettos, Nazis and, 630
Gia Long dynasty, 431
Gibbs, Philip, 565
Ginza (Tokyo), *561*
Gion district (Kyoto), *429*
Glasnost (openness), 678
Global economy: environment and, 776
Globalization, 667; of warfare, 449–450
Global village, 667
Global warming, 776
Glorious Revolution (England), 379
Goa, 339
Gobi Desert region, 545. *See also* Mongols
"Go East, Young Man" (Mahbubani), 774
Goh Chok Tong (Singapore), 774
Golan Heights, 739, 740
Gold, 373; in Africa, 336, 339, 346, 531; in Americas, 343, 444–445; Portugal and, 339; trade and, 443
Gold Coast, 339, 525, 529, 723. *See also* Ghana
Golden age: of English literature, 381; in Qing China, 411
Golden Horn, 387
Goodbye to All That (Graves), 569
Good Neighbor Policy, 611
Gorbachev, Mikhail, 666, 678–679
Gordon, Charles, 526, 528
Gorée (island near Senegal), *348*
Gothic literature, 505
Gottwald, Klement, 645
Gouges, Olympe de, 451
Government: of Afghanistan, 743; in Americas, 345; of Burma, 764; of China, 415; colonial, 516–517, 523, 533; of England, 379; of France, 451–452, 457, 484, 583; of Germany, 484, 618–619; of India, 400–401, 519–520, 753–756, 757; of Iran, 596, 741; of Japan, 427–428, 555, 556, 558, 605–608, 767–768; of Korea, 431; in Latin America, 609–611; of Mexico, 496, 611; in Middle East, 744; of Ottoman Empire, 389–390, 391; of Russia, 378; Safavid, 395; of South Africa, 532; in Southeast Asia, 761–762; of South Korea, 771–772; of Soviet Union, 584; of Spanish Empire, 342–343; of Taiwan, 772; totalitarian, 617–620; of United States, 447, 497; of Vietnam, 764. *See also* Absolutism; Colonies and colonization; Imperialism; Indirect rule; Politics
Government of India Act (1921), 593
Grain of Wheat, A (Ngugi Wa Thiong'o), 734
Grand Alliance (World War II), 626, 637, 644
Grand Army (Napoleon), 457–458, 458 (map)
Grand Canal (China), 544
Grand Duchy of Warsaw, 457

Grand Empire (Napoleon), 457–458, 458 (map)
Grand National Assembly (Turkey), 596
Grand vezir (Ottoman Empire), 391, 393
Grant, Ulysses S., 497
Graves, Robert, 569
Great Altar of Pergamum, *387*
Great Britain. *See* England (Britain)
Great Depression, *581,* 581–582, 609, 620, 706
Great East-Asia Co-Prosperity Sphere, 625, 627 (map)
Greater Japanese Women's Association, 635
Great Leap Forward (China), 681, 686
Great powers, after Napoleonic wars, 479
Great Proletarian Cultural Revolution (China), 549, 681–682, *682,* 683
Great Society, 704
Great Viet. *See* Dai Viet (Great Viet)
Great War. *See* World War I
Greece, 486; Anatolia and, 595; civil war in, 646; European unification and, 703; in World War II, 595
Green movements, 714
Grimmelshausen, Jakob von, 375
Guam, 498
Guangxu (Kuang Hsu) emperor, 545
Guangzhou (Canton), China. *See* Canton
Guaraní Indians, 446, *446*
Guatemala, 493, 496
Guerrilla warfare: in Nicaragua, 666; in Vietnam, *662*
Guianas, 609
Guided democracy, in Indonesia, 761
Guillotine (France), 454
Guinea, 725
Guiraldes, Ricardo, 611
Gulag Archipelago, The (Solzhenitsyn), 676
Gulf of Aqaba, 739
Gulf War. *See* Persian Gulf War
Gunpowder empires, 407–408
Guomindang (Kuomintang). *See* Nationalists (China)
Gutenberg, Johannes, 363
Gypsies, Nazi killings of, 631

Habibie, B. J. (Indonesia), 763
Habsburg dynasty, 566; Austrian Empire and, 378, 448, 482; Holy Roman Empire and, 364, 373
Hagia Sophia (Constantinople), 393
Haiti, 454, 491, 496
Hall of Mirrors (Versailles), *377,* 481, *481*
Hallucinogenic drugs, 710
Han (Japanese domains), 425
Hangul (spoken Korean), 431
Hanoi, *662. See also* Vietnam; Vietnam War
Harem: in Ottoman Empire, 390–391
Hargreaves, James, 465
Harijans (untouchables, India), 758
Harper, Stephen, 706
Harris, Townsend, 554
Hashemite clan, 738

Planetary motion, 436. *See also* Astronomy; Universe

Plantations: in Africa, 723; African slaves for, 346–347; in Americas, 345; environment and, 552; pepper, 351, *353*; rubber, *524*; trade and, 443; workers for, 524

Plassey, Battle of, 402

Playing for Thrills (Wang Shuo), 693

Please Don't Call Me Human (Wang Shuo), 693

PLO. *See* Palestine Liberation Organization

Poe, Edgar Allen, 505

Poets and poetry: in India, 406; in Japan, 428–429; Romantic, 505; Symbolists and, 510

Pogroms, against Jews, 509

Poison gas, 571, 631, 742

Poland, 703; after communism, 700, 701; Nazi Germany and, 622, 624, 631; protests in, 657; Soviet Union and, 645, 679; after World War I, 579, 580; after World War II, 629, 638

Polish people, 484, 629, 631

Politburo (Soviet Union), 584, 672

Political parties: in India, 754, 755; in Japan, 767–768; in Mexico, 709; in Nazi Germany, 618; in Russia, 484; socialist, 474–475; in Soviet-occupied states, 645; in Soviet Union, 678; in Taiwan, 773. *See also* specific parties

Politics: absolute rulers and, 375–379; in Africa, 350–351, 723, 725–727, 730–731, 736; in Canada, 706; in China, 414–415; in England, 583; after Enlightenment, 447–450; in Europe, 370; in France, 698–699; Green Parties and, 714–715; imperialism and, 515; in Japan, 605–608, 767–768; in Latin America, 495, 496, 609–611; Machiavelli on, 362; mass, 482–483; mass education and, 502; Ottoman, 389–390; in Reformation, 364–365; Safavid, 396–397; Scientific Revolution and, 438; in Southeast Asia, 761–762, 766–767; Thirty Years' War and, 373; in U.S., 703–706; women and, 501–502, 713; World War I and, 573

Pollock, Jackson, 715–716, *716*

Pollution, 689, 714–715, 758. *See also* Environment

Polo family: Marco, 335, 337; Niccolò and Maffeo, 337

Pol Pot (Cambodia), 765

Polygamy: in Africa, 532

Polynesia, 352

Popes: Napoleon and, 455; Reformation and, *365*; Renaissance, 363. *See also* specific popes

Popular culture, 442, 718–719; in East and West, *429*; after World War II, 710. *See also* Culture(s)

Popular Front (France), 583

Popular music, 716, 718, 719

Population: in Africa, 727, 728; in China, 418–419, 541, 687; in England, 468; in Europe, 371, 419, 443; explosion in (1700-1800), 419; in India, 419, 755, 758; industrialization and, 467–468; in Japan, 425–426; in Kenya, 728; in

Korea, 431; in New Zealand, 775; in Southeast Asia, 524; in Taiwan, 772; urban, 500

Porcelain: Chinese, 422

Port Arthur, 545, 558, 559

Port Hoogly: capture of, 402

Portolani (navigation charts), 338

Portugal: Africa and, 345–346, 724; Americas and, 341; Brazil and, 341, 445; China and, 340, 411; English, Dutch, and, 344–345; European unification and, 703; exploration by, 334, 338–341, 340 (map), 343; immigration from, 496; imperialism by, 529; India and, 334, 339, 401, 402; industrialization in, 471; Japan and, 423, *424*; Latin America and, 491; maritime empire of, 338–341; slave trade and, 339, 346–347; Southeast Asia and, 351; spice trade and, 339–341; trade and exploration by, 343

Post-Impressionism, 510

Postmodernism, 692, 715–716

Poststructuralism, 715

Potala Palace (Tibet), *684*

Potatoes, 343

Potosí mines, 343

Potsdam Conference, 638

Pottery. *See* Porcelain

Poverty: in Africa, 727; in China, 683; in India, 758

Power (energy). *See* Energy (power)

Power (political). *See* Politics; specific individuals, countries, and systems

Power looms, 465

Prague, 477

Predestination, 365–366

PRI. *See* Institutional Revolutionary Party

Primogeniture, in Japan, 428

Prince, The (Machiavelli), 362

Princess, The (Tennyson), 500–501

Principia (Newton), 437

Principle of intervention, 475

Principle of legitimacy, 475

Printing: in China, 412; Reformation and, 363

Prisoners of war: Japanese, 631

Private sector: in China, 687, 688, 690; in India, 755–756

Proclamation to French Troops in Italy (Napoleon), 456

Production: industrial, 471; systems of, 443; tributary mode of, 358

Progress, 439, 566

Progressive Conservative Party (Canada), 706

Progressive Era: in U.S., 498

Progressive Party (Japan), 555

Proletariat, 469, *473*, 473–474

Propaganda: in totalitarian states, 617

Property rights: in France, 457; of women, 501

Protectorates, in Africa, 526

Protest(s): in China, 683–684; in France, 698; in Mexico, 709; in Nigeria, 729; against nuclear weapons, 713; in Poland, 657; by university students, 710; in U.S. civil rights movement, 704–705

Protestantism, 361, *361*, 364–365, 366, 367; in England, 367, 370; evangelical, 730. *See also* specific groups

Protestant Reformation, 361–362, 364–369

Provinces: Canadian, 499

Provisional Government (Russia), 576

Prussia, 378, 449–450, 449 (map), 477; absolutism in, 377–378; and Concert of Europe, 475; enlightened absolutism in, 448; France and, 452, 481; German unification and, 480–481; Napoleon and, 457; after World War I, 579. *See also* Congress of Vienna

Psychoanalysis, 508

Ptolemy (astronomer), 436

Public opinion: in World War I, 573–574, *574*

Puddling, 466

Puerto Rico, United States and, 496, 498

Punjab, 755, 756. *See also* India; Pakistan

Purdah (India), 404

Pure Food and Drug Act (U.S.), 498

Purges, in Soviet Union, 620

Puritans, in England, 379

Pushtun people, 756

Putin, Vladimir, 702

Putting-out system, 443

Puyi (China), *549*

Qadhafi, Muammar, 726, 744

Qajar dynasty (Persia), 596

Qianlong (China), 414, 417, 540

Qing dynasty (China), 411, 413–418, 416 (map), 431, 540, 542 (map); arts of, 421–422; decline of, 541–550, 602; lifestyle under, 419–420

Qiu Jin (China), 552

Quadrant, 338

Quebec, 499

Queens. *See* Monarchs and monarchies; specific rulers

Quinine, 552

Quotations of Chairman Mao Zedong. See Little Red Book

Race and racism: in African colonies, 532; Holocaust and, 629–631, *630*; imperialism and, 515; Nazi Germany and, 619, 630; social Darwinism and, 508–509; in U.S., 704–705

Radar, 624, 716

Radiance of the King, The (Laye), 736

Radicalism: in China, 660, 681–682; in France, 453–455, 583; student, 710. *See also* Student protests

Radical Party (Argentina), 610

Radio, 471, 586

Radio Free Europe, 657

Radio Liberty, 657

Raffles, Stamford, 520

Railroads, 467, 472–473, 499, 519, 559

Raj (British), 519, 753

Raja (prince), 517

Rakosi, Matyas, 657

Rama (India), 757
Ramayana, 406
Ramcaritmanas (Tulsidas), 406
Rangoon (Yangon), Burma, *355*
Rap music, 718
Rasputin, 575
Raw materials, 523, 609
Reagan, Ronald, 665–666, 672, 705
Realism: in art, 381, 507, 510–511; in literature, 506–507
Realpolitik (Germany), 480
Rearmament, in Germany, 619, 620–621
Reason, in Enlightenment, 438–439, 502–504
Rebellions. *See* Revolts and rebellions
Red Army, 576–577, 638, 664
Red Fort, 401, 405–406
Red Guards (China), 681, 683
Red Sea, 665
Red Shirts (Italy), 480
"Red tide," 655
Reform(s). *See* Reformation; specific reforms and countries
Reform Act (England): of 1832, 478, 481
Reformation, 362–364; Catholic, 367–369; Protestant, 361–362, 364–369
Refugees: African, 732; Jewish, *599*, 737; Palestinian, 738
Regionalism: in Africa, 726
Reichstag, 364, 484, 618
Reign of Terror (France), 454, 455, 682
Relativity theory, 507–508
Relics, 364
Religion: of Abbas the Great, 396; in China, 690; European expansionism and, 337; French wars of, 365–367, 370; in German Reformation, 364–365; in India, 757; in Iran, 741; in Japan, 770; in Latin America, 445; in Mughal Empire, 399; nationalism and, 590–591; Nigerian disputes over, 729; in Ottoman Empire, 391; Protestant Reformation and, 361–362, 364–369; in Safavid Empire, 395; society and, 730, *730*; in Southeast Asia, 353; in Spanish colonies, 343; Thirty Years' War and, 373. *See also* Secularization; specific religions
Religious orders, Catholic, 369
Remarque, Erich Maria, 571
Reminiscences (Schurz), 478–479
Rémy, Nicholas, 371
Renaissance (Europe), 337, 362–363
Rentiers, 443
Reparations: after World War I, 579, 580–581; after World War II, 647
Representative government: in Southeast Asia, 764
Repression, Freud on, 508
Republic(s): in Brazil, 611; former Soviet, 672, 679; in France, 453–454, 455, 477, 484, 698; in Latin America, 494
Republic of China (ROC). *See* Taiwan
Republic of Korea (South Korea). *See* South Korea
Republic of Vietnam. *See* South Vietnam

Republic of Wine, The (Mo Yan), 693
Resistance. *See* Revolts and rebellions; specific movements
Resources. *See* Natural resources
Restoration: of Bourbons in France, 458, 475, 481–482; in England, 379; in Japan, 554–557
Reunification: of Germany, 680, 699; of Vietnam, 765
Reúnion, 527
Revisionism, 475, 649
Revive China Society, 548
Revolts and rebellions: in Africa, 726; anticolonial, 533–536; in China, 413, 414, *452*, 528, 544, 544 (map), 546, 546 (map), 603; in East Germany, 664; in Latin America, 491–494; by sepoys, 534. *See also* Protest(s)
Revolution(s): American, 447; Bolshevik (Russia), 573, 576; in China, *452*, 549–550, 601–605; in Cuba, 707, 708; of 1848, *477*, 477–479; in France, *435*, 435–436, 450–455, *452*; Great Proletarian Cultural Revolution (China), 681–682; in Haiti, 454; in Hungary, 477, 657, *657*; in Iran, 741, 747; in Mexico, 496; in non-Western societies, 599; in 17th century, 373–374. *See also* Revolts and rebellions; Scientific Revolution
Revolutionary Alliance (China), 548–549
Revolutionary socialism, 475
Reykjavik: U.S.-Soviet meeting in, 666
Reza Khan (shah of Iran), 596, 597
Rhee, Syngman, 771–772
Rhythm and blues, 718
Ricci, Matteo, 369, 412, 419
Rice: in China, 419, 687; Japan and, 631
Rifles, 534–535
Rigaud, Hyacinth, *376*
Rights: Enlightenment and, 447; in France, 451, 453, 455–457; in Latin America, 707. *See also* Women; specific rights
Right wing: anti-Semitism of, 509; in France, 698; in Germany, 618; terrorism by, 713; in U.S., 705
Riots: in East Pakistan, 754; in Hungary, 657
Rivera, Diego, 611
Rivers and river regions. *See* specific river regions
Riza-i-Abbasi (Persian artist), 397
Roads and highways: in China, 550; in India, 519
Robespierre, Maximilien, 453–454
Rock and roll music, 712, 718
Rococo style, 441–442
Roman Catholicism: Catholic Reformation and, 367–369; Church of England and, 367, 379; on contraception and abortion, 713; Copernican system and, 437; corruption of, 363–364; in East Timor, 764; French Revolution and, 451–452; in Latin America, 445, 446, *446*; Luther and, 364–365; Napoleon and, 455; Reformation of, 367–369; in Spain, 370; in

Spanish colonies, 343. *See also* Papacy; Popes; specific orders
Romania, 486, 624, 628, 645, 703
Romanians, 477
Romanov family, 378
Romanticism, in literature and art, 502–506, *506*
Rome (city): Italian unification and, 480; in World War II, 627
Rome, Treaty of, 703
Rome-Berlin Axis, 621
Rommel, Erwin, 626
Ronin (unemployed warriors), 426
Roosevelt, Franklin D.: death of, 629, 645; Great Depression and, 583; Japan and, 626; Mexico and, 611; social change and, 703; at Tehran, 637; at Yalta, 638, *644*, 644–645, 651
Rosas, Juan Manuel de, 495
Rousseau, Jean-Jacques, 440
Roy, Ram Mohan, 534
Rubber, *524*
Rubens, Peter Paul, *381*
Rugs: Ottoman, 394
Ruhr valley, French occupation of, 580–581
Rural areas: in Africa, 727, 732, *733*; in Asia, 534; in China, 550–551, 687, 688; colonization and, 524–525; in Europe, 443; in Japan, 555–556, 767
Rural responsibility system (China), 687
Rushdie, Salman, 759
Rusk, Dean, 659
Russia, 449 (map), 484, 486; absolutism in, 378, 484; Bolshevik Revolution in, 573; Catherine the Great in, 448; China and, 416, 545; civil war in, 576–577; and Concert of Europe, 475; Crimean War and, 479; economy in, 702; Germany and, 485–486; industrialization in, 467, 471, 472–473, 484, 634; Iran and, 596; Jews in, 509; military of, 566; Napoleon and, 457; Ottoman Empire and, 479; reforms in, 378, 482; Seven Years' War and, 450; society in, 676–678, 702; after Soviet Union, 702–703; war communism in, 577; after World War I, 580; World War I and, 486, 567–568, 569, 574, 576. *See also* Russian Revolutions; Soviet Union; specific wars
Russian Armenia, 576
Russian Revolutions, 573, 574–575, 576; Bolshevik Revolution, 573, 576, 599; of March, 1917, 575–576
Russo-Japanese War, 484, 486, 559
Rwanda: Burundi and, 729–730
Ryukyu Islands, 558

SA (Nazi Storm Troops), 618
Sacks: of Constantinople, 386–387, *388*; of Delhi, 401
"Sacred Edict" (Kangxi), 427
al -Sadat, Anwar, 739–740, 747
Saddam Hussein, 742–743, 744
Safavids, 388, 391, 394–397, 395 (map), *397*, 398

Safi al-Din, 394
Sahara Desert region, 346, 727, 729
Sahel, 552
Saigon, 662, 663. *See also* Vietnam War
Saikaku (Japanese novelist), 428
Sailing ships, 338, *338*
Saint-Domingue, 454, 490
Saint Helena, Napoleon on, 458
St. Petersburg, 575–576. *See also* Leningrad
Sakhalin Island, 559, 638, 767
Sakharov, Andrei, 675
Salinas, Carlos (Mexico), 709
Salt: trade in, 336
SALT I and II, 665
Samoa, 498
Samurai (Japan), *425*, 426, 428, 554, 555, 557
Sánchez Navarro family (Mexico), 495
Sanford, Elizabeth Poole, 503
Sanitation: in Africa, 727; in European cities, 469
San Martín, José de, 491, *492*, 492–493
Sarajevo, 566
Sardinia: Kingdom of, 477
Sarekat Islam (Association), 591
Sarkozy, Nicolas, 699
Saro-Wiwa, Ken, 729
Sarraut, Albert, 517, 523
Sartre, Jean-Paul, 715
Saskatchewan, 499
Satanic Verses, The (Rushdie), 759–760
Sat-Cho alliance (Japan), 554, 557
Satellites: communication, *717*
Satellite states: in Eastern Europe, 664, 666, 676. *See also* specific countries
Sati (India), 401, 404, 758, 759
Satrapi, Marjane, 742
Satyagraha, 591
Saudi Arabia, 598, 737, 744
Savoy, house of, 477, 480
Saya San, 534
Scandinavia: Lutheranism in, 364. *See also* specific countries
Schleswig, 480
Schlieffen Plan, 568, 568 (map)
Schönberg, Arnold, 585
Schools: Anglo-Indian, 520; in Japan, 769; for mass education, 502. *See also* Universities and colleges
Schroeder, Gerhard, 699
Schumacher, E. F., 717, 718
Schurz, Carl, 478–479
Sciences: after Industrial Revolution, 506; in Ottoman Empire, 392; before World War I, 507–508; after World War II, 716–718. *See also* Technology
Scientific laws: of motion, 437
Scientific method, 506
Scientific Revolution, 343, 436–438
Scotland, 367, *636*
Scott, Walter, 504
Secession: in U.S., 497
Second Battle of the Marne, 578
Second Class Citizen (Emecheta), 735

Second Continental Congress, 447
Second Empire (France), 482
Second Empire (Germany), 481
Second estate, 362, 450
"Second front": in World War II, 627–628
Second Indochina War, 660–663
Second Industrial Revolution, 469–475, *471, 472* (map)
Second International, 474
Second Republic (France), 477
Second Sex, The (de Beauvoir), 712
Second World War. *See* World War II
Secularization: in Enlightenment arts, 441–442; Muslim women and, 748; religion, society, and, 730; scientific method and, 506; of Turkey, 596
Security: in Cold War, 656; U.S. national security policy and, 653; after World War I, 580–582
Security Council (UN), 654, 655
Sedan, battle at, 481
Segregation: in South Africa, 724; in U.S., 704–705
Self-determination, 580
Self-Help (Smiles), 470
Self-strengthening policy (China), 545
Selim I (Ottoman Turks), 388, 395
Seljuk Turks, 394
Senegal, 529, 731
Seoul, Korea, 772
Separation of powers, 439
Sepoy Rebellion, 534–536, 591
September 11, 2001, terrorist attacks, 666, 667, 705, 713–714, *714, 737*
Serbia, 486, 566, 567, 569; ethnic cleansing by, 701–702; and Montenegro, 702; after World War I, 580
Serbs, 386, 477; nationalism among, 580; in Yugoslavia, 580, 701–702
Serfs and serfdom: in Europe, 373, 443; in France, 450, 455; in Japan, 555–556; in Russia, 482, 483
Servants: domestic, 501
Settlements: European, in Africa, 350–351; Jewish in occupied territories, 740
Seven Years' War, 443, 446, 447, 449–450
Sex and sexuality: in Africa, 532; in China, 605, 690; permissive society and, 710–711; after World War I, 584
Sexism: women's liberation and, 607
Shah: Ismail as, 394–395; Safavid, 396–397. *See also* Pahlavi dynasty (Iran)
Shakespeare, William, 381
Shamba (private farm), 727
Shandong peninsula, 545, 602, 609
Shanghai, China, *682*
Shanghai World Financial Center, 752
Shari'a (Islamic law), 391, 399, 596; in Nigeria, 729
Sharon, Ariel, 740
Shelley, Mary, 505
Shibusawa Eiichi, 470
Shidehara diplomacy, 609

Shi'ite Muslims, 747; in Iran, 596, 741, 742; in Iraq, 598, 742, 743, 743 (map); Safavids and, 388, 394, 396
Shikoku, 422, 423
Shimonoseki, Treaty of, 558–559
Ships and shipping: European warships and, *338*; exploration and, 338; Portuguese, 338, 340; in World War I, 573
Shogun and shogunate (Japan), 422–423
Shona peoples, 346
Shwedagon Pagoda (Rangoon), *355*
Siberia, 545
"Sick man of Europe," 479
Sideline industries: in China, 687
Siege weapons, 387
Sierra Leone, 350, 525, 731
Sikhs and Sikhism, 755, 757
Sikri, India, *406*
Silicon chip, 716
Silk and silk industry: in China, 417, *688*; in Japan, 557; in Ottoman Empire, 394, *394*; Persian weaving and, 397; women in, 552
Silk Road, *688*
Silver, 343, 373, 444–445; trade and, 412, 443
Simplicius Simplicissimus (Grimmelshausen), 375
Sinai Peninsula, 526, 739–740
Singapore, 335, 520, 521 (map), *522*, 765, 773–774, 773 (map)
Sino-Japanese War, Korea and, 545, 558–559, *560*
Sino-Soviet dispute, in Cold War, 660
Sipahis (Ottoman cavalry elite), 391
Siqueiros, David Alfaro, *612*
Six-Day War (1967), 739, 739 (map)
Sjahrir, Sutan, 591
Skyscrapers: in Southeast Asia, 752, *752*
Slave Coast, 351
Slavery: in Africa, 339, 349, *527,* 732; British abolition of, 528–529; in Haiti, 454; in Japan, 557; in Korea, 431; in Latin America, 495; in Ottoman Empire, 390, 391; sources of slaves, 348; in U.S., 483, 497–498, *498. See also* Slave trade
Slave trade, 339, 346–350, 347 (map), *348,* 525
Slavic peoples: Germans and, 484; Nazis and, 631; World War I and, 486, 567
SLORC (Burma), 764
Slovakia, 622, 703
Slovaks, 477
Slovenes: in Yugoslavia, 580
Slovenia, 378, 701, 703
Slums: in India, 758; in Southeast Asia, 765
Small Is Beautiful (Schumacher), 717, 718
Smallpox, 342, 419
Smiles, Samuel, 470
Smith, Adam, 440
Soccer, worldwide popularity of, *764*
Social classes. *See* Classes
Social Contract, The (Rousseau), 440
Social Darwinism, 508–509; colonialism and, 517; imperialism and, 515, 529

Stupas, *355*
Sublime Porte (grand vezir), 393
Submarine warfare: in World War I, 573
Sub-Saharan Africa. *See* Africa; specific countries
Subsistence farming, in Africa, 723
Sudan, 727, 731; Egypt and, 526; European imperialism and, 530–531; slavery and, 732
Sudetenland, 621–622
Suez Canal, 526, 526 (map), *527,* 738
Suffrage: universal male, 452; in U.S., 497. *See also* Voting and voting rights
Suffragists, 502
Sufism, 336, 391, 394
Sugar industry, 527
Suharto (Indonesia), 761–763
Suicide attacks: *kamikaze* as, 635
Sukarno (Indonesia), 761, 763
Sukarnoputri, Megawati (Indonesia), 763, 764
Sulawesi, 336
Suleyman I the Magnificent (Ottoman Turks), 385, 388, 390, *393*
Suleymaniye Mosque (Istanbul), *393*
Sultan(s), 386, 389, 391, 392–393
Sumatra, 335, 351, 525
Sun Kings, in France and China, *376*
Sunni Muslims: in Iraq, 598, 742, 743, 743 (map); in Ottoman Empire, 391
Sun Shines over the Sangan River, The (Ding Ling), 692
Sun Yat-sen, 548–549, 601, 602, 603
Superpowers, 639, 646, 672. *See also* Cold War; Soviet Union; United States
Supreme Court (U.S.), 497
Surat, India, 345
Surrealism, 584–585, *586*
Swahili coast: slave trade along, 525
Swahili culture, 351
Swan, Joseph, 471
Swaziland, 532
Sweden, 373, 378, 703, 710, 714
Swiss Republic, in Grand Empire, 457
Switzerland, 365–366, 714
Symbolists, 510
Syr Darya River region, 398
Syria, 526, 737; France and, 580, 598; government of, 744; Israel and, 738; socialism in, 600; terrorists and, 713; in United Arab Republic, 738

Tabriz, 395, 596
Tabula rasa (blank mind), Locke on, 439
Taille (French tax), 450
Taipei 101, 752, *773*
Taiping Rebellion (China), *452,* 528, 544, 544 (map)
Taiwan, 652, 656, 772–773; after Chiang Kai-shek, *773;* Chinese reunification with, 663; in Cold War, 654, 660; Japan and, 609, 767. *See also* Nationalists (China)
Taj Mahal, 394, 401, 405, *405*
Taliban, 714, 743, 756–757

Tamerlane, 394, 398
Tamil rebels, 755
Tanganyika, 530, 724. *See also* Tanzania; Zanzibar
Tannenberg, Battle of, 568
Tanzania, 351, 724, 725, 727. *See also* Tanganyika; Zanzibar
Taoism. *See* Daoism
Tariffs: in EEC, 703; Japan and, 616–617
Taxation: in China, 688; in England, 700; in Europe, 443; in France, 450; in India, 399, 403; in Japan, 556; in Ottoman Empire, 389; in U.S., 498
Teaching, 502
Team sports, 502
Technocratic society, 710
Technology: in China, 418–419, 550, 686; in cotton industry, 426; in India, 519, 756, 758; industrialization and, 717; in Industrial Revolution, 465–467; in Japan, 560; mass leisure and, 502; military, 386, 387, 530; in Ottoman Empire, 392; Scientific Revolution and, 438; after World War II, 716–718; before World War II, 617. *See also* Sciences
Tehran, 596
Tehran Conference, 637, 673
Telephone, 471
Telescope, 436–437, *438*
Television, 718, 719
Temple Mount (Jerusalem), *740*
Temple of Heaven (Beijing), *414*
Tenant farmers: in Japan, 426
Tennyson, Alfred (Lord), 500–501
Terror, The (France), 454
Terrorism: in Bali, *714;* coalition against, 700; in Europe, 713; in India, 756, 757; in Iran, 741; Islamic, 737; in Israel, 738; in Nazi Germany, 619; in U.S., 666, 667, 705, 713–714, *714*
Tetzel, Johann, 364
Textbooks: in Japan, 768
Textiles and textile industry, *466;* in Britain, 465, 467; child labor in, 469; in India, 403, 467, 519; in Japan, 557; in Ottoman Empire, 394; Safavid, 397; workers in, 469. *See also* Cotton; Silk and silk industry
Thailand, 351, 765; development in, 764; government of, 761, 763; imperialism and, 521; West and, 516; women in, 766
Thakin, in Burma, 591
Thatcher, Margaret, 699–700, *701*
Theater. *See* Drama
Theater of the Absurd, 715
Theology. *See* Religion
Things Fall Apart (Achebe), 734
Third Coalition, Napoleonic wars and, 457
Third estate, 362–363, 450, 451
Third Republic (France), 484
Third Wave, 717
Third World, 658, 665, 666
Thirteenth Amendment (U.S.), 498
Thirty-Six Views of Mount Fuji (Hokusai), 430

Thirty Years' War, 373, 374 (map)
Three People's Principles (Sun Yat-sen), 603
Thuggee, 518–519
Tiananmen Square (Beijing), 683; student protests in, 683–684
Tianjin (Tientsin), Treaty of, 544
Tibet, *684;* China and, 416, 545, 654, 684, 685
Timbuktu, 336
"Times They Are a-Changin', The" (Dylan), 712
Tito (Yugoslavia), 645, 646, 701
Tlaltelolco Square, Mexico: protests in, 709
Tobacco, 343, 392
Togo (Togoland), 351, 572
Tojo, Hideki, 635
Tokugawa shogunate (Japan), 422–430, 422 (map), 553; Tokugawa Ieyasu, 422, 423, 424
Tokyo, *423,* 425, 553, 554, *561;* earthquake in (1923), *608*
Tokyo School of Fine Arts, 561
Toleration: in Mughal Empire, 399; Voltaire on, 439–440
Tombs: of Chiang Kai-shek, *773;* Taj Mahal as, 401, *405*
Tongmenhui. *See* Revolutionary Alliance
Tonkin, king of, 354
Topkapi Palace (Istanbul), 391, 393
Tordesillas, Treaty of, 341
Totalitarianism, 617–619
Total war, World War I as, 573
Touré, Sékou, 725
Tourism, *688, 766*
Toussaint L'Ouverture, Pierre Dominique, 454, *490,* 490–491
Towns. *See* Cities and towns; Villages
Toynbee, Arnold, 566
Toyotomi Hideyoshi (Japan), 422, 423, 424, 425, 432
Trade: African, 725–726; in American products, 343; Canada-U.S., 706; in China, 411–412, 413 (map), *415,* 416–418, 540–541; European, 337, 443, 703; French, 377; in Great Depression, 581; in India, 399, 401; Islamic, 335–336; Japanese, 423, 424, *424,* 553; mercantilist, 373; Portuguese, *339;* Safavid, 396–397; in Southeast Asia, 355; trans-Saharan, 336; U.S.-Cuba, 707; worldwide, 357 (map); 471–472. *See also* Silk Road; Slave trade; Spices and spice trade; specific countries and regions
Trade unions, 473, 483, 618. *See also* Labor unions
Trade winds, 340 (map)
Transistors, 716
Trans-Jordan. *See* Jordan
Transportation: in Africa, 724; in China, 550; in India, 400, 519; power for, 471; steamboats as, 467; technology and, 717. *See also* specific types
Trans-Saharan trade, 336
Trans-Siberian Railway, 559
Transvaal, 529, *530,* 531, 532
Transylvania, 378, 392

Travels (Polo), 337

Travels of Sebastian Manrique, 1629-1649 (Cabral), 402

Treaties. *See* specific treaties

Trekkers: Boer, *530*

Trench warfare: in World War I, 569–572, *572*

Trent, Council of, 369

Trials: for witchcraft, 371, 372

Tribalism, in Africa, 726

Tribal law: in Ottoman Empire, 389

Tributary mode of production, 358

Tribute system, in China, 411, 416, 430

Trinh family: Louis XIV letter to, 354

Triple Alliance, 485, 485 (map), 486

Triple Entente, 485 (map), 486

Tripoli, 388, 527

Trotsky, Leon, 576–577, *577*, 584

Trudeau, Pierre (Canada), 706

Truman, Harry, 629, 635, 703; China and, 651, 652, 653; Cold War and, 655; Korean War and, 654–655; at Potsdam, 638; Taiwan and, 654

Truman Doctrine, 646

Tsar (Russia), 378. *See also* specific tsars

Tsunami: in Southeast Asia, 765

Tudor dynasty (England), 371, 378. *See also* specific rulers

Tulsidas (Hindi poet), 406

Tumasik, 335

Tunis, 388, 527

Tunisia, 527, 595, 627, 724

Turing, Alan, 716

Turkestan, 654

Turkey, 738; Cuban Missile Crisis and, 659; economy in, 596; government of, 744; Islam in, 747; modernization of, 595–596; Truman Doctrine and, 646

Turkic-speaking peoples: in Ottoman Empire, 391; Uzbeks and, 394

Turkish language, 596

Turks: Osman, 386; Ottoman, 386. *See also* Ottoman Empire; Turkey

Tutsi people, 729–730

Twentieth Party Congress (Soviet Union), 674

Typhus, 342

Uganda, 731; Kenya and, 726

Uhuru ("freedom"): African independence and, 723–724

Ukraine, 576, 624, 628, 631

Ulama (Muslim scholars), 391

Ulbricht, Walter, 647, 664

Ulianov, Vladimir. *See* Lenin, V. I.

Ultranationalism, in Japan, 607

Ulysses (Joyce), 586

Unbearable Lightness of Being, The (Kundera), 715

Unconscious: in arts, 585–586

Underdeveloped countries, 660, 683

Underdogs, The (Azuela), 611

Unemployment: in China, 686; in Great Depression, 581, 582, 583; in Nazi Germany,

618, 619. *See also* Employment; specific countries

Unification: of Europe, 702–703; of Germany, 477, 480–481, 480 (map), 485 (map); of Italy, 479–480, 480 (map)

Uninterrupted revolution: in China, 681, 682

Union (U.S. Civil War North), 497

Union of Malaysia, 761

Union of South Africa, 532

Union of Soviet Socialist Republics (USSR). *See* Soviet Union

Unions. *See* Labor unions; Trade unions

United Arab Republic (UAR), 738

United Fruit Company, 707

United Kingdom, 446. *See also* England (Britain)

United Nations (UN), 638; conferences on women's issues, 713; Darfur violence and, 729; Korean War and, 654–655; Millennium Declaration by, 731; peacekeeping in Africa, 731

United Provinces of the Netherlands, 370

United States, 447, 497–499; Arab-Israeli disputes and, 739–740; Austria, New Zealand, and, 775; China and, 663; economy in, 498, 705, 706; government of, 447; Great Depression in, 583; hostage crisis and, 705; industrialization in, 467, 498; Iran and, 740–741; isolationism in, 580; Japan and, 624–625, 767; Jews in, 509; Latin America and, 493–494, 496, 498–499, 609, 706, 707; national security policy in, 653; Nazis and, 626; Philippines and, 761; popular culture of, 718–719; postwar politics in, 703–706; Soviet Union and, 645–646, 663–666; as superpower, 703–706; terrorist attack on, 666, 667, 705, 713–714; Turkey and, 747; Vietnam and, 660; women in, 711; World War I and, 573; after World War II, 698; World War II and, 624. *See also* Western world

Universal male suffrage, 452, 477, 484

Universe: geocentric and heliocentric theories of, 436, 437; medieval conception of, *437*

Universities and colleges: higher education in West and, 710; women in, 502

Untouchables (India), 758

Urban areas: in China, 684, 688; in India, 758; mass society in, 500; population of, 363, 468. *See also* Cities and towns

Urbanization: industrialization and, 467–468

Urdu language, 756

Uruguay, 493

USSR. *See* Soviet Union

Utamaro (Japanese artist), 430

Uzbekistan, 679

Uzbeks, 394–395, 398

Vajpayee, A. B. (India), 755–756

Valois, house of (France), 370

Values: Islamic, 747; in Japan, 557; in Southeast Asia, 765–766

Van de Velde, Theodore, 584

Van Gogh, Vincent, 510, 561

Vargas, Getúlio (Brazil), 610–611

Veils: for Islamic women, 748

Venetia, 479, 480

Venezuela, 492, 493, 707

Venturi, Robert, 716

Verdun, battle at, 571

Vernacular languages: in Africa, 732

Versailles, 376–377; German unification at, 481, *481*; Hall of Mirrors at, *377*

Versailles Treaty, 579–580, 620

Vespucci, Amerigo, 340 (map), 341

Veterans: after World War I, 578

Viceroys, 342, 343, 445, 527

Vichy France, 624

Victor Emmanuel II (Italy), 480

Victor Emmanuel III (Italy), 617

Victoria (England), 481, *547*

Victorians: family ideals of, 501

Vienna, 477, 482; Congress of, 464, *464*; Ottomans in, 385, 388

Viet Cong, 660

Vietminh Front, 655

Vietnam, 351, 431; in ASEAN, 765; China and, 684; Christianity and, 431; colonialism in, 516, 520–521, 535; culture of, *521*; democracy and, 764; division of, 655–656; empire in, 431; France and, 431, 520–521, 545; government of, 764; Japan and, 631; nationalism in, 533–534, *600*; reunification of, 765; soccer in, *764*; United States and, 660; after World War II, 761. *See also* Indochina

Vietnam syndrome, 665

Vietnam War, 387, 660–663, *662*, 705

Villa, Pancho, 611

Villages: in China, 687; in Japan, 426–428. *See also* Cities and towns

Vindication of the Rights of Women (Wollstonecraft), 441

Violence: deaths from, 419

Vizier: Ottoman grand vezir as, 391

Voltaire (François-Marie Arouet), 439–440

Voting and voting rights: in France, 477; in Japan, 606, 769; in Latin America, 495, 496; in Turkey, 596; in U.S., 497, 704; for women, 501–502, 574, 711, 748

Voyages: of Columbus, 341; European, 337–338, 340 (map); Spanish, 341

Wade, Abdoulaye, 731

Wahhabi movement, 598

Waiting for Godot (Beckett), 715

Walesa, Lech, 679

Wallachia, 479

Walled cities, 387

Wang Jingwei, 623

Wang Shuo (China), 693

Wang Tao (Wang T'ao), on reform, 545

War communism, in Russia, 577, 583

War crimes: by Milosevic, 702

"War Girls" (poem), 574

War Guilt Clause: in Versailles Treaty, 579
War on Poverty, 704
Wars and warfare: changes in, 387; between 1870 and 1914, 484–485; in French Revolution, 453; Geneva Convention on, 631; global, 449–450; gunpowder empires and, 407–408; for Latin American independence, 491–494; Napoleon and, 457–458, 458 (map); in 17th century, 373–374, 375. *See also* Military; specific battles and wars
Warsaw Pact, 649, 650 (map), 657
Wars of religion, 365–367, 370
Washington, George, 447
Washington Conference (1922), 609
Water: in China, 688–689
Watergate scandal, 705
Waterloo, battle at, 458
Water pollution, 714, 758
Water power, 465
Watt, James, 465
Watteau, Antoine, 441, *442*
Watts riots, 704–705
Wealth and wealthy: in England, 467; in Japan, 556–557, 608; in Latin America, 495; in South Africa, 729; in U.S., 498, 705. *See also* specific locations
Wealth gap, 666; in India, 758
Weapons, 387; Enfield rifle as, 534–535; Gatling gun, 536; machine gun, 536, 565; nuclear test ban and, 659; population explosion and, 419; Portuguese and, 340–341; in World War I, 565, 571; in World War II, 632, 716. *See also* Atomic bomb; Firearms; Gunpowder
Weaving, 443; Safavid, 397. *See also* Textiles and textile industry
Weimar Republic, 583, 618
Welfare: in Canada, 706; in China, 690; in England, 699; in U.S., 705
West, the. *See* Western world
West Africa: Europeans and, 525; France and, 572; gold from, 339; imperialism in, 525, 529, 531; Islam in, 336, 727; slavery and, 339, 349; yams in, *419*
West Bank, 739, 740
Western Asia: Ottomans in, 387–388
Western Europe: democracy in, 483–484, 698–700; NATO in, 648–649
Western Front: in World War I, 568, *572*, 573. *See also* World War I
Western Hemisphere, 719; colonial empires in, 444–447; communism in, 666; decline of slave trade in, 525; plants and animals in, 344; trade and, 443. *See also* Americas; New World; specific countries
Westernization: in Asia and Africa, 599, 723
Western world: African education and, 732; China and, 684, 691, 693; colonialism by, *514*, 514–515; colonial resistance to, 533–536, 590–591; concept of nationalism and, 533; cultural life in, 502–507; East Asia and, 774; expansion by, 343–345, 401–403;

industrialization in, 465–475; Japanese culture and, 770; peaceful coexistence with Soviets, 656; Scientific Revolution in, 343, 436–438; society in, 709–714; trade and, 416–418; after World War II, 698–699, 709–719. *See also* specific countries and regions
West Germany, 647, 680, 699, 703. *See also* Germany; West Berlin
West India Company. *See* Dutch West India Company
West Indies, 454
West Pakistan, 756
Wet rice. *See* Rice
Whigs. *See* Liberal Party, in England
Whistler, James, 561
White-collar workers, 500
White forces, in Russian civil war, 576
White Lotus Rebellion (China), 414
White Man's Burden, The (Kipling), 518, 536
White Paper, on communism in China, 653
Whites: in South Africa, 728–729; in U.S., 705
White supremacy: in Africa, 529, 532; in U.S. South, 498
Widows: in China, 420; in India, 401, 404
William I (Germany), 480, *481*
William II (Germany), 484, 485, 573, 583
William and Mary (England), 379, 380
William of Nassau (prince of Orange), 370
Willis, Christopher, 552
Wilson, Woodrow, 498, 578, 580
Wind(s): exploration and, 340 (map)
Winkelmann, Maria, 441
Witchcraft, 371–372
"With Germany's Unemployed" (Hauser), 582
Witte, Sergei, 472–473
Wollstonecraft, Mary, 441
Woman in Her Social and Domestic Character (Sanford), 503
Women: in Africa, 532–533, 732–733; as African writers, 735–736; in China, 420, 551–553, *553*, 605, 689–690; education and, 553; in Egypt, 534; in Enlightenment, 440–441; in factories, 575; foot binding and, 551, *553*, *607*; in France, 451, 455–457; in India, 403–404, 593–594, 758–759; industrialization and, 469; 503; in Iran, 596, 741, 748, *748*; Islamic, 747–748; in Japan, 428, 557, 606, 635, 769–770; Koreans as Japanese "comfort women," 631, 768; in Latin America, 445; in mass society, 500–502; in middle classes, 501–502, 503; in 1920s, 584; in Ottoman Empire, 391–392; in Pakistan, 756; as rulers in East and West, *547*; in Russian Revolution, 575–576; in Southeast Asia, 355–357, 766; in Soviet Union, 620, 632–633, 672, 677; in Turkey, 596; voting rights for, 501–502, 574; witchcraft scare and, 371–372; as workers, 473; World War I and, 574, 711–713; World War II and, 632–634
Women of Algiers (Delacroix), 505, *506*
Women's liberation, 552, 607, 711–712
Women's rights: movements for, 501–502

Women's Social and Political Union (England), 502
Woodblock printing, 363; in Japan, 430, *430, 561*
Wordsworth, William, 505
Workers: in African colonies, 532; in China, 688, *688*; in Europe, 443; in France, 698; in industrial factories, 469; in Japan, 556, 767, 769; on plantations, 524, 552; in West, 710; women as, 473, 574, 575, 711, 713. *See also* Labor; Working classes
Work ethic, in Japan, 769
Working classes: housing reforms for, 500; industrial, 469; in Latin America, 495; organizing of, 473–475; women in, 501
Works Progress Administration (WPA), 583
World-machine (Newton), 437–438
World markets, 471–472
World of Yesterday, The (Zweig), 569
World power: Germany as, 621; U.S. as, 498–499
World Trade Center, destruction of, 713, *714*
World Trade Organization (WTO): Africa and, 731; China in, 688
World War I, *565*, 565–566, 568–574, 570 (map); culture and intellectual thought after, 584–586; events before, 486, 486 (map), 566; home front in, 573–574; interwar years and, 580–586; Latin America after, 590, 609–612; mandates after, 580; in 1918, 577–578; Ottoman Empire and, 595; outbreak of, 566–568; peace settlement after, 578–580; public opinion in, 573–574, *574*; Russia and, 576; Schlieffen Plan in, 568, 568 (map); territorial changes after, 579 (map); trench warfare in, 569–572, *572*; United States in, 573; Versailles Treaty after, 579–580; women and, 574. *See also* Peace; specific countries
World War II, 616–617, 624–638; African independence movements after, 723–724; Asia and, 622–624, 627 (map); costs of, 636–637; culture after, 715–716; dictatorships before, 617–620; in Europe, 620–622, 625 (map); Europe after, 636–637, 637 (map), *697*, 697–698; events leading to, 620–624; home front in, 631–635; Japan after, 767–769; Middle East after, 737; in North Africa, 625 (map); in Pacific region, 625, 626, 627 (map); prisoners of war in, 631; science and technology after, 716–718; Southeast Asia after, 761; turning point of, 626; United States after, 703–706; West after, 698–699, 709–719; women after, 711–713; women in, 632–633, 632–634. *See also* Fascism; Japan; Nazi Germany; specific countries
Wright, Orville and Wilbur, 471
Writers. *See* Literature; specific authors and works
Wrought iron, 466

Xavier, Francis, 369
Xinjiang, China, 416, 654, 685